SOCCER
YEARBOOK
2004-5 DAVID GOLDBLATT

THE COMPLETE GUIDE TO THE WORLD GAME

LONDON, NEW YORK, MUNICH, MELBOURNE, DELHI

Dorling Kindersley

Project Designer Purple Carol

Project Editors Sam Atkinson, Margaret Hynes

Digital Cartography and Graphics
Peter Winfield

Editorial and Design Assistance
Victoria Clark, Michelle Crane, Louise Dick,
Wim Jenkins, Simon Mumford, Julie Turner

Systems Co-ordinator Philip Rowles

Production Louise Daly

Editorial Director Andrew Heritage

Art Director Bryn Walls

Produced for Dorling Kindersley by Butler & Tanner

Caxton Road, Frome, Somerset, BA11 1DY

Project Editor Julian Flanders

Senior Designer Kathie Wilson

Editorial and Design Assistance
Helen Burge, Louise Cassell, Nick Heal,
Sue Lee, Sandra Morgan, Craig Stevens

www.butlerandtanner.com

Index by Indexing Specialists (UK) Ltd

Digital Cartography and Graphics
Encompass Graphics Limited
Tom Coulson, Martin Darlison
www.encompass-graphics.co.uk

First American Edition, 2002

04 05 10 9 8 7 6 5 4 3

Previously published as the World Soccer Yearbook 2002-3

Published in the United States by
DK Publishing, Inc., 375 Hudson Street, New York, NY 10014

ISBN: 0-7566-0426-5

Library of Congress CIP Data is available for this book

Printed and bound in the UK by Butler & Tanner, London and New York

See our complete catalog at
www.dk.com

Contents

THE CONMEBOL NATIONS

THE CAF NATIONS

THE AFC NATIONS

THE OFC NATIONS

THE CONCACAF NATIONS

Foreword

Welcome to the third edition of the Dorling Kindersley *Football Yearbook*. The 2003–04 season has been an immensely busy one. Alongside all the annual events and championships, 2003–04 will have seen the Women's World Cup, the African Cup of Nations, the European Championships, the Copa America, the Asian Cup and the Oceania Cup. Our deadlines, tied to the European football season, mean that we have not been able to cover the last three tournaments; but rest assured we will feature all of them in the next edition.

In the wake of Euro 2004 we have not only included expanded coverage of the tournament but devoted additional space to the football records and players and managers of many of the participants, including Bulgaria, Croatia, the Czech Republic, Denmark, Latvia, Greece, Russia and Sweden. We have also included the most recent records of the five FIFA affiliated countries that we had somehow managed to ignore in early versions of the book: Eritrea, Macao, North Korea, the Seychelles and Sri Lanka now have their spots. To make space for these new additions we have removed most of the World Themes section that came at the end of previous edition, but no doubt they will return in fully updated form some time in the future. As ever we have tried to cover the seasons, both on and off the pitch, in all the major footballing nations and regions in our annual reviews and updated and developed existing pages on fans and owners and football cities. Those of you who need to know which corporations and state governments own which top Nigerian football teams now have your answers.

Once again thank you to our many critics and correspondents who have pointed out our howlers and suggested improvements.

David Goldblatt

Introduction

IN 2004 FIFA CELEBRATED ITS CENTENARY. From its small European beginnings, founded by just seven national Football Associations in 1904, FIFA has grown to 204 members – considerably more than the United Nations – and is now one of the richest and most significant international NGOs on the planet. It would be hard to describe the accompanying celebrations as anything other than banal, yet FIFA controls the singularly most widespread, universal and popular cultural phenomenon in the modern world. Among the timid offerings were a dry celebratory game between France and Brazil and Pele's 125 greatest living soccer players – a document that displayed all the hallmarks of international committee interference and politicking. FIFA General Secretary Sepp Blatter did himself no favours with some of his more spontaneous suggestions – including the importance of designing revealing kits for women's soccer and his almost solo decision to declare Cameroon's one-piece strips (worn at the African Cup of Nations) illegal. Cameroon were deducted six points from their World Cup qualifying games, a decision thankfully rescinded at FIFA's centenary congress.

FIFA gets it right

However, in one key way FIFA got it absolutely right: 2004 was the year in which Africa was awarded its first great global sporting event and the World Cup will be held in South Africa in 2010. Africa is unquestionably the third continent in global soccer and the World Cup is reward for a century of soccer development completely against the odds and the prevailing power structures of the world.

The competition to host the event had already been restricted to Africa alone as recompense for Germany's last-minute victory for the 2006 hosting rights. Libya and Tunisia were never really in the running, Egypt failed to score a single vote and the fight came down to Morocco and South Africa. Behind the technocratic talk of infrastructure provision and tourist facilities, this was pure cultural politics. South Africa's opponents highlighted the crime rate and bizarrely the incidence of Aids (as if they were discussing the FIFA World Casual Sex Cup) while Morocco's opponents mused on issues of terrorism and fundamentalism. South Africa won the opening vote 14-10, carried by the arrival of three Nobel Prize winners (Mandela, De Klerk, and Tutu) in their bid team.

The underdogs and the unfancied also did well on the pitch this year with both the Copa Libertadores and the European Champions League going to small teams from smaller countries: Colombia's Once Caldas and Portugal's Porto respectively. Most amazing of all, Greece won the European Championships. After a hundred years of politicization and commercialization, the values of solidarity and teamwork can still spring unexpected surprises and ignite the imagination and that is something worth celebrating.

WORLD CLUB CUP
2003 FINAL

December 14 – Yokohama, Japan
Boca Juniors 1-1 Milan
(Argentina)   (Italy)
(Donnet 29)   *(Tomasson 23)*
h/t : 1-1 **Att:** 66,757
Ref: Ivanov (Russia)
Boca Juniors won 3-1 on penalties

Right: It only takes one corner and one header to win a game. Greece's Charisteas heads the ball home against Portugal and Greece are European Champions for the first time in their history.

The centenary of FIFA was suitably celebrated with a goalless draw at the Stade de France in May 2004. In historical garb for the occasion Brazil's Ronaldo steps past French captain Marcel Desailly.

FIFA General Secretary Sepp Blatter congratulates Nelson Mandela after South Africa was announced as the winner of the competition to host the 2010 World Cup.

Far left: *Two for the price of one: Boca Juniors' Diego Cagna and Guillermo Baros Schelotto hold aloft both of the trophies at stake in the World Club Cup.*

Left: *Who ate all the pies, all the hot dogs and the crisps? Maradona lets the crowds gathered outside the hospital know he is OK but no one believed him and he remains seriously ill.*

Bottom left: *Colombia's Once Caldas celebrate their victory in the Copa Libertadores after beating Boca Juniors on penalties.*

Bottom right: *Greek captain Theo Zagorakis accepts the Henry Delauney trophy from UEFA President Lennart Johannsson. Eusebio in the background can hardly bear to watch.*

England

SEASON OVERVIEW

NO ONE WAS ACTUALLY COUNTING but it is certain that during Euro 2004 England was bedecked by more St George flags than ever and more fans made the journey to Portugal for the tournament itself. As the meaning of Englishness becomes a more pressing matter, the England soccer team becomes an increasingly central vehicle for the expression of English nationalism. And there were some signs at least that this is changing – dire predictions of extensive trouble in Portugal came to almost nothing; English-Asian fans established their first significant presence in the crowds. On the other hand, attacks on Portuguese families in England after the Euro 2004 quarter-final suggested otherwise.

The sporting materials from which to construct a national identity were equally mixed. England under Sven Goran Eriksson have acquired a quiet, grim, even technocratic cautious professionalism. England played within themselves in their qualifying games. They saved their best for a tense and spiteful 0-0 draw in against Turkey in Istanbul from which England fans had been banned. Friendlies disintegrated into a tidal wave of substitutions and the dressing room has tried to assert its power – most notably over the exclusion of Rio Ferdinand.

In thrall to celebrity and money

In Portugal their caution saw them defend a narrow 1-0 lead against France for two-thirds of the game before being caught out by two late strikes from Zidane. Against Switzerland and Croatia they scored freely and Wayne Rooney belied his years by turning in the team's best performances. But against Portugal in the quarter-final Rooney's departure, a complete failure to attack or retain possession and almost robotic performances from David Beckham and Paul Scholes let Portugal back in. Beckham skied his third international penalty of the season (the other two were against Turkey and France) and the inevitable dawned. Do we get the soccer we deserve after a gruelling 11-month season? Perhaps the mundane reality of English national identity is captured here – an overworked and overcautious society in thrall to celebrity and money.

ENGLAND FRIENDLIES

Aug 20, 2003 – Portman Road, Ipswich
England 3-1 Croatia
(Beckham 9 pen,   (Mornar 77)
Owen 51,
Lampard 80)
h/t : 1-0 Att: 28,700
Ref: Larsen (Denmark)

Nov 16, 2003 – Old Trafford, Manchester
England 2-3 Denmark
(Rooney 4,   (Jorgensen 7,
Cole 8)   30 pen,
Tomasson 84)
h/t : 2-2 Att: 64,159
Ref: Hrinak (Slovakia)

Feb 18, 2004 – Estadio Algarve, Faro
Portugal 1-1 England
(Pauleta 71)   (King 48)
h/t : 0-0 Att: 27,000
Ref: Kassai (Hungary)

Mar 31, 2004 – Nea Ulevi, Gothenburg
Sweden 1-0 England
(Ibrahimovic 53)
h/t : 0-0 Att: 40,464
Ref: Ovrebo (Norway)

June 1, 2004 – City of Manchester Stadium
England 1-1 Japan
(Owen 25)   (Ono 53)
h/t : 1-0 Att: 38,581
Ref: Rosetti (Italy)

June 5, 2004 – City of Manchester Stadium
England 6-1 Iceland
(Lampard 24   (Helguson 41)
Rooney 26, 38,
Vassell 57, 76,
Bridge 68)
h/t : 3-1 Att: 43,500
Ref: Wegereef (Holland)

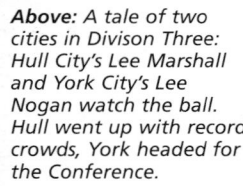

Above: A tale of two cities in Divison Three: Hull City's Lee Marshall and York City's Lee Nogan watch the ball. Hull went up with record crowds, York headed for the Conference.

Far left: The 20 million dollar goal: Neil Shipperley turns after scoring Crystal Palace's scrappy play-off winner that took them into the Premiership. Michael Carrick of West Ham can't believe it.

Left: Top scorer for the top club: Thierry Henry shows off his Player of the Year award.

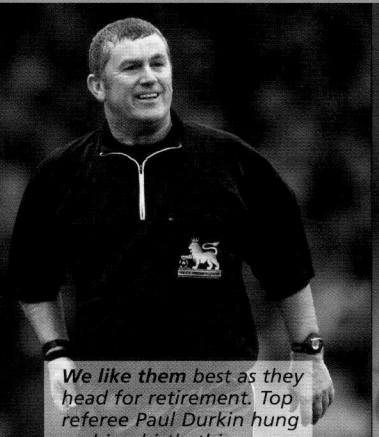

We like them best as they head for retirement. Top referee Paul Durkin hung up his whistle this season.

Above, right: *I'll just be two minutes, I'm going shopping. Manchester United's Rio Ferdinand excused himself from a drug test and received an eight-month ban for his troubles.*

Above, far right: *Confused nationalists? Despite fears to the contrary, England fans behaved well during Euro 2004 earning 9 out of 10 from UEFA for their efforts.*

EURO 2004
Qualifying Round Group Stage

Sep 6, 2003 – Gradski Stadium, Skopje
Macedonia 1-2 England
(Hristov 28)   (Rooney 52,
Beckham 63)
h/t : 1-0 **Att:** 20,500
Ref: de Bleeckere (Belgium)

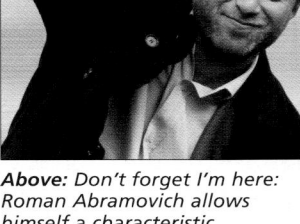

Above: *Don't forget I'm here: Roman Abramovich allows himself a characteristic weak smile.*

Right: *Wayne Rooney trudges off after breaking a bone in his foot during England's quarter-final defeat against Portugal at Euro 2004. Sven looks as though he knows that's the end of his team's chances.*

Sep 10, 2003 – Old Trafford, Manchester
England 2-0 Liechtenstein
(Owen 46
Rooney 52)
h/t : 0-0 **Att:** 64,931
Ref: Fisker (Denmark)

Oct 11, 2003 – Sukru Saracoglu Stadium, Istanbul
Turkey 0-0 England
h/t : 0-0 **Att:** 45,000
Ref: Collina (Italy)

GROUP 7

CLUB	P	W	D	L	F	A	Pts	
England	8	6	2	0	14	5	**20**	Qualified
Turkey	8	6	1	1	17	5	**19**	Play-off – lost to Latvia
Slovakia	8	3	1	4	11	9	**10**	
Macedonia	8	1	3	4	11	14	**6**	
Liechtenstein	8	0	1	7	2	22	**1**	

2004 EUROPEAN CHAMPIONSHIPS – PORTUGAL

June 13, 2004 – Estadio da Luz, Lisbon
England 1-2 France
(Lampard 38)   (Zidane 90, 91)
h/t: 1-0 **Att:** 62,487
Ref: Merk (Germany)

17 June 17, 2004 – Municipal, Coimbra
England 3-0 Switzerland
(Rooney 23, 75,
Gerrard 82)
h/t: 1-0 **Att:** 30,000
Ref: Ivanov (Russia)

June 21, 2004 – Estadio da Luz, Lisbon
England 4-2 Croatia
(Scholes 40,   (Kovac 5,
Rooney 45, 68,   Tudor 73)
Lampard 79)
h/t: 2-1 **Att:** 63,000
Ref: Collina (Italy)

June 24, 2004 – Estadio da Luz, Lisbon
England 2-2 Portugal
(Owen 3,   (Postiga 83,
Lampard 115)   Rui Costa 110)
(after extra time)
h/t: 1-0 **90 mins:** 1-1
Att: 65,000 **Ref:** Meier (Switzerland)
Portugal won 6-5 on penalties

The Premier League

SEASON REVIEW

AT THE START OF THIS SEASON all the talk was about Chelsea and Manchester United; the former transformed into the central bazaar of the global player market by Abramovich's money, the champions spending freely too. Arsenal, struggling to build a new stadium, had few reinforcements. But at the end, all the talk was about Arsenal. Yes, Chelsea lost some easy games and United self-destructed, losing to Wolves and Portsmouth, but Arsenal were magnificent. They became the first team since Preston North End in 1889 to go a full season unbeaten and they did it in some style. Thierry Henry, the league's top scorer, was inspired, the quality of Arsenal's movement was refined and their grit to come back when a goal down and to turn defeats into draws was immense.

League within a league

In the league within a league for the rest of the European places Liverpool and Newcastle eventually came good after deeply disappointing seasons of erratic and sometimes heartless play. Aston Villa, under David O'Leary, surprised everyone including themselves by creeping up to sixth. Just below them the Premiership's smaller but best managed clubs overperformed. Charlton, Birmingham, Fulham, Southampton and Bolton all looked in contention for a European place at one point or another. Portsmouth, under Harry Redknapp, were never challenging for Europe but 13th place in its first season in the top division constitutes a massive triumph. Only Middlesbrough can truly claim mid-table mediocrity and even they won the League Cup.

Further down, mismanagement, underperformance and defensive frailties were the order of the day with wretched seasons for Blackburn, Tottenham, Manchester City and, as ever, Everton. Below them come the financial morality tales. Wolves went down because it wouldn't spend anything; Leicester followed because they couldn't spend anything and Leeds finally sank because they had spent too much and couldn't pay it back.

Final Premier League Table 2003–04

CLUB	P	W	D	L	F	A	Pts	
Arsenal	38	26	12	0	73	26	90	Champions League
Chelsea	38	24	7	7	67	30	79	Champions League
Manchester United	38	23	6	9	64	35	75	Champions League
Liverpool	38	16	12	10	55	37	60	Champions League
Newcastle United	38	13	17	8	52	40	56	UEFA Cup
Aston Villa	38	15	11	12	48	44	56	
Charlton Athletic	38	14	11	13	51	51	53	
Bolton Wanderers	38	14	11	13	48	56	53	
Fulham	38	14	10	14	52	46	52	
Birmingham City	38	12	14	12	43	48	50	
Middlesbrough	38	13	9	16	44	52	48	UEFA Cup (League Cup winners)
Southampton	38	12	11	15	44	45	47	
Portsmouth	38	12	9	17	47	54	45	
Tottenham Hotspur	38	13	6	19	47	57	45	
Blackburn Rovers	38	12	8	18	51	59	44	
Manchester City	38	9	14	15	55	54	41	
Everton	38	9	12	17	45	57	39	
Leicester City	38	6	15	17	48	65	33	Relegated
Leeds United	38	8	9	21	40	79	33	Relegated
Wolverhampton Wanderers	38	7	12	19	38	77	33	Relegated

Promoted clubs: Norwich City, West Bromwich Albion, Crystal Palace.

Millwall earns UEFA Cup place as runners-up to Manchester United in FA Cup.

Top Goalscorers 2003–04

PLAYER	CLUB	NATIONALITY	GOALS
Thierry Henry	Arsenal	French	30
Alan Shearer	Newcastle United	English	22
Ruud van Nistelrooy	Manchester United	Dutch	20

Arsenal played with great fluidity and adventure, but at the core of its unbeaten season was a squad of players unmistakably playing for each other.

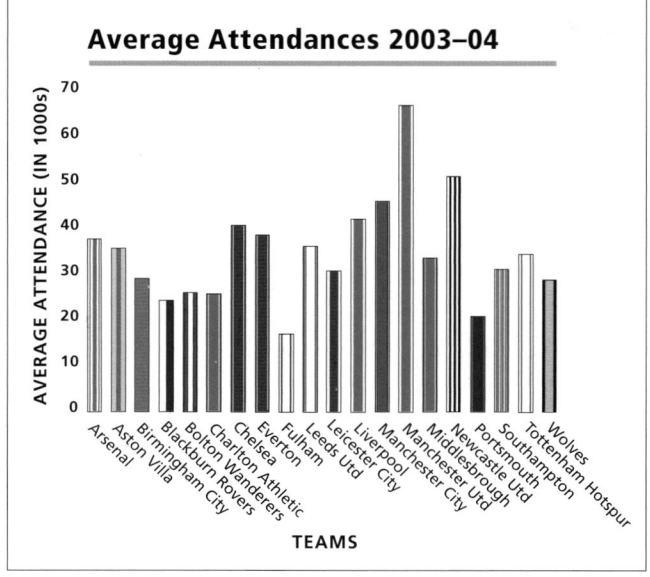

Average Attendances 2003–04

AVERAGE ATTENDANCE (IN 1000s)

TEAMS: Arsenal, Aston Villa, Birmingham City, Blackburn Rovers, Bolton Wanderers, Charlton Athletic, Chelsea, Everton, Fulham, Leeds Utd, Leicester City, Liverpool, Manchester City, Manchester Utd, Middlesbrough, Newcastle Utd, Portsmouth, Southampton, Tottenham Hotspur, Wolves

ENGLAND

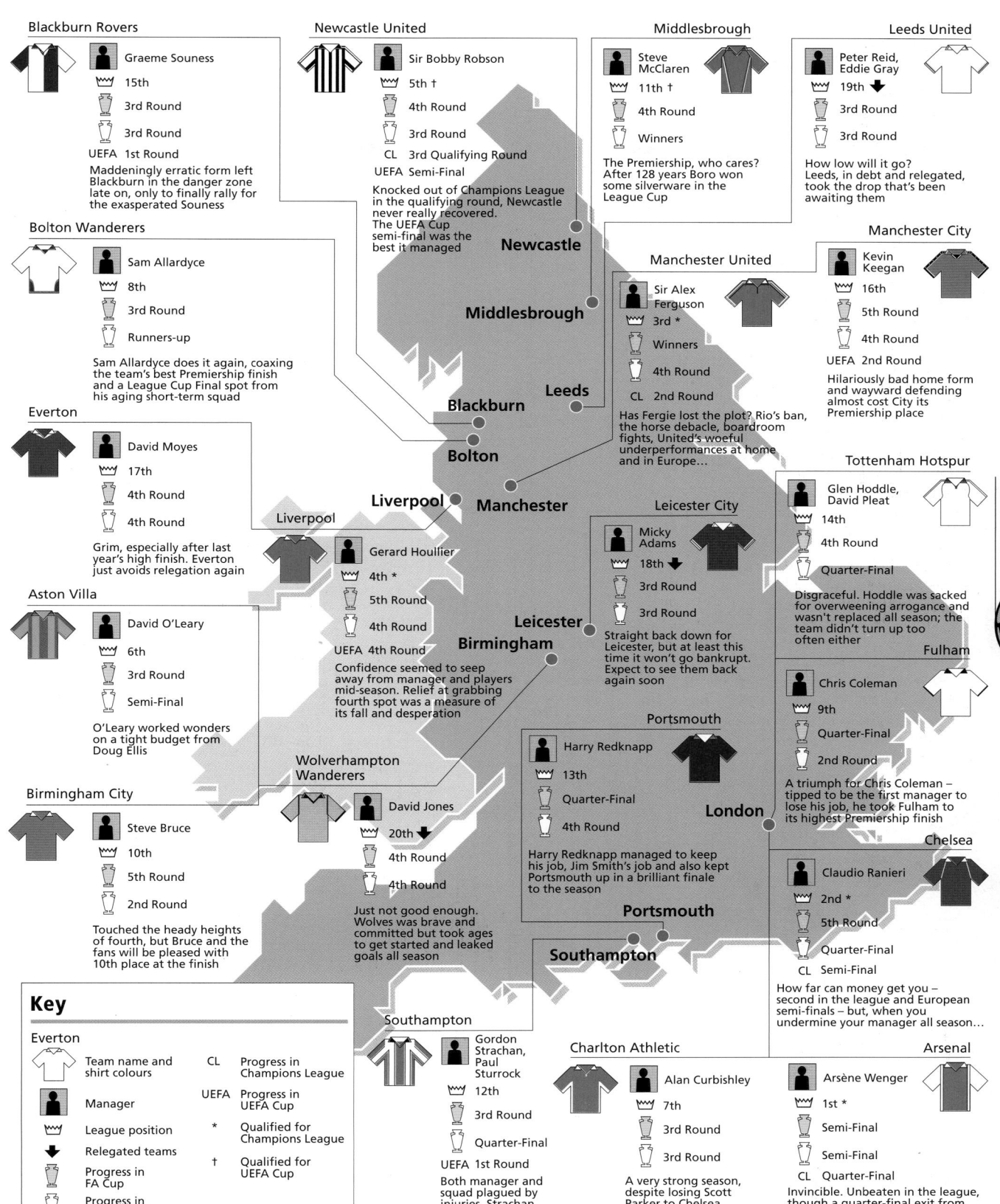

Blackburn Rovers

Graeme Souness

15th

3rd Round

3rd Round

UEFA 1st Round

Maddeningly erratic form left Blackburn in the danger zone late on, only to finally rally for the exasperated Souness

Bolton Wanderers

Sam Allardyce

8th

3rd Round

Runners-up

Sam Allardyce does it again, coaxing the team's best Premiership finish and a League Cup Final spot from his aging short-term squad

Everton

David Moyes

17th

4th Round

4th Round

Grim, especially after last year's high finish. Everton just avoids relegation again

Aston Villa

David O'Leary

6th

3rd Round

Semi-Final

O'Leary worked wonders on a tight budget from Doug Ellis

Birmingham City

Steve Bruce

10th

5th Round

2nd Round

Touched the heady heights of fourth, but Bruce and the fans will be pleased with 10th place at the finish

Newcastle United

Sir Bobby Robson

5th †

4th Round

3rd Round

CL 3rd Qualifying Round

UEFA Semi-Final

Knocked out of Champions League in the qualifying round, Newcastle never really recovered. The UEFA Cup semi-final was the best it managed

Liverpool

Gerard Houllier

4th *

5th Round

4th Round

UEFA 4th Round

Confidence seemed to seep away from manager and players mid-season. Relief at grabbing fourth spot was a measure of its fall and desperation

Wolverhampton Wanderers

David Jones

20th ↓

4th Round

4th Round

Just not good enough. Wolves was brave and committed but took ages to get started and leaked goals all season

Southampton

Gordon Strachan, Paul Sturrock

12th

3rd Round

Quarter-Final

UEFA 1st Round

Both manager and squad plagued by injuries. Strachan left while the team trod water

Middlesbrough

Steve McClaren

11th †

4th Round

Winners

The Premiership, who cares? After 128 years Boro won some silverware in the League Cup

Manchester United

Sir Alex Ferguson

3rd *

Winners

4th Round

CL 2nd Round

Has Fergie lost the plot? Rio's ban, the horse debacle, boardroom fights, United's woeful underperformances at home and in Europe…

Leicester City

Micky Adams

18th ↓

3rd Round

3rd Round

Straight back down for Leicester, but at least this time it won't go bankrupt. Expect to see them back again soon

Portsmouth

Harry Redknapp

13th

Quarter-Final

4th Round

Harry Redknapp managed to keep his job, Jim Smith's job and also kept Portsmouth up in a brilliant finale to the season

Charlton Athletic

Alan Curbishley

7th

3rd Round

3rd Round

A very strong season, despite losing Scott Parker to Chelsea. Just pipped for European places

Leeds United

Peter Reid, Eddie Gray

19th ↓

3rd Round

3rd Round

How low will it go? Leeds, in debt and relegated, took the drop that's been awaiting them

Manchester City

Kevin Keegan

16th

5th Round

4th Round

UEFA 2nd Round

Hilariously bad home form and wayward defending almost cost City its Premiership place

Tottenham Hotspur

Glen Hoddle, David Pleat

14th

4th Round

Quarter-Final

Disgraceful. Hoddle was sacked for overweening arrogance and wasn't replaced all season; the team didn't turn up too often either

Fulham

Chris Coleman

9th

Quarter-Final

2nd Round

A triumph for Chris Coleman – tipped to be the first manager to lose his job, he took Fulham to its highest Premiership finish

Chelsea

Claudio Ranieri

2nd *

5th Round

Quarter-Final

CL Semi-Final

How far can money get you – second in the league and European semi-finals – but, when you undermine your manager all season…

Arsenal

Arsène Wenger

1st *

Semi-Final

Semi-Final

CL Quarter-Final

Invincible. Unbeaten in the league, though a quarter-final exit from the Champions League leaves its European pedigree in question

ENGLAND

Newcastle

Middlesbrough

Leeds

Blackburn

Bolton

Liverpool

Manchester

Leicester

Birmingham

Portsmouth

London

Southampton

Key

Everton

Team name and shirt colours

Manager

League position

Relegated teams

Progress in FA Cup

Progress in League Cup

CL   Progress in Champions League

UEFA   Progress in UEFA Cup

*   Qualified for Champions League

†   Qualified for UEFA Cup

Division One

SEASON REVIEW

IN THE OCCASIONALLY UNSEEMLY AND often desperate struggle to claw one's way into the Premiership, Division One's top spots are often taken by a combination of one club that is steadily rising and one that is trying to go straight back up. This season was no different. The championship went to Nigel Worthington's Norwich on the back of two seasons of improvement and a rejuvenated Darren Huckerby up front, while West Bromwich Albion, relegated last season, gained automatic promotion at the first time of asking.

These two were top of the table at Christmas, but below them competition for play-off places went all the way down to Walsall in 13th position. In the latter stages of the season, Sheffield United, Wigan and Reading fell away, Sunderland and West Ham maintained their challenge and two sides that had skirted with relegation earlier on in the season – Ipswich and Crystal Place – crept into contention.

Play-off dramas

The play-off semi-finals proved real blood and guts affairs with West Ham and Crystal Palace showing more hunger if no more skill than their opponents. But the final was a nervy affair with neither side able to settle into a considered pattern of play. In the end the biggest pay day in European soccer was settled by a scrappy Neil Shipperly goal – scuffed into the net, but worth around £20 million.

Walsall, by contrast, headed down, losing its manager and last five games before tumbling into Division Two. Nottingham Forest and Derby hauled themselves up and past them, leaving Walsall to join Bradford, who teetered on the verge of administration and dissolution all season, and Wimbledon. The Dons, finally ensconced in their empty Milton Keynes franchise, were so broke they fielded an under-19 side for most of the season.

Top: *Norwich City director Delia Smith applauds another Canary victory.* ***Above:*** *Norwich goes two up against Crewe and into the Premiership.*

Final Division One Table 2003–04

CLUB	P	W	D	L	F	A	Pts	
Norwich City	46	28	10	8	79	39	**94**	Promoted
West Bromwich Albion	46	25	11	10	64	42	**86**	Promoted
Sunderland	46	22	13	11	62	45	**79**	Play-offs
West Ham United	46	19	17	10	67	45	**74**	Play-offs
Ipswich Town	46	21	10	15	84	72	**73**	Play-offs
Crystal Palace	46	21	10	15	72	61	**73**	Play-offs – promoted
Wigan Athletic	46	18	17	11	60	45	**71**	
Sheffield United	46	20	11	15	65	56	**71**	
Reading	46	20	10	16	55	57	**70**	
Millwall	46	18	15	13	55	48	**69**	UEFA Cup (FA Cup finalist)
Stoke City	46	18	12	16	58	55	**66**	
Coventry City	46	17	14	15	67	54	**65**	
Cardiff City	46	17	14	15	68	58	**65**	
Nottingham Forest	46	15	15	16	61	58	**60**	
Preston North End	46	15	14	17	69	71	**59**	
Watford	46	15	12	19	54	68	**57**	
Rotherham United	46	13	15	18	53	61	**54**	
Crewe Alexandra	46	14	11	21	57	66	**53**	
Burnley	46	13	14	19	60	77	**53**	
Derby County	46	13	13	20	53	67	**52**	
Gillingham	46	14	9	23	48	67	**51**	
Walsall	46	13	12	21	45	65	**51**	Relegated
Bradford City	46	10	6	30	38	69	**36**	Relegated
Wimbledon	46	8	5	33	41	89	**29**	Relegated

Promoted clubs: Plymouth Argyle, Queens Park Rangers, Brighton & Hove Albion.

Promotion Play-off Matches

SEMI-FINALS		
Crystal Palace	**3-2, 1-2** (2 legs)	Sunderland
	Crystal Palace won 5-4 on pens	
Ipswich Town	**1-0, 0-2** (2 legs)	West Ham United
	West Ham United won 2-1 on aggregate	

FINAL		
Crystal Palace	**1-0**	West Ham United

Top Goalscorers 2003–04

PLAYER	CLUB	NATIONALITY	GOALS
Andrew Johnson	Crystal Palace	English	22
Robert Earnshaw	Cardiff City	Welsh	21
Robbie Blake	Burnley	English	19

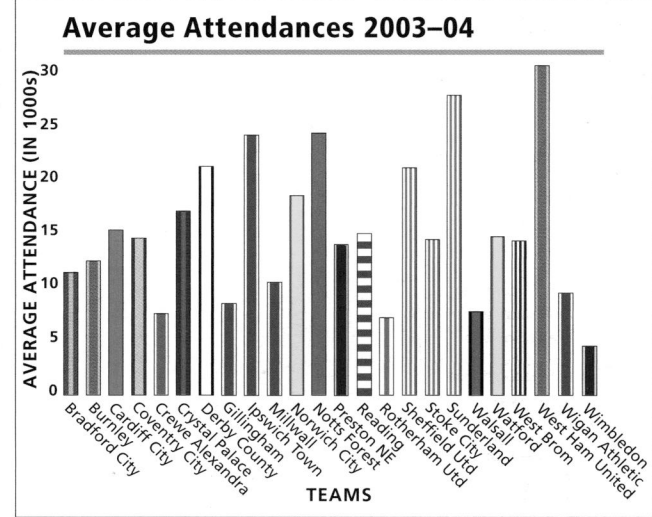

Average Attendances 2003–04

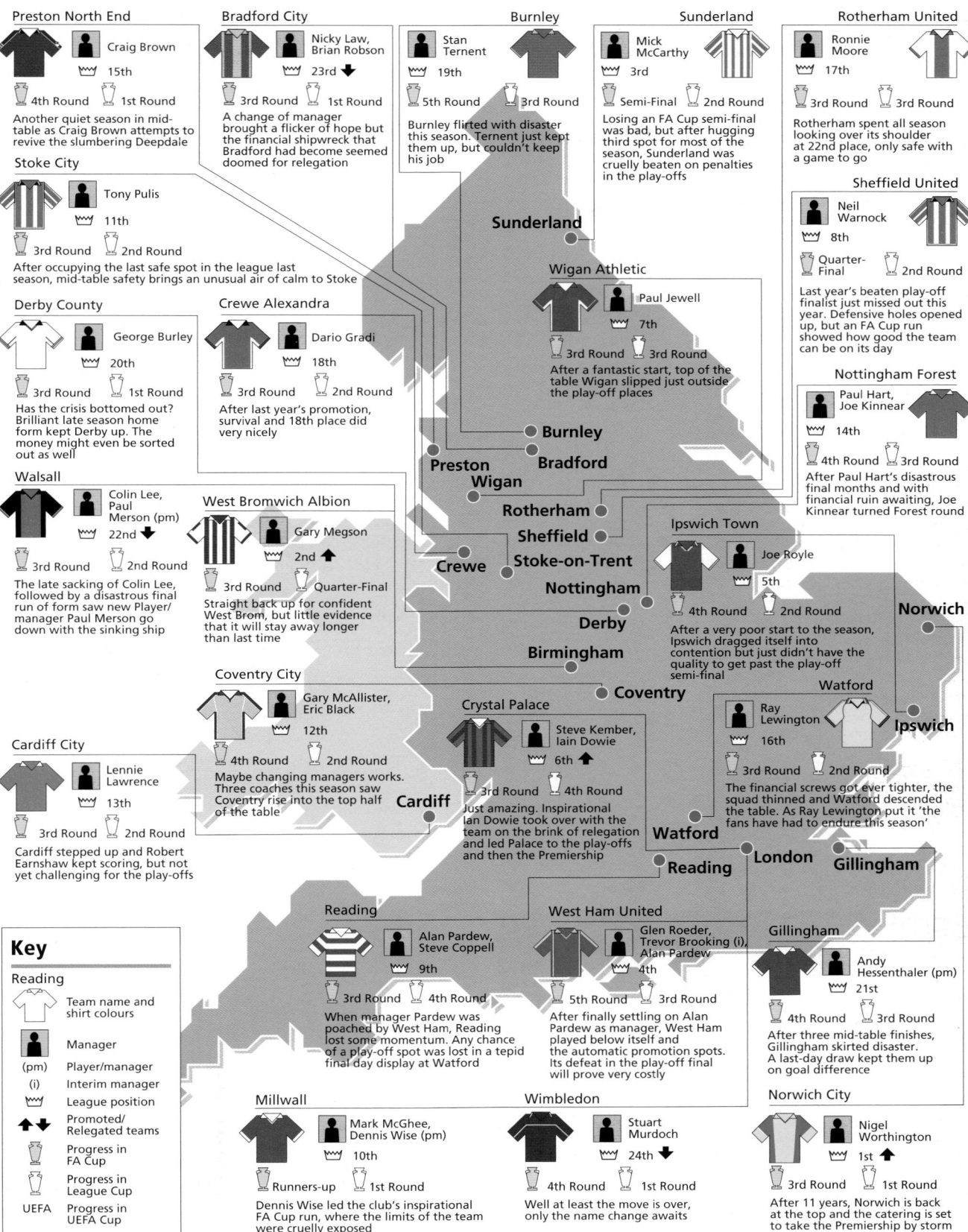

Preston North End
Craig Brown
15th
4th Round | 1st Round

Another quiet season in mid-table as Craig Brown attempts to revive the slumbering Deepdale

Stoke City
Tony Pulis
11th
3rd Round | 2nd Round

After occupying the last safe spot in the league last season, mid-table safety brings an unusual air of calm to Stoke

Derby County
George Burley
20th
3rd Round | 1st Round

Has the crisis bottomed out? Brilliant late season home form kept Derby up. The money might even be sorted out as well

Walsall
Colin Lee, Paul Merson (pm)
22nd
3rd Round | 2nd Round

The late sacking of Colin Lee, followed by a disastrous final run of form saw new Player/manager Paul Merson go down with the sinking ship

Cardiff City
Lennie Lawrence
13th
3rd Round | 2nd Round

Cardiff stepped up and Robert Earnshaw kept scoring, but not yet challenging for the play-offs

Bradford City
Nicky Law, Brian Robson
23rd
3rd Round | 1st Round

A change of manager brought a flicker of hope but the financial shipwreck that Bradford had become seemed doomed for relegation

Crewe Alexandra
Dario Gradi
18th
3rd Round | 2nd Round

After last year's promotion, survival and 18th place did very nicely

West Bromwich Albion
Gary Megson
2nd
3rd Round | Quarter-Final

Straight back up for confident West Brom, but little evidence that it will stay away longer than last time

Coventry City
Gary McAllister, Eric Black
12th
4th Round | 2nd Round

Maybe changing managers works. Three coaches this season saw Coventry rise into the top half of the table

Burnley
Stan Ternent
19th
5th Round | 3rd Round

Burnley flirted with disaster this season. Ternent just kept them up, but couldn't keep his job

Crystal Palace
Steve Kember, Iain Dowie
6th
3rd Round | 4th Round

Just amazing. Inspirational Iain Dowie took over with the team on the brink of relegation and led Palace to the play-offs and then the Premiership

Reading
Alan Pardew, Steve Coppell
9th
3rd Round | 4th Round

When manager Pardew was poached by West Ham, Reading lost some momentum. Any chance of a play-off spot was lost in a tepid final day display at Watford

Millwall
Mark McGhee, Dennis Wise (pm)
10th
Runners-up | 1st Round

Dennis Wise led the club's inspirational FA Cup run, where the limits of the team were cruelly exposed

Sunderland
Mick McCarthy
3rd
Semi-Final | 2nd Round

Losing an FA Cup semi-final was bad, but after hugging third spot for most of the season, Sunderland was cruelly beaten on penalties in the play-offs

Wigan Athletic
Paul Jewell
7th
3rd Round | 3rd Round

After a fantastic start, top of the table Wigan slipped just outside the play-off places

Ipswich Town
Joe Royle
5th
4th Round | 2nd Round

After a very poor start to the season, Ipswich dragged itself into contention but just didn't have the quality to get past the play-off semi-final

West Ham United
Glen Roeder, Trevor Brooking (i), Alan Pardew
4th
5th Round | 3rd Round

After finally settling on Alan Pardew as manager, West Ham played below itself and the automatic promotion spots. Its defeat in the play-off final will prove very costly

Wimbledon
Stuart Murdoch
24th
4th Round | 1st Round

Well at least the move is over, only the name change awaits

Rotherham United
Ronnie Moore
17th
3rd Round | 3rd Round

Rotherham spent all season looking over its shoulder at 22nd place, only safe with a game to go

Sheffield United
Neil Warnock
8th
Quarter-Final | 2nd Round

Last year's beaten play-off finalist just missed out this year. Defensive holes opened up, but an FA Cup run showed how good the team can be on its day

Nottingham Forest
Paul Hart, Joe Kinnear
14th
4th Round | 3rd Round

After Paul Hart's disastrous final months and with financial ruin awaiting, Joe Kinnear turned Forest round

Watford
Ray Lewington
16th
3rd Round | 2nd Round

The financial screws got ever tighter, the squad thinned and Watford descended the table. As Ray Lewington put it 'the fans have had to endure this season'

Gillingham
Andy Hessenthaler (pm)
21st
4th Round | 3rd Round

After three mid-table finishes, Gillingham skirted disaster. A last-day draw kept them up on goal difference

Norwich City
Nigel Worthington
1st
3rd Round | 1st Round

After 11 years, Norwich is back at the top and the catering is set to take the Premiership by storm

ENGLAND

Key

Reading
Team name and shirt colours

Manager

(pm) Player/manager

(i) Interim manager

League position

Promoted/Relegated teams

Progress in FA Cup

Progress in League Cup

UEFA Progress in UEFA Cup

Map labels: Sunderland, Burnley, Bradford, Preston, Wigan, Rotherham, Sheffield, Crewe, Stoke-on-Trent, Nottingham, Derby, Birmingham, Coventry, Cardiff, Crystal Palace, Watford, Reading, London, Gillingham, Ipswich, Norwich

Division Two

SEASON REVIEW

IT WAS HARD, SLIGHTLY SCRAPPY AND AMAZINGLY well supported lower division fare for most of the season and most of the clubs in Division Two. The top three at New Year – Plymouth, QPR and Bristol City – always looked a cut above the rest. Below them, another dozen clubs looked like they might have a chance of sixth spot and a play-off place.

Plymouth lost manager Paul Sturrock to Southampton in March, but, under new man Bobby Williamson, secured the title when it beat nearest challengers QPR 2-0 at home in late April. Despite some late wobbles, QPR, last year's losing promotion play-off finalists, finally made it back into Division One, with a decisive 3-1 final-day victory over struggling Sheffield Wednesday. The first play-off spot went to Bristol City, who had chased QPR hard all through the second half of the season, but the best defence in the league just couldn't score enough goals. Bristol was joined by Brighton, who had looked in with a chance all year, Swindon and Hartlepool, who had hauled themselves out of mid-table and squeezed out Port Vale on goal difference.

Semi-final excitement, final deadlock

The play-off semi-finals were dramatic. Bristol beat Hartlepool in a thriller at Ashton Gate. Bristol equalized with three minutes to go and scored the winner deep in added time. Brighton hacked its way past Swindon on a rainy night on the south coast. The final was played mainly in the air and was settled by a Brighton penalty – although Bristol never looked like scoring all game.

Notts County and Wycombe Wanderers were rooted to the bottom of the table for most of the season and County spent nearly all of that in agonizingly prolonged financial discussions. Rushden and Diamonds, newly promoted last season, went straight back down despite being in the top half of the table in January. Grimsby compounded the misery of last year's relegation from Division One by limping into the final relegation spot.

Top Goalscorers 2003–04

PLAYER	CLUB	NATIONALITY	GOALS
Leon Knight	Brighton & Hove Albion	English	24
Paul Heffernan	Notts County	English	19
Stephen McPhee	Port Vale	English	19
Tommy Mooney	Swindon Town	English	19

Plymouth Argyle won promotion and the championship under new manager Bobby Williamson.

Final Division Two Table 2003–04

CLUB	P	W	D	L	F	A	Pts	
Plymouth Argyle	46	26	12	8	85	41	90	Promoted
Queens Park Rangers	46	22	17	7	80	45	83	Promoted
Bristol City	46	23	13	10	58	37	82	Play-offs
Brighton & Hove Albion	46	22	11	13	64	43	77	Play-offs – promoted
Swindon Town	46	20	13	13	76	58	73	Play-offs
Hartlepool United	46	20	13	13	76	61	73	Play-offs
Port Vale	46	21	10	15	73	63	73	
Tranmere Rovers	46	17	16	13	59	56	67	
AFC Bournemouth	46	17	15	14	56	51	66	
Luton Town	46	17	15	14	69	66	66	
Colchester United	46	17	13	16	52	56	64	
Barnsley	46	15	17	14	54	58	62	
Wrexham	46	17	9	20	50	60	60	
Blackpool	46	16	11	19	58	65	59	
Oldham Athletic	46	12	21	13	66	60	57	
Sheffield Wednesday	46	13	14	19	48	64	53	
Brentford	46	14	11	21	52	69	53	
Peterborough United	46	12	16	18	58	58	52	
Stockport County	46	11	19	16	62	70	52	
Chesterfield	46	12	15	19	49	71	51	
Grimsby Town	46	13	11	22	55	81	50	Relegated
Rushden & Diamonds	46	13	9	24	60	74	48	Relegated
Notts County	46	10	12	24	50	78	42	Relegated
Wycombe Wanderers	46	6	19	21	50	75	37	Relegated

Promoted clubs: Doncaster Rovers, Hull City, Torquay United, Huddersfield Town.

Promotion Play-off Matches

SEMI-FINALS
Bristol City **1-1, 2-1** (2 legs) Hartlepool United
Bristol City won 3-2 on aggregate
Swindon **0-1, 2-1** (2 legs) Brighton & Hove Albion
Brighton & Hove Albion won 4-3 on pens

FINAL
Brighton & Hove Albion **1-0** Bristol City

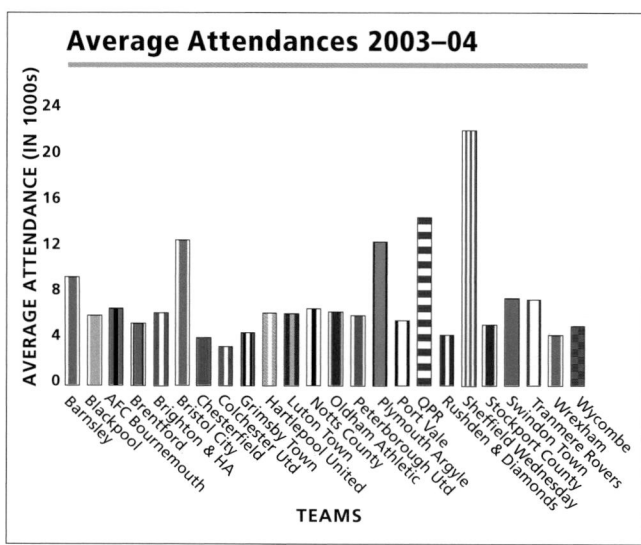

Average Attendances 2003–04

Stockport County

Carlton Palmer, Sammy McIlroy
19th
1st Round | 2nd Round

Carlton Palmer was eased out early in the season. McIlroy kept them up but that was about all

Port Vale

Brian Horton, Martin Foyle
7th
2nd Round | 1st Round

Jumped nearly ten places up from last year, but just missed the play-offs on goal difference

Notts County

Billy Dearden, Gary Mills
23rd ▼
3rd Round | 3rd Round

The financial disaster is not yet over, Second Division football is not. Notts County bow to the inevitable and go down

Tranmere Rovers

Ray Mathias, Brian Little
8th
Quarter-Final | 2nd Round

A great cup run but dismal away form kept them out of the play-offs

Swindon Town

Andy King
5th
1st Round | 2nd Round

Crept into the play-offs but was just off the pace in its rainy semi-final with Brighton

Blackpool

Steve McMahon
14th
3rd Round | 3rd Round

Knocked Birmingham out of the League Cup, but made no progress in the league itself

Oldham Athletic

Iain Dowie, John Sheridan, Brian Talbot
15th
2nd Round | 1st Round

Brian Talbot jumped ship from Rushden and just kept Oldham up when administration and relegation were looming

Sheffield Wednesday

Chris Turner
16th
2nd Round | 1st Round

Dismal. Wednesday is not a sleeping giant, it is comatose

Wrexham

Denis Smith ♛ 13th
1st Round | 1st Round

Not enough goals, not enough home wins, so no chance of a play-off place

Peterborough United

Barry Fry
18th
3rd Round | 1st Round

Last year Peterborough was in the top half, this year it was near the drop zone, but laughably bad home form was to blame

Bristol City

Danny Wilson
3rd
2nd Round | 3rd Round

Misery at Ashton Gate. A lack of goals all season kept Bristol out of the automatic promotion places and cost them the play-off final

Barnsley

Gudjon Thordarson, Paul Hart
12th
3rd Round | 1st Round

Barnsley came out of administration and out of relegation danger

Hartlepool United

Neale Cooper
6th
3rd Round | 2nd Round

A roller coaster of a season. Top of the table, out of the play-offs, back in at the last minute. The team was three minutes from Cardiff in the semi-finals till Bristol City hit the winner

Rushden and Diamonds

Brian Talbot, Barry Hunter (pm)
22nd ▼
1st Round | 1st Round

After a good start to the season and rumours of an Egyptian takeover, it was straight back down for Rushden

AFC Bournemouth

Sean O'Driscoll ♛ 9th
2nd Round | 1st Round

More than held its own after last year's play-off promotion

Brighton & Hove Albion

Steve Coppell, Mark McGhee ♛ 4th ▲
1st Round | 2nd Round

Straight back up for Brighton who hustled its way into the play-offs and won the final with a penalty. Maybe that nice Mr Prescott will let them build a stadium now

Chesterfield

Roy McFarland
20th
1st Round | 1st Round

Another season just missing the drop

Grimsby Town

Paul Groves (pm), Graham Roger (cm), Nicky Law
21st ▼
2nd Round | 1st Round

Those who saw its 8-1 defeat by Hartlepool knew what was coming. It's back-to-back relegations for Grimsby

Luton Town

Mike Newell
10th
4th Round | 2nd Round

A decent run but too many late goals conceded in too many games saw promotion hopes fade

Wycombe Wanderers

Lawrie Sanchez, Tony Adams
24th ▼
2nd Round | 2nd Round

The Sanchez era ended. The Adams era began with relegation. It can only get better

Colchester United

Phil Parkinson
11th
5th Round | 2nd Round

Steady in the league and a fine cup run

Queens Park Rangers

Ian Holloway
♛ 2nd ▲
1st Round | 3rd Round

At last QPR gets out of the Second Division. Last year's beaten play-off finalists made sure of going up on the last day

Brentford

Wally Downes, Martin Allen
17th
2nd Round | 1st Round

Looked like relegation candidates, but Martin Allen's late arrival energized Griffin Park

Plymouth Argyle

Paul Sturrock, Kevin Summerfield, Bobby Williamson
1st ▲
1st Round | 1st Round

Took top spot and never looked like relinquishing it. No wonder Southampton lured Sturrock down the road

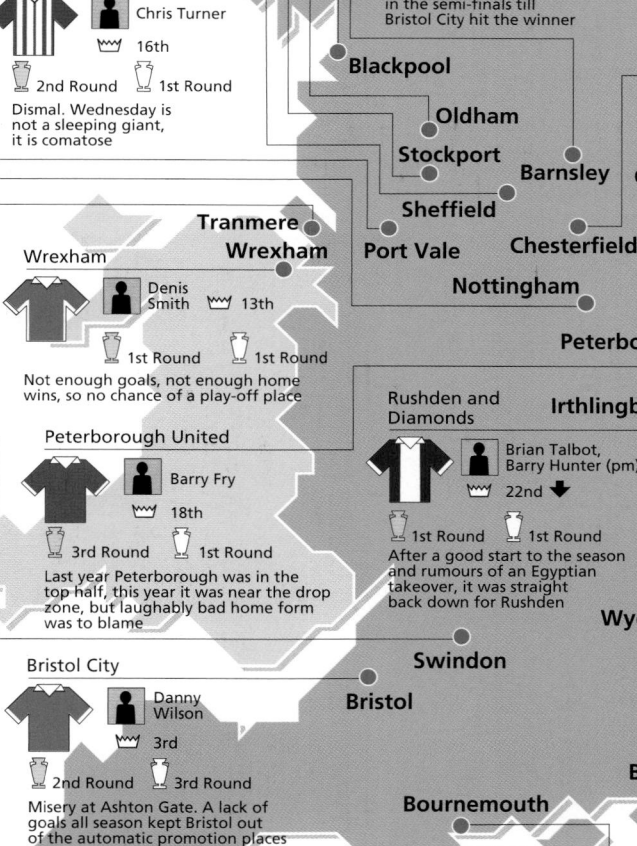

Blackpool
Oldham
Stockport
Sheffield
Barnsley
Grimsby
Chesterfield
Port Vale
Nottingham
Tranmere
Wrexham
Peterborough
Irthlingborough
Colchester
Luton
Wycombe
London
Swindon
Bristol
Brighton
Bournemouth
Plymouth
Hartlepool

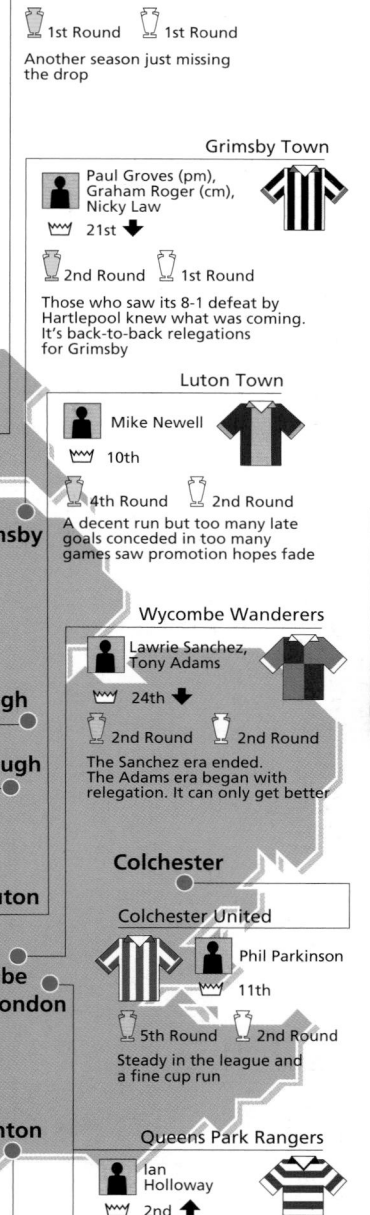

Key

Barnsley
 Team name and shirt colours

 Manager

(pm) Player manager

(cm) Caretaker manager

 League position

 Promoted/Relegated teams

 Progress in FA Cup

Progress in League Cup

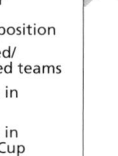

Division Three

SEASON REVIEW

THE STAKES MAY BE LOWER, but then fate is even crueller in the Third Division. Oxford United entered 2004 at the top of the table with only one defeat in 24 games. It finished the season ninth, outside the play-offs, with only four more wins to its name.

Oxford was replaced at the top by Doncaster Rovers, whose renaissance continues a year after promotion from the Conference. Yeovil, also newly promoted, only missed the play-offs on goal difference. Peter Taylor's Hull followed Doncaster, taking a stadium and a crowd with them that is as good as the lower reaches of the Premiership. Leroy Rosenior, on a minuscule budget, saw Torquay into the final automatic spot with a last-day win over Southend.

Play-off places went to Huddersfield, Mansfield, Lincoln, who had always been in the race, and Northampton, who had been hauled from mid-table by manager Colin Calderwood. Huddersfield and Mansfield played out a spirited but goalless final extended by poor finishing and great goalkeeping. Huddersfield, who had only missed promotion on goal difference, held its nerve in the penalty shootout as Mansfield missed two of its first three.

Carlisle United, once again, redefined the meaning of heroic battling against impossible odds. With only 12 points to its name at Christmas, it closed the gap through the spring, falling only four points short of safety. York City, by contrast, had come within touching distance of the play-off places in the New Year only to disintegrate. One win in five months left them bottom of the table and heading for a period of recuperation in the Conference.

Top Goalscorers 2003–04

PLAYER	CLUB	NATIONALITY	GOALS
Steven MacLean	Scunthorpe United	English	22
David Graham	Torquay United	English	20
Leon Constantine	Southend United	English	19

Final Division Three Table 2003–04

CLUB	P	W	D	L	F	A	Pts	
Doncaster Rovers	46	27	11	8	79	37	**92**	Promoted
Hull City	46	25	13	8	82	44	**88**	Promoted
Torquay United	46	23	12	11	68	44	**81**	Promoted
Huddersfield Town	46	23	12	11	68	52	**81**	Play-offs – promoted
Mansfield Town	46	22	9	15	76	62	**75**	Play-offs
Northampton Town	46	22	9	15	58	51	**75**	Play-offs
Lincoln City	46	19	17	10	68	47	**74**	Play-offs
Yeovil Town	46	23	5	18	70	57	**74**	
Oxford United	46	18	17	11	55	44	**71**	
Swansea City	46	15	14	17	58	61	**59**	
Boston United	46	16	11	19	50	54	**59**	
Bury	46	15	11	20	54	64	**56**	
Cambridge United	46	14	14	18	55	67	**56**	
Cheltenham Town	46	14	14	18	57	71	**56**	
Bristol Rovers	46	14	13	19	50	61	**55**	
Kidderminster Harriers	46	14	13	19	45	59	**55**	
Southend United	46	14	12	20	51	63	**54**	
Darlington	46	14	11	21	53	61	**53**	
Leyton Orient	46	14	11	19	48	65	**53**	
Macclesfield Town	46	13	13	20	54	69	**52**	
Rochdale	46	12	14	20	49	58	**50**	
Scunthorpe United	46	11	16	19	69	72	**49**	
Carlisle United	46	12	9	25	46	69	**45**	Relegated
York City	46	10	14	22	35	66	**44**	Relegated

Promoted clubs: Chester City, Shrewsbury Town.

Promotion Play-off Matches

SEMI-FINALS

Lincoln City **1-2, 2-2** (2 legs) Huddersfield Town
Huddersfield Town won 4-3 on aggregate

Northampton Town **0-2, 3-1** (2 legs) Mansfield Town
Mansfield Town won 5-4 on pens

FINAL

Huddersfield Town **0-0** Mansfield Town
Huddersfield Town won 4-1 on pens

Above left: Hull City players celebrate the team's automatic promotion place.

Above right: Leroy Rosenior issues instructions. He lifted Torquay to automatic promotion on the last day of the season.

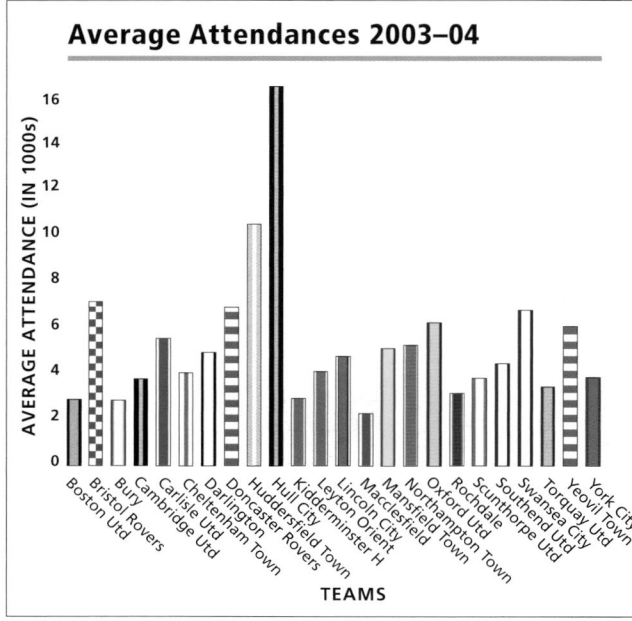

Average Attendances 2003–04

ENGLAND

Huddersfield Town
Peter Jackson
♛ 4th ▲
🏆 1st Round   🏆 3rd Round

Huddersfield dragged itself back into Division Two via the play-offs after giving up an automatic spot on the final day

Carlisle United
Paul Simpson (pm)
♛ 23rd ▼
🏆 1st Round   🏆 1st Round

The supply of miracles finally runs out in the North West and cash-strapped Carlisle succumbs to the Conference

York City
Chris Bass
♛ 24th ▼
🏆 1st Round   🏆 1st Round

With the youngest manager and the smallest wage bill, York was in real play-off contention at New Year. A record losing streak saw them fall all the way out of the league

Darlington
Mick Tait, Dave Hodgson
♛ 18th
🏆 1st Round   🏆 2nd Round

Steadily fell down the table in the second half of the season, saved like many by an easy win over a disintegrating Oxford

Doncaster Rovers
Dave Penny
♛ 1st ▲
🏆 1st Round   🏆 2nd Round

A brilliant season, as promotion follows promotion. Doncaster finished on an 18-game unbeaten run, Michael McIndoe was the division's player of the year

Rochdale
Alan Buckley, Steve Parkin
♛ 21st
🏆 2nd Round   🏆 1st Round

To be frank, Rochdale was very poor. A couple of late-season wins were the difference between staying up and going down

Lincoln City
Keith Alexander
♛ 7th
🏆 2nd Round   🏆 1st Round

Last year's losing finalists in the promotion play-offs went out in the semis this time

Hull City
Peter Taylor
♛ 2nd ▲
🏆 1st Round   🏆 1st Round

A late stutter and a run of draws sent the nerves jangling but Hull went up with crowds, a stadium and ambitions for higher things

Macclesfield Town
David Moss, John Askey, Brian Horton
♛ 20th
🏆 3rd Round   🏆 1st Round

Four wins out of seven under Brian Horton saved an otherwise awful season

Bury
Andy Preece, Graham Barrow
♛ 12th
🏆 1st Round   🏆 1st Round

In the play-off places at New Year but eight straight losses and crowds below 2,000 saw them tumble out of contention

Scunthorpe United
Brian Laws
♛ 22nd
🏆 4th Round   🏆 2nd Round

A chaotic season. Brian Laws fired and then reinstated, the club plummeting towards the bottom. A last day win over Darlington kept them up

Mansfield Town
Keith Curle
♛ 5th
🏆 3rd Round   🏆 1st Round

Performed above itself all season under the astute Keith Curle. It was cruelly beaten on penalties in the play-off final

Boston United
Neil Thompson, Jim Dodwell (cm)
♛ 11th
🏆 1st Round   🏆 1st Round

Another mid-table season, Boston is quietly creeping up the table

Northampton Town
Martin Wilkinson, Colin Calderwood
♛ 6th
🏆 4th Round   🏆 2nd Round

After a series of disastrous seasons, Northampton had something to shout about: an FA Cup clash with Manchester United and a stab at promotion

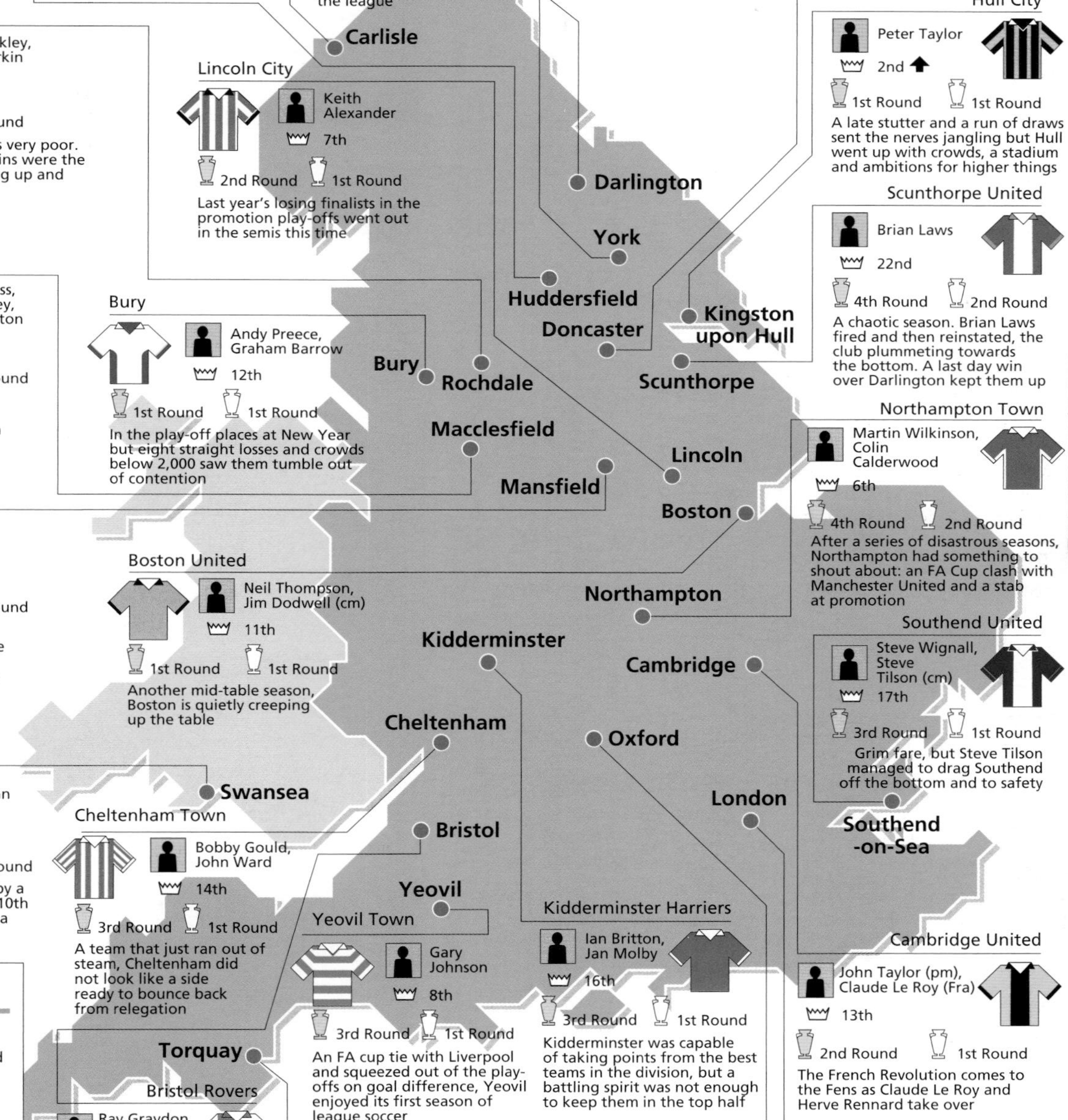

Swansea City
Brian Flynn
♛ 10th
🏆 5th Round   🏆 1st Round

A great cup run followed by a lot of league defeats, but 10th is a big step up for Swansea

Southend United
Steve Wignall, Steve Tilson (cm)
♛ 17th
🏆 3rd Round   🏆 1st Round

Grim fare, but Steve Tilson managed to drag Southend off the bottom and to safety

Cheltenham Town
Bobby Gould, John Ward
♛ 14th
🏆 3rd Round   🏆 1st Round

A team that just ran out of steam, Cheltenham did not look like a side ready to bounce back from relegation

Yeovil Town
Gary Johnson
♛ 8th
🏆 3rd Round   🏆 1st Round

An FA cup tie with Liverpool and squeezed out of the play-offs on goal difference, Yeovil enjoyed its first season of league soccer

Kidderminster Harriers
Ian Britton, Jan Molby
♛ 16th
🏆 3rd Round   🏆 1st Round

Kidderminster was capable of taking points from the best teams in the division, but a battling spirit was not enough to keep them in the top half

Cambridge United
John Taylor (pm), Claude Le Roy (Fra)
♛ 13th
🏆 2nd Round   🏆 1st Round

The French Revolution comes to the Fens as Claude Le Roy and Herve Rennard take over

Bristol Rovers
Ray Graydon, Phil Bater, Russell Osman and Kevin Broadhurst, Ian Atkins
♛ 15th
🏆 1st Round   🏆 1st Round

Well it wasn't pretty, but nondescript mid-table safety was a real improvement for the Gas

Torquay United
Leroy Rosenior
♛ 3rd ▲
🏆 1st Round   🏆 1st Round

Rosenior got Torquay to crawl its way up the table. Last day promotion was guaranteed by another goal from striking revelation David Graham

Oxford United
Ian Atkins, Graham Rix
♛ 9th
🏆 1st Round   🏆 2nd Round

Top of the table in January, Oxford lost its manager to Bristol Rovers and blew its promotion chances in a cataclysmic bad run of form

Leyton Orient
Paul Brush, Martin Ling
♛ 19th
🏆 2nd Round   🏆 1st Round

From mid-table in mid-season, Orient went on a 19-game run without a win. A late victory over York halted the slide ... just

Map labels: Carlisle · Darlington · York · Kingston upon Hull · Huddersfield · Doncaster · Scunthorpe · Bury · Rochdale · Lincoln · Macclesfield · Mansfield · Boston · Northampton · Cambridge · Kiddermister · Cheltenham · Oxford · London · Southend-on-Sea · Swansea · Bristol · Yeovil · Torquay

Key
York City

👕 Team name and shirt colours
👤 Manager
(pm) Player manager
(cm) Caretaker manager
♛ League position
▲▼ Promoted/Relegated teams
🏆 Progress in FA Cup
🏆 Progress in League Cup

The League Cup

TOURNAMENT REVIEW

ANOTHER SEASON, ANOTHER SPONSOR. In 2003–04 the English League Cup became the Carling Cup and everyone wondered whether the poor relative of English cup soccer would retain any significance. On the plus side, the fixture pressure that the tournament has caused was diminished this season by having all ties resolved on a one-game basis (except for the two-leg semi-finals).

'Middlesbrough fans expect to be let down,' said club captain Gareth Southgate. They have certainly had enough practice – 128 years without a major trophy of any kind. In the Premiership years, transformed by chairman Steve Gibson's personal fortune, the side has played three cup finals (the FA Cup and the League Cup in 1997 and the League Cup again the following year) and lost them all. Bolton, the other finalist, has not seen too much silverware either in recent years and, with a UEFA Cup place at stake, there was no doubting the significance of the match for both teams.

McClaren's lucky tracksuit

Neither finalist had an easy run. After seeing off Walsall and Gillingham, Bolton had to get past Liverpool, Southampton and Aston Villa, who it demolished 5-2 at home in the first leg of the semi-final. Middlesbrough came by way of Brighton, Wigan, Everton, Spurs and domestically unbeaten Arsenal. Middlesbrough began the Final like a team that had already comprehensively beaten the country's best – it tore into Bolton and was two up within seven minutes. Manager Steve McClaren missed the first goal as he was in the dressing room changing from lounge suit to lucky tracksuit. He contemplated staying there, but returned to see the slipping Zenden toe-poke a penalty home. The game went predictably haywire, hectic and scrappy. Djorkaeff missed three rapidly made chances before Kevin Davies managed to squeeze a shot home and make it 2-1. But a last-minute penalty appeal by Bolton for Ugo Ehiogu's handball aside, chances were rare. Middlesbrough's long wait was over.

Wigan sprung an early surprise, knocking Premiership side Fulham out in the Second Round. Here, Wigan's Nathan Ellington and Fulham's Martin Djetou clash.

THIRD ROUND

Arsenal **1-1** Rotherham United After extra time Arsenal won 9-8 on pens	Newcastle **1-2** West Bromwich United Albion After extra time
Aston Villa **1-0** Leicester City	Nottingham **2-4** Portsmouth Forest After extra time
Blackburn **3-4** Liverpool Rovers	QPR **0-3** Manchester City
Blackpool **1-3** Crystal Palace	Reading **1-0** Huddersfield Town
Bolton **2-0** Gillingham Wanderers	Tottenham **1-0** West Ham Hotspur United After extra time
Bristol City **0-3** Southampton	
Chelsea **4-2** Notts County	Wigan **1-2** Middlesbrough Athletic
Everton **1-0** Charlton Athletic	Wolverhampton **2-0** Burnley Wanderers
Leeds United **2-3** Manchester United After extra time	

FOURTH ROUND

Arsenal **5-1** Wolverhampton Wanderers	Reading **0-1** Chelsea
Aston Villa **3-0** Crystal Palace	Southampton **2-0** Portsmouth
Liverpool **2-3** Bolton Wanderers	Tottenham **3-1** Manchester Hotspur City
Middlesbrough **0-0** Everton After extra time Middlesbrough won 5-4 on pens	West **2-0** Manchester Bromwich United Albion

SECOND ROUND

Blackpool **1-0** Birmingham City	Middlesbrough **1-0** Brighton After extra time
Bolton **3-1** Walsall Wanderers	Notts County **2-1** Ipswich Town
Bristol City **1-0** Watford After extra time	Oxford United **1-3** Reading
Cardiff City **2-3** West Ham United	Portsmouth **5-2** Northampton Town
Charlton **4-4** Luton Town Athletic After extra time Charlton Athletic won 8-7 on pens	Rotherham **1-0** Colchester United United
	Scunthorpe Utd **2-3** Burnley
Coventry City **0-3** Tottenham Hotspur	Sheffield United **0-2** QPR
Crystal Palace **2-1** Doncaster Rovers	Stoke City **0-2** Gillingham
	Sunderland **2-4** Huddersfield Town
Everton **3-0** Stockport County	Tranmere **0-0** Nottingham Rovers Forest After extra time Nottingham Forest won 4-1 on pens
Hartlepool **1-2** West Bromwich United Albion	Wigan Athletic **1-0** Fulham
Leeds United **2-2** Swindon Town After extra time Leeds United won 4-3 on pens	Wolverhampton **2-0** Darlington Wanderers
Leicester City **1-0** Crewe Alexandra	Wycombe **0-5** Aston Villa Wanderers

Jay-Jay Okocha had a brilliant game as Bolton beats Liverpool 3-2 at Anfield in the Fourth Round.

ENGLAND

Right: Aston Villa showed its all-round improvement this season with a run to the semi-finals. Juan Pablo Angel celebrates the opening goal in the team's quarter-final victory over Chelsea.

Far right: Middlesbrough put Spurs out in the quarter-finals on penalties. Gareth Southgate takes on Tottenham's Freddie Kanoute.

Middle right: Gaizeka Mendieta slips past Arsenal's Gael Clichy and Ashley Cole as Boro completes its two-leg victory in the semi-finals.

QUARTER-FINALS

Aston Villa **2-1** Chelsea

Bolton **1-0** Southampton
Wanderers
After extra time

West Bromwich **0-2** Arsenal
Albion

Tottenham **1-1** Middlesbrough
Hotspur
After extra time
Middlesbrough won 5-4 on pens

SEMI-FINALS (2 legs)

Arsenal **0-1** Middlesbrough
(Juninho 55)

Middlesbrough **2-1** Arsenal
(Zenden 69,   (Edu 77)
Reyes o.g. 85)
Middlesbrough won 3-1
on aggregate

Bolton **5-2** Aston Villa
Wanderers   *(Angel 20, 56)*
(Okocha 2, 80,
Nolan 9,
Giannakopoulos
17, N'Gotty 74)

Aston Villa **2-0** Bolton
(Hitzlsperger 10,   Wanderers
Samuel 88)
Bolton Wanderers won
5-4 on aggregate

2003 FINAL

Feb 29 – Millennium Stadium, Cardiff
Bolton **1-2** Middlesbrough
Wanderers   *(Job 2,*
(Davies 21)   *Zenden 7 pen)*
h/t: 1-2   **Att:** 72,634
Ref: M. Riley

128 years in the making. The Middlesbrough team celebrates after its two-goal victory against Bolton. Boro had won the first-ever silverware in the club's history.

The FA Cup

TOURNAMENT REVIEW

THE STATUS OF THE FA CUP seems to be settling down. New prize money has helped the big clubs take it seriously. But, most importantly in an age of ludicrous financial and playing differentials between clubs and divisions, the one-leg, all-or-nothing cup game retains the capacity for surprise and opens paths of advancement to the most unlikely clubs. The Second Round this year was rich in non-league teams, though the majority of them – including Weston-Super-Mare, Woking, Hornchurch, Gravesend, Stevenage, Aldershot and Barnet – fell at this hurdle. The re-born Accrington Stanley, who departed the soccer league over 40 years ago, reappeared and beat Second Division Bournemouth in a penalty shootout. Scarborough lorded it over Port Vale and Telford ripped Second Division Brentford apart.

The arrival of the Premiership and First Division clubs in the Third Round always raises the casualty rate, but this year the competition was blessed with many encounters confined to top-flight clubs who, pleasingly, knocked each other out leaving the way open for others. Accrington Stanley finally departed after losing to Colchester in a replay, Kidderminster took Wolves to a second game, Tranmere Rovers overcame high-flying Bolton and Conference side Telford beat Crewe Alexandra from the First Division.

The Fourth Round was the end of the road for the real underdogs; Manchester United swept aside Northampton, Chelsea shut out Scarborough and Millwall showed great presence and composure to beat Telford away from home. But the match of the round, indeed the whole competition, was the replay between Spurs and Manchester City. Spurs, at home, were 3-0 up at half-time and City had gone down to ten men when midfielder Joey Barton was sent off for dissent. But then the impossible happened. Manchester City were on fire in the second half, Spurs wilted as all sense of composure and confidence disintegrated and City scored four times to win. They deserved better than a Fifth Round tie with Manchester United, which they lost. In the all-Premiership clashes, Portsmouth beat the faltering Liverpool, Arsenal beat Chelsea and Sunderland showed their quality in beating Birmingham 2-0 at St Andrews.

Back from the dead: *Accrington Stanley re-enter the national soccer consciousness. Andy Hollis can't believe it either.*

SECOND ROUND

Bournemouth **1-1** Accrington Stanley	Oldham **2-5** Blackpool Athletic
Replay	Peterborough **3-2** Grimsby Town United
Accrington **0-0** Bournemouth Stanley	Port Vale **0-1** Scarborough
After extra time	Rochdale **0-2** Luton Town
Accrington won 5-3 on pens	Scunthorpe **2-2** Sheffield United Wednesday
Bristol City **0-0** Barnsley	*Replay*
Replay	Sheffield **0-0** Scunthorpe
Barnsley **2-1** Bristol City	Wednesday United
Burton Albion **0-1** Hartlepool United	*After extra time*
Cheltenham **3-1** Leyton Orient Town	Scunthorpe won 3-1 on pens
Colchester United **1-0** Aldershot	Southend United **3-0** Lincoln City
Gravesend **1-2** Notts County & Northfleet	Swansea City **2-1** Stevenage Borough
Hornchurch **0-1** Tranmere Rovers	Telford **3-0** Brentford
Macclesfield **1-1** Cambridge Town United	Woking **0-3** Kidderminster Harriers
Replay	Wycombe **1-1** Mansfield Wanderers Town
Cambridge **2-2** Macclesfield United Town	*Replay*
After extra time	Mansfield **3-2** Wycombe Town Wanderers
Macclesfield won 4-2 on pens	Yeovil Town **5-1** Barnet
Northampton **4-1** Weston-super- Town Mare	

THIRD ROUND

Accrington **0-0** Colchester Stanley United	Northampton **1-1** Rotherham Town United
Replay	*Replay*
Colchester **2-1** Accrington United Stanley	Rotherham **1-2** Northampton United Town
Aston Villa **1-2** Manchester United	Nottingham **1-0** West Bromwich Forest Albion
Barnsley **0-0** Scunthorpe United	Portsmouth **2-1** Blackpool
Replay	Preston **3-3** Reading North End
Scunthorpe **2-0** Barnsley United	*Replay*
Birmingham **4-0** Blackburn City Rovers	Reading **1-2** Preston North End
Bradford City **1-2** Luton Town	Southampton **0-3** Newcastle United
Cardiff City **0-1** Sheffield United	Southend United **1-1** Scarborough
Coventry City **2-1** Peterborough United	*Replay*
Crewe **0-1** Telford United Alexandra	Scarborough **1-0** Southend United
Everton **3-1** Norwich City	Sunderland **1-0** Hartlepool United
Fulham **2-1** Cheltenham Town	Swansea City **2-1** Macclesfield Town
Gillingham **3-2** Charlton Athletic	Tottenham **3-0** Crystal Palace Hotspur
Ipswich Town **3-0** Derby County	Tranmere **1-1** Bolton Rovers Wanderers
Kidderminster **1-1** Wolverhampton Harriers Wanderers	*Replay*
Replay	Bolton **1-2** Tranmere Wanderers Rovers
Wolverhampton **2-0** Kidderminster Wanderers Harriers	*After extra time*
Leeds United **1-4** Arsenal	Watford **2-2** Chelsea
Manchester City **2-2** Leicester City	*Replay*
Replay	Chelsea **4-0** Watford
Leicester City **1-3** Manchester City	Wigan Athletic **1-2** West Ham United
Mansfield Town **0-2** Burnley	Wimbledon **1-1** Stoke City
Middlesbrough **2-0** Notts County	*Replay*
Millwall **2-1** Walsall	Stoke City **0-1** Wimbledon
	Yeovil Town **0-2** Liverpool

FOURTH ROUND

Arsenal **4-1** Middlesbrough	Manchester **1-1** Tottenham City Hotspur
Birmingham **1-0** Wimbledon City	*Replay*
Burnley **3-1** Gillingham	Tottenham **3-4** Manchester Hotspur City
Coventry City **1-1** Colchester United	Northampton **0-3** Manchester Town United
Replay Colchester United **3-1** Coventry City	Nottingham **0-3** Sheffield Forest United
Everton **1-1** Fulham	Portsmouth **2-1** Scunthorpe United
Replay Fulham **2-1** Everton *After extra time*	Scarborough **0-1** Chelsea
Ipswich Town **1-2** Sunderland	Swansea City **2-1** Preston North End
Liverpool **2-1** Newcastle United	Telford United **0-2** Millwall
Luton Town **0-1** Tranmere Rovers	Wolverhampton **1-3** West Ham Wanderers United

FIFTH ROUND

Arsenal **2-1** Chelsea	Millwall **1-0** Burnley
Fulham **0-0** West Ham United	Sheffield **1-0** Colchester United United
Replay West Ham **0-3** Fulham United	Sunderland **1-1** Birmingham City
Liverpool **1-1** Portsmouth	*Replay* Birmingham **0-2** Sunderland City
Replay Portsmouth **1-0** Liverpool	Tranmere **2-1** Swansea City Rovers
Manchester **4-2** Manchester United City	

Below: Comeback of the year? Manchester City's Jonathan Macken heads the winner in City's Fourth Round replay thriller against Spurs.

Below, middle: John Terry scores for Chelsea and Scarborough's FA Cup adventure is over in the Fourth Round.

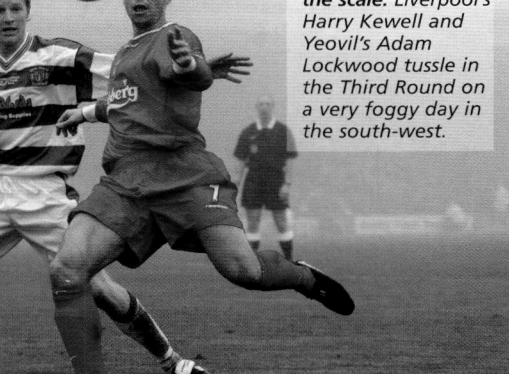

The groundstaff at Telford try to keep the rain off as their Fourth Round clash with Milwall is cancelled again.

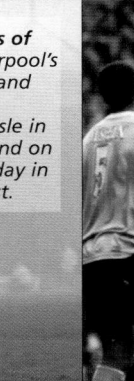

Opposite ends of the scale. Liverpool's Harry Kewell and Yeovil's Adam Lockwood tussle in the Third Round on a very foggy day in the south-west.

A rare goal for Paul Scholes, but it proved the opening shot in United's 4-2 defeat of City in their Fifth Round derby.

THE QUARTER-FINALS

Fate delivered a form of positive discrimination in the quarter-finals with four Premiership teams playing each other and four First Division teams playing each other, guaranteeing two of each in the semis. Millwall finally overcame Tranmere in an epic two-game battle to take the club's first semi-final place since 1937. In one of the most exhilarating displays of the season Arsenal thrashed Portsmouth 5-1. Sunderland got the better of last year's semi-finalists Sheffield United while Manchester United dispensed with Fulham; a brace of goals from van Nistelrooy was enough to counteract Malbranque's early penalty.

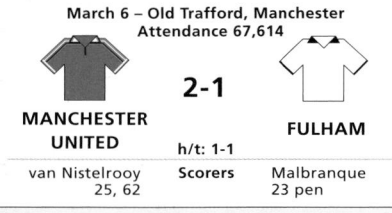

March 6 – Old Trafford, Manchester
Attendance 67,614

MANCHESTER UNITED **2-1** **FULHAM**
h/t: 1-1

| van Nistelrooy 25, 62 | Scorers | Malbranque 23 pen |

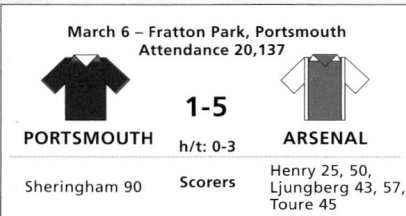

March 6 – Fratton Park, Portsmouth
Attendance 20,137

PORTSMOUTH **1-5** **ARSENAL**
h/t: 0-3

| Sheringham 90 | Scorers | Henry 25, 50, Ljungberg 43, 57, Toure 45 |

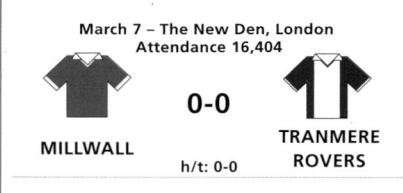

March 7 – The New Den, London
Attendance 16,404

MILLWALL **0-0** **TRANMERE ROVERS**
h/t: 0-0

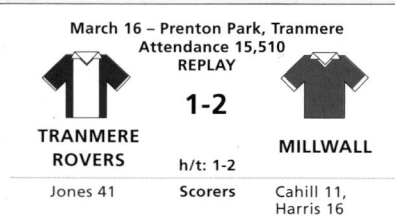

March 16 – Prenton Park, Tranmere
Attendance 15,510
REPLAY

TRANMERE ROVERS **1-2** **MILLWALL**
h/t: 1-2

| Jones 41 | Scorers | Cahill 11, Harris 16 |

March 7 – Stadium of Light, Sunderland
Attendance 37,115

SUNDERLAND **1-0** **SHEFFIELD UNITED**
h/t: 1-0

| Smith 15 | Scorers | |

THE SEMI-FINALS

The semi-finals threw up two brilliantly matched contests, both settled by a single first-half goal. In the battle of the First Division Sunderland faced Millwall and Tim Cahill's strike took the Londoners to their first ever FA Cup Final and, with Manchester United in the Champions League, a guaranteed place in the UEFA Cup. In the Premiership battle Arsenal faced Manchester United days after Chelsea had knocked them out of the Champions League. Amazingly, Arsenal started without Thierry Henry. They made and squandered chances in the first half hour: Dennis Bergkamp hit the bar and Kolo Toure saw a shot cleared off the line. They proved to be expensive misses and a single goal from Paul Scholes was enough to give United the win despite the late entry of both Henry and Reyes into the Arsenal attack.

April 3 – Villa Park, Birmingham
Attendance 39,939
Ref: Graham Barber

ARSENAL **0-1** **MANCHESTER UNITED**
h/t: 0-1

| | Scorers | Scholes 32 |

April 4 – Old Trafford, Manchester
Attendance 56,112
Ref: Paul Durkin

SUNDERLAND **0-1** **MILLWALL**
h/t: 0-1

| | Scorers | Cahill 26 |

Tim Cahill's goal against Sunderland took Millwall to their first ever FA Cup Final.

THE FINAL

The Final, pitching Manchester United against Millwall, recalled the similarly mismatched game between Liverpool and Wimbledon in 1988. Wimbledon won the game 1-0 and the team included Dennis Wise, the Millwall player manager, at the very start of his career. But 2004 was not to be a repeat. Millwall defended very deeply and effectively for 40 minutes. But, without an effective outlet up front, Manchester United retained possession and piled on the pressure. With a minute to go before half-time, Cristiano Ronaldo transformed the game, heading in from two metres from a Gary Neville cross. Millwall, despite immense support, could not get back in it. Livermore fouled the flying Ryan Giggs in the penalty area and van Nistelrooy made it 2-0 from the spot. His second goal a few minutes later was almost redundant.

Manchester United's *Cristiano Ronaldo heads the first goal just before half time.*

The Starting Line-Up

**May 22 – Millennium Stadium, Cardiff
Attendance 71,350**

MANCHESTER UNITED

Formation: 4-4-2

Manager

Sir Alex Ferguson

Substitutes

Carroll (13)

P. Neville (3)

Butt (8)

Djemba-Djemba (19)

Solskjaer (20)

Referee
Jeff Winter

MILLWALL

Formation: 4-5-1

Manager

Dennis Wise

Substitutes

(13) Gueret

(27) Dunne

(37) Cogan

(23) McCammon

(11) Weston

Manchester United's goalscorers Ruud van Nistelrooy and Cristiano Ronaldo celebrate with the FA Cup.

FA Cup first goal

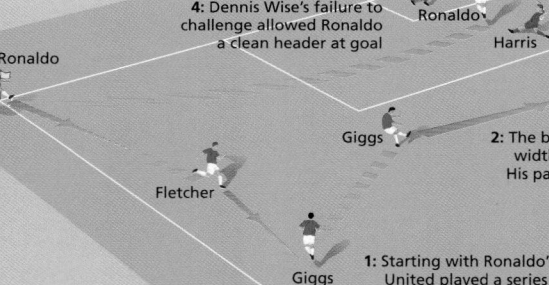

1: Starting with Ronaldo's corner, United played a series of short passes between Ronaldo, Fletcher and Giggs

2: The ball travelled right across the width of the pitch to Roy Keane. His pass sent Gary Neville running towards the byline

3: Neville's cross was perfectly flighted for Ronaldo who had made his way into the penalty area

4: Dennis Wise's failure to challenge allowed Ronaldo a clean header at goal

Highlights of the Game

KEY

Player booked — 🟦 | 🔄 — Substitution

Goal — ⚽

MANCHESTER UNITED

KICK OFF
0 mins

MILLWALL

5 min: United's first proper chance, van Nistelrooy heads wide from a Ronaldo cross

20 min: Livermore manages to break up a threatening attack by Fletcher and Scholes

22 min: Keane's volley from outside the area, just tipped over the crossbar

25 min: Milwall's first corner of the game

38 min: Ifill's first decent run into the box, but he shoots straight at Silvestre

41 min: Ronaldo's close range shot parried by Marshall and cleared off the line by Ward

43 min: Ronaldo heads home from 2 metres, on the end of a Gary Neville cross

45 mins
HALF-TIME: **1-0**

60 min: Dennis Wise booked after a wild tackle with studs showing on Ryan Giggs

64 min: Ryan Giggs goes on a brilliant run into the box. Brought down by Livermore. Van Nistelrooy steps up to blast the penalty home

65 min: Ryan and Harris off, Cogan and McCammon on

75 min: Wise off, Weston on

81 min: Giggs crosses behind the Millwall defence and van Nistelrooy is there to pounce on it and score

84 min: Ronaldo, Fletcher, Howard off: Solskjaer, Butt, Carrol on

90 mins

FULL-TIME: **3-0**

ENGLAND

The Origins of Soccer

THE ORIGINS OF SOCCER

THE IRRESISTIBLE URGE of children to kick things, and the general availability of round objects in the world, suggest that people have been playing some version of soccer since the beginning of history. Chinese archeologists have found stone balls from the Neolithic era (around 10,000 BC), and have claimed China to be the home of the global game. Reports from South America suggest that access to rubber in the Amazonian rainforest gave the region its head start in ball skills and control. Certainly there is evidence of various ball and kicking games among the indigenous Indian civilizations of Patagonia and the Andes.

Stronger records exist for a game called Tsu Chu played under the Han Empire of China (206 BC–221 AD), which spread into Japan and Korea with local variations and names. A stuffed animal-skin ball was kicked between large bamboo posts; some accounts suggest that it formed part of festivities, others that it was an element of military training. Frescoes from the era clearly indicate women playing the game.

Li Yu, a Chinese writer (c. 50–130 AD), wrote a eulogy to the game, which was intended to be hung on the goalposts:

> A round ball and a square goal
> Suggest the shape of the Yin and the Yang.
> The ball is like the full moon,
> And the two teams stand opposed:
> Captains are appointed and take their place.
> In the game make no allowance for relationship
> And let there be no partiality.
> Determination and coolness are essential
> And there must not be the slightest irritation for failure.
> Such is the game. Let its principles apply to life.

Folk football in Europe

Evidence of folk football in Europe dates from around the beginning of the second millennium. A variety of ball games were played by the Celtic periphery of Europe, such as Knappan in Wales and the game of Ba' in the Orkney Islands. First-hand reports from the 11th and 12th centuries mention a game called *La Soule*, popular among the peasantry of medieval Brittany and northern France, while a distinctive rule-bound game called *Calcio* was played by the ruling elites of Florence from the 16th century. But it is in England that the most regular and systematic reports of soccer come in the medieval period. William Fitzstephen, living in London between 1170 and 1183, wrote:

'After dinner all the youth of the city goes out into the fields for the very popular game of ball. The elders, the fathers and the men of wealth come on horseback to view the contests of their juniors.'

What the game of 'ball' seems to have consisted of was a very tough, often violent, unstructured brawling game in which two ill-defined and often ill-matched mobs moved a ball

Calcio, or Giuoco del calcio Fiorentino, was played in Florence and other parts of Northern Italy from the 16th century. This fresco by Giovanni Stradano, painted in 1555, shows a game in progress in the city's Piazza Santa Maria Novella.

The Origins of Soccer

		WALES	ORKNEY	ENGLAND
ENGLAND	Location	Knappan	ISLANDS	Mob or
Mob or	Early form	(1000)	**Ba'**	**folk football**
folk football	of soccer		(1000)	(1100)
(1100)	Approximate date			

WALES **Knappan** (1000)
ORKNEY ISLANDS **Ba'** (1000)
ENGLAND **Mob or folk football** (1100)
FRANCE (Brittany) **Soule** (1100)
ITALY **Giuoco del calcio Fiorentino** (1500) **Harpastum** (200 BC)
GREECE **Episkyros** (200 BC)
NORTH AMERICA **Passuckquakkohowog** (17th century)
MEXICO **Pok-ta-pok** (800 BC)
CHILE **Pilimatum** (1500 BC)
PATAGONIA **Tchoekah**

Passuckquakkohowog. This Native American word literally translates as 'those who gather to play football'. The earliest written reports of the game in North America come from 17th century English pilgrims.

Although a rudimentary form of soccer called Episkyros could be found in Classical Greece, it was of low status – the domain of women and children. No ball game was allowed into the prestigious ancient Olympic Games.

This ring is found on the wall of the Ball Court at the Mayan temple at Chichen-Itza in Mexico. Pok-ta-pok was just one of many games played by American Indians before the European conquest, along with Pilimatum in Chile and Tchoekah in Patagonia.

Though no codified forms of African soccer have been recorded, the San people of southern Africa played a vertical kickabout game. Modern soccer spread like wildfire during the colonization of the continent in the late 19th and early 20th centuries. This batik shows a game in contemporary Uganda.

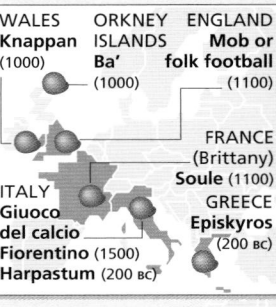

A 19th-century engraving of mob or folk football, England.

to some specified location by almost any means, and any limb, available. Reports abound of serious injuries and accidental stabbings, even deaths, during these games. More worrying for local elites, these games often led to, or turned into, acts of major social disturbance and riot. Not surprisingly, Edward II, King of England, issued a proclamation in 1314 banning the game, claiming that there was 'great uproar in the city through certain tumults arising from great footballs in the fields of the public, from which many evils may arise'. The ban was repeated in 1331 and 1365 in the hope of encouraging more archery, but without success.

Derby day

Shrove Tuesday was a particularly popular day for rural soccer matches – the game played in Derby between the parishes of St. Peter and All Saints was notorious for its unrestrained ferocity, and gave birth to the term for fiercely fought local contests – derbies. In the cities, soccer often accompanied rites of passage for journeymen and apprentices. An observer in 18th-century London wrote:

> *I spy the furies of the football war*
> *The Prentice quits his shop,*
> *To join the crew,*
> *Increasing crowds the flying*
> *Game pursue...*

These Chinese characters mean 'to kick with the foot' and 'a ball made of leather ... to allow it to be kicked around for recreation'.

足
球

JAPAN
Kemari
(400)

CHINA
Cuju or Tsu Chu
(200 BC)

Kemari, a Japanese variant of a Chinese ball game, was played from around the 5th century AD.

A fierce game called La Soule was popular in Normandy and Brittany in France during the 11th and 12th centuries.

Yet despite ruling class disapproval of folk football, it had begun to find a home in the schools and universities of England. Reports of soccer at Oxford and Cambridge date from the 16th century.

By the beginning of the 19th century, team sports had been enthusiastically adopted by England's elite public schools as an essential element of the practical and moral education of the ruling class. Soccer in a variety of forms and with a variety of rules was the predominant sport. Simultaneously, folk and mob football were in decline as the congested spaces and stricter policing of modern industrial cities made the game increasingly difficult to play. It would eventually disappear altogether, to be replaced by a game with fixed rules derived from the public school game *(see pages 26–27).*

The Global Game

CODIFICATION AND SPREAD

IN 19TH-CENTURY ENGLAND, there was no shortage of rules for the game of soccer. The elite public schools had embraced team sports as an essential component of ruling-class character formation, and each had created rules that suited their environment. Harrow's heavy ball favoured dribbling, while Winchester's narrow pitch suited kick and rush, and Westminster's cloisters the short pass. These rules collided when old boys played each other at university, so common soccer rules were drafted in 1846 at Cambridge University. A revised version of these rules formed the basis of the rules drawn up in 1863 by the newly created Football Association and representatives of 12 London clubs. The only dissenters from the rules were Blackheath, who opted to retain handling and hacking; they went on to play the newly codified game of rugby union in 1871.

In the English-speaking world local variations produced codified rules for American, Australian, Canadian and Gaelic soccer. Armed with the FA rules, an empire and the world's biggest trading network, Britons of every social class carried the game to Europe and the Americas. Sailors played in the ports of Chile and Germany, textile workers in the Netherlands, public schoolboy merchants in Rio and Barcelona. In Britain's formal Empire, in Asia and Africa, the colonial power was more reticent to spread the game, fearing the anti-colonial social organization that might emerge from soccer.

Caged into the tighter spaces of an urban environment, rural folk football acquired the rudiments of organized play, such as goals and duration, but violence and injury remained regular features of the game.

The global spread of soccer 1850–1930

Significant migrant communities playing soccer

- British
- Armenian
- French
- Spanish
- Greek
- Jewish

Date of formation of national Football Association

- By 1899
- 1900–39
- 1940–79
- After 1980

Reason for spread
(British, unless noted)

- Banking
- Cricket clubs
- Education
- Gymnastics
- Industrialists and workers
- Military
- Mining
- Missionaries
- Oil workers
- Railways
- Shipping
- Trading

Competing sports

- Football a minor sport
- American sports
- Australian Rules
- Cricket
- Gaelic football
- Ice hockey
- Rugby
- Tennis

The Evolution of Soccer

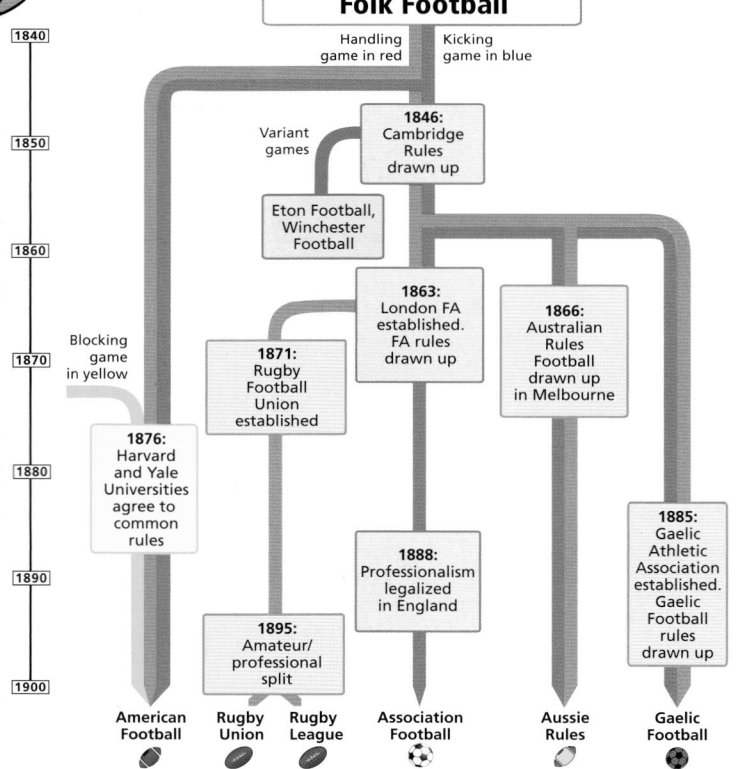

Folk Football

Handling game in red Kicking game in blue

1840

Variant games

1850

1846: Cambridge Rules drawn up

Eton Football, Winchester Football

1860

Blocking game in yellow

1863: London FA established. FA rules drawn up

1866: Australian Rules Football drawn up in Melbourne

1871: Rugby Football Union established

1870

1876: Harvard and Yale Universities agree to common rules

1880

1885: Gaelic Athletic Association established. Gaelic Football rules drawn up

1888: Professionalism legalized in England

1890

1895: Amateur/ professional split

1900

American Football Rugby Union Rugby League Association Football Aussie Rules Gaelic Football

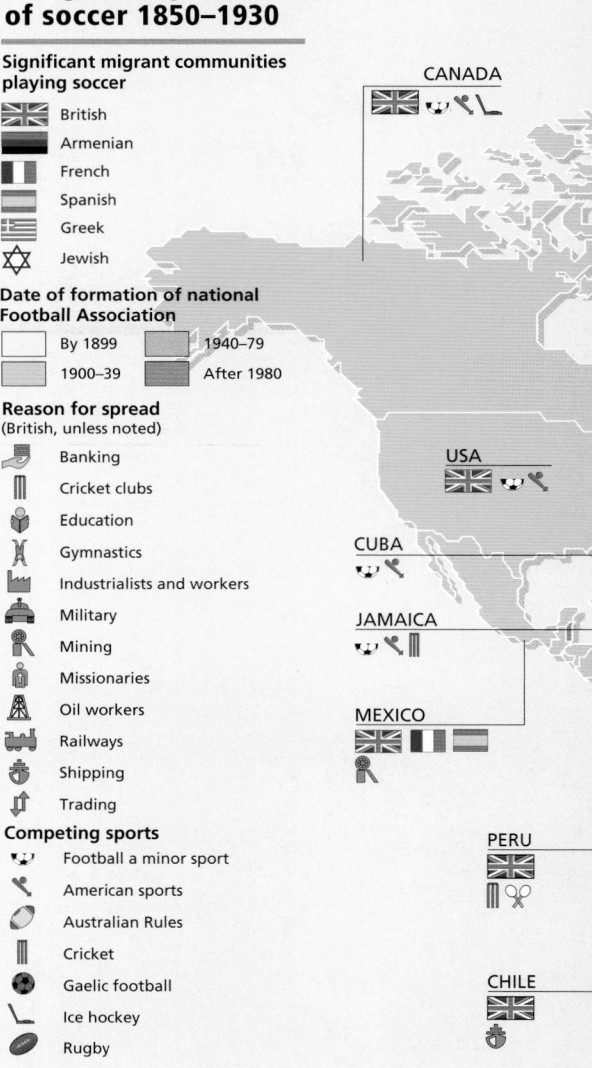

CANADA

USA

CUBA

JAMAICA

MEXICO

PERU

CHILE

Codification of the Rules

Shrewsbury
Birmingham
Rugby
E N G L A N D
Cambridge
Cambridge Rules
drawn up in 1846
and revised in 1863
Oxford
Harrow
Eton **Westminster**
Marlborough
London
FA founded
and rules
drawn up
in 1863
Charterhouse
Winchester

A competing set of rules was
established by Sheffield FC,
founded in 1857. The Sheffield
FA, innovators in the use of
free kicks and corner kicks,
brought its rules into line
with the FA in 1877.

Key

Cambridge University

Public school represented
at the rewriting of the
Cambridge Rules in 1863

Other public school

School with own rules

Rugby rules

Clubs involved in the formation of FA in 1863

Barnes
Blackheath (later withdrew)
Blackheath School
Charterhouse
Crusaders
Crystal Palace
Forest
Kensington School
No Names of Kilburn
Percival House
Surbiton
The War Office

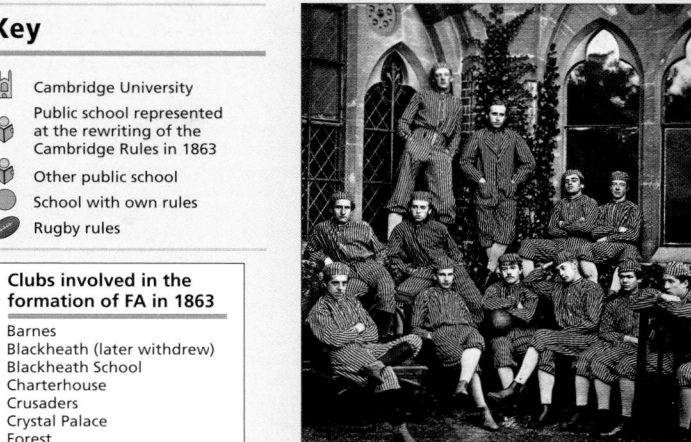

*Harrow School Soccer XI 1867.
Harrow's poorly drained fields
required a heavy leather ball and
encouraged dribbling rather than
hoofing the ball up the pitch.*

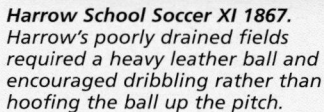

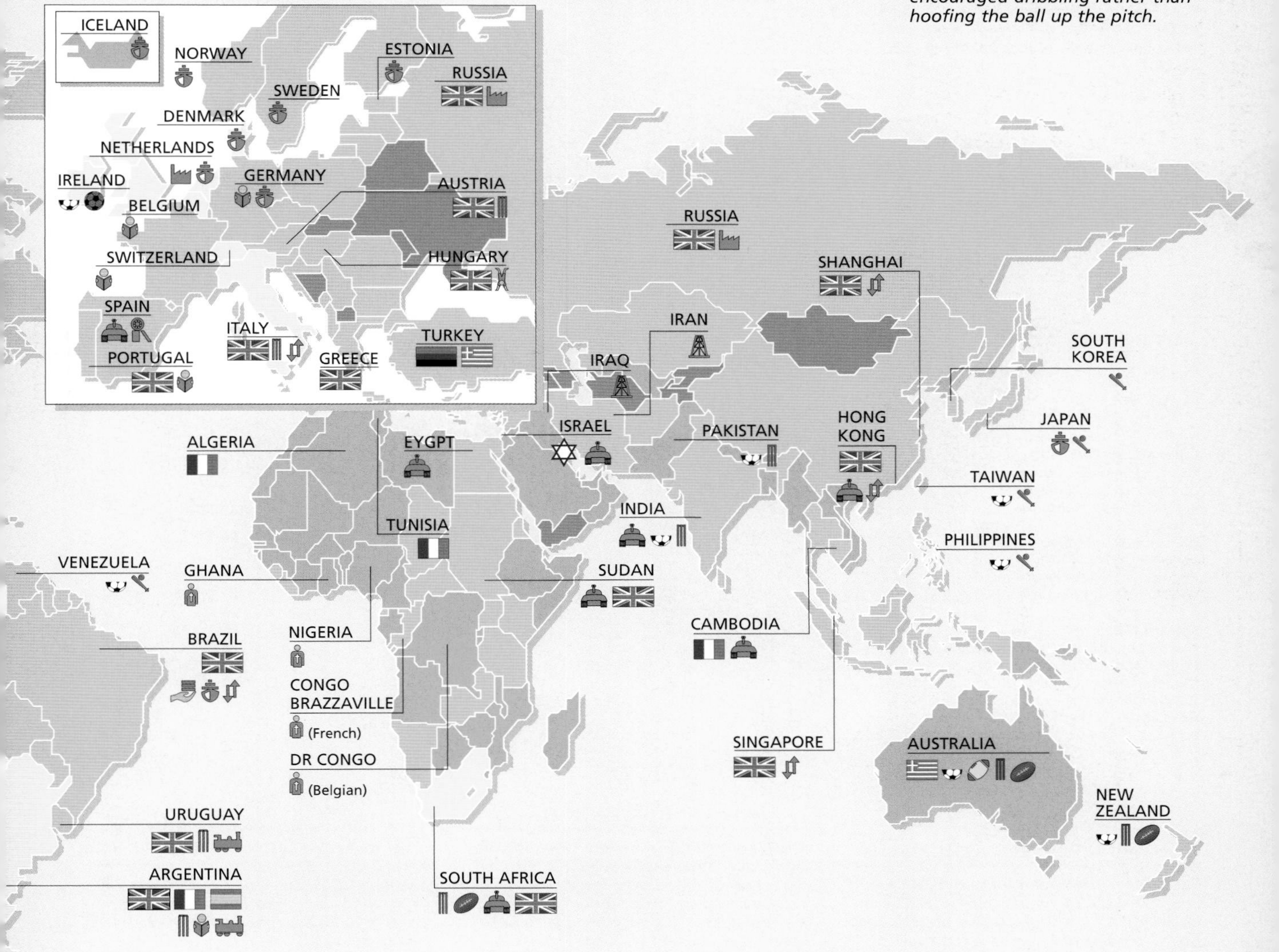

ICELAND
NORWAY
ESTONIA
RUSSIA
SWEDEN
DENMARK
NETHERLANDS
IRELAND
GERMANY
AUSTRIA
BELGIUM
SWITZERLAND
HUNGARY
SPAIN
ITALY
PORTUGAL
GREECE
TURKEY

RUSSIA
SHANGHAI
IRAN
SOUTH
KOREA
IRAQ
JAPAN
ISRAEL
PAKISTAN
HONG
KONG
TAIWAN
ALGERIA
EYGPT
PHILIPPINES
INDIA
TUNISIA
VENEZUELA
GHANA
SUDAN
BRAZIL
NIGERIA
CAMBODIA
CONGO
BRAZZAVILLE
(French)
DR CONGO
SINGAPORE
AUSTRALIA
(Belgian)
URUGUAY
NEW
ZEALAND
ARGENTINA
SOUTH AFRICA

The Laws of the Game

LAW I: FIELD OF PLAY

The field of play must be a rectangle of specific size (see diagram for length). The field must have clear lines marked on it: touchlines, goal lines, halfway line, centre circle, goal areas, goal area lines, goals, penalty areas, penalty spots, corner arcs and flagposts.

LAW II: BALL

The ball must be made of an approved material. At the start of the match the ball must be 68–70 cm in diameter, 410–450 grams in weight, and have an internal pressure of 0.6–1.1 atmospheres at sea level. It can only be changed by the referee. If the ball bursts during a game, play stops and restarts with a drop ball.

LAW III: PLAYERS

A match consists of two teams of not more than 11 players each including a goalkeeper. Any outfield player may change places with the goalkeeper during a stoppage. Teams need at least seven players to begin a game.

LAW V: REFEREE

The referee is the final arbiter on the interpretation and enforcement of the laws. They decide whether a game can be played and the duration of play. They can suspend and abandon a match, stop play to allow treatment of injured players, caution players (yellow card) for a range of misconduct and fouls or send off a player (red card) for serious foul play, violent conduct, offensive language and for two cautions. Referees make sure all equipment meets the relevant specifications and keeps a record of the match. They have a duty to allow play to flow and refrain from punishing insignificant or non-deliberate infringements.

LAW VI: ASSISTANT REFEREES

Formerly called the linesmen, the assistant referees help the referee primarily by signalling corner kicks, goal kicks, throw-ins and offsides. However, the referee's word is final.

LAW VIII: START & RESTART OF PLAY

Before the start of play a coin is tossed. The winning team chooses ends for the first half and the losing team takes the kick-off. This is reversed in the second half. Play begins after the referee has signalled. The kick-off is taken from the centre spot and the ball must move into the opposition's half of the field. All players must be in their half of the field and opposition players must be at least ten yards from the ball. The ball must be touched by another player before the kicker can touch it again.

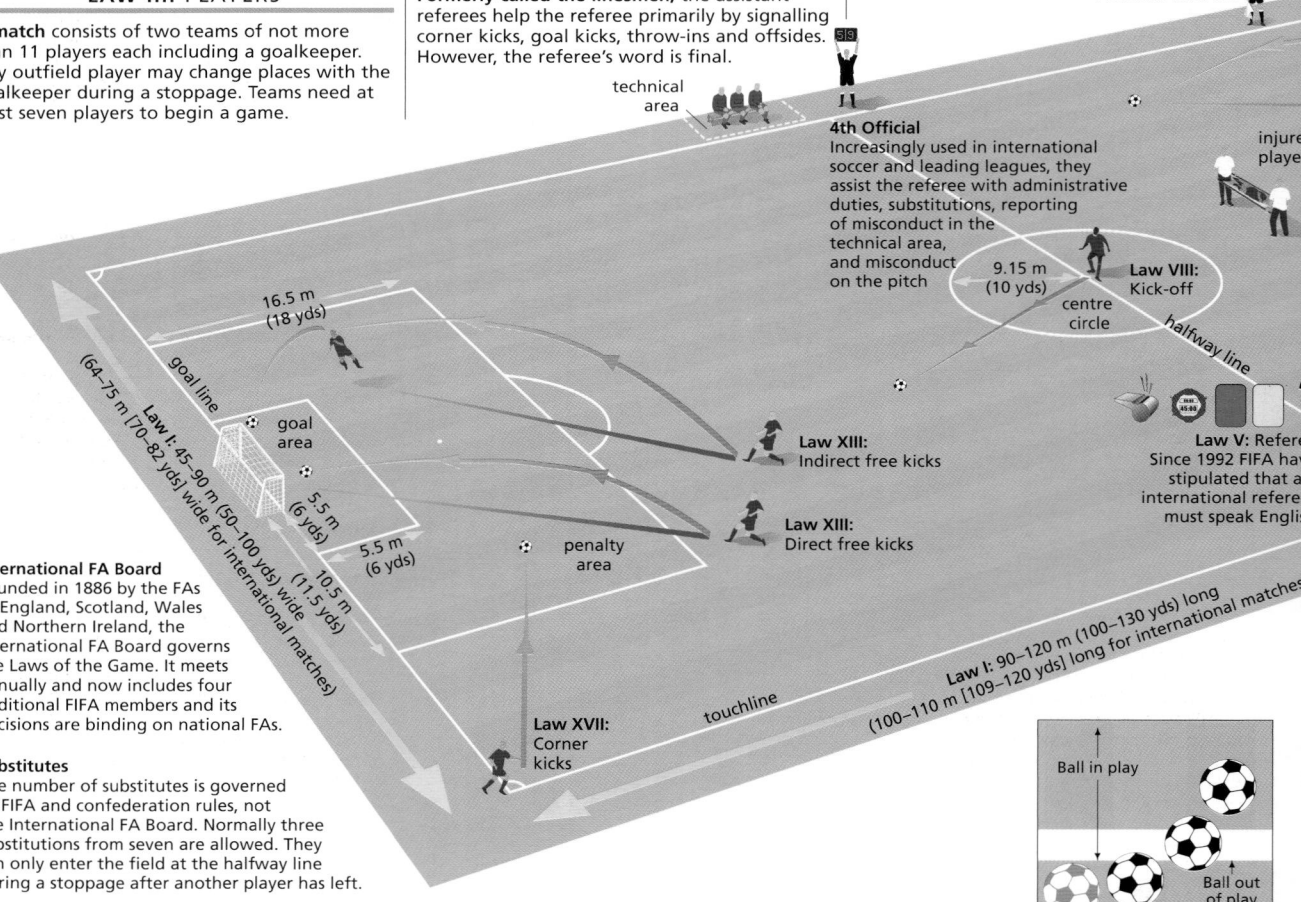

technical area

Law VI: Assistant referees

4th Official Increasingly used in international soccer and leading leagues, they assist the referee with administrative duties, substitutions, reporting of misconduct in the technical area, and misconduct on the pitch

injured player

9.15 m (10 yds)

Law VIII: Kick-off

centre circle

halfway line

16.5 m (18 yds)

goal line

goal area

5.5 m (6 yds)

10.5 m (11.5 yds)

5.5 m (6 yds)

penalty area

Law XIII: Indirect free kicks

Law XIII: Direct free kicks

Law V: Referee Since 1992 FIFA have stipulated that all international referees must speak English

Law I: 45–90 m (50–100 yds) wide (64–75 m [70–82 yds] wide for international matches)

Law XVII: Corner kicks

touchline

Law I: 90–120 m (100–130 yds) long (100–110 m [109–120 yds] long for international matches)

International FA Board
Founded in 1886 by the FAs of England, Scotland, Wales and Northern Ireland, the International FA Board governs the Laws of the Game. It meets annually and now includes four additional FIFA members and its decisions are binding on national FAs.

Substitutes
The number of substitutes is governed by FIFA and confederation rules, not the International FA Board. Normally three substitutions from seven are allowed. They can only enter the field at the halfway line during a stoppage after another player has left.

Ball in play

Ball out of play

LAW IV: PLAYERS' EQUIPMENT

Compulsory equipment for players are a shirt, shorts, socks, shin-guards and football boots. Goalkeepers must wear kit that distinguishes them from outfield players and officials.

LAW VII: DURATION OF PLAY

There are two equal periods of 45 minutes. Additional time may be added at the discretion of the referee for injuries, time-wasting and substitutions. Time can also be added to allow a penalty to be taken after the end of normal play.

LAW IX: IN & OUT OF PLAY

The game is in play when the ball is inside the field of play and the referee has not stopped play. The ball is out of play when the whole ball, whether in the air or on the ground, has crossed either touchlines or goal lines.

LAW X: SCORING

A goal has been scored when the whole of the ball has crossed the goal line between the goalposts and under the crossbar, provided no other infringements have taken place. The team with the most goals wins.

LAW XI: OFFSIDE

Offside is an illegal playing position taken up by a player relative to the ball, the field of play and opposition players at the moment when the ball is played by an attacking teammate. A player is offside when **a)** they are in the opposition's half of the field, **b)** they are closer to the opponent's goal line than the ball and **c)** there are fewer than two defenders, including the goalkeeper, who are closer to the goal line than the attacking player. A player will be penalized for being offside if they are interfering with play or with an opponent and they can gain some advantage from being in that position.

The Offside Rule

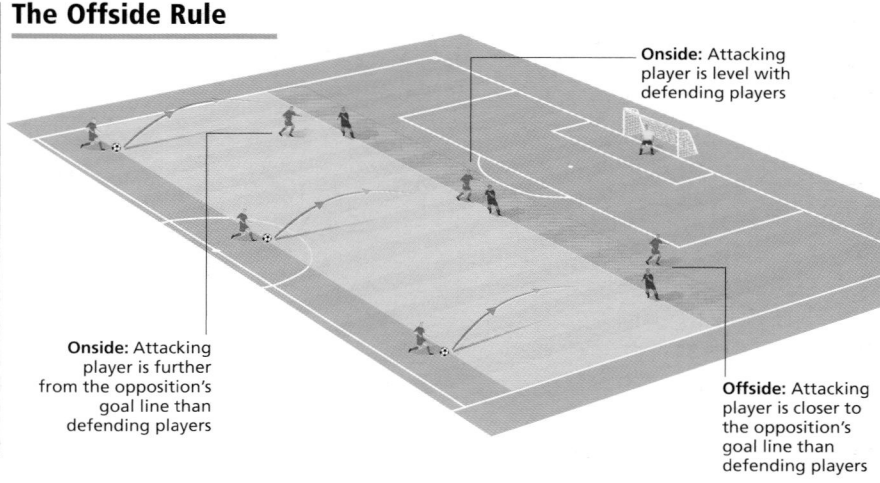

Onside: Attacking player is level with defending players

Onside: Attacking player is further from the opposition's goal line than defending players

Offside: Attacking player is closer to the opposition's goal line than defending players

Extra Time

00:00
45:00

Determined by the rules of the competition, but usually two periods of 15 minutes play after normal time where the scores are level. If the score remains level this often extends to a penalty shootout. In some competitions the 'golden goal' rule is applied to extra time. This means that during the period of extra time, the team which scores the first goal is declared the winner.

Law XVI: Goal kicks

Law XIV: Penalty kicks First introduced in 1891

penalty area

goalpost 2.44 m (2.67 yds)

Crossbar 7.32 m (8 yds) A cross tape was originally introduced between the posts by the FA in 1886.

penalty spot

corner arc

corner flag

Law XV: Throw-ins

Law VI: Assistant referees First introduced as linesmen in 1891

LAW XIII: FREE KICKS

Free kicks restart play after the game has been stopped for a foul or another act of misconduct. The referee will award the team which did not commit the offence with a direct free kick (from which a goal can be scored) or an indirect free kick (where the ball must touch another player before a goal can be scored). A free kick is usually taken from the point at which the offence was committed.

LAW XIV: PENALTY KICKS

A penalty is awarded for a foul by a defending player inside their own penalty area. A penalty kick is taken from the penalty spot. All other players, apart from the goalkeeper and penalty taker, must be at least ten yards from the spot and on the field of play. The ball is in play as soon as it is kicked. The penalty taker may touch the ball if it rebounds from the goalkeeper but not if it rebounds from the post or crossbar. Other players may touch the ball in that situation. The goalkeeper must face the penalty taker and stand on the goal line.

LAW XV: THROW-INS

A throw-in is awarded to a team when the ball has crossed the touchline and an opposition player was the last to touch it. The throw-in is taken from the point where the ball crossed the touchline. The taker must have both feet on the ground, use two hands, throw the ball from behind and over the head and be facing the field of play.

LAW XVI: GOAL KICKS

A goal kick is awarded to the defending team when the ball crosses its goal line, a goal has not been scored, and the last player to touch the ball was from the attacking team. Any player may take the goal kick by placing it within the team's own penalty area. The kick must go outside the penalty area or be retaken. The taker must not touch the ball again until another player has touched it. Opposition players must remain outside the penalty area while the kick is taken. A goal may be scored directly from a goal kick.

LAW XVII: CORNER KICKS

A corner kick is awarded to the attacking team when the ball was last touched by a member of the defending team and crosses its goal line without a goal being scored. A corner kick is also awarded if the ball enters the goal from a throw-in or an indirect free kick. The attacking team restarts the game with the ball placed in the corner arc nearest to where the ball crossed the goal line. Defending players must be at least 10 yards from the ball when it is kicked. The corner taker may not touch the ball after the corner kick until another player has touched it.

LAW XII: FOULS AND MISCONDUCT

A foul is committed if a player **(1)** trips, kicks, pushes, recklessly charges or uses excessive force against another player; **(2)** strikes, attempts to strike, or spits at an opponent; **(3)** makes a tackle but connects with their opponent before the ball; **(4)** deliberately handles the ball (except for goalkeepers inside their penalty area); **(5, 6)** obstructs an opponent or prevents the goalkeeper from releasing the ball. Goalkeepers commit a foul if they: fail to release the ball within six seconds of picking it up; release the ball into play and then handle it; handle a backpass or a throw-in from a teammate; or are guilty of time-wasting. An indirect free kick is awarded for the above.

FIFA and the Confederations

FIFA

**Fédération Internationale
de Football Association**
Founded: 1904
Headquarters: Zurich, Switzerland
President: Joseph Sepp Blatter (Switzerland)
General Secretary: Urs Linsi (Switzerland)
Members: 204
Competitions: World Cup
Women's World Cup
Under-17 World Championship
World Youth Championship
Club World Championship
Confederation's Cup
Awards: FIFA World Player of the Year
FIFA World Team of the Year
FIFA Fair Play Award

**NORTH &
CENTRAL AMERICA**
DOM REP DOMINICAN
REPUBLIC
NETH ANT NETHERLANDS
ANTILLES

CONCACAF

Founded: 1961
Headquarters: New York, USA
President: Jack Austin Warner
(Trinidad & Tobago)
General Secretary: Chuck Blazer (USA)
Members: 35
Competitions: CONCACAF Gold Cup
CONCACAF Women's
Gold Cup
CONCACAF
Champions Cup

**FIFA (FÉDÉRATION INTERNATIONALE DE FOOTBALL
ASSOCIATION)** is the global governing body of soccer. From its
headquarters in Switzerland it organizes and promotes the World
Cup, the Women's World Cup and a range of other tournaments
and prizes, as well as setting the legal and institutional framework
for global soccer. Founded in 1904 by representatives of seven
European nations, FIFA's early years were marked by struggles with
both the British soccer associations and other competing
international soccer groupings. The British nations in particular
were slow to join, reflecting both insecurity and indifference.
They were also quick to leave after the First World War when the
admission of Germany to FIFA was agreed. Similarly, the British
Home Countries remained individually represented on the
international rule-making Association Football Board, while FIFA
represented the rest of the world. Once the British had left and
the French visionary Jules Rimet had assumed the presidency, FIFA's
growth began. With the successful creation of the World Cup in
1930, FIFA's control of the global game was secured.

The confederations that make up FIFA vary widely: from the
fearsomely powerful UEFA to the marginal OFC (Oceanic Football
Confederation). All nations get a single vote at FIFA's biennial
conferences, but as usual, in the real corridors of power,
money and contacts talk.

SOUTH AMERICA
VENEZ VENEZUELA

CONMEBOL

**Confederación
Sudamericana de Fútbol**
Founded: 1916
Headquarters: Asunción, Paraguay
President: Dr Nicolas Leóz
(Paraguay)
General Secretary: Eduardo Deluca
(Argentina)
Members: 10
Competitions: Copa América
Copa Libertadores
Copa Sudamericana

UEFA

Union of European Football Associations

Founded: 1954
Headquarters: Nyon, Switzerland
President: Lennart Johansson (Sweden)
General Secretary: Lars-Christer Olsson (Denmark)
Members: 52
Competitions: European Championships
European Champions League
UEFA Cup
Intertoto Cup
European Super Cup
European Women's Championships

EUROPE
ARM ARMENIA
AUS AUSTRIA
AZER AZERBAIJAN
BEL BELGIUM
B-H BOSNIA-HERZEGOVINA
CZ REP CZECH REPUBLIC
ISR ISRAEL
LIECH LIECHTENSTEIN
LUX LUXEMBOURG
NETH NETHERLANDS
REP OF IRELAND REPUBLIC OF IRELAND
S&M SERBIA & MONTENEGRO
SWITZ SWITZERLAND

FIFA and the Confederations

☆ FIFA presidents
☐ FIFA headquarters
■ Confederation headquarters
⊙ Associate members
○ Non-members

Date of joining FIFA

	UEFA	CONMEBOL	CAF	AFC	OFC	CONCACAF
1900–20	⊙	⊙	⊙	■	⊙	⊙
1921–40	⊙	⊙	⊙	⊙	⊙	⊙
1941–60	⊙	⊙	⊙	⊙	⊙	⊙
1961–80	⊙	⊙	⊙	⊙	⊙	⊙
1981–present	☐	⊙	⊙	⊙	☐	⊙

AFC

Asian Football Confederation

Founded: 1954
Headquarters: Kuala Lumpur, Malaysia
President: Mohammed Bin Hammam (Qatar)
General Secretary: Peter Dato' Velappan (Malaysia)
Members: 44
Competitions: Asian Cup
Asian Games
Asian Champions League
Asian Women's Championship

ASIA
AFGHAN AFGHANISTAN
JOR JORDAN
LEB LEBANON
PAL PALESTINE
TAJ TAJIKISTAN
TURK TURKMENISTAN
UZBEK UZBEKISTAN

AFRICA
BF BURKINA FASO
CI CÔTE D'IVOIRE

CAF

Confédération Africaine de Football

Founded: 1957
Headquarters: Cairo, Eygpt
President: Issa Hayatou (Cameroon)
General Secretary: Mustapha Fahmy (Egypt)
Members: 52
Associate Members: 1
Competitions: African Cup of Nations
African Champions League
African Confederations Cup
CAF Super Cup

OFC

Oceania Football Confederation

Founded: 1966
Headquarters: Auckland, New Zealand
President: Reynald Temarii (Tahiti)
General Secretary: Tai Nicholas (Tahiti)
Members: 11
Associate Members: 1 (+1 Provisional)
Competitions: Oceania Nations Cup
OFC Club Championship
Oceania Women's Tournament

Seats on FIFA Executive

FIFA 2
AFC 4
CONMEBOL 3
CONCACAF 3
CAF 4
OFC 1
UEFA 8

Financial Affairs

EUROPE'S RICHEST CLUBS

SINCE THE ADVENT OF SATELLITE and pay-per-view television money has flooded into European soccer. It has not, however, been spread equally. Over the last decade the 20 richest clubs in the world, as measured by annual income by accountants Deloitte and Touche, have all been European. Within Europe money is concentrated in the five big leagues – England, France, Germany, Italy and Spain – from which 19 of the latest top 20 clubs are drawn; only Celtic is from outside these countries. In fact these leagues account for nearly 80 per cent of all the money in European soccer and the largest clubs – Manchester United and Real Madrid – have a higher annual turnover than the entire roster of the Swedish, Danish and Norwegian leagues put together.

No guarantee

Within the five big leagues a fairly stable set of very big clubs has emerged who make up most of the top 20. However, a permanent place in the top 20 is not guaranteed. Calamitous financial dealings, mountainous levels of debt and the collapse of affiliated companies have seen Leeds United and Lazio drop way down the list and Parma, Fiorentina and Marseille drop out altogether. Of those clubs that have retained their places, a number would not be included if real levels of debt rather than just income were taken into account. Barcelona and Valencia have debts close to 100 million Euros, as did Chelsea before the club was rescued by Roman Abramovich, the Russian industrialist.

While all of these clubs are rich, their forms of ownership vary greatly. In England in particular, clubs have been floated as public companies on the stock exchange – an option also pursued by the biggest Italian clubs, by Celtic and partially by Borussia Dortmund. In France and Germany, the disadvantages of stock market listing and stricter government control over clubs have seen them opt for private ownership with a limited amount of investment from very big corporations – for example Adidas's investment in Bayern München. In Spain, the two biggest clubs are actually owned by their paid up members – or socios – who also vote in elections for the club's president.

Biggest is best

All of these clubs have the advantage over the smaller clubs in their domestic markets, garnering a bigger share of sponsorship and television income as well having bigger stadiums and merchandising operations. But what lifts these clubs up onto a new level is their regular participation in the Champions League. With entry to the group stage now worth around £10 million whatever the results, and four times that going into the knockout stages, it is little wonder that entry into the competition's qualifying round is considered a more coveted prize than a domestic cup competition or even the UEFA Cup.

So much money is now at stake that the biggest clubs have banded together as the anomalously named G-14 (it now has 17 members) to press their interests with FIFA, UEFA and the European Union – including limiting international call-ups for their players, attempting to control the global soccer schedule and insisting on payment for internationals.

Olympique Lyonnais president *Jean Michel Aulas (right) with his 2003 signing Brazilian striker Giovane Elber. A downturn in the transfer and TV rights market has allowed French clubs to compete again for the world's best players.*

The World's Richest Clubs 2004

Club	Turnover
Manchester United 1 (1) =	
Juventus 2 (5) ▲	
Milan 3 (4) ▲	
Real Madrid 4 (2) ▼	
Bayern München 5 (3) ▼	
Internazionale 6 (9) ▲	
Arsenal 7 (11) ▲	
Liverpool 8 (19) ▲	
Newcastle United 9 (20) ▲	
Chelsea 10 (7) ▼	
AS Roma 11 (10) ▼	
Borussia Dortmund 12 (12) =	
Barcelona 13 (8) ▼	
FC Schalke 04 14 New	
Tottenham Hotspur 15 (17) ▲	
Leeds United 16 (13) ▼	
Lazio 17 (6) ▼	
Celtic 18 New	
Olympique Lyonnais 19 New	
Valencia 20 New	

TURNOVER MILLIONS (£): 0 50 100 150 200 250 300

Source: Deloitte and Touche Rich List 2003

Key

1 Position this year	▲ Moved up	= No movement
(1) Position in 2001	▼ Moved down	**New** New Entry

FINANCIAL AFFAIRS

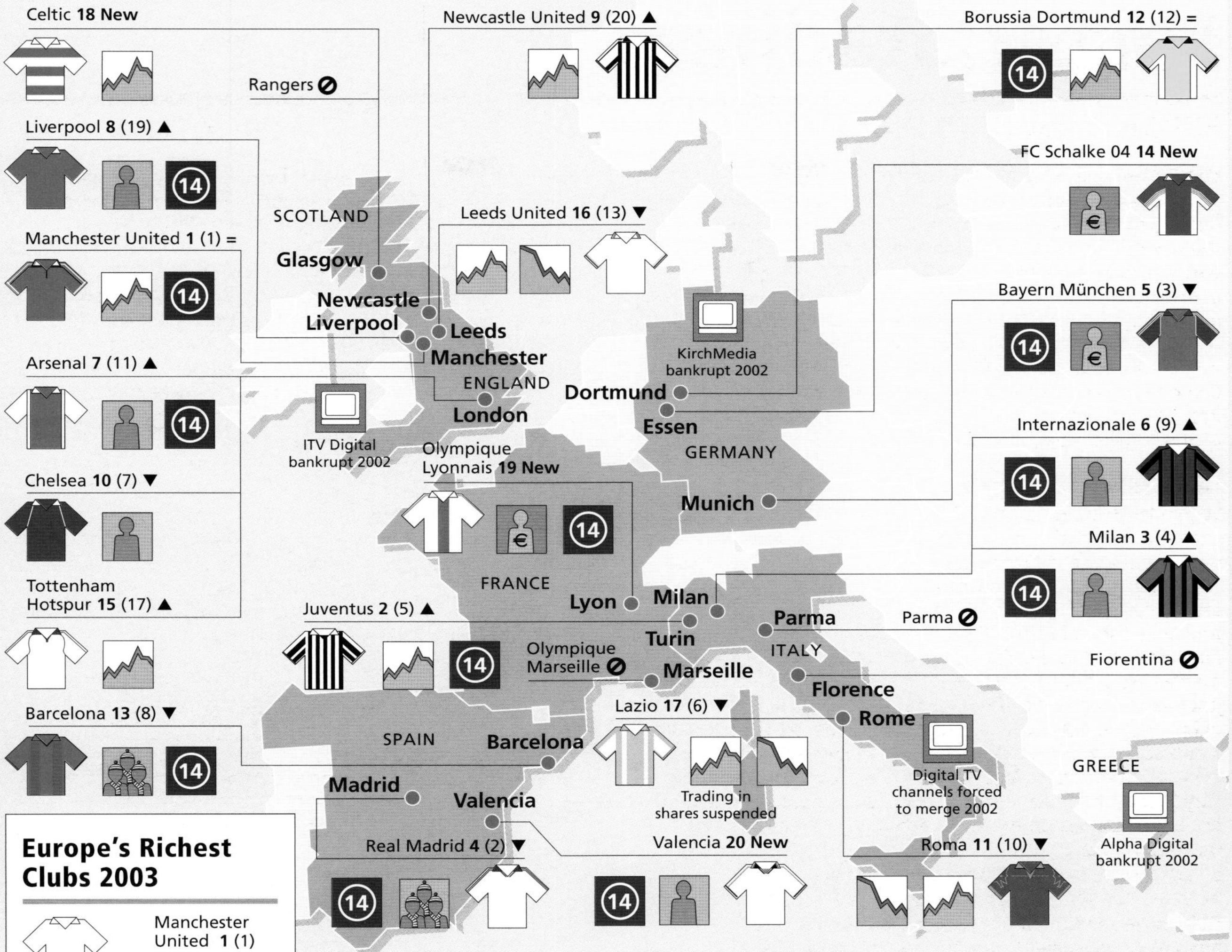

FINANCIAL AFFAIRS

Celtic **18 New**

Rangers ⊘

Newcastle United **9 (20)** ▲

Borussia Dortmund **12 (12)** =

Liverpool **8 (19)** ▲

(14)

FC Schalke 04 **14 New**

Manchester United **1 (1)** =

(14)

Leeds United **16 (13)** ▼

SCOTLAND

Glasgow

Newcastle
Liverpool **Leeds**
Manchester

ENGLAND

London

KirchMedia
bankrupt 2002

Bayern München **5 (3)** ▼

(14) €

Arsenal **7 (11)** ▲

(14)

ITV Digital
bankrupt 2002

Olympique
Lyonnais **19 New**

Dortmund

Essen

GERMANY

Internazionale **6 (9)** ▲

(14)

Chelsea **10 (7)** ▼

Tottenham
Hotspur **15 (17)** ▲

Juventus **2 (5)** ▲

(14) € (14)

Munich

FRANCE

Lyon **Milan**

Turin

Milan **3 (4)** ▲

(14)

Barcelona **13 (8)** ▼

(14)

Olympique
Marseille ⊘

Marseille

Lazio **17 (6)** ▼

Parma Parma ⊘

ITALY

Fiorentina ⊘

Florence

Rome

SPAIN

Barcelona

Madrid **Valencia**

Real Madrid **4 (2)** ▼

(14)

Trading in
shares suspended

Valencia **20 New**

(14)

Digital TV
channels forced
to merge 2002

Roma **11 (10)** ▼

GREECE

Alpha Digital
bankrupt 2002

Europe's Richest Clubs 2003

	Manchester United **1 (1)**
Team Shirt	Team name and **wealth ranking** (wealth ranking in 2001)

Privately Owned

Privately Owned with Major Commercial Investors

Socios

Flotation

(14) Group of 14

Failed TV Deal

Financial Crisis since 2001

⊘ Clubs that have dropped out of the Top 20 since 2001

Ajax, Bayer Leverkusen, Porto, PSG and PSV are also members of the Group of 14

Income from Champions League 1993–2002

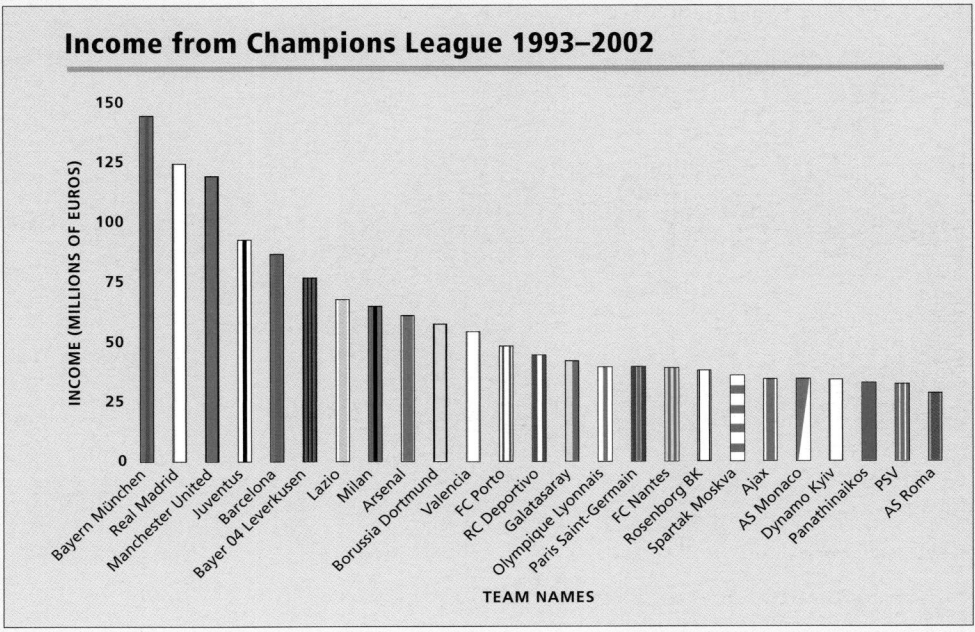

INCOME (MILLIONS OF EUROS)

150
125
100
75
50
25
0

Bayern München
Real Madrid
Manchester United
Juventus
Barcelona
Bayer 04 Leverkusen
Lazio
Milan
Arsenal
Borussia Dortmund
Valencia
FC Porto
RC Deportivo
Galatasaray
Olympique Lyonnais
Paris Saint-Germain
FC Nantes
Rosenborg BK
Spartak Moskva
Ajax
AS Monaco
Dynamo Kyiv
Panathinaikos
PSV
AS Roma

TEAM NAMES

Soccer Stadiums

THE LARGEST GROUNDS AND STADIUM DISASTERS

THE GREAT SOCCER STADIUMS OF THE WORLD are truly some of the most extraordinary structures of the 20th century. Enormous national stadiums have been built by governments hoping to benefit from the nationalism and grandeur generated by the international game. Modernist cathedrals have been created by the great clubs in pursuit of money and vanity. Yet although many stadiums are architectural triumphs, others are prime examples of appalling town planning.

While money has always been available for constructing stadiums to grand designs, the money and time necessary to make them safe has not. England and Scotland, the first countries to host truly enormous soccer crowds, have among the poorest stadium safety records of the Western nations. Outside of Europe, the precarious state of soccer's infrastructure compared to the size of crowds is most stark in Africa, where in 2001 alone four separate stadium disasters saw over 100 people killed. In Latin America and Africa persistent crowd trouble and undisciplined policing has added to this dangerous cocktail, making repeated disaster, death and injury at major soccer matches almost inevitable.

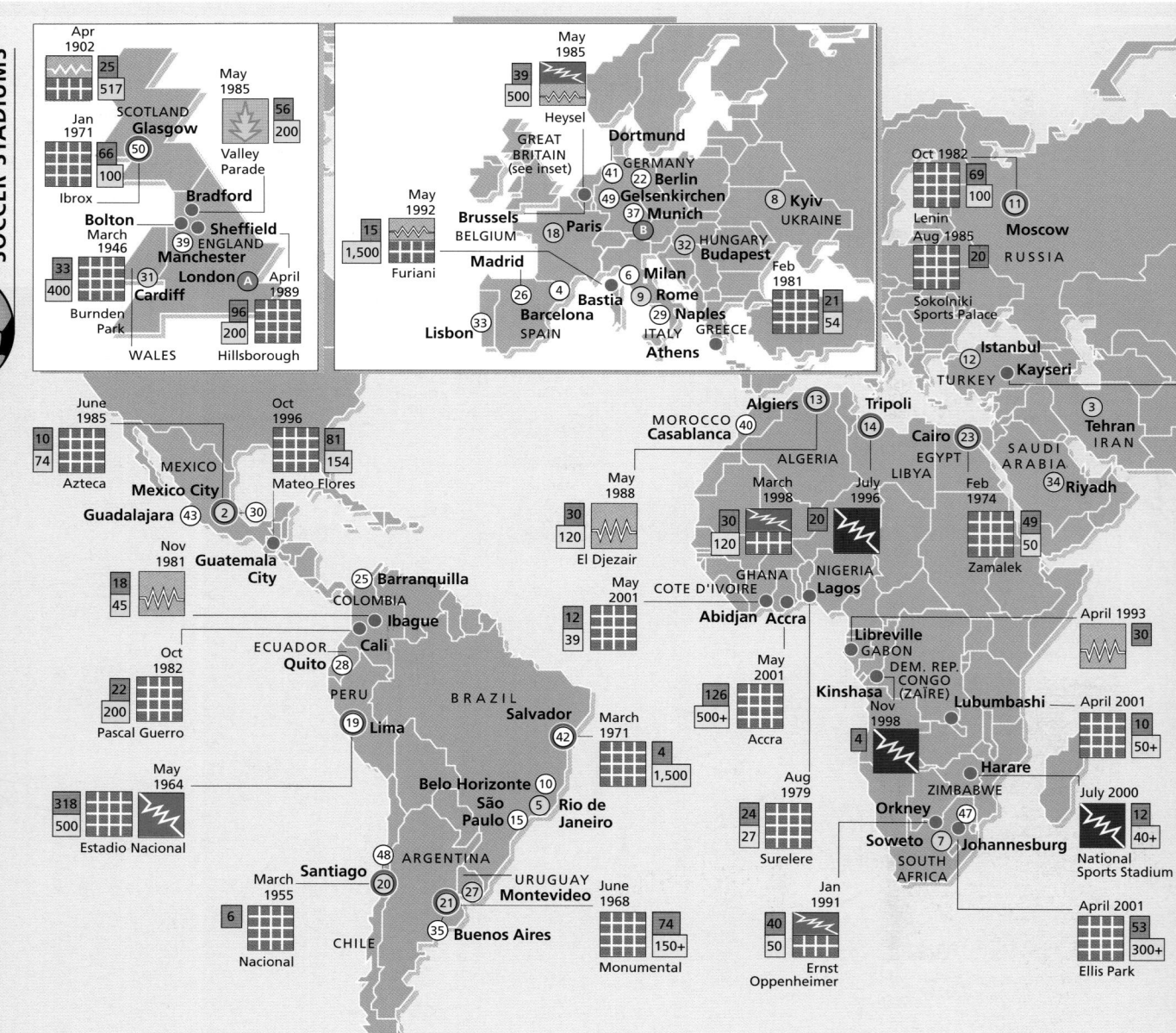

SOCCER STADIUMS

The tent-shaped, 70,000-seat, King Fahd II Stadium in Riyadh was built in 1987. Its roof is the largest stadium cover in the world and provides shade from the hot desert sun. The stadium also boasts some of the world's most luxurious sky boxes whose couch-filled lounges give deep-pocketed fans the chance to rub elbows with members of the Saudi royal family.

Key

Date

Fire | Police violence | Crowd violence | Building collapse | Crowd crush

| 33 | Dead |
| 400 | Injured |

① Ranking by stadium capacity

○ National stadium

● **Lima** Location of disaster

● Major stadium currently under construction

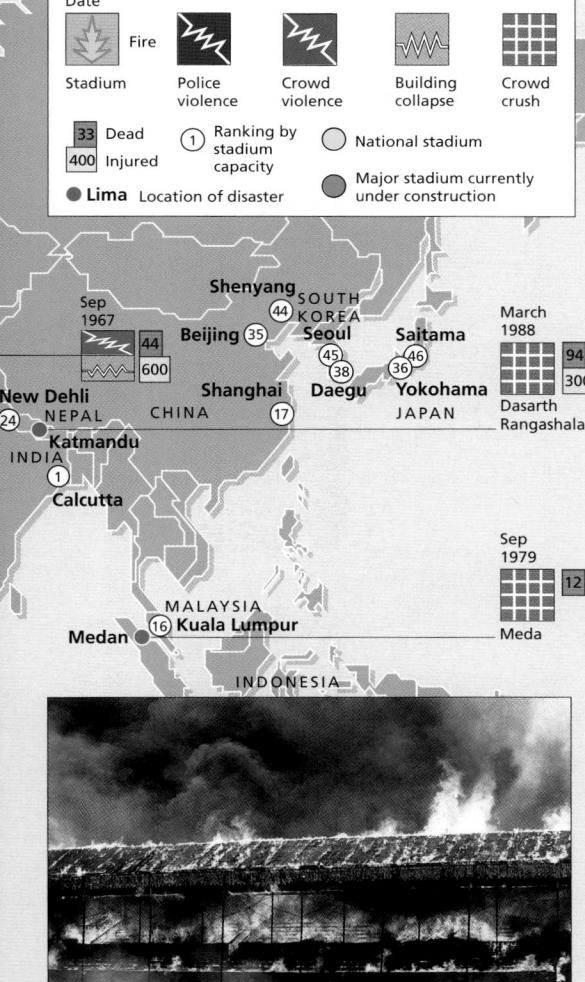

A fire at Bradford City's Valley Parade ground, England, in 1985 claimed the lives of 56 supporters and injured hundreds of others. This disaster led to new legislation governing the safety of British sports grounds.

World's Largest Stadiums (by capacity)

RANK	STADIUM	CAPACITY	TEAMS
①	Saltlake, Calcutta, India	120,000	Mohammedan FC, Mohun Bagan AC, East Bengal
②	Azteca, Mexico City, Mexico	106,000	América
③	Azadi, Tehran, Iran	100,000	Piroozi, Esteghlal, Pas, Saypa, Bank Melli
④	Camp Nou, Barcelona, Spain	98,600	Barcelona
⑤	Journalista Mario Filho, Rio, Brazil (Maracana)	95,095	Flamengo, Fluminense
⑥	Giuseppe Meazza, Milan, Italy (San Siro)	85,700	Milan, Internazionale
⑦	FNB, Soweto, South Africa (Soccer City)	85,000	Orlando Pirates
⑧	Olimpiyskiy, Kiev, Ukraine	83,160	Dynamo Kyiv
⑨	Olimpico, Rome, Italy	82,566	Roma, Lazio
⑩	Mineiro, Belo Horizonte, Brazil	81,897	Cruzeiro, Atlético Mineiro
⑪	Luzhniki, Moscow, Russia	80,800	Torpedo Moskva
⑫	Atatürk Olympic Stadium, Istanbul, Turkey	80,000	Turkey
⑬	5 Julliet 1962, Algiers, Algeria	80,000	MC Alger, Algeria
⑭	11 June Stadium, Tripoli, Libya	80,000	Libya
⑮	Cicero Pompeu De Toledo (Morumbi), São Paulo, Brazil	80,000	São Paulo
⑯	Shahalam, Kuala Lumpur, Malaysia	80,000	Selangor
⑰	Shanghai Stadium, Shanghai, China	80,000	Shanghai Shenhua
⑱	Stade de France, Paris	80,000	France
⑲	Theodoro Fernández, Lima, Peru	80,000	Universitario
⑳	Nacional, Santiago, Chile	77,000	Universidad de Chile
㉑	A.V. Liberti, Buenos Aires, Argentina (Monumental)	76,687	River Plate, Argentina
㉒	Olympiastadion, Berlin, Germany	76,243	Hertha BSC Berlin
㉓	Cairo International Stadium, Cairo, Egypt	75,750	Al Ahly, Zamalek
㉔	Jawaharlal Nehru, New Dehli, India	75,000	
㉕	Metropolitano, Barranquilla, Colombia	75,000	Atlético Júnior
㉖	Santiago Bernabeu, Madrid, Spain	74,300	Real Madrid
㉗	Centenario, Montevideo, Uruguay	73,609	Nacional, Peñarol, Uruguay
㉘	Monumental, Quito, Ecuador	73,000	Barcelona
㉙	San Paolo, Naples, Italy (Fuorigrotti)	72,810	Napoli
㉚	Olimpico Universitario, Mexico City, Mexico	72,449	UNAM
㉛	Millennium, Cardiff, Wales	72,000	Wales
㉜	Ferenc Puskas, Budapest, Hungary	71,000	Hungary
㉝	Estadio Da Luz, Lisbon, Portugal	70,000	Benfica
㉞	King Fahd II, Riyadh, Saudi Arabia	70,000	Saudi Arabia
㉟	Worker's Stadium, Beijing, China	70,000	Beijing Hyundai Cars
㊱	Yokohama International, Yokohama, Japan	70,000	Yokohama F. Marinos
㊲	Olympiastadion, Munich, Germany	69,000	Bayern München, TSV 1860 München
㊳	Daegu World Cup Stadium, Daegu, South Korea	68,014	Daegu FC
㊴	Old Trafford, Manchester, England	67,650	Manchester United
㊵	Mohammed V, Casablanca, Morocco	67,000	WAC Casablanca, Raja Casablanca
㊶	Westfalenstadion, Dortmund, Germany	67,000	Borussia Dortmund
㊷	Octavio Mangabeira, Salvador, Brazil	66,080	Bahia
㊸	Estadio Jalisco, Guadalajara, Mexico	66,000	Atlas
㊹	Wulihe Stadium, Shenyang, China	65,000	Shenyang Jinde
㊺	Seoul World Cup Stadium, Seoul, South Korea	64,667	
㊻	Saitama Stadium, Saitama, Japan	63,700	
㊼	Ellis Park, Johannesburg, South Africa	63,000	Kaiser Chiefs
㊽	David Arellano, Santiago, Chile	62,500	Colo Colo
㊾	Arena Aufschalke, Gelsenkirchen, Germany	61,027	FC Schalke 04
㊿	Celtic Park, Glasgow, Scotland (Parkhead)	60,506	Celtic
Ⓐ	Wembley, London, England	90,000	Under construction
Ⓑ	Allianz Arena, Munich, Germany	66,000	Under construction

Where capacities are the same, stadiums are listed alphabetically.

SOCCER STADIUMS

Playing Styles

THE EARLIEST STYLES OF SOCCER were overwhelmingly attack oriented, with the emphasis on individuals dribbling with the ball while protected by their teammates. The introduction of the offside rule in 1867 limited this system and also prevented the problem of long balls and 'goal hanging'. Early innovations in England and Scotland shifted the emphasis from dribbling and hoofing the ball to quick, short passes and the increased use of space and movement on the pitch. Early pioneers of this style included the Royal Engineers and the 12 clubs who founded the English FA, as well as Scottish professionals and coaches in England and throughout Europe.

Key to Abbreviations

(GK) - Goalkeeper
(FB) - Full-back
(LB) - Left-back
(RB) - Right-back
(3/4B) - 3/4-back
(CB) - Centre-back
(LCB) - Left centre-back

(RCB) - Right centre-back
(HB) - Half-back
(WH) - Wing-half
(M) - Midfielder
(F) - Forward

(IF) - Inside-forward
(CF) - Centre-forward
(C) - Centre
(W) - Winger
(LW) - Left-winger
(RW) - Right-winger
opp. - Opposition

Royal Engineers, 1872

FORMATION 1-2-7

The Royal Engineers are often credited with the development of the first innovative soccer formations and tactics. The standard 1-2-7 formation was subtly adapted with the seven forwards split into four wingers and three centre-forwards, and the long ball and charge supplemented with short passes.

FORMATION 2-3-5

With the advent of short passing, two forwards were brought back to protect the defence, exemplified by Preston North End's league winning 2-3-5 formation. Defenders covered attacking forwards, the half-backs patrolled the wings and the centre-back in midfield was free to move from defence to attack as required.

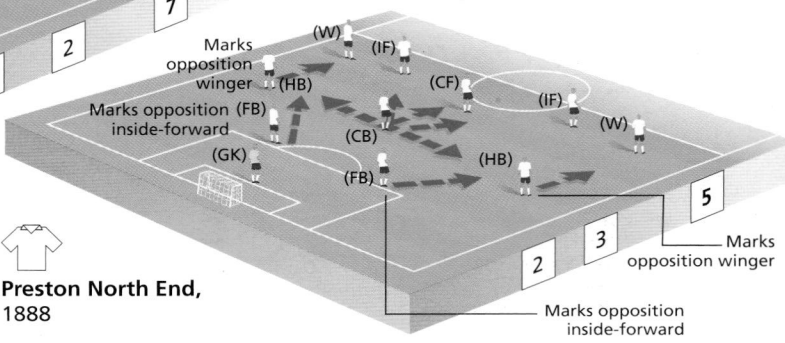

Preston North End, 1888

FORMATION M-W

M-W, **perfected by Herbert Chapman's Arsenal** team in the 1920s, was a response to the change in the offside rule. Strict man-marking in the back three and withdrawn inside-forwards were complemented by passing through the midfield to the centre-forward, inside-forwards and wingers.

Arsenal, 1926

FORMATION M-U

The great Hungarian side retained the old M formation at the back but innovated at the front. A deep-lying centre-forward pulled the opposition markers out of position leaving space for the inside-forwards to raid the opposition box, helped by the fact that they were not required to track back in defence.

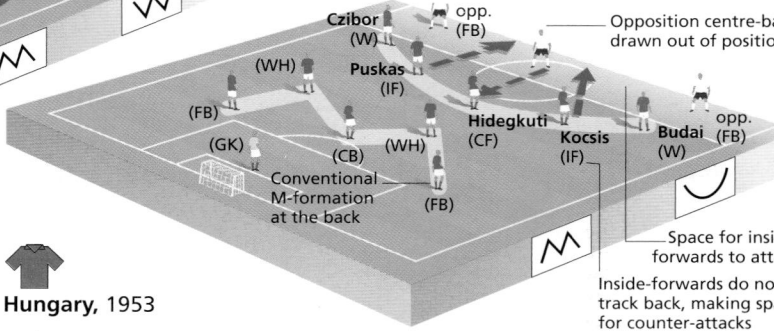

Hungary, 1953

The Development of Formations

1880s Passing game and wing play, developed particularly in Scotland, begin to transform the game and push more players into midfield

1925 Change in the offside rule

| 1860 | 1870 | 1880 | 1890 | 1920 | 1930 | 1940 |

Pre-1867 Pre-eminence of dribbling

1867 Offside rule first introduced

1870s First formations emerge – attributed to the Royal Engineers playing 1-2-7

1888–90 Preston North End (the Invincibles), win the first professional league with settled 2-3-5 formation

1934 Karl Rappan introduces the sweeper into the Swiss game

PLAYING STYLES

A new 2-3-5 formation was the mainstay of professional soccer at the start of the 20th century. However, its limits were soon discovered, and the offside rule gave ample opportunity for quick full-backs to exploit it. In response, play was often confined to a narrow strip near the halfway line. Revisions to the offside rule were capitalized on by Herbert Chapman's M-W formation, which became the standard formation for the next 30 years.

Outside Britain, tactical innovation continued in the inter-war era. Karl Rappan in Switzerland began to develop an early version of *catenaccio*, while the technical virtuosity of central Europeans encouraged a greater emphasis on midfield play and accurate passing. The rise of the European game was confirmed by Hungary's historic 6-3 victory over England at Wembley in 1953.

In the 1960s and 1970s the flat back four was introduced. *Catenaccio* was perfected by Helenio Herrera's Internazionale, and the sweeper role was given an attacking edge by Franz Beckenbauer's Bayern München. Most exciting of all, Ajax and then Holland played 'total football', in which all players were required to take up whatever position and role the play of the game dictated. In the 1990s, the 4-4-2 system has come to dominate the global game, with only the occasional side braving the reintroduction of wing-backs in flexible 3-5-2/5-3-2 systems.

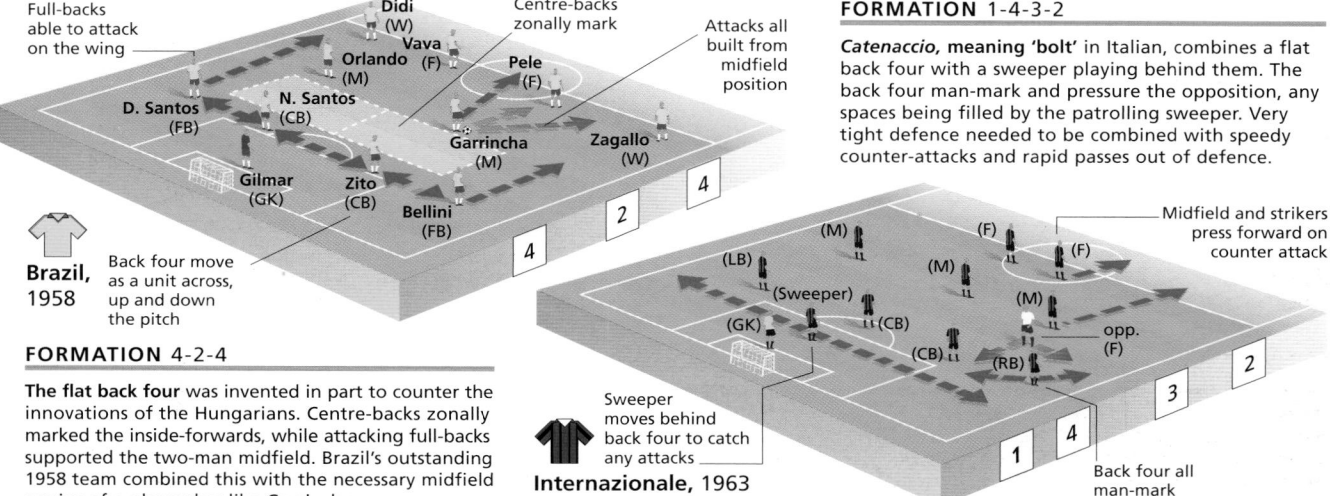

Brazil, 1958

FORMATION 4-2-4

The flat back four was invented in part to counter the innovations of the Hungarians. Centre-backs zonally marked the inside-forwards, while attacking full-backs supported the two-man midfield. Brazil's outstanding 1958 team combined this with the necessary midfield genius of a playmaker like Garrincha.

FORMATION 1-4-3-2

Catenaccio, **meaning 'bolt'** in Italian, combines a flat back four with a sweeper playing behind them. The back four man-mark and pressure the opposition, any spaces being filled by the patrolling sweeper. Very tight defence needed to be combined with speedy counter-attacks and rapid passes out of defence.

Internazionale, 1963

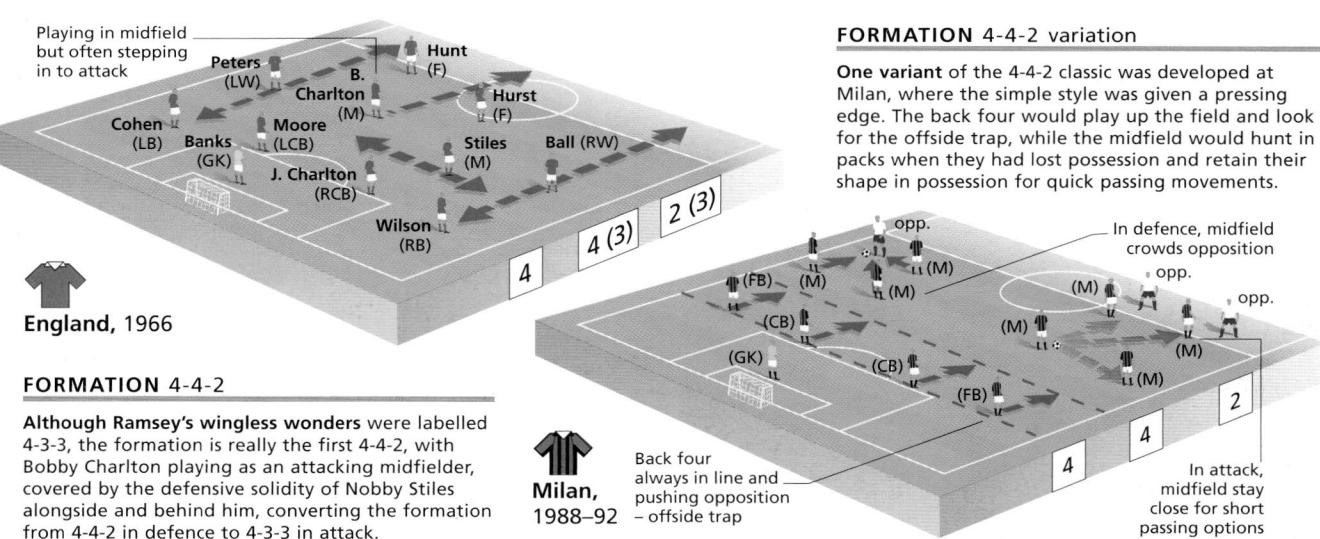

England, 1966

FORMATION 4-4-2

Although Ramsey's wingless wonders were labelled 4-3-3, the formation is really the first 4-4-2, with Bobby Charlton playing as an attacking midfielder, covered by the defensive solidity of Nobby Stiles alongside and behind him, converting the formation from 4-4-2 in defence to 4-3-3 in attack.

FORMATION 4-4-2 variation

One variant of the 4-4-2 classic was developed at Milan, where the simple style was given a pressing edge. The back four would play up the field and look for the offside trap, while the midfield would hunt in packs when they had lost possession and retain their shape in possession for quick passing movements.

Milan, 1988–92

World Players of the Year

THE SEASON IN REVIEW 2003

FOR THE THIRD TIME IN SIX YEARS Zinedine Zidane was voted FIFA World Footballer of the Year. FIFA asked the national team coaches of every FIFA nation who they would most want in their squad and, although 2003 only saw Zidane win the Spanish league with Real Madrid, his consistent quality, capacity to find space and orchestrate a game and, above all, his ability to make a telling pass made him irresistible.

The European Player of the Year, elected by a jury of journalists from *France Football*, went to the midfielder Pavel Nedved. Universally lauded for his energy, fitness and dynamism, Nedved showed his capacity to raise the game of his team-mates – most memorably in Juventus' victory over Real Madrid in the Champions League semi-final. Second in both polls was Thierry Henry, whose balletic artistry and deadly shooting have been so successful in the last few seasons.

Footballer of the Year in South America went to the 19-year-old Argentinian forward Carlos Tévez. After missing much of Boca's early season games due to international commitments, Tévez was the key man in taking Boca to another Argentinian title and the Copa Libertadores and Intercontinental Cup in 2003.

It's becoming a habit. The absurdly modest Zinedine Zidane picks up his third FIFA World Player of the Year award. He also announced that he would retire from international soccer after Euro 2004.

World Footballer of the Year (FIFA)

YEAR	PLAYER	CLUB	NATIONALITY
1991	Lothar Matthäus	Internazionale	German
1992	Marco van Basten	Milan	Dutch
1993	Roberto Baggio	Juventus	Italian
1994	Romario	Barcelona	Brazilian
1995	George Weah	Milan	Liberian
1996	Ronaldo	PSV/Barcelona	Brazilian
1997	Ronaldo	Barcelona/Inter	Brazilian
1998	Zinedine Zidane	Juventus	French
1999	Rivaldo	Barcelona	Brazilian
2000	Zinedine Zidane	Juventus	French
2001	Luis Figo	Real Madrid	Portuguese
2002	Ronaldo	Real Madrid	Brazilian
2003	Zinedine Zidane	Real Madrid	French

Elected by FIFA.

European Player of the Year

YEAR	PLAYER	CLUB	NATIONALITY
1956	Stanley Matthews	Stoke City	English
1957	Alfredo di Stefano	Real Madrid	Spanish
1958	Raymond Kopa	Real Madrid	French
1959	Alfredo di Stefano	Real Madrid	Spanish
1960	Luis Suárez	Barcelona	Spanish
1961	Omar Sivori	Juventus	Italian
1962	Josef Masopust	Dukla Praha	Czech
1963	Lev Yashin	Dinamo Moskva	Soviet
1964	Denis Law	Manchester United	Scottish
1965	Eusébio	SL Benfica	Portuguese
1966	Bobby Charlton	Manchester United	English
1967	Florian Albert	Ferencváros	Hungarian
1968	George Best	Manchester United	Northern Irish
1969	Gianni Rivera	Milan	Italian
1970	Gerd Müller	Bayern München	German
1971	Johan Cruyff	Ajax	Dutch
1972	Franz Beckenbauer	Bayern München	German
1973	Johan Cruyff	Ajax	Dutch
1974	Johan Cruyff	Ajax	Dutch
1975	Oleg Blokhin	Dynamo Kyiv	Soviet
1976	Franz Beckenbauer	Bayern München	German
1977	Allan Simonsen	Borussia M'gladbach	Danish
1978	Kevin Keegan	Hamburger SV	English
1979	Kevin Keegan	Hamburger SV	English
1980	Karl-Heinz Rummenigge	Bayern München	German
1981	Karl-Heinz Rummenigge	Bayern München	German
1982	Paolo Rossi	Juventus	Italian
1983	Michel Platini	Juventus	French
1984	Michel Platini	Juventus	French
1985	Michel Platini	Juventus	French
1986	Igor Belanov	Dynamo Kyiv	Soviet
1987	Ruud Gullit	Milan	Dutch
1988	Marco van Basten	Milan	Dutch
1989	Marco van Basten	Milan	Dutch
1990	Lothar Matthäus	Internazionale	German
1991	Jean-Pierre Papin	Olympique Marseille	French
1992	Marco van Basten	Milan	Dutch
1993	Roberto Baggio	Juventus	Italian
1994	Hristo Stoichkov	Barcelona	Bulgarian
1995	George Weah	Milan	Liberian
1996	Matthias Sammer	Borussia Dortmund	German
1997	Ronaldo	Barcelona	Brazilian
1998	Zinedine Zidane	Juventus	French
1999	Rivaldo	Barcelona	Brazilian
2000	Luis Figo	Barcelona	Portuguese
2001	Michael Owen	Liverpool	English
2002	Ronaldo	Real Madrid	Brazilian
2003	Pavel Nedved	Juventus	Czech

Elected by *France Football* magazine.

South American Footballer of the Year

YEAR	PLAYER	CLUB	NATIONALITY
1971	Tostão*	Cruzeiro	Brazilian
1972	Teofilio Cubillas*	Alianza Lima	Peruvian
1973	Pele*	Santos	Brazilian
1974	Elias Figueroa*	Internacional	Chilean
1975	Elias Figueroa*	Internacional	Chilean
1976	Elias Figueroa*	Internacional	Chilean
1977	Zico*	Flamengo	Brazilian
1978	Mario Kempes*	Valencia	Argentinian
1979	Diego Maradona*	Argentinos Juniors	Argentinian
1980	Diego Maradona*	Boca Juniors	Argentinian
1981	Zico*	Flamengo	Brazilian
1982	Zico*	Flamengo	Brazilian
1983	Socrates*	Corinthians	Brazilian
1984	Enzo Francescoli*	River Plate	Uruguayan
1985	Romero*	Fluminense	Paraguayan
1986	Ruben Paz*	Racing Club	Uruguayan
1986	Antonio Alzamendi*	River Plate	Uruguayan
1987	Diego Maradona*	Napoli	Argentinian
1987	Carlos Valderrama	Deportivo Cali	Colombian
1988	Diego Maradona*	Napoli	Argentinian
1988	Ruben Paz	Racing Club	Uruguayan
1989	Bebeto*	Vasco da Gama	Brazilian
1989	Gabriel Batistuta	Boca Juniors/ Fiorentina	Argentinian
1990	Diego Maradona*	Sevilla	Argentinian
1990	Raul Amarilla	Olimpia	Paraguayan
1991	Oscar Ruggeri	Vélez Sarsfield	Argentinian
1992	Rai	São Paulo	Brazilian
1993	Carlos Valderrama	Atlético Júnior	Colombian
1994	Cafu	São Paulo	Brazilian
1995	Enzo Francescoli	River Plate	Uruguayan
1996	Jose Luis Chilavert	Vélez Sarsfield	Paraguayan
1997	Marcelo Salas	River Plate	Chilean
1998	Martin Palermo	Boca Juniors	Argentinian
1999	Javier Saviola	River Plate	Argentinian
2000	Romario	Vasco da Gama	Brazilian
2001	Juan Román Riquelme	Boca Juniors	Argentinian
2002	Jose Cardozo	Toluca	Paraguayan
2003	Carlos Tévez	Boca Juniors	Argentinian

* Elected by *El Mundo*, Caracas; all others elected by *El Pais*, Montevideo.

Thierry Henry's form last season led to a groundswell in support of his claim on both World and European Player of the Year titles.

Boca Juniors' Carlos Tévez in characteristic tongue-biting mode. The latest in a long line of the 'next Maradona', he might just be the one.

Pavel Nedved goes past Barcelona's Carlos Puyol in the Champions League. Nedved's performances in the competition for Juventus were incomparable.

The World Cup

TOURNAMENT OVERVIEW

ALTHOUGH FIFA had given itself the right to organize a global soccer competition when created in 1904, it did not do so for some 25 years. Prior to this the tournament at the Olympics had functioned as the *de facto* world championships. However, as professionalism took hold in major soccer nations, the amateur ethos of the Olympic Games became a block on the appearance of the world's best players and teams. At the FIFA conference in Barcelona in 1929, Jules Rimet, the French general secretary of FIFA, proposed that an international championship be held within the next 12 months. Almost unanimous agreement saw the tournament established and destined for Uruguay, where on 13 July 1930, the very first World Cup fixture was played between France and Mexico.

The development of the competition parallels the global development of soccer. From only 13 entrants in 1930, all from Latin America or Europe, it now has over 200 from every corner of the globe in its qualifying stages. Since 1998, the finals have expanded to include 32 participants in a month-long event. The early domination of Europe and Latin America culminated in 1966 when FIFA allocated one place to Africa, Asia and Central America combined, prompting a widespread boycott. The steady shift in the balance of global soccer power saw 13 finalists from these confederations in 1998. From 2006 the champions will be forced to qualify. Most importantly, the finals are now one of the most significant televisual and media events in the calendar, as evidenced by the huge increase in the cost of acquiring TV broadcast rights and the astronomical viewing figures it achieves.

World Cup Finals (1930–2002)

YEAR	WINNERS	SCORE	RUNNERS-UP
1930	Uruguay	4-2	Argentina
1934	Italy	2-1 (aet)	Czechoslovakia
1938	Italy	4-2	Hungary
1950	Uruguay	2-1	Brazil
1954	West Germany	3-2	Hungary
1958	Brazil	5-2	Sweden
1962	Brazil	3-1	Czechoslovakia
1966	England	4-2 (aet)	West Germany
1970	Brazil	4-1	Italy
1974	West Germany	2-1	Netherlands
1978	Argentina	3-1 (aet)	Netherlands
1982	Italy	3-1	West Germany
1986	Argentina	3-2	West Germany
1990	West Germany	1-0	Argentina
1994	Brazil	0-0 (3-2 pens)	Italy
1998	France	3-0	Brazil
2002	Brazil	2-0	Germany

World Cup Soccer

Number of appearances at tournament 1930–98

- 12+ times
- 8–11 times
- 5–7 times
- 2–4 times
- 1 time
- 0 times

World Cup

- Winners
- **1954**, Winners in bold
- *66* Runners-up in italic
- 1999 Host country and year
- ● Rome Location of Final

REP OF IRELAND
WALES
PORTUGAL

CANADA

UNITED STATES OF AMERICA
1994

Pasadena ●

MEXICO
1970, 86
Mexico City

HAITI
CUBA
JAMAICA

EL SALVADOR
HONDURAS
COSTA RICA

COLOMBIA
ECUADOR

PERU
BOLIVIA
PARAGUAY

CHILE
1962 Montevideo

Buenos Aires

Santiago

ARGENTINA
1978

1930, 78, 86, 90

The World Cup Top Goalscorers (1930–2002)

YEAR	SCORER	NATIONALITY	GOALS
1930	Stabile	Argentina	8
1934	Nejedly	Czechoslovakia	5
1938	Leonidas	Brazil	8
1950	Ademir	Brazil	9
1954	Kocsis	Hungary	8
1958	Fontaine	France	13
1962	Ivanov	Soviet Union	4
	Sancjez	Chile	
	Garrincha	Brazil	
	Vava	Brazil	
	Albert	Hungary	
	Jerkovic	Yugoslavia	
1966	Eusebio	Portugal	9
1970	Müller	W. Germany	10
1974	Lato	Poland	7
1978	Kempes	Argentina	6
1982	Rossi	Italy	6
1986	Lineker	England	6
1990	Schillachi	Italy	6
1994	Salenko	Russia	6
	Stoichkov	Bulgaria	
1998	Suker	Croatia	6
2002	Ronaldo	Brazil	7

World Cup finals: number and origins of participants

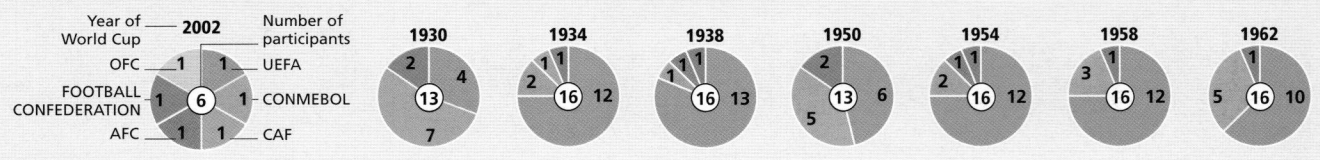

Year of World Cup — 2002 — Number of participants
OFC 1 | 1 UEFA
FOOTBALL CONFEDERATION 1 | 6 | 1 CONMEBOL
AFC 1 | 1 CAF

1930: 2, 4, 13, 7
1934: 2, 1, 1, 16, 12
1938: 1, 1, 1, 16, 13
1950: 2, 13, 6, 5
1954: 2, 1, 1, 16, 12
1958: 3, 1, 16, 12
1962: 1, 5, 16, 10

THE WORLD CUP

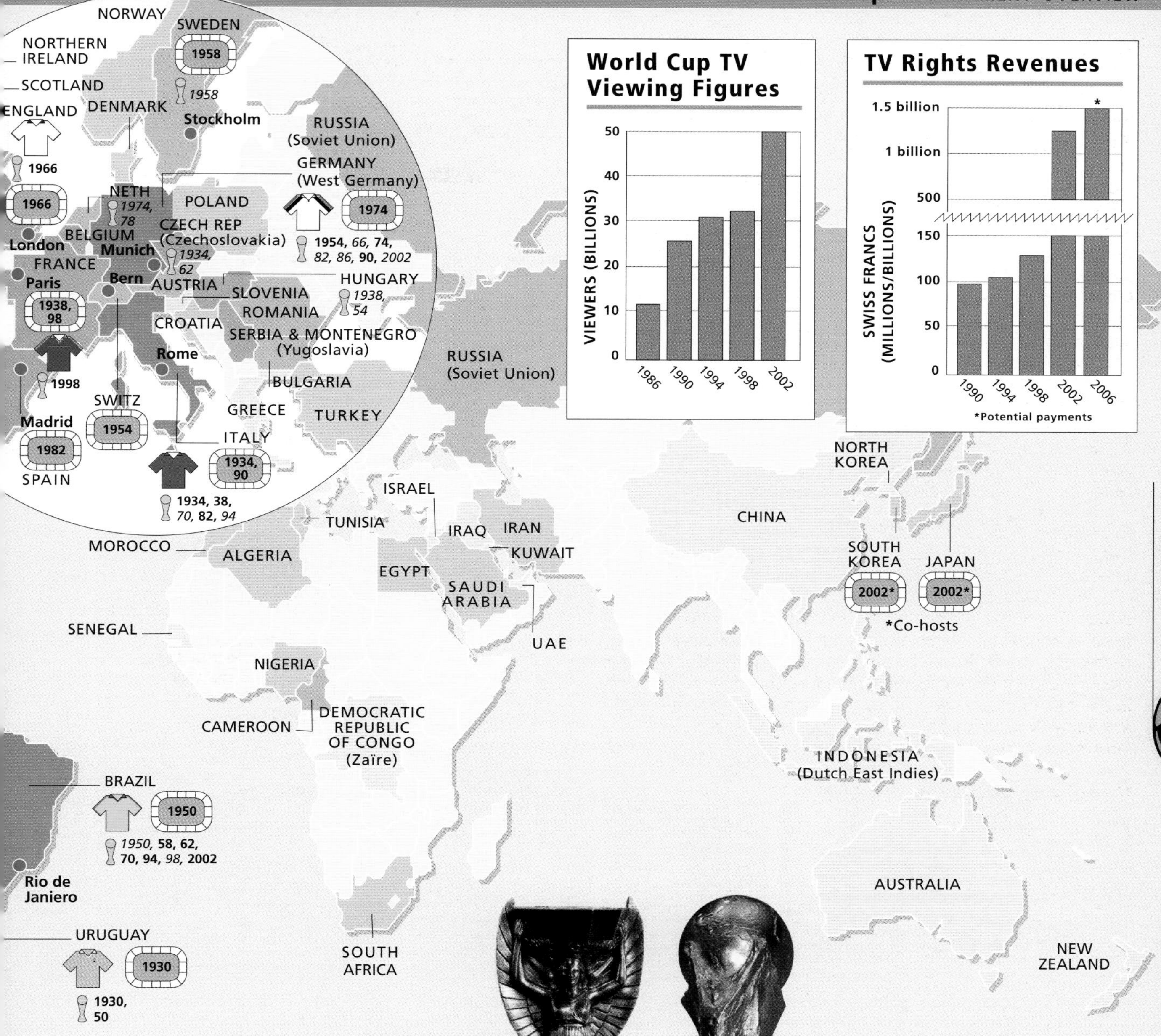

NORWAY
SWEDEN
NORTHERN
IRELAND
1958
1958
SCOTLAND
ENGLAND
DENMARK
Stockholm
RUSSIA
(Soviet Union)
1966
GERMANY
(West Germany)
1966
NETH
*1974,
78*
POLAND
1974
BELGIUM
CZECH REP
(Czechoslovakia)
*1954, 66, 74,
82, 86, 90, 2002*
London
Munich
*1934,
62*
FRANCE
AUSTRIA
HUNGARY
Paris
SLOVENIA
*1938,
54*
Bern
ROMANIA
**1938,
98**
CROATIA
SERBIA & MONTENEGRO
(Yugoslavia)
1998
Rome
RUSSIA
(Soviet Union)
Madrid
SWITZ
BULGARIA
1954
GREECE
1982
ITALY
TURKEY
SPAIN
**1934,
90**
*1934, 38,
70, 82, 94*
ISRAEL
NORTH
KOREA
MOROCCO
TUNISIA
IRAQ
IRAN
CHINA
ALGERIA
KUWAIT
EGYPT
SOUTH
KOREA
JAPAN
SAUDI
ARABIA
2002* **2002***
SENEGAL
UAE
*Co-hosts
NIGERIA
CAMEROON
DEMOCRATIC
REPUBLIC
OF CONGO
(Zaïre)
INDONESIA
(Dutch East Indies)
BRAZIL
1950
*1950, 58, 62,
70, 94, 98, 2002*
AUSTRALIA
**Rio de
Janiero**
URUGUAY
SOUTH
AFRICA
NEW
ZEALAND
1930
*1930,
50*

World Cup TV Viewing Figures

VIEWERS (BILLIONS)

50 — 40 — 30 — 20 — 10 — 0

1986 1990 1994 1998 2002

TV Rights Revenues

1.5 billion
1 billion
500
*
SWISS FRANCS (MILLIONS/BILLIONS)
150
100
50
0

1990 1994 1998 2002 2006

*Potential payments

The Coupe Jules Rimet was made by French sculptor Abel Lafleur and presented to Brazil on its third World Cup victory in 1970. It was stolen and recovered in England in 1966 and stolen again in Rio in 1983. It is believed to have been melted down.

The second World Cup trophy was made by Italian sculptor Silvio Gazzangia and is solid gold on a base of malachite. Copies are given to the victors but FIFA keeps the real thing.

1966	1970	1974	1978	1982	1986	1990	1994	1998	2002
1 1	2	1 1	1	1 2 1	2 2	1 2	2 2	4 3	4 3
4 (16) 10	1 (16) 9	1 (16) 9	1 (16) 10	2 (24) 14	2 (24) 14	2 (24) 14	3 (24) 13	3 (32) 15	3 (32) 15
	1 3	4	3	4	4	4	4	5	5

WORLD CUP FINALS (1930–2002)

The World Cup has invariably laid bare the distribution of power in world soccer. Only seven nations have won the tournament, three from Latin America (Argentina, Brazil and Uruguay) and four from Europe (England, France, Germany and Italy), and only four others have appeared in a Final, again all from Europe (Czechoslovakia, Hungary, Sweden, the Netherlands). Only the USA in 1930 and South Korea in 2002 have broken the presence of Latin Americans and Europeans in the semi-finals. Similarly, prior to 2002 no country

outside of Europe and the Americas has hosted the games. Home advantage has often proved decisive. Only Brazil has won a World Cup on a continent not their own (Sweden 1958) while home victories have been scored by Uruguay (1930), Italy (1934), England (1966), West Germany (1974), Argentina (1978) and France (1998).

A few World Cup Finals have ultimately disappointed. The fantastic play at Italia '90 was crowned with a bad-tempered and rather ugly game between West Germany and Argentina (including two

sending-offs for the Argentines). A tense, goalless 120 minutes between Brazil and Italy in the 1994 Final in Los Angeles was ultimately decided by the cruel lottery of a penalty shootout. On the other hand, most Finals have been exhilarating displays of soccer. The World Cup has delivered the pulsating 1986 Final between Argentina and West Germany in Mexico City, the drama of England's two extra-time goals in the 1966 Final, and the sublime majesty of Brazil's 1970 triumph against Italy, again in Mexico City.

1930: Pedro Cea of Uruguay makes it 2-2 in the 57th minute of the first-ever World Cup Final. The Uruguayans scored twice more to take the trophy.

1934: Italy's squad give the Fascist salute to Il Duce in the VIP box at the Flaminio Stadium, Rome. Italy went on to beat the Czechs 2-1 in extra time.

1938: Italy celebrates its second World Cup title after beating Hungary 4-2. Azzurri coach, Vittorio Pozzo (suited on the left), embraces his players.

1950: The Uruguayans pose before the final pool match against Brazil. In front of nearly 200,000 Brazilian fans, the Uruguayans found the strength to beat their hosts 2-1.

1954: Hidejkuti of Hungary shoots, watched by West Germany's Horst Eckel. The Germans won 3-2 in the Final, the only match the Magical Magyars lost between 1950 and 56.

1958: Just Fontaine celebrates 13 goals in the World Cup, a record that still stands. But France was decisively beaten in the semi-final against Brazil by 5-2.

1962: The battle of Santiago. The first round match between Italy and Chile descended into foul play and violence. The Italian David argues before being sent off.

1966: Wolfgang Weber equalizes for Germany in the dying seconds of normal time in the Final against England. Gordon Banks stretches to no avail.

1970: Pele's World Cup. In the 18th minute of the Final, Pele opens the scoring against Italy. He made two more goals as the Brazilians won 4-1.

1974: Captain Franz Beckenbauer (left) and manager Helmut Schön (right) exchange an embrace as West Germany wins its second World Cup title.

1978: Daniel Pasarella, Argentina's captain and defensive lynchpin, grasps the World Cup. Argentina beat the Netherlands 3-1 after extra time.

1982: Paulo Rossi opens the scoring for Italy in the 56th minute of the Final against West Germany. Harald Schumacher, the German goalkeeper, watches the ball in.

1986: Diego Maradona sets off on the electrifying run through the England midfield and defence for his second goal in Argentina's 2-1 victory in the quarter-finals.

1990: Roger Milla celebrates another Cameroon goal at Italia '90. In 1994, he became the oldest player to play and score during a World Cup finals tournament.

1994: Roberto Baggio (Italy) contemplates his missed penalty in the Final shootout. The Brazilians celebrate their fourth World Cup victory.

THE WORLD CUP

1998: Zinedine Zidane heads the opening goal for France in the team's crushing 3-0 defeat of a Brazilian team fatally weakened by an under par Ronaldo. The Brazilian centre-forward had been taken ill at the team's hotel but arrived moments before kick-off and was reinstated.

2002: Redemption at last as Ronaldo finally consigns his bizarre trance-like performance in the 1998 Final as Brazil triumphs over Germany in Yokohama.

The World Cup

THE IDEA OF THE WORLD CUP began with the establishment of FIFA in 1904, but for the first three decades of the century the soccer tournament at the Olympic Games served as the *de facto* soccer world championships. With the advent of professionalism in many European countries in the 1920s (and the resultant limit to participation in the amateur Olympic soccer tournament) the World Cup came into being.

The first tournament was held in Uruguay in 1930 as the Uruguayans were the current Olympic champions and promised to pay everybody's expenses. Despite this, only four European countries made the trip to a tournament dominated by South Americans. In Italy in 1934 and France in 1938, the early group rounds were dispensed with and the tournament became a knockout competition from the beginning. This format was tough on the Americans, Brazilians and Argentinians who often crossed an ocean for a single game.

After the Second World War, the World Cup settled into a 16-team final tournament, with a group phase followed by knockout stages. There were two exceptions: the 1950 tournament in Brazil had a league format for the final placing, and the 1954 competition in Switzerland saw 16 teams divided into four groups, with two teams in each group seeded. The two seeded teams didn't play each other in the group rounds.

The increasing financial attraction of the World Cup, and the increasing strength and numbers of soccer nations outside of Europe and Latin America, has led to a steady expansion of the tournament. There were 24 teams in 1982 (with four second round mini-leagues producing four semi-finalists); and 32 teams in 1998 and 2002 (reverting to opening groups and then knockout stages for the last 16).

1930 URUGUAY

POOL 1

France **4-1** Mexico
Argentina **1-0** France
Chile **3-0** Mexico
Chile **1-0** France
Argentina **6-3** Mexico
Argentina **3-1** Chile

	P	W	D	L	F	A	Pts
Argentina	3	3	0	0	10	4	6
Chile	3	2	0	1	5	3	4
France	3	1	0	2	4	3	2
Mexico	3	0	0	3	4	13	0

POOL 2

Yugoslavia **2-1** Brazil
Yugoslavia **4-0** Bolivia
Brazil **4-0** Bolivia

	P	W	D	L	F	A	Pts
Yugoslavia	2	2	0	0	6	1	4
Brazil	2	1	0	1	5	2	2
Bolivia	2	0	0	2	0	8	0

POOL 3

Romania **3-1** Peru
Uruguay **1-0** Peru
Uruguay **4-0** Romania

	P	W	D	L	F	A	Pts
Uruguay	2	2	0	0	5	0	4
Romania	2	1	0	1	3	5	2
Peru	2	0	0	2	1	4	0

POOL 4

USA **3-0** Belgium
USA **3-0** Paraguay
Paraguay **1-0** Belgium

	P	W	D	L	F	A	Pts
USA	2	2	0	0	6	0	4
Paraguay	2	1	0	1	1	3	2
Belgium	2	0	0	2	0	4	0

SEMI-FINALS

Argentina **6-1** USA
(Monti 20,   (Brown 88)
Scopello 56,
Stabile 69, 87,
Peucelle 80, 85)

Uruguay **6-1** Yugoslavia
(Cea 18, 67, 72,   (Sekulic 4)
Anselmo 20, 31,
Iriarte 60)

THIRD PLACE PLAY-OFF

not held

FINAL

July 30 – Centenario, Montevideo
Uruguay **4-2** Argentina
(Dorado 12,   (Peucelle 20,
Cea 58,   Stabile 37)
Iriarte 68,
Castro 89)
h/t: 1-2 **Att:** 93,000
Ref: Langenus (Belgium)

1934 ITALY

FIRST ROUND

Italy **7-1** USA
Czechoslovakia **2-1** Romania
Germany **5-2** Belgium
Austria **3-2** France
(after extra time)
Spain **3-1** Brazil
Switzerland **3-2** Netherlands
Sweden **3-2** Argentina
Hungary **4-2** Egypt

SECOND ROUND

Germany **2-1** Sweden
Austria **2-1** Hungary
Italy **1-1** Spain
(after extra time)
Replay
Italy **1-0** Spain
Czechoslovakia **3-2** Switzerland

SEMI-FINALS

Czechoslovakia **3-1** Germany
(Nejedly 19, 81,   (Noack 62)
Krcil 71)
Italy **1-0** Austria
(Guaita 19)

THIRD PLACE PLAY-OFF

Germany **3-2** Austria
(Lehner 1, 42,   (Horvath 28,
Conen 27)   Sesta 54)

FINAL

June 10 – Flaminio, Rome
Italy **2-1** Czechoslovakia
(Orsi 81,   (Puc 71)
Schiavio 95)
(after extra time)
h/t: 0-0 **90 mins:** 1-1
Att: 55,000 **Ref:** Eklind (Sweden)

1938 FRANCE

FIRST ROUND

Switzerland **1-1** Germany
(after extra time)
Replay
Switzerland **4-2** Germany
Cuba **3-3** Romania
(after extra time)
Replay
Cuba **2-1** Romania
Hungary **6-0** Dutch East Indies
Sweden **w/o** Austria
France **3-1** Belgium
Czechoslovakia **3-0** Netherlands
(after extra time)
Brazil **6-5** Poland
(after extra time)
Italy **2-1** Norway
(after extra time)

w/o denotes walk over

QUARTER-FINALS

Sweden **8-0** Cuba
Hungary **2-0** Switzerland
Italy **3-1** France
Brazil **1-1** Czechoslovakia
(after extra time)
Replay
Brazil **2-1** Czechoslovakia

SEMI-FINALS

Italy **2-1** Brazil
(Colaussi 55,   (Romeo 87)
Meazza 60)
Hungary **5-1** Sweden
(Zsengeller   (Nyberg 1)
18, 38, 86,
Titkos 26,
Sarosi 61)

THIRD PLACE PLAY-OFF

Brazil **4-2** Sweden
(Romeo 43,   (Jonasson 18,
Leonidas 63, 73,   Nyberg 38)
Peracio 80)

FINAL

June 19 – Stade Colombes, Paris
Italy **4-2** Hungary
(Colaussi 5, 35,   (Titkos 7,
Piola 16, 82)   Sarosi 70)
h/t: 3-1 **Att:** 55,000
Ref: Capdeville (France)

1950 BRAZIL

POOL 1

Brazil **4-0** Mexico
Yugoslavia **3-0** Switzerland
Yugoslavia **4-1** Mexico
Brazil **2-2** Switzerland
Brazil **2-0** Yugoslavia
Switzerland **2-1** Mexico

	P	W	D	L	F	A	Pts
Brazil	3	2	1	0	8	2	5
Yugoslavia	3	2	0	1	7	3	4
Switzerland	3	1	1	1	4	6	3
Mexico	3	0	0	3	2	10	0

POOL 2

Spain **3-1** USA
England **2-0** Chile
USA **1-0** England
Spain **2-0** Chile
Spain **1-0** England
Chile **5-2** USA

	P	W	D	L	F	A	Pts
Spain	3	3	0	0	6	1	6
England	3	1	0	2	2	2	2
Chile	3	1	0	2	5	6	2
USA	3	1	0	2	4	8	2

POOL 3

Sweden **3-2** Italy
Sweden **2-2** Paraguay
Italy **2-0** Paraguay

	P	W	D	L	F	A	Pts
Sweden	2	1	1	0	5	4	3
Italy	2	1	0	1	4	3	2
Paraguay	2	0	1	1	2	4	1

POOL 4

Uruguay **8-0** Bolivia

	P	W	D	L	F	A	Pts
Uruguay	1	1	0	0	8	0	2
Bolivia	1	0	0	1	0	8	0

FINAL POOL

Uruguay **2-2** Spain
Brazil **7-1** Sweden
Uruguay **3-2** Sweden

World Cup Winners

Uruguay
1930, 50

Italy
1934, 38, 82

West Germany
1954, 74, 90

Brazil
1958, 62, 70, 94, 2002

England
1966

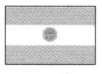
Argentina
1978, 86

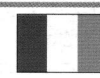
France
1998

Brazil **6-1** Spain
Sweden **3-1** Spain
Uruguay **2-1** Brazil

	P	W	D	L	F	A	Pts
Uruguay	3	2	1	0	7	5	**5**
Brazil	3	2	0	1	14	4	**4**
Sweden	3	1	0	2	6	11	**2**
Spain	3	0	1	2	4	11	**1**

THIRD PLACE
Sweden

FINAL
July 16 – Maracana, Rio de Janeiro
Uruguay **2-1** Brazil
(Schiaffino 66,   (Friaca 48)
Ghiggia 79)
h/t: 0-0   **Att:** 199,854
Ref: Reader (England)

1954 SWITZERLAND
POOL 1
Yugoslavia **1-0** France
Brazil **5-0** Mexico
France **3-2** Mexico
Brazil **1-1** Yugoslavia

	P	W	D	L	F	A	Pts
Brazil	2	1	1	0	6	1	**3**
Yugoslavia	2	1	1	0	2	1	**3**
France	2	1	0	1	3	3	**2**
Mexico	2	0	0	2	2	8	**0**

POOL 2
Hungary **9-0** South Korea
West Germany **4-1** Turkey
Hungary **8-3** West Germany
Turkey **7-0** South Korea

	P	W	D	L	F	A	Pts
Hungary	2	2	0	0	17	3	**4**
West Germany	2	1	0	1	7	9	**2**
Turkey	2	1	0	1	8	4	**2**
South Korea	2	0	0	2	0	16	**0**

PLAY-OFF
West Germany **7-2** Turkey

POOL 3
Austria **1-0** Scotland
Uruguay **2-0** Czechoslovakia
Austria **5-0** Czechoslovakia
Uruguay **7-0** Scotland

	P	W	D	L	F	A	Pts
Uruguay	2	2	0	0	9	0	**4**
Austria	2	2	0	0	6	0	**4**
Czechoslovakia	2	0	0	2	0	7	**0**
Scotland	2	0	0	2	0	8	**0**

POOL 4
England **4-4** Belgium
England **2-0** Switzerland
Switzerland **2-1** Italy
Italy **4-1** Belgium

	P	W	D	L	F	A	Pts
England	2	1	1	0	6	4	**3**
Italy	2	1	0	1	5	3	**2**
Switzerland	2	1	0	1	2	3	**2**
Belgium	2	0	1	1	5	8	**1**

PLAY-OFF
Switzerland **4-1** Italy

QUARTER-FINALS
West Germany **2-0** Yugoslavia
Hungary **4-2** Brazil
Austria **7-5** Switzerland
Uruguay **4-2** England

SEMI-FINALS
West Germany **6-1** Austria
(Schäfer 30,   (Probst 51)
Morlock 49,
F. Walter 54, 65,
O. Walter 60, 89)
Hungary **4-2** Uruguay
(Czibor 13,   (Hohberg 75, 86)
Hidegkuti 47,
Kocsis 111, 116)
(after extra time)

THIRD PLACE PLAY-OFF
Austria **3-1** Uruguay
(Stojaspal 16,   (Hohberg 21)
Cruz o.g. 59,
Ocwirk 79)

FINAL
July 4 – Wankdorf, Berne
West Germany **3-2** Hungary
(Morlock 11,   (Puskas 6,
Rahn 16, 83)   Czibor 8)
h/t: 2-2   **Att:** 60,000
Ref: Ling (England)

1958 SWEDEN
POOL 1
West Germany **3-1** Argentina
N. Ireland **1-0** Czechoslovakia
West Germany **2-2** Czechoslovakia
Argentina **3-1** N. Ireland
West Germany **2-2** N. Ireland
Czechoslovakia **6-1** Argentina

	P	W	D	L	F	A	Pts
West Germany	3	1	2	0	7	5	**4**
Czechoslovakia	3	1	1	1	8	4	**3**
N. Ireland	3	1	1	1	4	5	**3**
Argentina	3	1	0	2	5	10	**2**

PLAY-OFF
N. Ireland **2-1** Czechoslovakia

POOL 2
France **7-3** Paraguay
Yugoslavia **1-1** Scotland
Yugoslavia **3-2** France
Paraguay **3-2** Scotland
France **2-1** Scotland
Yugoslavia **3-3** Paraguay

	P	W	D	L	F	A	Pts
France	3	2	0	1	11	7	**4**
Yugoslavia	3	1	2	0	7	6	**4**
Paraguay	3	1	1	1	9	12	**3**
Scotland	3	0	1	2	4	6	**1**

POOL 3
Sweden **3-0** Mexico
Hungary **1-1** Wales
Wales **1-1** Mexico
Sweden **2-1** Hungary
Sweden **0-0** Wales
Hungary **4-0** Mexico

	P	W	D	L	F	A	Pts
Sweden	3	2	1	0	5	1	**5**
Hungary	3	1	1	1	6	3	**3**
Wales	3	0	3	0	2	2	**3**
Mexico	3	0	1	2	1	8	**1**

PLAY-OFF
Wales **2-1** Hungary

POOL 4
England **2-2** Soviet Union
Brazil **3-0** Austria
England **0-0** Brazil
Soviet Union **2-0** Austria
Brazil **2-0** Soviet Union
England **2-2** Austria

	P	W	D	L	F	A	Pts
Brazil	3	2	1	0	5	0	**5**
England	3	0	3	0	4	4	**3**
Soviet Union	3	1	1	1	4	4	**3**
Austria	3	0	1	2	2	7	**1**

PLAY-OFF
Soviet Union **1-0** England

QUARTER-FINALS
France **4-0** N. Ireland
West Germany **1-0** Yugoslavia
Sweden **2-0** Soviet Union
Brazil **1-0** Wales

SEMI-FINALS
Brazil **5-2** France
(Vava 2,   (Fontaine 8,
Didi 38,   Piantoni 83)
Pele 53, 64, 76)
Sweden **3-1** West Germany
(Skoglund 30,   (Schäfer 21)
Gren 81,
Hamrin 88)

THIRD PLACE PLAY-OFF
France **6-3** West Germany
(Fontaine   (Cieslarczyk 18,
16, 36, 78, 89,   Rahn 52,
Kopa 27,   Schäfer 83)
Douis 50)

FINAL
June 29 – Rasunda, Stockholm
Brazil **5-2** Sweden
(Vava 9, 32,   (Liedholm 4,
Pele 55, 89,   Simonsson 80)
Zagallo 68)
h/t: 2-1   **Att:** 49,737
Ref: Guigue (France)

1962 CHILE
GROUP 1
Uruguay **2-1** Colombia
Soviet Union **2-0** Yugoslavia
Yugoslavia **3-1** Uruguay
Soviet Union **4-4** Colombia
Soviet Union **2-1** Uruguay
Yugoslavia **5-0** Colombia

	P	W	D	L	F	A	Pts
Soviet Union	3	2	1	0	8	5	**5**
Yugoslavia	3	2	0	1	8	3	**4**
Uruguay	3	1	0	2	4	6	**2**
Colombia	3	0	1	2	5	11	**1**

GROUP 2
Chile **3-1** Switzerland
West Germany **0-0** Italy
Chile **2-0** Italy
West Germany **2-1** Switzerland
West Germany **2-0** Chile
Italy **3-0** Switzerland

	P	W	D	L	F	A	Pts
West Germany	3	2	1	0	4	1	**5**
Chile	3	2	0	1	5	3	**4**
Italy	3	1	1	1	3	2	**3**
Switzerland	3	0	0	3	2	8	**0**

GROUP 3
Brazil **2-0** Mexico
Czechoslovakia **1-0** Spain
Brazil **0-0** Czechoslovakia
Spain **1-0** Mexico
Brazil **2-1** Spain
Mexico **3-1** Czechoslovakia

	P	W	D	L	F	A	Pts
Brazil	3	2	1	0	4	1	**5**
Czechoslovakia	3	1	1	1	2	3	**3**
Mexico	3	1	0	2	3	4	**2**
Spain	3	1	0	2	2	3	**2**

GROUP 4
Argentina **1-0** Bulgaria
Hungary **2-1** England
England **3-1** Argentina
Hungary **6-1** Bulgaria
Argentina **0-0** Hungary
England **0-0** Bulgaria

	P	W	D	L	F	A	Pts
Hungary	3	2	1	0	8	2	**5**
England	3	1	1	1	4	3	**3**
Argentina	3	1	1	1	2	3	**3**
Bulgaria	3	0	1	2	1	7	**1**

QUARTER-FINALS
Yugoslavia **1-0** West Germany
Brazil **3-1** England
Chile **2-1** Soviet Union
Czechoslovakia **1-0** Hungary

SEMI-FINALS
Brazil **4-2** Chile
(Garrincha 9, 31,   (Toro 41,
Vava 49, 77)   L. Sanchez 61)
Czechoslovakia **3-1** Yugoslavia
(Kadraba 49,   (Jerkovic 69)
Scherer 80, 86)

THIRD PLACE PLAY-OFF
Chile **1-0** Yugoslavia
(Rojas 89)

FINAL
June 17 – Nacional, Santiago
Brazil **3-1** Czechoslovakia
(Amarildo 18,   (Masopust 16)
Zito 69,
Vava 77)
h/t: 1-1   **Att:** 68,679
Ref: Latishev (Soviet Union)

1966 ENGLAND

GROUP 1

England 0-0 Uruguay
France 1-1 Mexico
Uruguay 2-1 France
England 2-0 Mexico
Uruguay 0-0 Mexico
England 2-0 France

	P	W	D	L	F	A	Pts
England	3	2	1	0	4	0	5
Uruguay	3	1	2	0	2	1	4
Mexico	3	0	2	1	1	3	2
France	3	0	1	2	2	5	1

GROUP 2

West Germany 5-0 Switzerland
Argentina 2-1 Spain
Spain 2-1 Switzerland
Argentina 0-0 West Germany
Argentina 2-0 Switzerland
West Germany 2-1 Spain

	P	W	D	L	F	A	Pts
West Germany	3	2	1	0	7	1	5
Argentina	3	2	1	0	4	1	5
Spain	3	1	0	2	4	5	2
Switzerland	3	0	0	3	1	9	0

GROUP 3

Brazil 2-0 Bulgaria
Portugal 3-1 Hungary
Hungary 3-1 Brazil
Portugal 3-0 Bulgaria
Portugal 3-1 Brazil
Hungary 3-1 Bulgaria

	P	W	D	L	F	A	Pts
Portugal	3	3	0	0	9	2	6
Hungary	3	2	0	1	7	5	4
Brazil	3	1	0	2	4	6	2
Bulgaria	3	0	0	3	1	8	0

GROUP 4

Soviet Union 3-0 North Korea
Italy 2-0 Chile
Chile 1-1 North Korea
Soviet Union 1-0 Italy
North Korea 1-0 Italy
Soviet Union 2-1 Chile

	P	W	D	L	F	A	Pts
Soviet Union	3	3	0	0	6	1	6
North Korea	3	1	1	1	2	4	3
Italy	3	1	0	2	2	2	2
Chile	3	0	1	2	2	5	1

QUARTER-FINALS

England 1-0 Argentina
West Germany 4-0 Uruguay
Portugal 5-3 North Korea
Soviet Union 2-1 Hungary

SEMI-FINALS

West Germany 2-1 Soviet Union
(Haller 44,   (Porkuyan 88)
Beckenbauer 68)

England 2-1 Portugal
(R. Charlton   (Eusebio 82)
30, 79)

THIRD PLACE PLAY-OFF

Portugal 2-1 Soviet Union
(Eusebio 12,   (Metreveli 43)
Torres 88)

FINAL

July 30 – Wembley Stadium, London
England 4-2 West Germany
(Hurst   (Haller 13,
19, 100, 119,   Weber 89)
Peters 77)

(after extra time)

h/t: 1-1 90 mins: 2-2
Att: 96,924 Ref: Dienst (Switzerland)

1970 MEXICO

GROUP 1

Mexico 0-0 Soviet Union
Belgium 3-0 El Salvador
Soviet Union 4-1 Belgium
Mexico 4-0 El Salvador
Soviet Union 2-0 Belgium
Mexico 1-0 Belgium

	P	W	D	L	F	A	Pts
Soviet Union	3	2	1	0	6	1	5
Mexico	3	2	1	0	5	0	5
Belgium	3	1	0	2	4	5	2
El Salvador	3	0	0	3	0	9	0

GROUP 2

Uruguay 2-0 Israel
Italy 1-0 Sweden
Uruguay 0-0 Italy
Sweden 1-1 Israel
Sweden 1-0 Uruguay
Italy 0-0 Israel

	P	W	D	L	F	A	Pts
Italy	3	1	2	0	1	0	4
Uruguay	3	1	1	1	2	1	3
Sweden	3	1	1	1	2	2	3
Israel	3	0	2	1	1	3	2

GROUP 3

England 1-0 Romania
Brazil 4-1 Czechoslovakia
Romania 2-1 Czechoslovakia
Brazil 1-0 England
Brazil 3-2 Romania
England 1-0 Czechoslovakia

	P	W	D	L	F	A	Pts
Brazil	3	3	0	0	8	3	6
England	3	2	0	1	2	1	4
Romania	3	1	0	2	4	5	2
Czechoslovakia	3	0	0	3	2	7	0

GROUP 4

Peru 3-2 Bulgaria
West Germany 2-1 Morocco
Peru 3-0 Morocco
West Germany 5-2 Bulgaria
West Germany 3-1 Peru
Morocco 1-1 Bulgaria

	P	W	D	L	F	A	Pts
West Germany	3	3	0	0	10	4	6
Peru	3	2	0	1	7	5	4
Bulgaria	3	0	1	2	5	9	1
Morocco	3	0	1	2	2	6	1

QUARTER-FINALS

West Germany 3-2 England
(after extra time)
Brazil 4-2 Peru
Italy 4-1 Mexico
Uruguay 1-0 Soviet Union

SEMI-FINALS

Italy 4-3 West Germany
(Boninsegna 7,   (Schellinger 90,
Burgnich 99,   G. Müller 95, 110)
Riva 104,
Rivera 111)

(after extra time)

Brazil 3-1 Uruguay
(Clodoaldo 45,   (Cubilla 19)
Jairzinho 76,
Rivelino 88)

THIRD PLACE PLAY-OFF

West Germany 1-0 Uruguay
(Overath 26)

FINAL

June 21 – Azteca, Mexico City
Brazil 4-1 Italy
(Pele 18,   (Boninsegna 37)
Gerson 66,
Jairzinho 71,
Carlos Alberto 86)

h/t: 1-1 Att: 107,000
Ref: Glockner (East Germany)

1974 WEST GERMANY

GROUP 1

West Germany 1-0 Chile
East Germany 2-0 Australia
West Germany 3-0 Australia
East Germany 1-1 Chile
Australia 0-0 Chile
East Germany 1-0 West Germany

	P	W	D	L	F	A	Pts
East Germany	3	2	1	0	4	1	5
West Germany	3	2	0	1	4	1	4
Chile	3	0	2	1	1	2	2
Australia	3	0	1	2	0	5	1

GROUP 2

Brazil 0-0 Yugoslavia
Scotland 2-0 Zaïre
Brazil 0-0 Scotland
Yugoslavia 9-0 Zaïre
Yugoslavia 1-1 Scotland
Brazil 3-0 Zaïre

	P	W	D	L	F	A	Pts
Yugoslavia	3	1	2	0	10	1	4
Brazil	3	1	2	0	3	0	4
Scotland	3	1	2	0	3	1	4
Zaïre	3	0	0	3	0	14	0

GROUP 3

Netherlands 2-0 Uruguay
Bulgaria 0-0 Sweden
Netherlands 0-0 Sweden
Bulgaria 1-1 Uruguay
Netherlands 4-1 Bulgaria
Sweden 3-0 Uruguay

	P	W	D	L	F	A	Pts
Netherlands	3	2	1	0	6	1	5
Sweden	3	1	2	0	3	0	4
Bulgaria	3	0	2	1	2	5	2
Uruguay	3	0	1	2	1	6	1

GROUP 4

Italy 3-1 Haiti
Poland 3-2 Argentina
Argentina 1-1 Italy
Poland 7-0 Haiti
Argentina 4-1 Haiti
Poland 2-1 Italy

	P	W	D	L	F	A	Pts
Poland	3	3	0	0	12	3	6
Argentina	3	1	1	1	7	5	3
Italy	3	1	1	1	5	4	3
Haiti	3	0	0	3	2	14	0

SECOND ROUND - GROUP A

Brazil 1-0 East Germany
Netherlands 4-0 Argentina
Netherlands 2-0 East Germany
Brazil 2-1 Argentina
East Germany 1-1 Argentina
Netherlands 2-0 Brazil

	P	W	D	L	F	A	Pts
Netherlands	3	3	0	0	8	0	6
Brazil	3	2	0	1	3	3	4
East Germany	3	0	1	2	1	4	1
Argentina	3	0	1	2	2	7	1

SECOND ROUND - GROUP B

Poland 1-0 Sweden
West Germany 2-0 Yugoslavia
Poland 2-1 Yugoslavia
West Germany 4-2 Sweden
Sweden 2-1 Yugoslavia
West Germany 1-0 Poland

	P	W	D	L	F	A	Pts
West Germany	3	3	0	0	7	2	6
Poland	3	2	0	1	3	2	4
Sweden	3	1	0	2	4	6	2
Yugoslavia	3	0	0	3	2	6	0

THIRD PLACE PLAY-OFF

Poland 1-0 Brazil
(Lato 76)

FINAL

July 7 – Olympiastadion, Munich
West Germany 2-1 Netherlands
(Breitner 25 pen,   (Neeskens 2 pen)
G. Müller 43)

h/t: 2-1 Att: 77,833
Ref: Taylor (England)

1978 ARGENTINA

GROUP 1

Argentina 2-1 Hungary
Italy 2-1 France
Argentina 2-1 France
Italy 3-1 Hungary
Italy 1-0 Argentina
France 3-1 Hungary

	P	W	D	L	F	A	Pts
Italy	3	3	0	0	6	2	6
Argentina	3	2	0	1	4	3	4
France	3	1	0	2	5	5	2
Hungary	3	0	0	3	3	8	0

GROUP 2

West Germany 0-0 Poland
Tunisia 3-1 Mexico
Poland 1-0 Tunisia
West Germany 6-0 Mexico
Poland 3-1 Mexico
West Germany 0-0 Tunisia

	P	W	D	L	F	A	Pts
Poland	3	2	1	0	4	1	5
West Germany	3	1	2	0	6	0	4
Tunisia	3	1	1	1	3	2	3
Mexico	3	0	0	3	2	12	0

GROUP 3

Austria **2-1** Spain
Sweden **1-1** Brazil
Austria **1-0** Sweden
Brazil **0-0** Spain
Spain **1-0** Sweden
Brazil **1-0** Austria

	P	W	D	L	F	A	Pts
Austria	3	2	0	1	3	2	4
Brazil	3	1	2	0	2	1	4
Spain	3	1	1	1	2	2	3
Sweden	3	0	1	2	1	3	1

GROUP 4

Peru **3-1** Scotland
Netherlands **3-0** Iran
Scotland **1-1** Iran
Netherlands **0-0** Peru
Peru **4-1** Iran
Scotland **3-2** Netherlands

	P	W	D	L	F	A	Pts
Peru	3	2	1	0	7	2	5
Netherlands	3	1	1	1	5	3	3
Scotland	3	1	1	1	5	6	3
Iran	3	0	1	2	2	8	1

SECOND ROUND - GROUP A

Italy **0-0** West Germany
Netherlands **5-1** Austria
Italy **1-0** Austria
Austria **3-2** West Germany
Netherlands **2-1** Italy
Netherlands **2-2** West Germany

	P	W	D	L	F	A	Pts
Netherlands	3	2	1	0	9	4	5
Italy	3	1	1	1	2	2	3
West Germany	3	0	2	1	4	5	2
Austria	3	1	0	2	4	8	2

SECOND ROUND - GROUP B

Argentina **2-0** Poland
Brazil **3-0** Peru
Argentina **0-0** Brazil
Poland **1-0** Peru
Brazil **3-1** Poland
Argentina **6-0** Peru

	P	W	D	L	F	A	Pts
Argentina	3	2	1	0	8	0	5
Brazil	3	2	1	0	6	1	5
Poland	3	1	0	2	2	5	2
Peru	3	0	0	3	0	10	0

THIRD PLACE PLAY-OFF

Brazil **2-1** Italy
(Nelinho 64,   (Causio 38)
Dirceu 71)

FINAL

June 25 – Monumental, Buenos Aires
Argentina **3-1** Netherlands
(Kempes 37, 104,   (Nanninga 81)
Bertoni 114)
(after extra time)
h/t: 1-0 **90 mins:** 1-1 **Att:** 77,260
Ref: Gonella (Italy)

1982 SPAIN

GROUP 1

Italy **0-0** Poland
Peru **0-0** Cameroon
Italy **1-1** Peru
Poland **0-0** Cameroon
Poland **5-1** Peru
Italy **1-1** Cameroon

	P	W	D	L	F	A	Pts
Poland	3	1	2	0	5	1	4
Italy	3	0	3	0	2	2	3
Cameroon	3	0	3	0	1	1	3
Peru	3	0	2	1	2	6	2

GROUP 2

Algeria **2-1** West Germany
Austria **1-0** Chile
West Germany **4-1** Chile
Austria **2-0** Algeria
Algeria **3-2** Chile
West Germany **1-0** Austria

	P	W	D	L	F	A	Pts
West Germany	3	2	0	1	6	3	4
Austria	3	2	0	1	3	1	4
Algeria	3	2	0	1	5	5	4
Chile	3	0	0	3	3	8	0

GROUP 3

Belgium **1-0** Argentina
Hungary **10-1** El Salvador
Argentina **4-1** Hungary
Belgium **1-0** El Salvador
Belgium **1-1** Hungary
Argentina **2-0** El Salvador

	P	W	D	L	F	A	Pts
Belgium	3	2	1	0	3	1	5
Argentina	3	2	0	1	6	2	4
Hungary	3	1	1	1	12	6	3
El Salvador	3	0	0	3	1	13	0

GROUP 4

England **3-1** France
Czechoslovakia **1-1** Kuwait
England **2-0** Czechoslovakia
France **4-1** Kuwait
France **1-1** Czechoslovakia
England **1-0** Kuwait

	P	W	D	L	F	A	Pts
England	3	3	0	0	6	1	6
France	3	1	1	1	6	5	3
Czechoslovakia	3	0	2	1	2	4	2
Kuwait	3	0	1	2	2	6	1

GROUP 5

Spain **1-1** Honduras
N. Ireland **0-0** Yugoslavia
Spain **2-1** Yugoslavia
N. Ireland **1-1** Honduras
Yugoslavia **1-0** Honduras
N. Ireland **1-0** Spain

	P	W	D	L	F	A	Pts
N. Ireland	3	1	2	0	2	1	4
Spain	3	1	1	1	3	3	3
Yugoslavia	3	1	1	1	2	2	3
Honduras	3	0	2	1	2	3	2

GROUP 6

Brazil **2-1** Soviet Union
Scotland **5-2** New Zealand
Brazil **4-1** Scotland
Soviet Union **3-0** New Zealand
Scotland **2-2** Soviet Union
Brazil **4-0** New Zealand

	P	W	D	L	F	A	Pts
Brazil	3	3	0	0	10	2	6
Soviet Union	3	1	1	1	6	4	3
Scotland	3	1	1	1	8	8	3
New Zealand	3	0	0	3	2	12	0

SECOND ROUND - GROUP A

Poland **3-0** Belgium
Soviet Union **1-0** Belgium
Soviet Union **0-0** Poland

	P	W	D	L	F	A	Pts
Poland	2	1	1	0	3	0	3
Soviet Union	2	1	1	0	1	0	3
Belgium	2	0	0	2	0	4	0

SECOND ROUND - GROUP B

West Germany **0-0** England
West Germany **2-1** Spain
England **0-0** Spain

	P	W	D	L	F	A	Pts
West Germany	2	1	1	0	2	1	3
England	2	0	2	0	0	0	2
Spain	2	0	1	1	1	2	1

SECOND ROUND - GROUP C

Italy **2-1** Argentina
Brazil **3-1** Argentina
Italy **3-2** Brazil

	P	W	D	L	F	A	Pts
Italy	2	2	0	0	5	3	4
Brazil	2	1	0	1	5	4	2
Argentina	2	0	0	2	2	5	0

SECOND ROUND - GROUP D

France **1-0** Austria
N. Ireland **2-2** Austria
France **4-1** N. Ireland

	P	W	D	L	F	A	Pts
France	2	2	0	0	5	1	4
Austria	2	0	1	1	2	3	1
N. Ireland	2	0	1	1	3	6	1

SEMI-FINALS

Italy **2-0** Poland
(Rossi 22, 73)
West Germany **3-3** France
(Littbarski 18,   (Platini 27,
Rummenigge 102,   Tresor 93,
Fischer 107)   Giresse 97)
(after extra time)
West Germany won 5-4 on pens

THIRD PLACE PLAY-OFF

Poland **3-2** France
(Szarmach 41,   (Girard 14,
Majewski 44,   Couriol 75)
Kupcewicz 47)

FINAL

July 11 – Estadio Santiago Bernabeu, Madrid
Italy **3-1** West Germany
(Rossi 56,   (Breitner 82)
Tardelli 69,
Altobelli 80)
h/t: 0-0 **Att:** 90,080
Ref: Coelho (Brazil)

1986 MEXICO

GROUP A

Bulgaria **1-1** Italy
Argentina **3-1** South Korea
Italy **1-1** Argentina
Bulgaria **1-1** South Korea
Argentina **2-0** Bulgaria
Italy **3-2** South Korea

	P	W	D	L	F	A	Pts
Argentina	3	2	1	0	6	2	5
Italy	3	1	2	0	5	4	4
Bulgaria	3	0	2	1	2	4	2
South Korea	3	0	1	2	4	7	1

GROUP B

Mexico **2-1** Belgium
Paraguay **1-0** Iraq
Mexico **1-1** Paraguay
Belgium **2-1** Iraq
Paraguay **2-2** Belgium
Mexico **1-0** Iraq

	P	W	D	L	F	A	Pts
Mexico	3	2	1	0	4	2	5
Paraguay	3	1	2	0	4	3	4
Belgium	3	1	1	1	5	5	4
Iraq	3	0	0	3	1	4	0

GROUP C

Soviet Union **6-0** Hungary
France **1-0** Canada
Soviet Union **1-1** France
Hungary **2-0** Canada
France **3-0** Hungary
Soviet Union **2-0** Canada

	P	W	D	L	F	A	Pts
Soviet Union	3	2	1	0	9	1	5
France	3	2	1	0	5	1	5
Hungary	3	1	0	2	2	9	2
Canada	3	0	0	3	0	5	0

GROUP D

Brazil **1-0** Spain
N. Ireland **1-1** Algeria
Spain **2-1** N. Ireland
Brazil **1-0** Algeria
Spain **3-0** Algeria
Brazil **3-0** N. Ireland

	P	W	D	L	F	A	Pts
Brazil	3	3	0	0	5	0	6
Spain	3	2	0	1	5	2	4
N. Ireland	3	0	1	2	2	6	1
Algeria	3	0	1	2	1	5	1

GROUP E

West Germany **1-1** Uruguay
Denmark **1-0** Scotland
Denmark **6-1** Uruguay
West Germany **2-1** Scotland
Scotland **0-0** Uruguay
Denmark **2-0** West Germany

	P	W	D	L	F	A	Pts
Denmark	3	3	0	0	9	1	6
West Germany	3	1	1	1	3	4	3
Uruguay	3	0	2	1	2	7	2
Scotland	3	0	1	2	1	3	1

GROUP F

Morocco **0-0** Poland
Portugal **1-0** England
England **0-0** Morocco
Poland **1-0** Portugal
England **3-0** Poland
Morocco **3-1** Portugal

	P	W	D	L	F	A	Pts
Morocco	3	1	2	0	3	1	4
England	3	1	1	1	3	1	3
Poland	3	1	1	1	1	3	3
Portugal	3	1	0	2	2	4	2

SECOND ROUND

Mexico **2-0** Bulgaria
Belgium **4-3** Soviet Union
(after extra time)
Brazil **4-0** Poland
Argentina **1-0** Uruguay
France **2-0** Italy
West Germany **1-0** Morocco
England **3-0** Paraguay
Spain **5-1** Denmark

THE WORLD CUP

QUARTER-FINALS

France **1-1** Brazil
(after extra time)
France won 4-3 on pens

West Germany **0-0** Mexico
(after extra time)
West Germany won 4-1 on pens

Argentina **2-1** England
Belgium **1-1** Spain
(after extra time)
Belgium won 5-4 on pens

SEMI-FINALS

Argentina **2-0** Belgium
(Maradona
51, 62)

West Germany **2-0** France
(Brehme 9,
Völler 90)

THIRD PLACE PLAY-OFF

France **4-2** Belgium
(Ferreri 27,   (Ceulemans 10,
Papin 42,   Claesen 73)
Genghini 103,
Amoros 108)

FINAL

June 29 – Azteca, Mexico City
Argentina **3-2** West Germany
(Brown 22,   (Rummenigge 73,
Valdano 56,   Völler 82)
Burruchaga 84)
h/t: 1-0 **Att:** 114,590
Ref: Filho (Brazil)

1990 ITALY

GROUP A

Italy **1-0** Austria
Czechoslovakia **5-1** USA
Italy **1-0** USA
Czechoslovakia **1-0** Austria
Italy **2-0** Czechoslovakia
Austria **2-1** USA

	P	W	D	L	F	A	Pts
Italy	3	3	0	0	4	0	6
Czechoslovakia	3	2	0	1	6	3	4
Austria	3	1	0	2	2	3	2
USA	3	0	0	3	2	8	0

GROUP B

Cameroon **1-0** Argentina
Romania **2-0** Soviet Union
Argentina **2-0** Soviet Union
Cameroon **2-1** Romania
Argentina **1-1** Romania
Soviet Union **4-0** Cameroon

	P	W	D	L	F	A	Pts
Cameroon	3	2	0	1	3	5	4
Romania	3	1	1	1	4	3	3
Argentina	3	1	1	1	3	2	3
Soviet Union	3	1	0	2	4	4	2

GROUP C

Brazil **2-1** Sweden
Costa Rica **1-0** Scotland
Brazil **1-0** Costa Rica
Scotland **2-1** Sweden
Brazil **1-0** Scotland
Costa Rica **2-1** Sweden

	P	W	D	L	F	A	Pts
Brazil	3	3	0	0	4	1	6
Costa Rica	3	2	0	1	3	2	4
Scotland	3	1	0	2	2	3	2
Sweden	3	0	0	3	3	6	0

GROUP D

Colombia **2-0** UAE
West Germany **4-1** Yugoslavia
Yugoslavia **1-0** Colombia
West Germany **5-1** UAE
West Germany **1-1** Colombia
Yugoslavia **4-1** UAE

	P	W	D	L	F	A	Pts
West Germany	3	2	1	0	10	3	5
Yugoslavia	3	2	0	1	6	5	4
Colombia	3	1	1	1	3	2	3
UAE	3	0	0	3	2	11	0

GROUP E

Belgium **2-0** South Korea
Uruguay **0-0** Spain
Belgium **3-1** Uruguay
Spain **3-1** South Korea
Spain **2-1** Belgium
Uruguay **1-0** South Korea

	P	W	D	L	F	A	Pts
Spain	3	2	1	0	5	2	5
Belgium	3	2	0	1	6	3	4
Uruguay	3	1	1	1	2	3	3
South Korea	3	0	0	3	1	6	0

GROUP F

England **1-1** Rep. of Ireland
Netherlands **1-1** Egypt
England **0-0** Netherlands
Egypt **0-0** Rep. of Ireland
England **1-0** Egypt
Netherlands **1-1** Rep. of Ireland

	P	W	D	L	F	A	Pts
England	3	1	2	0	2	1	4
Netherlands	3	0	3	0	2	2	3
Rep. of Ireland	3	0	3	0	2	2	3
Egypt	3	0	2	1	1	2	2

SECOND ROUND

Cameroon **2-1** Colombia
(after extra time)
Czechoslovakia **4-1** Costa Rica
Argentina **1-0** Brazil
West Germany **2-1** Netherlands
Rep. of Ireland **0-0** Romania
(after extra time)
Rep. of Ireland won 5-4 on pens
Italy **2-0** Uruguay
Yugoslavia **2-1** Spain
(after extra time)
England **1-0** Belgium
(after extra time)

QUARTER-FINALS

Argentina **0-0** Yugoslavia
(after extra time)
Argentina won 3-2 on pens
Italy **1-0** Rep. of Ireland
West Germany **1-0** Czechoslovakia
England **3-2** Cameroon
(after extra time)

SEMI-FINALS

Argentina **1-1** Italy
(Caniggia 67)   (Schillaci 17)
(after extra time)
Argentina won 4-3 on pens
West Germany **1-1** England
(Brehme 59)   (Lineker 80)
(after extra time)
West Germany won 4-3 on pens

THIRD PLACE PLAY-OFF

Italy **2-1** England
(R. Baggio 71,   (Platt 80)
Schillaci 84)

FINAL

July 8 – Olimpico, Rome
West Germany **1-0** Argentina
(Brehme 84 pen)
h/t: 0-0 **Att:** 73,603
Ref: Codesal (Mexico)

1994 UNITED STATES

GROUP A

USA **1-1** Switzerland
Romania **3-1** Colombia
USA **2-1** Colombia
Switzerland **4-1** Romania
Romania **1-0** USA
Colombia **2-0** Switzerland

	P	W	D	L	F	A	Pts
Romania	3	2	0	1	5	5	6
Switzerland	3	1	1	1	5	4	4
USA	3	1	1	1	3	3	4
Colombia	3	1	0	2	4	5	3

GROUP B

Cameroon **2-2** Sweden
Brazil **2-0** Russia
Brazil **3-0** Cameroon
Sweden **3-1** Russia
Russia **6-1** Cameroon
Brazil **1-1** Sweden

	P	W	D	L	F	A	Pts
Brazil	3	2	1	0	6	1	7
Sweden	3	1	2	0	6	4	5
Russia	3	1	0	2	7	6	3
Cameroon	3	0	1	2	3	11	1

GROUP C

Germany **1-0** Bolivia
Spain **2-2** South Korea
Germany **1-1** Spain
South Korea **0-0** Bolivia
Spain **3-1** South Korea
Germany **3-2** South Korea

	P	W	D	L	F	A	Pts
Germany	3	2	1	0	5	3	7
Spain	3	1	2	0	6	4	5
South Korea	3	0	2	1	4	5	2
Bolivia	3	0	1	2	1	4	1

GROUP D

Argentina **4-0** Greece
Nigeria **3-0** Bulgaria
Argentina **2-1** Nigeria
Bulgaria **4-0** Greece
Nigeria **2-0** Greece
Bulgaria **2-0** Argentina

	P	W	D	L	F	A	Pts
Nigeria	3	2	0	1	6	2	6
Bulgaria	3	2	0	1	6	3	6
Argentina	3	2	0	1	6	3	6
Greece	3	0	0	3	0	10	0

GROUP E

Rep. of Ireland **1-0** Italy
Norway **1-0** Mexico
Italy **1-0** Norway
Mexico **2-1** Rep. of Ireland
Rep. of Ireland **0-0** Norway
Italy **1-1** Mexico

	P	W	D	L	F	A	Pts
Mexico	3	1	1	1	3	3	4
Rep. of Ireland	3	1	1	1	2	2	4
Italy	3	1	1	1	2	2	4
Norway	3	1	1	1	1	1	4

GROUP F

Belgium **1-0** Morocco
Netherlands **2-1** Saudi Arabia
Belgium **1-0** Netherlands
Saudi Arabia **2-1** Morocco
Netherlands **2-1** Morocco
Saudi Arabia **1-0** Belgium

	P	W	D	L	F	A	Pts
Netherlands	3	2	0	1	4	3	6
Saudi Arabia	3	2	0	1	4	3	6
Belgium	3	2	0	1	2	1	6
Morocco	3	0	0	3	2	5	0

SECOND ROUND

Germany **3-2** Belgium
Spain **3-0** Switzerland
Sweden **3-1** Saudi Arabia
Romania **3-2** Argentina
Netherlands **2-0** Rep. of Ireland
Brazil **1-0** USA
Italy **2-1** Nigeria
(after extra time)
Bulgaria **1-1** Mexico
(after extra time)
Bulgaria won 3-1 on pens

QUARTER-FINALS

Italy **2-1** Spain
Brazil **3-2** Netherlands
Bulgaria **2-1** Germany
Sweden **2-2** Romania
(after extra time)
Sweden won 5-4 on pens

SEMI-FINALS

Brazil **1-0** Sweden
(Romario 80)
Italy **2-1** Bulgaria
(R. Baggio 21, 26)   (Stoichkov 44 pen)

THIRD PLACE PLAY-OFF

Sweden **4-0** Bulgaria
(Brolin 8,
Mild 30,
H. Larsson 37,
K. Andersson 39)

FINAL

July 17 – Rose Bowl, Pasadena
Brazil **0-0** Italy
(after extra time)
Brazil won 3-2 on pens
h/t: 0-0 **90 mins:** 0-0 **Att:** 94,000
Ref: Puhl (Hungary)

1998 FRANCE

GROUP A

Brazil **2-1** Scotland
Morocco **2-2** Norway
Brazil **3-0** Morocco
Scotland **1-1** Norway
Norway **2-1** Brazil
Morocco **3-0** Scotland

	P	W	D	L	F	A	Pts
Brazil	3	2	0	1	6	3	6
Norway	3	1	2	0	5	4	5
Morocco	3	1	1	1	5	5	4
Scotland	3	0	1	2	2	6	1

GROUP B

Italy **2-2** Chile
Austria **1-1** Cameroon
Chile **1-1** Austria
Italy **3-0** Cameroon
Chile **1-1** Cameroon
Italy **2-1** Austria

	P	W	D	L	F	A	Pts
Italy	3	2	1	0	7	3	7
Chile	3	0	3	0	4	4	3
Austria	3	0	2	1	3	4	2
Cameroon	3	0	2	1	2	5	2

GROUP C

Denmark **1-0** Saudi Arabia
France **3-0** South Africa
France **4-0** Saudi Arabia
South Africa **1-1** Denmark
France **2-1** Denmark
South Africa **2-2** Saudi Arabia

	P	W	D	L	F	A	Pts
France	3	3	0	0	9	1	9
Denmark	3	1	1	1	3	3	4
South Africa	3	0	2	1	3	6	2
Saudi Arabia	3	0	1	2	2	7	1

GROUP D

Paraguay **0-0** Bulgaria
Nigeria **3-2** Spain
Nigeria **1-0** Bulgaria
Spain **0-0** Paraguay
Paraguay **3-1** Nigeria
Spain **6-1** Bulgaria

	P	W	D	L	F	A	Pts
Nigeria	3	2	0	1	5	5	6
Paraguay	3	1	2	0	3	1	5
Spain	3	1	1	1	8	4	4
Bulgaria	3	0	1	2	1	7	1

GROUP E

Mexico **3-1** South Korea
Netherlands **0-0** Belgium
Belgium **2-2** Mexico
Netherlands **5-0** South Korea
Belgium **1-1** South Korea
Netherlands **2-2** Mexico

	P	W	D	L	F	A	Pts
Netherlands	3	1	2	0	7	2	5
Mexico	3	1	2	0	7	5	5
Belgium	3	0	3	0	3	3	3
South Korea	3	0	1	2	2	9	1

GROUP F

Germany **2-0** USA
Yugoslavia **1-0** Iran
Germany **2-2** Yugoslavia
Iran **2-1** USA
Germany **2-0** Iran
Yugoslavia **1-0** USA

	P	W	D	L	F	A	Pts
Germany	3	2	1	0	6	2	7
Yugoslavia	3	2	1	0	4	2	7
Iran	3	1	0	2	2	4	3
USA	3	0	0	3	1	5	0

GROUP G

England **2-0** Tunisia
Romania **1-0** Colombia
Colombia **1-0** Tunisia
Romania **2-1** England
Romania **1-1** Tunisia
England **2-0** Colombia

	P	W	D	L	F	A	Pts
Romania	3	2	1	0	4	2	7
England	3	2	0	1	5	2	6
Colombia	3	1	0	2	1	3	3
Tunisia	3	0	1	2	1	4	1

GROUP H

Argentina **1-0** Japan
Croatia **3-1** Jamaica
Croatia **1-0** Japan
Argentina **5-0** Jamaica
Argentina **1-0** Croatia
Jamaica **2-1** Japan

	P	W	D	L	F	A	Pts
Argentina	3	3	0	0	7	0	9
Croatia	3	2	0	1	4	2	6
Jamaica	3	1	0	2	3	9	3
Japan	3	0	0	3	1	4	0

SECOND ROUND

Italy **1-0** Norway
Brazil **4-1** Chile
France **1-0** Paraguay
(after extra time)
Denmark **4-1** Nigeria
Germany **2-1** Mexico
Netherlands **2-1** Yugoslavia
Croatia **1-0** Romania
Argentina **2-2** England
(after extra time)
Argentina won 4-3 on pens

QUARTER-FINALS

France **0-0** Italy
(after extra time)
France won 4-3 on pens
Brazil **3-2** Denmark
Netherlands **2-1** Argentina
Croatia **3-0** Germany

SEMI-FINALS

Brazil **1-1** Netherlands
(Ronaldo 46) *(Kluivert 87)*
(after extra time)
Brazil won 4-2 on pens
France **2-1** Croatia
(Thuram 47, 70) *(Suker 46)*

THIRD PLACE PLAY-OFF

Croatia **2-1** Netherlands
(Prosinecki 13, *(Zenden 21)*
Suker 36)

FINAL

July 12 – Stade de France, Paris
France **3-0** Brazil
(Zidane 27, 45,
Petit 90)
h/t: 2-0 **Att:** 75,000
Ref: Belqola (Morocco)

2002 JAPAN/KOREA

GROUP A

Senegal **1-0** France
Denmark **2-1** Uruguay
Denmark **1-1** Senegal
France **0-0** Uruguay
Denmark **2-0** France
Senegal **3-3** Uruguay

	P	W	D	L	F	A	Pts
Denmark	3	2	1	0	5	2	7
Senegal	3	1	2	0	5	4	5
Uruguay	3	0	2	1	4	5	2
France	3	0	1	2	0	3	1

GROUP B

Paraguay **2-2** South Africa
Spain **3-1** Slovenia
Spain **3-1** Paraguay
South Africa **1-0** Slovenia
Spain **3-2** South Africa
Paraguay **3-1** Slovenia

	P	W	D	L	F	A	Pts
Spain	3	3	0	0	9	4	9
Paraguay	3	1	1	1	6	6	4
South Africa	3	1	1	1	5	5	4
Slovenia	3	0	0	3	2	7	0

GROUP C

Brazil **2-1** Turkey
Costa Rica **2-0** China
Brazil **4-0** China
Costa Rica **1-1** Turkey
Brazil **5-2** Costa Rica
Turkey **3-0** China

	P	W	D	L	F	A	Pts
Brazil	3	3	0	0	11	3	9
Turkey	3	1	1	1	5	3	4
Costa Rica	3	1	1	1	5	6	4
China	3	0	0	3	0	9	0

GROUP D

South Korea **2-0** Poland
USA **3-2** Portugal
South Korea **1-1** USA
Portugal **4-0** Poland
South Korea **1-0** Portugal
Poland **3-1** USA

	P	W	D	L	F	A	Pts
South Korea	3	2	1	0	4	1	7
USA	3	1	1	1	5	6	4
Portugal	3	1	0	2	6	4	3
Poland	3	1	0	2	3	7	3

GROUP E

Rep. of Ireland **1-1** Cameroon
Germany **8-0** Saudi Arabia
Germany **1-1** Rep. of Ireland
Cameroon **1-0** Saudi Arabia
Germany **2-0** Cameroon
Rep. of Ireland **3-0** Saudi Arabia

	P	W	D	L	F	A	Pts
Germany	3	2	1	0	11	1	7
Rep. of Ireland	3	1	2	0	5	2	5
Cameroon	3	1	1	1	2	3	4
Saudi Arabia	3	0	0	3	0	12	0

GROUP F

England **1-1** Sweden
Argentina **1-0** Nigeria
Sweden **2-1** Nigeria
England **1-0** Argentina
Sweden **1-1** Argentina
England **0-0** Nigeria

	P	W	D	L	F	A	Pts
Sweden	3	1	2	0	4	3	5
England	3	1	2	0	2	1	5
Argentina	3	1	1	1	2	2	4
Nigeria	3	0	1	2	1	3	1

Brazilian players celebrate by doing the samba after beating Germany in Japan 2002.

GROUP G

Mexico **1-0** Croatia
Italy **2-0** Ecuador
Croatia **2-1** Italy
Mexico **2-1** Ecuador
Italy **1-1** Mexico
Ecuador **1-0** Croatia

	P	W	D	L	F	A	Pts
Mexico	3	2	1	0	4	2	7
Italy	3	1	1	1	4	3	4
Croatia	3	1	0	2	2	3	3
Ecuador	3	1	0	2	2	4	3

GROUP H

Japan **2-2** Belgium
Russia **2-0** Tunisia
Japan **1-0** Russia
Tunisia **1-1** Belgium
Japan **2-0** Tunisia
Belgium **3-2** Russia

	P	W	D	L	F	A	Pts
Japan	3	2	1	0	5	2	7
Belgium	3	1	2	0	6	5	5
Russsia	3	1	0	2	4	4	3
Tunisia	3	0	1	2	1	5	1

SECOND ROUND

Germany **1-0** Paraguay
England **3-0** Denmark
Senegal **2-1** Sweden
(golden goal in extra time)
Spain **1-1** Rep. of Ireland
(after extra time)
Spain won 3-2 on pens
USA **2-0** Mexico
Brazil **2-0** Belgium
Turkey **1-0** Japan
South Korea **2-1** Italy
(golden goal in extra time)

QUARTER-FINALS

Brazil **2-1** England
Germany **1-0** USA
Spain **0-0** South Korea
(extra time)
South Korea won 5-3 on pens
Turkey **1-0** Senegal
(golden goal in extra time)

SEMI-FINALS

Germany **1-0** South Korea
(Ballack 78)
Brazil **1-0** Turkey
(Ronaldo 49)

THIRD PLACE PLAY-OFF

Turkey **3-2** South Korea
(Sukur 1, *(Lee Eul-yong 9,*
Mansiz 13, 32) *Song Chong-guk 93)*

FINAL

June 30 – Yokohama, Japan
Brazil **2-0** Germany
(Ronaldo 67, 79)
h/t: 0-0 **Att:** 69,029
Ref: Collina (Italy)

THE WORLD CUP

The Olympic Games

TOURNAMENT OVERVIEW

THE SOCCER TOURNAMENT at the Olympic Games has changed its status as a global tournament four or five times over its existence. As with all Olympic events, it began as a competition for national teams of amateurs only. As soccer became a professional sport all over the world, it inevitably collided with the Olympic amateur ethos. As soccer has acquired its own ruling body – FIFA – and its own global tournament – the World Cup – its relationship with the Olympics has become more complex.

At the earliest Olympics soccer was played as an exhibition sport. At the first modern Olympics in Athens in 1896, a tournament was played between a Danish XI, an Athenian XI and an Izmir XI (then a Greek area of Asian Turkey), but the records have been lost. In Paris in 1900 Upton Park FC (of east London) took on a French XI, while 1906 saw a rematch of the 1900 Games with the addition of a Thessaloniki XI (whose fixture with Athens descended into violence).

Soccer becomes official

Soccer became an official Olympic sport at the 1908 Games in London; it was in effect the first world championship. With the exception of Egypt, who played at the 1920 games, this was an exclusively European affair until 1924. Great Britain and Denmark set the early pace contesting two Finals (1908 and 1912). The 1924 games in Paris saw the arrival of the South Americans for the first time and a new global soccer power was revealed. The dazzling Uruguayans took the title with ease, while 1928 saw them triumph again, beating an equally fearsome Argentinian team in a replayed Final.

The 1932 Olympics in Los Angeles showed that the global spread of soccer had stopped at Ellis Island; there was no soccer tournament. By the time soccer returned to the Olympics in Berlin in 1936, professionalism had been legalized in most of the key soccer nations (England, Scotland, France, Uruguay, Argentina, Brazil, Italy and Spain) and two World Cups had been held; the status of Olympic soccer plummeted. For the next 30 years the tournament was effectively contested by the enduring amateur teams of Scandinavia and the state-sponsored amateurs of Eastern Europe; teams from these regions contested every Final from 1948 to 1980. This pattern was broken by FIFA's ban on players who had taken part in World Cup qualifiers from appearing at the Olympics – though this, of course, excluded some genuine amateurs.

The Africans are coming

The low to which the tournament had sunk has been redeemed by three changes. First, soccer's developing nations in Asia and Africa have taken an increasing interest and pride in Olympic performances and the global coverage it provides. Crowds for Olympic soccer at Seoul and Los Angeles were enormous and FIFA finally squared the amateurism circle by making the Olympic tournament an under-23 competition open to all players. Gold medals for Nigeria (1996) and Cameroon (2000) have kept global interest in the tournament alive.

In 1928 in Amsterdam the Uruguayans returned to the Olympics as holders. They were triumphant once again, beating the Netherlands 2-0, Germany 4-1 (pictured here, Uruguay in white), and Italy 3-2 on the way to the Final. There the team met its fellow South Americans from Argentina and triumphed 2-1 in a replay for which 250,000 people applied for tickets. This signalled a shift in the balance of power in world soccer from Europe to Latin America.

The Olympic Games Soccer Tournament

Number of appearances at Olympic Games		Olympic medals and date	
	10+ times	Gold	
	7–9 times	Silver	
	4–6 times	Bronze	
	1–3 times		
	none	VI* 1916*	Games cancelled

Host city and Olympiad number: **XIX**

Location and year of Games: **Sydney 2000**

Montreal 1976 — **XXI**

XXVI

Los Angeles 1932, 84 — **X, XXIII**

Atlanta 1996

GHANA 1992

Mexico City 1968 — **XIX**

BRAZIL 1984, 88 1996

CHILE 2000

URUGUAY 1924, 28

ARGENTINA 1928, 96

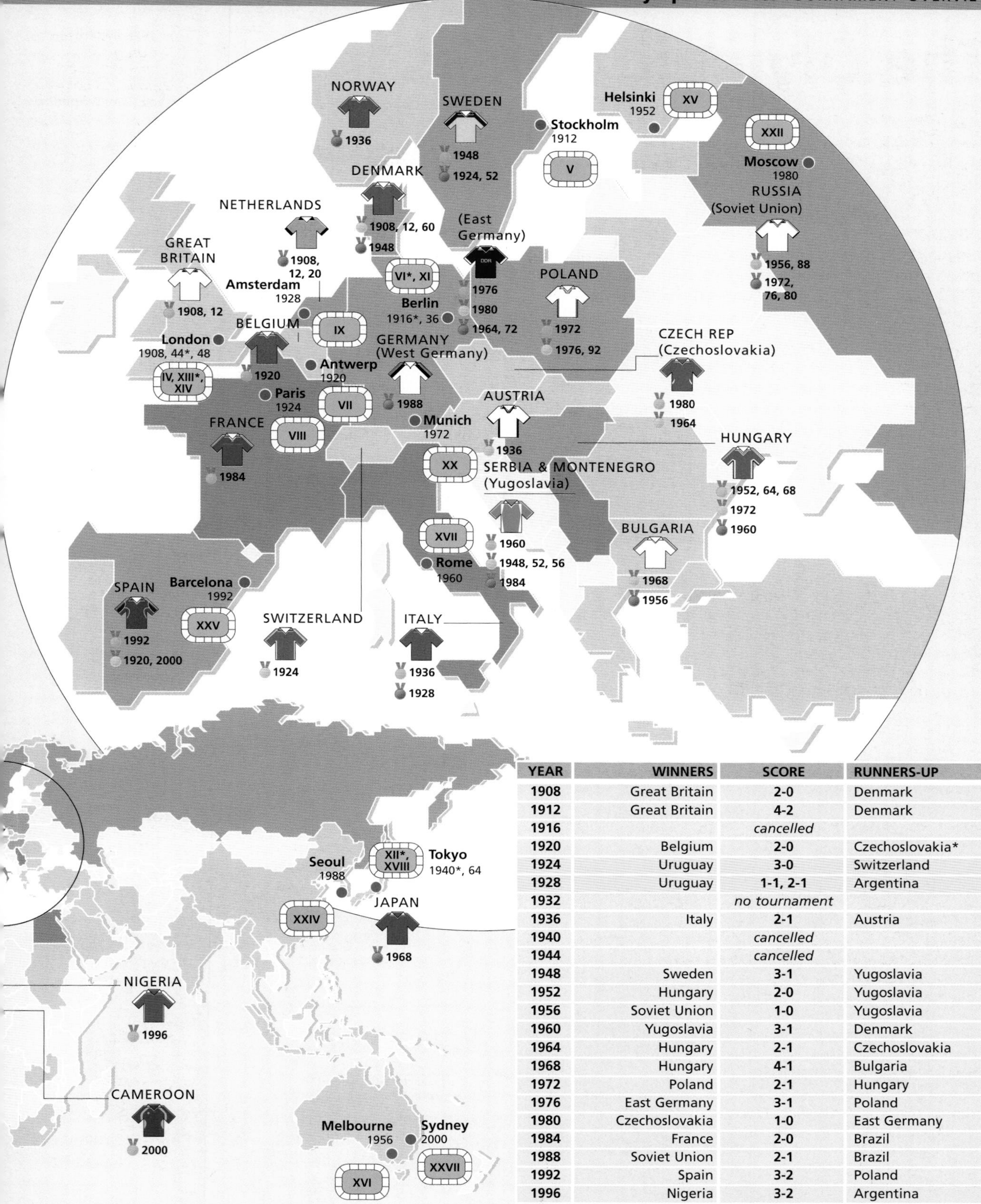

NORWAY
1936
SWEDEN
1948
1924, 52
Helsinki 1952
XV
Stockholm 1912
V
XXII
Moscow 1980
RUSSIA (Soviet Union)
1956, 88
1972, 76, 80
DENMARK
1908, 12, 60
1948
NETHERLANDS
1908, 12, 20
GREAT BRITAIN
1908, 12
Amsterdam 1928
IX
(East Germany)
DDR
1976
1980
1964, 72
VI*, XI
Berlin 1916*, 36
POLAND
1972
1976, 92
London 1908, 44*, 48
IV, XIII*, XIV
BELGIUM
1920
Antwerp 1920
GERMANY (West Germany)
1988
Paris 1924
VII
CZECH REP (Czechoslovakia)
1980
1964
FRANCE
1984
VIII
Munich 1972
AUSTRIA
1936
XX
HUNGARY
1952, 64, 68
1972
1960
SERBIA & MONTENEGRO (Yugoslavia)
1960
1948, 52, 56
1984
XVII
Rome 1960
BULGARIA
1968
1956
SPAIN
1992
1920, 2000
Barcelona 1992
XXV
SWITZERLAND
1924
ITALY
1936
1928
Seoul 1988
XII*, XVIII
Tokyo 1940*, 64
XXIV
JAPAN
1968
NIGERIA
1996
CAMEROON
2000
Melbourne 1956
Sydney 2000
XVI
XXVII

YEAR	WINNERS	SCORE	RUNNERS-UP
1908	Great Britain	2-0	Denmark
1912	Great Britain	4-2	Denmark
1916		*cancelled*	
1920	Belgium	2-0	Czechoslovakia*
1924	Uruguay	3-0	Switzerland
1928	Uruguay	1-1, 2-1	Argentina
1932		*no tournament*	
1936	Italy	2-1	Austria
1940		*cancelled*	
1944		*cancelled*	
1948	Sweden	3-1	Yugoslavia
1952	Hungary	2-0	Yugoslavia
1956	Soviet Union	1-0	Yugoslavia
1960	Yugoslavia	3-1	Denmark
1964	Hungary	2-1	Czechoslovakia
1968	Hungary	4-1	Bulgaria
1972	Poland	2-1	Hungary
1976	East Germany	3-1	Poland
1980	Czechoslovakia	1-0	East Germany
1984	France	2-0	Brazil
1988	Soviet Union	2-1	Brazil
1992	Spain	3-2	Poland
1996	Nigeria	3-2	Argentina
2000	Cameroon	2-2 (5-3 pens)	Spain

* In 1920 the silver medal was awarded to Spain after Czechoslovakia was disqualified. Please see over for further details.

The Olympic Games

AT THE FIRST THREE OLYMPIADS, between 1896 and 1904, the format for the soccer tournament was eclectic to say the least, and included exhibition games and mini-leagues with selected XIs and local clubs. For example, at the 1900 Games in France, Club Français of Paris represented the hosts against Upton Park FC from Great Britain and a Belgian Student XI; and at St. Louis in 1904 two local teams, St. Rose Kickers FC and Christian Brothers College, lost to the Canadian side Galt FC. A more formal knockout competition was played between eight teams at the 1908 games, though only after the rest of the Olympics had finished.

In 1912 a consolation tournament for first round losers was also played so that teams that crossed the world would get more than a single game. Sixteen teams, including Egypt – the first team to represent Africa in the Olympic soccer tournament – played in 1920 at Antwerp. This format was maintained, with the addition of various preliminary rounds to even out the numbers, until the 1956 Melbourne games in Australia.

The Melbourne Olympic tournament was preceded by a qualifying tournament, and this was formalized for the 1960 Olympics with places being allocated to each FIFA soccer confederation. However, the greater willingness of developing nations to compete at the Olympics saw Africa and Asia gain more places than they did in the World Cup.

Under FIFA regulations the tournament has become an Under-23's World competition since 1992, though a number of over-age players may be included in squads.

1908 LONDON
SEMI-FINALS
Great Britain **4-0** Netherlands
Denmark **17-1** France A
THIRD PLACE PLAY-OFF
Netherlands **2-0** Sweden
France A refused to play
FINAL
October 24 – White City
Great Britain **2-0** Denmark
(Chapman 20,
Woodward 46)
h/t: 1-0 **Att:** 15,000
Ref: Lewis (Great Britain)

1912 STOCKHOLM
SEMI-FINALS
Great Britain **4-0** Finland
Denmark **4-1** Netherlands
THIRD PLACE PLAY-OFF
Netherlands **9-0** Finland
FINAL
July 4 – Olympic Stadium
Great Britain **4-2** Denmark
(Walden 10,   (Olsen 27, 81)
Hoare 22, 41,
Berry 43)
h/t: 4-1 **Att:** 25,000
Ref: Groothoof (Netherlands)

1920 ANTWERP
SEMI-FINALS
Belgium **3-0** Netherlands
Czechoslovakia **4-1** France
SECOND PLACE PLAY-OFF*
Spain **3-1** Netherlands
FINAL
September 5 – Olympisch
Belgium **2-0** Czechoslovakia**
(Coppee 6 pen,
Larnoe 30)
h/t: n/a **Att:** 35,000
Ref: Lewis (Great Britain)

* Spain won the silver medal after a special mini tournament.
** Match abandoned after 39 minutes. Czechoslovakia left the pitch complaining of biased refereeing and were disqualified.

1924 PARIS
SEMI-FINALS
Uruguay **2-1** Netherlands
Switzerland **2-1** Sweden
THIRD PLACE PLAY-OFF
Sweden **3-1** Netherlands
FINAL
June 9 – Colombes
Uruguay **3-0** Switzerland
(Petrone 27,
Cea 63,
Romano 81)
h/t: 1-0 **Att:** 41,000
Ref: Slawick (France)

1928 AMSTERDAM
SEMI-FINALS
Uruguay **3-2** Italy
Argentina **6-0** Egypt
THIRD PLACE PLAY-OFF
Italy **11-3** Egypt
FINAL
June 10 – Olympic Stadium
Uruguay **1-1** Argentina
(Ferreira)   (Petrone)
(after extra time)
h/t: n/a **Att:** n/a
Ref: Lewis (Great Britain)
REPLAY
June 13 – Olympic Stadium
Uruguay **2-1** Argentina
(Figueroa,   (Monti)
H. Scarone)
h/t: n/a **Att:** n/a
Ref: Mutter (Netherlands)

1932 LOS ANGELES
no soccer tournament

1936 BERLIN
SEMI-FINALS
Italy **2-1** Norway
Austria **3-1** Poland
THIRD PLACE PLAY-OFF
Norway **3-2** Poland
FINAL
August 16 – Olympia Stadion
Italy **2-1** Austria
(Frossi 70, 92)   (Kainberger 80)
(after extra time)
h/t: 0-0 **90 mins:** 1-1 **Att:** 90,000
Ref: Bauwens (Germany)

1948 LONDON
SEMI-FINALS
Sweden **4-2** Denmark
Yugoslavia **3-1** Great Britain
THIRD PLACE PLAY-OFF
Denmark **5-3** Great Britain
FINAL
August 13 – Wembley Stadium
Sweden **3-1** Yugoslavia
(Gren 24, 67   (Bobek 42)
G. Nordahl 48)
h/t: 1-1 **Att:** 60,000
Ref: Ling (Great Britain)

1952 HELSINKI
SEMI-FINALS
Hungary **6-0** Sweden
Yugoslavia **3-1** West Germany
THIRD PLACE PLAY-OFF
Sweden **2-0** West Germany
FINAL
August 2 – Olympiastadion
Hungary **2-0** Yugoslavia
(Puskas 25,
Czibor 88)
h/t: 1-0 **Att:** 60,000
Ref: Ellis (Great Britain)

1956 MELBOURNE
SEMI-FINALS
Yugoslavia **4-1** India
Soviet Union **2-1** Bulgaria
THIRD PLACE PLAY-OFF
Bulgaria **3-0** India
FINAL
August 12 – Olympic Park
Soviet Union **1-0** Yugoslavia
(Ilyin 48)
h/t: 0-0 **Att:** 120,000
Ref: Wright (Australia)

1960 ROME
SEMI-FINALS
Yugoslavia **1-1** Italy
Yugoslavia won by drawing lots
Denmark **2-0** Hungary
THIRD PLACE PLAY-OFF
Hungary **2-1** Italy
FINAL
September 10 – Flaminio Stadium
Yugoslavia **3-1** Denmark
(Galic,   (F. Nielsen)
Matous,
Kostic)
h/t: n/a **Att:** 40,000
Ref: Lo Bello (Italy)

1964 TOKYO
SEMI-FINALS
Czechoslovakia **2-1** East Germany
Hungary **6-0** United Arab
Republic
THIRD PLACE PLAY-OFF
East Germany **3-1** United Arab
Republic
FINAL
October 23 – National Stadium
Hungary **2-1** Czechoslovakia
(Weiss 47,   (Brumousky 80)
Bene 59)
h/t: 1-0 **Att:** 75,000
Ref: Ashkenazi (Israel)

1968 MEXICO CITY
SEMI-FINALS
Hungary **5-0** Japan
Bulgaria **3-2** Mexico
THIRD PLACE PLAY-OFF
Japan **2-0** Mexico
FINAL
October 26 – Azteca Stadium
Hungary **4-1** Bulgaria
(Menczel 22,   (Dimitrov 40)
A. Dunai 41, 49,
Juhasz 62)
h/t: 2-1 **Att:** 75,000
Ref: Diego de Leo (Mexico)

Olympic Games Winners

 **Great Britain** 1908, 12
 **Belgium** 1920
 **Uruguay** 1924, 28
Italy 1936
 Sweden 1948
Hungary 1952, 64, 68
Soviet Union 1956, 88
 **Yugoslavia** 1960
Poland 1972

 East Germany 1976
 Czechoslovakia 1980
 France 1984
Spain 1992
Nigeria 1996
Cameroon 2000

1972 MUNICH

SECOND ROUND – GROUP A
Poland 2-1 Soviet Union
Poland 1-1 Denmark
Poland 5-0 Morocco
Soviet Union 4-0 Denmark
Soviet Union 3-0 Morocco
Denmark 3-1 Morocco

SECOND ROUND – GROUP B
Hungary 2-0 East Germany
Hungary 4-1 West Germany
Hungary 2-0 Mexico
East Germany 3-2 West Germany
East Germany 7-0 Mexico
West Germany 1-1 Mexico

THIRD PLACE PLAY-OFF
Soviet Union 2-2 East Germany
Bronze medal was shared

FINAL
September 10 – Olympic Stadium
Poland 2-1 Hungary
(Deyna 47, 68) (Varadi 42)
h/t: 0-1 Att: 50,000
Ref: Tschenscher (West Germany)

1976 MONTREAL

SEMI-FINALS
East Germany 2-1 Soviet Union
Poland 2-0 Brazil

THIRD PLACE PLAY-OFF
Soviet Union 2-0 Brazil

FINAL
July 31 – Olympic Stadium
East Germany 3-1 Poland
(Schade 7, (Lato 59)
Hoffmann 14,
Hafner 79)
h/t: 2-0 Att: 71,000
Ref: Barreto (Uruguay)

1980 MOSCOW

SEMI-FINALS
East Germany 1-0 Soviet Union
Czechoslovakia 2-0 Yugoslavia

THIRD PLACE PLAY-OFF
Soviet Union 2-0 Yugoslavia

FINAL
August 2 – Luzhniki Stadium
Czechoslovakia 1-0 East Germany
(Svoboda 77)
h/t: 0-0 Att: 70,000
Ref: Zade (Soviet Union)

1984 LOS ANGELES

SEMI-FINALS
France 4-2 Yugoslavia
Brazil 2-1 Italy

THIRD PLACE PLAY-OFF
Yugoslavia 2-1 Italy

FINAL
August 11 – Rose Bowl, Pasadena
France 2-0 Brazil
(Brisson 55,
Xuereb 62)
h/t: 0-0 Att: 101,000
Ref: Keizer (Netherlands)

1988 SEOUL

SEMI-FINALS
Soviet Union 3-2 Italy
Brazil 1-1 West Germany
Brazil won 3-2 on pens

THIRD PLACE PLAY-OFF
West Germany 3-0 Italy

FINAL
October 1 – Olympic Stadium
Soviet Union 2-1 Brazil
(Dobrovolski 61, (Romario 30)
Savichev 103)
(after extra time)
h/t: 0-1 90 mins: 1-1 Att: 73,000
Ref: Bignet (France)

1992 BARCELONA

SEMI-FINALS
Poland 6-1 Australia
Spain 2-0 Ghana

THIRD PLACE PLAY-OFF
Ghana 1-0 Australia

FINAL
August 8 – Nou Camp
Spain 3-2 Poland
(Abelardo 65, (Kowalczyk 44,
Quico 72, 90) Staniek 76)
h/t: 0-1 Att: 95,000
Ref: Torres (Colombia)

1996 ATLANTA

SEMI-FINALS
Argentina 2-0 Portugal
Nigeria 4-3 Brazil

THIRD PLACE PLAY-OFF
Brazil 5-0 Portugal

FINAL
August 3 – Sanford Stadium
Nigeria 3-2 Argentina
(Babayaro 27, (C. Lopez 3,
Amokachi 74, Crespo pen 50)
Amunike 89)
h/t: 1-1 Att: 86,000
Ref: Collina (Italy)

2000 SYDNEY

SEMI-FINALS
Spain 3-1 USA
Cameroon 2-1 Chile

THIRD PLACE PLAY-OFF
Chile 2-0 USA

FINAL
September 30 – Olympic Stadium
Cameroon 2-2 Spain
(Amaya o.g. 53, (Xavi 2,
Eto'o 58) Gabri 45)
h-t: 0-2 Att: n/a
Ref: Rizo (Mexico)
Cameroon won 5-3 on pens

The victorious Nigerian team proudly shows off its gold medals after winning the Olympic soccer tournament at the 1996 Games in Atlanta in the United States. It beat a powerful Argentinian team 3-2 in the Final having already beaten Brazil 4-3 in the semi-final.

THE OLYMPIC GAMES

53

The World Club Cup

TOURNAMENT OVERVIEW

THE WORLD CLUB CUP was originally known as the Copa Internacional in Latin America and the Intercontinental Cup in Europe. Henri Delaunay, the then general secretary of UEFA, originally proposed it in 1958 as an annual contest between the champions of the two major soccer continents. With the advent of the Copa Libertadores in Latin America in 1960, following the creation of the European Cup in 1956, an intercontinental championship was finally possible, and the first contest, between Real Madrid and Peñarol, was held in 1960 over two legs, Real winning 5-1 in Madrid after a 0-0 draw in Uruguay.

In the late 1960s and early 1970s, the World Club Cup began to acquire a reputation for on-field violence, particularly matches featuring the Argentinian team Estudiantes. As a consequence a number of European champions refused to take their place, which was then taken up by the European Cup runners-up – this included Panathinaikos instead of Ajax in 1971, Juventus over Ajax in 72, Atlético Madrid over Bayern München in 74, Borussia Mönchengladbach over Liverpool in 77 and Malmö rather than Nottingham Forest in 1979.

The potential demise of the fixture was halted by making it a single match, with extra time and penalties, played in Japan with the acquisition of Toyota as sponsors. Despite a poor run of performances in the 1990s Latin American clubs have accorded the game greater significance than their opponents. But with Real Madrid's victory in its centenary year attracting wide coverage, Europeans are acquiring a taste for the cup too.

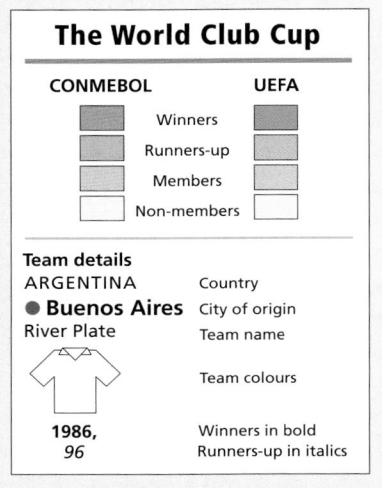

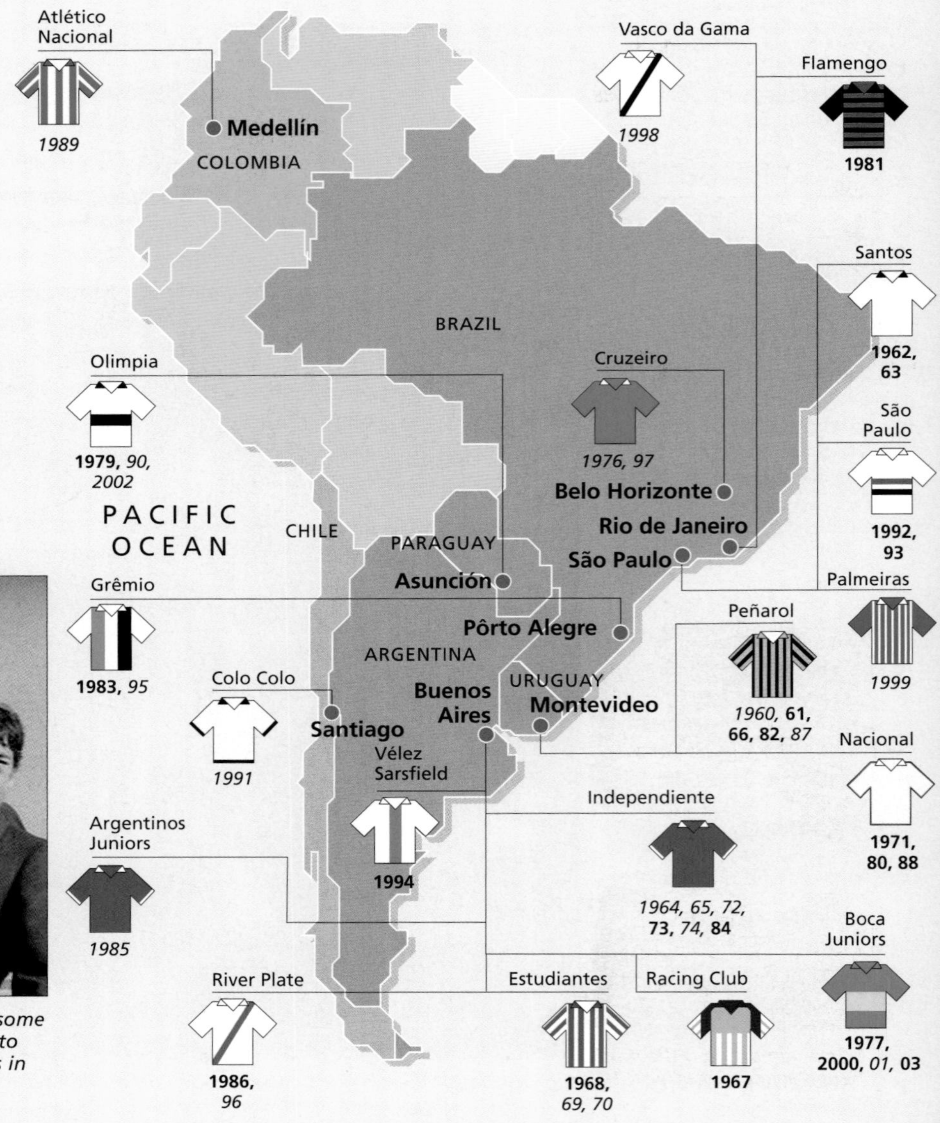

The World Club Cup

CONMEBOL		UEFA
	Winners	
	Runners-up	
	Members	
	Non-members	

Team details
ARGENTINA — Country
● **Buenos Aires** — City of origin
River Plate — Team name

— Team colours

1986, 96 — Winners in bold / Runners-up in italics

Atlético Nacional
● Medellín
COLOMBIA
1989

Vasco da Gama
1998

Flamengo
1981

Santos
1962, 63

São Paulo
1992, 93

Olimpia
1979, 90, *2002*

BRAZIL

Cruzeiro
1976, 97
Belo Horizonte

PACIFIC OCEAN

CHILE
PARAGUAY
Asunción

Rio de Janeiro
São Paulo

Palmeiras
1999

Grêmio
1983, *95*

Pôrto Alegre
ARGENTINA

Peñarol
1960, 61, 66, 82, 87

Colo Colo
1991

Buenos Aires
Santiago
Vélez Sarsfield
1994

URUGUAY
Montevideo

Nacional
1971, 80, 88

Argentinos Juniors
1985

Independiente
1964, 65, 72, 73, 74, 84

River Plate
1986, *96*

Estudiantes
1968, **69, 70**

Racing Club
1967

Boca Juniors
1977, 2000, *01, 03*

Members of the victorious Milan team, some showing signs of battle, on their return to Italy after their Final against Estudiantes in 1969, a match famous for its violence.

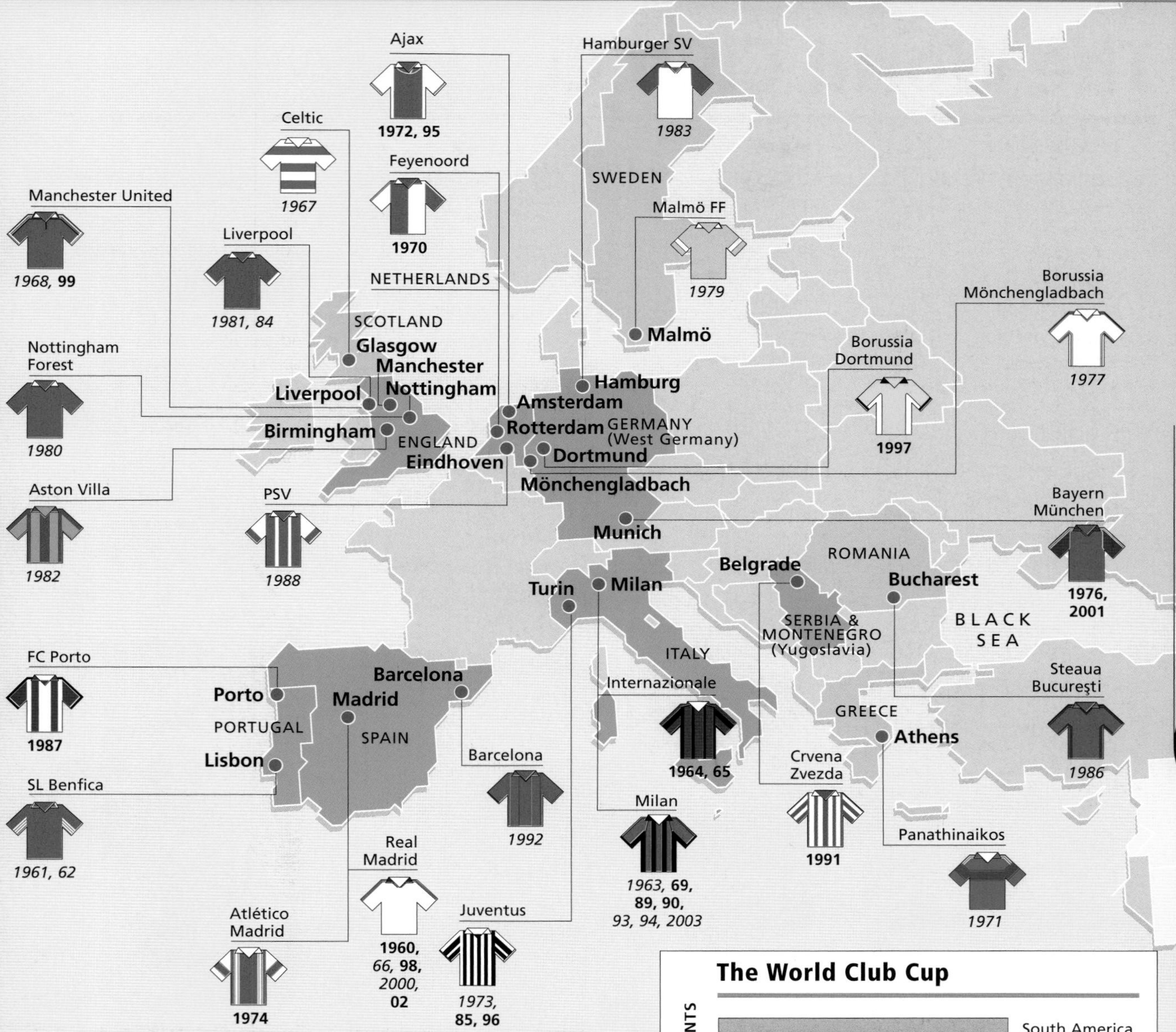

Ajax
1972, 95

Hamburger SV
1983

Celtic
1967

Feyenoord
1970

Borussia
Mönchengladbach
1977

Manchester United
1968, **99**

Liverpool
1981, 84

Malmö FF
1979

Borussia
Dortmund
1997

SWEDEN

NETHERLANDS

SCOTLAND
Glasgow
Manchester
Nottingham

Liverpool
Birmingham
ENGLAND
Eindhoven

Hamburg
Amsterdam
Rotterdam
GERMANY
(West Germany)
Dortmund
Mönchengladbach

Malmö

Nottingham
Forest
1980

Aston Villa
1982

PSV
1988

Munich

Turin **Milan**

Belgrade

ROMANIA
Bucharest

Bayern
München
1976,
2001

BLACK
SEA

FC Porto
1987

Porto

Barcelona
Madrid

PORTUGAL
SPAIN

Lisbon

Barcelona
1992

ITALY
Internazionale

SERBIA &
MONTENEGRO
(Yugoslavia)

GREECE
Athens

Steaua
Bucureşti
1986

SL Benfica
1961, 62

Real
Madrid
1960,
66, **98,**
2000,
02

Atlético
Madrid
1974

Juventus
1973,
85, 96

Milan
1963, **69,**
89, 90,
93, 94, 2003

Crvena
Zvezda
1991

Panathinaikos
1971

1964, 65

THE WORLD CLUB CUP

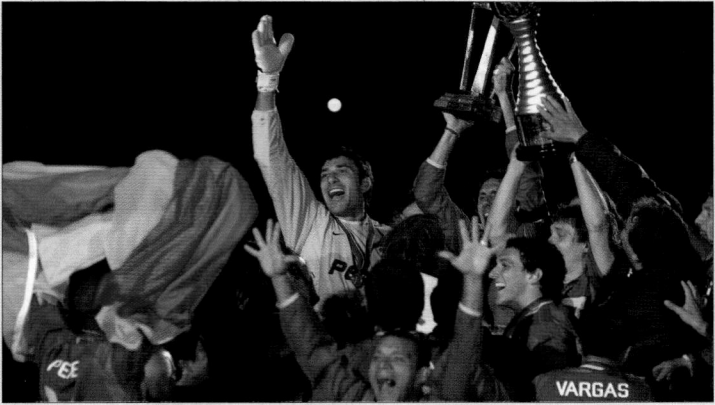

Boca Juniors won the World Club Cup *in 2003 beating Milan 3-1 in a
penalty shootout after a 1-1 draw. The Italians missed three penalties
and the trophy went to South America once again.*

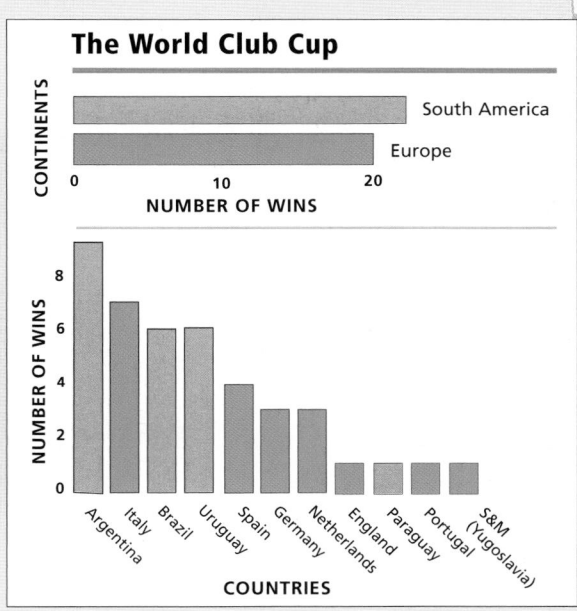

The World Club Cup

CONTINENTS

South America

Europe

0   10   20
NUMBER OF WINS

NUMBER OF WINS

8

4

2

0

Argentina
Italy
Brazil
Uruguay
Spain
Germany
Netherlands
England
Paraguay
Portugal
S&M
(Yugoslavia)

COUNTRIES

The World Club Cup

THE FORMAT OF THE WORLD CLUB CUP and its earlier incarnation the Intercontinental Cup has been changed on a number of occasions since 1960. However, in the event of a draw, the annual play-off between the European Champions League winners (formerly the European Cup) and the Copa Libertadores has always been decided by extra time or penalties. The Cup began as a two-leg affair at the two finalists' home grounds. If both sides had won one match, irrespective of aggregate scores, then a replay was deemed necessary to decide the winners (see 1961, 63, 64 and 67). The fixture acquired a well-deserved reputation for aggressive, even violent play, beginning with the Milan v Santos games in 1963 and peaking in the finals contested by Estudiantes of Argentina between 1968 and 1970.

Between 1969 and 1979 the two-leg format was retained, but aggregate scores determined the winner. However, this change of format couldn't help an ailing fixture that European champions refused to contest.

In 1980, with a new Japanese sponsor, the format shifted to a single match played at the national stadium in Tokyo. With the creation of the more global Club World Championship, the future of this competition looked uncertain, but the demise of the disappointing FIFA tournament has left it with no rival.

1960 FINAL (2 legs)
July 3 – Centenario, Montevideo
Peñarol 0-0 Real Madrid
(Uruguay)   (Spain)

September 4 – Santiago Bernabeu, Madrid
Real Madrid 5-1 Peñarol
(Puskas 3, 9,   (Borges 69)
di Stefano 4,
Herrera 44,
Gento 54)

Real Madrid won 5-1 on aggregate

1961 FINAL (2 legs)
September 17 – Estadio da Luz, Lisbon
SL Benfica 1-0 Peñarol
(Portugal)   (Uruguay)
(Coluna 60)

September 17 – Centenario, Montevideo
Peñarol 5-0 SL Benfica
(Sasia 10,
Joya 18, 28,
Spencer 42, 60)

PLAY-OFF
September 19 – Centenario, Montevideo
Peñarol 2-1 SL Benfica
(Sasia 6, 41)   (Eusebio 35)

1962 FINAL (2 legs)
September 19 – Maracana, Rio de Janeiro
Santos 3-2 SL Benfica
(Brazil)   (Portugal)
(Pele 31, 86,   (Santana 58, 87)
Coutinho 64)

October 11 – Estadio da Luz, Lisbon
SL Benfica 2-5 Santos
(Eusebio 87,   (Pele 17, 28, 64,
Santana 89)   Coutinho 49,
Pepe 77)

Santos won 8-4 on aggregate

1963 FINAL (2 legs)
October 16 – San Siro, Milan
Milan 4-2 Santos
(Italy)   (Brazil)
(Trappattoni 4,   (Pele 59, 87)
Amarildo 15, 65,
Mora 80)

November 14 – Maracana, Rio de Janeiro
Santos 4-2 Milan
(Pepe 50, 67,   (Altafini 12,
Almir 60,   Mora 17)
Lima 63)

PLAY-OFF
November 16 – Maracana, Rio de Janeiro
Santos 1-0 Milan
(Dalmo 26)

1964 FINAL (2 legs)
September 9 – Cordero, Avellaneda
Independiente 1-0 Internazionale
(Argentina)   (Italy)
(Rodriguez 60)

September 23 – San Siro, Milan
Internazionale 2-0 Independiente
(Mazzola 8,
Corso 39)

PLAY-OFF
September 26 – Santiago Bernabeu, Madrid
Internazionale 1-0 Independiente
(Corso 120)
(after extra time)

1965 FINAL (2 legs)
September 8 – San Siro, Milan
Internazionale 3-0 Independiente
(Italy)   (Argentina)
(Peiro 3,
Mazzola 23, 61)

September 15 – Cordero, Avellaneda
Independiente 0-0 Internazionale

Internazionale won 3-0 on aggregate

1966 FINAL (2 legs)
October 12 – Centenario, Montevideo
Peñarol 2-0 Real Madrid
(Uruguay)   (Spain)
(Spencer 39, 82)

October 26 – Santiago Bernabeu, Madrid
Real Madrid 0-2 Peñarol
(Rocha 28,
Spencer 37)

Peñarol won 4-0 on aggregate

1967 FINAL (2 legs)
October 18 – Hampden Park, Glasgow
Celtic 1-0 Racing Club
(Scotland)   (Argentina)
(McNeill 67)

November 1 – Mozart y Cuyo, Avellaneda
Racing Club 2-1 Celtic
(Raffo 32,   (Gemmell 20)
Cardenas 48)

PLAY-OFF
November 4 – Centenario, Montevideo
Racing Club 1-0 Celtic
(Cardenas 55)

1968 FINAL (2 legs)
September 25 –
Bombonera, Buenos Aires
Estudiantes 1-0 Manchester de la Plata United
(Argentina)   (England)
(Conigliaro 28)

October 16 – Old Trafford, Manchester
Manchester 1-1 Estudiantes United de la Plata
(Morgan 8)   (Veron 5)

Estudiantes de la Plata won 2-1 on aggregate

1969 FINAL (2 legs)
October 8 – San Siro, Milan
Milan 3-0 Estudiantes de la Plata
(Italy)   (Argentina)
(Sormani 8, 73,
Combin 44)

October 22 – Bombonera, Buenos Aires
Estudiantes 2-1 Milan de la Plata   (Rivera 30)
(Conigliaro 43,
Aguirre
Suarez 44)

Milan won 4-2 on aggregate

1970 FINAL (2 legs)
August 26 – Bombonera, Buenos Aires
Estudiantes 2-2 Feyenoord de la Plata
(Argentina)   (Netherlands)
(Echecopar 6,   (Kindvall 21,
Veron 10)   Van Hanegem 65)

September 9 –
Feyenoord Stadium, Rotterdam
Feyenoord 1-0 Estudiantes
(Van Daele 65)   de la Plata

Feyenoord won 3-2 on aggregate

1971 FINAL (2 legs)
December 15 – Karaiskakis, Piraeus
Panathinaikos 1-1 Nacional
(Greece)   Montevideo
(Filakouris 48)   (Uruguay)
      (Artime 50)

December 29 – Centenario, Montevideo
Nacional 2-1 Panathinaikos
Montevideo   (Filakouris 89)
(Artime 34, 75)

Nacional Montevideo won 3-2 on aggregate

1972 FINAL (2 legs)
September 6 – Mozart y Cuyo, Avellaneda
Independiente 1-1 Ajax
(Argentina)   (Netherlands)
(Sa 82)   (Cruyff 6)

September 28 –
Olympish Stadium, Amsterdam
Ajax 3-0 Independiente
(Neeskens 12,
Rep 16, 78)

Ajax won 4-1 on aggregate

1973 FINAL
November 28 – Stadio Olimpico, Rome
Independiente 1-0 Juventus
(Argentina)   (Italy)
(Bochini 40)

1974 FINAL (2 legs)
March 12 – Mozart y Cuyo, Avellaneda
Independiente 1-0 Atlético
(Argentina)   Madrid
(Balbuena 33)   (Spain)

April 10 – Vicente Calderon, Madrid
Atlético 2-0 Independiente
Madrid
(Irureta 21,
Ayala 86)

Atlético Madrid won 2-1 on aggregate

1975 FINAL
Bayern v Independiente
München   (Argentina)
(West Germany)
      not contested

1976 FINAL (2 legs)
November 23 – Olympiastadion, Munich
Bayern 2-0 Cruzeiro
München   (Brazil)
(West Germany)
(Müller 80,
Kappellmann 83)

December 21 – Mineirao, Belo Horizonte
Cruzeiro 0-0 Bayern München

Bayern München won 2-0 on aggregate

1977 FINAL (2 legs)
March 22 – Bombonera, Buenos Aires
Boca Juniors 2-2 Borussia
(Argentina)   Mönchen-
(Mastrangelo 16,   gladbach
Ribolzi 51)   (West Germany)
      (Hannes 24,
      Bonhof 29)

March 26 – Wildpark Stadion, Karlsruhe
Borussia **0-3** Boca
Mönchen-   Juniors
gladbach   *(Zanabria 2,*
                Mastrangelo 33,
                Salinas 35)

Boca Juniors won 5-2 on aggregate

1978 FINAL
Liverpool v Boca Juniors
(England)   (Argentina)
not contested

1979 FINAL (2 legs)
November 18 – Malmö Stadion, Malmö
Malmö FF **0-1** Olimpia
(Sweden)   (Paraguay)
            (Isasi 41)

March 3 – Manuel Ferreira, Asunción
Olimpia **2-1** Malmö FF
(Solalinde 40 pen,   *(Earlandsson 48)*
Michelagnoli 71)

Olimpia won 3-1 on aggregate

1980 FINAL
February 11 – National Stadium, Tokyo
Nacional **1-0** Nottingham
(Uruguay)   Forest
(Victorino 10)   (England)

1981 FINAL
December 13 – National Stadium, Tokyo
Flamengo **3-0** Liverpool
(Brazil)   (England)
(Nunes 13, 41,
Adilio 34)

1982 FINAL
December 12 – National Stadium, Tokyo
Peñarol **2-0** Aston Villa
(Uruguay)   (England)
(Jair 27,
Charrua 68)

1983 FINAL
December 11 – National Stadium, Tokyo
Grêmio **2-1** Hamburger SV
(Brazil)   (West Germany)
(Renato 37, 93)   *(Schröder 85)*

1984 FINAL
December 9 – National Stadium, Tokyo
Independiente **1-0** Liverpool
(Argentina)   (England)
(Percudiani 6)

1985 FINAL
December 8 – National Stadium, Tokyo
Juventus **2-2** Argentinos
(Italy)   Juniors
(Platini 63,   (Argentina)
M. Laudrup 82)   *(Ereros 45,*
                Castro 75)

Juventus won 4-2 on pens

1986 FINAL
December 14 – National Stadium, Tokyo
River Plate **1-0** Steaua
(Argentina)   Bucureşti
(Alzamendi 28)   (Romania)

1987 FINAL
December 13 – National Stadium, Tokyo
FC Porto **2-1** Peñarol
(Portugal)   (Uruguay)
(Gomes 41,   *(Viera 80)*
Madjer 108)

(after extra time)

1988 FINAL
December 11 – National Stadium, Tokyo
Nacional **2-2** PSV
(Uruguay)   (Netherlands)
(Ostolaza 7, 119)   *(Romario 75,*
                R. Koeman 109)

(after extra time)

Nacional won 7-6 on pens

1989 FINAL
December 17 – National Stadium, Tokyo
Milan **1-0** Atlético
(Italy)   Nacional
(Evani 118)   (Colombia)

1990 FINAL
December 9 – National Stadium, Tokyo
Milan **3-0** Olimpia
(Italy)   (Paraguay)
(Rijkaard 43, 65,
Stroppa 62)

1991 FINAL
December 8 – National Stadium, Tokyo
Crvena Zvezda **3-0** Colo Colo
(Yugoslavia)   (Chile)
(Jugovic 19, 58,
Pancev 72)

1992 FINAL
December 13 – National Stadium, Tokyo
São Paulo **2-1** Barcelona
(Brazil)   (Spain)
(Rai 26, 79)   *(Stoichkov 13)*

1993 FINAL
December 12 – National Stadium, Tokyo
São Paulo **3-2** Milan
(Brazil)   (Italy)
(Palinha 20,   *(Massaro 48,*
Cerezo 59,   *Papin 82)*
Müller 86)

1994 FINAL
December 1 – National Stadium, Tokyo
Vélez Sarsfield **2-0** Milan
(Argentina)   (Italy)
(Trotta 50 pen,
Asad 57)

1995 FINAL
November 28 – National Stadium, Tokyo
Ajax **0-0** Grêmio
(Netherlands)   (Brazil)
(after extra time)

Ajax won 4-3 on pens

1996 FINAL
November 26 – National Stadium, Tokyo
Juventus **1-0** River Plate
(Italy)   (Argentina)
(Del Piero 82)

1997 FINAL
December 2 – National Stadium, Tokyo
Borussia **2-0** Cruzeiro
Dortmund   (Brazil)
(Germany)
(Zorc 34,
Herrlich 85)

1998 FINAL
December 1 – National Stadium, Tokyo
Real Madrid **2-1** Vasco da Gama
(Spain)   (Brazil)
(Nasa o.g. 26,   *(Juninho 56)*
Raúl 82)

1999 FINAL
November 30 – National Stadium, Tokyo
Manchester **1-0** Palmeiras
United   (Brazil)
(England)
(Keane 35)

2000 FINAL
November 28 – National Stadium, Tokyo
Boca Juniors **2-1** Real Madrid
(Argentina)   (Spain)
(Palermo 2, 5)   *(Roberto Carlos 11)*

2001 FINAL
November 27 – National Stadium, Tokyo
Bayern **1-0** Boca Juniors
München   (Argentina)
(Germany)
(Kuffour 109)

(after extra time)

2002 FINAL
December 3 – Yokohama, Japan
Real **2-0** Olimpia
Madrid   (Paraguay)
(Spain)
(Ronaldo 14,
Guti 84)

2003 FINAL
December 14 – Yokohama, Japan
Boca **1-1** Milan
Juniors   (Italy)
(Argentina)   *(Tomasson 23)*
(Donnet 29)

(after extra time)

Boca Juniors won 3-1 on pens

Real Madrid's Roberto Carlos *(left, white shirt) shoots past Oscar Cordoba, the Boca Juniors goalkeeper, in the 11th minute of the 2000 World Club Cup Final. However, Boca, for whom Martin Palermo scored twice in the first five minutes, held on to win 2-1.*

Women's Soccer

WORLD CUP AND OLYMPIC SOCCER

PICTURES FROM CHINA during the Han Dynasty (206 BC–221 AD) clearly show women playing rudimentary forms of soccer, but other evidence of early participation in the game is rare. The male predominance at English public schools gave the boys a 30-year head start when the new codified rules were drawn up in 1863. The catch up began with the first recorded women's soccer match under FA rules played on 23 March 1895, at Crouch End in North London, when South of England beat North of England 7-1. However, the backlash soon arrived in the shape of systematic opposition to women's soccer from the male soccer establishment all over Europe.

In 1896, the Dutch soccer authority, KNVB, banned a women's match between a Sparta Rotterdam XI and an England XI and followed this up with a ban on women's games at any stadium of a club affiliated to it. Similar policies of exclusion were pursued by the English FA and by the German FA, the DFB, who banned women from affiliated stadiums in the 1950s. Medical, social and soccer commentators claimed that soccer was detrimental to the moral and physical health of women.

Despite all this, women's soccer grew in popularity and with the massive flow of European women into industrial employment during the First World War, players and teams multiplied. In fact, so great was the growth of women's soccer that the English FA moved to a stadium ban for women's teams in 1920, and the sport was forced into the world of exhibition matches and charity events. Dick Kerr's Ladies, a Preston-based factory team, played to large audiences in the 1920s, while Manchester Corinthians was the leading women's club in England in the 1940s and 50s.

The tide turns

Independent attempts to organize international women's soccer began with the creation of the International Ladies Football Association in 1957 and a Women's European Championship won by Manchester Corinthians. The Italian-based CIEFF was formed in 1969 and held informal women's world cups, the Mundialato, in Italy in 1970 and Mexico in 1971. Driven by fear of losing control and by some dim recognition that women's soccer was a significant sporting force, FIFA and UEFA acted. UEFA called for all member nation's FAs to incorporate women's soccer into the mainstream of the game (though in England this took until 1993).

In terms of participation and sporting success women's soccer has three strongholds: North America, China and Northern Europe. In America and China, the relative weakness of men's soccer has created the space in which women's soccer could grow. In northern Europe, the egalitarianism and social engineering of social democratic governments has helped promote women's soccer. Not surprisingly then these regions have hosted the official FIFA Women's World Cup and contested its Finals (as well as the Olympic Finals). Despite the growth of the grass roots game, 2003 was a difficult year for elite women's soccer. The SARS virus saw the World Cup hurriedly shifted from China to the USA, where two weeks beforehand WUSA, the world's first professional women's league, announced its closure.

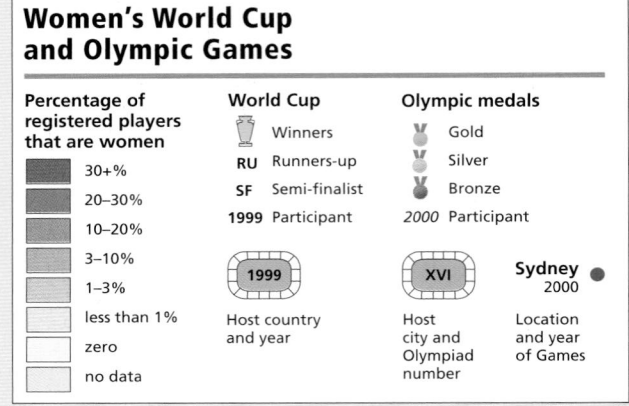

Women's World Cup and Olympic Games

Percentage of registered players that are women		
	30+%	
	20–30%	
	10–20%	
	3–10%	
	1–3%	
	less than 1%	
	zero	
	no data	

World Cup
- Winners
- RU Runners-up
- SF Semi-finalist
- 1999 Participant

Olympic medals
- Gold
- Silver
- Bronze
- 2000 Participant

1999 — Host country and year

XVI — Host city and Olympiad number

Sydney 2000 — Location and year of Games

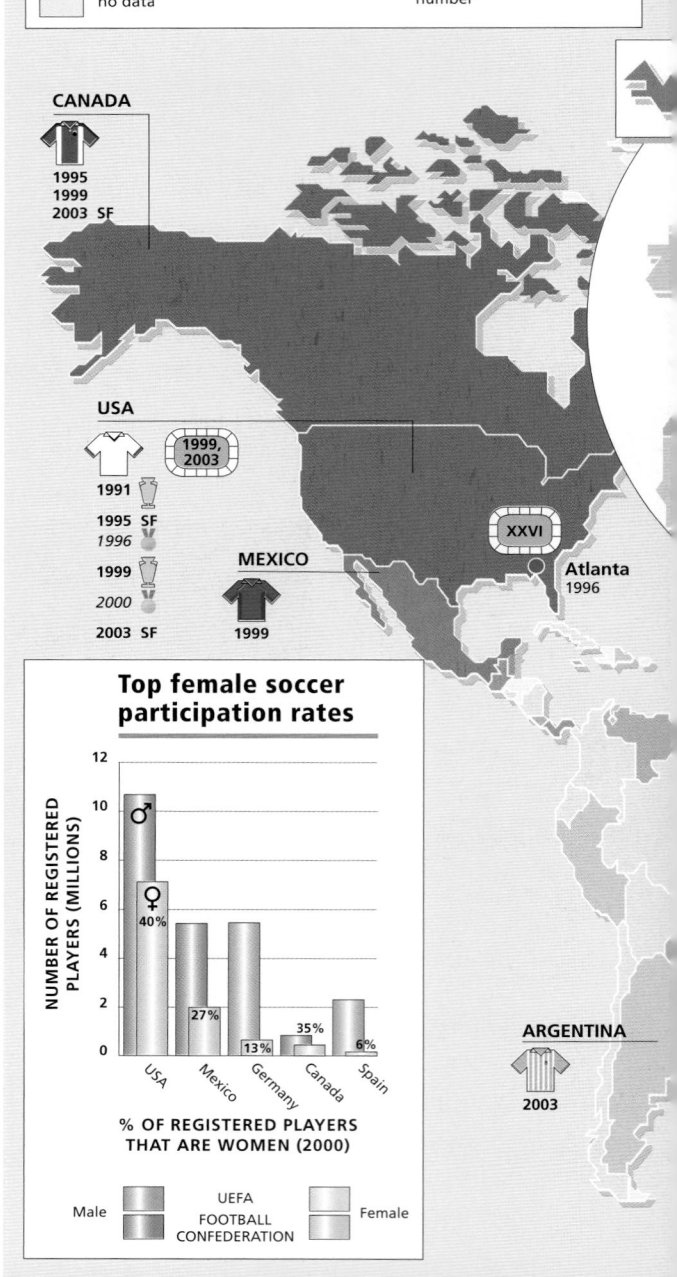

CANADA
1995
1999
2003 SF

USA
1999, 2003
1991
1995 SF
1996
1999
2000
2003 SF

MEXICO
1999

XXVI
Atlanta 1996

ARGENTINA
2003

Top female soccer participation rates

NUMBER OF REGISTERED PLAYERS (MILLIONS)

♂ 40%
USA ♀ 40%
Mexico 27%
Germany 13%
Canada 35%
Spain 6%

% OF REGISTERED PLAYERS THAT ARE WOMEN (2000)

Male — UEFA FOOTBALL CONFEDERATION — Female

The Preston Ladies soccer team prepares for a European tour at Bedford in 1939. Though women's soccer was confined to exhibition matches and charity events during the 1930s and 40s, it remained hugely popular with players and spectators, and tours such as this were regular events.

Semi-finalists in the first ever tournament in 1991, Germany finally triumphed in 2003, beating Sweden 2-1 in the Final. Here captain Bettina Wiegmann holds the trophy surrounded by her happy teammates.

WOMEN'S SOCCER

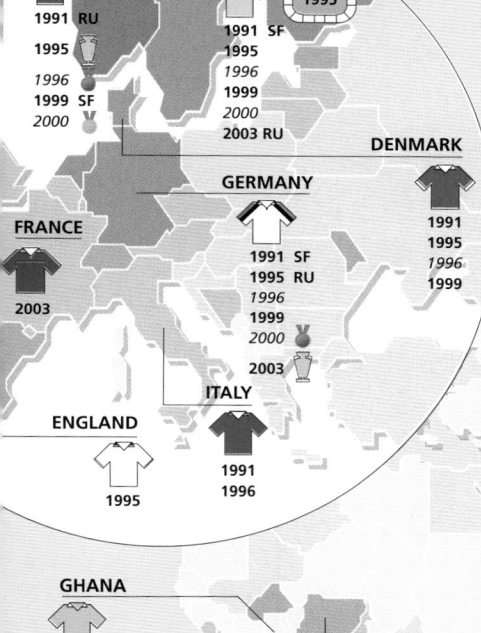

NORWAY
1991 RU
1995
1996
1999 SF
2000

SWEDEN
1995
1991 SF
1995
1996
1999
2000
2003 RU

DENMARK
1991
1995
1996
1999

GERMANY
1991 SF
1995 RU
1996
1999
2000
2003

FRANCE
2003

ENGLAND
1995

ITALY
1991
1996

RUSSIA
1999
2003

NORTH KOREA
1999
2003

SOUTH KOREA
2003

JAPAN
1991
1995
1996
1999
2003

TAIWAN
1991

GHANA
1999
2003

BRAZIL
1991
1995
1996
1999 SF
2000
2003

NIGERIA
1991
1995
1999
2000
2003

CHINA
1991
1991
1995 SF
1996
1999 RU
2000
2003

AUSTRALIA
1995
1999
2000
2003

Sydney
2000
XXVII

NEW ZEALAND
1991

Women's World Cup Finals (1991–2003)

YEAR	WINNERS	SCORE	RUNNERS-UP
1991	USA	2-1	Norway
1995	Norway	5-2	Germany
1999	USA	0-0 (5-4 pens)	China
2003	Germany	2-1	Sweden

Women's Olympic Finals (1996–2000)

YEAR	WINNERS	SCORE	RUNNERS-UP
1996	USA	2-1	China
2000	Norway	3-2	USA

THE UEFA NATIONS

ATLANTIC OCEAN

ICELAND
1947
The Football Association of Iceland
1954 (1929)

FAEROE ISLANDS
1979
Fotboltsamband Føroya
1992 (1988)

NORWAY
1902
Norges Fotballforbund
1954 (1908)

FINLAND
1907
Suomen Palloliitto/ Finlands Bollförbund
1954 (1908)

ESTONIA
1921
Eesti Jalgpalli Liit
1992 (1923–43, 1992)

SWEDEN
1904
Svenska Fotbollförbundet
1954 (1904)
1958

LATVIA
1921
Football Association of Latvia
1992 (1923–43, 1991)

SCOTLAND
1873
The Scottish Football Association
1954 (1910–20, 1924–28, 1946)

NORTHERN IRELAND
1880
The Irish Football Association
1954 (1911–20, 1924–28, 1946)

NETHERLANDS
1889
Koninklijke Nederlandse Voetbalbond
1954 (1904)
1974, 78
1988

DENMARK
1889
Dansk Boldspil Union
1954 (1904)
1992

LITHUANIA
1922
Lietuvos Futbolo Federacija
1992 (1923–43, 1992)

BELARUS
1989
Football Federation of the Republic of Belarus
1993 (1992)

ENGLAND
1863
The Football Association
1954 (1905–20, 1924–28, 1946)

GERMANY
1900
Deutscher Fussball-Bund
1954 (1904–46, 1950)
1954, 66, 74, 82, 86, 90, 2002
1972, 76, 80, 92, 96

CZECH REPUBLIC
1901
Českomoravský Fotbalový Svaz
1954 (1906)
1934, 62
1976, 96

POLAND
1919
Polski Związek Piłki Nożnej
1954 (1923)

SLOVAKIA
1938
Slovensky Futbalovy Zvaz
1993 (1994)

MOLDOVA
1990
Federaţia Moldoveneasca de Fotbal
1992 (1994)

WALES
1876
The Football Association of Wales
1954 (1910–20, 1924–28, 1946)
1966

REPUBLIC OF IRELAND
1921
The Football Association of Ireland
1954 (1923)

BELGIUM
1895
Union Royale des Sociétés de Football Association
1954 (1904)
1980

LUXEMBOURG
1908
Fédération Luxembourgeoise de Football
1954 (1910)

EAST GERMANY
1948
Deutsche Fussballverband
1954 (1904–46, 1950)
DDR

AUSTRIA
1904
Österreichischer Fussball-Bund
1954 (1905)

HUNGARY
1901
Magyar Labdarúgó Szövetség
1954 (1906)
1938, 54

ROMANIA
1908
Federaţia Româna de Fotbal
1954 (1930)

SLOVENIA
1920
Nogometna Zveza Slovenije
1993 (1992)

Nyon
UEFA Headquarters

CROATIA
1912, 1991
Croatian Football Federation
1993 (1992)

BULGARIA
1923
Bŭlgarski Futbolen Sŭyŭz
1954 (1924)

FRANCE
1918
Fédération Française de Football
1954 (1904)
1998
1984, 2000

ANDORRA
1994
Federació Andorrana de Futbol
1996 (1996)

LIECHTENSTEIN
1934
Liechtensteiner Fussballverband
1992 (1974)

ITALY
1898
Federazione Italiana Giuoco Calcio
1954 (1905)
1934, 38, 70, 82
1968, 2000

MACEDONIA
1908
Macedonian Football Union
1994 (1994)

SPAIN
1913
Real Federación Española de Fútbol
1954 (1904)
1964, 84

GREECE
1926
Hellenic Football Federation
1954 (1927)
2004

SERBIA & MONTENEGRO
1919
Football Association of Serbia & Montenegro
1993 (1919)
1960, 68

PORTUGAL
1914
Federação Portuguesa de Futebol
1954 (1923)
2004

SWITZERLAND
1895
Schweizerischer Fussballverband
1954 (1904)

SAN MARINO
1931
Federazione Sammarinese Giuoco Calcio
1988 (1988)

MALTA
1900
Malta Football Association
1960 (1959)

BOSNIA-HERZEGOVINA
1992
Nogometni Savez Bosne i Hercegovine
1996 (1996)

ALBANIA
1930
Federata Shqiptarë e Futbollit
1954 (1932)

MEDITERRANEAN SEA

The Development of European Soccer

1880 — 1890 — 1920 — 1930 — 1940 — 1950 — 1960 — 1970

1884 Home International Championship established

1924 Scandinavian Cup established

1929 Dr Gero Cup established

1940 Last Baltic Cup

1949 Latin Cup established

1954 UEFA founded

1957 Last Latin Cup

1960 European Cup-Winners' Cup begins, European Nations' Cup begins, Dr Gero Cup ends

1927 Mittropa Cup established

1928 Baltic Cup established

1932 Balkan Cup established

1939 Mittropa Cup suspended

1955 European Cup begins, Fairs Cup begins, Mittropa Cup revived

1956 European Footballer of the Year established

1968 European Nations' Cup renamed European Championships

60

The UEFA Nations

The UEFA Nations

Date of formation of the national Football Association		Formation of national FA —	COUNTRY 1916 Name of Football Association 1916 (1912)	Date of affiliation to FIFA
		Date of affiliation to UEFA —		— Date of affiliation to FIFA

Date of formation of the national Football Association

- Before 1899
- 1900–39
- 1940–79
- After 1980

Team colours

World Cup — **1990** — Winners in bold

European Championship — *1990* — Runners-up in italic

UEFA

European Tournaments and Cup Competitions:
European Championships
European Champions League
UEFA Cup
Intertoto Cup
European Super Cup
European Women's Championships

UKRAINE
1991
Football Federation of Ukraine
1992 (1992)

RUSSIA
1912, 1991
Rossiyskiy Futbol'nyy Soyuz
1954 (1912, 1992)
1960, 64, 72, 88

KAZAKHSTAN
1992
Football Union of Kazakhstan
(AFC 1994–2002)
2002 (1994)

BLACK SEA

CASPIAN SEA

GEORGIA
1990
Georgian Football Federation
1992 (1992)

TURKEY
1923
Türkiye Futbol Federasyonu
1962 (1923)

AZERBAIJAN
1992
Association of Football Federations of Azerbaijan
1994 (1994)

CYPRUS
1934
Kipriaki Omospondia Podosferu
1962 (1948)

ISRAEL
1928
Israel Football Association
(AFC 1956–75)
1992 (1929)

ARMENIA
1992
Football Federation of Armenia
1993 (1992)

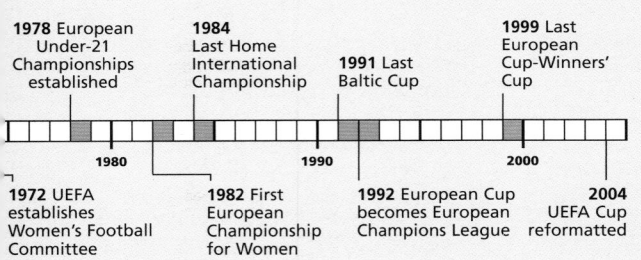

1978 European Under-21 Championships established

1984 Last Home International Championship

1991 Last Baltic Cup

1999 Last European Cup-Winners' Cup

1980

1990

2000

1972 UEFA establishes Women's Football Committee

1982 First European Championship for Women

1992 European Cup becomes European Champions League

2004 UEFA Cup reformatted

IN 1954, ALMOST 50 YEARS after the foundation of FIFA, and 38 years after the formation of CONMEBOL in South America, Europe acquired its own soccer federation in the form of UEFA: the Union of European Football Associations, based in Nyon, Switzerland. Soccer may have spread to every corner of the continent, but it took two world wars to overcome the Continent's divisions in order to reach agreement on the organization of soccer. UEFA had 35 founding members, and with the break-up of the Soviet Union and Yugoslavia it has grown to 52. Israel has transferred in from the Asian and Oceanic confederations as UEFA's contribution to global peacekeeping.

With the arrival of UEFA, the older international competitions, like the Scandinavian Cup organized by national FAs and ad hoc committees, were replaced by the European Nations' Championship. UEFA also spurred the development of European club competition in the 1950s and early 1960s, replacing the Latin Cup and Mittel Europa Cup with the European Cup. In the 1990s, UEFA had to fight to retain its political weight within world soccer, as FIFA, the European Community and the biggest European clubs have challenged its authority. At the turn of the century, its place was no more secure.

***Lennart Johansson**, the Swedish-born President of UEFA, was re-elected to the post in January 2002 as the sole nominee and will serve a further four years in the hot seat.*

Calendar of Events

Club Tournaments	European Champions League 2004–05 UEFA Cup 2004–05 Intertoto Cup 2005 European Super Cup 2005
International Tournaments	Qualifying Tournament for 2006 World Cup Qualifying Tournament for 2005 European Under–19 Championship

Europe

THE SEASONS IN REVIEW 2003, 2003–04

UEFA BEGAN ITS 50TH ANNIVERSARY CELEBRATIONS in a year that witnessed the triumph of soccer solidarity and teamwork over the power of money and influence. The economic overstretch that has left clubs across the continent, big and small, in deep financial trouble has helped limit the power of the biggest spenders – a fact only temporarily masked by the extraordinary infusion of cash that Roman Abramovich's Chelsea has injected into the European transfer market.

In Germany and Spain Valencia and Werder Bremen took their championships from under the noses of financial giants Bayern München and Real Madrid, while Arsenal, whose transfer budget was negligible, were unbeatable in England. Panathinaikos finally broke the web of power, money and status that has kept Olympiakos at the top of Greek soccer for seven years; Banik Ostrava were real outsiders and finished top of the Czech league. Leagues went with financial form in Italy, France, Portugal and the Netherlands, but Milan also played the most entertaining soccer in Serie A and Ajax were under pressure from the small team AZ from Alkmaar. French and Portuguese champions Lyon and Porto may be big teams at home but, for many years, they have been European minnows. The year also saw the biggest teams from the biggest leagues falter in Europe too. France, who have barely troubled the final stages of UEFA's tournaments, had finalists in both competitions this year (Monaco and Marseille) while the winners of both, Porto and Valencia, exemplified disciplined teams playing for themselves on restricted budgets.

If the power of money has been slightly blunted, the importance of naked power and manipulation appears to continue unabated. The otherwise squeaky-clean preparations for the World Cup in Germany in 2006 were given a dose of reality when it transpired that the President of TSV München (who's team will share the new Munich stadium after the tournament) had received unexplained monies from the winning contractors. Italian clubs are under financial scrutiny as never before, while in Portugal the biggest anti-corruption investigation in the country's history is underway. The Czech Republic has bristled with accounts of match fixing all season. Rumours abounded of referee corruption in Turkey and Serbia and both saw unexplained soccer-related shootings.

But in most leagues attendances are up. Ronaldinho at Barcelona gave us the most exuberant displays of trickery and pleasure. Thierry Henry, the continent's top scorer, showcased the games balletic athleticism. Perhaps best of all, the triumphs of Porto and Valencia have been eclipsed by the biggest upset of all – Greece winning Euro 2004 with a display of self-belief and hard work that can hardly be bettered in UEFA's 50-year history. Soccer's capacity to subvert its own ruling orders is perhaps its greatest asset.

UEFA Leagues

COUNTRY	CHAMPIONS	CUP WINNERS
Albania	SK Tirana	Partizani Tiranë
Andorra	Santa Coloma	Santa Coloma
Armenia	Pyunik Yerevan	Pyunik Yerevan
Austria	Grazer AK	Grazer AK
Azerbaijan	Neftçi Baku	Neftçi Baku
Belarus	FK Homel	Shakhtyosor Salihorsk
Belgium	RSC Anderlecht	Club Brugge KV
Bosnia-Herzegovina	Siroki Brijeg	Modrica Maksima
Bulgaria	Lokomotiv Plovdiv	Litex Lovetch
Croatia	Hajduk Split	Dinamo Zagreb
Cyprus	APOEL Nicosia	AEK Larnaca
Czech Republic	Baník Ostrava	Sparta Praha
Denmark	FC København	FC København
England	Arsenal	Manchester United
Estonia	FC Flora Tallinn	FC Levadia Tallinn
Faeroe Islands	HB	B36
Finland	HJK Helsinki	HJK Helsinki
France	Olympique Lyonnais	Paris Saint-Germain
Georgia	WIT Georgia	Dinamo Tbilisi
Germany	Werder Bremen	Werder Bremen
Greece	Panathinaikos	Panathinaikos
Hungary	Ferencváros	Ferencváros
Iceland	KR	IA Akranes
Israel	Maccabi Haifa	Hapoel Bnei Salchin
Italy	Milan	Lazio
Khazakhstan	Irtysh Pavlodar	Kairat Almaty
Latvia	Skonto Riga	FK Ventspils
Liechtenstein	no league	FC Vaduz
Lithuania	FBK Kaunas	Zalgiris Vilnius
Luxembourg	Jeunesse Esch	F91 Dudelange
Macedonia	Pobeda Prilep	Sloga Jugomagnat
Malta	Sliema Wanderers	Sliema Wanderers
Moldova	Serif Tiraspol	Zimbru Chişinău
Netherlands	Ajax	FC Utrecht
Northern Ireland	Linfield	Glentoran
Norway	Rosenborg BK	Rosenborg BK
Poland	Wisîa Kraków	Lech Poznaú
Portugal	FC Porto	SL Benfica
Republic of Ireland	Shelbourne	Longford Town
Romania	Dinamo Bucureşti	Dinamo Bucureşti
Russia	CSKA Moskva	Terek Grozny
San Marino	Pennarossa	Pennarossa
Scotland	Celtic	Celtic
Serbia & Montenegro	Crvena Zvezda	Crvena Zvezda
Slovakia	MSK Žilina	Artmedia Petrzalka
Slovenia	HIT Gorica	NK Maribor
Spain	Valencia	Real Zaragoza
Sweden	Djurgårdens IF	IF Elfsborg
Switzerland	FC Basel	FC Wil
Turkey	Fenerbahçe SK	Trabzonspor K
Ukraine	Dinamo Kyiv	Shakhtar Donetsk
Wales	Rhyl FC	Rhyl FC

Thierry Henry, winner of this year's European Golden Boot, dazzles the Portsmouth defence during yet another sparkling display for Arsenal.

EUROPE

European Super Cup

2003 FINAL

August 29 – Stade Louis II, Monaco

Milan 1-0 FC Porto
(Italy)   (Portugal)
(Shevchenko 10)
h/t : 1-0 **Att:** 18,500
Ref: Barber (England)

Left: Rejected by Real Madrid, Fernando Morientes carried Monaco to the Champions League Final against Porto. They lost the match but Morientes is said to have earned a recall to the troubled Spanish giants.

Far left: The man with a plan: Pinto da Costa, president of FC Porto for over three decades, will have his work cut out to maintain his club's recent success with the departure of manager José Mourinho and several of his top players.

Below: 'For peace, against terrorism. No more deaths': players from Barcelona and Murcia mourn those killed in the Madrid train bombings. There were similar scenes around all the Spanish grounds the weekend after the tragedy.

What's in the briefcase? Italian police leave the offices of the Italian soccer authority with financial documents in their long probe of the game's questionable finances.

POR LA PAZ, CONTRA EL TERRORISMO
NO MAS MUERTE

The biggest entertainer in European soccer this season was Barcelona's Ronaldinho.

'If this is a dream then I don't ever want to wake up': exuberant Greek players celebrate victory in Euro 2004.

The European Championships

TOURNAMENT OVERVIEW

HENRI DELAUNAY, head of the French FA, proposed the idea of a European nations tournament as early as 1927, but in the absence of a European soccer federation it failed to materialize. With the foundation of UEFA in 1954 Delaunay revived the idea. After much internal politics and the usual scepticism, UEFA announced that the first finals would be held in 1960. Though Delaunay died in 1955, he was honoured when the trophy was named the Henri Delaunay Cup. The format of the early tournaments was a series of two-leg qualifying rounds played home and away, producing four finalists who would contest semi-finals and a Final over a week in a single location.

The first finals, held in France, are best remembered for the controversial quarter-final between Spain and the USSR. Franco's love of soccer was more than matched by his hatred of Communism and he refused the Soviet team entry into Spain. UEFA awarded the tie to the Soviets. Under the inspirational Lev Yashin, the USSR won the Final beating Yugoslavia 2-1 in extra time. In 1964 Spain hosted the the tournament and, having allowed the Soviets in this time, beat them 2-1 in the Final. In 1968, Italy was host and beat Yugoslavia in a replayed Final.

Penalties and golden goals

In 1972, the Nations Cup was renamed the European Championships and West Germany thrashed the USSR 3-0. But in Yugoslavia in 1976, Eastern Europe struck back when the Czechs beat the Germans in a tense penalty shootout. In 1980, the tournament was expanded to eight teams and in 1996 to 16.

The 1980s saw two truly great teams take the trophy. In 1984, Platini's France swept to victory, while in 1988, the Dutch, with Gullit, van Basten and Rijkaard, triumphed. In 1992, Denmark, a late entrant in place of Yugoslavia (then embroiled in a civil war), made it to the Final and beat the favourites Germany 2-0. But the Germans were back four years later, defeating the English hosts in an excruciating penalty shootout before a rematch of the 1976 Final saw them beating the Czechs with a golden goal by Oliver Bierhoff – the first time an 'official' golden goal had decided the Final of a major competition. In 2000, France confirmed its then status as the world's No.1 team by beating Italy 2-1. By contrast, 2004 saw the most unexpected champions as Greece beat Portugal in the Final in Lisbon.

The European Championships (1960–2004)

YEAR	WINNERS	SCORE	RUNNERS-UP
1960	USSR	2-1	Yugoslavia
1964	Spain	2-1	USSR
1968	Italy	1-1, (replay) 2-0 (aet)	Yugoslavia
1972	West Germany	3-0	USSR
1976	Czechoslovakia	2-2 (5-3 pens)	West Germany
1980	West Germany	2-1	Belgium
1984	France	2-0	Spain
1988	Netherlands	2-0	USSR
1992	Denmark	2-0	Germany
1996	Germany	2-1 (golden goal)	Czech Republic
2000	France	2-1 (golden goal)	Italy
2004	Greece	1-0	Portugal

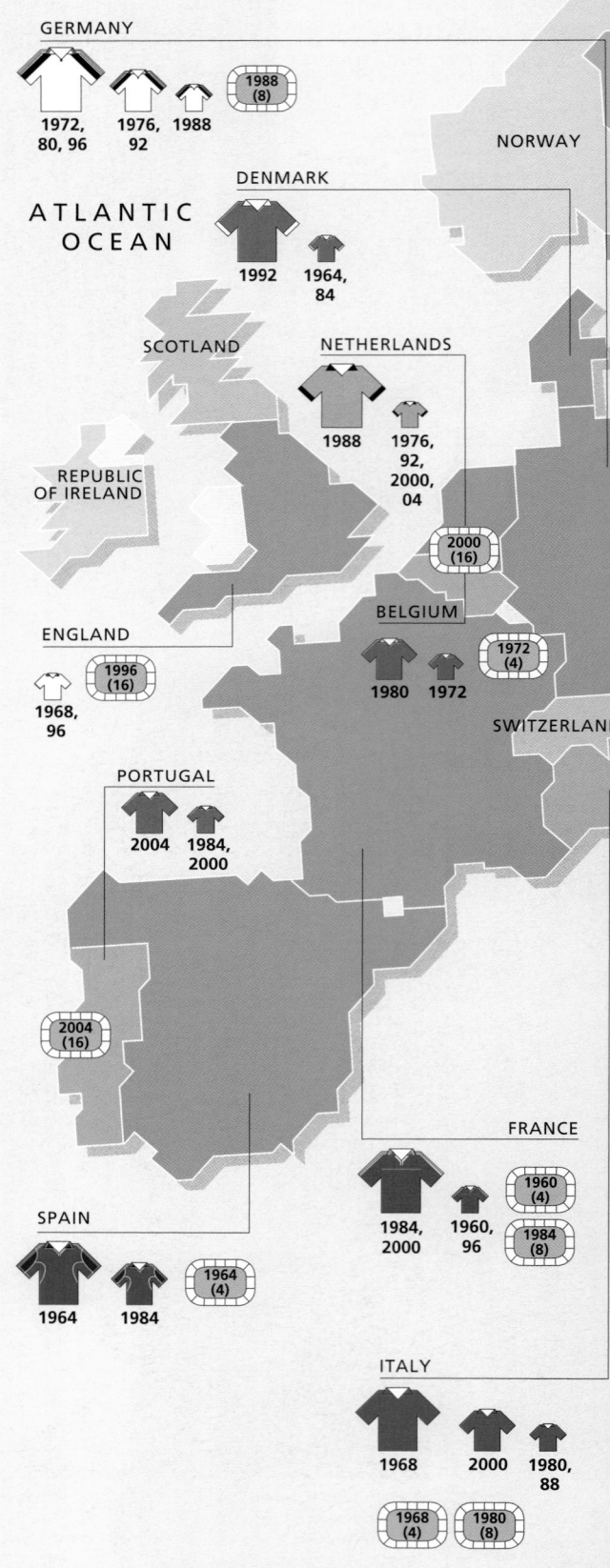

GERMANY
1972, 80, 96 · 1976, 92 · 1988 · 1988 (8)

ATLANTIC OCEAN

NORWAY

DENMARK
1992 · 1964, 84

SCOTLAND

NETHERLANDS
1988 · 1976, 92, 2000, 04 · 2000 (16)

REPUBLIC OF IRELAND

BELGIUM
1980 · 1972 · 1972 (4)

ENGLAND
1968, 96 · 1996 (16)

SWITZERLAND

PORTUGAL
2004 · 1984, 2000

2004 (16)

FRANCE
1984, 2000 · 1960, 96 · 1960 (4) · 1984 (8)

SPAIN
1964 · 1984 · 1964 (4)

ITALY
1968 · 2000 · 1980, 88 · 1968 (4) · 1980 (8)

The European Championships

Participation in the European Championships

- 6+ times
- 3–5 times
- 2 times
- 1 time
- 0 times

Winners, runners-up and semi-finalists with date

1996 1996 1996

Host country, with date in stadium and number of participants in brackets

ENGLAND 1996 (16)

SWEDEN
1992
1992 (8)

RUSSIA (includes USSR 1917–91)
1960 1964, 72, 88 1968

LATVIA

CZECH REPUBLIC
1976 1996 1960, 80, 2004

YUGOSLAVIA
1960, 68 1976 1976 (4)

HUNGARY
1964, 72

SLOVENIA

CROATIA

ROMANIA

BLACK SEA

BULGARIA

TURKEY

GREECE
2004

MEDITERRANEAN SEA

Czechoslovakia's Antonin Panenka chips his penalty over Sepp Maier in the German goal to win the 1976 tournament in Belgrade, Yugoslavia.

Germany's revenge against the Czech Republic for defeat in 1976 came at Wembley in 1996 when Oliver Bierhoff (in white) scored a precious golden goal winner in extra time.

The European Championships Top Goalscorers

YEAR	SCORER	NATIONALITY	GOALS
1960	Ivanov / Jerkovic	Russian / Yugoslavian	2
1964	Pereda / Novak	Spanish / Hungarian	2
1968	Drazij	Yugoslavian	2
1972	G. Müller	W. German	4
1976	D. Müller	W. German	4
1980	Allofs	W. German	3
1984	Platini	French	8
1988	van Basten	Dutch	5
1992	Bergkamp / Brolin / Larsen / Riedle	Dutch / Swedish / Danish / German	3
1996	Shearer	English	5
2000	Kluivert / Milosevic	Dutch / Yugoslavian	6
2004	Baros	Czech	5

Euro 2004

TOURNAMENT REVIEW

THE EUROPEAN CHAMPIONSHIPS

IN A PLEASING AND UTTERLY unexpected form of symmetry Euro 2004 opened with the Greeks beating the Portuguese and closed with the same result. Greece, who had only scored a single point in an international tournament before this, showed just how far you can go when you combine tactical nous with a willingness to work and play as a team. Marshalled by German coach Otto Rehhagel, the Greeks took advantage of the exhaustion and lassitude of better teams who just could not break them down.

Euro 2004 was notable for the failure of the biggest teams and biggest stars. Italian captain Totti only lasted a single game, banned for spitting in a Dane's face. As ever, Spain underperformed and none more so than Real Madrid's Raúl. His club mates, Zidane and Beckham, were almost as poor and seemed to lack energy and will. The Germans were just plain awful and uninspiring and the Dutch went as far as they did on luck rather than quality. Results and performances came from the smaller teams who showed organization, work and discipline. The Danes and the Swedes had plenty of both, and the Greeks had most of all, but even Latvia, Bulgaria and Russia showed that on their good days they could be a match for anyone.

The tournament did manage a few truly atmospheric matches and furnished space for some exceptional goals and independent performances. England's games with France and Portugal provided exceptional drama. Portugal's victory over Spain was a gritty, technical and heart-stopping affair. The Czech Republic at their best showed determination and the capacity to simply and intelligently split opposition defences apart. Wayne Rooney played at a level no one would have expected from the 18-year-old striker, and after hibernation at Liverpool for two seasons Milan Baros scored five goals in spectacular style. Less attractively there was a great deal of diving and acting that the referees could have been much harsher on.

England fans behave shock

Among the away fans, England provided by far and away the largest contingent with upwards of 50,000 present at England's opening game with France in Lisbon. If banners and flags are anything to go by, the English were pretty much present at every game of the tournament and in the case of France v Greece in the quarter-final estimates say they outnumbered both sets of fans. Dire predictions of violence and trouble proved unfounded. The Swedes and the Danes both brought disproportionately large crowds with them and, as ever, the Dutch orange hordes were impressively present. The Greeks grew as the tournament progressed and showed themselves to be awesome singers and unrepentant booers of the opposition. More might have been heard from all the fans if UEFA had not allowed so many incredibly distracting, noisy and irritating adverts in the stadiums before kick-off – the most insidious invasion of corporate power into the tournament.

Initially dispirited and downcast by their team's opening-game defeat the Portuguese fans rallied and provided huge support on the road to the Final. They were also exceptional hosts and the euphoria that overtook central Lisbon and other cities when they qualified for the final rounds of the tournament exhibited a warm and infectious exuberance. But the tournament belonged to Greece, and nothing that happened in Portugal can match the dizzying, wild partying of central Athens on the night of the Final and when the team returned in triumph to Panathinaikos' stadium in Athens the following week.

The indifferent and the extraordinary: David Beckham and Wayne Rooney offered very contrasting performances for England at Euro 2004.

Zinedine Zidane beat England single-handedly, scoring from a free kick and the penalty spot, but like the rest of Real Madrid's Galacticos he seemed tired and woefully out of sorts.

Qualification Groups

GROUP 1	GROUP 2	GROUP 3	GROUP 4	GROUP 5	GROUP 6	GROUP 7	GROUP 8	GROUP 9	GROUP 10
Cyprus	Bosnia-	Austria	Hungary	Faeroe	Armenia	England	Andorra	Azerbaijan	Albania
France	Herzegovina	Belarus	Latvia	Islands	Greece	Liechtenstein	Belgium	Finland	Georgia
Israel	Denmark	Czech	Poland	Germany	Northern	Macedonia	Bulgaria	Italy	Rep. of
Malta	Luxembourg	Republic	San Marino	Iceland	Ireland	Slovakia	Croatia	Serbia &	Ireland
Slovenia	Norway	Moldova	Sweden	Lithuania	Spain	Turkey	Estonia	Montenegro	Russia
	Romania	Netherlands		Scotland	Ukraine			Wales	Switzerland

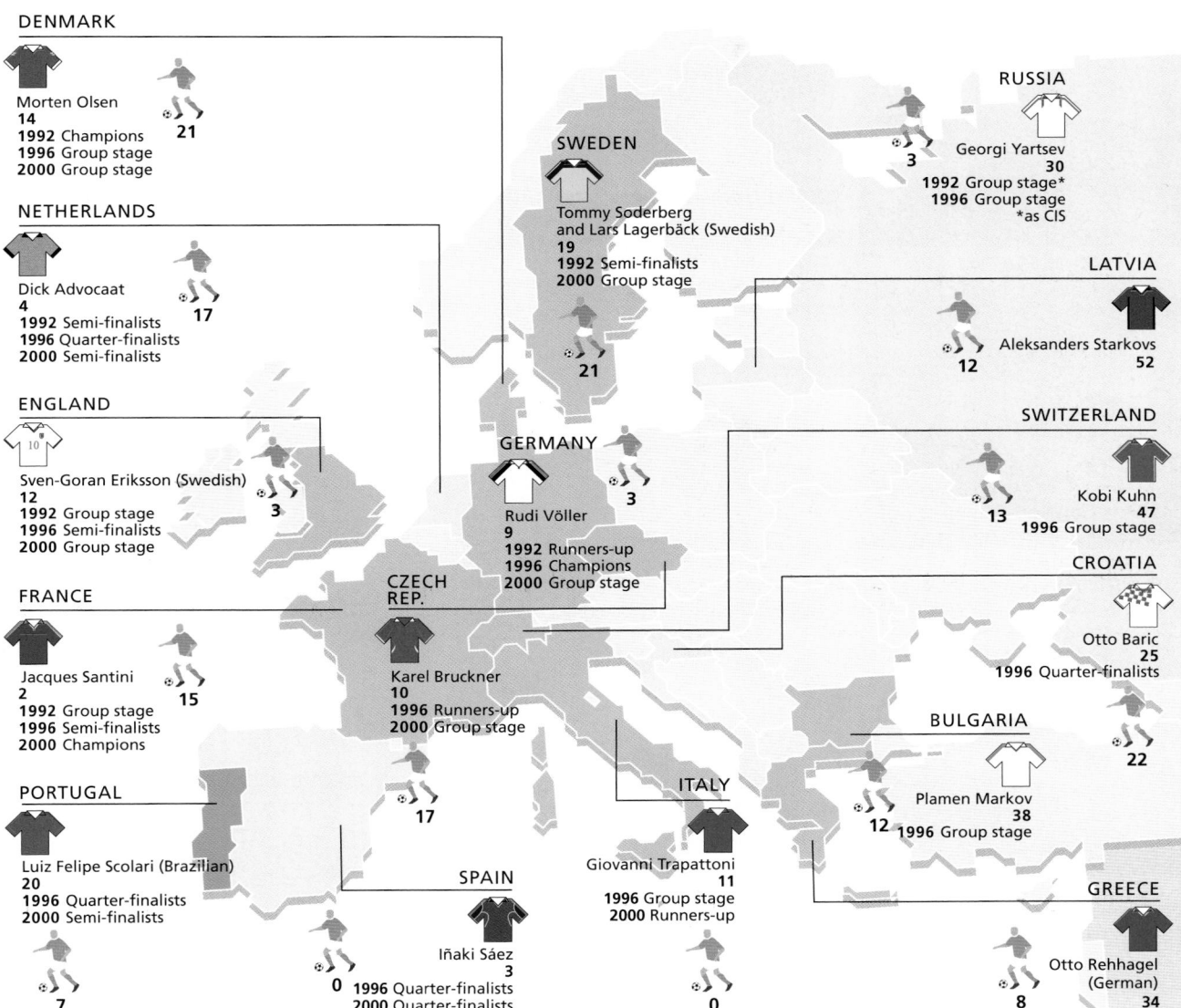

DENMARK
Morten Olsen
14
1992 Champions
1996 Group stage
2000 Group stage
21

NETHERLANDS
Dick Advocaat
4
1992 Semi-finalists
1996 Quarter-finalists
2000 Semi-finalists
17

ENGLAND
Sven-Goran Eriksson (Swedish)
12
1992 Group stage
1996 Semi-finalists
2000 Group stage
3

FRANCE
Jacques Santini
2
1992 Group stage
1996 Semi-finalists
2000 Champions
15

PORTUGAL
Luiz Felipe Scolari (Brazilian)
20
1996 Quarter-finalists
2000 Semi-finalists
7

SWEDEN
Tommy Soderberg
and Lars Lagerbäck (Swedish)
19
1992 Semi-finalists
2000 Group stage
21

GERMANY
Rudi Völler
9
1992 Runners-up
1996 Champions
2000 Group stage
3

CZECH REP.
Karel Bruckner
10
1996 Runners-up
2000 Group stage
17

SPAIN
Iñaki Sáez
3
0
1996 Quarter-finalists
2000 Quarter-finalists

ITALY
Giovanni Trapattoni
11
1996 Group stage
2000 Runners-up
0

RUSSIA
Georgi Yartsev
30
1992 Group stage*
1996 Group stage
*as CIS
3

LATVIA
Aleksanders Starkovs
52
12

SWITZERLAND
Kobi Kuhn
47
1996 Group stage
13

CROATIA
Otto Baric
25
1996 Quarter-finalists

BULGARIA
Plamen Markov
38
12   1996 Group stage
22

GREECE
Otto Rehhagel
(German)
34
8

Euro 2004 Qualification

Means by which the national team qualified

■	Host of Euro 2004
▨	Group winner
□	Play-off winner
▢	Did not qualify

National squads
GERMANY — Team name
Team colours
Manager — Manager's name (nationality – if different from team)
9 — FIFA ranking
1996 Champions — Performance in last three tournaments
21 — Number of squad members (out of 23) that play abroad

Top Goalscorers

PLAYER	NATIONALITY	GOALS
Milan Baros	Czech	5
Wayne Rooney	English	4
Ruud van Nistelrooy	Dutch	4
Frank Lampard	English	3
Henrik Larsson	Swedish	3
Jon-Dahl Tomasson	Danish	3
Zinedine Zidane	French	3

BRAGA MUNICIPAL

 30,000

Club: SC Braga
Matches: Group matches
Cost: £50m (€72m)
Architect: Eduardo Souta Moura

DO BESSA XXI

 30,000

Club: Boavista FC
Matches: Group matches
Cost: £29m (€41m)
Architect: Mario Moura

O DRAGÃO

 52,000

Club: FC Porto
Matches: Group matches, quarter-final, semi-final
Cost: £67m (€96m)
Architects: Somague

DR. MAGALHAES PESSOA

 30,000

Club: União Leiria
Matches: Group matches
Cost: £28m (€40m)
Architect: Tomas Taveira

JOSÉ ALVALADE XXI

 52,000

Club: Sporting CP
Matches: Group matches, quarter-final, semi-final
Cost: £51m (€74m)
Architects: Alves Ribeiro/ Tomas Taveira

DOM AFONSO HENRIQUES

 30,000

Club: Vitória SC Guimarães
Matches: Group matches
Cost: £17m (€24m)
Architect: Eduardo Guimarães

AVEIRO MUNICIPAL

 30,000

Club: SC Biera Mar
Matches: Group matches
Costs: £30m (€43m)
Architect: Tomas Taveira

COIMBRA MUNICIPAL

 52,000

Club: Academica
Matches: Group matches
Cost: £22m (€31m)
Architects: KSS Sports

DA LUZ

 30,000

Club: SL Benfica
Matches: Group matches, quarter-final, Final
Cost: £67m (€96m)
Architect: Tomas Taveira

ALGARVE

52,000

Clubs: SC Farense, Loulétano DC
Matches: Group matches, quarter-final
Cost: £22m (€31m)
Architects: HOK Sports

STADIUMS

PORTUGAL BUILT OR rebuilt ten stadiums for Euro 2004 and they represent the final flourish of nearly 20 years of infrastructural development in the country. In the Dragão and Da Luz the country has stadiums of a grandeur and architectural majesty to compete with anyone. The Bessa, although an ugly concrete box, proved an inferno of atmosphere with the crowd pressed as close to the action as possible. Braga and its rocky sides offered drama, the arcing ship-like stands of Faro gave sensational views and the Alvalade, Aveiro and Leiria were characteristically colourful and playful Portuguese post-modernist. Most incredible of all, the Portuguese built all ten for less than half the cost of the new Wembley.

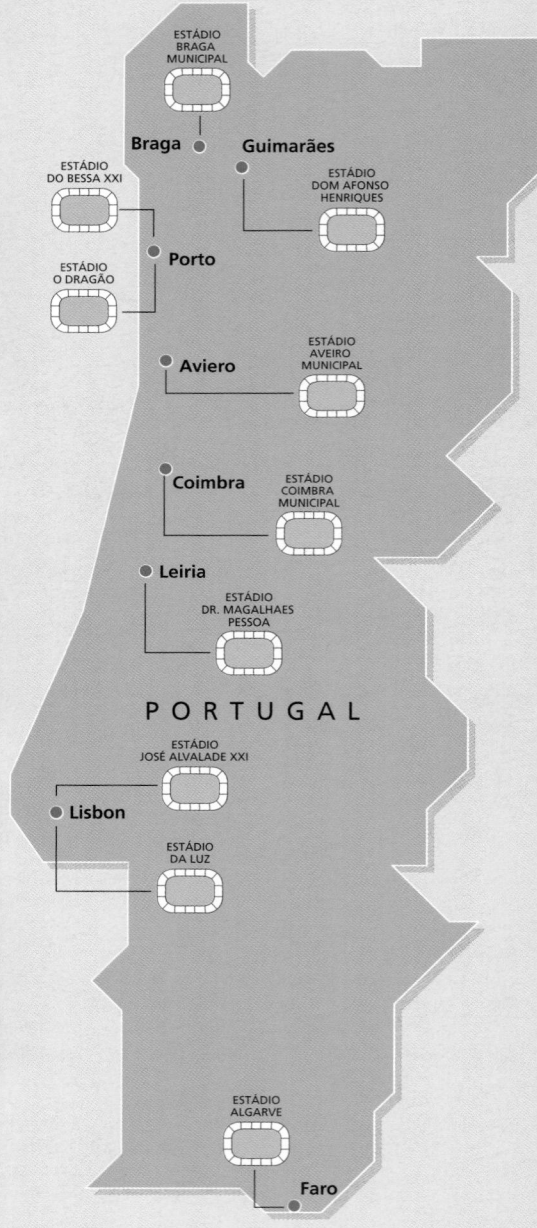

THE GROUP STAGES

AS WE NOW KNOW, Greece had not read the script and Euro 2004 opened with the shock defeat of the Portuguese in Porto. The Greeks proved it was no fluke when they went on to draw with the notoriously underperforming Spaniards. Portugal recovered their composure, beat the Russians and then in a tense and hard-fought encounter got a rare victory over their Spanish neighbours to take them into the quarter-finals. Group B opened with an epic encounter between France and England, Lampard's first-half goal only being overturned by a last-minute free kick from Zidane and a foolishly conceded penalty. England recovered and decisively beat both Croatia and Switzerland, but their opening defeat saw them consigned to a quarter-final against the hosts.

Italy were the favourites in Group C but turned in a series of disastrous, ill-tempered and mean spirited performances. A gruesome 0-0 draw with Denmark was followed by their game with Sweden who had uncharacteristically thrashed Bulgaria with élan. They sat on a 1-0 lead only to be undone by a brilliant twisting strike from Ibrahimovic. Despite beating the Bulgarians in their final game, Sweden and Denmark's 2-2 draw put them out. Cue the miserable Cassano collapsing on the touchline and hysterical claims of a fix (which were totally untrue).

Group D, which looked the toughest, was a breeze for the awesomely powerful-looking Czechs. They came from behind against both the Latvians and the Dutch – their 3-2 win being the game of the opening rounds. Then a reserve team dispensed with the Germans, who had looked well below par in both their previous games, allowing an equally unimpressive Dutch side to squeeze through.

Zlatan Ibrahimovic spins in the air to level the scores in the 85th minute of Sweden's first round game with Italy. Italy had played their best soccer of the tournament in the first half but sat back for the second with the inevitable consequences.

Rudi Völler shrugs having watched Germany beaten by the Czech Republic reserves and sent out of Euro 2004. He resigned two weeks later saying phlegmatically, 'I will take some time off but neither sulk nor emigrate'.

THE EUROPEAN CHAMPIONSHIPS

PORTUGAL	A	GREECE
SPAIN		RUSSIA

FRANCE	B	ENGLAND
SWITZERLAND		CROATIA

SWEDEN	C	BULGARIA
DENMARK		ITALY

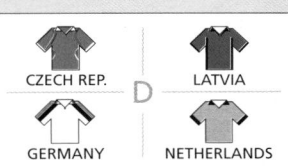

CZECH REP.	D	LATVIA
GERMANY		NETHERLANDS

GROUP A

Portugal **1-2** Greece
Spain **1-0** Russia
Greece **1-1** Spain
Russia **0-2** Portugal
Spain **0-1** Portugal
Russia **2-1** Greece

	P	W	D	L	F	A	Pts
Portugal	3	2	0	1	4	2	6
Greece	3	1	1	1	4	4	4
Spain	3	1	1	1	2	2	4
Russia	3	1	0	2	2	4	3

GROUP B

Switzerland **0-0** Croatia
France **2-1** England
England **3-0** Switzerland
Croatia **2-2** France
Croatia **2-4** England
Switzerland **1-3** France

	P	W	D	L	F	A	Pts
France	3	2	1	0	7	4	7
England	3	2	0	1	8	4	6
Croatia	3	0	2	1	4	6	2
Switzerland	3	0	1	2	1	6	1

GROUP C

Denmark **0-0** Italy
Sweden **5-0** Bulgaria
Bulgaria **0-2** Denmark
Italy **1-1** Sweden
Italy **2-1** Bulgaria
Denmark **2-2** Sweden

	P	W	D	L	F	A	Pts
Sweden	3	1	2	0	8	3	5
Denmark	3	1	2	0	4	2	5
Italy	3	1	2	0	3	2	5
Bulgaria	3	0	0	3	1	9	0

GROUP D

Czech Rep. **2-1** Latvia
Germany **1-1** Netherlands
Latvia **0-0** Germany
Netherlands **2-3** Czech Rep.
Netherlands **3-0** Latvia
Germany **1-2** Czech Rep.

	P	W	D	L	F	A	Pts
Czech Rep.	3	3	0	0	7	4	9
Netherlands	3	1	1	1	6	4	4
Germany	3	0	2	1	2	3	2
Latvia	3	0	1	2	1	5	1

THE EUROPEAN CHAMPIONSHIPS

THE QUARTER-FINALS

PORTUGAL V ENGLAND was the pick of the quarter-finals. An early goal from Michael Owen and the enforced departure of Wayne Rooney with a broken foot set the tone of the game. The next hour saw almost complete Portuguese possession as they chased an equalizer and it finally came from Postiga in the 82nd minute. Rui Costa and Frank Lampard hit late goals in extra time and England were denied a winner when Sol Campbell's header was disallowed. Inevitably it went to penalties and when David Beckham's opening strike soared high into the stands, England's demise seemed inevitable. France were hugely disappointing as the Greeks first stifled them and stole a winning goal from another set-piece. Sweden and Holland baked in the heat of the Algarve. Sweden provided the work-rate, the Dutch little but the colour of their fans. However, the Dutch held their nerve for once in a penalty shootout to book their semi-final place. Finally, after their usual slow start, the Czech Republic eventually cut loose to beat Denmark 3-0.

June 24 – Estadio da Luz, Lisbon
Attendance 65,000

PORTUGAL **2-2** **ENGLAND**

h/t: 0-1

	Scorers	
Postiga 83		Owen 3
Rui Costa 110		Lampard 115

Portugal won 6-5 on pens

June 25 – José Alvalade, Lisbon
Attendance 50,000

FRANCE **0-1** **GREECE**

h/t: 0-0

	Scorer	
		Charisteas 65

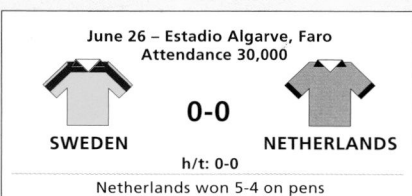

June 26 – Estadio Algarve, Faro
Attendance 30,000

SWEDEN **0-0** **NETHERLANDS**

h/t: 0-0

Netherlands won 5-4 on pens

June 27 – Drāgāo, Porto
Attendance 45,000

CZECH REP. **3-0** **DENMARK**

h/t: 0-0

	Scorers	
Koller 49		
Baros 63, 65		

THE SEMI-FINALS

IN THE FIRST SEMI-FINAL the lacklustre Dutch were finally found out, as their weak and uninspiring performance virtually handed the game to a Portuguese team that was truly fired up. A goal in each half gave the game to the hosts: a Ronaldo header after he was left virtually unmarked in the box, and a stunning, curling, long-distance strike from Maniche. The game was so clearly Portugal's they had time to give the Dutch a chance when defender Jorge Andrade delicately tipped a dangerous cross over the head of his own goalkeeper. The Czech Republic also seemed to have given their best by the time the semi-finals arrived as Greece's claustrophobic man-marking restricted the previously free-scoring Czechs to a tiny handful of chances, none better than Tomas Roziscky's shot that rattled off the bar in the opening minutes. It was 0-0 at 90 minutes and the stalemate was only broken when Greek defender Dellas rose to meet a looping corner and glance the ball home to go through on the silver goal rule.

Big Phil Scolari raises his hands in triumph as the hosts Portugal sweep through to the Final of Euro 2004.

June 30 – José Alvalade, Lisbon
Attendance 46,679

PORTUGAL **2-1** **NETHERLANDS**

h/t: 1-0

	Scorers	
Ronaldo 26		Andrade o.g. 62
Maniche 58		

July 1 – Drāgāo, Porto
Attendance 48,000

GREECE **1-0** **CZECH REP.**

h/t: 0-0

	Scorer	
Dallas 105		

Silver goal

THE FINAL

It was not a match to set the heart racing. As predicted, Portugal had the overwhelming majority of possession as the Greeks abandoned the ball to their opponents in their half, forming an impregnable series of defensive walls in their own. Super tight man-to-man marking on Portugal's most creative players – Ronaldo, Figo and Deco – served to limit the host's chances while the goalless striker, Pauleta, laboured in vain. The Greeks didn't get a corner until early in the second half, but that was enough. Once again a soaring ball came into the six-yard area; Portugal's goalkeeper Ricardo was woefully out of position and there was Charisteas to head home. Scolari's usually inspired substitutions failed to ignite the side and Greece, unbelievably, were European Champions.

Deco stakes his claim for an Oscar nomination. Dellas and the rest of the Greek defence ensured that there was no way through for him or the other Portuguese playmakers Figo and Cristian Ronaldo.

From zeroes to heroes: Greece, who had never even won a game in an international tournament before Euro 2004, just went out and won it with the minimum of fuss.

The Starting Line-Up

July 4 – Estadio da Luz, Lisbon
Attendance 62,685

PORTUGAL	Referee	**GREECE**
Formation: 4-1-4-1	M Merk (Germany)	Formation: 3-4-3
Manager		**Manager**
Luiz Felipe Scolari		Otto Rehhagel
Substitutes used		**Substitutes used**
Ferreira (2)		(2) Venetidis
Rui Costa (10)		(22) Papadopoulos
Nuno Gomes (21)		

PORTUGAL 0-1 GREECE

Match Statistics

Portugal		Greece
58%	Possession	42%
5	Shots on goal	1
2	Yellow Cards	4
23	Free kicks conceded	24
10	Corners won	1
4	Offsides	3

The Winning Goal

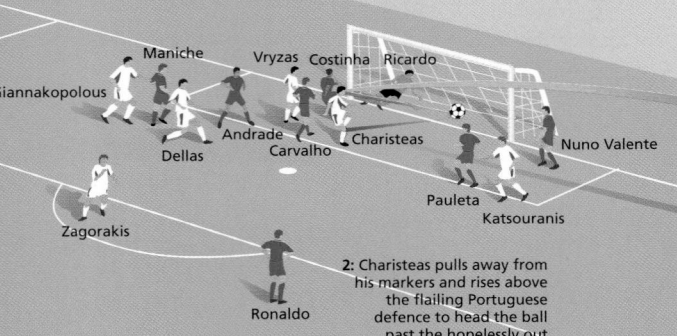

2: Charisteas pulls away from his markers and rises above the flailing Portuguese defence to head the ball past the hopelessly out of position Ricardo.

1: Basinas sends a simple looping ball from the corner into the centre of the penalty area.

Highlights of the Game

KEY

Player booked ▮▯ ⟲ Substitution
Goal ⚽▯

PORTUGAL   KICK OFF   **GREECE**
0 mins   *(played in white)*

12 min: Costinha booked for foul on Seitaridis

14 min: Miguel's low shot from outside of the area is just turned round the post by Nikopolidis

16 min: Last gasp save by Ricardo at the feet of Charisteas

17 min: Pauleta's best chance is covered by Nikolopidis at his near post

24 min: Maniche shapes to fire a perfect volley from the edge of the area but sent it wide

43 min: Miguel's rib injury is too much. Paulo Ferriera comes on in his place

45 mins
+2 min injury time

+2 min: Basinas booked for deliberate handball

HALF-TIME: **0-0**

60 min: Costinha off and Scolari throws on Rui Costa

57 min: Charisteas heads home from Greece's first corner of the game

63 min: Seitaridis booked for standing over Portugese free kick

74 min: At last Scolari takes of the goalless Pauleta and Nuno Gomes replaces him

67 min: Fyssas clatters Luis Figo

76 min: Giannakopolous off, Venetidis on

81 min: Greece swap strikers. Vyrzas off, Papadopoulos on

75 min: Rui Costa puts Ronaldo through but he sends his shot over the bar from 10 metres

85 min: Papadopoulos fouls Rui Costa

86 min: Game delayed for three minutes by a one-man Barcelona pitch invasion

90 min: Figo spins on the edge of the Greek area but his shot is just wide of the post

90 mins
+ 5 mins injury time

+4 min: Nuno Valente fouls Zagorakis

FULL-TIME: **0-1**

The European Championships

THE EUROPEAN CHAMPIONSHIPS

THE EUROPEAN CHAMPIONSHIPS are the most prestigious European national competition. Established in 1957, the first competition was held in 1960, and since then the Henri Delaunay Cup has been contested every four years, as with the World Cup. The Championship is open to the senior national representative teams of all UEFA's member associations, and the qualifying competition and final round are staged over the two-year period following every FIFA World Cup. The first tournaments comprised only semi-finals and Finals. In 1976 quarter-finals were added, and in 1980 eight teams competed in two mini-leagues before the semi-finals. Expansion in 1996 saw 16 teams compete in four leagues to produce eight quarter-finalists.

1960 FRANCE

SEMI-FINALS

Yugoslavia **5-4** France
(Galic 11,   (Vincent 12,
Zanetic 55,   Heutte 43, 62,
Knez 75,   Wisnieski 52)
Jerkovic 77, 79)

Soviet Union **3-0** Czechoslovakia
(V. Ivanov 34, 56,
Ponedelnik 65)

THIRD PLACE PLAY-OFF

Czechoslovakia **2-0** France

FINAL

July 10 – Parc des Princes, Paris
Soviet Union **2-1** Yugoslavia
(Metreveli 49,   (Galic 41)
Ponedelnik 113)
(after extra time)
h/t: 0-1 **90 mins:** 1-1
Att: 17,966 **Ref:** Ellis (England)

1964 SPAIN

SEMI-FINALS

Spain **2-1** Hungary
(Pereda 35,   (Bene 85)
Amancio 115)
(after extra time)

Soviet Union **3-0** Denmark
(Voronin 19,
Ponedelnik 40,
V. Ivanov 87)

THIRD PLACE PLAY-OFF

Hungary **3-1** Denmark
(after extra time)

FINAL

June 21 – Santiago Bernabeu, Madrid
Spain **2-1** Soviet Union
(Pereda 6,   (Khusainov 8)
Marcelino 84)
h/t: 1-1 **Att:** 105,000
Ref: Holland (England)

1968 ITALY

SEMI-FINALS

Yugoslavia **1-0** England
(Dzajic 86)

Italy **0-0** Soviet Union
(after extra time)
Italy won on toss of coin

THIRD PLACE PLAY-OFF

England **2-0** Soviet Union

FINAL

June 8 – Stadio Olimpico, Rome
Italy **1-1** Yugoslavia
(Domenghini 80)   (Dzajic 38)
(after extra time)
h/t: 0-1 **90 mins:** 1-1
Att: 85,000 **Ref:** Dienst (Switzerland)

REPLAY

June 10 – Stadio Olimpico, Rome
Italy **2-0** Yugoslavia
(Riva 11,
Anastasai 32)
h/t: 2-0 **Att:** 50,000
Ref: Ortiz (Spain)

1972 BELGIUM

SEMI-FINALS

Soviet Union **1-0** Hungary
(Konkov 53)

West Germany **2-1** Belgium
(G. Müller 24, 71)   (Polleunis 83)

THIRD PLACE PLAY-OFF

Belgium **2-1** Hungary

FINAL

June 18 – Stade Heysel, Brussels
West Germany **3-0** Soviet Union
(G. Müller 27, 58,
Wimmer 52)
h/t: 1-0 **Att:** 50,000
Ref: Marschall (Austria)

1976 YUGOSLAVIA

SEMI-FINALS

Czechoslovakia **3-1** Netherlands
(Ondrus 20,   (Ondrus o.g. 74)
Nehoda 115,
F. Vesely 118)
(after extra time)

West Germany **4-2** Yugoslavia
(Flohe 65,   (Popivoda 20,
D. Müller 82,   Dzajic 30)
114, 119)
(after extra time)

THIRD PLACE PLAY-OFF

Netherlands **3-2** Yugoslavia
(after extra time)

FINAL

June 20 – Crvena Zvezda, Belgrade
Czechoslovakia **2-2** West Germany
(Svehlík 8,   (D. Müller 28,
Dobiás 25)   Hölzenbein 89)
(after extra time)
h/t: 2-1 **90 mins:** 2-2
Att: 33,000 **Ref:** Gonella (Italy)
Czechoslovakia won 5-3 on pens

1980 ITALY

GROUP 1

West Germany **1-0** Czechoslovakia
Netherlands **1-0** Greece
West Germany **3-2** Netherlands
Czechoslovakia **3-1** Greece
Czechoslovakia **1-1** Netherlands
West Germany **0-0** Greece

	P	W	D	L	F	A	Pts
West Germany	3	2	1	0	4	2	5
Czechoslovakia	3	1	1	1	4	3	3
Netherlands	3	1	1	1	4	4	3
Greece	3	0	1	2	1	4	1

GROUP 2

England **1-1** Belgium
Italy **0-0** Spain
Belgium **2-1** Spain
Italy **1-0** England
England **2-1** Spain
Italy **0-0** Belgium

	P	W	D	L	F	A	Pts
Belgium	3	1	2	0	3	2	4
Italy	3	1	2	0	1	0	4
England	3	1	1	1	3	3	3
Spain	3	0	1	2	2	4	1

THIRD PLACE PLAY-OFF

Czechoslovakia **1-1** Italy
(after extra time)
Czechoslovakia won 9-8 on pens

FINAL

June 22 – Stadio Olimpico, Rome
West Germany **2-1** Belgium
(Hrubesch 10, 88)   (Vandereycken
72 pen)
h/t: 1-0 **Att:** 48,000
Ref: Rainea (Romania)

1984 FRANCE

GROUP 1

France **1-0** Denmark
Belgium **2-0** Yugoslavia
France **5-0** Belgium
Denmark **5-0** Yugoslavia
France **3-2** Yugoslavia
Denmark **3-2** Belgium

	P	W	D	L	F	A	Pts
France	3	3	0	0	9	2	6
Denmark	3	2	0	1	8	3	4
Belgium	3	1	0	2	4	8	2
Yugoslavia	3	0	0	3	2	10	0

GROUP 2

West Germany **0-0** Portugal
Spain **1-1** Romania
West Germany **2-1** Romania
Portugal **1-1** Spain
Spain **1-0** West Germany
Portugal **1-0** Romania

	P	W	D	L	F	A	Pts
Spain	3	1	2	0	3	2	4
Portugal	3	1	2	0	2	1	4
West Germany	3	1	1	1	2	2	3
Romania	3	0	1	2	2	4	1

SEMI-FINALS

France **3-2** Portugal

(Domergue 24, 114,   (Jordão 73, 97)
Platini 119)
(after extra time)

Spain **1-1** Denmark
(Maceda 66)   (Lerby 6)
(after extra time)
Spain won 5-4 on pens

FINAL

June 27 – Parc des Princes, Paris
France **2-0** Spain
(Platini 56,
Bellone 90)
h/t: 0-0 **Att:** 47,000
Ref: Christov (Czechoslovakia)

1988 WEST GERMANY

GROUP 1

West Germany **1-1** Italy
Spain **3-2** Denmark
West Germany **2-0** Denmark
Italy **1-0** Spain
West Germany **2-0** Spain
Italy **2-0** Denmark

	P	W	D	L	F	A	Pts
West Germany	3	2	1	0	5	1	5
Italy	3	2	1	0	4	1	5
Spain	3	1	0	2	3	5	2
Denmark	3	0	0	3	2	7	0

GROUP 2

Rep. of Ireland **1-0** England
Soviet Union **1-0** Netherlands
Netherlands **3-1** England
Soviet Union **1-1** Rep. of Ireland
Soviet Union **3-1** England
Netherlands **1-0** Rep. of Ireland

	P	W	D	L	F	A	Pts
Soviet Union	3	2	1	0	5	2	5
Netherlands	3	2	0	1	4	2	4
Rep. of Ireland	3	1	1	1	2	2	3
England	3	0	0	3	2	7	0

SEMI-FINALS

Netherlands **2-1** West Germany
(R. Koeman 74 pen,   (Matthäus
van Basten 89)   55 pen)

Soviet Union **2-0** Italy
(Litovchenko 60,
Protasov 62)

FINAL

June 25 – Olympiastadion, Munich
Netherlands **2-0** Soviet Union
(Gullit 33,
van Basten 54)
h/t: 1-0 **Att:** 72,300
Ref: Vautrot (France)

1992 SWEDEN

GROUP A

Sweden **1-1** France
Denmark **0-0** England
France **0-0** England
Sweden **1-0** Denmark
Denmark **2-1** France
Sweden **2-1** England

	P	W	D	L	F	A	Pts
Sweden	3	2	1	0	4	2	5
Denmark	3	1	1	1	2	2	3
France	3	0	2	1	2	3	2
England	3	0	2	1	1	2	2

European Championship Winners

Soviet Union 1960	Spain 1964	Italy 1968	West Germany 1972, 80	Czechoslovakia 1976	France 1984, 2000	Netherlands 1988	Denmark 1992	Germany 1996	Greece 2004

GROUP B

Netherlands 1-0 Scotland
Germany 1-1 CIS
Germany 2-0 Scotland
Netherlands 0-0 CIS
Netherlands 3-1 Germany
Scotland 3-0 CIS

	P	W	D	L	F	A	Pts
Netherlands	3	2	1	0	4	1	5
Germany	3	1	1	1	4	4	3
Scotland	3	1	0	2	3	3	2
CIS	3	0	2	1	1	4	2

SEMI-FINALS

Germany 3-2 Sweden
*(Hässler 11,   (Brolin 64,
Riedle 59, 88)   Andersson 89)*
Denmark 2-2 Netherlands
*(H. Larsen 5, 32)   (Bergkamp 23,
Rijkaard 85)*
(after extra time)
Denmark won 5-4 on pens

FINAL

June 26 – Nya Ullevi, Gothenburg
Denmark 2-0 Germany
*(Jensen 18,
Vilfort 78)*
h/t: 1-0 **Att:** 37,000
Ref: Galler (Switzerland)

1996 ENGLAND

GROUP A

England 1-1 Switzerland
Netherlands 0-0 Scotland
Netherlands 2-0 Switzerland
England 2-0 Scotland
Scotland 1-0 Switzerland
England 4-1 Netherlands

	P	W	D	L	F	A	Pts
England	3	2	1	0	7	2	7
Netherlands	3	1	1	1	3	4	4
Scotland	3	1	1	1	1	2	4
Switzerland	3	0	1	2	1	4	1

GROUP B

Spain 1-1 Bulgaria
France 1-0 Romania
Bulgaria 1-0 Romania
France 1-1 Spain
France 3-1 Bulgaria
Spain 2-1 Romania

	P	W	D	L	F	A	Pts
France	3	2	1	0	5	2	7
Spain	3	1	2	0	4	3	5
Bulgaria	3	1	1	1	3	4	4
Romania	3	0	0	3	1	4	0

GROUP C

Germany 2-0 Czech Rep.
Italy 2-1 Russia
Czech Rep. 2-1 Italy
Germany 3-0 Russia
Italy 0-0 Germany
Czech Rep. 3-3 Russia

	P	W	D	L	F	A	Pts
Germany	3	2	1	0	5	0	7
Czech Rep.	3	1	1	1	5	6	4
Italy	3	1	1	1	3	3	4
Russia	3	0	1	2	4	8	1

GROUP D

Denmark 1-1 Portugal
Croatia 1-0 Turkey
Portugal 1-0 Turkey
Croatia 3-0 Denmark
Portugal 3-0 Croatia
Denmark 3-0 Turkey

	P	W	D	L	F	A	Pts
Portugal	3	2	1	0	5	1	7
Croatia	3	2	0	1	4	3	6
Denmark	3	1	1	1	4	4	4
Turkey	3	0	0	3	0	5	0

QUARTER-FINALS

England 0-0 Spain
(after extra time)
England won 4-2 on pens
France 0-0 Netherlands
(after extra time)
France won 5-4 on pens
Germany 2-1 Croatia
*(Klinsmann   (Suker 51)
21 pen,
Sammer 59)*
Czech Rep. 1-0 Portugal
(Poborsky 53)

SEMI-FINALS

Czech Rep. 0-0 France
(after extra time)
Czech Rep. won 6-5 on pens
Germany 1-1 England
(Kuntz 16)   (Shearer 3)
(after extra time)
Germany won 6-5 on pens

FINAL

June 30 – Wembley, London
Germany 2-1 Czech Rep.
(Bierhoff 73, 94)   (Berger 58 pen)
h/t: 0-0 **90 mins:** 1-1
Att: 76,000 **Ref:** Pairetto (Italy)
Germany won on golden goal
in extra time

2000 BELGIUM AND THE NETHERLANDS

GROUP A

Germany 1-1 Romania
Portugal 3-2 England
Portugal 1-0 Romania
England 1-0 Germany
Romania 3-2 England
Portugal 3-0 Germany

	P	W	D	L	F	A	Pts
Portugal	3	3	0	0	7	2	9
Romania	3	1	1	1	4	4	4
England	3	1	0	2	5	6	3
Germany	3	0	1	2	1	5	1

GROUP B

Belgium 2-1 Sweden
Italy 2-1 Turkey
Italy 2-0 Belgium
Sweden 0-0 Turkey
Turkey 2-0 Belgium
Italy 2-1 Sweden

	P	W	D	L	F	A	Pts
Italy	3	3	0	0	6	2	9
Turkey	3	1	1	1	3	2	4
Belgium	3	1	0	2	2	5	3
Sweden	3	0	1	2	2	4	1

GROUP C

Norway 1-0 Spain
Yugoslavia 3-3 Slovenia
Spain 2-1 Slovenia
Yugoslavia 1-0 Norway
Spain 4-3 Yugoslavia
Slovenia 0-0 Norway

	P	W	D	L	F	A	Pts
Spain	3	2	0	1	6	5	6
Yugoslavia	3	1	1	1	7	7	4
Norway	3	1	1	1	1	1	4
Slovenia	3	0	2	1	4	5	2

GROUP D

France 3-0 Denmark
Netherlands 1-0 Czech Rep.
France 2-1 Czech Rep.
Netherlands 3-0 Denmark
Netherlands 3-2 France
Czech Rep. 2-0 Denmark

	P	W	D	L	F	A	Pts
Netherlands	3	3	0	0	7	2	9
France	3	2	0	1	7	4	6
Czech Rep.	3	1	0	2	3	3	3
Denmark	3	0	0	3	0	8	0

QUARTER-FINALS

Portugal 2-0 Turkey
(Nuno Gomes 44, 56)
Italy 2-0 Romania
*(Totti 33,
Inzaghi 43)*
Netherlands 6-1 Yugoslavia
*(Kluivert   Milosevic 90)
24, 38, 54,
Govedarica o.g. 51,
Overmars 78, 90)*
France 2-1 Spain
*(Zidane 33,   (Mendieta
Djorkaeff 44)   38 pen)*

SEMI-FINALS

France 2-1 Portugal
*(Henry 51,   (Nuno Gomes 19)
Zidane 117 pen)*
France won on golden goal in extra time
Italy 0-0 Netherlands
(after extra time)
Italy won 3-1 on pens

FINAL

July 2 – De Kuip, Rotterdam
France 2-1 Italy
*(Wiltord 90,   (Delvecchio 55)
Trezeguet 103)*
France won on golden goal in extra time
h/t: 0-0 **90 mins:** 1-1
Att: 55,000 **Ref:** Frisk (Sweden)

2004 PORTUGAL

GROUP A

Portugal 1-2 Greece
Spain 1-0 Russia
Greece 1-1 Spain
Portugal 2-0 Russia
Russia 2-1 Greece
Portugal 1-0 Spain

	P	W	D	L	F	A	Pts
Portugal	3	2	0	1	4	2	6
Greece	3	1	1	1	4	4	4
Spain	3	1	1	1	2	2	4
Russia	3	1	0	2	2	4	3

GROUP B

Switzerland 0-0 Croatia
France 2-1 England
England 3-0 Switzerland
Croatia 2-2 France
Croatia 2-4 England
Switzerland 1-3 France

	P	W	D	L	F	A	Pts
France	3	2	1	0	7	4	7
England	3	2	0	1	8	4	6
Croatia	3	0	2	1	4	6	2
Switzerland	3	0	1	2	1	6	1

GROUP C

Denmark 0-0 Italy
Sweden 5-0 Bulgaria
Bulgaria 0-2 Denmark
Italy 1-1 Sweden
Italy 2-1 Bulgaria
Denmark 2-2 Sweden

	P	W	D	L	F	A	Pts
Sweden	3	1	2	0	8	3	5
Denmark	3	1	2	0	4	2	5
Italy	3	1	2	0	3	2	5
Bulgaria	3	0	0	3	1	9	0

GROUP D

Czech Rep 2-1 Latvia
Germany 1-1 Netherlands
Latvia 0-0 Germany
Netherlands 2-3 Czech Rep
Netherlands 3-0 Latvia
Germany 1-2 Czech Rep

	P	W	D	L	F	A	Pts
Czech Rep	3	3	0	0	7	4	9
Netherlands	3	1	1	1	6	4	4
Germany	3	0	2	1	2	3	2
Latvia	3	0	1	2	1	5	1

QUARTER-FINALS

England 2-2 Portugal
*(Owen 3,   (Postiga 83,
Lampard 115)   Rui Costa 110)*
(after extra time)
Portugal won 6-5 on pens
France 0-1 Greece
(Charisteas 65)
Netherlands 0-0 Sweden
(after extra time)
Netherlands won 5-4 on pens
Czech Rep. 3-0 Denmark
*(Koller 49,
Baros 63, 65)*

SEMI-FINALS

Czech Rep. 0-1 Greece
(Dellas 106)
(silver goal)
Portugal 2-1 Netherlands
*(Ronaldo 26,   (Andrade o.g. 63)
Maniche 58)*

FINAL

July 4 – Estadio da Luz, Lisbon
Portugal 0-1 Greece
(Charisteas 56)
h/t: 0-0 **Att:** 62,865
Ref: Merk (Germany)

The European Champions League

TOURNAMENT REVIEW 2003–04

FOR THE FIRST TIME SINCE 1991, when Red Star Belgrade beat Marseille, the European Cup Final did not feature a team from one of the big four leagues. Monaco, France's first representatives for 13 years, had never made the final before. Porto was the last Portuguese team to have appeared when the club won the title in 1987. Neither of the other semi-finalists – Chelsea and Deportivo la Coruña – had made it that far before and, of the eight quarter-finalists, there were only two previous winners – Milan and Real Madrid. Perhaps a hint of things to come was given in the last qualifying round of the tournament. Newcastle United were hustled and bundled out of the competition by a muscular and determined Partizan Belgrade, while Club Brugge took Borussia Dortmund to penalties and held its nerve to initiate a season of discord and decline for the Ruhr giants. Later on in the tournament, UEFA's decision to scrap the second group stage of the competition and replace its six games with a two-leg knockout round for the last 16 teams created greater opportunities for upsets and reversals of form.

The Aegean's expanding presence

Partizan were one of only four clubs from Eastern and Central Europe to make the group stage, alongside Lokomotiv Moskva, Dynamo Kyiv and Sparta Praha. There were no Scandinavian representatives this season as both Rosenborg and FC København went out in the qualifiers. Last year's surprise participants from Israel and Switzerland were not followed up this year. Both of the Scottish Old Firm made the group stage but five qualifiers from Greece and Turkey maintained the Aegean's expanding presence in the group stage of the competition.

Newcastle United's income for the season was transformed by losing out on penalties to Partizan Belgrade in the tournament's qualifying round. Here Partizan's Damir Cakar takes on Shay Given in the Newcastle goal.

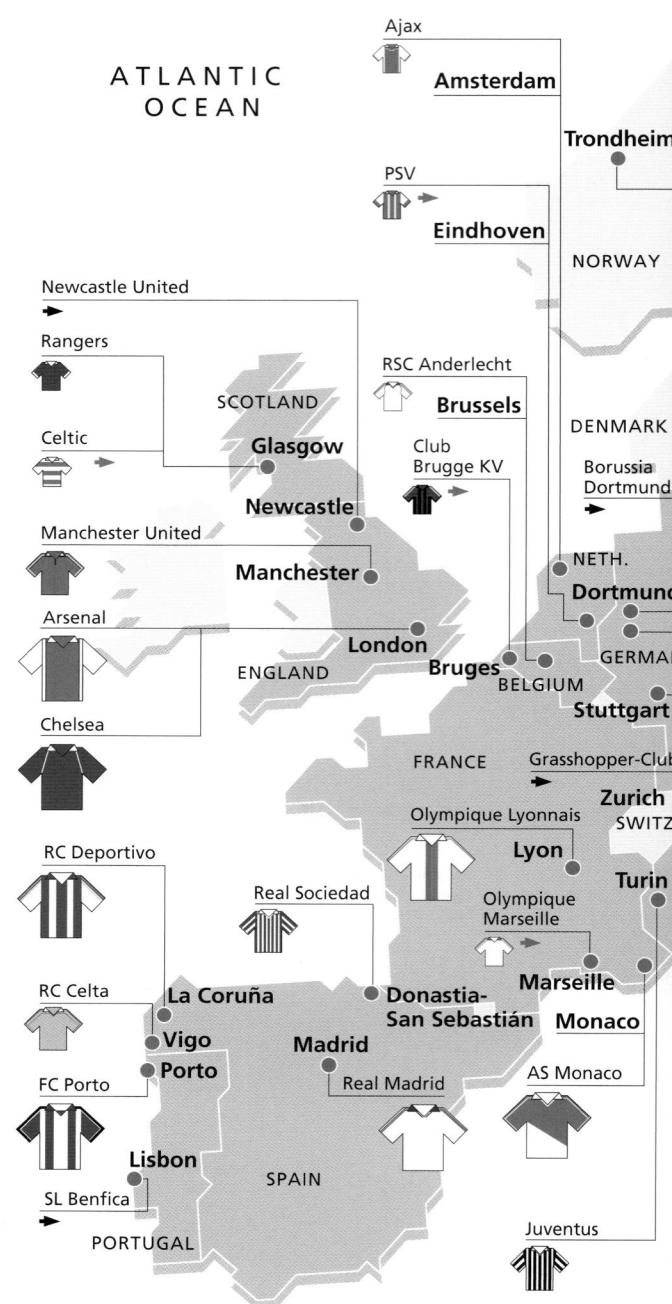

ATLANTIC OCEAN

Ajax — Amsterdam

Trondheim

PSV — Eindhoven

NORWAY

Newcastle United

Rangers

SCOTLAND

Celtic

Glasgow

RSC Anderlecht — Brussels

DENMARK

Club Brugge KV

Newcastle

Borussia Dortmund

Manchester United

Manchester

NETH.

Dortmund

Arsenal

London

ENGLAND

Bruges

BELGIUM

GERMANY

Chelsea

Stuttgart

FRANCE

Grasshopper-Club

Olympique Lyonnais

Zurich

SWITZ.

RC Deportivo

Lyon

Real Sociedad

Olympique Marseille

Turin

RC Celta

La Coruña

Donastia-San Sebastián

Marseille

Vigo

Madrid

Monaco

FC Porto

Porto

Real Madrid

AS Monaco

Lisbon

SPAIN

SL Benfica

Juventus

PORTUGAL

The European Champions League 2003–04

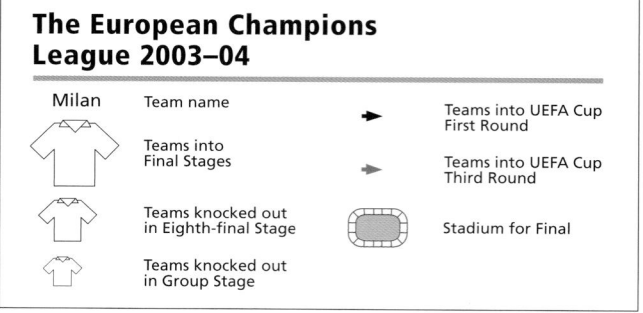

Milan	Team name		Teams into UEFA Cup First Round
Teams into Final Stages		Teams into UEFA Cup Third Round
Teams knocked out in Eighth-final Stage		Stadium for Final
Teams knocked out in Group Stage		

Teams Eliminated in Qualifying Round 1

Barry Town	Wales
FC BATE Borisov	Belarus
Glentoran	Northern Ireland
CS Grevenmacher	Luxembourg
HB	Faeroe Islands
KR	Iceland
Irtysh Pavlodar	Kazakhstan
Skonto Riga	Latvia
FC Flora Tallinn	Estonia
Dinamo Tbilisi	Georgia

Teams Eliminated in Qualifying Round 2

Bohemians	Republic of Ireland
Rapid Bucureşti	Romania
Djurgårdens IF	Sweden
HJK Helsinki	Finland
FBK Kaunas	Lithuania
FK Leotar	Bosnia
Maccabi Tel-Aviv	Israel
NK Maribor	Slovenia
CSKA Moskva	Russia
Osmonia Nicosia	Cyprus
Serif Tiraspol	Moldova
Sliema Wanderers	Malta
SK Tirana	Albania
Pyunik Yerevan	Armenia

Rosenborg BK

FC København
Copenhagen

VfB Stuttgart

Gelsenkirchen
ARENA AUFSCHALKE
60,215

Bayern München

Sparta Praha

POLAND

Slavia Praha

Wisla Kraków

Moscow

Lokomotiv Moskva

Kiev

Dynamo Kyiv

CZECH REPUBLIC
Prague **Kraków**
Zilina
Vienna MSK Zilina
SLOVAKIA

UKRAINE

Shakhtar Donetsk

Donetsk

Munich
FK Austria Wien
AUSTRIA **Graz**
Grazer AK HUNGARY

MTK Hungária

Budapest

Zagreb CROATIA

Partizan Beograd

Milan
Dinamo Zagreb

Lazio

Belgrade
SERBIA & MONTENEGO
Sofia
CSKA Sofia

BULGARIA BLACK SEA

Rome
ITALY

MACEDONIA **Skopje**
Vardar Skopje

Istanbul
Beşiktaş

TURKEY

Internazionale

Galatasaray SK

GREECE **Athens**

AEK

Milan

MEDITERRANEAN SEA

Olympiakos

Panathinaikos

Champions League Top Goalscorers 2003–04

PLAYER	CLUB	NATIONALITY	GOALS
Fernando Morientes	AS Monaco	Spanish	9
Dado Prso	AS Monaco	Croatian	7
Roy Makaay	Bayern München	Dutch	6
Walter Pandiani	RC Deportivo	Uruguayan	6
Didier Drogba	Olympique Marseille	French	5

At the end of the 2003–04 season Borussia Dortmund announced the club was parting company with manager Matthias Sammer, who had been at the helm since 1993. Matters were not helped when Dortmund crashed out of the lucrative Champions League in the third qualifying round beaten in a penalty shootout by Club Brugge.

Group Stage

The Group Stage went broadly with expected form but not without some close and absorbing contests. In Group A Bayern München again looked well below its European best. After winning their opening game with Celtic, Bayern were held to three draws and beaten in Lyon with a brilliant goal from striker Giovanni Elber whose services the club had dispensed with at the end of the previous season. In the end Bayern needed both a narrow home victory against Anderlecht and the excellent Lyon to finish above Celtic to creep into the second round. In Group B Arsenal, again looking to turn domestic promise into European results, opened the campaign with a humiliating home defeat by Inter and took a single point from away games in Moscow and Kiev. However, the club qualified top of their group with three imperious victories, most notably a sensational 5-1 thrashing of a dispirited Inter at the San Siro.

Group C was an absorbing three-way fight between Monaco, Deportivo and PSV. Monaco's exuberant 8-3 defeat of Deportivo, which included four goals for Croatian striker Dado Prso, gave them the edge in the table, while Deportivo squeaked past PSV by virtue of a marginally better goal difference. A similar tussle took place in Group H where all four clubs were in contention on the final match day and both Celta and Club Brugge were good enough to beat last year's champions Milan.

Above: *3-0 to Inter at Highbury – Andy Van de Meyde and the Inter midfield hail their second goal of the night.*

Below: *5-1 to Arsenal at the San Siro – Thierry Henry scores Arsenal's third of five on the night in a total turnaround from their first game with Inter.*

GROUP STAGE

GROUP A
Olym. Lyonnais	**1-0**	RSC Anderlecht
Bayern München	**2-1**	Celtic
Celtic	**2-0**	Olym. Lyonnais
RSC Anderlecht	**1-1**	Bayern München
RSC Anderlecht	**1-0**	Celtic
Olym. Lyonnais	**1-1**	Bayern München
Celtic	**3-1**	RSC Anderlecht
Bayern München	**1-2**	Olym. Lyonnais
RSC Anderlecht	**1-0**	Olym. Lyonnais
Celtic	**0-0**	Bayern München
Olym. Lyonnais	**3-2**	Celtic
Bayern München	**1-0**	RSC Anderlecht

GROUP B
Dynamo Kyiv	**2-0**	Lokomotiv Moskva
Arsenal	**0-3**	Internazionale
Internazionale	**2-1**	Dynamo Kyiv
Lokomotiv Moskva	**0-0**	Arsenal
Lokomotiv Moskva	**3-0**	Internazionale
Dynamo Kyiv	**2-1**	Arsenal
Internazionale	**1-1**	Lokomotiv Moskva
Arsenal	**1-0**	Dynamo Kyiv
Lokomotiv Moskva	**3-2**	Dynamo Kyiv
Internazionale	**1-5**	Arsenal
Dynamo Kyiv	**1-1**	Internazionale
Arsenal	**2-0**	Lokomotiv Moskva

GROUP C
AEK	**1-1**	RC Deportivo
PSV	**1-2**	AS Monaco
AS Monaco	**4-0**	AEK
RC Deportivo	**2-0**	PSV
RC Deportivo	**1-0**	AS Monaco
AEK	**0-1**	PSV
AS Monaco	**8-3**	RC Deportivo
PSV	**2-0**	AE
RC Deportivo	**3-0**	AEK
AS Monaco	**1-1**	PSV
AEK	**0-0**	AS Monaco
PSV	**3-2**	RC Deportivo

GROUP D
Juventus	**2-1**	Galatasaray
Real Sociedad	**1-0**	Olympiakos
Olympiakos	**1-2**	Juventus
Galatasaray	**1-2**	Real Sociedad
Galatasaray	**1-0**	Olympiakos
Juventus	**4-2**	Real Sociedad
Olympiakos	**3-0**	Galatasaray
Real Sociedad	**0-0**	Juventus
Olympiakos	**2-2**	Real Sociedad
Galatasaray	**2-0**	Juventus FC
Juventus	**7-0**	Olympiakos
Real Sociedad	**1-1**	Galatasaray

GROUP E
Rangers	**2-1**	VfB Stuttgart
Manchester Utd	**5-0**	Panathinaikos
Panathinaikos	**1-1**	Rangers
VfB Stuttgart	**2-1**	Manchester Utd
VfB Stuttgart	**2-0**	Panathinaikos
Rangers	**0-1**	Manchester Utd
Panathinaikos	**1-3**	VfB Stuttgart
Manchester Utd	**3-0**	Rangers
VfB Stuttgart	**1-0**	Rangers
Panathinaikos	**0-1**	Manchester Utd
Rangers	**1-3**	Panathinaikos
Manchester Utd	**2-0**	VfB Stuttgart

GROUP F
Real Madrid	**4-2**	Olym. Marseille
Partizan Beograd	**1-1**	FC Porto
FC Porto	**1-3**	Real Madrid
Olym. Marseille	**3-0**	Partizan Beograd
Olym. Marseille	**2-3**	FC Porto
Real Madrid	**1-0**	Partizan Beograd
FC Porto	**1-0**	Olym. Marseille
Partizan Beograd	**0-0**	Real Madrid
Olym. Marseille	**1-2**	Real Madrid
FC Porto	**2-1**	Partizan Beograd
Real Madrid	**1-1**	FC Porto
Partizan Beograd	**1-1**	Olym. Marseille

GROUP G
Sparta Praha	**0-1**	Chelsea
Beşiktaş	**0-2**	Lazio
Lazio	**2-2**	Sparta Praha
Chelsea	**0-2**	Beşiktaş
Chelsea	**2-1**	Lazio
Sparta Praha	**2-1**	Beşiktaş
Lazio	**0-4**	Chelsea
Beşiktaş	**1-0**	Sparta Praha
Chelsea	**0-0**	Sparta Praha
Lazio	**1-1**	Beşiktaş
Sparta Praha	**1-0**	Lazio
Beşiktaş	**0-2**	Chelsea

GROUP H
Milan	**1-0**	Ajax
Club Brugge KV	**1-1**	RC Celta
RC Celta	**0-0**	Milan AC
Ajax	**2-0**	Club Brugge KV
Ajax	**1-0**	RC Celta
Milan AC	**0-1**	Club Brugge KV
RC Celta	**3-2**	Ajax
Club Brugge KV	**0-1**	Milan AC
Ajax	**0-1**	Milan AC
RC Celta	**1-1**	Club Brugge KV
Milan AC	**1-2**	RC Celta
Club Brugge KV	**2-1**	Ajax

GROUP A

CLUB	P	W	D	L	F	A	Pts	
Olympique Lyonnais (France)	6	3	1	2	7	7	10	Knockout Stage
Bayern München (Germany)	6	2	3	1	6	5	9	Knockout Stage
Celtic (Scotland)	6	2	1	3	8	7	7	UEFA Cup
RSC Anderlecht (Belgium)	6	2	1	3	4	6	7	

GROUP B

CLUB	P	W	D	L	F	A	Pts	
Arsenal (England)	6	3	1	2	9	6	10	Knockout Stage
Lokomotiv Moskva (Russia)	6	2	2	2	7	7	8	Knockout Stage
Internazionale (Italy)	6	2	2	2	8	11	8	UEFA Cup
Dynamo Kyiv (Ukraine)	6	2	1	3	8	8	7	

GROUP C

CLUB	P	W	D	L	F	A	Pts	
AS Monaco (France)	6	3	2	1	15	6	11	Knockout Stage
RC Deportivo (Spain)	6	3	1	2	12	12	10	Knockout Stage
PSV (Netherlands)	6	3	1	2	8	7	10	UEFA Cup
AEK (Greece)	6	0	2	4	1	11	2	

GROUP D

CLUB	P	W	D	L	F	A	Pts	
Juventus (Italy)	6	4	1	1	15	6	13	Knockout Stage
Real Sociedad (Spain)	6	2	3	1	8	8	9	Knockout Stage
Galatasaray (Turkey)	6	2	1	3	6	8	7	UEFA Cup
Olympiakos (Greece)	6	1	1	4	6	13	4	

GROUP E

CLUB	P	W	D	L	F	A	Pts	
Manchester United (England)	6	5	0	1	13	2	15	Knockout Stage
VfB Stuttgart (Germany)	6	4	0	2	9	6	12	Knockout Stage
Panathinaikos (Greece)	6	1	1	4	5	13	4	UEFA Cup
Rangers (Scotland)	6	1	1	4	4	10	4	

GROUP F

CLUB	P	W	D	L	F	A	Pts	
Real Madrid (Spain)	6	4	2	0	11	5	14	Knockout Stage
FC Porto (Portugal)	6	3	2	1	9	8	11	Knockout Stage
Olympique Marseille (France)	6	1	1	4	9	11	4	UEFA Cup
Partizan Beograd (S&M)	6	0	3	3	3	8	3	

GROUP G

CLUB	P	W	D	L	F	A	Pts	
Chelsea (England)	6	4	1	1	9	3	13	Knockout Stage
Sparta Praha (Czech Republic)	6	2	2	2	5	5	8	Knockout Stage
Beşiktaş (Turkey)	6	2	1	3	5	7	7	UEFA Cup
Lazio (Italy)	6	1	2	3	6	10	5	

GROUP H

CLUB	P	W	D	L	F	A	Pts	
Milan (Italy)	6	3	1	2	4	3	10	Knockout Stage
RC Celta (Spain)	6	2	3	1	7	6	9	Knockout Stage
Club Brugge KV (Belgium)	6	2	2	2	5	6	8	UEFA Cup
Ajax (Netherlands)	6	2	0	4	6	7	6	

Chelsea's Frank Lampard sends one of the goals of the season rocketing over the head of Lazio keeper Angelo Peruzzi.

Above: Monaco's Dado Prso scored four goals in his side's comprehensive 8-3 defeat of Deportivo.

Below, left: Manchester United's Phil Neville opens the scoring in their comprehensive 3-0 defeat of Rangers at Old Trafford.

Below, middle: Fabrizio Miccoli of Juventus scores one of seven goals his team put passed Olympiakos.

Below: Lokomotiv Moskva proved one of the Group Stage surprises, beating both Inter and Dynamo Kyiv.

Elsewhere Juventus and Real Sociedad made short work of Galatasaray and Olympiakos; the latter had the misfortune of losing 7-0 to Juventus. Manchester United and Stuttgart were rarely troubled by Rangers or Panathinaikos. The latters' clash was notable for the strange cross-border club alliances of the new Europe: Panathinaikos fans in Celtic strips and Rangers fans in Olympiakos colours. Real Madrid made it look easy as did Porto, though Partizan Belgrade offered some stiff resistance, while Chelsea and Sparta had more energy and organization that the often dispirited and disorganised-looking Beşiktaş and Lazio.

1st Knockout Round

The first knockout stage duly delivered some upsets, with three previous champions swept aside. Manchester United had lost 2-1 in Porto, but when Paul Scholes made it 1-0 at Old Trafford, United were through on aggregate. But in the dying minutes of the game, Costinha latched onto the end of a fumbled ball from the United keeper Howard to score and send United out. José Mourinho's celebration on the touchline was nothing less than extravagant. Real Madrid had salvaged a 1-1 draw at Bayern München when Roberto Carlos' shot found its way under a flailing Oliver Kahn. In Madrid, despite having little possession, Zidane's goal was enough to dispense with the Germans. An ailing and injury-ridden Juventus were beaten and comprehensively outplayed, home and away, by Deportivo. Milan looked for a moment like they might suffer a similar fate. Resolute defending by Sparta Praha had forced a 0-0 draw in the Czech Republic and Sparta led at the San Siro until Kaka and Shevchenko combined to put Milan through with a comprehensive display and a 4-1 victory.

French and English clubs prospered in the other ties. Chelsea beat Stuttgart courtesy of a single own goal from Fernando Miera in the first leg. Stuttgart often had the lion's share of possession and space over the two games, but the team desperately lacked attacking options. Arsenal were in inspirational form against Celta Vigo. A 3-2 victory in Spain, the club's first European victory in the country, gave them an immense advantage and they cruised home in the return leg, winning 2-0 and crowned by two assured goals from Thierry Henry. Lyon made their way to their first European cup quarter-final with two 1-0 victories over the misfiring Real Sociedad; Monaco went to Lokomotiv Moskva and found themselves trailing 2-0 until Fernando Morientes grabbed a late and vital away goal, heading home after Lokomotiv had failed to clear a late Monaco free kick. In the return leg Monaco were lucky to see Lokomotiv captain Loskov controversially dismissed after a quarter of the game. Monaco's Prso missed a penalty before getting a second-half winner.

FIRST KNOCKOUT ROUND (2 legs)

February 24 – Olympiastadion, Munich
Bayern 1-1 Real Madrid
München   (Roberto
(Makaay 75)   Carlos 83)
h/t: 0-0 Att: 59,000
Ref: Terje Hauge (Norway)

March 10 – Santiago Bernabeu, Madrid
Real Madrid 1-0 Bayern
(Zidane 32)   München
h/t: 1-0 Att: 78,000
Ref: Meier (Switzerland)
Real Madrid won 2-1 on aggregate

February 24 – Balaidos Stadium, Vigo
RC Celta 2-3 Arsenal
(Luis Edu 27,   (Edu 18, 58,
Ignacio 64)   Pires 80)
h/t: 1-1 Att: 21,000
Ref: Frisk (Sweden)

March 10 – Highbury, London
Arsenal 2-0 RC Celta
(Henry 14, 34)
h/t: 2-0 Att: 35,402
Ref: Collina (Italy)
Arsenal won 5-2 on aggregate

February 24 – Lokomotiv Stadium, Moscow
Lokomotiv 2-1 AS Monaco
Moskva   (Morientes 69)
(Izmailov 32,
Maminov 59)
h/t: 1-0 Att: 26,000
Ref: Gonzalez (Spain)

March 10 – Stade Louis II, Monaco
AS Monaco 1-0 Lokomotiv
(Prso 60)   Moskva
h/t: 0-0 Att: 18,000
Ref: Batista (Portugal)
Monaco won on away goals rule

February 24 – Toyota Arena, Prague
Sparta Praha 0-0 Milan
Att: 20,640
Ref: Poll (England)

March 10 – San Siro, Milan
Milan 4-1 Sparta Praha
(Inzaghi 45,   (Jun 59)
Shevchenko
66, 79,
Gattuso 85)
h/t: 1-0 Att: 50,000
Ref: Merk (Germany)
Milan won 4-1 on aggregate

February 25– Gottlieb-Daimler Stadium,
Stuttgart
VfB Stuttgart 0-1 Chelsea
(Meira o.g. 12)
h/t: 0-1 Att: 42,000
Ref: Vassaras (Greece)

March 9 – Stamford Bridge, London
Chelsea 0-0 VfB Stuttgart
h/t: 0-0 Att: 36,657
Ref: Nielsen (Denmark)
Chelsea won 1-0 on aggregate

February 25 – Riazor, La Coruña
RC Deportivo 1-0 Juventus
(Luque 38)
h/t: 1-0 Att: 28,000
Ref: Veissiere (France)

March 9 – Stadio delle Alpi, Turin
Juventus 0-1 RC Deportivo
(Pandiani 12)
h/t: 0-1 Att: 24,680
Ref: Michel (Slovakia)
Deportivo won 2-0 on aggregate

February 25 – Anoeta, San Sebastian
Real Sociedad 0-1 Olympique
Lyonnais
(Schurrer o.g. 18)
h/t: 0-1 Att: 28,000
Ref: De Santis (Italy)

March 9 – Stade Gerland, Lyon
Olympique 1-0 Real Sociedad
Lyonnais
(Pernambucano 77)
h/t: 0-0 Att: 38,914
Ref: Riley (England)
Olympique Lyonnais won 2-0
on aggregate

February 25 – Estadio do Dragao, Porto
FC Porto 2-1 Manchester
(McCarthy 29, 78)   United
(Fortune 14)
h/t: 1-1 Att: 49,977
Ref: Fandel (Germany)

March 9 – Old Trafford, Manchester
Manchester 1-1 FC Porto
United   (Costinha 90)
(Scholes 32)
h/t: 1-0 Att: 67,029
Ref: Ivanov (Russia)
FC Porto won 3-2 on aggregate

Oliver Kahn looks despairingly *behind him. His terrible blunder has let Roberto Carlos' free kick squirm under him. Real put Bayern out in the 1st knockout round, winning the second leg 1-0.*

Deportivo La Coruña's *Walter Pandiani can't believe it. Having won the first leg of their 1st Knockout Round match in Turin, they were now one up at home to Juventus.*

The quarter-finals

The quarter-finals provided the most open and dramatic games of the year. Porto beat Lyon at home and always looked in command in the second leg. Arsenal appeared to have the upper hand after the first leg encounter with Chelsea at Stamford Bridge. The home side had taken the lead through a piece of opportunism from Gudjohnsen, only to yield the lead to a characteristic Arsenal goal on the break six minutes later. Reyes put Arsenal 1-0 up on the stroke of half time in the return game, but Chelsea responded with the team's best 45 minutes of the year; an early equalizer from Lampard and a winner three minutes from time from Wayne Bridge.

Performances of the season were also in evidence in the other quarter-finals. Imperious Milan had beaten Deportivo 4-1 at the San Siro but in the return leg at the Riazor, Deportivo were a whirlwind. By half time it was 4-4 on and a goal from Fran halfway through the second half shook the stadium as Deportivo made it 5-4. No less a comeback was enacted in Monaco. Real Madrid, 4-1 up at the Bernabeu in the first leg, had let Morientes in for a late goal and 4-2. In the return leg it stood at 1-1 at half time, but second-half goals from Morientes and Giuly made it 3-1 on the night and 5-5 overall. Real were out on away goals.

Wayne Bridge slots the ball past Arsenal keeper Jens Lehmann to earn Chelsea their first victory against the Gunners in 17 attempts.

QUARTER-FINALS (2 legs)

March 23 – San Siro, Milan
Milan 4-1 RC Deportivo
*(Kaka 45, 49,   (Pandiani 11)
Shevchenko 46,
Pirlo 53)*
h/t: 1-1 **Att:** 60,335
Ref: Ivanov (Russia)

April 7 – Riazor, La Coruña
RC Deportivo 4-0 Milan
*(Pandiani 5,
Valeron 35,
Luque 44,
Fran 76)*
h/t: 3-0 **Att:** 29,000
Ref: Meier (Switzerland)
RC Deportivo won 5-4 on aggregate

March 23 – Estadio do Dragao, Porto
FC Porto 2-0 Olympique
*(Deco 44,   Lyonnais
Carvalho 71)*
h/t: 1-0 **Att:** 46,910
Ref: Hauge (Norway)

April 7 – Stade Gerland, Lyon
Olympique 2-2 FC Porto
Lyonnais   *(Ribeiro 6, 47)*
*(Luyindula 14,
Elber 90)*
h/t: 1-1 **Att:** 40,000
Ref: Frisk (Sweden)
Porto won 4-2 on aggregate

March 24 – Santiago Bernabeu, Madrid
Real 4-2 AS Monaco
Madrid   *(Squillaci 42,
(Helguera 51,   Morientes 83)*
Zidane 70,
Figo 77,
Ronaldo 81)*
h/t: 0-1 **Att:** 70,000
Ref: Michel (Slovakia)

April 6, Stade Louis II, Monaco
Monaco 3-1 Real
*(Giuly 45, 66,   Madrid
Morientes 48)   (Raúl 36)*
h/t: 1-1 **Att:** 18,500
Ref: Collina (Italy)
Monaco won on away goals rule

March 24 – Stamford Bridge, London
Chelsea 1-1 Arsenal
(Gudjohnsen 53)   (Pires 59)
h/t: 0-0 **Att:** 40,778
Ref: Gonzalez (Spain)

April 6 – Highbury, London
Arsenal 1-2 Chelsea
*(Reyes 45)   (Lampard 51,
Bridge 87)*
h/t: 1-0 **Att:** 35,486
Ref: Merk (Germany)
Chelsea won 3-2 on aggregate

Above: *Last minute hope – Fernando Morientes grabs a goal against Real Madrid to reduce Monaco's arrears in their quarter-final, first leg. Monaco won the second leg 3-1 and advanced on the away goals rule.*

Left: *Unbelievable but true – Juan Valeron and Victor celebrate Deportivo's second goal in the quarter-final home leg against Milan. Deportivo won 4-0 on the night, and 5-4 on aggregate.*

Far left: *Claudio Ranieri plays it very straight as Chelsea squeeze past Stuttgart in the 1st Knockout Round.*

The semi-finals

The semi-finals were contrasting affairs. Monaco and Chelsea provided open, attacking and risky soccer, sharing eight goals over the two legs. Deportivo and Porto were separated by a single penalty over 180 minutes in a gruelling tactical duel. In Monaco Dada Prso opened the scoring with a looping header. Chelsea immediately responded with an equalizer from Hernan Crespo and for most of the game looked like they might go home with a precious away goal advantage. Chelsea sought to extend that advantage even further when Monaco's Akis Zikos was sent off following the most disgraceful play-acting of the season from Claude Makelele. But justice was done as ten-man Monaco were electrifying. Claudio Ranieri's bizarre substitutions all backfired and Moirentes and Nonda made it 3-1. In the return leg Chelsea again took the game to Monaco going 2-0 up. But a goal from Morientes on the stroke of half time seemed to deflate Chelsea who just could not find a riposte.

Porto and Deportivo ground out a 0-0 draw in Portugal marked by a cagey opening, few chances, some tough tackling and the late exit of Deportivo's Andrade. Maniche's volley hit the crossbar for Porto but the stalemate could not be broken. In the second leg Porto continued to press and harry, closing down Deportivo playmaker Valeron. Derlei put them ahead with a 60th-minute penalty and there was no way back for Deportivo.

SEMI-FINALS (2 legs)	
April 20 – Stade Louis II, Monaco **Monaco 3-1 Chelsea** *(Prso 16,* *(Crespo 22)* *Morientes 77,* *Nonda 83)* **h/t:** 1-1 **Att:** 15,000 **Ref:** Meier (Switzerland)	April 21 – Estadio do Dragao, Porto **FC Porto 0-0 RC Deportivo** **h/t:** 0-0 **Att:** 50,818 **Ref:** Merk (Germany)
May 5 – Stamford Bridge, London **Chelsea 2-2 AS Monaco** *(Gronkjaer 22,* *(Ibarra 45,* *Lampard 44)* *Morientes 60)* **h/t:** 2-1 **Att:** 37,132 **Ref:** Frisk (Sweden) Monaco won 5-3 on aggregate	May 4 – Riazor, La Coruña **RC Deportivo 0-1 FC Porto** *(Derlei 60 pen)* **h/t:** 0-0 **Att:** 34,600 **Ref:** Collina (Italy) Porto won 1-0 on aggregate

The Final

It was a measure of the two squads and their modes of play that the Champions League Final was billed as much as a duel between managers José Mourinho and Didier Deschamps as it was between their players. Porto's played their allotted if limited roles to perfection. The back four's positioning and offside traps were faultless. Costinha and Maniche in central midfield broke up, delayed and impeded every thrust from Monaco. And when their chances came, and there were precious few, the almost abandoned striker Carlos Alberto and playmaker Deco did not fail to take them. Monaco's counterattacking flair and invention was never given an opening and the loss of Ludovic Giuly blunted what attack that remained. The vanquished giants of European soccer were pouring over the squads on show in Gelsenkirchen and making their bids for players and coaches even before the trophy was presented.

Deco makes it look easy as he slots home Porto's second goal against Monaco.

Last year the UEFA Cup, this year the Champions League, Porto are entitled to celebrate.

Morientes exuberant and unbound. Down to ten men against Chelsea in the semi-final Moirentes somehow found a late winner.

The Starting Line-Up

May 26 – Aufschlake Arena, Gelsinkirchen
Attendance 52,000

2 Jorge Costa
22 Paulo Ferreira
3 Evra
10 Deco
27 Rodriguez
10 Morientes
4 Ricardo Carvalho
4 Ibarra
99 Vítor Baía
11 Derlei
19 Carlos Alberto
25 Rothen
14 Cissé
30 Roma
6 Costinha
7 Bernardi
18 Maniche
23 Mendes
32 Givet
15 Zikos
8 Giuly
8 Nuno Valente

FC PORTO	Referee	AS MONACO
Formation: 4-3-1-2	●	Formation: 4-3-3
Manager	Kim Milton Nielsen (Denmark)	**Manager**
José Mourinho		Didier Deschamps
Substitutes		**Substitutes**

FC PORTO Substitutes		AS MONACO Substitutes	
Nuno	**13**	Sylva	**29**
Pedro Emanuel	**3**	Plasil	**6**
Ricardo Costa	**5**	Prso	**9**
Jankauskas	**9**	Nonda	**18**
Alenitchev	**15**	Squillaci	**19**
Bosingwa	**17**	Adebayor	**24**
McCarthy	**77**	El Fakiri	**35**

Match Statistics

FC Porto		AS Monaco
44%	Possession	56%
3	Shots on goal	0
3	Yellow Card	0
14	Fouls conceded	10
2	Corners won	6
8	Offside	12

Highlights of the Game

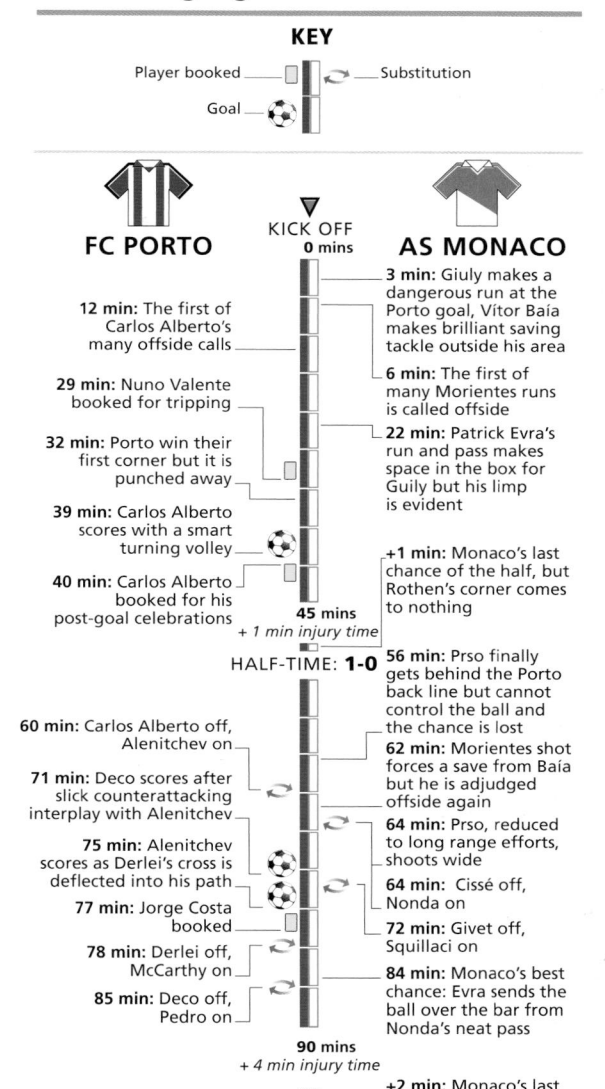

KEY

Player booked ▢ ↩ Substitution
Goal ⚽

FC PORTO — KICK OFF 0 mins — **AS MONACO**

3 min: Giuly makes a dangerous run at the Porto goal, Vítor Baía makes brilliant saving tackle outside his area

12 min: The first of Carlos Alberto's many offside calls

6 min: The first of many Morientes runs is called offside

29 min: Nuno Valente booked for tripping

22 min: Patrick Evra's run and pass makes space in the box for Guily but his limp is evident

32 min: Porto win their first corner but it is punched away

39 min: Carlos Alberto scores with a smart turning volley

+1 min: Monaco's last chance of the half, but Rothen's corner comes to nothing

40 min: Carlos Alberto booked for his post-goal celebrations

45 mins
+ 1 min injury time

HALF-TIME: 1-0

56 min: Prso finally gets behind the Porto back line but cannot control the ball and the chance is lost

60 min: Carlos Alberto off, Alenitchev on

62 min: Morientes shot forces a save from Baía but he is adjudged offside again

71 min: Deco scores after slick counterattacking interplay with Alenitchev

64 min: Prso, reduced to long range efforts, shoots wide

75 min: Alenitchev scores as Derlei's cross is deflected into his path

64 min: Cissé off, Nonda on

77 min: Jorge Costa booked

72 min: Givet off, Squillaci on

78 min: Derlei off, McCarthy on

84 min: Monaco's best chance: Evra sends the ball over the bar from Nonda's neat pass

85 min: Deco off, Pedro on

90 mins
+ 4 min injury time

+2 min: Monaco's last chance as Squillaci heads over from a late corner

FULL-TIME: 3-0

Porto's second goal

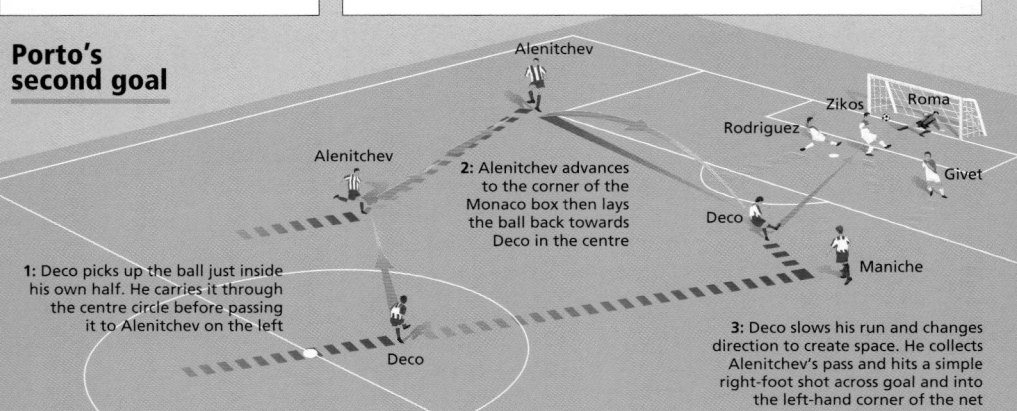

Alenitchev
Alenitchev
Zikos
Roma
Rodriguez
Deco
Givet
Deco
Maniche

1: Deco picks up the ball just inside his own half. He carries it through the centre circle before passing it to Alenitchev on the left

2: Alenitchev advances to the corner of the Monaco box then lays the ball back towards Deco in the centre

3: Deco slows his run and changes direction to create space. He collects Alenitchev's pass and hits a simple right-foot shot across goal and into the left-hand corner of the net

The European Champions League

TOURNAMENT OVERVIEW

ORGANIZED EUROPEAN CLUB COMPETITIONS began in 1927 with the Mittel Europa Cup, contested by the leading teams in Austria, Hungary, Italy and Czechoslovakia. Although it was revived after the Second World War, Cold War divisions made the logistics difficult. Moreover, the power base of club soccer had shifted west and the Latin Cup was established in 1949 among the champions of France, Italy, Spain and Portugal. Based on this model of two aggregate legs and a single-match Final, Gabriel Hunot, editor of French sports paper *L'Equipe*, proposed the creation of a European Cup, contested by its national champions in 1955. Formally sanctioned by FIFA, the cup was first contested in 1956. But Chelsea, the English champions at the time, was not allowed to compete by the FA.

Real win five in a row

Thus the European Cup began as a small affair with no sponsors, and barely any television coverage. The first Final was won by Real Madrid beating Stade de Reims 4-3 in Paris. The following year, against the wishes of the English FA, Manchester United entered the tournament. On the flight home from a successful quarter-final second-leg match against Red Star Belgrade the core of the squad was killed in an air crash in Munich. Fatally weakened, United was put out in the semi-finals by Real Madrid who went on to win the Final against Fiorentina. Madrid won a further three consecutive titles, culminating in their extraordinary 7-3 demolition of Eintracht Frankfurt in the 1960 Final at Hampden Park in Glasgow, thought by many who saw it to have been the finest match ever seen.

With Real on the slide, the next five cups fell two apiece to Benfica and Internazionale, with a win for Milan in between, before a sixth Real victory in 1966. A shift of soccer-playing power northward soon followed with British victories in 1967 and 1968 (Celtic and Manchester United). Four Dutch victories, three for Ajax, began the 1970s followed by three victories for Bayern München. Liverpool's triumph in 1977 began a series of six consecutive English victories. Liverpool's last Final, in 1985, was the occasion of the Heysel Stadium disaster after which English clubs were banned from European competition for six years. In their absence, the cup went east for the first time to Steaua Bucureşti of Romania.

Birth of the Champions League

Under considerable pressure from big clubs and TV companies the tournament was steadily expanded and reformatted during the late 1990s as the European Champions League, with winning teams playing at least 16 matches to get to the Final and more clubs from the bigger leagues getting into the tournament. The huge sums of TV and sponsorship money the Champions League generates has made it the biggest soccer event outside the World Cup.

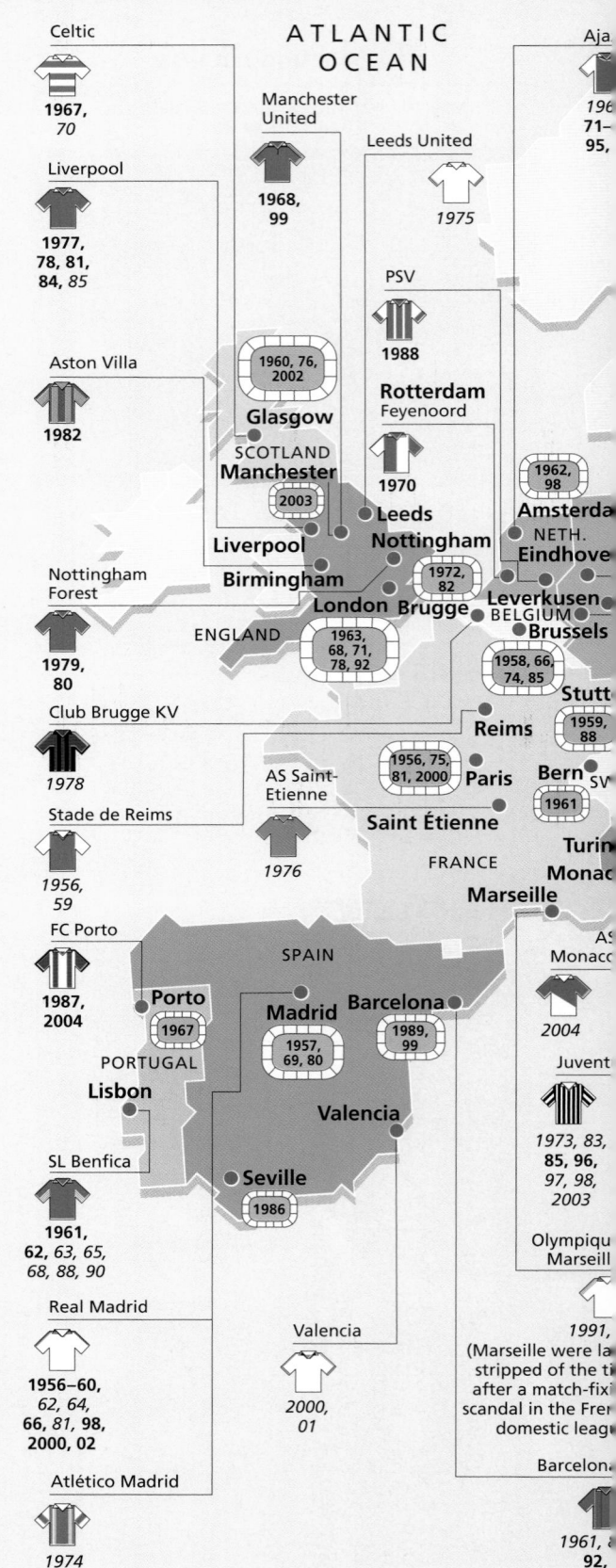

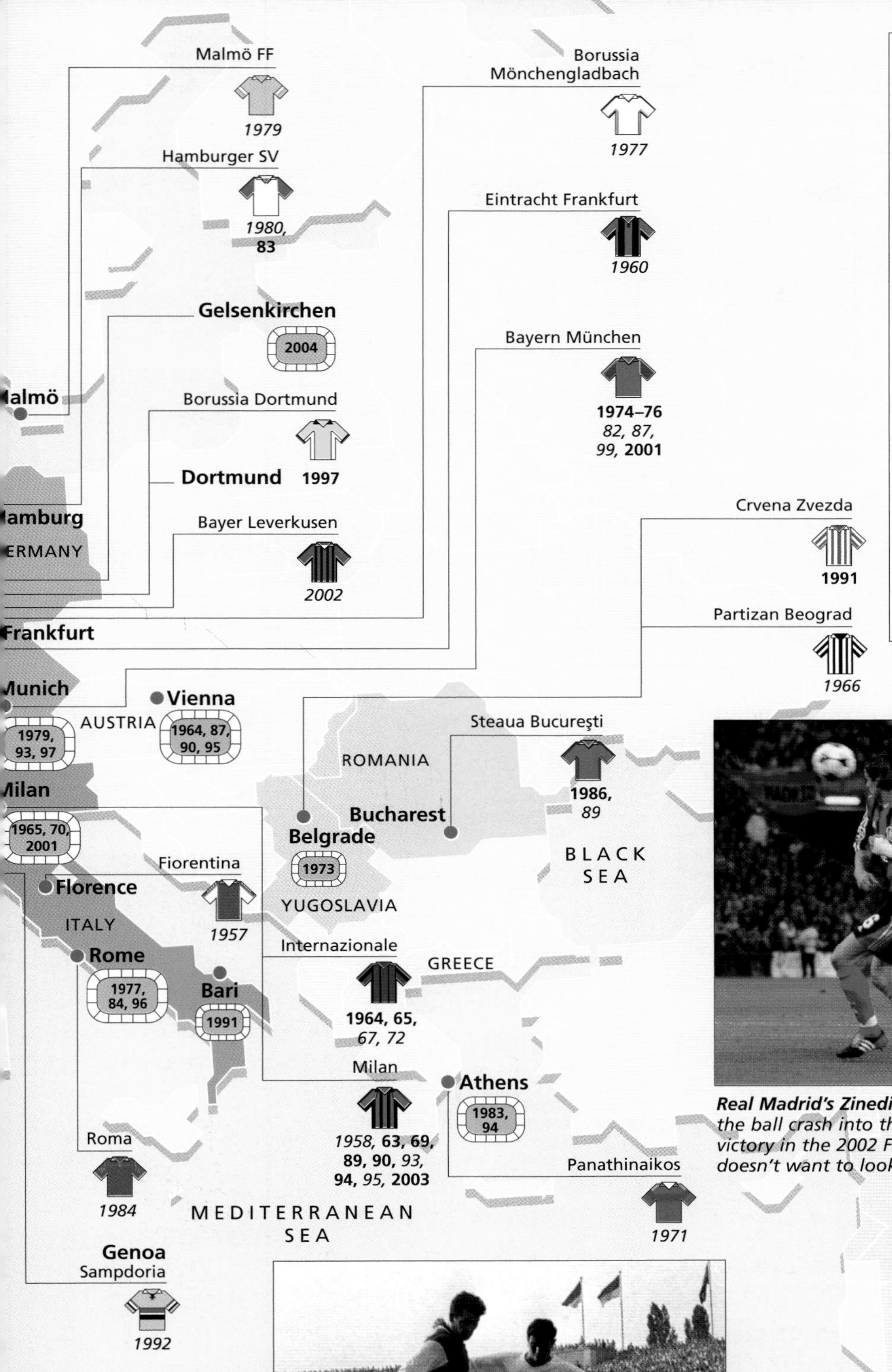

Malmö FF
1979

Hamburger SV
1980,
83

Gelsenkirchen
2004

Borussia Dortmund
1997

Dortmund 1997

Bayer Leverkusen
2002

Borussia
Mönchengladbach
1977

Eintracht Frankfurt
1960

Bayern München
1974–76
82, 87,
99, **2001**

Crvena Zvezda
1991

Partizan Beograd
1966

lalmö

1amburg
ERMANY

Frankfurt

Munich
1979,
93, 97

Vienna
1964, 87,
90, 95
AUSTRIA

Milan
1965, 70,
2001

Fiorentina
1957

Florence
ITALY

Rome
1977,
84, 96

Bari
1991

Internazionale
1964, 65,
67, 72
Milan

Roma
1984

AC Milan
1958, 63, 69,
89, 90, 93,
94, 95, **2003**

Belgrade
1973
YUGOSLAVIA

Steaua Bucureşti
1986,
89

ROMANIA

Bucharest

B L A C K
S E A

GREECE

Athens
1983,
94

Panathinaikos
1971

Genoa
Sampdoria
1992

M E D I T E R R A N E A N
S E A

The European Champions League

Number of wins in the European Champions League (by country)

■	8+ times
■	5–7 times
■	2–4 times
■	1 time
□	0 times

Team details

PORTUGAL	Country
● **Lisbon**	City of origin
Benfica	Team name
👕	Team colours
1961, 62 *63, 65, 68, 88, 90*	Winners in bold Runners-up in italic
● **Belgrade**	
1973	Host city of Final and year

Real Madrid's Zinedine Zidane *swivels, volleys and watches the ball crash into the roof of the net to seal the team's victory in the 2002 Final. Bayer Leverkusen's Michael Ballack doesn't want to look.*

Just Fontaine *of Stade de Reims (dark shirt) challenges Real Madrid's Domingues during the 1959 Final in Stuttgart – Real's fourth victory in the first four years of the competition.*

The European Champions League 1956–2004

COUNTRY	WINNERS	RUNNERS-UP
Italy	10	13
Spain	10	9
England	9	2
Germany	6	7
Netherlands	6	2
Portugal	4	5
France	1	5
Romania	1	1
Scotland	1	1
Yugoslavia	1	1
Belgium	0	1
Greece	0	1
Sweden	0	1

The European Champions League

THE EUROPEAN CHAMPIONS LEAGUE

THE EUROPEAN CUP was established in 1955 after a meeting called by Gabriel Hunot, then editor of the French sports newspaper *L'Equipe*. Although the initial tournament had an eclectic mix of national champions and other big clubs, it was soon codified and run by UEFA with entry restricted to national champions and the previous year's winner. Two-leg matches in each round were played with a single final match at a neutral venue. In 1992, mini-leagues were played to produce the finalists. In 1995, there was a shift back to two-leg quarter- and semi-finals, but the really big change in the competition's format came in 1996. Under pressure from the big clubs for more games and more money, UEFA created qualifying rounds for smaller countries and a first round of four mini-leagues of four to produce eight quarter-finalists.

In 2000 the tournament was expanded even further, with two places guaranteed to the strongest leagues in Europe and extra routes in for clubs via a longer qualifying round. The first round consisted of eight groups of four clubs with 16 progressing into the second round. Teams defeated in the preliminary stages were entered into the first round of the UEFA Cup, while third-placed teams from the first group stage qualified for the third round. The final 16 played in four groups of four to produce eight quarter-finalists. Two-legged matches determined the finalists, who still play a single match at a neutral venue. As a consequence teams may have needed to play more than 20 matches to win the tournament. However, with UEFA worried by fatigue amongst TV audiences and fixture congestion, the second group stage ended in 2003. In 2004 it was replaced with two-leg knockout second round matches.

1955–56 FINAL
June 13 – Parc des Princes, Paris
Real Madrid 4-3 Stade de Reims
(Spain) (France)
(di Stefano 15, (Leblond 6,
Rial 30, 79, Templin 10,
Marquitos 71) Hidalgo 62)
h/t: 2-2 **Att:** 38,239
Ref: Ellis (England)

1956–57 FINAL
May 30 – Santiago Bernabeu, Madrid
Real Madrid 2-0 Fiorentina
(Spain) (Italy)
(di Stefano
70 pen,
Gento 76)
h/t: 0-0 **Att:** 120,000
Ref: Horn (Netherlands)

1957–58 FINAL
May 29 – Heysel, Brussels
Real Madrid 3-2 Milan
(Spain) (Italy)
(di Stefano 74, (Schiaffino 69,
Rial 79, Grillo 78)
Gento 107)
(after extra time)
h/t: 0-0 **90 mins:** 2-2
Att: 70,000 **Ref:** Alsteen (Belgium)

1958–59 FINAL
June 3 – Neckar, Stuttgart
Real Madrid 2-0 Stade de Reims
(Spain) (France)
(Mateos 2,
di Stefano 47)
h/t: 1-0 **Att:** 72,000
Ref: Dusch (France)

1959–60 FINAL
May 18 – Hampden Park, Glasgow
Real Madrid 7-3 Eintracht
(Spain) **Frankfurt**
(di Stefano (West Germany)
26, 29, 74, (Kress 18,
Puskas 44, 56, Stein 72, 76)
60 pen, 71)
h/t: 3-1 **Att:** 127,621
Ref: Mowat (Scotland)

1960–61 FINAL
May 31 – Wankdorf, Bern
SL Benfica 3-2 Barcelona
(Portugal) (Spain)
(Aguas 30, (Kocsis 20,
Ramallets o.g. 31, Czibor 75)
Coluna 54)
h/t: 2-1 **Att:** 33,000
Ref: Dienst (Switzerland)

1961–62 FINAL
May 2 – Olympic, Amsterdam
SL Benfica 5-3 Real Madrid
(Portugal) (Spain)
(Aguas 25, (Puskas
Cavem 34, 17, 23, 38)
Coluna 61,
Eusebio
68 pen, 78)
h/t: 2-3 **Att:** 68,000
Ref: Horn (Netherlands)

1962–63 FINAL
May 22 – Wembley, London
Milan 2-1 SL Benfica
(Italy) (Portugal)
(Altafini 58, 66) (Eusebio 18)
h/t: 0-1 **Att:** 45,000
Ref: Holland (England)

1963–64 FINAL
May 27 – Prater, Vienna
Internazionale 3-1 Real Madrid
(Italy) (Spain)
(Mazzola 43, 76, (Felo 69)
Milani 62)
h/t: 1-0 **Att:** 72,000
Ref: Stoll (Austria)

1964–65 FINAL
May 27 – San Siro, Milan
Internazionale 1-0 SL Benfica
(Italy) (Portugal)
(Jair 42)
h/t: 1-0 **Att:** 80,000
Ref: Dienst (Switzerland)

1965–66 FINAL
May 11 – Heysel, Brussels
Real Madrid 2-1 Partizan
(Spain) **Beograd**
(Amancio 70, (Yugoslavia)
Serena 76) (Vasovic 55)
h/t: 0-0 **Att:** 55,000
Ref: Kreitlein (West Germany)

1966–67 FINAL
May 25 – Estadio da Luz, Lisbon
Celtic 2-1 Internazionale
(Scotland) (Italy)
(Gemmell 62, (Mazzola 6 pen)
Chalmers 83)
h/t: 0-1 **Att:** 55,000
Ref: Tschenscher (West Germany)

1967–68 FINAL
May 29 – Wembley, London
Manchester 4-1 SL Benfica
United (Portugal)
(England) *(Jaime Graca 78)*
(Charlton 54, 98,
Best 92, Kidd 95)
(after extra time)
h/t: 0-0 **90 mins:** 1-1
Att: 100,000 **Ref:** Lo Bello (Italy)

1968–69 FINAL
May 28 – Santiago Bernabeu, Madrid
Milan 4-1 Ajax
(Italy) (Netherlands)
(Prati 7, 39, 74, (Vasovic 61 pen)
Sormani 66)
h/t: 2-0 **Att:** 50,000
Ref: Ortiz (Spain)

1969–70 FINAL
May 6 – San Siro, Milan
Feyenoord 2-1 Celtic
(Netherlands) (Scotland)
(Israel 29, (Gemmell 31)
Kindvall 116)
(after extra time)
h/t: 1-1 **90 mins:** 1-1
Att: 53,187 **Ref:** Lo Bello (Italy)

1970–71 FINAL
June 2 – Wembley, London
Ajax 2-0 Panathinaikos
(Netherlands) (Greece)
(Van Dijk 5,
Haan 87)
h/t: 1-0 **Att:** 90,000
Ref: Taylor (England)

1971–72 FINAL
May 31 – De Kuip, Rotterdam
Ajax 2-0 Internazionale
(Netherlands) (Italy)
(Cruyff 48, 77)
h/t: 0-0 **Att:** 61,000
Ref: Helies (France)

1972–73 FINAL
May 30 – Crvena Zvezda, Belgrade
Ajax 1-0 Juventus
(Netherlands) (Italy)
(Rep 4)
h/t: 1-0 **Att:** 93,000
Ref: Gugulovic (Yugoslavia)

1973–74 FINAL
May 15 – Heysel, Brussels
Bayern 1-1 Atlético
München Madrid
(West Germany) (Spain)
(Schwarzenbeck (Luis Aragones
120) 113)
(after extra time)
h/t: 0-0 **90 mins:** 0-0
Att: 65,000 **Ref:** Loraux (Belgium)

REPLAY
May 17 – Heysel, Brussels
Bayern 4-0 Atlético
München Madrid
(Hoeness 28, 81,
Müller 57, 70)
h/t: 1-0 **Att:** 23,000
Ref: Delcourt (Belgium)

1974–75 FINAL
May 28 – Parc des Princes, Paris
Bayern 2-0 Leeds
München United
(West Germany) (England)
(Roth 71,
Müller 81)
h/t: 0-0 **Att:** 48,000
Ref: Kitabdjian (France)

1975–76 FINAL
May 12 – Hampden Park, Glasgow
Bayern 1-0 AS Saint-
München Etienne
(West Germany) (France)
(Roth 57)
h/t: 0-0 **Att:** 54,684
Ref: Palotai (Hungary)

1976–77 FINAL
May 25 – Olimpico, Rome
Liverpool 3-1 Borussia
(England)   Mönchen-
(McDermott 27,   gladbach
Smith 65,   (West Germany)
Neal 82 pen)   *(Simonsen 51)*
h/t: 1-0 **Att:** 57,000
Ref: Wurtz (France)

1977–78 FINAL
May 10 – Wembley, London
Liverpool 1-0 Club Brugge KV
(England)   (Belgium)
(Dalglish 64)
h/t: 0-0 **Att:** 92,000
Ref: Corver (Netherlands)

1978–79 FINAL
May 30 – Olympiastadion, Munich
Nottingham 1-0 Malmö FF
Forest   (Sweden)
(England)
(Francis 44)
h/t: 1-0 **Att:** 57,500
Ref: Linemayr (Austria)

1979–80 FINAL
May 28 – Santiago Bernabeu, Madrid
Nottingham 1-0 Hamburger SV
Forest   (West Germany)
(England)
(Robertson 19)
h/t: 1-0 **Att:** 51,000
Ref: Garrido (Portugal)

1980–81 FINAL
May 27 – Parc des Princes, Paris
Liverpool 1-0 Real Madrid
(England)   (Spain)
(A. Kennedy 82)
h/t: 0-0 **Att:** 48,360
Ref: Palotai (Hungary)

1981–82 FINAL
May 26 – De Kuip, Rotterdam
Aston Villa 1-0 Bayern
(England)   München
(Withe 67)   (West Germany)
h/t: 0-0 **Att:** 45,000
Ref: Konrath (France)

1982–83 FINAL
May 25 – Olympic, Athens
Hamburger SV 1-0 Juventus
(West Germany)   (Italy)
(Magath 9)
h/t: 1-0 **Att:** 73,500
Ref: Rainea (Romania)

1983–84 FINAL
May 30 – Olimpico, Rome
Liverpool 1-1 Roma
(England)   (Italy)
(Neal 15)   *(Pruzzo 38)*
(after extra time)
h/t: 1-1 **90 mins:** 1-1
Att: 69,693 **Ref:** Fredriksson (Sweden)
Liverpool won 4-2 on pens

1984–85 FINAL
May 29 – Heysel, Brussels
Juventus 1-0 Liverpool
(Italy)   (England)
(Platini 57 pen)
h/t: 0-0 **Att:** 60,000
Ref: Daina (Switzerland)

1985–86 FINAL
May 7 – Sanchez Pizjuan, Seville
Steaua 0-0 Barcelona
Bucureşti   (Spain)
(Romania)
(after extra time)
h/t: 0-0 **90 mins:** 0-0
Att: 75,000 **Ref:** Vautrot (France)
Steaua Bucureşti won 2-0 on pens

1986–87 FINAL
May 27 – Prater, Vienna
FC Porto 2-1 Bayern
(Portugal)   **München**
(Madjer 77,   (West Germany)
Juary 81)   *(Kogl 25)*
h/t: 0-1 **Att:** 62,000
Ref: Ponnet (Belgium)

1987–88 FINAL
May 25 – Neckar, Stuttgart
PSV 0-0 SL Benfica
(Netherlands)   (Portugal)
(after extra time)
h/t: 0-0 **90 mins:** 0-0
Att: 68,000 **Ref:** Agnolin (Italy)
PSV won 6-5 on pens

1988–89 FINAL
May 24 – Nou Camp, Barcelona
Milan 4-0 Steaua
(Italy)   **Bucureşti**
(Gullit 18, 38,   (Romania)
van Basten 27, 46)
h/t: 3-0 **Att:** 100,000
Ref: Tritschler (West Germany)

1989–90 FINAL
May 23 – Prater, Vienna
Milan 1-0 SL Benfica
(Italy)   (Portugal)
(Rijkaard 67)
h/t: 0-0 **Att:** 58,000
Ref: Kohl (Austria)

1990–91 FINAL
May 29 – San Nicola, Bari
Crvena Zvezda 0-0 Olympique
(Yugoslavia)   **Marseille**
(France)
(after extra time)
h/t: 0-0 **90 mins:** 0-0
Att: 58,000 **Ref:** Lanese (Italy)
Crvena Zvezda won 5-3 on pens

1991–92 FINAL
May 20 – Wembley, London
Barcelona 1-0 Sampdoria
(Spain)   (Italy)
(Koemann 111)
(after extra time)
h/t: 0-0 **90 mins:** 0-0 **Att:** 70,827
Ref: Schmidhuber (Germany)

1992–93 FINAL
May 26 – Olympiastadion, Munich
Olympique 1-0 Milan
Marseille   (Italy)
(France)
(Boli 43)
h/t: 1-0 **Att:** 64,400
Ref: Rothlisberger (Switzerland)
Marseille later stripped of title

1993–94 FINAL
May 18 – Olympic, Athens
Milan 4-0 Barcelona
(Italy)   (Spain)
(Massaro 22, 45,
Savicevic 47,
Desailly 59)
h/t: 2-0 **Att:** 70,000
Ref: Don (England)

1994–95 FINAL
May 24 – Ernst-Happel Stadion, Vienna
Ajax 1-0 Milan
(Netherlands)   (Italy)
(Kluivert 83)
h/t: 0-0 **Att:** 49,500
Ref: Craciunescu (Romania)

1995–96 FINAL
May 22 – Olimpico, Rome
Juventus 1-1 Ajax
(Italy)   (Netherlands)
(Ravanelli 12)   *(Litmanen 40)*
(after extra time)
h/t: 1-1 **90 mins:** 1-1
Att: 70,000 **Ref:** Diaz Vega (Spain)
Juventus won 4-2 on pens

1996–97 FINAL
May 28 – Olympiastadion, Munich
Borussia 3-1 Juventus
Dortmund   (Italy)
(Germany)   *(Del Piero 64)*
(Riedle 29, 34,
Ricken 71)
h/t: 2-0 **Att:** 65,000
Ref: Puhl (Hungary)

1997–98 FINAL
May 20 – Arena, Amsterdam
Real Madrid 1-0 Juventus
(Spain)   (Italy)
(Mijatovic 66)
h/t: 0-0 **Att:** 50,000
Ref: Krug (Germany)

1998–99 FINAL
May 26 – Nou Camp, Barcelona
Manchester 2-1 Bayern
United   **München**
(England)   (Germany)
(Sheringham 89,   *(Basler 6)*
Solskjaer 90)
h/t: 0-1 **Att:** 90,000
Ref: Collina (Italy)

1999–2000 FINAL
May 24 – Stade St Denis, Paris
Real Madrid 3-0 Valencia
(Spain)   (Spain)
(Morientes 39,
McManaman 67,
Raúl 75)
h/t: 1-0 **Att:** 78,000
Ref: Braschi (Italy)

2000–01 FINAL
May 23 – San Siro, Milan
Bayern 1-1 Valencia
München   (Spain)
(Germany)   *(Mendieta 3 pen)*
(Effenberg
51 pen)
(after sudden death extra time)
h/t: 0-1 **90 mins:** 1-1 **Att:** 74,000
Ref: Jol (Netherlands)
Bayern München won 5-4 on pens

2001–02 FINAL
May 15 – Hampden Park, Glasgow
Real Madrid 2-1 Bayer
(Spain)   **Leverkusen**
(Raúl 8,   (Germany)
Zidane 45)   *(Lucio 14)*
h/t: 2-1 **Att:** 52,000
Ref: Meier (Switzerland)

2002–03 FINAL
May 28 – Old Trafford, Manchester
Milan 0-0 Juventus
(Italy)   (Italy)
(after extra time)
h/t: 0-0 **90 mins:** 0-0
Att: 68,000 **Ref:** Markus (Germany)
Milan won 3-2 on pens

2003–04 FINAL
May 26 – Arena Aufschalke, Gelsenkirchen
FC Porto 3-0 AS Monaco
(Portugal)   (France)
(Carlos Alberto 39,
Deco 71,
Alenitchev 75)
h/t: 1-0 **Att:** 52,000
Ref: Nielsen (Denmark)

Experts seldom agree on much,
but many pundits concur that
the 1959–60 European Cup
Final between Real Madrid and
Eintracht Frankfurt at Hampden
Park was the finest match ever
seen. Here, Ferenc Puskas makes
it 5-1 from the penalty spot on the
hour. Real went on to win 7-3.

The UEFA Cup

TOURNAMENT REVIEW 2003–04

THE UEFA CUP MAY LACK SOME OF the prestige of the Champions League and certainly its income, but, for the two teams that contested the 2004 Final, there was no doubting its importance. After a disappointing exit from the Champions League Group Stage and the collapse of their domestic title challenge in the spring, the UEFA Cup became Marseille's only chance of a trophy and their only route back into Europe next season. A Didier Drogba penalty saw them squeeze past Ukraine's Dnipro in the Third Round after which they consistently raised their game to dispense with Liverpool, Inter and Newcastle. Eleven years since Marseille won and lost the European Cup after match fixing allegations were proved true, the opportunity to open a new account in Europe had arrived.

Valencia were also looking to change the course of its European destiny as this was the club's third European final in five years and it had lost two Champions League Finals in 2000 and 2001. In keeping with the team's profile as hard-working honest artisans, Valencia had battled all the way from the First Round, eliminating Stockholm's AIK, Maccabi Haifa, the two Turkish sides Beşiktaş and Gençlerbirligi, Bordeaux and Villareal on the way. The semi-final against Villareal, another east coast Spanish city, was a particularly tight affair settled by a single penalty.

Howling wind

The Final, played in the howling spring winds of Gothenburg's Nea Ullevi stadium, was settled by a single moment of madness. Deep into injury time at the end of the first half of a match that Marseille had controlled, Valencia's Mista ran dangerously into their penalty area. Fabien Barthez, Marseille's goalkeeper, rushed off his

line and, diving for a ball just pulled round him, clattered into the Spaniard and brought him and Marseille's chances down. Referee Collina harshly, but correctly, sent Barthez off and inevitably, the first touch for the reserve goalkeeper was to pick Vicente's penalty out of his net. In the second half Valencia were just too smart and too polished for ten-man Marseille. They held onto possession and made Marseille work. Early in the second half, a fabulous strike from Mista, on his weaker foot, made it 2-0 and comfortable for the Spaniards. With a Spanish championship this season as well, Valencia can look forward to a new European venture next year. However, 2004–05 will be a strictly domestic affair for Marseille.

Sonny Anderson (left) of Villareal scores against AS Roma during their Fourth Round, second leg match in Rome. Anderson's goal saw the Spanish team through to the next round.

THIRD ROUND (2 legs)

Brøndby IF **0-1** Barcelona
(Denmark)   (Spain)
Barcelona **2-1** Brøndby IF
Barcelona won 3-1 on aggregate

Galatasaray **2-2** Villareal
(Turkey)   (Spain)
Villareal **3-0** Galatasaray
Villareal won 5-2 on aggregate

Parma **0-1** Gençlerbirligi
(Italy)   (Turkey)
Gençlerbirligi **3-0** Parma
Gençlerbirligi won 4-0 on aggregate

Club Brugge KV **1-0** Debreceni
(Belgium)   (Hungary)
Debreceni **0-0** Club Brugge KV
Club Brugge won 1-0 on aggregate

SL Benfica **1-0** Rosenborg BK
(Portugal)   (Norway)
Rosenborg BK **2-1** Benfica
SL Benfica won on away goals rule

FC Sochaux- **2-2** Internazionale
Montbéliard   (Italy)
(France)
Internazionale **0-0** FC Sochaux-
Montbéliard
Internazionale won on away goals rule

Olympique **1-0** Dnipro
Marseille   Dnipropetrovsk
(France)   (Ukraine)
Dnipro **0-0** Olympique
Dnipropetrovsk   Marseille
Olympique Marseille won 1-0
on aggregate

Liverpool **2-0** Levski Sofia
(England)   (Bulgaria)
Levski Sofia **2-4** Liverpool
Liverpool won 6-2 on aggregate

Celtic **3-0** FK Teplice
(Scotland)   (Czech Republic)
FK Teplice **1-0** Celtic
Celtic won 3-1 on aggregate

Spartak **0-3** RCD Mallorca
Moskva   (Spain)
(Russia)
RCD Mallorca **0-1** Spartak
Moskva
RCD Mallorca won 3-1 on aggregate

Perugia **0-0** PSV
(Italy)   (Netherlands)
PSV **3-1** Perugia
PSV won 3-1 on aggregate

Gaziantepspor **1-0** Roma
(Turkey)   (Italy)
Roma **2-0** Gaziantepspor
Roma won 2-1 on aggregate

Groclin **0-1** Girondins
Grodzisk   de Bordeaux
(Poland)   (France)
Girondins **4-1** Groclin
de Bordeaux   Grodzisk
Girondins de Bordeaux won 5-1
on aggregate

AJ Auxerre **0-0** Panathinaikos
(France)   (Greece)
Panathinaikos **0-1** AJ Auxerre
AJ Auxerre won 1-0 on aggregate

Valencia **3-2** Beşiktaş
(Spain)   (Turkey)
Beşiktaş **0-2** Valencia
Valencia won 5-2 on aggregate

Vålerenga IF **1-1** Newcastle
(Norway)   United
(England)
Newcastle **3-1** Vålerenga IF
United
Newcastle United won 4-2 on aggregate

FOURTH ROUND (2 legs)

Celtic **1-0** Barcelona
Barcelona **0-0** Celtic
Celtic won 1-0 on aggregate

AJ Auxerre **1-1** PSV
PSV **3-0** AJ Auxerre
PSV won 4-1 on aggregate

Gençlerbirligi **1-0** Valencia
Valencia **2-0** Gençlerbirligi
Valencia won 2-1 on aggregate

SL Benfica **0-0** Internazionale
Internazionale **4-3** SL Benfica
Internazionale won 4-3
on aggregate

Girondins **3-1** Club Brugge KV
de Bordeaux
Club Brugge KV **0-1** Girondins
de Bordeaux
Girondins de Bordeaux won 4-1
on aggregate

Liverpool **1-1** Olympique
Marseille
Olympique **2-1** Liverpool
Marseille
Olympique Marseille won 3-2
on aggregate

Newcastle **4-1** RCD Mallorca
United
RCD Mallorca **0-3** Newcastle
United
Newcastle United won 7-1 on aggregate

Villareal **2-0** Roma
Roma **2-1** Villareal
Villareal won 3-2 on aggregate

THE UEFA CUP

QUARTER-FINALS (2 legs)

Girondins **1-2** Valencia
de Bordeaux
Valencia **2-1** Girondins
de Bordeaux
Valencia won 4-2 on aggregate

Olympique **1-0** Internazionale
Marseille
Internazionale **0-1** Olympique
Marseille
Olympique Marseille won 2-0 on aggregate

Celtic **1-1** Villareal
Villareal **2-0** Celtic
Villareal won 3-1 on aggregate

PSV **1-1** Newcastle
United
Newcastle **2-1** PSV
United
Newcastle United won 3-2 on aggregate

SEMI-FINALS (2 legs)

April 22 – St James' Park, Newcastle
Newcastle **0-0** Olympique
United   Marseille

May 6 – Vélodrome, Marseille
Olympique **2-0** Newcastle
Marseille   United
(Drogba 18, 82)
Olympique Marseille won 2-0 on aggregate

April 22 – El Madrigal, Villareal
Villareal **0-0** Valencia

May 6 – Mestalla, Valencia
Valencia **1-0** Villareal
(Mista 16 pen)
Valencia won 1-0 on aggregate

2004 FINAL

May 19 – Nea Ullevi Stadium, Gothenburg
Valencia **2-0** Olympique
(Vicente 45 pen,   Marseille
Mista 58)
h/t: 1-0 **Att:** 43,000
Ref: Collina (Italy)
Valencia won 2-0 on aggregate

PSV Eindhoven's Mateja Kezman *celebrates scoring the opening goal against Auxerre in their Fourth Round clash.*

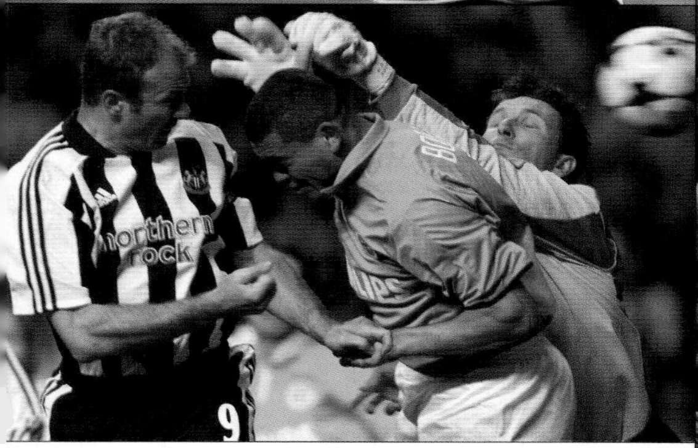

Above: *Newcastle United's Alan Shearer opens the scoring in the second leg of their quarter-final against PSV.*

Right, top: *Inter Milan's Gamarra (top) challenges Pereira of Benfica during their Fourth Round second leg match which the Italian team won 4-3.*

Right: *Valencia supporters celebrate their semi-final victory over Villareal.*

Below: *Valencia's veteran defender Amedeo Carboni lifts the UEFA Cup.*

Olympique Marseille's *Didier Drogba (centre) scores his second goal of the semi-final second leg against Newcastle.*

The UEFA Cup

TOURNAMENT OVERVIEW

IN 1950, THE SWISS VICE-PRESIDENT of FIFA, Ernst Thommen, proposed a competition between select XIs from European cities with industrial fairs. Bizarre as the concept may seem it was strongly supported by Sir Stanley Rous, president of FIFA. Representatives from 12 cities met in Basle to draw up rules for the competition with matches planned to coincide with the industrial fairs. As a consequence, the first edition of the Fairs Cup took nearly three years to complete (1955–58) and was won by Barcelona who beat a London XI over two legs.

Fixture congestion forced the tournament into a single season alongside the European Cup in 1960–61 and Barcelona found itself competing in both. The team went out in the quarter-finals leaving the way for Roma to take the trophy. The rest of the 1960s saw Spanish dominance, initially maintained by Valencia and Real Zaragoza, before giving way to four successive English victories (1968–71).

In 1971, UEFA finally took the competition over, renamed it the UEFA Cup, and awarded places systematically to the highest-placed league clubs not entering other competitions. In the mid-1990s, the disintegration of the Soviet Union saw the competition contested by over 100 clubs with additional places available via UEFA Fair Play awards and the Intertoto Cup.

The 1970s were dominated by English (five winners), German (two) and Dutch (two) teams. The 1980s saw clubs from smaller leagues doing well: RSC Anderlecht from Belgium won it once and IFK Göteborg from Sweden won it twice.

In the 1990s, however, it was the Italian sides who dominated. Between 1989 and 99, Italian clubs took the title eight times, including four all-Italian finals. However, new challengers have risen: 2000 saw Galatasaray win Turkey's first European victory, 2001 saw the return of Liverpool to winning ways and in 2003 Porto won its first trophy for 16 years.

THE UEFA CUP

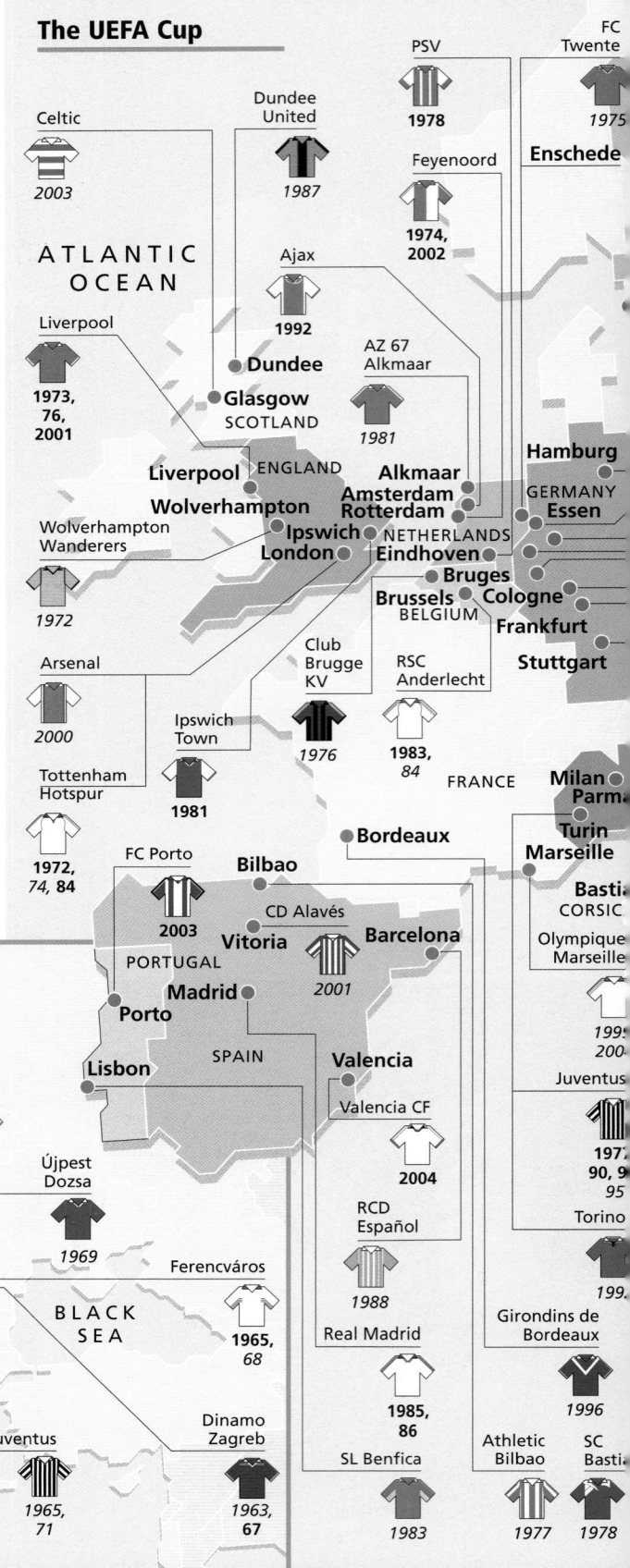

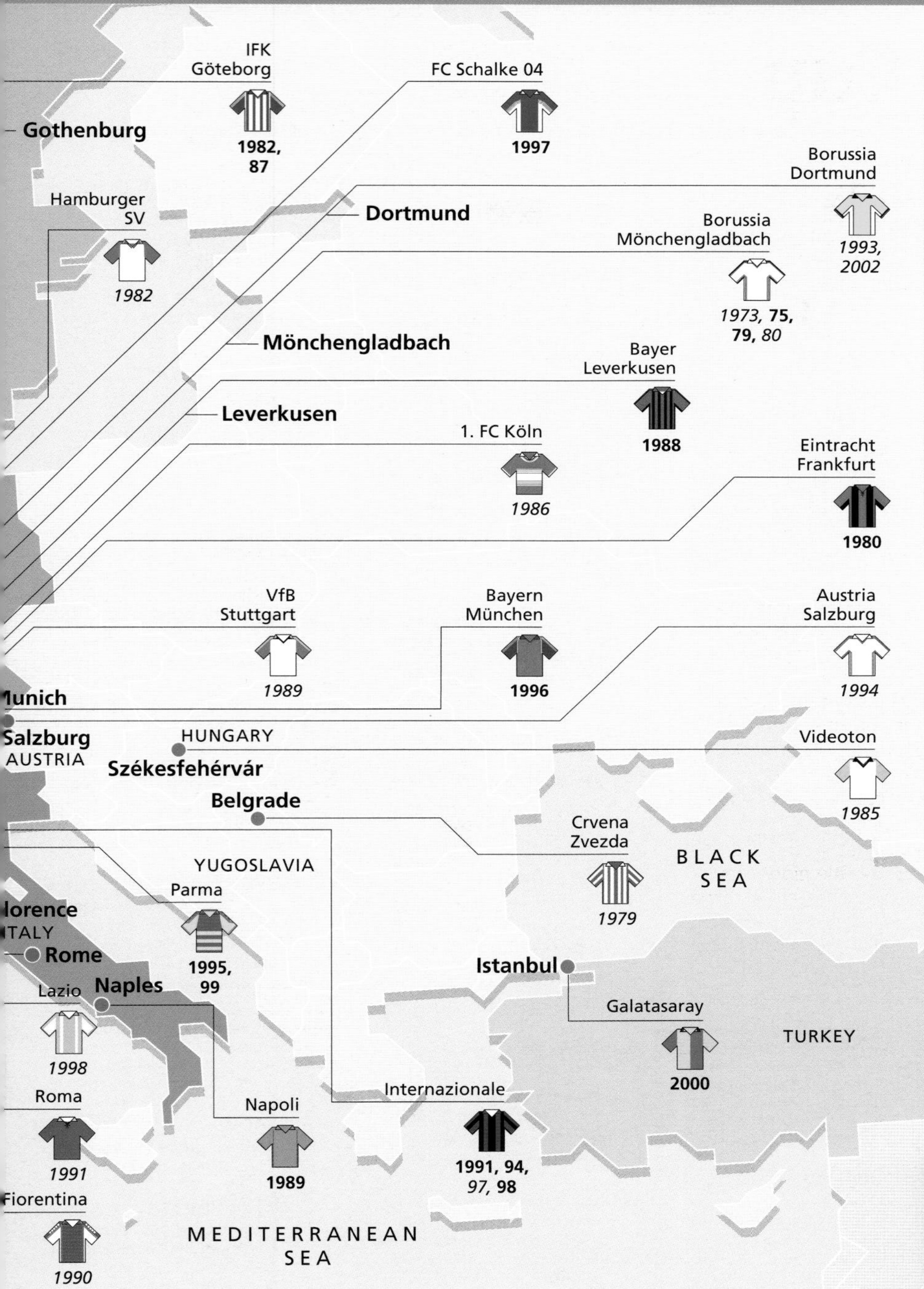

IFK
Göteborg
**1982,
87**

FC Schalke 04
1997

Borussia
Dortmund
*1993,
2002*

Gothenburg

Hamburger
SV
1982

Dortmund

Borussia
Mönchengladbach
**1973, 75,
79**, *80*

Mönchengladbach

Bayer
Leverkusen
1988

Leverkusen

1. FC Köln
1986

Eintracht
Frankfurt
1980

VfB
Stuttgart
1989

Bayern
München
1996

Austria
Salzburg
1994

Munich

Salzburg
AUSTRIA

HUNGARY
Székesfehérvár

Videoton
1985

Belgrade

Crvena
Zvezda
1979

BLACK
SEA

YUGOSLAVIA

Parma
**1995,
99**

Florence
ITALY
Rome

Lazio **Naples**
1998

Roma
1991
Fiorentina

Napoli
1989

Istanbul

Galatasaray
2000

TURKEY

Internazionale
**1991, 94,
97, 98**

MEDITERRANEAN
SEA

The Fairs Cup and the UEFA Cup

Number of wins (by country)

The Fairs Cup	The UEFA Cup
5+ times	9+ times
2–4 times	6–8 times
1 time	2–5 times
0 times	1 time
	0 times

Team details

HUNGARY — Country
● **Budapest** — City of origin
Ferencváros — Team name

— Team colours

1965,
68 — Winners in bold
Runners-up in italic

The UEFA Cup 1958–2004

COUNTRY	WINNERS	RUNNERS-UP
Italy	9	6
Germany	6	7
England	6	3
Netherlands	4	2
Spain	3	3
Sweden	2	0
Belgium	1	2
Portugal	1	1
Turkey	1	0
France	0	4
Scotland	0	2
Austria	0	1
Hungary	0	1
Yugoslavia	0	1

Pierre van Hooijdonk viciously curves the ball over the Borussia Dortmund wall for his and Feyenoord's second goal in 2002's frantic, entertaining Final.

Consecutive participation

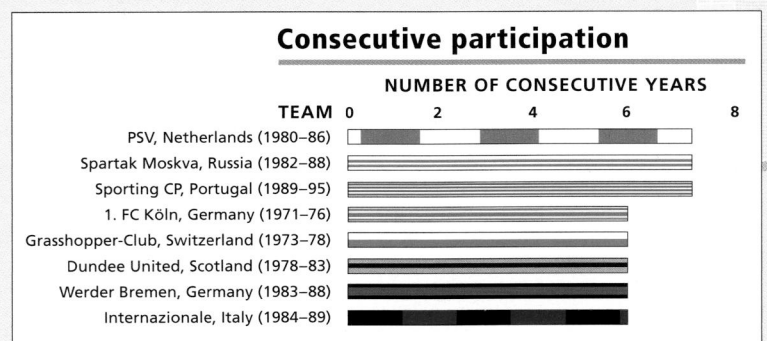

	NUMBER OF CONSECUTIVE YEARS				
TEAM	0	2	4	6	8
PSV, Netherlands (1980–86)					
Spartak Moskva, Russia (1982–88)					
Sporting CP, Portugal (1989–95)					
1. FC Köln, Germany (1971–76)					
Grasshopper-Club, Switzerland (1973–78)					
Dundee United, Scotland (1978–83)					
Werder Bremen, Germany (1983–88)					
Internazionale, Italy (1984–89)					

The UEFA Cup

ERNST THOMMEN'S International Industrial Fairs Inter City Cup was open to teams from cities that had hosted international trade fairs. The first tournament, in 1955, had ten entrants from ten cities. Two-leg, home and away rounds were played over three years to produce the first winner of the (now abbreviated) Fairs Cup. The away goals rule was first introduced into the tournament in 1967, and, in 1971, penalties replaced the toss of a coin for drawn matches. In 1972 it became the UEFA Cup. In 1998 the two-leg final was replaced by a single match at a neutral venue.

From 1961 the tournament spread its net, with three places allocated to each UEFA nation. Places are now allocated on a nation's past performance in European competition, though national associations can allocate those places as they choose. With the merger of the Cup-Winners' Cup into an expanded UEFA Cup in 2000, national cup winners are generally awarded a place and preliminary rounds have been added. Defeated teams from the preliminary round of the Champions League now enter the first round, and third-place teams from the Champions League first-round mini-leagues enter the third round.

1955–58 FINAL (2 legs)

March 5 – Stamford Bridge, London
London 2-2 Barcelona
Select XI (Spain)
(England) (Tejada 7,
(Greaves 10, Martinez 35)
Langley 88 pen)

May 1 – Nou Camp, Barcelona
Barcelona 6-0 London
(Suarez 6, 8, **Select XI**
Evaristo 52, 75,
Martinez 43,
Verges 63)

Barcelona won 8-2 on aggregate

1958–60 FINAL (2 legs)

March 29 – St. Andrew's, Birmingham
Birmingham 0-0 Barcelona
City (Spain)
(England)

May 4 – Nou Camp, Barcelona
Barcelona 4-1 Birmingham
(Czibor 6, 48, **City**
Martinez 43, (Hooper 82)
Coll 78)

Barcelona won 4-1 on aggregate

1960–61 FINAL (2 legs)

September 27 – St. Andrew's, Birmingham
Birmingham 2-2 Roma
City (Italy)
(England) (Manfredini
(Hellawell 78, 30, 56)
Orritt 85)

October 11 – Stadio Olimpico, Rome
Roma 2-0 Birmingham
(Farmer o.g. 56, **City**
Pestrin 90)

Roma won 4-2 on aggregate

1961–62 FINAL (2 legs)

August 9 – Luis Casanova, Valencia
Valencia 6-2 Barcelona
(Spain) (Spain)
(Yosu 14, 42, (Kocsis 4, 20)
Guillot 35, 54, 67,
Nunez 74)

September 9 – Nou Camp, Barcelona
Barcelona 1-1 Valencia
(Kocsis 46) (Guillot 87)

Valencia won 7-3 on aggregate

1962–63 FINAL (2 legs)

June 12 – Dinamo Stadion, Zagreb
Dinamo Zagreb 1-2 Valencia
(Yugoslavia) (Spain)
(Zambata 13) (Waldo 64,
Urtiaga 67)

June 25 – Mestalla, Valencia
Valencia 2-0 Dinamo Zagreb
(Manio 68,
Nunez 78)

Valencia won 4-1 on aggregate

1963–64 FINAL

June 25 – Nou Camp, Barcelona
Real Zaragoza 2-1 Valencia
(Spain) (Spain)
(Villa 40, (Urtiaga 41)
Marcelino 83)

1964–65 FINAL

June 23 – Communale, Turin
Ferencváros 1-0 Juventus
(Hungary) (Italy)
(Fenyvesi 74)

1965–66 FINAL (2 legs)

September 14 – Nou Camp, Barcelona
Barcelona 0-1 Real Zaragoza
(Spain) (Spain)
(Canario 30)

September 21 – La Romareda, Zaragoza
Real Zaragoza 2-4 Barcelona
(Marcelino (Pujol 3, 86, 119,
24, 87) Zaballa 89)
(after extra time)

Barcelona won 4-3 on aggregate

1966–67 FINAL (2 legs)

August 30 – Dinamo Stadion, Zagreb
Dinamo Zagreb 2-0 Leeds United
(Yugoslavia) (England)
(Cercek 39, 59)

September 6 – Elland Road, Leeds
Leeds United 0-0 Dinamo Zagreb

Dinamo Zagreb won 2-0 on aggregate

1967–68 FINAL (2 legs)

September 7 – Elland Road, Leeds
Leeds United 1-0 Ferencváros
(England) (Hungary)
(Jones 41)

September 11 – Nep, Budapest
Ferencváros 0-0 Leeds United

Leeds United won 1-0 on aggregate

1968–69 FINAL (2 legs)

May 29 – St. James' Park, Newcastle
Newcastle 3-0 Újpest Dozsa
United (Hungary)
(England)
(Moncur 63, 72,
Scott 83)

June 11 – Nep, Budapest
Újpest Dozsa 2-3 Newcastle
(Bene 31, **United**
Gorocs 44) (Moncur 46,
Arentoft 50,
Foggon 74)

Newcastle United won 6-2 on aggregate

1969–70 FINAL (2 legs)

April 22 – Parc Astrid, Brussels
RSC Anderlecht 3-1 Arsenal
(Belgium) (England)
(Devrindt 25, (Kennedy 82)
Mulder 30, 74)

April 28 – Highbury, London
Arsenal 3-0 RSC Anderlecht
(Kelly 25,
Radford 75,
Sammels 76)

Arsenal won 4-3 on aggregate

1970–71 FINAL (2 legs)

May 26 – Communale, Turin
Juventus 0-0 Leeds United
(Italy) (England)

Match abandoned after 51 mins
due to waterlogged pitch

REPLAY

May 28 – Communale, Turin
Juventus 2-2 Leeds United
(Bettega 27, (Madeley 48,
Capello 55) Bates 77)

June 3 – Communale, Turin
Leeds United 1-1 Juventus
(Clarke 12) (Anastasi 20)

Leeds United won on away goals rule

1971–72 FINAL (2 legs)

May 3 – Molineux, Wolverhampton
Wolverhampton 1-2 Tottenham
Wanderers **Hotspur**
(England) (England)
(McCalliog 72) (Chivers 57, 87)

May 17 – White Hart Lane, London
Tottenham 1-1 Wolverhampton
Hotspur **Wanderers**
(Mullery 30) (Wagstaffe 41)

Tottenham Hotspur won 3-2
on aggregate

1972–73 FINAL (2 legs)

May 9 – Anfield, Liverpool
Liverpool 0-0 Borussia
(England) **Mönchen-**
gladbach
(West Germany)

Match abandoned after 27 mins
due to waterlogged pitch

REPLAY

May 10 – Anfield, Liverpool
Liverpool 3-0 Mönchen-
(Keegan 21, 32, **gladbach**
Lloyd 61)

May 23 – Bokelberg, Mönchengladbach
Borussia 2-0 Liverpool
Mönchen-
gladbach
(Heynckes 29, 40)

Liverpool won 3-2 on aggregate

1973–74 FINAL (2 legs)

May 21 – White Hart Lane, London
Tottenham 2-2 Feyenoord
Hotspur (Netherlands)
(England) (Van Hanegem 43,
(England 39, De Jong 85)
Van Daele o.g. 64)

May 28 – Feyenoord, Rotterdam
Feyenoord 2-0 Tottenham
(Rijsbergen 43, **Hotspur**
Ressel 84)

Feyenoord won 4-2 on aggregate

1974–75 FINAL (2 legs)

May 7 – Rheinstadion, Düsseldorf
Borussia 0-0 FC Twente
Mönchen- (Netherlands)
gladbach
(West Germany)

September 11 – Arke, Enschede
FC Twente 1-5 Borussia
(Drost 76) **Mönchen-**
gladbach
(Simonsen 2, 86,
Heynckes
9, 50, 60)

Borussia Mönchengladbach won 5-1
on aggregate

1975–76 FINAL (2 legs)

April 28 – Anfield, Liverpool
Liverpool 3-2 Club Brugge KV
(England) (Belgium)
(Kennedy 59, (Lambert 5,
Case 61, Cools 15)
Keegan 65)

May 19 – Olympiastadion, Bruges
Club Brugge KV 1-1 Liverpool
(Lambert 11) (Keegan 15)

Liverpool won 4-3 on aggregate

1976–77 FINAL (2 legs)

May 4 – Communale, Turin
Juventus 1-0 Athletic Bilbao
(Italy) (Spain)
(Tardelli 15)

May 18 – San Mames, Bilbao
Athletic Bilbao 2-1 Juventus
(Churruca 11, (Bettega 7)
Carlos 78)

Juventus won on away goals rule

1977–78 FINAL (2 legs)

April 26 – Furiani, Bastia
SC Bastia **0-0** PSV
(France)   (Netherlands)

May 9 – Philips, Eindhoven
PSV **3-0** SC Bastia
*(W. Van der
Kerkhof 24,
Deijkers 67,
Van der Kuijlen 69)*

PSV Eindhoven won 3-0 on aggregate

1978–79 FINAL (2 legs)

May 9 – Crvena Zvezda, Belgrade
Crvena Zvezda **1-1** Borussia
(Yugoslavia)   Mönchen-
(Sestic 21)   gladbach
                 (West Germany)
                 (Jurisic o.g. 60)

May 23 – Rheinstadion, Düsseldorf
Borussia **1-0** Crvena Zvezda
Mönchen-
gladbach
(Simonsen 15)

Borussia Mönchengladbach won 2-1
on aggregate

1979–80 FINAL (2 legs)

May 7 – Bokelberg, Mönchengladbach
Borussia **3-2** Eintracht
Mönchen-   Frankfurt
gladbach   (West Germany)
(West Germany) *(Karger 37,
(Kulik 44, 88, Hlzenbein 71)*
Matthäus 76)*

May 21 – Waldstadion, Frankfurt
Eintracht **1-0** Borussia
Frankfurt   Mönchen-
(Schaub 81)   gladbach

Eintracht Frankfurt won on away
goals rule

1980–81 FINAL (2 legs)

May 6 – Portman Road, Ipswich
Ipswich Town **3-0** AZ 67 Alkmaar
(England)   (Netherlands)
*(Wark 28,
Thijssen 46,
Mariner 56)*

May 20 – Alkmaarderhout, Alkmaar
AZ 67 Alkmaar **4-2** Ipswich Town
*(Welzl 7,   (Thijssen 4,
Metgod 25,   Wark 32)*
Tol 40, Jonker 74)*

Ipswich Town won 5-4 on aggregate

1981–82 FINAL (2 legs)

May 5 – Nea Ullevi, Gothenburg
IFK Göteborg **1-0** Hamburger SV
(Sweden)   (West Germany)
*(Tord Holmgren
87)*

May 19 – Volksparkstadion, Hamburg
Hamburger SV **0-3** IFK Göteborg
               *(Nilsson 6,
               Corneliusson 26,
               Fredriksson 63)*

IFK Göteborg won 4-0 on aggregate

1982–83 FINAL (2 legs)

May 4 – Heysel, Brussels
RSC Anderlecht **1-0** Benfica
(Belgium)   (Portugal)
(Brylle 29)

May 18 – Estadio da Luz, Lisbon
Benfica **1-1** RSC Anderlecht
(Sheu 36)   *(Lozana 38)*

RSC Anderlecht won 2-1 on aggregate

1983–84 FINAL (2 legs)

May 9 – Parc Astrid, Brussels
RSC Anderlecht **1-1** Tottenham
(Belgium)   Hotspur
(Olsen 85)   (England)
               (Miller 57)

May 23 – White Hart Lane, London
Tottenham **1-1** RSC Anderlecht
Hotspur   *(Czerniatynski 60)*
(Roberts 84)
(after extra time)
Tottenham Hotspur won 4-3 on pens

1984–85 FINAL (2 legs)

May 8 – Sostol, Székesfehérvár
Videoton **0-3** Real Madrid
(Hungary)   (Spain)
               *(Michel 31,
               Santillana 77,
               Valdano 89)*

May 22 – Santiago Bernabeu, Madrid
Real Madrid **0-1** Videoton
               (Majer 86)

Real Madrid won 3-1 on aggregate

1985–86 FINAL (2 legs)

April 30 – Santiago Bernabeu, Madrid
Real Madrid **5-1** 1. FC Köln
(Spain)   (West Germany)
*(Sanchez 38,   *(Allofs 29)*
Gordillo 42,
Valdano 51, 84,
Santillana 89)*

May 6 – Olympiastadion, Berlin
1. FC Köln **2-0** Real Madrid
*(Bein 22,
Geilenkirchen 72)*

Real Madrid won 5-3 on aggregate

1986–87 FINAL (2 legs)

May 6 – Nea Ullevi, Gothenburg
IFK Göteborg **1-0** Dundee
(Sweden)   United
(Pettersson 38) (Scotland)

May 20 – Tannadice Park, Dundee
Dundee **1-1** IFK Göteborg
United   *(Nilsson 22)*
(Clark 60)

IFK Göteborg won 2-1 on aggregate

1987–88 FINAL (2 legs)

May 4 – Sarria, Barcelona
RCD Español **3-0** Bayer
(Spain)   Leverkusen
*(Losada 45, 56, (West Germany)
Soler 49)*

May 18 – Haberland Stadion, Leverkusen
Bayer **3-0** RCD Español
Leverkusen
*(Tita 57,
Götz 63,
Cha Bumkun 81)*
(after extra time)
Bayer Leverkusen won 3-2 on pens

1988–89 FINAL (2 legs)

May 3 – San Paolo, Naples
Napoli **2-1** VfB Stuttgart
(Italy)   (West Germany)
*(Maradona 68,   *(Gaudino 17)*
Careca 87)*

May 17 – Neckarstadion, Stuttgart
VfB Stuttgart **3-3** Napoli
*(Klinsmann 27, (Alemo 18,
De Napoli o.g. 70, Ferrara 39,
Schmäler 89)*   Careca 62)*

Napoli won 5-4 on aggregate

1989–90 FINAL (2 legs)

May 2 – Stadio Communale, Turin
Juventus **3-1** Fiorentina
(Italy)   (Italy)
*(Galia 3,   *(Buso 10)*
Casiraghi 59,
De Agostini 73)*

May 16 – Partenio, Avellino
Fiorentina **0-0** Juventus

Juventus won 3-1 on aggregate

1990–91 FINAL (2 legs)

May 8 – Guiseppe Meazza, Milan
Internazionale **2-0** Roma
(Italy)   (Italy)
*(Mätthaus 55,
Berti 67)*

May 22 – Stadio Olimpico, Rome
Roma **1-0** Internazionale
(Rizzitelli 81)

Internazionale won 2-1 on aggregate

1991–92 FINAL (2 legs)

April 29 – Stadio Delle Alpi, Turin
Torino **2-2** Ajax
(Italy)   (Netherlands)
*(Casagrande   *(Jonk 17,
65, 82)*   Pettersson 73)*

May 13 – Olympisch Stadion, Amsterdam
Ajax **0-0** Torino

Ajax won on away goals rule

1992–93 FINAL (2 legs)

May 5 – Westfalenstadion, Dortmund
Borussia **1-3** Juventus
Dortmund   (Italy)
(Germany)   *(D. Baggio 27,
(M. Rummenigge 2)* R. Baggio 31, 74)*

May 19 – Delle Alpi, Turin
Juventus **3-0** Borussia
*(D. Baggio 5, 40, Dortmund
Möller 65)*

Juventus won 6-1 on aggregate

1993–94 FINAL (2 legs)

April 26 – Ernst-Happel-Stadion, Vienna
Austria **0-1** Internazionale
Salzburg   (Italy)
(Austria)   *(Berti 35)*

May 11 – Giuseppe Meazza, Milan
Internazionale **1-0** Austria
(Jonk 63)   Salzburg

Internazionale won 2-0 on aggregate

1994–95 FINAL (2 legs)

May 3 – Tardini, Parma
Parma **1-0** Juventus
(Italy)   (Italy)
(D. Baggio 5)

May 17 – Guiseppe Meazza, Milan
Juventus **1-1** Parma
(Vialli 33)   *(D. Baggio 54)*

Parma won 2-1 on aggregate

1995–96 FINAL (2 legs)

May 1 – Olympia, Munich
Bayern **2-0** Girondins de
München   Bordeaux
(Germany)   (France)
*(Helmer 35,
Scholl 60)*

May 15 – Bordeaux
Girondins de **1-3** Bayern
Bordeaux   München
(Dutuel)   *(Scholl 53,
               Kostadinov 65,
               Klinsmann 79)*

Bayern München won 5-1 on aggregate

1996–97 FINAL (2 legs)

May 7 – Parkstadion, Gelsenkirchen
FC Schalke 04 **1-0** Internazionale
(Germany)   (Italy)
(Wilmots 70)

May 21 – Guiseppe Meazza, Milan
Internazionale **1-0** FC Schalke 04
(Zamorano 84)
(after extra time)
FC Schalke 04 won 4-1 on pens

1997–98 FINAL

May 6 – Parc des Princes, Paris
Lazio **0-3** Internazionale
(Italy)   (Italy)
               *(Zamorano 5,
               Zanetti 60,
               Ronaldo 70)*

1998–99 FINAL

May 12 – Luzhniki, Moscow
Parma **3-0** Olympique
(Italy)   Marseille
*(Crespo 26,   (France)
Vanoli 36,
Chiesa 55)*

1999–2000 FINAL

May 17 – Parken, Copenhagen
Galatasaray **0-0** Arsenal
(Turkey)   (England)
(after extra time)
Galatasaray won 4-1 on pens

2000–01 FINAL

May 16 – Westfalenstadion, Dortmund
Liverpool **5-4** CD Alavés
(England)   (Spain)
*(Babbel 4,   (Alonzo 27,
Gerrard 16,   Moreno 48, 51,
McAllister 41 pen, Cruyff 89)*
Fowler 73,
Gelí o.g. 116)*
(after extra time)

2001–02 FINAL

May 8 – De Kuip, Rotterdam
Feyenoord **3-2** Borussia
(Netherlands) Dortmund
*(van Hooijdonk (Germany)
33 pen, 40,   (Amoroso 47 pen,
Tomasson 50)*   Koller 58)*

2002–03 FINAL

May 21 – Olimpico, Seville
Celtic **2-3** FC Porto
(Scotland)   (Portugal)
(Larsson 47, 56) *(Derlei 45, 115,
               Alenitchev 54)*

2003–04 FINAL

May 19 – Nea Ullevi Stadium, Gothenburg
Valencia **2-0** Olympique
(Spain)   Marseille
*(Vincente 45 pen, (France)
Mista 58)*

The European Cup-Winners' Cup

TOURNAMENT OVERVIEW

WITH THE SUCCESS OF THE EUROPEAN CUP clear to all, and entry to the Fairs Cup initially restricted to certain cities, pressure built up for a further European club competition. The European Cup-Winners' Cup was officially set up in February 1960 at a meeting in Vienna, and was originated by the organizing committee of the now tiring Mittel Europa Cup. Based on the same format as the European Cup, the tournament was open to the winners of national knockout competitions (or losing finalists, if the winners were going to compete in the European Cup). Of course, not all European nations possessed a domestic cup, but with the establishment of the tournament, they all soon acquired one. Only ten teams entered the first tournament, which was won by Fiorentina, beating Glasgow Rangers 4-1 on aggregate – Italy's first European club triumph. The tournament was taken over and expanded by UEFA for the 1961–62 competition and that final saw Atlético Madrid beat champions Fiorentina 3-0 in a replay. In 1963, Atlético Madrid lost 5-1 to Tottenham Hotspur in a single match Final in Rotterdam.

Over the next ten years British clubs won the cup four times, German clubs twice, with Slovan Bratislava's victory over Barcelona in 1969 the first win for an Eastern European club in the competition. The rest of the 1970s saw further Eastern European success (1. FC Magdeburg, Dinamo Kiev) and RSC Anderlecht's run of three consecutive finals 1976–78 (of which the team won the first and last).

The late 1980s and 90s saw a much wider spread of teams getting to the Final, with some smaller clubs securing victory: Belgium's KV Mechelen beat Ajax in 1988, with Sampdoria beating RSC Anderlecht in 1990. Barcelona, winners in 1997, chose to enter the newly expanded Champions League the following year. This was perhaps the death knell for the tournament, whose significance appeared to be slipping. The final tournament was held in 1999 and won by Lazio before the whole show was wrapped up into the newly-expanded UEFA Cup.

West Ham captain Bobby Moore shakes hands with TSV 1860 München's Rudi Brunnenmeier before the start of the 1965 European Cup-Winners' Cup Final at Wembley. West Ham won the cup with two goals in two minutes from Alan Sealey.

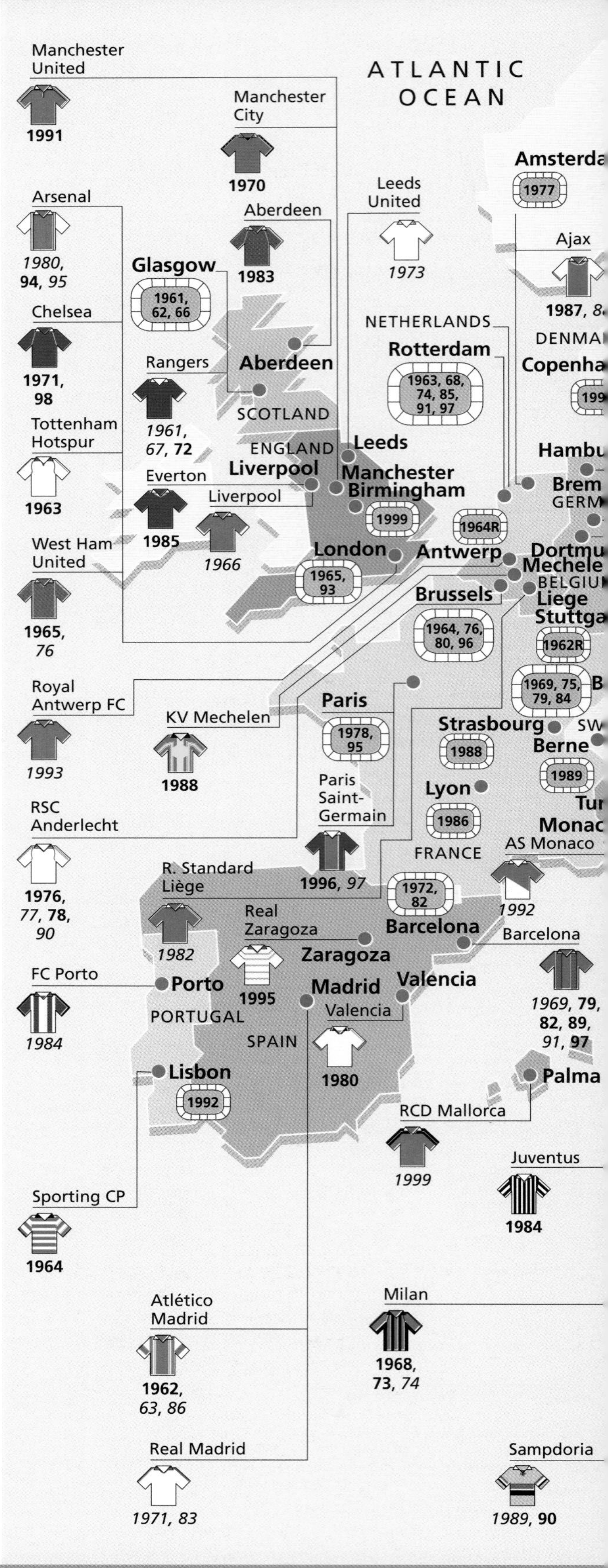

Map labels

Manchester United — **1991**

Manchester City — **1970**

Arsenal — *1980, 94, 95*

Aberdeen — **1983**

Leeds United — *1973*

Amsterdam — 1977

Ajax — **1987, 8.**

Chelsea — **1971, 98**

Glasgow — 1961, 62, 66

Rangers — *1961, 67, 72*

Rotterdam — 1963, 68, 74, 85, 91, 97

Copenha. — 199.

NETHERLANDS

DENMA.

Tottenham Hotspur — **1963**

Everton — **1985**

Leeds

Liverpool — *1966*

Manchester Birmingham

Hambu.

Brem — **1999**

GERM.

West Ham United — **1965, 76**

London — 1965, 93

Antwerp

1964R

Dortmu. / Mechele.

BELGIU.

Liege / Stuttga.

Brussels — 1964, 76, 80, 96

1962R

Royal Antwerp FC — *1993*

KV Mechelen — **1988**

Paris — 1978, 95

Strasbourg — 1988

Berne — 1989

SW.

RSC Anderlecht — *1976, 77, 78, 90*

Paris Saint-Germain — **1996, 97**

Lyon — 1986

Tu.

Monac.

AS Monaco — *1992*

FRANCE

R. Standard Liège — *1982*

Real Zaragoza — **1995**

Barcelona — 1972, 82

Barcelona

FC Porto — *1984*

Porto

Madrid

Valencia

1969, 79, 82, 89, 91, 97

PORTUGAL

SPAIN

Zaragoza

Valencia — *1980*

Palma

Lisbon — 1992

RCD Mallorca — *1999*

Juventus — **1984**

Sporting CP — **1964**

Atlético Madrid — **1962, 63, 86**

Milan — **1968, 73, 74**

Real Madrid — *1971, 83*

Sampdoria — *1989, **90***

ATLANTIC OCEAN

SCOTLAND

ENGLAND

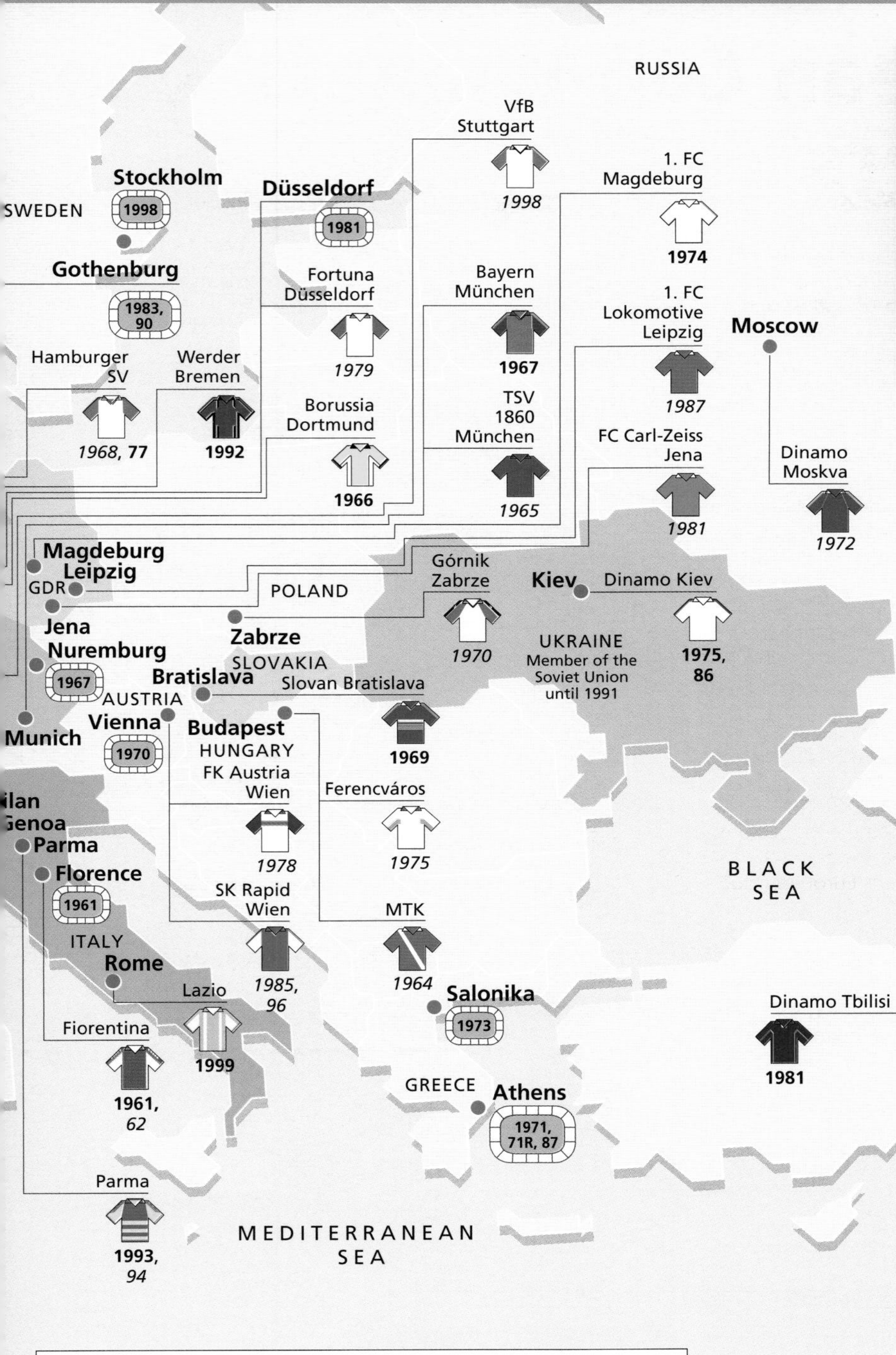

SWEDEN

Stockholm
1998

Gothenburg
1983, 90

Hamburger
SV
1968, **77**

Werder
Bremen
1992

Düsseldorf
1981

Fortuna
Düsseldorf
1979

Borussia
Dortmund
1966

VfB
Stuttgart
1998

Bayern
München
1967

TSV
1860
München
1965

RUSSIA

1. FC
Magdeburg
1974

1. FC
Lokomotive
Leipzig
1987

FC Carl-Zeiss
Jena
1981

Moscow

Dinamo
Moskva
1972

Pavel Nedved *of Lazio strikes home the winning goal against Mallorca in the 81st minute of the last-ever Cup-Winners' Cup Final at Villa Park in Birmingham, England, in May 1999.*

Magdeburg
Leipzig
GDR

Jena
Nuremburg
1967
AUSTRIA

Munich

Vienna
1970

Milan
Genoa
Parma

Florence
1961

ITALY
Rome

Lazio
1999

Fiorentina
1961,
62

Parma
1993,
94

Zabrze
Bratislava
SLOVAKIA
Slovan Bratislava
1969

Budapest
HUNGARY
FK Austria
Wien
1978

SK Rapid
Wien
1985,
96

POLAND

Górnik
Zabrze
1970

Ferencváros
1975

MTK
1964

Kiev

Dinamo Kiev
1975,
86

UKRAINE
Member of the
Soviet Union
until 1991

Salonika
1973

GREECE
Athens
1971,
71R, 87

MEDITERRANEAN
SEA

BLACK
SEA

Dinamo Tbilisi

GEORGIA
Member of the
Soviet Union
until 1991

T'bilisi

Dinamo Tbilisi
1981

Clubs that won without winning their domestic cup

YEAR	TEAM
1961	Fiorentina
1972	Rangers
1978	RSC Anderlecht
1981	Dinamo Tbilisi
1997	Barcelona

The European Cup-Winners' Cup

Number of wins in the European Cup-Winners' Cup (by country)

- 8+ times
- 5–7 times
- 2–4 times
- 1 time
- 0 times

Team details

ITALY	Country
● **Florence**	City of origin
Fiorentina	Team name
(shirt)	Team colours
1961, *62*	Winners in bold / Runners-up in italic
● **Amsterdam**	
1977R	Host city of Final and year, R means replay

Consecutive participation

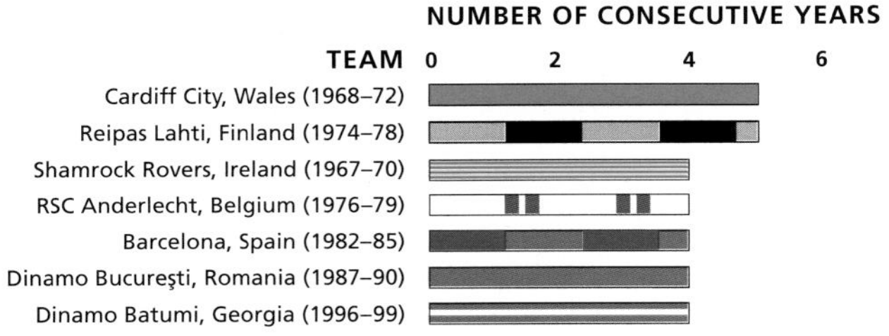

NUMBER OF CONSECUTIVE YEARS

TEAM 0   2   4   6

Cardiff City, Wales (1968–72)
Reipas Lahti, Finland (1974–78)
Shamrock Rovers, Ireland (1967–70)
RSC Anderlecht, Belgium (1976–79)
Barcelona, Spain (1982–85)
Dinamo Bucureşti, Romania (1987–90)
Dinamo Batumi, Georgia (1996–99)

The European Cup-Winners' Cup

THE EUROPEAN CUP-WINNERS' CUP

THE CUP-WINNERS' CUP was the last of the major European tournaments to be established, and the first to be completely abandoned. It was first organized by UEFA in 1960–61, and ran for 39 years. The competition was open to the previous year's winners and the winners of national cup competitions. Throughout the whole of the tournament's history the same format was used: two-leg home and away rounds, with away goals counting double, and penalties to decide drawn matches. Apart from the first year the Final has always been a single match played at a neutral venue.

When the tournament was first created, many UEFA nations had no national cup competition, and if nothing else, the Cup-Winners' Cup ensured that knockout-format cup soccer would spread right across the continent. In its final years, preliminary rounds were introduced to produce 17 entrants from among the weaker soccer nations for a 32-club first round. Fourteen places were reserved for the strongest national leagues and one for the previous year's winner. The last Final was played in 1999. The cup has been effectively merged with the expanded UEFA cup, as national cup winners now enter that competition.

1960–61 FINAL (2 legs)
May 17 – Ibrox, Glasgow
Rangers 0-2 Fiorentina
(Scotland) (Italy)
  (Milani 12, 88)
h/t: 0-1 **Att:** 80,000
Ref: Steiner (Austria)

May 27 – Communale, Florence
Fiorentina 2-1 Rangers
*(Milani 12, (Scott 60)
Hamrin 88)*
h/t: 1-0 **Att:** 50,000
Ref: Hernadi (Hungary)

Fiorentina won 4-1 on aggregate

1961–62 FINAL
May 10 – Hampden Park, Glasgow
Atlético 1-1 Fiorentina
Madrid (Italy)
(Spain) *(Hamrin 27)*
(Peiro 11)
h/t: 1-1 **Att:** 27,000
Ref: Wharton (Scotland)

REPLAY
September 5 –
Neckarstadion, Stuttgart
Atlético 3-0 Fiorentina
Madrid
*(Jones 8,
Mendonca 27,
Peiro 59)*
h/t: 2-0 **Att:** 38,000
Ref: Tschenscher (West Germany)

1962–63 FINAL
May 15 – De Kuip, Rotterdam
Tottenham 5-1 Atlético
Hotspur Madrid
(England) (Spain)
*(Greaves 16, 80, (Collar 47)
White 35,
Dyson 67, 85)*
h/t: 2-0 **Att:** 49,000
Ref: Van Leuwen (Netherlands)

1963–64 FINAL
May 13 – Heysel, Brussels
Sporting CP 3-3 MTK
(Portugal) (Hungary)
*(Mascarenhas 40, (Sandor 18, 75,
Figueiredo 45, 80) Kuti 73)*
(after extra time)
h/t: 2-1 **Att:** 3,000
Ref: Van Nuffel (Belgium)

REPLAY
May 15 – Bosuilstadion, Antwerp
Sporting CP 1-0 MTK
(Morais 19)
h/t: 1-0 **Att:** 19,000
Ref: Versyp (Belgium)

1964–65 FINAL
May 19 – Wembley, London
West Ham 2-0 TSV 1860
United München
(England) (West Germany)
(Sealey 70, 72)
h/t: 0-0 **Att:** 100,000
Ref: Zsolt (Hungary)

1965–66 FINAL
May 5 – Hampden Park, Glasgow
Borussia 2-1 Liverpool
Dortmund (England)
(West Germany) *(Hunt 68)*
*(Held 62,
Libuda 109)*
(after extra time)
h/t: 0-0 **90 mins:** 1-1
Att: 41,000 **Ref:** Schwinte (France)

1966–67 FINAL
May 31 – Frankenstadion, Nüremberg
Bayern 1-0 Rangers
München (Scotland)
(West Germany)
(Roth 108)
(after extra time)
h/t: 0-0 **90 mins:** 0-0
Att: 69,000 **Ref:** Lo Bello (Italy)

1967–68 FINAL
May 23 – De Kuip, Rotterdam
Milan 2-0 Hamburger SV
(Italy) (West Germany)
(Hamrin 3, 19)
h/t: 2-0 **Att:** 53,000
Ref: Ortiz (Spain)

1968–69 FINAL
May 21 – St Jakob, Basle
Slovan 3-2 Barcelona
Bratislava (Spain)
(Czechoslovakia) *(Zaldua 16,
(Cvetler 2, Rexach 52)
Hrivnak 30,
Jan Capkovic 42)*
h/t: 3-1 **Att:** 19,000
Ref: Van Raven (Netherlands)

1969–70 FINAL
May 29 – Prater, Vienna
Manchester 2-1 Górnik
City Zabrze
(England) (Poland)
*(Young 11, (Oslizlo 70)
Lee 43)*
h/t: 2-0 **Att:** 10,000
Ref: Schiller (Austria)

1970–71 FINAL
May 19 – Karaiskakis, Piraeus
Chelsea 1-1 Real Madrid
(England) (Spain)
(Osgood 55) (Zoco 30)
h/t: 0-0 **90 mins:** 1-1 **Att:** 42,000
Ref: Scheurer (Switzerland)

REPLAY
May 21 – Karaiskakis, Piraeus
Chelsea 2-1 Real Madrid
*(Dempsey 31, (Fleitas 75)
Osgood 39)*
h/t: 2-0 **Att:** 19,917
Ref: Bucheli (Switzerland)

1971–72 FINAL
May 24 – Nou Camp, Barcelona
Rangers 3-2 Dinamo
(Scotland) **Moskva**
*(Stein 23, (Soviet Union)
W. Johnston (Estrekov 60,
40, 49) Makovikov 87)*
h/t: 2-0 **Att:** 24,000
Ref: Ortiz (Spain)

1972–73 FINAL
May 16 – Kaftantzoglio, Salonica
Milan 1-0 Leeds United
(Italy) (England)
(Chiarugi 5)
h/t: 1-0 **Att:** 45,000
Ref: Michas (Greece)

1973–74 FINAL
May 8 – De Kuip, Rotterdam
1. FC 2-0 Milan
Magdeburg (Italy)
(East Germany)
*(Lanzi o.g. 40,
Seguin 74)*
h/t: 1-0 **Att:** 4,000
Ref: Van Gemert (Netherlands)

1974–75 FINAL
May 14 – St Jakob, Basle
Dinamo Kiev 3-0 Ferencváros
(Soviet Union) (Hungary)
*(Onischenko
18, 39,
Blokhin 67)*
h/t: 2-0 **Att:** 10,000
Ref: Davidson (Scotland)

1975–76 FINAL
May 5 – Heysel, Brussels
RSC Anderlecht 4-2 West Ham
(Belgium) **United**
*(Rensenbrink (England)
42, 73, (Holland 28,
Van der Elst Robson 68)
48, 87)*
h/t: 1-1 **Att:** 58,000
Ref: Wurtz (France)

1976–77 FINAL
May 11 – Olympisch, Amsterdam
Hamburger SV 2-0 RSC Anderlecht
(West Germany) (Belgium)
*(Volkert 78,
Magath 88)*
h/t: 0-0 **Att:** 66,000
Ref: Partridge (England)

1977–78 FINAL
May 3 – Parc des Princes, Paris
RSC Anderlecht 4-0 FK Austria
(Belgium) **Wien**
*(Rensenbrink (Austria)
13, 41,
Van Binst 45, 80)*
h/t: 2-1 **Att:** 48,000
Ref: Alginder (West Germany)

1978–79 FINAL
May 16 – St Jakob, Basle
Barcelona 4-3 Fortuna
(Spain) **Düsseldorf**
*(Sanchez 5, (West Germany)
Asensi 34, (T. Allofs 8,
Rexach 104, Seel 41, 114)
Krankl 111)*
(after extra time)
h/t: 2-2 **90 mins:** 2-2
Att: 58,000 **Ref:** Palotai (Hungary)

1979–80 FINAL

May 15 – Heysel, Brussels
Valencia **0-0** Arsenal
(Spain)   (England)
(after extra time)
h/t: 0-0 **90 mins:** 0-0
Att: 36,000
Ref: Christov (Czechoslovakia)
Valencia won 5-4 on pens

1980–81 FINAL

May 13 – Rheinstadion, Düsseldorf
Dinamo **2-1** FC Carl-Zeiss
Tbilisi   Jena
(Soviet Union) (East Germany)
(Gutsayev 67,   (Hoppe 63)
Daraselia 86)
h/t: 0-0 **Att:** 9,000
Ref: Lattanzi (Italy)

1981–82 FINAL

May 12 – Nou Camp, Barcelona
Barcelona **2-1** R. Standard
(Spain)   Liège
(Simonsen 44, (Belgium)
Quini 63)   (Vandersmissen 7)
h/t: 1-1 **Att:** 100,000
Ref: Eschweller (West Germany)

1982–83 FINAL

May 11 – Nya Ullevi, Gothenburg
Aberdeen **2-1** Real Madrid
(Scotland)   (Spain)
(Black 4,   (Juanito 15)
Hewitt 112)
(after extra time)
h/t: 1-1 **90 mins:** 1-1
Att: 17,000 **Ref:** Menegali (Italy)

1983–84 FINAL

May 16 – St Jakob, Basle
Juventus **2-1** FC Porto
(Italy)   (Portugal)
(Vignola 12,   (Sousa 29)
Boniek 41)
h/t: 2-1 **Att:** 60,000
Ref: Procop (East Germany)

1984–85 FINAL

May 15 – De Kuip, Rotterdam
Everton **3-1** SK Rapid Wien
(England)   (Austria)
(Gray 57,   (Krankl 85)
Steven 72,
Sheedy 85)
h/t: 0-0 **Att:** 50,000
Ref: Casarin (Italy)

1985–86 FINAL

May 2 – Gerland, Lyon
Dinamo Kiev **3-0** Atlético
(Soviet Union)   Madrid
(Zavarov 4,   (Spain)
Blokhin 85,
Yevtushenko 87)
h/t: 1-0 **Att:** 50,000
Ref: Wohrer (Austria)

1986–87 FINAL

May 13 – Olympic, Athens
Ajax **1-0** 1. FC
(Netherlands)   Lokomotive
(van Basten 21)   Leipzig
                   (East Germany)
h/t: 1-0 **Att:** 35,000
Ref: Agnolin (Italy)

1987–88 FINAL

May 11 – Meinau, Strasbourg
KV Mechelen **1-0** Ajax
(Belgium)   (Netherlands)
(Den Boer 53)
h/t: 0-0 **Att:** 40,000
Ref: Pauly (West Germany)

1988–89 FINAL

May 10 – Wankdorf, Berne
Barcelona **2-0** Sampdoria
(Spain)   (Italy)
(Salinas 4,
Rekarte 79)
h/t: 1-0 **Att:** 45,000
Ref: Courtney (England)

1989–90 FINAL

May 9 – Nya Ullevi, Gothenburg
Sampdoria **2-0** RSC Anderlecht
(Italy)   (Belgium)
(Vialli 105, 107)
(after extra time)
h/t: 0-0 **90 mins:** 0-0
Att: 20,000 **Ref:** Galler (Switzerland)

1990–91 FINAL

May 15 – De Kuip, Rotterdam
Manchester **2-1** Barcelona
United   (Spain)
(England)   (Koeman 79)
(Hughes 69, 74)
h/t: 0-0 **Att:** 48,000
Ref: Karlsson (Sweden)

1991–92 FINAL

May 6 – Estadio da Luz, Lisbon
Werder Bremen **2-0** AS Monaco
(Germany)   (France)
(K. Allofs 41,
Rufer 54)
h/t: 1-0 **Att:** 15,000
Ref: D'Elia (Italy)

1992–93 FINAL

May 12 – Wembley, London
Parma **3-1** Royal
(Italy)   Antwerp FC
(Minotti 9,   (Belgium)
Melli 30,   (Severeyns 11)
Cuoghi 83)
h/t: 2-1 **Att:** 37,000
Ref: Assenmacher (Germany)

1993–94 FINAL

May 4 – Park Stadion, Copenhagen
Arsenal **1-0** Parma
(England)   (Italy)
(Smith 19)
h/t: 1-0 **Att:** 33,765
Ref: Krondl (Czechoslovakia)

1994–95 FINAL

May 10 – Parc des Princes, Paris
Real Zaragoza **2-1** Arsenal
(Spain)   (England)
(Esnaider 68, (Hartson 77)
Nayim 119)
(after extra time)
h/t: 0-0 **90 mins:** 1-1
Att: 42,424 **Ref:** Ceccarini (Italy)

1995–96 FINAL

May 8 – King Baudoui, Brussels
Paris Saint- **1-0** SK Rapid
Germain   Wien
(France)   (Austria)
(N'Gotty 28)
h/t: 1-0 **Att:** 37,500
Ref: Pairetto (Italy)

1996–97 FINAL

May 14 – De Kuip, Rotterdam
Barcelona **1-0** Paris Saint-
(Spain)   Germain
(Ronaldo 37 pen) (France)
h/t: 1-0 **Att:** 50,000
Ref: Merk (Germany)

1997–98 FINAL

May 13 – Rasunda, Stockholm
Chelsea **1-0** VfB Stuttgart
(England)   (Germany)
(Zola 71)
h/t: 0-0 **Att:** 30,216
Ref: Braschi (Italy)

1998–99 FINAL

May 19 – Villa Park, Birmingham
Lazio **2-1** RCD Mallorca
(Italy)   (Spain)
(Vieri 7,   (Dani 11)
Nedved 81)
h/t: 1-1 **Att:** 33,000
Ref: Benko (Austria)

***The 1982–83 European Cup-Winners' Cup** Final was played in Gothenburg, Sweden, in appalling weather conditions. Both Real Madrid and Aberdeen scored in the first 15 minutes, but the match was level after 90. In the 112th minute, Aberdeen's substitute John Hewitt dived forward to head the ball past the Real keeper and clinch the cup for the only time in the Scottish club's history.*

England

THE SEASON IN REVIEW 2003–04

RARELY CAN ONE TEAM and one person have so dominated the summer break in England. When it was announced that Russian oligarch Roman Abramovich had bought Chelsea and all its debts, and planned an unprecedented wave of buying, it seemed as if English soccer would be utterly transformed. Perhaps it will be yet. But for all the bluster and the hype in West London there is no doubt that the season belonged to North London and to Arsenal. Not since Preston North End, 115 years ago, in the very first season of professional soccer in England, has a team gone through a season undefeated, and Arsenal did it with a matchless grace, style, invention and fluidity. The club's domestic greatness is now assured and only the summit of the European Champions League awaits them as unexplored territory.

Buying frenzy

But in August all eyes were on Stamford Bridge, where an immense war chest was opened. Over £100 million was spent. Arsenal, it seemed, had nothing to spend and a new stadium to fund. But Arsène Wenger conjured an amazing revival from the team that threw away the championship last season. Thierry Henry was simply the best forward in Europe, scoring and making goals that won games and warmed the soul. Patrick Vieira was at his best, orchestrating the team in defence and attack, while Dennis Bergkamp, despite his years, was full of invention and guile.

Manchester United's challenge faltered in the New Year and was all but extinguished by the early spring. Rio Ferdinand's failure to attend a drug test saw the defender banned for the rest of the season. Behind the scenes the battle for control over the club's shareholding intensified. Most worryingly, the dispute between J.P. McManus and Sir Alex Ferguson over the ownership and breeding rights of the horse Rock of Gibraltar brought manager and major

Final Premier League Table 2003–04

CLUB	P	W	D	L	F	A	Pts	
Arsenal	38	26	12	0	73	26	**90**	Champions League
Chelsea	38	24	7	7	67	30	**79**	Champions League
Manchester United	38	23	6	9	64	35	**75**	Champions League
Liverpool	38	16	12	10	55	37	**60**	Champions League
Newcastle United	38	13	17	8	52	40	**56**	UEFA Cup
Aston Villa	38	15	11	12	48	44	**56**	
Charlton Athletic	38	14	11	13	51	51	**53**	
Bolton Wanderers	38	14	11	13	48	56	**53**	
Fulham	38	14	10	14	52	46	**52**	
Birmingham City	38	12	14	12	43	48	**50**	
Middlesbrough	38	13	9	16	44	52	**48**	UEFA Cup (League Cup winners)
Southampton	38	12	11	15	44	45	**47**	
Portsmouth	38	12	9	17	47	54	**45**	
Tottenham Hotspur	38	13	6	19	47	57	**45**	
Blackburn Rovers	38	12	8	18	51	59	**44**	
Manchester City	38	9	14	15	55	54	**41**	
Everton	38	9	12	17	45	57	**39**	
Leicester City	38	6	15	17	48	65	**33**	Relegated
Leeds United	38	8	9	21	40	79	**33**	Relegated
Wolverhampton Wanderers	38	7	12	19	38	77	**33**	Relegated

Promoted clubs: Norwich City, West Bromwich Albion, Crystal Palace.

Contrasting fortunes in the Midlands: Wolves' Alex Rae tries to get past Villa's Gareth Barry.

Above, middle: *Ruud van Nistelrooy's penalty ricochets off the Arsenal bar in their early season clash at Old Trafford.*

Above: *Martin Keown lets van Nistelrooy know just how pleased he is with the miss. Keown, Parlour and Lauren all received bans and fines for their part in the fracas. United's Giggs and Ronaldo received minor fines for their involvement.*

ENGLAND

Chelsea's best striker scores again. It was another season on loan at Birmingham for Mikael Forssell this year where he continued to score, this one past flailing Bolton keeper Jussi Jaaskelainen.

Left: The first of five Arsenal/Chelsea encounters this season. Chelsea's keeper Carlo Cudicini uncharacteristically fumbles and Thierry Henry pounces to score the winner at Highbury.

Below, left: Wish you'd retired now? Sir Alex resides over Manchester United's worst season in a decade: players banned and off form, the team out of Europe laughably early and only third in the Premiership.

Below, left middle: Bolton and Nigerian captain Jay-Jay Okocha. His free kicks were brilliant and in the club's League Cup semi-final victory over Aston Villa he gave one of the performances of the season.

Below: Paolo Di Canio's penalty makes it Charlton 2 Leicester 2 and sends the Midlands club back down to the First Division.

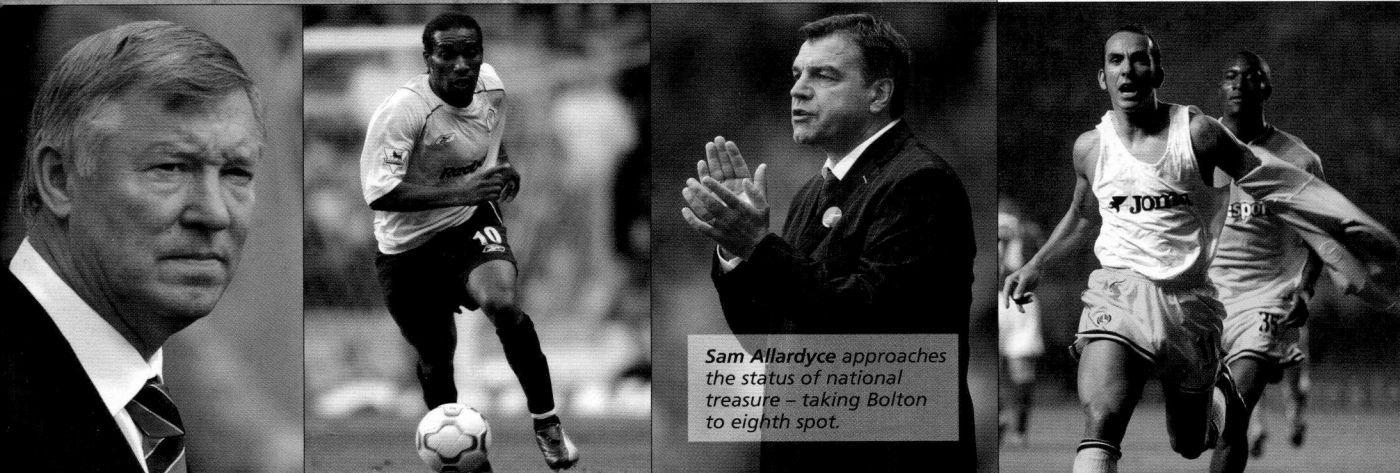

Sam Allardyce approaches the status of national treasure – taking Bolton to eighth spot.

shareholder into open legal conflict. Above all, this was a Manchester United that had remembered how to lose, and defeats to Portsmouth and Wolverhampton were just the most startling of a series of draws and losses that would have been considered inconceivable in recent seasons. United roused itself to beat Arsenal in their FA Cup semi-final clash, but it was a Pyrrhic victory. United's total domination of Millwall in the Final could barely compensate for its decline in both the league and Europe.

Chelsea's challenge to Arsenal lasted longer and in their titanic struggle in the quarter-finals of the Champions League Chelsea finally triumphed, only to squander the opportunity in the semi-finals with Monaco. Its defeat exemplified the limits of the Abramovich revolution in the Premiership as well as Europe: a remaining tactical naivety in the team, some bizarre substitutions from a manager placed under intolerable and undignified pressure all season and too many failures among the new signings. But Arsenal, despite losing two-thirds of its treble ambitions in a ten-day streak, was not deflected from its task, winning the title at White Hart Lane and completing its unbeaten run with a win over Leicester at Highbury.

Gerrard's monumental performance

With the top three so far in front of the rest, the contest for fourth and a shot at the Champions League became effectively a separate contest. Although Liverpool and Newcastle always looked the most likely candidates for the spot, they were consistently challenged by a raft of smaller clubs who, in budgetary terms at any rate, should not have come near them. Aston Villa, Fulham, Birmingham, Charlton, Southampton and Bolton all had ambitions of a European spot. In the end, Newcastle saved its best for the UEFA Cup until Marseille's Drogba put them out in the semi-finals. At Anfield, awash with despair, Steven Gerrard's monumental season-long performance finally got Liverpool to fourth – but it was not enough to keep Gérard Houllier in his job and after six years he departed.

Middlesbrough's mid-table mediocrity was made irrelevant when victory over Bolton in the League Cup Final brought the club its first-ever major trophy. The erratic, the maddening and the underperforming included the usual subjects. Spurs, of course, came top of the list. Glenn Hoddle's departure early in the season left Director of Football David Pleat in temporary charge and the question of the succession ominously looming

Top: There were some good things about Manchester City's season. Shaun Wright-Phillips, the club's best player, keeps the ball away from United's Cristiano Ronaldo in a rare derby win for City.

Right: Wayne Rooney shows poise and balance as Everton record a rare three-goal victory over Southampton; he and Everton could do with some support on the pitch.

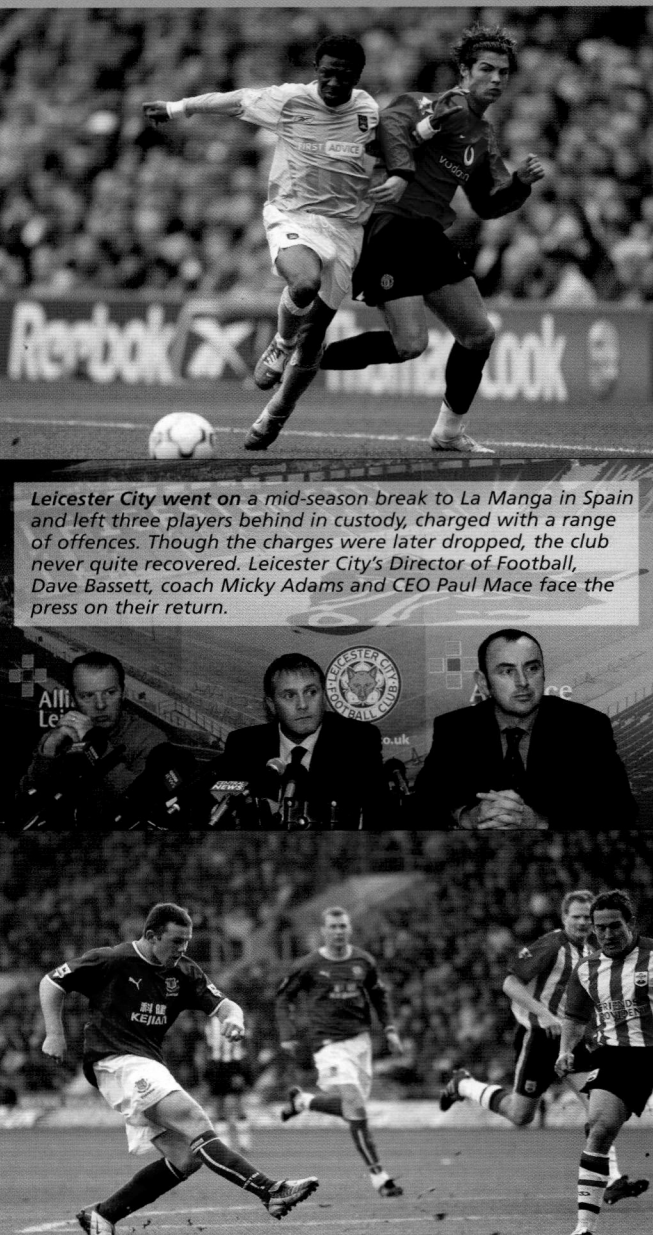

Leicester City went on a mid-season break to La Manga in Spain and left three players behind in custody, charged with a range of offences. Though the charges were later dropped, the club never quite recovered. Leicester City's Director of Football, Dave Bassett, coach Micky Adams and CEO Paul Mace face the press on their return.

ENGLAND

Arsenal's unbeaten run

	1 Aug 4	3	2 Aug 24	6	3 Aug 27	9	4 Aug 31	12	5 Sep 13	13	6 Sep 21	14	7 Sep 26	17	8 Oct 4	20	9 Oct 18	23	10 Oct 26	24
No. / Pts	Everton		Middlesbrough		Aston Villa		Manchester City		Portsmouth		Manchester United		Newcastle United		Liverpool		Chelsea		Charlton Athletic	
	2-1		4-0		2-0		2-1		1-1		0-0		3-2		2-1		2-1		1-1	
	Henry, Pires		Henry, Gilberto, Wiltord 2		Campbell, Henry		Wiltord, Ljungberg		Henry				Henry, Gilberto 2		Pires, Hyypia (og)		Edu, Henry		Henry	

Above: *A fantastic season from Southampton's goalkeeper Antti Neimi kept them safely mid-table.*

Above, left: *Fulham's Sean Davis volleys home one of the goals of the season; Charlton's defence runs for cover.*

Far left: *Gérard Houllier eyes the clock as time and patience run out at Anfield. Houllier left Liverpool at the end of the season.*

Left: *Sol Campbell shields the ball as Arsenal battles to squeeze a draw out of its home tie with Charlton. Arsenal's defence was as important to its unbeaten run as its attack.*

11	Nov 1	27	12	Nov 8	30	13	Nov 22	33	14	Nov 30	34	15	Dec 6	35	16	Dec 14	38	17	Dec 20	39	18	Dec 26	42	19	Dec 29	45
No.		Pts	No.		Pts	No.		Pts	No.		Pts	No.		Pts	No.		Pts	No.		Pts	No.		Pts	No.		Pts
	Leeds United			Tottenham Hotspur			Birmingham City			Fulham			Leicester City			Blackburn Rovers			Bolton Wanderers			Wolverhampton Wanderers			Southampton	
	4-1			2-1			3-0			0-0			1-1			1-0			1-1			3-0			1-0	
	Henry 2, Pires, Gilberto			Pires, Ljungberg			Ljungberg, Bergkamp, Pires						Gilberto			Bergkamp			Pires			Henry 2, Craddock (og)			Pires	

Key

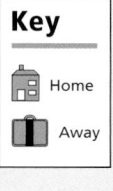 Home

Away

continued on next page

over the club all season. Although there was talent in abundance – especially with Kanoute, Defoe and Keane in attack – consistency, discipline, rigour and spirit were in scant supply. Manchester City followed close behind. Both Blackburn and Everton spent nearly the whole season perilously placed above the relegation zone.

Two of the relegation places went to newly-promoted teams. Wolves started so badly on its return to the Premiership that it was almost inconceivable that it could recover. Leicester, who had shown its usual tenacity for most of the season, slipped away quietly, undone by its mid-season madness in La Manga. The final twist in the morality tale of Leeds United was played out this season. The vast accumulated debts of the Ridsdale-O'Leary era hung ever more heavily over the club. Peter Reid presided over an appalling opening spell and, after losing 6-1 to Portsmouth, was shown the door. His replacement, Eddie Gray, never looked or sounded convincing and began his reign with a 2-0 defeat to Bolton. The rematch at the end of the year was the final straw. Leeds was rent asunder 4-1, displaying the shambolic defending that was the team's trademark during the campaign. Mark Viduka, whose disinterest in playing had moved in exact parallel with Leeds' relegation chances, unforgivably got himself sent off for his petulant kicking.

At last: after 128 years Middlesbrough wins something. Boudewijn Zenden celebrates after putting Middlesbrough two up.

Left: Going down: Paul Robinson (now at Spurs) consoles Alan Smith (now at Manchester United) as Leeds is relegated at Bolton.

Below, left: Steven Gerrard saved Liverpool's season with consistent displays of leadership, running and fantastic long passes.

Below: Harry Redknapp conjured an amazing final run of form from Portsmouth to keep them comfortably in the Premiership and somehow almost lost his job for doing so until chairman Mandaric came to his senses.

League Cup

2003–04 FINAL

February 29 – Millennium Stadium, Cardiff
Middlesbrough 2-1 Bolton
(Job 2, Wanderers
Zenden 7 pen) *(Davies 21)*
h/t: 2-1   **Att:** 72,634
Ref: M. Riley

FA Cup

2003–04 FINAL

May 22 – Millennium Stadium, Cardiff
Manchester 3-0 Millwall
United
(Ronaldo 44,
van Nistelrooy
65 pen, 80)
h/t: 1-0   **Att:** 71,350
Ref: Winter

International Club Performances 2003–04

CLUB	COMPETITION	PROGRESS
Arsenal	Champions League	Quarter-finals
Chelsea	Champions League	Semi-finals
Manchester United	Champions League	First Knockout Round
Newcastle United	Champions League	Qualifying Phase 3
	UEFA Cup	Semi-finals
Blackburn Rovers	UEFA Cup	1st Round
Liverpool	UEFA Cup	4th Round
Manchester City	UEFA Cup	2nd Round
Southampton	UEFA Cup	1st Round

Top Goalscorers 2003–04

PLAYER	CLUB	NATIONALITY	GOALS
Thierry Henry	Arsenal	French	30
Alan Shearer	Newcastle United	English	22
Ruud van Nistelrooy	Manchester United	Dutch	20

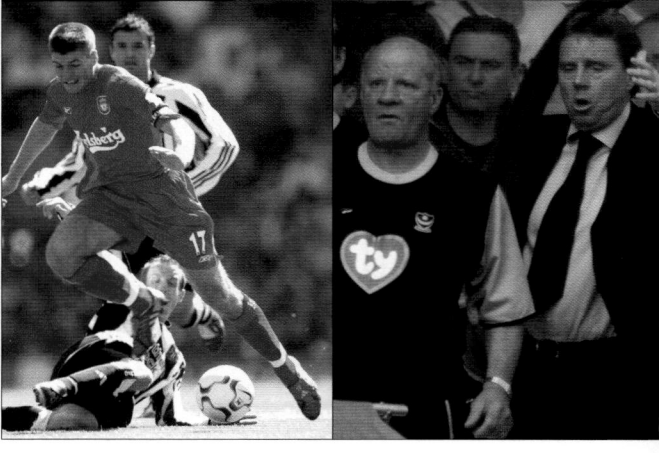

Arsenal's unbeaten run

continued from previous page

20 Jan 7 46	21 Jan 10 49	22 Jan 18 52	23 Feb 1 55	24 Feb 7 58	25 Feb 10 61	26 Feb 21 64	27 Feb 28 67	28 Mar 13 70	29 Mar 20 73
No. Pts	No. Pts	No. Pts	No. Pts	No. Pts	No. Pts	No. Pts	No. Pts	No. Pts	No. Pts
Everton	Middlesbrough	Aston Villa	Manchester City	Wolverhampton Wanderers	Southampton	Chelsea	Charlton Athletic	Blackburn Rovers	Bolton Wanderers
1-1	**4-1**	**2-0**	**2-1**	**3-1**	**2-0**	**2-1**	**2-1**	**2-0**	**2-1**
Kanu	Henry, Pires, Ljungberg, Queudrue (og)	Henry 2	Tarnat (og), Henry	Bergkamp, Henry, Toure	Henry 2	Vieira, Edu	Pires, Henry	Henry, Pires	Pires, Bergkamp

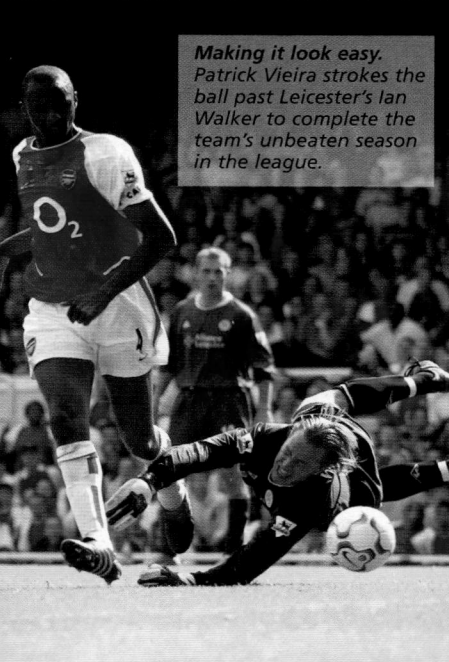

Making it look easy. Patrick Vieira strokes the ball past Leicester's Ian Walker to complete the team's unbeaten season in the league.

Above: *For a man who had clearly got his eye on the ball, Roman Abramovich does seem to stare into space a lot. Peter Kenyon does his serious soccer executive look.*

Left: *Claudio Ranieri takes a standing ovation on the last day at Stamford Bridge. Rarely can any manager have been treated so poorly for so long by his club.*

Below: *United relief. Manchester United celebrates with the FA Cup, its only silverware of a disappointing season.*

Arsenal celebrates its championship and unveils its unorthodox new signing, top left with baseball cap.

30	Mar 28	74	31	Apr 9	77	32	Apr 11	78	33	Apr 16	81	34	Apr 25	82	35	May 1	83	36	May 4	84	37	May 9	87	38	May 15	90	**Key**	
No.	🏠	Pts	No.	🏠	Pts	No.	💼	Pts	No.	🏠	Pts	No.	🏠	Pts	No.	🏠	Pts	No.	💼	Pts	No.	💼	Pts	No.	🏠	Pts	🏠	Home
Manchester United			Liverpool			Newcastle United			Leeds United			Tottenham Hotspur			Birmingham City			Portsmouth			Fulham			Leicester City			💼	Away
1-1			**4-2**			**0-0**			**5-0**			**2-2**			**0-0**			**1-1**			**1-0**			**2-1**				
Henry			Henry 3, Pires						Pires, Henry 4			Vieira, Pires						Reyes			Reyes			Henry, Vieira				

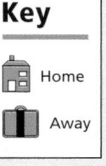

ENGLAND

Soccer in England

1846: Cambridge Rules drawn up	1845
	1850
1863: Formation of FA. First game under new rules played 19 December, Richmond v Barnes, drawn 0-0	1855
	1860
1870: First unofficial international, v Scotland, drawn 1-1, venue: London	1865
	1870
1872: First FA Cup Final First official international, v Scotland, drawn 0-0, venue: Partick	1875
	1880
1885: Professionalism legalized	1885
1888: First league championship	1890
1892: Second Division established	1895
1905: Affiliation to FIFA	1900
1908: Great Britain wins Olympic soccer tournament in London	1905
1912: Great Britain wins Olympic soccer tournament in Stockholm	1910
1923: Wembley Stadium opened and hosts its first FA Cup Final	1915
1924: Reaffiliation to FIFA	1920
1928: Resigned from FIFA	1925
	1930
	1935
1946: Reaffiliation to FIFA	1940
1949: Burnden Park, Bolton, 33 die and 500 injured in terrace crush	1945
1954: Affiliation to UEFA	1950
1961: League Cup first played	1955
1963: Tottenham Hotspur win the European Cup-Winners' Cup – a British club's first European prize	1960
1969: Women's Football Association formed	1965
1970: FA ban on women's teams lifted	1970
	1975
1989: Hillsborough disaster, 95 killed by crushing. Taylor report calls for all-seater stadiums	1980
1991: Ban on English clubs in Europe lifted	1985
1992: Premier League breaks away from FA	1990
1993: WFA dissolved. Women's soccer incorporated into FA	1995
	2000
1996: England hosts European Championships	2005

English soccer's finest hour – Bobby Moore holds up the 1966 World Cup.

1916–19: Seasons cancelled for war

1920: Resigned from FIFA. Third Division established

1921: English Ladies' FA founded. FA bans women's teams from FA member grounds. Fourth Division added, bottom division renamed Third Division North and South

1940–46: Football reduced to regional leagues for duration of war

1953: England beaten 6-3 at Wembley by Hungary

1958: Third Division North and South became Third and Fourth Divisions

1966: England hosts and wins World Cup

1972: First women's international, v Scotland, won 3-2, venue: Greenock

1983: WFA affiliated to FA

1985: Bradford fire, 56 killed. Heysel disaster, 39 killed after crowd disturbances, Liverpool v Juventus, European Cup Final. Beginning of five-year ban on English clubs in European football

2002: Demolition of Wembley Stadium begins

Key

	International soccer
	Affiliation to FIFA
	Affiliation to UEFA
	Women's soccer
	War
	Disaster

England: The main clubs

Arsenal
1886 — Team name with year of formation

● Club formed before 1912

★ Founder members of League (1888)

Champions (1888–1915)

Champions (1920–39)

Originated from a military institution

Originated from a cricket club

Originated from a school or college

Teachers' Association

Originated from a hockey club

Singers Cycle factory

Railway workers

Salter's Spring Works

Thames Ironworks

Originated from a church

Originated from a rugby club

Blackburn Rovers 1875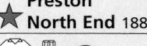

Bolton Wanderers 1874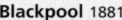
Christ Church (1874–77)

Preston North End 1881

Blackpool 1881
Formed after the break-up of Blackpool St. John's club Combined with South Shore (1899)

Blackpool

Liverpool 1892

Tranmere Rovers 1884
Belmont AFC (1884–85)

Everton 1878

Liverpool

St Domingo (1878–79)

Crewe Alexandra 18...

Manchester City 1887
Ardwick FC (1887–94) Amalgamation of West Gorton and Gorton Athletic

Manchester United 1878
Newton Heath LYR (1878–80), Newton Heath (1880–1902)

Stockport County 1883
Heaton Norris Rovers (1883–88), Heaton Norris (1888–90)

Stoke City 1863
Stoke Ramblers (1868–70), Stoke (1870–1925)

Derby County 1884

Wolverhampton Wanderers 1879
Merger of St Lukes (1877) and Wanderers Cricket Club

West Bromwich Albion 1879
West Bromwich Strollers (1878–81)

E N G L A N D

England

ORIGINS AND GROWTH OF SOCCER

ENGLISH SOCCER EMERGED from the coincidence of a rural folk soccer tradition and the sporting enthusiasm of England's upper-class public schools. Team games became a central part of the culture of these schools and soccer was the favourite sport. The wide variety of rules of the game at the time were settled with the formation of the world's first FA (1863). While many of the earliest clubs grew out of these schools, they were soon joined by clubs founded by works' teams, churches and boys' clubs from the industrial cities of the West Midlands and Lancashire. The amateur traditions of the south were surpassed in the 1880s by the alliance of working-class fans and players and middle-class directors leading to the creation of the world's first professional league in 1888.

Before the First World War all of today's leading clubs were in existence. However, the security of a hugely popular domestic game left England uninterested in international soccer. England had reluctantly joined FIFA in 1905 but withdrew in 1920 and again in 1928. The illusion of English dominance was crushed by failure at the 1950 World Cup and a 6-3 thrashing by Hungary at Wembley in 1953.

Pride was partly restored by World Cup victory in 1966 and a good record in Europe for English clubs in the 1970s and early 1980s. But the process of catch up seems to continue unabated.

ENGLAND

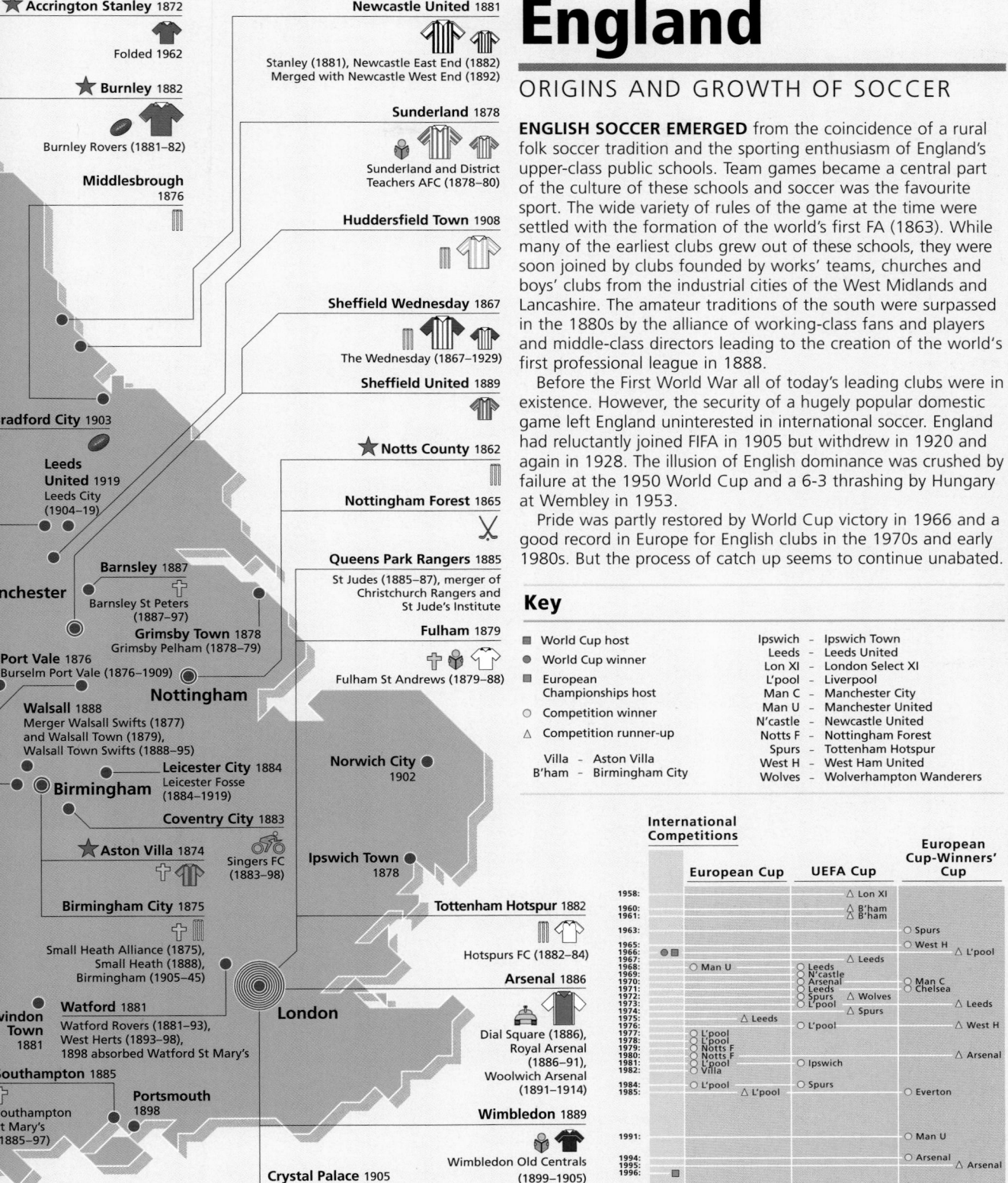

Accrington Stanley 1872
Folded 1962

Burnley 1882
Burnley Rovers (1881–82)

Middlesbrough 1876

Bradford City 1903

Leeds United 1919
Leeds City (1904–19)

anchester

Barnsley 1887
Barnsley St Peters (1887–97)

Grimsby Town 1878
Grimsby Pelham (1878–79)

Port Vale 1876
Burslem Port Vale (1876–1909)

Nottingham

Walsall 1888
Merger Walsall Swifts (1877) and Walsall Town (1879), Walsall Town Swifts (1888–95)

Leicester City 1884
Leicester Fosse (1884–1919)

Birmingham

Coventry City 1883

Aston Villa 1874
Singers FC (1883–98)

Birmingham City 1875
Small Heath Alliance (1875), Small Heath (1888), Birmingham (1905–45)

windon Town 1881

Watford 1881
Watford Rovers (1881–93), West Herts (1893–98), 1898 absorbed Watford St Mary's

Southampton 1885
Southampton St Mary's (1885–97)

Portsmouth 1898

West Ham United 1895
Thames Ironworks (1895–1900)

Newcastle United 1881
Stanley (1881), Newcastle East End (1882) Merged with Newcastle West End (1892)

Sunderland 1878
Sunderland and District Teachers AFC (1878–80)

Huddersfield Town 1908

Sheffield Wednesday 1867
The Wednesday (1867–1929)

Sheffield United 1889

Notts County 1862

Nottingham Forest 1865

Queens Park Rangers 1885
St Judes (1885–87), merger of Christchurch Rangers and St Jude's Institute

Fulham 1879
Fulham St Andrews (1879–88)

Norwich City 1902

Ipswich Town 1878

Tottenham Hotspur 1882
Hotspurs FC (1882–84)

Arsenal 1886
Dial Square (1886), Royal Arsenal (1886–91), Woolwich Arsenal (1891–1914)

Wimbledon 1889
Wimbledon Old Centrals (1899–1905)

Crystal Palace 1905

Charlton Athletic 1905

Chelsea 1905

London

Key

- ■ World Cup host
- ● World Cup winner
- ■ European Championships host
- ○ Competition winner
- △ Competition runner-up

Villa – Aston Villa
B'ham – Birmingham City

Ipswich – Ipswich Town
Leeds – Leeds United
Lon XI – London Select XI
L'pool – Liverpool
Man C – Manchester City
Man U – Manchester United
N'castle – Newcastle United
Notts F – Nottingham Forest
Spurs – Tottenham Hotspur
West H – West Ham United
Wolves – Wolverhampton Wanderers

International Competitions

	European Cup	UEFA Cup	European Cup-Winners' Cup
1958:		△ Lon XI	
1960:		△ B'ham	
1961:		△ B'ham	
1963:			○ Spurs
1965:			○ West H
1966:	■ ●		△ L'pool
1967:			
1968:	○ Man U	○ Leeds	○ Man C
1969:		△ Leeds	
1970:		○ N'castle	○ Man C
1971:		○ Arsenal	○ Chelsea
1972:		○ Leeds	
1973:		○ Spurs	△ Leeds
1974:		○ L'pool	
1975:		△ Wolves	
1977:	○ L'pool	△ Spurs	
1978:	○ L'pool		△ West H
1979:	○ Notts F	○ L'pool	
1980:	○ Notts F		
1981:	○ L'pool		△ Arsenal
1982:	○ Villa	○ Ipswich	
1984:	○ L'pool	○ Spurs	
1985:		△ L'pool	○ Everton
1991:			○ Man U
1994:			○ Arsenal
1995:			△ Arsenal
1996:	■		
1998:			○ Chelsea
1999:	○ Man U		
2000:			
2001:		○ L'pool	△ Arsenal

ENGLAND

Port Vale
(1950–)
VALE PARK
A53

HANLEY
Birthplace of
Stanley Matthews
VICTORIA GROUND

STOKE-ON-TRENT
BRITANNIA STADIUM

RECREATION GROUND
Port Vale
(1913–1950)

Stoke City
(1878–1997)

Stoke City
(1997–)

22,546

28,000

A50

A34

The Midlands

22,350	Capacity of stadium
	Stadium no longer in use for top-flight soccer
	Cricket ground
	Team colours
M8	Motorway
A82	Major road
1900	Champions
2000	Runners-up

Sir Stanley Matthews was born in Hanley, Stoke-on-Trent on 1 February 1915. He retired 50 years later. He is rightly regarded as the first great soccer player of the modern era.

DERBY COUNTY 1884

League	*1896, 1930, 36,* **72, 75**
FA Cup	*1898, 99, 1903,* **46**

Derby County
(1997–)
PRIDE PARK

THE BASEBALL GROUND

Derby County
(1895–1997)

Derby County
(1884–95)
Venue for the first FA Cup Final replay in 1886 between Blackburn Rovers and West Bromwich Albion

DERBY
THE RACECOURSE GROUND

33,597

STOKE CITY 1863

League Cup	*1964,* **72**

ASTON VILLA 1874

League	**1889, 94, 96, 97, 99, 1900, 03, 08, 10, 11, 13, 14, 31, 33, 81, 90, 93**
FA Cup	**1887,** *92,* **95, 97, 1905, 13, 20, 24,** *57,* **2000**
League Cup	**1961,** *63,* **71,** *75,* **77, 94, 96**
European Cup	**1982**
World Club Cup	*1982*

BIRMINGHAM CITY 1875

FA Cup	*1931, 56*
League Cup	**1963,** *2001*
Fairs Cup	*1960, 61*

Burton Wanderers
Members of the Football League 1894–97

BURTON UPON TRENT
DERBY TURN
PEEL CROFT

FA NATIONAL TRAINING CENTRE
Currently under construction

Burton Swifts
Members of the Football League 1892–1901

Burton United
Members of the Football League 1901–07. Merger of Burton Swifts and Burton Wanderers

A51

A518

WOLVERHAMPTON WANDERERS 1879

League	*1938, 39, 50,* **54,** *55,* **58, 59, 60**
FA Cup	*1889, 93, 96,* **1908,** *21, 39, 49, 60*
League Cup	**1974,** *80*
UEFA Cup	*1972*

A5

Wolverhampton Wanderers
M54
MOLINEUX
28,525

WOLVERHAMPTON

WEST BROMWICH
SALTER'S SPRING WORKS
West Bromwich Albion started as the works' team here. Originally called West Bromwich Strollers

Walsall
WALSALL
BESCOT STADIUM
M6
11,300

Aston Villa
VILLA PARK
43,275

M6

West Bromwich Albion
THE HAWTHORNS
M5
25,400

A458

DUDLEY

WEST BROMWICH ALBION 1879

League	**1920,** *25,* **54**
FA Cup	*1886, 87,* **88,** *92,* **95,** *1912,* **31,** *35,* **54, 68**
League Cup	**1966,** *67, 70*

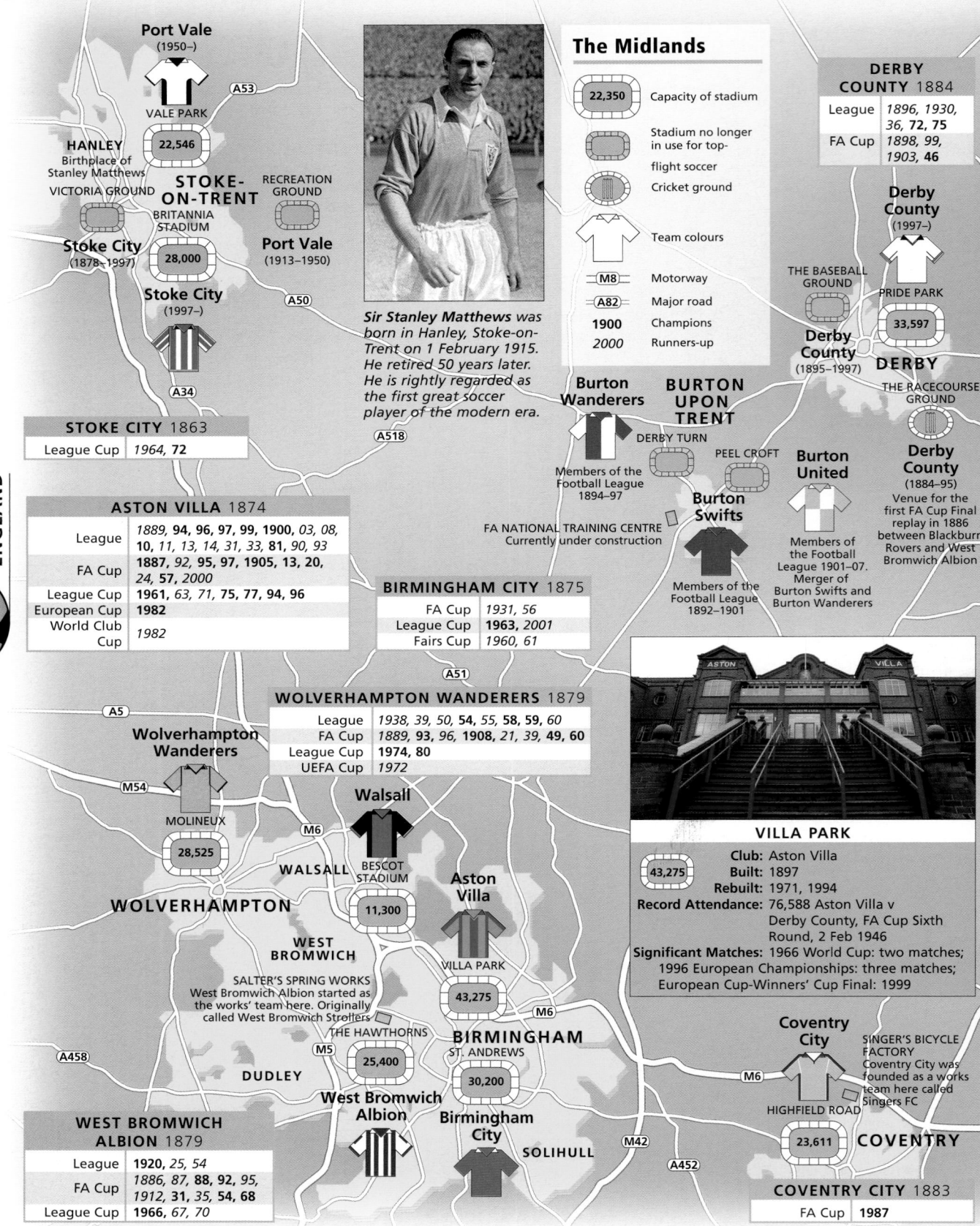

VILLA PARK

43,275

Club: Aston Villa
Built: 1897
Rebuilt: 1971, 1994
Record Attendance: 76,588 Aston Villa v Derby County, FA Cup Sixth Round, 2 Feb 1946
Significant Matches: 1966 World Cup: two matches; 1996 European Championships: three matches; European Cup-Winners' Cup Final: 1999

Coventry City
SINGER'S BICYCLE FACTORY
Coventry City was founded as a works team here called Singers FC
HIGHFIELD ROAD
23,611
COVENTRY

BIRMINGHAM
ST. ANDREWS
Birmingham City
30,200
SOLIHULL

M42
A452

COVENTRY CITY 1883

FA Cup	**1987**

The Midlands

SOCCER CENTERS

NOTTS COUNTY 1862	
FA Cup	*1891*, **94**

NOTTINGHAM FOREST 1865	
League	*1967*, **78**, *79*
FA Cup	**1898**, *1959*, **91**
League Cup	**1978**, **79**, *80*, **89**, **90**, **92**
European Cup	**1979**, **80**
World Club Cup	*1980*

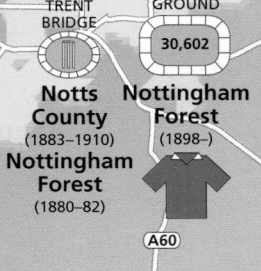

Notts County (1910–)
MEADOW LANE
M1
21,300
TRENT BRIDGE

NOTTINGHAM
CITY GROUND
30,602

Notts County (1883–1910)
Nottingham Forest (1880–82)

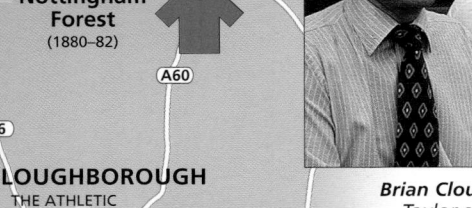

Nottingham Forest (1898–)
A60

A6

LOUGHBOROUGH
THE ATHLETIC GROUND

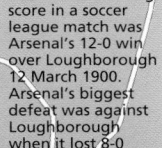

Loughborough Athletic

Members of the Football League 1895–1900

The record-winning score in a soccer league match was Arsenal's 12-0 win over Loughborough 12 March 1900. Arsenal's biggest defeat was against Loughborough when it lost 8-0 12 December 1896

LEICESTER
M1
FILBERT STREET

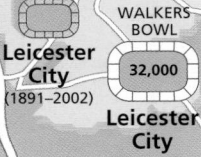

WALKERS BOWL
32,000

Leicester City (1891–2002)
M69

Leicester City (2002–)

M1

THE CLUSTER OF CITIES that make up the English Midlands are home to some of the oldest professional clubs in England; six were founder members of the Football League in 1888 (Stoke City, West Bromwich Albion, Aston Villa, Notts County, Derby County and Wolverhampton Wanderers). By the turn of the century, Leicester Fosse (later Leicester City), Nottingham Forest, Small Heath (later Birmingham City) and Loughborough had joined them. Although Loughborough was unable to cut it in the professional leagues, and became defunct in 1900, Coventry's entry into the Second Division in 1919 kept the Midlands' numbers up. The industrial economy of the region provided both works' teams and a large number of spectators. Coventry City was founded as a works' team at the Singer's bicycle factory, West Bromwich at a spring factory in Smethwick, while Birmingham, Aston Villa, Wolves and Derby emerged out of cricket clubs.

Villa dominant

Across the last 120 years Aston Villa has been the dominant team in the region. In the first 12 years of English professional soccer, Villa won five league championships and three FA Cups, including the double in 1897. Villa remained a force in the First Division for three decades before its first relegation in 1936, after which followed a spiral of decline, culminating in relegation to the Third Division in 1970. But revival came in the shape of manager Ron Saunders who led the team to the title in 1981 and the European Cup in 1982. Wolves (in the 1950s), Derby and Nottingham Forest in the 1970s have all risen to the top of the English game, and under the unique direction of Brian Clough, Forest took the European Cup back-to-back in 1979 and 1980. But the 1990s and beyond have been harder times for the region's clubs. Under the Doug Ellis regime of recent years, Villa has remained on the fringe of the title race despite considerable spending; but it is now being challenged by Birmingham City as the region's top team.

Brian Clough (left) and Peter Taylor steered Nottingham Forest to back-to-back European Cup victories in 1979 and 1980.

LEICESTER CITY 1884	
League	*1929*
FA Cup	*1949, 61, 63, 69*
League Cup	**1964**, *65*, **97**, *99*, **2000**

West Bromwich Albion began life as West Bromwich Strollers – the works' team of Salter's Spring Works in the Smethwick area of the city.

London

SOCCER CENTER

AS SOCCER EMERGED out of the public school and university system in England in the 1850s, old boy and graduate networks created teams all over Victorian London, where their players were busy staffing the hub of the British Empire. When the FA was founded in 1863 in Central London, the representatives of the clubs all came from the city. Replays aside, London has hosted all but eight of the FA Cup Finals since the first was played at Kennington Oval in 1872. For a moment in the late 19th century it looked as if London might be displaced as the soccer capital of the country. The newly professional Soccer League was a distinctly northern institution, with its headquarters in Lancashire, and not a single London team appeared in the First Division until Woolwich Arsenal in 1904. However, the size, wealth and power of London has steadily brought more clubs into contention: Chelsea made its debut in 1907, Tottenham in 1909, West Ham in 1922. London's place was sealed with the opening of the national stadium – Wembley – in 1923 (see Wembley box overleaf). More recently, the breakaway Premier League has based itself in London alongside the other key institutions in modern English soccer – the stock market in the City of London and the headquarters of the major television stations.

Despite great strength in depth (with half a dozen London teams in the Premiership at any one time) London's soccer strength has been concentrated for most of the 20th century in the north London rivals Arsenal and Tottenham (see North London box overleaf). Beyond this, constant success has been thin on the ground. South of the river, Crystal Palace have struggled to survive economically while Wimbledon's owners have abandoned the fight and moved the club to Milton Keynes. In the east, West Ham has ridden the modern wave of soccer money well, but has yet to replicate its cup successes of the mid-1960s. In the west, Chelsea, buoyed up on the combined fortunes of Ken Bates and Matthew Harding, turned on the style to take domestic and European cups in the 1990s. The club is now in the hands of Russian billionaire Roman Abramovich and aiming higher. Its neighbour Fulham is on the rise, care of Mohamed Al Fayed, while QPR remains mired in lower division debt.

ENGLAND

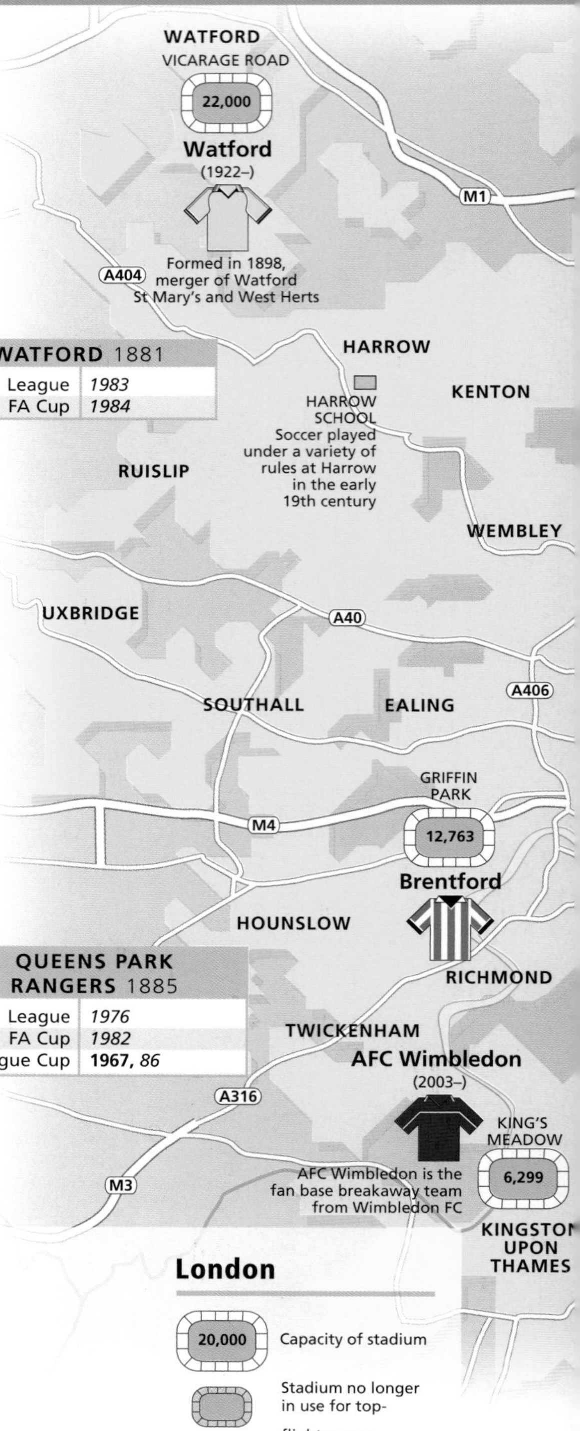

WATFORD — Vicarage Road

22,000

Watford
(1922–)

Formed in 1898, merger of Watford St Mary's and West Herts

WATFORD 1881	
League	*1983*
FA Cup	*1984*

HARROW

KENTON

HARROW SCHOOL
Soccer played under a variety of rules at Harrow in the early 19th century

WEMBLEY

RUISLIP

UXBRIDGE

SOUTHALL

EALING

GRIFFIN PARK

12,763

Brentford

HOUNSLOW

RICHMOND

QUEENS PARK RANGERS 1885	
League	*1976*
FA Cup	*1982*
League Cup	**1967**, 86

TWICKENHAM

AFC Wimbledon
(2003–)

KING'S MEADOW

6,299

AFC Wimbledon is the fan base breakaway team from Wimbledon FC

KINGSTON UPON THAMES

London

20,000	Capacity of stadium
	Stadium no longer in use for top-flight soccer
	Cricket ground
	Team colours
M1	Motorway
A20	Major road
1900	Champions
2000	Runners-up

Queens Park Rangers has played at 12 different grounds during its history – including White City during 1962–63 – more than any other Football League Club.

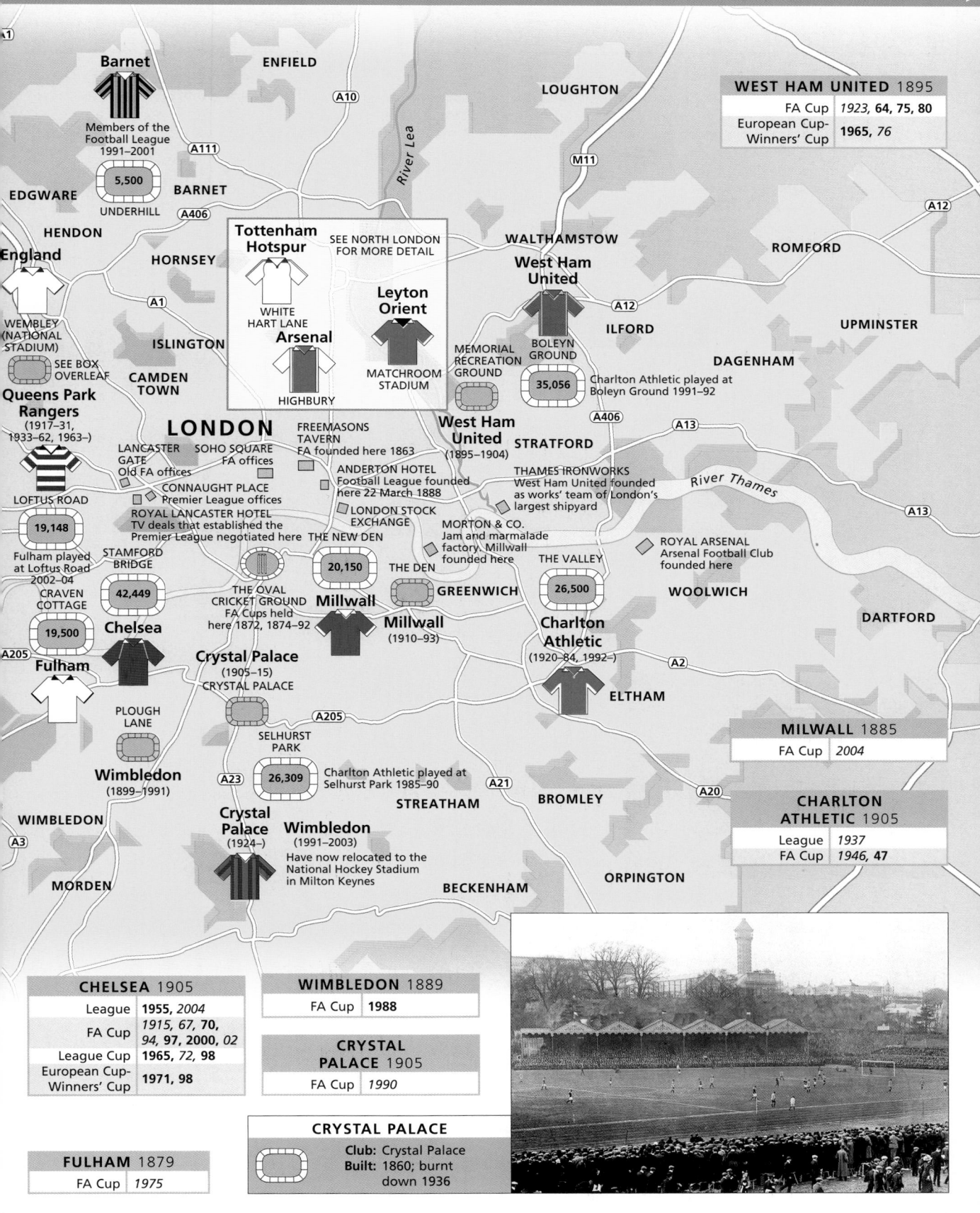

Barnet

Members of the Football League 1991–2001

5,500

UNDERHILL

WEST HAM UNITED 1895

FA Cup	*1923*, 64, 75, 80
European Cup-Winners' Cup	1965, *76*

ENFIELD

LOUGHTON

A10

WALTHAMSTOW

EDGWARE

BARNET

A111

A406

ROMFORD

HENDON

HORNSEY

M11

West Ham United

England

A1

ILFORD

A12

UPMINSTER

WEMBLEY (NATIONAL STADIUM)

SEE BOX OVERLEAF

ISLINGTON

CAMDEN TOWN

Tottenham Hotspur

WHITE HART LANE

SEE NORTH LONDON FOR MORE DETAIL

Leyton Orient

MATCHROOM STADIUM

BOLEYN GROUND

35,056

DAGENHAM

Charlton Athletic played at Boleyn Ground 1991–92

Queens Park Rangers

(1917–31, 1933–62, 1963–)

Arsenal

HIGHBURY

MEMORIAL RECREATION GROUND

STRATFORD

A406

A13

LONDON

FREEMASONS TAVERN
FA founded here 1863

West Ham United

(1895–1904)

A13

LANCASTER GATE
Old FA offices

SOHO SQUARE
FA offices

ANDERTON HOTEL
Football League founded here 22 March 1888

River Thames

LOFTUS ROAD

19,148

CONNAUGHT PLACE
Premier League offices

ROYAL LANCASTER HOTEL
TV deals that established the Premier League negotiated here

LONDON STOCK EXCHANGE

THAMES IRONWORKS
West Ham United founded as works' team of London's largest shipyard

Fulham played at Loftus Road 2002–04

STAMFORD BRIDGE

THE NEW DEN

MORTON & CO.
Jam and marmalade factory. Millwall founded here

THE VALLEY

ROYAL ARSENAL
Arsenal Football Club founded here

CRAVEN COTTAGE

42,449

20,150

THE DEN

26,500

WOOLWICH

19,500

Chelsea

THE OVAL CRICKET GROUND
FA Cups held here 1872, 1874–92

Millwall

GREENWICH

Millwall

(1910–93)

Charlton Athletic

(1920–84, 1992–)

DARTFORD

A205

Fulham

PLOUGH LANE

Crystal Palace

(1905–15)
CRYSTAL PALACE

ELTHAM

A2

MILWALL 1885

FA Cup	*2004*

19,500

Wimbledon

(1899–1991)

SELHURST PARK

A205

26,309

Charlton Athletic played at Selhurst Park 1985–90

A21

A20

CHARLTON ATHLETIC 1905

League	*1937*
FA Cup	*1946*, 47

A3

WIMBLEDON

Crystal Palace

(1924–)

A23

Wimbledon

(1991–2003)
Have now relocated to the National Hockey Stadium in Milton Keynes

STREATHAM

BROMLEY

MORDEN

BECKENHAM

ORPINGTON

CHELSEA 1905

League	**1955**, *2004*
FA Cup	*1915*, 67, **70**, 94, **97**, **2000**, *02*
League Cup	**1965**, *72*, **98**
European Cup-Winners' Cup	**1971**, **98**

WIMBLEDON 1889

FA Cup	**1988**

CRYSTAL PALACE 1905

FA Cup	*1990*

CRYSTAL PALACE

Club: Crystal Palace
Built: 1860; burnt down 1936

FULHAM 1879

FA Cup	*1975*

NORTH LONDON

London's soccer-playing power has been gathered in north London for almost a century. To the east of both clubs are the great stretches of Hackney Marshes where amateur soccer flourishes on a Sunday, but on Saturdays attention turns west. Local schoolboys founded Tottenham Hotspur in 1882. The club first played at Northumberland Park, close to the ancestral home of Henry Percy (nicknamed Harry Hotspur by Shakespeare) before settling at White Hart Lane in 1899. Arsenal began life south of the river in 1886 as Dial Square FC, a works' team from the Royal Arsenal in Woolwich. The team soon turned professional, changing its name to Royal Arsenal in 1891 before migrating north to settle at Highbury in 1913. Tottenham was the first to win a major trophy, but it was Arsenal in the early 1930s under Herbert Chapman that first won the league and, for a time, dominated English soccer. Tottenham has regularly achieved cup success at home and abroad, as well as winning the first double of the 20th century in 1961, but it is Arsenal that has pulled ahead in its consistent capacity to challenge for the title (winning the double in 1971, 98 and 2002). Tottenham is often cast as London's Jewish team, and the area is certainly one of the strongholds of English Jewry, but in reality Arsenal's fans and board of directors seem to draw on London's Jews in equal number.

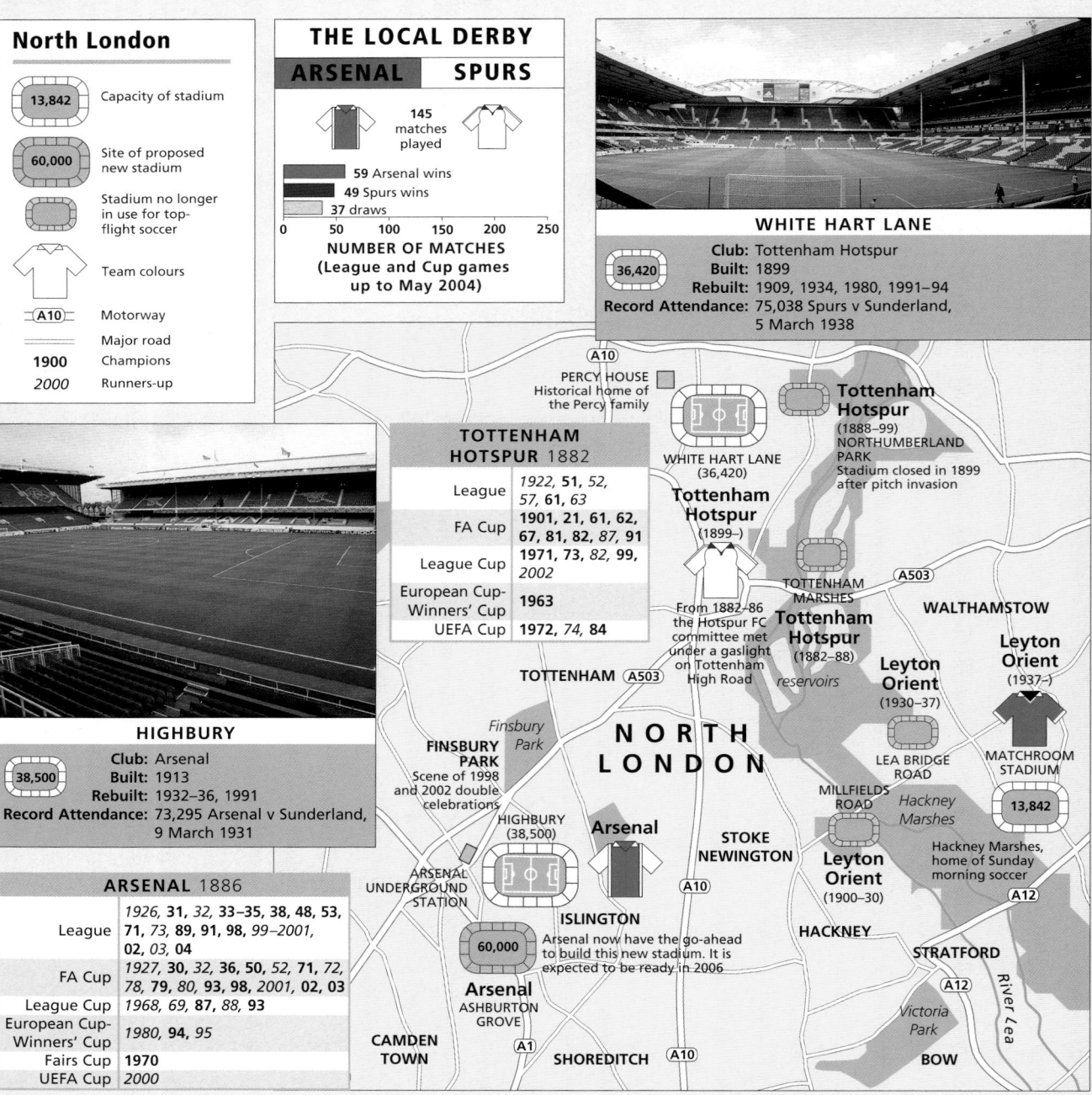

North London

13,842	Capacity of stadium
60,000	Site of proposed new stadium
	Stadium no longer in use for top-flight soccer
	Team colours
A10	Motorway
	Major road
1900	Champions
2000	Runners-up

THE LOCAL DERBY

ARSENAL — **SPURS**

145 matches played

59 Arsenal wins
49 Spurs wins
37 draws

0   50   100   150   200   250

NUMBER OF MATCHES
(League and Cup games up to May 2004)

WHITE HART LANE

36,420
Club: Tottenham Hotspur
Built: 1899
Rebuilt: 1909, 1934, 1980, 1991–94
Record Attendance: 75,038 Spurs v Sunderland, 5 March 1938

ENGLAND

HIGHBURY

38,500
Club: Arsenal
Built: 1913
Rebuilt: 1932–36, 1991
Record Attendance: 73,295 Arsenal v Sunderland, 9 March 1931

TOTTENHAM HOTSPUR 1882

League	1922, **51**, *52*, *57*, **61**, *63*
FA Cup	**1901**, **21**, **61**, **62**, **67**, **81**, **82**, *87*, **91**
League Cup	**1971**, **73**, *82*, **99**, **2002**
European Cup-Winners' Cup	**1963**
UEFA Cup	**1972**, **74**, **84**

ARSENAL 1886

League	1926, **31**, *32*, 33–35, **38**, **48**, **53**, **71**, *73*, **89**, **91**, **98**, *99–2001*, **02**, *03*, **04**
FA Cup	*1927*, **30**, *32*, **36**, **50**, *52*, **71**, *72*, *78*, *79*, **80**, **93**, **98**, *2001*, **02**, **03**
League Cup	*1968*, **69**, *87*, **88**, *93*
European Cup-Winners' Cup	**1980**, **94**, *95*
Fairs Cup	**1970**
UEFA Cup	*2000*

PERCY HOUSE
Historical home of the Percy family

WHITE HART LANE
(36,420)

Tottenham Hotspur
(1888–99)
NORTHUMBERLAND PARK
Stadium closed in 1899 after pitch invasion

Tottenham Hotspur
(1899–)

A10

A503

TOTTENHAM MARSHES

Tottenham Hotspur
(1882–88)

reservoirs

From 1882–86 the Hotspur FC committee met under a gaslight on Tottenham High Road

TOTTENHAM **A503**

WALTHAMSTOW

Leyton Orient
(1937–)

MATCHROOM STADIUM

13,842

Leyton Orient
(1930–37)

LEA BRIDGE ROAD

N O R T H   L O N D O N

Finsbury Park

FINSBURY PARK
Scene of 1998 and 2002 double celebrations

HIGHBURY
(38,500)

Arsenal

ARSENAL UNDERGROUND STATION

ISLINGTON

60,000
Arsenal now have the go-ahead to build this new stadium. It is expected to be ready in 2006

Arsenal
ASHBURTON GROVE

CAMDEN TOWN

A1

SHOREDITCH

A10

STOKE NEWINGTON

A10

MILLFIELDS ROAD

Hackney Marshes

Leyton Orient
(1900–30)

HACKNEY

Hackney Marshes, home of Sunday morning soccer

A12

STRATFORD

A12

Victoria Park

BOW

River Lea

WEMBLEY

Club:	None; national stadium
Built:	1923
Original Capacity:	100,000 approx
Rebuilt:	1948, 1963, 1990
Record Attendance:	Approx 200,000, Bolton v West Ham, FA Cup Final, 1923
Significant Matches:	1966 World Cup: nine matches including semi-final, 3rd place play-off, Final; 1996 European Championships: six matches, including semi-final, Final; European Cup Final: 1963, 68, 71, 78, 92; European Cup-Winners' Cup Final: 1965, 93

Closed

PC Scorey and his legendary horse Billy organize the huge crowd at Wembley in April 1923. The first-ever FA Cup Final at the new stadium, between West Ham and Bolton, attracted some 250,000 spectators – and only the self-discipline of the fans and the police, led by the white horse, averted a possible disaster.

WEMBLEY STADIUM

Designed by Sir John Simpson and Maxwell Ayrton, Wembley, opened in 1923, was originally the centrepiece of the British Empire Exhibition. It took a mere 300 days to build, cost £750,000 and staged its first soccer match – the 'White Horse' FA Cup – in April that year. But internationals and the FA Cup Final were not enough to sustain the vast stadium, and it was only saved by the investment of Arthur Elvin, who brought greyhound racing and speedway to Wembley. In its lifetime, Wembley also hosted the 1948 Olympic Games, and sports such as boxing, American soccer, and rugby league, as well as music concerts.

But it is for soccer that Wembley is best known: 77 FA Cup Finals, innumerable internationals, as well as the finals of the 1966 World Cup, the 1996 European Championships and numerous European Cup Finals. Nostalgia aside, the stadium's facilities, sightlines and atmosphere have been in steady decline, and the decision to rebuild Wembley with a mixture of government, lottery and private money saw it stage its last match in 2000. However, the enormous cost of the proposed rebuild, including the demolition of the iconic twin towers, has foundered in cost overruns and hubris. After innumerable financial reassessments and the abandonment of plans for hotels and offices, the redevelopment plan was rescued by the intervention of a German bank. The financial future of Wembley Stadium hinges on the successful sale of a considerable number of premium priced seats. While this may secure the balance sheet its impact on the atmosphere inside the stadium on a matchday remains to be seen.

February 2003: the most iconic buildings in world soccer are summarily torn down. The demolition and rebuilding of the stadium has proved so controversial that no one, including the architects, are allowed on to the demolition site.

Merseyside

SOCCER CENTER

AT THE CENTRE of the Merseyside region is the city of Liverpool, and close to its heart is Stanley Park, site of the stadiums of the city's eternal rivals, Everton and Liverpool. In their great shadow, smaller teams (like Bootle and South Liverpool) have withered, and only Tranmere Rovers on the Wirral peninsula across the Mersey has survived. In the city's hinterland, soccer has been abandoned and rugby league has grown up in the available sporting spaces. Everton was founded in 1878 out of a church team playing as St. Domingo's. Immediate popularity made the club a founder member of the Football League in 1888. In 1892 the club split, with John Houlding, owner of the Anfield ground at which they played, forming Liverpool, while the rest of the club headed to the other side of the park to play at Goodison Park.

Fierce and bitter rivalry

Both teams have garnered fanatical support across the city, and although Houlding was an active member of the Protestant Orange order, no sectarian (Catholic-Protestant) division between the clubs has ever emerged. Nonetheless, rivalry is fierce and bitter. Everton was the stronger side for the first half of the 20th century, its peak coming when it won the 1928 league title courtesy of a record-breaking 60 goals from its centre-forward Dixie Dean. But in the modern era, it is Liverpool that has been dominant. With Bill Shankly's arrival in 1959, successive dynasties of players and managers were created, and style and success were intertwined at Anfield. As the city declined through grim years of de-industrialization and unemployment, the team surged, winning ten league titles and four European Cups between 1976 and 1990. But the Heysel and Hillsborough disasters seemed to bring an end to that glorious era. Over a decade on from Hillsborough, Liverpool has risen again, Everton has rediscovered its form under David Moyes and both clubs are looking to build new stadiums.

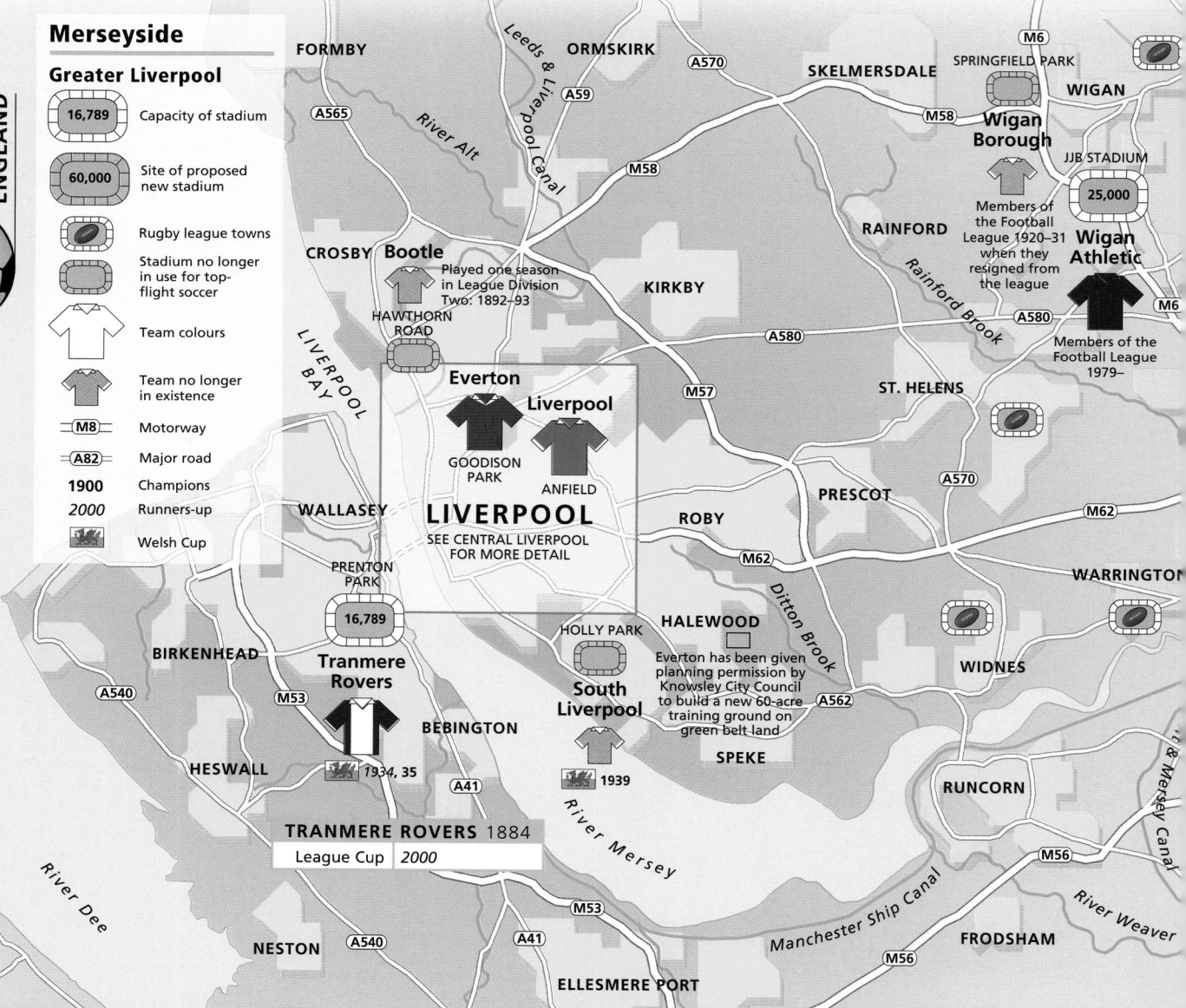

Merseyside

Greater Liverpool

16,789	Capacity of stadium
60,000	Site of proposed new stadium
	Rugby league towns
	Stadium no longer in use for top-flight soccer
	Team colours
	Team no longer in existence
M8	Motorway
A82	Major road
1900	Champions
2000	Runners-up
	Welsh Cup

ENGLAND

FORMBY · ORMSKIRK · SKELMERSDALE · SPRINGFIELD PARK · WIGAN · Wigan Borough · JJB STADIUM · Wigan Athletic · 25,000

Members of the Football League 1920–31 when they resigned from the league

Members of the Football League 1979–

A565 · A570 · A59 · River Alt · Leeds & Liverpool Canal · M58 · M6 · M58 · RAINFORD · Rainford Brook · A580 · A580 · M6

CROSBY · Bootle · HAWTHORN ROAD · Played one season in League Division Two: 1892–93 · KIRKBY · ST. HELENS

LIVERPOOL BAY · Everton · GOODISON PARK · Liverpool · ANFIELD · **LIVERPOOL** · SEE CENTRAL LIVERPOOL FOR MORE DETAIL · M57 · ROBY · PRESCOT · A570 · M62

WALLASEY · M62 · HALEWOOD · Ditton Brook · WARRINGTON

PRENTON PARK · 16,789 · HOLLY PARK · Everton has been given planning permission by Knowsley City Council to build a new 60-acre training ground on green belt land · WIDNES

BIRKENHEAD · Tranmere Rovers · M53 · South Liverpool · A562 · SPEKE · RUNCORN

A540 · 1934, 35 · BEBINGTON · 1939 · Manchester Ship Canal · FRODSHAM · River Weaver

HESWALL · A41 · River Mersey

TRANMERE ROVERS 1884

League Cup	2000

River Dee · NESTON · A540 · A41 · M53 · ELLESMERE PORT · M56

GOODISON PARK

40,260

Club: Everton
Built: 1892
Original Capacity: 11,000
Rebuilt: 1906–9, 1926, 1938, 1994
Record Attendance: 78,299 Everton v Liverpool, 18 Sept 1948. Record for women's match: 53,000 for Dick Kerr's Ladies v St Helens, 26 Dec 1920
Significant Matches: 1966 World Cup: three matches including semi-final

Policemen help a fan out of the Anfield Kop before a league match in 1966 – when full during those years, the Kop had a capacity of 28,000 people, all standing.

ENGLAND

ANFIELD

45,362

Club: Liverpool
Built: 1884
Original Capacity: Approximately 10,000
Rebuilt: 1906 (the Kop), 1963, 1990–98
Record Attendance: 61,905 Liverpool v Wolverhampton Wanderers, FA Cup 4th Round, 2 Feb 1952
Significant Matches: 1996 European Championships: three matches

EVERTON 1878	
League	*1890,* **91,** *95, 1902, 05, 09, 12,* **15, 28, 32, 39, 63, 70, 85, 86, 87**
FA Cup	*1893, 97,* **1906,** *07, 33, 66, 68,* **84,** *85,* **86,** *89,* **95**
League Cup	*1977, 84*
European Cup-Winners' Cup	**1985**

THE LOCAL DERBY

EVERTON   LIVERPOOL

172 matches played

■ 54 Everton wins
■ 63 Liverpool wins
□ 55 draws

0 50 100 150 200 250
NUMBER OF MATCHES
(League only up to May 2004)

BOOTLE

Everton
GOODISON PARK (40,260)

KIRKDALE

In a post-Hillsborough display of solidarity, a chain of soccer scarves was hung between the two stadiums

WALTON

Liverpool
NEW ANFIELD
A5058
60,000
Stanley Park

A580

LITTLEWOODS POOLS
Owned by the Moores family, major shareholders at Liverpool, Littlewoods have made a fortune from the Pools, a soccer betting system

NORRIS GREEN

MELWOOD
Liverpool training ground

SANDON HOTEL
In 1892 Everton and Liverpool split into two clubs at a meeting in this hotel

ST. DOMINGO'S METHODIST HALL
Everton began life here as St. Domingo's

ANFIELD (45,362)
Everton at Anfield 1884–92

Liverpool

CENTRAL LIVERPOOL

BELLEFIELD
Everton training ground. Due to close in 2006 when new training ground opens in Halewood

EVERTON

EVERTON BROW
The tower on Everton's badge is based on the single tower prison built on Everton Brow in 1787

STONEYCROFT
A57

Town Hall and St George's Hall are both sites of the clubs' victory celebrations

TOWN HALL

ST. GEORGE'S HALL

METROPOLITAN CATHEDRAL (Catholic)

Memorial plaques to the Hillsborough victims were laid in both cathedrals

River Mersey

55,000

Everton
KING'S DOCK
Everton have been forced to abandon their plans for King's Dock for financial reasons

LIVERPOOL CATHEDRAL (Anglican)
A562

TOXTETH

BIRKENHEAD

LIVERPOOL 1892	
League	*1899,* **1901,** *06, 10, 22, 23, 47, 64, 66,* **73, 74, 75, 76, 77,** *78,* **79, 80,** *82–84,* **85, 86, 87, 88,** *89,* **90, 91,** *2002*
FA Cup	*1914, 50,* **65,** *71,* **74,** *77,* **86, 88, 89, 92, 96, 2001**
League Cup	*1978,* **81–84,** *87,* **95,** *2001, 03*
European Cup	**1977, 78, 81, 84, 85**
European Cup-Winners' Cup	*1966*
UEFA Cup	**1973, 76, 2001**
World Club Cup	*1981, 84*

Manchester

SOCCER CENTER

ALTHOUGH SOCCER WAS FIRST DEVELOPED and codified in the public schools and universities of southern England, its transformation into a professional mass-spectator sport was centred on Lancashire – and on the periphery of Manchester and a little further north are many of the country's first professional teams. Some of the key meetings that preceded the Football League's creation took place in Manchester, as did the formation of the Professional Footballers' Association.

The heart and soul of the city
Within Manchester itself, the game took longer to mature. Manchester United began life as a railway works' team in Newton Heath to the north-east of the city centre, while Manchester City was formed from the merger of small teams in the Ardwick area

to the south-east. The rivalry between the two has taken on a religious dimension, with United inclined towards the Catholic community and regularly fielding Scottish and Irish players and City towards the Protestant community. But those sectarian undertones have been lost in what has become a conflict for the soul of the city. United, the richest and most famous club in the world, garners support from every continent, its stands filled with out-of-towners. City, Manchester's own authentic, local team, has stands filled by the Moss Side faithful, where resilience in the face of disaster on and off the pitch is worn as a badge of honour.

Although City has had moments of ascendancy – between the wars, and in the early 1970s when it sent United down with a Denis Law backheel – United has cast an awesome shadow over its rival, with two league titles before the First World War, three in the 1950s before the Munich air disaster, two in the 60s, Sir Matt Busby's European Cup triumph in 1968 and, under Alex Ferguson, seven league titles and the European Cup as one third of a treble in 1999. Nonetheless, City appears to be on its way back, with more stable finances, an unflinching fan base and a move to the City of Manchester Stadium in August 2003.

ENGLAND

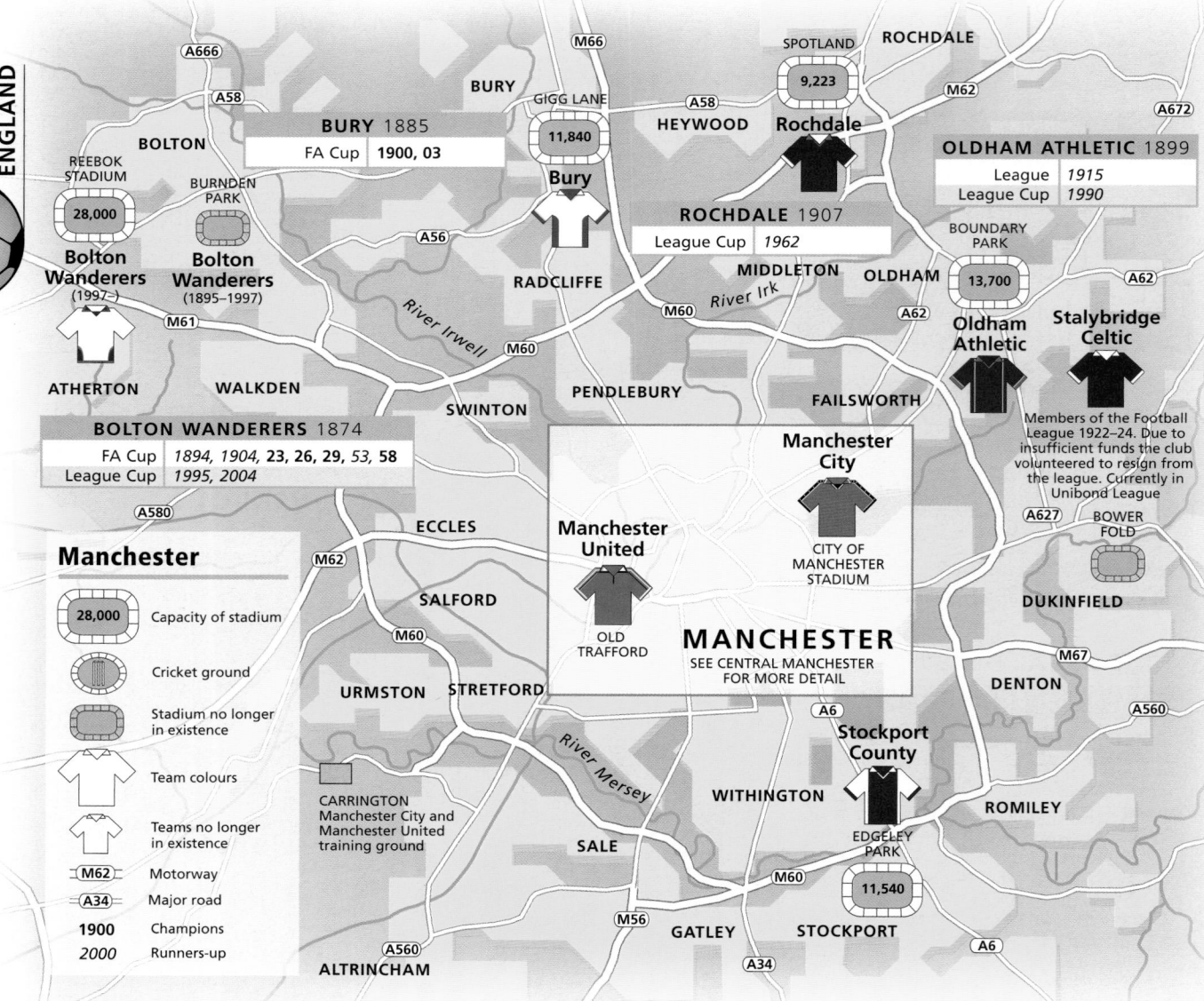

BURY 1885

FA Cup	1900, 03

ROCHDALE 1907

League Cup	1962

OLDHAM ATHLETIC 1899

League	1915
League Cup	1990

BOLTON WANDERERS 1874

FA Cup	1894, 1904, 23, 26, 29, 53, 58
League Cup	1995, 2004

Stalybridge Celtic — Members of the Football League 1922–24. Due to insufficient funds the club volunteered to resign from the league. Currently in Unibond League

Manchester

28,000	Capacity of stadium
	Cricket ground
	Stadium no longer in existence
	Team colours
	Teams no longer in existence
M62	Motorway
A34	Major road
1900	Champions
2000	Runners-up

CARRINGTON Manchester City and Manchester United training ground

Manchester United — OLD TRAFFORD

Manchester City — CITY OF MANCHESTER STADIUM

MANCHESTER SEE CENTRAL MANCHESTER FOR MORE DETAIL

Stockport County — EDGELEY PARK

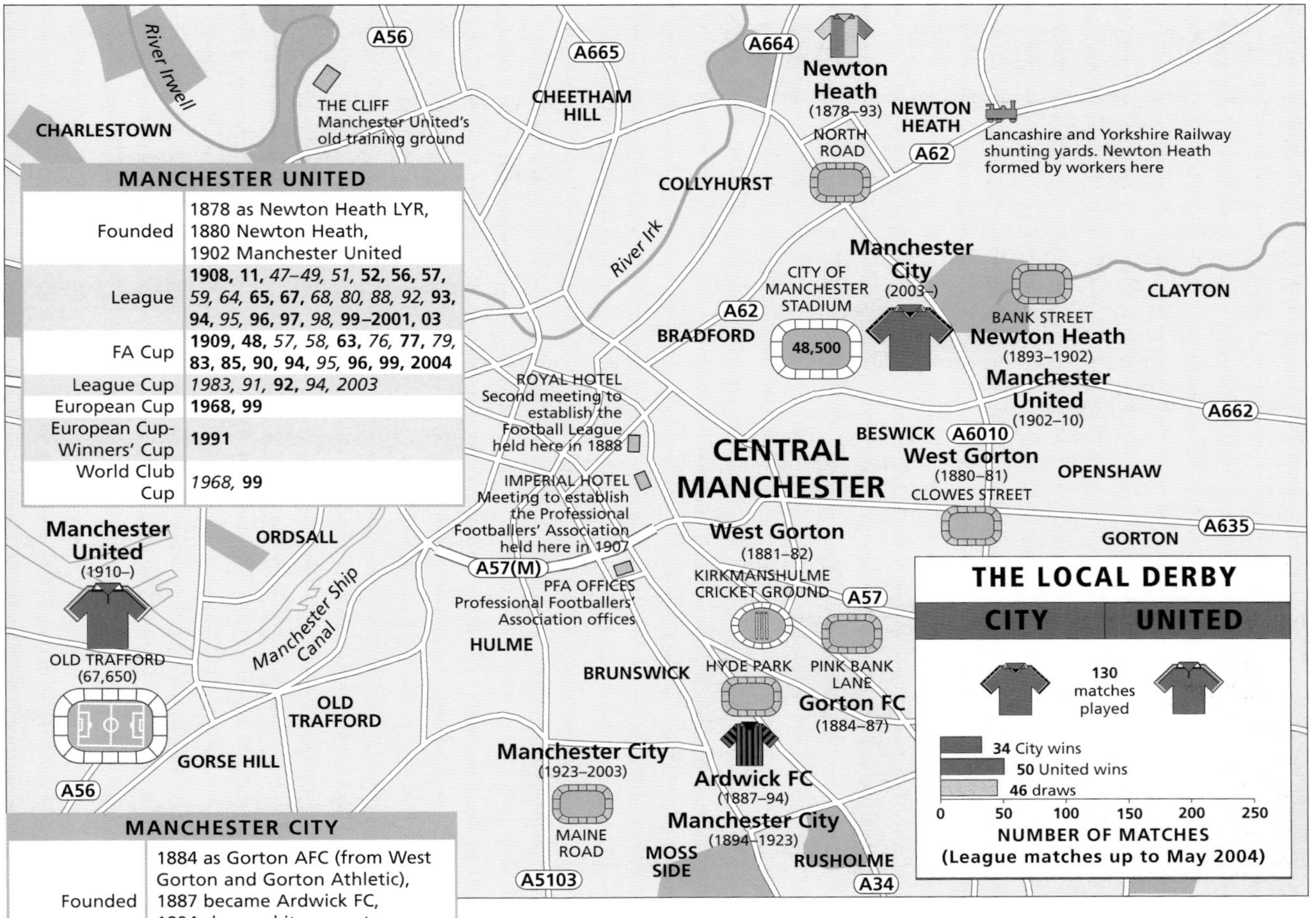

MANCHESTER UNITED

Founded	1878 as Newton Heath LYR, 1880 Newton Heath, 1902 Manchester United
League	1908, 11, *47–49, 51,* **52, 56, 57,** *59, 64,* **65, 67,** *68, 80,* **88, 92, 93, 94, 95, 96, 97, 98, 99–2001,** *03*
FA Cup	**1909,** *48, 57, 58,* **63,** *76,* **77,** *79, 83,* **85, 90, 94,** *95,* **96, 99, 2004**
League Cup	*1983,* **91,** *92,* **94,** *2003*
European Cup	**1968, 99**
European Cup-Winners' Cup	**1991**
World Club Cup	*1968,* **99**

MANCHESTER CITY

Founded	1884 as Gorton AFC (from West Gorton and Gorton Athletic), 1887 became Ardwick FC, 1894 changed its name to Manchester City
League	*1904, 21,* **37,** *68,* **77**
FA Cup	**1904,** *26, 33,* **34,** *55,* **56,** *69,* **81**
League Cup	**1970,** *74,* **76**
European Cup-Winners' Cup	**1970**

Map labels:

River Irwell · CHARLESTOWN · THE CLIFF Manchester United's old training ground · A56 · A665 · CHEETHAM HILL · A664 · Newton Heath (1878–93) · NEWTON HEATH · NORTH ROAD · A62 · Lancashire and Yorkshire Railway shunting yards. Newton Heath formed by workers here · COLLYHURST · River Irk · Manchester City (2003–) · CITY OF MANCHESTER STADIUM · 48,500 · BANK STREET · CLAYTON · A62 · BRADFORD · Newton Heath (1893–1902) · Manchester United (1902–10) · A662 · ROYAL HOTEL Second meeting to establish the Football League held here in 1888 · BESWICK · A6010 · West Gorton (1880–81) CLOWES STREET · OPENSHAW · IMPERIAL HOTEL Meeting to establish the Professional Footballers' Association held here in 1907 · CENTRAL MANCHESTER · West Gorton (1881–82) · KIRKMANSHULME CRICKET GROUND · GORTON · A635 · Manchester United (1910–) · ORDSALL · Manchester Ship Canal · A57(M) · PFA OFFICES Professional Footballers' Association offices · A57 · HYDE PARK · PINK BANK LANE · HULME · BRUNSWICK · Gorton FC (1884–87) · OLD TRAFFORD (67,650) · OLD TRAFFORD · Manchester City (1923–2003) · Ardwick FC (1887–94) · GORSE HILL · A56 · MAINE ROAD · Manchester City (1894–1923) · MOSS SIDE · RUSHOLME · A5103 · A34

THE LOCAL DERBY

CITY	UNITED
130 matches played	
34 City wins	
50 United wins	
46 draws	

NUMBER OF MATCHES
(League matches up to May 2004)
0 50 100 150 200 250

CITY OF MANCHESTER STADIUM

Club: Manchester City
Built: 2002
Original Capacity: 50,000
Record Attendance: 47,201 v Liverpool, Premier League, 28 December 2003
Significant Matches: Commonwealth Games held here in 2002

On 11 March 1941 Old Trafford was badly damaged by German bombs. United played home games at Maine Road until repairs were complete.

OLD TRAFFORD

Club: Manchester United
Built: 1910
Original Capacity: 80,000
Rebuilt: Bombed 1940–41, rebuilt 1948–49; rebuilt with Europe's first executive boxes, mid-1966; fully covered 1973; 1992–2000 constant rebuilding
Record Attendance: 76,962 Wolves v Grimsby FA Cup semi-final, 25 Mar 1939
Significant Matches: FA Cup Final: 1915; FA Cup Final replays: 1911, 1970; 1966 World Cup: three group matches; 1996 European Championships: three group matches, quarter-final and semi-final; England internationals: 1926, 97, 2001

The North East

SOCCER CENTER

Although professional soccer arrived in the North East slightly later than its Lancastrian and Midlands heartlands, the region soon made up for it. Sunderland was founded by students at a teacher training college in 1879, but soon opened its doors to everyone and entered the Football League in 1890. The 'team of all talents' as it was known won three titles in four years and saw off the threat of the splinter club, Sunderland Albion, who played in the league for a year before folding.

Newcastle and the wider Tyneside region threw up a number of clubs in the 1880s before the fusion of Newcastle East End (previously Stanley) – who had fans and players but no ground – and Newcastle West End who just had the lease of what is now St. James' Park. The two teams fused to create Newcastle United in 1892, joined the league the following year and won its first title in 1905. Sunderland took the title in the 1930s and Newcastle peaked with its 1950s FA Cup wins and triumph in the Fairs Cup. But league titles eluded it and all the region's clubs have spent long periods in the lower divisions.

Economic boom of the 1990s

The advent of the economic boom in soccer in the 1990s has allowed the region's big clubs to capitalize on massive and fervent support. With the personal fortune of Sir John Hall at Newcastle combined with massive sponsorship, merchandise and TV money, St. James' Park has been transformed almost out of recognition. Both the Riverside in Middlesbrough and the Stadium of Light in Sunderland have architecturally announced the erosion of the region's industrial heritage.

Beyond the professional game, the North East boasts among the strongest semi-professional and amateur leagues in the country which have helped nurture a steady flow of nationally recognized talent: Jackie Milburn and his nephews the Charlton brothers and Paul Gascoigne among others. Non-league Blyth Spartans, formed in 1899, almost reached the sixth round of the FA Cup in 1978 after its Fifth Round tie with Wrexham went to a replay at St. James' Park. Over 42,000 people saw them lose 2-1. How many other regions can even begin to imagine that level of support for such a club?

Roker Park is long gone to the developers now, but at its height in the 1930s, it could accommodate 75,000 spectators.

SUNDERLAND 1879	
League	1892, 93, 94, 95, 98, 1901, 02, 13, 23, 35, 36
FA Cup	1913, 37, 73, 92
League Cup	1985

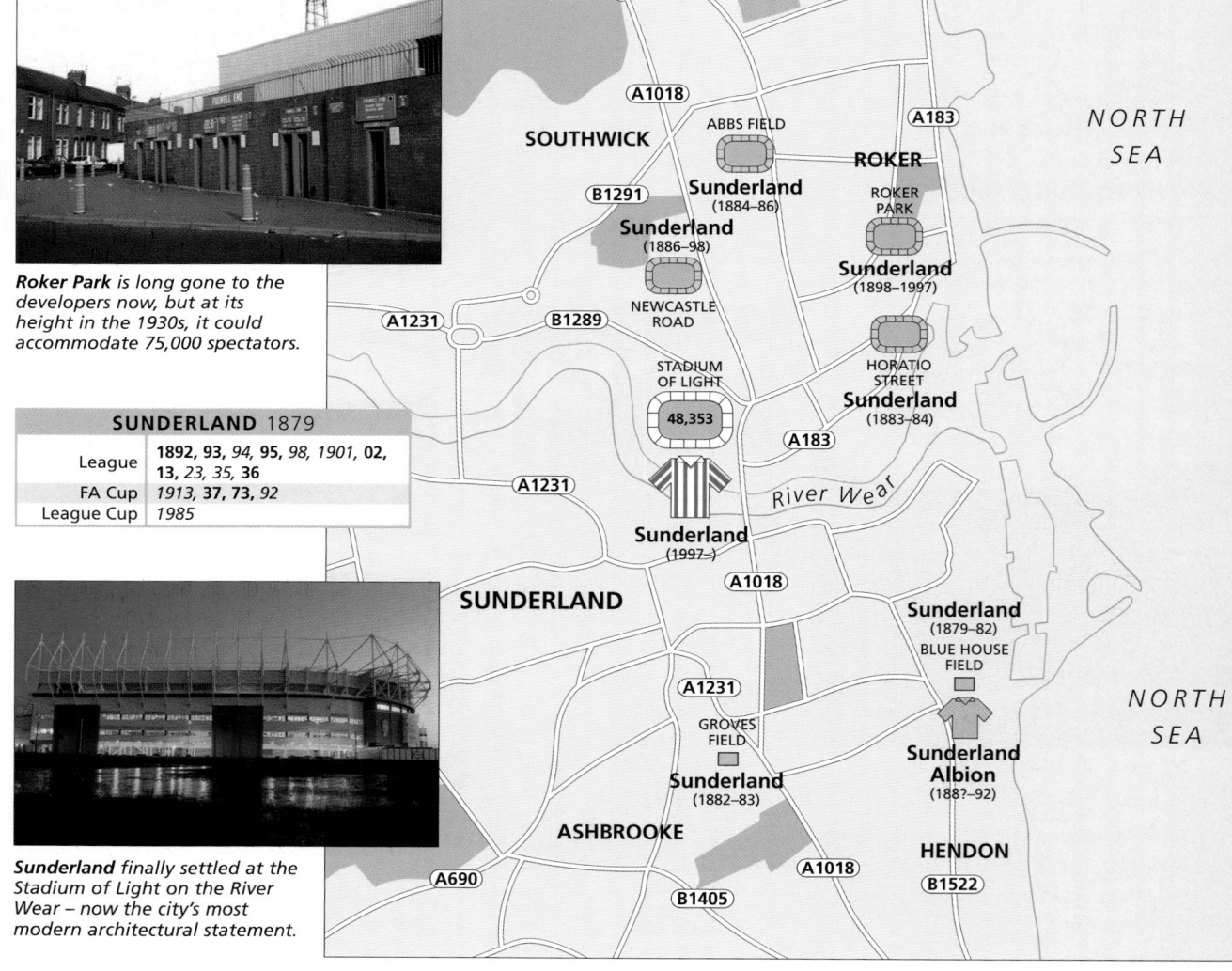

Sunderland finally settled at the Stadium of Light on the River Wear – now the city's most modern architectural statement.

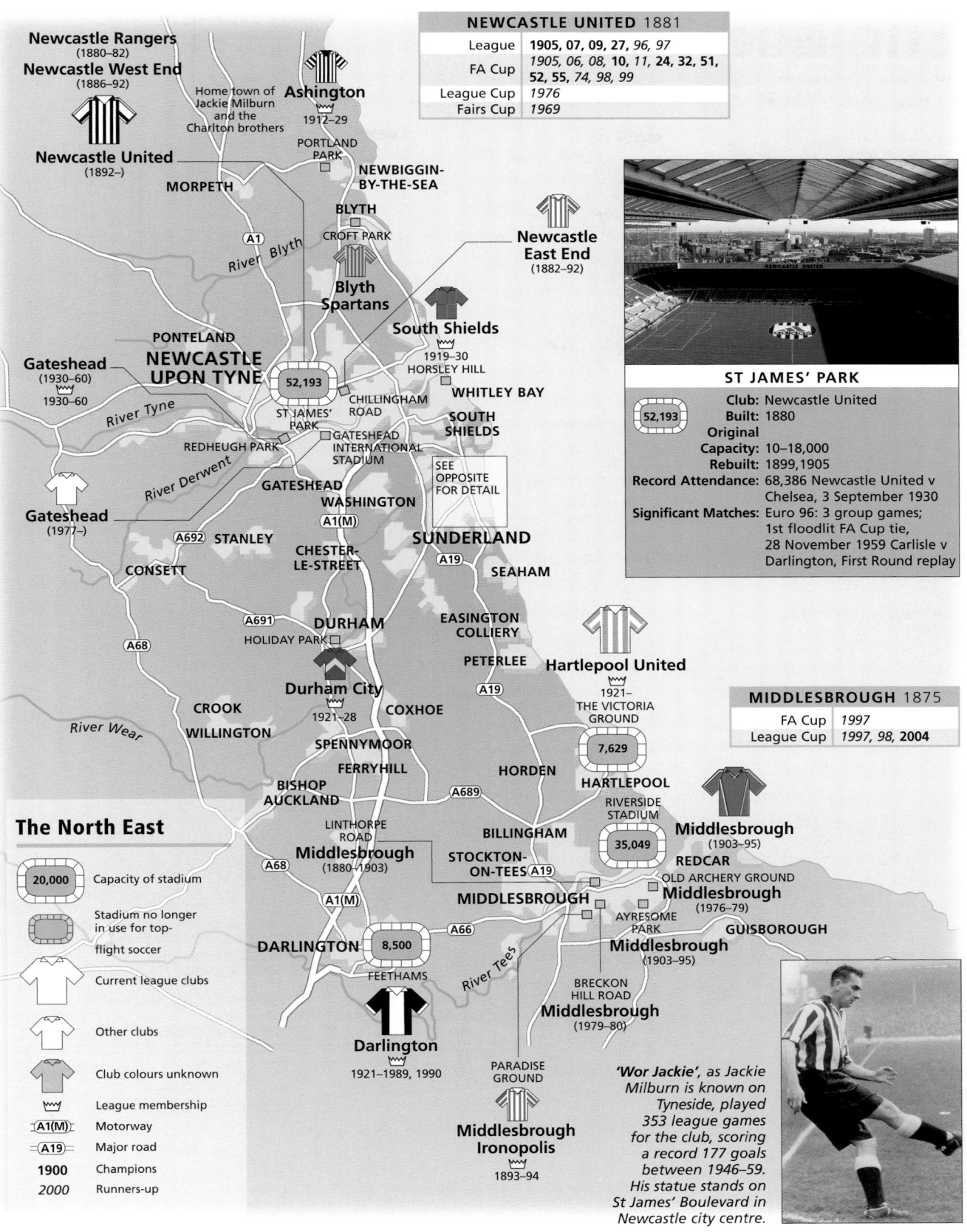

Newcastle Rangers
(1880–82)

Newcastle West End
(1886–92)

Home town of
Jackie Milburn
and the
Charlton brothers

Ashington
1912–29

Newcastle United
(1892–)

MORPETH

PORTLAND
PARK

NEWBIGGIN-
BY-THE-SEA

A1

River Blyth

BLYTH

CROFT PARK

Blyth
Spartans

Newcastle
East End
(1882–92)

NEWCASTLE UNITED 1881	
League	**1905, 07, 09, 27,** *96, 97*
FA Cup	*1905, 06, 08,* **10, 11, 24, 32, 51, 52, 55,** *74, 98, 99*
League Cup	*1976*
Fairs Cup	*1969*

ST JAMES' PARK

52,193	**Club:** Newcastle United
	Built: 1880
	Original
	Capacity: 10–18,000
	Rebuilt: 1899,1905
	Record Attendance: 68,386 Newcastle United v Chelsea, 3 September 1930
	Significant Matches: Euro 96: 3 group games; 1st floodlit FA Cup tie, 28 November 1959 Carlisle v Darlington, First Round replay

ENGLAND

PONTELAND

NEWCASTLE
UPON TYNE

52,193

ST JAMES'
PARK

CHILLINGHAM
ROAD

South Shields

1919–30
HORSLEY HILL

WHITLEY BAY

SOUTH
SHIELDS

SEE
OPPOSITE
FOR DETAIL

Gateshead
(1930–60)
1930–60

River Tyne

REDHEUGH PARK

GATESHEAD
INTERNATIONAL
STADIUM

River Derwent

GATESHEAD

Gateshead
(1977–)

WASHINGTON

A692 STANLEY

A1(M)

CONSETT

CHESTER-
LE-STREET

SUNDERLAND

A19

SEAHAM

A691

A68

DURHAM

HOLIDAY PARK

EASINGTON
COLLIERY

PETERLEE

Hartlepool United

1921–
THE VICTORIA
GROUND

Durham City

1921–28 COXHOE

A19

7,629

River Wear

CROOK

WILLINGTON

SPENNYMOOR

FERRYHILL

HORDEN

HARTLEPOOL

MIDDLESBROUGH 1875	
FA Cup	*1997*
League Cup	*1997, 98,* **2004**

BISHOP
AUCKLAND

A689

RIVERSIDE
STADIUM

35,049

Middlesbrough
(1903–95)

REDCAR

The North East

20,000	Capacity of stadium
	Stadium no longer in use for top-flight soccer
	Current league clubs
	Other clubs
	Club colours unknown
	League membership
A1(M)	Motorway
A19	Major road
1900	Champions
2000	Runners-up

LINTHORPE
ROAD

Middlesbrough
(1880–1903)

A68

A1(M)

STOCKTON-
ON-TEES A19

MIDDLESBROUGH

OLD ARCHERY GROUND
Middlesbrough
(1976–79)

AYRESOME
PARK

GUISBOROUGH

A66

Middlesbrough
(1903–95)

DARLINGTON 8,500

FEETHAMS

River Tees

BRECKON
HILL ROAD

Middlesbrough
(1979–80)

Darlington
1921–1989, 1990

PARADISE
GROUND

Middlesbrough
Ironopolis

1893–94

*'Wor Jackie', as Jackie
Milburn is known on
Tyneside, played
353 league games
for the club, scoring
a record 177 goals
between 1946–59.
His statue stands on
St James' Boulevard in
Newcastle city centre.*

England

FANS AND OWNERS

SINCE THE FORMATION of the Premiership, patterns of club ownership in English soccer have changed. A core of top clubs continue to be owned privately by rich individuals, either directly (the Moores at Liverpool) or indirectly through trusts and offshore arrangements (Freddy Shepherd at Newcastle, Al Fayed at Fulham). Others have floated as public companies on one of the British stock exchanges. Finance companies and media companies (Granada, BSkyB and NTL) have taken the lead in buying stakes in clubs. However, since the collapse of ITV Digital and the global transfer market in 2002, share prices have plummeted and there are few takers for shares in most clubs. However, Roman Abramovich's purchase of Chelsea bucked the trend.

Numbers up, volume down

Whoever the fans are, there are more of them. Gates in all divisions, but especially the Premiership, have steadily risen since the lows of the early 1980s. Since then, all-seater stadiums have become compulsory, private boxes and corporate hospitality have become integral features of club incomes, and crowd trouble has all but been eliminated within the grounds (although it has been partially displaced to outside the ground, to the lower division clubs and to the national team's following). The concern remains that these changes have come at a price, as the noise and passion of the crowd has been sanitized.

Old fans, new fans

Inside the stands, the traditional long-term soccer fans remain but they have been joined by a wave of new fans. These are, on average, wealthier than the older fans and include significantly more women. The enormous number of domestic and foreign black players is not, however, mirrored on the terraces. Unsurprisingly, fans from the north of England tend to be lower earners than fans from the south, and are much more likely to have been born locally to the club.

ENGLAND

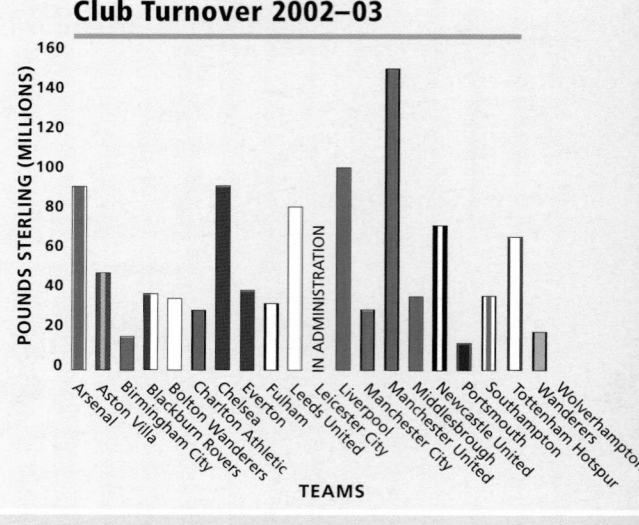

Club Turnover 2002–03

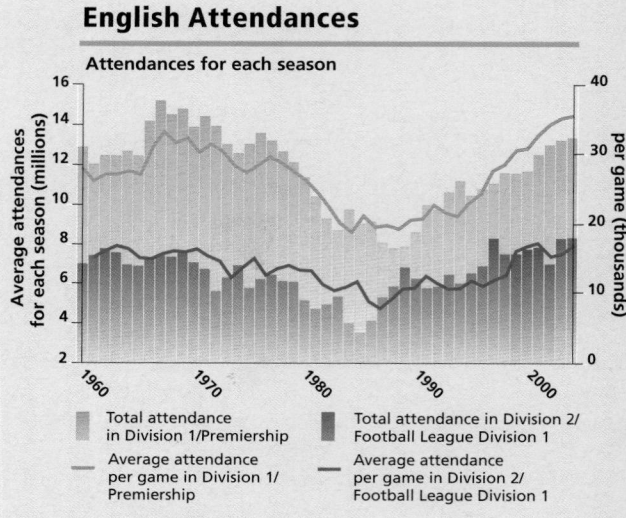

English Attendances

Attendances for each season

Total attendance in Division 1/Premiership
Total attendance in Division 2/Football League Division 1
Average attendance per game in Division 1/Premiership
Average attendance per game in Division 2/Football League Division 1

Fans Income

% of season ticket holders earning over £50,000 PA

40% 30% 20% 10% 0%

TEAMS

Arsenal
Aston Villa
Chelsea
Everton
Leeds United
Liverpool
Manchester United
Middlesbrough
Newcastle United
Southampton
Sunderland
Tottenham Hotspur
West Ham United

Fans Origins

% of season ticket holders who were born locally

40% 45% 50% 55% 60% 65% 70% 75% 80% 85%

Details from season 2002–03

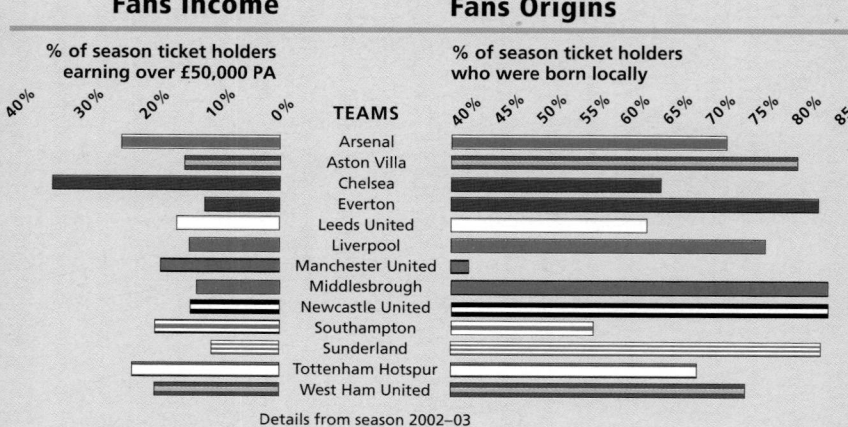

The Toon Army on tour: Newcastle's devoted following are unique in their capacity to brave the cold. They are a truly home grown audience with 85 per cent of their season ticket holders born locally.

Newcastle United

| Freddy Shepherd 24.5% | Hall Family 48% | LSE 1997 |

Middlesbrough

| NTL 5.5% | Steve Gibson 94.5% |

Leeds United

| LSE 1996 | Adulant Force Ltd 100% |

Liverpool

| David Moores 51% | Stephen Morgan 5% | Granada 9.9% |

Blackburn Rovers

| BRFC Investments (Trustees of Jack Walker) 99% |

Leicester City

| New Fox Plc 100% |

Everton

| Bill Kenwright 71.4% | Lord Granchester 7.9% |

Arsenal

| Offex 1999 | Granada 5% | Danny Fiszman 26.6% | David Dein 15.4% | Lady Bracewell Smith 16.8% |

Bolton Wanderers

| WB Warburton 8.1% | Eddie Davies 29.8% | Gartside Holdings 3.3% | Gordon's (Bolton) Ltd 10.7% | LSE 1997 |

Tottenham Hotspur

| LSE 1983 | ENIC 29.9% | Alan Sugar 13.2% |

Manchester United

| Harry Dobson 6.5% | Malcolm Glaser 18.2% | Cubic Expression Company 28.9% | Legal and General 3% | UBS Global Asset Management 4.7% | LSE 1991 |

Charlton Athletic

| AIM 1997 | Richard Murray 28.5% | Robert Whitehand 11.4% | Martin Simons 6.4% | David Sumners 5.7% |

Manchester City

| Walbrook Trustees 18.8% | Makin and Wardle Trusts 30% | Francis Lee 7.1% | BSkyB 9.9% |

Wolverhampton Wanderers

| Sir Jack Hayward 100% |

Birmingham City

| Media Group Sports Newspapers 78% |

Chelsea

| AIM 1996 | Roman Abramovich 90% |

Aston Villa

| Ellis Family 33.6% | Merril Lynch 9% | AXA Sun Life 3.1% | Hargreaves Landsdowne 4.1% | LSE 1997 |

Southampton

| LSE 1997 | Waterhead 5.2% | Amvescap 13.2% | Board Members 20% | Michael Withers 4.4% |

Fulham

| Ruxley Holdings 25% | Mohamed Al Fayed 75% |

Portsmouth

| Milan Manderic 100% |

ENGLAND

E N G L A N D

Newcastle ● **Middlesbrough** ● **Blackburn** ● **Bolton** ● **Leeds** ● **Liverpool** ● **Manchester** ● **Leicester** ● **Birmingham** ● **London** ● **Portsmouth** ● **Southampton** ●

Majority and Leading Shareholders

| Team | Personal share | Family share | Multi-person consortium | Telecommunications company | Media company | Car company | Sports company | Financial company | Flotation |

LSE – London Stock Exchange   AIM – Alternative Investment Market
Teams shown were members of the Premiership 2003–04

England

PLAYERS AND MANAGERS

THE CULTURE OF ENGLISH PROFESSIONAL soccer has changed over the last hundred years, particularly since professionalism was legalized. Before that it had been solidly working class, simultaneously tough and impassioned on the pitch and apparently deferential to authority off it. It was only in the 1960s that money began to move into the game, the maximum wage for players was abolished and contractual freedom was obtained. In the shape of Bobby Moore, Geoff Hurst and Bobby Charlton, a new generation of talent emerged.

But, to the surprise and horror of many of the foreign players that arrived in England in the early 1990s, little else has changed. Heart and lungs are still often valued over technique and training. Scientific analysis, nutritional care and tactical preparation have been disdained in favour of rough and ready measures, fried breakfasts and just getting 'stuck into them'. Above all, the drinking and nightlife culture of professional soccer players has not gone away; if anything, the riches of the Premiership have intensified it. For every clean-cut dedicated Michael Owen there seems to be an unruly Stan Collymore, the wasted talent of Paul Gascoigne or the headlining antics of Jonathan Woodgate.

Motivation over technique

The limit of the motivation over technique school of English management was reached with the demise of Kevin Keegan as England manager and his replacement with the national team's first foreign manager, Sven-Göran Eriksson. Although Bobby Robson continues to hang on in the Premiership, the bulk of the league's top teams are coached by Scots (Alex Ferguson at Manchester United, David Moyes at Everton and Graeme Souness at Blackburn), a Frenchman (Arsène Wenger at Arsenal) or Iberians (Rafa Benitez at Liverpool and José Mourinho at Chelsea). The influx of foreign players appears to have peaked as the current financial crisis limits clubs' wage bills (Chelsea aside). However, while some foreign players are coming to the Premiership early in their careers, many arrive for a lucrative end-of-career payday.

Top 20 International Caps

PLAYER	CAPS	GOALS	FIRST MATCH	LAST MATCH
Peter Shilton	125	0	1970	1990
Bobby Moore	108	2	1962	1973
Bobby Charlton	106	49	1958	1970
Billy Wright	105	3	1946	1959
Bryan Robson	90	26	1980	1991
Kenny Sansom	86	1	1979	1988
Ray Wilkins	84	3	1976	1986
Gary Lineker	80	48	1984	1992
John Barnes	79	11	1983	1995
Stuart Pearce	78	5	1987	1999
Terry Butcher	77	3	1980	1990
Tom Finney	76	30	1946	1958
David Seaman	75	0	1988	2003
Alan Ball	72	8	1965	1975
Gordon Banks	72	0	1963	1972
David Beckham*	72	13	1996	2004
Gary Neville*	67	0	1995	2004
Martin Peters	67	20	1966	1974
Tony Adams	66	5	1987	2000
Paul Scholes*	66	14	1997	2004

Top 10 International Goalscorers

PLAYER	GOALS	CAPS	FIRST MATCH	LAST MATCH
Bobby Charlton	49	106	1958	1970
Gary Lineker	48	80	1984	1992
Jimmy Greaves	43	57	1959	1967
Nat Lofthouse	30	33	1950	1958
Alan Shearer*	30	63	1991	2000
Tom Finney	30	76	1946	1958
Vivian Woodward	29	23	1903	1911
Stephen Bloomer	28	23	1895	1907
David Platt	27	62	1989	1996
Michael Owen*	26	60	1998	2004
Bryan Robson	26	90	1980	1991
Geoff Hurst	24	49	1966	1972
Stan Mortensen	23	25	1947	1953

* Indicates players still playing at least at club level.

England International Managers

DATES	NAME	GAMES	WON	DRAWN	LOST
1946–62	Walter Winterbottom	139	78	33	28
1963–74	Alf Ramsey	113	69	27	17
1974	Joe Mercer	7	3	3	1
1974–77	Don Revie	29	14	8	7
1977–82	Ron Greenwood	55	33	12	10
1982–90	Bobby Robson	95	47	30	18
1990–93	Graham Taylor	38	18	13	7
1994–96	Terry Venables	23	11	11	1
1996–99	Glenn Hoddle	28	17	6	5
1999	Howard Wilkinson	2	0	1	1
1999–2000	Kevin Keegan	18	7	7	4
2000	Peter Taylor	1	0	0	1
2000–	Sven Goran Eriksson	42	22	13	7

All figures correct as of 28 June 2004.

Foreign Players in England (in top division squads)

2003–04

13 CONCACAF
4 AFC
31 CAF
17 CONMEBOL
10 OFC
229 UEFA
Total: 304

Key: Total Players / Foreign Players / %

Player of the Year

YEAR	PLAYER	CLUB
1948	Matthews	Blackpool
1949	Carey	Manchester United
1950	Mercer	Arsenal
1951	Johnston	Blackpool
1952	Wright	Wolverhampton W
1953	Lofthouse	Bolton Wanderers
1954	Finney	Preston North End
1955	Revie	Manchester City
1956	Trautmann	Manchester City
1957	Finney	Preston North End
1958	Blanchflower	Tottenham Hotspur
1959	Owen	Luton Town
1960	Slater	Wolverhampton W
1961	Blanchflower	Tottenham Hotspur
1962	Adamson	Burnley
1963	Matthews	Stoke City
1964	Moore	West Ham United
1965	Collins	Leeds United
1966	R. Charlton	Manchester United
1967	J. Charlton	Leeds United
1968	Best	Manchester United
1969	Mackay	Derby County
1969	Book	Manchester City
1970	Bremner	Leeds United
1971	McLintock	Arsenal
1972	Banks	Stoke City
1973	Jennings	Tottenham Hotspur
1974	Callaghan	Liverpool
1975	Mullery	Fulham
1976	Keegan	Liverpool

Player of the Year (continued)

YEAR	PLAYER	CLUB
1977	Hughes	Liverpool
1978	Burns	Nottingham Forest
1979	Dalglish	Liverpool
1980	McDermott	Liverpool
1981	Thijssen	Ipswich Town
1982	Perryman	Tottenham Hotspur
1983	Dalglish	Liverpool
1984	Rush	Liverpool
1985	Southall	Everton
1986	Lineker	Everton
1987	Allen	Tottenham Hotspur
1988	Barnes	Liverpool
1989	Nicol	Liverpool
1990	Barnes	Liverpool
1991	Strachan	Leeds United
1992	Lineker	Tottenham Hotspur
1993	Waddle	Sheffield Wednesday
1994	Shearer	Blackburn Rovers
1995	Klinsmann	Tottenham Hotspur
1996	Cantona	Manchester United
1997	Zola	Chelsea
1998	Bergkamp	Arsenal
1999	Ginola	Tottenham Hotspur
2000	Keane	Manchester United
2001	Sheringham	Manchester United
2002	Pires	Arsenal
2003	Henry	Arsenal
2004	Henry	Arsenal

Awarded by the English Football Writers' Association.

The legendary Dixie Dean presents the Player of the Year trophy to Liverpool's Kevin Keegan in 1976.

The late Walter Winterbottom, England's first international manager, remained in charge of the team from 1946 to 1962.

Top Goalscorers by Season 1947–2004

SEASON	PLAYER	CLUB	GOALS
1947–48	Rooke	Arsenal	33
1948–49	Moir	Bolton W	25
1949–50	Davies	Sunderland	25
1950–51	Mortensen	Blackpool	30
1951–52	Robledo	Newcastle Utd	33
1952–53	Wayman	Preston NE	24
1953–54	Glazzard	Huddersfield T	29
1954–55	Allen	WBA	27
1955–56	Lofthouse	Bolton W	33
1956–57	Charles	Leeds United	38
1957–58	Smith	Spurs	36
1958–59	Greaves	Chelsea	33
1959–60	Viollet	Manchester U	32
1960–61	Greaves	Chelsea	41
1961–62	Crawford	Ipswich Town	33
1961–62	Kevan	WBA	33
1962–63	Greaves	Spurs	37
1963–64	Greaves	Spurs	35
1964–65	Greaves	Spurs	29
1964–65	McEvoy	Blackburn R	29
1965–66	Irvine	Burnley	29
1966–67	Davies	Southampton	37
1967–68	Best	Manchester U	28
1967–68	Davies	Southampton	28
1968–69	Greaves	Spurs	27
1969–70	Astle	WBA	25
1970–71	Brown	WBA	28
1971–72	Lee	Manchester C	33
1972–73	Robson	West Ham U	28
1973–74	Channon	Southampton	21
1974–75	Macdonald	Newcastle Utd	21
1975–76	MacDougall	Norwich City	23
1976–77	Macdonald	Newcastle Utd	25
1976–77	Gray	Aston Villa	25
1977–78	Latchford	Everton	30
1978–79	Worthington	Bolton W	24
1979–80	Boyer	Southampton	23

SEASON	PLAYER	CLUB	GOALS
1980–81	Withe	Aston Villa	20
1980–81	Archibald	Spurs	20
1981–82	Keegan	Southampton	26
1982–83	Blisset	Watford	27
1983–84	Rush	Liverpool	32
1984–85	Dixon	Chelsea	24
1984–85	Lineker	Leicester City	24
1985–86	Lineker	Everton	30
1986–87	Allen	Spurs	33
1987–88	Aldridge	Liverpool	26
1988–89	Smith	Arsenal	23
1989–90	Lineker	Spurs	24
1990–91	Chapman	Leeds United	31
1991–92	Wright	Crystal Palace/ Arsenal	29
1992–93	Sheringham	Nottingham F/ Spurs	22
1993–94	Cole	Newcastle Utd	34
1994–95	Shearer	Blackburn R	35
1995–96	Shearer	Blackburn R	31
1996–97	Shearer	Newcastle Utd	25
1997–98	Owen	Liverpool	18
1997–98	Sutton	Blackburn R	18
1997–98	Dublin	Coventry City	18
1998–99	Yorke	Manchester U	18
1998–99	Owen	Liverpool	18
1998–99	Hasselbaink	Leeds United	18
1999–2000	Phillips	Sunderland	30
2000–01	Hasselbaink	Chelsea	23
2001–02	Henry	Arsenal	24
2001–02	Shearer	Newcastle	24
2002–03	van Nistelrooy	Manchester United	25
2003–04	Henry	Arsenal	30

With 49 goals in 106 appearances, Bobby Charlton (right) is one of England's greatest players. His brother Jack (left) also played 35 times for England, and both were members of the 1966 World Cup-winning team.

England

THE PREMIERSHIP 1992–2003

IN 1992, THE ENGLISH PREMIER LEAGUE was established by the country's 22 leading clubs, breaking away from the control of the English FA and the Football League. Correctly anticipating an enormous increase in TV income for soccer, the Premier League was primarily a device for keeping that income at the top and excluding both non-league and lower division soccer from the goldrush; to that extent it has succeeded. The most recent TV deal (2004–2007) has brought in more than a billion pounds over four years, though this is down on the previous deal. Combined with rising gate income, sponsorship deals and intensive merchandising, the English Premier League is the richest in global soccer.

Where does the money go?

Yet as fast as the money comes in, it goes out, drained by the explosive rise in player's wages and the increasingly large transfer budgets of Premiership clubs. Most of the latter have been spent overseas. Clubs have brought players from all over Europe, as well as South America, the Caribbean, Africa and Asia. The increasing financial muscle of the Premiership can be seen in the gradual acquisition of players from the strongest European leagues (Italy, Germany and the Netherlands) – and not just players coming to the end of their career (Klinsmann, Gullit, Vialli) but players in their prime (van Nistelrooy, Mutu, Viera).

Below the Premiership, the English lower divisions have seen transfer income steadily diminish while wage bills rise, a situation exacerbated by the ITV Digital disaster, which has forced many clubs close to the wall. The enormous foreign presence in the Premiership (both among players and, increasingly, managers as well) has raised the technical and tactical sophistication of the game immeasurably, but it remains to be seen what the consequence of this will be for the development of indigenous English talent.

Unite and rule

Financial and sporting success has become increasingly concentrated at the top end of the Premiership. In ten seasons, Alex Ferguson's Manchester United has taken seven championships; in 2000–01 it won at a canter. Ferguson has built a series of teams at United based on an attacking and aggressive 4-4-2 play. Passing, moving and possessed of an unquenchable confidence, his team persistently dominated the weaker teams when its challengers have shown inconsistency. Only Blackburn Rovers, fuelled by Jack Walker's personal fortune and Alan Shearer's best year (1995), and Arsenal, under the cerebral Arsène Wenger (1998 and 2002), have broken the Mancunian monopoly. In all three seasons, United still came in a close second. Challenges from Leeds, Liverpool, Chelsea and Kevin Keegan's Newcastle were all seen off.

Life at the bottom

Financial imbalances have created a whole category of clubs that are too strong for Division One but too weak to sustain their place in the Premiership. Manchester City, West Bromwich Albion, Crystal Palace, Leicester City and others have been condemned to a cycle of relegation and promotion. Excluded from significant TV income while in the First Division, a single year in the Premiership does not deliver enough money to sufficiently strengthen the team. Outspending resources in a gamble to stay up can see clubs left deep in debt. Others constantly teeter on the edge of the relegation precipice, like Everton, Southampton and, in the case of Coventry and Sunderland, eventually fall over it. Even clubs with bigger resources, such as Tottenham Hotspur and Aston Villa, have been reduced to mid-table scrapping and the fight for a place in the UEFA Cup.

Number seven, but will there be any more? Manchester United players celebrate their championship in 2002-03.

Under Alan Curbishley's *old school management and the board's parsimonious wage policy Charlton Athletic has been one of the few clubs to make the transition from yo-yo team to perennial member of the Premiership.*

The shift of power begins? Arsenal wins the 2002 Premiership and the first leg of its double after beating Manchester United at Old Trafford.

Player Salaries 1995–2001

Total wage bill of Premiership clubs

Annual TV Rights Income

YEAR	POUNDS STERLING (MILLIONS)
1983	(2.6 BBC/ITV)
1984	(2.6 BBC/ITV)
1985	(1.3 BBC/ITV)
1986	(3.1 BBC/ITV)
1987	(3.1 BBC/ITV)
1988	(11 ITV)
1989	(11 ITV)
1990	(11 ITV)
1991	(11 ITV)
1992	(38.3 BskyB)
1993	(38.3 BskyB)
1994	(38.3 BskyB)
1995	(38.3 BskyB)
1996	(38.3 BskyB)
1997	(168 BskyB)
1998	(168 BskyB)
1999	(168 BskyB)
2000	(168 BskyB)
2001	(367 BskyB)
2002	(367 BskyB)
2003	(367 BskyB)
2004	(256 BskyB)
2005	(256 BskyB)
2006	(256 BskyB)
2007	(256 BskyB)

Above: The financial morality tale of the decade. Leeds United rode high at home and in Europe on an ocean of short-term debt. The team's failure to regularly qualify for the Champions League saw the club's accounts, squad and league position disintegrate in 2002 and 2003.

Right: In October 2002 Alan Shearer scored his 300th Premiership goal playing for Newcastle United against his old club Blackburn Rovers.

ENGLAND

Champions' Winning Margin 1992–2003

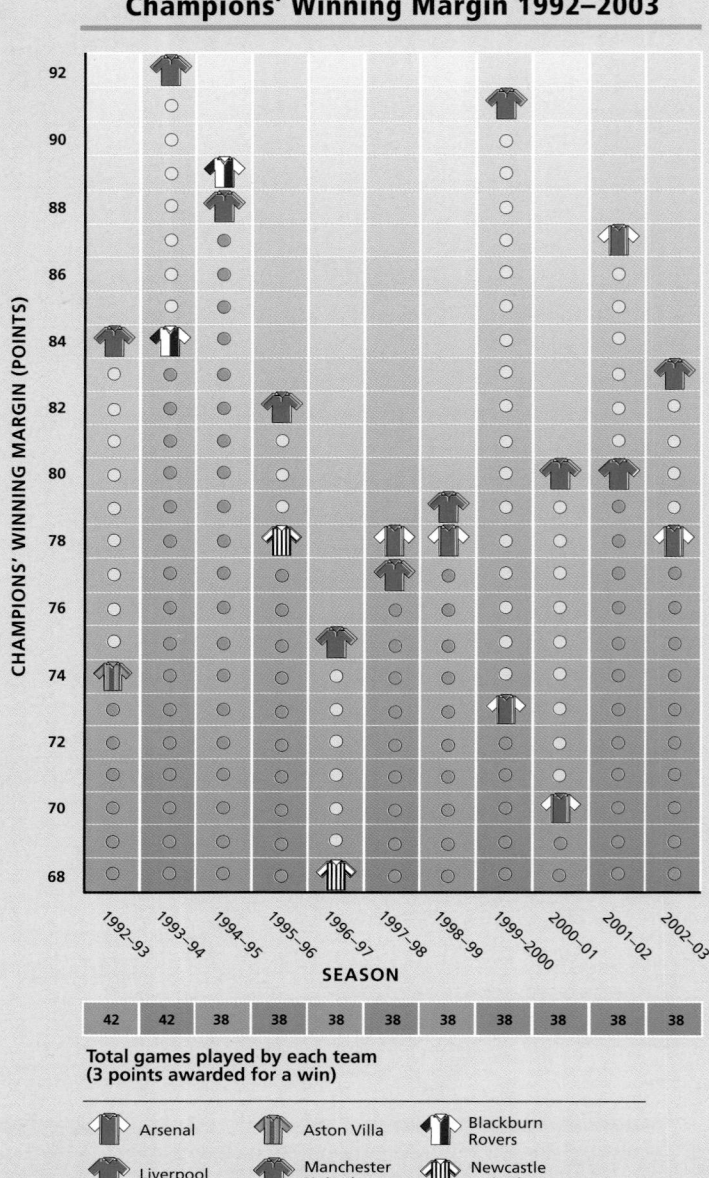

CHAMPIONS' WINNING MARGIN (POINTS)

SEASON: 1992-93, 1993-94, 1994-95, 1995-96, 1996-97, 1997-98, 1998-99, 1999-2000, 2000-01, 2001-02, 2002-03

| 42 | 42 | 38 | 38 | 38 | 38 | 38 | 38 | 38 | 38 | 38 |

Total games played by each team (3 points awarded for a win)

Key: Arsenal · Aston Villa · Blackburn Rovers · Liverpool · Manchester United · Newcastle United

Chelsea midfielder *Gianfranco Zola was voted best foreign player in the first decade of the Premiership. The league was graced by his considerable talent and sportsmanship.*

Key to League Positions Table

- League champions
- Season of relegation from league
- Season of promotion to league
- Other teams playing in league
- 5 — Final position in league

English League Positions 1992–2003

TEAM	1992-93	1993-94	1994-95	1995-96	1996-97	1997-98	1998-99	1999-2000	2000-01	2001-02	2002-03
Arsenal	10	4	12	5	3	1	2	2	2	1	2
Aston Villa	2	10	18	4	5	7	6	6	8	8	16
Barnsley						19					
Birmingham City											13
Blackburn Rovers	4	2	1	7	13	6	19			10	6
Bolton Wanderers			20			18				16	17
Bradford City								17	20		
Charlton Athletic							18		9	14	12
Chelsea	11	14	11	11	6	4	3	5	6	6	4
Coventry City	15	11	16	16	17	11	15	14	19		
Crystal Palace	20		19			20					
Derby County					12	9	8	16	17	19	
Everton	13	17	15	6	15	17	14	13	16	15	7
Fulham										13	14
Ipswich Town	16	19	22						5	18	
Leeds United	17	5	5	13	11	5	4	3	4	5	15
Leicester City			21		9	10	10		13	20	
Liverpool	6	8	4	3	4	3	7	4	3	2	5
Manchester City	9	16	17	18					18		9
Manchester United	1	1	2	1	1	2	1	1	1	3	1
Middlesbrough	21			12	19		9	12	14	12	11
Newcastle United		3	6	2	2	13	13	11	11	4	3
Norwich City	3	12	20								
Nottingham Forest	22		3	9	20		20				
Oldham Athletic	19	21									
Portsmouth											
Queens Park Rangers	5	9	8	19							
Sheffield United	14	20									
Sheffield Wednesday	7	7	13	15	7	16	12	19			
Southampton	18	18	10	17	16	12	17	15	10	11	8
Sunderland					18			7	7	17	20
Swindon Town		22									
Tottenham Hotspur	8	15	7	8	10	14	11	10	12	9	10
Watford								20			
West Bromwich Albion											19
West Ham United		13	14	10	14	8	5	9	15	7	18
Wimbledon	12	6	9	14	8	15	16	18			
Wolverhampton Wanderers											

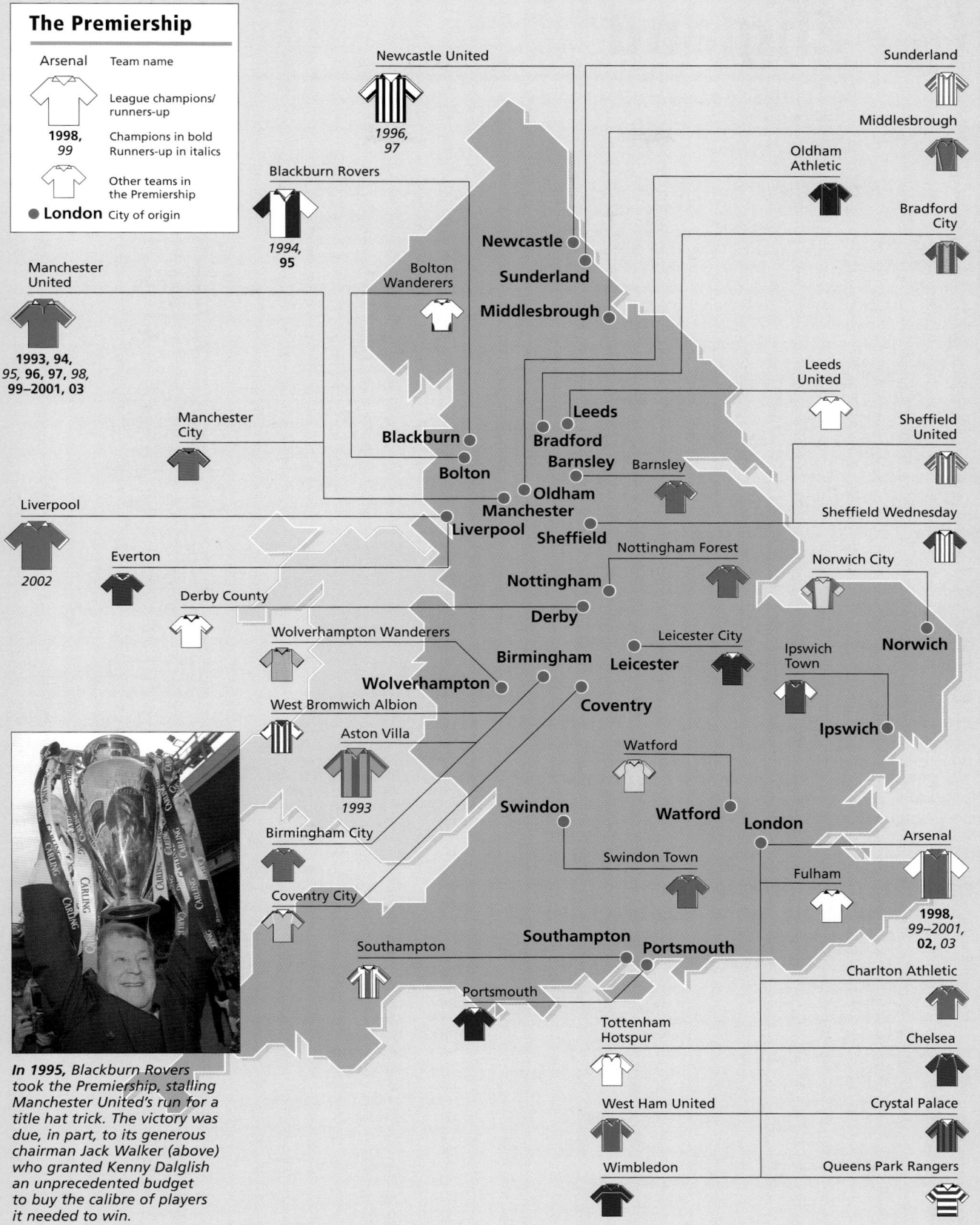

The Premiership

Arsenal — Team name

League champions/runners-up

1998, *99* — Champions in bold Runners-up in italics

Other teams in the Premiership

● **London** — City of origin

Newcastle United
1996, **97**

Blackburn Rovers
1994, **95**

Manchester United
1993, 94, 95, 96, 97, 98, 99–2001, 03

Manchester City

Liverpool

Everton
2002

Derby County

Wolverhampton Wanderers

West Bromwich Albion

Aston Villa
1993

Birmingham City

Coventry City

Southampton

Portsmouth

Bolton Wanderers

Newcastle ●
Sunderland ●
Middlesbrough ●

Blackburn ●
Bolton ●
Oldham ●
Manchester ●
Liverpool ●

Leeds ●
Bradford ●
Barnsley ●

Sheffield ●
Nottingham ●

Derby ●

Birmingham ●
Wolverhampton ●

Coventry ●

Swindon ●

Leicester ●

Watford ●

Southampton ●
Portsmouth ●

Sunderland

Middlesbrough

Oldham Athletic

Bradford City

Leeds United

Sheffield United

Sheffield Wednesday

Nottingham Forest

Norwich City

Norwich ●

Leicester City

Ipswich Town

Ipswich ●

Watford

London ●

Arsenal
1998, 99–2001, 02, *03*

Fulham

Charlton Athletic

Chelsea

Crystal Palace

Queens Park Rangers

Barnsley

Swindon Town

Tottenham Hotspur

West Ham United

Wimbledon

In 1995, Blackburn Rovers took the Premiership, stalling Manchester United's run for a title hat trick. The victory was due, in part, to its generous chairman Jack Walker (above) who granted Kenny Dalglish an unprecedented budget to buy the calibre of players it needed to win.

ENGLAND

 # England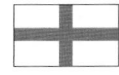

The Football Association
Founded: 1863
Joined FIFA: 1905–20, 1924–28, 1946
Joined UEFA: 1954

ENGLAND

IN ENGLAND, UNLIKE MOST NATIONS, national soccer competitions began with the cup rather than the league. The Football Association Challenge Cup, or FA Cup as it is usually known, began in 1872, and is the oldest formal soccer tournament in the world. It was open to amateur clubs and, after legalization in 1885, to professional teams as well. The Final found a permanent home at Wembley in 1923, but moved to the Millennium Stadium in Cardiff in 2001. Currently, over 500 non-league teams compete in preliminary rounds before the bottom two league divisions join in the first round, and the First Division and Premiership teams join in the third round. Each year the competition takes ten months to complete.

A separate League Cup, not open to amateur teams, was created in 1961. For the first six years, the Final was decided over two legs, home and away, before finding a new home at Wembley in 1967. Despite rather low attendances, often gruelling two-leg rounds, and endless changes of name and sponsor, the lure of a UEFA Cup place for the winners has retained interest in the competition.

The Football League was established in 1888 by a core of 12 professional clubs from the Midlands and the north of England. A second division was added in 1892, a third in 1920 and a fourth in 1921, when the lower division was divided into Third Division North and South. These were amalgamated to create a Third and Fourth Division in 1950. The national leagues were replaced by regional competitions for most of the First and Second World Wars. The FA Cup competition was suspended between 1916 and 1919, and again between 1940 and 1945, though a War Cup, with a Final at Wembley, was hastily organized in 1941 and contested for the next few years.

In 1992, the top 22 clubs broke away from the FA's control to create an independently administered Premiership. Three teams are relegated from the now 20-team league, and three come up from Division One (two automatically and one by play-off).

English League Record 1889–2004

SEASON	CHAMPIONS	RUNNERS-UP
1889	Preston North End	Aston Villa
1890	Preston North End	Everton
1891	Everton	Preston North End
1892	Sunderland	Preston North End
1893	Sunderland	Preston North End
1894	Aston Villa	Sunderland
1895	Sunderland	Everton
1896	Aston Villa	Derby County
1897	Aston Villa	Sheffield United
1898	Sheffield United	Sunderland
1899	Aston Villa	Liverpool
1900	Aston Villa	Sheffield United
1901	Liverpool	Sunderland
1902	Sunderland	Everton
1903	Sheffield Wednesday	Aston Villa
1904	Sheffield Wednesday	Manchester City
1905	Newcastle United	Everton
1906	Liverpool	Preston North End
1907	Newcastle United	Bristol City

English League Record (*continued*)

SEASON	CHAMPIONS	RUNNERS-UP
1908	Manchester United	Aston Villa
1909	Newcastle United	Everton
1910	Aston Villa	Liverpool
1911	Manchester United	Aston Villa
1912	Blackburn Rovers	Everton
1913	Sunderland	Aston Villa
1914	Blackburn Rovers	Aston Villa
1915	Everton	Oldham Athletic
1916–19	*no championship*	
1920	West Bromwich Albion	Burnley
1921	Burnley	Manchester City
1922	Liverpool	Tottenham Hotspur
1923	Liverpool	Sunderland
1924	Huddersfield Town	Cardiff City
1925	Huddersfield Town	West Bromwich Albion
1926	Huddersfield Town	Arsenal
1927	Newcastle United	Huddersfield Town
1928	Everton	Huddersfield Town
1929	Sheffield Wednesday	Leicester City
1930	Sheffield Wednesday	Derby County
1931	Arsenal	Aston Villa
1932	Everton	Arsenal
1933	Arsenal	Aston Villa
1934	Arsenal	Huddersfield Town
1935	Arsenal	Sunderland
1936	Sunderland	Derby County
1937	Manchester City	Charlton Athletic
1938	Arsenal	Wolverhampton Wanderers
1939	Everton	Wolverhampton Wanderers
1940–46	*no championship*	
1947	Liverpool	Manchester United
1948	Arsenal	Manchester United
1949	Portsmouth	Manchester United
1950	Portsmouth	Wolverhampton Wanderers
1951	Tottenham Hotspur	Manchester United
1952	Manchester United	Tottenham Hotspur
1953	Arsenal	Preston North End
1954	Wolverhampton Wanderers	West Bromwich Albion
1955	Chelsea	Wolverhampton Wanderers
1956	Manchester United	Blackpool
1957	Manchester United	Tottenham Hotspur
1958	Wolverhampton Wanderers	Preston North End
1959	Wolverhampton Wanderers	Manchester United
1960	Burnley	Wolverhampton Wanderers
1961	Tottenham Hotspur	Sheffield Wednesday
1962	Ipswich Town	Burnley
1963	Everton	Tottenham Hotspur
1964	Liverpool	Manchester United
1965	Manchester United	Leeds United
1966	Liverpool	Leeds United
1967	Manchester United	Nottingham Forest
1968	Manchester City	Manchester United
1969	Leeds United	Liverpool
1970	Everton	Leeds United
1971	Arsenal	Leeds United
1972	Derby County	Leeds United
1973	Liverpool	Arsenal
1974	Leeds United	Liverpool
1975	Derby County	Liverpool
1976	Liverpool	Queens Park Rangers
1977	Liverpool	Manchester City
1978	Nottingham Forest	Liverpool

English League Record (continued)

SEASON	CHAMPIONS	RUNNERS-UP
1979	Liverpool	Nottingham Forest
1980	Liverpool	Manchester United
1981	Aston Villa	Ipswich Town
1982	Liverpool	Ipswich Town
1983	Liverpool	Watford
1984	Liverpool	Southampton
1985	Everton	Liverpool
1986	Liverpool	Everton
1987	Everton	Liverpool
1988	Liverpool	Manchester United
1989	Arsenal	Liverpool
1990	Liverpool	Aston Villa
1991	Arsenal	Liverpool
1992	Leeds United	Manchester United
1993	Manchester United	Aston Villa
1994	Manchester United	Blackburn Rovers
1995	Blackburn Rovers	Manchester United
1996	Manchester United	Newcastle United
1997	Manchester United	Newcastle United
1998	Arsenal	Manchester United
1999	Manchester United	Arsenal
2000	Manchester United	Arsenal
2001	Manchester United	Arsenal
2002	Arsenal	Liverpool
2003	Manchester United	Arsenal
2004	Arsenal	Chelsea

English League Summary

TEAM	TOTALS	CHAMPIONS & RUNNERS-UP (BOLD) (ITALICS)
Liverpool	18, 11	*1899,* **1901, 06, 10, 22, 23, 47, 64, 66, 69, 73, 74, 75, 76, 77, 78, 79, 80, 82–84,** *85,* **86,** *87,* **88, 89, 90, 91, 2002**
Manchester United	15, 12	**1908, 11,** *47–49, 51,* **52, 56, 57,** *59, 64, 65, 67, 68, 80,* **88,** *92,* **93, 94, 95, 96, 97, 98, 99–2001, 03**
Arsenal	13, 7	*1926, 31, 32,* **33–35, 38, 48, 53, 71,** *73,* **89, 91,** *98,* **99–2001, 02, 03, 04**
Everton	9, 7	*1890,* **91,** *95, 1902, 05, 09, 12,* **15,** *28,* **32, 39, 63, 70, 85,** *86,* **87**
Aston Villa	7, 10	**1889,** *94,* **96, 97, 99, 1900,** *03, 08, 10, 11, 13, 14, 31, 33,* **81,** *90, 93*
Sunderland	6, 5	**1892,** *93,* **94,** *95,* **98,** *1901,* **02,** *13, 23, 35,* **36**
Newcastle United	4, 2	**1905, 07, 09, 27,** *96, 97*
Sheffield Wednesday	4, 1	**1903, 04, 29, 30,** *61*
Leeds United	3, 5	*1965, 66,* **69,** *70–72,* **74,** *92*
Wolverhampton Wanderers	3, 5	*1938, 39, 50,* **54, 55,** *58, 59, 60*
Huddersfield Town	3, 3	**1924–26,** *27, 28,* **34**
Blackburn Rovers	3, 1	**1912, 14,** *94,* **95**
Preston North End	2, 6	**1889, 90,** *91–93, 1906, 53, 58*
Tottenham Hotspur	2, 4	*1922,* **51,** *52, 57,* **61,** *63*
Derby County	2, 3	*1896, 1930, 36,* **72,** *75*
Manchester City	2, 3	*1904, 21,* **37, 68,** *77*
Burnley	2, 2	*1920,* **21,** *60,* **62**
Portsmouth	2, 0	**1949, 50**
Ipswich Town	1, 2	**1962,** *81, 82*
Nottingham Forest	1, 2	**1967,** *78, 79*
Sheffield United	1, 2	*1897,* **98,** *1900*
West Bromwich Albion	1, 2	**1920,** *25, 54*
Chelsea	1, 1	**1955,** *2004*
Blackpool	0, 1	*1956*
Bristol City	0, 1	*1907*
Cardiff City	0, 1	*1924*
Charlton Athletic	0, 1	*1937*
Leicester City	0, 1	*1929*

English League Summary (continued)

TEAM	TOTALS	CHAMPIONS & RUNNERS-UP (BOLD) (ITALICS)
Oldham Athletic	0, 1	*1915*
Queens Park Rangers	0, 1	*1976*
Southampton	0, 1	*1984*
Watford	0, 1	*1983*

English FA Cup Record 1872–2004

YEAR	WINNERS	SCORE	RUNNERS-UP
1872	Wanderers	1-0	Royal Engineers
1873	Wanderers	2-0	Oxford University
1874	Oxford University	2-0	Royal Engineers
1875	Royal Engineers	1-1 (aet), (replay) 2-0	Old Etonians
1876	Wanderers	1-1 (aet), (replay) 3-0	Old Etonians
1877	Wanderers	2-1 (aet)	Oxford University
1878	Wanderers	3-1	Royal Engineers
1879	Old Etonians	1-0	Clapham Rovers
1880	Clapham Rovers	1-0	Oxford University
1881	Old Carthusians	3-0	Old Etonians
1882	Old Etonians	1-0	Blackburn Rovers
1883	Blackburn Olympic	2-1 (aet)	Old Etonians
1884	Blackburn Rovers	2-1	Queen's Park
1885	Blackburn Rovers	2-0	Queen's Park
1886	Blackburn Rovers	0-0, (replay) 2-0	West Bromwich Albion
1887	Aston Villa	2-0	West Bromwich Albion
1888	West Bromwich Albion	2-1	Preston North End
1889	Preston North End	3-0	Wolverhampton Wanderers
1890	Blackburn Rovers	6-1	Sheffield Wednesday
1891	Blackburn Rovers	3-1	Notts County
1892	West Bromwich Albion	3-0	Aston Villa
1893	Wolverhampton Wanderers	1-0	Everton
1894	Notts County	4-1	Bolton Wanderers
1895	Aston Villa	1-0	West Bromwich Albion
1896	Sheffield Wednesday	2-1	Wolverhampton Wanderers
1897	Aston Villa	3-2	Everton
1898	Nottingham Forest	3-1	Derby County
1899	Sheffield United	4-1	Derby County
1900	Bury	4-0	Southampton
1901	Tottenham Hotspur	2-2, (replay) 3-1	Sheffield United
1902	Sheffield United	1-1, (replay) 2-1	Southampton
1903	Bury	6-0	Derby County
1904	Manchester City	1-0	Bolton Wanderers
1905	Aston Villa	2-0	Newcastle United
1906	Everton	1-0	Newcastle United
1907	Sheffield Wednesday	2-1	Everton
1908	Wolverhampton Wanderers	3-1	Newcastle United
1909	Manchester United	1-0	Bristol City
1910	Newcastle United	1-1, (replay) 2-0	Barnsley
1911	Bradford City	0-0, (replay) 1-0	Newcastle United
1912	Barnsley	0-0, (replay) 1-0 (aet)	West Bromwich Albion
1913	Aston Villa	1-0	Sunderland
1914	Burnley	1-0	Liverpool
1915	Sheffield United	3-0	Chelsea
1916–19	no competition		

ENGLAND

English FA Cup Record (continued)

YEAR	WINNERS	SCORE	RUNNERS-UP
1920	Aston Villa	1-0 (aet)	Huddersfield Town
1921	Tottenham Hotspur	1-0	Wolverhampton Wanderers
1922	Huddersfield Town	1-0	Preston North End
1923	Bolton Wanderers	2-0	West Ham United
1924	Newcastle United	2-0	Aston Villa
1925	Sheffield United	1-0	Cardiff City
1926	Bolton Wanderers	1-0	Manchester City
1927	Cardiff City	1-0	Arsenal
1928	Blackburn Rovers	3-1	Huddersfield Town
1929	Bolton Wanderers	2-0	Portsmouth
1930	Arsenal	2-0	Huddersfield Town
1931	West Bromwich Albion	2-1	Birmingham City
1932	Newcastle United	2-1	Arsenal
1933	Everton	3-0	Manchester City
1934	Manchester City	2-1	Portsmouth
1935	Sheffield Wednesday	4-2	West Bromwich Albion
1936	Arsenal	1-0	Sheffield United
1937	Sunderland	3-1	Preston North End
1938	Preston North End	1-0 (aet)	Huddersfield Town
1939	Portsmouth	4-1	Wolverhampton Wanderers
1940–45		no competition	
1946	Derby County	4-1 (aet)	Charlton Athletic
1947	Charlton Athletic	1-0 (aet)	Burnley
1948	Manchester United	4-2	Blackpool
1949	Wolverhampton Wanderers	3-1	Leicester City
1950	Arsenal	2-0	Liverpool
1951	Newcastle United	2-0	Blackpool
1952	Newcastle United	1-0	Arsenal
1953	Blackpool	4-3	Bolton Wanderers
1954	West Bromwich Albion	3-2	Preston North End
1955	Newcastle United	3-1	Manchester City
1956	Manchester City	3-1	Birmingham City
1957	Aston Villa	2-1	Manchester United
1958	Bolton Wanderers	2-0	Manchester United
1959	Nottingham Forest	2-1	Luton Town
1960	Wolverhampton Wanderers	3-0	Blackburn Rovers
1961	Tottenham Hotspur	2-0	Leicester City
1962	Tottenham Hotspur	3-1	Burnley
1963	Manchester United	3-1	Leicester City
1964	West Ham United	3-2	Preston North End
1965	Liverpool	2-1 (aet)	Leeds United
1966	Everton	3-2	Sheffield Wednesday
1967	Tottenham Hotspur	2-1	Chelsea
1968	West Bromwich Albion	1-0 (aet)	Everton
1969	Manchester City	1-0	Leicester City
1970	Chelsea	2-2 (aet), (replay) 2-1 (aet)	Leeds United
1971	Arsenal	2-1 (aet)	Liverpool
1972	Leeds United	1-0	Arsenal
1973	Sunderland	1-0	Leeds United
1974	Liverpool	3-0	Newcastle United
1975	West Ham United	2-0	Fulham
1976	Southampton	1-0	Manchester United
1977	Manchester United	2-1	Liverpool
1978	Ipswich Town	1-0	Arsenal
1979	Arsenal	3-2	Manchester United

English FA Cup Record (continued)

YEAR	WINNERS	SCORE	RUNNERS-UP
1980	West Ham United	1-0	Arsenal
1981	Tottenham Hotspur	1-1 (aet), (replay) 3-2	Manchester City
1982	Tottenham Hotspur	1-1 (aet), (replay) 1-0	Queens Park Rangers
1983	Manchester United	2-2 (aet), (replay) 4-0	Brighton & Hove Albion
1984	Everton	2-0	Watford
1985	Manchester United	1-0 (aet)	Everton
1986	Liverpool	3-1	Everton
1987	Coventry City	3-2 (aet)	Tottenham Hotspur
1988	Wimbledon	1-0	Liverpool
1989	Liverpool	3-2 (aet)	Everton
1990	Manchester United	3-3 (aet), (replay) 1-0	Crystal Palace
1991	Tottenham Hotspur	2-1 (aet)	Nottingham Forest
1992	Liverpool	2-0	Sunderland
1993	Arsenal	1-1 (aet), (replay) 2-1 (aet)	Sheffield Wednesday
1994	Manchester United	4-0	Chelsea
1995	Everton	1-0	Manchester United
1996	Manchester United	1-0	Liverpool
1997	Chelsea	2-0	Middlesbrough
1998	Arsenal	2-0	Newcastle United
1999	Manchester United	2-0	Newcastle United
2000	Chelsea	1-0	Aston Villa
2001	Liverpool	2-1	Arsenal
2002	Arsenal	2-0	Chelsea
2003	Arsenal	1-0	Southampton
2004	Manchester United	3-0	Millwall

English FA Cup Summary

TEAM	TOTALS	WINNERS & RUNNERS-UP (BOLD) (ITALICS)
Manchester United	11, 5	**1909, 48, 57, 58, 63, 76, 77, 79, 83, 85, 90, 94, 95, 96, 99, 2004**
Arsenal	9, 7	*1927, 30, 32, 36, 50, 52, 71, 72, 78, 79, 80, 93, 98,* **2001, 02, 03**
Tottenham Hotspur	8, 1	**1901, 21, 61, 62, 67, 81, 82, 87, 91**
Aston Villa	7, 3	**1887,** *92,* **95, 97,** *1905, 13, 20, 24, 57, 2000*
Newcastle United	6, 7	*1905, 06, 08,* **10, 11, 24, 32, 51, 52, 55,** *74, 98, 99*
Liverpool	6, 6	*1914, 50,* **65, 71,** *74, 77,* **86, 88, 89, 92, 96, 2001**
Blackburn Rovers	6, 2	**1882, 84–86, 90, 91, 1928,** *60*
Everton	5, 7	*1893, 97,* **1906,** *07, 33,* **66,** *68, 84, 85,* **86,** *89,* **95**
West Bromwich Albion	5, 5	*1886, 87,* **88,** *92,* **95, 1912,** *31,* **35, 54, 68**
Wanderers	5, 0	**1872, 73, 76–78**
Manchester City	4, 4	**1904,** *26, 33,* **34,** *55,* **56,** *69, 81*
Wolverhampton Wanderers	4, 4	*1889, 93,* **96, 1908,** *21, 39,* **49, 60**
Bolton Wanderers	4, 3	*1894,* **1904,** *23,* **26, 29,** *53,* **58**
Sheffield United	4, 2	*1899,* **1901,** *02,* **15, 25,** *36*
Chelsea	3, 4	*1915,* **67,** *70,* **94,** *97,* **2000,** *02*
Sheffield Wednesday	3, 3	*1890,* **96, 1907,** *35,* **66,** *93*
West Ham United	3, 1	*1923,* **64, 75,** *80*
Preston North End	2, 5	*1888,* **89,** *22, 37,* **38,** *54, 64*
Old Etonians	2, 4	**1875,** *76,* **79,** *81, 82, 83*
Sunderland	2, 2	*1913,* **37,** *73,* **92**
Nottingham Forest	2, 1	**1898, 1959,** *91*

English FA Cup Summary (*continued*)

TEAM	TOTALS	WINNERS & RUNNERS-UP (BOLD) (*ITALICS*)
Bury	2, 0	**1900, 03**
Huddersfield Town	1, 4	*1920,* **22,** *28, 30, 38*
Derby County	1, 3	*1898, 99, 1903,* **46**
Leeds United	1, 3	**1965,** *70,* **72,** *73*
Oxford University	1, 3	**1873,** *74,* **77,** *80*
Royal Engineers	1, 3	**1872,** *74,* **75,** *78*
Southampton	1, 3	*1900, 02,* **76,** *03*
Blackpool	1, 2	*1948, 51,* **53**
Burnley	1, 2	**1914,** *47, 62*
Portsmouth	1, 2	*1929, 34,* **39**
Barnsley	1, 1	*1910,* **12**
Cardiff City	1, 1	*1925,* **27**
Charlton Athletic	1, 1	**1946,** *47*
Clapham Rovers	1, 1	*1879,* **80**
Notts County	1, 1	**1891,** *94*
Blackburn Olympic	1, 0	**1883**
Bradford City	1, 0	**1911**
Coventry City	1, 0	**1987**
Ipswich Town	1, 0	**1978**
Old Carthusians	1, 0	**1881**
Wimbledon	1, 0	**1988**
Leicester City	0, 4	*1949, 61, 63, 69*
Birmingham City	0, 2	*1931, 56*
Queen's Park	0, 2	*1884, 85*
Brighton & Hove Albion	0, 1	*1983*
Bristol City	0, 1	*1909*
Crystal Palace	0, 1	*1990*
Fulham	0, 1	*1975*
Luton Town	0, 1	*1959*
Middlesbrough	0, 1	*1997*
Millwall	0, 1	*2004*
Queens Park Rangers	0, 1	*1982*
Watford	0, 1	*1984*

English League Cup Record 1961–2004

YEAR	WINNERS	SCORE	RUNNERS-UP
1961	Aston Villa	0-2, 3-0 (aet) (2 legs)	Rotherham United
1962	Norwich City	3-0, 1-0 (2 legs)	Rochdale
1963	Birmingham City	3-1, 0-0 (2 legs)	Aston Villa
1964	Leicester City	1-1, 3-2 (2 legs)	Stoke City
1965	Chelsea	3-2, 0-0 (2 legs)	Leicester City
1966	West Bromwich Albion	1-2, 4-1 (2 legs)	West Ham United
1967	Queens Park Rangers	3-2	West Bromwich Albion
1968	Leeds United	1-0	Arsenal
1969	Swindon Town	3-1 (aet)	Arsenal
1970	Manchester City	2-1 (aet)	West Bromwich Albion
1971	Tottenham Hotspur	2-0	Aston Villa
1972	Stoke City	2-1	Chelsea
1973	Tottenham Hotspur	1-0	Norwich City
1974	Wolverhampton Wanderers	2-1	Manchester City
1975	Aston Villa	1-0	Norwich City
1976	Manchester City	2-1	Newcastle United
1977	Aston Villa	0-0, (replay) 1-1 (aet), (replay) 3-2 (aet)	Everton
1978	Nottingham Forest	0-0 (aet), (replay) 1-0	Liverpool
1979	Nottingham Forest	3-2	Southampton
1980	Wolverhampton Wanderers	1-0	Nottingham Forest
1981	Liverpool	1-1 (aet), (replay) 2-1	West Ham United

English League Cup Record (*continued*)

YEAR	WINNERS	SCORE	RUNNERS-UP
1982	Liverpool	3-1 (aet)	Tottenham Hotspur
1983	Liverpool	2-1 (aet)	Manchester United
1984	Liverpool	0-0 (aet), (replay) 1-0	Everton
1985	Norwich City	1-0	Sunderland
1986	Oxford United	3-0	Queens Park Rangers
1987	Arsenal	2-1	Liverpool
1988	Luton Town	3-2	Arsenal
1989	Nottingham Forest	3-1	Luton Town
1990	Nottingham Forest	1-0	Oldham Athletic
1991	Sheffield Wednesday	1-0	Manchester United
1992	Manchester United	1-0	Nottingham Forest
1993	Arsenal	2-1	Sheffield Wednesday
1994	Aston Villa	3-1	Manchester United
1995	Liverpool	2-1	Bolton Wanderers
1996	Aston Villa	3-0	Leeds United
1997	Leicester City	1-1 (aet), (replay) 1-0 (aet)	Middlesbrough
1998	Chelsea	2-0 (aet)	Middlesbrough
1999	Tottenham Hotspur	1-0	Leicester City
2000	Leicester City	2-1	Tranmere Rovers
2001	Liverpool	1-1 (aet)(5-4 pens)	Birmingham City
2002	Blackburn Rovers	2-1	Tottenham Hotspur
2003	Liverpool	2-0	Manchester United
2004	Middlesbrough	2-1	Bolton Wanderers

English League Cup Summary

TEAM	TOTALS	WINNERS & RUNNERS-UP (BOLD) (*ITALICS*)
Liverpool	7, 2	*1978,* **81–84,** *87,* **95, 2001, 03**
Aston Villa	5, 2	**1961,** *63,* **71,** *75, 77,* **94,** *96*
Nottingham Forest	4, 2	**1978, 79, 80, 89, 90,** *92*
Leicester City	3, 2	**1964,** *65,* **97,** *99,* **2000**
Tottenham Hotspur	3, 2	**1971,** *73,* **82,** *99,* **2002**
Arsenal	2, 3	*1968, 69,* **87, 88,** *93*
Norwich City	2, 2	**1962,** *73,* **75,** *85*
Chelsea	2, 1	**1965,** *72,* **98**
Manchester City	2, 1	**1970,** *74,* **76**
Wolverhampton Wanderers	2, 0	**1974, 80**
Manchester United	1, 4	*1983, 91,* **92,** *94, 2003*
Middlesbrough	1, 2	*1997, 98,* **2004**
West Bromwich Albion	1, 2	**1966,** *67, 70*
Birmingham City	1, 1	**1963,** *2001*
Leeds United	1, 1	**1968,** *96*
Luton Town	1, 1	**1988,** *89*
Queens Park Rangers	1, 1	**1967,** *86*
Sheffield Wednesday	1, 1	**1991,** *93*
Stoke City	1, 1	**1964,** *72*
Blackburn Rovers	1, 0	**2002**
Oxford United	1, 0	**1986**
Swindon Town	1, 0	**1969**
Bolton Wanderers	0, 2	*1995, 2004*
Everton	0, 2	*1977, 84*
Newcastle United	0, 1	*1976*
Oldham Athletic	0, 1	*1990*
Rochdale	0, 1	*1962*
Rotherham United	0, 1	*1961*
Southampton	0, 1	*1979*
Sunderland	0, 1	*1985*
Tranmere Rovers	0, 1	*2000*

Scotland

THE SEASON IN REVIEW 2003–04

ONCE AGAIN THE PENDULUM OF SCOTTISH SOCCER has swung. Last year Rangers took the treble, this year it was Celtic's season. The club won the league at a canter with six games to spare, and beat Rangers in every one of the Old Firm derbies; it also established the longest winning streak in top flight Scottish soccer. In Europe, the Celts only made the quarter-finals of the UEFA Cup this year, but were good enough to beat Barcelona in the competition. Celtic also won the Scottish Cup (and had the pleasure of knocking Rangers out in the quarter-finals) and bid an emotional goodbye to the club's favourite son Henrik Larsson, who once again scored freely all season. But beyond Celtic Park there was a distinct and pervading sense of gloom in Scottish soccer.

Grim realities

The national team's capitulation to the Dutch, losing 6-0 in the Euro 2004 play-offs, was grim, as are the finances of the SPL. Indeed, so poor is the situation in the lower reaches of the SPL that this season's first division champions – Inverness Caledonian Thistle – expressed serious doubts before taking up their promotion spot. Aside from the SPL's self-imposed idiocy of having to play in a minimum of a 10,000-seat stadium (a figure likely to be reduced to 6,000 from 2005–06 onwards) in a league where only four clubs have average gates in excess of that figure, Inverness are well aware of what a poisoned chalice the SPL can be.

The internal fighting of the last few years over control of television rights has seen the SPL forced to settle for a poor deal with the BBC. The decline in TV revenues has hit hard at clubs already overspending and underperforming. The combined debts of the SPL stand at £190 million. Three clubs have gone into administration over the last two years – Motherwell, Dundee and this season's League Cup winners Livingston. Hearts are desperate to sell their old Tynecastle ground and will go anywhere and share with anyone. Dunfermline's players have been forced to take a pay cut despite grabbing a place in the UEFA Cup. Rangers alone have debts of £60 million and until they clear that the pendulum may be stuck in Celtic Park.

Scottish Premier League Table 2003–04

CLUB	P	W	D	L	F	A	Pts	
Celtic	38	31	5	2	105	25	**98**	Champions League
Rangers	38	25	6	7	76	33	**81**	Champions League
Hearts	38	19	11	8	56	40	**68**	UEFA Cup
Dunfermline Athletic	38	14	11	13	45	52	**53**	UEFA Cup (cup finalists)
Dundee United	38	13	10	15	47	60	**49**	
Motherwell	38	12	10	16	42	49	**46**	
Dundee	38	12	10	16	48	57	**46**	
Hibernian	38	11	11	16	41	60	**44**	
Livingston	38	10	13	15	48	57	**43**	
Kilmarnock	38	12	6	20	51	74	**42**	
Aberdeen	38	9	7	22	39	63	**34**	
Partick Thistle	38	6	8	24	39	67	**26**	Relegated

Promoted club: Inverness Caledonian Thistle (who will play home games at Aberdeen's Pittodrie Stadium for 2004–05 season).

Scottish League Cup

2004 FINAL

March 14 – Hampden Park, Glasgow
Livingston 2-0 Hibernian
(Lilley 50,
McAllister 52)
h/t: 0-0   Att: 45,500
Ref: Young

Scottish FA Cup

2004 FINAL

May 22 – Hampden Park, Glasgow
Celtic 3-1 Dunfermline
(Larsson 58, 71,   Athletic
Petrov 84)   (Skerla 40)
h/t: 0-1   Att: 50,846
Ref: Dougal

Top Goalscorers 2003–04

PLAYER	CLUB	NATIONALITY	GOALS
Henrik Larsson	Celtic	Swedish	30
Steven MacLean	Rangers	Scottish	23
Nacho Novo	Dundee	Spanish	19
Chris Sutton	Celtic	English	19

International Club Performances 2003–04

CLUB	COMPETITION	PROGRESS
Celtic	Champions League	Group Stage
	UEFA Cup	Quarter-finals
Rangers	Champions League	Group Stage
Dundee	UEFA Cup	1st Round
Hearts	UEFA Cup	2nd Round

Going up. *Players and fans of Inverness Caledonian Thistle celebrate Liam Keogh's opening goal in the game with Clyde. Despite doubts the highland club will take their place in the SPL in August 2004.*

Motherwell's Steve Hammell *clears the ball under pressure from Rangers' Shota Arveladze. Motherwell clawed their way out of financial danger this year and finished in the top six.*

Henrik Larsson heads the ball past Rangers' Michael Ball and scores the opening goal of Celtic's 2-1 league victory at Ibrox.

Far left, top: Rangers manager Alex McLeish estimates the size of the gap between his team's performance this season and last.

Far left, middle: Partick Thistle's Stephane Bonnes in action against Livingston. But it was too little too late. Partick never recovered from a dismal start and went straight back down.

Far left, bottom: Administration is good for you. Imperilled by financial problems all season Livingston rose above it to win the CIS Insurance Cup Final. Jamie McAllister lifts the trophy.

Left: They made it look easy. Celtic celebrate their 39th Scottish League title.

Celtic make it a double. In his last game for Celtic Henrik Larsson lifts the Scottish Cup after Celtic had outplayed Dunfermline in the Final.

Soccer in Scotland

1867: Queen's Park FC, Scotland's oldest club founded

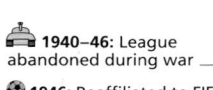 **1872:** First official international, v England, drawn 0-0, venue: Glasgow

1873: Formation of Scottish FA

1874: First Scottish Cup Final

1891: First league championship

1893: Professionalism adopted, Scottish Second Division created

1902: Ibrox disaster. Stand collapses at Scotland v England match, 29 killed, 500 injured

1910: Affiliation to FIFA

1920: Withdrew from FIFA

1924: Reaffiliated to FIFA

1928: Withdrew from FIFA

1929: Scotland play first foreign international, beating Norway 7-3 in Oslo

1940–46: League abandoned during war

1946: Reaffiliated to FIFA

1947: First Scottish League Cup Final

1954: Affiliation to UEFA

1968: First women's league formed

1971: Ibrox disaster. Crush during Rangers v Celtic match, 66 killed

1972: Scottish Women's Football Association founded. First international, v England, lost 2-3, venue: Greenock

1975: Scottish league reorganization, creating ten-team Premier League, First and Second Divisions

1994: Two lower leagues turned into three with addition of two new clubs from the Highlands

1997: Scottish Premier League separates from Scottish FA

1999: Scottish Women's FA affiliates to SFA

2002: Ten non-Old Firm clubs resign from SPL and threaten to establish breakaway league

Timeline: 1865, 1870, 1875, 1880, 1885, 1890, 1895, 1900, 1905, 1910, 1915, 1920, 1925, 1930, 1935, 1940, 1945, 1950, 1955, 1960, 1965, 1970, 1975, 1980, 1985, 1990, 1995, 2000, 2005

SCOTLAND

In March 1878, the annual Scotland v England match ended in a convincing 7-2 victory for the Scots at Queen's Park, Glasgow.

Key

International soccer		○	Competition winner
Affiliation to FIFA		△	Competition runner-up
Affiliation to UEFA		Dons	– Aberdeen
Women's soccer		Dun U	– Dundee United
Disaster		Gers	– Rangers
War			

International Competitions

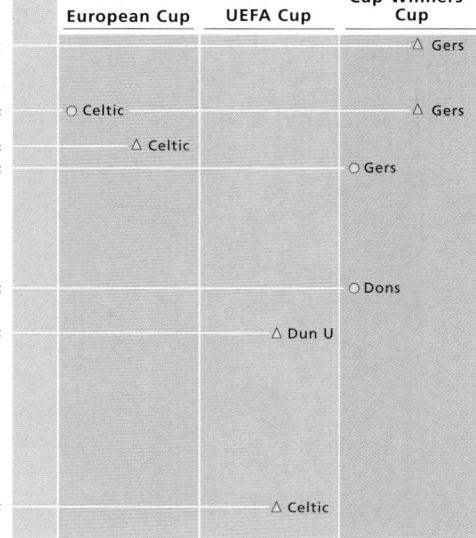

	European Cup	UEFA Cup	European Cup-Winners' Cup
1961:			△ Gers
1967:	○ Celtic		△ Gers
1970:	△ Celtic		
1972:			○ Gers
1983:			○ Dons
1987:		△ Dun U	
2003:			△ Celtic

Scotland: The main clubs

Clyde 1878	Team name with year of formation
●	Club formed before 1912
●	Club formed 1912–25
●	Club formed 1925–50
○	Club formed after 1950
★	Founder members of league (1890)
	Pre-1914 champions
⊞	English origins
	Originated from a military institution
	Originated from a cricket club
	Originated from a school or college
	Mining origins
✝	Catholic allegiances
✝	Protestant allegiances
	YMCA

★ Third Lanark 1872

Founded by members of Third Lanark Rifle Volunteers, changed name to Third Lanark (1878). Dissolved 1966

Renton 1872

Left league 1898

Hamilton Academical 1874

★ Cambuslang 1875

Left league 1892

★ Cowlairs 1876

Left league 1891

Queen's Park 1867

Clydebank 1965

Played one year (1964–65) as ES Clydebank, merger with East Stirlingshire

Partick Thistle 1876

★ Rangers 1873

★ Celtic 1888

Clydebank 1914

Dissolved 1931

★ Abercorn 1870s

Left league 1915

★ St. Mirren 1877

Founded in 1867, Queen's Park is Scotland's oldest club. The team is shown here in action during a friendly match with the English club Corinthians in 1901.

Scotland

ORIGINS AND GROWTH OF SOCCER

SCOTTISH SOCCER FOLLOWED RAPIDLY on the heels of its English counterpart. Its first club, Queen's Park, was formed in Glasgow in 1867 by members of the YMCA and went on to compete in the English FA Cups of the era. Along with the other home countries Scotland is a political region that has nation status in international soccer, and in 1872 the first-ever international, against England, was played in Glasgow. The following year saw the establishment of the Scottish FA in Glasgow and the first Scottish Cup competition. In the following decade soccer swept through the working-class communities of Scotland's central belt. Clubs and followings were often established around Protestant and Irish immigrant/Catholic neighbourhoods and identities, especially in the cities of Glasgow, Edinburgh and Dundee.

The price of success

The world's second oldest national league began in 1890 and professionalism arrived in 1893. But more significant was the fact that Scottish soccer provided much of the manpower for the early English professional league, also exporting players, missionaries and coaches of the game to Europe and Latin America. They pioneered the passing game – a style at odds with the dreary solo dribbling and long balls of the emerging English game – where players moved the ball on the ground in structured passing and running moves.

But the explosive growth of Scottish soccer came at a cost. In 1902, 29 people died and over 500 were injured when a new stand at Rangers' Ibrox stadium collapsed during a Scotland v England international match. In 1909, a Celtic v Rangers fixture at Hampden Park descended into soccer's first full-scale stadium riot.

The economics of failure

Like England, Scotland's international performance during the early World Cups was limited by the SFA's disinterest or active opposition to FIFA. It has yet to recover. In the postwar era, the economic and soccer dominance of Celtic and Rangers has increased, their domestic strength bringing European success in the late 1960s and early 1970s. However, the economics of soccer in a small country since then has meant that both clubs have failed to repeat those successes.

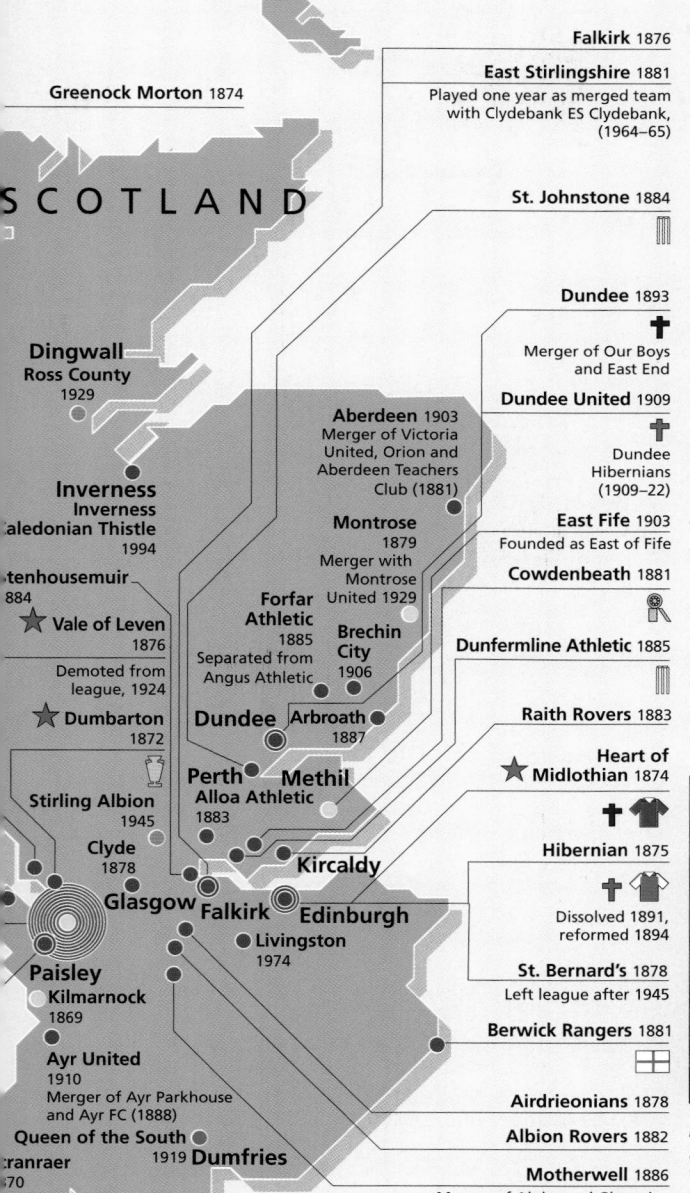

Falkirk 1876

East Stirlingshire 1881
Played one year as merged team with Clydebank ES Clydebank, (1964–65)

Greenock Morton 1874

S C O T L A N D

St. Johnstone 1884

Dundee 1893
Merger of Our Boys and East End

Dundee United 1909
Dundee Hibernians (1909–22)

Dingwall
Ross County
1929

Aberdeen 1903
Merger of Victoria United, Orion and Aberdeen Teachers Club (1881)

East Fife 1903
Founded as East of Fife

Montrose
1879
Merger with Montrose United 1929

Cowdenbeath 1881

Inverness
Inverness Caledonian Thistle
1994

Forfar Athletic
1885
Separated from Angus Athletic

Brechin City
1906

Dunfermline Athletic 1885

tenhousemuir
884

Vale of Leven
1876
Demoted from league, 1924

Raith Rovers 1883

Dumbarton
1872

Dundee   **Arbroath**
1887

Heart of Midlothian 1874

Perth   **Methil**
Alloa Athletic
1883

Stirling Albion
1945

Hibernian 1875
Dissolved 1891, reformed 1894

Clyde
1878

Kircaldy

St. Bernard's 1878
Left league after 1945

Glasgow   **Falkirk**   **Edinburgh**
Livingston
1974

Paisley

Berwick Rangers 1881

Kilmarnock
1869

Ayr United
1910
Merger of Ayr Parkhouse and Ayr FC (1888)

Airdrieonians 1878

Albion Rovers 1882

Queen of the South
1919   **Dumfries**
tranraer
70

Motherwell 1886
Merger of Alpha and Glencairn

In 1902, at a friendly match between Scotland and England at Ibrox Park, seven rows of wooden planking on the newly-built eastern terrace collapsed under the weight of spectators. Hundreds plunged 40 feet to the ground below, resulting in 29 deaths.

SCOTLAND

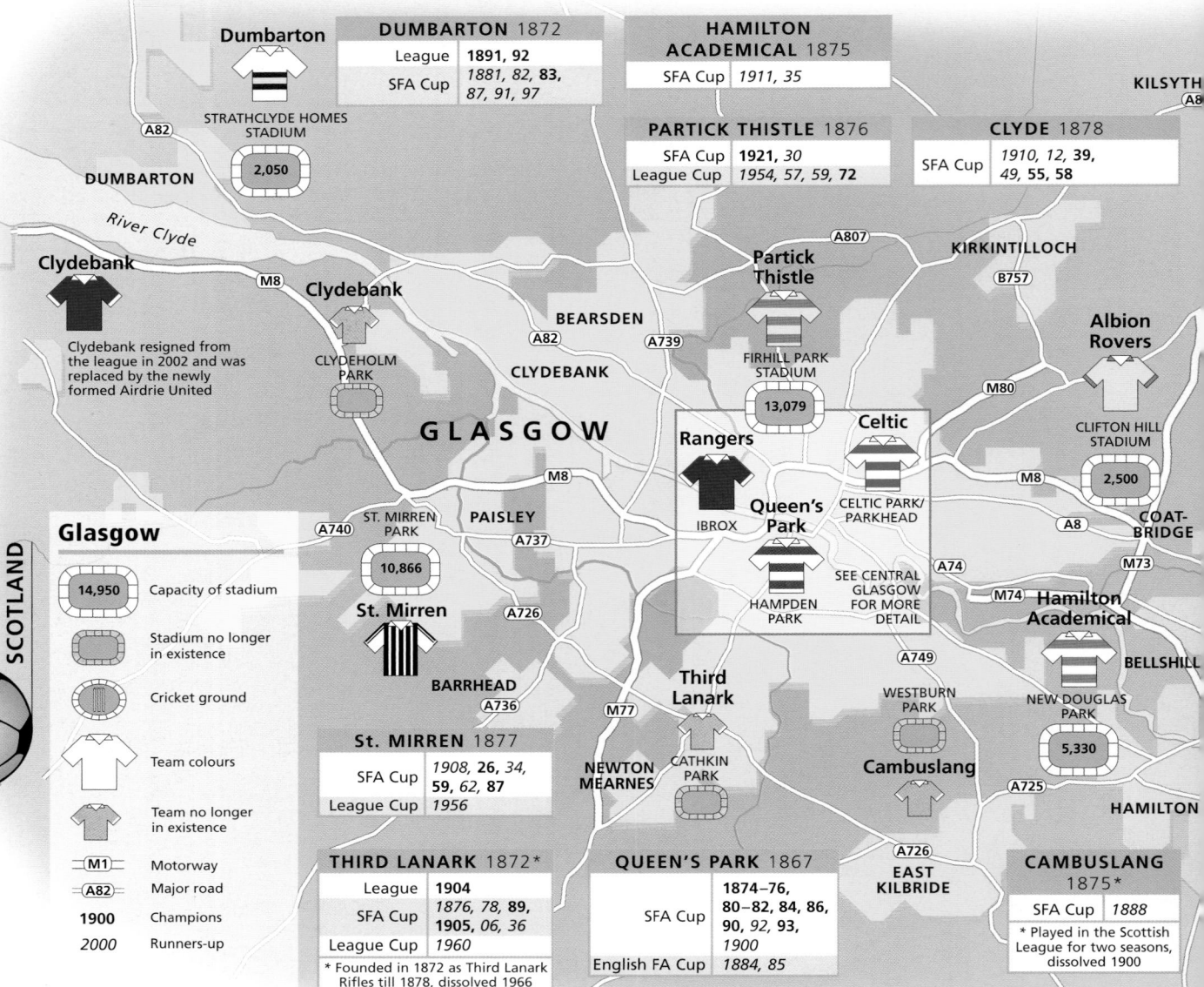

SCOTLAND

Dumbarton

STRATHCLYDE HOMES STADIUM

2,050

DUMBARTON 1872	
League	**1891, 92**
SFA Cup	*1881, 82,* **83,** *87, 91, 97*

HAMILTON ACADEMICAL 1875	
SFA Cup	*1911, 35*

KILSYTH

PARTICK THISTLE 1876	
SFA Cup	**1921,** *30*
League Cup	**1954, 57, 59, 72**

CLYDE 1878	
SFA Cup	*1910, 12, 39, 49, 55, 58*

Clydebank

Clydebank resigned from the league in 2002 and was replaced by the newly formed Airdrie United

Clydebank

CLYDEHOLM PARK

CLYDEBANK

BEARSDEN

Partick Thistle

FIRHILL PARK STADIUM

13,079

KIRKINTILLOCH

Albion Rovers

CLIFTON HILL STADIUM

2,500

G L A S G O W

Rangers

IBROX

Celtic

CELTIC PARK/ PARKHEAD

Queen's Park

HAMPDEN PARK

SEE CENTRAL GLASGOW FOR MORE DETAIL

COAT-BRIDGE

Hamilton Academical

NEW DOUGLAS PARK

5,330

BELLSHILL

HAMILTON

Glasgow

14,950	Capacity of stadium
	Stadium no longer in existence
	Cricket ground
	Team colours
	Team no longer in existence
M1	Motorway
A82	Major road
1900	Champions
2000	Runners-up

ST. MIRREN PARK

PAISLEY

10,866

St. Mirren

BARRHEAD

Third Lanark

CATHKIN PARK

NEWTON MEARNES

WESTBURN PARK

Cambuslang

EAST KILBRIDE

St. MIRREN 1877	
SFA Cup	*1908,* **26,** *34, 59, 62, 87*
League Cup	*1956*

THIRD LANARK 1872*	
League	**1904**
SFA Cup	*1876, 78,* **89,** **1905,** *06, 36*
League Cup	*1960*
Founded in 1872 as Third Lanark Rifles till 1878, dissolved 1966	

QUEEN'S PARK 1867	
SFA Cup	**1874–76, 80–82, 84, 86, 90, 92, 93,** *1900*
English FA Cup	*1884, 85*

CAMBUSLANG 1875*	
SFA Cup	*1888*
Played in the Scottish League for two seasons, dissolved 1900	

Glasgow

SOCCER CENTER

GLASGOW MAY NOT BE the political capital of Scotland, but there was no question that the Scottish FA would be located anywhere but in the country's soccer-playing capital. Scotland's first club, Queen's Park, was founded in the south of the city in 1867. Glasgow saw the world's first international, played in Partick in 1872, the world's first penalty in 1891; the world's first stadium collapse in 1902; and the first stadium riot in 1909.

In the late 19th century, Glasgow's booming heavy industries drew heavily on rural Scottish Protestant and Irish Catholic immigrants. In the following two decades, soccer clubs sprang up all over greater Glasgow as this divided working class embraced Scottish soccer. However, the centre of the city was dominated by the rivalry between Celtic and Rangers – the 'Old Firm'.

The origins of the Old Firm

Celtic was founded in 1888 by Brother Walfrid of the Marist Order as both a soccer club and a social service for Catholic boys. The club's affiliations have remained clear: a shamrock emblem and the flying of the Irish tricolor at the stadium. Rangers was formed over a decade earlier out of a rowing club north of the River Clyde, but soon settled among the docks and Protestant dockworkers of the Govan area. Rangers' affiliation to Unionism and Protestantism, always present, grew with the emergence of Celtic as sporting and cultural rivals. By 1910, Rangers would no longer sign Catholic players, and its strip, predominantly blue, had acquired red and white trimmings. Persistent conflict on and off the pitch has been tempered in recent years by the geographical dispersal of the old religious ghettoes and concerted official efforts to challenge sectarianism, including Rangers' signing of the Catholic Mo Johnston in 1989. But, like the issue of sectarianism in wider Scottish society, it remains largely unexamined and intact.

SCOTLAND

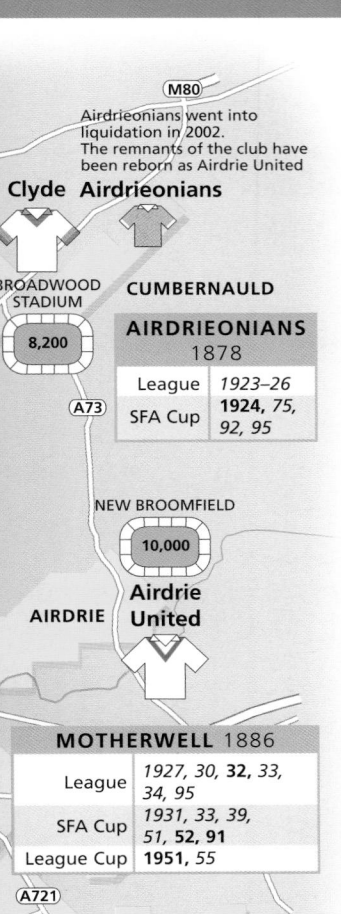

Airdrieonians went into liquidation in 2002. The remnants of the club have been reborn as Airdrie United

Clyde Airdrieonians

BROADWOOD STADIUM | CUMBERNAULD

8,200

A73

AIRDRIEONIANS 1878

League	1923–26
SFA Cup	**1924**, 75, 92, 95

NEW BROOMFIELD

10,000

Airdrie United

AIRDRIE

MOTHERWELL 1886

League	1927, 30, **32**, 33, 34, 95
SFA Cup	1931, 33, 39, 51, **52**, **91**
League Cup	**1951**, 55

A721

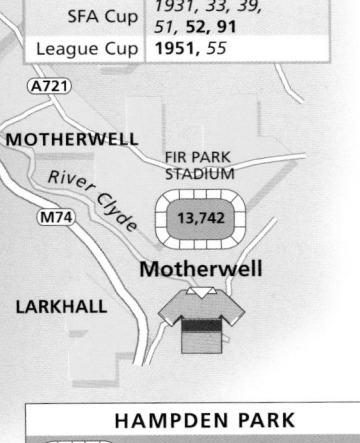

MOTHERWELL

FIR PARK STADIUM

River Clyde

M74

13,742

Motherwell

LARKHALL

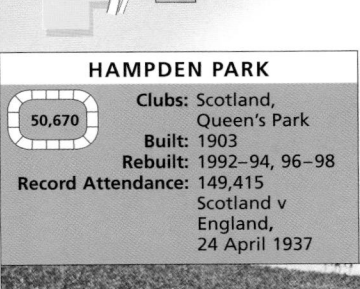

HAMPDEN PARK

50,670

Clubs: Scotland, Queen's Park
Built: 1903
Rebuilt: 1992–94, 96–98
Record Attendance: 149,415 Scotland v England, 24 April 1937

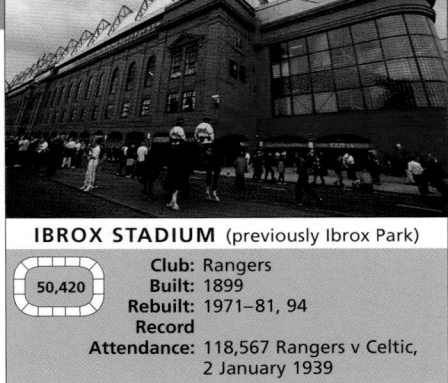

IBROX STADIUM (previously Ibrox Park)

50,420

Club: Rangers
Built: 1899
Rebuilt: 1971–81, 94
Record Attendance: 118,567 Rangers v Celtic, 2 January 1939

RANGERS 1873

League	1891, 93, 96, 98, 99–1902, 05, 11–13, 14, 16, **18**, 19, 20, 21, 22, 23–25, 27–31, 32, 33–35, 36, 37, 39, 47, 48, 49, 50, 51, 52, 53, 56, 57, 58, 59, 61, 62, 63, 64, 66–70, 73, 75, 76, 77, 78, 79, 87, 89–97, 98, 99, 2000, 01, 02, 03, 04
SFA Cup	1877, 79, 94, 97, 98, 99, 1903, 04, 05, 21, 22, **28**, 29, 30, 32, 34–36, 48–50, 53, 60, 62–64, 66, 69, 71, 73, 76, 77, 78, 79, 80, 81, 82, 83, 89, 92, 93, 94, 96, 98, 99, 2000, 02, 03
League Cup	1947, 49, 52, 58, 61, 62, 64, 65, 66, 67, 71, 76, 78, 79, 82, 83, 84, 85, 87–89, 90, 91, 93, 94, 97, 99, 2002, 03
European Cup-Winners' Cup	1961, 67, **72**

CELTIC 1888

League	1892, 93, 94, 95, 96, 98, 1900–02, 05–10, 12, 13, **14–17**, 18, **19**, 20, 21, **22**, 26, 28, 29, 31, 35, 36, 38, 39, 54, 55, 66–74, 76, 77, 79, 80, 81, 82, 83–85, 86, 87, 88, 96, 97, 98, 99, 2000, 01, 02, 03, 04
SFA Cup	1889, 92, 93, 94, 99, 1900, 01, 02, 04, 07, 08, 11, 12, 14, 23, 25, 26, 27, 28, 31, 33, 37, 51, 54, 55, 56, 61, 63, 65, 66, 67, 69, 70, 71, 72, 73, 74, 75, 77, 80, 84, 85, 88, 89, 90, 95, 99, 2001, 02, 04
League Cup	1957, 58, 65, 66–70, 71–74, 75, 76–78, 83, 84, 87, 91, 95, 98, 2000, 01, 03
European Cup	**1967**, 70
UEFA Cup	2003
World Club Cup	1967

CELTIC PARK/PARKHEAD

60,506

Club: Celtic
Built: 1892
Rebuilt: 1995
Record Attendance: 92,000 Celtic v Rangers, 1 January 1938

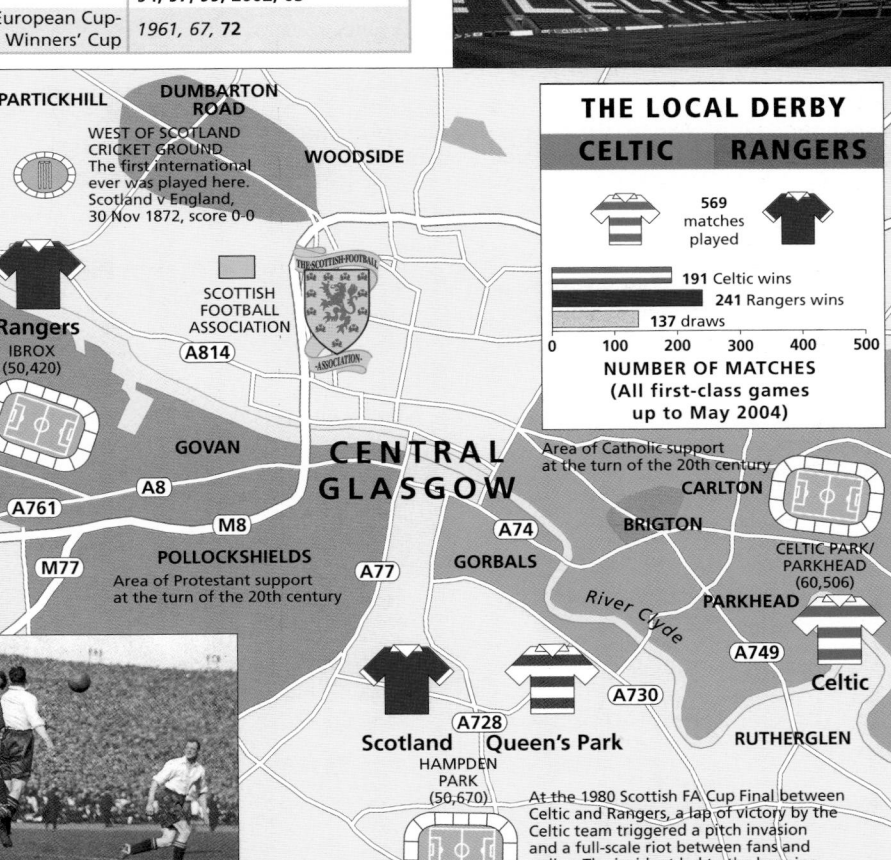

PARTICKHILL   DUMBARTON ROAD

WEST OF SCOTLAND CRICKET GROUND
The first international ever was played here. Scotland v England, 30 Nov 1872, score 0-0

WOODSIDE

SCOTTISH FOOTBALL ASSOCIATION

Rangers
IBROX (50,420)

A814

GOVAN

A8

A761   M8

POLLOCKSHIELDS
Area of Protestant support at the turn of the 20th century

M77

CENTRAL GLASGOW

Area of Catholic support at the turn of the 20th century

CARLTON

BRIGTON

A74

A77   GORBALS

CELTIC PARK/ PARKHEAD (60,506)

River Clyde

PARKHEAD

A749

Celtic

A730

RUTHERGLEN

A728

Scotland Queen's Park
HAMPDEN PARK (50,670)

At the 1980 Scottish FA Cup Final between Celtic and Rangers, a lap of victory by the Celtic team triggered a pitch invasion and a full-scale riot between fans and police. The incident led to the banning of alcohol from Scottish grounds

THE LOCAL DERBY

CELTIC   RANGERS

569 matches played

191 Celtic wins
241 Rangers wins
137 draws

0 100 200 300 400 500

NUMBER OF MATCHES (All first-class games up to May 2004)

Scotland

PLAYERS AND MANAGERS

ALMOST INEVITABLY SCOTTISH soccer has been a great exporter of talent. Among the earliest players of the game and the earliest professionals, Scottish players and managers have constantly found themselves outgrowing their small and economically limited leagues. In the late 19th century, Scots were central to the spread of the game in Latin America and continental Europe, while Scottish teams pioneered the short passing game as it was known, displacing the kick and rush that was dominant south of the border. Scots took their talents and their style to Germany, Central Europe and, above all, to England, for it is the old enemy that has most consistently provided the better wages and the bigger stage that Scottish soccer talent has demanded. It is the same logic that has seen a steady influx of foreign talent not only to the big two Glasgow teams, but also to the smallest Premier Division sides.

Working-class politics

The great Scottish managers of the modern era – Sir Matt Busby, Sir Alex Ferguson and Bill Shankly – have all really made their mark south of the border, not only winning trophies but building teams and clubs that lasted. Only Jock Stein (a disastrous month at Leeds United aside) built his career in Scotland at Celtic and as national team manager. The working-class and often political roots of these men has provided a context in which their special kind of leadership and management talent could be awakened. Similarly, among the greatest players of the modern era it has often been an English club that has provided the home in which their talent could fully mature: Denis Law at Manchester United, and Kenny Dalglish, Alan Hansen and Graeme Souness at Liverpool.

In the early years of the soccer league Preston North End redefined the style of professional soccer in a team stuffed with Scots. Sunderland, another dominant team of the era, also drew heavily on Scottish players. The same logic of labour migration has transformed contemporary Scottish soccer. In the last decade, a flood of foreign players has gone to Scotland.

It is arguable that the decline of the national team in recent years can be attributed to the squeezing out of domestic talent, a situation made starker by the appointment of the German coach Berti Vogts as national team manager.

Top 10 International Caps

PLAYER	CAPS	GOALS	FIRST MATCH	LAST MATCH
Kenny Dalglish	102	30	1972	1987
Jim Leighton	91	0	1983	1999
Alex McLeish	77	1	1980	1993
Paul McStay	76	9	1984	1997
Tommy Boyd*	73	1	1991	2001
Willie Miller	65	1	1975	1990
Danny McGrain	62	0	1973	1982
Richard Gough	61	6	1983	1993
Ally McCoist	61	19	1986	1998
John Collins*	58	12	1988	2000
Roy Aitken	57	1	1980	1992
Gary McAllister*	57	5	1990	1999

Top 10 International Goalscorers

PLAYER	GOALS	CAPS	FIRST MATCH	LAST MATCH
Denis Law	30	55	1959	1974
Kenny Dalglish	30	102	1972	1987
Hugh Gallacher	23	53	1924	1935
Lawrie Reilly	22	38	1949	1957
Ally McCoist	19	61	1986	1998
Robert Cumming Hamilton	14	11	1899	1911
Mo Johnston	14	38	1984	1992
John Smith	13	10	1877	1884
Andrew Nesbit Wilson	13	12	1920	1923
Robert Smyth McColl	13	13	1896	1908

* Indicates players still playing at least at club level.

Scotland International Managers

DATES	NAME	GAMES	WON	DRAWN	LOST
1954	Andy Beattie	6	2	1	3
1958	Matt Busby	2	1	1	0
1959–60	Andy Beattie	12	3	3	6
1960–65	Ian McColl	28	17	3	8
1965	Jock Stein	7	3	1	3
1966	John Prentice	4	0	1	3
1966	Malcolm McDonald	2	1	1	0
1967–71	Bobby Brown	28	9	8	11
1971–72	Tommy Docherty	12	7	2	3
1973–77	Willie Ormond	38	18	8	12
1977–78	Ally McLeod	17	7	5	5
1978–85	Jock Stein	61	26	12	23
1985–86	Alex Ferguson	10	3	4	3
1986–93	Andy Roxburgh	61	23	19	19
1993–2001	Craig Brown	70	32	18	20
2002–	Berti Vogts	27	9	5	13

All figures correct as of 28 June 2004.

Foreign Players in Scotland (in top division squads)

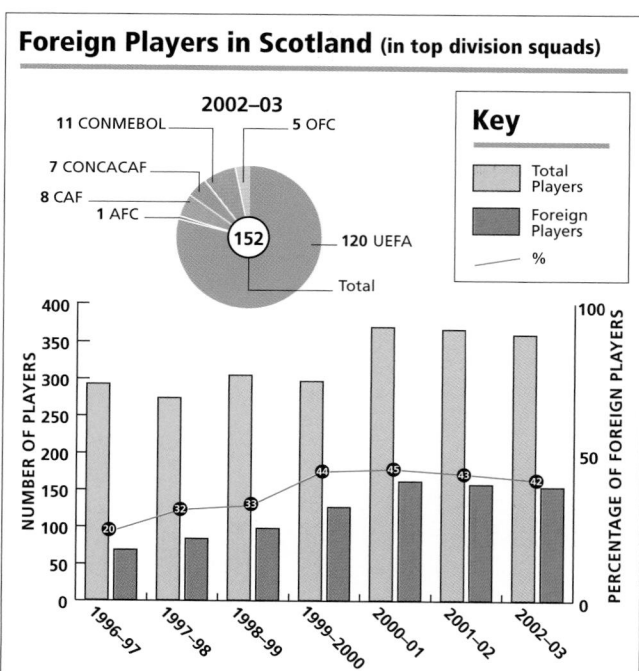

2002–03

11 CONMEBOL
5 OFC
7 CONCACAF
8 CAF
1 AFC
152
120 UEFA
Total

Key
- Total Players
- Foreign Players
- %

SCOTLAND

Player of the Year

YEAR	PLAYER	CLUB
1965	McNeill	Celtic
1966	Greig	Rangers
1967	Simpson	Celtic
1968	Wallace	Raith Rovers
1969	Murdoch	Celtic
1970	Stanton	Hibernian
1971	Buchan	Aberdeen
1972	Smith	Rangers
1973	Connelly	Celtic
1974	Scotland World Cup Squad	
1975	Jardine	Rangers
1976	Greig	Rangers
1977	McGrain	Celtic
1978	Johnstone	Rangers
1979	Ritchie	Morton
1980	Strachan	Aberdeen
1981	Rough	Partick Thistle
1982	Sturrock	Dundee United
1983	Nicholas	Celtic
1984	Miller	Aberdeen
1985	McAlpine	Dundee United
1986	Jardine	Heart of Midlothian
1987	McClair	Celtic
1988	McStay	Celtic
1989	Gough	Rangers
1990	McLeish	Aberdeen
1991	Malpas	Dundee United
1992	McCoist	Rangers
1993	Goram	Rangers
1994	Hateley	Rangers
1995	Laudrup	Rangers
1996	Gascoigne	Rangers
1997	Laudrup	Rangers
1998	Burley	Celtic
1999	Larsson	Celtic
2000	B. Ferguson	Rangers
2001	Larsson	Celtic
2002	Lambert	Celtic
2003	B. Ferguson	Rangers
2004	McNamara	Celtic

Awarded by the Scottish Football Writers' Association.

Manager of the Year

YEAR	MANAGER	CLUB
1987	Jim McLean	Dundee United
1988	Billy McNeill	Celtic
1989	Graeme Souness	Rangers
1990	Andy Roxburgh	Scotland
1991	Alex Totten	St. Johnstone
1992	Walter Smith	Rangers
1993	Walter Smith	Rangers
1994	Walter Smith	Rangers
1995	Jimmy Nichol	Raith Rovers
1996	Walter Smith	Rangers
1997	Walter Smith	Rangers
1998	Wim Jansen	Celtic
1999	Dick Advocaat	Rangers
2000	Dick Advocaat	Rangers
2001	Martin O'Neill	Celtic
2002	John Lambie	Partick Thistle
2003	Alex McLeish	Rangers
2004	Martin O'Neill	Celtic

Awarded by Tennents.

Celtic's Billy McNeill is held up by his teammates after their victory in the 1965 Scottish Cup Final against Dunfermline. McNeill's efforts that season earned him the Scottish Player of the Year award.

Top Goalscorers by Season 1965–2004

SEASON	PLAYER	CLUB	GOALS	SEASON	PLAYER	CLUB	GOALS
1965–66	McBride	Celtic	31	1995–96	Hooijdonk	Celtic	26
1965–66	A. Ferguson	Dunfermline Athletic	31	1996–97	Cadete	Celtic	25
1966–67	Chalmers	Celtic	21	1997–98	Negri	Rangers	32
1967–68	Lennox	Celtic	32	1998–99	Larsson	Celtic	29
1968–69	Cameron	Dundee United	26	1999–2000	Viduka	Celtic	25
1969–70	Stein	Rangers	24	2000–01	Larsson	Celtic	35
1970–71	Hood	Celtic	22	2001–02	Larsson	Celtic	29
1971–72	Harper	Aberdeen	33	2002–03	Larsson	Celtic	28
1972–73	Gordon	Hibernian	27	2003–04	Larsson	Celtic	30
1973–74	Deans	Celtic	26				
1974–75	Gray	Dundee United	20				
1974–75	Pettigrew	Motherwell	20				
1975–76	Dalglish	Celtic	24				
1976–77	Pettigrew	Motherwell	21				
1977–78	Johnstone	Rangers	25				
1978–79	Ritchie	Morton	22				
1979–80	Somner	St. Mirren	25				
1980–81	McGarvey	Celtic	23				
1981–82	McCluskey	Celtic	21				
1982–83	Nicholas	Celtic	29				
1983–84	McClair	Celtic	23				
1984–85	McDougall	Dundee	22				
1985–86	McCoist	Rangers	24				
1986–87	McClair	Celtic	35				
1987–88	Coyne	Dundee	33				
1988–89	McGhee	Celtic	16				
1988–89	Nicholas	Aberdeen	16				
1989–90	Robertson	Heart of Midlothian	17				
1990–91	Coyne	Celtic	18				
1991–92	McCoist	Rangers	34				
1992–93	McCoist	Rangers	34				
1993–94	Hateley	Rangers	22				
1994–95	Coyne	Motherwell	16				

Despite limited resources, *Craig Brown presided over one of the most successful periods of Scottish soccer playing history between 1993 and 2001: with a record of 32 wins, 18 draws and 20 defeats in 70 matches he is also Scotland's longest-serving manager.*

Scotland

SCOTTISH PREMIER LEAGUE 1975–2003

IN THE LAST 25 YEARS the Scottish League has been through three reorganizations (two under the auspices of the Scottish FA in 1975 and 1994, and then again in 1997 with the establishment of the Scottish Premier League). Each time the issue has been the same – how to create a competitive, financially viable league when two clubs are so much bigger than the others. The last couple of years have seen an increasingly bitter battle between the Old Firm and the rest of the SPL. Celtic and Rangers have actively explored the possibility of joining the English leagues or a pan-European Atlantic league.

Rangers revolution, Celtic dominance

The era began with the usual Glasgow monopoly on the title, including Jock Stein's last championship with Celtic. Post-Stein, Billy McNeill's team continued to win, but Rangers went into a decade of decline. Into the vacuum stepped Alex Ferguson's Aberdeen and, for a glorious season in 1983, Dundee United. But with the arrival of businessman David Murray at Rangers, the vacuum was filled again. Money was spent on the squad, first in England and then in Europe and, shortly after the appointment of Graeme Souness as manager, the sectarian ban on signing Catholic players was ended.

Under Souness, Walter Smith and Dick Advocaat, Rangers then won 11 out of 12 titles (1989–2000) – a sequence broken by a revived Celtic under Wim Jansen and then by Martin O'Neill's team in 2000, Celtic's best squad for two decades. Beyond these two, only Hearts, Aberdeen and Motherwell have been regular members of the Premier League but none of them have mounted a sustained challenge to the Old Firm's dominance on the field. It may require the entire league to do so off the field.

SCOTLAND

Scottish League Positions 1975–2003

TEAM	1975-76	1976-77	1977-78	1978-79	1979-80	1980-81	1981-82	1982-83	1983-84	1984-85	1985-86	1986-87	1987-88	1988-89	1989-90	1990-91	1991-92	1992-93	1993-94	1994-95	1995-96	1996-97	1997-98	1998-99	1999-2000	2000-01	2001-02	2002-03
Aberdeen	7	3	2	4	1	2	2	3	1	1	4	4	4	2	2	2	6	2	2	9	3	6	6	8	10	7	4	8
Airdrieonians						7	10										7	12										
Ayr United	6	8	9																									
Celtic	2	1	5	1	2	1	1	2	2	2	1	2	1	3	5	3	3	3	4	4	2	2	1	2	2	1	1	2
Clydebank		10									10	11																
Dumbarton									9																			
Dundee	9						8	6	8	6	6	6	7	8	10			10	12					5	7	6	9	6
Dundee United	8	4	3	3	4	5	4	1	3	3	3	3	5	4	4	4	4	6	10			3	7	9	8	11	8	11
Dunfermline Athletic												11		8	8	12					5	8	10			9	6	5
Falkirk												10	10				9	11		5	10							
Hamilton Academical												12		10														
Heart of Midlothian	5	9		9		10			5	7	2	5	2	6	3	5	2	5	7	6	4	4	3	6	3	5	5	3
Hibernian	3	6	4	5	10		6	7	7	8	8	9	6	5	7	9	5	7	5	3	5	9	10		6	3	10	7
Kilmarnock		10			8	9		10											8	7	7	7	4	4	9	4	7	4
Livingston																											3	9
Morton				7	6	8	7	9		10			12															
Motherwell	4	7	6	10		8	10		9	8	8	9	6	6	10	9	3	2	8	8	9	7	4	8			11	12*
Partick Thistle		5	7	8	7	6	9										8	9	8	9								10
Raith Rovers																			11		6	10						
Rangers	1	2	1	2	5	3	3	4	4	4	5	1	3	1	1	1	1	1	1	1	1	1	2	1	2	1	2	1
St. Johnstone	10			9				9									7	8	6	10			5	3	5	10	12	
St. Mirren			8	6	3	4	5	5	5	6	5	7	7	9	7	9	10	11								12		

* Though Motherwell finished bottom of the SPL it was not relegated because the facilities at First Division champions Falkirk's Brockville Park stadium were deemed unsuitable for Premiership crowds.

Rangers turns the screw in 1990: another goal, another Old Firm derby, another Rangers championship. Mo Johnston, Ally McCoist and Ian Ferguson celebrate.

Despite winning the Scottish First Division in 2002–03 Falkirk were denied their place in the SPL because their Brockville Park ground did not meet Premier League standards.

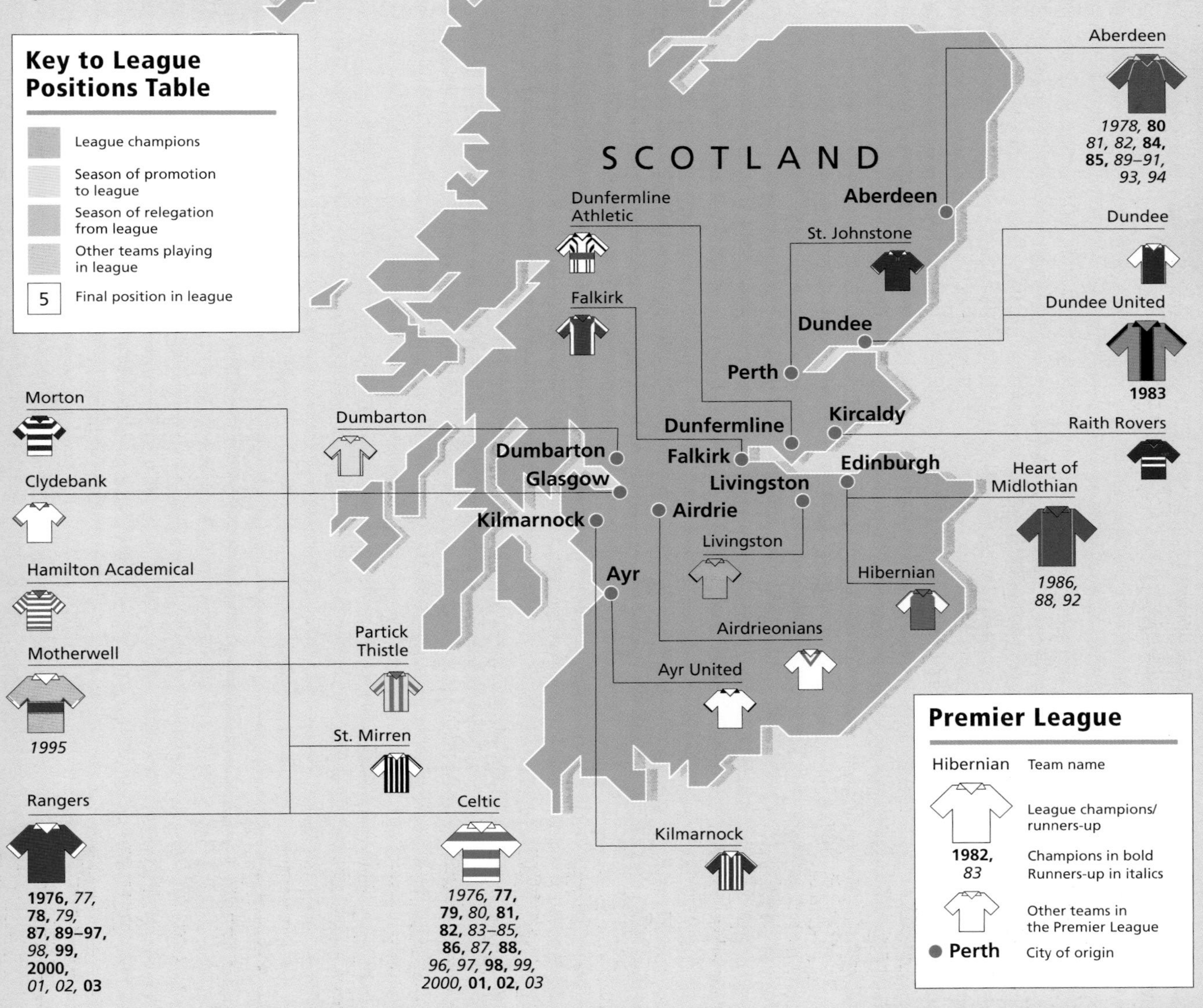

SCOTLAND

Key to League Positions Table

- League champions
- Season of promotion to league
- Season of relegation from league
- Other teams playing in league
- 5   Final position in league

SCOTLAND

Aberdeen
1978, **80** **81**, **82**, **84**, **85**, 89–91, **93**, **94**

Dunfermline Athletic

Aberdeen

St. Johnstone

Dundee

Dundee
Perth

Dundee United
1983

Falkirk
Dundee

Dumbarton
Glasgow

Dumbarton

Dunfermline
Falkirk

Kircaldy

Raith Rovers

Morton

Clydebank

Hamilton Academical

Motherwell
1995

Partick Thistle

St. Mirren

Kilmarnock

Ayr

Livingston
Airdrie

Livingston

Airdrieonians

Ayr United

Edinburgh

Heart of Midlothian
1986, 88, 92

Hibernian

Kilmarnock

Rangers
1976, *77*, **78**, *79*, **87**, **89–97**, **98**, **99**, **2000**, *01*, *02*, **03**

Celtic
1976, *77*, *79*, **80**, *81*, **82**, *83–85*, **86**, *87*, **88**, *96*, *97*, **98**, *99*, **2000**, **01**, **02**, *03*

Premier League

Hibernian	Team name
	League champions/runners-up
1982, *83*	Champions in bold Runners-up in italics
	Other teams in the Premier League
● Perth	City of origin

Scotland

The Scottish Football Association
Founded: 1873
Joined FIFA: 1910–20, 1924–28, 1946
Joined UEFA: 1954

SCOTLAND

SCOTLAND'S SOCCER INSTITUTIONS are the second oldest in the world. Even before the establishment of the Scottish FA in 1873, Glasgow club Queen's Park was competing in the English FA Cup. With the creation of the SFA came the Scottish Cup, first played in 1874. A national league was created in 1890, rapidly followed by the arrival of professionalism in 1893 and the creation of a second division for the 1893–94 season.

Both these tournaments and the Scottish League Cup, first played in 1947, have been dominated by the Glasgow 'Old Firm' – Celtic and Rangers. There has been an occasional look in for Aberdeen, the two Dundee sides and the two Edinburgh teams – Hibernian and Heart of Midlothian.

During the Second World War, national championships were abandoned and teams played in smaller regional leagues. The continued dominance of the Old Firm led to a reorganization of the league structure for the 1975–76 season. A ten-team Premiership was created, with the big teams playing each other four times a year. Two lower divisions of 14 teams were also created. In 1994–95 the lower divisions were reorganized again, the two being expanded into three, with the addition of two teams from the Highland League. In 1997 the Scottish top flight followed the lead of the English first division, creating a separate and independent Premiership.

However, none of these structural changes can mask the basic problem that the two big Glasgow teams are economically and sportingly in a different class from the rest of the country. The Scottish Premiership continues, but the Old Firm has explored the possibility of forming an Atlantic league with other small European nations (an idea which has been blocked by UEFA) and has continued to pursue the preferred option of joining the English Premiership.

The Old Firm derby between Celtic and Rangers is one of the most keenly contested fixtures in the world.

Scottish League Record 1891–2004

SEASON	CHAMPIONS	RUNNERS-UP
1891	Dumbarton/Rangers*	
1892	Dumbarton	Celtic
1893	Celtic	Rangers
1894	Celtic	Heart of Midlothian
1895	Heart of Midlothian	Celtic
1896	Celtic	Rangers
1897	Heart of Midlothian	Hibernian
1898	Celtic	Rangers
1899	Rangers	Heart of Midlothian
1900	Rangers	Celtic
1901	Rangers	Celtic
1902	Rangers	Celtic
1903	Hibernian	Dundee
1904	Third Lanark	Heart of Midlothian
1905	Celtic	Rangers
1906	Celtic	Heart of Midlothian
1907	Celtic	Dundee
1908	Celtic	Falkirk
1909	Celtic	Dundee
1910	Celtic	Falkirk
1911	Rangers	Aberdeen
1912	Rangers	Celtic
1913	Rangers	Celtic
1914	Celtic	Rangers
1915	Celtic	Heart of Midlothian
1916	Celtic	Rangers
1917	Celtic	Morton
1918	Rangers	Celtic
1919	Celtic	Rangers
1920	Rangers	Celtic
1921	Rangers	Celtic
1922	Celtic	Rangers
1923	Rangers	Airdrieonians
1924	Rangers	Airdrieonians
1925	Rangers	Airdrieonians
1926	Celtic	Airdrieonians
1927	Rangers	Motherwell
1928	Rangers	Celtic
1929	Rangers	Celtic
1930	Rangers	Motherwell
1931	Rangers	Celtic
1932	Motherwell	Rangers
1933	Rangers	Motherwell
1934	Rangers	Motherwell
1935	Rangers	Celtic
1936	Celtic	Rangers
1937	Rangers	Aberdeen
1938	Celtic	Heart of Midlothian
1939	Rangers	Celtic
1940–46	*no championship*	
1947	Rangers	Hibernian
1948	Hibernian	Rangers
1949	Rangers	Dundee
1950	Rangers	Hibernian
1951	Hibernian	Rangers
1952	Hibernian	Rangers
1953	Rangers	Hibernian
1954	Celtic	Heart of Midlothian
1955	Aberdeen	Celtic
1956	Rangers	Aberdeen
1957	Rangers	Heart of Midlothian
1958	Heart of Midlothian	Rangers

Scottish League Record (*continued*)

SEASON	CHAMPIONS	RUNNERS-UP
1959	Rangers	Heart of Midlothian
1960	Heart of Midlothian	Kilmarnock
1961	Rangers	Kilmarnock
1962	Dundee	Rangers
1963	Rangers	Kilmarnock
1964	Rangers	Kilmarnock
1965	Kilmarnock	Heart of Midlothian
1966	Celtic	Rangers
1967	Celtic	Rangers
1968	Celtic	Rangers
1969	Celtic	Rangers
1970	Celtic	Rangers
1971	Celtic	Aberdeen
1972	Celtic	Aberdeen
1973	Celtic	Rangers
1974	Celtic	Hibernian
1975	Rangers	Hibernian
1976	Rangers	Celtic
1977	Celtic	Rangers
1978	Rangers	Aberdeen
1979	Celtic	Rangers
1980	Aberdeen	Celtic
1981	Celtic	Aberdeen
1982	Celtic	Aberdeen
1983	Dundee United	Celtic
1984	Aberdeen	Celtic
1985	Aberdeen	Celtic
1986	Celtic	Heart of Midlothian
1987	Rangers	Celtic
1988	Celtic	Heart of Midlothian
1989	Rangers	Aberdeen
1990	Rangers	Aberdeen
1991	Rangers	Aberdeen
1992	Rangers	Heart of Midlothian
1993	Rangers	Aberdeen
1994	Rangers	Aberdeen
1995	Rangers	Motherwell
1996	Rangers	Celtic
1997	Rangers	Celtic
1998	Celtic	Rangers
1999	Rangers	Celtic
2000	Rangers	Celtic
2001	Celtic	Rangers
2002	Celtic	Rangers
2003	Rangers	Celtic
2004	Celtic	Rangers

* Both teams had equal points, and the title was held jointly.

Scottish League Summary

TEAM	TOTALS	CHAMPIONS & RUNNERS-UP (BOLD) (*ITALICS*)
Rangers	50, 27	**1891**, *93*, *96*, *98*, **1899–1902**, *05*, **11–13**, *14*, **16**, *18*, **19**, **20**, **21**, *22*, **23–25**, **27–31**, *32*, **33–35**, *36*, **37**, **39**, **47**, **48**, **49**, **50**, *51*, *52*, **53**, **56**, **57**, *58*, **59**, **61**, *62*, **63**, **64**, **66–70**, *73*, **75**, **76**, **77**, *78*, *79*, **87**, **89–97**, *98*, **99**, **2000**, *01*, *02*, **03**, **04**
Celtic	39, 27	*1892*, *93*, *94*, *95*, **96**, *98*, *1900–02*, *05–10*, *12*, *13*, **14–17**, *18*, **19**, *20*, *21*, **22**, *26*, *28*, *29*, **31**, *35*, **36**, *38*, **39**, **54**, *55*, **66–74**, *76*, **77**, *79*, **80**, **81**, **82**, *83–85*, **86**, *87*, **88**, *96*, *97*, **98**, *99*, *2000*, **01**, **02**, **03**, **04**
Aberdeen	4, 13	*1911*, *37*, *55*, *56*, *71*, *72*, *78*, **80**, **81**, **82**, *84*, **85**, *89–91*, *93*, *94*
Heart of Midlothian	4, 13	*1894*, **95**, *97*, *99*, *1904*, *06*, *15*, *38*, *54*, *57*, **58**, *59*, **60**, *65*, *86*, *88*, *92*
Hibernian	4, 6	*1897*, **1903**, *47*, *48*, *50*, **51**, **52**, *53*, *74*, *75*
Dumbarton	2, 0	**1891, 92**
Motherwell	1, 5	*1927*, *30*, *32*, *33*, *34*, **95**

Scottish League Summary (*continued*)

TEAM	TOTALS	CHAMPIONS & RUNNERS-UP (BOLD) (*ITALICS*)
Dundee	1, 4	*1903*, *07*, *09*, *49*, **62**
Kilmarnock	1, 4	*1960*, *61*, *63*, *64*, **65**
Dundee United	1, 0	**1983**
Third Lanark	1, 0	**1904**
Airdrieonians	0, 4	*1923–26*
Falkirk	0, 2	*1908, 10*
Morton	0, 1	*1917*

Scottish Cup Record 1874–2004

YEAR	WINNERS	SCORE	RUNNERS-UP
1874	Queen's Park	2-0	Clydesdale
1875	Queen's Park	3-0	Renton
1876	Queen's Park	1-1, (replay) 2-0	Third Lanark
1877	Vale of Leven	0-0, (replay) 1-1, (replay) 3-2	Rangers
1878	Vale of Leven	1-0	Third Lanark
1879	Vale of Leven	1-1, (replay) w/o	Rangers
1880	Queen's Park	3-0	Thornley Bank
1881	Queen's Park	3-1*	Dumbarton
1882	Queen's Park	2-2, (replay) 4-1	Dumbarton
1883	Dumbarton	2-2, (replay) 2-1	Vale of Leven
1884	Queen's Park	w/o	Vale of Leven
1885	Renton	0-0, (replay) 3-1	Vale of Leven
1886	Queen's Park	3-1	Renton
1887	Hibernian	2-1	Dumbarton
1888	Renton	6-1	Cambuslang
1889	Third Lanark	2-1**	Celtic
1890	Queen's Park	1-1, (replay) 2-2	Vale of Levan
1891	Heart of Midlothian	1-0	Dumbarton
1892	Celtic	5-1	Queen's Park
1893	Queen's Park	2-1	Celtic
1894	Rangers	3-1	Celtic
1895	St. Bernard's	2-1	Renton
1896	Heart of Midlothian	3-1	Hibernian
1897	Rangers	5-1	Dumbarton
1898	Rangers	2-0	Kilmarnock
1899	Celtic	2-0	Rangers
1900	Celtic	4-3	Queen's Park
1901	Heart of Midlothian	4-3	Celtic
1902	Hibernian	1-0	Celtic
1903	Rangers	1-1, (replay) 0-0, (replay) 2-0	Heart of Midlothian
1904	Celtic	3-2	Rangers
1905	Third Lanark	0-0, (replay) 3-1	Rangers
1906	Heart of Midlothian	1-0	Third Lanark
1907	Celtic	3-0	Heart of Midlothian
1908	Celtic	5-1	St. Mirren
1909	*cup withheld* †	2-2, (replay) 1-1	Celtic v Rangers
1910	Dundee	0-0, (replay) 2-2, (replay) 2-1	Clyde
1911	Celtic	0-0, (replay) 2-0	Hamilton Academical
1912	Celtic	2-0	Clyde
1913	Falkirk	2-0	Raith Rovers
1914	Celtic	0-0, (replay) 4-1	Hibernian
1915–19	*no competition*		
1920	Kilmarnock	3-2	Albion Rovers
1921	Partick Thistle	1-0	Rangers
1922	Morton	1-0	Rangers
1923	Celtic	1-0	Hibernian
1924	Airdrieonians	2-0	Hibernian
1925	Celtic	2-1	Dundee
1926	St. Mirren	2-0	Celtic
1927	Celtic	3-1	East Fife
1928	Rangers	4-0	Celtic
1929	Kilmarnock	2-0	Rangers
1930	Rangers	0-0, (replay) 2-1	Partick Thistle
1931	Celtic	2-2, (replay) 4-2	Motherwell

SCOTLAND

Scottish Cup Record (*continued*)

YEAR	WINNERS	SCORE	RUNNERS-UP
1932	Rangers	1-1, (replay) 3-0	Kilmarnock
1933	Celtic	1-0	Motherwell
1934	Rangers	5-0	St. Mirren
1935	Rangers	2-1	Hamilton Academical
1936	Rangers	1-0	Third Lanark
1937	Celtic	2-1	Aberdeen
1938	East Fife	1-1, (replay) 4-2 (aet)	Kilmarnock
1939	Clyde	4-0	Motherwell
1940–46		*no competition*	
1947	Aberdeen	2-1	Hibernian
1948	Rangers	1-1, (replay) 1-0 (aet)	Morton
1949	Rangers	4-1	Clyde
1950	Rangers	3-0	East Fife
1951	Celtic	1-0	Motherwell
1952	Motherwell	4-0	Dundee
1953	Rangers	1-1, (replay) 1-0	Aberdeen
1954	Celtic	2-1	Aberdeen
1955	Clyde	1-1, (replay) 1-0	Celtic
1956	Heart of Midlothian	3-1	Celtic
1957	Falkirk	1-1, (replay) 2-1 (aet)	Kilmarnock
1958	Clyde	1-0	Hibernian
1959	St. Mirren	3-1	Aberdeen
1960	Rangers	2-0	Kilmarnock
1961	Dunfermline Athletic	0-0, (replay) 2-0	Celtic
1962	Rangers	2-0	St. Mirren
1963	Rangers	1-1, (replay) 3-0	Celtic
1964	Rangers	3-1	Dundee
1965	Celtic	3-2	Dunfermline Athletic
1966	Rangers	0-0, (replay) 1-0	Celtic
1967	Celtic	2-0	Aberdeen
1968	Dunfermline Athletic	3-1	Heart of Midlothian
1969	Celtic	4-0	Rangers
1970	Aberdeen	3-1	Celtic
1971	Celtic	1-1, (replay) 2-1	Rangers
1972	Celtic	6-1	Hibernian
1973	Rangers	3-2	Celtic
1974	Celtic	3-0	Dundee United
1975	Celtic	3-1	Airdrieonians
1976	Rangers	3-1	Heart of Midlothian
1977	Celtic	1-0	Rangers
1978	Rangers	2-1	Aberdeen
1979	Rangers	0-0, (replay) 0-0, (replay) 3-2 (aet)	Hibernian
1980	Celtic	1-0 (aet)	Rangers

Scottish Cup Record (*continued*)

YEAR	WINNERS	SCORE	RUNNERS-UP
1981	Rangers	0-0, (replay) 4-1	Dundee United
1982	Aberdeen	4-1 (aet)	Rangers
1983	Aberdeen	1-0 (aet)	Rangers
1984	Aberdeen	2-1	Celtic
1985	Celtic	2-1 (aet)	Dundee United
1986	Aberdeen	3-0	Heart of Midlothian
1987	St. Mirren	1-0 (aet)	Dundee United
1988	Celtic	2-1	Dundee United
1989	Celtic	1-0	Rangers
1990	Aberdeen	0-0 (9-8 pens)	Celtic
1991	Motherwell	4-3 (aet)	Dundee United
1992	Rangers	2-1	Airdrieonians
1993	Rangers	2-1	Aberdeen
1994	Dundee United	1-0	Rangers
1995	Celtic	1-0	Airdrieonians
1996	Rangers	5-1	Heart of Midlothian
1997	Kilmarnock	1-0	Falkirk
1998	Heart of Midlothian	2-1	Rangers
1999	Rangers	1-0	Celtic
2000	Rangers	4-0	Aberdeen
2001	Celtic	3-0	Hibernian
2002	Rangers	3-2	Celtic
2003	Rangers	1-0	Dundee
2004	Celtic	3-1	Dunfermline Athletic

w/o denotes walk over

* Dumbarton protested result of first game.

** SFA ordered replay due to playing conditions.

† Cup withheld due to riots.

Scottish Cup Summary

TEAM	TOTALS	WINNERS & RUNNERS-UP (**BOLD**) (*ITALICS*)
Celtic	32, 18	*1889*, **92**, *93*, *94*, *99*, **1900**, *01*, *02*, *04*, *07*, *08*, **11**, **12**, *14*, **23**, **25**, *26*, *27*, **28**, *31*, **33**, **37**, **51**, **54**, *55*, *56*, *61*, *63*, **65**, *66*, **67**, **69**, **70**, **71**, **72**, **73**, **74**, **75**, **77**, **80**, *84*, **85**, **88**, **89**, **90**, *95*, *99*, **2001**, *02*, **04**
Rangers	31, 17	**1877**, *79*, **94**, **97**, **98**, *99*, **1903**, *04*, *05*, *21*, *22*, *28*, *29*, **30**, **32**, **34–36**, **48–50**, **53**, **60**, **62–64**, *66*, **69**, **71**, **73**, *76*, **77**, *78*, *79*, *80*, **81**, **82**, **83**, **89**, **92**, **93**, **94**, **96**, *98*, **99**, **2000**, **02**, **03**
Queen's Park	10, 2	**1874–76**, **80–82**, **84**, **86**, **90**, *92*, **93**, *1900*
Aberdeen	7, 8	*1937*, **47**, *53*, *54*, *59*, *67*, **70**, *78*, **82–84**, **86**, *90*, *93*, **2000**
Heart of Midlothian	6, 6	**1891**, **96**, **1901**, *03*, *06*, *07*, **56**, *68*, *76*, *86*, *96*, **98**
Kilmarnock	3, 5	**1898**, **1920**, *29*, *32*, *38*, *57*, *60*, **97**
Vale of Leven	3, 4	**1877–79**, *83-85*, *90*
Clyde	3, 3	**1910**, *12*, **39**, *49*, **55**, *58*
St. Mirren	3, 3	**1908**, *26*, *34*, **59**, *62*, **87**
Hibernian	2, 9	**1887**, *96*, **1902**, *14*, *23*, *24*, *47*, *58*, *72*, *79*, *2001*
Motherwell	2, 4	*1931*, *33*, *39*, *51*, **52**, **91**
Third Lanark	2, 4	*1876*, *78*, **89**, **1905**, *06*, *36*
Renton	2, 3	*1875*, **85**, *86*, **88**, *95*
Dunfermline Athletic	2, 2	**1961**, **65**, *68*, *2004*
Falkirk	2, 1	**1913**, **57**, *97*
Dundee United	1, 6	**1974**, *81*, *85*, *87*, *88*, *91*, *94*
Dumbarton	1, 5	*1881*, **82**, **83**, *87*, *91*, *97*
Dundee	1, 4	**1910**, *25*, *52*, *64*, *2003*
Airdrieonians	1, 3	**1924**, *75*, *92*, *95*
East Fife	1, 2	**1927**, *38*, *50*
Morton	1, 1	**1922**, *48*
Partick Thistle	1, 1	**1921**, *30*
St. Bernard's	1, 0	**1895**
Hamilton Academical	0, 2	*1911*, *35*

Dundee United's Craig Brewster beats Rangers' David McPherson to score in Dundee United's 1994 Scottish Cup Final victory.

Scottish Cup Summary (*continued*)

TEAM	TOTALS	WINNERS & RUNNERS-UP
		(BOLD) (*ITALICS*)
Albion Rovers	0, 1	*1920*
Cambuslang	0, 1	*1888*
Clydesdale	0, 1	*1874*
Raith Rovers	0, 1	*1913*
Thornley Bank	0, 1	*1880*

Scottish League Cup Record 1947–2004

YEAR	WINNERS	SCORE	RUNNERS-UP
1947	Rangers	4-0	Aberdeen
1948	East Fife	0-0, (replay) 4-1	Falkirk
1949	Rangers	2-0	Raith Rovers
1950	East Fife	3-0	Dunfermline Athletic
1951	Motherwell	3-0	Hibernian
1952	Dundee	3-2	Rangers
1953	Dundee	2-0	Kilmarnock
1954	East Fife	3-2	Partick Thistle
1955	Heart of Midlothian	4-2	Motherwell
1956	Aberdeen	2-1	St. Mirren
1957	Celtic	3-0	Partick Thistle
1958	Celtic	7-1	Rangers
1959	Heart of Midlothian	5-1	Partick Thistle
1960	Heart of Midlothian	2-1	Third Lanark
1961	Rangers	2-0	Kilmarnock
1962	Rangers	1-1, (replay) 3-1	Heart of Midlothian
1963	Heart of Midlothian	1-0	Kilmarnock
1964	Rangers	5-0	Morton
1965	Rangers	2-1	Celtic
1966	Celtic	2-1	Rangers
1967	Celtic	1-0	Rangers
1968	Celtic	5-3	Dundee
1969	Celtic	6-2	Hibernian
1970	Celtic	1-0	St. Johnstone
1971	Rangers	1-0	Celtic
1972	Partick Thistle	4-1	Celtic
1973	Hibernian	2-1	Celtic
1974	Dundee	1-0	Celtic
1975	Celtic	6-3	Hibernian
1976	Rangers	1-0	Celtic
1977	Aberdeen	2-1 (aet)	Celtic
1978	Rangers	2-1 (aet)	Celtic
1979	Rangers	2-1	Aberdeen
1980	Dundee United	0-0, (replay) 3-0	Aberdeen
1981	Dundee United	3-0	Dundee
1982	Rangers	2-1	Dundee United
1983	Celtic	2-1	Rangers
1984	Rangers	3-2 (aet)	Celtic
1985	Rangers	1-0	Dundee United
1986	Aberdeen	3-0	Hibernian
1987	Rangers	2-1	Celtic
1988	Rangers	3-3 (aet)(5-3 pens)	Aberdeen
1989	Rangers	3-2	Aberdeen
1990	Aberdeen	2-1 (aet)	Rangers
1991	Rangers	2-1 (aet)	Celtic
1992	Hibernian	2-0	Dunfermline Athletic
1993	Rangers	2-1	Aberdeen
1994	Rangers	2-1	Hibernian
1995	Raith Rovers	2-2 (aet)(6-5 pens)	Celtic
1996	Aberdeen	2-0	Dundee
1997	Rangers	4-3	Heart of Midlothian
1998	Celtic	3-0	Dundee United
1999	Rangers	2-1	St. Johnstone
2000	Celtic	2-0	Aberdeen
2001	Celtic	3-0	Kilmarnock
2002	Rangers	4-0	Ayr United
2003	Rangers	2-1	Celtic
2004	Livingston	2-0	Hibernian

Scottish League Cup Summary

TEAM	TOTALS	WINNERS & RUNNERS-UP
		(BOLD) (*ITALICS*)
Rangers	23, 6	**1947, 49,** *52, 58,* **61, 62, 64, 65,** *66, 67,* **71, 76, 78, 79, 82, 83,** *84,* **85,** *87–89,* *90,* **91,** *93, 94,* **97,** *99,* **2002,** *03*
Celtic	11, 13	**1957,** *58,* **65,** *66–70, 71–74,* **75,** *76–78,* **83,** *84, 87, 91, 95,* **98, 2000, 01,** *03*
Aberdeen	5, 7	*1947,* **56, 77,** *79, 80,* **86,** *88, 89,* **90,** *93,* **96,** *2000*
Heart of Midlothian	4, 2	**1955, 59, 60,** *62,* **63,** *97*
Dundee	3, 3	**1952, 53, 68, 74, 81,** *96*
East Fife	3, 0	**1948, 50, 54**
Hibernian	2, 6	*1951, 69,* **73,** *75, 86,* **92,** *94,* **2004**
Dundee United	2, 3	**1980, 81,** *82,* **85,** *98*
Partick Thistle	1, 3	*1954,* **57,** *59, 72*
Motherwell	1, 1	**1951,** *55*
Raith Rovers	1, 1	**1949,** *95*
Livingston	1, 0	**2004**
Kilmarnock	0, 4	*1953, 61, 63, 2001*
Dunfermline Athletic	0, 2	*1950, 92*
St. Johnstone	0, 2	*1970, 99*
Ayr United	0, 1	*2002*
Falkirk	0, 1	*1948*
Morton	0, 1	*1964*
St. Mirren	0, 1	*1956*
Third Lanark	0, 1	*1960*

It's not often that a major Scottish trophy is won by anyone outside the 'Old Firm'. When it is, it's a major cause for celebration, as Aberdeen's Stewart McKimmie shows as he lifts the Scottish League Cup after the team's victory over Dundee in 1996.

SCOTLAND

Ireland
(Republic of)

The Football Association of Ireland
Founded: 1921
Joined FIFA: 1923
Joined UEFA: 1954

PRIOR TO PARTITION AND INDEPENDENCE in 1921, few clubs from the south of Ireland had made much impression in national competitions. With independence and the creation of a separate league and cup competition in 1922, domestic soccer improved, but Ireland has never been able to sustain a professional league as money, fans and players cross the Irish Sea to England and Scotland.

Ireland League Record 1922–2003

SEASON	CHAMPIONS	SEASON	CHAMPIONS
1922	St. James' Gate	1964	Shamrock Rovers
1923	Shamrock Rovers	1965	Drumcondra
1924	Bohemians	1966	Waterford
1925	Shamrock Rovers	1967	Dundalk
1926	Shelbourne	1968	Waterford
1927	Shamrock Rovers	1969	Waterford
1928	Bohemians	1970	Waterford
1929	Shelbourne	1971	Cork Hibernians
1930	Bohemians	1972	Waterford
1931	Shelbourne	1973	Waterford
1932	Shamrock Rovers	1974	Cork Celtic
1933	Dundalk	1975	Bohemians
1934	Bohemians	1976	Dundalk
1935	Dolphin	1977	Sligo Rovers
1936	Bohemians	1978	Bohemians
1937	Sligo Rovers	1979	Dundalk
1938	Shamrock Rovers	1980	Limerick United
1939	Shamrock Rovers	1981	Athlone Town
1940	St. James' Gate	1982	Dundalk
1941	Cork United	1983	Athlone Town
1942	Cork United	1984	Shamrock Rovers
1943	Cork United	1985	Shamrock Rovers
1944	Shelbourne	1986	Shamrock Rovers
1945	Cork United	1987	Shamrock Rovers
1946	Cork United	1988	Dundalk
1947	Shelbourne	1989	Derry City
1948	Drumcondra	1990	St. Patrick's Athletic
1949	Drumcondra	1991	Dundalk
1950	Cork Athletic	1992	Shelbourne
1951	Cork Athletic	1993	Cork City
1952	St. Patrick's Athletic	1994	Shamrock Rovers
1953	Shelbourne	1995	Dundalk
1954	Shamrock Rovers	1996	St. Patrick's Athletic
1955	St. Patrick's Athletic	1997	Derry City
1956	St. Patrick's Athletic	1998	St. Patrick's Athletic
1957	Shamrock Rovers	1999	St. Patrick's Athletic
1958	Drumcondra	2000	Shelbourne
1959	Shamrock Rovers	2001	Bohemians
1960	Limerick	2002	Shelbourne
1961	Drumcondra	2002-03	Bohemians
1962	Shelbourne	2003*	Shelbourne
1963	Dundalk		

* Ireland changed from an autumn/spring to a spring/autumn season.

Ireland Cup Record 1922–2003

YEAR	WINNERS	YEAR	WINNERS
1922	St. James' Gate	1926	Fordsons
1923	Alton United	1927	Drumcondra
1924	Athlone Town	1928	Bohemians
1925	Shamrock Rovers	1929	Shamrock Rovers

Ireland Cup Record (*continued*)

YEAR	WINNERS	YEAR	WINNERS
1930	Shamrock Rovers	1968	Shamrock Rovers
1931	Shamrock Rovers	1969	Shamrock Rovers
1932	Shamrock Rovers	1970	Bohemians
1933	Shamrock Rovers	1971	Limerick
1934	Cork	1972	Cork Hibernians
1935	Bohemians	1973	Cork Hibernians
1936	Shamrock Rovers	1974	Finn Harps
1937	Waterford	1975	Home Farm
1938	St. James' Gate	1976	Bohemians
1939	Shelbourne	1977	Dundalk
1940	Shamrock Rovers	1978	Shamrock Rovers
1941	Cork United	1979	Dundalk
1942	Dundalk	1980	Waterford
1943	Drumcondra	1981	Dundalk
1944	Shamrock Rovers	1982	Limerick United
1945	Shamrock Rovers	1983	Sligo Rovers
1946	Drumcondra	1984	UCD
1947	Cork United	1985	Shamrock Rovers
1948	Shamrock Rovers	1986	Shamrock Rovers
1949	Dundalk	1987	Shamrock Rovers
1950	Transport	1988	Dundalk
1951	Cork Athletic	1989	Derry City
1952	Dundalk	1990	Bray Wanderers
1953	Cork Athletic	1991	Galway United
1954	Drumcondra	1992	Bohemians
1955	Shamrock Rovers	1993	Shelbourne
1956	Shamrock Rovers	1994	Sligo Rovers
1957	Drumcondra	1995	Derry City
1958	Dundalk	1996	Shelbourne
1959	St. Patrick's Athletic	1997	Shelbourne
1960	Shelbourne	1998	Cork City
1961	St. Patrick's Athletic	1999	Bray Wanderers
1962	Shamrock Rovers	2000	Shelbourne
1963	Shelbourne	2001	Bohemians
1964	Shamrock Rovers	2002	Dundalk
1965	Shamrock Rovers	2002-03	Derry City
1966	Shamrock Rovers	2003*	Longford Town
1967	Shamrock Rovers		

* Ireland changed from an autumn/spring to a spring/autumn season.

Northern Ireland

The Irish Football Association
Founded: 1880
Joined FIFA: 1911–20, 1924–28, 1946
Joined UEFA: 1954

NORTHERN IRELAND'S league and cup competitions are the third oldest in the world. The cup dates from 1881 and the league from 1890. These all-Ireland competitions organized from Belfast became purely Northern Irish in 1921 after the partition of the island. Derry City, a team based in Catholic Londonderry, withdrew from both competitions in 1972 and joined the FA south of the border.

Northern Ireland League Record 1891–2004

SEASON	CHAMPIONS	SEASON	CHAMPIONS
1891	Linfield	1898	Linfield
1892	Linfield	1899	Distillery
1893	Linfield	1900	Celtic
1894	Glentoran	1901	Distillery
1895	Linfield	1902	Linfield
1896	Distillery	1903	Distillery
1897	Glentoran	1904	Linfield

Northern Ireland League Record (*continued*)

SEASON	CHAMPIONS	SEASON	CHAMPIONS
1905	Glentoran	1960	Glenavon
1906	Cliftonville	1961	Linfield
1907	Linfield	1962	Linfield
1908	Linfield	1963	Distillery
1909	Linfield	1964	Glentoran
1910	Cliftonville	1965	Derry City
1911	Linfield	1966	Linfield
1912	Glentoran	1967	Glentoran
1913	Glentoran	1968	Glentoran
1914	Linfield	1969	Linfield
1915	Celtic	1970	Glentoran
1916–19	*no championship*	1971	Linfield
1920	Celtic	1972	Glentoran
1921	Glentoran	1973	Crusaders
1922	Linfield	1974	Coleraine
1923	Linfield	1975	Linfield
1924	Queen's Island	1976	Crusaders
1925	Glentoran	1977	Glentoran
1926	Celtic	1978	Linfield
1927	Celtic	1979	Linfield
1928	Celtic	1980	Linfield
1929	Celtic	1981	Glentoran
1930	Linfield	1982	Linfield
1931	Glentoran	1983	Linfield
1932	Linfield	1984	Linfield
1933	Celtic	1985	Linfield
1934	Linfield	1986	Linfield
1935	Linfield	1987	Linfield
1936	Celtic	1988	Glentoran
1937	Celtic	1989	Linfield
1938	Celtic	1990	Portadown
1939	Celtic	1991	Portadown
1940	Celtic	1992	Glentoran
1941–47	*no championship*	1993	Linfield
1948	Celtic	1994	Linfield
1949	Linfield	1995	Crusaders
1950	Linfield	1996	Portadown
1951	Glentoran	1997	Crusaders
1952	Glentoran	1998	Cliftonville
1953	Glentoran	1999	Glentoran
1954	Linfield	2000	Linfield
1955	Linfield	2001	Linfield
1956	Linfield	2002	Portadown
1957	Glenavon	2003	Glentoran
1958	Ards	2004	Linfield
1959	Linfield		

Northern Ireland Cup Record 1881–2004

YEAR	WINNERS	YEAR	WINNERS
1881	Moyola Park	1903	Distillery
1882	Queen's Island	1904	Linfield
1883	Cliftonville	1905	Distillery
1884	Distillery	1906	Shelbourne
1885	Distillery	1907	Cliftonville
1886	Distillery	1908	Bohemians
1887	Ulster	1909	Cliftonville
1888	Cliftonville	1910	Distillery
1889	Distillery	1911	Shelbourne
1890	Gordon Highlanders	1912	Linfield
1891	Linfield	1913	Linfield
1892	Linfield	1914	Glentoran
1893	Linfield	1915	Linfield
1894	Distillery	1916	Linfield
1895	Linfield	1917	Glentoran
1896	Distillery	1918	Celtic
1897	Cliftonville	1919	Linfield
1898	Linfield	1920	Shelbourne
1899	Linfield	1921	Glentoran
1900	Cliftonville	1922	Linfield
1901	Cliftonville	1923	Linfield
1902	Linfield	1924	Queen's Island

Northern Ireland Cup Record (*continued*)

YEAR	WINNERS	YEAR	WINNERS
1925	Distillery	1966	Glentoran
1926	Celtic	1967	Crusaders
1927	Ards	1968	Crusaders
1928	Willowfield	1969	Ards
1929	Ballymena United	1970	Linfield
1930	Linfield	1971	Distillery
1931	Linfield	1972	Coleraine
1932	Glentoran	1973	Glentoran
1933	Glentoran	1974	Ards
1934	Linfield	1975	Coleraine
1935	Glentoran	1976	Carrick Rangers
1936	Linfield	1977	Coleraine
1937	Celtic	1978	Linfield
1938	Celtic	1979	Cliftonville
1939	Linfield	1980	Linfield
1940	Ballymena United	1981	Ballymena United
1941	Celtic	1982	Linfield
1942	Linfield	1983	Glentoran
1943	Celtic	1984	Ballymena United
1944	Celtic	1985	Glentoran
1945	Linfield	1986	Glentoran
1946	Linfield	1987	Glentoran
1947	Celtic	1988	Glentoran
1948	Linfield	1989	Ballymena United
1949	Derry City	1990	Glentoran
1950	Linfield	1991	Portadown
1951	Glentoran	1992	Glenavon
1952	Ards	1993	Bangor
1953	Linfield	1994	Linfield
1954	Derry City	1995	Linfield
1955	Dundela	1996	Glentoran
1956	Distillery	1997	Glenavon
1957	Glenavon	1998	Glentoran
1958	Ballymena United	1999	Portadown
1959	Glenavon	2000	Glentoran
1960	Linfield	2001	Glentoran
1961	Glenavon	2002	Linfield
1962	Linfield	2003	Coleraine
1963	Linfield	2004	Glentoran
1964	Derry City		
1965	Coleraine		

Wales

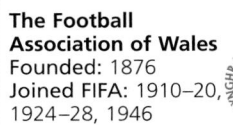

The Football Association of Wales
Founded: 1876
Joined FIFA: 1910–20, 1924–28, 1946
Joined UEFA: 1954

In Wales, the strength of rugby and the allure of the English game have seen a weak and often fragmented soccer culture. The largest clubs (Swansea, Cardiff and Wrexham) play their league soccer in England, though the Welsh Cup has provided a convenient route for the holders into European soccer via the Cup-Winners' Cup and now the UEFA Cup. In 1992 a unified semi-professional league was established.

SEASON	LEAGUE CHAMPIONS
2000	Total Network Solutions
2001	Barry Town
2002	Barry Town
2003	Barry Town
2004	Rhyl FC

YEAR	CUP WINNERS
2000	Bangor City
2001	Barry Town
2002	Barry Town
2003	Barry Town
2004	Rhyl FC

YEAR	LEAGUE CUP WINNERS
2000	Bangor City
2001	Caersws
2002	Caersws
2003	Wrexham
2004	Rhyl FC

NORTHERN IRELAND, WALES

Scandinavia

THE SEASONS IN REVIEW 2003, 2003–04

ALTHOUGH SCANDINAVIAN NATIONAL TEAMS CONTINUE to perform well in international tournaments, and Scandinavian players are in the top leagues all over Europe, the region's clubs have found progress in European competition very hard to come by. In an effort to improve standards and give the best teams more exposure to stronger opposition, Norway, Sweden and Denmark have created the Royal League. It will feature the top four clubs in each country playing through the winter break – some of it indoors. There is considerable commercial support and UEFA has sanctioned the experiment, as the competition will not lead to UEFA tournament places. In the meantime, the regions' leading clubs continue to control their domestic leagues.

In Norway Rosenborg made it 12 titles in a row. With four games to go, the team needed to beat its nearest challengers Bodø/Glimt to claim the championship. Rosenborg looked emphatic, coming out 4-0 up at the start of the second half, but Bodø mounted an amazing comeback to 4-4, before Rosenborg's Strand grabbed a winner. Stockholm's Djurgårdens is not quite in Rosenborg's league, but it did make it two in a row, retaining the Swedish league championship. The Cup went to Elfsborg, who beat Assyriaka, a team that has sprung from Stockholm's new migrant communities, and this year the team was good enough to thrash champions Djurgårdens 4-0 in their cup semi-final. HJK Helsinki followed the trend by also winning a second consecutive league championship; a fantastic late run of unbeaten games pushing them past the long-time league leaders Haka.

In Denmark it looked for a moment that an outsider might win the league. After the end of the winter break Esjberg beat the league leaders Brøndby 6-1 and made the title race a three-way affair with Brøndby and Copenhagen. In the final run Esjberg collapsed, losing four games in a row, but a UEFA Cup spot is a massive achievement for this small team. The big two continued to battle it out, but Brøndby let vital points slip. The Danish Cup was the first trophy to be decided and Copenhagen won it by a single goal from Aalborg. The following week, Copenhagen won its penultimate game to retain an unbeatable four point lead over Brøndby and the double was secured.

The Rosenborg players *celebrate winning the Norwegian league championship after the team's epic 5-4 victory over Bodø/Glimt.*

Danish League Table 2003–04

CLUB	P	W	D	L	F	A	Pts	
FC København	33	20	8	5	56	27	68	Champions League
Brøndby IF	33	20	7	6	55	29	67	UEFA Cup
Esjberg fB	33	18	8	7	71	42	62	
OB Odense	33	16	9	8	66	46	57	
AaB Aalborg	33	16	9	8	55	41	57	UEFA Cup (cup runners-up)
FC Midtjylland	33	14	6	13	65	51	48	
Viborg FF	33	11	9	13	47	44	42	
AGF Aarhus	33	11	3	19	45	67	36	
FC Nordsjælland*	33	7	11	15	35	59	32	
Herfølge BK	33	8	7	18	34	57	31	
BK Frem	33	8	3	22	38	65	27	Relegated
AB	33	8	2	23	31	70	17†	Relegated

Promoted clubs: Silkeborg, Randers FC.
* Farum BK was renamed FC Nordsjælland † 9 points deducted for irregularities.

Finnish Premier Division Table 2003

CLUB	P	W	D	L	F	A	Pts	
HJK Helsinki	26	17	6	3	51	15	57	Champions League
Haka Valkeakoski	26	16	5	5	54	16	53	UEFA Cup
United Tampere	26	14	5	7	39	21	47	
MyPa Anjalankoski	26	13	4	9	46	29	43	
FC Lahti	26	11	8	7	40	31	41	
Allianssi Vantaa	26	10	6	10	43	44	36	UEFA Cup (cup runners-up)
Inter Turku	26	10	5	11	43	41	35	
Jaro Pietarsaari	26	9	8	9	36	38	35	
TPS Turku	26	8	8	10	30	35	32	
Jokerit Helsinki	26	7	7	12	29	37	28	
FC Hämeenlinna	26	7	7	12	25	48	28	
Jazz Pori	26	7	7	12	31	55	28	
KooTeePee Kotka	26	6	4	16	28	53	22	Relegated (via play-off)
KuPS Kuopio	26	4	6	16	25	57	18	Relegated

Promoted clubs: TP-47 Tornio, RoPS Rovaniemi (via play-off).

Norwegian League Table 2003

CLUB	P	W	D	L	F	A	Pts	
Rosenborg BK	26	19	4	3	68	28	61	Champions League
Bodø/Glimt	26	14	5	7	45	30	47	UEFA Cup (cup runners-up)
Stabæk Fotball	26	11	9	6	51	35	42	UEFA Cup
Odd Grenland	26	11	5	10	46	43	38	UEFA Cup
Viking FK	26	9	10	7	46	34	37	
SK Brann	26	10	7	9	45	47	37	
Lillestrøm SK	26	10	7	9	33	35	37	
Sogndal IL	26	9	8	9	43	46	35	
Molde FK	26	9	4	13	32	41	31	
SFK Lyn	26	8	6	12	34	45	30	
Tromsø IL	26	8	5	13	30	52	29	
Vålerenga IF	26	6	10	10	30	33	28	Relegation play-off*
Aalesund FK	26	7	7	12	30	43	28	Relegated
Bryne IL	26	7	1	18	35	56	22	Relegated

Promoted clubs: Hamarkameratene, Fredrikstad.
* Vålerenga IF defeated Sandefjord 5-3 in the two-leg relegation play-off and therefore retains its place in the top division.

Top Goalscorers 2003, 2003–04

COUNTRY	PLAYER	CLUB	GOALS
Denmark	Mwape Miti	OB Odense	19
Denmark	Mohammed Zidan	FC Midtjylland	19
Denmark	Steffen Hojer	OB Odense	19
Denmark	Tommy Bechmann	Esjberg fB	19
Finland	Saka Puhakainen	Mypa Anjalankoski	14
Norway	Harald Brattbakk	Rosenborg BK	17
Sweden	Niklas Skoog	Malmö FF	22

SCANDINAVIA

Swedish League Table 2003

CLUB	P	W	D	L	F	A	Pts	
Djurgårdens IF	26	19	1	6	62	26	**58**	Champions League
Hammarby IF	26	15	6	5	50	30	**51**	UEFA Cup
Malmö FF	26	14	6	6	50	23	**48**	
Örgryte IS	26	14	3	9	42	40	**45**	
AIK	26	11	6	9	39	34	**39**	
Helsingborgs IF	26	11	5	10	35	36	**38**	
IFK Göteborg	26	10	7	9	37	28	**37**	
Örebro SK	26	10	7	9	29	33	**37**	
Halmstads BK	26	11	3	12	41	37	**36**	
Elfsborg IF	26	9	7	10	29	34	**34**	UEFA Cup (cup winners)
Landskrona BoIS	26	8	8	10	26	39	**32**	
GIF Sundsvall	26	3	10	13	25	43	**19**	
Östers IF	26	3	8	15	31	56	**17**	Relegated UEFA Cup (Fair Play)
Enköpings SK	26	3	5	18	22	59	**14**	Relegated

Promoted clubs: Kalmar FF, Trelleborgs FF.

International Club Performances 2003–04

CLUB	COMPETITION	PROGRESS
FC København (Den)	Champions League	3rd Qualifying Round
	UEFA Cup	2nd Round
Rosenborg BK (Nor)	Champions League	3rd Qualifying Round
	UEFA Cup	2nd Round
Djurgårdens IF (Swe)	Champions League	2nd Qualifying Round
HJK Helsinki (Fin)	Champions League	2nd Qualifying Round
AIK (Swe)	UEFA Cup	1st Round
Brøndby (Den)	UEFA Cup	3rd Round
Esjberg fB (Den)	UEFA Cup	1st Round
Haka Valkeakoski (Fin)	UEFA Cup	Qualifying Phase
SFK Lyn (Nor)	UEFA Cup	1st Round
Malmö FF (Swe)	UEFA Cup	1st Round
Molde FK (Nor)	UEFA Cup	2nd Round
MyPa Anjalankoski (Fin)	UEFA Cup	1st Round
FC Nordsjaelland (Den)	UEFA Cup	1st Round
OB Odense (Den)	UEFA Cup	1st Round
Vålerenga IF (Nor)	UEFA Cup	3rd Round

National Cup Finals 2003, 2003–04

COUNTRY	WINNERS	SCORE	RUNNERS-UP
Denmark	FC København	**1-0**	AaB Aalborg
Finland	HJK Helsinki	**2-1** (aet)	Allianssi Vantaa
Norway	Rosenborg	**3-1** (aet)	Bodø/Glimt
Sweden	IF Elfsborg	**1-0**	Assyriska Förening AIK

Above: *FC København fans turn out in numbers at a city centre reception to congratulate their team who clinched the Danish league and cup double.*

Above, left: *Djurgårdens' Kim Kallstrom (centre) and Jesper Blomqvist (right) celebrate their Swedish league title triumph after the final game against Östers.*

Left: *Iiro Aalto opens the scoring for Finnish champions HJK Helsinki on its way to a 3-0 home victory against FC Hämeenlinna.*

Soccer in Sweden

SWEDEN

1870s: Soccer introduced to Sweden by British workers and diplomats

1887: Ögryte IS, Sweden's oldest club formed

1895: Swedish Sports and Athletics Association formed, soccer's first governing body

1896: Gothenburg League begins

1900: Stockholm clubs allowed into Gothenburg League

1904: Formation of FA: Svenska Fotbollförbundet. Affiliation to FIFA

1908: First international, v Norway, won 11-3, venue: Gothenburg

1920: First women's soccer charity matches

1925: League format replaces play-offs for championship

1934: Sweden play in World Cup in Italy

1941: First Swedish Cup Final

1948: Sweden wins gold medal at London Olympics

1954: Affiliation to UEFA

1958: Professionals allowed to play for national team

1973: First women's international, v Finland, drawn 0-0

1978: National FA incorporates women's soccer

1982: League decided by final play-off

1990: League reverts to simple format

1870 1875 1880 1885 1890 1895 1900 1905 1910 1915 1920 1925 1930 1935 1940 1945 1950 1955 1960 1965 1970 1975 1980 1985 1990 1995 2000 2005

Gunnar Nordahl moved from IFK Norrköping to Milan in 1949 to become part of an all-Swedish forward line with Gunnar Gren and Nils Liedholm.

Key

 International soccer
Affiliation to FIFA
Affiliation to UEFA
Women's soccer
World Cup host
World Cup runner-up
European Championships host
○ Competition winner
△ Competition runner-up
IFK – IFK Göteborg
Mal – Malmö FF

International Competitions

	European Cup	UEFA Cup	European Cup-Winners' Cup
1958:	△ ■		
1979:	△ Mal		
1982:		○ IFK	
1987:		○ IFK	
1992:	■		

Sweden: The main clubs

IFK Elfsborg 1905 Team name with year of formation

● Club formed before 1912
● Club formed 1912–25
● Club formed 1925–50
○ Club formed after 1950
★ Founder members of League (1925)
Pre-1925 champions
Champions (1925–55)
Colours and date unknown

★ **Örgryte IS** 1887

★ **IFK Göteborg** 1904

Gunnilse

Västra Frölunda 1930

★ **GAIS** 1894

Göteborg IF

BK Häcken 1940

Fässbergs IF 1916

★ **Helsingborgs IF** 1907

Råå IF Helsingborg 1921

★ **Landskrona** 1915

★ **IFK Malmö** 1899

Malmö FF 1887

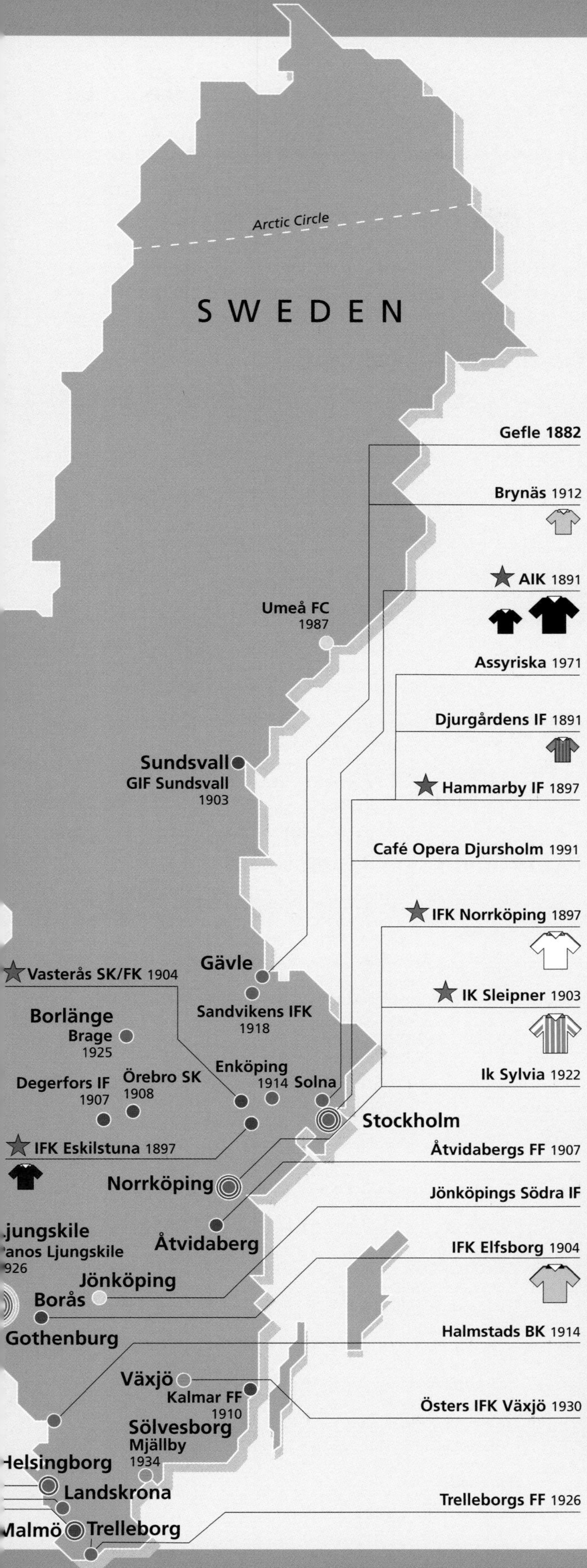

Sweden

ORIGINS AND GROWTH OF SOCCER

SOCCER ARRIVED IN SWEDEN IN THE 1870s by a variety of routes: Scottish riveters and English sailors in Gothenburg, British engineers and railway workers, as well as British embassy staff in the parks of Stockholm. Swedish soccer's centre of gravity was quickly established in Gothenburg with the formation of Ögryte (1887) and GAIS Gothenburg (1894). In 1895 a Gothenburg-based tournament was set up. Stockholm clubs joined in 1900 and a national league was created in 1925. Sweden absorbed soccer influences from Britain and Continental Europe, both providing coaches and managers to leading club sides and the national teams prior to the Second World War.

Swedes in Milan

The development of Swedish soccer has obvious parallels with wider Swedish society, most clearly an active international presence out of all proportion with the strength of its domestic soccer. Sweden was a founder member of FIFA, won the gold medal at the 1948 Olympics, has been third or fourth at three World Cups (1938, 1950, 1994) and was runner-up and host at the 1958 World Cup. Domestically, the persistence of amateurism saw the best players migrate south, most famously the forward line of Gren, Nordahl and Liedholm to Milan in 1949. This move was met by the exclusion of professionals from the national team until 1958. Limited economic resources combined with a continuing exodus of talent left Swedish clubs weak in postwar European competitions until the de facto arrival of professionalism at the bigger clubs and the UEFA Cup triumphs of IFK Gothenburg in the 1980s.

Women on top

The egalitarian and anti-commercial ethos of much of Swedish society may have been barriers to the success of Swedish men's soccer but it has certainly encouraged the relatively early adoption and active promotion of women's soccer in Sweden. The Swedish women's team won the inaugural Women's European Championships in 1984 and was runner-up in the first Women's World Cup in 1988 and again in 2003.

SWEDEN

Gefle 1882

Brynäs 1912

AIK 1891

Umeå FC 1987

Assyriska 1971

Djurgårdens IF 1891

Sundsvall
GIF Sundsvall 1903

Hammarby IF 1897

Café Opera Djursholm 1991

IFK Norrköping 1897

Vasterås SK/FK 1904   Gävle

IK Sleipner 1903

Borlänge
Brage 1925

Sandvikens IFK 1918

Degerfors IF 1907   Örebro SK 1908

Enköping 1914   Solna

Ik Sylvia 1922

IFK Eskilstuna 1897

Stockholm

Åtvidabergs FF 1907

Norrköping

Jönköpings Södra IF

jungskile
anos Ljungskile
926   Åtvidaberg

IFK Elfsborg 1904

Jönköping

Borås

Gothenburg

Halmstads BK 1914

Växjö
Kalmar FF 1910

Östers IFK Växjö 1930

Sölvesborg
Mjällby 1934

Helsingborg

Landskrona

Trelleborgs FF 1926

Malmö   Trelleborg

The Swedish Women's team won the first-ever Women's European Championships in 1984 beating England in the Final.

Sweden

PLAYERS AND MANAGERS

DESPITE THE STRENGTH AND DEPTH of its soccer-playing culture and its apparent insularity Swedish soccer has remained open to a stream of foreign coaches and ideas. The country's persistence with amateur soccer until the 1980s saw the leading players created in this environment move abroad to play their sport. The wealth of talent in Swedish soccer was first revealed at the London Olympics in 1948 where the national team boasted the amazing forward line of Gunnar Gren, Gunnar Nordhal and Niels Liedholm – known still as 'Gre-No-Li'. They won the tournament, beating Yugoslavia 3-1 in the final at Wembley. All three left to play in Italy for the next decade only returning to Sweden and the national team for the 1958 World Cup finals. Here they were joined by a new generation of players including Agne Simonsen, Kurt Hamrin and Lennart Skoglund. In the wake of their run to the Final, where they lost 5-2 to Brazil, all three of these new players made their way overseas. Both these successful national teams were coached by an Englishman – George Raynor.

Double act in the hot seat

It was not until the 1990s and particularly Sweden's 1994 showcase World Cup campaign that Swedish players of a similar quality emerged and began to play aboard in numbers. Some did so with great success, like Kennet Andersson at Bologna and Fenerbahçe, while others like Tomas Brolin went overseas with much less success. The most eye-catching players of recent times have been striker Henrik Larsson and playmaker Zlatan Ibrahimovic – the first leading player to emerge from the substantial immigrant population in Sweden from the former Yugoslavia. Today, almost uniquely in international soccer, Sweden boasts a double act in the top job. Tommy Söderberg and Lars Lagerbäck have managed to share the hot seat now for over seven years.

Top 20 International Caps

PLAYER	CAPS	GOALS	FIRST MATCH	LAST MATCH
Thomas Ravelli	143	0	1981	1997
Roland Nilsson	116	2	1986	2000
Björn Nordqvist	115	0	1963	1978
Patrik Andersson*	96	3	1991	2002
Örvar Bergmark	94	0	1951	1965
Kennet Andersson	83	31	1990	2000
Henrik Larsson*	78	28	1993	2004
Ronnie Hellström	77	0	1968	1980
Joachim Björklund	75	0	1991	2000
Jonas Thern	75	6	1987	1997
Håkan Mild	74	8	1991	2001
Karl Svensson	73	0	1949	1958
Bosse Larsson	70	17	1964	1978
Ingemar Erlandsson	69	2	1978	1985
Stefan Schwarz*	69	6	1989	2001
Niclas Alexandersson*	68	7	1993	2003
Glenn Hysén	68	6	1981	1990
Teddy Lukic*	61	0	1995	2004
Martin Dahlin	60	29	1991	2000
Roger Ljung	59	3	1988	1995

Top 10 International Goalscorers

PLAYER	GOALS	CAPS	FIRST MATCH	LAST MATCH
Sven Rydell	49	43	1923	1932
Gunnar Nordahl	43	33	1942	1948
Gunnar Gren	32	57	1940	1958
Kennet Andersson	31	83	1990	2000
Martin Dahlin	29	60	1991	2000
Henrik Larsson*	28	78	1993	2004
Agne Simonsson	27	51	1957	1967
Tomas Brolin	26	47	1990	1995
Per Kaufeldt	23	33	1922	1929
Karl Gustafsson	22	32	1908	1918

* Indicates players still playing at least at club level.

Sweden International Managers

DATES	NAME	GAMES	WON	DRAWN	LOST
1943–56	Rudolf Kock	110	61	20	29
1957–61	Eric Persson	39	26	4	9
1962–65	Lennart Nyman	36	14	13	9
1966–70	Orvar Bergmark	49	26	11	12
1971–79	Georg Ericson	91	39	19	33
1980–85	Lars Arnesson	59	27	13	19
1986–90	Olle Nordin	45	23	12	10
1990	Nils Andersson	4	2	0	2
1991–97	Tommy Svensson	87	44	23	20
1997	Tommy Svensson and Tommy Söderberg	9	5	2	2
1998–	Tommy Söderberg and Lars Lagerbäck	43	25	11	7

All figures correct as of 28 June 2004.

'Gre-No-Li': In the wake of their 1948 Olympic gold medal, Gunnar Gren, Gunnar Nordhal and Niels Liedholm all moved to Milan.

Player of the Year

YEAR	PLAYER	CLUB
1946	Gren	IFK Göteborg
1947	G. Nordahl	IFK Norrköping
1948	B. Nordahl	Degerfors IF
1949	K. Nordahl	IFK Norrköping
1950	Nilsson	Malmv FF
1951	Åhlund	Degerfors IF
1952	K. Svensson	Helsingborgs IF
1953	Gustavsson	IFK Norrköping
1954	S-O Svensson	Helsingborgs IF
1955	Löfgren	Motala AIF
1956	Sandberg	Djurgårdens IF
1957	Johansson	IFK Norrköping
1958	Bergmark	Örebro SK
1959	Simonsen	Örgryte IS
1960	Jonsson	IFK Norrköping

Player of the Year *(continued)*

YEAR	PLAYER	CLUB
1961	Nyholm	IFK Norrköping
1962	Öberg	Malmö FF
1963	Bild	IFK Norrköping
1964	Mild	Djurgårdens IF
1965	Larsson	Malmö FF
1966	Kindvall	IFK Norrköping/ Feyenoord
1967	Svahn	Malmö FF
1968	Nordqvist	IFK Norrköping
1969	T. Svensson	Östers IF
1970	Olsson	VfB Stuttgart
1971	Hellström	Hammarby IF
1972	Edström	Åtvidabergs FF
1973	Larsson	Malmö FF
1974	Edström	PSV Eindhoven

Player of the Year *(continued)*

YEAR	PLAYER	CLUB
1975	Karlsson	Åtvidabergs FF
1976	Linderoth	Östers IF
1977	Andersson	Malmö FF
1978	Hellström	1.FC Kaiserslautern
1979	Möller	Malmö FF
1980	Zetterlund	IK Brage
1981	Ravelli	Östers IF
1982	Nilsson	IFK Göteborg/ 1.FC Kaiserslautern
1983	Hysén	IFK Göteborg
1984	Dahlkvist	AIK
1985	Strömberg	Atalanta
1986	Prytz	BSC Young Boys
1987	Peter Larsson	IFK Göteborg
1988	Hysén	AC Fiorentina
1989	Thern	Malmö FF/ SL Benfica
1990	Brolin	IFK Norrköping/ Parma
1991	Limpár	Arsenal
1992	Eriksson	IFK Norrköping/ 1.FC Kaiserslautern
1993	Dahlin	VfL Borussia Mönchengladbach
1994	Brolin	Parma
1995	Andersson	VfL Borussia Mönchengladbach
1996	Nilsson	Helsingborgs IF
1997	Zetterberg	RSC Anderlecht
1998	Larsson	Celtic
1999	Schwarz	Sunderland
2000	Hedman	Coventry City
2001	Andersson	FC Bayern München
2002	Ljungberg	Arsenal
2003	Mellberg	Aston Villa

One of the revelations of the 1958 World Cup, Agne Simonsen went to Real Madrid as Di Stefano's proposed successor. But it seems that Di Stefano was not ready to retire and Simonsen moved on to Italy.

SWEDEN

Top Goalscorers by Season 1947–2003

SEASON	PLAYER	CLUB	GOALS
1947	Gren	IFK Göteborg	18
1948	Nordahl	IFK Norrköping	18
1949	Franck	Helsingborgs IF	19
1950	Rydell	Malmö FF	22
1951	Jeppson	Djurgårdens	17
1952	Jakobsson	GAIS	17
1953	Jakobsson	GAIS	24
1954	Jakobsson	GAIS	21
1955	Hamrin	AIK	22
1956	Bengtsson	Halmstads Bk	22
1957	Bild	IFK Norrköping	19
1958	Johansson	IFK Göteborg	27
1958	Källgren	IFK Norrköping	27
1959	Börjesson	Örgryte IS	21
1960	Börjesson	Örgryte IS	24
1961	Johansson	IFK Göteborg	20
1962	Skiöld	Djurgårdens	21
1963	Larsson	Malmö FF	17
1963	Heinemann	Degerfors FF	17
1964	Granbom	Helsingborgs IF	22
1965	Larsson	Malmö FF	28
1966	Kindvall	IFK Norrköping	20
1967	Szepanski	Malmö FF	22
1968	Eklund	Åtvidabergs FF	16
1969	Almqvist	IFK Göteborg	16
1970	Larsson	Malmö FF	16
1971	Sandberg	Åtvidabergs FF	17
1972	Edström	Åtvidabergs FF	16
1972	Sandberg	Åtvidabergs FF	16
1973	Mattsson	Östers IF	20

SEASON	PLAYER	CLUB	GOALS
1974	Mattsson	Östers IF	22
1975	Mattsson	Östers IF	31
1976	Backe	Halmstads	21
1977	Almqvist	IFK Landskrona	15
1977	Aronsson	BoIS	15
1978	Berggren	Djurgårdens	19
1979	Werner	Hammarby IF	14
1980	Ohlsson	Hammarby IF	19
1981	Nilsson	IFK Göteborg	20
1982	Corneliusson	IFK Göteborg	12
1983	Ahlström	IF Elfsborg	16
1984	Ohlsson	Hammarby IF	14
1985	Börjesson	Örgryte IS	10
1985	Lansdowne	Kalmar FF	10
1985	Karlsson	Kalmar FF	10
1986	Ekström	IFK Göteborg	13
1987	Larsson	Malmö FF	19
1988	Dahlin	Malmö FF	17
1989	Hellström	IFK Norrköping	16
1990	Eskelinen	IFK Göteborg	10
1991	K. Andersson	IFK Göteborg	13
1992	Eklund	Östers IF	16
1993	Lilienberg	Trelleborgs FF	18
1993	Bertilsson	Halmstads BK	18
1994	Kindvall	IFK Norrköping	23
1995	Skoog	Västra Frölunda	17
1996	A. Andersson	IFK Göteborg	19
1997	Mattiasson	IF Elfsborg	14
1997	Sahlin	Örebro SK	14
1997	Lilienberg	Halmstads BK	14

SEASON	PLAYER	CLUB	GOALS
1998	Stavrum	Helsingborgs IF	18
1999	Allbäck	Örgryte IS	15
2000	Berglund	IF Elfsborg	18
2001	Selakovic	Halmstads	15
2002	Ijeh	Malmö FF	24
2003	Skoog	Malmö FF	22

After exporting *players for decades, Swedish soccer has finally begun to import players from Eastern Europe and Africa. Nigerian striker Peter Ijeh was top scorer in the league for Malmö in 2002.*

Sweden

Svenska Fotbollförbundet
Founded: 1904
Joined FIFA: 1904
Joined UEFA: 1954

SWEDEN

THE FIRST SWEDISH league championship was played in 1896 and was restricted to clubs from Gothenburg. In 1900, the league was expanded to include teams from Stockholm and the final rounds were played as a knockout competition until 1925, when a normal league format was adopted (this accounts for the two championships awarded that year).

The Swedish Cup was established in 1941, and ran fitfully over the next couple of decades until European qualification for the winners made it a more pressing engagement. Despite this, Finals have attracted crowds of less than 2,000.

Swedish League Record 1896–2003

SEASON	CHAMPIONS	RUNNERS-UP
1896	Örgryte IS	IV Göteborg
1897	Örgryte IS	Örgryte II
1898	Örgryte IS	AIK
1899	Örgryte IS	Göteborg FF
1900	AIK	Örgryte IS
1901	AIK	Örgryte II
1902	Örgryte IS	Jönköpings AIF
1903	Göteborg IF	Göteborg FF
1904	Örgryte IS	Djurgårdens IF
1905	Örgryte IS	IFK Stockholm
1906	Örgryte IS	Djurgårdens IF
1907	Örgryte IS	IFK Uppsala
1908	IFK Göteborg	IFK Uppsala
1909	Örgryte IS	Djurgårdens IF
1910	IFK Göteborg	Djurgårdens IF
1911	AIK	IFK Uppsala
1912	Djurgårdens IF	Örgryte IS
1913	Örgryte IS	Djurgårdens IF
1914	AIK	Helsingborgs IF
1915	Djurgårdens IF	AIK
1916	AIK	Djurgårdens IF
1917	Djurgårdens IF	AIK
1918	IFK Göteborg	Helsingborgs IF
1919	GAIS	Djurgårdens IF
1920	Djurgårdens IF	IK Sleipner
1921	IFK Eskilstuna	IK Sleipner
1922	GAIS	Hammarby IF
1923	AIK	IFK Eskilstuna
1924	Fassbergs IF	Sirius Uppsala
1925	Brynas IF Gävle	Derby BK Linköping
1925	GAIS	IFK Göteborg
1926	Örgryte IS	GAIS
1927	GAIS	IFK Göteborg
1928	Örgryte IS	Helsingborgs IF
1929	Helsingborgs IF	Örgryte IS
1930	Helsingborgs IF	IFK Göteborg
1931	GAIS	AIK
1932	AIK	Örgryte IS
1933	Helsingborgs IF	GAIS
1934	Helsingborgs IF	GAIS
1935	IFK Göteborg	AIK
1936	IF Elfsborg	AIK
1937	AIK	IK Sleipner
1938	IK Sleipner	Helsingborgs IF
1939	IF Elfsborg	AIK
1940	IF Elfsborg	IFK Göteborg
1941	Helsingborgs IF	Degerfors IF
1942	IFK Göteborg	GAIS
1943	IFK Norrköping	IF Elfsborg

Swedish League Record (*continued*)

SEASON	CHAMPIONS	RUNNERS-UP
1944	Malmö FF	IF Elfsborg
1945	IFK Norrköping	IF Elfsborg
1946	IFK Norrköping	Malmö FF
1947	IFK Norrköping	AIK
1948	IFK Norrköping	Malmö FF
1949	Malmö FF	Helsingborgs IF
1950	Malmö FF	Jonköpings Södra
1951	Malmö FF	Råå IF Helsingborg
1952	IFK Norrköping	Malmö FF
1953	Malmö FF	IFK Norrköping
1954	GAIS	Helsingborgs IF
1955	Djurgårdens IF	Halmstads BK
1956	IFK Norrköping	Malmö FF
1957	IFK Norrköping	Malmö FF
1958	IFK Göteborg	IFK Norrköping
1959	Djurgårdens IF	IFK Norrköping
1960	IFK Norrköping	IFK Malmö
1961	IF Elfsborg	IFK Norrköping
1962	IFK Norrköping	Djurgårdens IF
1963	IFK Norrköping	Degerfors IF
1964	Djurgårdens IF	Malmö FF
1965	Malmö FF	IF Elfsborg
1966	Djurgårdens IF	IFK Norrköping
1967	Malmö FF	Djurgårdens IF
1968	Östers IF Växjö	Malmö FF
1969	IFK Göteborg	Malmö FF
1970	Malmö FF	Åtvidabergs FF
1971	Malmö FF	Åtvidabergs FF
1972	Åtvidabergs FF	AIK
1973	Åtvidabergs FF	Östers IF Växjö
1974	Malmö FF	AIK
1975	Malmö FF	Östers IF Växjö
1976	Halmstads BK	Malmö FF
1977	Malmö FF	IF Elfsborg
1978	Östers IF Växjö	Malmö FF
1979	Halmstads BK	Malmö FF
1980	Östers IF Växjö	Malmö FF
1981	Östers IF Växjö	IFK Göteborg
1982	IFK Göteborg	Hammarby IF
1983	IFK Göteborg	Östers IF Växjö
1984	IFK Göteborg	IFK Norrköping
1985	Örgryte IS	IFK Göteborg
1986	Malmö FF	AIK
1987	IFK Göteborg	Malmö FF
1988	Malmö FF	Djurgårdens IF
1989	IFK Norrköping	Malmö FF
1990	IFK Göteborg	IFK Norrköping
1991	IFK Göteborg	IFK Norrköping
1992	AIK	IFK Norrköping
1993	IFK Göteborg	IFK Norrköping
1994	IFK Göteborg	Örebro SK
1995	IFK Göteborg	Helsingborgs IF
1996	IFK Göteborg	Malmö FF
1997	Halmstads BK	IFK Göteborg
1998	AIK	Helsingborgs IF
1999	Helsingborgs IF	AIK
2000	Halmstads BK	Helsingborgs IF
2001	Hammarby IF	Djurgårdens IF
2002	Djurgårdens IF	Malmö FF
2003	Djurgårdens IF	Hammarby IF

Swedish League Summary

TEAM	TOTALS	CHAMPIONS & RUNNERS-UP (BOLD)　　(ITALICS)
IFK Göteborg	17, 7	**1908, 10, 18,** 25, 27, 30, **35, 40, 42, 58, 69, 81, 82–84, 85, 87, 90, 91, 93–96,** 97
Malmö FF	14, 16	**1944,** 46, 48, **49–51,** 52, 53, 56, 57, 64, 65, 67, 68, 69, 70, 71, 74, 75, 76, 77, 78–80, 86, 87, **88,** 89, 96, 2002
Örgryte IS	14, 4	**1896–99,** 1900, **02, 04–07, 09,** 12, **13,** 26, 28, 29, 32, 85
IFK Norrköping	12, 10	**1943, 45–48, 52, 53, 56, 57, 58, 59, 60,** 61, 62, **63,** 66, 84, 89, **90–93**
AIK	10, 12	1898, **1900, 01, 11, 14,** 15, **16, 17, 23,** 31, **32, 35, 36, 37,** 39, 47, 72, 74, 86, **92, 98,** 99
Djurgårdens IF	10, 11	1904, 06, 09, 10, **12, 13, 15, 16, 17, 19, 20,** 55, **59,** 62, 64, 66, 67, 88, 2001, **02, 03**
Helsingborgs IF	6, 9	1914, 18, 28, **29, 30, 33, 34,** 38, 41, 49, 54, 95, 98, 99, 2000
GAIS	6, 4	**1919, 22, 25,** 26, 27, **31,** 33, 34, 42, 54
IF Elfsborg	4, 5	**1936, 39, 40, 43–45,** 61, **65,** 77
Östers IF Växjö	4, 3	**1968,** 73, **75, 78, 80, 81,** 83
Halmstads BK	4, 1	**1955,** 76, **79, 97, 2000**
Åtvidabergs FF	2, 2	1970, 71, **72, 73**
Hammarby IF	1, 3	1922, 82, **2001,** 03
IK Sleipner	1, 3	1920, 21, **37,** 38
IFK Eskilstuna	1, 1	**1921,** 23
Brynas IF Gävle	1, 0	**1925**
Fassbergs IF	1, 0	**1924**
Göteborg IF	1, 0	**1903**
IFK Uppsala	0, 3	1907, 08, 11
Degerfors	0, 2	1941, 63
Göteborg FF	0, 2	1899, 1903
Örgryte II	0, 2	1897, 1901
Derby BK Linköping	0, 1	1925
IFK Malmö	0, 1	1960
IFK Stockholm	0, 1	1905
IV Göteborg	0, 1	1896
Jönköpings Södra	0, 1	1950
Jönköpings AIF	0, 1	1902
Örebro SK	0, 1	1994
Råå IF Helsingborg	0, 1	1951
Sirius Uppsala	0, 1	1924

Swedish Cup Record 1941–2003

YEAR	WINNERS	SCORE	RUNNERS-UP
1941	Helsingborgs IF	3-1	IK Sleipner
1942	GAIS	2-1	IK Elfsborg
1943	IFK Norrköping	0-0, (replay) 5-2	AIK
1944	Malmö FF	4-3 (aet)	IFK Norrköping
1945	IFK Norrköping	4-1	Malmö FF
1946	Malmö FF	3-0	Åtvidabergs FF
1947	Malmö FF	3-2	AIK
1948	Råå IF Helsingborg	6-0	BK Kenty Linköping
1949	AIK	1-0	Landskrona BoIS
1950	AIK	3-2	Helsingborgs IF
1951	Malmö FF	2-1	Djurgårdens IF
1952		no competition	
1953	Malmö FF	3-2	IFK Norrköping
1954–66		no competition	
1967	Malmö FF	2-0	IFK Norrköping
1968		no competition	
1969	IFK Norrköping	1-0	AIK
1970	Åtvidabergs FF	2-0	Sandvikens IF
1971	Åtvidabergs FF	3-2	Malmö FF
1972	Landskrona BoIS	0-0, (replay) 3-2 (aet)	IFK Norrköping
1973	Malmö FF	7-0	Åtvidabergs FF

Swedish Cup Record (*continued*)

YEAR	WINNERS	SCORE	RUNNERS-UP
1974	Malmö FF	2-0	Östers IF Växjö
1975	Malmö FF	1-0	Djurgårdens IF
1976	AIK	1-1, (replay) 3-0	Landskrona BoIS
1977	Östers IF Växjö	1-0	Hammarby IF
1978	Malmö FF	2-0 (aet)	Kalmar FF
1979	IFK Göteborg	6-1	Åtvidabergs FF
1980	Malmö FF	3-3 (aet)(4-3 pens)	IK Brage
1981	Kalmar FF	4-0	IF Elfsborg
1982	IFK Göteborg	3-2	Östers IF Växjö
1983	IFK Göteborg	1-0 (aet)	Hammarby IF
1984	Malmö FF	1-0	Landskrona BoIS
1985	AIK	1-1 (aet)(3-2 pens)	Östers IF Växjö
1986	Malmö FF	2-1	IFK Göteborg
1987	Kalmar FF	2-0	GAIS
1988	IFK Norrköping	3-1	Örebro SK
1989	Malmö FF	3-0	Djurgårdens IF
1990	Djurgårdens IF	2-0	Hacken BK Göteborg
1991	IFK Norrköping	4-1	Östers IF Växjö
1992	IFK Göteborg	3-2 (aet)	AIK
1993	Degerfors IF	3-0	Landskrona BoIS
1994	IFK Norrköping	4-3 (gg)	Helsingborgs IF
1995	Halmstads BK	3-1	AIK
1996	AIK	1-0 (gg)	Malmö FF
1997	AIK	2-1	IF Elfsborg
1998	Helsingborgs IF	1-1, 1-1 (aet) (3-0 pens)(2 legs)	Örgryte IS
1999	AIK	1-0, 0-0 (2 legs)	IFK Göteborg
2000	Örgryte IS	2-0, 0-1 (2 legs)	AIK
2001	IF Elfsborg	1-1 (aet)(9-8 pens)	AIK
2002	Djurgårdens IF	1-0 (aet)	AIK
2003	IF Elfsborg	2-0	Assyriska Föreningen

(gg) denotes victory on golden goal

Swedish Cup Summary

TEAM	TOTALS	WINNERS & RUNNERS-UP (BOLD)　　(ITALICS)
Malmö FF	14, 3	**1944,** 45, **46, 47, 51, 53, 67,** 71, **73–75, 78,** 80, **84,** 86, **89,** 96
AIK	7, 8	1943, 47, **49, 50,** 69, 76, 85, 92, 95, **96,** 97, 99, 2000–02
IFK Norrköping	6, 4	**1943,** 44, **45,** 53, 57, **69,** 72, **88, 91, 94**
IFK Göteborg	4, 2	**1979, 82, 83,** 86, **92,** 99
Åtvidabergs FF	2, 3	1946, **70, 71,** 73, 79
Djurgårdens IF	2, 3	1951, 75, 89, **90, 2002**
IF Elfsborg	2, 2	**1981,** 97, **2001,** 03
Helsingborgs IF	2, 2	**1941,** 50, 94, **98**
Kalmar FF	2, 1	1978, **81, 87**
Landskrona BoIS	1, 4	1949, **72,** 76, 84, 93
Östers IF Växjö	1, 4	1974, **77,** 82, 85, 91
GAIS	1, 1	**1942,** 87
Örgryte IS	1, 1	1998, **2000**
Degerfors IF	1, 0	**1993**
Halmstads BK	1, 0	**1995**
Råå IF Helsingborg	1, 0	**1948**
Hammarby IF	0, 2	1977, 83
Assyriska Föreningen	0, 1	2003
BK Kenty Linköping	0, 1	1948
Hacken BK Göteborg	0, 1	1990
IK Brage	0, 1	1980
IK Elfsborg	0, 1	1942
IK Sleipner	0, 1	1941
Örebro SK	0, 1	1988
Sandvikens IF	0, 1	1970

DENMARK

Soccer in Denmark

1876: Continental Europe's oldest club, København Boldklub, established — 1875

1880

1885

1889: Formation of FA: Dansk Boldspil Union — 1890

1895

⚽ **1904:** Affiliation to FIFA — 1900

🇩🇰 **1908:** First international, v France, won 9-0, venue: London. Runners-up in Olympic tournament — 1905

1912: Runners-up in Olympic tournament — 1910

1913: National League established — 1915

🏛 **1915:** League abandoned during war — 1920

1925

1930

1935

1940

1945

⚽ **1954:** Affiliation to UEFA — 1950

1955: First Danish Cup Final — 1955

♀ **1972:** Women's committee established by Danish FA — 1960

♀ **1973:** Women's National League established — 1965

♀🇩🇰 **1974:** First women's international, v Sweden — 1970

1976: Law banning Danes who played overseas from the national side ended — 1975

1978: Professionalism introduced — 1980

1991: Professional Premier League, the Superliga, formed — 1985

1990

1992: Victory over Germany made Denmark European Champions — 1995

1995: Superliga expanded to 12 clubs — 2000

2005

Nils Bohr, the first Dane to win the Nobel Prize for Physics, was also reserve goalkeeper for AB, one of the teams from Copenhagen.

Jan Molby was transferred from Molding to Liverpool in 1984. His success in England paved the way for a generation of other Danish exports.

Key

🇩🇰	International soccer
⚽	Affiliation to FIFA
⚽	Affiliation to UEFA
♀	Women's soccer
●	European Championships winner
🏛	War

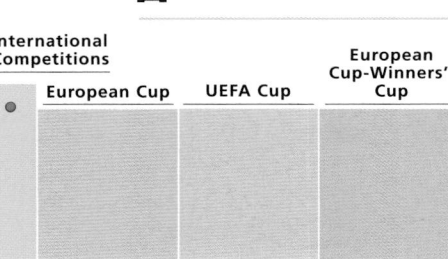

International Competitions	European Cup	UEFA Cup	European Cup-Winners' Cup
1992: ●			

Denmark: The main clubs

Skive 1901 Team name with year of formation

● Club formed before 1912

● Club formed 1912–25

● Club formed 1925–50

○ Club formed after 1950

★ Founder members of League (1927)

☆ Founder members of Superliga (1991)

👕 Champions (1913–45)

👕 Champions (1946–91)

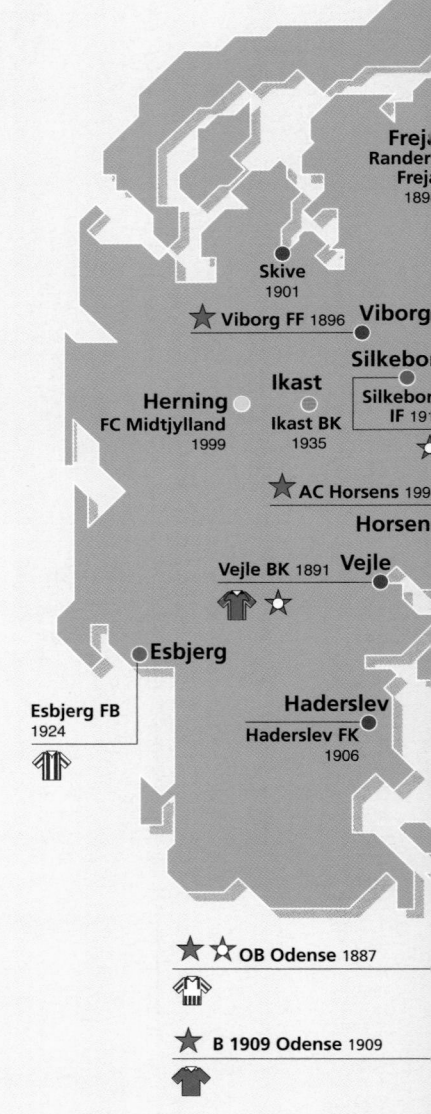

Frej Rander Frej 189.

Skive 1901

★ Viborg FF 1896 **Viborg**

Silkebo

Herning FC Midtjylland 1999

Ikast Ikast BK 1935

Silkebor Silkebor IF 19

★ AC Horsens 199

Horsen

Vejle BK 1891 **Vejle** 👕 ☆

● **Esbjerg**

Esbjerg FB 1924 👕

Haderslev Haderslev FK 1906

★ ☆ OB Odense 1887 👕

★ B 1909 Odense 1909 👕

Lyngby BFC 1921

AB (Akademisk Boldklub) 1889

Moved to Gladsaxe (1965)

Skovshoved IF 1909

B 1903 København 1903–92

Merged into FC København

FC København 1992

Merger of B 1903 København
and KB København

Brønshøj 1919

COPENHAGEN

AB
1885

Aalborg

Frem København 1886

Hvidovre BK 1925

B 93 København 1893

KB København 1876–1992

Merged into FC København

Fremad Amager 1910

FC Aarhus 1918

AGF 1880

Brøndby IF 1964

Aarhus

Farum

FC Nordsjaelland
1991
Formerly
Farum BK

COPENHAGEN
(see inset)

DENMARK

Køge

Herfølge

Naestved

Køge BK 1927

Herfølge
1921

Odense

Næstved IF
1939

B 1913 Odense 1913

Denmark

ORIGINS AND GROWTH OF SOCCER

PERHAPS IT WAS JUST PROXIMITY and the regular flow of British sailors and ships through Danish ports that explains Denmark's early enthusiasm for soccer. The dockside games recorded in the 1860s were soon followed by the foundation of Europe's oldest continental soccer club, København Boldklub, in 1876. KB was soon joined by Copenhagen teams Akademisk, Frem and B93, who played together as Staevnet against touring top British club sides. A national FA was formed in 1889 and four clubs were founded in provincial cities: AGF Aarhus in 1880, AAB in Aalborg in 1885, OB Odense in 1887 and Viborg FF in 1896. Denmark was also a founder member of FIFA in 1904.

Early enthusiasm and organization brought international success as Denmark took the silver medal at the Olympic tournaments in 1908 and 1912 (losing both Finals to Great Britain, 2-0 and 4-2). Despite this the game remained unequivocally amateur in Denmark. In the wake of this success a league was established in 1913 which has run ever since, but for a single season in 1915.

Ups and downs

However, it was not a professional league and the standard of Danish soccer steadily fell relative to the rest of Europe and Latin America. Each crop of promising players (including the Olympic squads of 1948 and 1960) were spirited away to foreign clubs as the Danish FA insisted on banning foreign-based professionals from the national side. Change came in the 1970s as a new generation of Danes, like Allan Simonsen at Barcelona and Jan Molby at Liverpool, played at the highest level in Europe. The national team ban was lifted and Denmark qualified for its first World Cup in 1986. In 1992, as late entrants to the European Championships, it took the title, beating Germany in the Final.

This success helped encourage a transformation of the domestic scene, and in 1991, a professional Premier League was finally established. Since then, a wave of mergers and club reorganizations have attempted to modernise Danish soccer but the recent financial crisis has seen many top clubs teeter on the verge of bankruptcy.

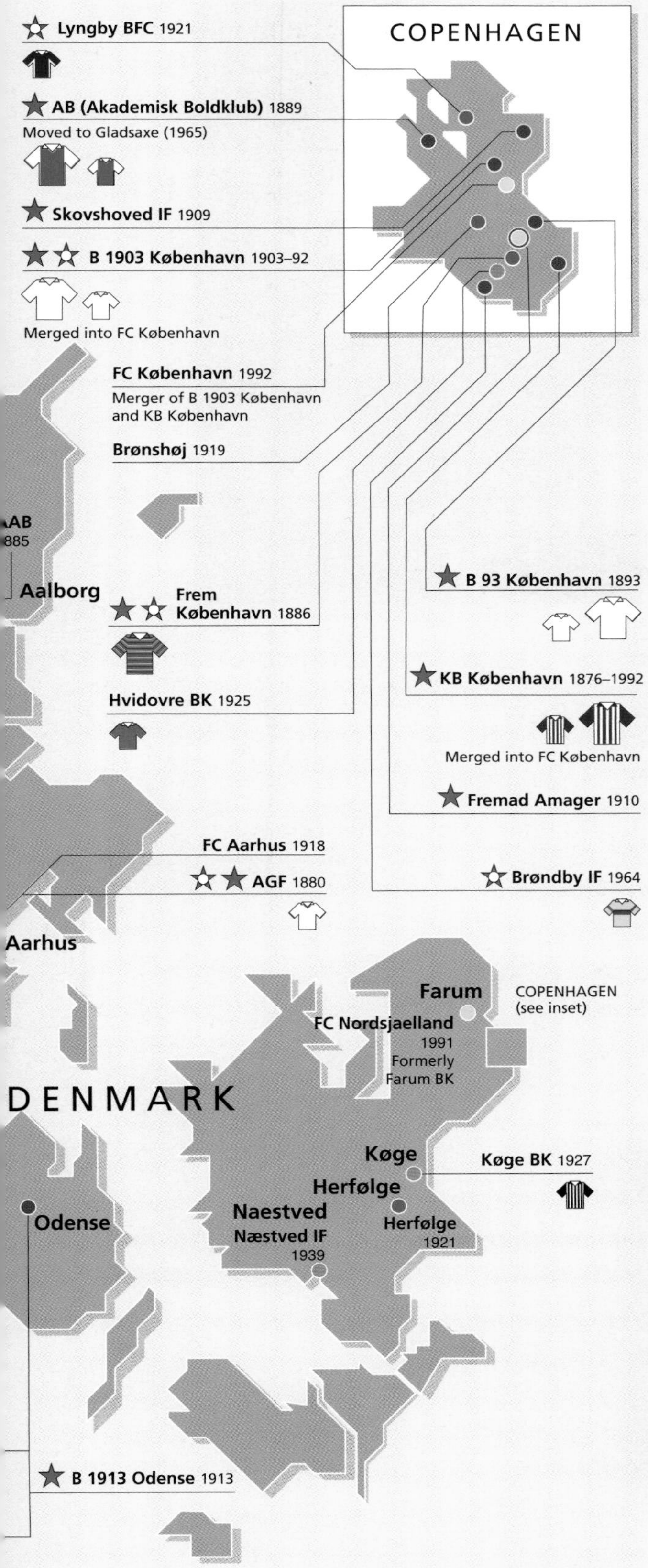

John Jensen is buried underneath a pile of his teammates after giving Denmark the lead in the 1992 European Championships Final against Germany in Gothenburg. Denmark won the match 2-0.

Denmark

PLAYERS AND MANAGERS

DENMARK'S EARLY AND ELITE soccer-playing history saw working-class Copenhagen boys rub shoulders with university-educated students in the ranks of the leading clubs. But for most of the 20th century the strength of a fierce and unbending amateur tradition kept talent either away from the game or sent it abroad, like Nils Middleboe who had a long and successful spell with Chelsea between 1913 and 1921. In 1948 the Danish team took the silver medal at the London Olympics and the three leading players in the team, Karl Praest and brothers Karl and John Hansen, were promptly signed by Juventus. Having taken up professional contracts they would not be allowed to play for the national team again.

Breaking the mould

The player that broke the mould of Danish amateurism was Allan Simonsen – a slight and speedy striker – who left the Danish provincial club Velje for Borussia Mönchengladbach in the mid-1970s. With Mönchengladbach he won domestic and European honours as well as being voted European Footballer of the Year in 1977. He followed Mönchengladbach's coach Neenes Weisweller to Barcelona before finishing his career with a short spell in South London at Charlton and finally back to Velje again. His progress inspired the generation of Danish players that would take Denmark to the World Cup finals in 1986 and peak when they won the 1992 European Championships. All, like Simonsen, developed their game abroad.

The altogether chunkier Jan Molby prospered at Liverpool, one of the top sides in Europe in the 1980s, while Peter Schmeichel graduated from Brøndby to Manchester United in the 1990s. The leading figures, though, were the Laudrup brothers.

Flemming Povlsen – unobtrusive but part of the backbone of the Danish national team for a decade – celebrates with the European Championships trophy in 1992.

The Laudrups' father, Finn, had played as a Danish international and was a key part of the team that revived Copenhagen club Brøndby. Both brothers played there before embarking on extended European club tours. Brian to Bayern München, Milan, Fiorentina, Rangers and Chelsea amongst others; Michael, the younger and more gifted of the pair, to Lazio, Juventus, Barcelona, Real Madrid, Vissel Kobe in Japan and Ajax.

Top 20 International Caps

PLAYER	CAPS	GOALS	FIRST MATCH	LAST MATCH
Peter Schmeichel	129	1	1987	2001
Michael Laudrup	104	37	1982	1998
Morten Olsen	102	4	1970	1989
Thomas Helveg*	88	2	1994	2004
John Sivebaek	87	1	1982	1992
Jan Heintze	86	4	1987	2002
Lars Olsen	84	4	1986	1996
Brian Laudrup	82	21	1987	1998
Kim Vilfort	77	14	1983	1996
Per Røntved	75	11	1970	1982
Jens Jørn Bertelsen	69	2	1976	1987
Preben Elkjaer-Larsen	69	38	1977	1988
John 'Faxe' Jensen	69	4	1986	1995
Søren Lerby	67	10	1978	1989
René Henriksen*	66	0	1998	2004
Brian Steen Nielsen	66	3	1990	2002
Ebbe Sand*	66	22	1998	2004
Jon Dahl Tomasson*	64	31	1997	2004
Henning Munk Jensen	62	1	1966	1978
Flemming Povlsen	62	21	1987	1994
Søren Busk	61	2	1979	1988
Marc Rieper	61	2	1990	2000
Bent Hansen	59	1	1958	1965
Jes Høgh	57	1	1991	2000
Allan Simonsen	56	21	1972	1986
Henning Enoksen	54	29	1958	1966
Kent Nielsen	54	3	1983	1992

Top 10 International Goalscorers

PLAYER	GOALS	CAPS	FIRST MATCH	LAST MATCH
Poul 'Tist' Nielsen	52	38	1912	1925
Pauli Jørgensen	44	44	1925	1939
Ole Madsen	42	51	1958	1969
Preben Elkjaer-Larsen	38	69	1977	1988
Michael Laudrup	37	104	1982	1998
Jon Dahl Tomasson*	31	64	1997	2003
Henning Enoksen	29	54	1958	1966
Michael Rohde	22	40	1915	1931
Ebbe Sand*	22	66	1998	2004
Brian Laudrup	21	82	1987	1998
Flemming Povlsen	21	62	1987	1994
Allan Simonsen	21	56	1972	1986
Jens Peder Hansen	18	38	1949	1961

* Indicates players still playing at least at club level.

Denmark International Managers (1956–2004)

DATES	NAME	GAMES	WON	DRAWN	LOST
1956–61	Arne Sørensen	41	20	8	13
1962–66	Paul Petersen	47	17	8	22
1967	Ernst Netuka & Erik Hansen	8	4	2	2
1968–69	Henry Form, Erik Hansen & John Hansen	20	9	2	9
1970–75	Rudi Strittich	60	20	11	29
1976–79	Kurt Nielsen	31	13	6	12
1979–90	Sepp Piontek	115	52	24	39
1990–96	Richard Møller Nielsen	67	37	17	13
1996–2000	Bo Johansson	40	17	9	14
2000–	Morten Olsen	47	27	13	7

All figures correct as of 28 June 2004.

DENMARK

Player of the Year

YEAR	PLAYER	CLUB
1963	Petersen	Esbjerg FB
1964	Madsen	HIK
1965	Poulsen	Vejle BK
1966	L. Nielsen	Frem København
1967	J. Hansen	Vejle BK
1968	H.M. Jensen	AaB Aalborg
1969	Michaelsen	B 1903 København
1970	Larsen	Akademisk
1971	Pedersen	Hvidovre BK
1972	Røntved	Brøshøj
1973	Aabech	Hvidovre BK
1974	Holmstrøm	KB København
1975	H.M. Jensen	AaB Aalborg
1976	Ahlberg	Frem København
1977	A. Hansen	OB Odense
1978	Kjaer	Esbjerg FB
1979	Bertelsen	Esbjerg FB
1980	Bastrup	AGF Aarhus
1981	A. Hansen	OB Odense
1982	M. Laudrup	Brøndby IF
1983	M. Olsen	RSC Anderlecht
1984	Elkjaer	Hellas Verona
1985	M. Laudrup	Juventus

Player of the Year (continued)

YEAR	PLAYER	CLUB
1986	M. Olsen	1. FC Köln
1987	J. Jensen	Brøndby IF
1988	L. Olsen	Brøndby IF
1989	B. Laudrup	Brøndby IF/ Bayer Uerdingen
1990	Schmeichel	Brøndby IF
1991	Vilfort	Brøndby IF
1992	B. Laudrup	Bayern München/ Fiorentina
1993	Schmeichel	Manchester United
1994	Helveg	Udinese
1995	B. Laudrup	Rangers
1996	A. Nielsen	Brøndby IF/ Tottenham Hotspur
1997	B. Laudrup	Rangers
1998	Sand	Brøndby IF
1999	Schmeichel	Manchester United
2000	Henriksen	Panathinaikos
2001	Sand	FC Schalke 04
2002	Tomasson	Feyenoord/Milan
2003	Wieghorst	Brøndby IF

***Sepp Piontek** – the German manager of the Danish national team in the 1980s – who finally welded the Danish Diaspora into a quality team who qualified for their first European Championships in 1984.*

Top Goalscorers by Season 1945–2004

SEASON	PLAYER	CLUB	GOALS
1945–46	Sorensen	B 93 København	16
1946–47	Bronee	OB Odense	21
1947–48	J. Hansen	Frem København	20
1948–49	Sorensen	OB Odense	16
1949–50	Ronvang	AB København	15
1950–51	Bjerregaard	B 93 København	11
1950–51	J.P. Hansen	Esbjerg FB	11
1950–51	Ronvang	AB København	11
1951–52	Kendzior	Skovshoved IF	13
1951–52	P.E. Petersen	Køge BK	13
1952–53	Kendzior	Skovshoved IF	17
1953–54	J.C. Christensen	AB København	12
1954–55	H. Jensen	Frem København	17
1955–56	Kjeldberg	AGF Aarhus	18
1956–57	S. Andersen	Frem København	27
1958	Enoksen	Vejle BK	27
1959	P. Jensen	KB København	20
1960	H. Nielsen	Frederikshavn	19
1961	Ravn	KB København	26
1962	Enoksen	AGF Aarhus	24
1962	C.E. Christiansen	Esbjerg FB	24
1963	Haastrup	B 1909 Odense	21
1964	Ravn	KB København	21
1965	P. Petersen	B 1903 København	18
1966	Enoksen	AGF Aarhus	16
1967	L. Nielsen	Frem København	15
1968	Holmstrom	KB København	23
1969	S.R. Larsen	B 1903 København	15
1970	Forsing	B 1903 København	18
1971	Brage	KB København	19
1971	J. Nielsen	B 1901 Nykøbing	19
1972	J. Nielsen	B 1901 Nykøbing	16
1972	Lund	Vejle BK	16

SEASON	PLAYER	CLUB	GOALS
1973	Aabech	Hvidovre FB	28
1974	Holmstrom	KB København	24
1975	B. Petersen	KB København	25
1976	Jespersen	AaB Aalborg	22
1977	A. Hansen	OB Odense	23
1978	Eriksen	OB Odense	22
1979	Eriksen	OB Odense	20
1980	Aabech	KB København	19
1981	A. Hansen	OB Odense	28
1982	Jacquet	Vejle BK	20
1983	V.M. Nielsen	OB Odense	20
1984	Thychosen	Vejle BK	24
1985	Bastrup	Ikast BK	20
1986	C. Nielsen	Brøndby IF	16
1987	C. Nielsen	Brøndby IF	20
1988	B. Christensen	Brøndby IF	21
1989	Jacobsen	OB Odense	14
1989	Molnar	Frem København	14
1989	F. Christensen	Lyngby FC	14
1990	B. Christensen	Brøndby IF	17

SEASON	PLAYER	CLUB	GOALS
1991	B. Christensen	Brøndby IF	11
1991–92	Moller	AaB Aalborg	17
1992–93	Moller	AaB Aalborg	20
1993–94	Frederiksen	Silkeborg IF	18
1994–95	E.B. Andersen	AaB Aalborg	24
1995–96	Thorninger	AGF Aarhus	20
1996–97	Molnar	Lyngby FC	26
1997–98	Sand	Brøndby IF	28
1998–99	Fernandez	Viborg FF	23
1999–2000	Lassen	Silkeborg IF	16
2000–01	Graulund	Brøndby IF	21
2001–02	Madsen	Brøndby IF	22
2001–02	Dalgas	OB Odense	22
2002–03	Kristiansen	Esbjerg FB	18
2002–03	Frederiksen	Viborg FF	18
2003–04	Bechmann	Esbjerg FB	19
2003–04	Hojer	OB Odense	19
2003–04	Miti	OB Odense	19
2003–04	Zidan	FD Midtjylland	19

DENMARK

***Back together:** the Laudrup Brothers in training with the national team in 1993. Michael Laudrup (left) had been dropped from the 1992 European Championships squad after a protracted quarrel with the coach.*

Denmark

Dansk Boldspil Union
Founded: 1889
Joined FIFA: 1904
Joined UEFA: 1954

SOCCER ARRIVED EARLY IN DENMARK, making its way into Scandinavia through the ports. KB København, the first Danish club, was founded in 1876, considerably in advance of most English and Scottish clubs. Despite this early enthusiasm, the formation of a national soccer association in 1889, and becoming a founder member of FIFA, organized domestic competition lagged behind. Nonetheless, Denmark made it to the Finals of the first two Olympic Games with a soccer competition (1908 and 1912). Future international successes were limited by the DBU's fierce amateurism, as Danes playing professionally overseas were excluded from the national team. In 1913 a national league was established and it has run uninterrupted since 1916. The championship was won by Copenhagen clubs until the 1950s, when Køge, Aarhus and Vejle broke the capital's stronghold.

A Danish Cup competition was created in 1955 and professionalism arrived in 1978. In 1976 the DBU allowed players playing outside Denmark to play for the national teams for the first time which, combined with the advent of professionalism, led to the beginnings of an exodus of Danish talent. In response to this, and the uneven quality of Danish soccer clubs, the Danish league was reorganized in 1991 with the creation of an eight-team, wholly professional, Superliga, with clubs playing each other four times a year. In 1992, these changes seemed to have borne fruit, as Denmark were crowned unexpected winners of the European Championship. In 1995 the Superliga was expanded to 12 teams playing each other three times a season. There is a standard two-up/two-down promotion/relegation system between the Superliga and the second division.

Danish League Record 1913–2004

SEASON	CHAMPIONS	RUNNERS-UP
1913	KB København	B93 København
1914	KB København	B93 København
1915	*no championship*	
1916	B93 København	KB København
1917	KB København	Akademisk
1918	KB København	Frem København
1919	Akademisk	B93 København
1920	B1903 København	KB København
1921	Akademisk	B1903 København
1922	KB København	Frem København
1923	Frem København	B93 København
1924	B1903 København	KB København
1925	KB København	Akademisk
1926	B1903 København	B93 København
1927	B93 København	B1903 København
1928	B93 København	Frem København
1929	B93 København	KB København
1930	B93 København	Frem København
1931	Frem København	KB København
1932	KB København	Akademisk
1933	Frem København	B1903 København
1934	B93 København	B1903 København
1935	B93 København	Frem København
1936	Frem København	Akademisk
1937	Akademisk	Frem København
1938	B1903 København	Frem København

Danish League Record (*continued*)

SEASON	CHAMPIONS	RUNNERS-UP
1939	B93 København	KB København
1940	KB København	Fremad Amager
1941	Frem København	Fremad Amager
1942	B93 København	Akademisk
1943	Akademisk	KB København
1944	Frem København	Akademisk
1945	Akademisk	AGF Aarhus
1946	B93 København	KB København
1947	Akademisk	KB København
1948	KB København	Frem København
1949	KB København	Akademisk
1950	KB København	Akademisk
1951	Akademisk	OB Odense
1952	Akademisk	Køge BK
1953	KB København	Skovshoved IF
1954	Køge BK	KB København
1955	AGF Aarhus	Akademisk
1956	AGF Aarhus	Esbjerg FB
1957	AGF Aarhus	Akademisk
1958	Vejle BK	Frem København
1959	B1909 Odense	KB København
1960	AGF Aarhus	KB København
1961	Esbjerg FB	KB København
1962	Esbjerg FB	B1913 Odense
1963	Esbjerg FB	B1913 Odense
1964	B1909 Odense	AGF Aarhus
1965	Esbjerg FB	Vejle BK
1966	Hvidovre BK	Frem København
1967	Akademisk	Frem København
1968	KB København	Esbjerg FB
1969	B1903 København	KB København
1970	B1903 København	Akademisk
1971	Vejle BK	Hvidovre BK
1972	Vejle BK	B1903 København
1973	Hvidovre BK	Randers Freja
1974	KB København	Vejle BK
1975	Køge BK	Holbaek BK
1976	B1903 København	Frem København
1977	OB Odense	B1903 København
1978	Vejle BK	Esbjerg FB
1979	Esbjerg FB	KB København
1980	KB København	Naestved IF
1981	Hvidovre BK	Lyngby FC
1982	OB Odense	AGF Aarhus
1983	Lyngby FC	OB Odense
1984	Vejle BK	AGF Aarhus
1985	Brøndby IF	Lyngby FC
1986	AGF Aarhus	Brøndby IF
1987	Brøndby IF	Ikast BK
1988	Brøndby IF	Naestved IF
1989	OB Odense	Brøndby IF
1990	Brøndby IF	B1903 København
1991	Brøndby IF	Lyngby FC
1992	Lyngby FC	B1903 København
1993	FC København	OB Odense
1994	Silkeborg IF	FC København
1995	AaB Aalborg	Brøndby IF
1996	Brøndby IF	AGF Aarhus
1997	Brøndby IF	Vejle BK
1998	Brøndby IF	Silkeborg IF
1999	AaB Aalborg	Brøndby IF
2000	Herfølge	Brøndby IF

Danish League Record (*continued*)

SEASON	CHAMPIONS	RUNNERS-UP
2001	FC København	Brøndby IF
2002	Brøndby IF	FC København
2003	FC København	Brøndby IF
2004	FC København	Brøndby IF

Danish League Summary

TEAM	TOTALS	CHAMPIONS & RUNNERS-UP (BOLD) (*ITALICS*)
KB København	15, 15	**1913, 14, 16, 17, 18, 20, 22, 24, 25,** *29, 31,* **32,** *39,* **40,** *43,* **46, 47, 48–50,** *53, 54, 59–61,* **68, 69, 74, 79, 80**
B93 København	10, 5	*1913, 14,* **16,** *19, 23, 26,* **27–30, 34,** *35,* **39, 42,** *46*
Akademisk	9, 11	*1917,* **19, 21,** *25,* **32,** *36,* **37,** *42,* **43, 44,** *45, 47, 49, 50,* **51, 52, 55, 57,** *67, 70*
Brøndby IF	9, 8	**1985,** *86,* **87, 88,** *89,* **90, 91,** *95,* **96–98, 1999–2001,** *02, 03, 04*
B1903 København	7, 8	**1920,** *21,* **24,** *26, 27,* **33, 34, 38,** *69, 70,* **72,** *76, 77,* **90,** *92*
Frem København	6, 12	*1918,* **22,** *23,* **28, 30, 31, 33,** *35,* **36,** *37, 38,* **41,** *44,* **48,** *58,* **66,** *67, 76*
AGF Aarhus	5, 5	*1945,* **55–57, 60, 64,** *82,* **84,** *86, 96*
Esbjerg FB	5, 3	**1956,** *61–63,* **65,** *68,* **78,** *79*
Vejle BK	5, 3	**1958,** *65,* **71, 72,** *74,* **78, 84,** *97*
FC København*	4, 2	**1993,** *94,* **2001,** *02, 03, 04*
OB Odense	3, 3	**1951,** *77,* **82, 83,** *89, 93*
Hvidovre BK	3, 1	**1966,** *71,* **73, 81**
Lyngby FC	2, 3	*1981,* **83,** *85,* **91,** *92*
Køge BK	2, 1	*1952,* **54,** *75*
AaB Aalborg	2, 0	**1995, 99**
B1909 Odense	2, 0	**1959, 64**
Silkeborg IF	1, 1	**1994,** *98*
Herfølge	1, 0	**2000**
B1913 Odense	0, 2	*1962, 63*
Naestved IF	0, 2	*1980, 88*
Fremad Amager	0, 2	*1940, 41*
Randers Freja	0, 1	*1973*
Ikast BK	0, 1	*1987*
Holbaek BK	0, 1	*1975*
Shovshoved IF	0, 1	*1953*

* Formed in 1993 after a merger of KB København and B1903 København.

Danish Cup Record 1955–2004

YEAR	WINNERS	SCORE	RUNNERS-UP
1955	AGF Aarhus	4-0	Aalborg Chang
1956	Frem København	1-0	Akademisk
1957	AGF Aarhus	2-0	Esbjerg FB
1958	Vejle BK	3-2	AGF Aarhus
1959	Vejle BK	1-1 (aet), (replay) 2-0	AGF Aarhus
1960	AGF Aarhus	2-0	Frem Sakskøbing
1961	AGF Aarhus	2-0	KB København
1962	B1909 Odense	1-0	Esbjerg FB
1963	B1913 Odense	2-1	Køge BK
1964	Esbjerg FB	2-1	Odense KFUM
1965	AGF Aarhus	1-0	KB København
1966	AaB Aalborg	3-1 (aet)	KB København
1967	Randers Freja	1-0	AaB Aalborg
1968	Randers Freja	3-1	Vejle BK
1969	KB København	3-0	Frem København
1970	AaB Aalborg	2-1	Lyngby FC
1971	B1909 Odense	1-0	Frem København
1972	Vejle BK	2-0	Fremad Amager
1973	Randers Freja	2-0	B1901 Nykøbing
1974	Vanlose BK	5-2	OB Odense
1975	Vejle BK	1-0	Holbaek BK

Danish Cup Record (*continued*)

YEAR	WINNERS	SCORE	RUNNERS-UP
1976	Esbjerg FB	2-1	Holbaek BK
1977	Vejle BK	2-1	B1909 Odense
1978	Frem København	1-1 (aet), (replay) 1-1 (aet) (6-5 pens)	Esbjerg FB
1979	B1903 København	1-0	Køge BK
1980	Hvidovre BK	5-3	Lyngby FC
1981	Vejle BK	2-1	Frem København
1982	B93 København	3-3 (aet), (replay) 1-0	B1903 København
1983	OB Odense	3-0	B1901 Nykøbing
1984	Lyngby FC	2-1	KB København
1985	Lyngby FC	3-2	Esbjerg FB
1986	B1903 København	2-1	Ikast BK
1987	AGF Aarhus	3-0	AaB Aalborg
1988	AGF Aarhus	2-1 (aet)	Brøndby IF
1989	Brøndby IF	6-3 (aet)	Ikast BK
1990	Lyngby FC	0-0 (aet), (replay) 6-1	AGF Aarhus
1991	OB Odense	0-0 (aet), (replay) 0-0 (aet) (4-3 pens)	AaB Aalborg
1992	AGF Aarhus	3-0	B1903 København
1993	OB Odense	2-0	AaB Aalborg
1994	Brøndby IF	0-0 (aet)(4-3 pens)	Naestved IF
1995	FC København	5-0	Akademisk
1996	AGF Aarhus	2-0	Brøndby IF
1997	FC København	2-0	Ikast BK
1998	Brøndby IF	4-1	FC København
1999	Akademisk	2-1	AaB Aalborg
2000	Viborg FF	1-0	AaB Aalborg
2001	Silkeborg IF	4-1	Akademisk
2002	OB Odense	2-1	FC København
2003	Brøndby IF	3-0	FC Midtjylland
2004	FC København	1-0	AaB Aalborg

Danish Cup Summary

TEAM	TOTALS	WINNERS & RUNNERS-UP (BOLD) (*ITALICS*)
AGF Aarhus	9, 3	**1955, 57,** *58, 59,* **60, 61, 65, 87,** *88,* **90, 92, 96**
Vejle BK	6, 1	**1958, 59,** *68,* **72, 75, 77, 81**
Brøndby IF	4, 2	*1988,* **89, 94,** *96,* **98, 2003**
OB Odense	4, 1	**1974, 83, 91, 93,** *2002*
FC København	3, 2	**1995,** *98,* **97,** *2002,* **04**
Lyngby FC	3, 2	*1970,* **80, 84, 85,** *90*
Randers Freja	2, 0	**1967, 68, 73**
AaB Aalborg	2, 7	**1966,** *67,* **70,** *87, 91, 93, 99, 2000, 04*
Esbjerg FB	2, 4	*1957,* **62,** *64,* **76,** *78, 85*
Frem København	2, 3	**1956,** *69,* **71,** *78, 81*
B1903 København	2, 2	**1979,** *82,* **86,** *92*
B1909 Odense	2, 1	**1962, 71,** *77*
KB København	1, 4	*1961, 65, 66,* **69,** *84*
Akademisk	1, 3	*1956,* **95,** *99, 2001*
B1913 Odense	1, 0	**1963**
Vanlose BK	1, 0	**1974**
Viborg FF	1, 0	**2000**
Hvidovre BK	1, 0	**1980**
Silkeborg IF	1, 0	**2001**
Ikast BK	0, 3	*1986, 89, 97*
B1901 Nykøbing	0, 2	*1973, 83*
Holbaek BK	0, 2	*1975, 76*
Køge BK	0, 2	*1963, 79*
Aalborg Chang	0, 1	*1955*
Frem Sakskøbing	0, 1	*1960*
Fremad Amager	0, 1	*1972*
FC Midtjylland	0, 1	*2003*
Naestved IF	0, 1	*1994*
Odense KFUM	0, 1	*1964*

Soccer in Norway

1892: Kongsvinger IL formed, Norway's oldest club

1902: Formation of FA: Norges Fotballforbund. First Norwegian Cup Final

1905: Independence from Sweden

1908: Affiliation to FIFA. First international, v Sweden, lost 11–3, venue: Gothenburg

1938: First national championship. Norway plays in World Cup in France

1940–45: Norwegian sport strike against German occupation. Cup abandoned 1941–44

1954: Affiliation to UEFA

1962: National championship reorganized as full league

1975: National FA incorporates women's soccer

1978: First women's international, v Sweden

1991: Women's World Cup runners-up. Premier League formed

1995: Women's World Cup winners

1997: Rosenborg reaches quarter-finals of the Champions League – the best performance ever by a Norwegian team in European competition

1998: Men's team qualify for the World Cup – its first major international tournament

2000: Women's team win Olympic gold medal

1890
1895
1900
1905
1910
1915
1920
1925
1930
1935
1940
1945
1950
1955
1960
1965
1970
1975
1980
1985
1990
1995
2000
2005

Key

- International soccer
- Affiliation to FIFA
- Affiliation to UEFA
- Women's soccer
- War

Extreme weather *presents a considerable problem for regular soccer in Norway. Alfheim Stadium (above), home of Tromsø IL, is above the Arctic Circle.*

Since the advent of *the Premier League in 1991, teams like Rosenborg BK from Trondheim (in white, playing against Feyenoord from the Netherlands) have appeared regularly in the Champions League.*

Norway: The main clubs

Moss FK 1906 Team name with year of formation

- Club formed before 1912
- Club formed 1912–25
- Club formed 1925–50
- Club formed after 1950

★ Founder members of Premier League (1991)

Leading clubs in 1938 national championship

Colours unknown

Steinkjer IFK 1919

Rosenborg BK 1917

Fyllingen 1946

SK Brann Bergen 1908

Steinkjer

Trondheim

Molde

Molde FK 1911

Gjøvik Lyn 1902

Sogndal IL 1926

Bergen

Drammen
IF Strømsgodset 1907

Kongsvinger

Lillestrøm

FK Haugesund 1993

Moss

Stavanger

Horten

Skien

Viking FK Stavanger 1899

Larvik

Kristiansand

IK Start 1892

Odd Grenland 1894
Formerly Odd SK Skien

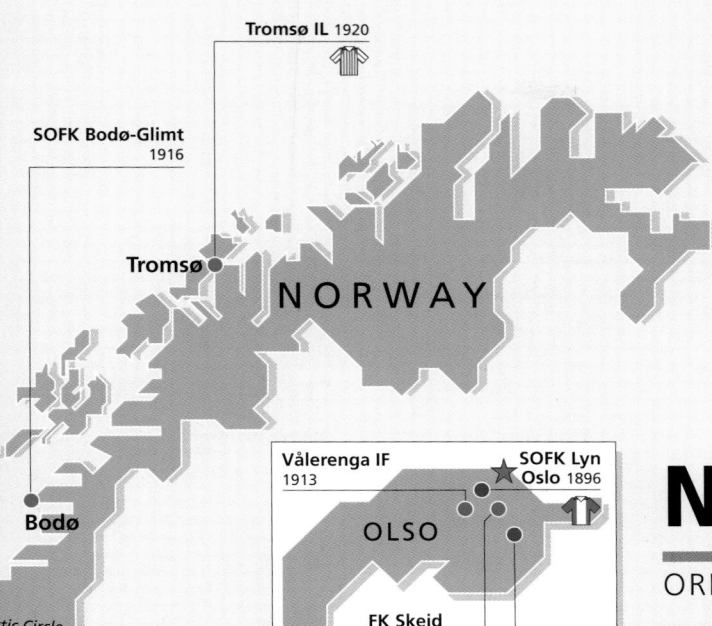

Tromsø IL 1920

SOFK Bodø-Glimt 1916

Tromsø

NORWAY

Bodø

rctic Circle

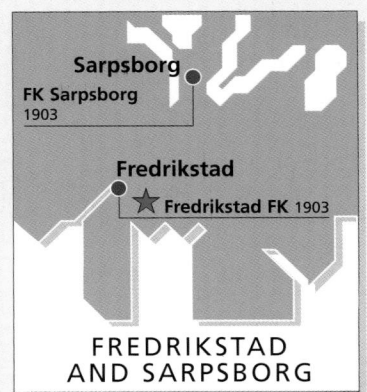

Vålerenga IF 1913

SOFK Lyn Oslo 1896

OLSO

FK Skeid Oslo 1915

Frigg SK Oslo 1904

Stabaek 1912

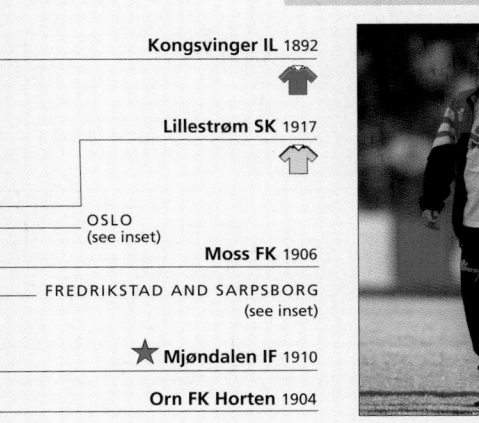

Sarpsborg

FK Sarpsborg 1903

Fredrikstad

Fredrikstad FK 1903

FREDRIKSTAD AND SARPSBORG

Kongsvinger IL 1892

Lillestrøm SK 1917

OSLO
(see inset)

Moss FK 1906

FREDRIKSTAD AND SARPSBORG
(see inset)

Mjøndalen IF 1910

Orn FK Horten 1904

IF Fram 1894

Larvik Turn IF 1906

The Norwegian national women's team is one of the strongest in the world. It is shown here sporting its Olympic gold medals from Sydney 2000. The team beat the USA 3-2 in a memorable Final.

Norway

ORIGINS AND GROWTH OF SOCCER

LIKE ITS SCANDINAVIAN NEIGHBOURS Norway was exposed to soccer in the late 19th century, and proved an early and enthusiastic adopter of the game. Clubs emerged all over the country in the years up to and including the First World War, some of the earliest being Kongsvinger IL (1892), Odd SK Skien (1894), SOFK Lyn Oslo (1896) and Viking FK Stavanger (1899).

The cost of amateurism

A national FA was set up in 1902, joining FIFA in 1908. However, the development of the sport was always constrained by weather and sentiment. The extremes of cold and snow present a considerable problem for regular soccer, and make the competing attractions of winter sports and games compelling. This aside, the prevailing amateurism of Norwegian soccer has ensured that little money or development could take place in the game relative to the international competition. A national league was not actually created until 1937 and it was decided by play-offs until 1961 when a more conventional league was created. Despite all of this, Oslo, the capital city, has yet to produce a consistently powerful team and leading clubs and players continue to come from small towns and rural Norway.

Norwegian soccer's finest hour was during the Second World War. After the German invasion and occupation in 1940, Quislings (or collaborators) were placed in charge of every Norwegian club and sports association. Players refused to play, fans refused to attend and the national league effectively collapsed. Tournaments organized by the Norwegian resistance were played in secret deep in the countryside.

Powerful women

In the 1990s Norwegian soccer began to change with the arrival of significant government support for elite sports, the installation of the tough-minded Egil Olsen as national team manager and an increasing place for professionals in the leading clubs. A national premier league has been created, and at European level Rosenborg and SK Brann have performed creditably. By contrast to the men's game, Norwegian women's soccer is a strong force on the global stage, with the national team winning the inaugural FIFA Women's World Cup in China in 1988 and the Olympic gold in Sydney 2000.

Egil Olsen (professor of economics and national team manager 1990–98) brought a new tactical awareness.

NORWAY

Norway

Norges Fotballforbund
Founded: 1902
Joined FIFA: 1908
Joined UEFA: 1954

NORWAY

NORWEGIAN DOMESTIC SOCCER began with the establishment of the Norges Fotballforbund in 1902 when a national cup competition was set up; this has run every year since, only stopping between 1941 and 1944 in the midst of the Second World War. However, antiquity does not guarantee popularity, and attendances at some Finals have dipped below the 2,000 mark. A national league arrived later, and the first championships took place in 1938. Until 1961, the title was decided by a knockout phase, but since 1962 it has kept a simplified league format.

Norwegian League Record 1938–2003

SEASON	CHAMPIONS	RUNNERS-UP
1938	Fredrikstad FK	SOFK Lyn Oslo
1939	Fredrikstad FK	FK Skeid Oslo
1940–47	*no championship*	
1948	Freidig SK	Sparta Sarpsborg
1949	Fredrikstad FK	Vålerenga IF
1950	Fram Larvik	Fredrikstad FK
1951	Fredrikstad FK	Odd SK Skien
1952	Fredrikstad FK	SK Brann Bergen
1953	Larvik Turn IF	FK Skeid Oslo
1954	Fredrikstad FK	FK Skeid Oslo
1955	Larvik Turn IF	Fredrikstad FK
1956	Larvik Turn IF	Fredrikstad FK
1957	Fredrikstad FK	Odd SK Skien
1958	Viking FK Stavanger	FK Skeid Oslo
1959	Lillestrøm SK	Fredrikstad FK
1960	Fredrikstad FK	Lillestrøm SK
1961	Fredrikstad FK	IF Eik
1962	SK Brann Bergen	Steinkjer IFK
1963	SK Brann Bergen	SOFK Lyn Oslo
1964	SOFK Lyn Oslo	Fredrikstad FK
1965	Vålerenga IF	SOFK Lyn Oslo
1966	FK Skeid Oslo	Fredrikstad FK
1967	Rosenborg BK	FK Skeid Oslo
1968	SOFK Lyn Oslo	Rosenborg BK
1969	Rosenborg BK	Fredrikstad FK
1970	IF Strømgodset	Rosenborg BK
1971	Rosenborg BK	SOFK Lyn Oslo
1972	Viking FK Stavanger	Fredrikstad FK
1973	Viking FK Stavanger	Rosenborg BK
1974	Viking FK Stavanger	Molde FK
1975	Viking FK Stavanger	SK Brann Bergen
1976	Lillestrøm SK	Mjøndalen IF
1977	Lillestrøm SK	SOFK Bodø-Glimt
1978	Start Kristiansand	Lillestrøm SK
1979	Viking FK Stavanger	Moss FK
1980	Start Kristiansand	Bryne FK
1981	Vålerenga IF	Viking FK Stavanger
1982	Viking FK Stavanger	Bryne FK
1983	Vålerenga IF	Lillestrøm SK
1984	Vålerenga IF	Viking FK Stavanger
1985	Rosenborg BK	Lillestrøm SK
1986	Lillestrøm SK	Mjøndalen IF
1987	Moss FK	Molde FK
1988	Rosenborg BK	Lillestrøm SK
1989	Lillestrøm SK	Rosenborg BK
1990	Rosenborg BK	Tromsø IL
1991	Viking FK Stavanger	Rosenborg BK
1992	Rosenborg BK	Viking FK Stavanger
1993	Rosenborg BK	SOFK Bodø-Glimt

Norwegian League Record (*continued*)

SEASON	CHAMPIONS	RUNNERS-UP
1994	Rosenborg BK	Lillestrøm SK
1995	Rosenborg BK	Molde FK
1996	Rosenborg BK	Lillestrøm SK
1997	Rosenborg BK	SK Brann Bergen
1998	Rosenborg BK	Molde FK
1999	Rosenborg BK	Molde FK
2000	Rosenborg BK	SK Brann Bergen
2001	Rosenborg BK	Lillestrøm SK
2002	Rosenborg BK	Molde FK
2003	Rosenborg BK	SOFK Bodø-Glimt

Norwegian League Summary

TEAM	TOTALS	CHAMPIONS & RUNNERS-UP (BOLD) (*ITALICS*)
Rosenborg BK	18, 5	**1967, 68, 69, 70, 71, 73, 85, 88, 89, 90, 91, 1992–2003**
Fredrikstad FK	9, 8	**1938, 39, 49, 50, 51, 52, 54,** *55, 56, 57, 59, 60, 61, 64, 66, 69, 72*
Viking FK Stavanger	8, 3	**1958,** *72–75,* **79,** *81,* **82,** *84,* **91,** *92*
Lillestrøm SK	5, 8	*59, 60,* **76, 77,** *78, 83, 85,* **86,** *88,* **89,** *94, 96, 2001*
Vålerenga IF	4, 1	*1949,* **65,** *81,* **83, 84**
Larvik Turn IF	3, 0	**1953, 55, 56**
SK Brann Bergen	2, 4	*1952,* **62, 63,** *75, 97, 2000*
SOFK Lyn Oslo	2, 4	*1938,* **63,** *64, 65,* **68,** *71*
Start Kristiansand	2, 0	**1978, 80**
FK Skeid Oslo	1, 5	*1939, 53, 54, 58,* **66,** *67*
Moss FK	1, 1	*1979,* **87**
Fram Larvik	1, 0	**1950**
Freidig SK	1, 0	**1948**
IF Strømgodset	1, 0	**1970**
Molde FK	0, 6	*1974, 87, 95, 98, 99, 2002*
SOFK Bodø-Glimt	0, 3	*1977, 93, 2003*
Bryne FK	0, 2	*1980, 82*
Mjøndalen IF	0, 2	*1976, 86*
Odd Grenland (includes Odd Sk Skien)	0, 2	*1951, 57*
IF Eik	0, 1	*1961*
Sparta Sarpsborg	0, 1	*1948*
Steinkjer IFK	0, 1	*1962*
Tromsø IL	0, 1	*1990*

Norwegian Cup Record 1902–2003

YEAR	WINNERS	SCORE	RUNNERS-UP
1902	Grand Nordstrand	2-0	Odd SK Skien
1903	Odd SK Skien	1-0	Grand Nordstrand
1904	Odd SK Skien	4-0	IF Uraed
1905	Odd SK Skien	2-1	Akademisk FK Oslo
1906	Odd SK Skien	1-0	FK Sarpsborg
1907	Mercantile	3-0	FK Sarpsborg
1908	SOFK Lyn Oslo	3-2	Odd SK Skien
1909	SOFK Lyn Oslo	4-3	Odd SK Skien
1910	SOFK Lyn Oslo	4-2	Odd SK Skien
1911	SOFK Lyn Oslo	5-2	IF Uraed

Norwegian Cup Record (*continued*)

YEAR	WINNERS	SCORE	RUNNERS-UP
1912	Mercantile	6-0	Fram Larvik
1913	Odd SK Skien	2-1	Mercantile
1914	Frigg SK Oslo	4-0	Gjøvik Lyn
1915	Odd SK Skien	2-1	Kvik Halden
1916	Frigg SK Oslo	2-0	Orn FK Horten
1917	FK Sarpsborg	4-1	SK Brann Bergen
1918	Kvik Halden	4-0	SK Brann Bergen
1919	Odd SK Skien	1-0	Frigg SK Oslo
1920	Orn FK Horten	1-0	Frigg SK Oslo
1921	Frigg SK Oslo	2-0	Odd SK Skien
1922	Odd SK Skien	5-1	Kvik Halden
1923	SK Brann Bergen	2-1	SOFK Lyn Oslo
1924	Odd SK Skien	3-0	Mjøndalen IF
1925	SK Brann Bergen	3-0	FK Sarpsborg
1926	Odd SK Skien	3-0	Orn FK Horten
1927	Orn FK Horten	4-0	Drafn SK
1928	Orn FK Horten	2-1	SOFK Lyn Oslo
1929	FK Sarpsborg	2-1	Orn FK Horten
1930	Orn FK Horten	4-2	Drammens BK
1931	Odd SK Skien	3-1	Mjøndalen IF
1932	Fredrikstad FK	6-1	Orn FK Horten
1933	Mjøndalen IF	3-1	Viking FK Stavanger
1934	Mjøndalen IF	2-1	FK Sarpsborg
1935	Fredrikstad FK	4-0	FK Sarpsborg
1936	Fredrikstad FK	2-0	Mjøndalen IF
1937	Mjøndalen IF	4-2	Odd SK Skien
1938	Fredrikstad FK	3-2	Mjøndalen IF
1939	FK Sarpsborg	2-1	FK Skeid Oslo
1940	Fredrikstad FK	3-0	FK Skeid Oslo
1941–44		*no competition*	
1945	SOFK Lyn Oslo	1-1, (replay) 1-1, (replay) 4-0	Fredrikstad FK
1946	SOFK Lyn Oslo	3-2	Fredrikstad FK
1947	FK Skeid Oslo	2-0	Viking FK Stavanger
1948	FK Sarpsborg	1-0	Fredrikstad FK
1949	FK Sarpsborg	3-1	FK Skeid Oslo
1950	Fredrikstad FK	3-0	SK Brann Bergen
1951	FK Sarpsborg	3-2	Asker
1952	Sparta Sarpsborg	3-2	Solberg
1953	Viking FK Stavanger	2-1	Lillestrøm SK
1954	FK Skeid Oslo	3-0	Fredrikstad FK
1955	FK Skeid Oslo	5-0	Lillestrøm SK
1956	FK Skeid Oslo	2-1	Larvik Turn IF
1957	Fredrikstad FK	4-0	Sandefjord BK
1958	FK Skeid Oslo	1-0	Lillestrøm SK
1959	Viking FK Stavanger	2-1	Sandefjord BK
1960	Rosenborg BK	3-3, (replay) 3-2	Odd SK Skien
1961	Fredrikstad FK	7-0	SK Hauger
1962	Gjøvik Lyn	2-0	SK Vard Haugesund
1963	FK Skeid Oslo	2-1	Fredrikstad FK
1964	Rosenborg BK	2-1	FK Sarpsborg
1965	FK Skeid Oslo	2-2, (replay) 1-1, (replay) 2-1	Frigg SK Oslo
1966	Fredrikstad FK	3-2	SOFK Lyn Oslo
1967	SOFK Lyn Oslo	4-1	Rosenborg BK
1968	SOFK Lyn Oslo	3-0	Mjøndalen IF
1969	IF Strømgodset	2-2, (replay) 5-3	Fredrikstad FK
1970	IF Strømgodset	4-2	SOFK Lyn Oslo
1971	Rosenborg BK	4-1	Fredrikstad FK
1972	SK Brann Bergen	1-0	Rosenborg BK
1973	IF Strømgodset	1-0	Rosenborg BK
1974	FK Skeid Oslo	3-1	Viking FK Stavanger
1975	SOFK Bodø-Glimt	2-0	SK Vard Haugesund
1976	SK Brann Bergen	2-1	Sogndal IL
1977	Lillestrøm SK	1-0	SOFK Bodø-Glimt
1978	Lillestrøm SK	2-1	SK Brann Bergen
1979	Viking FK Stavanger	2-1	SK Hauger
1980	Vålerenga IF	4-1	Lillestrøm SK
1981	Lillestrøm SK	3-1	Moss FK
1982	SK Brann Bergen	3-2	Molde FK
1983	Moss FK	2-0	Vålerenga IF
1984	Fredrikstad FK	3-3, (replay) 3-2	Viking FK Stavanger
1985	Lillestrøm SK	4-1	Vålerenga IF

Norwegian Cup Record (*continued*)

YEAR	WINNERS	SCORE	RUNNERS-UP
1986	Tromsø IL	4-1	Lillestrøm SK
1987	Bryne FK	1-0	SK Brann Bergen
1988	Rosenborg BK	2-2, (replay) 2-0	SK Brann Bergen
1989	Viking FK Stavanger	2-2, (replay) 2-1	Molde FK
1990	Rosenborg BK	5-1	Fyllingen
1991	IF Strømgodset	3-2	Rosenborg BK
1992	Rosenborg BK	3-2	Lillestrøm SK
1993	SOFK Bodø-Glimt	2-0	IF Strømgodset
1994	Molde FK	3-2	Lyn
1995	Rosenborg BK	1-1, (replay) 3-1	SK Brann Bergen
1996	Tromsø IL	2-1	SOFK Bodø-Glimt
1997	Vålerenga IF	4-2	IF Strømgodset
1998	Stabaek	3-1	Rosenborg BK
1999	Rosenborg BK	2-0	SK Brann Bergen
2000	Odd Grenland	2-1	Viking FK Stavanger
2001	Viking FK Stavanger	3-0	Bryne FK
2002	Vålerenga IF	1-0	Odd Grenland
2003	Rosenborg BK	3-1	SOFK Bodø-Glimt

Norwegian Cup Summary

TEAM	TOTALS	WINNERS & RUNNERS-UP (BOLD) (*ITALICS*)
Odd Grenland (includes Odd Sk Skien)	12, 8	*1902,* **03–06,** *08–10,* **13, 15, 19,** *21, 22,* **24,** *26,* **31,** *37, 60,* **2000,** *02*
Fredrikstad FK	10, 7	**1932, 35, 36, 38, 40,** *45, 46,* **48, 50,** *54,* **57, 61,** *63,* **66,** *69,* **71, 84**
Rosenborg BK	9, 5	**1960, 64, 67, 71,** *72, 73,* **88, 90,** *91,* **92, 95, 98, 99, 2003**
SOFK Lyn Oslo	8, 4	**1908–11,** *23,* **28,** *45,* **46,** *66,* **67, 68,** *70*
FK Skeid Oslo	8, 3	*1939,* **40,** *47,* **49,** *54–56,* **58,** *63,* **65,** *74*
FK Sarpsborg	6, 6	*1906, 07,* **17,** *25,* **29,** *34, 35,* **39, 48,** *49,* **51,** *64*
SK Brann Bergen	5, 8	**1917,** *18,* **23, 25,** *50,* **72,** *76,* **78,** *82, 87, 88, 95, 99*
Viking FK Stavanger	5, 5	*1933,* **47, 53,** *59,* **74, 79,** *84,* **89, 2000,** *01*
Lillestrøm SK	4, 6	*1953, 55, 58,* **77,** *78,* **80, 81, 85,** *86, 92*
Orn FK Horten	4, 4	*1916,* **20,** *26,* **27, 28,** *29,* **30,** *32*
IF Strømgodset	4, 2	**1969, 70, 73, 91,** *93,* **97**
Mjøndalen IF	3, 5	*1924, 31,* **33, 34,** *36,* **37,** *38, 68*
Frigg SK Oslo	3, 3	**1914, 16,** *19, 20,* **21,** *65*
Vålerenga IF	3, 2	**1980,** *83,* **85, 97, 2002**
SOFK Bodø-Glimt	2, 3	**1975,** *77,* **93,** *96,* **2003**
Mercantile	2, 1	*1907,* **12,** *13*
Tromsø IL	2, 0	**1986, 96**
Kvik Halden	1, 2	*1915,* **18,** *22*
Molde FK	1, 2	*1982,* **89,** *94*
Bryne FK	1, 1	**1987,** *2001*
Gjøvik Lyn	1, 1	*1914,* **62**
Grand Nordstrand	1, 1	**1902,** *03*
Moss FK	1, 1	*1981,* **83**
Sparta Sarpsborg	1, 0	**1952**
Stabaek	1, 0	**1998**
IF Uraed	0, 2	*1904, 11*
Sandefjord	0, 2	*1957, 59*
SK Hauger	0, 2	*1961, 79*
SK Vard Haugesund	0, 2	*1962, 75*
Akademisk FK Oslo	0, 1	*1905*
Asker	0, 1	*1951*
Drafn SK	0, 1	*1927*
Drammens BK	0, 1	*1930*
Fram Larvik	0, 1	*1912*
Fyllingen	0, 1	*1990*
Larvik Turn IF	0, 1	*1956*
Lyn	0, 1	*1994*
Sogndal IL	0, 1	*1976*
Solberg	0, 1	*1952*

Finland

Suomen Palloliitto/Finlands Bollförbund
Founded: 1907
Joined FIFA: 1908
Joined UEFA: 1954

FINLAND'S OLDEST CLUB – Reipas Lahti – was founded in 1891, and its association was founded in 1907. A regular league, based in Helsinki, started almost immediately, and gradually spread to include the rest of the country. Until 1929, the title was decided via a play-off, after which a league format was adopted. A national cup competition was established in 1955.

Finnish League Record 1908–2003

SEASON	CHAMPIONS	RUNNERS-UP
1908	Unitas Helsinki	PUS Helsinki
1909	PUS Helsinki	HIFK Helsinki
1910	ÅIFK Turku	Reipas Viipuri
1911	HJK Helsinki	HIFK Helsinki
1912	HJK Helsinki	HIFK Helsinki
1913	KIF Helsinki	ÅIFK Helsinki
1914	*no championship*	
1915	KIF Helsinki	ÅIFK Turku
1916	KIF Helsinki	ÅIFK Turku
1917	HJK Helsinki	ÅIFK Turku
1918	HJK Helsinki	Reipas Viipuri
1919	HJK Helsinki	Reipas Viipuri
1920	ÅIFK Turku	HPS Helsinki
1921	HPS Helsinki	HJK Helsinki
1922	HPS Helsinki	Reipas Viipuri
1923	HJK Helsinki	TPS Turku
1924	ÅIFK Turku	HPS Helsinki
1925	HJK Helsinki	TPS Turku
1926	HPS Helsinki	TPS Turku
1927	HPS Helsinki	Reipas Viipuri
1928	TPS Turku	HIFK Helsinki
1929	HPS Helsinki	HIFK Helsinki
1930	HIFK Helsinki	TPS Turku
1931	HIFK Helsinki	HPS Helsinki
1932	HPS Helsinki	VPS Vaasa
1933	HIFK Helsinki	HJK Helsinki
1934	HPS Helsinki	HIFK Helsinki
1935	HPS Helsinki	HIFK Helsinki
1936	HJK Helsinki	HPS Helsinki
1937	HIFK Helsinki	HJK Helsinki
1938	HJK Helsinki	TPS Turku
1939	TPS Turku	HJK Helsinki
1940	Sudet Viipuri	TPS Turku
1941	TPS Turku	VPS Vaasa
1942	HT Helsinki	Sudet Viipuri
1943	*no championship*	
1944	VIFK Vaasa	TPS Turku
1945	VPS Vaasa	HPS Helsinki
1946	VIFK Vaasa	TPV Tampere
1947	HIFK Helsinki	TuTo Turku
1948	VPS Vaasa	TPS Turku
1949	TPS Turku	VPS Vaasa
1950	Ikissat Tampere	KuPS Kuopio
1951	KTP Kotka	VIFK Vaasa
1952	KTP Kotka	VIFK Vaasa
1953	VIFK Vaasa	Jäntevä Kotka
1954	Pyrkivä Turku	KuPS Kuopio
1955	KIF Helsinki	Haka Valkeakoski
1956	KuPS Kuopio	HJK Helsinki
1957	HPS Helsinki	Haka Valkeakoski
1958	KuPS Kuopio	HPS Helsinki
1959	HIFK Helsinki	RU-38 Pori
1960	Haka Valkeakoski	TPS Turku
1961	HIFK Helsinki	KIF Helsinki

Finnish League Record (*continued*)

SEASON	CHAMPIONS	RUNNERS-UP
1962	Haka Valkeakoski	Reipas Lahti
1963	Reipas Lahti	Haka Valkeakoski
1964	HJK Helsinki	KuPS Kuopio
1965	Haka Valkeakoski	KuPS Kuopio
1966	KuPS Kuopio	HJK Helsinki
1967	Reipas Lahti	KuPS Kuopio
1968	TPS Turku	Reipas Lahti
1969	KPV Kokkola	KuPS Kuopio
1970	Reipas Lahti	MP Mikkeli
1971	TPS Turku	HIFK Helsinki
1972	TPS Turku	MP Mikkeli
1973	HJK Helsinki	KPV Kokkola
1974	KuPS Kuopio	Reipas Lahti
1975	TPS Turku	KuPS Kuopio
1976	KuPS Kuopio	Haka Valkeakoski
1977	Haka Valkeakoski	KuPS Kuopio
1978	HJK Helsinki	KPT Kuopio
1979	OPS Oulu	KuPS Kuopio
1980	OPS Oulu	Haka Valkeakoski
1981	HJK Helsinki	KPT Kuopio
1982	Kuusysi Lahti	HJK Helsinki
1983	Ilves Tampere	HJK Helsinki
1984	Kuusysi Lahti	TPS Turku
1985	HJK Helsinki	Ilves Tampere
1986	Kuusysi Lahti	TPS Turku
1987	HJK Helsinki	Kuusysi Lahti
1988	HJK Helsinki	Kuusysi Lahti
1989	Kuusysi Lahti	TPS Turku
1990	HJK Helsinki	Kuusysi Lahti
1991	Kuusysi Lahti	MP Mikkeli
1992	HJK Helsinki	Kuusysi Lahti
1993	Jazz Pori	MyPa Anjalankoski
1994	TPV Tampere	MyPa Anjalankoski
1995	Haka Valkeakoski	MyPa Anjalankoski
1996	Jazz Pori	MyPa Anjalankoski
1997	HJK Helsinki	VPS Vaasa
1998	Haka Valkeakoski	VPS Vaasa
1999	Haka Valkeakoski	HJK Helsinki
2000	Haka Valkeakoski	Jokerit Helsinki
2001	Tampere United	HJK Helsinki
2002	HJK Helsinki	MyPa Anjalankoski
2003	HJK Helsinki	Haka Valkeakoski

Finnish League Summary

TEAM	TOTALS	CHAMPIONS & RUNNERS-UP (BOLD) (ITALICS)
HJK Helsinki	21, 10	**1911, 12, 17–19**, *21*, **23**, *25*, **33**, *36, 37, 38, 39*, **56**, *64*, **66**, *73*, **78**, *81*, **82, 83, 85, 87, 88, 90, 92, 97**, *99*, **2001**, *2002*, **03**
HPS Helsinki	9, 6	*1920*, **21, 22**, *24*, **26, 27, 29**, *31*, **32, 34, 35**, *36*, **36**, *58*
TPS Turku	8, 12	*1923, 25, 26*, **28**, *30*, **38**, *39, 40, 41, 44, 48, 49*, **60**, *68*, **71, 72, 75**, *84, 86, 89*
Haka Valkeakoski	8, 6	*1955, 57*, **60**, *62*, **63**, *65*, **76, 77**, *80*, **95**, *98, 99*, **2000**, *03*
HIFK Helsinki	7, 8	*1909*, **11, 12**, *28, 29*, **30, 31, 33**, *34, 35*, **37**, *47*, **59**, *61*, **71**
KuPS Kuopio	5, 9	*1950*, **54**, *56, 58*, **64**, *65, 66, 67*, **69**, *74, 75*, **76**, *77, 79*
Kuusysi Lahti	5, 4	**1982, 84, 86**, *87, 88*, **89**, *90*, **91**, *92*
KIF Helsinki	4, 1	**1913**, *15*, **16, 55**, *61*
ÅIFK Turku	3, 3	**1910**, *15, 16, 17*, **20, 24**
Reipas Lahti	3, 3	*1962*, **63, 67**, *68*, **70**, *74*
VIFK Vaasa	3, 2	**1944, 46**, *51, 52*, **53**
VPS Vaasa	2, 5	*1932, 41*, **45, 48**, *49, 97, 98*

FINLAND

Finnish League Summary (*continued*)

TEAM	TOTALS	CHAMPIONS & RUNNERS-UP (BOLD) (*ITALICS*)
Tampere United (includes Ikissat Tampere, Ilves Tampere)	3, 1	**1950, 83,** *85,* **2001**
Jazz Pori	2, 0	**1993, 96**
KTP Kotka	2, 0	**1951, 52**
OPS Oulu	2, 0	**1979, 80**
KPV Kokkola	1, 1	**1969,** *73*
PUS Helsinki	1, 1	**1908,** *09*
Sudet Viipuri	1, 1	**1940,** *42*
TPV Tampere	1, 1	*1946,* **94**
HT Helsinki	1, 0	**1942**
Pyrkivä Turku	1, 0	**1954**
Unitas Helsinki	1, 0	**1908**

This summary only features clubs that have won the Finnish League. For a full list of league champions and runners-up please see the League Record opposite.

Finnish Cup Record 1955–2003

YEAR	WINNERS	SCORE	RUNNERS-UP
1955	Haka Valkeakoski	5-1	HPS Helsinki
1956	PPojat Helsinki	2-1	TKT Tampere
1957	Drott Pietarsaari	2-1 (aet)	KPT Kuopio
1958	KTP Kotka	4-1	KIF Helsinki
1959	Haka Valkeakoski	2-1	HIFK Helsinki
1960	Haka Valkeakoski	3-1 (aet)	RU-38 Pori
1961	KTP Kotka	5-2	PPojat Helsinki
1962	HPS Helsinki	5-0	RoPS Rovaniemi
1963	Haka Valkeakoski	1-0	Reipas Lahti
1964	Reipas Lahti	1-0	LaPa Lappeenranta
1965	ÅIFK Turku	1-0	TPS Turku
1966	HJK Helsinki	6-1	KTP Kotka
1967	KTP Kotka	2-0	Reipas Lahti
1968	KuPS Kuopio	2-1	KTP Kotka
1969	Haka Valkeakoski	2-0	Honka Espoo
1970	MP Mikkeli	4-1 (aet)	Reipas Lahti
1971	MP Mikkeli	4-1	Sport Vaasa
1972	Reipas Lahti	2-0	VPS Vaasa
1973	Reipas Lahti	1-0	SePS Seinäjoki
1974	Reipas Lahti	1-0	OTP Oulu
1975	Reipas Lahti	6-2 (aet)	HJK Helsinki
1976	Reipas Lahti	2-0	Ilves Tampere
1977	Haka Valkeakoski	3-1	SePS Seinäjoki
1978	Reipas Lahti	3-1, 1-1 (2 legs)	KPT Kuopio
1979	Ilves Tampere	2-0	TPS Turku
1980	KTP Kotka	3-2	Haka Valkeakoski
1981	HJK Helsinki	4-0	Kuusysi Lahti
1982	Haka Valkeakoski	3-2	KPV Kokkola
1983	Kuusysi Lahti	2-0	Haka Valkeakoski
1984	HJK Helsinki	2-1	Kuusysi Lahti
1985	Haka Valkeakoski	2-2 (aet)(2-1 pens)	HJK Helsinki
1986	RoPS Rovaniemi	2-0	KePS Kemi
1987	Kuusysi Lahti	5-4	OTP Oulu
1988	Haka Valkeakoski	1-0	OTP Oulu
1989	KuPS Kuopio	3-2	Haka Valkeakoski
1990	Ilves Tampere	2-1	HJK Helsinki
1991	TPS Turku	0-0 (aet)(5-3 pens)	Kuusysi Lahti
1992	MyPa Anjalankoski	2-0	Jaro Pietarsaari
1993	HJK Helsinki	2-0	RoPS Rovaniemi
1994	TPS Turku	2-1	HJK Helsinki
1995	MyPa Anjalankoski	1-0	Jazz Pori
1996	HJK Helsinki	0-0 (aet)(4-3 pens)	TPS Turku
1997	Haka Valkeakoski	2-1 (aet)	TPS Turku
1998	HJK Helsinki	3-2	PK-35 Helsinki
1999	Jokerit Helsinki	2-1	Jaro Pietarsaari
2000	HJK Helsinki	1-0	KTP Kotka
2001	Atlantis Helsinki	1-0	Tampere United
2002	Haka Valkeakoski	4-1	FC Lahti
2003	HJK Helsinki	2-1 (aet)	Allianssi Vantaa

Finnish Cup Summary

TEAM	TOTALS	WINNERS & RUNNERS-UP (BOLD) (*ITALICS*)
Haka Valkeakoski	11, 3	**1955, 59, 60, 63, 69, 77,** *80,* **82, 83, 85, 88, 89, 97, 2002**
HJK Helsinki	8, 4	**1966,** *75,* **81, 84,** *85,* **90, 93,** *94* **96, 98, 2000,** *03*
Reipas Lahti	7, 3	*1963,* **64,** *67,* **70,** *72–76,* **78**
KTP Kotka	4, 3	**1958,** *61,* **66, 67, 68,** *80, 2000*
FC Lahti (includes Kuusysi Lahti)	2, 4	*1981,* **83, 84,** *87,* **91,** *2002*
TPS Turku	2, 4	*1965,* **79,** *91,* **94,** *96, 97*
Tampere United (includes Ilves Tampere)	2, 2	*1976,* **79, 90,** *2001*
KuPS Kuopio	2, 0	**1968, 89**
MP Mikkeli	2, 0	**1970, 71**
MyPa Anjalankoski	2, 0	**1992, 95**
Jaro Pietarsaari (includes Drott Pietarsaari)	1, 2	**1957,** *92, 99*
RoPS Rovaniemi	1, 2	*1962,* **86,** *93*
FC Jokerit (includes PK-35 Helsinki and Jokerit Helsinki)	1, 1	*1998,* **99**
HPS Helsinki	1, 1	**1955,** *62*
PPojat Helsinki	1, 1	**1956,** *61*
ÅIFK Turku	1, 0	**1965**
Atlantis Helsinki	1, 0	**2001**

This summary only features clubs that have won the Finnish Cup. For a full list of cup winners and runners-up please see the Cup Record left.

Faeroe Islands

Fotboltssamband Føroya
Founded: 1979
Joined FIFA: 1988
Joined UEFA: 1992

The tiny Faeroe Islands have played regular league soccer since 1942. The national team played their first competitive international in 1990, beating a lacklustre and complacent Austrian side. In 2002 they famously drew with Scotland.

SEASON	LEAGUE CHAMPIONS
1999	KÍ
2000	VB
2001	GÍ
2002	HB
2003	HB

YEAR	CUP WINNERS
1999	KÍ
2000	GÍ
2001	B36
2002	NSi
2003	B36

Iceland

The Football Association of Iceland
Founded: 1947
Joined FIFA: 1929
Joined UEFA: 1954

The first Icelandic football club, KR of Reykjavík, was set up in 1899. Soccer formalized in Iceland in 1912 with the creation of a Reykjavik league, though the national soccer association was not formed until 1947. A cup was established in 1960, ensuring a berth in the Cup-Winners' Cup for the victors.

SEASON	LEAGUE CHAMPIONS
1999	KR
2000	KR
2001	ÍA
2002	KR
2003	KR

YEAR	CUP WINNERS
1999	KR
2000	ÍA
2001	Fylkir
2002	Fylkir
2003	IA Akranes

LOW COUNTRIES

Soccer in the Netherlands

Soccer in Belgium

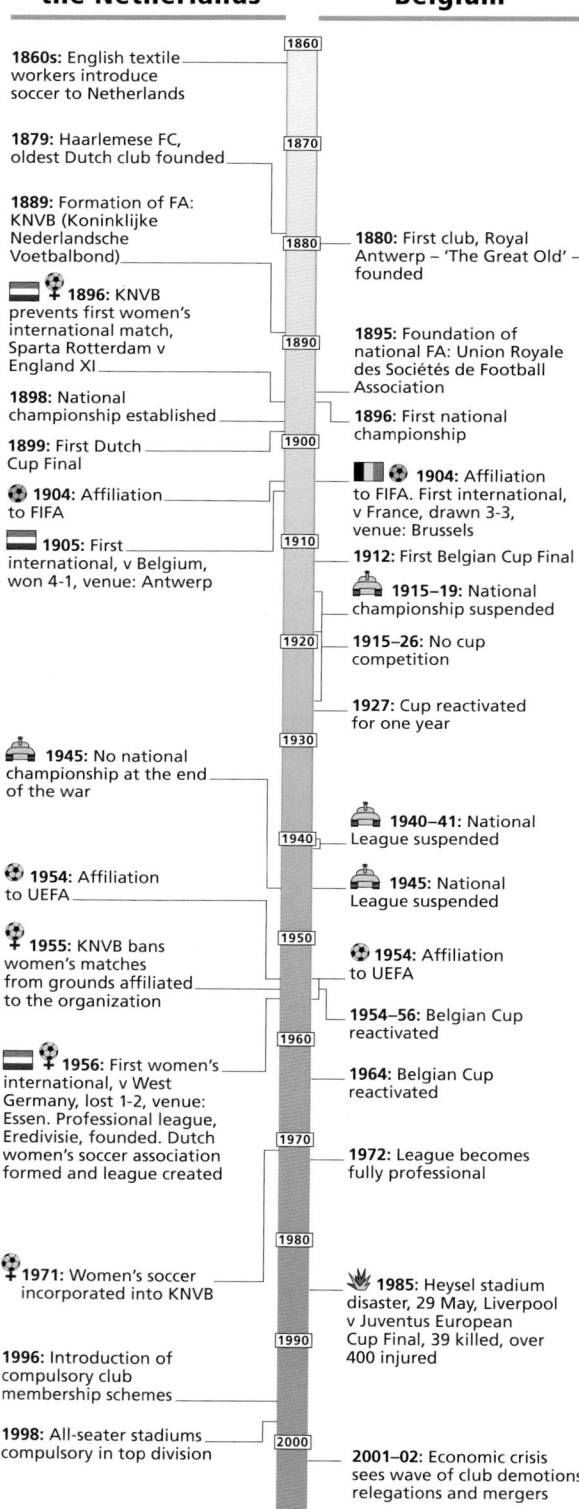

1860s: English textile workers introduce soccer to Netherlands — **1860**

1879: Haarlemese FC, oldest Dutch club founded — **1870**

1889: Formation of FA: KNVB (Koninklijke Nederlandse Voetbalbond) — **1880**

1896: KNVB prevents first women's international match, Sparta Rotterdam v England XI — **1890**

1898: National championship established

1899: First Dutch Cup Final — **1900**

1904: Affiliation to FIFA

1905: First international, v Belgium, won 4-1, venue: Antwerp — **1910**

— **1920**

— **1930**

1945: No national championship at the end of the war

— **1940**

1954: Affiliation to UEFA

1955: KNVB bans women's matches from grounds affiliated to the organization — **1950**

— **1960**

1956: First women's international, v West Germany, lost 1-2, venue: Essen. Professional league, Eredivisie, founded. Dutch women's soccer association formed and league created — **1970**

— **1980**

1971: Women's soccer incorporated into KNVB

— **1990**

1996: Introduction of compulsory club membership schemes

1998: All-seater stadiums compulsory in top division — **2000**

— **2010**

1880: First club, Royal Antwerp – 'The Great Old' – founded

1895: Foundation of national FA: Union Royale des Sociétés de Football Association

1896: First national championship

 1904: Affiliation to FIFA. First international, v France, drawn 3-3, venue: Brussels

1912: First Belgian Cup Final

1915–19: National championship suspended

1915–26: No cup competition

1927: Cup reactivated for one year

1940–41: National League suspended

1945: National League suspended

1954: Affiliation to UEFA

1954–56: Belgian Cup reactivated

1964: Belgian Cup reactivated

1972: League becomes fully professional

1985: Heysel stadium disaster, 29 May, Liverpool v Juventus European Cup Final, 39 killed, over 400 injured

2001–02: Economic crisis sees wave of club demotions, relegations and mergers

Low Countries: The main clubs

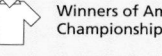 **Ajax** 1900 — Team name with year of formation

● Club formed before 1912

● Club formed 1912–25

● Club formed 1925–50

○ Club formed after 1950

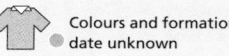 Winners of Amateur Championship

Runners-up in Amateur Championship

Colours and formation date unknown

Dordrecht 90 1904

DFC Dodrecht (1904–74). Merged with SVV Schiedamse Voetbal Vvereniging (1904) in 1991

Club Brugge KV 1899

Cercle Brugge 1899

NAC Breda 1912

K Lierse SK 1908

Royal Antwerp FC 1880

Beerschot VAV 1899–1999

KV Oostende 1981
Merger of AS Oostende and KVG Oostende

Germinal Beerschot Antwerpen 1999

FC Germinal Ekiren 1942–99

Berchem Sport 1906

KSV Waregem 1946
Merger of Red Star Waregem and Sportif

R Excelsior Mouscron 1964
Merger of ARA Mouscronnois and R. Stade Mouscron

RC Jet Wavre 1970
Merger of Racing Stade de Bruxelles and RC Jette. Racing Jet de Bruxelles (1970–88)

RSC Anderlecht 1908

Merged with Brussels D' 71 in 1994

RWD Molenbeek 1973
Merger of Racing White Brussels (1963) and Daring CB (1895)

KV Kortrijk 1971
Merger of Kortrijk Sport (1901) and Stade Kortrijk

Union FC d'Ixelles 1896

(Folded)

White Star FC 1910–63

Leopold Club de Bruxelles 1893–1990

Union St Gilloise 1899

HBS Den Haag 1893

HVV Den Haag 1885

Quick Den Haag 1896

ADO Den Haag 1971

Merger of ADO Den Hagg (1905) and Holland Sport (1954) in 1971 as FC Den Haag new name 1996

Sparta Rotterdam 1888

Excelsior 1902

Feyenoord 1908

KRC Harlebeke 1930

AA Gent 1896

KSC Eendracht Aalst 1919
Merger of Amical and Standard

KSC Lokeren 1970
Merger of Racing Lokeren and Standard Lokeren

Ajax 1900

De Volewijckers 1920

Merged with DWS and Blauwit in 1972 to form FC Amsterdam, demerge in 1983

RAP Amsterdam 1887

(Folded)

BVC Amsterdam 1954

(Folded)

Haarlem 1889

Telstar 19 **Ijmuide**

Haarlem

Haarlemese FC 1879

RCH Haarlem

The Hagu

Rotterdam

Breda

RBS Roosendaal 1912

SK Beveren 1935

K. ST Niklase SK 1920

Antwerp

Lier

Mechelen

Aalst

Daring Club Brussels 1895–1973

Racing Club Brussels 1891–1963

Brussels

Royal Charleroi FC 1904

Charleroi

Bruges

Ostend

Waregem

Kortrijk

Mouscron

Low Countries

ORIGINS AND GROWTH OF SOCCER

THE TRAJECTORIES OF soccer in Belgium and the Netherlands have clear parallels – early arrival through British influences, the establishment of national FAs and leagues before the end of the 19th century, followed by decades of weak domestic soccer due to the persistence of amateurism. In Belgium, English colleges in Brussels and Bruges and English workers in Antwerp were the main points of arrival. In the Netherlands, English textile workers in Enschede were playing soccer in the late 1860s. Pim Mulier, an English-educated journalist, established the country's first club, Haarlemese FC, in 1879.

Professionalism came to the Netherlands in 1956, while in Belgium semi-professionalism began in the late 1950s and full professionalism in 1972. In both countries there has been a massive concentration of soccer strength into a few big clubs, followed by waves of small club mergers in an attempt to keep up. In Belgium the balance of power has shifted to Brussels, Anderlecht and French-speaking Belgium and away from Flemish-speaking areas in the North. In the Netherlands the big three, Ajax, Feyenoord and PSV, have been dominant.

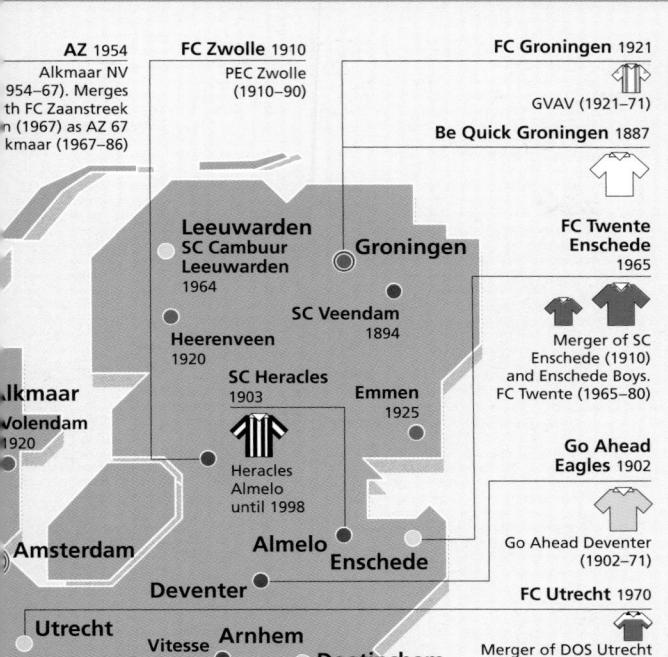

AZ 1954
Alkmaar NV
954–67). Merges
th FC Zaanstreek
n (1967) as AZ 67
kmaar (1967–86)

FC Zwolle 1910
PEC Zwolle
(1910–90)

FC Groningen 1921
GVAV (1921–71)
Be Quick Groningen 1887

Leeuwarden
SC Cambuur
Leeuwarden
1964

Groningen

FC Twente
Enschede
1965

SC Veendam
1894

Heerenveen
1920

Merger of SC
Enschede (1910)
and Enschede Boys.
FC Twente (1965–80)

SC Heracles
1903

Emmen
1925

lkmaar
/olendam
1920

Heracles
Almelo
until 1998

Go Ahead
Eagles 1902

Amsterdam

Almelo
Enschede

Go Ahead Deventer
(1902–71)

Deventer

Utrecht

FC Utrecht 1970

Vitesse
Arnhem 1892

Arnhem

Merger of DOS Utrecht
(1902) and Vleox and
Elinkwijk (1919)

ETHERLANDS

Doetinchem
De Graafschap
1954

KC
Vaalwijk
940

NEC Nijmegen
1900

Willem II Tilburg 1896

Oss

TOP Oss 1928
Top until 1994

's-Hertogen-
bosch

FC Den Bosch 1906

Tilburg

Helmond

Helmond Sport 1967
Splits from Helmondia 55

dhoven
C Verbr.
el 1924

VVV Venlo 1920

BVV Den Bosch
(1906–67) merges
with Willhelmia (1967)

Lommel

Geel

PSV 1913

Beringen
Royal Beringen FC

Heerlen

/C
esterlo
64

Maastricht

Geleen
1902

Eindhoven 1909

Hasselt

MVV

Racing
Club
Mechelen
1904

Liège

Roda JC Kerkrade 1914

KV
Mechelen
1904

KSK
Tongeren
1969
Merger of
Tongerse
SV Cercle
and K. Patria
FC Tongeren

Roda Sport merged with
Rapid JC (1954) in 1962

Fortuna Sittard 1968

BELGIUM

Merger of Fortuna 54 Geleen
and Sittardia (1950) in 1968.
FSC (1968–79)

K. Waterschei SV
Thor Genk
1925–88

RFC Seresien

FC Winterslag
1923–88

R. Standard Liège 1898

SC Hasselt 1964
Merger of Excelsior Hasselt
and K. Hasselt VV

RFC Liège 1892

Racing Club Genk 1988
Merger of FC Winterslag
and Waterschei Thor

RFC Leiegois (1892–1989)

Key

International soccer (Netherlands)	●	European Championships winner
International soccer (Belgium)	▲	European Championships runner-up
Affiliation to FIFA	○	Netherlands competition winner
Affiliation to UEFA	△	Netherlands competition runner-up
Women's soccer	◉	Belgian competition winner
War	▲	Belgian competition runner-up
Disaster		
▲ World Cup runner-up		
■ European Championships host		

Alk – AZ Alkmaar
And – Anderlecht
Ant – Royal Antwerp FC
Brug – Club Brugge
Feyn – Feyenoord
Liege – Standard Liège
Mech – KV Mechelen
Twen – FC Twente

International Competitions

Year		European Cup	UEFA Cup	European Cup-Winners' Cup
1969:		△ Ajax		
1970:		○ Feyn		
1971:		○ Ajax		
1972:	■	○ Ajax		
1973:		○ Ajax		
1974:	▲		○ Feyn	
1975:				▲ Twen
1976:				▲ Brug
1977:				● And
1978:	▲	▲ Brug	○ PSV	▲ And
1980:	▲			● And
1981:	▲		△ Alk	
1982:				▲ Liege
1983:			● And	
1984:			▲ And	
1987:	◉			▲ Ajax
1988:	◉	○ PSV		● Mech △ Ajax
1990:				▲ And
1992:			○ Ajax	
1993:				▲ Ant
1995:		○ Ajax		
1996:			△ Ajax	
2000:	■			
2002:			○ Feyn	

Belgium

THE SEASON IN REVIEW 2003–04

THIS YEAR ANDERLECHT WON ITS THIRD Belgian title in six years and its 27th in total. The Brussels club played its best soccer in the first half of the season, though it wasn't good enough to stay in the Champions League. At home Anderlecht were invincible, going unbeaten in the league through to March. The club's young defender Vincent Kompany was outstanding, as was striker Aruna Dindane – the two topping the polls for Belgian player of the year.

Club Brugge, the reigning champions, never quite had enough to take on Anderlecht and the team saved its best for the early rounds of the Champions League; most notably in a fantastic 1-0 defeat of Milan at the San Siro. Finishing third in the group, the club went on to the UEFA Cup where it lost out in the Fourth Round to Bordeaux. A Champions League qualifying spot following a brilliant run of late form, and a decisive victory in the Belgian Cup Final over Beveren, were Brugge's compensations. Its domination of the Cup Final was so great that the team not only scored its own four goals but managed two own goals for Beveren as well.

Frustration boils over

The only other club to challenge Anderlecht was Standard Liège who had played very well for much of the early season, including a defeat of Anderlecht. But Standard let an 11-point lead over chasing third place Club Brugge evaporate as the team fell away in the second half of the year. The brooding frustration in the camp spilt over after a frustrating goalless draw with Genk. After having a penalty appeal refused, Luciano D'Onofrio, the brother of coach Dominique, knocked a steward out and verbally threatened the referee on leaving the pitch. He told a press conference that he had said 'I will put a bullet through your head'. Star striker Emile Mpenza kicked a hole in a dressing room door afterwards.

Anderlecht's Vincent Kompany (left), one of Europe's most accomplished young defenders, presses Andres Mendoza of Club Brugge.

Jupiler League Table 2003–04

CLUB	P	W	D	L	F	A	Pts	
RSC Anderlecht	34	25	6	3	77	27	81	Champions League
Club Brugge KV	34	22	6	6	77	31	72	Champions League
Standard Liège	34	18	11	5	68	31	65	UEFA Cup
KRC Genk	34	17	8	9	58	40	59	
R Excelsior Mouscron	34	15	14	5	64	42	59	
KVC Westerlo	34	14	10	10	51	45	52	
G Beerschot Antwerpen	34	11	11	12	34	40	44	
RAA Louviéroise	34	10	14	10	45	46	44	
RAA Gent	34	8	16	10	33	34	40	
Sporting Lokeren SNW	34	10	9	15	45	54	39	
Lierse SK*	34	8	15	11	33	40	39	
SK Beveren Waas	34	11	5	18	45	58	38	UEFA Cup (cup finalists)
St Truidense	34	9	11	14	36	50	38	
KSV Cercle Brugge	34	7	14	13	28	52	35	
RSC Charleroi	34	8	9	17	35	47	33	
RAEC Mons	34	7	12	15	29	52	33	
K Heusden-Zolder	34	7	7	20	36	68	28	Relegated
Royal Antwerp FC	34	7	6	21	30	67	27	Relegated

* Lierse has had its playing licence for 2004–05 withdrawn due to unpaid taxes. The club can appeal but should that appeal be rejected they will be relegated to the third division.
Promoted clubs: FC Brussels, KV Oostende.

Top Goalscorers 2003–04

PLAYER	CLUB	NATIONALITY	GOALS
Luigi Pieroni	R Excelsior Mouscron	Belgian	28
Emile Mpenza	Standard Liège	Belgian	21
Tosin Dosunmu	KVC Westerlo	Nigerian	16
Aruna Dindane	RSC Anderlecht	Cote d'Ivoirean	15
Gert Verheyen	Club Brugge KV Antwerpen	Belgian	15

International Club Performances 2003–04

CLUB	COMPETITION	PROGRESS
RSC Anderlecht	Champions League	Group Stage
Club Brugge KV	Champions League	Group Stage
	UEFA Cup	4th Round
KSC Lokeren	UEFA Cup	1st Round
RAA Louviéroise	UEFA Cup	1st Round

Belgian Cup

2004 FINAL

May 23 – King Boudewin, Brussels
Club Brugge KV 4-2 KSK Beveren
(Verheyen 23, Ceh 47, Mendoza 74, van der Heyden 79) (Verlinden 37 o.g., Maertens 61 o.g.)
h/t: 1-1 **Att:** 37,000
Ref: ver Eecke

Club Brugge captain Danny Verlinden holds the Belgian Cup after Brugge's 4-2 victory over Beveren in the Final.

A key man for the champions: Aruna Dindane celebrates a goal for Anderlecht against Charleroi.

Emile Mpenza, Standard's fiery striker, chases down the ball, but his 21 goals could not lift his side higher than third.

Right: Genk goalkeeper Jan Moons tested a radio device linking him to the bench this season in their game with Brugge – for the record Genk won 1-0.

Far right: Heusden Zolder's Brian Priske just keeps the ball from the chasing Genk players, but Heusden couldn't keep above the relegation zone.

Below: RAEC Mons coach Sergio Brio shrugs his shoulders as his team are thrashed 9-0 by Club Brugge in their final game of the season. However, results elsewhere meant that the club had done well enough to stay up.

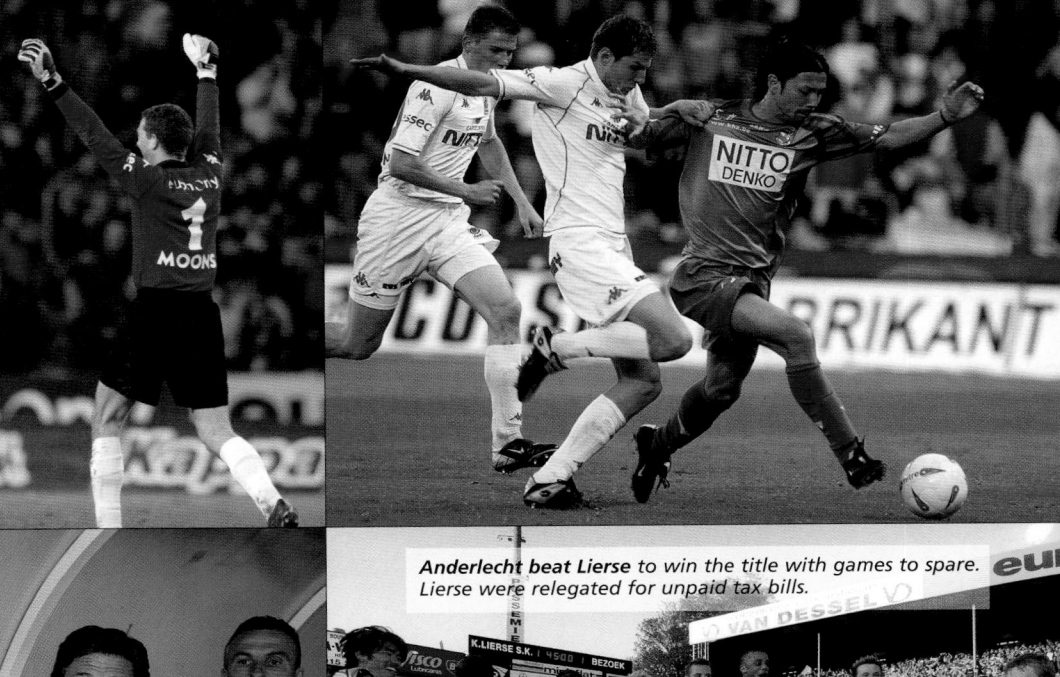

Anderlecht beat Lierse to win the title with games to spare. Lierse were relegated for unpaid tax bills.

Belgium

THE JUPILER LEAGUE 1982–2003

THE LAST 20 YEARS of Belgian soccer have been dominated by three teams: Standard Liège, who opened the 1980s with a couple of titles; Club Brugge KV, who has consistently challenged for the title and took a string of them in the late 1980s under former player Jan Ceulemans; and the biggest club of all, Anderlecht. Beyond these teams only four minnows have taken the title: Lierse, Beveren, Mechelen and Genk.

Anderlecht has risen to the top under the control of Constant Vanden Stock. Previously a player with the club and national team manager, he made an enormous fortune in the brewing industry. Under his control the club won three titles in a row in the mid-1980s, built the first executive boxes in a European

stadium and brought the leading Belgian player of the era – Enzo Schifo – to the club. In the mid-1990s, the championship-winning team was built around Luc Nilis and Marc Degryse.

Competition has consistently come from the likes of Gent, Antwerpen and Charleroi, but most clubs are struggling to survive, and the league has seen a wave of mergers forced on the smaller sides, while older established clubs, like Cercle Brugge, have disappeared from view. In 2002, two top-flight clubs were relegated on financial rather than sporting grounds as Eendracht Aalst failed to pay its players and RWD Molenbeek collapsed under its debts. Lommelse and Mechelen went the same way in 2003.

BELGIUM

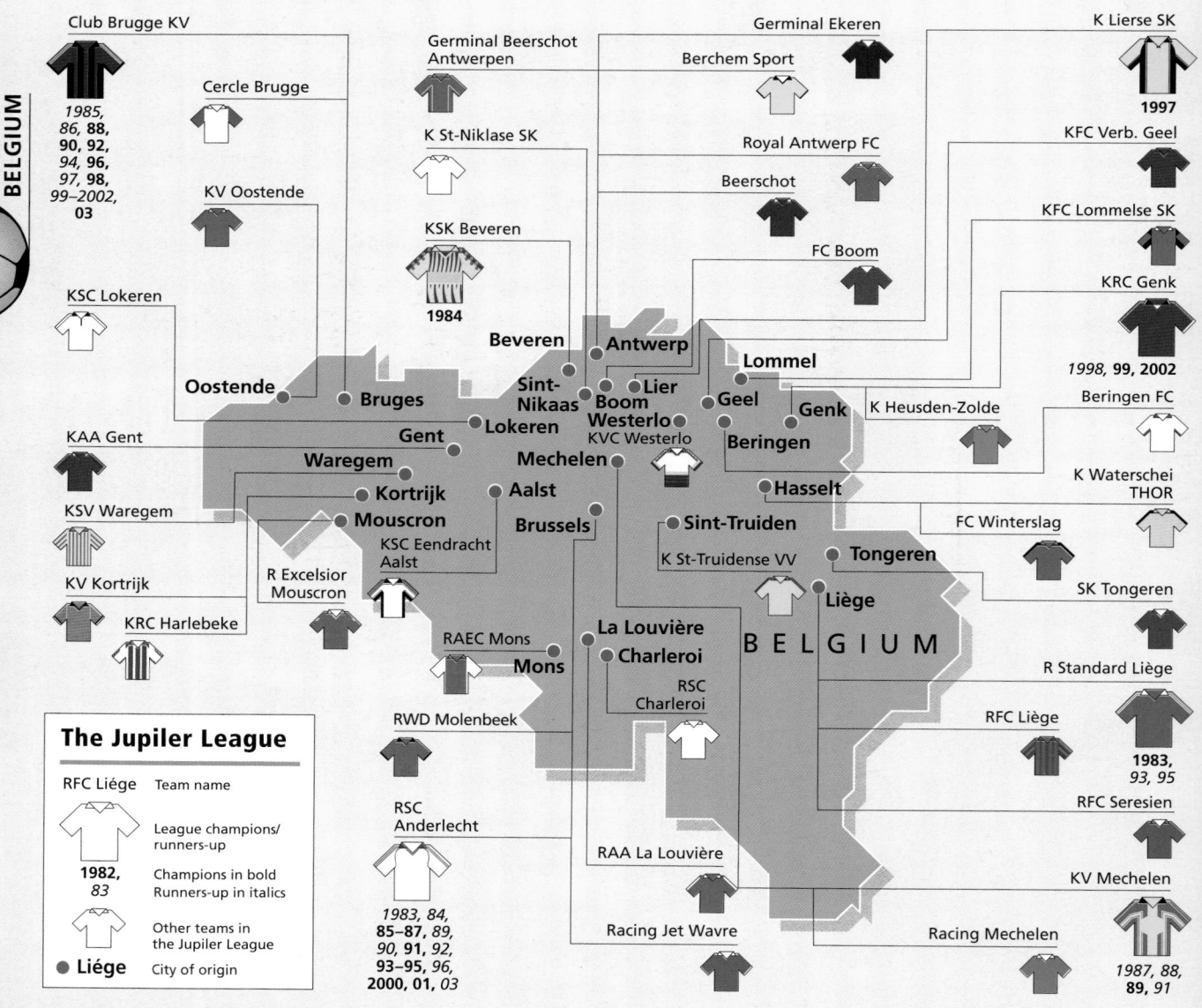

Key to League Positions Table

▮	League champions
▮	Other team playing in league
▮	Season promoted to league
▮	Season of relegation from league
5	Final positition in league
▮	Merger between teams

FC Winterslag and K Waterschei THOR merged to form KRC Genk for the 1988–99 season

R Standard Liège and RFC Seresien merged to form R Standard Liège for the 1996–97 season

Germinal Ekeren and Beerschot merged to form Germinal Beerschot Antwerpen for the 1999–2000 season

Patrick Zoundi and Ibrahima Sory of Lokeren celebrate. Lokeren has at times fielded 11 African players for a league match.

Enzo Schifo, the most gifted Belgian player ever and an inspiration for RSC Anderlecht.

Belgian League Positions 1982–2003

SEASON

TEAM	82-83	83-84	84-85	85-86	86-87	87-88	88-89	89-90	90-91	91-92	92-93	93-94	94-95	95-96	96-97	97-98	98-99	99-2000	00-01	01-02	02-03
KSC Eendracht Aalst										18			4	10	15	15	13	12	16	17	
RSC Anderlecht	2	2	1	1	1	4	2	2	1	2	1	1	1	2	4	4	3	1	1	3	2
Royal Antwerp FC	3	8	7	9	14	3	5	4	7	5	5	5	16	13	6	18			12	16	12
Germinal Beerschot Antwerpen																		7	6	9	14
Beerschot	15	16	16	7	9	13	16	8	18												
Berchem Sport					18																
Beringen FC		18																			
KSK Beveren	6	1	5	5	5	14	12	17		12	8	9	10	17		16	15	15	14	18*	11
FC Boom											18										
Cercle Brugge	12	11	11	10	11	7	15	9	16	9	13	12	15	8	18						
Club Brugge KV	5	3	2	2	3	1	4	1	4	1	6	2	3	1	2	1	2	2	2	2	1
RSC Charleroi		12	7	8	11	14	8	13	7	4	13	7	13	13	14	16			9	12	16
Germinal Ekeren							13	5	8	14	10	6	3	10	3	10					
KRC Genk							18		14	16	15	18			8	2	1	8	11	1	6
KFC Verb. Geel																		17			
KAA Gent	4	15	6	4	16	17		6	3	6	9	15	14	14	8	8	3	5	4	8	
KRC Harlebeke															12	9	5	11	14	17	
K Heusden-Zolde																					
KV Kortrijk	11	12	13	15	15	9	8	7	15	17						17					
RFC Liège	9	13	3	6	6	5	3	12	10	15	12	13	18								
R Standard Liège	1	4	8	3	10	10	6	5	6	3	2	6	2	6	7	9	6	5	3	5	7
K Lierse SK	14	14	15	18			10	10	11	7	14	5	5		1	7	7	9	10	15	5
KSC Lokeren	8	10	10	14	4	16	14	11	9	14	17				12	6	5	10	4	7	3
KFC Lommelse SK											16	11	7	9	5	11	16	18		13	†
RAA La Louvière																			15	11	15
KV Mechelen		6	12	11	2	2	1	3	2	4	3	8	11	11	17			11	18		17†
Racing Mechelen						13	18														
RWD Molenbeek	10	17		13	13	12	17		12	11	11	16	12	4	16	17			10*		
RAEC Mons																					9
R Excelsior Mouscron															3	10	4	4	7	6	13
KV Oostende											7	17					18				
K St-Niklase SK		17																			
K St-Truidense VV					11	7	15	17					8	15	11	14	9	13	13	8	4
RFC Seresien	13	5	14	16	17							3	9	16							
SK Tongeren	17																				
KSV Waregem	16	7	4	8	8	6	9	16	13	10	4			18							
K Waterschei THOR	7	9	9	17																	
Racing Jet Wavre		18			12	18															
KVC Westerlo																12	12	6	8	14	10
FC Winterslag	18				15																

*Despite finishing bottom, Beveren were spared relegation as RWD Molenbeek were relegated for financial reasons.

† Both Lommelse and Mechelen went into liquidation and were relegated. Lommelse had its league record annulled.

Belgium

Union Royale des Sociétés de Football Association
Founded: 1895
Joined FIFA: 1904
Joined UEFA: 1954

BELGIUM SHARES WITH Sweden the honour of having Europe's oldest soccer league outside the British Isles. Established in 1895 across both French- and Flemish-speaking Belgium, the league has run for over 100 years, breaking only for the First World War and the beginning and the end of the Second World War. Power in the league has shifted from the early dominance of Brussels-based teams such as Union St. Gilloise and Racing CB, to include the clubs of Antwerp, Bruges and Liège. By contrast, the Belgian Cup has been a sporadic and low-key affair and was played only once between 1915 and 1954. Interest has risen since the early 1960s when the winners were awarded a place in European competitions. The current league has 18 teams with two relegated each year and two promoted from the lower league in a complex series of play-offs.

Belgian League Record 1896–2004

SEASON	CHAMPIONS	RUNNERS-UP
1896	RFC Liège	Royal Antwerp FC
1897	Racing CB	RFC Liège
1898	RFC Liège	Racing CB
1899	RFC Liège	Racing CB
1900	Racing CB	Royal Antwerp FC
1901	Racing CB	Beerschot
1902	Racing CB	Leopold CB
1903	Racing CB	Union St. Gilloise
1904	Union St. Gilloise	Racing CB
1905	Union St. Gilloise	Racing CB
1906	Union St. Gilloise	Club Brugge KV
1907	Union St. Gilloise	Racing CB
1908	Racing CB	Union St. Gilloise
1909	Union St. Gilloise	Daring CB
1910	Union St. Gilloise	Club Brugge KV
1911	Cercle Brugge	Club Brugge KV
1912	Daring CB	Union St. Gilloise
1913	Union St. Gilloise	Daring CB
1914	Daring CB	Union St. Gilloise
1915–19	*no championship*	
1920	Club Brugge KV	Union St. Gilloise
1921	Daring CB	Union St. Gilloise
1922	Beerschot	Union St. Gilloise
1923	Union St. Gilloise	Beerschot
1924	Beerschot	Union St. Gilloise
1925	Beerschot	Royal Antwerp FC
1926	Beerschot	R Standard Liège
1927	Cercle Brugge	Beerschot
1928	Beerschot	R Standard Liège
1929	Royal Antwerp FC	Beerschot
1930	Cercle Brugge	Royal Antwerp FC
1931	Royal Antwerp FC	KV Mechelen
1932	K Lierse SK	Royal Antwerp FC
1933	Union St. Gilloise	Royal Antwerp FC
1934	Union St. Gilloise	Daring CB
1935	Union St. Gilloise	K Lierse SK
1936	Daring CB	R Standard Liège
1937	Daring CB	Beerschot
1938	Beerschot	Daring CB
1939	Beerschot	K Lierse SK
1940–41	*no championship*	
1942	K Lierse SK	Beerschot
1943	KV Mechelen	Beerschot

Belgian League Record (*continued*)

SEASON	CHAMPIONS	RUNNERS-UP
1944	Royal Antwerp FC	RSC Anderlecht
1945	*no championship*	
1946	KV Mechelen	Royal Antwerp FC
1947	RSC Anderlecht	Olympic Charleroi
1948	KV Mechelen	RSC Anderlecht
1949	RSC Anderlecht	Berchem Sport
1950	RSC Anderlecht	Berchem Sport
1951	RSC Anderlecht	Berchem Sport
1952	RFC Liège	Racing Mechelen
1953	RFC Liège	RSC Anderlecht
1954	RSC Anderlecht	KV Mechelen
1955	RSC Anderlecht	AA Gent
1956	RSC Anderlecht	Royal Antwerp FC
1957	Royal Antwerp FC	RSC Anderlecht
1958	R Standard Liège	Royal Antwerp FC
1959	RSC Anderlecht	RFC Liège
1960	K Lierse SK	RSC Anderlecht
1961	R Standard Liège	RFC Liège
1962	RSC Anderlecht	R Standard Liège
1963	R Standard Liège	Royal Antwerp FC
1964	RSC Anderlecht	FC Beringen
1965	RSC Anderlecht	R Standard Liège
1966	RSC Anderlecht	St. Truidense
1967	RSC Anderlecht	Club Brugge KV
1968	RSC Anderlecht	Club Brugge KV
1969	R Standard Liège	RSC Charleroi
1970	R Standard Liège	Club Brugge KV
1971	R Standard Liège	Club Brugge KV
1972	RSC Anderlecht	Club Brugge KV
1973	Club Brugge KV	R Standard Liège
1974	RSC Anderlecht	Royal Antwerp FC
1975	RWD Molenbeek	Royal Antwerp FC
1976	Club Brugge KV	RSC Anderlecht
1977	Club Brugge KV	RSC Anderlecht
1978	Club Brugge KV	RSC Anderlecht
1979	KSK Beveren	RSC Anderlecht
1980	Club Brugge KV	R Standard Liège
1981	RSC Anderlecht	KSC Lokeren
1982	R Standard Liège	RSC Anderlecht
1983	R Standard Liège	RSC Anderlecht
1984	KSK Beveren	RSC Anderlecht
1985	RSC Anderlecht	Club Brugge KV
1986	RSC Anderlecht	Club Brugge KV
1987	RSC Anderlecht	KV Mechelen
1988	Club Brugge KV	KV Mechelen
1989	KV Mechelen	RSC Anderlecht
1990	Club Brugge KV	RSC Anderlecht
1991	RSC Anderlecht	KV Mechelen
1992	Club Brugge KV	RSC Anderlecht
1993	RSC Anderlecht	Standard Liège
1994	RSC Anderlecht	Club Brugge KV
1995	RSC Anderlecht	Standard Liège
1996	Club Brugge KV	RSC Anderlecht
1997	K Lierse SK	Club Brugge KV
1998	Club Brugge KV	KRC Genk
1999	KRC Genk	Club Brugge KV
2000	RSC Anderlecht	Club Brugge KV
2001	RSC Anderlecht	Club Brugge KV
2002	KRC Genk	Club Brugge KV
2003	Club Brugge KV	RSC Anderlecht
2004	RSC Anderlecht	Club Brugge KV

Belgian League Summary

TEAM	TOTALS	CHAMPIONS & RUNNERS-UP (BOLD) (ITALICS)
RSC Anderlecht	27, 17	*1944, 47, 48,* **49–51,** *53,* **54–56,** *57, 59, 60,* **62,** *64–68,* **72,** *74,* **76–79, 81,** *82–84,* **85–87, 89, 90, 91, 92, 93–95,** *96,* **2000, 01,** *03,* **04**
Club Brugge KV	12, 17	*1906, 10, 11,* **20,** *67, 68, 70–72,* **73,** *76–78,* **80,** *85, 86,* **88, 90, 92,** *94, 96, 97, 98,* **99–2002,** *03, 04*
Union St. Gilloise	11, 8	*1903,* **04–07,** *08,* **09, 10,** *12,* **13,** *14,* **20–22,** *23,* **24,** *33–35*
R Standard Liège	8, 9	*1926, 28, 36,* **58,** *61,* **62,** *63,* **65, 69–71,** *73,* **80,** *82, 83,* **93,** *95*
Beerschot	7, 7	*1901,* **22, 23,** *24–26,* **27,** *28,* **29,** *37, 38,* **39,** *42, 43*
Racing CB	6, 5	**1897,** *98, 99,* **1900–03,** *04, 05,* **07,** *08*
Daring CB	5, 4	*1909,* **12, 13,** *14,* **21,** *34,* **36, 37,** *38*
RFC Liège	5, 3	**1896,** *97, 98,* **99,** *1952,* **53,** *59,* **61**
Royal Antwerp FC	4, 12	*1896, 1900, 25,* **29,** *30,* **31,** *32, 33,* **44,** *46, 56,* **57,** *58, 63, 74, 75*
KV Mechelen	4, 5	*1931,* **43,** *46, 48, 54,* **87,** *88,* **89,** *91*
K Lierse SK	4, 2	**1932,** *35,* **39,** *42,* **60, 97**
Cercle Brugge	3, 0	**1911, 27, 30**
KRC Genk	2, 1	**1998,** *99,* **2002**
KSK Beveren	2, 0	**1979, 84**
RWD Molenbeek	1, 0	**1975**

This summary only features clubs that have won the Belgian League. For a full list of league champions and runners-up please see the League Record opposite.

Belgian Cup Record 1912–2004

YEAR	WINNERS	SCORE	RUNNERS-UP
1912	Racing CB	1-0	Racing Gent
1913	Union St. Gilloise	3-2	Cercle Brugge
1914	Union St. Gilloise	4-1	Club Brugge KV
1915–26		no competition	
1927	Cercle Brugge	2-1	Tubantia Borgerhout
1928–53		no competition	
1954	R Standard Liège	3-1	Racing Mechelen
1955	Royal Antwerp FC	4-0	Waterschei THOR
1956	Racing Tournai	2-1	CS Verviers
1957–63		no competition	
1964	KAA Gent	4-2	FC Diest
1965	RSC Anderlecht	3-2 (aet)	R Standard Liège
1966	R Standard Liège	1-0	RSC Anderlecht
1967	R Standard Liège	3-1 (aet)	KV Mechelen
1968	Club Brugge KV	1-1, (replay) 4-4 (4-2 pens)	Beerschot
1969	K Lierse SK	2-0	Racing White
1970	Club Brugge KV	6-1	Daring CB
1971	Beerschot	2-1	St. Truidense
1972	RSC Anderlecht	1-0	R Standard Liège
1973	RSC Anderlecht	2-1	R Standard Liège
1974	KSV Waregem	4-1	SK Tongeren
1975	RSC Anderlecht	1-0	Royal Antwerp FC
1976	RSC Anderlecht	4-0	K Lierse SK
1977	Club Brugge KV	4-3	RSC Anderlecht
1978	KSK Beveren	2-0	RSC Charleroi
1979	Beerschot	1-0	Club Brugge KV
1980	Waterschei THOR	2-1	KSK Beveren
1981	R Standard Liège	4-0	KSC Lokeren
1982	Waterschei THOR	2-0	KSV Wagerem
1983	KSK Beveren	3-1	Club Brugge KV
1984	KAA Gent	2-0	R Standard Liège
1985	Cercle Brugge	1-1 (aet)(5-4 pens)	KSK Beveren
1986	Club Brugge KV	3-0	Cercle Brugge
1987	KV Mechelen	1-0	RFC Liège
1988	RSC Anderlecht	2-0	R Standard Liège
1989	RSC Anderlecht	2-0	R Standard Liège
1990	RFC Liège	2-1	Germinal Ekeren

Belgian Cup Record (*continued*)

YEAR	WINNERS	SCORE	RUNNERS-UP
1991	Club Brugge KV	3-1	KV Mechelen
1992	Royal Antwerp FC	2-2 (aet)(9-8 pens)	KV Mechelen
1993	R Standard Liège	2-0	RSC Charleroi
1994	RSC Anderlecht	2-0	Club Brugge KV
1995	Club Brugge KV	3-1	Germinal Ekeren
1996	Club Brugge KV	2-1	Cercle Brugge
1997	Germinal Ekeren	4-2 (aet)	RSC Anderlecht
1998	Racing Genk	4-0	Club Brugge KV
1999	K Lierse SK	3-1	R Standard Liège
2000	Racing Genk	4-1	R Standard Liège
2001	KVC Westerlo	1-0	Lommel
2002	Club Brugge KV	3-1	Excelsior Mouscron
2003	La Louvière	3-1	St. Truidense
2004	Club Brugge KV	4-2	KSK Beveren

Belgian Cup Summary

TEAM	TOTALS	WINNERS & RUNNERS-UP (BOLD) (ITALICS)
Club Brugge KV	9, 5	*1914,* **68,** *70,* **77,** *79,* **83,** *86,* **91,** *94,* **95, 96,** *98,* **2002,** *04*
RSC Anderlecht	8, 3	**1965,** *66,* **72, 73,** *75,* **76,** *77,* **88, 89, 94,** *97*
R Standard Liège	5, 8	**1954,** *65,* **66, 67,** *72, 73,* **81,** *84, 88, 89, 93,* **99,** *2000*
KSK Beveren	2, 3	**1978,** *80,* **83,** *85,* **2004**
Cercle Brugge	2, 3	*1913,* **27,** *85,* **86,** *96*
Beerschot	2, 1	*1968,* **71,** *79*
K Lierse SK	2, 1	**1969,** *76,* **99**
Racing Genk	2, 1	*1912,* **98, 2000**
Royal Antwerp FC	2, 1	**1955,** *75,* **92**
Waterschei THOR	2, 1	*1955,* **80, 82**
KAA Gent	2, 0	**1964, 84**
Union St. Gilloise	2, 0	**1913, 14**
KV Mechelen	1, 3	*1967,* **87,** *91, 92*
Germinal Ekeren	1, 2	*1990, 95,* **97**
KSV Waregem	1, 1	**1974,** *82*
RFC Liège	1, 1	**1987,** *90*
La Louvière	1, 0	**2003**
KVC Westerlo	1, 0	**2001**
Racing CB	1, 0	**1912**
Racing Tournai	1, 0	**1956**

This summary only features clubs that have won the Belgian Cup. For a full list of cup winners and runners-up please see the Cup Record left.

Luxembourg

Fédération Luxembourgeoise de Football
Founded: 1908
Joined FIFA: 1910
Joined UEFA: 1954

Soccer in Luxembourg is almost as old as in Belgium, with a league established in 1910 and a cup in 1922.

A new system of play-offs for the top four teams was introduced in 1999–2000 to decide the championship with the remaining teams involved in relegation play-offs.

SEASON	LEAGUE CHAMPIONS
2000	F91 Dudelange
2001	F91 Dudelange
2002	F91 Dudelange
2003	CS Grevenmacher
2004	Jeunesse Esch

YEAR	CUP WINNERS
2000	Jeunesse Esch
2001	Etzella Ettelbruck
2002	Avenir Beggen
2003	CS Grevenmacher
2004	F91 Dudelange

Netherlands

THE SEASON IN REVIEW 2003–04

AS EVER, SCUFFLING, FIGHTING AND more serious incidents of disorder continued throughout the Dutch soccer season. A game in Amsterdam between Feyenoord and Ajax Reserves saw Ajax fans invade the pitch and attack Feyenoord's Jorge Acuna. But violence between these two sets of fans is almost expected; the previous week had seen widespread fighting and arrests in Rotterdam after the senior teams met in a 1-1 draw. A riot by hundreds of NEC Nijmegen supporters at the central station in Amsterdam after the team's game with Ajax was also predictable but, unbelievably, the fans of tiny village team Heerenveen got in on the act as well. The previously unblemished record of its fans was tarnished after incidents among away supporters on the train to Arnhem saw a number of arrests. The club's president has since insisted that all fans going to away games travel on the official bus. While the Dutch police have yet to crack the hooligan problem, they did manage to foil a plot to kidnap and ransom PSV's Serbian star Mateja Kezman.

AZ joins the big three

Ajax and PSV were the inevitable front-runners in the first half of the season. Ronald Koeman dispelled rumours of a move to Barcelona by signing an extended contract as coach and set about building a new Ajax team around another generation of youthful stars: John Heitinga in defence, Rafael van der Vaart and Wesley Sneijder in midfield and, up front, Swede Zlatan Ibrahimovic and South African Steve Pienaar. Both teams had poor Champions League campaigns, with Ajax going out altogether at the Group Stage and PSV creeping into the UEFA Cup. Such European distractions created space for AZ, the biggest surprise of the season. Under ex-Ajax coach Co Adriaanse, AZ's attacking soccer and in-form strikers, Ali El Khattabi, Kenneth Perez and Stein Huysegems, saw them actually take top spot in the autumn and keep pace with Ajax and PSV into the New Year.

By this time Feyenoord was fourth and already out of serious contention for the title. The team was dumped out of the UEFA Cup as well. The Rotterdam side had lost the core of its squad over the summer, including van Hooijdonk, Emerton and Bosvelt, and their replacements had not proved up to the mark. Coach Bert van Marwijk announced that he would be stepping down at the end of the year after which Ruud Gullit will be taking over the job.

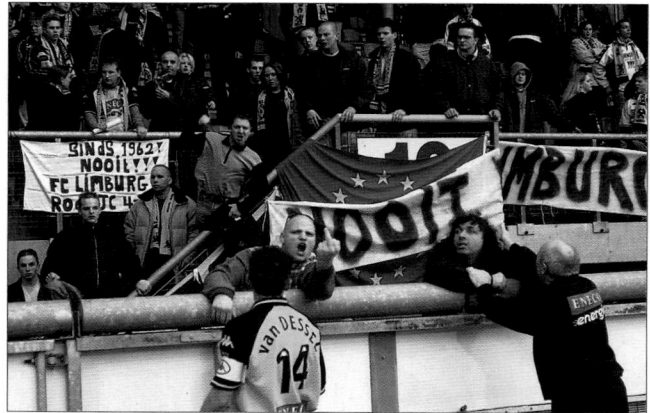

Eredivisie Table 2003–04

CLUB	P	W	D	L	F	A	Pts	
Ajax	34	25	5	4	79	31	80	Champions League
PSV	34	23	5	6	92	30	74	Champions League
Feyenoord	34	20	8	6	71	38	68	UEFA Cup
Heerenveen	34	17	7	10	45	35	58	UEFA Cup
AZ Alkmaar	34	17	6	11	65	42	57	UEFA Cup
Roda JC Kerkrade	34	14	11	9	60	41	53	
Willem II	34	13	10	11	47	54	49	
FC Twente	34	15	3	16	56	53	48	
FC Utrecht	34	13	7	14	42	52	46	UEFA (cup winners)
NAC Breda	34	12	10	12	58	55	46	
RKC Waalwijk	34	10	10	14	47	55	40	
RBC Roosendaal	34	10	10	14	34	47	40	
FC Groningen	34	9	10	15	38	53	37	
NEC Nijmegen	34	10	4	20	44	62	34	
ADO Den Haag	34	9	7	18	36	61	34	
Vitesse Arnhem	34	4	16	14	39	56	28	*Play-offs – winners
FC Volendam	34	7	6	21	31	79	27	*Play-offs – relegated
FC Zwolle	34	5	11	18	27	67	26	Relegated

* Vitesse Arnhem, FC Volendam and six teams from Eerste Divisie (Second Division) were involved in a mini leagues play-off where the two winners would play in the Eredivisie the next season. Vitesse Arnhem and De Graafschap were group winners.

Promoted clubs: FC Den Bosch, De Graafschap.

Top: NAC's highpoint of the year, putting the mighty Ajax out of the Cup in a decisive 2-0 victory.

Above: Vitesse Arnhem fans gather more in hope than expectation to discuss the club's perilous finances.

Left: Roda JC players and officials try to calm down another outbreak of trouble at the team's game with Heerenveen.

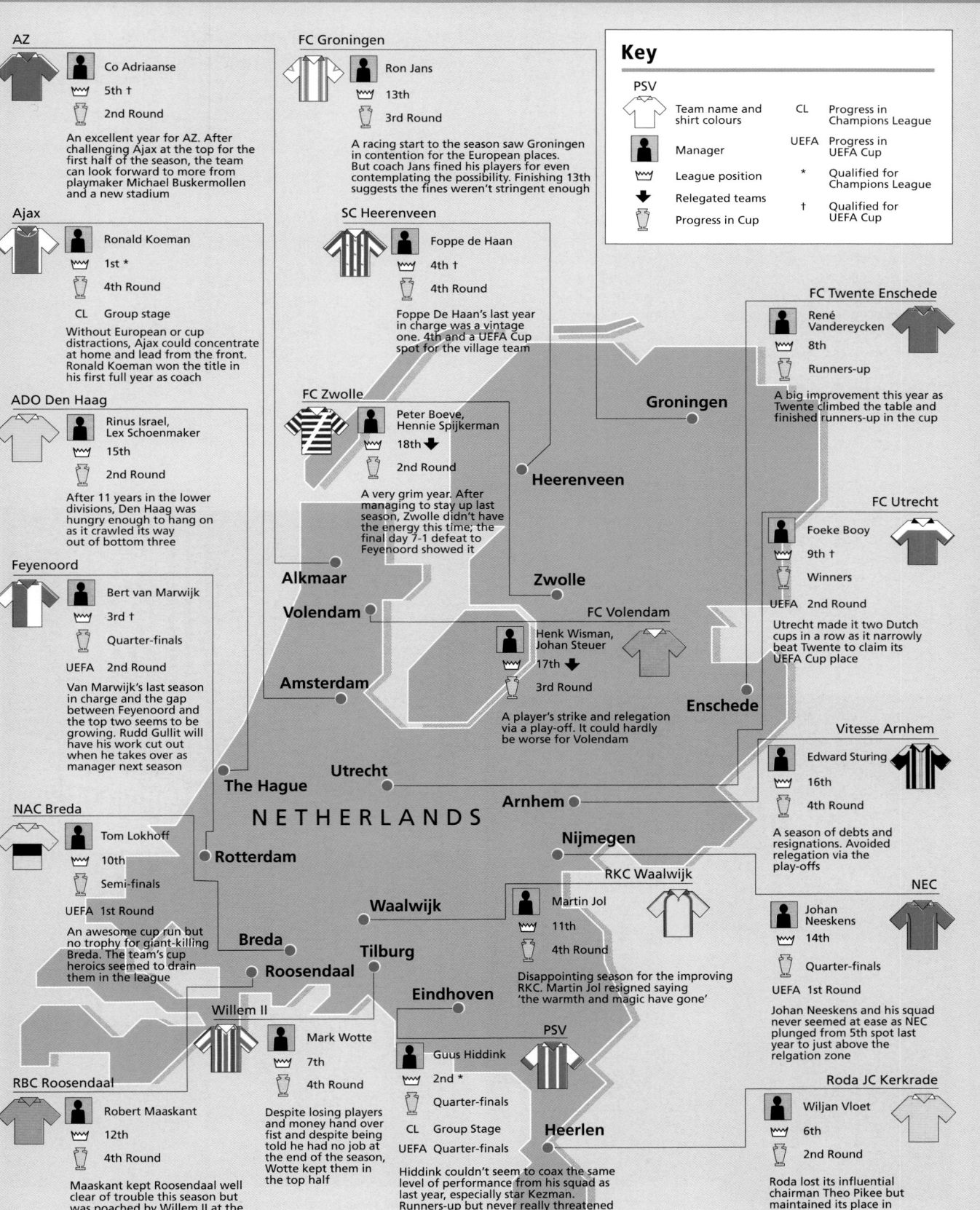

AZ

Co Adriaanse

👑 5th †

🏆 2nd Round

An excellent year for AZ. After challenging Ajax at the top for the first half of the season, the team can look forward to more from playmaker Michael Buskermollen and a new stadium.

Ajax

Ronald Koeman

👑 1st *

🏆 4th Round

CL Group stage

Without European or cup distractions, Ajax could concentrate at home and lead from the front. Ronald Koeman won the title in his first full year as coach.

ADO Den Haag

Rinus Israel, Lex Schoenmaker

👑 15th

🏆 2nd Round

After 11 years in the lower divisions, Den Haag was hungry enough to hang on as it crawled its way out of bottom three

Feyenoord

Bert van Marwijk

👑 3rd †

🏆 Quarter-finals

UEFA 2nd Round

Van Marwijk's last season in charge and the gap between Feyenoord and the top two seems to be growing. Rudd Gullit will have his work cut out when he takes over as manager next season

NAC Breda

Tom Lokhoff

👑 10th

🏆 Semi-finals

UEFA 1st Round

An awesome cup run but no trophy for giant-killing Breda. The team's cup heroics seemed to drain them in the league

RBC Roosendaal

Robert Maaskant

👑 12th

🏆 4th Round

Maaskant kept Roosendaal well clear of trouble this season but was poached by Willem II at the end. RBC may struggle without him

FC Groningen

Ron Jans

👑 13th

🏆 3rd Round

A racing start to the season saw Groningen in contention for the European places. But coach Jans fined his players for even contemplating the possibility. Finishing 13th suggests the fines weren't stringent enough

SC Heerenveen

Foppe de Haan

👑 4th †

🏆 4th Round

Foppe De Haan's last year in charge was a vintage one. 4th and a UEFA Cup spot for the village team

FC Zwolle

Peter Boeve, Hennie Spijkerman

👑 18th ⬇

🏆 2nd Round

A very grim year. After managing to stay up last season, Zwolle didn't have the energy this time; the final day 7-1 defeat to Feyenoord showed it

FC Volendam

Henk Wisman, Johan Steuer

👑 17th ⬇

🏆 3rd Round

A player's strike and relegation via a play-off. It could hardly be worse for Volendam

Willem II

Mark Wotte

👑 7th

🏆 4th Round

Despite losing players and money hand over fist and despite being told he had no job at the end of the season, Wotte kept them in the top half

PSV

Guus Hiddink

👑 2nd *

🏆 Quarter-finals

CL Group Stage

UEFA Quarter-finals

Hiddink couldn't seem to coax the same level of performance from his squad as last year, especially star Kezman. Runners-up but never really threatened to win it

FC Twente Enschede

René Vandereycken

👑 8th

🏆 Runners-up

A big improvement this year as Twente climbed the table and finished runners-up in the cup

FC Utrecht

Foeke Booy

👑 9th †

🏆 Winners

UEFA 2nd Round

Utrecht made it two Dutch cups in a row as it narrowly beat Twente to claim its UEFA Cup place

Vitesse Arnhem

Edward Sturing

👑 16th

🏆 4th Round

A season of debts and resignations. Avoided relegation via the play-offs

RKC Waalwijk

Martin Jol

👑 11th

🏆 4th Round

Disappointing season for the improving RKC. Martin Jol resigned saying 'the warmth and magic have gone'

NEC

Johan Neeskens

👑 14th

🏆 Quarter-finals

UEFA 1st Round

Johan Neeskens and his squad never seemed at ease as NEC plunged from 5th spot last year to just above the relgation zone

Roda JC Kerkrade

Wiljan Vloet

👑 6th

🏆 2nd Round

Roda lost its influential chairman Theo Pikee but maintained its place in the top six

Key

PSV — Team name and shirt colours

Manager

👑 League position

⬇ Relegated teams

🏆 Progress in Cup

CL — Progress in Champions League

UEFA — Progress in UEFA Cup

* — Qualified for Champions League

† — Qualified for UEFA Cup

Map labels:
Groningen
Heerenveen
Alkmaar
Volendam
Zwolle
Amsterdam
Enschede
Utrecht
Arnhem
The Hague
Nijmegen
Rotterdam
Waalwijk
NEC
Breda
Tilburg
Roosendaal
Eindhoven
Heerlen

N E T H E R L A N D S

Among the smaller clubs, Heerenveen had another excellent season in what was the last year for the longest-serving coach in the Netherlands – Foppe de Haan. The Dutch Cup provided considerable entertainment and giant-killing opportunities. NAC Breda beat first Ajax and then PSV to set up a semi-final clash with Twente Enschede, who had already beaten Feyenoord. The tie was predictably close and Twente squeezed into the Final after a penalty shoot-out. In the Final, Twente met last year's cup winners Utrecht, who had found its lower league opposition in the cup – Heracles and Sparta Rotterdam – difficult to negotiate.

The Cup Final was won for the second year running by Utrecht in a tense meeting with FC Twente. A goalless first half was followed by a controversial second. Twente's Jereon Heubach kicked the ball into touch to allow a player to get medical attention and, when Utrecht restarted, rather than returning the ball to Twente, kept it, allowing a beautiful shot from Van den Bergh. It was enough, and the Twente players lost their heads, went down to ten men and took a flurry of bookings.

Dismal end for PSV

In the final run in PSV could never quite put enough pressure on Ajax, who just kept on winning. PSV's big chance came in the spring when it met Ajax, just three points ahead of them. However, PSV coach Guus Hiddink's contract negotiations had reached a critical impasse prior to the game and the uncertainty seemed to affect the squad who limply lost 2-1. The team then went to Heerenveen and lost again, leaving Ajax six points ahead. RBC Roosendaal managed to finally break Ajax's 23-game streak of home wins with a 1-1 draw at the end of the season, but, by then, PSV had managed to consecutively lose to Feyenoord, draw with NAC and lose to Willem II. Ajax was now 12 points clear and only mathematically stoppable. The team duly won its 29th Dutch championship. Whether this talented squad will stay together and whether it can step up onto the European stage next season remains to be seen.

International Club Performances 2003–04

CLUB	COMPETITION	PROGRESS
Ajax	Champions League	Group Stage
PSV	Champions League	Group Stage
	UEFA Cup	Quarter-finals
NAC Breda	UEFA Cup	1st Round
Feyenoord	UEFA Cup	2nd Round
NEC	UEFA Cup	1st Round
FC Utrecht	UEFA Cup	2nd Round

Top Goalscorers 2003–04

PLAYER	CLUB	NATIONALITY	GOALS
Mateja Kezman	PSV	Serbian	19
Ali Elkhattabi	AZ Alkmaar	Moroccan	15
Thomas Buffel	Feyenoord	Dutch	13
Dirk Kuyt	Feyenoord	Dutch	12
Blaise N'Kufo	FC Twente	DR Congo	12

Dutch Cup

2004 FINAL

May 23 – De Kuip, Rotterdam
FC Utrecht 1-0 FC Twente
*(van den Bergh
66)*
h/t: 0-0 **Att:** 42,000
Ref: Luinge

Back in charge. Ruud Gullit enjoys the view from the box after his appointment as Feyenoord's coach for the 2004–05 season.

The top two clash. Ajax's Nigel de Jong takes on PSV's Wilfred Bouma.

An excellent season for Ajax's ever-improving Swede Zlatan Ibrahimovic, here celebrating a goal against Feyenoord.

Left: AZ's Ali El Khattabi (right) had a fine season, scoring freely and taking the club to the top fo the table in the autumn. Here they are seeing off minnows ADO Den Haag.

Below, middle left: FC Twente's brillant striker Blaise N'Kufo's (left) goals got his team to the Cup Final. But it was not enough to overcome the holders FC Utrecht.

Below: Feyenoord's Hossam Ghaly in action during his team's 1-1 draw with Ajax in Rotterdam.

Bottom, left: And that makes two. FC Utrecht are getting used to celebrating cup victories.

Bottom, right: Ajax captain Rafael van der Vaart holds up the Dutch Eredivise trophy. The celebrations followed a 2-0 victory in the team's final home game against NAC Breda, clinching its 29th title.

Amsterdam

SOCCER CENTER

NETHERLANDS

FOR THE MOST PART, Amsterdam is a city of footballing ghosts. RAP Amsterdam won the city's first league title in 1898 and the double a year later, but has left no mark. In 1972, a new professional club was formed – FC Amsterdam (from the fusion of three amateur clubs: Blauwit, De Volewijckers and DWS) – only to return to obscurity in 1982. The Olympic Stadium that housed the team sits empty. De Meer, the site of Ajax's greatest years, has gone. The old Jewish areas which provided a significant share of Ajax's support and players have shrunk. Jordaan, home to Surinamese immigrants and their families (including Ruud Gullit), has been gentrified.

Only on the south-eastern edge of the city at the Amsterdam Arena does football have its single, gigantic material expression. And even here Ajax must share it with a weekly roster of concerts and commercial events. Formed in 1900, Ajax has gradually migrated from its first playing field in Amsterdam Noord, down to the south-eastern edge of the city, settling at De Meer in the 1930s. A rash of league titles followed, but the club remained small and intensely local in its connections; a relationship so close that a special area has been set aside in the Westtergaarde Cemetery and laid with De Meer turf, where ashes can continue to be scattered long after the pitch has gone.

In its curiously rural setting, the De Meer had ivy-covered cottages in three of its corners which housed the stadium staff.

The total football revolution

What transformed Amsterdam and Ajax were the 1960s, Johan Cruyff and Rinus Michels. An outburst of political situationism and light anarchic protest erupted in the mid-1960s, bringing first inept police violence and then the elite acceptance that made Amsterdam a bohemian paradise. Out of this peculiar Dutch brew of playful anti-authoritarianism and liberation, Cruyff on the field and Michels off it added technical virtuosity and iron discipline to create the unstable but unstoppable 'total football'. In less than a decade, Ajax had gone from near relegation to triple European champions. Cruyff left in 1972 and the club eventually imploded, though its awesome youth training system (now a global phenomenon) created the team under Louis van Gaal who won the 1995 European Cup. However, the iron laws of post-Bosman economics saw the squad scattered to the richest clubs in Europe.

OLYMPISCH STADIUM

22,500	**Club:** Previously Ajax, FC Amsterdam
	Built: 1928
	Original Capacity: 24,700
	Rebuilt: 2000
	Significant Matches: 1928 Amsterdam Olympics; Ajax European matches; European Cup Final 1962; European Cup-Winners' Cup Final 1977

SPIERINGHORN

DWS

OSDORP

WESTTERGAARDE CEMETERY

Ringvaart

A9

BADHOEVEDOR

A4

The old Jewish areas of Amsterdam have shrunk, but many Ajax supporters identify themselves and the club with Amsterdam's Jewish legacy, and have taken the Star of David as their symbol.

AMSTERDAM ARENA

51,324	**Club:** Ajax
	Built: 1996
	Significant Matches: 2000 European Championships: four matches including quarter-final and semi-final; European Cup Final: 1998

Haarlemmermeer

NETHERLANDS

Amsterdam

51,324	Capacity of stadium
	Amateur club stadium
	Stadium no longer in use for top-flight soccer
	Team colours
	Amateur teams
M8	Motorway
A82	Major road
1900	Champions
2000	Runners-up

ZAANSTAD

LANDSMEER

Noordhollands Kanaal

A10

TUINDORP OOSTZAAN

A10

Het IJ

BUIKSLOTER-BANNE

AMSTERDAM NOORD

De Volewijckers

Ajax
(1900–07)

Het IJ

AMSTERDAM STOCK EXCHANGE
Ajax partially floated on Amsterdam Stock Exchange in 1998

JORDAAN

THE HEART OF OLD JEWISH AMSTERDAM
Amsterdam's substantial Jewish community was decimated by German deportations during the Second World War

LEIDSEPLEIN
Traditional location for Ajax victory celebration and site of surreal 'happenings' in 1960s

CAFE OOST INDIË
Ajax founded here in Kalverstraat, 18 March 1900

FC Amsterdam
(1972–83)

A M S T E R D A M

HET HOUTEN STADION

A1

Ajax
(1907–34)

DIEMEN

...LOTERVAART

...ORTPARK ...SLOTEN

OLYMPISCH STADION

JEWISH BUTCHERS
In the late 1960s and early 70s Ajax players ritually ate Kosher salami before home games from a Jewish butchers in Beethovenstraat

DE MEER

...auwit

22,500

OUDE STADION
The Netherlands' first purpose built stadium was situated here and opened in 1914. It was demolished in 1928 to make way for the Olympish Stadion

Ajax
(1934–96)

BUITENVELDERT

Amstel

THE NATIONAL DERBY 'De Klassieker'

AJAX	FEYENOORD
	Feyenoord play in Rotterdam

150 matches played

63 Ajax wins
50 Feyenoord wins
37 draws

0   50   100   150   200   250

**NUMBER OF MATCHES
(All first-class games up to May 2004)**

AMSTELVEEN

AMSTERDAM ARENA

AMSTERDAM ZUIDOOST

DE TOEKOMST
Ajax's youth academy

51,324

Ajax
(1996–)

OUDERKERK AAN DE AMSTEL

A2

Amstel

A9

	AJAX 1900
League	**1918, 19,** *28, 30,* **31, 32, 34,** *36,* **37, 39,** *46,* **47, 57, 60, 61, 63,** *66–68,* **69, 70, 71, 72, 73, 77,** *78,* **79, 80, 81, 82, 83, 85,** *86–89,* **90, 91, 92, 94–96, 98, 2002,** *03,* **04**
Cup	*1900,* **17, 43, 61, 67, 68, 70–72,** *78,* **79, 80, 81, 83, 86, 87, 93, 98, 99, 2002,** *1969,* **71–73, 95,** *96*
European Cup	*1969,* **71–73, 95,** *96*
European Cup-Winners' Cup	**1987,** *88*
UEFA Cup	**1992**
World Club Cup	**1972, 95**

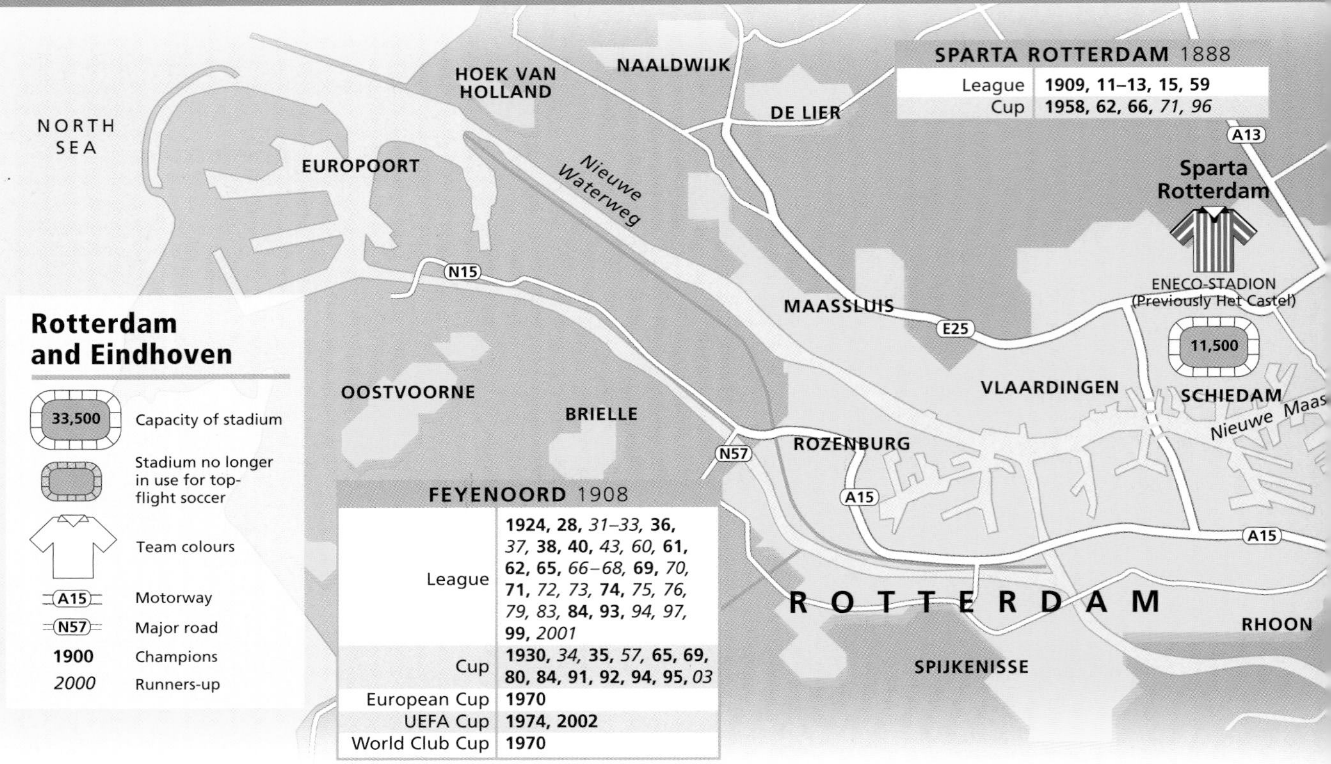

NETHERLANDS

Sparta
Rotterdam

ENECO-STADION
(Previously Het Castel)

11,500

**Rotterdam
and Eindhoven**

33,500	Capacity of stadium
	Stadium no longer in use for top-flight soccer
	Team colours
A15	Motorway
N57	Major road
1900	Champions
2000	Runners-up

FEYENOORD 1908

League	**1924, 28,** 31–33, **36, 37, 38, 40,** 43, 60, **61, 62, 65,** 66–68, **69,** 70, **71,** 72, 73, **74,** 75, 76, 79, 83, **84, 93, 94, 97, 99,** 2001
Cup	**1930,** 34, **35,** 57, **65, 69,** 80, **84, 91, 92, 94, 95,** 03
European Cup	**1970**
UEFA Cup	**1974, 2002**
World Club Cup	**1970**

R O T T E R D A M

Rotterdam and Eindhoven

SOCCER CENTERS

IF THE DUTCH are the Brazilians of European soccer, then Rotterdam is São Paulo – hard working, industrial, no-nonsense, perpetually comparing itself to bohemian glamorous Amsterdam. In soccer terms, the same comparison is made between Feyenoord and Ajax, a fact well demonstrated by the bitterness of their derby matches. Although Feyenoord can claim championships in every decade since the 1960s, and a European Cup in 1970, the team has always remained in Ajax's shadow.

Feyenoord was founded in 1908 in the heart of the old docks area, and there the club remains. Its stadium, De Kuip, was opened in 1937, surviving the carpet bombing of the docks during the Second World War only to disintegrate through neglect before renovation turned it into a venue for the 2000 European Championships.

Bitterness erupts

Feyenoord fans don't all come from Rotterdam, but from right across the Brabant and Zeeland regions as well. In the 1990s a hooligan element emerged; Ajax v Feyenoord matches were often seen as an excuse for organized violence, and fans fought street battles with the police after the Rotterdam club's 1999 championship victory.

The city's second club, Sparta, has scraped along in the top division for most of the century, apart from two golden eras of success in the years before the First World War and in the late 1950s. The city's third team, Excelsior, is as much Feyenoord's nursery club as anything else.

Southeast of Rotterdam, Eindhoven is a prosperous company town. The electronics giant Philips is headquartered there, employing 20 per cent of the population; it founded PSV in 1913 after a company sports event held to celebrate Holland's independence. Considerable sponsorship has seen PSV rise to the top of Dutch soccer. Across town, tiny Eindhoven ekes out an existence in the lower divisions.

Feyenoord was founded in 1908 in the old docks area of Rotterdam close to where its stadium, De Kuip, stands today.

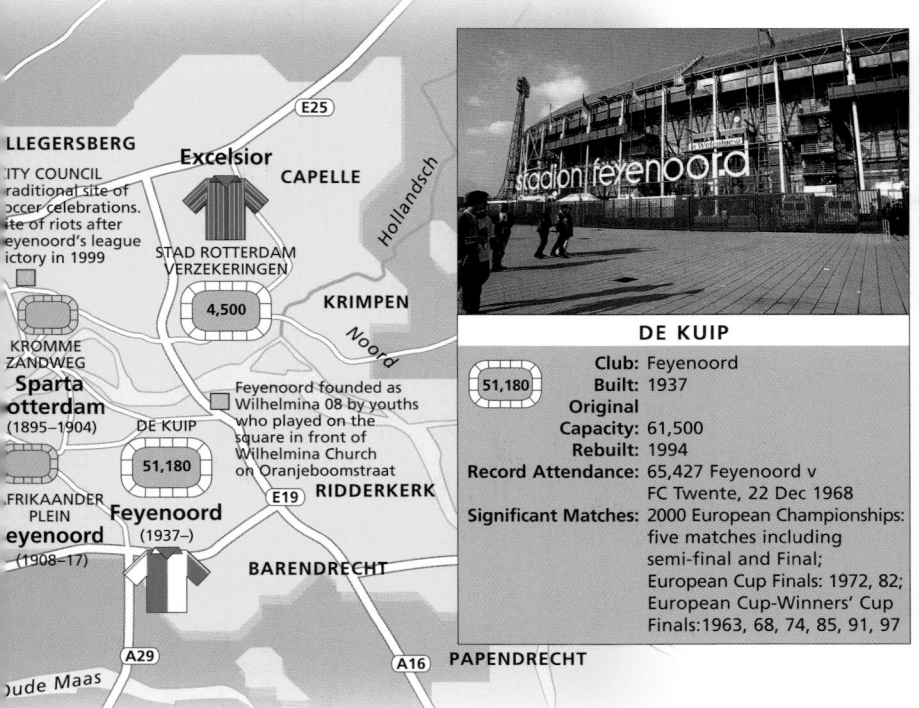

LLEGERSBERG

ITY COUNCIL
raditional site of
occer celebrations.
ite of riots after
eyenoord's league
ictory in 1999

Excelsior

CAPELLE

STAD ROTTERDAM
VERZEKERINGEN

4,500

KRIMPEN

Hollandsch

Noord

KROMME
ZANDWEG

Sparta
otterdam
(1895–1904)

DE KUIP

51,180

Feyenoord founded as
Wilhelmina 08 by youths
who played on the
square in front of
Wilhelmina Church
on Oranjeboomstraat

RIDDERKERK

FRIKAANDER
PLEIN
eyenoord
(1908–17)

Feyenoord
(1937–)

BARENDRECHT

A29

Oude Maas

A16

PAPENDRECHT

DE KUIP

51,180

Club:	Feyenoord
Built:	1937
Original Capacity:	61,500
Rebuilt:	1994
Record Attendance:	65,427 Feyenoord v FC Twente, 22 Dec 1968
Significant Matches:	2000 European Championships: five matches including semi-final and Final; European Cup Finals: 1972, 82; European Cup-Winners' Cup Finals:1963, 68, 74, 85, 91, 97

Heavy policing has been frequent at
*De Kuip stadium since the rise of hooligan
activity among Feyenoord fans in the 1990s.*

NETHERLANDS

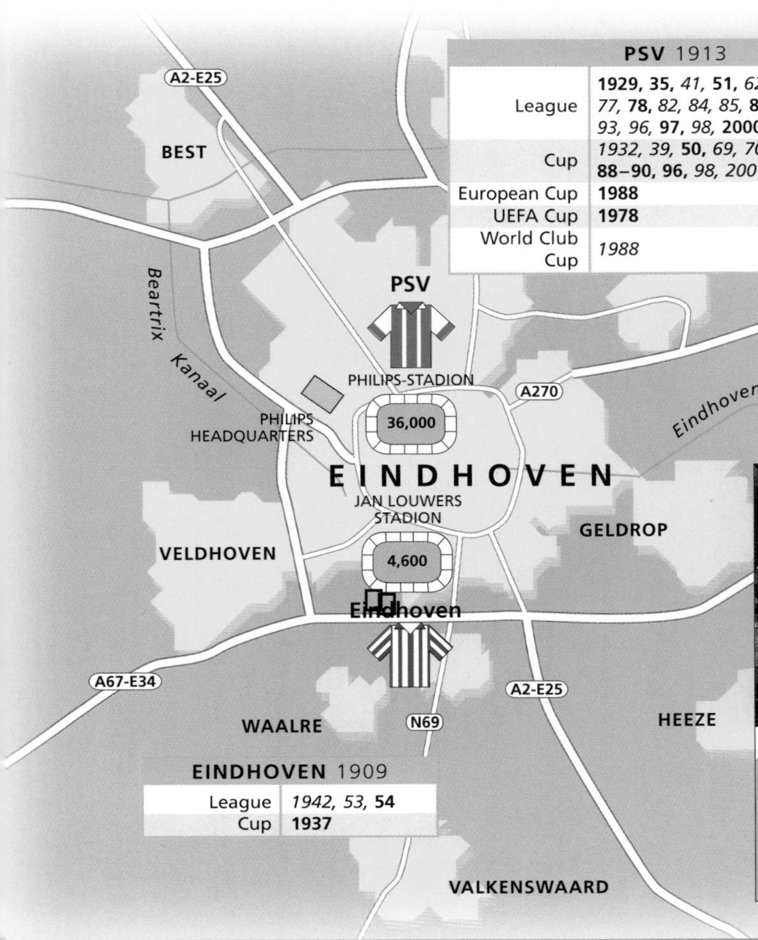

PSV 1913	
League	**1929**, **35**, **41**, **51**, *62*, **63**, **64**, **75**, **76**, *77*, **78**, **82**, **84**, **85**, **86–89**, **90**, **91**, **92**, *93*, *96*, **97**, **98**, **2000**, **01**, *02*, **03**, *04*
Cup	*1932*, **39**, **50**, *69*, *70*, **74**, **76**, **88–90**, **96**, *98*, *2001*
European Cup	**1988**
UEFA Cup	**1978**
World Club Cup	*1988*

A2-E25

BEST

Beartrix

Kanaal

PSV

PHILIPS-STADION

36,000

PHILIPS
HEADQUARTERS

E I N D H O V E N

A270

Eindhovensch Kanaal

JAN LOUWERS
STADION

4,600

VELDHOVEN

GELDROP

A67-E34

Eindhoven

A67-E34

WAALRE

N69

A2-E25

HEEZE

DE BRAAK

4,000

Helmond Sport

HELMOND

N270

N270

ASTEN

Zuid-Willensvaart

EINDHOVEN 1909	
League	*1942*, *53*, **54**
Cup	**1937**

PHILIPS-STADION

36,000

Club:	PSV
Built:	1913
Rebuilt:	1999
Significant Matches:	2000 European Championships: three first-round matches

VALKENSWAARD

Netherlands

FANS AND OWNERS

PROFESSIONALISM AND COMMERCIALISM arrived late in Dutch soccer (1956 was the first professional season) and the ownership of Dutch clubs still reflects the amateur and social club character of the past. While many clubs continue as small membership associations, private investors have begun to take more significant shares in some clubs. PSV remains the property of the electronics giant Philips. Only Ajax has so far explored a further option – partial flotation. In 1997, Ajax was allowed to separate out its membership association and commercial activities. The club retained 70 per cent of the Ajax NV and the rest was sold on the stock market.

These three clubs are in a different league. Their income and attendances dwarf the remaining Dutch clubs though they remain small by European standards. Dutch TV income is particularly low compared to the big leagues. The current economic crisis in Dutch soccer has plunged many clubs into debt and several city councils have been forced to act as lenders of last resort to keep the clubs in operation.

The not-so-jolly orange ranks

Dutch fan culture has many sides: from the newly-fashionable executive boxes of the Ajax Arena to the tiny, windswept stands of the small provincial clubs; from the absurdly jolly, mass-orange ranks that follow the national team; to the organized and violent *ultras* of Feyenoord and Ajax. An early occurrence of violence in Dutch soccer first appeared in the 1970s, when Tottenham fans started fighting at a UEFA Cup tie with Feyenoord. Since then, violence has been concentrated among Ajax, Feyenoord and Den Haag supporters. The peak of trouble was the mid-1980s, and led to intensive and complex policing measures and hefty bans from the courts. The problem has continued to simmer. In March 1997, Feyenoord and Ajax fans fought on an area of wasteland, resulting in one death. In 1999, Feyenoord fans celebrating the club's victory in the league began rioting and fighting with the police in the city streets. In the Netherlands Euro 2000 saw a further development of Dutch policing methods, including highly visible preventative work, which was rewarded with the absence of trouble during the tournament.

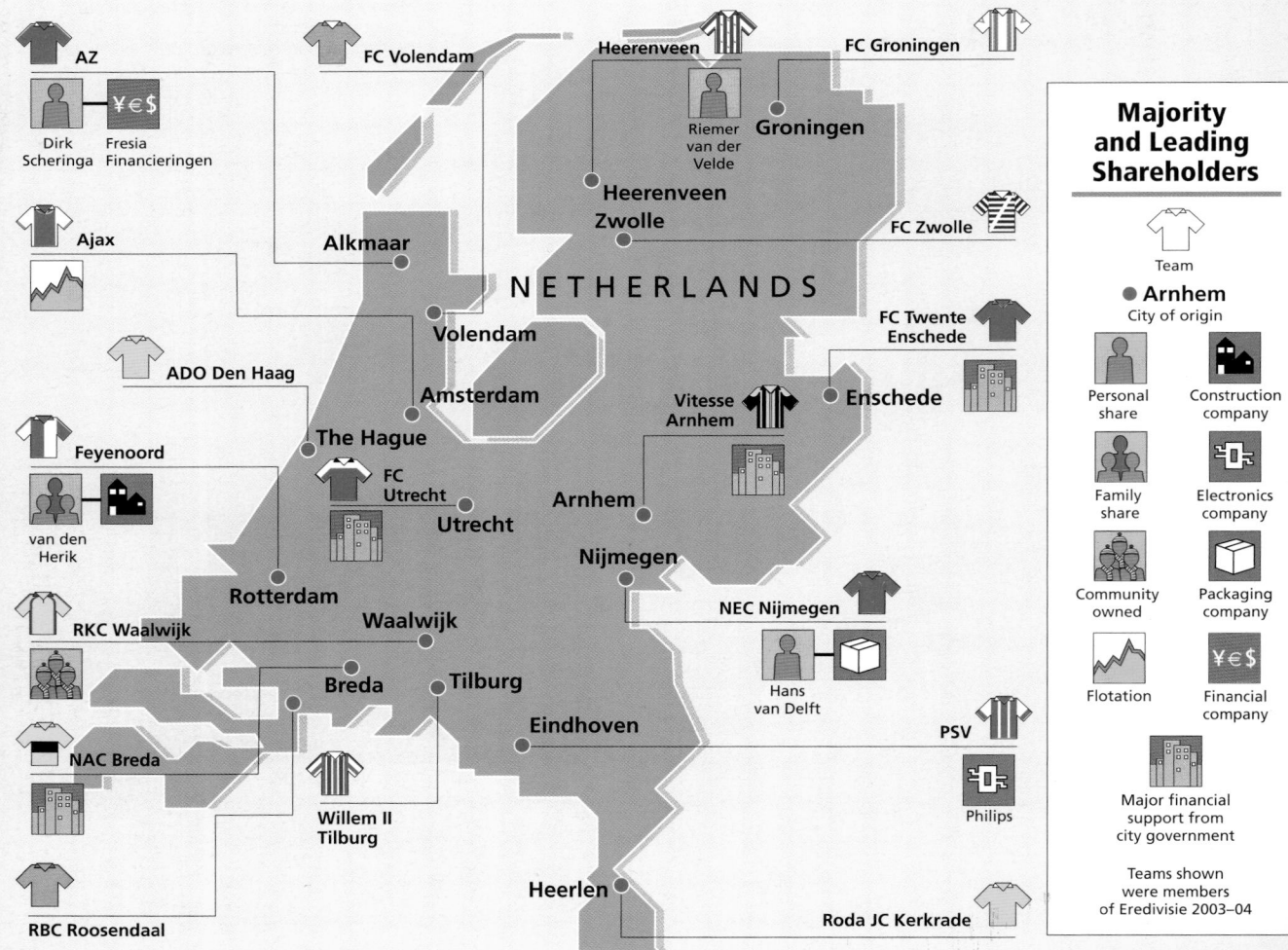

The sight of thousands of orange-clad Dutch fans is common at the Netherlands' international matches.

Club Budgets 2003–04

EUROS (MILLIONS)

TEAMS

Ajax, Vitesse Arnhem, AZ, NAC Breda, ADO Den Haag, Feyenoord, FC Groningen, Heerenveen, Roda JC Kerkrade, NEC Nijmegen, PSV, RBS Roosendaal, FC Twente Enschede, FC Utrecht, FC Volendam, RKC Waalwijk, Willem II Tilburg, FC Zwolle

Rotterdam police arrest a fan after trouble at Feyenoord. In 2002 there has been a resurgence of trouble at Ajax as well, with the club threatening to lock fans out of the Amsterdam Arena.

Dutch Attendances

Attendances for each season

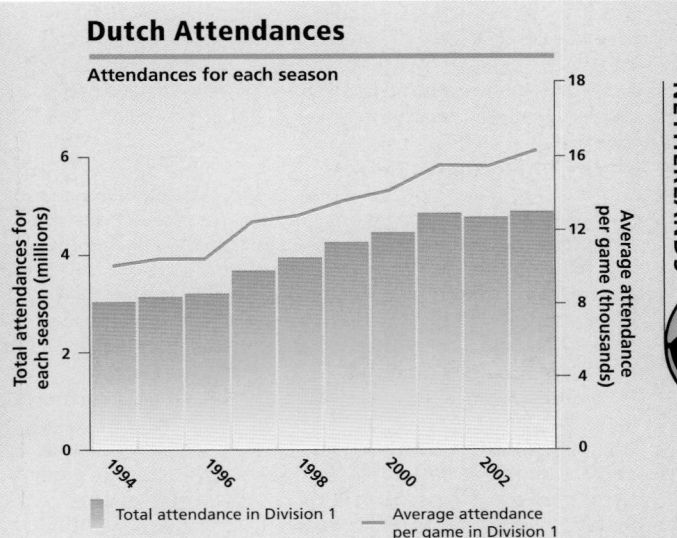

Total attendances for each season (millions)

Average attendance per game (thousands)

1994 1996 1998 2000 2002

Total attendance in Division 1   Average attendance per game in Division 1

NETHERLANDS

Average Attendance

Average attendance for season 2003–04 (thousands)

50 40 30 20 10 0

Capacity

Attendance as a percentage of capacity for season 2003–04 (capacity in brackets)

60% 70% 80% 90% 100%

TEAMS	Capacity
Ajax	(51,324)
Vitesse Arnhem	(29,000)
AZ	(8,320)
NAC Breda	(16,400)
ADO Den Haag	(11,000)
Feyenoord	(51,180)
FC Groningen	(13,000)
Heerenveen	* (14,300)
Roda JC Kerkrade	(19,500)
NEC Nijmegen	(13,500)
PSV	(33,500)
RBC Roosendaal	(4,995)
FC Twente Enschede	(13,350)
FC Utrecht	(25,000)**
FC Volendam	(6,200)
RKC Waalwijk	(7,500)
Willem II	(14,700)
FC Zwolle	(6,800)

* Stadium at Heerenveen is currently undergoing expansion, with the capacity set to increase from 14,300 to 28,000 over the next three years, some expansion has already taken place

** Stadium subject to redevelopment programme 2002–04, 25,000 will be the finished capacity

Riemer van der Velde, president of Heerenveen, has seen attractive small-town soccer pull almost sell-out crowds at home.

Netherlands

PLAYERS AND MANAGERS

ALTHOUGH SOCCER ARRIVED EARLY in the Netherlands, the game did not go professional until 1956, and the only truly great players of this long era were the suitably named Kick Smit and the Italian-suited Faas Wilkes, the dribble-king, whose departure to Valencia triggered the start of professionalism.

In their wake, Dutch soccer was transformed by the social and sporting innovations of the 1960s. From the Ajax crucible of total soccer and the anti-authoritarian politics of the time a new kind of Dutch footballer was born. Exemplified by Johan Cruyff, Dutch soccer players have come to prize technique and tactics above all else. Individual artistry, speed of thought, movement and accurate perception of space have become the hallmark of two generations of Dutch players since the amateur era. Along with Cruyff in the first wave of total soccer players were Ruud Krol, Johan Neeskens and Johnny Rep. But self-possession, self-belief and ardent individualism among Dutch players has also been nurtured, and this has made for loose and fragmented teams.

More players overseas

In the 1980s, players of Surinamese origin, like Ruud Gullit and Frank Rijkaard, began to take their place in the Dutch team, and in the 1990s the ethnic divisions within the Dutch national squad boiled over into open conflict. With the advent of Cruyff, Dutch players started playing abroad in significant numbers and today their leading players are more likely to play overseas than those of any other leading European soccer nation: Edgar Davids, Dennis Bergkamp, Patrick Kluivert, Marc Overmars and the de Boer brothers have all played the bulk of their careers in Spain, Italy and Britain. Ruud van Nistelrooy, now of Manchester United, is just the latest in a long line of homegrown players whose exceptional performances in the Netherlands have seen them transfer overseas. Sadly for a country whose players possess so much talent, the national team has become the biggest underachiever in Europe.

Dutch coaches have proved almost as cosmopolitan as their players – Dick Advocaat coached Glasgow Rangers, Johan Cruyff coached Barcelona, Guus Hiddink won tremendous praise for his coaching of the South Korean national team at the 2002 World Cup, while Leo Beenhakker has recently made his way to Mexico's biggest club, América.

Top 15 International Caps

PLAYER	CAPS	GOALS	FIRST MATCH	LAST MATCH
Frank de Boer*	112	13	1990	2004
Edwin van der Sar*	89	0	1995	2004
Marc Overmars*	86	17	1993	2004
Phillip Cocu*	84	7	1996	2004
Aron Winter	84	6	1987	2000
Ruud Krol	83	4	1969	1983
Dennis Bergkamp*	79	37	1990	2000
Patrick Kluivert*	79	40	1994	2004
Ronald Koeman	77	14	1983	1994
Clarence Seedorf*	77	11	1994	2004
Hans van Breukelen	73	0	1980	1992
Frank Rijkaard	73	10	1981	1994
Michael Reiziger*	72	2	1994	2004
Jan Wouters	70	4	1982	1994
Edgar Davids*	68	6	1994	2004

Top 10 International Goalscorers

PLAYER	GOALS	CAPS	FIRST MATCH	LAST MATCH
Patrick Kluivert*	40	79	1994	2004
Dennis Bergkamp*	37	79	1990	2000
Faas Wilkes	35	38	1946	1961
Johan Cruyff	33	47	1966	1977
Abe Lenstra	33	48	1940	1959
Bep Bakhuys	28	23	1928	1937
Kick Smit	26	29	1934	1946
Marco van Basten	23	58	1983	1992
Leen Vente	19	21	1933	1940
Ruud van Nistelrooy*	19	38	1998	2004

* Indicates players still playing at least at club level.

Netherlands International Managers

DATES	NAME	GAMES	WON	DRAWN	LOST
1973	Frantisek Fadrhonc	5	3	2	0
1974	Rinus Michels	10	6	3	1
1974–76	Georg Knobel	15	9	1	5
1976–77	Jan Zwartkruis	5	4	1	0
1977–78	Ernst Happel and Jan Zwartkruis	13	8	3	2
1978–81	Jan Zwartkruis	22	8	6	8
1981	Rob Baan	3	3	0	0
1981–84	Kees Rijvers	19	9	3	7
1984–85	Rinus Michels	34	19	8	7
1985–86	Leo Beenhakker	7	4	1	2
1986–88	Rinus Michels	20	12	5	3
1988–90	Thijs Lijbregts	13	6	4	3
1990	Leo Beenhakker	6	1	3	2
1990–92	Rinus Michels	19	11	4	4
1992–95	Dick Advocaat	26	15	5	6
1995–98	Guus Hiddink	37	22	7	8
1998–2000	Frank Rijkaard	22	11	8	3
2000–02	Louis van Gaal	14	8	4	2
2002–	Dick Advocaat	28	15	7	6

All figures correct as of 30 June 2004.

Foreign Players in the Netherlands
(in top division squads)

2003–04

16 CONMEBOL
2 CONCACAF
32 CAF
5 AFC
4 OFC
110 UEFA
169
Total

Key
Total Players
Foreign Players
%

The Dutch national team has had little success during the last 30 years despite the amount of talent available. The most successful team was this one that won the European Championships in 1988 and which included (back row, left to right) van Basten, R. Koeman, Rijkaard, E. Koeman, Gullit, van Breukelen; (front row) van Tiggelen, Muhren, van Aerle, Wouters, Vaneburg.

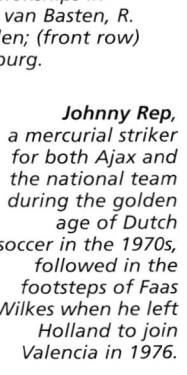

Johnny Rep, a mercurial striker for both Ajax and the national team during the golden age of Dutch soccer in the 1970s, followed in the footsteps of Faas Wilkes when he left Holland to join Valencia in 1976.

Player of the Year

YEAR	PLAYER	CLUB
1984	Gullit	Feyenoord
1985	van Basten	Ajax
1986	Gullit	PSV
1987	R. Koeman	PSV
1988	R. Koeman	PSV
1989	Romario	PSV
1990	Wouters	Ajax
1991	Bergkamp	Ajax
1992	Bergkamp	Ajax
1993	Litmanen	Ajax
1994	R. de Boer	Ajax
1995	Nilis	PSV
1996	R. de Boer	Ajax
1997	Stam	PSV
1998–99	van Nistelrooy	PSV
1999–2000	van Nistelrooy	PSV
2000–01	van Bommel	PSV
2001–02	van Hooijdonk	Feyenoord
2002–03	Kezman	PSV
2003–04	Maxwell	Ajax

Manager of the Year

YEAR	MANAGER	CLUB
1996	Louis van Gaal	Ajax
1997	Foppe de Haan	Heerenveen
1998–99	Leo Beenhakker	Feyenoord
1999–2000	Foppe de Haan	Heerenveen
2000–01	Martin Jol	RKC Wallwijk
2001–02	Bert van Marwijk	Feyenoord
2002–03	Ronald Koeman	Ajax
2003–04	Co Adriaanse	AZ

Awarded by the Dutch Professional Footballers' Association.

Top Goalscorers by Season 1956–2004

SEASON	PLAYER	CLUB	GOALS
1956–57	Dillen	PSV	43
1957–58	Canjels	NAC Breda	32
1958–59	Canjels	NAC Breda	34
1959–60	Henk Groot	Ajax	38
1960–61	Henk Groot	Ajax	41
1961–62	Tol	Volendam	27
1962–63	Kerkhoffs	PSV	22
1963–64	Guertsen	DWS	28
1964–65	Guertsen	DWS	23
1965–66	van der Kuijlen	PSV	23
1965–66	Kruiver	Feyenoord	23
1966–67	Cruyff	Ajax	33
1967–68	Kindvall	Feyenoord	28
1968–69	van Dijk	FC Twente	30
1969–70	van der Kuijlen	PSV	26
1970–71	Kindvall	Feyenoord	24
1971–72	Cruyff	Ajax	25
1972–73	Janssens	NEC	18
1972–73	Brokamp	MVV	18
1973–74	van der Kuijlen	PSV	27
1974–75	Geels	Ajax	30
1975–76	Geels	Ajax	29
1976–77	Geels	Ajax	34
1977–78	Geels	Ajax	30
1978–79	Kist	AZ 67 Alkmaar	34
1979–80	Kist	AZ 67 Alkmaar	27

SEASON	PLAYER	CLUB	GOALS
1980–81	Geels	Sparta R	22
1981–82	Kieft	Ajax	32
1982–83	Houtman	Feyenoord	30
1983–84	van Basten	Ajax	28
1984–85	van Basten	Ajax	22
1985–86	van Basten	Ajax	37
1986–87	van Basten	Ajax	31
1987–88	Kieft	PSV	29
1988–89	Romario	PSV	19
1989–90	Romario	PSV	23
1990–91	Romario	PSV	25
1991–92	Bergkamp	Ajax	24
1992–93	Bergkamp	Ajax	26
1993–94	Litmanen	Ajax	26
1994–95	Ronaldo	PSV	30
1995–96	Nilis	PSV	21
1996–97	Nilis	PSV	21
1997–98	Machlas	Vitesse Arnhem	34
1998–99	van Nistelrooy	PSV	31
1999–2000	van Nistelrooy	PSV	29
2000–01	Kezman	PSV	24
2001–02	van Hooijdonk	Feyenoord	24
2002–03	Kezman	PSV	35
2003–04	Kezman	PSV	31

Netherlands

EREDIVISIE 1982–2003

IN 1981, THE SMALL PROVINCIAL CLUB AZ Alkmaar finally broke the stranglehold of the big three – Ajax, Feyenoord and PSV – by taking the Dutch league title. It was not to last, however, and the next 20 seasons have all gone to one of the big three. Ajax was the first to revive when Johan Cruyff came home from his foreign travels and took the club to two consecutive titles, including a league and cup double in 1983. Alongside Cruyff, the next generation of Dutch internationals was maturing, including the gangly 17-year-old Marco van Basten, Frank Rijkaard, Dennis Bergkamp and Aron Winter. Cruyff left Ajax in 1984, to manage its old rival Feyenoord. There he joined the young Ruud Gullit in a magical display of intelligent and zestful soccer. But financial decline and poor attendances followed, and the club was close to bankruptcy before being rejuvenated in the early 1990s by the money of building magnate Jorein van den Herik.

The rise of PSV

A further title for Ajax in 1985 was a prelude to the dominance of PSV. A top three spot for the team in the previous five seasons was finally converted into a title in 1986. PSV would go on to win another five titles in six years; only Ajax in 1990 under Leo Beenhakker could stop them. PSV was initially led by Hans Kraay, who systematically bought the leading players of the other top clubs in the country: Ruud Gullit came in from Feyenoord, Ronald Koeman from Ajax; two titles and a European Cup in 1987 followed. New manager Guus Hiddink added the goalscoring Wim Kieft and Dutch international goalkeeper Hans van Breukelen, and the titles kept coming. Gullit was eventually sold to Milan and with the proceeds PSV bought Brazilian striker Romario. He delivered over 100 goals in five seasons before leaving for Barcelona.

Ajax before Bosman

The rejuvenated Feyenoord under manager Wim Jansen took a surprise title in 1993. Then the new Ajax of Louis van Gaal, previously the club's youth coach, burst on the scene. Drawing on the legendary youth scouting and coaching system at the club, van Gaal nurtured and drilled a new generation of young Dutch internationals: Davids, Seedorf, Overmars, Bogarde, the De Boer brothers and Patrick Kluivert. Fast passing, awesome team play and deadly striking brought three titles and a European Cup. But with the Bosman ruling on transfers coming into force and the perennial pressures of money on the club, the squad was quickly scattered across Europe's biggest clubs. In the late 1990s, with no single dominant club, titles were split between PSV, Ajax and Feyenoord. The lack of competition

In 1984 the Feyenoord team featured Johan Cruyff, in his final playing year, and the rising star Ruud Gullit. The team took an unexpected and unforgettable title. This picture shows Ruud Gullit in action for Feyenoord against Fortuna Sittard.

Key to Champions' Winning Margin

Ajax · Feyenoord · SC Heerenveen · PSV · Roda JC · Willem II

lower down the league, and the meagre income from gates and television compared to the bigger European leagues, has left the big three looking for an alternative league to play in: Ajax and PSV have been leading forces in campaigning for the creation of either an Atlantic League (with the biggest clubs from western Europe's smaller nations) or a joint league with Belgium.

Ruud's roots

Among the challengers, the tiny SC Heerenveen has been the most surprising. Under a new president and coach in the early 1990s, Riemer van der Velde and Foppe de Haan respectively, the club has seen regular European competition. Clever buys from smaller soccer nations like Denmark, Finland and Romania were combined with nurturing and selling its own talent: Ruud van Nistlerooy being the greatest success. Vitesse Arnhem, under chairman Karel Aalbers, avoided bankruptcy in 1991, built the new Gelredrome stadium, but has yet to do better than third. Regular Eredivisie members include the solidly supported but limited charms of FC Twente Enschede, Roda JC Kerkrade, AZ from Alkmaar and FC Utrecht. While down at the bottom, a range of clubs come up and down the divisions and contemplate mergers and reorganizations in an effort to stay afloat.

CARS
BATAVU

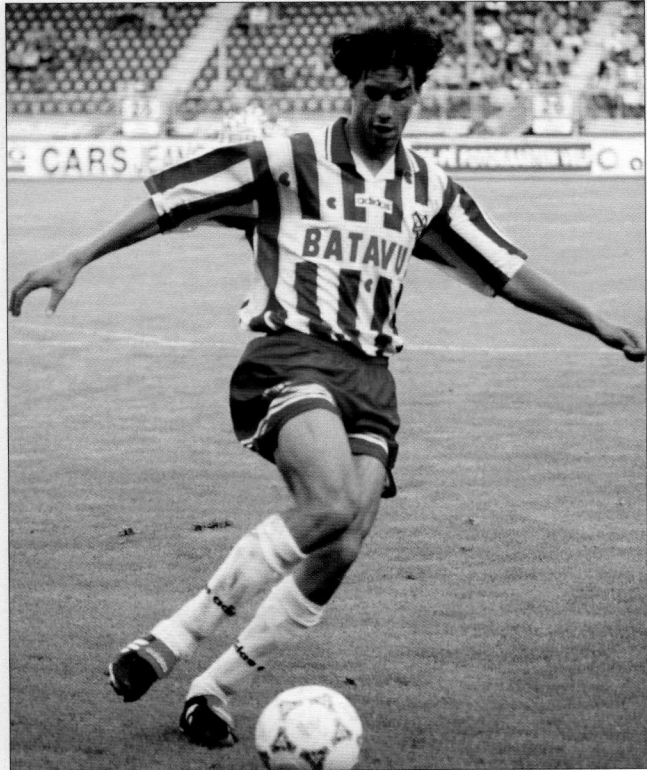

Ruud van Nistelrooy's *career typifies the dilemmas of Dutch soccer. A ruthless striker, he has migrated from tiny SC Heerenveen to PSV and on to Manchester United. He is one of many great players lost by a Dutch domestic game which cannot currently pay them enough.*

Champions' Winning Margin 1993–2003

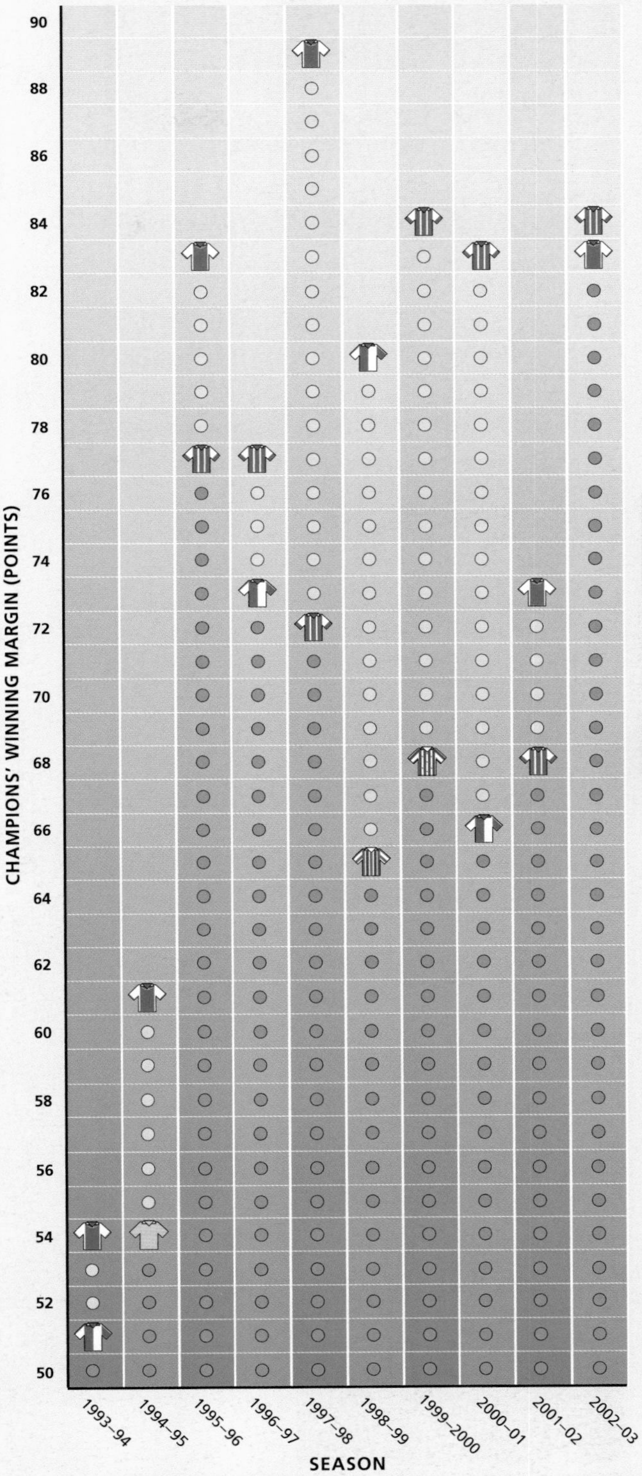
CHAMPIONS' WINNING MARGIN (POINTS)
90
88
86
84
82
80
78
76
74
72
70
68
66
64
62
60
58
56
54
52
50
1993–94
1994–95
1995–96
1996–97
1997–98
1998–99
1999–2000
2000–01
2001–02
2002–03
SEASON

34	34	34	34	34	34	34	34	34	34

Total games played by each team
(2 points awarded for a win until 1996, when 3 points awarded)

NETHERLANDS

The strongest side in the Netherlands in the late 1990s, PSV is the model of a medium-sized modern club: it has corporate backing; it is careful in its transfer dealings; it has had huge domestic success, but has a poor record in Europe.

NETHERLANDS

Louis van Gaal, whose great young Ajax squads of the mid-1990s climbed the peaks of Dutch and European soccer, only to be dismembered in the transfer market, with van Gaal himself moving to Barcelona.

Ronald Koeman made a mid-season switch in 2001–02 from Vitesse Arnhem to Ajax and took the club from a mid-table wobble to a league and cup double.

Key to League Positions Table

- League champions
- Season of promotion to league
- Season of relegation from league
- Other teams playing in league
- 5 — Final position in league

Dutch League Positions 1982–2003

TEAM	1982-83	1983-84	1984-85	1985-86	1986-87	1987-88	1988-89	1989-90	1990-91	1991-92	1992-93	1993-94	1994-95	1995-96	1996-97	1997-98	1998-99	1999-2000	2000-01	2001-02	2002-03
Ajax	1	3	1	2	2	2	2	1	2	2	3	1	1	1	4	1	6	5	3	1	2
Vitesse Arnhem								4	5	4	4	4	6	5	5	3	4	4	6	5	14
AZ	11	5	13	9	15	16									18		9	7	13	10	10
FC Den Bosch		10	6	6	10	7	7	17			17							18		16	
NAC Breda	17		17								7	10	8	9	12	18			9	6	4
Dordrecht '90									16	15	18		18								
DS '79		18				18															
Excelsior	9	13	12	15	18																17
Feyenoord	2	1	3	3	3	6	4	11	8	3	1	2	4	3	2	4	1	3	2	3	3
Go Ahead Eagles	12	12	15	10	16						15	12	17	18							
De Graafschap										17				14	8	11	13	14	15	14	18
FC Groningen	5	7	5	4	13	11	6	9	3	5	12	15	13	9	10	17			14	15	15
ADO Den Haag					14	17		10	14	16											
Haarlem	7	4	9	11	12	9	10	18													
SC Heerenveen									17			13	9	7	7	6	7	2	10	4	7
Helmond Sport	15	16																			
SC Heracles				18																	
Roda JC Kerkrade	6	9	11	5	4	15	5	5	10	9	11	6	2	4	6	14	5	8	4	13	6
SC Cambuur Leeuwarden											14	18					15	17			
MVV		14	16			14	15	15	7	7	10	16					15	14	16		
NEC	18		17						16	18			15	17	17	8	11	15	12	9	5
PSV	3	2	2	1	1	1	1	2	1	1	2	3	3	2	1	2	3	1	1	2	1
RBC Roosendaal																			18		13
Sparta Rotterdam	4	6	4	7	8	12	12	12	13	8	13	9	14	6	13	13	17	13	17	17	
Fortuna Sittard	8	11	7	8	9	8	8	7	12	14	16				13	11	7	10	12	16	18
FC Twente Enschede	16		8	14	7	3	3	6	6	5	5	5	10	3	9	8	6		11	12	12
FC Utrecht	10	8	10	12	6	10	13	14	4	11	8	14	12	15	12	10	12	10	5	7	8
BV Veendam					17		18														
VVV Venlo				13	5	5	17			18		17									
FC Volendam		15	16				14	9	6	9	13	6	11	11	16	14	18				
RKC Waalwijk							11	8	7	10	9	16	8	11	16	16	16	11	7	8	9
Willem II	14	17				4	15	13	11	12	10	8	7	12	15	5	2	9	8	11	11
FC Zwolle	13	14	18		11	13	16														16

Since the mid-1990s it is Eindhoven rather than Amsterdam that has hosted the majority of championship celebrations as PSV has taken over the mantle of the top team in the Netherlands. In 2002–03 the city's replica championship plate sellers had a field day.

Eredivisie

Ajax — Team name

League champions/runners-up

1985, *86* — Champions in bold Runners-up in italics

Other teams in the Eredivisie

● **Amsterdam** — City of origin

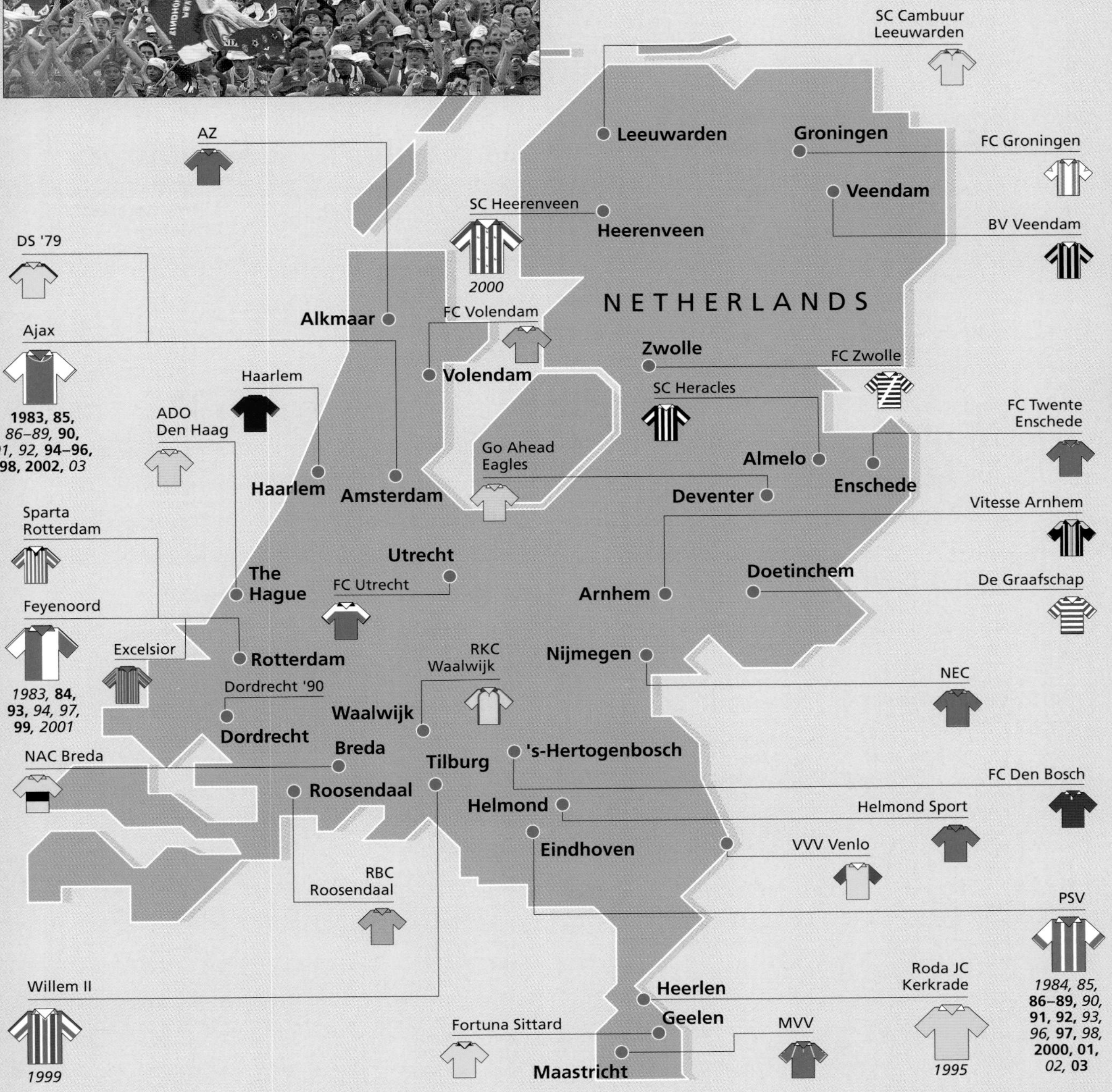

NETHERLANDS

N E T H E R L A N D S

SC Cambuur Leeuwarden

● Leeuwarden
Groningen
FC Groningen

AZ

● **Veendam**
BV Veendam

SC Heerenveen
2000

● **Heerenveen**

DS '79

Ajax

1983, 85, 86–89, 90, 91, 92, 94–96, 98, 2002, *03*

● **Alkmaar**
FC Volendam

● **Volendam**

Zwolle ●
FC Zwolle

SC Heracles

FC Twente Enschede

Haarlem

ADO Den Haag

● **Haarlem**

Go Ahead Eagles

● **Almelo**

● Deventer

● **Enschede**

Vitesse Arnhem

Sparta Rotterdam

● Amsterdam

Utrecht ●
FC Utrecht

● Doetinchem
De Graafschap

Feyenoord

1983, 84, 93, 94, 97, 99, *2001*

Excelsior

● **The Hague**

● **Rotterdam**

RKC Waalwijk

● Nijmegen
NEC

Dordrecht '90

● **Waalwijk**

NAC Breda

● **Dordrecht**

● **Breda**

● Tilburg

● 's-Hertogenbosch
FC Den Bosch

● **Roosendaal**

● Helmond
Helmond Sport

RBC Roosendaal

● **Eindhoven**
VVV Venlo

PSV

Willem II

1999

● **Heerlen**

● Geelen

MVV

Roda JC Kerkrade
1995

1984, 85, 86–89, 90, 91, 92, 93, 96, *97,* **98, 2000, 01,** *02,* **03**

Fortuna Sittard

● **Maastricht**

Netherlands

Koninklijke Nederlandsche Voetbalbond
Founded: 1889
Joined FIFA: 1904
Joined UEFA: 1954

SOCCER ARRIVED EARLY in the Netherlands with the first clubs being set up in the late 1870s. But somehow it took until 1956 for a fully-fledged national league to develop. The amateur era in Dutch soccer ran from the first national competition in 1898 until the legalization of professionalism in 1956.

It is truly extraordinary that despite being enveloped by two world wars the Netherlands has only lost one league season (1945) to social and political chaos.

Dutch Amateur League Record 1898–1956

SEASON	CHAMPIONS	RUNNERS-UP
1898	RAP Amsterdam	Vitesse Arnhem
1899	RAP Amsterdam	PW Enschede
1900	HVV Den Haag	Victoria Wageningen
1901	HVV Den Haag	Victoria Wageningen
1902	HVV Den Haag	Victoria Wageningen
1903	HVV Den Haag	Vitesse Arnhem
1904	HBS Den Haag	Velocitas Breda
1905	HVV Den Haag	PW Enschede
1906	HBS Den Haag	PW Enschede
1907	HVV Den Haag	PW Enschede
1908	Quick Den Haag	UD
1909	Sparta Rotterdam	Wilhelmina
1910	HVV Den Haag	Quick Nijmegen
1911	Sparta Rotterdam	GVC
1912	Sparta Rotterdam	GVC
1913	Sparta Rotterdam	Vitesse Arnhem
1914	HVV Den Haag	Vitesse Arnhem
1915	Sparta Rotterdam	Vitesse Arnhem
1916	Willem II	Go Ahead Deventer
1917	Go Ahead Deventer	UVV
1918	Ajax	Go Ahead Deventer
1919	Ajax	Go Ahead Deventer
1920	Be Quick Groningen	VOC Rotterdam
1921	NAC Breda	Be Quick Groningen
1922	Go Ahead Deventer	Blauw-Wit Amsterdam
1923	RCH Haarlem	Be Quick Groningen
1924	Feyenoord	Stormvogels Velsen
1925	HBS Den Haag	NAC Breda
1926	SC Enschede	MVV Maastricht
1927	Heracles Almelo	NAC Breda
1928	Feyenoord	Ajax
1929	PSV	Go Ahead Deventer
1930	Go Ahead Deventer	Ajax
1931	Ajax	Feyenoord
1932	Ajax	Feyenoord
1933	Go Ahead Deventer	Feyenoord
1934	Ajax	KFC Alkmaar
1935	PSV	Go Ahead Deventer
1936	Feyenoord	Ajax
1937	Ajax	Feyenoord
1938	Feyenoord	Heracles Almelo
1939	Ajax	DWS Amsterdam
1940	Feyenoord	Blauw-Wit Amsterdam
1941	Heracles Almelo	PSV
1942	ADO Den Haag	Eindhoven
1943	ADO Den Haag	Feyenoord
1944	De Volewijckers	VUC Den Haag
1945	*no championship*	
1946	Haarlem	Ajax
1947	Ajax	SC Heerenveen
1948	BVV Hertogenbosch	SC Heerenveen

Dutch Amateur League Record (*continued*)

SEASON	CHAMPIONS	RUNNERS-UP
1949	SVV Schiedam	BVV Hertogenbosch
1950	Limburg Brunssue	Blauw-Wit Amsterdam
1951	PSV	DWS Amsterdam
1952	Willem II	Hermes Schiedam
1953	RCH Haarlem	Eindhoven
1954	Eindhoven	DOS Utrecht
1955	Willem II	NAC Breda
1956	Rapid JC Heerlen	NAC Breda

Dutch Professional League Record 1957–2004

SEASON	CHAMPIONS	RUNNERS-UP
1957	Ajax	Fortuna '54 Geleen
1958	DOS Utrecht	SC Enschede
1959	Sparta Rotterdam	Rapid JC Heerlen
1960	Ajax	Feyenoord
1961	Feyenoord	Ajax
1962	Feyenoord	PSV
1963	PSV	Ajax
1964	DWS Amsterdam	PSV
1965	Feyenoord	DWS Amsterdam
1966	Ajax	Feyenoord
1967	Ajax	Feyenoord
1968	Ajax	Feyenoord
1969	Feyenoord	Ajax
1970	Ajax	Feyenoord
1971	Feyenoord	Ajax
1972	Ajax	Feyenoord
1973	Ajax	Feyenoord
1974	Feyenoord	FC Twente
1975	PSV	Feyenoord
1976	PSV	Feyenoord
1977	Ajax	PSV
1978	PSV	Ajax
1979	Ajax	Feyenoord
1980	Ajax	AZ 67 Alkmaar
1981	AZ 67 Alkmaar	Ajax
1982	Ajax	PSV
1983	Ajax	Feyenoord
1984	Feyenoord	PSV
1985	Ajax	PSV
1986	PSV	Ajax
1987	PSV	Ajax
1988	PSV	Ajax
1989	PSV	Ajax
1990	Ajax	PSV
1991	PSV	Ajax
1992	PSV	Ajax
1993	Feyenoord	PSV
1994	Ajax	Feyenoord
1995	Ajax	Roda JC
1996	Ajax	PSV
1997	PSV	Feyenoord
1998	Ajax	PSV
1999	Feyenoord	Willem II
2000	PSV	SC Heerenveen
2001	PSV	Feyenoord
2002	Ajax	PSV
2003	PSV	Ajax
2004	Ajax	PSV

Dutch League Summary

TEAM	TOTALS	CHAMPIONS & RUNNERS-UP (BOLD) (ITALICS)
Ajax	29, 17	**1918, 19,** *28, 30,* **31, 32, 34,** *36,* **37, 39, 46, 47, 57, 60, 61, 63,** *66–68,* **69, 70, 71,** *72,* **73, 77, 78, 79, 80, 81, 82, 83, 85,** *86–89,* **90,** *91, 92,* **94–96, 98, 2002,** *03,* **04**
PSV	17, 13	**1929,** *35,* **41,** *51,* **62,** *63,* **64, 75, 76, 77, 78,** *82,* **84,** *85,* **86–89, 90, 91, 92,** *93, 96, 97, 98,* **2000,** *01, 02, 03,* **04**
Feyenoord	14, 19	**1924,** *28, 31–33,* **36,** *37,* **38,** *40, 43, 60,* **61,** *62,* **65,** *66–68,* **69,** *70, 71, 72, 73,* **74, 75,** *76,* **79,** *83,* **84,** *93, 94,* **97,** *99,* **2001**
HVV Den Haag	8, 0	**1900–03, 05, 07, 10, 14**
Sparta Rotterdam	6, 0	**1909, 11–13, 15, 59**
Go Ahead Deventer	4, 5	*1916,* **17,** *18, 19,* **22,** *29, 30, 33,* **35**
Willem II	3, 1	**1916,** *52,* **55,** *99*
HBS Den Haag	3, 0	**1904, 06, 25**

This summary only features clubs that have won the Dutch League three times or more. For a full list of league champions and runners-up please see the League Records opposite.

Dutch Cup Record 1899–2004

YEAR	WINNERS	SCORE	RUNNERS-UP
1899	RAP Amsterdam	1-0 (aet)	HVV Den Haag
1900	Velocitas Breda	3-1	Ajax
1901	HBS Den Haag	4-3	RAP Amsterdam
1902	Haarlem	2-1	HBS Den Haag
1903	HVV Den Haag	6-1	HBS Den Haag
1904	HFC Haarlem	3-1	HVV Den Haag
1905	VOC Rotterdam	3-0	HBS Den Haag
1906	Concordia	3-2	Volharding
1907	VOC Rotterdam	4-3 (aet)	Voolwaarts
1908	HBS Den Haag	3-1	VOC Rotterdam
1909	Quick Den Haag	2-0	VOC Rotterdam
1910	Quick Den Haag	2-0	HVV Den Haag
1911	Quick Den Haag	1-0	Haarlem
1912	Haarlem	2-0	Vitesse Arnhem
1913	HFC Haarlem	4-1	DFC Dordrecht
1914	DFC Dordrecht	3-2	Haarlem
1915	HFC Haarlem	1-0	HBS Den Haag
1916	Quick Den Haag	2-1 (aet)	HBS Den Haag
1917	Ajax	5-0	VSV Velsen
1918	RCH Haarlem	2-1	VVA
1919		no competition	
1920	CVV	2-1	VUC Den Haag
1921	Schoten	2-1	RFC
1922–24		no competition	
1925	ZFC	5-1	Xerxes
1926	LONGA Lichtenvoorde	5-2	De Spartan
1927	VUC Den Haag	3-1	Vitesse Arnhem
1928	RCH Haarlem	2-0	PEC Zwolle
1929		no competition	
1930	Feyenoord	1-0	Excelsior
1931		no competition	
1932	DFC Dordrecht	5-4 (aet)	PSV
1933		no competition	
1934	Velocitas Groningen	3-2 (aet)	Feyenoord
1935	Feyenoord	5-2	Helmondia
1936	Roermond	4-2	KFC Alkmaar
1937	Eindhoven	1-0	De Spartan
1938	VSV Velsen	4-1	AGOVV
1939	Wageningen	2-1 (aet)	PSV
1940–42		no competition	
1943	Ajax	3-2	DFC Dordrecht
1944	Willem II	9-2	Groene Star
1945–47		no competition	
1948	Wageningen	0-0 (aet)(2-1 pens)	DWV
1949	Quick Nijmegen	1-1 (aet)(2-1 pens)	Helmondia
1950	PSV	4-3	Haarlem
1951–56		no competition	

Dutch Cup Record (continued)

YEAR	WINNERS	SCORE	RUNNERS-UP
1957	Fortuna '54 Geelen	4-2	Feyenoord
1958	Sparta Rotterdam	4-3	Volendam
1959	VVV Venlo	4-1	ADO Den Haag
1960		no competition	
1961	Ajax	3-0	NAC Breda
1962	Sparta Rotterdam	1-0 (aet)	DHC
1963	Willem II	3-0	ADO Den Haag
1964	Fortuna '54 Geelen	0-0 (aet)(4-3 pens)	ADO Den Haag
1965	Feyenoord	1-0	Go Ahead Deventer
1966	Sparta Rotterdam	1-0	ADO Den Haag
1967	Ajax	2-1 (aet)	NAC Breda
1968	ADO Den Haag	2-1	Ajax
1969	Feyenoord	1-1 (aet), (replay) 2-0	PSV
1970	Ajax	2-0	PSV
1971	Ajax	2-2 (aet), (replay) 2-1	Sparta Rotterdam
1972	Ajax	3-2	FC Den Haag
1973	NAC Breda	2-0	NEC Nijmegen
1974	PSV	6-0	NAC Breda
1975	FC Den Haag	1-0	FC Twente
1976	PSV	1-0 (aet)	Roda JC Kerkrade
1977	FC Twente	3-0 (aet)	PEC Zwolle
1978	AZ 67 Alkmaar	1-0	Ajax
1979	Ajax	1-1 (aet), (replay) 3-0	FC Twente
1980	Feyenoord	3-1	Ajax
1981	AZ 67 Alkmaar	3-1	Ajax
1982	AZ 67 Alkmaar	5-1, 0-1 (2 legs)	FC Utrecht
1983	Ajax	3-1, 3-1 (2 legs)	NEC Nijmegen
1984	Feyenoord	1-0	Fortuna Sittard
1985	FC Utrecht	1-0	Helmond Sport
1986	Ajax	3-0	RBC Roosendaal
1987	Ajax	4-2	FC Den Haag
1988	PSV	3-2	Roda JC Kerkrade
1989	PSV	4-1	FC Groningen
1990	PSV	1-0	Vitesse Arnhem
1991	Feyenoord	1-0	BVV Den Bosch
1992	Feyenoord	3-0	Roda JC Kerkrade
1993	Ajax	6-2	SC Heerenveen
1994	Feyenoord	2-1	NEC Nijmegen
1995	Feyenoord	2-1	Volendam
1996	PSV	5-2	Sparta Rotterdam
1997	Roda JC Kerkrade	4-2	SC Heerenveen
1998	Ajax	5-0	PSV
1999	Ajax	2-0	Fortuna Sittard
2000	Roda JC Kerkrade	2-0	NEC Nijmegen
2001	FC Twente	0-0 (aet)(4-3 pens)	PSV
2002	Ajax	3-2 (aet)	FC Utrecht
2003	FC Utrecht	4-1	Feyenoord
2004	FC Utrecht	1-0	FC Twente Enschede

Dutch Cup Summary

TEAM	TOTALS	WINNERS & RUNNERS-UP (BOLD) (ITALICS)
Ajax	15, 5	*1900,* **17, 43,** *61, 67, 68,* **70–72,** *78,* **79, 80, 81, 83, 86, 87, 93, 98,** *99,* **2002**
Feyenoord	10, 3	**1930,** *34,* **35,** *57,* **65, 69, 80, 84, 91, 92, 94, 95,** *2003*
PSV	7, 6	*1932, 39,* **50,** *69, 70,* **74, 76, 88–90,** *96, 98,* **2001**
Quick Den Haag	4, 0	**1909–11, 16**
Sparta Rotterdam	3, 2	**1958,** *62,* **66,** *71,* **96**
FC Utrecht	3, 2	*1982,* **85,** *2002,* **03, 04**
AZ 67 Alkmaar	3, 0	**1978, 81, 82**
HFC Haarlem	3, 0	**1904, 13, 15**

This summary only features clubs that have won the Dutch Cup three times or more. For a full list of cup winners and runners-up please see the Cup Record above.

Germany

THE SEASON IN REVIEW 2003–04

GERMANS LIKE THEIR SOCCER as this year's record attendances in the Bundesliga show. They also like their beer and sausages and they are not getting enough. The German Football Federation asked FIFA to consider lengthening half time to 20 minutes to allow more time for fans to slake their thirst. FIFA said no and so supporters had to make do with the usual half-time crush throughout this year's season.

In the first half of the year the pacesetters were last year's runners-up Stuttgart. At home and away, in Germany and in Europe, their defence was watertight and married with a capacity to snatch a winning goal – exemplified by their 2-1 victory over Manchester United at Old Trafford in the Group Stage of the Champions League. The normally reticent coach Felix Magath was prompted to say 'This is one of the best days of my life'. Something, however, was not quite right at last year's champions Bayern München. The arrival of Dutch striker Roy Makaay from Spanish club Deportivo promised a new attacking edge, but a sense of gloom appeared to envelop the club; most notably their key midfielder Sebastian Deisler took nine months out to deal with an intense bout of clinical depression. Before Christmas Bayern did just enough. They scraped into the knockout rounds of the Champions League after scares at Celtic and Anderlecht, and kept themselves at or near the top of the Bundesliga. But, as an exasperated Bayern president Franz Beckenbauer bemoaned, 'They can't run. They just stand there. I see no energy, no will, no motion'. And they needed some energy and motion because hard on their heels in the league were a rejuvenated Bayer Leverkusen and a highly improved Werder Bremen. By the winter break Werder had crept into the lead and they were never to relinquish it.

Werder's nerveless consistency

Thomas Schaaf's Werder played with a nerveless consistency. French midfielder Johan Micoud orchestrated their attacks, while Brazilian Ailton and a late arrival, Croat forward Ivan Klasnic, both scored freely. Valerien Ismael was the lynchpin of a mean defence in front of goalkeeper Andreas Reinke who was having

Bundesliga Table 2003–04

CLUB	P	W	D	L	F	A	Pts	
Werder Bremen	34	22	8	4	79	38	**74**	Champions League
Bayern München	34	20	8	6	70	39	**68**	Champions League
Bayer Leverkusen	34	19	8	7	73	39	**65**	Champions League
VfB Stuttgart	34	18	10	6	52	24	**64**	UEFA Cup
VfL Bochum	34	15	11	8	57	39	**56**	UEFA Cup
Borussia Dortmund	34	16	7	11	59	48	**55**	
FC Schalke 04	34	13	11	10	49	42	**50**	
Hamburger SV	34	14	7	13	47	60	**49**	
Hansa Rostock	34	12	8	14	55	54	**44**	
VfL Wolfsburg	34	13	3	18	56	61	**42**	
Borussia Mönchengladbach	34	10	9	15	40	49	**39**	
Hertha BSC Berlin	34	9	12	13	42	59	**39**	
SC Freiburg	34	10	8	16	42	67	**38**	
Hannover 96	34	9	10	15	49	63	**37**	
1.FC Kaiserslautern*	34	11	6	17	39	62	**36***	
Eintracht Frankfurt	34	9	5	20	36	53	**32**	Relegated
TSV 1860 München	34	8	8	18	32	55	**32**	Relegated
1.FC Köln	34	6	5	23	32	57	**23**	Relegated

* Kaiserslautern had 3 points deducted for financial irregularities.
Promoted Clubs: TSV Alemannia Aachen, Arminia Bielefeld, FSV Mainz 05.

Above: Bayern's big buy of the summer was Dutch striker Roy Makaay who arrived from Deportivo La Coruña. He scored 23 Bundesliga goals and six in the Champions League.

Left: It's 50 years since West Germany re-entered the soccer world internationally and won the 1954 World Cup. The country has been awash with football nostalgia captured by the phenomenally successful movie Das Wunder von Bern. *The film tells the story of that West German World Cup-winning team. Here the cast show off their hats.*

Key

VfB Stuttgart

	Team name and shirt colours	CL	Progress in Champions League
👤	Manager	UEFA	Progress in UEFA Cup
👑	League position	*	Qualified for Champions League
⬇	Relegated teams	†	Qualified for UEFA Cup
🏆	Progress in Cup		

Hamburger SV

Kurt Jara, Klaus Toppmöller
👑 8th
UEFA 1st Round

Beer and cigarette time at Hamburg. Toppi is back and inspirationally led them up the table after a dismal start under Jara

Werder Bremen

Thomas Schaaf
👑 1st *
🏆 Winners

A brilliant and sustained triumph for Schaff and his squad without stars

FC Hansa Rostock

Armin Veh, Juri Schluenz
👑 9th
🏆 2nd Round

After an appalling start under Veh, ex-player Schluenz got the best from Hansa – their best finish for seven years

Borussia Dortmund

Matthias Sammer
👑 6th
🏆 2nd Round
CL 3rd Qualifying Round
UEFA 2nd Round

The biggest crowds in Europe, and they need them. After losing their Champions League qualifier, Dortmund were in financial crisis all season

Hannover 96

Ralf Rangnick, Ewald Linen
👑 14th
🏆 2nd Round

A late change of coach and Hannover managed to haul themselves to safety

VfL Wolfsburg

Jurgen Rober, Eric Gerets
👑 10th
🏆 2nd Round

Despite the immense ambitions of their owners, Wolfsburg remained marooned in the upper mid-table again. A mid-season collapse in form saw Rober out and Gerets in

Hertha BSC Berlin

Huub Stevens, Hans Meyer
👑 12th
🏆 3rd Round
UEFA 1st Round

Very disappointing. Hertha flirted with relegation when they should have been challenging at the top. Meyer pulls them round after Hubb Stevens was thrown out

FC Schalke 04

Jupp Heynckes
👑 7th
🏆 2nd Round
UEFA 2nd Round

Schalke's dilemma is having a stadium fit for the Champions League Final but a team not good enough to qualify for it, let alone win it. Seventh again in the Bundesliga

VfL Bochum

Peter Neururer
👑 5th †
🏆 1st Round

A great season brings European football and the satisfaction of being the top side in the Ruhr. Bochum's attacking soccer on a non-existent budget was a triumph

Borussia Mönchengladbach

Ewald Lienen, Holger Fach
👑 11th
🏆 Semi-finals

Holger Fach lifted his depressed squad and not only made them safe in the league but took them to the cup semi-finals

Bayer Leverkusen

Klaus Augenthaler
👑 3rd *
🏆 3rd Round

After last year's near disaster, third place and a Champions League spot shows that Leverkusen – albeit without Toppmöller's flair – are back

1.FC Köln

Friedhelm Funkel, Marcel Koller
👑 18th ⬇
🏆 3rd Round

Rooted to bottom spot for most of the season, its straight back down for Köln

Eintracht Frankfurt

Willi Reimann
👑 16th ⬇
🏆 2nd Round

Another very short stay in the Bundesliga for promoted Frankfurt; just not enough money, quality or luck

VfB Stuttgart

Felix Magath
👑 4th †
🏆 3rd Round
CL 1st Knockout Round

Set the pace early on. A watertight defence took Stuttgart close, but a lack of goals was the problem both at home and in Europe

SC Freiburg

Volker Finke
👑 13th
🏆 3rd Round

Comfortable survival constituted an immense achievement for tiny Freiburg in their first year back in the Bundesliga

TSV 1860 München

Falko Gotz, Gerald Vanenburg
👑 17th
🏆 2nd Round

An awful season. TSV's president resigned after the Allianz Arena bribe scandal broke and the team just kept heading down

Bayern München

Ottmar Hitzfeld
👑 2nd *
🏆 Quarter-finals
CL 1st Knockout Round

Humiliating and disgraceful, and that was the best of it. Never in contention in the league, bundled out of the cup by lowly Aachen and the Champions League by Real Madrid. Hitzfeld was inevitably fired

1. FC Kaiserslautern

Eric Gerets, Kurt Jara
👑 15th
🏆 1st Round
UEFA 1st Round

Staying up, but only just, a final day draw with Dortmund kept them in the Bundesliga

GERMANY

Rostock
Hamburg
Bremen
Hannover
Braunschweig
Dortmund
Essen
Mönchengladbach
Leverkusen
Cologne
Berlin
Frankfurt
Kaiserslautern
Stuttgart
Freiburg am Breisgau
Munich

the best season of his career. By March they were 11 points in front, while both Stuttgart and Bayern were losing games they should have drawn and drawing games they should have won; both were eliminated from the First Knockout Round of the Champions League by Chelsea and Real Madrid respectively. Werder sealed their title first by holding an electric Stuttgart to a 4-4 draw and then, with three games to go, they finished off the faltering Bayern by imperiously beating them 3-1 at the Olympiastadion. The game was over by half time as Werder scored three goals in 35 minutes including a humiliating flick from Micoud over the head of Oliver Kahn. It was similar story in the cup as Werder dispensed with top flight and lower league opposition alike, beating Alemannia Aachen 3-2 in the Final to complete the double. Bayern by contrast were knocked out of the quarter-finals by the lowly second division side Alemannia Aachen. As Bild Zeitung put it in their own inimitable way, 'Bayern: Ha Ha Ha! The whole of Germany is laughing itself sick about you'.

Fight for the UEFA Cup

Just below the top four the fight for UEFA Cup places was confined to three teams from the Ruhr. Fifth and seventh spots went to Bochum and Schalke while the region's biggest team, Borussia Dortmund, had a season wracked by problems with money. The club, despite attracting the largest average crowd in European soccer in their enormous and brilliantly appointed Westfalenstadion, began the season with considerable debts. A bad situation turned into a crisis when they failed to qualify for the Champions League Group Stages; they were beaten in a penalty shootout by Club Brugge. The income from the competition was so central to their budget that the players were asked to take around a 20 per cent pay cut. When the team lost 1-0 at Stuttgart fans organised a sit-down protest that prevented the team bus from leaving the stadium. Defeat in the Second Round of the UEFA Cup by the French club Sochaux depressed both share values and squad morale even further. Deutsche Bank, one of the club's main shareholders, disposed of its equity. With the obvious prospect of large-scale

Left: Where the two million euros accidentally went. Karl Heinz Wildmoser, ex-president of Munich club TSV 1860, shows off a plan of the city's new stadium. He is currently under investigation on charges of corruption in the tendering process.

Below, left: Eric Gerets saved Kaiserslautern last year when relegation seemed certain. This year a more comfortable finish was not good enough and Gerets got the sack.

Below: Sebastian Diesler, Bayern Munich's brilliant midfielder, prepares for his comeback game against Stuttgart. Diesler missed most of the season with a long bout of depression.

How was that? Erik Meijer of second divison Alemannia Aachen celebrates the winning goal with team-mate Alexander Kitzpera in their giant-killing cup quarter-final against Bayern München.

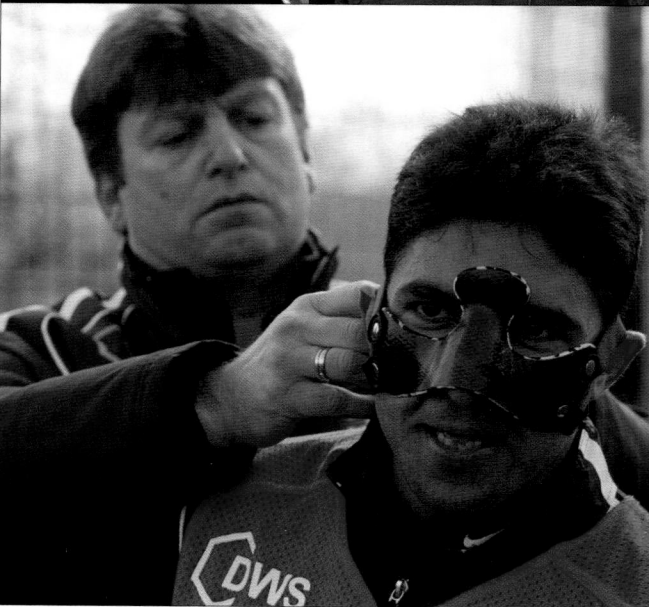

Vahid Hashemain, VfL Bochum's Iranian striker, tries on his nose protector. During a game against Hansa Rostock, team-mate Sunday Oliseh had broken his nose. Oliseh was fired for his efforts.

GERMANY

Oliver Kahn provided enormous entertainment on and off the pitch. The best player at the 2002 World Cup fumbled balls, gave away crucial goals, and spent a great deal of time in the country's gossip columns.

Race for the Championship

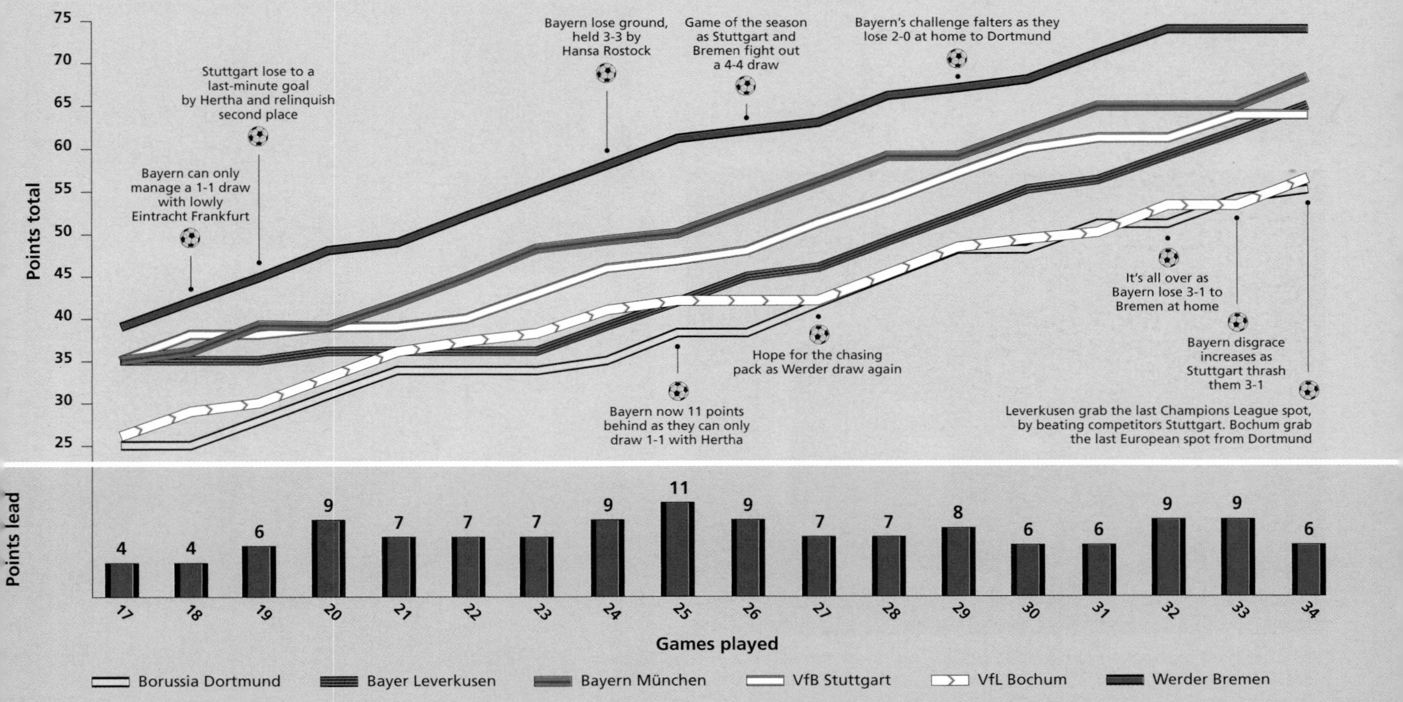

Bayern can only manage a 1-1 draw with lowly Eintracht Frankfurt

Stuttgart lose to a last-minute goal by Hertha and relinquish second place

Bayern lose ground, held 3-3 by Hansa Rostock

Game of the season as Stuttgart and Bremen fight out a 4-4 draw

Bayern's challenge falters as they lose 2-0 at home to Dortmund

Bayern now 11 points behind as they can only draw 1-1 with Hertha

Hope for the chasing pack as Werder draw again

It's all over as Bayern lose 3-1 to Bremen at home

Bayern disgrace increases as Stuttgart thrash them 3-1

Leverkusen grab the last Champions League spot, by beating competitors Stuttgart. Bochum grab the last European spot from Dortmund

Points total (axis: 25–75)

Points lead

Games played	17	18	19	20	21	22	23	24	25	26	27	28	29	30	31	32	33	34
Points lead	4	4	6	9	7	7	7	9	11	9	7	7	8	6	6	9	9	6

Legend: Borussia Dortmund — Bayer Leverkusen — Bayern München — VfB Stuttgart — VfL Bochum — Werder Bremen

GERMANY

sales to come much of the squad seemed to be more worried by their next job than the next match and Dortmund became a shadow of their former selves.

Finishing just behind Dortmund came Hamburg. A desperate start under Kurt Jara saw them drop into the relegation zone. Jara's job was, of course, secure and then he was fired. Enter Klaus Toppmöller and Hamburg began a charge up the table that took them to eighth. In mid-table the ambitious Wolfsburg failed to improve, Hansa Rostock and Mönchengladbach changed coaches and survived. Kaiserslautern remained mired in financial crisis and Hertha Berlin almost inexplicably, with the sixth-largest budget in the league, skirted relegation all season. Two of last year's promoted teams took the drop back down: Köln were rooted to the bottom from almost the first game and never looked like getting off it, and Eintracht Frankfurt fared little better. The final spot went to TSV München whose mediocre form was made immeasurably worse by the crisis that engulfed the club in the spring. It was revealed that the club's president, Karl Heinz Wildmoser, had been involved in some decidedly dodgy financial transactions with the construction company who won the contract to build the new Allianz Arena in Munich. The stadium will host the opening games of the 2006 World Cup and provide a new home for TSV and Bayern. TSV were always going to be pushed to even half-fill the 66,000-seat arena. In the lower divisions it will be unbearably empty. At least the queues for beer and sausage will be more manageable.

Bundesliga Top Goalscorers 2003–04

PLAYER	CLUB	NATIONALITY	GOALS
Ailton	Werder Bremen	Brazilian	27
Roy Makaay	Bayern München	Dutch	23
Marin Max	Hansa Rostock	German	20

International Club Performances 2003–04

CLUB	COMPETITION	PROGRESS
Bayern München	Champions League	1st Knockout Round
VfB Stuttgart	Champions League	1st Knockout Round
Borussia Dortmund	Champions League	3rd Qualifying Round
	UEFA Cup	2nd Round
FC Schalke 04	UEFA Cup	2nd Round
1.FC Kaiserslautern	UEFA Cup	1st Round
Hertha BSC Berlin	UEFA Cup	1st Round
Hamburger SV	UEFA Cup	1st Round

German Cup

2004 FINAL

May 29 – Olympiastadion, Berlin

Werder **3-2** TSV
Bremen   Alemannia
(Borowski 31, 84,   Aachen
Klasnic 45)   *(Blank 51,*
        Meijer 90)

h/t: 2-0 **Att:** 71,682
Ref: Fandel

Above: Werder Bremen captain Frank Baumann lifts the German Cup after just beating Alemannia Aachen 3-2 in a tight Final.

Below: Werder Bremen's Ivan Klasnic keeps the ball out of the reach of Bayern's Oliver Kahn and scores the opening goal in their end-of-season clash. Werder won 3-1 and the title was effectively theirs.

VfB Stuttgart manager Felix Magath tells his side to tighten up in defence – which they did. Goals however, proved more of a problem.

The meanest defence in the league: Stuttgart defenders Fernando Meira and Jurica Vranjes squeeze out Cologne's Marius Ebbers.

Thank you fans. 1.FC Köln's Dirk Lottner applauds the suffering stands in Köln's last home game of a season in which relegation looked and proved inevitable.

Werder waited until their home game with Bayer Leverkusen to claim the Bundesliga crown. With the trophy are Paul Stalteri, Fabian Ernst and the Cherubic Brazilian striker Ailton.

Soccer in Germany

1887: First soccer only club created – SC Germania Hamburg

1898: First regional leagues – Southern Germany and Berlin

1900: Formation of FA: Deutscher Fussball-Bund

1902: First national championships

1904: Affiliation to FIFA. First international, v Switzerland, won 1-0, venue: Stuttgart

1911: German army introduces soccer into its physical education programme

1930: Schalke 04 banned by DFB for professionalism

1933: German government ban Jews from soccer club membership

1935: German Cup established

1945–48: No national championships

1946: Expelled from FIFA

1938: Anschluss with Austria, Austrian teams played in German championships until 1944

1944: German Cup abandoned

1948: East German FA created, national championships begin in East and West

1950: West German FA readmitted to FIFA

1952: East German FA readmitted to FIFA

1953: East German Cup abandoned due to Berlin uprising. West German Cup re-established

1954: East and West German affiliation to UEFA

1955: DFB bans affiliated clubs from letting women use their grounds. West German Women's Football Association founded in Essen

1956: First women's international, v Netherlands, won 2-1, venue: Essen

1961: East German Cup and League abandoned. Berlin wall erected

1963: West German Bundesliga established

1970: DFB ban on women at affiliated clubs lifted

1990: East German FA dissolved into all German FA, two Bundesliga places only for eastern teams

1997: Borussia Dortmund become first German club partially floated on stock exchange

2002: Kirch Media collapses causing financial crisis. Germany awarded 2006 World Cup finals

Timeline years: 1885, 1890, 1895, 1900, 1905, 1910, 1915, 1920, 1925, 1930, 1935, 1940, 1945, 1950, 1955, 1960, 1965, 1970, 1975, 1980, 1985, 1990, 1995, 2000, 2005

Key

- International soccer
- Affiliation to FIFA
- Affiliation to UEFA
- Women's soccer
- War
- ■ World Cup host
- ● World Cup winner
- ▲ World Cup runner-up
- ■ European Championships host
- ● European Championships winner
- ▲ European Championships runner-up
- ○ Competition winner
- △ Competition runner-up

BayL – Bayer Leverkusen
BayM – Bayern München
BorD – Borussia Dortmund
BorM – Borussia Mönchengladbach
Carl – Carl Zeiss Jena
Ein – Eintracht Frankfurt
For – Fortuna Düsseldorf
Ham – Hamburger SV
Köln – 1.FC Köln
Loko – Lokomotive Leipzig
Mag – FC Magdeburg
Schl – FC Schalke 04
Stutt – VfB Stuttgart
TSV – TSV 1860 München
Wer – Werder Bremen

International Competitions

Year	European Cup	UEFA Cup	European Cup-Winners' Cup
1954: ●			
1960:	△ Ein		
1965:			△ TSV
1966:			○ BorD
1967:			○ BayM
1968:			△ Ham
1972: ●			△ BorM
1973:			
1974: ● ■	○ BayM		△ BorM
1975: ▲	○ BayM	○ BorM	○ Mag
1976:	○ BayM		
1977: ▲	○ BorM		○ Ham
1979:	△ Ham	○ BorM	
1980: ●		○ Ein	○ BorM	△ For
1981:			△ Carl
1982: ▲	○ BayM	△ Ham	
1983:	○ Ham		
1986: ▲		△ Köln	
1987:	△ BayM		
1988: ■		○ BayL	△ Loko
1989:		△ Stutt	
1990: ●			
1992: ▲			○ Wer
1993:		△ BorD	
1996: ●	○ BorD	○ BayM	
1997:		○ Schl	
1999:		△ BayM	△ Stutt
2001:	○ BayM		
2002: ▲	△ BayL	○ BorD	

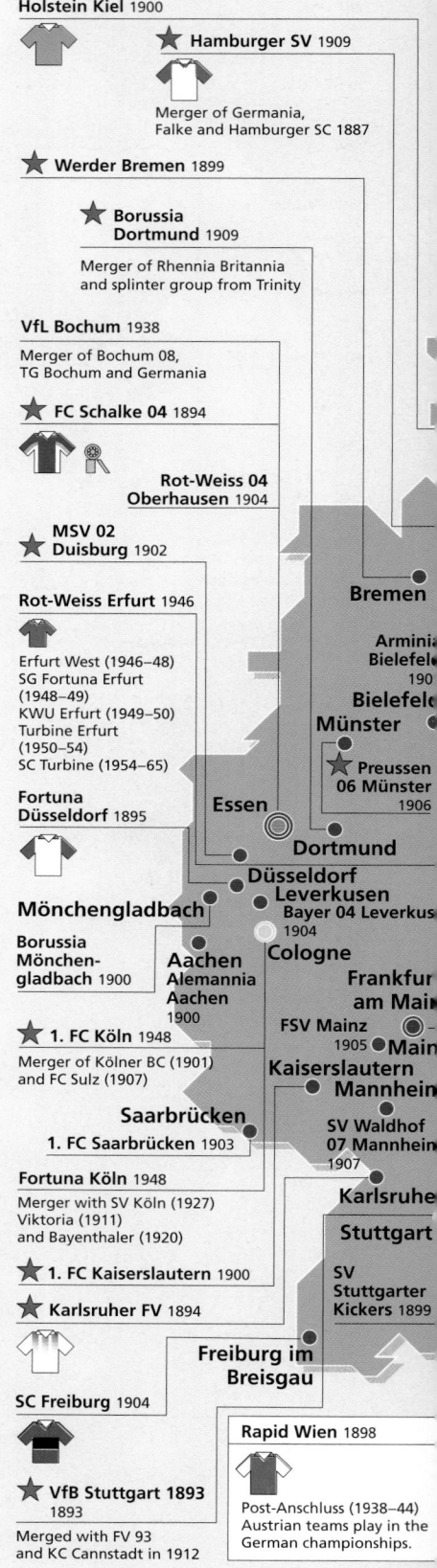

Holstein Kiel 1900

Hamburger SV 1909
Merger of Germania, Falke and Hamburger SC 1887

Werder Bremen 1899

Borussia Dortmund 1909
Merger of Rhennia Britannia and splinter group from Trinity

VfL Bochum 1938
Merger of Bochum 08, TG Bochum and Germania

FC Schalke 04 1894

Rot-Weiss 04 Oberhausen 1904

MSV 02 Duisburg 1902

Rot-Weiss Erfurt 1946
Erfurt West (1946–48)
SG Fortuna Erfurt (1948–49)
KWU Erfurt (1949–50)
Turbine Erfurt (1950–54)
SC Turbine (1954–65)

Fortuna Düsseldorf 1895

Borussia Mönchengladbach 1900

1. FC Köln 1948
Merger of Kölner BC (1901) and FC Sulz (1907)

Fortuna Köln 1948
Merger with SV Köln (1927) Viktoria (1911) and Bayenthaler (1920)

1. FC Kaiserslautern 1900

Karlsruher FV 1894

SC Freiburg 1904

VfB Stuttgart 1893
1893
Merged with FV 93 and KC Cannstadt in 1912

Bremen

Arminia Bielefeld 190

Bielefeld

Münster

Preussen 06 Münster 1906

Essen

Dortmund

Düsseldorf
Leverkusen
Bayer 04 Leverkus 1904

Aachen
Alemannia Aachen 1900

Cologne

Frankfurt am Main

FSV Mainz 1905
Mainz

Kaiserslautern
Mannheim

SV Waldhof 07 Mannheim 1907

Karlsruhe

Stuttgart

SV Stuttgarter Kickers 1899

Saarbrücken
1. FC Saarbrücken 1903

Freiburg im Breisgau

Rapid Wien 1898
Post-Anschluss (1938–44) Austrian teams play in the German championships.

VfB Leipzig 1893

Dissolved in GDR after WWII
Refounded 1945 SG Probstheida

**FC Sachsen
Leipzig 1990** 1945

Founded as SG Leipzig
Leutzsch (1945–48)
ZSG Industrie (1948–50)
BSG Chemie (1950–54)
SC Lokomotive (1954–63)
BSG Chemie Leipzig (1963–90)

**Eintracht
Braunschweig** 1895

Kiel
St Pauli
1910

Rostock
**FC Hansa
Rostock** 1949

Rostock (1949),
Empor Lauter
(1949–54)
SC Empor
(1954–65)
FC Rostock
(1965–66)

Hamburg
Hannover 96
1896

VfL Wolfsburg
1945

Braunschweig
Magdeburg
SC Magdeburg 1951

Leipzig
Halle

Berlin

**Frankfurt
an der Oder**
Energie Cottbus
1966
Cottbus

G E R M A N Y

Erfurt **Jena** **Dresden**

**Eintracht
Frankfurt** 1899

Merged with Kicker,
Victoria Frankfurt and
Frankfurter FV in 1911

Kickers Offenbach 1901

**SpVgg Greuther
Furth** 1903
Fürth

**1. FC
Nürnberg**
1900

Munich
SSV
Ulm
1846
1970
**SpVgg
Unterhaching**
1925

**FC Bayern
München** 1900

**TSV 1860
München** 1900

Chemnitz
Zwickau
Aue

FSV Zwickau 1949

Founded as SG Planitz
Horch Zwickau (1949–65)
Motor Zwickau (1950–67)
BSG Sachsenring
Zwickau (1967–90)

---

1. FC Union Berlin 1945

SG Union Oberschönweide (1945–51)
BSG Motor Berlin (1951–55)
SC Motor Berlin (1955–57)
TSC Oberschönweide (1957–63)
TSC Berlin (1963–66)

Hertha BSC Berlin 1892

Viktoria 98
1889
Formerly
Viktoria Berlin

Founded as Hertha 92
Merged with
Berliner BC 99
in 1923

Berliner FC 1952

Dynamo Berlin (1952–90)
Offshoot of Dynamo
Dresden

**Tennis Club
Borussia
Berlin** 1902

FC Victoria 91 1951

Vorwärts Leipzig (1951–54)
Vorwärts Berlin (1954–71)
Vorwärts Frankfurt/
Oder (1971–91)

Hallescher FC 1945

Founded as SG
Frelimfelde Halle (1945–49)
ZSG Union Halle (1949–50)
BSG Turbine Halle (1950–54)
SC Chemie Halle-Leuna
(1958–66)
HFC Chemie (1966–91)

**FC Carl Zeiss
Jena** 1946

Founded as
SG Ernst Abbe
Motor Jena (1951–56)

1. FC Dynamo Dresden 1953

Dynamo Dresden (1953–90)

Dresdener FC 1898

Dissolved in
GDR after WWII

Chemnitzer FC 1965

SG Chemnitzer Nord till 1950
BSG Fewa (1950–51)
BSG Chemie Chemnitz (1951–53)
Chemie Karl Marx Stadt (1953–56)
Motor Karl Marx Stadt (1956–63)
SC Karl Marx Stadt (1963–65)
FC Karl Marx Stadt (1965–90)

FC Wismut Aue 1946

Founded as
Pneumatik Aue (1946–49)
Zentra Wismu Aue (1949–51)
Wismut Aue (1951–54)
Wismut Karl Marx Stadt (1954–63)
BSG Wismut Aue (1963–90)

Germany

ORIGINS AND GROWTH OF SOCCER

DESPITE AN EARLY START, soccer was a late developer in Germany. In the early 1870s, English students and traders played the game in Berlin and the northern ports. Oxford University toured in 1875 and the country's first club, SC Germania Hamburg, was founded in 1887. However, soccer faced considerable athletic and political opposition. It was viewed by German nationalists as a foreign import and a threat to *Turnen*, the Prussian tradition of individual athleticism. It was excluded from Prussian schools and the armed forces and was socially frowned upon by both Protestant and Catholic church leaders.

White-collar success

Despite the foundation of a national FA in 1900, soccer remained a predominantly lower middle class amateur game. However, it found favour with the white-collar workers of Germany's new cities. For them it was a perfect vehicle for social mixing. By 1911, the army lifted its ban on the game and it became a huge element of life in the armed forces during the First World War. In the postwar era crowds and players became progressively more working class. This phenomenon culminated in 1934, when a miners' team from the Ruhr – Schalke 04 – won the championship.

The Nazi takeover saw the collapse of semi-professionalism and a dismal performance on the international stage. After the war, in 1946, Germany was excluded from FIFA. Partition followed and both West and East Germany rejoined FIFA separately in 1950 and 1952. In East Germany, soccer remained a relatively minor sport carved up among state agencies, but West German soccer bloomed. An extraordinary victory in the 1954 World Cup against the unbeatable Hungarians encouraged the gradual introduction of professionalism and the eventual establishment of a national league – the Bundesliga – in 1963.

The world stage

Since then, Germany at all levels has remained a major player on the world soccer scene, with regular victories at both club and international level. Reunification in 1991 saw a merger of East and West German soccer, but East German teams were only given two places in the top division.

Despite some poor performances by the national team in the late 1990s Germany reached the 2002 World Cup Final and was chosen as host for the 2006 finals. It remains one of the world's most powerful soccer nations.

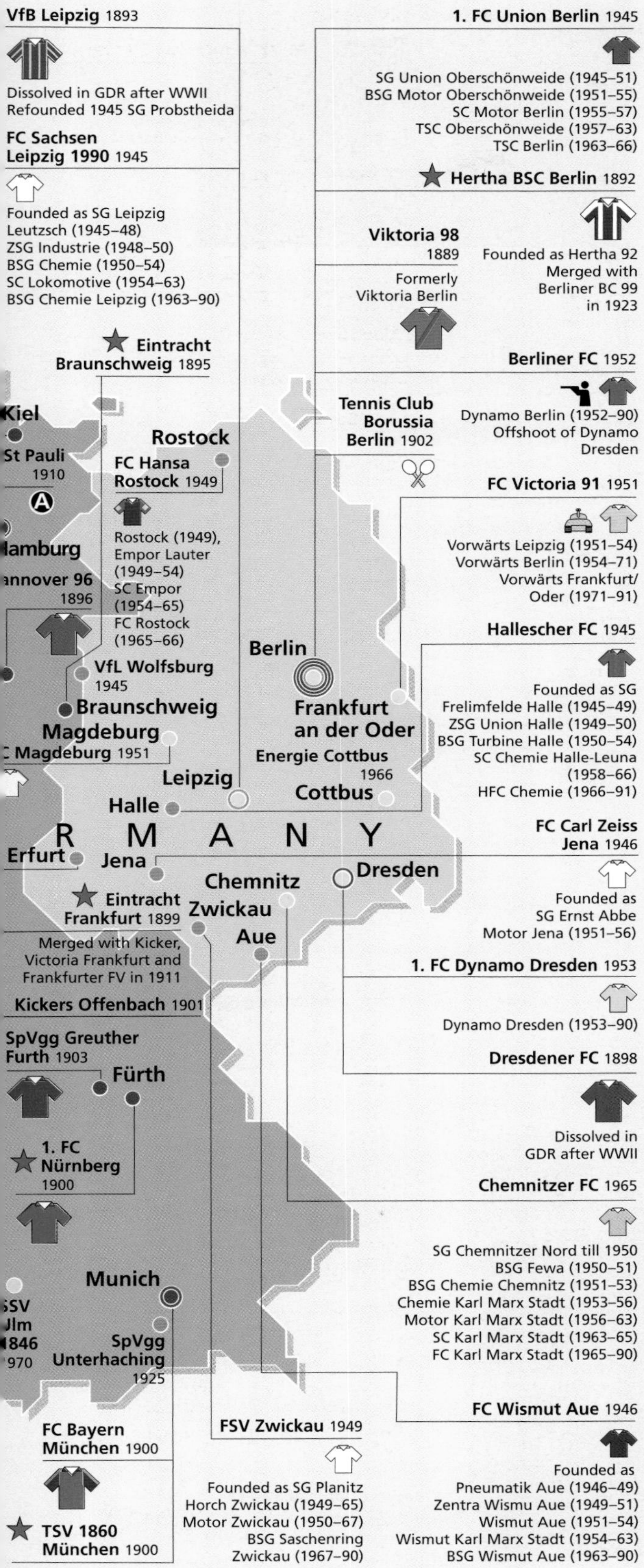

Germany: The main clubs

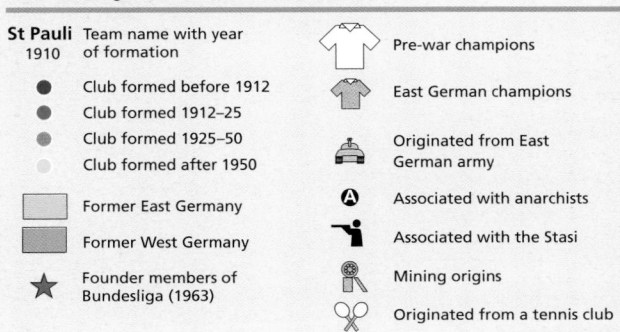

St Pauli 1910 — Team name with year of formation	Pre-war champions
● Club formed before 1912	East German champions
● Club formed 1912–25	
● Club formed 1925–50	Originated from East German army
○ Club formed after 1950	
Former East Germany	Ⓐ Associated with anarchists
Former West Germany	Associated with the Stasi
★ Founder members of Bundesliga (1963)	Mining origins
	Originated from a tennis club

The Ruhr

SOCCER CENTERS

GERMAN INDUSTRIALIZATION and German soccer were both late developers which rose to world-class status towards the end of the 20th century. The heartland of both is the Ruhr valley in the north-west of the country. The connections are intimate: FC Schalke grew out of a mining community with Polish immigrant roots; Borussia Dortmund remains actively involved in the struggles of the region's steelworkers; Bayer Leverkusen has been owned and run by the chemical giant Bayer since its foundation in 1904. A hundred years later, the post-industrial economy of the Ruhr is churning out vast new stadiums and arenas all over the area.

Changing balance of power

The region's earliest soccer-based power lay in the north: in Essen, Bochum, Duisburg and Dortmund. Strong traditions were given a practical boost with the fusion in 1924 of two small teams, FC Westfalia 04 and TV 1877 Schalke, to create FC Schalke 04. The soccer authority's strict insistence on amateur regulations were used to exclude Schalke and its squad (made up of miners) from competition, but the team forced its way into the national championships, winning six titles in the 1930s and 40s. The postwar era was altogether harder for the club, and it was only in the 1990s that Schalke started to fill the Parkstadion and challenge for the country's major honours.

Borussia Dortmund was formed from the fusion in 1909 of three clubs: Trinity, Rhenania and Britannia. It remained in the shadow of Schalke until its first national championship in 1956. However, no dynasty was established, and only the shock of a relegation play-off in 1986 raised the club from its torpor. A decade of commercial growth peaked in 1997 when Ottmar Hitzfeld's team took the European Cup. A public flotation soon followed and success eventually returned with a Bundesliga title in 2002.

To the south of the region, Mönchengladbach, a small industrial town, produced the surprise package of the 1970s, when Borussia became a force both at home and in Europe. Cologne's teams were born from the bombed-out wreckage of the city in the 1940s, when small teams were amalgamated to create two sustainable clubs: 1. FC Köln was formed from KBC and Sülz 07, while its poorer neighbour Fortuna Köln was raised from the ashes of Bayernthaler and SV Köln.

GERMANY

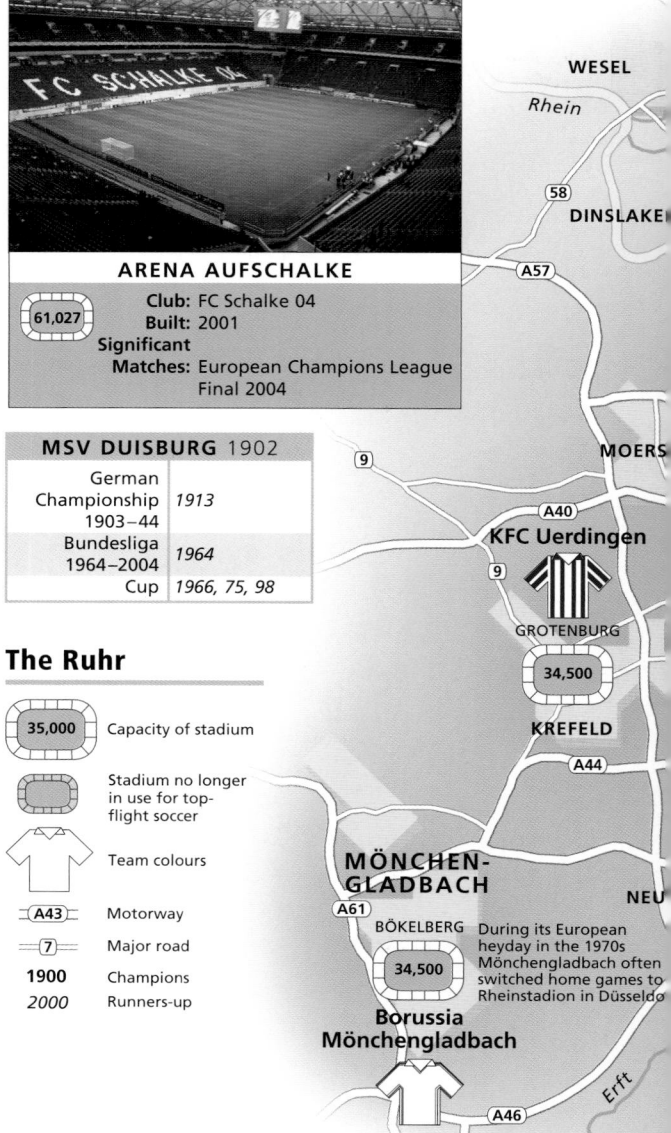

ARENA AUFSCHALKE

61,027

Club: FC Schalke 04
Built: 2001
Significant Matches: European Champions League Final 2004

MSV DUISBURG 1902	
German Championship 1903–44	1913
Bundesliga 1964–2004	1964
Cup	1966, 75, 98

The Ruhr

35,000	Capacity of stadium
	Stadium no longer in use for top-flight soccer
	Team colours
A43	Motorway
7	Major road
1900	Champions
2000	Runners-up

KFC Uerdingen

GROTENBURG

34,500

KREFELD

MÖNCHEN-GLADBACH

BÖKELBERG

34,500

Borussia Mönchengladbach

During its European heyday in the 1970s Mönchengladbach often switched home games to Rheinstadion in Düsseldorf

WESEL

DINSLAKE

MOERS

NEU

BORUSSIA MÖNCHENGLADBACH 1900	
Bundesliga 1964–2004	**1970**, **71**, *74*, **75–77**, *78*
Cup	**1960**, **73**, *84*, *92*, *95*
European Cup	*1977*
UEFA Cup	*1973*, **75**, **79**, *80*
World Club Cup	*1977*

FORTUNA KÖLN 1948	
Cup	*1983*

The Bayer Chemical Works: *the German Parliament passed a special law, the 'Lex Leverkusen', allowing Bayer to retain 100 per cent ownership of Bayer Leverkusen.*

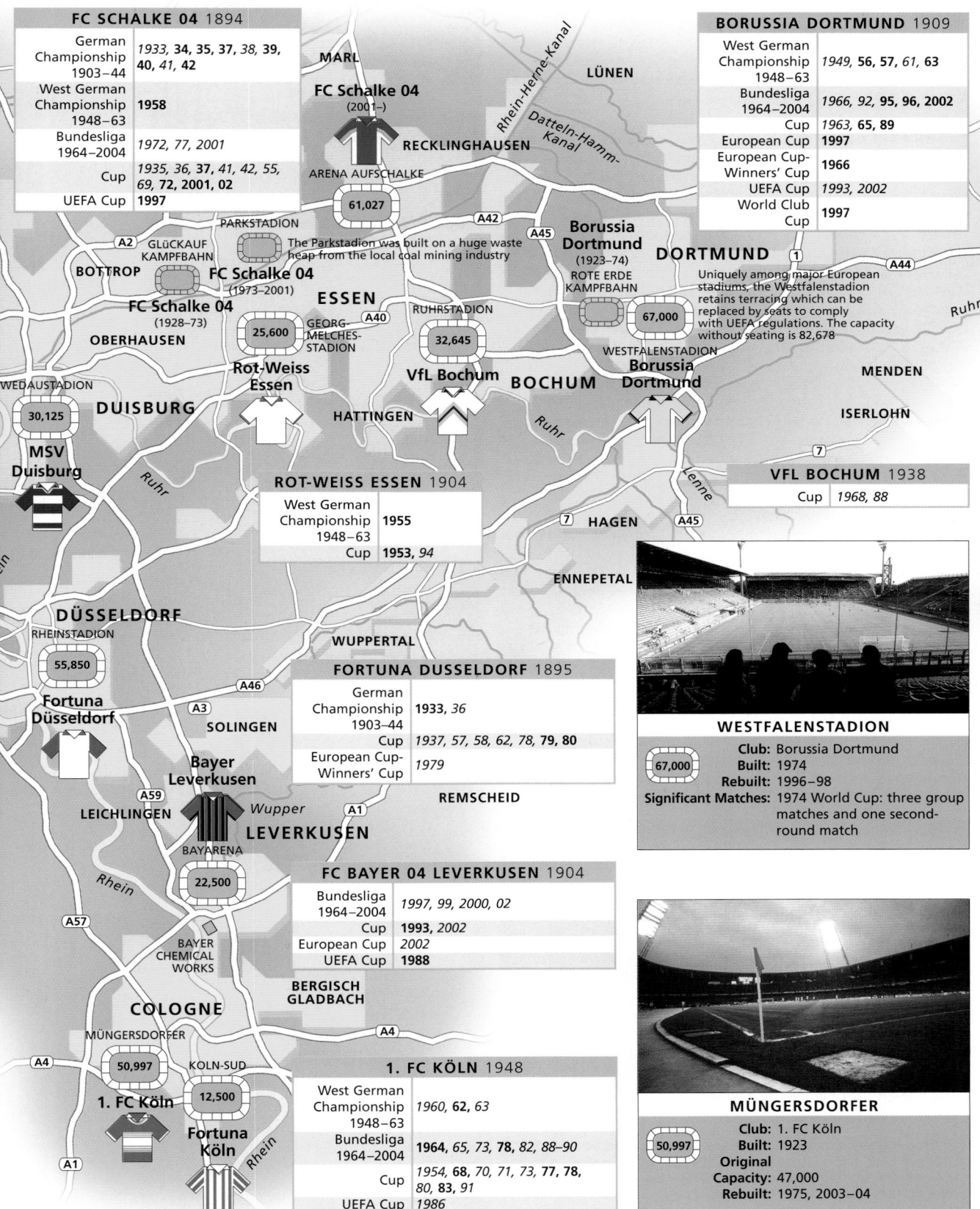

FC SCHALKE 04 1894

German Championship 1903–44	*1933,* **34, 35, 37,** *38, 39,* **40,** *41,* **42**
West German Championship 1948–63	**1958**
Bundesliga 1964–2004	*1972, 77, 2001*
Cup	*1935, 36,* **37,** *41, 42, 55, 69,* **72, 2001, 02**
UEFA Cup	**1997**

MARL

LÜNEN

FC Schalke 04 (2001–)

ARENA AUFSCHALKE

61,027

RECKLINGHAUSEN

A42

A45

BORUSSIA DORTMUND 1909

West German Championship 1948–63	*1949,* **56, 57,** *61,* **63**
Bundesliga 1964–2004	*1966, 92,* **95, 96, 2002**
Cup	*1963,* **65, 89**
European Cup	**1997**
European Cup-Winners' Cup	**1966**
UEFA Cup	*1993, 2002*
World Club Cup	**1997**

Borussia Dortmund (1923–74)

ROTE ERDE KAMPFBAHN

DORTMUND

1

A44

Ruhr

PARKSTADION

A2

The Parkstadion was built on a huge waste heap from the local coal mining industry

GLÜCKAUF KAMPFBAHN

BOTTROP

FC Schalke 04 (1973–2001)

FC Schalke 04 (1928–73)

OBERHAUSEN

25,600

GEORG-MELCHES-STADION

ESSEN

A40

RUHRSTADION

32,645

67,000

WESTFALENSTADION

Uniquely among major European stadiums, the Westfalenstadion retains terracing which can be replaced by seats to comply with UEFA regulations. The capacity without seating is 82,678

Borussia Dortmund

MENDEN

WEDAUSTADION

30,125

DUISBURG

Rot-Weiss Essen

VfL Bochum

BOCHUM

ISERLOHN

MSV Duisburg

Ruhr

HATTINGEN

Ruhr

Lenne

7

ROT-WEISS ESSEN 1904

West German Championship 1948–63	**1955**
Cup	**1953,** *94*

VFL BOCHUM 1938

Cup	*1968, 88*

HAGEN

A45

7

ENNEPETAL

DÜSSELDORF

RHEINSTADION

55,850

Fortuna Düsseldorf

A46

A3

SOLINGEN

WUPPERTAL

FORTUNA DUSSELDORF 1895

German Championship 1903–44	**1933,** *36*
Cup	*1937, 57, 58, 62, 78,* **79, 80**
European Cup-Winners' Cup	*1979*

Bayer Leverkusen

A59

LEICHLINGEN

Wupper

A1

REMSCHEID

LEVERKUSEN

BAYARENA

22,500

WESTFALENSTADION

67,000	
Club:	Borussia Dortmund
Built:	1974
Rebuilt:	1996–98
Significant Matches:	1974 World Cup: three group matches and one second-round match

FC BAYER 04 LEVERKUSEN 1904

Bundesliga 1964–2004	*1997, 99, 2000, 02*
Cup	**1993,** *2002*
European Cup	*2002*
UEFA Cup	**1988**

A57

BAYER CHEMICAL WORKS

Rhein

BERGISCH GLADBACH

COLOGNE

MÜNGERSDORFER

A4

A4

50,997

KOLN-SUD

1. FC Köln

12,500

Fortuna Köln

A1

Rhein

1. FC KÖLN 1948

West German Championship 1948–63	*1960,* **62,** *63*
Bundesliga 1964–2004	**1964,** *65, 73,* **78,** *82,* **88–90**
Cup	*1954,* **68,** *70, 71, 73,* **77, 78,** *80,* **83,** *91*
UEFA Cup	*1986*

MÜNGERSDORFER

50,997	
Club:	1. FC Köln
Built:	1923
Original Capacity:	47,000
Rebuilt:	1975, 2003–04

GERMANY

Munich

SOCCER CENTER

IN THE EARLY 20TH CENTURY, Bavaria was a German byword for inept conservatism and peasant values, and Munich was its antiquated capital. In the 21st century, the city has become the new hub of German industrial and commercial success, and in Bayern München, it has the team that has dominated German football for a quarter of a century. Bayern was born in the working-class Schwabing district of the city in 1900, and was bold enough to win a national championship title in 1932. But its provincial obscurity was such that when the professional Bundesliga was formed in 1963, the club chosen to represent Munich was its rival TSV 1860 München. TSV was founded in the south of the city as a gymnastics club that later took up football. Its early inclusion in professional football seemed justified when it won the cup in 1964 and then the league two years later, but a steady decline saw the team lose its licence in 1981 and it only returned to the top flight a decade later. Even further down the footballing ladder is SpVgg Unterhaching on the southern edge of the city – this relative newcomer made it to the Bundesliga in 1999.

Bayern rise to the top

Despite the snub from the Bundesliga, Bayern went professional anyway and gained quick promotion, successive cup victories and then the 1967 European Cup-Winners' Cup. The team now emerging around Sepp Maier, Franz Beckenbauer and Gerd Müller would eventually win three European Cups and sustain a decade of unbroken dominance in German football. In the 1990s, under Beckenbauer, Trapattoni and Hitzfeld, Bayern has returned to the very top of European football. In 1972 Bayern moved to the Olympiastadion and TSV joined the team, having abandoned its old Grunwalderstrasse stadium on its return to the top flight. While Bayern fills the stadium with fans from all across Germany, TSV's defiantly local supporters leave it almost two-thirds empty. Both are due to move to the new Allianz Arena in the city's northern suburbs, which will open in time to host the World Cup Finals tournament in 2006.

OLYMPIASTADION

69,000

Clubs: Bayern München, TSV 1860 München
Built: 1972
Significant Matches: 1974 World Cup: five matches including 3rd place play-off, Final; 1972 Munich Olympics: Final; 1988 European Championships: Final; European Cup Final: 1979, 93

Bayern win again. The traditional victory celebrations took place in Marienplatz as Bayern took their sixth Bundesliga title in ten years in May 2003.

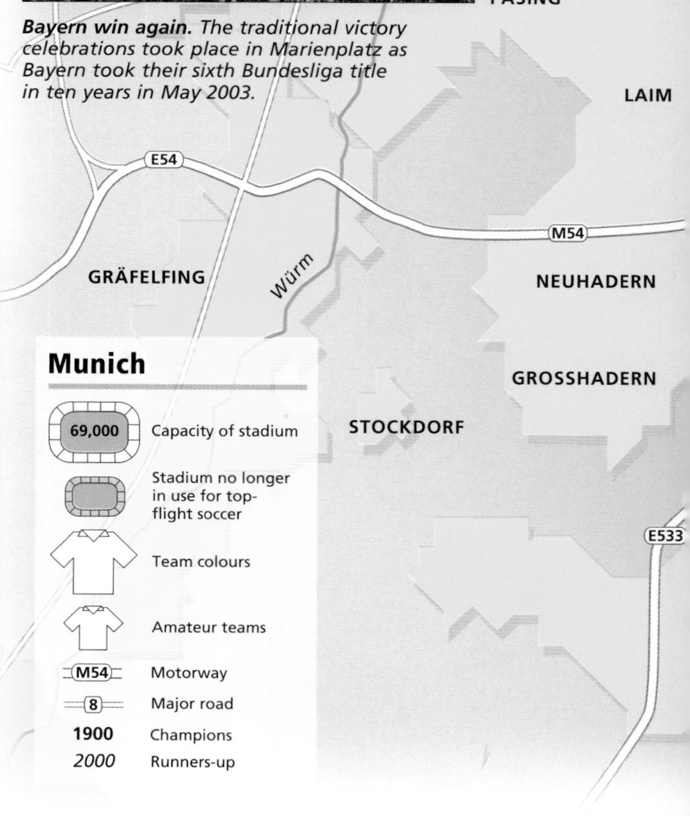

The Grunwalder Strasse is the old and now empty heart of soccer in Munich. A classic rectangular stadium with open teraces behind the goals, the stadium hosted both TSV and Bayern's debut matches in the Bundesliga. Many TSV fans would prefer to return to this cosy venue where their smaller crowds could actually fill the place.

GERMANY

Munich

69,000	Capacity of stadium
	Stadium no longer in use for top-flight soccer
	Team colours
	Amateur teams
M54	Motorway
8	Major road
1900	Champions
2000	Runners-up

KARLSFELD

304

ALLACH

UNTERMENZING

Nymphenburger Ka

NYMPHENBURG

PASING

LAIM

E54

GRÄFELFING

Würm

M54

NEUHADERN

GROSSHADERN

STOCKDORF

E533

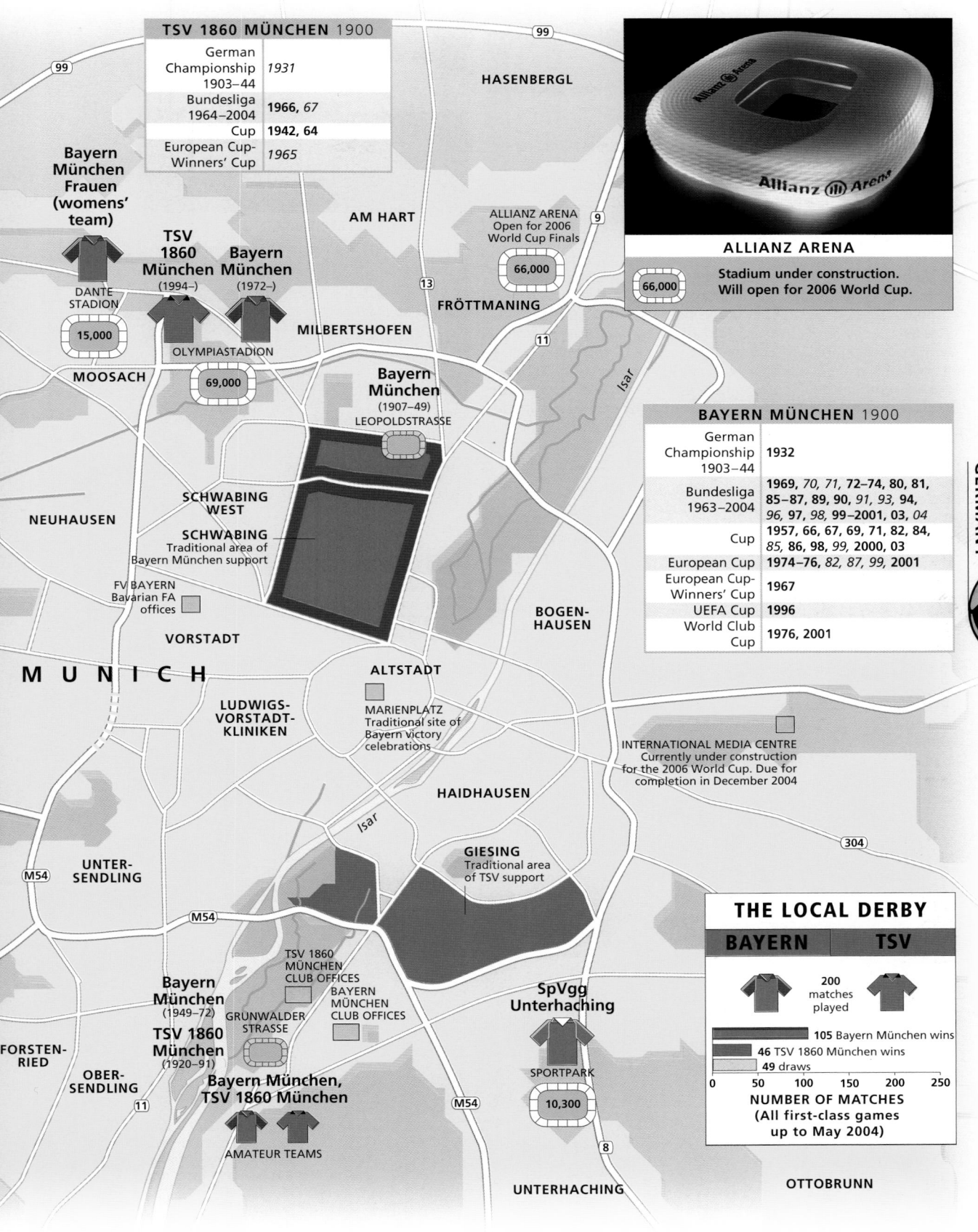

GERMANY

TSV 1860 MÜNCHEN 1900

German Championship 1903–44	*1931*
Bundesliga 1964–2004	**1966,** *67*
Cup	**1942, 64**
European Cup-Winners' Cup	*1965*

HASENBERGL

AM HART

MILBERTSHOFEN

Bayern München Frauen (womens' team)

DANTE STADION
15,000

TSV 1860 München (1994–)

Bayern München (1972–)

OLYMPIASTADION
69,000

MOOSACH

ALLIANZ ARENA
Open for 2006 World Cup Finals
66,000

FRÖTTMANING

ALLIANZ ARENA

66,000

Stadium under construction. Will open for 2006 World Cup.

Bayern München (1907–49) LEOPOLDSTRASSE

SCHWABING WEST

SCHWABING
Traditional area of Bayern München support

NEUHAUSEN

FV BAYERN Bavarian FA offices

VORSTADT

M U N I C H

LUDWIGS-VORSTADT-KLINIKEN

ALTSTADT

MARIENPLATZ
Traditional site of Bayern victory celebrations

BOGEN-HAUSEN

BAYERN MÜNCHEN 1900

German Championship 1903–44	**1932**
Bundesliga 1963–2004	**1969,** *70, 71,* **72–74, 80, 81, 85–87, 89, 90,** *91, 93,* **94,** *96, 97, 98, 99–2001,* **03,** *04*
Cup	**1957, 66, 67, 69, 71, 82, 84, 85,** *86,* **98, 99, 2000, 03**
European Cup	**1974–76,** *82, 87, 99,* **2001**
European Cup-Winners' Cup	**1967**
UEFA Cup	**1996**
World Club Cup	**1976, 2001**

INTERNATIONAL MEDIA CENTRE
Currently under construction for the 2006 World Cup. Due for completion in December 2004

HAIDHAUSEN

GIESING
Traditional area of TSV support

UNTER-SENDLING

Bayern München (1949–72)

TSV 1860 München (1920–91)

TSV 1860 MÜNCHEN CLUB OFFICES

BAYERN MÜNCHEN CLUB OFFICES

GRUNWALDER STRASSE

FORSTEN-RIED

OBER-SENDLING

Bayern München, TSV 1860 München

AMATEUR TEAMS

SpVgg Unterhaching

SPORTPARK
10,300

THE LOCAL DERBY

BAYERN		TSV
	200 matches played	

105 Bayern München wins
46 TSV 1860 München wins
49 draws

0   50   100   150   200   250

NUMBER OF MATCHES (All first-class games up to May 2004)

UNTERHACHING

OTTOBRUNN

Berlin

SOCCER CENTER

BERLIN TOOK TO SOCCER more quickly than much of Germany, and produced early national champions like Viktoria Berlin (which still survives as amateur outfit Viktoria 98). But the city did not create a team of sufficient size and working-class popularity until Hertha 92 and Berliner BC 99 combined in 1923 to create Hertha Berlin. Runners-up for four consecutive years in the national championships, Hertha finally took the prize in 1930 and 31. But the winning streak was soon over and the club languished throughout the Nazi era and in the divided, isolated West Berlin of the postwar era. With the erection of the Berlin Wall in 1961, the club was severed from its supporters in the East and the move to the Olympiastadion saw its old fans in Wedding drift away. Berlin's post-unification boom has seen money and sponsors flow in, but fans and trophies are thinner on the ground. West Berlin's other teams to have made the Bundesliga have all fared poorly, though the city's new immigrant communities are making their mark in the lower leagues with clubs like Croatia Berlin and Türkiyemspor Berlin.

Decline in the East

In the East, Vorwärts Berlin, the East German army club, moved into the city from Leipzig, where the immediate postwar team had played. But in the internal struggles of the East German state, Vorwärts and the army lost out. The team was expelled to Frankfurt-an-der-Oder in 1971, where it has declined and now plays in amateur leagues. In its place, and in its now empty stadium, rose Dynamo Berlin, a team staffed, supported and funded by the *Stasi* – the East German secret police. Two decades of bizarre and biased decisions and questionable triumphs followed. As for the rest of the East Berlin teams, 1. FC Union was the people's team of choice and its loyal fan base has seen it survive the post-unification collapse of East German institutions, especially in a glorious Cup run in 2001. Dynamo by contrast has, like its masters, changed its name to Berliner FC, and sunk into grim suburban, lower-league obscurity at the bleak Sportpark Forum.

OLYMPIASTADION

76,243	
Clubs:	Blau-Weiss 90, Hertha BSC Berlin, Tasmania Berlin
Built:	1936
Rebuilt:	1974
Record Attendance:	88,075 Hertha BSC Berlin v 1. FC Köln, Bundesliga, 26 Sep 1969
Significant Matches:	1936 Berlin Olympics; 1974 World Cup: three group matches; German Cup Final 1992–2001

HERTHA BSC BERLIN 1892

German Championship 1903–44	1926–29, **30, 31**
Bundesliga 1964–2004	*1975*
Cup	*1977, 79, 93*

HENNINGSDORF

FALKENSEE

Blau-Weiss 90

Hertha BSC Berlin (1971–)

SPANDAU

Tasmania Berlin

OLYMPIASTADION

76,243

Havel

Tegele See

KLADOW

Havel

ZEHLENDORF

A115

TELTOW

POTSDAM

A115

Nuthe

The building of the Berlin Wall in 1961 separated Hertha Berlin from many of its fans. Legend has it that many of them assembled by the wall on match days to hear the roar of the crowd.

GERMANY

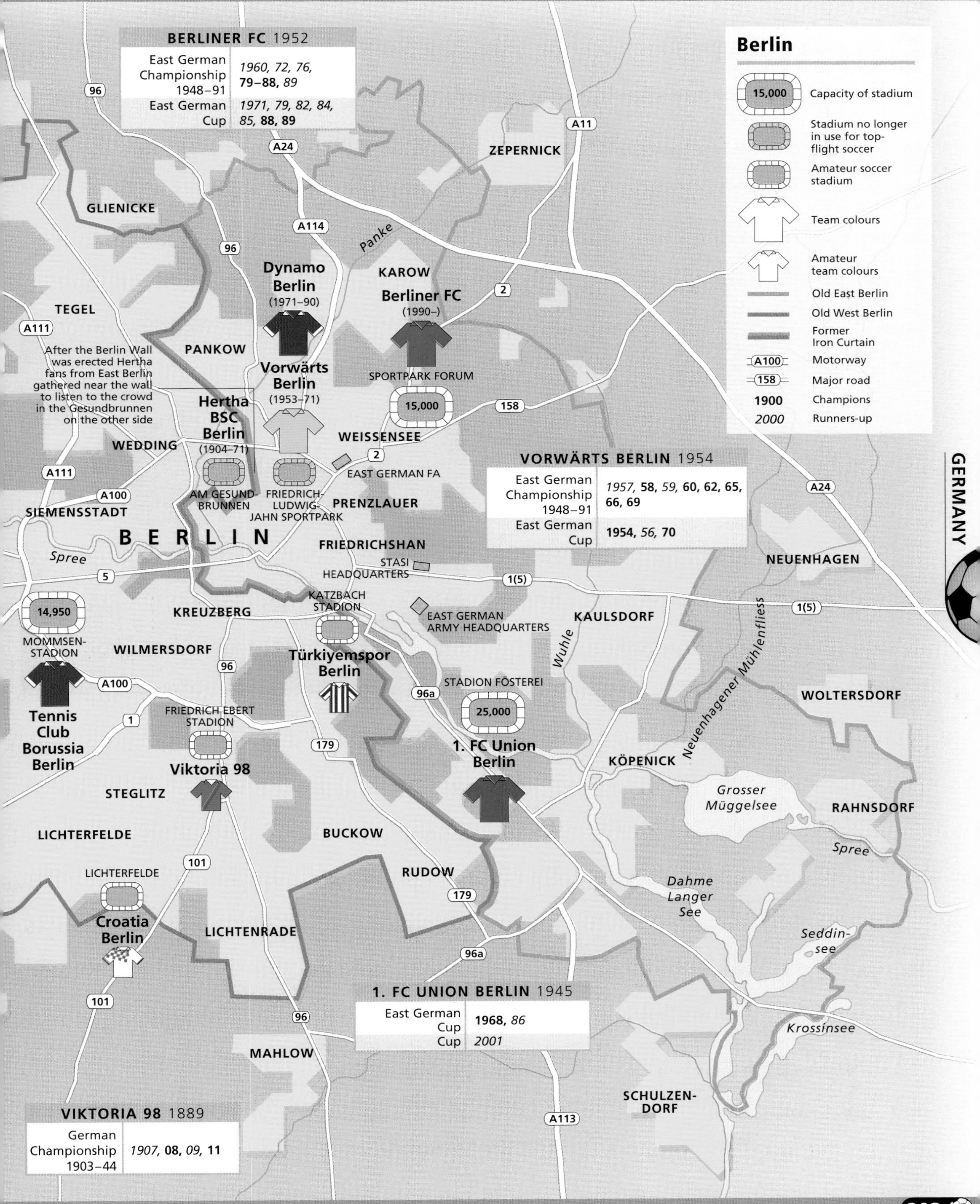

BERLINER FC 1952

East German Championship 1948–91	1960, 72, 76, 79–88, 89
East German Cup	1971, 79, 82, 84, 85, 88, 89

Berlin

15,000	Capacity of stadium
	Stadium no longer in use for top-flight soccer
	Amateur soccer stadium
	Team colours
	Amateur team colours
	Old East Berlin
	Old West Berlin
	Former Iron Curtain
A100	Motorway
158	Major road
1900	Champions
2000	Runners-up

ZEPERNICK

GLIENICKE

TEGEL

PANKOW

Dynamo Berlin (1971–90)

KAROW

Berliner FC (1990–)

Panke

Vorwärts Berlin (1953–71)

SPORTPARK FORUM

15,000

After the Berlin Wall was erected Hertha fans from East Berlin gathered near the wall to listen to the crowd in the Gesundbrunnen on the other side

Hertha BSC Berlin (1904–71)

WEDDING

WEISSENSEE

EAST GERMAN FA

AM GESUND-BRUNNEN

FRIEDRICH-LUDWIG-JAHN SPORTPARK

PRENZLAUER

SIEMENSSTADT

B E R L I N

Spree

FRIEDRICHSHAN

STASI HEADQUARTERS

VORWÄRTS BERLIN 1954

East German Championship 1948–91	1957, 58, 59, 60, 62, 65, 66, 69
East German Cup	1954, 56, 70

NEUENHAGEN

KREUZBERG

KATZBACH STADION

EAST GERMAN ARMY HEADQUARTERS

KAULSDORF

Wuhle

MOMMSEN-STADION

14,950

WILMERSDORF

Türkiyemspor Berlin

STADION FÖSTEREI

25,000

Neuenhagener Mühlenfliess

WOLTERSDORF

Tennis Club Borussia Berlin

FRIEDRICH EBERT STADION

1. FC Union Berlin

KÖPENICK

Grosser Müggelsee

RAHNSDORF

Viktoria 98

STEGLITZ

BUCKOW

Spree

LICHTERFELDE

RUDOW

Dahme Langer See

Seddin-see

LICHTERFELDE

Croatia Berlin

LICHTENRADE

179

Krossinsee

1. FC UNION BERLIN 1945

East German Cup	**1968**, *86*
Cup	*2001*

MAHLOW

SCHULZEN-DORF

A113

VIKTORIA 98 1889

German Championship 1903–44	*1907*, **08**, *09*, **11**

Germany

FANS AND OWNERS

THE LEGAL STRUCTURE OF GERMAN CLUBS has been very tightly regulated, leaving control with the elected boards of sports and social clubs. Although German sides have appeared to prosper on smaller turnovers than the giants of Italy, Spain and England, the economic limits of this kind of structure have seen the government allow clubs to either float on the stock exchange or to spin off their professional soccer activities into a separate public company. That is, as long as the social club continues to holds 51 per cent of the equity. Borussia Dortmund was the first to convert, partially floating the club. Bayer 04 Leverkusen became a plc in 1999, but under a special regulation, the 'Lex Leverkusen', the club is 100 per cent owned by Bayer AG, the chemical company that has run the club for nearly 100 years. Borussia Mönchenglabdach, FC Schalke 04 and Hertha BSC Berlin have all considered floating but have so far declined. More likely, they will follow the path of 1. FC Köln, TSV 1860 München and FC Bayern München, which have opted to take Aktien Gesellschaft status, in which the commercial and amateur sporting components of the club are separated, the latter holding a majority stake in the former, but with the option of external private investment taking the rest. In Bayern's case, Adidas took a 10 per cent stake in 2001, valuing the club at the time at £475 million.

Alternative fans

There are recognizable tribes of German fans. The mainstream combines an older and younger generation, boisterous and noisy but very peaceful. A handful of clubs can claim a following beyond their immediate locality: Bayern München, Dortmund, Schalke and FC Hansa Rostock in particular. Many of the smaller teams, like Berlin's smaller clubs and St. Pauli in Hamburg, attract the alternative scene in Germany: punks, anarchists, Greens and hippies. In the east, skinhead gangs have clustered around some old East German clubs, and have made a speciality of following the national team, causing extensive trouble at France 98, where a policeman was seriously injured in an encounter with German fans. In response, policing has been tightened and, with a characteristic German mixture of incorporation and social reasonability, clubs have set up *fanprojekts*. These bring autonomous supporters' groups, local authority youth projects and the clubs together in a range of activities, including a chance for fans to meet and quiz clubs' directors.

Despite poor performances in recent seasons, attendances at Borussia Dortmund's impressive Westfalenstadion continue to rise. The club has the largest average attendance of any team in Europe.

Average Attendance

Average attendance for season 2003–04 (thousands)

80 70 60 50 40 30 20 10 0

Capacity

Attendance as a percentage of capacity for season 2003–04 (capacity in brackets)

40% 50% 60% 70% 80% 90% 100%

TEAMS	Capacity
Hertha BSC Berlin	(76,243)
VfL Bochum	(33,000)
Werder Bremen	(39,800)
Borussia Dortmund	(82,700)
Eintracht Frankfurt	(61,146)
SC Frieburg	(25,000)
Hamburger SV	(55,000)
Hannover 96	(50,423)
1. FC Kaiserslautern	(41,582)
1. FC Koln	(47,000)
Bayer 04 Leverkusen	(22,500)
Borussia Mönchengladbach	(34,500)
FC Bayern München	(69,000)
TSV 1860 München	(69,256)
FC Hansa Rostock	(30,000)
FC Schalke 04	(62,000)
VfB Stuttgart	(53,072)
VfL Wolfsburg	(30,122)

VfL Bochum

FC Schalke 04

Esse

Mönchengladbach

Borussia Mönchengladbach

AG

1. FC Kaiserslautern

AG

VfB Stuttgart

SC Freiburg

Club Budgets 2000–01, 2001–02

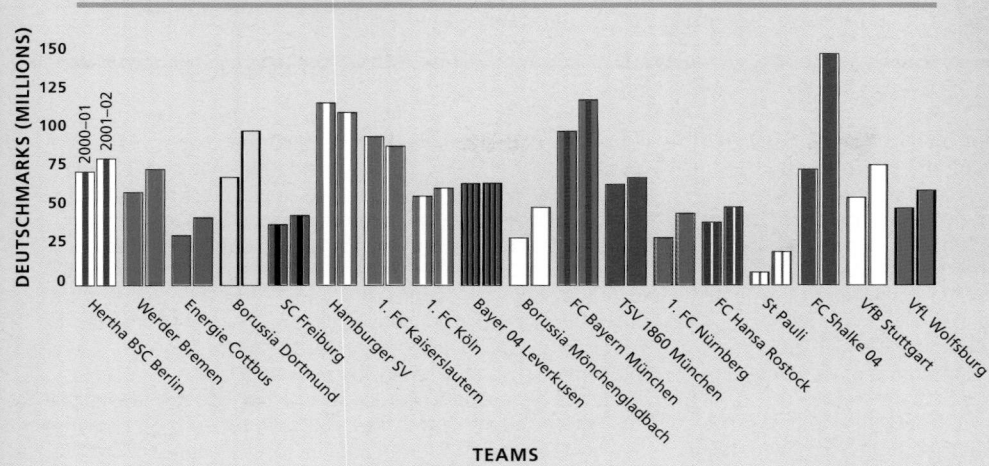

DEUTSCHMARKS (MILLIONS)

2000–01
2001–02

TEAMS

Hertha BSC Berlin · Werder Bremen · Energie Cottbus · Borussia Dortmund · SC Freiburg · Hamburger SV · 1. FC Kaiserslautern · 1. FC Köln · Bayer 04 Leverkusen · Borussia Mönchengladbach · FC Bayern München · TSV 1860 München · 1. FC Nürnberg · FC Hansa Rostock · St Pauli · FC Shalke 04 · VfB Stuttgart · VfL Wolfsburg

Leo Kirch created a media empire that paid enormous sums for the Bundesliga's TV rights. The collapse of the Kirch group in 2002 with debts of £10 billion is likely to see budgets in the Bundesliga slashed.

Majority and Leading Shareholders

Team · ● Berlin City of origin · Sportswear company · Car company · AG Aktien Gesellschaft · GMBH Public limited company

Partial flotation

Teams shown were members of Bundesliga 2003–04

Borussia Dortmund
FC Hansa Rostock
Rostock
Hamburger SV
Bremen · Hamburg · GMBH
Volkswagen 90%
VfL Wolfsburg
Werder Bremen
AG
Hannover · Wolfsburg · Hertha BSC Berlin
Hannover 96 · Berlin
Dortmund · Bayer 04 Leverkusen
everkusen · AG
1.FC Köln
ologne
Frankfurt am Main · Eintracht Frankfurt
Kaiserslautern · AG
G E R M A N Y · TSV 1860 München
Stuttgart · AG
FC Bayern München
Freiburg im Breisgau · Munich · AG
Adidas 10%

Income from Sponsorship 2001–02

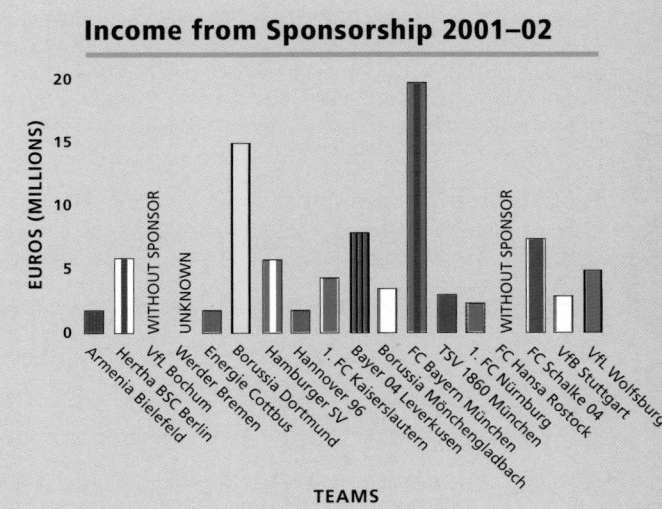

EUROS (MILLIONS)

WITHOUT SPONSOR
UNKNOWN
WITHOUT SPONSOR

TEAMS

Armenia Bielefeld · Hertha BSC Berlin · VfL Bochum · Werder Bremen · Energie Cottbus · Borussia Dortmund · Hamburger SV · Hannover 96 · 1. FC Kaiserslautern · Bayer 04 Leverkusen · Borussia Mönchengladbach · FC Bayern München · TSV 1860 München · 1. FC Nürnberg · FC Hansa Rostock · FC Schalke 04 · VfB Stuttgart · VfL Wolfsburg

German Attendances

Attendances for each season

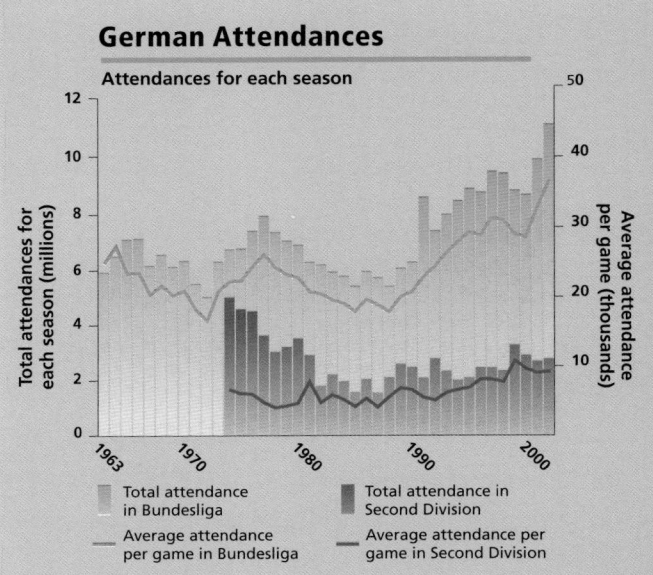

Total attendances for each season (millions)

Average attendance per game (thousands)

1963 · 1970 · 1980 · 1990 · 2000

Total attendance in Bundesliga
Total attendance in Second Division
Average attendance per game in Bundesliga
Average attendance per game in Second Division

Germany

PLAYERS AND MANAGERS

GERMAN SOCCER BEGAN LATER than in many European countries, and remained an amateur and regional affair for longer than in any other leading soccer nation. Originally a middle-class sport, it took two generations to reach the huge German urban working-class and to begin to significantly draw on its pool of talent. From the pre-Second World War generation two names stand out: Fritz Walter and Uwe Seeler. Walter captained the 1954 World Cup-winning side; Seeler the side that lost in 1966. Both played for a single club their whole career: Kaiserslautern and Hamburger SV respectively.

Arrival of the Bundesliga

But Germany's greatest players emerged from the new national professional league – the Bundesliga – formed in 1963. These players would win the 1974 World Cup, and those at Bayern München would come to dominate the national and European game in the mid-1970s: Gerd Müller, whose goalscoring record is almost unsurpassable; Paul Brietner, Bayern's midfield intellectual and bearded radical; and the Kaiser himself, Franz Beckenbauer, Germany's greatest player, manager and soccer politician.

In the 1990s, German players spread their wings and began to play abroad; Kohler, Klinsmann and Matthäus – the spine of the 1990 World Cup side – have all played in Italy, and displayed consistency, quiet intelligence and longevity. Matthias Sammer, one of the few East Germans to make it to the highest level after unification, picked up Beckenbauer's mantle as sweeper. Simultaneously, the growing wealth of the Bundesliga has seen a steady expansion in its overseas players, with strong African and Eastern European contingents. However, the current crisis in German soccer finances, and its relative weakness compared to Europe's other big leagues, means that the biggest talents from Africa and Latin America go elsewhere.

German soccer is also remarkable for the degree of stability and longevity in the coaching of the national squad. From Otto Nerz's appointment in 1926 to Rudi Völler's in 2000, there have been only eight coaches in over 70 years; a point worth pondering when you're trying to work out just why the national team has been so phenomenally successful despite the weaknesses of the domestic league.

Germany International Managers

DATES	NAME	GAMES	WON	DRAWN	LOST
1926–36	Otto Nerz	70	42	10	18
1936–63	Sepp Herberger	162	92	26	44
1963–78	Helmut Schön	139	87	30	22
1978–84	Jupp Derwall	67	45	11	11
1984–90	Franz Beckenbauer	66	36	17	13
1990–98	Berti Vogts	102	67	23	12
1998–2000	Erich Ribbeck	24	10	6	8
2000–04	Rudi Völler	53	29	11	13

All figures correct as of 28 June 2004.

Top 20 International Caps

PLAYER	CAPS	GOALS	FIRST MATCH	LAST MATCH
Lothar Matthäus	150	23	1980	2000
Jürgen Klinsmann	108	47	1987	1998
Jürgen Kohler*	105	2	1986	1998
Franz Beckenbauer	103	14	1965	1977
Thomas Hässler*	101	11	1988	2000
Hans-Hubert Vogts	96	1	1967	1978
Sepp Maier	95	0	1966	1979
Karl-Heinz Rummenigge	95	45	1976	1986
Rudi Völler	90	47	1982	1994
Andreas Brehme	86	8	1984	1994
Andreas Möller*	85	29	1988	1999
Karl Heinz Forster	81	2	1978	1986
Wolfgang Overath	81	17	1963	1974
Guido Buchwald	76	4	1984	1994
Harald Schumacher	76	0	1979	1986
Pierre Littbarski	73	18	1981	1990
Hans Peter Briegel	72	4	1979	1986
Oliver Kahn*	72	0	1995	2004
Uwe Seeler	72	43	1954	1970
Christian Ziege*	72	9	1993	2004

Top 10 International Goalscorers

PLAYER	GOALS	CAPS	FIRST MATCH	LAST MATCH
Gerd Müller	68	62	1966	1974
Rudi Völler	47	90	1982	1994
Jürgen Klinsmann	47	108	1987	1998
Karl-Heinz Rummenigge	45	95	1976	1986
Uwe Seeler	43	72	1954	1970
Oliver Bierhoff*	35	70	1996	2002
Fritz Walter	33	61	1940	1958
Klaus Fischer	32	45	1977	1982
Ernst Lehner	31	65	1933	1942
Andreas Möller*	29	85	1988	1999

* Indicates players still playing at least at club level.

Foreign Players in Germany (in top division squads)

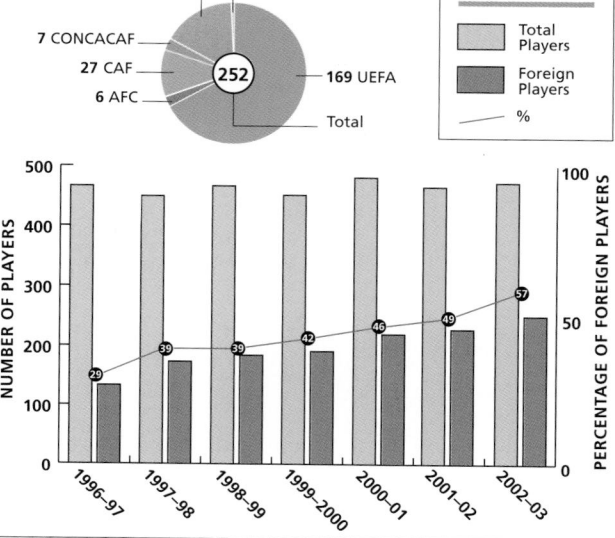

2003–04

41 CONMEBOL
2 OFC
7 CONCACAF
27 CAF
6 AFC
252
169 UEFA
Total

Key

Total Players
Foreign Players
%

GERMANY

Places in the Top 20 International Caps and Top 10 International Goalscorers tables (left) make Rudi Völler the perfect choice as manager of the German national team. The wisdom of the appointment was confirmed when Völler took an unfancied German team to the Final of the 2002 World Cup.

Player of the Year

YEAR	PLAYER	CLUB
1963	Schäfer	1. FC Köln
1964	Seeler	Hamburger SV
1965	Tilkowski	Borussia Dortmund
1966	Beckenbauer	Bayern München
1967	G. Müller	Bayern München
1968	Beckenbauer	Bayern München
1969	G. Müller	Bayern München
1970	Seeler	Hamburger SV
1971	Vogts	Borussia Mönchengladbach
1972	Netzer	Borussia Mönchengladbach
1973	Netzer	Borussia Mönchengladbach
1974	Beckenbauer	Bayern München
1975	Maier	Bayern München
1976	Beckenbauer	Bayern München
1977	Maier	Bayern München
1978	Maier	Bayern München

YEAR	PLAYER	CLUB
1979	Vogts	Borussia Mönchengladbach
1980	Rummenigge	Bayern München
1981	Breitner	Bayern München
1982	Förster	VfB Stuttgart
1983	Völler	Werder Bremen
1984	Schumacher	1. FC Köln
1985	Briegel	Hellas Verona [Ita]
1986	Schumacher	1. FC Köln
1987	Rahn	Borussia Mönchengladbach
1988	Klinsmann	VfB Stuttgart
1989	Hässler	1. FC Köln
1990	Matthäus	Internazionale [Ita]
1991	Kuntz	1. FC Kaiserslautern
1992	Hässler	Roma [Ita]
1993	Köpke	1. FC Nürnberg
1994	Klinsmann	Tottenham Hotspur [Eng]
1995	Sammer	Borussia Dortmund
1996	Sammer	Borussia Dortmund
1997	Kohler	Borussia Dortmund
1998	Bierhoff	Udinese/Milan [Ita]
1999	Matthäus	Bayern München
2000	Kahn	Bayern München
2001	Kahn	Bayern München
2002	Ballack	Bayer Leverkusen
2003	Ballack	Bayern München

Awarded by *Kicker* magazine.

Top Goalscorers by Season 1963–2004

SEASON	PLAYER	CLUB	GOALS
1963–64	Seeler	Hamburger SV	30
1964–65	Brunnen-meier	TSV 1860 München	24
1965–66	Emmerich	Borussia Dortmund	31
1966–67	G. Müller	Bayern München	28
1966–67	Emmerich	Borussia Dortmund	28
1967–68	Lohr	1. FC Köln	27
1968–69	G. Müller	Bayern München	30
1969–70	G. Müller	Bayern München	38
1970–71	Kobluhn	Rot-Weiss Oberhausen	24
1971–72	G. Müller	Bayern München	40
1972–73	G. Müller	Bayern München	36
1973–74	G. Müller	Bayern München	30
1973–74	Heynckes	Borussia M'gladbach	30
1974–75	Heynckes	Borussia M'gladbach	29
1975–76	Fischer	FC Schalke 04	29
1976–77	D. Müller	1. FC Köln	34
1977–78	D. Müller	1. FC Köln	24
1977–78	G. Müller	Bayern München	24
1978–79	K. Allofs	Fortuna Dusseldorf	22
1979–80	Rummenigge	Bayern München	26
1980–81	Rummenigge	Bayern München	29
1981–82	Hrubesch	Hamburger SV	27
1982–83	Völler	Werder Bremen	23
1983–84	Rummenigge	Bayern München	26
1984–85	K. Allofs	1. FC Köln	26
1985–86	Kuntz	VfL Bochum	22
1986–87	Rahn	Borussia M'gladbach	24

SEASON	PLAYER	CLUB	GOALS
1987–88	Klinsmann	VfB Stuttgart	18
1988–89	T. Allofs	1. FC Köln	17
1988–89	Wohlfahrth	Bayern München	17
1989–90	Andersen	Eintracht Frankfurt	18
1990–91	Wohlfahrth	Bayern München	21
1991–92	Walter	VfB Stuttgart	22
1992–93	Kirsten	Bayer Leverkusen	20
1992–93	Yeboah	Eintracht Frankfurt	20
1993–94	Kuntz	1. FC Kaiserslautern	18
1993–94	Yeboah	Eintracht Frankfurt	18
1994–95	Bassler	Werder Bremen	20
1994–95	Herrlich	Borussia M'gladbach	20
1995–96	Bobic	VfB Stuttgart	17
1996–97	Kirsten	Bayer Leverkusen	22
1997–98	Kirsten	Bayer Leverkusen	22
1998–99	Preetz	Hertha Berlin	23
1999–2000	Max	TSV 1860 München	19
2000–01	Barbarez	Hamburger SV	22
2000–01	Sand	FC Schalke 04	22
2001–02	Amoroso	Borussia Dortmund	18
2001–02	Max	TSV 1860 München	18
2002–03	Christiansen	VfL Bochum	21
2002–03	Elber	Bayern München	21
2003–04	Ailton	Werder Bremen	28

One of Germany's first exports was naturally one of its finest players. Jürgen Klinsmann left VfB Stuttgart to join Italian giants Internazionale in 1989. He had three successful years in Milan before moving to AS Monaco of France in 1992.

Germany

BUNDESLIGA 1981–2003

IN THE 1970s, GERMAN SOCCER was dominated by Bayern München and an unlikely small-town team from the Ruhr called Borussia Mönchengladbach. However, by the beginning of the 1980s, Hamburger SV was the power in the land. Even without the departed Kevin Keegan (European Footballer of the Year in 1978 and 79) the team from Hamburg was formidable: the side was managed by Austrian warhorse Ernst Happel, Horst Hrubesch led the line and sweeper Manni Kaltz kept it tidy at the back. Hamburger took back-to-back titles (1982 and 83) and was pipped for a third by a revived Stuttgart in 1984.

The rest of the decade saw a reversion to old form as a newly constructed Bayern München, under manager Udo Lattek and captain Lothar Mätthaus, took five of the next six championships. The only constant challenge came from Werder Bremen under Otto Rehhagel (who stayed a record 14 years at the club). With very little income Werder fielded a compact, clever and hardworking team, and nurtured future German internationals like Rudi Völler and Karlheinz Riedle. The team became famed for its *Wesermiracles*, as it consistently demonstrated its ability to come back from behind at its home, Weserstadion. Together, the mix allowed Bremen to take two championships (1988 and 93), as well as finding European success.

Formation of the modern Bundesliga

As the Berlin Wall was dismantled in 1991, and East Germany was effectively liquidated by the Federal Republic, the Bundesliga of the newly unified Germany dutifully offered two places to the top East German league sides, Hansa Rostock and Dynamo Dresden. Leipzig came up a year later only to go straight back down, and Dresden lasted only four seasons before relegation. Hansa was immediately relegated only to return in the mid-1990s. With a couple of sixth place finishes, Hansa Rostock is easily the most successful team from the East. Geographically Eastern, but politically and economically from West Berlin, Hertha BSC has made a comeback in the last five years. Buoyed by the money flooding into the new Berlin, it has made the top six regularly. Similarly strong challenges have come from two teams from the Ruhr with substantial crowds and financial support: FC Schalke and Bayer Leverkusen.

Bayern went off the boil in the years immediately after reunification and the title was more evenly spread with Borussia Dortmund, Kaiserslautern, Stuttgart and Bremen all winning the top prize. Dortmund, under inspirational president Gerd Niebaum and manager Ottmar Hitzfeld, was the most consistent team. With a massive programme of redevelopment and commercialization (culminating in partial flotation on the German stock exchange), Hitzfeld brought in the Brazilian César from under the noses of Bayern, and a number of German internationals who had been playing abroad, like Andy Möller and Jurgen Kohler; together they won two Bundesliga titles and the European Cup. But with Hitzfeld moving upstairs the side began to creak and break up. Kaiserslautern, under Otto

Rehhagel, won the title on the last day of the 1998 season by beating Borussia Mönchengladbach 3-2.

Despite fearsome competition and perennial feuding between its leading players, Bayern still managed two titles in the mid-1990s. In 1998, Beckenbauer, now president of the club, recalled manager Trapattoni for his second spell in charge, and the first of three titles duly came back to the Olympiastadion. Two more followed with Ottmar Hitzfeld at the helm. Hitzfeld's Bayern has included leading German internationals (like Steffan Effenberg, Oliver Khan, Jens Jeremies and Mehmet Scholl) as well as clever buys in the foreign transfer market (the Brazilian Giovane Elber and French defender Bixente Lizarazu) and one of the strictest wage policies in European soccer.

The collapse of Kirch

While sponsorship and attendance money has been rising in the Bundesliga, the strict controls on the commercialization of German clubs have left them heavily dependent on TV income. TV money has poured into the Bundesliga in the last decade, but a reality check may be in store. The Kirch group – holder of the Bundesliga TV rights – went spectacularly bankrupt in 2002. With some clubs at the bottom end of the table dependent for 60 per cent of their income on this money, their prospects look bleak; so bleak that the German government has been considering a very expensive safety net for the clubs and their players.

Out with the old, in with the new. Giovanni Trapattoni (left) of Bayern München and Ottmar Hitzfeld of Borussia Dortmund in 1997. A year later, Hitzfeld replaced Trapattoni at the helm of Germany's most famous club.

GERMANY

Top: *Karlheinz Riedle (on ground) scores for Werder Bremen, performing one of its Wesermiracles, at home to Hamburger SV in 1988.*

Above: *The Borussia Dortmund squad that won the Champions League and successive Bundesliga titles in the mid-1990s celebrate winning the European Supercup in 1995.*

Players' Salaries 1996–2002

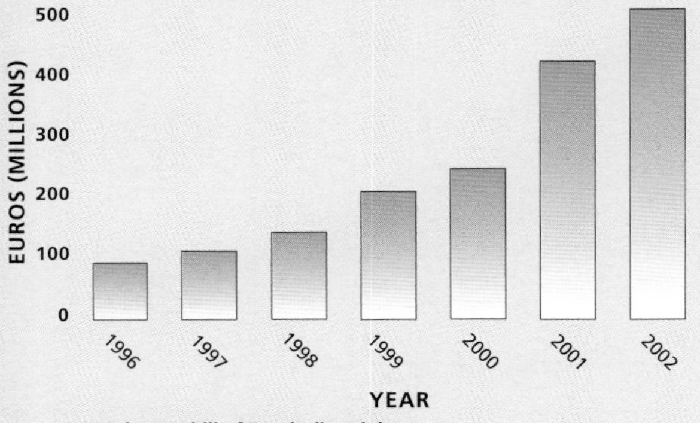

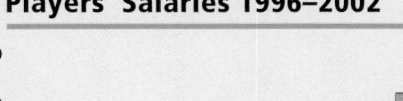

Total wage bill of Bundesliga clubs

Champions' Winning Margin 1993–2003

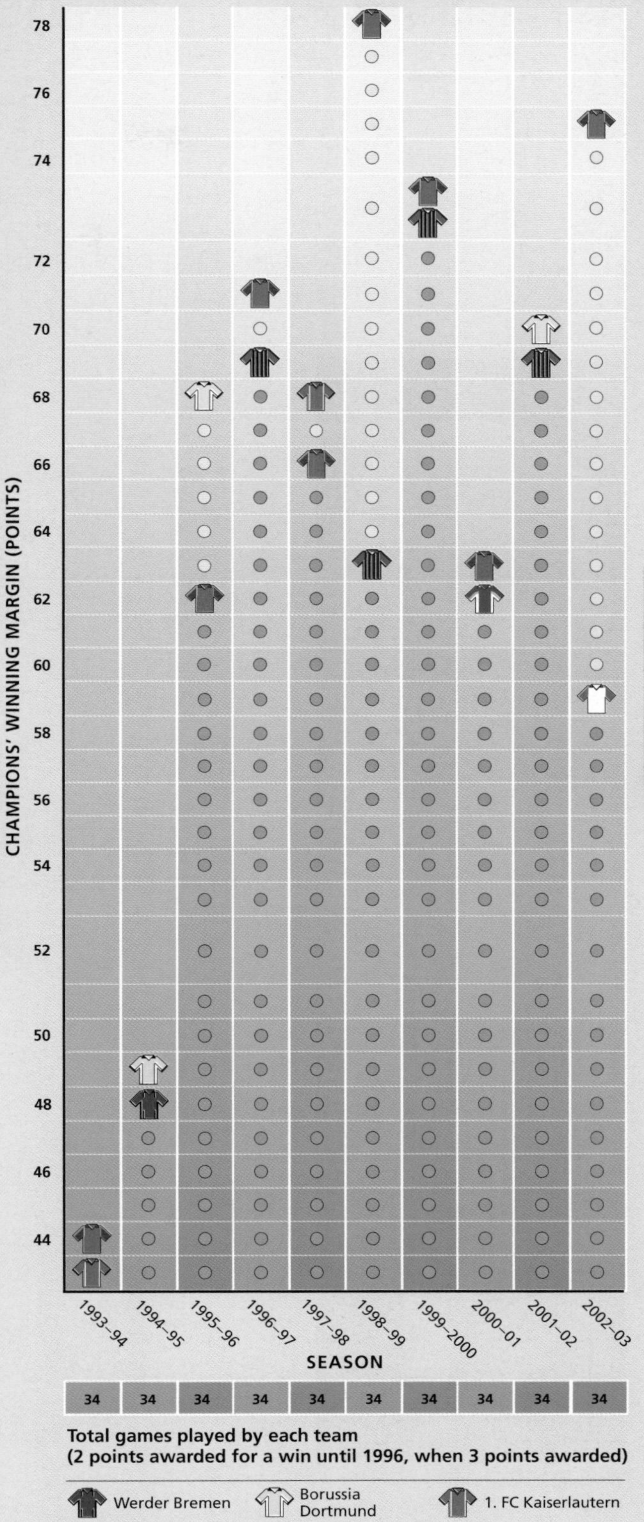

CHAMPIONS' WINNING MARGIN (POINTS)

SEASON

34	34	34	34	34	34	34	34	34	34

Total games played by each team
(2 points awarded for a win until 1996, when 3 points awarded)

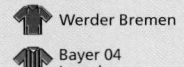 Werder Bremen

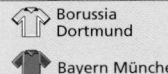 Borussia Dortmund

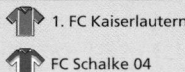 1. FC Kaiserlautern

Bayer 04 Leverkusen

Bayern München

FC Schalke 04

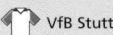 VfB Stuttgart

GERMANY

Key to League Positions Table

- League champions
- Season of promotion to league
- Season of relegation from league
- Other teams playing in league
- 5   Final position in league

German League Positions 1981–2003

Since retiring from playing, Franz Beckenbauer has coached both the national team and Bayern München, and become president of both Bayern and Germany's World Cup bidding committees.

The nearly man, the nearly team. Klaus Toppmöller, now at Hamburg, led Bayer Leverkusen to defeat in the German Cup Final, Champions League Final and Bundesliga in 2001–02.

SEASON

TEAM	1981–82	1982–83	1983–84	1984–85	1985–86	1986–87	1987–88	1988–89	1989–90	1990–91	1991–92	1992–93	1993–94	1994–95	1995–96	1996–97	1997–98	1998–99	1999–2000	2000–01	2001–02	2002–03
Blau-Weiss 90 Berlin						18																
Hertha BSC Berlin		18							18								11	3	6	5	4	5
Arminia Bielefeld	12	8	8	16												15	18	17				16
VfL Bochum	10	13	15	8	9	12	12	15	16	14	15	16		16		5	12	17		18		9
Eintracht Braunschweig	11	15	9	18																		
Werder Bremen	5	2	5	2	2	4	1	3	7	3	9	1	9	2	9	8	7	14	9	7	6	6
Energie Cottbus																				14	13	18
Darmstadt 98	17																					
Borussia Dortmund	6	7	13	14	16	5	14	7	4	10	2	4	3	1	1	3	10	4	11	3	1	3
1. FC Dynamo Dresden										14	15	12	18									
MSV Duisburg	18										19		8	17		9	8	8	18			
Fortuna Düsseldorf	15	9	14	15	14	17			9	12	20			13	16							
Eintracht Frankfurt	8	10	16	12	15	15	10	16	3	5	3	3	5	9	17		15	14	17			
SC Freiburg													15	3	11	17		11	12	6	16	
Hamburger SV	1	1	2	5	7	2	6	4	11	4	12	11	13	13	5	13	9	7	3	13	11	4
Hannover 96						18			11	18												11
FC Homburg						16	17		18													
1. FC Kaiserslautern	4	6	12	11	11	7	15	9	13	1	5	8	2	4	16		1	5	5	8	7	14
Karlsruher SC	14	17	17				13	11	10	13	8	6	6	8	7	6	16					
1. FC Köln	2	5	6	3	13	10	3	2	2	7	4	12	11	10	12	10	17			10	17	
VfB Leipzig													18									
Bayer 04 Leverkusen	16	11	7	13	6	6	8	8	6	5	4	7	15	2	3	2	4	2	2	4	2	15
SV Waldhof Mannheim		11	6	8	14	16	12	17														
Borussia Mönchengladbach	7	12	3	4	4	3	7	6	15	9	13	9	10	6	4	11	15	18			12	12
Bayern München	3	4	4	1	1	1	2	1	2	2	10	2	1	5	2	1	2	1	1	1	3	1
TSV 1860 München														14	8	7	13	10	4	11	9	10
1. FC Nürnberg	13	14	18		12	9	5	14	8	15	7	14	16				16				15	17
Kickers Offenbach		17																				
FC Hansa Rostock											18				6	14	6	13	15	12	14	13
1. FC Saarbrücken					17							18										
St Pauli								10	12	16					14	18					18	
FC Schalke 04		16			9	10	13	18			11	10	14	11	3	12	5	9	13	2	5	7
VfB Stuttgart	9	3	1	10	5	11	4	5	6	6	1	7	7	12	10	4	4	12	8	15	8	2
Stuttgarter Kickers								17			17											
KFC Uerdingen		10	7	3	8		9	13	14	17				15	18							
SV Ulm																		16				
SpVgg Unterhaching																			10	16		
Wattenscheid 09										11	16	13	17									
VfL Wolfsburg																	14	6	7	9	10	8

Coach Otto Rehhagel celebrates as newly-promoted club 1. FC Kaiserslautern wins the Bundesliga in 1998. It was the first and only time a newly-promoted side had won the championship.

Otmar Hitzfeld claims Bayern München's third consecutive Bundesliga title in 2001. Victory in the European Cup Final followed soon afterwards.

GERMANY

Bundesliga

Hamburger SV	Team name
	League champions/ runners-up
1983, *84*	Champions in bold Runners-up in italics
	Other teams in the Bundesliga
● **Hamburg**	City of origin
	Former East Germany
	Former West Germany

St Pauli

Hamburger SV

1982, 83, 84, 87

FC Schalke 04

2001

Borussia Dortmund

1992, 95, 96, 2002 Dortmund

Essen

MSV Duisburg

KFC Uerdingen

Krefeld

Duisburg

Düsseldorf

Mönchengladbach

Borussia Mönchengladbach

Leverkusen

Cologne

Bayer 04 Leverkusen

1997, 99, 2000, 02

1. FC Köln

FC Homburg

Homburg

1982, 89, 90

1. FC Saarbrücken

Saarbrücken

VfB Stuttgart

Darmstadt 98

Kaiserslautern

SV Waldhof Mannheim

Mannheim

Karlsruher SC

Karlsruher

1. FC Kaiserslautern

1991, 94, 98

1984, 92, 2003

SC Freiburg

Freiburg im Breisgau

Stuttgart

Darmstadt

Frankfurt am Main

Hamburg

Werder Bremen

Bremen

Arminia Bielefeld

1983, 85, 86, 88, 93, 95

Hannover

Bielefeld

Wattenscheid 09

VfL Bochum

VfL Wolfsburg

Hannover 96

GERMANY

Fortuna Düsseldorf

SV Ulm

Ulm

Stuttgarter Kickers

Rostock

Eintracht Braunschweig

Braunschweig

Berlin

Leipzig

Dresden

Cottbus

Nürnberg

1. FC Nürnberg

Munich

FC Hansa Rostock

Blau-Weiss 90 Berlin

Hertha BSC Berlin

VfB Leipzig

Energie Cottbus

1. FC Dynamo Dresden

Eintracht Frankfurt

Kickers Offenbach

TSV 1860 München

Bayern München

SpVgg Unterhaching

1985–87, 88, 89, 90, 91, 93, 94, 96, 97, 98, 99–2001, 03

Germany (including former East and West Germany)

Deutscher Fussball-Bund
Founded: 1900
Joined FIFA: 1904–46, 1950
Joined UEFA: 1954

LOCAL, CITY AND INTER-CITY LEAGUE matches were being played all across Germany in the late 19th century. In 1898 the first national championship was awarded after a play-off between the winners of the two strongest regional leagues: Southern Germany and Berlin. With the formation of the Deutscher Fussball-Bund in 1900 a more systematic play-off system was introduced between the winners of all the regional leagues in 1902. The format remained the same while the German state grew and shrank. Between 1938 and 1944 Austrian teams were included, and after 1948, when the format was recreated, East Germany and its teams had been separated off.

East Germany retained the format until 1949, before moving to a conventional national league format. In 1963–64 the old championship was abandoned and a national professional league – the Bundesliga – was established. Its format has remained broadly the same since, with two teams from the former East Germany being awarded a place after German unification in 1991. There are now two national leagues of 18 teams, with a standard three up, three down promotion system.

The German Cup was set up in 1935 and it too has seen Austrians join and East Germans depart and return.

German National Championship Record 1903–44

SEASON	CHAMPIONS	SEASON	CHAMPIONS
1903	VfB Leipzig	1926	SpVgg Furth
1904	*	1927	1. FC Nürnberg
1905	Union 92 Berlin	1928	Hamburger SV
1906	VfB Leipzig	1929	SpVgg Furth
1907	SC Freiburg	1930	Hertha BSC Berlin
1908	Viktoria Berlin	1931	Hertha BSC Berlin
1909	Phoenix Karlsruhe	1932	Bayern München
1910	Karlsruher FV	1933	Fortuna Düsseldorf
1911	Viktoria Berlin	1934	FC Schalke 04
1912	Holstein Keil	1935	FC Schalke 04
1913	VfB Leipzig	1936	1. FC Nürnberg
1914	SpVgg Furth	1937	FC Schalke 04
1915–19	no championship	1938	Hannover 96
1920	1. FC Nürnberg	1939	FC Schalke 04
1921	1. FC Nürnberg	1940	FC Schalke 04
1922	**	1941	Rapid Wien
1923	Hamburger SV	1942	FC Schalke 04
1924	1. FC Nürnberg	1943	Dresdener FC
1925	1. FC Nürnberg	1944	Dresdener FC

* Final not played after a dispute over semi-final venues.
** Hamburger SV awarded championship but declined it following an appeal by FC Nürnberg.

West German League Record 1948–63

SEASON	CHAMPIONS	SEASON	CHAMPIONS
1948	1. FC Nürnberg	1956	Borussia Dortmund
1949	VfR Mannheim	1957	Borussia Dortmund
1950	VfB Stuttgart	1958	FC Schalke 04
1951	1. FC Kaiserslautern	1959	Eintracht Frankfurt
1952	VfB Stuttgart	1960	Hamburger SV
1953	1. FC Kaiserslautern	1961	1. FC Nürnberg
1954	Hannover 96	1962	1. FC Köln
1955	Rot-Weiss Essen	1963	Borussia Dortmund

East German League Record 1948–91

SEASON	CHAMPIONS	SEASON	CHAMPIONS
1948	SG Planitz	1970	Carl-Zeiss Jena
1949	ZGS Halle	1971	Dynamo Dresden
1950	Horch Zwickau	1972	1. FC Magdeberg
1951	Chemie Leipzig	1973	Dynamo Dresden
1952	Turbine Halle	1974	1. FC Magdeberg
1953	Dynamo Dresden	1975	1. FC Magdeberg
1954	Turbine Erfurt	1976	Dynamo Dresden
1955	Turbine Erfurt	1977	Dynamo Dresden
1956	Wismut KMS	1978	Dynamo Dresden
1957	Wismut KMS	1979	Dynamo Berlin
1958	Vorwärts Berlin	1980	Dynamo Berlin
1959	Wismut KMS	1981	Dynamo Berlin
1960	Vorwärts Berlin	1982	Dynamo Berlin
1961	no championship	1983	Dynamo Berlin
1962	Vorwärts Berlin	1984	Dynamo Berlin
1963	Motor Jena	1985	Dynamo Berlin
1964	Chemie Leipzig	1986	Dynamo Berlin
1965	Vorwärts Berlin	1987	Dynamo Berlin
1966	Vorwärts Berlin	1988	Dynamo Berlin
1967	FC Karl-Marx-Stadt	1989	Dynamo Dresden
1968	Carl-Zeiss Jena	1990	Dynamo Dresden
1969	Vorwärts Berlin	1991	Hansa Rostock

East German Cup Record 1949–91

YEAR	WINNERS	YEAR	WINNERS
1949	BSG Waggonbau Dessau	1971	SG Dynamo Dresden
1950	BSG EHW Thale	1972	FC Carl-Zeiss Jena
1951	no competition	1973	1. FC Magdeburg
1952	SG Volkspolizei Dresden	1974	FC Carl-Zeiss Jena
1953	no competition	1975	BSG Sachsenring Zwickau
1954	Vorwärts Berlin	1976	1. FC Lokomotive Leipzig
1955	no competition	1977	SG Dynamo Dresden
1956	SC Chemie Halle	1978	1. FC Magdeburg
1957	SC Lokomotive Leipzig	1979	1. FC Magdeburg
1958	SC Einheit Dresden	1980	FC Carl-Zeiss Jena
1959	SC Dynamo Berlin	1981	1. FC Lokomotive Leipzig
1960	SC Motor Jena	1982	SG Dynamo Dresden
1961	no competition	1983	1. FC Magdeburg
1962	SC Chemie Halle	1984	SG Dynamo Dresden
1963	BSC Motor Zwickau	1985	SG Dynamo Dresden
1964	SC Aufbau Magdeburg	1986	1. FC Lokomotive Leipzig
1965	SC Aufbau Magdeburg	1987	1. FC Lokomotive Leipzig
1966	BSG Motor Leipzig	1988	Berliner FC Dynamo
1967	BSC Motor Zwickau	1989	Berliner FC Dynamo
1968	1. FC Union Berlin	1990	SG Dynamo Dresden
1969	1. FC Magdeburg	1991	FC Hansa Rostock
1970	Vorwärts Berlin		

Bundesliga Record 1964–2004

SEASON	CHAMPIONS	RUNNERS-UP
1964	1. FC Köln	MSV Duisburg
1965	Werder Bremen	1. FC Köln
1966	TSV 1860 München	Borussia Dortmund
1967	Eintracht Braunschweig	TSV 1860 München
1968	1. FC Nürnberg	Werder Bremen
1969	Bayern München	Alemania Aachen
1970	Borussia Mönchengladbach	Bayern München
1971	Borussia Mönchengladbach	Bayern München
1972	Bayern München	FC Schalke 04
1973	Bayern München	1. FC Köln
1974	Bayern München	Borussia Mönchengladbach
1975	Borussia Mönchengladbach	Hertha BSC Berlin
1976	Borussia Mönchengladbach	Hamburger SV
1977	Borussia Mönchengladbach	FC Schalke 04

GERMANY

Bundesliga Record (*continued*)

SEASON	CHAMPIONS	RUNNERS-UP
1978	1. FC Köln	Borussia Mönchengladbach
1979	Hamburger SV	VfB Stuttgart
1980	Bayern München	Hamburger SV
1981	Bayern München	Hamburger SV
1982	Hamburger SV	1. FC Köln
1983	Hamburger SV	Werder Bremen
1984	VfB Stuttgart	Hamburger SV
1985	Bayern München	Werder Bremen
1986	Bayern München	Werder Bremen
1987	Bayern München	Hamburger SV
1988	Werder Bremen	Bayern München
1989	Bayern München	1. FC Köln
1990	Bayern München	1. FC Köln
1991	1. FC Kaiserslautern	Bayern München
1992	VfB Stuttgart	Borussia Dortmund
1993	Werder Bremen	Bayern München
1994	Bayern München	1. FC Kaiserslautern
1995	Borussia Dortmund	Werder Bremen
1996	Borussia Dortmund	Bayern München
1997	Bayern München	Bayer Leverkusen
1998	1. FC Kaiserslautern	Bayern München
1999	Bayern München	Bayer Leverkusen
2000	Bayern München	Bayer Leverkusen
2001	Bayern München	FC Schalke 04
2002	Borussia Dortmund	Bayer Leverkusen
2003	Bayern München	VfB Stuttgart
2004	Werder Bremen	Bayern München

Bundesliga Summary

TEAM	TOTALS	CHAMPIONS & RUNNERS-UP (BOLD) (*ITALICS*)
Bayern München	17, 7	**1969**, *70, 71, 72–74, 80, 81, 85–87,* *89, 90,* **91,** *93,* **94,** *96,* **97,** *98,* *99–2001,* **03,** *04*
Borussia Mönchengladbach	5, 2	**1970, 71, 74,** *75–77, 78*
Werder Bremen	4, 5	**1965,** *68, 83, 85, 86,* **88, 93, 95, 2004**
Hamburger SV	3, 5	*1976, 79, 80, 81,* **82, 83,** *84, 87*
Borussia Dortmund	3, 2	**1966,** *92,* **95, 96,** *2002*
1. FC Köln	2, 6	**1964,** *65, 73,* **78,** *82, 88–90*
VfB Stuttgart	2, 2	*1979,* **84,** *92,* **2003**
1. FC Kaiserslautern	2, 1	**1991,** *94,* **98**
TSV 1860 München	1, 1	**1966,** *67*
1. FC Nürnberg	1, 0	**1968**
Eintracht Braunschweig	1, 0	**1967**
Bayer Leverkusen	0, 4	*1997, 99, 2000, 02*
FC Schalke 04	0, 3	*1972, 77, 2001*
Alemania Aachen	0, 1	*1969*
Hertha BSC Berlin	0, 1	*1975*
MSV Duisberg	0, 1	*1964*

German Cup Record 1935–2004

YEAR	WINNERS	SCORE	RUNNERS-UP
1935	1. FC Nürnberg	2-0	FC Schalke 04
1936	VfB Leipzig	2-1	FC Schalke 04
1937	FC Schalke 04	2-1	Fortuna Düsseldorf
1938	SK Rapid Wien	3-1	FSV Frankfurt
1939	1. FC Nürnberg	2-0	SV Waldhof Mannheim
1940	Dresdener SC	2-1 (aet)	1. FC Nürnberg
1941	Dresdener SC	2-1	FC Schalke 04
1942	TSV 1860 München	2-0	FC Schalke 04
1943	First Vienna FC	3-2 (aet)	Hamburger SV
1944–52	*no competition*		
1953	Rot-Weiss Essen	2-1	Alemania Aachen
1954	VfB Stuttgart	1-0 (aet)	1. FC Köln
1955	Karlsruher SC	3-2	FC Schalke 04

German Cup Record (*continued*)

YEAR	WINNERS	SCORE	RUNNERS-UP
1956	Karlsruher SC	3-1	Hamburger SV
1957	Bayern München	1-0	Fortuna Düsseldorf
1958	VfB Stuttgart	4-3	Fortuna Düsseldorf
1959	Schwarz Weiss Essen	5-2	Borussia Neunkirchen
1960	Borussia Mönchengladbach	3-2	Karlsruher FC
1961	Werder Bremen	2-0	1. FC Kaiserslautern
1962	1. FC Nurnberg	2-1 (aet)	Fortuna Düsseldorf
1963	Hamburger SV	3-0	Borussia Dortmund
1964	TSV 1860 München	2-0	Eintracht Frankfurt
1965	Borussia Dortmund	2-0	Alemania Aachen
1966	Bayern München	4-2	MSV Duisburg
1967	Bayern München	4-0	Hamburger SV
1968	1. FC Köln	4-1	VfL Bochum
1969	Bayern München	2-1	FC Schalke 04
1970	Kickers Offenbach	2-1	1. FC Köln
1971	Bayern München	2-1 (aet)	1. FC Köln
1972	FC Schlake 04	5-0	1. FC Kaiserslautern
1973	Borussia Mönchengladbach	2-1 (aet)	1. FC Köln
1974	Eintracht Frankfurt	3-1 (aet)	Hamburger SV
1975	Eintracht Frankfurt	1-0	MSV Duisburg
1976	Hamburger SV	2-0	1. FC Kaiserslautern
1977	1. FC Köln	1-1 (aet), (replay) 1-0	Hertha BSC Berlin
1978	1. FC Köln	2-0	Fortuna Düsseldorf
1979	Fortuna Düsseldorf	1-0 (aet)	Hertha BSC Berlin
1980	Fortuna Düsseldorf	2-1	1. FC Köln
1981	Eintracht Frankfurt	3-1	1. FC Kaiserslautern
1982	Bayern München	4-2	1. FC Nürnberg
1983	1. FC Köln	1-0	Fortuna Köln
1984	Bayern München	1-1 (aet)(7-6 pens)	Borussia Mönchengladbach
1985	Bayer Uerdingen	2-1	Bayern München
1986	Bayern München	5-2	VfB Stuttgart
1987	Hamburger SV	3-1	Stuttgarter Kickers
1988	Eintracht Frankfurt	1-0	VfL Bochum
1989	Borussia Dortmund	4-1	Werder Bremen
1990	1. FC Kaiserslautern	3-2	Werder Bremen
1991	Werder Bremen	1-1 (aet)(4-3 pens)	1. FC Köln
1992	Hannover 96	0-0 (aet)(4-3 pens)	Borussia Mönchengladbach
1993	Bayer 04 Leverkusen	1-0	Hertha BSC Berlin
1994	Werder Bremen	3-1	Rot-Weiss Essen
1995	Borussia Mönchengladbach	3-0	Wolfsburg
1996	1. FC Kaiserslautern	1-0	Karlsruher FC
1997	VfB Stuttgart	2-0	Energie Cottbus
1998	Bayern München	2-1	MSV Duisburg
1999	Werder Bremen	1-1 (aet)(5-4 pens)	Bayern München
2000	Bayern München	3-0	Werder Bremen
2001	FC Schalke 04	2-0	1. FC Union Berlin
2002	FC Schalke 04	4-2	Bayer Leverkusen
2003	Bayern München	3-1	1. FC Kaiserslautern
2004	Werder Bremen	3-2	Alemannia Aachen

German Cup Summary

TEAM	TOTAL	WINNERS & RUNNERS-UP (BOLD) (*ITALICS*)
Bayern München	11, 2	**1957, 66, 67, 69, 71, 82, 84,** *85,* **86,** **98,** *99,* **2000,** *03*
Werder Bremen	5, 3	**1961,** *89, 90,* **91, 94, 99,** *2000,* **04**
1. FC Köln	4, 6	*1954,* **68,** *70, 71, 73,* **77, 78,** *80,* *83,* **91**
FC Schalke 04	4, 6	**1935,** *36,* **37,** *41, 42, 55, 69,* **72, 2001, 02**
Eintracht Frankfurt	4, 1	*1964,* **74, 75, 81,** *88*

This summary only features clubs that have won the German Cup four times or more. For a full list of cup winners and runners-up please see the Cup Record above.

France

THE SEASON IN REVIEW 2003–04

ALMOST A DECADE HAD PASSED since a French club contested a European final, but 2004 saw Marseille in the UEFA Cup Final and Monaco in the Champions League Final. Olympique Lyonnais made the quarter-finals of the Champions League as well. Although all three could count notable scalps on their European adventures, neither Lyon nor Monaco could get past the organizational and tactical precision of Porto, while Marseille could match Valencia with 11 players but were always going to lose with only 10. This improvement in French fortunes coincides with the recent decline in the value of the European transfer market. French clubs, relying on smaller incomes than the other big leagues and paying higher taxes, are able to both attract and retain more talent than before, though the vast majority of the national team continues to play outside France. Monaco, Lyon and Marseille are examples of French soccer's continuing capacity to nurture domestic talent, both in terms of players and coaches. They have also cannily attracted cast-offs from bigger clubs in bigger leagues, Monaco's Morientes and Lyon's Giovane Elber being deemed surplus to requirements at Real Madrid and Bayern München respectively.

The Monaco anomaly

How quickly things can change. At the start of the season the presidents of the clubs that make up the top division in France were complaining about Monaco's place in the Champions League. Olympique Marseille president Christoph Bouchet said, 'They take a Champions League place away from other French clubs'. Monaco is certainly an anomaly, being the only club from an independent state who plays in the league of another state. Of course, the presidents had no intention of kicking Monaco out of the league, but they were looking to pressurise

FRANCE

Le Championnat League Table 2003–04

CLUB	P	W	D	L	F	A	Pts	
Olympique Lyonnais	38	24	7	7	64	26	79	Champions League
Paris Saint-Germain	38	22	10	6	50	28	76	Champions League
AS Monaco	38	21	12	5	59	30	75	Champions League
AJ Auxerre	38	19	8	11	60	34	65	UEFA Cup
FC Sochaux	38	18	9	11	54	42	63	UEFA Cup (League Cup winners)
FC Nantes	38	17	9	12	47	35	60	
Olympique Marseille	38	17	6	15	51	45	57	
RC Lens	38	15	8	15	34	48	53	
Stade Rennais	38	14	10	14	56	44	52	
Lille OSC	38	14	9	15	41	41	51	
OGC Nice	38	11	17	10	42	39	50	
Bordeaux	38	13	11	14	40	43	50	
RC Strasbourg	38	10	13	15	43	50	43	
FC Metz	38	11	9	18	34	42	42	
AC Ajaccio	38	10	10	18	33	55	40	
Toulouse FC	38	9	12	17	31	44	39	
SC Bastia	38	9	12	17	33	49	39	
Guingamp	38	10	8	20	36	58	38	Relegated
Le Mans UC72	38	9	11	18	35	57	38	Relegated
Montpellier HSC	38	8	7	23	41	74	31	Relegated

Promoted clubs: AS Saint-Etienne, Stade Malherbe Caen, FC Istres.
Châteauroux take the 3rd UEFA Cup place as French Cup runners-up (the winners, Paris Saint-Germain, having qualified for the Champions League).

One of the best buys in European soccer? Giovane Elber's move from Bayern München to Olympique Lyonnais gave the French champions another powerful option up front. Here Elber takes on Ajaccio's Frederic Danjou.

James Fanchone of Le Mans looks to break through the Lens defence, but try as they might Le Mans could not pull themselves out of the relegation zone.

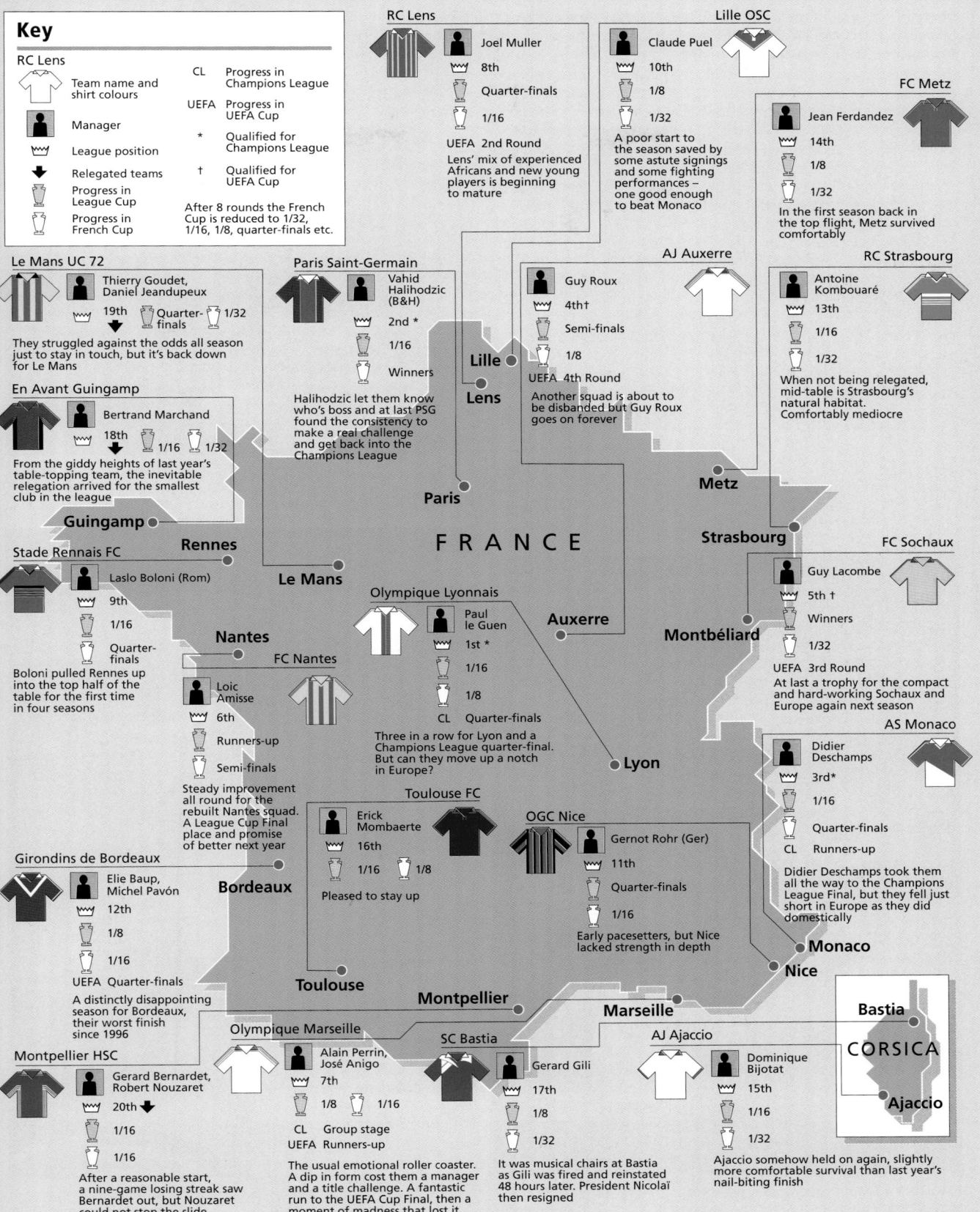

Key

RC Lens — Team name and shirt colours

Manager

League position

Relegated teams

Progress in League Cup

Progress in French Cup

CL — Progress in Champions League

UEFA — Progress in UEFA Cup

* — Qualified for Champions League

† — Qualified for UEFA Cup

After 8 rounds the French Cup is reduced to 1/32, 1/16, 1/8, quarter-finals etc.

RC Lens
Joel Muller
8th
Quarter-finals
1/16
UEFA 2nd Round
Lens' mix of experienced Africans and new young players is beginning to mature

Lille OSC
Claude Puel
10th
1/8
1/32
A poor start to the season saved by some astute signings and some fighting performances – one good enough to beat Monaco

FC Metz
Jean Ferdandez
14th
1/8
1/32
In the first season back in the top flight, Metz survived comfortably

Le Mans UC 72
Thierry Goudet, Daniel Jeandupeux
19th
Quarter-finals
1/32
They struggled against the odds all season just to stay in touch, but it's back down for Le Mans

Paris Saint-Germain
Vahid Halilodzic (B&H)
2nd *
1/16
Winners
Halilodzic let them know who's boss and at last PSG found the consistency to make a real challenge and get back into the Champions League

AJ Auxerre
Guy Roux
4th†
Semi-finals
1/8
UEFA 4th Round
Another squad is about to be disbanded but Guy Roux goes on forever

RC Strasbourg
Antoine Kombouaré
13th
1/16
1/32
When not being relegated, mid-table is Strasbourg's natural habitat. Comfortably mediocre

En Avant Guingamp
Bertrand Marchand
18th
1/16
1/32
From the giddy heights of last year's table-topping team, the inevitable relegation arrived for the smallest club in the league

Stade Rennais FC
Laslo Boloni (Rom)
9th
1/16
Quarter-finals
Boloni pulled Rennes up into the top half of the table for the first time in four seasons

FC Nantes
Loic Amisse
6th
Runners-up
Semi-finals
Steady improvement all round for the rebuilt Nantes squad. A League Cup Final place and promise of better next year

Olympique Lyonnais
Paul le Guen
1st *
1/16
1/8
CL Quarter-finals
Three in a row for Lyon and a Champions League quarter-final. But can they move up a notch in Europe?

FC Sochaux
Guy Lacombe
5th †
Winners
1/32
UEFA 3rd Round
At last a trophy for the compact and hard-working Sochaux and Europe again next season

AS Monaco
Didier Deschamps
3rd*
1/16
Quarter-finals
CL Runners-up
Didier Deschamps took them all the way to the Champions League Final, but they fell just short in Europe as they did domestically

Girondins de Bordeaux
Elie Baup, Michel Pavón
12th
1/8
1/16
UEFA Quarter-finals
A distinctly disappointing season for Bordeaux, their worst finish since 1996

Toulouse FC
Erick Mombaerte
16th
1/16 1/8
Pleased to stay up

OGC Nice
Gernot Rohr (Ger)
11th
Quarter-finals
1/16
Early pacesetters, but Nice lacked strength in depth

Montpellier HSC
Gerard Bernardet, Robert Nouzaret
20th
1/16
1/16
After a reasonable start, a nine-game losing streak saw Bernardet out, but Nouzaret could not stop the slide

Olympique Marseille
Alain Perrin, José Anigo
7th
1/8 1/16
CL Group stage
UEFA Runners-up
The usual emotional roller coaster. A dip in form cost them a manager and a title challenge. A fantastic run to the UEFA Cup Final, then a moment of madness that lost it

SC Bastia
Gerard Gili
17th
1/8
1/32
It was musical chairs at Bastia as Gili was fired and reinstated 48 hours later. President Nicolaï then resigned

AJ Ajaccio
Dominique Bijotat
15th
1/16
1/32
Ajaccio somehow held on again, slightly more comfortable survival than last year's nail-biting finish

FRANCE

Lille · Lens · Paris · Le Mans · Guingamp · Rennes · Nantes · Bordeaux · Toulouse · Montpellier · Marseille · Lyon · Auxerre · Metz · Strasbourg · Montbéliard · Nice · Monaco · Bastia · Ajaccio

CORSICA

FRANCE

UEFA into changing their regulations and offer a separate place to Monaco while retaining current levels of French representation. The idea must have seemed all the more attractive to the rest of the league as Monaco took an early lead in the championship. Last year's top scorer Shabani Nonda suffered a very serious knee ligament injury early on and was out for seven months of the season. Deschamps was able to replace him with Fernando Morientes who, alongside captain Ludovic Giuly and Croat Dado Prso, formed a fast and effective strike force.

Auxerre were the only other club who looked to compete with the top three for the title. But, in the space of a month in the early spring, they were knocked out of the League Cup, beaten on penalties by Nantes, knocked out of the French Cup by fourth division Brive in a humiliating 1-0 defeat, and lost any chance of mounting a real challenge for the championship as Lyon beat them 2-1 at home. Finally, PSV swept them out of the UEFA Cup Fourth Round. Yet Guy Roux managed to rally his dispirited squad, many of whom are destined for bigger clubs in other countries next season, and kept them in fourth spot, sealed with a final day victory over Nantes who had been pushing them for a European place. Sochaux, who finished in fifth, rounded off a brilliant season with a trophy – the League Cup – beating Nantes on penalties to win the club's first major trophy since 1938.

Mid-table was mixture of bigger clubs in internal turmoil – including Bordeaux, Bastia and, Europe aside, Marseille. Indeed Marseille threw away their lead at the top of the table after eleven games when the dressing room erupted with discontent and coach Perrin was sacked. Metz and Rennes were pleased to

PSG sealed their revival in the league with a hard fought but clear-cut 2-1 victory over Marseille in April. Here PSG striker Pedro Pauleta is hustled off the ball by Marseille's Manuel Dos Santos.

PSG were a team transformed, with goals coming from across the squad. Juan Pablo Sorin takes the ball past Ajaccio's Yohan Demont.

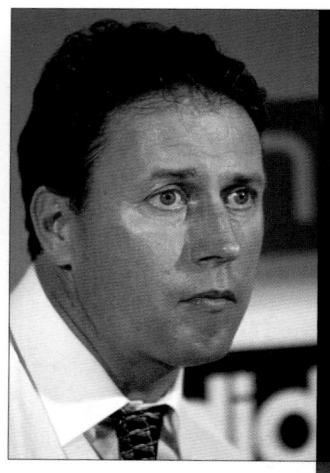

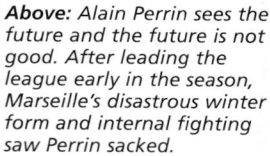

Above: Alain Perrin sees the future and the future is not good. After leading the league early in the season, Marseille's disastrous winter form and internal fighting saw Perrin sacked.

Above, right: With a third title in a row and a Champions League quarter-final place, Olympique Lyonnais coach Paul le Guen has more than delivered on the promise of Jacques Santini's team.

Right: Djibril Cisse played his last season for the club that nurtured him – Auxerre. He starts with Liverpool in summer 2004.

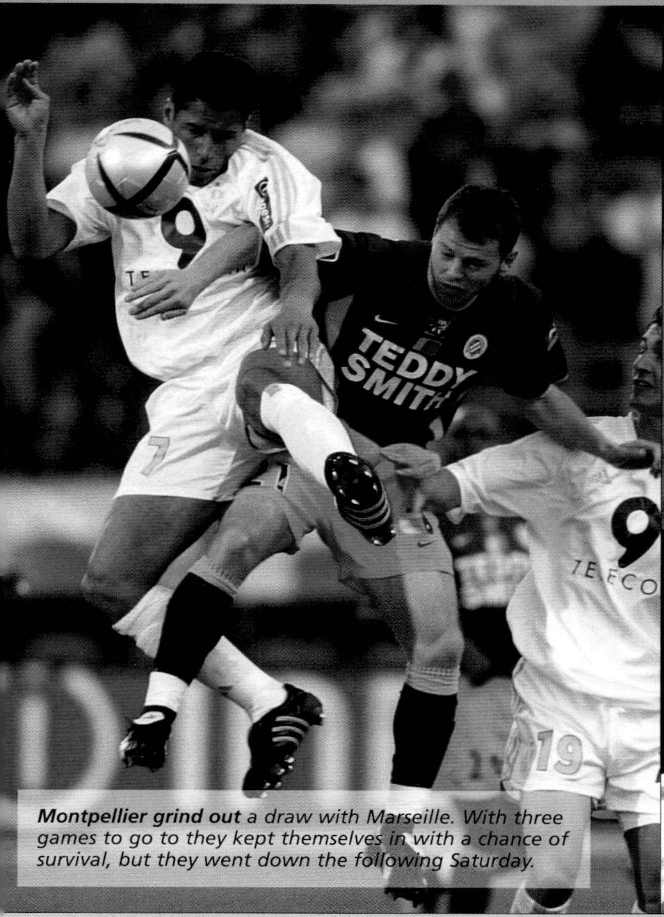
TEDDY SMITH

Montpellier grind out *a draw with Marseille. With three games to go to they kept themselves in with a chance of survival, but they went down the following Saturday.*

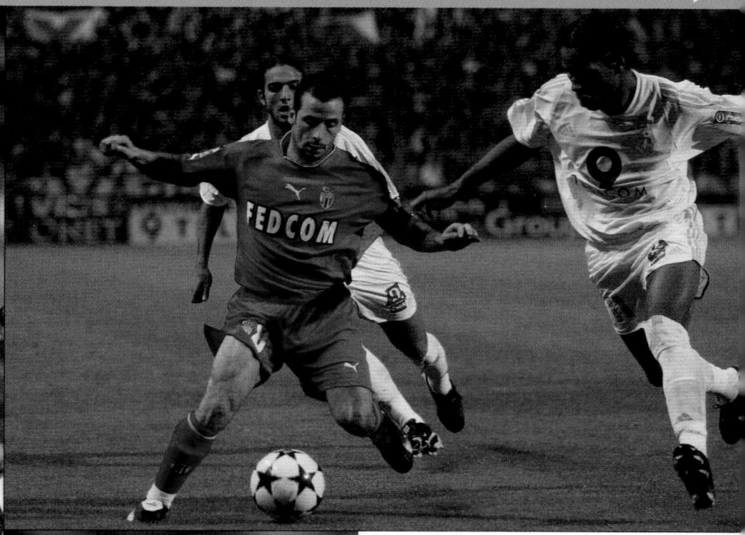
FEDCOM

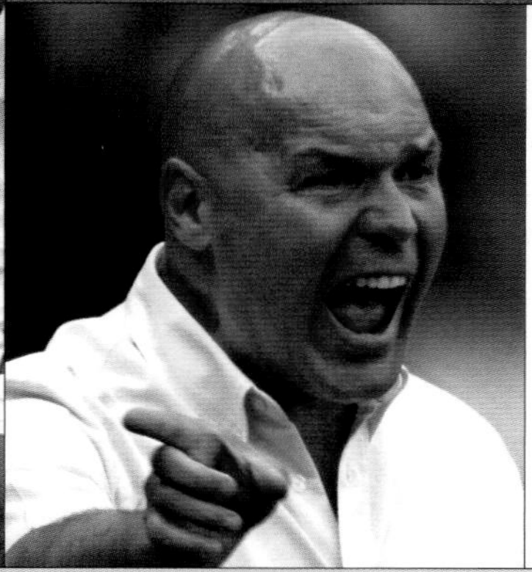

Above: *Two giants clash as Monaco's Ludovic Giuly (left) is closed down by Olympique Marseille's Didier Drogba.*

Left: *Jose Angio took over from Alain Perrin at Marseille this year. The ex-player had plenty to say at some volume and it got them to the UEFA Cup Final, but they never managed to recover their league position and miss out on Europe in 2004–05.*

Race for the Championship

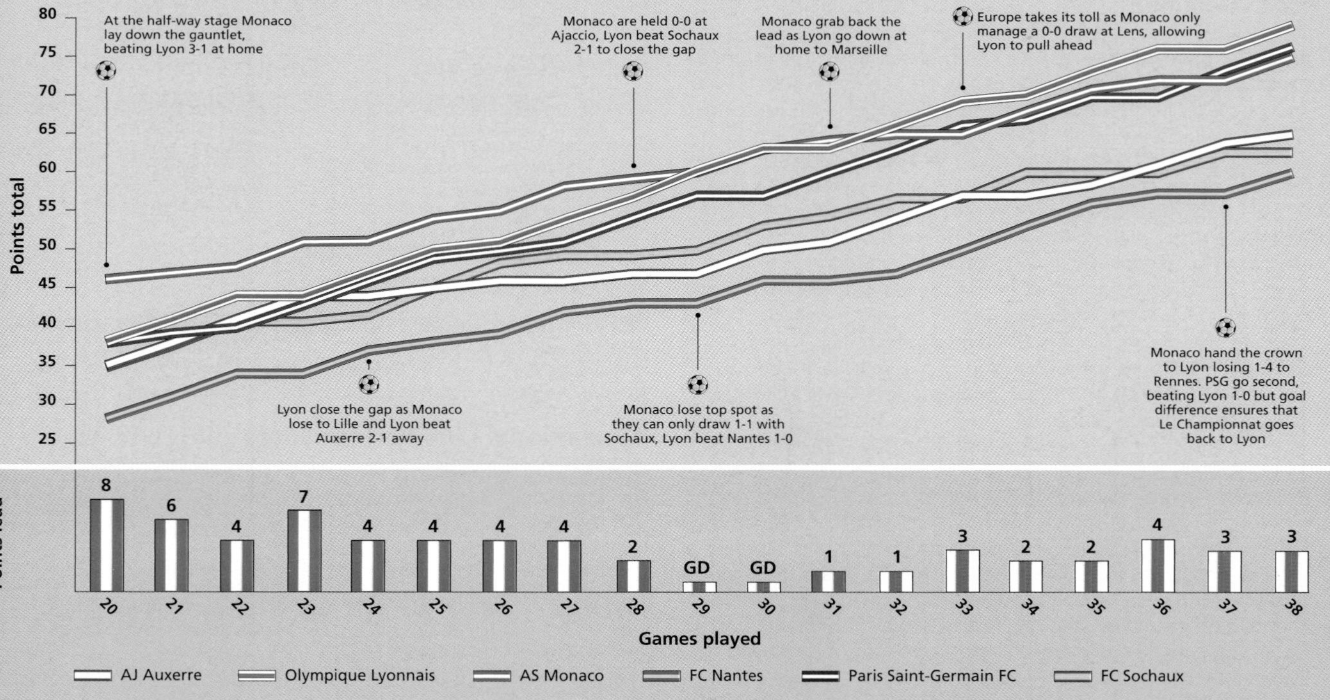
Points total
80
75
70
65
60
55
50
45
40
35
30
25
At the half-way stage Monaco lay down the gauntlet, beating Lyon 3-1 at home
Monaco are held 0-0 at Ajaccio, Lyon beat Sochaux 2-1 to close the gap
Monaco grab back the lead as Lyon go down at home to Marseille
Europe takes its toll as Monaco only manage a 0-0 draw at Lens, allowing Lyon to pull ahead
Lyon close the gap as Monaco lose to Lille and Lyon beat Auxerre 2-1 away
Monaco lose top spot as they can only draw 1-1 with Sochaux, Lyon beat Nantes 1-0
Monaco hand the crown to Lyon losing 1-4 to Rennes. PSG go second, beating Lyon 1-0 but goal difference ensures that Le Championnat goes back to Lyon
Points lead
8 6 4 7 4 4 4 4 2 GD GD 1 1 3 2 2 4 3 3
20 21 22 23 24 25 26 27 28 29 30 31 32 33 34 35 36 37 38
Games played
AJ Auxerre
Olympique Lyonnais
AS Monaco
FC Nantes
Paris Saint-Germain FC
FC Sochaux

keep out of trouble of all kinds. Montpellier were the first club to be relegated having descended to the bottom half of the table in the second half of the season. The final placings were decided on the last day with Toulouse and Ajaccio just managing to get themselves out of trouble while two of the smallest clubs took the tumble: Le Mans and En Avant Guingamp.

Champions League responsibilities

The defining game of the title race came just after the end of the winter break. Monaco, already five points ahead of their nearest challengers, went to Lyon and comprehensively beat them 3-0 to take an eight-point lead at the top. Ten games later Lyon had crawled their way back into contention, taking top spot on goal difference as Monaco dropped points once again in a goalless draw with Ajaccio. Lyon, by contrast, had stolen a single goal to take all the points at Nantes. In the final run, Lyon maintained their edge over Monaco and the hard chasing PSG. Monaco, clearly strained by their Champions League responsibilities, quietly slipped away with three games to go as they could only manage a goalless draw with Strasbourg. They let second place slip to PSG who seem finally to have acquired some of the form, organization and consistency that has eluded squad after squad and coach after coach. New coach Vahid Halilhodzic arrived with a reputation for miracles having taken tiny Lille from nowhere to the Champions League and saved Stade Rennais from certain relegation. PSG presented a different task and the year began with very early morning training and unambiguous ultimatums to the players. Once again, Halilhodzic hit the right notes. PSG became extremely difficult to beat; their meanness built around captain and central defender Frédéric Déhu and their outstanding goalkeeper Jérôme Alonzo. Goals have come via the prolific Danijel Ljuboja and Pedro Pauleta. It was Pauleta who scored PSG's only goal in the French Cup Final that saw them beat second division Châteauroux and round off a season of immense improvement with their first trophy since 1998.

It's Lyon again

Olympique Lyonnais achieved what only two other clubs have managed in French soccer – to win the championship in three consecutive years. Their predecessors, St Etienne in the 1970s and Marseille in the early 1990s, stamped their authority and character on their eras. St Etienne were the last of the hard-working teams of small-town industrial France. Marseille were the cosmopolitan showmen of the Mitterrand years – forever tarnished by their legacy of corruption. And Olympique Lyonnais? What era do they reflect or are they making? They are certainly capable of a comeback as, like last season, they made up a large point deficit in the second half of their season. Key players like French international Péguy Luyindula or Brazilian playmaker Juninho Pernambucano bring a flash of style, but consistency and focus on the league have been their hallmarks on the pitch. Off the pitch president Jean-Michel Aulas offered this explanation: 'Seventeen years ago, the club was in the second division with a budget of 2.3 million euros and yearly debts of one million euros. Today, we have an 80 million euros revenue, with a 35 million profit.' Olympique Lyonnais is, unquestionably, the best funded and staffed club in France. It is organized and run more explicitly as a business than any French club before – most of which exist in the grey zones of semi-commercial social clubs and personal local fiefdoms. The question remains whether this new business model for French soccer can compete in the uneven playing fields of European competition.

Oh yes. Sochaux captain Benoit Pedretti lifts the French League Cup and roars after Sochaux beat Nantes on penalties.

French League Cup

2004 FINAL

April 17 – Stade de France, Paris
FC Nantes **1-1** FC Sochaux
(Pujol 14) *(Monsoreau 19)*
(after extra time)
h/t: 1-1 **Att:** 78,409
Ref: Garibian
FC Sochaux won 5-4 on pens

French Cup

2004 FINAL

May 29 – Stade de France, Paris
Paris Saint- **1-0** LB Châteauroux
Germain
(Pauleta 65)
h/t: 0-0 **Att:** 78,000
Ref: Bré

Top Goalscorers 2003–04

PLAYER	CLUB	NATIONALITY	GOALS
Djibril Cisse	AJ Auxerre	French	26
Alexander Frei	Stade Rennais	Swiss	19
Didier Drogba	Olympique Marseille	Cote d'Ivoirean	18

International Club Performances 2003–04

CLUB	COMPETITION	PROGRESS
AS Monaco	Champions League	Runners-up
Olympique Lyonnais	Champions League	Quarter-finals
Olympique Marseille	Champions League	Group Stage
Bordeaux	UEFA Cup	Runners-up
AJ Auxerre	UEFA Cup	Quarter-finals
FC Sochaux	UEFA Cup	4th Round
RC Lens	UEFA Cup	3rd Round
	UEFA Cup	2nd Round

FRANCE

Top: An old head on a relatively young body. In only his second season at Monaco, Didier Deschamps managed to get the best from his small squad and played tactically astute soccer.

Top, left: Sochaux's Monsoreau grabs their 18th-minute equalizer in the French League Cup Final against Nantes.

Above: They lost the game but won the league. Lyon celebrate three titles in a row after their game against Lille. From left to right: Juninho, Michael Essien and Sidney Govou.

Left: Pedro Pauleta's single headed goal was enough to give PSG their first trophy since 1998, beating Châteauroux in the French Cup Final.

Soccer in France

FRANCE

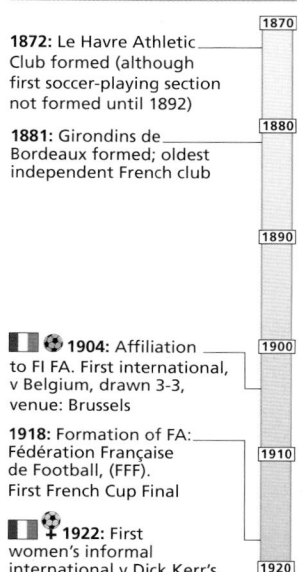

1870

1872: Le Havre Athletic Club formed (although first soccer-playing section not formed until 1892)

1880

1881: Girondins de Bordeaux formed; oldest independent French club

1890

1900

1904: Affiliation to FI FA. First international, v Belgium, drawn 3-3, venue: Brussels

1918: Formation of FA: Fédération Française de Football, (FFF). First French Cup Final

1910

1922: First women's informal international v Dick Kerr's Ladies (England), drawn 1-1, venue: Paris

1920

1923: First edition of *France Football* published

1932: National league established; professionalism legalized

1930

1940–45: During war league championship played as play-offs between regions, cup continued

1940

1950

1954: Affiliation to UEFA

1955–56: Inspired by the French press, the first European Cup competition is held with the Final played in Paris

1960

1958: France reach semi-finals of the World Cup. French Algerians withdraw from French soccer to form independent Algerian team

1970

1986: France reach semi-finals of the World Cup

1980

1992: Cup abandoned after Bastia disaster, a temporary stand collapsed in Cup semi-final, Bastia v Olympique Marseille, over 1,500 injured

1990

1993: Olympique Marseille stripped of European Cup and French League title for match-fixing

2000

2001: France play Algeria in Paris in the first post-independence meeting of the teams – match abandoned due to crowd trouble

2010

Jules Rimet (left) – lawyer, first President of FIFA and pioneer of the World Cup – hands its first-ever trophy to Dr Paul Jude, President of the Uruguayan FA. Uruguay beat Argentina 4-2 in the Final in Montevideo on 30 July 1930.

Key

🇫🇷	International soccer	◼	European Championships host
⚽	Affiliation to FIFA	●	European Championships winner
⚽	Affiliation to UEFA	○	Competition winner
⚽	Women's soccer	△	Competition runner-up
🏆	War		
🌿	Disaster	Bas	– Bastia
		Bor	– Bordeaux
◼	World Cup host	Mon	– Monaco
●	World Cup winner	OM	– Olympique Marseille
		PSG	– Paris Saint-Germain
		St-E	– St-Etienne
		St R	– Stade de Reims

International Competitions

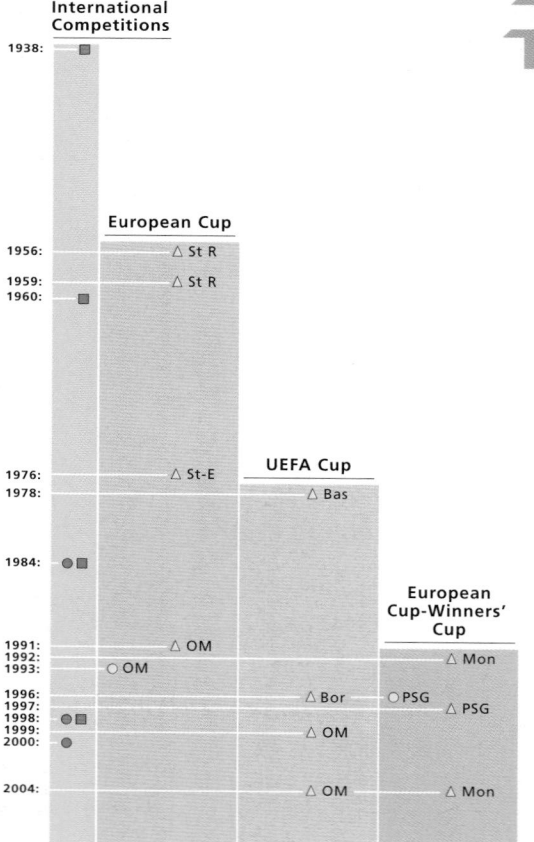

1938: ◼

European Cup

1956: △ St R
1959: △ St R
1960: ◼

1954: Affiliation to UEFA

1976: △ St-E
1978: **UEFA Cup** △ Bas

1984: ● ◼

European Cup-Winners' Cup

1991: △ OM
1992: ○ OM
1993:

1996: △ Bor ○ PSG
1997: ○ PSG
1998: ● ◼
1999: △ OM
2000: ●

2004: △ OM △ Mon

Stade Français 1883
Stade Red Star (1948–50). Dissolved 1985

⭐ **CA Charenton** 1891

🏆 ⭐ **Club Français Paris** 1892

🏆

⭐ **Red Star 93** 1897

🏆 🏆 🏆

Merged with Olympique de Paris to form Red Star Olympique, (1926–46)
Merged with Stade Français to form Stade Red Star, (1948–50)
Red Star Olympique Audonien, (1950–67)
Merged with Tolouse to form Red Star Tolouse, (1967–70)
Red Star 93, (1970–present)

Paris Saint-Germain FC 1970

Merger of Paris FC and St-Germain En Laye

⭐ **Racing Club de Paris** 1932

👕 ⬆

(Folded 1965)

CAS Généraux
⬆

Caen
SM Caen
1913

Le Havre
Le Havre A
1872

Guingamp ● **En Avant Guingamp** 1912

Brest
● **Brest-Armorique FC** 1912

Rennes
Stade Rennais FC 1901

Laval
Stade Lavallois MFC 1902

Lorient
FC Lorient 1926

Le M
Le Ma
UC 72

Tours
FC Tours 1951

Angers
● SCO Angers 1919

Nantes

FC Nantes Atlantique 1943

👕

Merger of St Pierre, Mellenet, Loire, ASO Nantes and Stade Nantes (1943)

Niort
● Chamois Niortais FC 1925

Angoulême
AS Angoulême ● 1925

FC Girondins de Bordeaux 1881

👕

● **Bordeaux**
F R

⭐ **Nîmes OSC** 1901

SC Nîmes (1901–1937)

Toulouse
Toulouse FC 1970

⭐ **FC Sète** 1914

👕 🏆

⭐ **Montpellier HSC** 1919/1974

🏆

Founded as Sports Olympique Montpellier, dissolved 1969

FC Martigues 1921

France: The main clubs

RC Lens 1906	Team name with year of formation
●	Club formed before 1912
●	Club formed 1912–25
●	Club formed 1925–50
○	Club formed after 1950
★	Founder members of League
👕	Champions (1933–50)
👕	Champions (1951–80)
🏆	Cup winners (1918–33)
	Formed by Jules Rimet
†	Church origins
⬆	Elite origins
	Fan donor origins
🏭	Hardware factory origins
	Mining origins
🚗	Car factory
●	Date unknown

Map labels

RC Lens 1906

★ CO Roubaix-Tourcoing 1945

Merger of Racing, Excelsior and US Tourcoing

★ Lille OSC 1944

Merger of SC Fives (1908) and Olympique Lillois (1910)

Roubaix
RC Roubaix 1895

Valenciennes FC 1913

Lille
Lens

Amiens SCF 1901

Sedan
FC Sedan 1919

Reims
★ Stade de Reims 1931

Paris

Créteil
US Créteil 1937

Troyes
Troyes-Aube 1986

Auxerre
AJ Auxerre 1905 †

Châteauroux
LB Châteauroux 1883

Limoges
FC Limoges 1947

St-Étienne

Grenoble
FC Grenoble 1892

C E

Alès
FC Olympique Alèsien 1923

Nîmes

Montpellier
AS Béziers 1913

Sète

Martigues

Marseille
SC Toulon-Var 1945

★ Olympique Marseille 1899

Metz
★ FC Metz 1932

Strasbourg
RC Strasbourg 1906

Nancy

SR Colmar 1930

Colmar

Mulhouse
FC Mulhouse 1893

Montbéliard

RC Franc Comtois 1905

AS Nancy-Lorraine 1935

FC Nancy (1935–67)

★ FC Sochaux-Montbéliard 1928

Gueugnon
FC Gueugnonnais 1940

Formed from merger of FC Sochaux and FC Montbéliard (1935)

Lyon
Olympique Lyonnais 1950

AS Saint-Etienne 1933

AS Monaco 1924

Royal House

Olympiques Avignonnais 1929

★ OGC Nice 1904

Avignon

Aix-en-Provence
AS Aixoise 1941

Monaco
Nice

Cannes

Toulon

Hyères

★ AS Cannes 1902

Hyères FC 1912

Bastia
SC Bastia 1905

Ajaccio
AC Ajaccien 1910

CORSICA

France

ORIGINS AND GROWTH OF SOCCER

THE DEVELOPMENT OF French domestic soccer was slow. Rugby was significantly more popular than soccer in 19th-century France, and early soccer clubs often grew up out of rugby clubs or other sport and athletic associations. For example, Le Havre was founded in 1872, but did not play soccer until 1892. Prior to the First World War, five different organizations claimed the mantle of the national FA before the creation of single institution, the FFF, in 1918. Though a national cup competition began almost immediately, it was only after considerable resistance that professionalism was acceptedand a national league was not contested until 1932.

Rimet and Hunot

However, domestic disorganization and weakness was paralleled by international inventiveness. France was a founder member of FIFA and supplied its first president, Jules Rimet. Rimet was instrumental in establishing the World Cup, and Gabriel Hunot, editor of sports paper *L'Équipe*, was the inspiration behind the European Cup. However, it is only since the 1950s that French soccer has seen signs of sporting rather than organizational life. Stade de Reims' European adventures in the 1950s, Platini and the national team in the 1980s, Olympique Marseille and Monaco in the 1990s have been the high points in an era of otherwise mediocre performances and small crowds.

Exceeding all of these, however, is the extraordinary recent success of the national team and the massive financial and organizational investment in soccer's infrastructure by the French government. So far, this has delivered the World Cup in 1998 and the European Championships in 2000. In 2001, France finally displaced Brazil as the world's number one team in the FIFA rankings. But it was short-lived as a depleted French team crashed out in the first round of the 2002 World Cup.

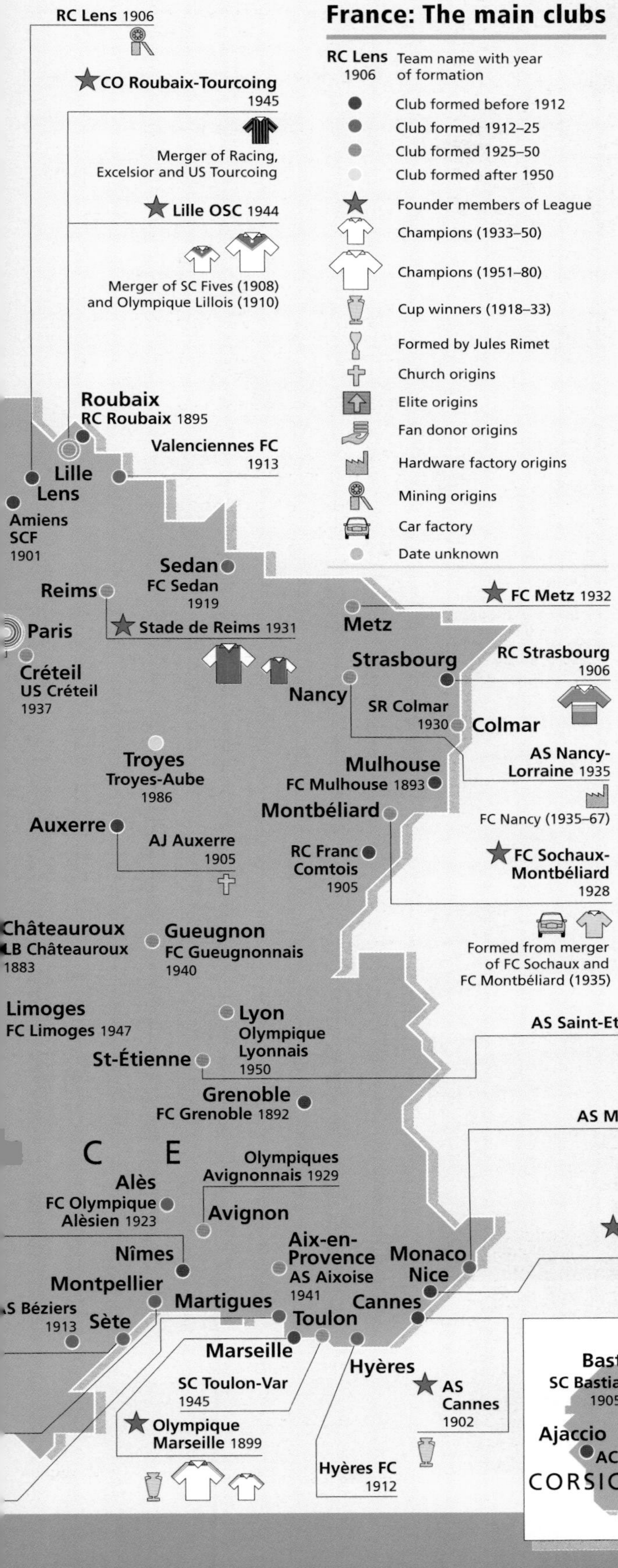

Just Fontaine challenges Real Madrid's goalkeeper in the 1959 European Cup Final. Fontaine's Stade de Reims was the brightest star in French soccer between the war and the rise of Tapie's Olympique Marseille in the early 1990s.

FRANCE

France

SOCCER CENTERS

THE GEOGRAPHY OF FRANCE'S soccer teams reflects the peculiar geography of French urbanization: late to develop, slow in coming and massively concentrated on Paris. No French city outside of Paris has been able to sustain two top-flight clubs for very long and even in Paris, where this has happened for a short period, no sustainable derby of the intensity of the Italian or English cities has been created. Paris produced two major clubs in the amateur era: Red Star 93, founded in 1897 by Jules Rimet and based in the Bauer district of the city, and Racing Club, which occupied the exclusive and stylish Colombes ground in the north-west of the city.

The professional era has been unkind to both, and Red Star has been forced to leave its Bauer heartland for the peripheral wastelands of Marville, while the Colombes ground may have hosted the 1938 World Cup but cannot currently sustain even Second Division soccer. This vacuum in Parisian soccer was finally filled by the creation of Paris Saint-Germain from FC Paris and Saint-Germain-en-Laye in the early 70s. Basing itself in Racing's old ground, the newly renovated Parc des Princes, PSG has climbed into the upper echelon of French soccer without ever dominating it.

One city, one team

Outside of Paris, it is one city, one team – Saint-Etienne, Stade Rennais, Girondins de Bordeaux, Olympique Marseille, Nice, Lyon, Nantes, Lens and Auxerre, although in the case of Monaco, it is one principality, one team. That said, in all of these cities, the connection with the soccer club is intimate: in Marseille, different districts of the town have their own *ultra* (fan group), each with its own space in the Stade Vélodrome, while in Bordeaux, Nantes and other provincial towns the city and regional governments have taken special care of their soccer clubs.

PARIS SAINT-GERMAIN 1970		
League	1986, *89*, *93*, **94**, *96*, *97*, *2000*, *04*	
Cup	**1982**, *83*, *85*, **93**, *95*, **98**, *2003*, **04**	
European Cup-Winners' Cup	**1996**, *97*	

RACING CLUB PARIS 1932	
League	**1936**, *61*, *62*
Cup	**1936**, *39*, *40*, *45*, *49*, *50*, *90*

RED STAR 93 1897	
Cup	**1921**–23, 28, 42, 46

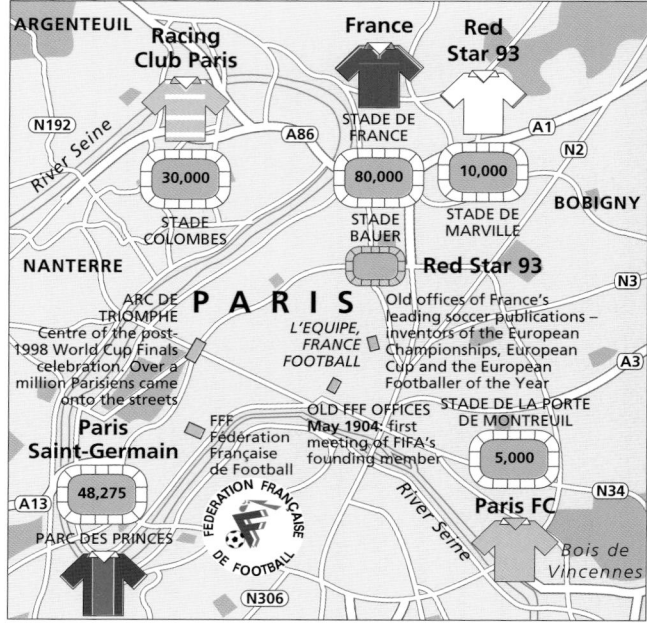

PARC DES PRINCES

Club: Paris Saint-Germain
Built: 1897
Original Capacity: 50,000
Rebuilt: 1932, 1972
Significant Matches: 1938 World Cup: three matches; 1998 World Cup: six matches; 1984 European Championships: Final; European Cup Finals: 1956, 75, 81; European Cup-Winners' Cup Final: 1978, 95; UEFA Cup Final: 1998; French Cup Final: 1919, 38, 43, 44, 65–97

48,275

STADE DE FRANCE

Club: National team
Built: 1998
Significant Matches: 1998 World Cup: nine matches including quarter-final, semi-final and Final; French Cup Final 1998–present

80,000

STADE COLOMBES (Yves de Manoir)

Club: Racing Club Paris
Built: 1907
Original Capacity: 45,000
Rebuilt:
Record Attendance: 62,145 France v Soviet Union, 21 Oct 1965
Significant Matches: 1924 Paris Olympics; 1983 World Cup: three matches including quarter-final and Final; French Cup Final: 1925–39, 42–64

30,000

STADE RENNAIS 1901

Cup	*1922, 35,* **65, 71**

FC NANTES 1943

League	**1965, 66, 67, 73, 74, 77, 78, 79, 80, 81, 83, 85, 86, 95, 2001**
Cup	*1966, 70, 73, 79, 83, 93,* **99, 2000**
League Cup	*2004*

GIRONDINS DE BORDEAUX 1881

League	**1950,** *52,* **65, 66,** *69, 83,* **84, 85, 87, 88, 90, 99**
Cup	**1941,** *43, 52, 55, 64, 68, 69,* **86, 87**
League Cup	*1997, 98,* **2002**
UEFA Cup	*1996*

RC LENS 1906

League	*1956, 57, 77,* **98,** *2002*
Cup	*1948, 75, 98*
League Cup	**1999**

AJ AUXERRE 1905

League	**1996**
Cup	*1979, 94,* **96, 2003**

LILLE OSC 1944

League	**1946,** *48–51,* **54**
Cup	*1945, 46–48, 49* **53, 55**

STADE DE REIMS 1931

League	*1947,* **49, 53, 54, 55,** *58,* **60,** *62, 63*
Cup	**1950,** *58,* **77**
European Cup	*1956, 59*

AS SAINT-ETIENNE 1933

League	*1946,* **57, 64, 67–70,** *71,* **74–76,** *81, 82*
Cup	*1960, 62,* **68,** *70,* **74, 75, 77,** *81, 82*
European Cup	*1976*

FÉLIX-BOLLAERT

41,649

Lens

GRIMONPREZ-JOORIS

21,128

Lille

Lille OSC

Lens

A26

Stade Rennais

ROUTE DE LORIENT

19,555

Reims

STADE DE REIMS CHAMPAGNE

A31 A4

18,000

Rennes

Paris

A13

A11 A10

Auxerre

Stade de Reims

A1

Nantes

ABBÉ-DES-CHAMPS

21,000

AJ Auxerre

FRANCE

Olympique Lyonnais

A6

GERLAND

41,852

AS Monaco

38,220

LA BEAUJOIRE-LOUIS-FONTENEAU

FC Nantes

St-Étienne

Lyon

A7

LOUIS II

18,250

PARC LESCURE

Bordeaux

34,088

A62

AS Saint-Étienne

GEOFFROY-GUICHARD

35,600

Monaco

Nice

OGC Nice

Girondins de Bordeaux

A61

Marseille

Olympique Marseille

MUNICIPAL DU RAY

17,415

VÉLODROME

60,000

France

34,088	Capacity of stadium

Stadium no longer in use for top-flight soccer

Team colours

M6 — Motorway

1900 — Champions

2000 — Runners-up

OLYMPIQUE MARSEILLE 1899

League	**1937,** *38, 39,* **48,** *70,* **71, 72,** *75,* **87,** *89–92, 94, 99*
Cup	*1924, 26, 27, 34, 35,* **38,** *40, 43, 54,* **69, 72, 76,** *86, 87,* **89,** *91*
European Cup	*1991,* **93**
UEFA Cup	*1999, 2004*

OGC NICE 1904

League	**1951,** *52,* **56, 59,** *68, 73, 76*
Cup	**1952, 54,** *78, 97*

OLYMPIQUE LYONNAIS 1950

League	*1995, 2001,* **02-04**
Cup	*1963, 64, 67,* **71,** *73, 76*
League Cup	*1996,* **2001**

AS MONACO 1924

League	**1961,** *63, 64,* **78, 82,** *84,* **88,** *91, 92,* **97, 2000,** *03*
Cup	*1960,* **63,** *74, 80,* **84, 85,** *89,* **91**
League Cup	*2001, 03*
European Cup	*2004*
European Cup-Winners' Cup	*1992*

Marseille's last league title was 1992, but it remains the best supported club in France. No other stadium can match the flags and flares of the Stade Vélodrome.

France

FRANCE

FANS AND OWNERS

DESPITE HAVING BEEN World and European champions, France is less financially strong than the other big nations in Europe in terms of domestic soccer. Attendances and TV revenues have been lower, and the game is generally less commercialized. French clubs also face much larger tax bills, and the big clubs continue to subsidize smaller and amateur clubs. Little wonder that almost the entire French national squad plays overseas, and France's challenge at club level in Europe has been so limited in the last decade.

Rising income, rising debts

French club owners have been lobbying for some time to be allowed to raise more money. The FFF and the government have refused to allow them to float on the stock market but have introduced two categories of ownership: SAOS (*Société Anonyme à Objet Sportif*) and SASP (*Société Anonyme Sportive Professionelle*). The SAOS model is the status quo, leaving the clubs in the hands of private investors and the supporters' association. The SASP allows the clubs to distribute dividends to shareholders, pay salaries to elected officials and reduce the supporters' association share of the club below one-third. This second option is being pursued by the bigger clubs and large companies are beginning to take stakes in some of them. However, it is still risky; the clubs in the top division in 2002 were collectively in debt to the tune of £82.2 million.

Although France has little of the *ultra* culture of Italy or Spain, in Marseille, Lens, Bastia and Metz the marginal status of the cities, geographically and socially, gives support a peculiar intensity. Marseille's many *ultra* groups, who come from different parts of the city, have their places in the stands clearly marked. There is very little violence in French soccer, but OM's fans can and do get pretty terse with their club. At the other end of the scale, the executive boxes built during the stadium refurbishment programme for the 1998 World Cup seem full as soccer acquires an elite glamour it has lacked in France for a long time.

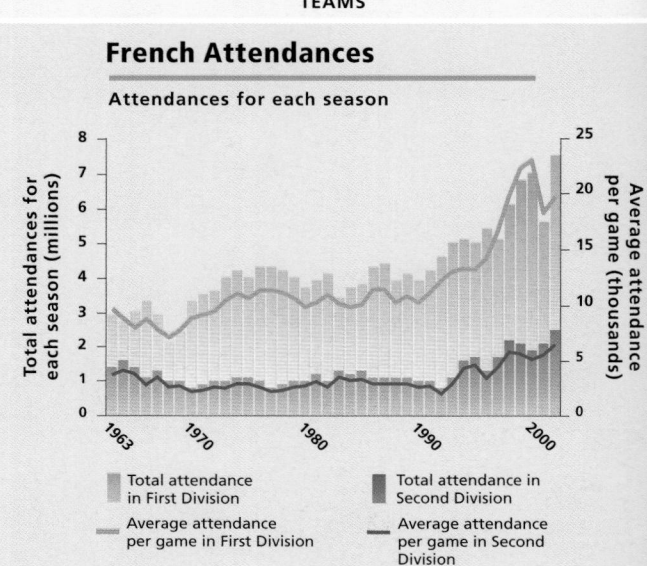

French Attendances

Attendances for each season

Key:
- Total attendance in First Division
- Average attendance per game in First Division
- Total attendance in Second Division
- Average attendance per game in Second Division

Prince Rainier of Monaco's money took the club to the first division in 1953. Since then the Grimaldi family's subventions have been augmented by a FF50 million subsidy from Monaco's national council. However, the club's debts continue to grow.

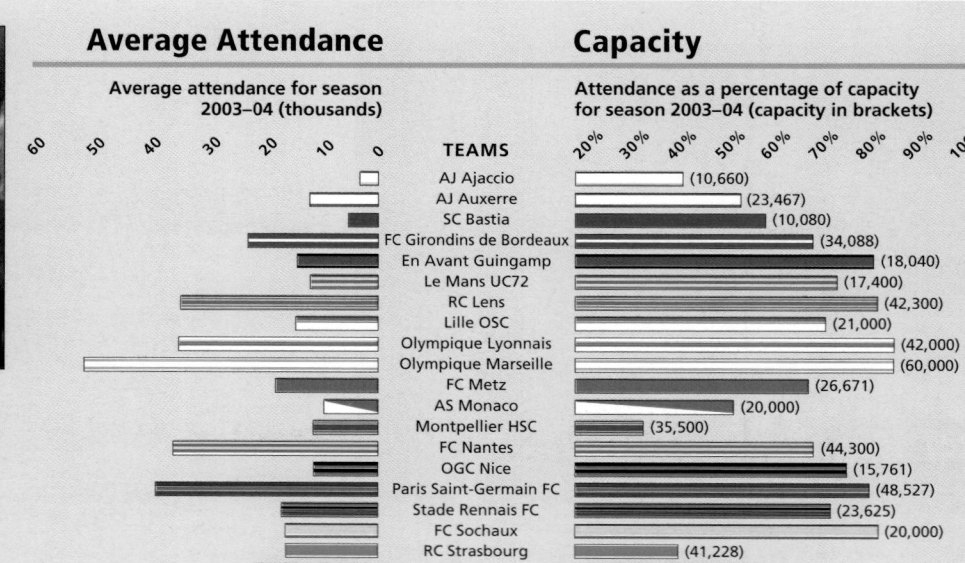

Average Attendance

Average attendance for season 2003–04 (thousands)

Capacity

Attendance as a percentage of capacity for season 2003–04 (capacity in brackets)

TEAMS	Capacity
AJ Ajaccio	(10,660)
AJ Auxerre	(23,467)
SC Bastia	(10,080)
FC Girondins de Bordeaux	(34,088)
En Avant Guingamp	(18,040)
Le Mans UC72	(17,400)
RC Lens	(42,300)
Lille OSC	(21,000)
Olympique Lyonnais	(42,000)
Olympique Marseille	(60,000)
FC Metz	(26,671)
AS Monaco	(20,000)
Montpellier HSC	(35,500)
FC Nantes	(44,300)
OGC Nice	(15,761)
Paris Saint-Germain FC	(48,527)
Stade Rennais FC	(23,625)
FC Sochaux	(20,000)
RC Strasbourg	(41,228)
Toulouse FC	(37,000)

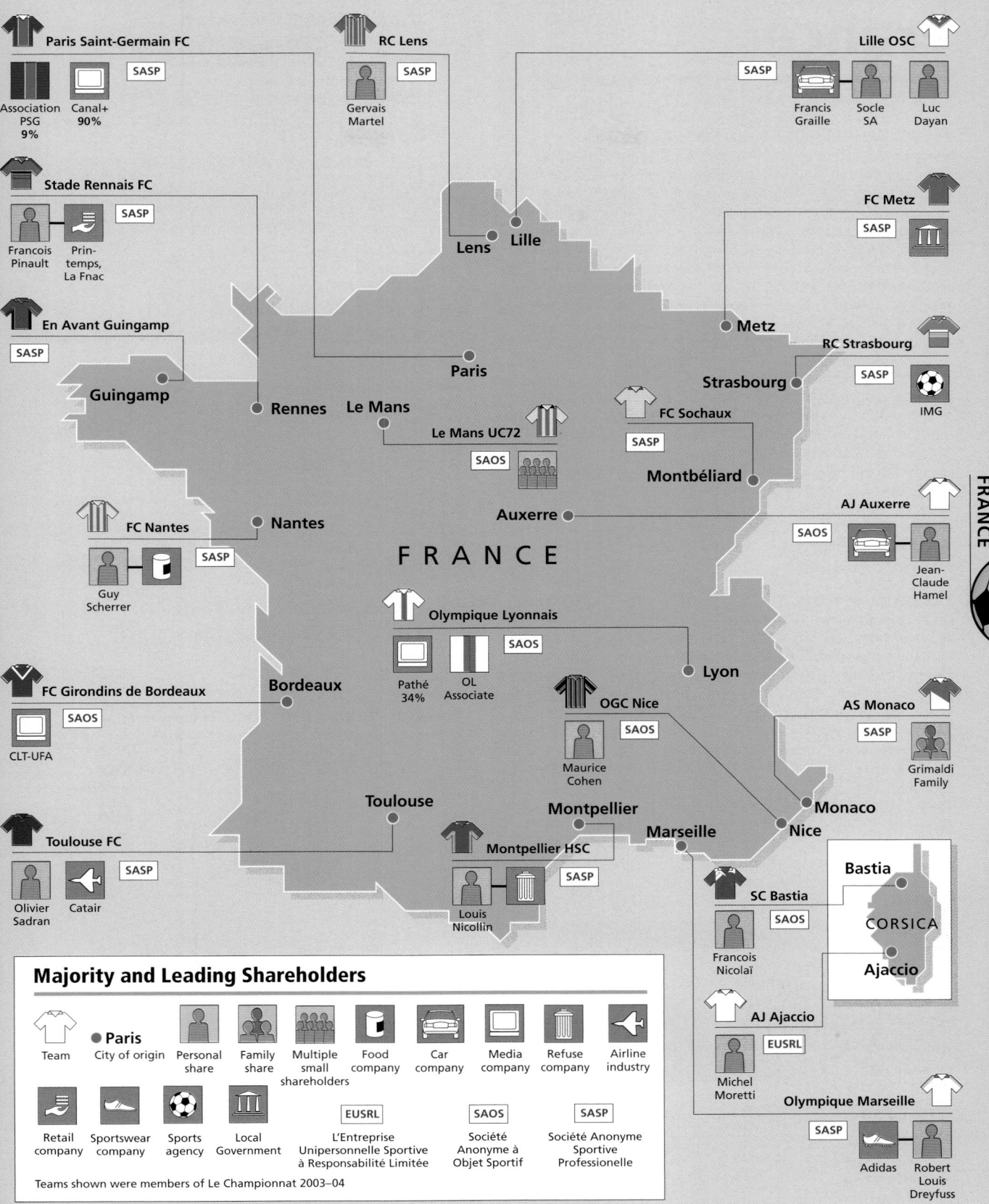

Paris Saint-Germain FC — SASP — Association PSG 9% — Canal+ 90%

RC Lens — SASP — Gervais Martel

Lille OSC — SASP — Francis Graille — Socle SA — Luc Dayan

Stade Rennais FC — SASP — Francois Pinault — Printemps, La Fnac

FC Metz — SASP

En Avant Guingamp — SASP — Guingamp

RC Strasbourg — SASP — IMG

FC Sochaux — SASP — Montbéliard

Le Mans UC72 — SAOS

AJ Auxerre — SAOS — Jean-Claude Hamel

FC Nantes — SASP — Guy Scherrer

Olympique Lyonnais — SAOS — Pathé 34% — OL Associate — Lyon

OGC Nice — SAOS — Maurice Cohen

AS Monaco — SASP — Grimaldi Family

FC Girondins de Bordeaux — SAOS — CLT-UFA — Bordeaux

Toulouse FC — SASP — Olivier Sadran — Catair

Montpellier HSC — SASP — Louis Nicollin

SC Bastia — SAOS — Francois Nicolaï — CORSICA — Bastia — Ajaccio

AJ Ajaccio — EUSRL — Michel Moretti

Olympique Marseille — SASP — Adidas — Robert Louis Dreyfuss

Lens, Lille, Paris, Rennes, Le Mans, Metz, Strasbourg, Auxerre, Nantes, Montbéliard, Toulouse, Montpellier, Marseille, Monaco, Nice

FRANCE

Majority and Leading Shareholders

- Team
- ● Paris — City of origin
- Personal share
- Family share
- Multiple small shareholders
- Food company
- Car company
- Media company
- Refuse company
- Airline industry
- Retail company
- Sportswear company
- Sports agency
- Local Government
- **EUSRL** — L'Entreprise Unipersonnelle Sportive à Responsabilité Limitée
- **SAOS** — Société Anonyme à Objet Sportif
- **SASP** — Société Anonyme Sportive Professionelle

Teams shown were members of Le Championnat 2003–04

France

PLAYERS AND MANAGERS

FRENCH SOCCER WENT PROFESSIONAL in the 1930s, but it was not until the postwar era that the first generation of international stars began to emerge. Just Fontaine (who holds the record for the most goals at a single World Cup Finals tournament) was among the first and like many to follow was born in French colonial North Africa – Morocco in his case. Playing alongside Fontaine at Reims was Raymond Kopa. Born of a Polish immigrant family, Raymond Kopaszeweski was the leading centre-forward of the era. France's next wave of great players emerged in the 1980s, built around the prodigious talent of Michel Platini. Platini's midfield colleagues Alain Giresse and Jean Tigana also stand out from this era and both have gone on to successful managerial careers. This era also saw the beginning of a transformation in the organization of training, management and scouting in France, with massive investment from government and clubs in talent and education.

However, France's coaching philosophy has older roots. Albert Batteux, generally acknowledged to be the father of the profession in France, coached the most successful clubs of the 1950s and 60s – Reims and St Etienne – as well as the national team at the 1958 World Cup. Nantes has also continued to provide players who become leading coaches – in the 2001–02 season one quarter of all top-flight clubs were coached by Nantes graduates.

Fantastic success

The leading players of the early 21st century are a product of this earlier era and again they reflect France's internal diversity and the continuing waves of African and Arabic immigration: Zidane, the outstanding player of his generation, was born of Algerian parents; Patrick Vieira transferred from Senegalese to French citizenship; Youri Djorkaeff has Armenian roots and Marcel Desailly was born in Ghana. The fantastic success of the French team in recent years has seen the leading players head for Italy, Spain and, increasingly, England. French managers have followed them, with Arsène Wenger presiding over Arsenal in the English Premiership. Jean Tigana and Gèrard Houllier both did stints in England with Fulham and Liverpool respectively. Simultaneously, there has been a huge influx of Africans in particular to the leading French clubs.

Top 10 International Caps

PLAYER	CAPS	GOALS	FIRST MATCH	LAST MATCH
Marcel Desailly*	116	3	1993	2004
Didier Deschamps	103	4	1989	2000
Lilian Thuram*	103	2	1994	2004
Laurent Blanc	97	16	1989	2000
Bixente Lizarazu*	97	2	1992	2004
Zinedine Zidane*	93	26	1994	2004
Manuel Amoros	82	1	1982	1992
Youri Djorkaeff*	82	28	1993	2002
Maxime Bossis	76	1	1976	1986
Robert Pires*	74	14	1996	2004
Michel Platini	72	41	1976	1987
Patrick Vieira*	72	4	1997	2004
Fabien Barthez*	70	0	1994	2004
Marius Trésor	65	4	1971	1983
Silvain Wiltord*	65	22	1999	2004

Top 10 International Goalscorers

PLAYER	GOALS	CAPS	FIRST MATCH	LAST MATCH
Michel Platini	41	72	1976	1987
Just Fontaine	30	21	1953	1960
Jean-Pierre Papin	30	54	1986	1995
Youri Djorkaeff*	28	82	1993	2002
Thierry Henry*	27	63	1997	2004
Zinedine Zidane*	26	93	1994	2004
David Trezeguet*	22	43	1998	2003
Jean Vincent	22	46	1953	1961
Silvain Wiltord*	22	65	1999	2004
Jean Nicolas	21	25	1933	1938

* Indicates players still playing at least at club level.

France International Managers

DATES	NAME	GAMES	WON	DRAWN	LOST
1960–64	Georges Verniet, Henri Guerin	24	4	6	14
1964–65	Henri Guerin	15	5	4	6
1966	Jean Snella, Jose Arribas	4	2	0	2
1967	Just Fontaine	9	2	3	4
1967–68	Louis Dugauquez	31	15	5	11
1969–73	Georges Boulogne	15	6	4	5
1973–75	Stefan Kovacs	15	6	4	5
1976–84	Michel Hidalgo	75	41	16	18
1984–88	Henri Michel	36	16	12	8
1988–92	Michel Platini	29	16	8	5
1992–93	Gérard Houllier	12	7	1	4
1994–98	Aime Jacquet	53	34	16	3
1998–2002	Roger Lemerre	53	34	11	8
2002–04	Jacques Santini	28	22	4	2

All figures correct as of 28 June 2004.

Foreign Players in France (in top division squads)

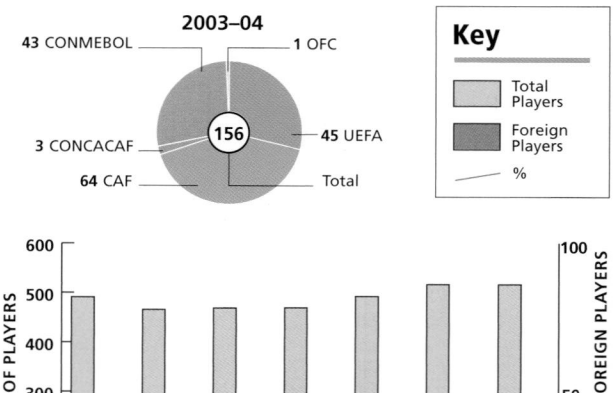

2003–04

43 CONMEBOL
1 OFC
3 CONCACAF
64 CAF
156
45 UEFA
Total

Key
Total Players
Foreign Players
%

Player of the Year*

YEAR	PLAYER	CLUB
1963	Douis	AS Monaco
1964	Artelesa	AS Monaco
1965	Gondet	FC Nantes
1966	Gondet	FC Nantes
1967	Bosquier	AS Saint-Etienne
1968	Bosquier	AS Saint-Etienne
1969	Revelli	AS Saint-Etienne
1970	Carnus	AS Saint-Etienne
1971	Carnus	AS Saint-Etienne/ Olympique Marseille
1972	Trésor	Ajaccio/ Olympique Marseille
1973	Bereta	AS Saint-Etienne
1974	Bereta	AS Saint-Etienne
1975	Guillou	Angers/OGC Nice
1976	Platini	FC Nancy
1977	Platini	FC Nancy
1978	Petit	AS Monaco
1979	Bossis	FC Nantes
1980	Larios	AS Saint-Etienne
1981	Bossis	FC Nantes
1982	Giresse	Girondins de Bordeaux
1983	Giresse	Girondins de Bordeaux
1984	Tigana	Girondins de Bordeaux
1985	Fernandez	Paris Saint-Germain
1986	Amoros	AS Monaco
1987	Giresse	Olympique Marseille
1988	Paille	FC Sochaux
1989	Papin	Olympique Marseille
1990	Blanc	Montpellier
1991	Papin	Olympique Marseille
1992	Roche	Paris Saint-Germain
1993	Ginola	Paris Saint-Germain
1994	Lama	Paris Saint-Germain
1995	Guérin	Paris Saint-Germain
1996	Deschamps	Juventus [Ita]
1997	Thuram	Parma [Ita]
1998	Zidane	Juventus [Ita]
1999	Wiltord	Girondins de Bordeaux
2000	Henry	Arsenal [Eng]
2001	Vieira	Arsenal [Eng]
2002	Zidane	Real Madrid [Spain]
2003	Henry	Arsenal [Eng]

Never a favourite of the French national team manager, Eric Cantona raised the profile of French soccer when he left France for England in 1992. Hugely successful, both at Leeds and Manchester United, Cantona remains one of the finest players of the 1990s.

Manager of the Year*

YEAR	MANAGER	CLUB
1970	Batteux	AS Saint-Etienne
1970	Zatelli	O Marseille
1971	Firoud	Nîmes Olympique
1971	Prouff	Stade Rennais
1972	Snella	OGC Nice
1973	Herbin	AS Saint-Etienne
1974	Cahuzac	SC Bastia
1975	Huart	FC Metz
1976	Herbin	AS Saint-Etienne
1977	Cahuzac	SC Bastia
1978	Gress	RC Strasbourg
1979	Le Milinaire	Laval
1980	Hauss	FC Sochaux
1980	Vincent	FC Nantes
1981	Jacquet	Girondins de Bordeaux
1982	Hidalgo	France
1983	Le Milinaire	Laval
1984	Jacquet	Girondins de Bordeaux
1985	Suaudeau	FC Nantes
1986	Roux	AJ Auxerre
1987	Fernandez	AS Cannes
1988	Roux	AJ Auxerre
1989	Gili	O Marseille
1990	Kasperczak	SCP Montpelier
1991	Jeandupeux	Caen
1992	Suaudeau	FC Nantes
1993	Fernandez	AS Cannes
1994	Suaudeau	FC Nantes
1995	Smerecki	Guingamp
1996	Roux	AJ Auxerre
1997	Tigana	AS Monaco
1998	Jacquet	France
1999	Baup	Girondins de Bordeaux
2000	Dupont	FC Sedan
2001	Halilhodzic	Lille OSC
2002	Santini	O Lyonnais
2003	Deschamps	AS Monaco

Elected by France Football magazine.

***Jean Tigana was** an integral part of the legendary French midfield of the 1980s along with Michel Platini and Alain Giresse.*

Top Goalscorers 1963–2004

SEASON	PLAYER	CLUB	GOALS
1962–63	Masnaghetti	Valenciennes	35
1963–64	Oudjani	RC Lens	30
1964–65	Simon	FC Nantes	24
1965–66	Gondet	FC Nantes	36
1966–67	Revelli	Saint-Etienne	31
1967–68	Sansonetti	Ajaccio	26
1968–69	Guy	FC Lyon	25
1969–70	Revelli	Saint-Etienne	28
1970–71	Skoblar	O Marseille	44
1971–72	Skoblar	O Marseille	30
1972–73	Skoblar	O Marseille	26
1973–74	Bianchi	Stade Reims	30
1974–75	Onnis	AS Monaco	30
1975–76	Bianchi	Stade Reims	34
1976–77	Bianchi	Stade Reims	28
1977–78	Bianchi	Paris SG	37
1978–79	Bianchi	Paris SG	27
1979–80	Onnis	AS Monaco	21
1979–80	Kostedde	Laval	21
1980–81	Onnis	Tours	24
1981–82	Onnis	Tours	29
1982–83	Halilhodzic	FC Nantes	27
1983–84	Garande	AJ Auxerre	21
1983–84	Onnis	Toulon	21
1984–85	Halilhodzic	FC Nantes	28
1985–86	Bocandé	FC Metz	23
1986–87	Zénier	FC Metz	18
1987–88	Papin	O Marseille	19
1988–89	Papin	O Marseille	22
1989–90	Papin	O Marseille	30
1990–91	Papin	O Marseille	23
1991–92	Papin	O Marseille	27
1992–93	Boksic	O Marseille	22
1993–94	Djorkaeff	AS Monaco	20
1993–94	Boli	RC Lens	20
1993–94	Ouédec	FC Nantes	20
1994–95	Loko	FC Nantes	22
1995–96	Anderson	AS Monaco	21
1996–97	Guivarc'h	Stade Rennais	22
1997–98	Guivarc'h	AJ Auxerre	21
1998–99	Wiltord	Girondins de Bordeaux	22
1999–2000	Anderson	AS Monaco	23
2000–01	Anderson	Lyon	22
2001–02	Cisse	AJ Auxerre	22
2001–02	Pauleta	Bordeaux	22
2002–03	Nonda	AS Monaco	26
2003–04	Cisse	AJ Auxerre	26

FRANCE

France

LE CHAMPIONNAT 1982–2003

AT THE BEGINNING OF THE 1980s, the French championship was evenly distributed between clubs built with old money and clubs built with new money. The new money came in the shape of Claude Bez, Girondins de Bordeaux's ambitious president. Without a title since 1950 and with its Lescure stadium devoted mainly to rugby and cycling, Bordeaux was transformed by Bez's injection of money and energy. In the early 1980s a new stadium and training centre were constructed, a considerable deal done with the newly emergent cable TV company Canal Plus, and a stylish team assembled under future national team coach Aimé Jacquet, including Jean Tigana and Alain Giresse. Those years belonged to Bordeaux with three league titles and a top four place for seven seasons. But Bez was accused and convicted of fraud and mismanagement, and Bordeaux was relegated by the league in 1991. The new money at Paris Saint-Germain brought in Luis Fernandez and Osvaldo Ardiles and saw the team finally take its first title in 1986. The old money and old form came in the shape of titles for Monaco, under Arsène Wenger, and for Nantes.

Further south, Olympique Marseille began the 1980s bankrupt and in the second division. But the potential of the biggest and most fiercely supported club in the country was in no doubt. Enter Bernard Tapie, then boss of Adidas, who bought the club in 1985. Tapie brought money, energy and connections as well as players of the calibre of Jean-Pierre Papin, Chris Waddle, Didier Deschamps and Abedi Pele. Elected as a socialist MP, Tapie was described as the 'Red Berlusconi', and he drove the right-wingers mad as five league titles and three tilts at the European Cup followed. Finally, in 1993, Tapie's Marseille beat Berlusconi's Milan 1-0 to take Europe's top club prize. The day afterwards it was revealed in the French press that there was serious evidence of match-fixing in Marseille's league game against US Valenciennes

that season. The floodgates opened, accusations turned to convictions for match-fixing and illegal payments in the transfer market. Tapie was imprisoned, the club relegated and eventually made insolvent. Since then, despite considerable investment from Adidas's new boss Robert Louis Dreyfuss, the team has yet to show the form of the Tapie years.

TV and its money

In the mid-1990s money began to pour into French soccer from new TV deals, and salaries and transfers began to rise. But given France's high employment taxes and the relatively lower percentage incomes from sponsorship and TV available to French clubs (in comparison with Spain, Italy and England), the leading French players of the era, including nearly all of the 1998 World Cup-winning squad, played outside France. In their wake, French clubs have drawn extensively on African and Eastern European players, and none have been able to establish any kind of dominance.

In the late 1990s there have been titles for PSG, AJ Auxerre, RC Lens, Monaco and Nantes. At Auxerre, long-standing coach Guy Roux finally hit the jackpot with the club's youth academy. Nantes rose on money from Guy Scherrer, a millionaire in the food industry. Monaco took the 2000 title by a length with an attacking side including David Trezeguet and Marco Simeone. But European success has eluded French clubs, and the struggle to survive at the rarefied level of European competition has left them seriously in debt. Their competitors at the bottom of the league are equally troubled. The only serious new challenger to have emerged from the era of TV money has been Olympique Lyonnais, while for many of the old guard times have been even harder; Saint-Etienne, Stade de Reims, Racing Club Paris, SM Caen and OGC Nice have all found themselves slipping out of the top flight.

Sonny Anderson, Olympique Lyonnais' Brazilian talisman, splits the Lens line of Fredrick Colly (left) and Jean Guy Wallemme as Lyon steals the title from under Lens' nose on the final day of the 2001–02 season.

Jean Tigana in his prime running the midfield for Bordeaux during the early 1980s.

The irrepressible Bernard Tapie and friends celebrate. Despite his downfall in 1993, Tapie has clawed his way back into French soccer with a short spell behind the scenes at Marseille in 2002.

French League Income (in euros)

SEASON	1996–97	1997–98	1998–99	1999–2000	2000–01	2001–02
Income	292,630	322,714	393,183	607,194	608,424	643,090
Costs	300,070	368,313	462,721	570,866	646,847	740,821
Gross profit	-7,440	-45,599	-69,537	36,328	-38,422	-97,731
Net profit	25,077	51,075	65,885	8,135	-19,341	-68,080

Total for all top division clubs

Sources of Income 2002

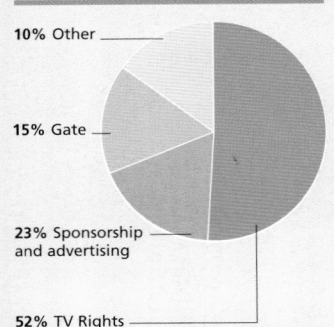

10% Other

15% Gate

23% Sponsorship and advertising

52% TV Rights

Income of French first division clubs in season 2001–02

Player Salaries 1996–2001

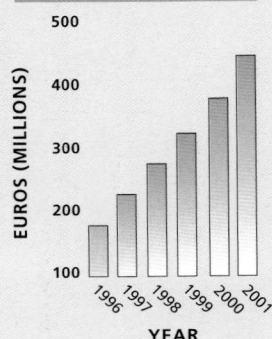

EUROS (MILLIONS)

YEAR

Total wage bill of French first division clubs

FRANCE

Champions' Winning Margin 1993–2003

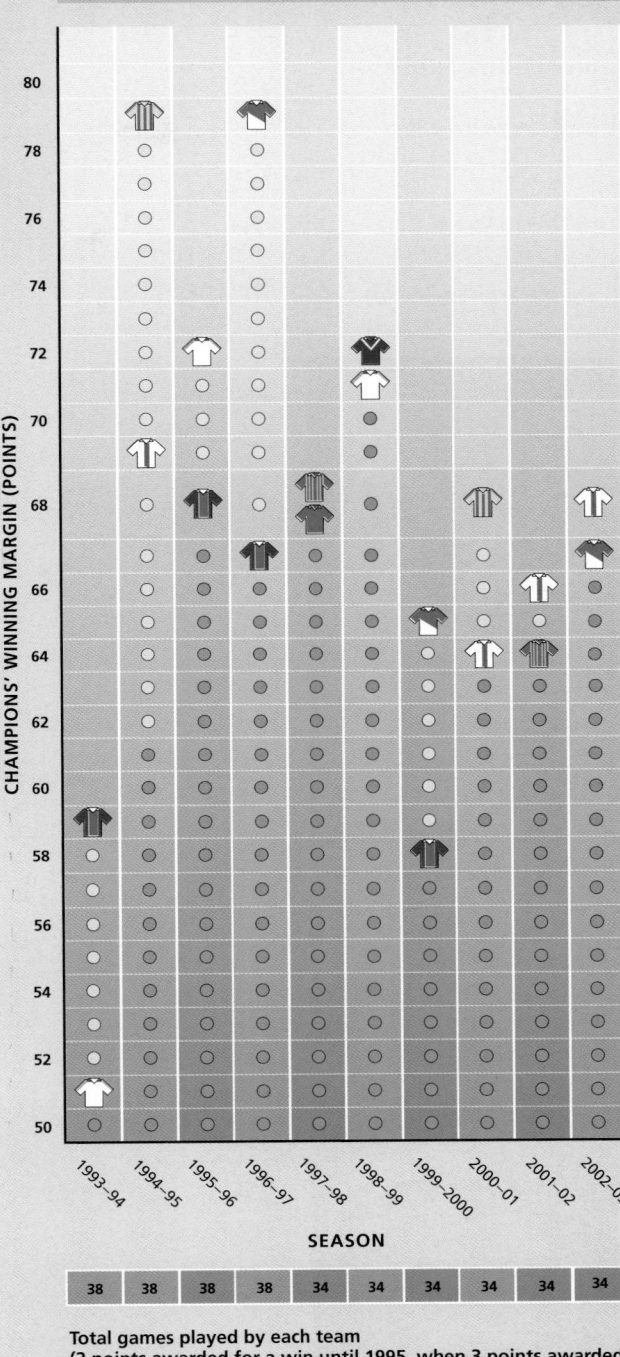

CHAMPIONS' WINNING MARGIN (POINTS)

SEASON

| 38 | 38 | 38 | 38 | 34 | 34 | 34 | 34 | 34 | 34 |

Total games played by each team
(2 points awarded for a win until 1995, when 3 points awarded)

AJ Auxerre   Girondins de Bordeaux   RC Lens

Olympique Lyonnais   Olympique Marseille   FC Metz

AS Monaco   FC Nantes   Paris Saint-Germain

French League Positions 1982–2003

Key to League Positions Table

- ◻ League champions
- ◻ Season of promotion to league
- ◻ Season of relegation from league
- ◻ Other teams playing in league
- 5 Final position in league

FRANCE

A young Thierry Henry provided the firepower to take Jean Tigana's AS Monaco to the French championship in 1997.

Guy Roux has been at Auxerre for almost four decades, nurturing talents like Eric Cantona. The club's scouting and youth network is second to none.

TEAM	82-83	83-84	84-85	85-86	86-87	87-88	88-89	89-90	90-91	91-92	92-93	93-94	94-95	95-96	96-97	97-98	98-99	99-2000	00-01	01-02	02-03
AJ Ajaccio																					17
SCO Angers											20										
AJ Auxerre	8	3	4	7	4	9	5	6	3	4	6	3	4	1	6	7	14	8	13	3	6
SC Bastia	17	11	14	20									15	15	7	9	13	10	8	11	12
Berrichonne Chat																17					
Girondins de Bordeaux	2	1	1	3	1	2	13	2	10†		4	4	7	16	4	5	1	4	4	6	4
Brest-Armorique FC	10	17	9	14	8	19		10	11†												
SM Caen								16	16	8	5	11	16	19		17					
AS Cannes								12	12	11	4	19		6	9	14	15	18			
FC Gueugnonnais														18							
En Avant Guingamp														10	12	16			10	16	7
Le Havre AC				17	17	20					7	15	17	12	13	14	10	15	17		18
Stade Lavallois MFC	5	10	10	11	9	14	19														
Le Mans UC72																					
RC Lens	4	13	7	5	10	17	20			8	9	10	5	5	13	1	6	5	14	2	8
Lille OSC	13	9	15	10	14	11	8	17	6	13	17	15	14	17	19				3	5	14
FC Lorient																	16		18		
Olympique Lyonnais	19							8	5	16	14	8	2	11	8	6	3	3	2	1	1
Olympique Marseille		17	12	2	6	1	1	1	1	1*	2**				11	4	2	15	15	9	3
FC Martigues												18	11	20							
FC Metz	9	12	5	6	6	8	15	14	12	12	12	12	8	4	5	2	10	11	12	17	
AS Monaco	6	2	3	9	5	1	3	3	2	2	3	9	6	3	1	3	4	1	11	15	2
Montpellier HSC						3	9	13	7	6	10	7	17	6	10	12	8	18		13	16
FC Mulhouse	20							20													
AS Nancy-Lorraine	7	15	12	18	19				17	20						18		11	16		
FC Nantes	1	6	2	2	12	10	7	7	15	9	5	5	1	7	3	11	7	12	1	10	9
OGC Nice				8	11	16	6	18	14†						16	12	20				10
Nîmes Olympique		19									15	20									
Chamois Niortais FC						18															
Paris Saint-Germain	3	4	13	1	7	15	2	5	9	3	2	1	3	2	2	8	9	2	9	4	11
Racing Club de Paris			20		13	7	17	19													
AS Saint-Etienne	14	18			16	4	14	15	13	10	7	11	18	19				6	17		
CS Sedan Ardennes																		7	5	14	19
Stade Rennais FC		20		13	20			20	18				13	8	16	14	5	13	6	12	15
FC Rouen	16	14	18																		
FC Sochaux	12	7	8	15	18		4	4	18	17	16	14	20			17				8	5
RC Strasbourg	15	8	16	19			18				8	13	10	9	9	13	12	9	18		13
SC Toulon-Var		16	6	16	15	5	11	12	16	14	19										
Toulouse FC	11	5	11	4	3	13	10	4	19	11	13	19			15	18			16		
FC Tours	18		19																		
A Troyes AC																		14	7	7	20
US Valenciennes											18										

Le Championnat

FC Nantes
Atlantique — Team name

League champions/
runners-up

1983,
85 — Champions in bold
Runners-up in italics

Other teams in
Le Championnat

● **Nantes** — City of origin

Luis Fernandez was another managerial casualty of PSG's unsated search for success. He was summarily dismissed in 2003 after the team's 11th-place finish.

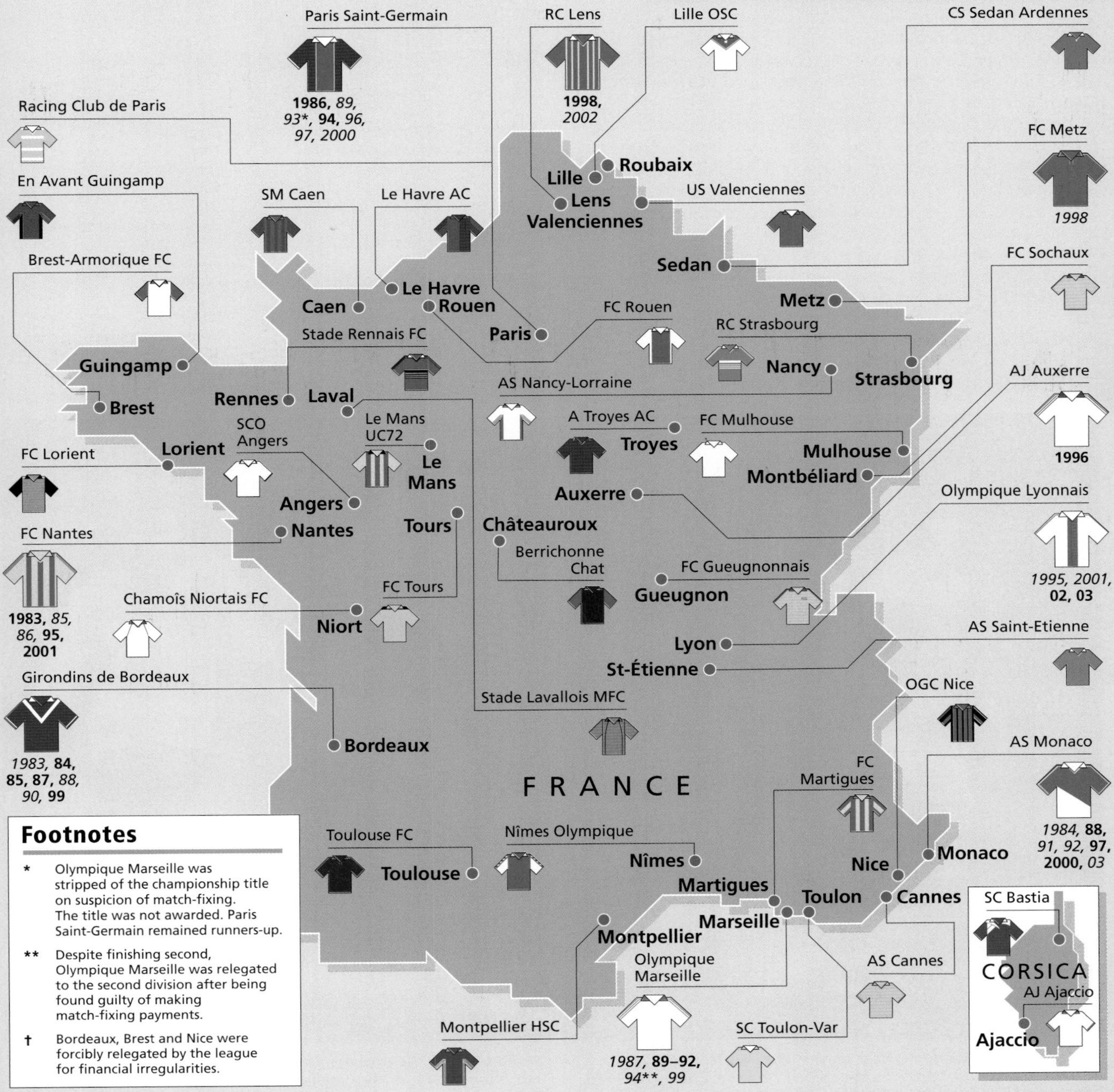

Footnotes

* Olympique Marseille was stripped of the championship title on suspicion of match-fixing. The title was not awarded. Paris Saint-Germain remained runners-up.

** Despite finishing second, Olympique Marseille was relegated to the second division after being found guilty of making match-fixing payments.

† Bordeaux, Brest and Nice were forcibly relegated by the league for financial irregularities.

FRANCE

Paris Saint-Germain
1986, *89,* *93*,* **94,** *96,* *97,* **2000**

RC Lens
1998, *2002*

Lille OSC

CS Sedan Ardennes

Racing Club de Paris

FC Metz
1998

En Avant Guingamp

SM Caen

Le Havre AC

US Valenciennes

FC Sochaux

Brest-Armorique FC

FC Metz

Roubaix
Lille
Lens
Valenciennes
Sedan
Metz

FC Metz

FC Rouen

RC Strasbourg

AJ Auxerre
1996

Stade Rennais FC

Guingamp
Brest
Rennes
Laval

Rouen
Paris

Caen
Le Havre

AS Nancy-Lorraine

Nancy
Strasbourg

A Troyes AC

FC Mulhouse

FC Lorient

SCO Angers

Le Mans UC72

Lorient
Angers
Nantes
Le Mans
Tours

Troyes
Mulhouse
Montbéliard

Olympique Lyonnais
1995, **2001,** **02,** **03**

FC Nantes
1983, *85,* **86,** *95,* **2001**

Chamoîs Niortais FC

Châteauroux
Berrichonne Chat

FC Gueugnonnais

Auxerre

Niort
FC Tours

Gueugnon

AS Saint-Etienne

Girondins de Bordeaux
1983, **84,** **85,** **87,** **88,** **90,** *99*

Stade Lavallois MFC

Lyon
St-Étienne

OGC Nice

AS Monaco
1984, **88,** **91,** **92,** *97,* **2000,** *03*

Bordeaux

Toulouse FC

Nîmes Olympique

FC Martigues

Toulouse
Nîmes
Martigues
Montpellier
Marseille
Toulon
Cannes
Nice
Monaco

AS Cannes

SC Bastia

Olympique Marseille

Montpellier HSC
1987, **89–92,** *94**,* *99*

SC Toulon-Var

CORSICA
AJ Ajaccio
Ajaccio

FRANCE

France

Fédération Française de Football
Founded: 1918
Joined FIFA: 1904
Joined UEFA: 1954

DESPITE BEING AT THE FOREFRONT of the global organization of soccer, French domestic soccer began in a chaotic manner. In the early part of the 20th century five different soccer federations vied to organize the national game and each established a separate national league.

With the creation of the Fédération Française de Football in 1918, the first national cup competition was established. The French Cup has been played for every year since, except for 1992, when tragic events on the terraces overshadowed the French game. In a semi-final match between the Corsican club SC Bastia and Olympique Marseille, a temporary stand collapsed, leaving 15 dead and over 1,500 injured. As a result of the tragedy the tournament was abandoned. In 2000, Calais, an amateur team from the fourth division, reached the Cup Final, only to lose 2-1 to FC Nantes, who scored the winner in the 90th minute.

A national league was formed in 1926 and was solidified by the advent of professionalism in 1932. The national championships acquired a different format during the Second World War with the champions of different zones (North [Occupied], South and Central) playing off against each other. In 1993 Olympique Marseille won the league, but was stripped of its title for alleged match fixing.

French League Record 1933–2004

SEASON	CHAMPIONS	RUNNERS-UP
1933	Olympique Lille	AS Cannes
1934	FC Sète	SC Fives
1935	FC Sochaux	RC Strasbourg
1936	Racing Club Paris	Olympique Lille
1937	Olympique Marseille	FC Sochaux
1938	FC Sochaux	Olympique Marseille
1939	FC Sète	Olympique Marseille
1940–45	*no championship*	
1946	Lille OSC	AS Saint-Etienne
1947	CO Roubaix	Stade de Reims
1948	Olympique Marseille	Lille OSC
1949	Stade de Reims	Lille OSC
1950	Girondins de Bordeaux	Lille OSC
1951	OGC Nice	Lille OSC
1952	OGC Nice	Girondins de Bordeaux
1953	Stade de Reims	FC Sochaux
1954	Lille OSC	Stade de Reims
1955	Stade de Reims	FC Toulouse
1956	OGC Nice	RC Lens
1957	AS Saint-Etienne	RC Lens
1958	Stade de Reims	Nîmes Olympique
1959	OGC Nice	Nîmes Olympique
1960	Stade de Reims	Nîmes Olympique
1961	AS Monaco	Racing Club Paris

One of France's greatest soccer players was Michel Platini. His career started with Nancy, but he joined AS Saint-Etienne in 1979. Almost at the end of its golden era, having won the league title seven times in the previous ten years, Saint-Etienne's fortunes were reignited by Platini. The team won the title again in 1981, and finished second in 1982, before Platini moved to Juventus in Italy.

The legendary Raymond Kopa. He was born to a Polish immigrant family in inter-war France – similar origins to many French players of the era. His goals made Stade de Reims one of the most successful teams in France during the late 1950s. He moved to Real Madrid in 1956, but returned to Reims as European Footballer of the Year two years later.

French League Summary

TEAM	TOTALS	CHAMPIONS & RUNNERS-UP (BOLD) (ITALICS)
AS Saint-Etienne	10, 3	*1946,* **57, 64, 67–70,** *71,* **74–76, 81, 82**
FC Nantes	8, 7	**1965, 66, 67, 73, 74, 77, 78, 79, 80,** *81,* **83,** *85, 86,* **95, 2001**
Olympique Marseille	8, 7	**1937,** *38, 39,* **48,** *70,* **71, 72,** *75,* **87,** *89–92,* **94,** *99*
AS Monaco	7, 5	**1961,** *63,* **64,** *78,* **82,** *84,* **88,** *91, 92,* **97, 2000,** *03*
Stade de Reims	6, 3	*1947,* **49,** *53, 54,* **55, 58, 60, 62,** *63*
Girondins de Bordeaux	5, 7	*1950, 52, 65, 66, 69,* **83, 84, 85,** *87, 88, 90,* **99**
OGC Nice	4, 3	**1951, 52, 56, 59,** *68, 73, 76*
Olympique Lyonnais	3, 2	*1995, 2001,* **02–04**
Paris Saint-Germain	2, 6	**1986,** *89, 93,* **94,** *96, 97, 2000, 04*
Lille OSC	2, 4	**1946,** *48–51,* **54**
FC Sochaux	2, 3	**1935,** *37,* **38,** *53, 80*
FC Sète	2, 0	**1934, 39**
RC Lens	1, 4	*1956, 57, 77,* **98,** *2002*
Racing Club Paris	1, 2	**1936,** *61, 62*
Olympique Lille	1, 1	**1933,** *36*
RC Strasbourg	1, 1	*1935,* **79**
AJ Auxerre	1, 0	**1996**
CO Roubaix	1, 0	**1947**
Nîmes Olympique	0, 4	*1958–60, 72*
AS Cannes	0, 1	*1933*
FC Metz	0, 1	*1998*
FC Toulouse	0, 1	*1955*
SC Fives	0, 1	*1934*

French League Record (*continued*)

SEASON	CHAMPIONS	RUNNERS-UP
1962	Stade de Reims	Racing Club Paris
1963	AS Monaco	Stade de Reims
1964	AS Saint-Etienne	AS Monaco
1965	FC Nantes	Girondins de Bordeaux
1966	FC Nantes	Girondins de Bordeaux
1967	AS Saint-Etienne	FC Nantes
1968	AS Saint-Etienne	OGC Nice
1969	AS Saint-Etienne	Girondins de Bordeaux
1970	AS Saint-Etienne	Olympique Marseille
1971	Olympique Marseille	AS Saint-Etienne
1972	Olympique Marseille	Nîmes Olympique
1973	FC Nantes	OGC Nice
1974	AS Saint-Etienne	FC Nantes
1975	AS Saint-Etienne	Olympique Marseille
1976	AS Saint-Etienne	OGC Nice
1977	FC Nantes	RC Lens
1978	AS Monaco	FC Nantes
1979	RC Strasbourg	FC Nantes
1980	FC Nantes	FC Sochaux
1981	AS Saint-Etienne	FC Nantes
1982	AS Monaco	AS Saint-Etienne
1983	FC Nantes	Girondins de Bordeaux
1984	Girondins de Bordeaux	AS Monaco
1985	Girondins de Bordeaux	FC Nantes
1986	Paris Saint-Germain	FC Nantes
1987	Girondins de Bordeaux	Olympique Marseille
1988	AS Monaco	Girondins de Bordeaux
1989	Olympique Marseille	Paris Saint-Germain
1990	Olympique Marseille	Girondins de Bordeaux
1991	Olympique Marseille	AS Monaco
1992	Olympique Marseille	AS Monaco
1993	Olympique Marseille*	Paris Saint-Germain
1994	Paris Saint-Germain	Olympique Marseille**
1995	FC Nantes	Olympique Lyonnais
1996	AJ Auxerre	Paris Saint-Germain
1997	AS Monaco	Paris Saint-Germain
1998	RC Lens	FC Metz
1999	Girondins de Bordeaux	Olympique Marseille
2000	AS Monaco	Paris Saint-Germain
2001	FC Nantes	Olympique Lyonnais
2002	Olympique Lyonnais	RC Lens
2003	Olympique Lyonnais	AS Monaco
2004	Olympique Lyonnais	Paris Saint-Germain

* Title won by Olympique Marseille but taken away from them for alleged match-fixing payments. Title not awarded.

** Despite finishing second Olympique Marseille was relegated to the Second Division after being found guilty of match-fixing payments.

Another brilliant striker rolls off the Auxerre production line. Djibril Cisse was a key member of Auxerre's 2003 cup winning team.

FRANCE

George Weah signed *for AS Monaco in 1988, bought from Tonnerre Yaoundé of Cameroon by manager Arsène Wenger. He went on to become one of the finest players in the world, also appearing for PSG, Milan, Chelsea, Manchester City and Olympique Marseille.*

French Cup Record 1918–2004

YEAR	WINNERS	SCORE	RUNNERS-UP
1918	Olympique de Pantin	3-0	FC Lyon
1919	CAS Généraux	3-2 (aet)	Olympique Paris
1920	CA Paris	2-1	Le Havre AC
1921	Red Star Paris	2-1	Olympique Paris
1922	Red Star Paris	2-0	Stade Rennais
1923	Red Star Paris	4-2	FC Sète
1924	Olympique Marseille	3-2	FC Sète
1925	CAS Généraux	1-1 (aet), (replay) 3-2	FC Rouen
1926	Olympique Marseille	4-1	AS Valentigney
1927	Olympique Marseille	3-0	US Quevilly
1928	Red Star Paris	3-1	CA Paris
1929	SO Montpellier	2-0	FC Sète
1930	FC Sète	3-1	Racing Club France
1931	Club Français	3-0	SO Montpellier
1932	AS Cannes	1-0	Racing Club Roubaix
1933	Excelsior Roubaix	3-1	Racing Club Roubaix
1934	FC Sète	2-1	Olympique Marseille
1935	Olympique Marseille	3-0	Stade Rennais
1936	Racing Club Paris	1-0	US Charleville
1937	FC Sochaux	2-1	RC Strasbourg
1938	Olympique Marseille	2-1 (aet)	FC Metz

French Cup Record (*continued*)

YEAR	WINNERS	SCORE	RUNNERS-UP
1939	Racing Club Paris	3-1	Olympique Lille
1940	Racing Club Paris	2-1	Olympique Marseille
1941	Girondins de Bordeaux	2-0	SC Fives
1942	Red Star Paris	2-0	FC Sète
1943	Olympique Marseille	2-2 (aet), (replay) 4-0	Girondins de Bordeaux
1944	Nancy-Lorraine XI	4-0	Reims-Champagne XI
1945	Racing Club Paris	3-0	Lille OSC
1946	Lille OSC	4-2	Red Star Paris
1947	Lille OSC	2-0	RC Strasbourg
1948	Lille OSC	3-2	RC Lens
1949	Racing Club Paris	5-2	Lille OSC
1950	Stade de Reims	2-0	Racing Club Paris
1951	RC Strasbourg	3-0	US Valenciennes
1952	OGC Nice	5-3	Girondins de Bordeaux
1953	Lille OSC	2-1	FC Nancy
1954	OGC Nice	2-1	Olympique Marseille
1955	Lille OSC	5-2	Girondins de Bordeaux
1956	FC Sedan	3-1	FC Troyes-Aube
1957	FC Toulouse	6-3	SC Angers
1958	Stade de Reims	3-1	Nîmes Olympique
1959	Le Havre AC	2-2 (aet), (replay) 3-0	FC Sochaux
1960	AS Monaco	4-2 (aet)	AS Saint-Etienne
1961	FC Sedan	3-1	Nîmes Olympique
1962	AS Saint-Etienne	1-0	FC Nancy
1963	AS Monaco	0-0 (aet), (replay) 2-0	Olympique Lyonnais
1964	Olympique Lyonnais	2-0	Girondins de Bordeaux
1965	Stade Rennais	2-2 (aet), (replay) 3-1	FC Sedan
1966	RC Strasbourg	1-0	FC Nantes
1967	Olympique Lyonnais	3-1	FC Sochaux
1968	AS Saint-Etienne	2-1	Girondins de Bordeaux
1969	Olympique Marseille	2-0	Girondins de Bordeaux
1970	AS Saint-Etienne	5-0	FC Nantes
1971	Stade Rennais	1-0	Olympique Lyonnais
1972	Olympique Marseille	2-1	SC Bastia
1973	Olympique Lyonnais	2-1	FC Nantes
1974	AS Saint-Etienne	2-1	AS Monaco
1975	AS Saint-Etienne	2-0	RC Lens
1976	Olympique Marseille	2-0	Olympique Lyonnais
1977	AS Saint-Etienne	2-1	Stade de Reims
1978	AS Nancy	1-0	OGC Nice
1979	FC Nantes	4-1 (aet)	AJ Auxerre
1980	AS Monaco	3-1	US Orléans
1981	SC Bastia	2-1	AS Saint-Etienne
1982	Paris Saint-Germain	2-2 (aet)(6-5 pens)	AS Saint-Etienne
1983	Paris Saint-Germain	3-2	FC Nantes
1984	FC Metz	2-0 (aet)	AS Monaco
1985	AS Monaco	1-0	Paris Saint-Germain
1986	Girondins de Bordeaux	2-1 (aet)	Olympique Marseille
1987	Girondins de Bordeaux	2-0	Olympique Marseille
1988	FC Metz	1-1 (aet)(5-4 pens)	FC Sochaux
1989	Olympique Marseille	4-3	AS Monaco
1990	SCP Montpellier	2-1 (aet)	Racing Club Paris
1991	AS Monaco	1-0	Olympique Marseille
1992*		*no final*	
1993	Paris Saint-Germain	3-0	FC Nantes
1994	AJ Auxerre	3-0	SCP Montpellier
1995	Paris Saint-Germain	1-0	RC Strasbourg
1996	AJ Auxerre	1-0	Nîmes Olympique
1997	OGC Nice	1-1 (aet)(4-3 pens)	Guingamp
1998	Paris Saint-Germain	2-1	RC Lens
1999	FC Nantes	1-0	FC Sedan
2000	FC Nantes	2-1	Calais
2001	RC Strasbourg	0-0 (aet)(5-4 pens)	Amiens
2002	FC Lorient	1-0	SC Bastia
2003	AJ Auxerre	2-1	Paris Saint-Germain
2004	Paris Saint-Germain	1-0	LB Châteauroux

* No final was held in 1992 following the collapse of a temporary stand at the SC Bastia v Olympique Marseille semi-final.

Victorious FC Nantes players celebrate in front of their fans after overcoming fourth division amateurs Calais 2-1 in the Final of the French Cup in 2000. Nantes won with a last-minute goal.

French Cup Summary

TEAM	TOTALS	WINNERS & RUNNERS-UP (BOLD) (ITALICS)
Olympique Marseille	10, 6	**1924, 26, 27,** *34,* **35, 38, 40, 43,** *54,* **69,** *72,* **76,** *86, 87,* **89,** *91*
AS Saint-Etienne	6, 3	*1960, 62,* **68, 70, 74, 75, 77,** *81, 82*
Paris Saint-Germain	6, 2	**1982, 83, 85, 93, 95, 98,** *2003,* **04**
AS Monaco	5, 3	**1960,** *63,* **74, 80,** *84,* **85,** *89,* **91**
Lille OSC	5, 2	*1945,* **46–48,** *49,* **53, 55**
Racing Club Paris	5, 2	**1936, 39, 40, 45,** *49,* **50,** *90*
Red Star Paris	5, 1	**1921–23, 28, 42,** *46*
Girondins de Bordeaux	3, 6	**1941,** *43, 52, 55, 64, 68,* **69,** *86,* **87**
FC Nantes	3, 5	*1966, 70, 73,* **79,** *83,* **93,** *99,* **2000**
Olympique Lyonnais	3, 3	*1963,* **64, 67,** *71,* **73,** *76*
RC Strasbourg	3, 3	*1937, 47,* **51, 66,** *95,* **2001**
AJ Auxerre	3, 1	**1979,** *94,* **96, 2003**
OGC Nice	3, 1	**1952, 54,** *78,* **97**
FC Sète	2, 4	*1923, 24, 29,* **1930,** *34, 42*
FC Sedan	2, 2	**1956,** *61,* **65,** *99*
Stade Rennais	2, 2	*1922, 35,* **65, 71**
FC Metz	2, 1	*1938,* **84, 88**
Stade de Reims	2, 1	**1950,** *58,* **77**
CAS Généraux	2, 0	**1919, 25**
FC Sochaux	1, 3	**1937,** *59, 67, 88*
SC Bastia	1, 2	*1972,* **81,** *2002*
CA Paris	1, 1	*1920,* **28**
Le Havre AC	1, 1	*1920,* **59**
SCP Montpellier	1, 1	**1990,** *94*
SO Montpellier	1, 1	**1929,** *31*
AS Cannes	1, 0	**1932**
AS Nancy	1, 0	**1978**
Club Français	1, 0	**1931**
Excelsior Roubaix	1, 0	**1933**
FC Lorient	1, 0	**2002**
FC Toulouse	1, 0	**1957**
Nancy-Lorraine XI	1, 0	**1944**
Olympique de Pantin	1, 0	**1918**
Nîmes Olympique	0, 3	*1958, 61, 96*
RC Lens	0, 3	*1948, 75, 98*
FC Nancy	0, 2	*1953, 62*
Olympique Paris	0, 2	*1919, 21*
Racing Club Roubaix	0, 2	*1932, 33*
Amiens	0, 1	*2001*
AS Valentigney	0, 1	*1926*
Calais	0, 1	*2000*

French Cup Summary (*continued*)

TEAM	TOTALS	WINNERS & RUNNERS-UP (BOLD) (ITALICS)
FC Lyon	0, 1	*1918*
FC Rouen	0, 1	*1925*
FC Troyes-Aube	0, 1	*1956*
Guingamp	0, 1	*1997*
LB Châteauroux	0, 1	*2004*
Olympique Lille	0, 1	*1939*
Racing Club France	0, 1	*1930*
Reims-Champagne XI	0, 1	*1944*
SC Angers	0, 1	*1957*
SC Fives	0, 1	*1941*
US Charleville	0, 1	*1936*
US Orléans	0, 1	*1980*
US Quevilly	0, 1	*1927*
US Valenciennes	0, 1	*1951*

French League Cup Record 1995–2004

YEAR	WINNERS	SCORE	RUNNERS-UP
1995	Paris Saint-Germain	2-0	SC Bastia
1996	RC Metz	0-0 (aet)(5-4 pens)	Olympique Lyonnais
1997	RC Strasbourg	0-0 (aet)(6-5 pens)	Girondins de Bordeaux
1998	Paris Saint-Germain	2-2 (aet)(4-2 pens)	Girondins de Bordeaux
1999	RC Lens	1-0	FC Metz
2000	Gueugnon	2-0	Paris Saint-Germain
2001	Olympique Lyonnais	2-1 (aet)	AS Monaco
2002	Girondins de Bordeaux	3-0	FC Lorient
2003	AS Monaco	4-1	FC Sochaux
2004	FC Sochaux	1-1 (aet)(5-4 pens)	FC Nantes

French League Cup Summary

TEAM	TOTALS	WINNERS & RUNNERS-UP (BOLD) (ITALICS)
Paris Saint-Germain	2, 1	**1995, 98,** *2000*
Girondins de Bordeaux	1, 2	*1997, 98,* **2002**
AS Monaco	1, 1	*2001,* **03**
RC Metz	1, 1	**1996,** *99*
Olympique Lyonnais	1, 1	*1996,* **2001**
FC Sochaux	1, 1	*2003,* **04**
RC Lens	1, 0	**1999**
Strasbourg	1, 0	**1997**
Gueugnon	1, 0	**2000**
FC Lorient	0, 1	*2002*
SC Bastia	0, 1	*1995*
FC Nantes	0, 1	*2004*

Andorra

Federació Andorrana de Futbol
Founded: 1994
Joined FIFA: 1996
Joined UEFA: 1996

Better late than never, tiny Andorra became UEFA's 51st member in 1996, equipped with a fledgling league and a national stadium that holds 1,000 people. The team's first victory was 2-0 in a friendly against Belarus in April 2000.

SEASON	LEAGUE CHAMPIONS
2000	Constelació Esportiva
2001	FC Santa Coloma
2002	Encamp Dicoansa
2003	Don Pernil Santa Coloma
2004	Don Pernil Santa Coloma

YEAR	CUP WINNERS
2000	Constelació Esportiva
2001	FC Santa Coloma
2002	Lusitanos
2003	Don Pernil Santa Coloma
2004	Don Pernil Santa Coloma

Portugal

THE SEASON IN REVIEW 2003–04

FROM THE OUTSIDE PORTUGUESE SOCCER this season was all about Euro 2004; the stadiums and their cost, security and the lack of it, and the fate of the national team. But domestically it was all Porto. Jose Mourinho's team imperiously took its second consecutive championship. Despite the poor form and injury of the midfield stars Deco and Derlei, Porto's tenacity and strength in depth was immense. Costinha, Maniche and Alenitchev were consistently good and South African striker Benni McCarthy was rejuvenated. The team won the league with two games to go as nearest challengers Sporting, from Lisbon, lost to União Lieria. A month later, Porto crowned two years of organized and intelligent soccer by winning the European Champions League.

Have some shame and work

Sporting seemed the most likely challengers when it went on a long winning streak through the autumn driven by Brazilian playmaker Rochemback and goals from compatriot Liedson. Benfica kept up, improving all season under Antonio Camacho, and honourably dealt with the tragic death of the Hungarian midfielder Miklos Feher, who collapsed and died from a cardiac arrest during a match at Guimarães. Second place in the league was decided by the Sporting-Benfica clash in their penultimate game. Benfica won 1-0 with a goal from Geovanni, which prompted a pitch invasion from a group of Sporting ultras. Benfica confirmed its spot the following week with a nervy 0-0 draw at home to Leiria. The team finished the season by winning its first trophy in eight years. In the Portuguese Cup Final it beat Porto 2-1 with the winner coming from Simão in extra time.

Beyond the big three Nacional, Braga and Marítimo, all performed well and Rio Ave did better than it could ever have imagined. Despite finishing fifth and in a UEFA Cup spot, the club had considered the possibility so remote that it had failed to register properly with FIFA. Guimarães, by contrast, had a disastrous year, with home form so bad that a male witch was called in to cast a spell at its stadium. Fans harassed the squad at the training ground, with one man running up to the team and screaming, 'I'm 51 and I've never seen Vitória in the Second Division. Have some shame and work!' On a number of occasions tempers frayed and fights broke out at games, leading to bans and stadium closures.

1 Divisão League Table 2003–04

CLUB	P	W	D	L	F	A	Pts	
FC Porto	34	25	7	2	63	19	82	Champions League
SL Benfica	34	22	8	4	62	28	74	Champions League
Sporting CP	34	23	4	7	60	33	73	UEFA Cup
CD Nacional	34	17	5	12	56	35	56	UEFA Cup
SC Braga	34	15	9	10	36	38	54	UEFA Cup
Rio Ave FC	34	12	12	10	42	37	48	
CS Marítimo	34	12	12	10	35	33	48	UEFA Cup
Boavista FC	34	12	11	11	32	31	47	
Moreirense FC	34	12	10	12	33	33	46	
União Leiria	34	11	12	11	43	45	45	
SC Beira-Mar	34	11	8	15	36	45	41	
Gil Vicente FC	34	10	10	14	43	40	40	
Acádemica de Coimbra	34	11	5	18	40	42	38	
Vitória Guimarães	34	9	10	15	31	40	37	
CF Os Belenenses	34	8	11	15	35	54	35	
FC Alverça	34	10	5	19	33	49	35	Relegated
Paços de Ferreira	34	8	4	22	27	53	28	Relegated
CF Estrela Amadora	34	4	5	25	22	74	17	Relegated

Promoted clubs: Estoril, Vitóra Sebúbal, FC Penafiel.

International Club Performances 2003–04

CLUB	COMPETITION	PROGRESS
FC Porto	Champions League	Winners
SL Benfica	Champions League	3rd Qualifying Round
	UEFA Cup	4th Round
Sporting CP	UEFA Cup	2nd Round
União de Leiria	UEFA Cup	1st Round

Top Goalscorers 2003–04

PLAYER	CLUB	NATIONALITY	GOALS
Benni McCarthy	FC Porto	South African	20
Adriano	CD Nacional	Brazilian	19
Evandro	Rio Ave FC	Brazilian	15
Liedson	Sporting CP	Brazilian	15

Portuguese Cup

2004 FINAL

May 16 – National Stadium, Lisbon

SL Benfica **2-1** FC Porto
*(Fyssas 58,   (Derlei 45)
Simão 103)*

(after extra time)

h/t: 0-1 **Att:** 38,000
Ref: Lucilio Baptista

Left: Sporting Lisbon moved into the new Estadio Jose Alvalade, rebuilt for Euro 2004, but barely half full for most domestic games.

Right: The most wanted man in European soccer. The enigmatic José Mourinho made Porto champions of Portugal and Europe with a disciplined, canny, tactical team. His move to Chelsea has made him the best-paid manager in European club soccer.

Top left: *Tragedy struck Portuguese soccer when Benfica's Hungarian midfielder Miklos Feher collapsed during its game at Guimarães. He later died of a heart condition.*

Top right: *Portuguese League President Valentim Loureiro is led from a hearing at Gondomar Court in Lisbon as the long saga of corruption and match fixing in Portugal continues. During Operation Golden Whistle, police raided over 60 premises arresting and charging referees and soccer executives from numerous clubs.*

Middle left: *Nacional's Adriano takes on Porto's Dmitri Alenitchev. Adriano scored 19 goals this season and was one of the main reasons that the Nacional could take fourth spot and a UEFA Cup place.*

Middle right: *Porto celebrates its league championship by playing at home with its faces painted in club colours. From left to right: Sérgio Conceição, Benni McCarthy and Dmitri Alenitchev.*

Below: *Benfica won the cup, but there's no sign of coach Camacho; he was probably already in talks with Florentine Perez arranging his move to Real Madrid.*

Soccer in Portugal

1903: Boavista formed, Portugal's oldest major existing club

— 1900

— 1910

1914: Formation of FA: Federação Portuguesa de Futebol

— 1920

1921: First international, v Spain, lost 1-3, venue: Madrid

1922: First Portuguese Cup Final

1923: Affiliation to FIFA

— 1930

1935: National league established

— 1940

1944: National stadium at Caxias, Lisbon inaugurated

1946: OS Belenenses win the Championship, the first time one of the big three did not win it

— 1950

1954: Affiliation to UEFA

— 1960

1961: Eusebio joins Benfica

1965: Eusebio given European Footballer of the Year award

— 1970

1974–76: Portuguese Revolution took place. Soccer continued, but stadiums were regularly used for political rallys

— 1980

1986–88: Saltillo affair: Portuguese internationals refused to play in conflict over appearance fees

— 1990

2000: Boavista win league championship, breaking 54-year domination of Benfica, Sporting and Porto

— 2000

2004: Portugal host European Championships and finish as runners-up. Porto win Champions League

— 2010

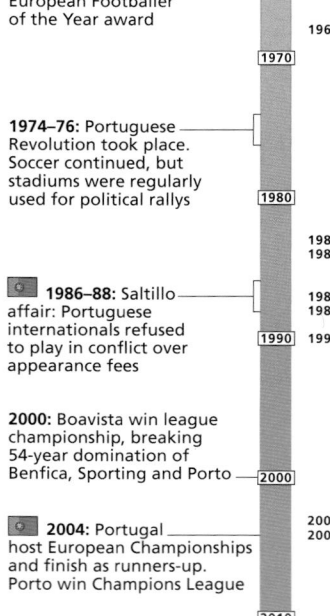
PORTUGAL

In 1961, a young player from Mozambique, named Eusebio, joined Benfica and started a golden era in Portuguese soccer.

Key

▣ International soccer	○ Competition winner
◉ Affiliation to FIFA	△ Competition runner-up
◉ Affiliation to UEFA	■ European Championships host
Ben – Benfica Porto – FC Porto Sport – Sporting CP	▲ European Championships runner-up

International Competitions

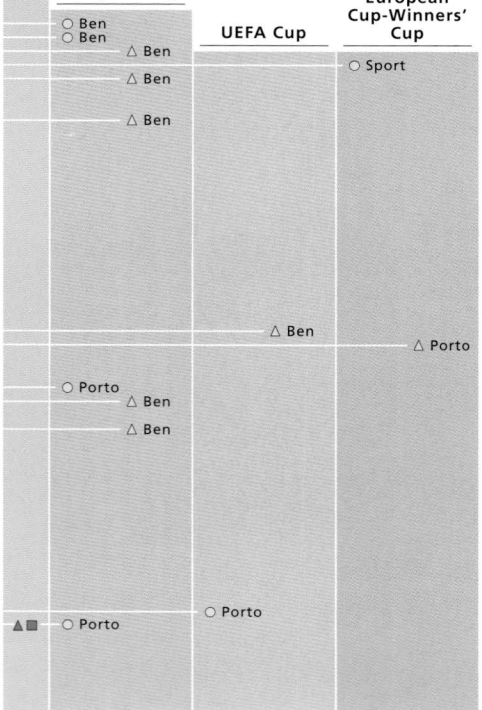

	European Cup	UEFA Cup	European Cup-Winners' Cup
1961:	○ Ben		
1962:	○ Ben		
1963:	△ Ben		
1964:			○ Sport
1965:	△ Ben		
1968:	△ Ben		
1983:		△ Ben	
1984:			△ Porto
1987:	○ Porto		
1988:	△ Ben		
1990:	△ Ben		
2003:		○ Porto	
2004:	▲■ ○ Porto	○ Porto	

Portugal: The main clubs

Chaves
1949 — Team name with year of formation

● Club formed before 1912
● Club formed 1912–25
● Club formed 1925–50
○ Club formed after 1950
● Date unknown
★ Founder members of National League 1934–35
👕 Champions (1935–80)
👕 Cup winners (1929–80)

Leça FC 1923

★ **Academico do Porto** 1911

★ **FC Porto** 1906

SC Salgueiros 1911

Boavista FC 1903

Leixões SC 1907

THE AZORES

Ponta Delgada ●
CD Santa Clara 1921

★ **Sporting CP** 1906

★ **CF Os Belenenses** 1919

★ **Atletico CP** 1942

Merger of Carcavelinhos and União (founded league as União)

Amadora

Cascais
GD Estoril Praia 1939

Lisbon

MADEIRA

Funchal ●

CS Marítimo 1910

Portugal

ORIGINS AND GROWTH OF SOCCER

IN THE LATE 19th century, Portugal was part of an informal British Empire, with extensive British communities trading and sailing from Lisbon and Porto. University students were recorded playing the game as early as 1866, and the first recorded club, Lisbon FC, was founded in 1875. By the 1890s Portuguese students returning from England started forming their own teams.

The popularity of the sport gathered pace and the country's four biggest clubs were formed in the first decade of the 20th century; in Lisbon, Benfica and Sporting Lisbon in 1904, and in Porto, Boavista in 1903 and Porto in 1906. By 1914, major teams were being established in the provinces and in the smaller cities. A national FA was set up in 1914 and professional league and cup competitions were running by the 1930s.

The golden era

After the Second World War, the Portuguese game was significantly boosted by the arrival of players from Portugal's African empire – Angola, Mozambique and Guinea-Bissau. Above all, the arrival of Eusebio from Mozambique to play for Benfica heralded a short golden era. Benfica, triumphant at home, also broke Real Madrid's monopoly on the European Cup, winning the tournament in 1961 and 1962. The following year, the Portuguese team made it to the semi-finals of the World Cup only to go out to the host and eventual winner, England.

Despite the talent at home, this period represents the country's peak international performance, having only qualified for two World Cups since 1934. The rather dormant Portuguese soccer scene of the 1970s was lifted by Porto's success in the European Cup in 1987, the arrival of many Brazilian players, the recent promise of the national team – semi-finalists at Euro 2000 – and Porto's victory in the UEFA Cup in 2003. However, their abject performance at the 2002 World Cup and the persistent accusations of corruption in the game overshadow the prospects of success.

Porto striker Derlei *shoots past Rab Douglas in the Celtic goal to win the UEFA Cup in 2003, becoming the first Portuguese club to win this particular competition.*

Barcelos
Gil Vicente FC
1924

SC Braga 1921

Chaves
1949

CD Aves 1930

Desportivo Aves 1930

Vitória Guimarães
1922

Felgueiras 1934

Varzim FC 1915

Rio Ave FC 1939

Aves

voa de rzim

Maia
1954

Penafiel 1951

FC Paços Ferreira 1950

SC Freamunde

Porto

São João da Madeira
Espinho
1944

Aviero
SC Beira Mar
1922

Covilhã
SC Covilhã
1923

Coimbra ★ Académica 1876

Figueira da Foz
Naval 1
de Maio
1893

União Lamas
1932

Leiria
União Leiria
1966

P O R T U G A L

CF Estrela Amadora 1932

FC Marco
1929

C Alverca
939

★ SL Benfica 1904

Campo Maior
SC Campomaiorense
1926

arreiro

FC Barreirense

GD Quimigal

★ Vitória Setúbal 1910

Casa Pia 1920

Amora FC 1921

Oriental Lisboa

FC Seixal

SC Olhãnense 1912

Faro
SC Farense
1910

Albufeira
Imortal DC
1920

Olhão

PORTUGAL

SL BENFICA 1904

League 1935–2004 (including Campionata de Portugal 1922–38)	**1930**, **31**, **35***, **36–38**, *38**, **42**, **43**, *44*, **45**, *46–49*, **50**, *52*, **53**, **55**, **56**, **57**, *59*, **60**, **61**, *63–65*, *66*, *67–69*, **70**, **71–73**, *74*, **75–77**, **78**, *79*, **81**, **82**, **83**, **84**, *86*, **87**, *88*, **89**, *90*, **91**, *92*, *93*, **94**, **96**, *98*, **03**, **04**
Cup	*1939*, *40*, **43**, **44**, *49*,**51–53**, **55**, **57**, *58*, **59**, **62**, **64**, **65**, **69**, **70**, **71**, **72**, **74**, **75**, **80**, **81**, **83**, **85–87**, **89**, **93**, **96**, *97*, **2004**
European Cup	**1961**, **62**, *63*, *65*, *68*, *88*, *90*
UEFA Cup	*1983*
World Club Cup	*1961*, *62*

SPORTING CP 1906

League 1935–2004 (including Campionata de Portugal 1922–38)	*1922*, *23*, *25*, *28*, *33*, **34**, **35**, **35***, **36***, *37**, **38***, *39*, **40**, **41**, *42*, *43*, **44**, **45**, **47–49**, **50**, **51–54**, *58*, **60**, **61**, *62*, **66**, **68**, **70**, **71**, **74**, **77**, **80**, **82**, **85**, *95*, *97*, **2000**, **02**
Cup	**1941**, **45**, **46**, **48**, **52**, **54**, **55**, **60**, **63**, **70**, **71**, **72**, **73**, **74**, **78**, **79**, **82**, **87**, **94**, **95**, **96**, **2000**, **02**
European Cup-Winners' Cup	**1964**

ESTADIO DA LUZ

70,000

Club:	SL Benfica
Built:	2003
Original Capacity:	70,000
Significant Matches:	European Championships 2004; three group games, quarter-final and Final

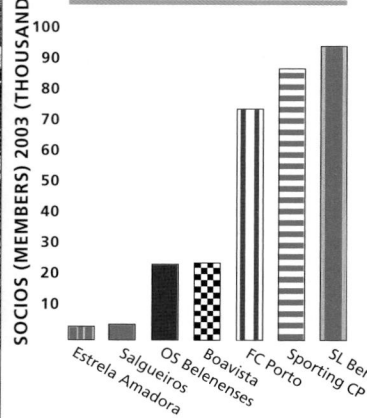
CF OS BELENENSES 1919

League 1935–2004 (including Campionata de Portugal 1922–38)	*1926*, **27**, **29**, *32*, **33**, *36**, *37*, **46**, *55*, *73*
Cup	*1940*, *41*, **42**, *48*, *60*, *86*, *89*

Estrela Amadora
PONTINHA
JOSÉ GOMES
25,000

CAMPO DA FEITEIRA
Benfica played here (1908–12)

BRANDOA
AVENIDA GOMES PEREIRA
BENFICA

SL Benfica (1917–25)
BURACA
ESTASIO PINA MANIQUE
IC19

Casa Pia

Sporting CP (1945–56)
EN117

A5
A5

Parque
Florestal
de Monsanto

CARAMÃO
RESTELO
40,000
OS Belenenses
BELÉM

SANTO AMARO
TAPADINHA
E01
Atletico Lisbon
Sporting CP (1945–56)
E01

ESTÁDIO JOSÉ ALVALADE
Sporting CP (1956–2003)
ESTÁDIO JOSÉ ALVALADE
52,000

QUINTA DOS LILAZES

ESTÁDIO DA LUZ
SL Benfica (1954–2003)
ESTÁDIO DA LUZ
70,000
SL Benfica (2003–)

Sporting CP (2003–)
SL Benfica (1941–54)
Sporting CP (1917–45)
SETE RIOS

SL Benfica (1913–17)

Parque
CAMPOLIDE

Parque Eduardo VII
ESTADIO AMOREIRAS
SÃO SEBASTIÃO
SL Benfica (1915–40)

ALCÂNTARA
MADRAGOA

CAMPO GRANDE
Until the 1960s this was a large area of open ground where many of the city's teams had pitches or small stadiums

A1

CIDADE UNIVERSITARIA

L I S B O N

ARCO CEGO
ALTO DO PINA

ESTEFÂNIA

PORTUGUESE STOCK EXCHANGE
FC Porto and Sporting CP have both partially floated on the Portuguese Stock Exchange

FEDERAÇÃO PORTUGUESA DE FUTEBOL HEADQUARTERS

CAMINHOS DE FERRO

Oriental Lisboa
CAMPO CARLOS SALEMA
CHELAS

Rio Tejo

Rio Tejo

ESTADIO NACIONAL
Built in Caxias, 10km west of Lisbon, in 1944, this stadium hosted many of Benfica and Sporting CP's big games between 1945 and 1954

Lisbon and Porto

 40,000 Capacity of stadium

 Stadium no longer in use for top-flight football

 Team colours

 Semi-professional or amateur team colours

 M1 Motorway

A82 Major road

1900 Champions

2000 Runners-up

* Denotes honours in Campionata de Portugal

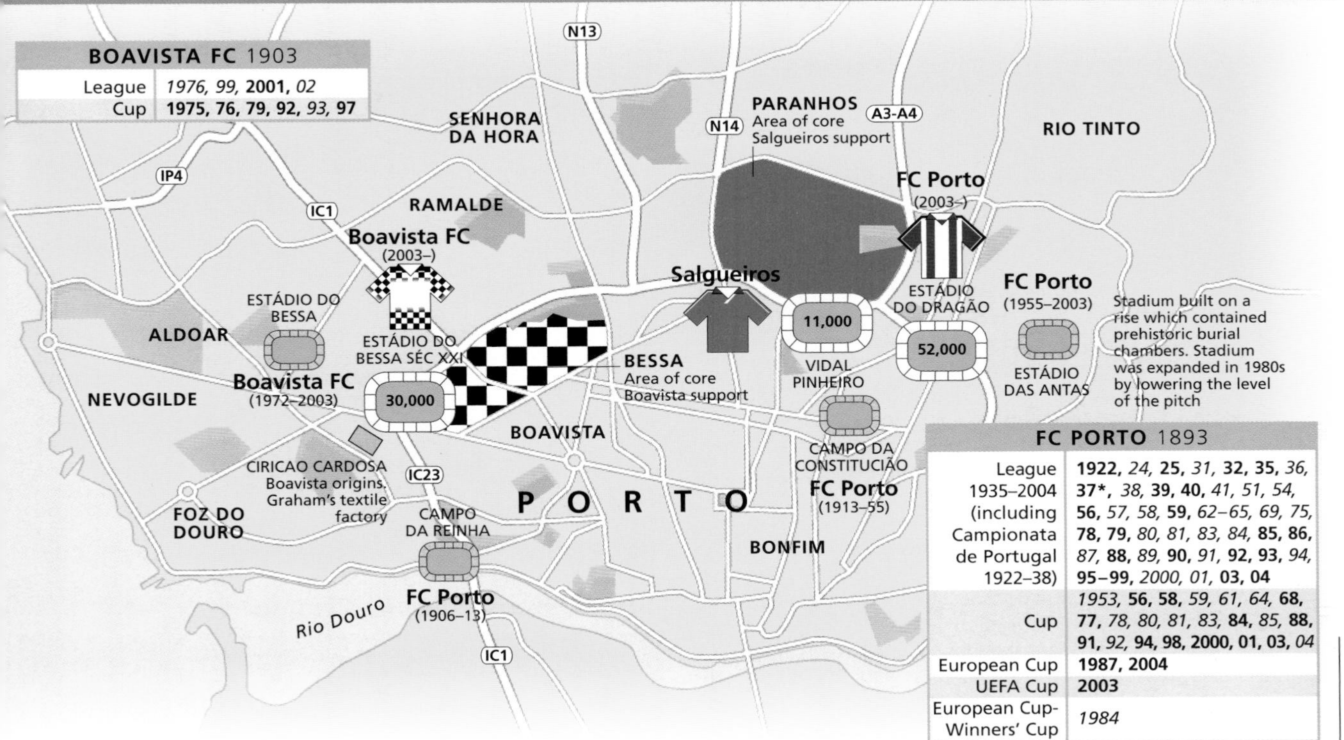

BOAVISTA FC 1903

League	1976, 99, **2001**, 02
Cup	**1975, 76, 79, 92, 93, 97**

SENHORA
DA HORA

N13

PARANHOS A3-A4
Area of core
Salgueiros support

RIO TINTO

N14

IP4

IC1

RAMALDE

Boavista FC
(2003–)

FC Porto
(2003–)

**ESTÁDIO DO
BESSA**

ESTÁDIO DO
BESSA SÉC XXI

Salgueiros

ESTÁDIO
DO DRAGÃO

FC Porto
(1955–2003)

Stadium built on a
rise which contained
prehistoric burial
chambers. Stadium
was expanded in 1980s
by lowering the level
of the pitch

ALDOAR

Boavista FC
(1972–2003)

11,000

52,000

ESTÁDIO
DAS ANTAS

NEVOGILDE

30,000

BESSA
Area of core
Boavista support

VIDAL
PINHEIRO

BOAVISTA

P O R T O

CIRICAO CARDOSA
Boavista origins;
Graham's textile
factory

IC23

CAMPO DA
CONSTITUCIÃO
FC Porto
(1913–55)

**FOZ DO
DOURO**

CAMPO
DA REINHA

BONFIM

FC Porto
(1906–13)

Rio Douro

IC1

FC PORTO 1893	
League 1935–2004 (including Campionata de Portugal 1922–38)	**1922**, 24, **25**, 31, **32, 35, 36, 37***, 38, **39, 40**, 41, 51, 54, **56, 57, 58, 59**, 62–65, 69, 75, **78, 79, 80, 81**, 83, **84, 85, 86, 87, 88**, 89, **90, 91, 92, 93**, 94, **95–99**, 2000, 01, **03, 04**
Cup	1953, **56, 58**, 59, 61, 64, 68, 77, 78, 80, 81, 83, **84, 85**, 88, 91, 92, **94**, 98, **2000, 01**, 03, 04
European Cup	**1987, 2004**
UEFA Cup	**2003**
European Cup-Winners' Cup	1984
World Club Cup	**1987**

PORTUGAL

Lisbon and Porto

SOCCER CENTERS

PORTUGUESE SOCCER IS CONCENTRATED in two cities –
Lisbon and Porto – and although both have their local derbies
(SL Benfica v Sporting CP and FC Porto v Boavista) neither can
match the intensity of the clashes between teams from the two
cities. Similar to the contrast between Rio and São Paulo or
Amsterdam and Rotterdam, Lisbon is the city of glamour and
irresponsible hedonism; Porto is the city that gets up and goes to
work. Porto makes things and sells them; Lisbon lives off its cut.

Lisbon has a scattering of small clubs who have on occasion
made it to the top flight, like Casa Pia and Oriental, a medium-
sized club in Os Belenenses, who sit in the historic suburb of
Bélem to the west of the city, and a penumbra of teams in its
distant suburbs. However, there are only two really big clubs:
Benfica and Sporting, who both roamed the city before finally
settling in the north. Benfica was founded in 1904 in Bélem
with a nationalist, Portuguese-only policy – but this policy was
bent to allow Portuguese colonial citizens from Africa into the
squad. Led by Eusebio and accruing massive support, the team
peaked in the 1960s and won two European Cups, famously
breaking Real Madrid's stranglehold on the competition.
Sporting drew on the land and finances of the Viscount of
Alvalade and built the best team in postwar Portugal, though
titles have been thinner on the ground in recent years. Both
cities have seen extensive stadium redevelopments in
anticipation of the 2004 European Championships.

The rise of Boavista

Porto's soccer has for a long time been dominated by FC Porto,
who started off at the Campo da Constituciã̃o before moving to
the enormous Estádio das Antas in the 1950s. However, Porto's
monopoly on the city's soccer triumphs and affections is being
challenged. Boavista, the inner-city team from Bessa,
is gaining ground. Founded by the English managers and
Portuguese workers of Graham's textile factory, by 1905 the
team had acquired a stadium, and in 1909 it changed its
name from Boavista Footballers to Boavista Futebol Clube.
After many years of obscurity, Boavista finally rose to take a
well-deserved championship victory in 2001. The big Porto
clubs are joined by tiny club Salgueiros from the working-class
Paranhos district of the city.

Political rally at the Das Antas in 1975. During the
Portuguese Revolution (1974–76) soccer stadiums all
over the country hosted enormous political rallies.

Portugal

PLAYERS AND MANAGERS

PERHAPS, BEFORE ANY OTHER EUROPEAN colonial power, Portugal took advantage of its imperial domains to find and recruit talent for its soccer. South Americans and Eastern Europeans had already begun to appear in the Portuguese league in the 1940s and 1950s. The earliest recruits were the Angolan Miguel Arcanjo, the son of a colonial civil servant, and the working-class Lucas Figueiredo 'Matateu' – who played for Porto and Belenenses respectively – both were capped for Portugal. Most famously Mario Coluna and Eusebio Ferreira came to Benfica in the late 1950s and early 1960s and took the team to their highest achievement – winning the European Cup in 1961.

The 'golden generation'

More recently Portugal has produced a great crop of players of its own – the so-called 'golden generation' – who won the 1991 World Youth Cup, including Luis Figo, Rui Costa and João Pinto. At the same time, the flow of foreign coaches into the country continues. Bela Guttman, the legendary Hungarian, led Benfica to the European Cup, Bobby Robson was in charge at Porto when they repeated the feat in 1987, and Sven-Goran Eriksson cut his teeth in big club management at Benfica in the early 1990s. The latest arrival is Luis Felipe Scolari who won the World Cup with Brazil in 2002 before taking charge of the national team.

The core of the memorable 1960s Portuguese national team in New York for the Cup of Champions: (left to right) Antonio Simoes, José Augusto, José Torres, Eusebio, Mario Coluna, Graca.

Top 20 International Caps

PLAYER	CAPS	GOALS	FIRST MATCH	LAST MATCH
Fernando Couto*	110	7	1990	2004
Luis Figo*	110	31	1991	2004
Rui Costa*	94	26	1993	2004
João Viera Pinto*	81	23	1991	2002
Vitor Baia*	80	0	1990	2002
Joao Silva Pinto	70	1	1983	1996
Tamagnini 'Nene'	66	22	1971	1984
Eusebio	64	41	1961	1973
Humberto Coelho	64	6	1968	1983
Manuel Bento	63	0	1976	1986
Pedro 'Pauleta'*	62	30	1997	2004
Mario Coluna	57	8	1955	1968
Serio Conceição*	56	12	1996	2003
Oceano Cruz	54	8	1985	1998
Paulo Sousa	51	0	1991	2002
Jorge Costa*	50	2	1992	2002
Fernando Gomes	48	13	1975	1988
Antonio Simoes da Costa	46	3	1962	1973
Jose Augusto	45	9	1958	1968
Ricardo Sa Pinto*	45	10	1994	2001

Top 10 International Goalscorers

PLAYER	GOALS	CAPS	FIRST MATCH	LAST MATCH
Eusebio	41	64	1961	1973
Luis Figo*	31	110	1991	2004
Pedro 'Pauleta'*	30	62	1997	2004
Rui Costa*	26	94	1993	2004
João Vieira Pinto*	23	81	1991	2002
Tamagnini 'Nené'	22	66	1971	1984
Nuno Gomes'*	21	46	1996	2004
Fernando Peyroteo	15	20	1938	1949
Rui Jordão	15	43	1972	1989
José Torres	14	33	1963	1973
Fernando Gomes	13	48	1975	1988
Sebastião 'Matateu'	13	27	1952	1960

* indicates players still playing at least at club level.

Portugal International Managers

DATES	NAME	GAMES	WON	DRAWN	LOST
1964–66	Otto Glyria, Manuel da Luz Afonso	20	15	2	3
1967	José Gomes da Silva	6	2	3	1
1968–69	José Maria Antunes	9	1	3	5
1970–71	José Gomes da Silva	7	3	1	3
1972–73	José Augusto	15	9	4	2
1974–76	José Maria Pedroto	16	6	4	6
1977–78	Júlio Cernadas Pereira	5	3	1	1
1978–80	Mário Wilson	10	5	2	3
1980–82	Júlio Cernadas Pereira	18	6	3	9
1982–83	Otto Glória	7	3	1	3
1983–84	Fernando Cabrita, António Morais, António Oliveira, José Augusto	9	5	2	2
1984–86	José Torres	17	8	1	8
1986–87	Rui Seabra	6	1	4	1
1987–89	Júlio Cernadas Pereira	10	6	3	1
1989	Artur Jorge	7	2	2	3
1990–93	Carlos Queiroz	31	14	11	6
1994	Eduardo Vingada	2	0	2	0
1994–96	António Oliveira	22	13	5	4
1996–97	Artur Jorge	12	5	5	2
1998–2000	Humberto Coelho	11	8	1	2
2000–02	António Oliveira	22	13	5	4
2002–03	Agostinho Oliviera	4	2	2	0
2003–	Luis Felipe Scolari	23	13	5	5

All figures correct as of 4 July 2004.

PORTUGAL

Player of the Year

YEAR	PLAYER	CLUB
1970	Eusebio***	Benfica
1971	Nene	Benfica
1972	Toni	Benfica
1973	Eusebio	Benfica
1974	Coelho	Benfica
1975	Alves	Benfica
1976	Chalana	Benfica
1977	Bento	Benfica
1978	Oliveira	FC Porto
1979	Costa	FC Porto
1980	Jordão	Sporting CP
1981	Oliveira	FC Porto
1982	Oliveira	FC Porto
1983	Gomes	FC Porto
1984	Chalana	Benfica
1985	Manuel	Benfica
1986	Futre**	FC Porto
1987	Futre**	FC Porto/ Atlético Madrid
1988	Barros	FC Porto/Juventus
1989	Baía	FC Porto
1989	Ricardo [Bra]*	Benfica
1990	Domingos	FC Porto
1990	Cadete*	Sporting CP
1991	Vitor	FC Porto
1991	Domingos*	FC Porto

Player of the Year (*continued*)

YEAR	PLAYER	CLUB
1992	João Pinto	Benfica
1992	Baía*	FC Porto
1993	João Pinto	Benfica
1993	Couto*	FC Porto
1994	João Pinto**	Benfica
1995	João Pinto	Sporting/Barcelona
1995	Figo*	Sporting CP
1996	Figo	Barcelona
1996	Baía*	FC Porto
1997	Figo	Barcelona
1997	Jardel [Bra]*	FC Porto
1998	Figo	Barcelona
1998	Conceição*	FC Porto
1999	Figo	Barcelona
1999	Jardel [Bra]*	FC Porto
2000	Figo	Real Madrid
2000	Acosta [Arg]*	Sporting
2001	Petit*	Boavista FC
2002	Jardel [Bra]*	Sporting CP

* Awarded by *Record*. All others awarded by CNID.
** Awarded by both *Record* and CNID.
*** Awarded by *Diário Popular*.

Luis Figo, leader of Portugal's 'golden generation', had to settle for silver as the national team finished as runners-up in Euro 2004 beaten by Greece in the Final.

Top Goalscorers by Season 1938–2004

SEASON	PLAYER	CLUB	GOALS
1938–39	Monteiro	FC Porto	18
1939–40	Peyroteo	Sporting CP	29
1939–40	Kordnya	FC Porto	29
1940–41	Peyroteo	Sporting CP	29
1941–42	Dias	FC Porto	36
1942–43	Silva	SL Benfica	24
1943–44	Rodrigues	Vitória FC Setúbal	28
1944–45	Rodrigues	Vitória FC Setúbal	21
1945–46	Peyroteo	Sporting CP	37
1946–47	Peyroteo	Sporting CP	43
1947–48	Araújo	FC Porto	36
1948–49	Peyroteo	Sporting CP	40
1949–50	Silva	SL Benfica	28
1950–51	Vasques	Sporting CP	29
1951–52	Águas	SL Benfica	28
1952–53	Fonseca	CF Os Belenenses	29
1953–54	Martins	Sporting CP	31
1954–55	Fonseca	CF Os Belenenses	32
1955–56	Águas	SL Benfica	28
1956–57	Águas	SL Benfica	30
1957–58	Duarte	GD CUF Barreiro	23
1958–59	Águas	SL Benfica	26
1959–60	Ribeiro	Vitória SC Guimarães	25
1960–61	Águas	SL Benfica	27
1961–62	Veríssimo	FC Porto	23
1962–63	Torres	SL Benfica	26
1963–64	Eusebio	SL Benfica	28
1964–65	Eusebio	SL Benfica	28
1965–66	Eusebio	SL Benfica	25
1965–66	Figueiredo	Sporting CP	25
1966–67	Eusebio	SL Benfica	31
1967–68	Eusebio	SL Benfica	42
1968–69	António	Académica Coimbra	19
1969–70	Eusebio	SL Benfica	20

SEASON	PLAYER	CLUB	GOALS
1970–71	Jorge	SL Benfica	23
1971–72	Jorge	SL Benfica	27
1972–73	Eusebio	SL Benfica	40
1973–74	Yazalde	Sporting CP	46
1974–75	Yazalde	Sporting CP	30
1975–76	Jordão	SL Benfica	30
1976–77	Gomes	FC Porto	26
1977–78	Gomes	FC Porto	25
1978–79	Gomes	FC Porto	27
1979–80	Jordão	Sporting CP	31
1980–81	Nené	SL Benfica	20
1981–82	Pereira	FC Porto	27
1982–83	Gomes	FC Porto	36
1983–84	Gomes	FC Porto	21
1983–84	Nené	SL Benfica	21
1984–85	Gomes	FC Porto	39
1985–86	Fernandes	Sporting CP	30
1986–87	Cascavel'	Vitória SC Guimarães	22
1987–88	Cascavel'	Sporting CP	23
1988–89	Garcia	SL Benfica	16
1989–90	Magnusson	SL Benfica	33
1990–91	Águas	SL Benfica	25
1991–92	Owubokiri	Boavista FC/ FC Porto	30
1992–93	Cadete	Sporting CP	18
1993–94	Yekini	Vitória FC Setúbal	21
1994–95	Nader SC	SC Farense	21
1995–96	Oliveira	FC Porto	25
1996–97	Jardel	FC Porto	30
1997–98	Jardel	FC Porto	26
1998–99	Jardel	FC Porto	36
1999–2000	Jardel	FC Porto	37
2000–01	Jesus	FC Porto	22
2001–02	Jardel	Sporting CP	42
2002–03	Sabrosa	SL Benfica	18
2002–03	Faye	SC Beira Mar	18
2003–04	McCarthy	FC Porto	20

Ricardo Carvalho, one of the new generation of Portuguese players nurtured at FC Porto where his play is characterised by cultured and mature defending.

Portugal

1 DIVISÃO 1990–2003

IN 1982, SPORTING CP from Lisbon took the title under the eccentric English manager Malcolm Allison, after which the Portuguese championship was shared between SL Benfica and FC Porto for 19 seasons. Under Sven-Göran Eriksson, Benfica showed something of its old dominance, winning five titles and going to two European Cup Finals. Porto, revived under coach and former player José María Pedroto and striker Fernando Gomes, took three titles in the mid-1980s and two in the early 1990s. Benfica continued to challenge, but was progressively diminished by escalating debts and incredible inconsistency in managers and squads. By contrast, Porto was rock solid, taking a record-breaking five titles in a row in the 1990s, first under Bobby Robson, then Antonio Oliveira, and finally Fernando Santos. The club was unstoppable and in Brazilian Mario Jardel it had one of the greatest goalscorers of the time.

The Boavista surprise

A briefly revived Benfica, under manager Juup Heynckes, looked a threat to the Porto monopoly, but the swirling mists of corruption overtook the club and president João Vale e Azevedo was arrested and later tried and convicted on embezzlement charges. Instead, the challenge came first from Sporting, who, despite managerial changes and boardroom reshuffles, took the title in 2000 with talismanic Dane Peter Schmeichel in goal and again in 2002. In 2001, the real surprise package was Porto's Boavista FC. Gradually improving throughout the 1990s, the team took the lead early in the tournament and held it over Porto, showing outstanding discipline and tenacity across the whole season.

Beyond the charmed circle, who have held on to nearly all the money available from European qualification, the composition of the league has been very unstable. The only additional permanent members of the top flight are Vitória SC Guimarães, SC Braga and more recently CS Marítimo, SC Farense and SC Salgueiros. In order to survive, Farense has sold itself to a Spanish businessman, and Braga has floated on the stock exchange. However, the truth is that neither strategy looks likely to upset the *status quo* at the top of the Portuguese soccer ladder.

Boavista FC celebrates entry to the Champions League after its spectacular league championship in 2001. The club's budget is one-tenth of that available to rivals FC Porto and Sporting CP.

Portuguese League Positions 1990–2003

TEAM	1990–91	1991–92	1992–93	1993–94	1994–95	1995–96	1996–97	1997–98	1998–99	1999–2000	2000–01	2001–02	2002–03
Academica								15	18				15
FC Alverca									15	11	12	18	
CD Aves										17			
SC Beira Mar	6	8	8	14	17				16		8	11	13
CF Os Belenenses	19		7	13	12	6	13	18		12	7	5	9
SL Benfica	1	2	2	1	3	2	3	2	3	3	6	4	2
Boavista FC	4	3	4	4	9	4	7	6	2	4	1	2	10
SC Braga	7	11	12	15	10	8	4	10	9	9	4	9	14
SC Campomaiorense							17	11	13	13	16		
GD Chaves	8	9	18		14	15	10	16	17				
Espinho		17				16							
GD Estoril Praia		10	13	18									
CF Estrela Amadora	18		9	15	11	9	7	8	8	8			
FC Famalicão	14	14	14	17									
SC Farense	11	6	6	8	5	13	11	14	11	14	13	17	
FC Felgueiras						16							
FC Paços Ferreira		12	10	16							9	8	6
Gil Vicente FC	13	13	9	10	13	12	18			5	14	13	8
Vitória SC Guimarães	9	5	11	7	4	5	5	3	7	5	10	4	
Leça FC							14	14	12				
União Leiria						6	7	17	6	10	5	7	5
CD Nacional Madeira	20												11
CF União Madeira	12	18		12	16								
CS Marítimo	10	7	5	5	7	9	8	5	10	6	11	6	7
FC Moreirense													12
FC Penafiel	15	17											
FC Porto	2	1	1	2	1	1	1	1	1	2	2	3	1
Rio Ave FC								15	9	14	17		
SC Salgueiros	5	15	15	11	11	10	6	8	12	15	10	16	
CD Santa Clara											18	14	17
Vitória Setúbal	17		6	18		12	13	5	16			12	18
Sporting CP	3	4	3	3	2	3	2	4	4	1	3	1	3
FC Tirsense	16		16		8	18							
SCU Torreense		16											
Varzim FC										17		15	16

Key to League Positions Table

- League champions
- Other teams playing in league
- Season promoted to league
- Season of relegation from league
- 5 — Final position in league

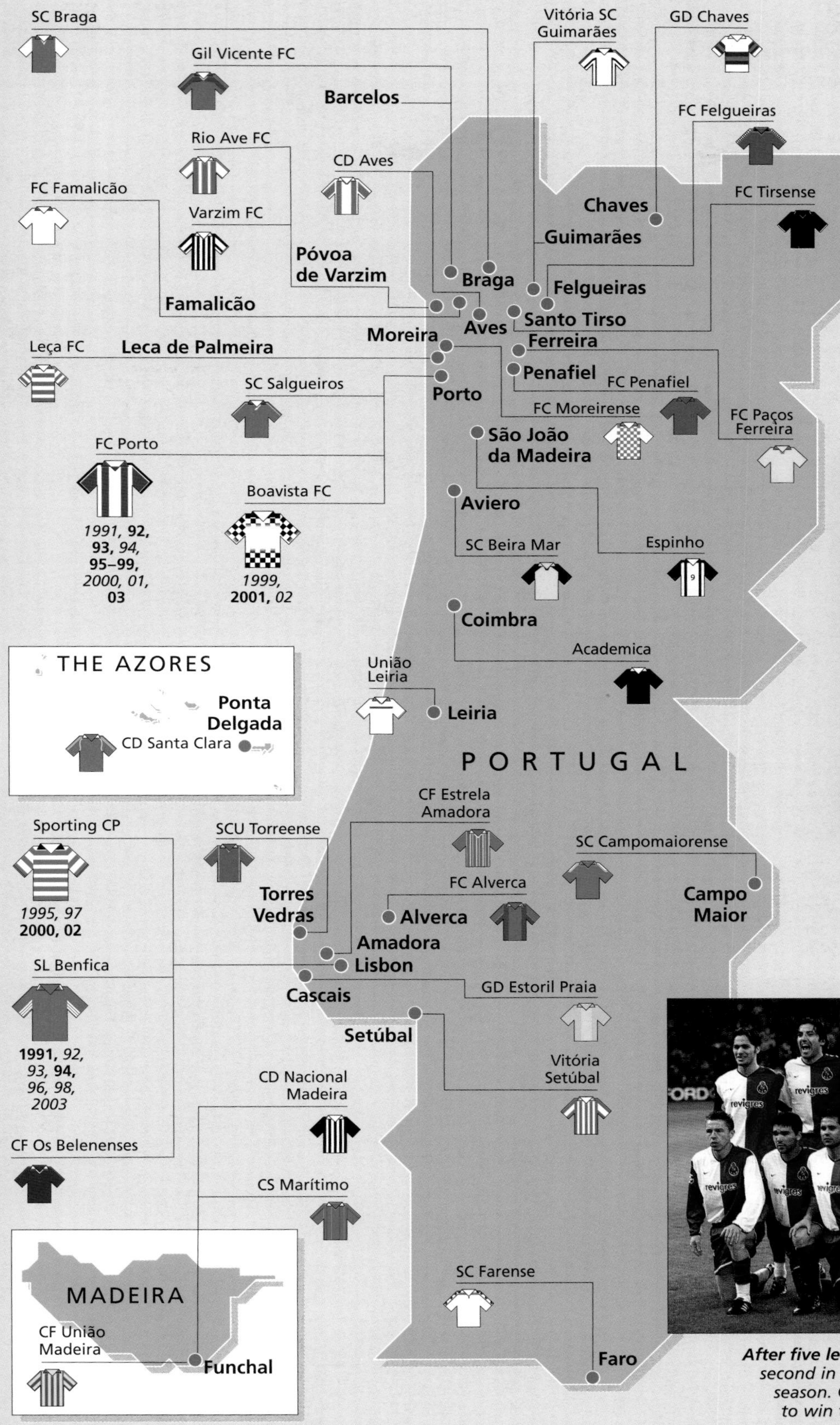

PORTUGAL

1 Divisão

Boavista FC	Team name
	League champions/ runners-up
1999, *2001*	Champions in bold Runners-up in italics
	Other teams in the 1 Divisão
● **Porto**	City of origin

SC Braga

Gil Vicente FC

Barcelos

Vitória SC Guimarães

GD Chaves

FC Felgueiras

FC Tirsense

Rio Ave FC

CD Aves

Chaves

Guimarães

FC Famalicão

Varzim FC

Póvoa de Varzim

Braga

Felgueiras

Famalicão

Moreira

Aves

Santo Tirso Ferreira

Leça FC

Leça de Palmeira

SC Salgueiros

Porto

Penafiel

FC Penafiel

FC Porto

1991, **92,** **93,** *94,* **95–99,** *2000,* **01,** **03**

Boavista FC

1999, **2001,** *02*

FC Moreirense

FC Paços Ferreira

São João da Madeira

Aviero

SC Beira Mar

Espinho

9

Coimbra

Academica

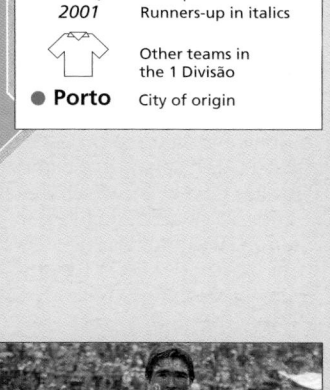

Porto's mercurial midfielder
Deco is one of the many Brazilian players to take Portuguese citizenship in order to further their careers.

THE AZORES

Ponta Delgada

CD Santa Clara

União Leiria

Leiria

P O R T U G A L

Sporting CP

1995, 97 **2000, 02**

SCU Torreense

CF Estrela Amadora

Torres Vedras

FC Alverca

SC Campomaiorense

Campo Maior

SL Benfica

1991, *92,* **93,** **94,** *96, 98,* **2003**

Alverca

Amadora

Lisbon

Cascais

GD Estoril Praia

Setúbal

Vitória Setúbal

CF Os Belenenses

CD Nacional Madeira

CS Marítimo

MADEIRA

CF União Madeira

Funchal

SC Farense

Faro

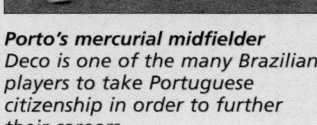

After five league titles in five years, Porto came second in 1999–2000 and again the following season. Coach José Mourinho was delighted to win the championship again in 2002–03.

Portugal

Federação Portuguesa de Futebol
Founded: 1914
Joined FIFA: 1923
Joined UEFA: 1954

PORTUGUESE SOCCER WAS ESTABLISHED in the early years of the 20th century, but no national league championship was properly organized until 1935. Prior to this, local tournaments centred on Lisbon and Oporto had been played and, in 1922, a national cup competition, the Campionata de Portugal, had been established. The winners of this cup were considered to be national champions.

Since 1935, the league championship has been dominated by three clubs – Benfica, FC Porto and Sporting CP from Lisbon –

with only CF Os Belenenses and Boavista FC occasionally making waves. Unlike most of mainland Europe, Portuguese neutrality ensured that league soccer continued throughout the Second World War. The league currently consists of 18 teams with a standard three up, three down promotion and relegation system.

The entrance to the old Stadium of Light, home to SL Benfica of Lisbon until 2003. A new Stadium of Light has been constructed next door.

Campionata de Portugal 1922–38

YEAR	WINNERS	SCORE	RUNNERS-UP
1922	FC Porto	3-1	Sporting CP
1923	Sporting CP	3-0	Academica
1924	SC Olhãnense	4-2	FC Porto
1925	FC Porto	2-1	Sporting CP
1926	CS Marítimo	2-0	CF Os Belenenses
1927	CF Os Belenenses	3-0	Vitória Setúbal
1928	Carcavelinhos	3-1	Sporting CP
1929	CF Os Belenenses	2-1	União de Lisboa
1930	SL Benfica	3-1	FC Barreirense
1931	SL Benfica	3-0	FC Porto
1932	FC Porto	2-0	CF Os Belenenses
1933	CF Os Belenenses	3-1	Sporting CP
1934	Sporting CP	4-3	FC Barreirense
1935	SL Benfica	2-1	Sporting CP
1936	Sporting CP	3-1	CF Os Belenenses
1937	FC Porto	3-2	Sporting CP
1938	Sporting CP	3-1	SL Benfica

Portuguese League Record 1935–2004

SEASON	CHAMPIONS	RUNNERS-UP
1935	FC Porto	Sporting CP
1936	SL Benfica	FC Porto
1937	SL Benfica	CF Os Belenenses
1938	SL Benfica	FC Porto
1939	FC Porto	Sporting CP
1940	FC Porto	Sporting CP
1941	Sporting CP	FC Porto
1942	SL Benfica	Sporting CP
1943	SL Benfica	Sporting CP

Portuguese League Record (*continued*)

SEASON	CHAMPIONS	RUNNERS-UP
1944	Sporting CP	SL Benfica
1945	SL Benfica	Sporting CP
1946	CF Os Belenenses	SL Benfica
1947	Sporting CP	SL Benfica
1948	Sporting CP	SL Benfica
1949	Sporting CP	SL Benfica
1950	SL Benfica	Sporting CP
1951	Sporting CP	FC Porto
1952	Sporting CP	SL Benfica
1953	Sporting CP	SL Benfica
1954	Sporting CP	FC Porto
1955	SL Benfica	CF Os Belenenses
1956	FC Porto	SL Benfica
1957	SL Benfica	FC Porto
1958	Sporting CP	FC Porto
1959	FC Porto	SL Benfica
1960	SL Benfica	Sporting CP
1961	SL Benfica	Sporting CP
1962	Sporting CP	FC Porto
1963	SL Benfica	FC Porto
1964	SL Benfica	FC Porto
1965	SL Benfica	FC Porto
1966	Sporting CP	SL Benfica
1967	SL Benfica	Academica
1968	SL Benfica	Sporting CP
1969	SL Benfica	FC Porto
1970	Sporting CP	SL Benfica
1971	SL Benfica	Sporting CP
1972	SL Benfica	Vitória Setúbal
1973	SL Benfica	CF Os Belenenses
1974	Sporting CP	SL Benfica
1975	SL Benfica	FC Porto
1976	SL Benfica	Boavista FC
1977	SL Benfica	Sporting CP
1978	FC Porto	SL Benfica
1979	FC Porto	SL Benfica
1980	Sporting CP	FC Porto
1981	SL Benfica	FC Porto
1982	Sporting CP	SL Benfica
1983	SL Benfica	FC Porto
1984	SL Benfica	FC Porto
1985	FC Porto	Sporting CP
1986	FC Porto	SL Benfica
1987	SL Benfica	FC Porto
1988	FC Porto	SL Benfica
1989	SL Benfica	FC Porto
1990	FC Porto	SL Benfica
1991	SL Benfica	FC Porto
1992	FC Porto	SL Benfica
1993	FC Porto	SL Benfica
1994	SL Benfica	FC Porto
1995	FC Porto	Sporting CP
1996	FC Porto	SL Benfica
1997	FC Porto	Sporting CP
1998	FC Porto	SL Benfica
1999	FC Porto	Boavista FC
2000	Sporting CP	FC Porto
2001	Boavista FC	FC Porto
2002	Sporting CP	Boavista FC
2003	FC Porto	SL Benfica
2004	FC Porto	SL Benfica

PORTUGAL

Portuguese League Summary

TEAM	TOTALS	CHAMPIONS & RUNNERS-UP (BOLD) (ITALICS)
SL Benfica	33, 25	**1930, 31, 35*, 36–38,** *38*,* **42, 43, 44, 45,** *46–49,* **50,** *52, 53,* **55, 56, 57,** *59,* **60, 61, 63–65, 66, 67–69,** *70,* **71–73,** *74,* **75–77,** *78, 79,* **81, 82, 83, 84,** *86,* **87,** *88,* **89, 90, 91, 92, 93, 94,** *96, 98, 2003,* **04**
FC Porto	24, 25	*1922, 24,* **25,** *31, 32,* **35,** *36,* **37*,** *38, 39,* **40, 41, 51, 54, 56, 57, 58,** *59, 62–65, 69, 75,* **78, 79, 80, 81, 83, 84, 85, 86, 87, 88, 89, 90, 91, 92, 93, 94, 95–99, 2000, 01,** *03,* **04**
Sporting CP	22, 21	*1922,* **23,** *25, 28, 33,* **34,** *35*, 35, 36*, 37*, 38*, 39,* **40, 41, 42, 43, 44, 45, 47–49,** *50,* **51–54,** *58, 60, 61, 62,* **66,** *68, 70, 71,* **74,** *77,* **80, 82,** *85, 95, 97,* **2000,** *02*
CF Os Belenenses	4, 6	*1926, 27, 29, 32,* **33,** *36*,* **37,** *46, 55, 73*
Boavista FC	1, 3	*1976, 99,* **2001,** *02*
Carcavelinhos	1, 0	**1928**
CS Marítimo	1, 0	**1926**
SC Olhãnense	1, 0	**1924**
Academica	0, 2	*1923, 67*
FC Barreirense	0, 2	*1930, 34*
Vitória Setúbal	0, 2	*1927, 72*
União de Lisboa	0, 1	*1929*

* denotes honours in Campionata de Portugal.

Portuguese Cup Record 1939–2004

YEAR	WINNERS	SCORE	RUNNERS-UP
1939	Academica	4-3	SL Benfica
1940	SL Benfica	3-1	CF Os Belenenses
1941	Sporting CP	4-1	CF Os Belenenses
1942	CF Os Belenenses	2-0	Vitória SC Guimarães
1943	SL Benfica	5-1	Vitória Setúbal
1944	SL Benfica	8-0	GD Estoril Praia
1945	Sporting CP	1-0	SC Olhãnense
1946	Sporting CP	4-2	Atletico CP
1947		no competition	
1948	Sporting CP	3-1	CF Os Belenenses
1949	SL Benfica	2-1	Atletico CP
1950		no competition	
1951	SL Benfica	5-1	Academica
1952	SL Benfica	5-4	Sporting CP
1953	SL Benfica	5-0	FC Porto
1954	Sporting CP	3-2	Vitória Setúbal
1955	SL Benfica	2-1	Sporting CP
1956	FC Porto	3-0	SCU Torreense
1957	SL Benfica	3-1	SC Covilhã
1958	FC Porto	1-0	SL Benfica
1959	SL Benfica	1-0	FC Porto
1960	CF Os Belenenses	2-1	Sporting CP
1961	Leixões SC	2-0	FC Porto
1962	SL Benfica	3-0	Vitória Setúbal
1963	Sporting CP	4-0	Vitória SC Guimarães
1964	SL Benfica	6-2	FC Porto
1965	Vitória Setúbal	3-1	SL Benfica
1966	SC Braga	1-0	Vitória Setúbal
1967	Vitória Setúbal	3-2	Academica
1968	FC Porto	2-1	Vitória Setúbal
1969	SL Benfica	2-1	Academica
1970	SL Benfica	3-1	Sporting CP
1971	Sporting CP	4-1	SL Benfica
1972	SL Benfica	3-2	Sporting CP
1973	Sporting CP	3-2	Vitória Setúbal
1974	Sporting CP	2-1	SL Benfica
1975	Boavista FC	2-1	SL Benfica
1976	Boavista FC	2-1	Vitória SC Guimarães

Portuguese Cup Record (*continued*)

YEAR	WINNERS	SCORE	RUNNERS-UP
1977	FC Porto	2-1	SC Braga
1978	Sporting CP	1-1, (replay) 2-1	FC Porto
1979	Boavista FC	1-1, (replay) 1-0	Sporting CP
1980	SL Benfica	1-0	FC Porto
1981	SL Benfica	3-1	FC Porto
1982	Sporting CP	4-0	SC Braga
1983	SL Benfica	1-0	FC Porto
1984	FC Porto	4-1	Rio Ave FC
1985	SL Benfica	3-1	FC Porto
1986	SL Benfica	2-0	CF Os Belenenses
1987	SL Benfica	2-1	Sporting CP
1988	FC Porto	1-0	Vitória SC Guimarães
1989	CF Os Belenenses	2-1	SL Benfica
1990	CF Estrela Amadora	3-1 (aet)	SC Farense
1991	FC Porto	3-1	SC Beira Mar
1992	Boavista FC	2-1	FC Porto
1993	SL Benfica	5-2	Boavista FC
1994	FC Porto	2-1 (aet)	Sporting CP
1995	Sporting CP	2-0	CS Marítimo
1996	SL Benfica	3-1	Sporting CP
1997	Boavista FC	3-2	SL Benfica
1998	FC Porto	3-1	SC Braga
1999	SC Beira Mar	1-0	SC Campomaiorense
2000	FC Porto	3-1 (aet)	Sporting CP
2001	FC Porto	2-0	CS Marítimo
2002	Sporting CP	1-0	Lexiões SC
2003	FC Porto	1-0	União Leiria
2004	SL Benfica	2-1	FC Porto

Portuguese Cup Summary

TEAM	TOTALS	WINNERS & RUNNERS-UP (BOLD) (ITALICS)
SL Benfica	24, 8	*1939,* **40, 43, 44, 49, 51–53, 55, 57, 58, 59, 62, 64, 65, 69, 70, 71, 72,** *74, 75,* **80, 81, 83, 85–87,** *89, 93, 96, 97,* **2004**
Sporting CP	13, 10	**1941, 45, 46, 48,** *52,* **54,** *55, 60,* **63,** *70,* **71,** *72,* **73, 74, 78, 79,** *82,* **87, 94, 95,** *96,* **2000,** *02*
FC Porto	12, 11	*1953,* **56,** *58, 59, 61, 64,* **68,** *77,* **78,** *80, 81, 83,* **84, 85,** *88,* **91,** *92,* **94, 98, 2000, 01, 03,** *04*
Boavista FC	5, 1	**1975, 76, 79, 92,** *93,* **97**
CF Os Belenenses	3, 4	*1940, 41,* **42,** *48,* **60,** *86,* **89**
Vitória Setúbal	2, 6	*1943, 54, 62,* **65,** *66, 67,* **68,** *73*
Academica	1, 3	**1939,** *51,* **67,** *69*
SC Braga	1, 3	**1966,** *77, 82, 98*
Leixões SC	1, 1	**1961,** *2002*
SC Beira Mar	1, 1	*1991,* **99**
CF Estrela Amadora	1, 0	**1990**
Vitória SC Guimarães	0, 4	*1942, 63, 76, 88*
Atletico CP	0, 2	*1946, 49*
CS Marítimo	0, 2	*1995, 2001*
GD Estoril Praia	0, 1	*1944*
Rio Ave FC	0, 1	*1984*
SC Campomaiorense	0, 1	*1999*
SC Covilhã	0, 1	*1957*
SC Farense	0, 1	*1990*
União Leiria	0, 1	*2003*
SC Olhãnense	0, 1	*1945*
SCU Torreense	0, 1	*1956*

PORTUGAL

247

Spain

THE SEASON IN REVIEW 2003–04

'MONEY ISN'T EVERYTHING. This is the league of humility. We are a TEAM with capital letters,' exclaimed Valencia's captain David Albelda after the team won La Liga for the second time in three years. The season had begun to the contrary, with the expectation that money would indeed be everything. Real Madrid sacked Vicente Del Bosque, who had only won them La Liga and taken them to a Champions League semi-final, installed Carlos Queiroz as coach and signed David Beckham from Manchester United for £25 million. The latest addition to the Galacticos generated more coverage and more shirt sales then even Figo, Ronaldo and Zidane's arrivals. Barcelona welcomed Ronaldinho, but, that aside, the rest of Spanish soccer nursed its debts. However, almost unnoticed at the time, Real Madrid had not only dispensed with Del Bosque, but also retired captain Hierro, sold defensive midfielders Gérémi and Makelele and sent its talented striker Fernando Morientes into exile on loan at Monaco.

Predictably enough Real Madrid began the season in imperious style at home and in Europe. Beckham's work rate and seriousness won the approval of team-mates and the Madrid public. Iker Casillas continued to produce impossible saves on a regular basis and, although he seemed to be getting bigger by the game, Ronaldo was scoring regularly. Deportivo and Valencia kept within touching distance of Madrid, but Barcelona, who had begun well enough under new coach Frank Rijkaard, hit a miserable run of form, which saw them plummet as low as 12th in the league. Worse still, Real Madrid came to the Nou Camp and won for the first time in 20 years. Rijkaard was lambasted not only for losing, but, worse, for beginning the game in a negative and defensive formation. Meanwhile, Real Madrid seemed to step up another gear as it dispensed with Deportivo, Atlético and Murcia and built up an 8-point lead.

Primera Liga Table 2003–04

CLUB	P	W	D	L	F	A	Pts	
Valencia CF	38	23	8	7	71	27	77	Champions League
Barcelona	38	21	9	8	63	39	72	Champions League
RC Deportivo	38	21	8	9	60	34	71	Champions League
Real Madrid	38	21	7	10	72	54	70	Champions League
Athletic Bilbao	38	15	11	12	53	49	56	UEFA Cup
Sevilla FC	38	15	10	13	56	45	55	UEFA Cup
Atlético Madrid	38	15	10	13	51	53	55	
Villareal CF	38	15	9	14	47	49	54	
Real Betis	38	13	13	12	46	43	52	
Málaga CF	38	15	6	17	50	55	51	
RCD Mallorca	38	15	6	17	54	66	51	
Real Zaragoza	38	13	9	16	46	55	48	UEFA Cup (cup winners)
CA Osasuna	38	11	15	12	38	37	48	
Albacete Balompié	38	13	8	17	40	48	47	
Real Sociedad	38	11	13	14	49	53	46	
RCD Espanyol	38	13	4	21	48	64	43	
Racing Santander	38	11	10	17	48	63	42*	
Real Valladolid	38	10	11	17	46	56	41	Relegated
RC Celta	38	9	12	17	48	68	39	Relegated
Real Murcia	38	5	11	22	29	57	26	Relegated

* Racing had one point deducted for fielding one non-EU player too many in its match v Osasuna on 14 December.

Promoted clubs: Levante UD, Getafe CF, CD Numancia.

Above: Osasuna's fine form at the start of the season saw them in contention for the European places, but the team fell away during the second half of the campaign.

Below: David Beckham meets his adoring fans after signing for Real Madrid.

Above, left: Spanish Prime Minister Jose Luis Rodriguez is the first Barcelona supporter to take the top job since the end of the dictatorship.

Above: Javier Irureta coaxed another season of disciplined team play from Deportivo la Coruña.

Left: Joan Laporta, Barca's new president, seems finally to have stopped the rot.

SPAIN

Key

Barcelona

👕 Team name and shirt colours

👤 Manager

♔ League position

⬇ Relegated teams

🏆 Progress in Cup

CL Progress in Champions League

UEFA Progress in UEFA Cup

* Qualified for Champions League

† Qualified for UEFA Cup

📺 G12 Member
(TV consortium that has secured the lion's share of TV income for the big teams)

Athletic Bilbao

👤 Ernesto Valverde

♔ 5th †

🏆 2nd Round

Steady improvement from Bilbao, its best finish for six seasons and a place in Europe

Real Sociedad

👤 Raynald Denoueix (Fra)

♔ 15th

🏆 3rd Round

CL 1st Knockout Round

Last year's runners-up was a pale shadow of its former self. The pressure of the Champions League and La Liga was too much for the squad

Barcelona

👤 Frank Rijkaard (Neth)

♔ 2nd *

🏆 Quarter-final

UEFA 4th Round

A terrible run of form in the late autumn saw Barca drop into the lower half of the table. The Ronaldinho-inspired run that followed was simply breathtaking

CA Osasuna

👤 Javier Aguirre (Mex)

♔ 13th

🏆 4th Round

Pressing for a European place in the first half of the season, beating both Real and Barcelona. Fell away in the second half

RCD Espanyol

👤 Javier Clemente, Luis Fernandez

♔ 16th

🏆 3rd Round

After spending nearly the whole season in the bottom three, Espanyol finally pulled itself to safety on the last day – ecstasy at Montjuic

RC Deportivo

👤 Javier Irureta

♔ 3rd *

🏆 4th Round

CL Semi-final

There or thereabouts all season, Deportivo was as compact and as competitive as ever; after its bond issue it may even be solvent

Racing Santander

👤 Lucas Alcarez

♔ 17th

🏆 3rd Round

Another season flirting with relegation, Santander just stayed safe

RC Celta

👤 Miguel Angel Lotina, Radomir Antic (S&M), Ramón Carnero

♔ 19th ⬇

🏆 Quarter-final

CL 1st Knockout Stage

Good enough to make the last 16 of the Champions League but Celta's home form completely disintegrated and relegation surely followed

Real Valladolid

👤 Fernando Vasquez, Santos

♔ 18th ⬇

🏆 4th Round

A long slide into trouble saw the club fire Vasquez, but assistant Santos couldn't stop them going down after ten season in the top flight

Real Zaragoza

👤 Paco Flores, Victor Munoz

♔ 12th † 🏆 Winners

Disappointing in the league, but had a great cup run and a famous victory over Real Madrid in the Final

Atlético Madrid

👤 Gregorio Manzano

♔ 7th

🏆 Quarter-final

Atletico's inconsistency kept them out of the European spots, but will the team ever be the same again after Jesus Gil's death?

Real Madrid

👤 Carlos Queiroz (Por)

♔ 4th *

🏆 Runners-up

CL Quarter-final

After Monaco knocked them out of the Champions League, Real seemed to disintegrate; the treble turned into nothing

RCD Mallorca

👤 Jaime Pacheco, Luis Aragones

♔ 11th

🏆 3rd Round

UEFA 4th Round

Picked up well after a poor start to the season. A quarter-final in the UEFA Cup was good, but its 3-2 crushing of Real Madrid was the death knell for the Galacticos' title challenge

Albacete Balompié

👤 Cesar Ferrando

♔ 14th 🏆 2nd Round

A great season for the newly promoted club. Fourteenth place, like the team, was a comfortable performance

Valencia

👤 Rafael Benitez

♔ 1st *

🏆 Quarter-final

UEFA Winners

Champions for the second time in three years and the UEFA Cup as well – a victory for teamwork and spirit

Real Betis

👤 Victor Fernández

♔ 9th

🏆 4th Round

Just outside the European spots. However, Betis' best result was holding on to star midfielder Joaquin

Sevilla FC

👤 Joaquin Caparros

♔ 6th †

🏆 Semi-final

A poor start to the season followed by a steady rise up La Liga. A European spot was clinched on the final day

Málaga CF

👤 Juan de Dios Ramos

♔ 10th

🏆 4th Round

Still not quite good enough to trouble the top spots, Malaga hovered outside the European zone again

Real Murcia

👤 Joaquin Peiró, John Toshack (Wal)

♔ 20th ⬇

🏆 3rd Round

When you don't win for four months you get relegated, John Toshack or not

Villareal CF

👤 Benito Floro, Pacquito Gomez

♔ 8th

🏆 4th Round

UEFA Winners

Just outside the European places, Villareal's highlight was a semi-final clash with Valencia in the UEFA Cup

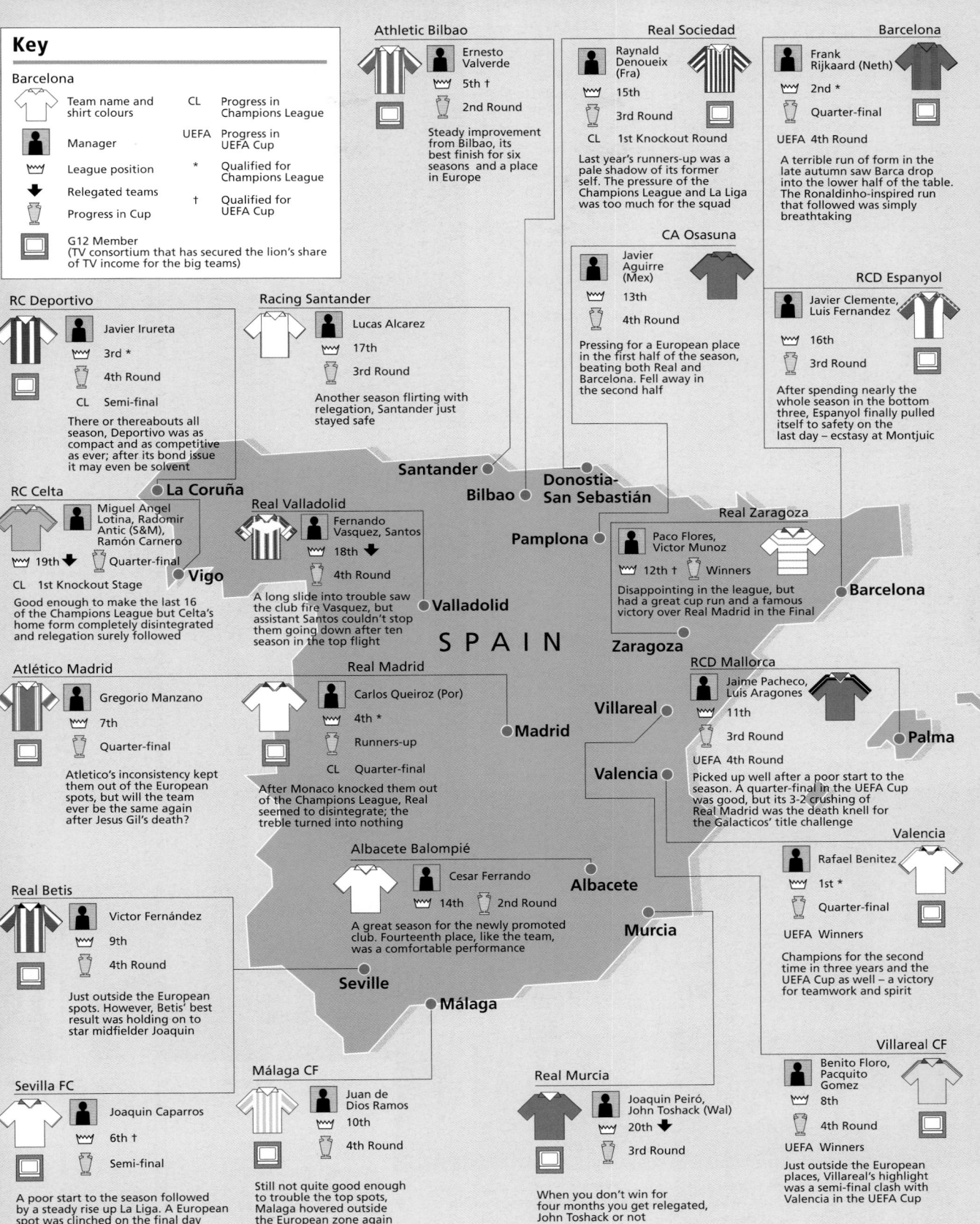

SPAIN

Santander
Bilbao
Donostia-San Sebastián
La Coruña
Pamplona
Vigo
Valladolid
Zaragoza
Barcelona
Madrid
Villareal
Valencia
Palma
Albacete
Murcia
Seville
Málaga
Valencia

SPAIN

Real unravel

Real Madrid's season began to unravel in the spring. The team squeezed its way past Bayern München in the First Knockout Round of the Champions League and then beat Monaco 4-2 in the first leg of its quarter-final – Monaco's Morientes having grabbed a last-minute goal. The return leg was the defining moment of its season as Monaco and Morientes took the game to them, winning 3-1 on the night and going through on away goals. It was reported that on leaving the pitch at half time when it was still 1-1, Zidane turned to Morientes and said, 'Can't you see we're shattered?' And so they were. In the cup final, Real abdicated to Zaragoza, and in La Liga its 8-point lead was surrendered as it could only manage a draw with cup nemesis Zaragoza, then lost to Bilbao, Osasuna and Barcelona. Real Madrid's strongest team was indeed the best in the league, but the bench was desperately thin and the loss of defensively inclined players simply couldn't be remedied by the team's goalscoring.

The Ronaldinho factor

Barcelona too was a different team in the second half of the season, going on a 19-game unbeaten run that carried them from mid-table to second in the final weeks of the season. The arrival of Edgar Davids from Juventus during the winter break bought some security and bite to the midfield, but it was the impetuous, inventive, dazzling talent of Ronaldinho that drove them up the table. For sheer exuberance and entertainment there was nothing better in European soccer this year. His dummies, sly feints and trickery were beguiling, his gargantuan smile infectious.

As Real Madrid fell to pieces it was Valencia, week in and week out, who won the points that took them to the top of the table. Coach Benitez had feared that he had precious little new talent to infuse his side. He had cryptically said that Jesus Garcia Pitarch, Valencia's director of soccer, 'brought me a lamp when I asked for a sofa'. It didn't seem to matter. Valencia played with all its traditional hallmarks. Its defence was simply magnificent, conceding a miserly 24 goals in 38 games. It was equally mean in its UEFA Cup run as well. In goal Canizares was back to his fiery best. Across the year hard work, team play, discipline, accuracy and quiet intelligence were the team's defining

Edgar Davids' mid-season arrival from Juventus helped transform Barcelona's campaign.

Real Madrid held a minute's silence days after the train bombings in the city killed over a hundred people. A minute's silence was observed at Spanish soccer grounds across the country.

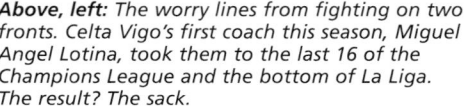

Above, left: The worry lines from fighting on two fronts. Celta Vigo's first coach this season, Miguel Angel Lotina, took them to the last 16 of the Champions League and the bottom of La Liga. The result? The sack.

Above, right: Goodbye Jesus Gil. Atlético Madrid's long-serving president passed away in 2004. His volcanic anger, rough talking and shady manoeuvrings will be sorely missed.

Above: *The Valencia team protests the award of a deeply controversial penalty with referee Tristante Oliva in its draw with Real in Madrid.*

Left: *Ronaldinho tries to lift the ball over Real Madrid's wall in Barca's historic 2-1 defeat of Real at the Bernabeu.*

Race for the Championship

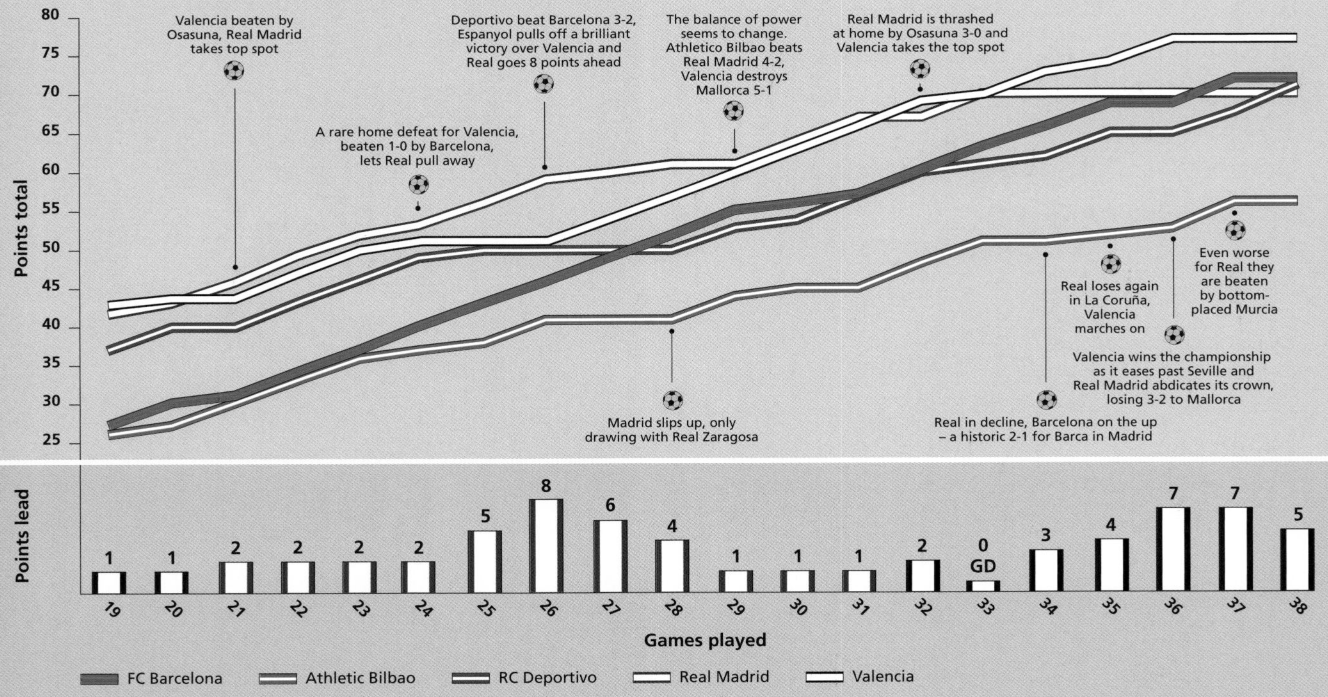

Valencia beaten by Osasuna, Real Madrid takes top spot

A rare home defeat for Valencia, beaten 1-0 by Barcelona, lets Real pull away

Deportivo beat Barcelona 3-2, Espanyol pulls off a brilliant victory over Valencia and Real goes 8 points ahead

The balance of power seems to change. Athletico Bilbao beats Real Madrid 4-2, Valencia destroys Mallorca 5-1

Real Madrid is thrashed at home by Osasuna 3-0 and Valencia takes the top spot

Real loses again in La Coruña, Valencia marches on

Even worse for Real they are beaten by bottom-placed Murcia

Valencia wins the championship as it eases past Seville and Real Madrid abdicates its crown, losing 3-2 to Mallorca

Madrid slips up, only drawing with Real Zaragosa

Real in decline, Barcelona on the up – a historic 2-1 for Barca in Madrid

Points total

80
75
70
65
60
55
50
45
40
35
30
25

Points lead

1	1	2	2	2	2	5	8	6	4	1	1	1	2	0 GD	3	4	7	7	5

Games played

19 20 21 22 23 24 25 26 27 28 29 30 31 32 33 34 35 36 37 38

▬ FC Barcelona   ▭ Athletic Bilbao   ▭ RC Deportivo   ▭ Real Madrid   ▭ Valencia

251 ⚽

characteristics. Carboni and Ayala were mature, wise heads in defence. Albelda and Baraja ran the midfield. And there was no shortage of goals either. As Roberto Ayala said, 'We may not have stars, but we do have players that can make a difference at a given moment.' Vicente, Angulo, Olivera and Mista all had their moments.

Valencia's ruthless composure

With five games to go Valencia held the lead over Real by three points. But a challenge never came as Real disintegrated. It was beaten at home by Barcelona and could not raise itself against Osasuna and had all title hopes extinguished by Mallorca who beat them 3-2 in Madrid. Worse was to come as it successively capitulated to bottom of the table Murcia and, on the final day, lost 4-1 to Real Sociedad in an embittered and almost empty Bernabeu. Valencia cruised past Sevilla to clinch the title and then demonstrated its composure and ruthlessness by taking the UEFA Cup from 10-man Marseille.

Outside the big four, Athletic Bilbao won a well-deserved UEFA Cup spot for a season of attacking soccer and Sevilla grabbed the last European place behind them. Atlético Madrid was occasionally brilliant and often not. In Fernando Torres Atlético retains one of La Liga's most exciting and prolific strikers. After the death of ex-president Jesus Gil, it has lost one of Spanish soccer's most newsworthy characters. Murcia, who at one point went without a win for four months, was relegated long before the end of the season. It was joined by Valladolid and Celta Vigo. Celta's season had been truly wretched. Although it made it to the knockout stages of the Champions League, its form at home was simply appalling and it never shook the losing habit. Espanyol, who had spent nearly the entire season in the bottom three, engineered an amazing late comeback to stay in La Liga, while newly-promoted Albacete did well to finish 14th.

International Club Performances 2003–04

CLUB	COMPETITION	PROGRESS
RC Celta	Champions League	1st Knockout Round
Real Sociedad	Champions League	1st Knockout Round
Real Madrid	Champions League	Quarter-finals
RC Deportivo	Champions League	Semi-finals
Barcelona	UEFA Cup	4th round
RCD Mallorca	UEFA Cup	4th round
Villareal	UEFA Cup	Semi-finals
Valencia CF	UEFA Cup	Winners

Top Goalscorers 2003–04

PLAYER	CLUB	NATIONALITY	GOALS
Ronaldo	Real Madrid	Brazilian	24
Julio Baptista	Sevilla FC	Brazilian	20
Salva Ballesta	Málaga CF	Spanish	19
Miguel Mista	Valencia CF	Spanish	19
Raul Tamudo	RCD Espanyol	Spanish	19
Fernando Torres	Atlético Madrid	Spanish	19

Spanish Cup

2004 FINAL

March 17 – Olympic Stadium, Barcelona
Real 3-2 Real Madrid
Zaragoza
(Dani 28,
Villa pen 44,
Galletti 111)
(Beckham 23,
Roberto
Carlos 47)

(after extra time)
h/t: 2-1 90 mins: 2-2
Att: 56,000
Ref: Mendez

Real Zaragoza celebrates its victory over Real Madrid in the Copa del Rey Final.

CAMPEON | **COPA'04**

Top right: Samuel Eto'o (Real Mallorca) takes the ball past Real Madrid's Iker Casillas to score. Mallorca won 3-2 and Real abdicated its championship throne to Valencia.

Right: Real's decline continues. Deportivo beats them in La Coruña; Juan Capdevila celebrates.

SPAIN

Left: *The end is nigh. Real have lost La Liga, they are losing to lowly Murcia and David Beckham is about to be sent off.*

Left, middle: *Real changes tack. As Carlos Quieroz departed, Florentine Perez (president) and Jorge Valdano (director of soccer) welcome a new coach, the dour and defensive-minded Antonio Camacho.*

Left, bottom: *Valencians celebrate the team's triumph outside the city's town hall.*

Below: *Headers, free kicks, dummies, assists – he did them all. Ronaldinho heads home against Espanyol.*

Valencia's 19-goal striker *Miguel Mista lifts the La Liga trophy as the champions celebrate at the Mestalla.*

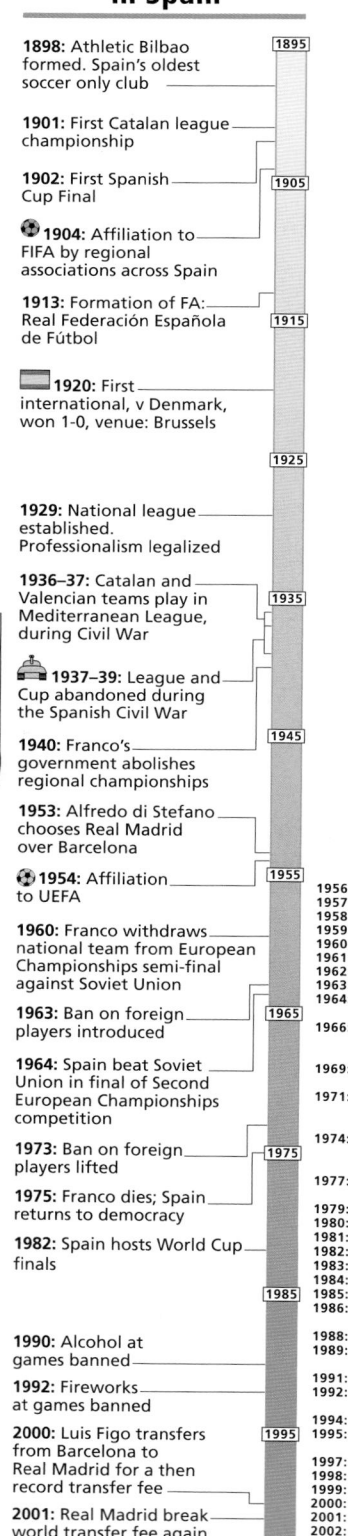

SPAIN

Soccer in Spain

1898: Athletic Bilbao formed. Spain's oldest soccer only club

1901: First Catalan league championship

1902: First Spanish Cup Final

1904: Affiliation to FIFA by regional associations across Spain

1913: Formation of FA: Real Federación Española de Fútbol

1920: First international, v Denmark, won 1-0, venue: Brussels

1929: National league established. Professionalism legalized

1936–37: Catalan and Valencian teams play in Mediterranean League, during Civil War

1937–39: League and Cup abandoned during the Spanish Civil War

1940: Franco's government abolishes regional championships

1953: Alfredo di Stefano chooses Real Madrid over Barcelona

1954: Affiliation to UEFA

1960: Franco withdraws national team from European Championships semi-final against Soviet Union

1963: Ban on foreign players introduced

1964: Spain beat Soviet Union in final of Second European Championships competition

1973: Ban on foreign players lifted

1975: Franco dies; Spain returns to democracy

1982: Spain hosts World Cup finals

1990: Alcohol at games banned

1992: Fireworks at games banned

2000: Luis Figo transfers from Barcelona to Real Madrid for a then record transfer fee

2001: Real Madrid break world transfer fee again for Zinedine Zidane from Juventus

1895
1905
1915
1925
1935
1945
1955
1965
1975
1985
1995
2005

Real Madrid, Spanish champions for the fourth consecutive year in 1964, included almost the entire Spanish national team: (back row left to right) Vicente, Isidro, Santamaria (from Uruguay), Casado, Muller (from France), Zoco; (front row) Amancio, Felo, di Stefano, Puskas (from Hungary) and Gento.

Key

⬛ International soccer
⚽ Affiliation to FIFA
⚽ Affiliation to UEFA
🚂 War

⬛ World Cup host
● World Cup winner
▲ World Cup runner-up
⬛ European Championships host
● European Championships winner
▲ European Championships runner-up

○ Competition winner
△ Competition runner-up

Alav – CD Alavés
Atl B – Athletic Bilbao
Atl M – Atlético Madrid
Barca – Barcelona
Esp – RCD Español
RCD – RCD Mallorca
Real M – Real Madrid
Val – Valencia
Zara – Real Zaragoza

International Competitions

	European Cup	UEFA Cup	European Cup-Winners' Cup
1956:	○ Real M		
1957:	○ Real M		
1958:	○ Real M		
1959:	○ Real M		
1960:	○ Real M		
1961:	△ Barca		
1962:	△ Real M	○ Val △ Barca	○ Atl M
1963:		○ Val	△ Atl M
1964:	●⬛⬛ △ Real M	○ Zara △ Val	
1966:	○ Real M	△ Barca △ Zara	
1969:			△ Barca
1971:			△ Real M
1974:	△ Atl M		
1977:		△ Atl B	
1979:		○ Barca	
1980:		○ Val	
1981:	△ Real M		
1982:	⬛	○ Barca	
1983:			△ Real M
1984:	▲		
1985:	△ Barca	○ Real M	△ Atl M
1986:		○ Real M	
1988:		△ Esp	
1989:			○ Barca
1991:			△ Barca
1992:	○ Barca		
1994:	△ Barca		
1995:		○ Zara	
1997:		○ Barca	
1998:	○ Real M		
1999:	○ Real M△ Val		△ RCD
2000:	○ Real M△ Val		
2001:		△ Alav	
2002:	○ Real M		
2004:		○ Val	

The Royal House in Spain has played a big part in the nation's soccer-playing history. Many of the big clubs bear the name 'Real' meaning 'royal', and the Copa del Rey (Cup of the King) is named after King Alfonso XIII (1886–1931).

⭐ Athletic Bilbao **1898**

Sporting Gijón 1905

RC Deportivo **1904**

La Coruña
Santiago
SD Compostela 1962

Celta Vigo **1923**
Merger of Fortuna and Sporting

Pontevedra 1928
● Vigo

Spain: The main clubs

Cadiz 1910 — Team name with year of formation

● Club formed before 1912
● Club formed 1912–25
● Club formed 1925–50
○ Club formed after 1950
⭐ Founder members of National League (1929)
👕 Winners Copa del Rey 1902–29
⊞ English origins
⊞ Swiss origins
▤ Catalonian regional identity
◩ Galician regional identity
⊞ Basque regional identity
Foreign student origins
Mining origins
Originated from a cycling club
Student origins
Railway workers
⛑ Royal house

Spain

ORIGINS AND GROWTH OF SOCCER

SPAIN'S OLDEST SOCCER CLUB, Real Club Recreativo de Huelva, was founded in 1889 as an informal sports club with a soccer team based around the British presence of railway and copper-mine workers. Over the next decade clubs formed in Madrid, the Basque Country, Barcelona and Seville. British influences through sailors, miners and expatriate traders were significant in Seville, Barcelona and Bilbao.

Modern Spanish history is dominated by the political and cultural struggles between the centre (especially Madrid and Castille) and the regions of Spain. This was immediately reflected in the organization of Spanish soccer. Strong regional leagues were established in the first years of the 20th century, the first in Catalonia in 1901. These continued despite the establishment

of a national professional league in 1929. The Spanish monarchy's concern with centralizing power extended to the establishment of the Copa del Rey in 1902 by King Alfonso XIII – a national championship among regional champions. The Royal House had also seen fit to bestow its patronage on clubs across the country.

The Spanish Civil War (1936–39) was a struggle between right and left but also between the centre and the regions. With the victory of Franco's centralizing nationalist forces, regional leagues were abolished, foreign influences in club origins played down and the Copa del Rey renamed the Copa del Generalisimo. Atlético Madrid was forced to change name – to Atlético Aviación – but received the crack Air Force soccer squad as part of the deal. Strict control of the press and most social and political institutions saw soccer clubs become an even more significant symbol of regional identities. With the death of Franco in 1975, Spain returned to democracy and a revived regionalism. Spanish club performances in European tournaments have been second only to Italy, but the national team continues to underperform in major tournaments.

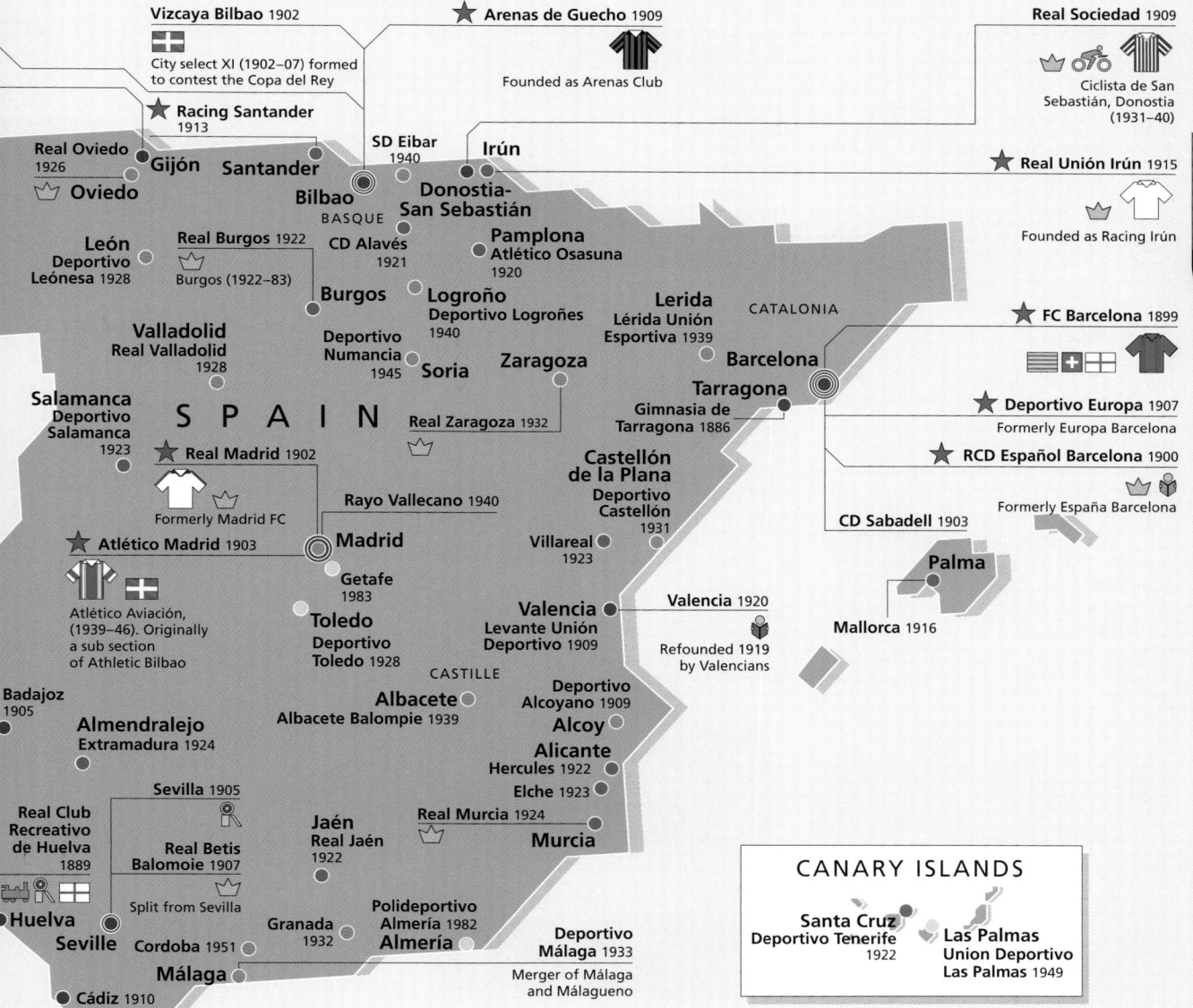

SPAIN

Vizcaya Bilbao 1902
City select XI (1902–07) formed to contest the Copa del Rey

Arenas de Guecho 1909
Founded as Arenas Club

Real Sociedad 1909
Ciclista de San Sebastián, Donostia (1931–40)

Racing Santander 1913

SD Eibar 1940

Irún

Real Oviedo 1926
Gijón
Oviedo
Santander
Bilbao
BASQUE

Donostia-San Sebastián

Real Unión Irún 1915
Founded as Racing Irún

León
Deportivo Leónesa 1928

Real Burgos 1922
Burgos (1922–83)

CD Alavés 1921

Pamplona
Atlético Osasuna 1920

Valladolid
Real Valladolid 1928

Burgos

Logroño
Deportivo Logroñes 1940

Lerida
Lérida Unión Esportiva 1939

CATALONIA

FC Barcelona 1899

Deportivo Numancia 1945

Soria

Zaragoza

Salamanca
Deportivo Salamanca 1923

SPAIN

Real Zaragoza 1932

Tarragona
Gimnasia de Tarragona 1886

Barcelona

Deportivo Europa 1907
Formerly Europa Barcelona

Real Madrid 1902
Formerly Madrid FC

Rayo Vallecano 1940

Castellón de la Plana
Deportivo Castellón 1931

RCD Español Barcelona 1900
Formerly España Barcelona

CD Sabadell 1903

Atlético Madrid 1903
Atlético Aviación, (1939–46). Originally a sub section of Athletic Bilbao

Madrid
Getafe 1983

Villareal 1923

Toledo
Deportivo Toledo 1928

CASTILLE

Valencia
Levante Unión Deportivo 1909

Valencia 1920
Refounded 1919 by Valencians

Palma

Mallorca 1916

Badajoz 1905

Deportivo Alcoyano 1909

Almendralejo
Extramadura 1924

Albacete
Albacete Balompie 1939

Alcoy

Alicante
Hercules 1922

Real Club Recreativo de Huelva 1889

Sevilla 1905

Jaén
Real Jaén 1922

Elche 1923

Real Murcia 1924

Real Betis Balomoie 1907
Split from Sevilla

Murcia

Huelva
Seville
Cordoba 1951
Granada 1932

Polideportivo Almería 1982
Almería

Deportivo Málaga 1933
Merger of Málaga and Málagueno

Málaga

Cádiz 1910

CANARY ISLANDS

Santa Cruz
Deportivo Tenerife 1922

Las Palmas
Union Deportivo Las Palmas 1949

255

Barcelona

SOCCER CENTER

SPAIN

ALTHOUGH FC BARCELONA was one of the key institutions in the creation of Catalan nationalism in the 20th century, it was founded and initially run by a Swiss, Hans Gamper, and an Englishman, Arthur Witty, both expatriate businessmen attracted by the city's dynamic economic growth. The team's first game was played on Christmas Eve 1899 at the racetrack in Bonanova against FC Catala and, while the team's opponents were Catalan, Barcelona's team was overwhelmingly foreign. But the Catalan nationalism that was growing rapidly at the turn of the century could absorb foreign influences: Barcelona was coached by foreigners throughout the 1920s and 1930s and had regularly fielded foreign players. On top of that, Andalusian immigrants, attracted to the booming industrial estates of the city in the 1950s, swelled its support. The club's cosmopolitanism was matched by success and, by the early 1930s, the club had acquired a major stadium in Les Corts, a series of national and regional titles, a massive following and a fierce, politically-charged rivalry with Real Madrid.

Barça and Catalan nationalism

The weight of these nationalist identities was given a massive boost by the outcome of the Spanish Civil War (1936–39). Centralist and right-wing forces under General Franco brutally suppressed the regional, left-wing forces that included most of Barcelona, Catalonia and FC Barcelona. In the 1940s and 1950s, Madrid's political domination of Catalonia, interference in the running of the club, and repression of nearly all forms of political opposition, made the connection between supporting FC Barcelona and Catalan nationalism even clearer, a connection that has remained in the years since Franco's death and the subsequent democratization and devolution of Spain.

In the long shadow cast by Barça sits the city's second club, RCD Espanyol. The club was founded by a group of students with the Castilian name Español – an attempt to wind up the Catalan nationalists down the road – and it traditionally attracts state employees and those migrant workers from Andalusia with Castilian sentiments. But with only two cup wins and some near misses in the late 1980s and early 1990s to its name, its challenge has been symbolic rather than sporting. Time and tastes have forced even this bastion of Royalism and Centralism to take the Catalan spelling for its name. To make matters worse, the club was forced to clear an enormous debt by selling its Sarria stadium and moving into the large but unatmospheric Olympic stadium on Montjuïc.

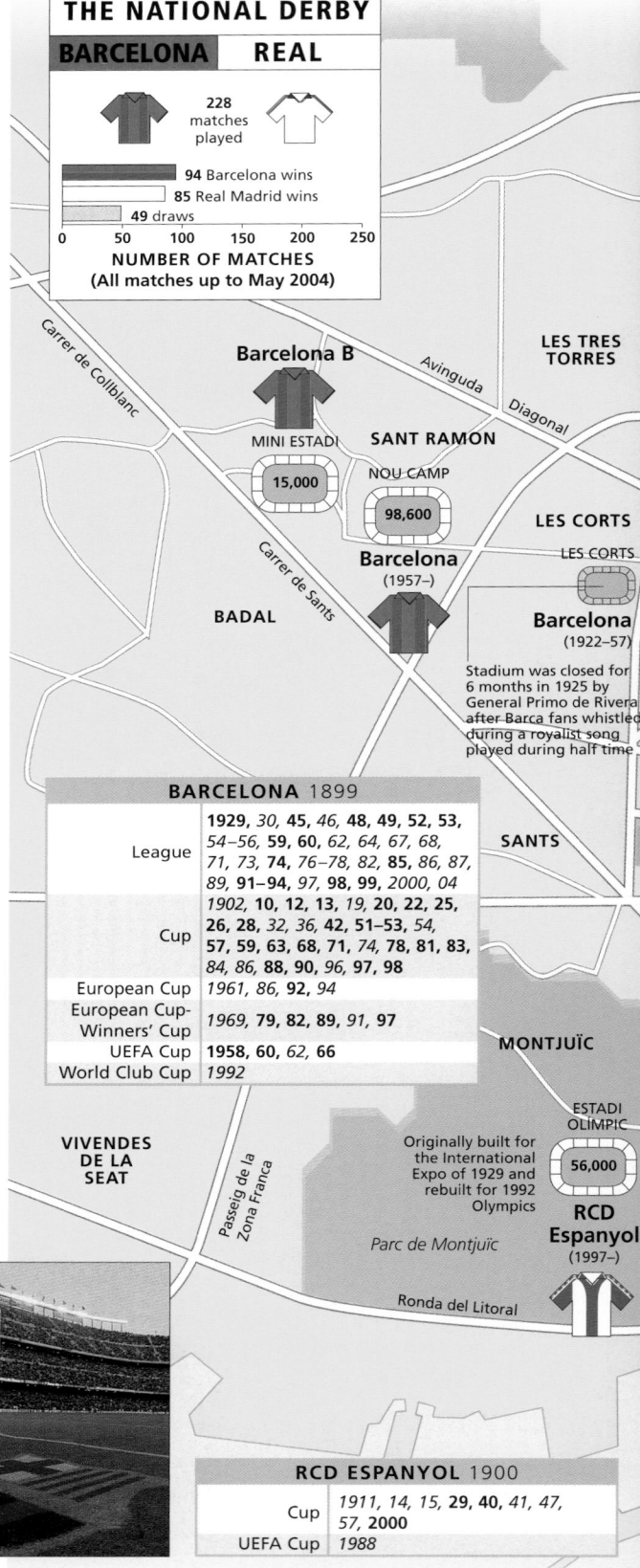

THE NATIONAL DERBY

BARCELONA	REAL

228 matches played

94	Barcelona wins
85	Real Madrid wins
49	draws

NUMBER OF MATCHES
(All matches up to May 2004)

0 50 100 150 200 250

Barcelona B
MINI ESTADI
15,000

SANT RAMON
NOU CAMP
98,600
Barcelona (1957–)

LES TRES TORRES

LES CORTS
LES CORTS
Barcelona (1922–57)

BADAL

Stadium was closed for 6 months in 1925 by General Primo de Rivera after Barca fans whistled during a royalist song played during half time

Carrer de Collblanc

Avinguda Diagonal

Carrer de Sants

SANTS

BARCELONA 1899	
League	1929, 30, **45**, **46**, **48**, **49**, **52**, **53**, 54–56, **59**, **60**, 62, 64, 67, 68, 71, 73, **74**, 76–78, 82, **85**, 86, 87, 89, **91–94**, 97, **98**, 99, 2000, 04
Cup	1902, 10, 12, 13, 19, 20, 22, 25, 26, 28, 32, 36, 42, **51–53**, 54, 57, 59, 63, 68, 71, 74, 78, 81, 83, 84, 86, **88**, 90, 96, 97, 98
European Cup	1961, 86, **92**, **94**
European Cup-Winners' Cup	1969, **79**, **82**, **89**, **91**, 97
UEFA Cup	**1958**, **60**, 62, 66
World Club Cup	1992

MONTJUÏC

VIVENDES DE LA SEAT

Passeig de la Zona Franca

Parc de Montjuïc

Ronda del Litoral

ESTADI OLIMPIC
56,000
RCD Espanyol (1997–)

Originally built for the International Expo of 1929 and rebuilt for 1992 Olympics

NOU CAMP

98,600

Club: Barcelona
Built: 1957
Original Capacity: 90,000
Rebuilt: 1982
Significant Matches: 1982 World Cup: five matches; 1992 Barcelona Olympics: opening ceremony, football Final; European Cup Final: 1989, 1999; European Cup-Winners' Cup Final: 1982

RCD ESPANYOL 1900	
Cup	1911, 14, 15, **29**, 40, 41, 47, 57, **2000**
UEFA Cup	1988

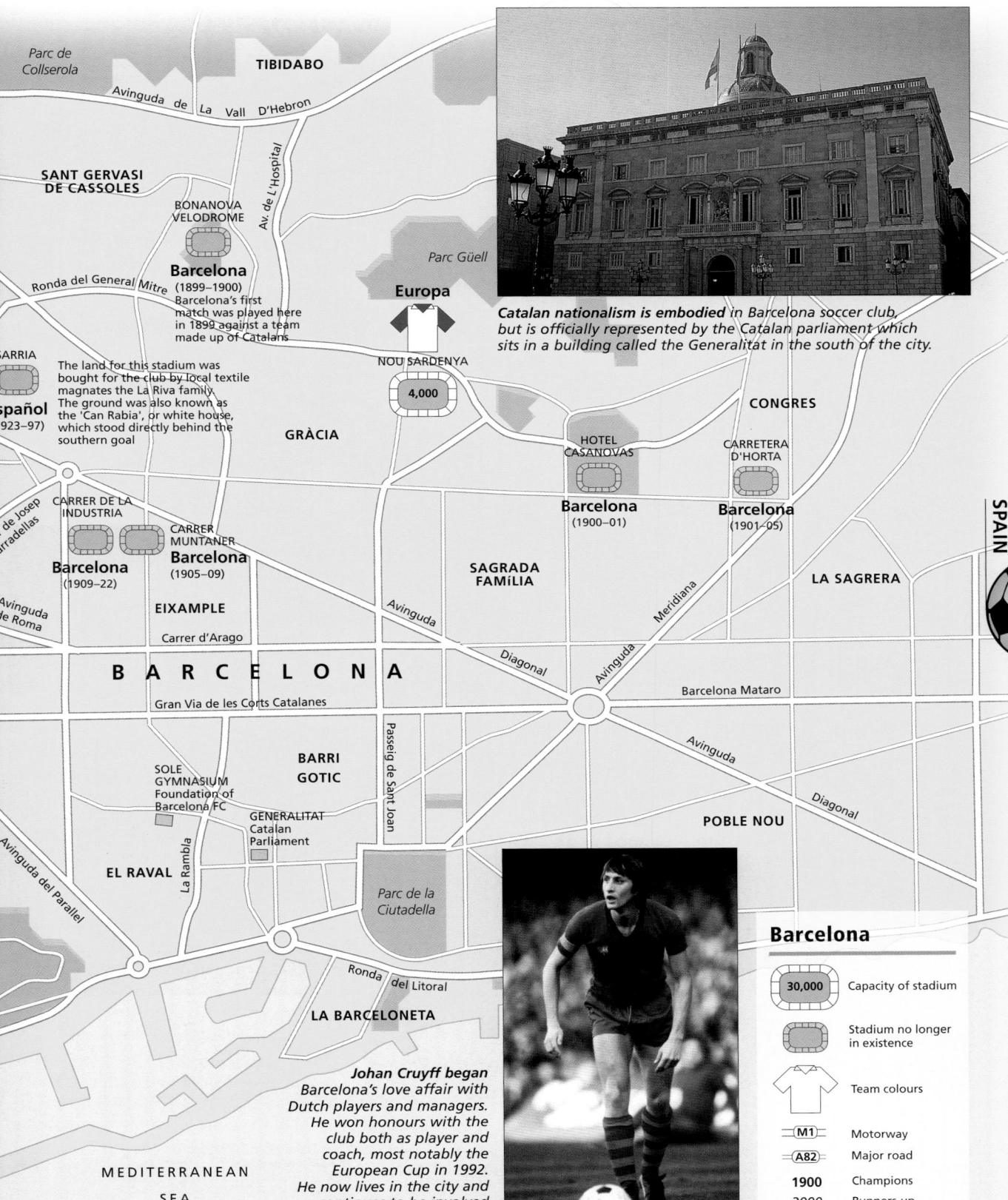

Parc de Collserola

TIBIDABO

Avinguda de La Vall D'Hebron

SANT GERVASI DE CASSOLES

BONANOVA VELODROME

Av. de l'Hospital

Parc Güell

Europa

Ronda del General Mitre

Barcelona
(1899–1900)
Barcelona's first match was played here in 1899 against a team made up of Catalans

Catalan nationalism is embodied in Barcelona soccer club, but is officially represented by the Catalan parliament which sits in a building called the Generalitat in the south of the city.

SARRIA

spañol
923–97

The land for this stadium was bought for the club by local textile magnates the La Riva family. The ground was also known as the 'Can Rabia', or white house, which stood directly behind the southern goal

NOU SARDENYA

4,000

GRÀCIA

CONGRES

HOTEL CASANOVAS

CARRETERA D'HORTA

Barcelona
(1900–01)

Barcelona
(1901–05)

CARRER DE LA INDUSTRIA

de Josep arradellas

CARRER MUNTANER

Barcelona
(1905–09)

Barcelona
(1909–22)

Avinguda de Roma

EIXAMPLE

Carrer d'Arago

SAGRADA FAMÍLIA

LA SAGRERA

Avinguda

Meridiana

SPAIN

B A R C E L O N A

Gran Via de les Corts Catalanes

Diagonal

Avinguda

Barcelona Mataro

Passeig de Sant Joan

SOLE GYMNASIUM
Foundation of Barcelona FC

BARRI GOTIC

Avinguda

Diagonal

GENERALITAT
Catalan Parliament

POBLE NOU

EL RAVAL

La Rambla

Parc de la Ciutadella

Avinguda del Parallel

Ronda del Litoral

LA BARCELONETA

Johan Cruyff began Barcelona's love affair with Dutch players and managers. He won honours with the club both as player and coach, most notably the European Cup in 1992. He now lives in the city and continues to be involved in club politics.

MEDITERRANEAN SEA

Barcelona

30,000	Capacity of stadium
	Stadium no longer in existence
	Team colours
M1	Motorway
A82	Major road
1900	Champions
2000	Runners-up

Madrid

SOCCER CENTER

REAL MADRID GREW OUT OF AN ELITE CLUB called Football Sky, which was founded in 1895. A team split in 1900 saw Español de Madrid emerge, which transmuted into Madrid FC in 1902. When King Alfonso XIII accepted the offer of royal patronage in 1920, the team became known as Real. Although Real Madrid was successful in the national championships in the first decade of the 20th century, it did not acquire a permanent home until the construction of the Campo O'Donnell in 1912, and a proper stadium had to await the construction of Chamartîn in 1924.

Located in the most exclusive financial and residential district of Madrid, Real was transformed by the arrival of Santiago Bernabéu as president and the Franco regime at the end of the Spanish Civil War. Although Franco was undoubtedly a Real fan, and his regime benefited hugely from the successful international exposure the great Real team of the 1950s brought, his real influence on the club is probably less than Bernabéu and the network of financiers and bankers he amassed. Constant access to funds has allowed Real to build one of the world's largest stadiums, fund record-breaking transfers, and return after two

quiet decades to dominant ways, winning three European Cups (1998, 2000 and 2002). This has also allowed Real to accumulate the biggest debts in global soccer, only paid off by the sale of its training ground in 2001 for massive real estate development.

Hard-won success

Atlético was founded in 1903 by three Basques studying in Madrid as an offshoot of their home team, Athletic Bilbao. The team played in Athletic's blue and white stripes before switching to its current red and white stripes in 1911. The club performed poorly before the Civil War, only returning to the league afterwards because Oviedo's ground had been destroyed and they could no longer play in the league. It merged with the air force's brilliant side, Atlético Aviacion, which brought it two immediate titles. Although historically it is among the most successful teams in Spain, Atlético is better known for the fanaticism of its *ultras* (fans) and the erratic and financially dubious behaviour of the team's long term president, Jesus Gil. The club's recent poor fortunes have often left it behind the tiny Rayo Vallecano, which survives on a shoestring in the city's rough southern suburbs.

The Royal Palace in Madrid: the Spanish Royal House has played a big part in the history of Spanish soccer. Madrid FC became Real or 'Royal' Madrid in 1920, when King Alphonso XIII accepted the offer of royal patronage of the team. General Franco too was a Real fan, and with such supporters as this it is little wonder that Real has come to be associated with the elite elements of Spanish society.

VICENTE CALDERÓN

57,500

Club: Atlético Madrid
Built: 1966
Rebuilt: 1982
Significant Matches: 1982 World Cup: three group matches

SANTIAGO BERNABÉU

74,300

Club: Real Madrid
Built: 1947
Original Capacity: 75,000
Record Attendance: 124,000, Real Madrid v Fiorentina, European Cup Final, 1957
Rebuilt: 1982, 1998
Significant Matches: 1964 European Championships: Final; 1982 World Cup: three group matches; European Cup Finals: 1957, 69, 80

PEÑA GRANDE

TETUÁN

CIUDAD LINEAL

VELODROME

Real Madrid
(1920–23)

M40

M30

CIUDAD DEPORTIVO
Real Madrid's old training ground

CHAMARTÍN

Real Madrid
(1948–)

Real Madrid
(1923–47)

RACE COURSE
16 April 1905
First international game played in Spain: Real Madrid v Gallia Sport, result: 1–1

REAL MADRID 1902

League	*1929*, **32, 33**, *34–36, 42, 45, 54, 55, 57, 58, 59, 60*, **61–65**, *66, 67–69, 72, 75, 76, 78–80, 81, 83, 84*, **86–90**, *92, 93, 95, 97, 99*, **2001**, *03*
Cup	*1903, 05–08, 16, 17, 18, 24, 29, 30, 33*, **34, 36, 40, 43, 46, 47, 58, 60, 61, 62, 68, 70, 74, 75, 79, 80, 82, 83, 89, 90, 92, 93**, *2002*, **04**
European Cup	**1956–60**, *62*, **64**, *66*, **81, 98, 2000, 02**
European Cup-Winners' Cup	*1971, 83*
UEFA Cup	**1985, 86**
World Club Cup	**1960**, *66*, **98**, *2000*, **02**

SANTIAGO BERNABÉU

74,300

Atlético Madrid played here for one season while the Metropolitano underwent a refit

Atlético Madrid
(1964–65)

Real Madrid
(pre-1912)

CHAMARTÍN

Offices of La Liga

CIUDAD UNIVERSITARIA

Real Madrid's first games were played here on the fields of Mocloa

METROPOLITANO

Atlético Madrid
(1923–66)

PLAZA DE TOROS

M30

M30

A6

M30

A5

M A D R I D

CAMPO DE LA ESTRADA

Real Madrid
(pre-1912)

Offices of *Marca*, Madrid's leading sports daily and significant supporters of Real

ARGÜELLES

SPAIN

Río Manzanares

CHAMBERÍ

SALAMANCA

CAMPO O'DONNELL

Casa de Campo

LA PLAZA DE CIBELES
Traditional site of victory celebrations

Real Madrid
(1912–20)

Atlético Madrid
(1913–23)

ROYAL PALACE

CENTRO

REAL FEDERACIÓN ESPAÑOLA DE FÚTBOL HEADQUARTERS

RETIRO

PALACIO

ESTADIO VICENTE CALDERÓN
(previously Estadio Manzanares)

57,500

Atlético Madrid
(1966–)

ARGANZUELA

A3

PUENTE DE VALLECAS

NUEVO VALLECAS
MARIA TERESA
RIVERO SÁNCHEZ

RONDA DE VALLECAS

15,500

Rayo Vallecano

Atlético Madrid
(1903–13)

USERA

Madrid

57,500	Capacity of stadium
	Stadium no longer in existence
	Team colours
A5	Motorway
	Major road
1900	Champions
2000	Runners-up

ATLÉTICO MADRID 1903

League	**1940, 41**, *44*, **50, 51**, *58*, **61**, *63*, **65, 66, 70, 73**, *74*, **77**, *85*, **91, 96**
Cup	*1921, 26, 56*, **60, 61**, *64*, **65, 72**, *75*, **76, 85**, *87*, **91, 92, 96**, *99*, **2000**
European Cup	*1974*
European Cup-Winners' Cup	**1962**, *63*, **86**
World Club Cup	**1974**

Spain

FANS AND OWNERS

THERE IS A MIXED ECONOMY in the ownership of clubs in Spain; some are run as sporting and social clubs, others are private limited companies, some with a single dominant investor and others with multiple-share ownership. The two biggest clubs in the country, Real Madrid and Barcelona, are owned by their members, or *socios*, who select the paid officials that run the clubs in highly politicized and expensive elections. The biggest incomes and highest attendances of Spain's top teams are concentrated among the big five – Real, Barcelona, Valencia, Athletic Bilbao and RC Deportivo from La Coruña, although when Atlético Madrid is in the top flight, it joins that elite group.

The rising tide of debt

But despite huge TV income, other investments, and a lot of European success, Spanish clubs are heavily indebted. Real has recently escaped from a crippling debt of around $150 million by selling its city-centre training ground, though the legality of the sale is currently being contested. In the last couple of seasons, smaller clubs with smaller assets have seen board resignations, unpaid creditors and a search for new investors. Worse still, the bankruptcy of Atlético Madrid in 2002 led to an investigation by the Spanish treasury which has revealed unpaid taxes among the top clubs for the years 1996–99 of £129 million. Clubs with debts of more than one third of their capital are technically bankrupt in Spain – and this would apply to about a third of the Primera Liga if the debts were immediately enforced. Barcelona, Deportivo and Valencia have debts of around 100 milion Euros.

Spanish fans were traditionally organized in *peñas* or supporters' clubs, often based around a particular bar, which arranged away trips and social events. With the passing of Franco's authoritarian regime and the development of a distinctive youth culture in Spain, it was inevitable that the *ultra* model would be imported from Italy by a new generation of supporters. The first *ultra* groups emerged in Madrid in 1982 at both Real (*Ultras Sur*) and Atlético (*El Frente Atlético*) and they have more recently been joined by groups at Barcelona (*ICC – Inter City Cules*), Sevilla (*Peña Biri-Biri*) and Athletic Bilbao. Although there has been some violence between groups outside the stadiums, the phenomenon appears to have peaked since a Real Sociedad fan was stabbed outside Atlético Madrid's Vincente Calderón stadium in 1998. The death of a fan at Deportivo in 2004 saw the main ultra group disband itself.

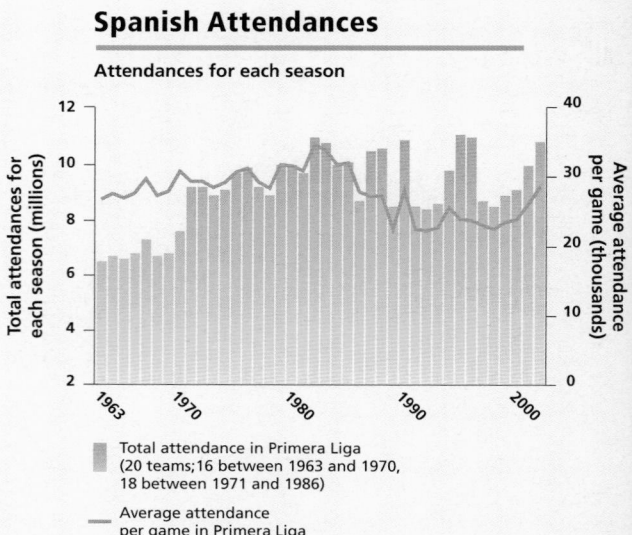

Spanish Attendances

Attendances for each season

- Total attendance in Primera Liga (20 teams; 16 between 1963 and 1970, 18 between 1971 and 1986)
- Average attendance per game in Primera Liga

SPAIN

Average Attendance

Average attendance for season 2003–04 (thousands)

Capacity

Attendance as a percentage of capacity for season 2003–04 (capacity in brackets)

TEAMS	Capacity
Albacete Balompié	(16,362)
FC Barcelona	(98,000)
Real Betis	(56,500)
Athletic Bilbao	(40,300)
RC Deportivo	(35,800)
RCD Espanyol	(55,000)
Atlético Madrid	(57,500)
Real Madrid	(90,000)
Deportivo Málaga	(33,000)
RCD Mallorca	(26,500)
Real Murcia	(15,805)
Atlético Osasuna	(19,553)
Racing Santander	(22,124)
Sevilla	(55,000)
Real Sociedad	(32,000)
Real Valladolid	(26,512)
Valencia	(53,000)
RC Celta	(31,800)
Villareal	(22,000)
Real Zaragoza	(34,596)

Ukrainian businessman *Dimitri Pieterman owned and tried to coach Racing Santander in 2002-03. He gave up in 2004 and sold his stake.*

Majority and Leading Shareholders

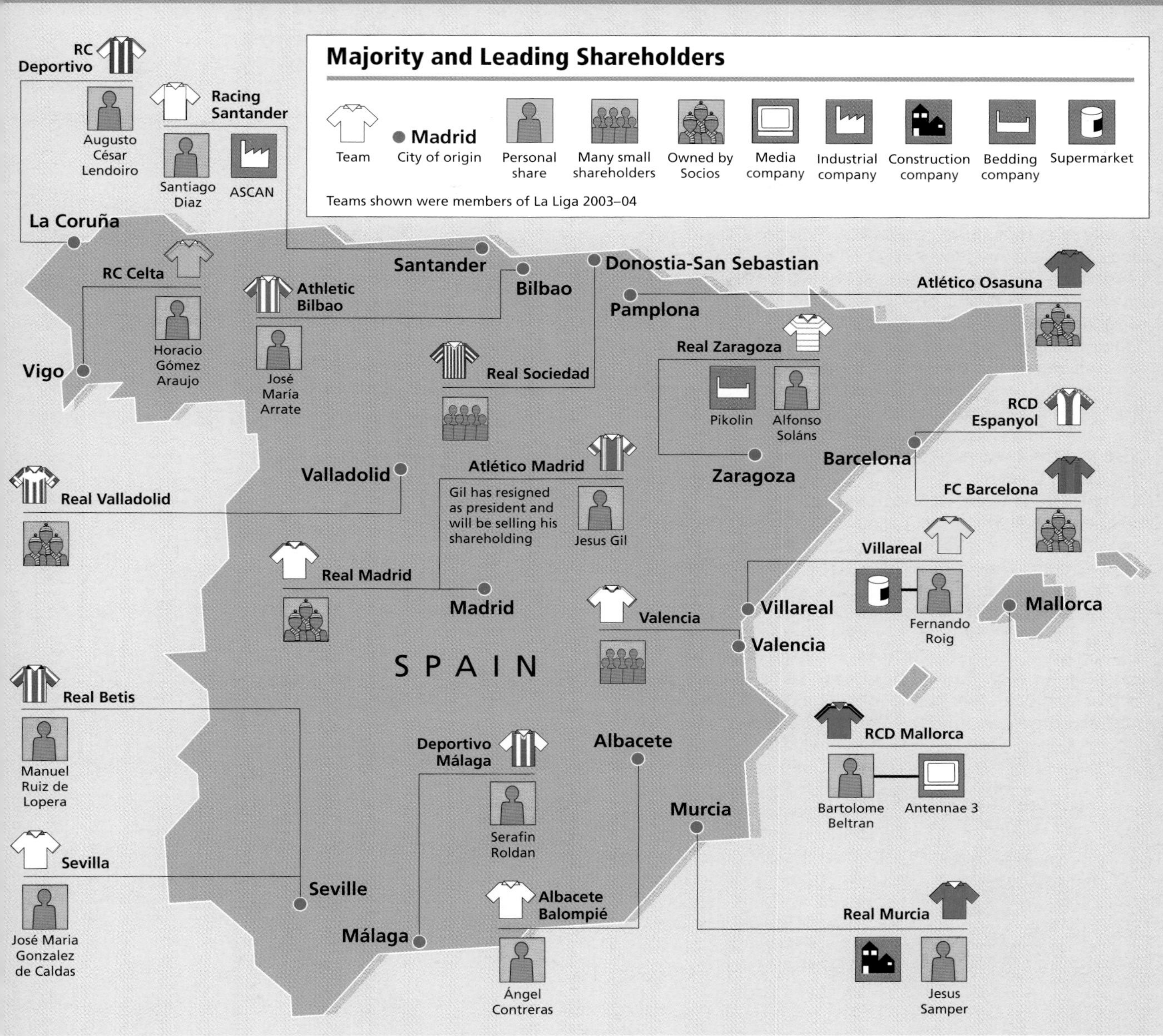

- Team
- ● **Madrid** City of origin
- Personal share
- Many small shareholders
- Owned by Socios
- Media company
- Industrial company
- Construction company
- Bedding company
- Supermarket

Teams shown were members of La Liga 2003–04

RC Deportivo
Augusto César Lendoiro
La Coruña

Racing Santander
Santiago Diaz — ASCAN

RC Celta
Horacio Gómez Araujo
Vigo

Athletic Bilbao
José María Arrate
Santander — **Bilbao**

Donostia-San Sebastian
Pamplona

Real Sociedad

Atlético Osasuna

Real Zaragoza
Pikolin — Alfonso Soláns
Zaragoza

RCD Espanyol
Barcelona

FC Barcelona

Real Valladolid
Valladolid

Atlético Madrid
Gil has resigned as president and will be selling his shareholding
Jesus Gil

Real Madrid
Madrid

Valencia
Valencia

Villareal
Fernando Roig
Villareal

Mallorca

S P A I N

Real Betis
Manuel Ruiz de Lopera

Sevilla
José Maria Gonzalez de Caldas

Albacete

Deportivo Málaga
Serafin Roldan

RCD Mallorca
Bartolome Beltran — Antennae 3

Seville

Albacete Balompié
Ángel Contreras

Murcia

Real Murcia
Jesus Samper

Málaga

SPAIN

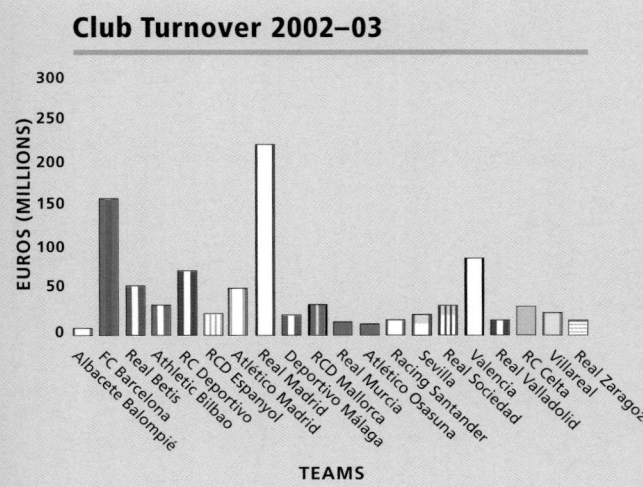

Club Turnover 2002–03

EUROS (MILLIONS)

300
250
200
150
100
50
0

TEAMS

Albacete Balompié, FC Barcelona, Real Betis, Athletic Bilbao, RC Deportivo, RCD Espanyol, Atlético Madrid, Real Madrid, Deportivo Málaga, RCD Mallorca, Real Murcia, Atlético Osasuna, Racing Santander, Sevilla, Real Sociedad, Valencia, Real Valladolid, RC Celta, Villareal, Real Zaragoza

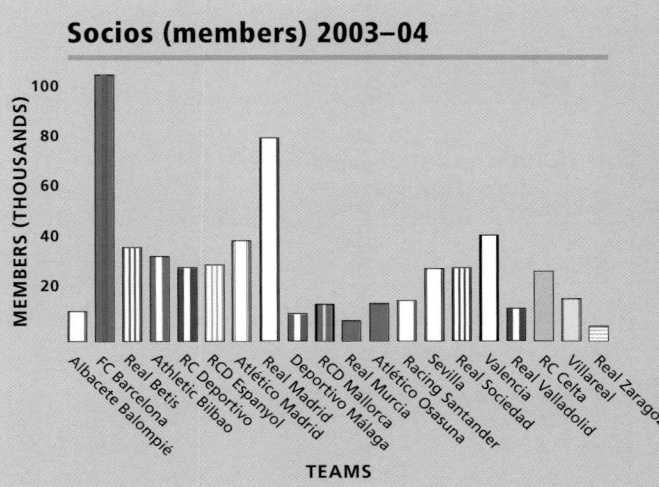

Socios (members) 2003–04

MEMBERS (THOUSANDS)

100
80
60
40
20

TEAMS

Albacete Balompié, FC Barcelona, Real Betis, Athletic Bilbao, RC Deportivo, RCD Espanyol, Atlético Madrid, Real Madrid, Deportivo Málaga, RCD Mallorca, Real Murcia, Atlético Osasuna, Racing Santander, Sevilla, Real Sociedad, Valencia, Real Valladolid, RC Celta, Villareal, Real Zaragoza

Spain

PLAYERS AND MANAGERS

WHILE FITNESS IS ASSUMED among Spanish soccer players, a certain professional craftiness is required to be regarded as a real player, and the possession of *calidad* ('quality of technique') is a Spanish soccer's most prized asset. This style is exemplified by the magisterial Raúl at today's Real Madrid. Of course, you also need a good nickname to get on. The leading goalscorer in Spanish soccer is known as 'Pichichi', named in honour of Rafael Moreno Aranzadi, the great Basque centre-forward who played for Athletic Bilbao in the 1920s. In his wake, Spain's great strikers have included Emilio Butragueño, nicknamed 'the Vulture' for his capacity to pick up and devour chances in the box, and Francisco Gento, 'El Supersonico', the only man to win six European Cup winner's medals.

Nationalism v cosmopolitanism

The roster of great Spanish players and managers expresses both the country's inward-looking nationalism and its outward-looking cosmopolitanism. On the playing side (and recently on the managerial side as well), Spanish soccer has drawn widely and deeply on the pool of foreign talent. In the postwar era, Franco's Spain was pleased to accept Alfredo di Stefano from Argentina and Ferenc Puskas from Hungary, and award Spanish citizenship to both. In the 1960s, nationalist paranoia saw a decade-long ban on foreign players until a new wave of talent arrived in the shape of Johan Cruyff at Barcelona in the 1970s

and then Diego Maradona in the early 1980s. However, at Athletic Bilbao the strict Basque-only policy on players remains in place. In recent years, the enormous amount of money in the Spanish game has seen a steady rise in the number of overseas players, especially from Latin America, with Brazilians, Argentinians and Uruguayans flooding the top division.

Born on the first day of the 20th century, legendary keeper Ricardo Zamora was known as 'El Divino'.

Top 10 International Caps

PLAYER	CAPS	GOALS	FIRST MATCH	LAST MATCH
Andoni Zubizarreta	129	0	1985	1998
Fernando Ruiz Hierro*	90	29	1989	2003
José Antonio Camacho	81	0	1975	1988
Raúl González Blanco*	75	38	1996	2004
Rafael Gordillo	75	3	1978	1988
Emilio Butragueño	69	26	1984	1992
Luis Miguel Arconada	68	0	1977	1985
Miguel González 'Michel'	66	21	1985	1992
Miguel Angel Nadal*	63	3	1991	2001
Luis Enrique*	62	12	1991	2002
Victor Muñoz	60	3	1981	1988

Top 10 International Goalscorers

PLAYER	GOALS	CAPS	FIRST MATCH	LAST MATCH
Raúl González Blanco*	38	75	1996	2004
Fernando Ruiz Hierro*	29	90	1989	2003
Emilio Butragueño	26	69	1984	1992
Alfredo di Stefano	23	31	1957	1961
Fernando Morientes*	23	36	1998	2004
Julio Salinas Fernández	22	56	1986	1996
Miguel González 'Michel'	21	66	1985	1992
Telmo Zarraonandia 'Zarra'	20	20	1945	1951
Isidro Lángara	17	12	1932	1936
Luis Regueiro	16	25	1927	1936
José Martínez 'Pirri'	16	41	1966	1978
Carlos Alonso 'Santillana'	15	56	1975	1985

* Indicates players still playing at least at club level.
Nicknames are indicated between inverted commas.

Spain International Managers

DATES	NAME	GAMES	WON	DRAWN	LOST
1955–56	Guillermo Eizaguirre	3	0	1	2
1957–59	Manuel Meana	12	7	3	2
1959–60	José Luis Costa, Ramón Gabilondo, José Luis Lasplazas	5	4	0	1
1961	Pedro Escartin	7	5	2	0
1962	Pablo Hernandez	3	1	0	2
1962–66	Jose Villalonga	22	9	5	8
1966–68	Domingo Balmanya	11	4	3	4
1968–69	Eduardo Toba	4	1	2	1
1969	Salvador Artigas, Luis Molowny, Miguel Munoz	4	2	1	1
1969–80	Ladislao Kubala	68	32	21	15
1980–82	José Santamaria	23	10	6	7
1982–88	Miguel Munoz	59	31	13	15
1988–91	Luis Suárez	27	15	4	8
1991–92	Vincente Miera	8	4	2	2
1992–98	Javier Clemente	62	36	19	7
1998–2002	José Antonio Camacho	44	28	9	7
2002–04	Iñaki Saez	23	15	6	2

All figures correct as of 28 June 2004.

Foreign Players in Spain (in top division squads)

2003–04

1 OFC
86 CONMEBOL
66 UEFA
164
Total
5 CONCACAF
6 CAF

Key

Total Players

Foreign Players

%

(Bar chart: Number of Players vs Percentage of Foreign Players, 1996–97 to 2002–03, with values 53, 38, 39, 38, 34, 34, 30)

Player of the Year

YEAR	PLAYER	CLUB
1976	Ángel	Real Madrid
1977	'Juanito'	Real Burgos
1978	'Migueli'	Barcelona
1979	'Quini'	Sporting Gijón
1980	Gordillo	Real Betis
1981	'Urruti'	RCD Español
1982	Tendillo	Valencia
1983	Señor	Real Zaragoza
1984	Cervantes	Real Murcia
1985	'Migueli'	Barcelona
1986	'Míchel'	Real Madrid
1987	Zubizarreta	Barcelona
1988	Larrañaga	Real Sociedad
1989	Fernando	Valencia
1990	Martín Vázquez	Real Madrid
1991	Goikoetxea	Barcelona
1992	Elduayen	Real Burgos
1993	'Fran'	RC Deportivo
1994	Guerrero	Athletic Bilbao
1995	Amavisca	Real Madrid
1996	Caminero	Atlético Madrid
1997	Raúl	Real Madrid
1998	Alfonso	Real Betis
1999	Raúl	Real Madrid
2000	Raúl	Real Madrid
2001	Marino	Alavés
2002	Raúl	Real Madrid
2003	Xabi Alonso	Real Sociedad

Awarded by *Don Balon* magazine.

Foreign Player of the Year

PLAYER	CLUB	NATIONALITY
Neeskens	Barcelona	Dutch
Cruyff	Barcelona	Dutch
Cruyff	Barcelona	Dutch
Stielike	Real Madrid	German
Stielike	Real Madrid	German
Stielike	Real Madrid	German
Stielike	Real Madrid	German
Barbas	Real Zaragoza	Argentinian
Barbas	Real Zaragoza	Argentinian
Schuster	Barcelona	German
Valdano	Real Madrid	Argentinian
Hugo Sánchez	Real Madrid	Mexican
Alemão	Atlético Madrid	Brazilian
Ruggeri	CD Logroñés	Argentinian
Hugo Sánchez	Real Madrid	Mexican
Schuster	Atlético Madrid	German
Laudrup	Barcelona	Danish
Dujkic	RC Deportivo	Yugoslavian
Stoichkov	Barcelona	Bulgarian
Zamorano	Real Madrid	Chilean
Mijatovic	Valencia	Yugoslavian
Ronaldo	Barcelona	Brazilian
Rivaldo	Barcelona	Brazilian
Figo	Barcelona	Portuguese
Figo	Barcelona	Portuguese
Figo	Barcelona	Portuguese
Zidane	Real Madrid	French
Nihat	Real Sociedad	Turkish

Manager of the Year

MANAGER	CLUB	NATIONALITY
Miljanic	Real Madrid	Yugoslavian
Aragonés	Atlético Madrid	Spanish
Molowny	Real Madrid	Spanish
Molowny	Real Madrid	Spanish
Molowny	Real Madrid	Spanish
Ormachea	Real Sociedad	Spanish
Ormachea	Real Sociedad	Spanish
Clemente	Athletic Bilbao	Spanish
Clemente	Athletic Bilbao	Spanish
Venables	Barcelona	English
Molowny	Real Madrid	Spanish
Clemente	RCD Español	Spanish
Beenhakker	Real Madrid	Dutch
Toshack	Real Sociedad	Welsh
Toshack	Real Madrid	Welsh
Cruyff	Barcelona	Dutch
Cruyff	Barcelona	Dutch
Inglesias	RC Deportivo	Spanish
Fernandez	Real Zaragoza	Spanish
Inglesias	RC Deportivo	Spanish
Antic	Atlético Madrid	Yugoslavian
Cantatore	Real Valladolid	Uruguayan
'Irureta'	RC Celta	Spanish
Cúper	RCD Mallorca	Argentinian
'Irureta'	RC Deportivo	Spanish
Mane	Alavés	Spanish
Benitez	Valencia	Spanish
Denoueix	Real Sociedad	French

Top Goalscorers by Season 1975–2004

SEASON	PLAYER	CLUB	GOALS
1975–76	'Quini'	Real Sporting	18
1976–77	Kempes	Valencia	24
1977–78	Kempes	Valencia	28
1978–79	Krankl	Barcelona	26
1979–80	'Quini'	Real Sporting	24
1980–81	'Quini'	Barcelona	20
1981–82	'Quini'	Barcelona	26
1982–83	Rincón	Real Betis	20
1983–84	Da Silva	Real Valladolid	17
1983–84	'Juanito'	Real Madrid	17
1984–85	Sánchez	Atlético Madrid	19
1985–86	H. Sánchez	Real Madrid	22
1986–87	H. Sánchez	Real Madrid	34
1987–88	H. Sánchez	Real Madrid	29
1988–89	Baltazar	Atlético Madrid	35
1989–90	H. Sánchez	Real Madrid	38
1990–91	Butragueño	Real Madrid	19
1991–92	Manolo	Atlético Madrid	27
1992–93	Bebeto	RC Deportivo	29
1993–94	Romario	Barcelona	30
1994–95	Zamorano	Real Madrid	28
1995–96	Pizzi	Tenerife	31
1996–97	Ronaldo	Barcelona	34
1997–98	Vieri	Atlético Madrid	24
1998–99	Raúl	Real Madrid	25
1999–2000	Salva	Racing Santander	27
2000–01	Raúl	Real Madrid	24
2001–02	Tristan	RC Deportivo	21
2002–03	Makaay	RC Deportivo	29
2003–04	Ronaldo	Real Madrid	24

Emilio Butragueño's 26 international goals included four in Spain's five-goal thrashing of Denmark in the second round of the 1986 World Cup Finals in Mexico.

Spain

PRIMERA LIGA 1983–2003

THE EARLY 1980s saw the Basque country rise to prominence in Spain, with titles for Real Sociedad and Athletic Bilbao. Both fielded Basque-only squads and in the relative freedom of the post-Franco years an intense Basque nationalism pervaded the mood of the crowds. At Bilbao, Javier Clemente built a tough, fiery team with Andoni Goikoetxea, the 'Butcher of Bilbao', leading a mean defensive line on Spain's wettest, slowest pitch. Although both teams have been permanent members of La Liga since then, neither has been able to sustain more than a season's serious challenge for the title. Most recently, Athletic, under Luis Fernandez, came second to Barcelona in 1998. Real Sociedad has abandoned its Basque-only policy and Athletic has been through a slew of foreign coaches including Howard Kendall, Guus Hiddink and Jupp Heynckes.

The 'Vulture Squad' v the 'Dream Team'

The Basque stranglehold on the title was broken by Barcelona in 1985 under English coach Terry Venables, only for the centre to reassert itself in the shape of Real Madrid and *La Quinta Del Buitre* – the 'Vulture Squad'. Despite an enormous turnover of managers and increasingly hysterical financial and administrative practices, Real had an inspired and disciplined spine in Emilio Butragueño (the 'Vulture'), Michel, Sanchis and Martín Vásquez. That was enough to take five straight titles in the 1980s.

At Barcelona, president José Luis Núñez lured ex-player and local hero Johan Cruyff back to the Bernabeu stadium as manager in 1988. Cruyff created a team made up of both homegrown players, like the young Pep Guardiola, and foreign internationals like Ronald Koeman, Hirsto Stoichkov and Michael Laudrup. The 'Dream Team', as it became known, took four titles in a row, though, rather ironically, two of them required lowly Tenerife to beat Real Madrid on the final day of the season to ensure the title went to Barça. The 1994 title came courtesy of Miroslav Djukic's last-minute penalty miss for the chasing RC Deportivo from La Coruña.

Despite the chaos and rising debts of Ramón Mendoza's Real Madrid, 1995 saw the club back at the top under Argentinian Jorge Valdano. Valdano was, of course, promptly fired, and in 1996 Atlético Madrid took its first title for over 20 years under its eccentric and improbable president Jesús Gil. Mayor of Marbella and inveterate dealer and fixer, Gil would eventually be convicted on a range of corruption charges in the late 1990s, and Atlético would plummet into the lower divisions, where it

After 31 years of waiting, Valencia won La Liga in 2001–02 with a final day victory over Málaga at home in the Mestalla. Major celebrations followed.

remained for several years. Over at Real, Mendoza was toppled by new president Lorenzo Sans. Sans brought in coach Fabio Capello, fresh from his success with Milan, and authorized a massive spend on the squad, bringing in Clarence Seedorf, Roberto Carlos and Davor Suker. It was enough to take the title in 1997 and the team went on to win the European Champions League the following season. However, a ridiculous turnover of managers once again saw the club unable to provide the consistency required to win the league title.

The arrival of the Dutchmen

That consistency was delivered by the new-look Barcelona who, having dispensed with both Bobby Robson and Ronaldo, brought in the architect of the new Ajax, Louis van Gaal. The core of the Dutch national squad, including the De Boers, Kluivert, Overmars, Cocu, Zenden and Reiziger, were purchased to play alongside Rivaldo and Luis Figo. Barcelona stormed the table in 1998 and 99. A triple was blocked by Deportivo La Coruña who finally made good on its promise throughout the 1990s and won in 2000. Real was back the following year, now augmented by Luis Figo, who'd been 'stolen' from Barcelona at the beginning of the season.

Competition in Spanish soccer has been fierce, with good sustainable sides built at RCD Mallorca under Hector Cuper in the mid-1990s, and Valencia (also led by Cuper) who contested two consecutive Champions League finals. The tiny Basque team CD Alavés, Galician RC Celta from Vigo and Real Zaragoza have also all proved tough regular competitors. The big southern clubs, Real Betis and Sevilla FC, have proved less successful, and both have tasted lower division soccer. However, despite the healthy competition, clubs in the lower reaches of the league are beset by debt, and demands from the Spanish treasury in 2002 for unpaid taxes threatened to bankrupt half the teams in La Liga.

Despite a few seasons in the second division Seville's two clubs, Real Betis (in stripes) and Sevilla, play out one of the most fearsome derbies in the Spanish league.

SPAIN

***Sociedad returns.** Goals from Darko Kovacevic helped Real Sociedad to second place in 2002–03, the club's best season in 20 years.*

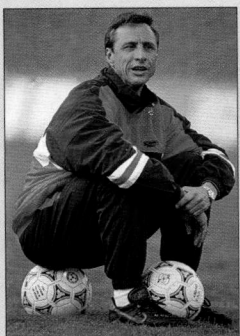

***Above:** Johan Cruyff returned to Barcelona as coach, winning four consecutive league titles between 1991 and 94.*

***Right:** José Núñez was elected president of Barcelona in 1978 after a bruising campaign. He ruled the club as something close to a fiefdom before his shock defeat to Joan Gaspart in the 2001 presidential elections.*

Champions' Winning Margin 1995–2003

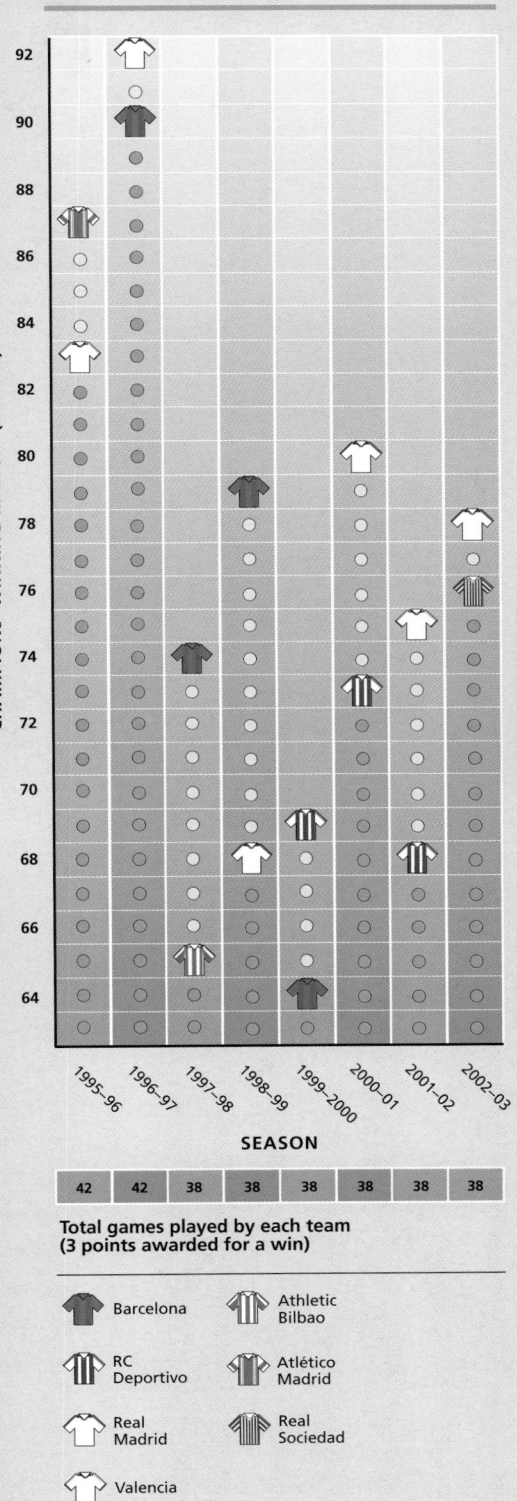

SPAIN

CHAMPIONS' WINNING MARGIN (POINTS)

SEASON

42	42	38	38	38	38	38	38

**Total games played by each team
(3 points awarded for a win)**

- Barcelona
- Athletic Bilbao
- RC Deportivo
- Atlético Madrid
- Real Madrid
- Real Sociedad
- Valencia

SPAIN

Key to League Positions Table

- League champions
- Season of promotion to league
- Season of relegation from league
- Other teams playing in league
- 5 — Final position in league

Pablo Aimar was the engine room in midfield for Valencia during its championship-winning season in 2001–02.

Dutch striker Roy Makaay helped Deportivo to top three finishes in each of the last four years.

Spanish League Positions 1983–2003

SEASON

TEAM	1983-84	1984-85	1985-86	1986-87	1987-88	1988-89	1989-90	1990-91	1991-92	1992-93	1993-94	1994-95	1995-96	1996-97	1997-98	1998-99	1999-2000	2000-01	2001-02	2002-03
CD Alavés																16	6	10	7	19
Albacete Balompié								7	17	13	17	20								
Barcelona	3	1	2	2	6	2	3	1	1	1	1	4	3	2	1	1	2	4	4	6
Real Betis	5	14	8	9	16	18		20				3	8	4	8	11	18		6	8
Athletic Bilbao	1	3	3	13	4	7	12	12	14	8	5	8	15	6	2	8	11	12	9	7
Real Burgos							11	9	20											
Cádiz	16		15	18	12	15	15	18	18	19										
Deportivo Castellón							14	19												
RC Celta			18			7	8	19		11	15	13	11	16	6	5	7	6	5	4
SD Compostela												16	10	11	17					
RC Deportivo									17	3	2	2	9	3	12	6	1	2	2	3
Elche CF			17			20														
RCD Espanyol	10	8	11	3	15	17		16	16	18		6	4	12	10	7	14	9	14	17
CF Extremadura														19		17				
Sporting Gijón	13	4	6	4	9	13	13	5	8	12	14	18	18	15	20					
Hércules		15	17												21					
RC Recreativo de Huelva																				18
Unión Deportivo Las Palmas				13	14	20												11	18	
Lérida Unión Esportiva										19										
Deportivo Logroñes					13	14	7	10	10	15	16	20		22						
Atlético Madrid	4	2	5	7	3	4	2	3	6	12	14	1	5	7	13	19				11
Real Madrid	2	5	1	1	1	1	1	3	2	2	4	1	6	1	4	2	5	1	3	1
Deportivo Málaga	9	16			16	17											12	8	10	14
RCD Mallorca	17			6	18		10	15	20						5	3	10	3	16	9
CP Mérida													21		19					
Real Murcia	11	18		11	17	19														
CD Numancia																	17	20		
Atlético Osasuna	15	6	14	16	5	10	8	4	15	10	20							15	17	12
Real Oviedo						12	11	6	11	16	9	9	14	17	18	14	16	18		
CD Sabadell				15	19															
Deportivo Salamanca	18												22		15	20				
Racing Santander		11	12	17							8	12	17	13	14	15	15	19		16
Sevilla FC	8	12	9	12	10	9	6	8	12	7	6	5	12	20			20		8	10
Real Sociedad	6	7	7	8	2	11	4	5	13	11	11	7		3	10	13	13	13		2
Deportivo Tenerife							18	14	13	5	10	15	5	9	16	19			19	
Valencia	12	9	16			14	3	2	7	4	7	10	2	10	9	4	3	5	1	5
Real Valladolid	14	13	10	10	8	6		19			18	19	16	7	11	12	8	16	12	13
Rayo Vallecano							20		14	17			19	18			9	14	11	20
Villareal																18		7	15	15
Real Zaragoza	7	10	4	5	11	5	9	17	5		3	7	13	14	13	9	4	17	20	

Primera Liga

Real Madrid — Team name

League champions/
runners-up

1990,
92 — Champions in bold
Runners-up in italics

Other teams in the
Primera Liga

● **Madrid** — City of origin

Money doesn't buy you
success? Real Madrid's
expensively assembled
squad, Los Galacticos,
celebrates its title
victory in 2002–03.
(Left to right) Ronaldo,
Steve McManaman,
Zinedine Zidane and
Iker Cassillas.

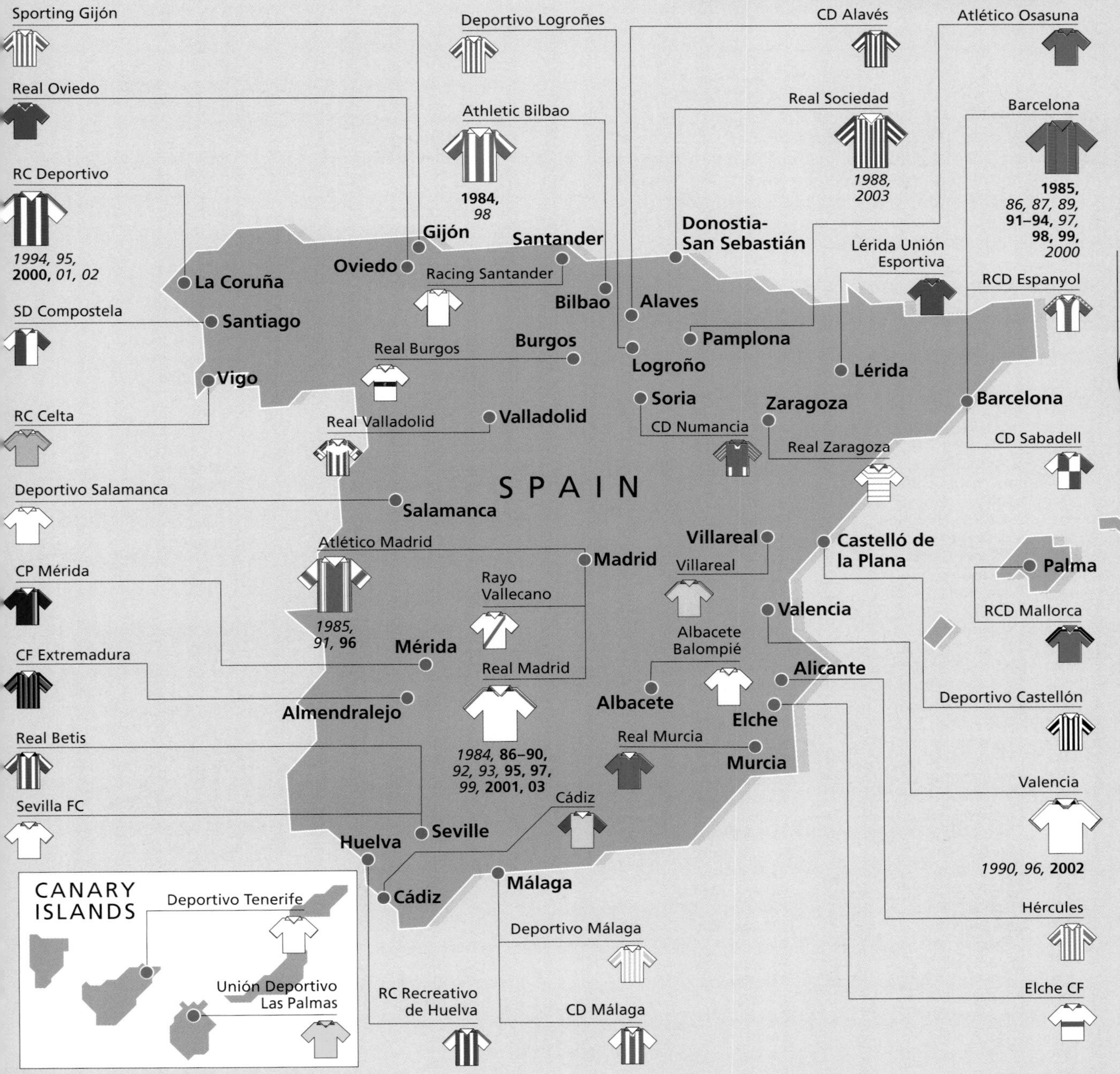

SPAIN

Sporting Gijón

Real Oviedo

RC Deportivo

1994, 95,
2000, 01, 02

SD Compostela

RC Celta

Deportivo Salamanca

CP Mérida

CF Extremadura

Real Betis

Sevilla FC

Deportivo Logroñes

Athletic Bilbao

1984,
98

Racing Santander

Real Burgos

Real Valladolid

Atlético Madrid

1985,
91, 96

Rayo
Vallecano

Real Madrid

1984, 86–90,
92, 93, 95, 97,
99, **2001, 03**

CD Alavés

Real Sociedad

1988,
2003

CD Numancia

Villareal

Albacete
Balompié

Real Murcia

Atlético Osasuna

Barcelona

1985,
86, 87, 89,
91–94, *97,*
98, 99,
2000

RCD Espanyol

Real Zaragoza

CD Sabadell

RCD Mallorca

Deportivo Castellón

Valencia

1990, 96, **2002**

Hércules

Elche CF

Lérida Unión
Esportiva

● **La Coruña**
Oviedo ●
Gijón ●
● Santander
Santiago ●
● **Vigo**
● **Valladolid**
Burgos ●
● **Alaves**
Bilbao ●
Donostia-
San Sebastián ●
● **Pamplona**
● **Logroño**
● **Soria**
● **Lérida**
Zaragoza ●
● **Barcelona**
Salamanca ●

S P A I N

Mérida ●
● **Madrid**
Villareal ●
● **Castelló de**
la Plana
● **Valencia**
● **Palma**
Almendralejo ●
● **Albacete**
● **Alicante**
● **Elche**
● **Murcia**
Huelva ●
● **Seville**
● Cádiz
● **Málaga**
● **Cádiz**

Deportivo Málaga

CD Málaga

RC Recreativo
de Huelva

CANARY ISLANDS

Deportivo Tenerife

Unión Deportivo
Las Palmas

Spain

Real Federación Española de Fútbol
Founded: 1913
Joined FIFA: 1904
Joined UEFA: 1954

FROM ITS EARLIEST DAYS, SPANISH SOCCER had a strong regional character. A Catalonian league was up and running by 1901, and the first years of the 20th century saw the establishment of regional leagues all over the country. The first national league began in 1929 comprising ten clubs. It grew steadily to a peak of 22 clubs in the 1990s, but has now decreased in size to just 20.

The first national competition, the Copa del Rey, was created in 1902. Not surprisingly given its title, it was supported by the centralizing monarchy in the person of King Alfonso XIII. The name, if not the format, of the cup has shifted with Spain's constitution. In 1934 it became the short-lived Copa del Republica, but was halted by the civil war, and reinvented under Franco's regime as the Copa del Generalisimo. With the return of the monarchy after Franco's death, the name of the competition reverted to its original title, the Copa del Rey.

Spanish League Record 1929–2004

SEASON	CHAMPIONS	RUNNERS-UP
1929	Barcelona	Real Madrid
1930	Athletic Bilbao	Barcelona
1931	Athletic Bilbao	Racing Santander
1932	Real Madrid	Athletic Bilbao
1933	Real Madrid	Athletic Bilbao
1934	Athletic Bilbao	Real Madrid
1935	Real Betis	Real Madrid
1936	Athletic Bilbao	Real Madrid
1937–39	no championship	
1940	Atlético Aviación	Sevilla
1941	Atlético Aviación	Athletic Bilbao
1942	Valencia	Real Madrid
1943	Athletic Bilbao	Sevilla
1944	Valencia	Atlético Aviación
1945	Barcelona	Real Madrid
1946	Sevilla	Barcelona
1947	Valencia	Athletic Bilbao
1948	Barcelona	Valencia
1949	Barcelona	Valencia
1950	Atlético Madrid	RC Deportivo
1951	Atlético Madrid	Sevilla
1952	Barcelona	Athletic Bilbao
1953	Barcelona	Valencia
1954	Real Madrid	Barcelona
1955	Real Madrid	Barcelona
1956	Athletic Bilbao	Barcelona
1957	Real Madrid	Sevilla
1958	Real Madrid	Atlético Madrid
1959	Barcelona	Real Madrid
1960	Barcelona	Real Madrid
1961	Real Madrid	Atlético Madrid
1962	Real Madrid	Barcelona
1963	Real Madrid	Atlético Madrid
1964	Real Madrid	Barcelona
1965	Real Madrid	Atlético Madrid
1966	Atlético Madrid	Real Madrid
1967	Real Madrid	Barcelona
1968	Real Madrid	Barcelona
1969	Real Madrid	Las Palmas
1970	Atlético Madrid	Athletic Bilbao
1971	Valencia	Barcelona

Spanish League Record (continued)

SEASON	CHAMPIONS	RUNNERS-UP
1972	Real Madrid	Valencia
1973	Atlético Madrid	Barcelona
1974	Barcelona	Atlético Madrid
1975	Real Madrid	Real Zaragoza
1976	Real Madrid	Barcelona
1977	Atlético Madrid	Barcelona
1978	Real Madrid	Barcelona
1979	Real Madrid	Sporting Gijón
1980	Real Madrid	Real Sociedad
1981	Real Sociedad	Real Madrid
1982	Real Sociedad	Barcelona
1983	Athletic Bilbao	Real Madrid
1984	Athletic Bilbao	Real Madrid
1985	Barcelona	Atlético Madrid
1986	Real Madrid	Barcelona
1987	Real Madrid	Barcelona
1988	Real Madrid	Real Sociedad
1989	Real Madrid	Barcelona
1990	Real Madrid	Valencia
1991	Barcelona	Atlético Madrid
1992	Barcelona	Real Madrid
1993	Barcelona	Real Madrid
1994	Barcelona	RC Deportivo
1995	Real Madrid	RC Deportivo
1996	Atlético Madrid	Valencia
1997	Real Madrid	Barcelona
1998	Barcelona	Athletic Bilbao
1999	Barcelona	Real Madrid
2000	RC Deportivo	Barcelona
2001	Real Madrid	RC Deportivo
2002	Valencia	RC Deportivo
2003	Real Madrid	Real Sociedad
2004	Valencia	Barcelona

Spanish League Summary

TEAM	TOTALS	CHAMPIONS & RUNNERS-UP (BOLD) (ITALICS)
Real Madrid	29, 15	*1929*, **32, 33**, *34–36, 42, 45*, **54, 55, 57, 58, 59, 60, 61–65**, *66*, **67–69, 72, 75, 76, 78–80**, *81*, **83**, *84*, **86–90**, *92, 93*, **95, 97, 99, 2001**, *03*
Barcelona	16, 21	**1929**, *30, 45, 46, 48, 49, 52, 53, 54–56, 59*, **60**, *62, 64, 67, 68, 71, 73*, **74**, *76–78, 82*, **85**, *86, 87, 89*, **91–94**, *97*, **98, 99**, *2000*, **04**
Atlético Madrid (including Atlético Aviación)	9, 8	**1940, 41, 44, 50, 51**, *58*, **61**, *63, 65*, **66**, *70*, **73**, *74*, **77**, *85, 91*, **96**
Athletic Bilbao	8, 7	**1930, 31**, *32, 33*, **34**, *36*, **41**, *43*, **47**, *52*, **56**, *70*, **83, 84**, *98*
Valencia	6, 6	**1942**, *44*, **47**, *48, 49*, **53, 71**, *72*, **90**, *96*, **2002, 04**
Real Sociedad	2, 3	*1980*, **81, 82**, *88*, **2003**
RC Deportivo	1, 5	*1950, 94, 95*, **2000**, *01, 02*
Sevilla	1, 4	**1940**, *43*, **46**, *51, 57*
Real Betis	1, 0	**1935**

This summary only features clubs that have won the Spanish League. For a full list of league champions and runners-up please see the League Record above.

SPAIN

Spanish Cup Record 1902–2004

YEAR	WINNERS	SCORE	RUNNERS-UP
1902	Vizcaya Bilbao	2-1	Barcelona
1903	Athletic Bilbao	3-2	Real Madrid
1904	Athletic Bilbao	w/o	
1905	Real Madrid	1-0	Athletic Bilbao
1906	Real Madrid	4-1	Athletic Bilbao
1907	Real Madrid	1-0	Vizcaya Bilbao
1908	Real Madrid	2-1	Vigo Sporting
1909	Ciclista San Sebastián	3-1	Español Madrid
1910	Athletic Bilbao	1-0*	Basconia
1910	Barcelona	3-2**	Español Madrid
1911	Athletic Bilbao	3-1	RCD Español
1912	Barcelona	2-0	Gimnastica Madrid
1913	Barcelona	2-2, (replay) 0-0, (replay) 2-1*	Real Sociedad
1913	Racing Irún	2-2, (replay) 1-0**	Athletic Bilbao
1914	Athletic Bilbao	2-1	España Barcelona
1915	Athletic Bilbao	5-0	RCD Español
1916	Athletic Bilbao	4-0	Real Madrid
1917	Real Madrid	0-0, (replay) 2-1	Arenas Guecho Bilbao
1918	Real Unión Irún	2-0	Real Madrid
1919	Arenas Guecho Bilbao	5-2 (aet)	Barcelona
1920	Barcelona	2-0	Athletic Bilbao
1921	Athletic Bilbao	4-1	Atlético Madrid
1922	Barcelona	5-1	Real Unión Irún
1923	Athletic Bilbao	1-0	Europa Barcelona
1924	Real Unión Irún	1-0	Real Madrid
1925	Barcelona	2-0	Arenas Guecho Bilbao
1926	Barcelona	3-2 (aet)	Atlético Madrid
1927	Real Unión Irún	1-0 (aet)	Arenas Guecho Bilbao
1928	Barcelona	1-1, (replay) 1-1, (replay) 3-1	Real Sociedad
1929	RCD Español	2-1	Real Madrid
1930	Athletic Bilbao	3-2 (aet)	Real Madrid
1931	Athletic Bilbao	3-1	Real Betis
1932	Athletic Bilbao	1-0	Barcelona
1933	Athletic Bilbao	2-1	Real Madrid
1934	Real Madrid	2-1	Valencia
1935	Sevilla	3-0	Sabadell
1936	Real Madrid	2-1	Barcelona
1937–38	*no competition*		
1939	Sevilla	6-2	Racing Ferrol
1940	RCD Español	3-2 (aet)	Real Madrid
1941	Valencia	3-1	RCD Español
1942	Barcelona	4-3 (aet)	Athletic Bilbao
1943	Athletic Bilbao	1-0 (aet)	Real Madrid
1944	Athletic Bilbao	2-0	Valencia
1945	Athletic Bilbao	3-2	Valencia
1946	Real Madrid	3-1	Valencia
1947	Real Madrid	2-0 (aet)	RCD Español
1948	Sevilla	4-1	RC Celta
1949	Valencia	1-0	Athletic Bilbao
1950	Athletic Bilbao	4-1 (aet)	Valladolid
1951	Barcelona	3-0	Real Sociedad
1952	Barcelona	4-2 (aet)	Valencia
1953	Barcelona	2-1	Athletic Bilbao
1954	Valencia	3-0	Barcelona
1955	Athletic Bilbao	1-0	Sevilla
1956	Athletic Bilbao	2-1	Atlético Madrid
1957	Barcelona	1-0	RCD Español
1958	Athletic Bilbao	2-0	Real Madrid
1959	Barcelona	4-1	Granada
1960	Atlético Madrid	3-1	Real Madrid
1961	Atlético Madrid	3-2	Real Madrid
1962	Real Madrid	2-1	Sevilla
1963	Barcelona	3-1	Real Zaragoza
1964	Real Zaragoza	2-1	Atlético Madrid
1965	Atlético Madrid	1-0	Real Zaragoza
1966	Real Zaragoza	2-0	Athletic Bilbao
1967	Valencia	2-1	Athletic Bilbao

Spanish Cup Record (*continued*)

YEAR	WINNERS	SCORE	RUNNERS-UP
1968	Barcelona	1-0	Real Madrid
1969	Athletic Bilbao	1-0	Elche
1970	Real Madrid	3-1	Valencia
1971	Barcelona	4-3	Valencia
1972	Atlético Madrid	2-1	Valencia
1973	Athletic Bilbao	2-0	Castellón
1974	Real Madrid	4-0	Barcelona
1975	Real Madrid	0-0 (aet)(4-3 pens)	Atlético Madrid
1976	Atlético Madrid	1-0	Real Zaragoza
1977	Real Betis	2-2 (aet)(8-7 pens)	Athletic Bilbao
1978	Barcelona	3-1	Las Palmas
1979	Valencia	2-0	Real Madrid
1980	Real Madrid	6-1	Castilla
1981	Barcelona	3-1	Sporting Gijón
1982	Real Madrid	2-1	Sporting Gijón
1983	Barcelona	2-1	Real Madrid
1984	Athletic Bilbao	1-0	Barcelona
1985	Atlético Madrid	2-1	Athletic Bilbao
1986	Real Zaragoza	1-0	Barcelona
1987	Real Sociedad	2-2 (aet)(4-2 pens)	Atlético Madrid
1988	Barcelona	1-0	Real Sociedad
1989	Real Madrid	1-0	Valladolid
1990	Barcelona	2-0	Real Madrid
1991	Atlético Madrid	1-0 (aet)	Mallorca
1992	Atlético Madrid	2-0	Real Madrid
1993	Real Madrid	2-0	Real Zaragoza
1994	Real Zaragoza	0-0 (aet)(5-4 pens)	RC Celta
1995	RC Deportivo	2-1†	Valencia
1996	Atlético Madrid	1-0 (aet)	Barcelona
1997	Barcelona	3-2 (aet)	Real Betis
1998	Barcelona	1-1 (aet)(5-4 pens)	Mallorca
1999	Valencia	3-0	Atlético Madrid
2000	RCD Espanyol	2-1	Atlético Madrid
2001	Real Zaragoza	3-1	RC Celta
2002	RC Deportivo	2-1	Real Madrid
2003	RCD Mallorca	3-0	Recreativo Huelva
2004	Real Zaragoza	3-2	Real Madrid

w/o denotes walk over
  * Copa de la Federación Española de Fútbol.
 ** Copa de la Unión Española de Clubs de Fútbol.
  † Match was abandoned in the 80th minute due to torrential rain (at 1-1) and finished a few days later.

Spanish Cup Summary

TEAM	TOTALS	WINNERS & RUNNERS-UP (BOLD) (ITALICS)
Barcelona	24, 9	*1902*, **10, 12, 13, 19, 20, 22, 25, 26, 28,** *32, 36,* **42,** *51–53, 54,* **57, 59, 63, 68, 71,** *74, 78,* **81, 83,** *84,* **86, 88, 90, 96, 97, 98**
Athletic Bilbao	23, 11	**1903,** *04,* **05, 06,** *10, 11,* **13,** *14–16,* **20, 21, 23, 30–33,** *42,* **43–45, 49, 50,** *53,* **55, 56,** *58, 66, 67,* **69, 73,** *77,* **84, 85**
Real Madrid	17, 19	*1903,* **05–08,** *16, 17, 18, 24, 29, 30, 33,* **34,** *36,* **40,** *43,* **46, 47,** *58,* **60, 61, 62,** *68,* **70,** *74, 75,* **79, 80, 82,** *83,* **89,** *90, 92,* **93,** *2002,* **04**
Atlético Madrid	9, 8	*1921, 26, 56,* **60, 61,** *64,* **65,** *72, 75,* **76, 85,** *87,* **91, 92, 96,** *99,* **2000**
Valencia	6, 9	*1934,* **41,** *44–46,* **49,** *52,* **54,** *67, 70–72,* **79,** *95,* **99**
Real Zaragoza	6, 4	*1963,* **64,** *65,* **66,** *76,* **86,** *93,* **94, 2001, 04**
Real Unión Irún (includes Racing Irún)	4, 1	**1913, 18, 22, 24, 27**
RCD Espanyol (includes RCD Español, España Barcelona)	3, 6	*1911, 14, 15,* **29,** *40, 41, 47, 57,* **2000**
Sevilla	3, 2	**1935, 39, 48,** *55, 62*

This summary only features clubs that have won the Spanish Cup three or more times. For a full list of cup winners and runners-up please see the Cup Record above.

Italy

THE SEASON IN REVIEW 2003–04

THE ITALIAN SEASON OPENED WITH the Super Cup, this time held in New York. The match was a replay of last year's Champions League Final – Milan v Juventus. But before a single ball had been kicked, the administrative, legal and political soap opera that usually accompanies an Italian season had already begun. A minor spat between Juventus and Nike occurred as the American company could not, under US federal law, manufacture or distribute Juventus' Champions League shirts because they bore the logo of the Libyan oil company Tamoil. US law forbids its companies to deal with Libyan corporations in any way. Four clubs, including Roma, who had received financial guarantees from a company endorsed by the nation's leading sporting body – Covisoc – turned out to have been backed with false and forged documents. The Italian government announced that not only were the country's clubs in significant debt to their banks, but also that most of them had huge unpaid tax bills and massive pension contributions still to be fulfilled (around 500 million Euros). But Italy's soccer elite is not distracted by such minor government interference when it has its own extraordinary disputes to deal with.

Domestic disputes

More conflict came in the opening weeks of the season, firstly about the composition of Serie B and then about something that really matters to the clubs: television rights and money. The Italian league had decided to expand Serie B to 24 teams – readmitting the three teams relegated last season as well as Fiorentina. As a result 19 of the 20 teams already in Serie B declared a boycott of the league's fixtures, while their fans hurled eggs and shouted abuse outside the league headquarters. The problem began when Sicilian club Catania, who had just been relegated from Serie B to Serie C1, argued that it should not have been relegated because of a technicality. It took its case to a Sicilian court, which duly found in its favour and ordered that the relegation be rescinded. Pretty soon everyone else who had been relegated was seeking similar judgements in local courts, and with home advantage got the right result. Prime Minister Berlusconi interrupted his Sardinian holiday in an effort to sort the chaos out and decreed that clubs had to accept the rulings of the Football Federation and not the local courts. The federation then decided to readmit Catania and two other relegated clubs from last season – Genoa and Salernitana – but the fourth relegated side, Cosenza, could not come back due to its terminal financial health. Amazingly, on the grounds of 'sporting merit', Fiorentina was to leapfrog from Serie C1, to which it had just won promotion, straight into Serie B. The boycott duly followed and was sustained for two weeks into the season; a compromise was finally agreed in which five teams would be allowed up from Serie B to Serie A this year creating a 20-team Serie A and a 22-team Serie B for next season. The television dispute was between Sky Italia, which holds the TV rights for the big clubs' games and own the main satellite platform in Italy, and Gioco Calcio, a smaller company that holds the TV rights for the smaller Serie A clubs. Gioco Calcio planned to use Sky's platform for broadcasting its own subscription service – but Sky refused to let them. The dispute was finally resolved only for another strike to be threatened when the league was late in paying the small clubs their TV money.

Serie A League Table 2003–04

CLUB	P	W	D	L	F	A	Pts	
Milan	34	25	7	2	65	24	82	Champions League
Roma	34	21	8	5	68	19	71	Champions League
Juventus	34	21	6	7	67	42	69	Champions League
Internazionale	34	17	8	9	59	37	59	Champions League
Parma	34	16	10	8	57	46	58	UEFA Cup
Lazio	34	16	8	10	52	38	56	UEFA Cup (cup winners)
Udinese	34	13	11	10	44	40	50	UEFA Cup
Sampdoria	34	11	13	10	40	42	46	
Chievo	34	11	11	12	36	37	44	
Lecce	34	11	8	15	43	56	41	
Brescia	34	9	13	12	52	57	40	
Bologna	34	10	9	15	45	53	39	
Siena	34	8	10	16	41	54	34	
Reggina	34	6	16	12	29	45	34	
Perugia	34	6	14	14	44	56	32	Relegated (play-off)
Modena	34	6	12	16	27	46	30	Relegated
Empoli	34	7	9	18	26	54	30	Relegated
Ancona	34	2	7	25	21	70	13	Relegated

Serie A is to be extended to 20 clubs for 2004–05, with three clubs being relegated directly, five promoted automatically, and the team placed 15th in Serie A to play-off against the team placed 6th in Serie B.
Promoted clubs: Atalanta, Cagliary, Livorno, Messina, Palermo, Fiorentina.

Top: The odd couple. Perugia's occasional midfielder Saad Gaddafi and quixotic president Luciano Gaucci watch their team draw with Milan.

Above: Inter's Julio Cruz sends the ball past Juve's Gianluigi Buffon as Inter record a rare 3-1 victory in the Derby d'Italia.

Milan

Carlo Ancelotti

👑 1st *

🏆 Semi-final

CL Quarter-final

Imperious, electric and inventive. Ancelotti's Milan played fabulous and consistent attacking soccer

Internazionale

Héctor Cúper, Alberto Zaccheroni

👑 4th *

🏆 Semi-final

CL Group Stage

UEFA Quarter-final

The word erratic was invented for Inter. First Cúper was sacked, then President Moratti resigned. Dismal mid-season form in the league and bundled out of Europe. Hauled itself into the Champions League but only just

Brescia

Giovanni de Biasi

👑 11th

🏆 2nd Round

Another mid-table finish for Brescia. Roberto Baggio was outstanding in his farewell season. How will the team manage without him?

Udinese

Luciano Spalletti

👑 7th †

🏆 Quarter-final

UEFA 1st Round

Strong, businesslike Udinese squeezed into Europe

Chievo

Luigi del Neri

👑 9th

🏆 3rd Round

Chievo is now firmly established in Serie A just below the European places, but Italy's best-run small club has been accused of match fixing

Modena

Alberto Malesani

👑 16th ⬇

🏆 3rd Round

No repeat of last year's escape from relegation, back down to Serie B for Modena

Bologna

Francesco Guidolin, Carlo Mazzone

👑 12th

🏆 3rd Round

Mazzone, Serie A's oldest coach, nursed his team to safety as injuries and retirements took their toll

Juventus

Marcello Lippi

👑 3rd *

🏆 Runners-up

CL 1st Knockout Round

A deeply disappointing season for the Old Lady. Its early season form dissolved. Defeated in Europe and repeatedly trounced by the big clubs in Serie A, Lippi was inevitably forced to go

Ancona

Leonardo Menichini, Nedo Sonetti, Giovanni Galeone

👑 18th ⬇

🏆 1st Round

Two wins, three managers and relegation added up to an utterly dismal year for Ancona. Thankfully Galeone described the fans as 'civilized and compassionate'

Siena

Giuseppe Papadopoulo

👑 13th

🏆 3rd Round

Staying up. Papadopoulo guided his charges to safety on a shoestring budget

Sampdoria

Walter Novellino

👑 8th

🏆 3rd Round

Its first year back in Serie A since 1999 and Sampdoria looked the part

SARDINIA

ITALY

Empoli

Silvio Baldini

👑 17th ⬇

🏆 2nd Round

After two seasons in Serie A, Empoli was consigned to Serie B

Parma

Cesare Prandelli

👑 5th †

🏆 Quarter-final

UEFA 3rd Round

Parmalat, the team's sponsors, became Europe's Enron as it dissolved in a mountain of debt. Yet so far the team remains a going concern, with young striker Gilardino the revelation of the season

Perugia

Serse Cosmi

👑 15th ⬇

🏆 Quarter-final

UEFA 3rd Round

No shortage of entertainment at Perugia – Saadi Gaddafi made his Serie A debut, the president Luciano Gaucci plans to sign a woman and the team went down after a relegation play-off against Fiorentina

Lecce

Delio Rossi

👑 10th

🏆 1st Round

10th was a brilliant finish for newly promoted Lecce, Ernesto Chevanton's goals made all the difference

Roma

Fabio Capello

👑 2nd *

🏆 Quarter-final

UEFA 4th Round

After last year's disaster this was the real Roma. Totti was magnificent but two defeats against Milan lost them the crown

Reggina Calcio

Franco Colomba, Giancarlo Camolese, Bortollo Mutti

👑 14th

🏆 3rd Round

A late run of form with its third manager of the season kept Reggina safe

Lazio

Roberto Mancini

👑 6th †

🏆 Winners

CL Group Stage

The money situation at Lazio never seemed to be resolved but somehow Mancini kept the team focused on soccer. Beating Juve in the Cup Final was sweet reward

Milan ·

Turin ·

Brescia ·

Verona ·

Genoa ·

Parma ·

Modena ·

Bologna ·

Udine ·

Empoli ·

Siena ·

Perugia ·

Ancona ·

Rome ·

Lecce ·

Reggio di Calabria ·

SICILY

Key

Milan

👕 Team name and shirt colours

🧑 Manager

👑 League position

⬇ Relegated teams

🏆 Progress in Cup

🤝 Under investigation for match fixing

CL Progress in Champions League

UEFA Progress in UEFA Cup

* Qualified for Champions League

† Qualified for UEFA Cup

ITALY

Problems off and on the pitch

When the soccer finally got under way, Juventus, Roma and Milan made the early running, with Roma just ahead at the winter break. Inter had started well, but a series of reverses, including another derby defeat against Milan, saw president Massimo Moratti lose patience with coach Cuper and sack him. Moratti himself resigned as president, Alberto Zaccheroni replaced Cuper and club legend Giacinto Facchetti became president – although Moratti continued to own and fund the club. The owners of Parma – the Tanzi family – also stepped down over the winter break. The problem here was not match results but financial ones. Parmalat, the multinational food company owned by the Tanzi family, of which Parma was a part, was revealed as Europe's Enron – a huge and apparently successful company kept afloat by illegal accounting practices. The company's real debt was over 3 billion euros and the arrest of the Tanzi family saw Parma placed in the hands of administrators. Despite this, Parma played well all season and after an injury to its star striker, Adriano, it uncovered the brilliant young Italian Alberto Gilardino, who ended up with an amazing 23 goals.

Although there was significantly less trouble in Italian soccer this year, the season saw two deaths, possibly suicides, as fans fell from the top tier of Lazio and Inter's stadiums during games. At Napoli's match with Avellino another fan died after falling from the stands. Moments later the Napoli fans invaded the pitch and fought running battles with the police in which over 30 people were injured. The power of Italian fans was amply displayed at the second Rome derby of the season when rumours began among the Roma supporters that a fan had been killed by the police. The rumours spread, fans informed a number of players and, after much discussion in the centre circle, the game was abandoned. It later transpired that no one had been killed or injured.

Oh yes, the soccer

The sporting shape of the season was soon clarified in the New Year. Despite a flurry of signings, Ancona was relegated early. Modena and Empoli followed them. Reggina, who looked ready for the drop and without a home win since January, got out of jail late by beating Milan 2-1 at the San Siro, and then Roma. Perugia, who had struggled all year, hit an amazing seam of late form to drag itself into the relegation play-off, only to lose to the rejuvenated Fiorentina. The European prowess of Italian

Above: The insolvent and the irreconcilable. Parma's Daniele Bonera and Inter's Christian Vieri clash. Vieri's face barely cracked a smile all season, his team-mates seemingly more reluctant to pass to him as the year wore on.

Right: John Charles, the brilliant Welsh centre forward, was a favourite in the mighty Juventus sides of the 1950s. He died in 2004.

Below: Inter seeks some steel. Giacinto Facchetti, the legendary defender, was appointed Inter president after Moratti resigned.

Above: Life's tough at the bottom: Ancona's Dario Hubner and Siena's Leandro Cufre battle for the ball.

Above, right: Marcello Lippi wonders why his aging squad just can't quite cut it at the top anymore.

Above: With typical poise and balance Kaka scores for Milan against Inter.

Above, left: Rome captain, Francesco Totti, and Lazio captain, Sinisa Mihailovic, discuss whether to play on in the second half of the Rome derby.

Far left: Lazio's Claudio Lopez has the beating of Milan's Paolo Maldini.

Left: The last straight man in Italian soccer? Bologna's president Giuseppe Gazzoni Frascara blew the whistle on match-fixing in Serie A this season.

Race for the Championship

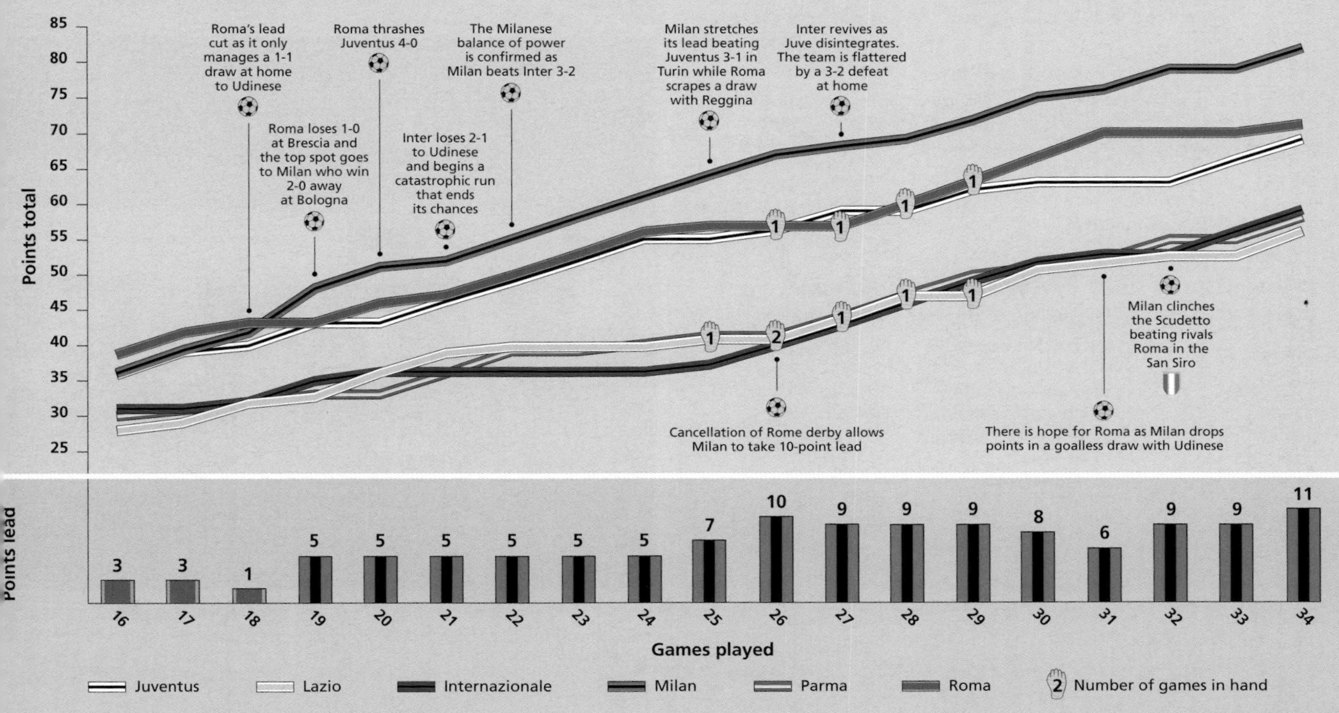

Roma's lead cut as it only manages a 1-1 draw at home to Udinese

Roma loses 1-0 at Brescia and the top spot goes to Milan who win 2-0 away at Bologna

Roma thrashes Juventus 4-0

Inter loses 2-1 to Udinese and begins a catastrophic run that ends its chances

The Milanese balance of power is confirmed as Milan beats Inter 3-2

Milan stretches its lead beating Juventus 3-1 in Turin while Roma scrapes a draw with Reggina

Inter revives as Juve disintegrates. The team is flattered by a 3-2 defeat at home

Milan clinches the Scudetto beating rivals Roma in the San Siro

Cancellation of Rome derby allows Milan to take 10-point lead

There is hope for Roma as Milan drops points in a goalless draw with Udinese

Points total (y-axis): 85, 80, 75, 70, 65, 60, 55, 50, 45, 40, 35, 30, 25

Points lead (bar values): 3, 3, 1, 5, 5, 5, 5, 5, 5, 7, 10, 9, 9, 9, 8, 6, 9, 9, 11

Games played (x-axis): 16, 17, 18, 19, 20, 21, 22, 23, 24, 25, 26, 27, 28, 29, 30, 31, 32, 33, 34

Legend: Juventus | Lazio | Internazionale | Milan | Parma | Roma | ② Number of games in hand

teams last season was not to be repeated this term. Spanish side Deportivo La Coruña knocked Juventus out of the Champions League in the first knockout round and followed this up by beating Milan in the quarter-finals. Roma and Inter were the only sides left in the UEFA Cup. Neither seemed entirely bothered and both went out before Easter. Domestically, the championship race narrowed to two teams: Roma and Milan. Juve's challenge steadily disintegrated as a tired and out of sorts squad lost comprehensively to Milan and Inter at home. Lazio, Inter and Parma scrapped it out below them for the last Champions League spot and, in the final run-in, Inter at last found some form to take the precious place. Lazio was consoled by a brilliant victory over Juve in the Coppa d'Italia.

Milan turn on the style

Roma had ceded its lead to Milan early in the New Year after losing to Brescia. But it kept chasing, driven by playmaker, captain and top scorer, Francesco Totti. His goals from free-kicks and long-range shots were spectacular and his pinpoint crossfield passes a key element in Roma's attacks. But in the end the team could not match the consistency and class of Milan. Andrei Schevchenko, the league's top scorer, was at his very best. New Brazilian signing Kaka brought inspiration and directness to the midfield, but the entire cast was excellent. Milan made its move in April when it effectively wrapped up the title by beating Roma 2-1 at the San Siro.

But, just when it looked like the season might be concluded on an essentially sporting note, the Italian authorities announced a massive investigation into match-fixing in Serie A with five of the league's clubs under serious investigation. Like most Italian investigations it is unlikely to deliver a conclusive result, but its presence is a reminder that the Italian soccer season happens as much, if not more, off the pitch than on it.

Antonio Cassano, Roma's scoring revelation this season, puts another goal past Juventus as Roma chased Milan in the final weeks of the season.

ITALY

Coppa d'Italia

2004 FINAL (2 legs)
March 17 – Olimpico, Rome
Lazio 2-0 Juventus
(Fiore 59, 80)
h/t: 0-0 **Att:** 62,204
Ref: Collina

May 19 – Stadio delle Alpi, Turin
Juventus 2-2 Lazio
(Trezeguet 20,   (Corradi 74,
Del Piero 47)   Fiore 83)
h/t: 1-0 **Att:** 38,849
Ref: Paparesta
Lazio won 4-2 on aggregate

Relegation play-off

2004 PLAY-OFF (2 legs)
June 16 – Stadio Renato Curi, Perugia
Perugia 0-1 Fiorentina
(Fantini 9)
h/t: 0-1 **Att:** 27,660
Ref: Trefoloni

June 20 – Stadio Franchi, Florence
Fiorentina 1-1 Perugia
(Fantini 47)   (Do Prado 81)
h/t: 0-0 **Att:** 40,000
Ref: Rosetti
Fiorentina won on 2-1 on aggregate
Perugia relegated

International Club Performances 2003–04

CLUB	COMPETITION	PROGRESS
Internazionale	Champions League	Group Stage
	UEFA Cup	Quarter-finals
Juventus	Champions League	1st Knockout Round
Lazio	Champions League	Group Stage
Milan	Champions League	Quarter-finals
Parma	UEFA Cup	3rd Round
Perugia	UEFA Cup	3rd Round
Roma	UEFA Cup	4th Round
Udinese	UEFA Cup	1st Round

Top Goalscorers 2003–04

PLAYER	CLUB	NATIONALITY	GOALS
Andrei Shevchenko	Milan	Ukrainian	24
Alberto Gilardino	Parma	Italian	23
Francesco Totti	Roma	Italian	20

Above, middle: Bernado Corradi grabs a goal back for Lazio in its second leg Coppa d'Italia Final against Juventus and puts Lazio into the lead on aggregate.

Above: Lazio celebrates its Coppa d'Italia victory.

Above, top: *Andrei Shevchenko proves too quick for even Roma's superb defender Walter Samuel. His two goals sealed Milan's 2-0 victory over Roma at the San Siro and with it the Scudetto.*

Above, right: *Roberto Baggio kisses the captain's armband and says goodbye to Serie A as he finished his career playing for Brescia against Milan on the last day of the season.*

Above: *Francesco Totti, the most complete player in Italian football this season, scores against Sampdoria.*

Right: *Milan celebrates its title triumph. (From left to right) Cafu, Shevchenko and Kaka were all key elements in its success during the season.*

ITALY

Soccer in Italy

1887: Palestra Ginnastica Libertas, Italy's oldest club formed (later merged into Fiorentina) — 1885 / 1890

1898: Formation of FA: Federazione Italiana Giuoco Calcio. First national championship — 1895 / 1900

1905: Affiliation to FIFA — 1905

1910: First international, v France, won 6–2, venue: Milan — 1910

1916–19: League abandoned during war — 1915 / 1920

1922: First Italian Cup Final
1929: Mussolini de-anglicizes name changes for Genoa and Inter who become Genova and Ambrosiana Inter — 1925

1930: National championship reorganized into national league; professionalism legalized — 1930 / 1935

1944–45: League abandoned during war — 1940 / 1945

1949: Torino, dominant team of the decade, killed in Mount Superga air crash — 1950

1954: Affiliation to UEFA
1964: Foreign players banned — 1955

1968: FICF, Federazione Italiana Calcio Femminile founded. — 1960

First women's international, v Czechoslovakia, won 2–0, venue: Viareggio — 1965

1970: Breakaway Women's FA formed – FFIGC — 1970

1972: Reunification of women's association to form the FIGCF, Federazione Italiana Giuoco Calcio Femminile — 1975

1980: Ban on foreign players lifted. FIGCF becomes associate member of FIGC (national FA) — 1980 / 1985

1986: FIGCF fully incorporated into FIGC — 1990

1997: Clubs required to convert themselves into limited companies — 1995

1998: Lazio is first Italian club to float on the stock exchange — 2000

2002: Italian Supercup played in Libya for first time — 2005

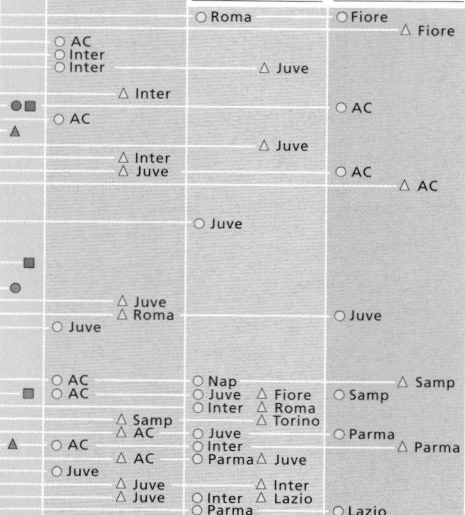

Valentino Mazzola leads out *Il Grande Torino*; four-time consecutive champions (1946–49), backbone of the national team, tragically killed in the Mount Superga air crash.

Key

International soccer
Affiliation to FIFA
Affiliation to UEFA
Women's soccer
War
Disaster
World Cup host
World Cup winner
World Cup runner-up
European Championships host
European Championships winner
European Championships runner-up
Competition winner
Competition runner-up

Fiore – Fiorentina
Inter – Internazionale
Juve – Juventus
Nap – Napoli
AC – Milan
Samp – Sampdoria

International Competitions

Year	European Cup	UEFA Cup	European Cup-Winners' Cup
1934:	☐ ●		
1938:	●		
1957:	△ Fiore		
1958:	△ AC		
1961:		○ Roma	
1962:			○ Fiore
1963:	○ AC		△ Fiore
1964:	○ Inter		
1965:	○ Inter		△ Juve
1967:	△ Inter		
1968:	● ☐		○ AC
1969:	○ AC		
1970:			△ Juve
1971:			
1972:	△ Inter		○ AC
1973:	△ Juve		
1974:			△ AC
1977:		○ Juve	
1980:	☐		
1982:	●		
1983:	△ Juve		
1984:	△ Roma		○ Juve
1985:	○ Juve		
1989:	○ AC	○ Nap	
1990:	☐ ○ AC	○ Juve	△ Fiore	○ Samp	△ Samp
1991:		○ Inter	△ Roma
1992:			○ Torino
1993:	△ Samp	○ Juve	○ Parma
1994:	▲ ○ AC	△ AC	○ Inter	△ Parma
1995:	△ AC	○ Parma	△ Juve
1996:	○ Juve		
1997:		△ Inter	△ Juve
1998:	△ Juve	○ Inter	△ Lazio
1999:	△ Juve	○ Parma	○ Lazio
2000:	▲		
2003:	○ AC	△ Juve	

Milan 1899

Milan Cricket and Football Club (1899–1905). Milan Football Club (1905–38)

Pro Vercelli 1892

Juventus 1897

Originated from the Massimo d'Azeglio Grammar School

Torino 1906

Merger FC Torinese and splinter group from Juventus (in 1901 FC Torinese founded 1887, merged with Internazionale Torino)

Casale 1909

Alessandria 1920

Merger of US Alessandria and Alessandria FC

Genoa 1893*

Genoa Football and Cricket Club (1893–99), Genoa FC (1899–1929), Genova (1893, 1929–45)

Sampierdarenese 1901

Merged with Andrea Doria to become Sampdoria in 1946

Con Cal 19

Vare F 19

Gallaratese 1909

Novara Calcio 1908

Vercel
Casal

Turin ● **Alessandria**

Novese 1908

Genoa

Vado 1908

Parma 1938

Began in 1913 as Verdi, then Parma. Bankr in 1968 and re-established

Italy: The main clubs

Cagliari 1920 — Team name with year of formation

●	Club formed before 1912
●	Club formed 1912–25
●	Club formed 1925–50
○	Club formed after 1950
	Winners of Amateur Championship (1899–1929)
	Runners-up in Amateur Championship
⊞	English origins
⊞	Swiss origins
⫼	Originated from a cricket club
	Originated from a school or college
★	10 Scudettos†
★★	20 Scudettos
*	Shirts shown are in teams' original colours

†*Scudetto = Italian Championship*
1 star awarded & worn for 10 Scudettos
2 stars awarded & worn for 20 Scudettos

SARDIN

Cagliari 1920

Italy

ORIGINS AND GROWTH OF SOCCER

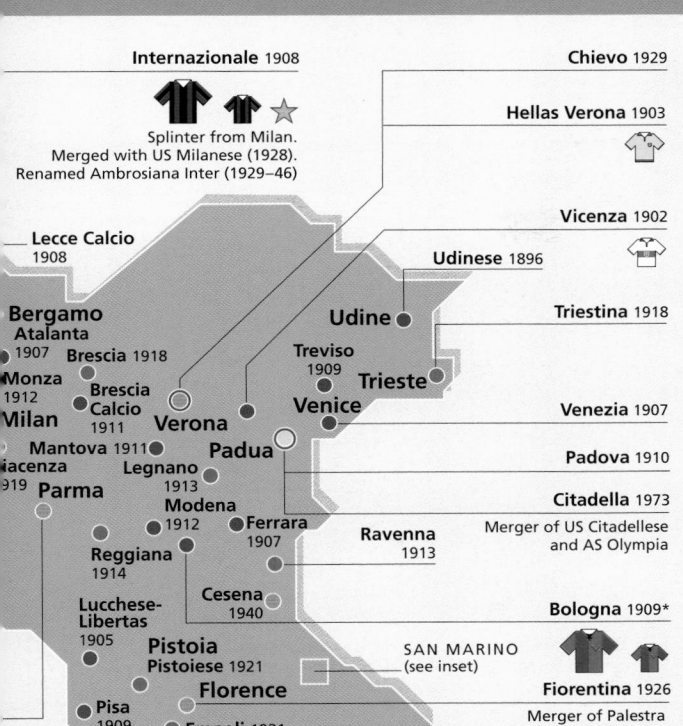

Internazionale 1908

Splinter from Milan.
Merged with US Milanese (1928).
Renamed Ambrosiana Inter (1929–46)

Chievo 1929

Hellas Verona 1903

Lecce Calcio
1908

Vicenza 1902

Udinese 1896

Bergamo
Atalanta
1907   **Brescia** 1918
Monza   **Udine**
1912   **Brescia**
Milan   **Calcio**   **Treviso**
1911   **Verona**   1909
Mantova 1911   **Padua**   **Venice**   **Trieste**
iacenza **Legnano**
919   **Parma**   1913
         Modena   **Ferrara**
            1912   1907
Reggiana
1914

Triestina 1918

Venezia 1907

Padova 1910

Citadella 1973
Merger of US Citadellese
and AS Olympia

Ravenna
1913

Lucchese-
Libertas
1905
Pistoia
Pistoiese 1921
Florence

Pisa
1909   **Empoli** 1921

Livorno
Siena
1904

Livorno
1915

Cesena
1940

Bologna 1909*

SAN MARINO
(see inset)

Fiorentina 1926
Merger of Palestra
Ginnastica Libertas,
Sportive and CS Firenze.
Club liquidated in 2002.
Refounded as
Fiorentina Viola

Ancona
1905

Ascoli Calcio
1898

Perugia   **Terni**
1905   **Ternana** 1925

Pescara
1936

Roma 1927

Merger in 1927
of Fortitudo,
Pro Roma,
Roma FBC and Alba

Rome

I T A L Y

Lazio 1900

SP Lazio
(1900–25)

Napoli 1926

Merger of Internaples
and Naples

Savoia 1908 1908

Naples

Foggia
1920

Avellino
1912

Salerno
Salernitana
1919

Bari 1928
Merger of FC Bari
and US Ideale
as US Bari (1928–45)

Lecce
1908

Cosmos 1979
Folgore Falciano
1972
         Juvenes
            1953
Libertas
1928   **Domagnano**
Tre   1966
Penne   **Calcio**
1956   **Faetano**
   SAN   1962
MARINO
         Tre
Fiorita **Fiori**
1967   1949

Cosenza
1914

Crotone
1923

Catanzaro
1929

Reggina
Calcio
1914

Palermo 1899
JS Palermo (1892–1942)
Palermo Juvem (1942–45)
SSC Palermo (1945–87)

Messina
1945

SICILY

Catania 1946
Merger of Virtus
and US Cantanese

Italy

ORIGINS AND GROWTH OF SOCCER

UNLIKE MUCH OF CONTINENTAL EUROPE, Italy had its own traditions of folk soccer – the Florentine *Calcio* and the Roman *Harpastum* – to draw upon when association soccer first arrived in the late 19th century. British influences combined with domestic interests to produce a flourishing soccer scene in Northern Italy around Genoa, Turin and Milan. English expatriate cricket clubs started Genoa and AC Milan, while the first organized game of soccer is said to have been arranged by Edorado Bosio of Turin, a businessman with extensive connections in Britain.

The first leagues

The early organization of Italian soccer reflected the divided geographical loyalties of the nation and the weakness of national institutions. The national Football Association was set up in 1898; it changed location four times before settling in Rome in the 1920s. It also faced challenges to its authority from the clubs and rival organizations. Regional leagues and championships were early to form, and remained so strong that, despite the creation of a national championship as early as 1898, it was a rather low-key and disorganized affair. With the advent of professionalism the national league finally became the dominant competition in 1930. Soccer continued to be dominated by teams from the industrial cities of the north, with only Rome and Naples able to sustain teams of sufficient weight to challenge them.

The national game

The popularity of Italian soccer with the public, politicians and business exceeded that of almost any other nation in the first half of the 20th century. Industrialists, like Pirelli (tyres and AC Milan) and Agnelli (cars and Juventus), were very active participants in the game. Italy won two of its three World Cups in the 1930s. In the postwar era Italian domestic soccer's sophistication, politicization and wealth continued to develop and expand, delivering from the early 1960s onwards an extraordinary catalogue of European club success.

*Vittorio Pozzo
(1886–1968)* was Italy's
first great coach. He was
active in the management
of Torino over two decades
and coach of the national
side that won the World
Cup in 1934 and 1938.

ITALY

Turin

SOCCER CENTER

MILAN MAY HAVE GLAMOUR AND STYLE, but when it comes to the hard grit of winning, Turin has no equal. Between them the city's two clubs, Torino and Juventus, have won over 30 Scudetti. In 1887, Eduardo Bosio went back to Turin after a trip to England and took a soccer with him. Soon after, clubs began to form: Internazionale Torino and FC Torinese were up and running and competing in the fledgling national championships. They fused in 1906 as Torino. Juventus was founded by students in 1897, and took its first title in 1905. The teams settled in the south of the city, their stadiums separated by a single road. The amateur era was quiet for both sides, but with the coming of professionalism Turin's economic and demographic weight really began to count. Juventus has been tied to the Agnelli family and Fiat for over 50 years; its support is strong among southern Italian immigrants to the city and also has a national and international dimension. Torino, by contrast, has claimed deeper and wider roots in the city itself and in its people, not least among Fiat's workforce.

Success and tragedy

Juve, *la Vecchia Signora* (the 'Old Lady') as the club is known, has an extraordinary record. In every decade since the 1920s it has won the domestic championship; it has won every European competition going; and along with the glory, the club has earned the distaste and envy of every other team in the country. Torino, by contrast, has had only one truly great era, that of Il Grand Torino when the team won four successive *Scudetti* from 1946 to 1949. Under coach Vittorio Pozzo, Il Grand Torino was led by the charismatic striker Valentino Mazzola. In May 1949, following a friendly match, the entire squad was killed in the Superga air crash (see box). This tragedy saw the heart torn from Torino and two decades of mid-table soccer followed. Only in 1976 was the club able to lay a few ghosts to rest when it won the championship once more under Gigi Radice. Since then a cycle of relegation and promotion has been Torino's fate. Both clubs moved to the Stadio delle Alpi on the northern outskirts of town after the 1990 World Cup. Unloved and sterile, it is barely ever half full, even for big games. Juventus has finally bought the stadium from the city council and is planning a complete redevelopment.

The scene after the aircrash on the mountain of Superga, on the outskirts of Turin, which killed all 31 passengers when a plane came down in mist and torrential rain on 4 May 1949.

THE SUPERGA AIRCRASH

On 4 May 1949, a Fiat G212 airliner left Lisbon with the Torino squad on board. They had been playing a friendly match against Benfica in honour of the great Portuguese player Franciso Ferriera. The plane carried 31 passengers, including 18 Torino squad members, two club directors, four other club staff and three journalists. In mist and torrential rain, the plane, heading for the Aeritalia airfield, was seen emerging from a bank of cloud and crashing into an embankment below the Superga Basilica, a church and monastic complex set on the hills rising to the east of the city. There were no survivors. Two days later, funerals were held at the Palazzo Madama. Half a million people lined the streets of the city centre to pay their last respects, led by the youth teams of Torino and Juventus in full kit.

Cars being tested on the roof of the Fiat factory in Turin in 1929. Despite its sponsorship of Juventus, the company's workforce is split in its support of the city's two big clubs.

STADIO DELLE ALPI

69,041

Clubs: Juventus, Torino
Built: 1990
Original Capacity: 71,000
Record Attendance: 71,010 Juventus v Internazionale, 28 Apr 1998
Significant Matches: 1990 World Cup: five matches including semi-final

STADIO COMMUNALE

Club: Currently Juventus' training ground. Torino is likely to play here in 2006
Built: 1933
Original Capacity: 55,000
Significant Matches: 1934 World Cup: two matches

ITALY

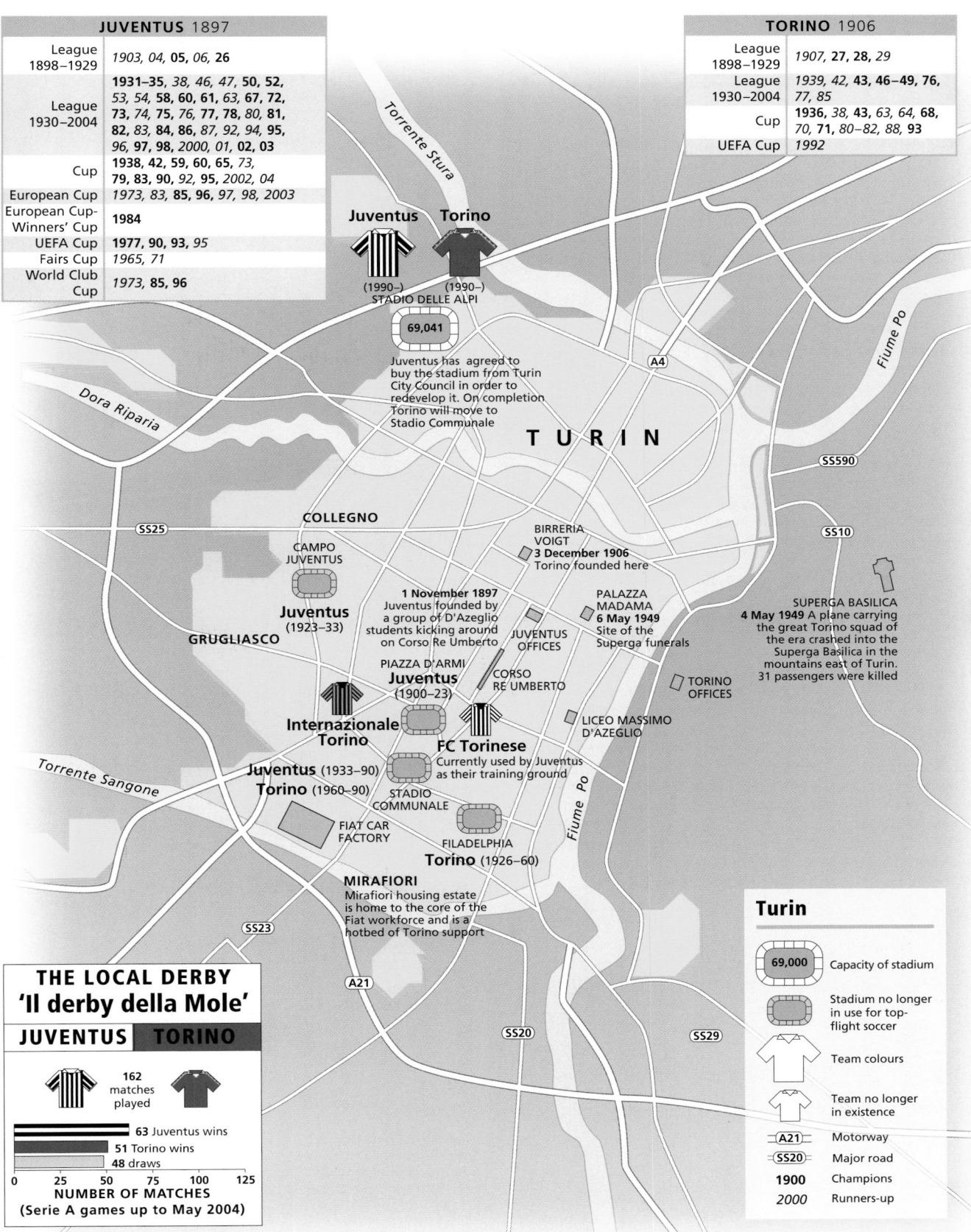

JUVENTUS 1897	
League 1898–1929	*1903, 04,* **05,** *06,* **26**
League 1930–2004	**1931–35,** *38,* **46, 47, 50, 52, 53,** *54,* **58, 60, 61, 63, 67, 72, 73, 74, 75, 76, 77, 78, 80, 81, 82, 83, 84, 86,** *87,* **92, 94, 95, 96, 97, 98, 2000, 01, 02, 03**
Cup	**1938, 42, 59, 60, 65,** *73,* **79, 83, 90,** *92,* **95, 2002, 04**
European Cup	*1973, 83,* **85,** *96, 97, 98, 2003*
European Cup-Winners' Cup	**1984**
UEFA Cup	**1977, 90, 93,** *95*
Fairs Cup	*1965, 71*
World Club Cup	*1973,* **85, 96**

TORINO 1906	
League 1898–1929	*1907,* **27, 28,** *29*
League 1930–2004	*1939, 42,* **43,** *46–49,* **76, 77,** *85*
Cup	**1936,** *38,* **43,** *63, 64,* **68,** *70,* **71,** *80–82,* **88,** *93*
UEFA Cup	*1992*

Juventus Torino

(1990–) (1990–)
STADIO DELLE ALPI

69,041

Juventus has agreed to buy the stadium from Turin City Council in order to redevelop it. On completion Torino will move to Stadio Communale

T U R I N

A4

Torrente Stura

Fiume Po

SS590

SS10

Dora Riparia

SS25

COLLEGNO

CAMPO JUVENTUS

Juventus
(1923–33)

GRUGLIASCO

1 November 1897
Juventus founded by a group of D'Azeglio students kicking around on Corso Re Umberto

PIAZZA D'ARMI

Juventus
(1900–23)

BIRRERIA VOIGT
3 December 1906
Torino founded here

JUVENTUS OFFICES

PALAZZA MADAMA
6 May 1949
Site of the Superga funerals

CORSO RE UMBERTO

TORINO OFFICES

SUPERGA BASILICA
4 May 1949 A plane carrying the great Torino squad of the era crashed into the Superga Basilica in the mountains east of Turin. 31 passengers were killed

LICEO MASSIMO D'AZEGLIO

Internazionale Torino

Juventus (1933–90)
Torino (1960–90)
STADIO COMMUNALE

FIAT CAR FACTORY

FC Torinese
Currently used by Juventus as their training ground

FILADELPHIA

Torino (1926–60)

MIRAFIORI
Mirafiori housing estate is home to the core of the Fiat workforce and is a hotbed of Torino support

Torrente Sangone

SS23

A21

SS20

SS29

ITALY

Turin

69,000	Capacity of stadium
	Stadium no longer in use for top-flight soccer
	Team colours
	Team no longer in existence
A21	Motorway
SS20	Major road
1900	Champions
2000	Runners-up

THE LOCAL DERBY
'Il derby della Mole'

JUVENTUS	TORINO

162 matches played

63 Juventus wins
51 Torino wins
48 draws

0   25   50   75   100   125
NUMBER OF MATCHES
(Serie A games up to May 2004)

Milan

SOCCER CENTER

THE MILAN SOCCER AND CRICKET CLUB was founded in 1899 by a mixture of English and Swiss expatriate businessmen led by the Englishman Alfred Edwards. Milan FC achieved early success, winning three national championships before 1907. In 1908, disaffected members of the club, resenting its Anglo dominance, split to form a new club called Internazionale. Rivalry between the two clubs has consumed the city ever since, although the social meaning of the conflict has changed. At first Inter attracted the elite and middle class, and Milan the working class, though over time this relationship seems to have shifted.

Class divide

Milan moved to the San Siro in 1926, financed by the millions of tyre magnate Piero Pirelli. Internazionale played in the Arena in the centre of town. With the arrival of Fascism, Inter's cosmopolitan leanings looked suspect, and the club was forced to merge with US Milanese and change its name to Ambrosiana-Inter. Despite its name, the team proved brilliant, with a forward line led by the great Giuseppe Meazza. In 1946, it joined its city rival at the San Siro. Milan's English connections made the team even more suspicious to the Fascist authorities and it was only after the Second World War that the club really flourished: four *Scudetti* in the 1950s, followed by two in the 1960s as well as two great European Cup victories. Inter took the European Cup twice (1964 and 65) under the charismatic Helenio Herrera who brought the playing style of *catenaccio* (see page 37) and strict squad discipline to the city, and helped encourage the first organized fan clubs, or *tifosi*, who would travel to Inter's away games in Europe.

In the 1980s and 1990s it was Milan that prospered. Money flooded into the club from the Berlusconi fortune and, under Arrigo Sacchi and Fabio Capello, Milan became the dominant force in European soccer. Inter has countered with the oil-based fortunes of Massimo Moratti (whose father had owned the club in the 1950s). Inter's spending in the transfer market has been phenomenal (including the purchase of Christian Vieri and Ronaldo for almost £50 million), but so far only one UEFA Cup trophy sits in the cabinet under the Moratti regime. Indeed the frustration finally got to him in the spring of 2003 and he resigned from the club presidency.

ITALY

MILAN 1899	
League 1898–1929	**1901**, *02*, **06, 07**
League 1930–2004	*1948, 50,* **51,** *52,* **55, 56, 57,** *59,* **61, 62,** *65,* **68,** *71–73,* **79, 88, 90, 91, 92–94, 96, 99, 2004**
Cup	*1942,* **67,** *68,* **71, 72, 73,** *75,* **77,** *85, 90, 98,* **2003**
European Cup	*1958,* **63, 69, 89, 90,** *93,* **94, 95, 2003**
European Cup-Winners' Cup	**1968, 73,** *74*
World Club Cup	*1963,* **69, 89, 90,** *93,* **94**

STADIO GIUSEPPE MEAZZA (SAN SIRO)

85,700

Clubs: Internazionale, Milan
Built: 1926
Original Capacity: 35,000
Rebuilt: 1955, 1990
Significant Matches: 1934 World Cup: three matches; 1990 World Cup: five matches; European Cup Finals: 1965, 70, 2001

INTERNAZIONALE 1908	
League 1898–1929	**1910, 20**
League 1930–2004	**1930,** *33–35,* **38, 40, 41, 49, 51, 53, 54,** *62,* **63,** *64,* **65, 66,** *67,* **70, 71, 80, 89,** *93,* **98, 2003**
Cup	**1939,** *59,* **65,** *77,* **78, 82,** *2000*
European Cup	**1964, 65,** *67,* **72**
UEFA Cup	**1991, 94,** *97,* **98**
World Club Cup	**1964, 65**

The Piazza del Duomo in the centre of the city is the traditional location of victory celebrations for fans of both Milan and Internazionale.

SS233

A8

SS33

A4

PERO

BAGGIO

CESANO BOSCONE

CÓRSICO

BUCCINASCO

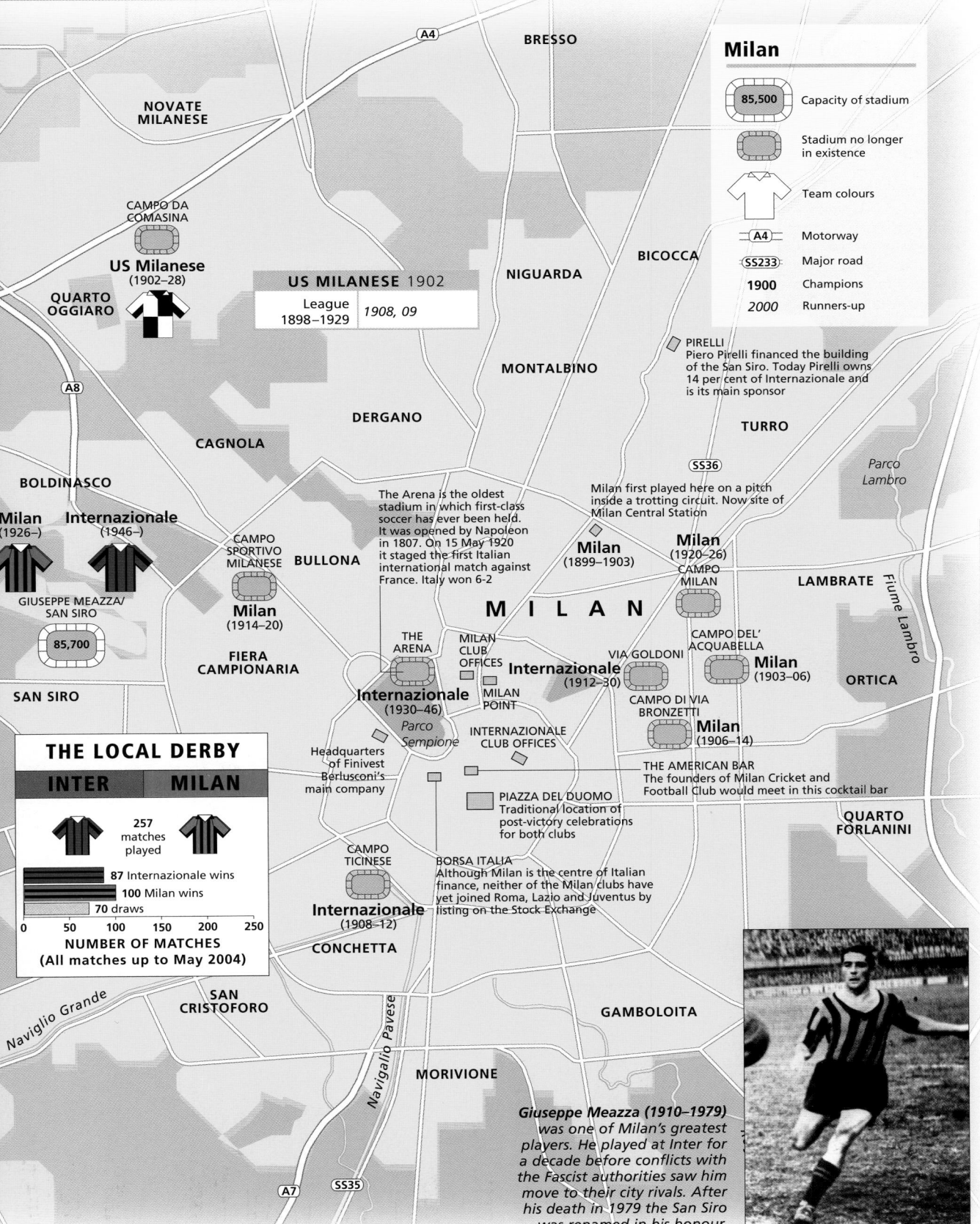

Milan

85,500	Capacity of stadium
	Stadium no longer in existence
	Team colours
A4	Motorway
SS233	Major road
1900	Champions
2000	Runners-up

BRESSO

NOVATE MILANESE

CAMPO DA COMASINA

US Milanese
(1902–28)

QUARTO OGGIARO

US MILANESE 1902

League 1898–1929	1908, 09

NIGUARDA

BICOCCA

MONTALBINO

PIRELLI
Piero Pirelli financed the building of the San Siro. Today Pirelli owns 14 per cent of Internazionale and is its main sponsor

DERGANO

TURRO

CAGNOLA

Parco Lambro

BOLDINASCO

Milan
(1926–)

Internazionale
(1946–)

CAMPO SPORTIVO MILANESE

BULLONA

The Arena is the oldest stadium in which first-class soccer has ever been held. It was opened by Napoleon in 1807. On 15 May 1920 it staged the first Italian international match against France. Italy won 6-2

Milan first played here on a pitch inside a trotting circuit. Now site of Milan Central Station

Milan
(1899–1903)

Milan
(1920–26)

CAMPO MILAN

LAMBRATE

GIUSEPPE MEAZZA/ SAN SIRO

85,700

Milan
(1914–20)

M I L A N

CAMPO DEL' ACQUABELLA

SS36

Fiume Lambro

FIERA CAMPIONARIA

THE ARENA

MILAN CLUB OFFICES

Internazionale
(1912–30)

VIA GOLDONI

Milan
(1903–06)

ORTICA

SAN SIRO

Internazionale
(1930–46)

MILAN POINT

Parco Sempione

CAMPO DI VIA BRONZETTI

Milan
(1906–14)

INTERNAZIONALE CLUB OFFICES

Headquarters of Finivest Berlusconi's main company

THE AMERICAN BAR
The founders of Milan Cricket and Football Club would meet in this cocktail bar

QUARTO FORLANINI

PIAZZA DEL DUOMO
Traditional location of post-victory celebrations for both clubs

THE LOCAL DERBY

INTER	MILAN

257 matches played

87 Internazionale wins

100 Milan wins

70 draws

0	50	100	150	200	250

NUMBER OF MATCHES
(All matches up to May 2004)

CAMPO TICINESE

Internazionale
(1908–12)

CONCHETTA

BORSA ITALIA
Although Milan is the centre of Italian finance, neither of the Milan clubs have yet joined Roma, Lazio and Juventus by listing on the Stock Exchange

GAMBOLOITA

Naviglio Grande

SAN CRISTOFORO

Naviglio Pavese

MORIVIONE

A7   SS35

Giuseppe Meazza (1910–1979) was one of Milan's greatest players. He played at Inter for a decade before conflicts with the Fascist authorities saw him move to their city rivals. After his death in 1979 the San Siro was renamed in his honour.

ITALY

Rome

SOCCER CENTER

LAZIO WAS FOUNDED IN 1900 by an Italian army officer, Luigi Bigarelli, and adopted Greek colours and secluded itself in the wealthy northern suburbs of the city. The team soon acquired the well-appointed Rondinella stadium to play in and Benito Mussolini as a fan. But Il Duce's plans for the capital of the new Roman Empire extended to its soccer stadium, and he moved Lazio to his monumental and bombastic Fascist Party stadium (the PNF) in the 1930s, and strutted around the city when Italy hosted and won the 1934 World Cup.

Lazio acquired a proper rival with the creation of Roma in 1927 from the fusion of four small clubs (Alba, Fortitudo, ProRoma and Roma FBC). Roma settled in the working-class streets of Testaccio, where it built the extraordinary all-wooden Campo Testaccio. The area still remains the club's spiritual heartland. Roma too was shipped out to the PNF until after the war, and both clubs moved again to the new Olympic stadium built across the Tiber in the north-east of the city in the early 1950s.

Investment pays off

Although prosperity and geographical mobility have fractured the old core areas of club support, Roma's fans are more working-class, left-wing and urban in origin, while Lazio has drawn on middle-class support in the city along with fans from across the Lazio region. Recently it has attracted more vociferous, right-wing *ultras* from the city's southern housing projects. These new fans first made their presence felt when Lazio won its first *Scudetto* in 1974, with a rough, tough squad schooled in the Estudiantes sides of the 1960s and inspired by Argentinian coach Juan Carlos Lorenzo.

Since the late 1990s, Rome has at last become the country's soccer capital. Under the presidencies of Sensi and Cragnotti, Roma and Lazio became the first Italian clubs to float on the stock exchange, and both have spent hugely to create cosmopolitan and powerful squads. Lazio's double in 1999 (managed by Sven Goran Eriksson), and Roma's first *Scudetto* for almost 20 years in 2001 (managed by Fabio Capello), have been the pay-off.

However, Rome's fall from soccer grace has been as fast as its ascent. Sergio Cragnotti has been forced to put Lazio on the market after suffering financial difficulties at his Cirio food company. The club's unsustainable wage bill has seen many of its stars sold on. Roma's finances are in equally bad shape, with regular visits to the club's offices by the Italian tax authorities and rumours, in spring 2003, of a Russian takeover at the club.

ITALY

This aerial shot of Rome was taken just before the 1960 Olympic Games and shows the Olimpico (centre left) and other smaller arenas which were also used for the Games.

OLIMPICO

82,566

Club: Lazio, Roma, Italy
Built: 1952
Original
Capacity: 80,000
Rebuilt: 1989–90
Significant Matches: 1990 World Cup: six matches
including Final; 1968
European Championships:
Final and replay;
1980 European Championships:
Final; European Cup
Finals: 1977, 84, 96

LAZIO 1900

League 1898–1929	*1913, 14, 23*
League 1930–2004	*1937,* **74, 95, 99, 2000**
Cup	**1958,** *61,* **98, 2000, 04**
European Cup-Winners' Cup	**1999**
UEFA Cup	*1998*

ROMA 1927

League 1930–2004	*1931, 36,* **42,** *81,* **83, 84, 86, 2001,** *02,* **04**
Cup	*1937, 41,* **64, 69, 80, 81, 84, 86, 91,** *93, 2003*
European Cup	*1984*
UEFA Cup	*1991*
Fairs Cup	**1961**

FLAMINIO

24,500

Club: Lodigiani (major games; others
are played at Tre Fontane in
the southern suburbs). Roma
and Lazio played here in 1989
during rebuilding of Olimpico
Built: 1953
Original Capacity: 55,000
Significant Matches: 1934 World Cup: Final (as
PNF); 1960 Rome Olympics

Roma (1953–)   **Lazio** (1953–)

FORO ITALICO

River Tiber

Italy

OLIMPICO   82,566

Italian national
team plays every
third home
match here

Lazio (1931–53)
Roma (1940–53)
PNF

RONDINELLA

Villa Ada

MONTE MARIO

DUE PINI

24,500

Alba

Lazio (1914–31)

PARIOLI
Area of traditional
Lazio support

PIAZZA D'ARMI

FLAMINIO

Roma FBC

Lodigiani

CAMPO DEI DAINI

Prior to its fusion
with Roma, Fortitudo
also played at the
Madonna del Riposo

Lazio (1900–06)
This was their
first ground

This stadium occupied
the site currently taken
by the Flaminio. Built
in 1911 as the Stadium
Nazionale, Mussolini
turned it into the Stadio
PNF (Partito Nazionale
Fascisti) in 1927.
It was renamed twice
after the war and
demolished in 1953

Villa Borghese

Fortitudo

PINCIO

SALARIO

Lazio (1906–13)

LAZIO'S OFFICES

LUDOVISI

CORRIERE DELLO
SPORT OFFICES

COLONNA

TREVI

VATICAN CITY

The Vatican City,
which runs its own
5-a-side league, has
recently considered
an application to
join FIFA

UFFICE DEL VICARIO
Roma founded in an
apartment here on
22 July 1927

R O M E

FIGC
Federazione
Italiana
Giuoco Calcio

PONTE PARIONE

REGOLA

FEDERAZIONE
ITALIANA
GIUOCO CALCIO

Villa Doria Pamphili

GIANICOLO

COLOSSEUM

TRASTEVERE

ProRoma

CAMPO DELLA PIRAMIDE

TESTACCIO

Roma (1929–40)
Between 1927–29
Roma played in the
south-eastern suburbs
at the Moto Velodromo

TESTACCIO
Traditional
Roma support

GARBATELA

OSTIENSE

Rome

24,500	Capacity of stadium
	Stadium no longer in existence
	Team colours
	Teams fused to form Roma in 1927
	Vatican City border
	Major road
1900	Champions
2000	Runners-up

THE LOCAL DERBY 'Il Derby Capitale'

LAZIO	ROMA

141 matches played

37 Lazio wins
51 Roma wins
53 draws

| 0 | 50 | 100 | 150 | 200 | 250 |

NUMBER OF MATCHES
(All Matches to May 2004)

ITALY

Italy

FANS AND OWNERS

UNTIL RECENTLY, nearly every club in Italy was privately owned by a single dominant figure on the board and linked to a large company with which it had made its fortune. This is still the case at the Milan giants, Internazionale and Milan, and the clubs of the smaller northern cities. But in the last few years the enormous demand for capital that success in Italian soccer requires has led Roma, Lazio and Juventus to the stock market for partial flotation, although in each case, a majority shareholder remains in charge. Equally enormous wage bills have swallowed the astronomical income of Italian clubs. Attendances have stagnated or fallen, TV income is jeopardized by the pirating of satellite channels on a massive scale, and the recent merger of Italy's main pay-per-view TV companies. Not surprisingly, the debt of many clubs has risen substantially. The crisis in Italian soccer is biting hardest at the clubs that have failed to deliver on ambitious expenditures: Napoli, Sampdoria and Genoa have all changed hands as owners' finances and patience have run out. Fiorentina was declared bankrupt and dissolved in 2002. The collapse of Lazio's and Parma's corporate backers has destabilized both clubs and Roma teeters on a precipice of debt.

Italy's lay religion

The huge, working-class crowds that gathered on a Sunday afternoon for Italian soccer always had an element of ritual and religion to them. In the 1970s, young Italian fans organized themselves into groups called *ultras* which specialized in the construction of vast banners, choreographed displays of colours, drumming, singing and chanting. The fierce localism of these groups means that no similar following for the national team exists. By 1983, symbolic contest turned to organized violence and the earlier left-wing bent of some *ultra* groups was replaced by the presence of the far right. In the 1990s, a new generation of *ultras* have emerged, older groups have fragmented, and increased policing has subdued the scene. However, since 2000 there has been a renewed spate of violence outside grounds and attacks by fans on poorly performing players and coaches.

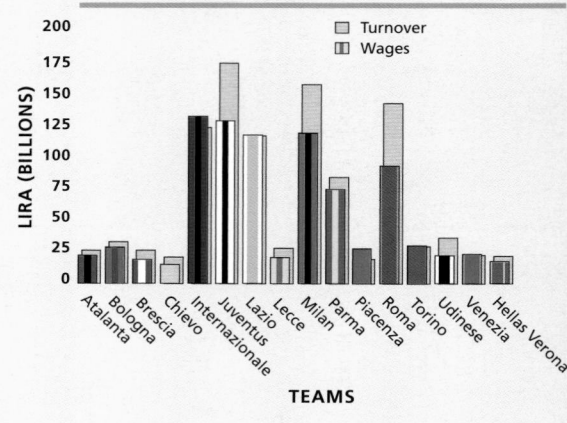

Club Wages and Turnover 2002

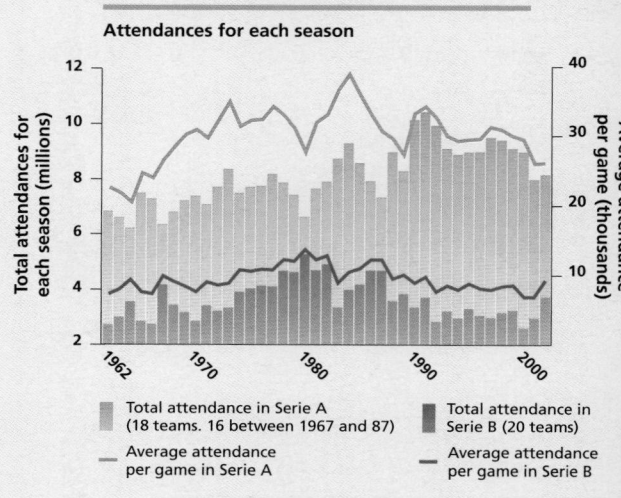

Italian Attendances

Attendances for each season

AS Roma's fans clash with police before its match against Juventus at Olympic stadium in Rome 1 December 2002.

Average Attendance

Average attendance for season 2003–04 (thousands)

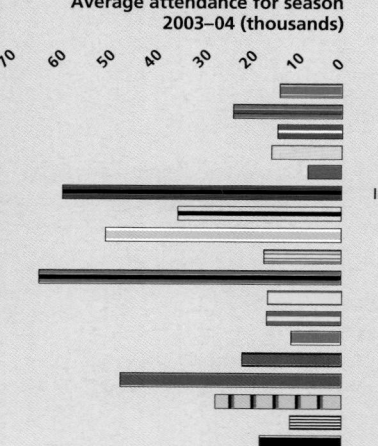

Capacity

Attendance as a percentage of capacity for season 2003–04 (capacity in brackets)

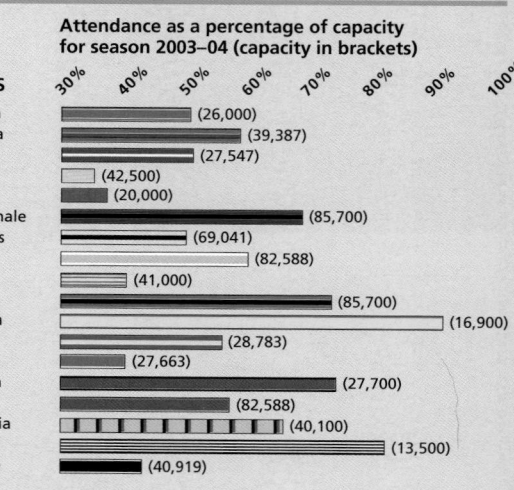

TEAMS: Ancona, Bologna (39,387), Brescia (27,547), Chievo (42,500), Empoli (20,000), Internazionale (85,700), Juventus (69,041), Lazio (82,588), Lecce (41,000), Milan (85,700), Modena (16,900), Parma (28,783), Perugia (27,663), Reggina (27,700), Roma (82,588), Sampdoria (40,100), Siena (13,500), Udinese (40,919)

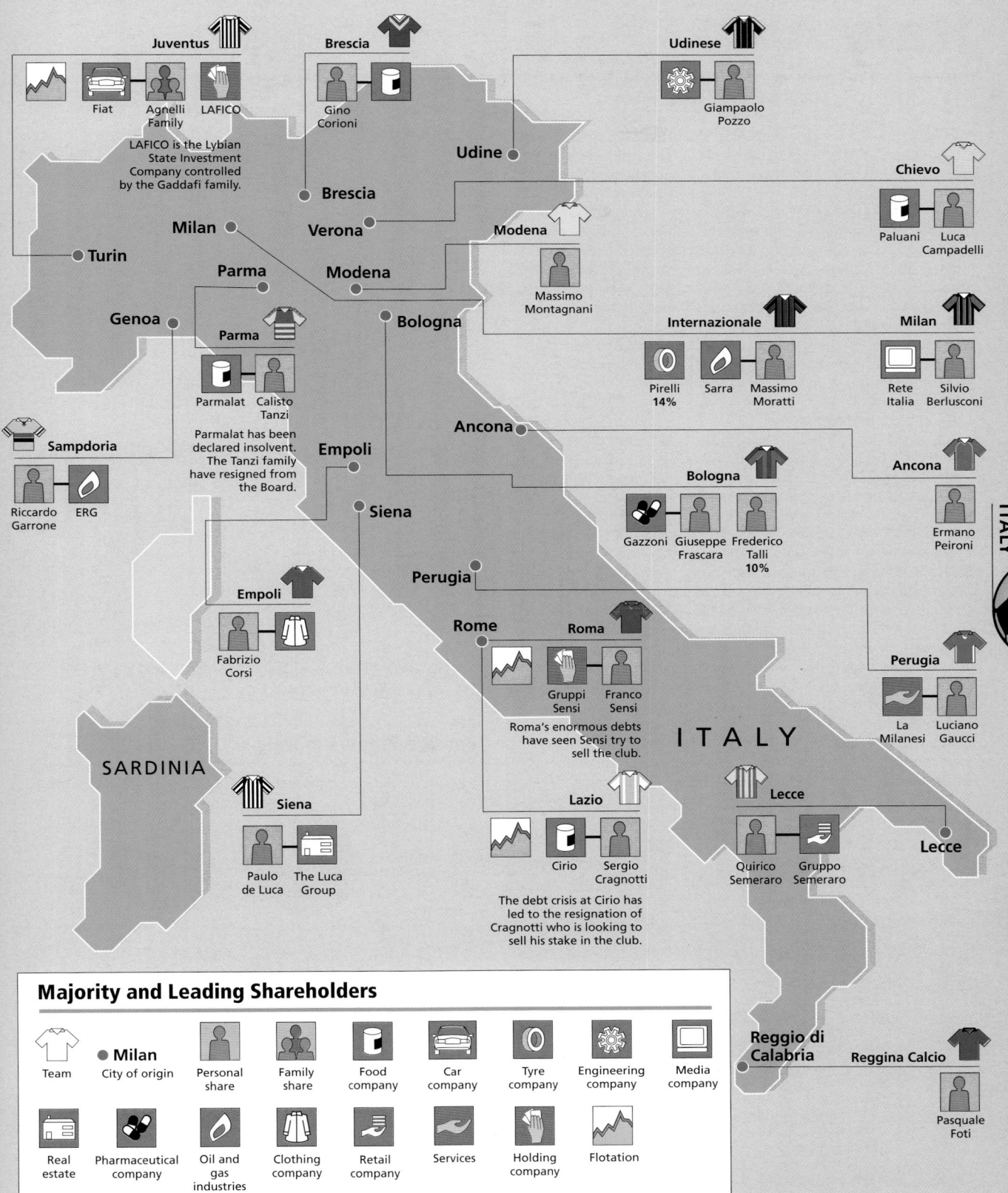

Juventus

Fiat — Agnelli Family — LAFICO

LAFICO is the Lybian State Investment Company controlled by the Gaddafi family.

Brescia

Gino Corioni

Udine

Brescia

Verona

Milan

Turin

Parma

Genoa

Parma

Parmalat — Calisto Tanzi

Parmalat has been declared insolvent. The Tanzi family have resigned from the Board.

Sampdoria

Riccardo Garrone — ERG

Empoli

Siena

Empoli

Fabrizio Corsi

Udinese

Giampaolo Pozzo

Chievo

Paluani — Luca Campadelli

Modena

Massimo Montagnani

Bologna

Internazionale

Pirelli **14%** — Sarra — Massimo Moratti

Milan

Rete Italia — Silvio Berlusconi

Ancona

Bologna

Gazzoni — Giuseppe Frascara — Frederico Talli **10%**

Ancona

Ermano Peironi

Perugia

Rome

Roma

Gruppi Sensi — Franco Sensi

Roma's enormous debts have seen Sensi try to sell the club.

Lazio

Cirio — Sergio Cragnotti

The debt crisis at Cirio has led to the resignation of Cragnotti who is looking to sell his stake in the club.

Perugia

La Milanesi — Luciano Gaucci

Lecce

Quirico Semeraro — Gruppo Semeraro

Lecce

ITALY

I T A L Y

SARDINIA

Siena

Paulo de Luca — The Luca Group

Reggio di Calabria

Reggina Calcio

Pasquale Foti

Majority and Leading Shareholders

Team	● Milan City of origin	Personal share	Family share	Food company	Car company	Tyre company	Engineering company	Media company
Real estate	Pharmaceutical company	Oil and gas industries	Clothing company	Retail company	Services	Holding company	Flotation	

Teams shown were members of Serie A 2003–04

Italy

PLAYERS AND MANAGERS

ITALIAN PLAYERS AND MANAGERS HAVE perhaps the most intensely pressurized and scrutinized soccer careers in the world. Italy's extraordinarily voracious and dedicated sporting press leaves no stone unturned in analyzing performance, rumour, gossip and behaviour. Of course, there are salaries and adulation to match, tied to an obsessive culture of training, discipline and, in many cases, the prescription of pre-match sex. In the 1990s, foreigners have come in increasing numbers into the Italian game, with many of the very best Germans, Dutch, Yugoslavs, Argentinians and Brazilians finding their way to Serie A. Similarly, foreign coaches have begun to find their way at the top of the Italian game. As a consequence, the capacity of Italian teams to absorb and deal with pressure and grind out results has been formidable.

The art of defence

What marks out Italian soccer culture from many others is that it is perhaps the only nation where defenders are not only regarded with a respect usually reserved for strikers, but that defending is considered an art form full of technical virtuosity and perfect timing that has no superior. Gianni Facchetti redefined the role of the modern sweeper and full-back at Internazionale in the 1960s, where man-marking left him free to build and join attacks and score freely. His modern descendents include Claudio Gentile, Gaetano Scirea, Franco Baresi, Giuseppe Bergomi, Paolo Maldini, and more recently Alessandro Nesta. Scirea in particular was noted for the grace rather than the viciousness of his tackling. That said, Italian strikers have proved their enduring worth in the guise of Giuseppe Meazza, Gianni Rivera, Paolo Rossi and Roberto Baggio. Nicknamed '*il condino divino*', or the divine ponytail, Baggio was the leading forward of his era, noted not only for his hair but also for his quiet Buddhism and ferocious goalscoring. Riots broke out in the streets of Florence when his transfer to Juventus was announced in 1990.

Top 20 International Caps

PLAYER	CAPS	GOALS	FIRST MATCH	LAST MATCH
Paolo Maldini*	126	7	1988	2003
Dino Zoff	112	0	1968	1983
Giacinto Fachetti	94	3	1963	1977
Franco Baresi	81	1	1982	1994
Giuseppe Bergomi	81	6	1982	1998
Marco Tardelli	81	6	1976	1985
Fabio Cannavaro*	80	0	1997	2004
Demitrio Albertini*	79	2	1991	2002
Gaetano Scirea	78	2	1975	1986
Giancarlo Antognoni	73	7	1974	1983
Antonio Cabrini	73	9	1978	1987
Claudio Gentile	71	1	1975	1984
Alessandro Mazzola	70	22	1963	1974
Tarcisio Burgnich	66	2	1963	1974
Alessandro Del Piero*	66	22	1995	2004
Francesco Graziani	64	23	1975	1983
Franco Causio	63	6	1972	1983
Roberto Donadoni	63	5	1986	1996
Alessandro Nesta*	62	0	1996	2004
Alessandro Altobelli	61	25	1980	1988

Top 10 International Goalscorers

PLAYER	GOALS	CAPS	FIRST MATCH	LAST MATCH
Luigi Riva	35	42	1965	1974
Giuseppe Meazza	33	53	1930	1939
Silvio Piola	30	34	1935	1952
Roberto Baggio*	27	55	1988	1999
Adolfo Baloncieri	25	47	1920	1930
Alessandro Altobelli	25	61	1980	1988
Francesco Graziani	23	64	1975	1983
Alessandro Del Piero*	22	66	1995	2004
Alessandro Mazzola	22	70	1963	1974
Christian Vieri*	22	43	1997	2004
Filipo Inzaghi*	21	47	1997	2004
Paolo Rossi	20	48	1977	1986
Roberto Bettega	19	42	1975	1983

* Indicates players still playing at least at club level.

Italy International Managers

DATES	NAME	GAMES	WON	DRAWN	LOST
1960	Gipo Viani	3	1	1	1
1960–62	Giovanni Ferrari	16	7	5	4
1962–66	Edmondo Fabbri	29	18	6	5
1966–67	Helenio Herrera	4	3	1	0
1967–74	Ferruccio Valcareggi	58	31	21	6
1974–77	Fulvio Bemardini	22	12	4	6
1977–86	Enzo Bearzot	104	51	28	25
1986–92	Azeglio Vicini	54	32	15	7
1992–96	Arrigo Sacchi	53	34	11	8
1996–98	Cesare Maldini	20	10	8	2
1998–2000	Dino Zoff	23	11	7	5
2000–04	Giovanni Trapattoni	46	25	14	7

All figures correct as of 28 June 2004.

Foreign Players in Italy (in top division squads)

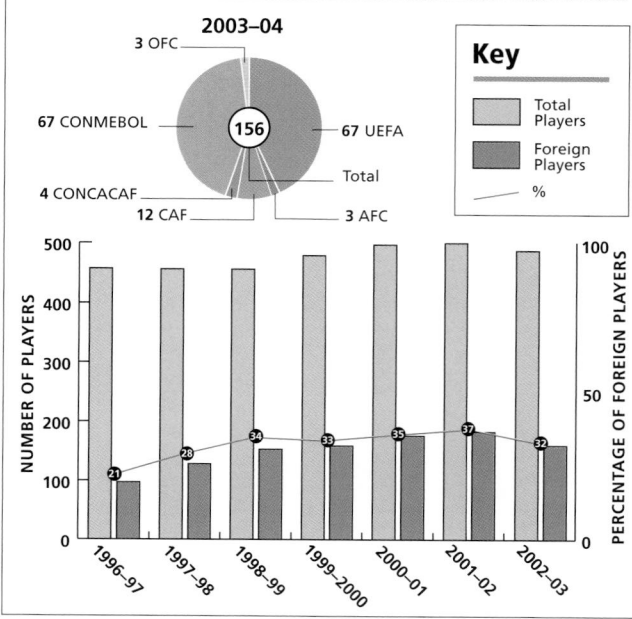

2003–04

3 OFC
67 CONMEBOL
156
67 UEFA
Total
4 CONCACAF
12 CAF
3 AFC

Key
Total Players
Foreign Players
%

Player of the Year

YEAR	PLAYER	CLUB
1976	Sala	Torino
1977	Sala	Torino
1978	Filippi	Vicenza
1979	Filippi	Napoli
1980	Castellini	Napoli
1981	Krol	Napoli
1982	Causio	Udinese
1983	Vierchowod	Roma
1984	Platini	Juventus
1985	Maradona	Napoli
1986	Renato	Torino
1987	Zenga	Internazionale
1988	Mancini	Sampdoria
1989	Brehme	Internazionale
1990	Baresi	Milan
1991	Mancini	Sampdoria
1992	Rijkaard	Milan
1993	Signori	Lazio
1994	Massaro	Milan
1995	Sousa	Juventus
1996	Chiesa	Sampdoria
1997	Pagliuca	Internazionale
1997	Peruzzi	Juventus
1997	Thuram	Parma
1998	Totti	Roma
1999	Almeyda	Lazio
2000	Frey	Verona
2001	R. Baggio	Brescia
2002	Vieri	Internazionale
2003	Nedved	Juventus

Awarded by *Guerin Sportivo* magazine.

Championship-Winning Managers

YEAR	MANAGER	CLUB
1976	Radice	Torino
1977	Trappatoni	Juventus
1978	Trappatoni	Juventus
1979	Liedholm [Swe]	Milan
1980	Bersellini	Internazionale
1981	Trappatoni	Juventus
1982	Trappatoni	Juventus
1983	Liedholm [Swe]	Roma
1984	Trappatoni	Juventus
1985	Bagnoli	Verona
1986	Trappatoni	Juventus
1987	Bianchi	Napoli
1988	Sacchi	Milan
1989	Trappatoni	Internazionale
1990	Bigon	Napoli
1991	Boskov [Yugo]	Sampdoria
1992	Capello	Milan
1993	Capello	Milan
1994	Capello	Milan
1995	Lippi	Juventus
1996	Capello	Milan
1997	Lippi	Juventus
1998	Lippi	Juventus
1999	Zaccheroni	Milan
2000	Ericksson [Swe]	Lazio
2001	Capello	Roma
2002	Lippi	Juventus
2003	Lippi	Juventus
2004	Ancelotti	Milan

Marco Tardelli turns in triumph after scoring for Italy in the 1982 World Cup Final against West Germany. Tardelli is one of only a select few players to have won every major domestic European honour, as well as a World Cup winner's medal.

Top Goalscorers 1929–2004

SEASON	PLAYER	CLUB	GOALS
1929–30	Meazza	Internazionale	31
1930–31	Volk	Roma	29
1931–32	Petrone	Fiorentina	25
1931–32	Schiavio	Bologna	25
1932–33	Borel II	Juventus	29
1933–34	Borel II	Juventus	32
1934–35	Guaita	Roma	28
1935–36	Meazza	Internazionale	25
1936–37	Piola	Lazio	21
1937–38	Meazza	Internazionale	20
1938–39	Boffi	Milan	19
1938–39	Puricelli	Bologna	19
1939–40	Boffi	Milan	24
1940–41	Puricelli	Bologna	22
1941–42	Boffi	Milan	22
1942–43	Piola	Lazio	21
1943–45	*no competition*		
1945–46	Castiglione	Torino	13
1946–47	V. Mazzola	Torino	29
1947–48	Boniperti	Juventus	27
1948–49	Nyers	Internazionale	26
1949–50	Nordahl	Milan	35
1950–51	Nordahl	Milan	34
1951–52	J. Hansen	Juventus	30
1952–53	Nordahl	Milan	26
1953–54	Nordahl	Milan	23
1954–55	Nordahl	Milan	27
1955–56	Pivatelli	Bologna	29
1956–57	Da Costa	Roma	22
1957–58	Charles	Juventus	28
1958–59	Angelillo	Internazionale	33
1959–60	Sivori	Juventus	27
1960–61	Brighenti	Sampdoria	27
1961–62	Altafini	Milan	22
1961–62	Milani	Fiorentina	22
1962–63	Manfredini	Roma	19
1962–63	Nielsen	Bologna	19
1963–64	Nielsen	Bologna	21
1964–65	A. Mazzola	Internazionale	17
1964–65	Orlando	Fiorentina	17
1965–66	Vinicio	Vicenza	25
1966–67	Riva	Cagliari	18
1967–68	Prati	Milan	15
1968–69	Riva	Cagliari	20
1969–70	Riva	Cagliari	21
1970–71	Boninsegna	Inter	24
1971–72	Boninsegna	Internazionale	22
1972–73	P. Pulici	Torino	17
1972–73	Rivera	Milan	17
1972–73	I. Savoldi	Bologna	17
1973–74	Chignaglia	Lazio	24
1974–75	P. Pulici	Torino	18

Top Goalscorers (*continued*)

SEASON	PLAYER	CLUB	GOALS
1975–76	P. Pulici	Torino	21
1976–77	Graziani	Torino	21
1977–78	P. Rossi	Vicenza	24
1978–79	Giordano	Lazio	19
1979–80	Bettega	Juventus	16
1980–81	Pruzzo	Roma	18
1981–82	Pruzzo	Roma	15
1982–83	Platini	Juventus	16
1983–84	Platini	Juventus	20
1984–85	Platini	Juventus	18
1985–86	Pruzzo	Roma	19
1986–87	Virdis	Milan	17
1987–88	Maradona	Napoli	15
1988–89	Serena	Internazionale	22
1989–90	van Basten	Milan	19
1990–91	Vialli	Sampdoria	17
1991–92	van Basten	Milan	25
1992–93	Signori	Lazio	26
1993–94	Signori	Lazio	23
1994–95	Batistuta	Fiorentina	26
1995–96	Signori	Lazio	24
1995–96	Protti	Bari	24
1996–97	Inzaghi	Atalanta	24
1997–98	Bierhoff	Udinese	27
1998–99	Amoroso	Udinese	22
1999–2000	Schevchenko	Milan	24
2000–01	Crespo	Lazio	26
2001–02	Hubner	Piacenza	24
2001–02	Trezeguet	Juventus	24
2002–03	Vieri	Internazionale	24
2003–04	Shevchenko	Milan	24

Five championships in *Italy, and one in Spain with Real Madrid in 1997, have made Fabio Capello one of Europe's most sought-after managers.*

ITALY

Italy

SERIE A 1984–2003

THE 1980s BEGAN IN Serie A as the 1970s had ended: with Juventus, under Giovanni Trapattoni, fielding the core of the Italian national squads for the 1978 and 1982 World Cups, playing with an iron defence and spring-loaded counterattacks, and winning the *Scudetto*. As foreigners were allowed back into the Italian game, Juventus scooped up Liam Brady and the sublime Michel Platini, winning the *Scudetto* again in 1984 and 86. But between these triumphs the title went to smaller, battling sides. Roma won in 1983 under Swede Nils Liedholm and the inspirational Brazilian Falcão. Hellas Verona, under Osvaldo Bagnoli, was promoted from Serie B in 1982 with a core of good Italian players. The team added foreigners Elkjaer and Briegel, pushed hard and took its first and only *Scudetto* in 1985. A burst of money and stars followed, only to see the club disappear from Serie A for most of the 1990s.

Off the field, the legal and economic framework of Italian soccer was beginning to change, and 1981 saw the introduction of contract freedom for players and the first bidding war for TV rights between the state-owned RAI and Silvio Berlusconi's private channels. RAI won the first round but the steady ratcheting up of the value of TV rights had begun: simultaneously, transfer and wages costs began their inexorable rise.

When Trapattoni and Platini left Juventus in 1986, a power vacuum opened in Serie A and the next five years saw four clubs take the title. First off the mark was Napoli. Under president Ferlaino Corrado, Napoli signed Diego Maradona from Barcelona for a record-breaking fee of £5 million. When the club couldn't find the cash to pay, an appeal for donations saw fans queuing up at the San Paolo stadium to contribute. Coming off his extraordinary performance at the 1986 World Cup, Maradona and coach Ottavio Bianchi took Napoli to its first *Scudetto* (the most southerly in the league's history) and a second three years later in 1990, although accusations of playacting in a crucial game at Atalanta have tarnished the triumph. Maradona's departure saw the side in steady decline until its relegation in 1998.

Berlusconi arrives

Milan had been a shadow of the team's former self, relegated in 1981 after accusations of match-fixing against its president Felice Colombo; the club bounced back only to be relegated again in 1983. In 1986, TV and property magnate Silvio Berlusconi bought the club and its debts, and began turning Milan into a serious business. Installing Arrigo Sacchi as manager, Milan combined a skilled but tough back four (Baresi, Maldini, Tassoti and Costacurta) with Saachi's aggressive pressing game in midfield. The team took the title in 1988 and, adding the star quality of Dutch imports Gullit, van Basten and Rijkaard, went on to take two European Cups. Titles also went to the old money at Internazionale in 1989, and the new money at Sampdoria in 1990. Genoa's second team finally acquired some serious

Lazio President Sergio Cragnotti celebrates with his team after winning the league championship in 2000.

*AS Roma's **Vincenzo Montella** celebrates after scoring against Parma during the team's final match of the 2000–01 season. Roma's 3-1 victory saw them claim its first Scudetto since 1984.*

Growth of Turnover and Wages

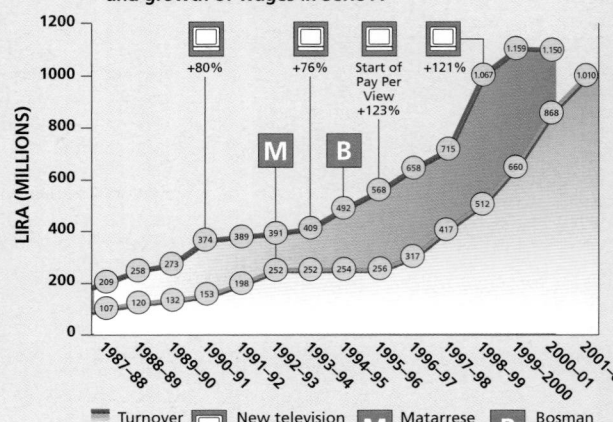

Relationship between growth of turnover and growth of wages in Serie A

+80%   +76%   Start of Pay Per View +123%   +121%

Turnover	New television contract	M Matarrese reform*
Wages		B Bosman ruling

* Matarrese reform allowed clubs to sign as many players with EU passports as they wanted plus two non-EU passport holders

backing in the form of oil magnate Paolo Mantovani, who astutely built a team around Roberto Mancini and Gianluca Vialli.

The avalanche of TV money and increased attendances that followed the success of Italia '90 saw the old order reassert itself. At Milan, Sacchi had given way to his junior Fabio Capello and the Dutch masters to a new generation of foreign stars (Desailly, Weah, Boban and Savicevic). They duly delivered four out of the next five titles, including an amazing run of 58 unbeaten matches (1991–93) and an entire season (1991–92) undefeated in Serie A. Juventus ended almost a decade without titles, winning under Marcello Lippi in 1995 and again in 1997 and 98. Lippi's squad included Zidane, Davids and Del Piero.

Hysterical spending

Challenges to the big two came from Internazionale, whose hysterical spending in the transfer market, and its turnover of managers, has been second to none. Parma and Fiorentina have also spent big, but cup and European success have not been matched by success in the gruelling league battle. Fiorentina has since gone bankrupt and the collapse of Parma's owners Parmalat may see them do the same. Atalanta, Udinese and Bologna have all established themselves as regular mid-table stayers. The presence of clubs from the south has steadily diminished and only Lecce and Bari have been able to sustain more than a season in the top flight.

The Milan-Juventus monopoly was finally broken by the capital's two big clubs, Lazio and Roma in 2000 and 2001. But the financial bubble burst in 2002 as clubs' income was eaten up by ever increasing salaries and accumulating debt. In 2002 and 2003 there was a return to form by the old guard with *Scudettos* for Juventus and Milan.

Italian League Income (in million lire)

SEASON	1997–98	1998–99	1999–2000	2000–01
Revenue	650	714	1059	1151
Costs	872	1049	1465	1861
Gross profit	-222	-335	-406	-710
Net profit	-38	-11	35	-133

Total for all Serie A clubs

La Vecchia Signora, *the 'Old Lady': after a barren spell in the early 1990s, Juventus has come back and has finished in the top two in all but one season since 1994.*

Champions' Winning Margin 1993–2003

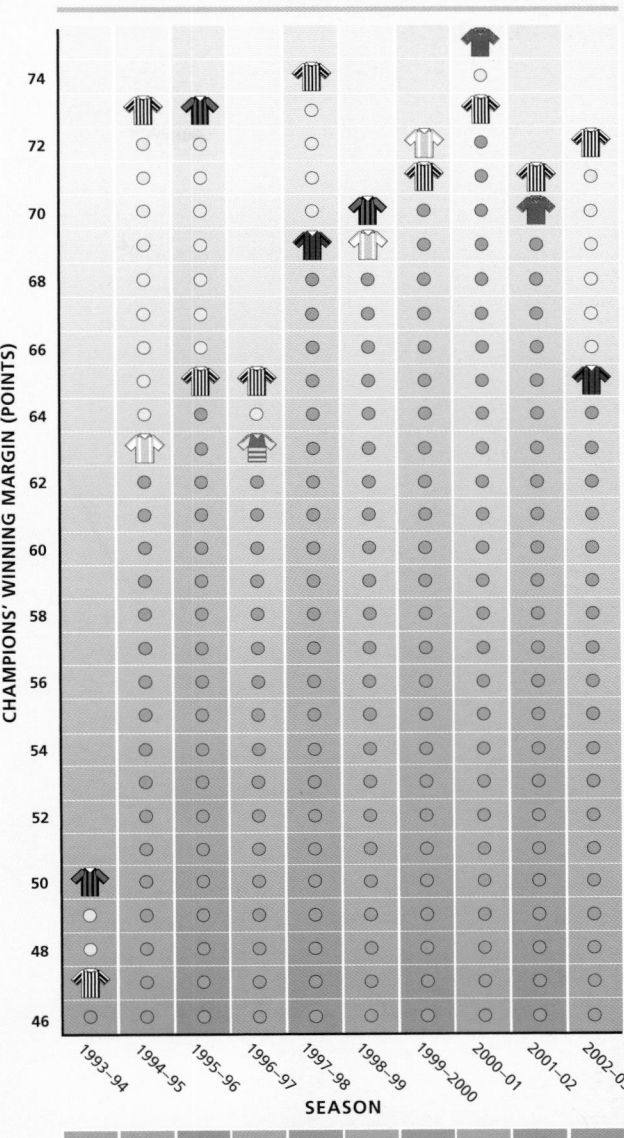

CHAMPIONS' WINNING MARGIN (POINTS)

SEASON

1993–94 · 1994–95 · 1995–96 · 1996–97 · 1997–98 · 1998–99 · 1999–2000 · 2000–01 · 2001–02 · 2002–03

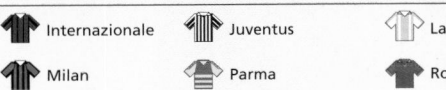

Total games played by each team
(2 points awarded for a win until 1995, when 3 points awarded)

Internazionale　　Juventus　　Lazio

Milan　　Parma　　Roma

Sources of Income 2001

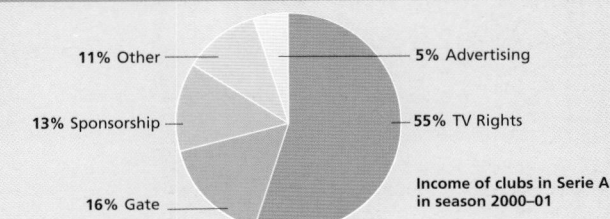

11% Other — 5% Advertising

13% Sponsorship — 55% TV Rights

16% Gate

Income of clubs in Serie A in season 2000–01

ITALY

ITALY

Key to League Positions Table

- ▇ League champions
- ▤ Season of promotion to league
- ▩ Season of relegation from league
- ▨ Other teams playing in league
- | 5 | Final position in league

Gianluca Vialli helped Sampdoria to the very top of Italian soccer in the early 1990s. A decade later Vialli was sacked by Watford and Sampdoria had a spell in Serie B.

Fabio Capello, Scudetto *winner with both Milan and Roma, works on his worry lines.*

Italian League Positions 1984–2003

TEAM	1984-85	1985-86	1986-87	1987-88	1988-89	1989-90	1990-91	1991-92	1992-93	1993-94	1994-95	1995-96	1996-97	1997-98	1998-99	1999-2000	2000-01	2001-02	2002-03
Ancona								17											
Ascoli Calcio	14		12	12	12	18		18											
Atalanta	10	8	15		6	7	10	11	7	17		13	10	16			7	9	14*
Avellino	13	12	8	15															
Bari		15			10	13	15				12	15		11	10	14	18		
Bologna			14		14	8	18						7	8	9	11	10	7	11
Brescia									14		18			15			8	13	9
Cagliari							14	13	6	12	9	10	15		12	17			
Cesena				9	13	14	17												
Chievo																		5	7
Como Calcio	11	9	9	11	18														17
Cremonese	16		13		17		17			10	13	17							
Empoli			16										12	18					13
Fiorentina	9	4	10	8	7	12	12	12	16		10	4	9	5	3	7	9	17	
Foggia									9	11	9	16							
Genoa							11	4	14	13	11	14							
Internazionale	3	6	3	5	1	3	3	8	2	13	6	7	3	2	8	4	5	3	2
Juventus	6	1	2	6	4	4	7	2	4	2	1	2	1	1	6	2	2	1	1
Lazio	15				10	9	11	10	5	4	2	3	4	7	2	1	3	6	4
Lecce		16		9	13	15					18			17		13	13	16	
Milan	5	7	5	1	3	2	2	1	1	1	4	1	11	10	1	3	6	4	3
Modena																			12
Napoli	8	3	1	2	2	1	8	4	11	6	7	12	13	18		17			
Padova											15	18							
Parma							6	7	3	5	3	6	2	6	4	5	4	10	5
Perugia													16		14	10	11	8	10
Pescara			14	16				18											
Piacenza											15		14	14	13	13	18	12	16
Pisa		14		13	17		16												
Reggiana										14	17		18						
Reggina Calcio																12	14		15*
Roma	7	2	7	3	8	6	9	5	10	7	5	5	12	4	5	6	1	2	8
Salernitana															15				
Sampdoria	4	11	6	4	5	5	1	6	7	3	8	8	6	9	16				
Siena																			
Torino	2	5	11	7	15		5	3	9	8	11	16			15			11	18
Udinese	12	13	16		15				14	16		11	5	3	7	8	12	14	6
Venezia															11	16		18	
Hellas Verona	1	10	4	10	11	16		16						17		9	15	15	
Vicenza												9	8	14	17		16		

* Reggina beat Atalanta in a 2-legged relegation play-off

Internazionale
1989, *93,*
98, **2003**

Milan
1988, *90,*
91, **92–94,**
96, *99*

Torino
1985

Piacenza

Juventus
1986, *87,*
92, *94,* **95,**
96, *97,* **98,**
2000, *01,*
02, **03**

Parma
1997

Sampdoria
1991

Genoa

Reggiana

Roma
1986,
2001, *02*

Lazio
1995, *99,*
2000

Cagliari

Como Calcio

Atalanta

Cremonese

Hellas Verona
1985

Chievo

Brescia

Vicenza

Udinese

Modena

Padova

Bologna

Cesena

Fiorentina

Empoli

Ascoli Calcio

Pisa

Siena

Perugia

Pescara

Ancona

Avellino

Foggia

Bari

Napoli
1987, *88,*
89, **90**

Salernitana

Lecce

Reggina Calcio

ITALY

Como
Bergamo
Milan
Cremona
Verona
Vicenza
Venice
Padua
Piacenza
Parma
Reggio Emilia
Modena
Bologna
Turin
Genoa
Brescia
Udine
Cesena
Pisa
Florence
Empoli
Siena
Ascoli Piceno
Perugia
Pescara
Ancona
Rome
Avellino
Naples
Salerno
Foggia
Bari
Lecce
Reggio Calabria

SARDINIA

SICILY

Cagliari

Serie A

| Lazio | Team name |

League champions/
runners-up

1988,
99 — Champions in bold
Runners-up in italics

Other teams
in Serie A

● **Rome** — City of origin

Italy

FEDERAZIONE ITALIANA GIUOCO CALCIO

Federazione Italiana Giuoco Calcio
Founded: 1898
Joined FIFA: 1905
Joined UEFA: 1954

REGULAR COMPETITIVE SOCCER LEAGUES had been established in Italy in the 1890s, and the national championship was created in 1898. However, like most things national in Italy, it was in reality rather fragmented and regional. Until 1910 the national component of the championship consisted of various play-off rounds between champions from the north, centre and south of the country and it was only in 1910, and for one season, that a single national league format was used. Indeed, the regional component grew so large that there were 18 separate regional leagues of wildly different standards.

With the advent of professionalism, a single national league was re-established in 1930, and this formed the basis of today's Serie A, the top national division. The title is known as *Lo Scudetto*, and refers to the tricolor shield that the previous year's champions are entitled to wear on their shirts. During the 1980s and 90s Serie A was regarded by many as the most exciting league in Europe.

The Copa Italia, a national cup competition, is a rather more low-key affair, played first in 1922 and again for a few years in the 1930s before being re-established in 1958 to provide an Italian entrant for the Cup-Winners' Cup. The bottom clubs in Serie A do not join until the second round, and the top eight join in the third round.

Soccer is a team game and one player does not always make a difference. However, Diego Maradona inspired Napoli to two Italian championships and UEFA Cup glory during his seven-year stay.

Italian Amateur League Record 1898–1929

SEASON	CHAMPIONS	RUNNERS-UP
1898	Genoa	Internazionale Torino
1899	Genoa	Internazionale Torino
1900	Genoa	FC Torinese
1901	Milan	Genoa
1902	Genoa	Milan
1903	Genoa	Juventus
1904	Genoa	Juventus
1905	Juventus	Genoa
1906	Milan	Juventus
1907	Milan	Torino
1908	Pro Vercelli	US Milanese
1909	Pro Vercelli	US Milanese
1910	Internazionale	Pro Vercelli
1911	Pro Vercelli	Vicenza
1912	Pro Vercelli	Vicenza
1913	Pro Vercelli	Lazio
1914	Casale	Lazio
1915	Genoa*	
1916–19	no championship	
1920	Internazionale	Livorno
1921	Pro Vercelli	Pisa
1922	Novese	Sampierdarenese
1922	Pro Vercelli**	Fortitudo
1923	Genoa	Lazio
1924	Genoa	Savoia
1925	Bologna	Alba
1926	Juventus	Alba
1927	Torino†	Bologna
1928	Torino	Genoa
1929	Bologna	Torino

* Genoa awarded title after league suspended at start of First World War.
** CCI organized championship.
† Torino's title was revoked because of alleged payments to a Juventus player before its match which Torino won 2-1.

Italian Professional League Record 1930–2004

SEASON	CHAMPIONS	RUNNERS-UP
1930	Ambrosiana Inter	Genoa
1931	Juventus	Roma
1932	Juventus	Bologna
1933	Juventus	Ambrosiana Inter
1934	Juventus	Ambrosiana Inter
1935	Juventus	Ambrosiana Inter
1936	Bologna	Roma
1937	Bologna	Lazio
1938	Ambrosiana Inter	Juventus
1939	Bologna	Torino
1940	Ambrosiana Inter	Bologna
1941	Bologna	Ambrosiana Inter
1942	Roma	Torino
1943	Torino	Livorno
1944–45	no championship	
1946	Torino	Juventus
1947	Torino	Juventus
1948	Torino	Milan
1949	Torino	Internazionale
1950	Juventus	Milan
1951	Milan	Internazionale
1952	Juventus	Milan
1953	Internazionale	Juventus
1954	Internazionale	Juventus
1955	Milan	Udinese
1956	Fiorentina	Milan

Italian Professional League Record (*continued*)

SEASON	CHAMPIONS	RUNNERS-UP
1957	Milan	Fiorentina
1958	Juventus	Fiorentina
1959	Milan	Fiorentina
1960	Juventus	Fiorentina
1961	Juventus	Milan
1962	Milan	Internazionale
1963	Internazionale	Juventus
1964	Bologna	Internazionale
1965	Internazionale	Milan
1966	Internazionale	Bologna
1967	Juventus	Internazionale
1968	Milan	Napoli
1969	Fiorentina	Cagliari
1970	Cagliari	Internazionale
1971	Internazionale	Milan
1972	Juventus	Milan
1973	Juventus	Milan
1974	Lazio	Juventus
1975	Juventus	Napoli
1976	Torino	Juventus
1977	Juventus	Torino
1978	Juventus	Vicenza
1979	Milan	Perugia
1980	Internazionale	Juventus
1981	Juventus	Roma
1982	Juventus	Fiorentina
1983	Roma	Juventus
1984	Juventus	Roma
1985	Verona	Torino
1986	Juventus	Roma
1987	Napoli	Juventus
1988	Milan	Napoli
1989	Internazionale	Napoli
1990	Napoli	Milan
1991	Sampdoria	Milan
1992	Milan	Juventus
1993	Milan	Internazionale
1994	Milan	Juventus
1995	Juventus	Lazio
1996	Milan	Juventus
1997	Juventus	Parma
1998	Juventus	Internazionale
1999	Milan	Lazio
2000	Lazio	Juventus
2001	Roma	Juventus
2002	Juventus	Roma
2003	Juventus	Internazionale
2004	Milan	Roma

Italian League Summary

TEAM	TOTALS	CHAMPIONS & RUNNERS-UP (BOLD) (*ITALICS*)
Juventus	27, 19	*1903, 04,* **05, 06, 26, 31–35, 38, 46, 47, 50, 52, 53, 54, 58, 60, 61,** *63,* **67,** *72, 73, 74, 75, 76, 77, 78,* **80, 81, 82, 83, 84,** *86,* **87,** *92,* **94, 95, 96, 97,** *99,* **2000,** *01,* **02,** *03*
Milan	17, 12	**1901,** *02,* **06,** *07, 48,* **50, 51, 52, 55, 56, 57, 59, 61, 62,** *65,* **68,** *71–73,* **79,** *88,* **90,** *91,* **92–94, 96, 99, 2004**
Internazionale (includes Ambrosiana Inter)	13, 13	**1910, 20, 30,** *33–35,* **38, 40,** *41, 49,* **51,** *53, 54,* **62, 63,** *64,* **65, 66,** *67, 70,* **71, 80, 89,** *93, 98, 2003*
Genoa	9, 4	**1898–1900,** *01,* **02–04,** *05,* **15,** *23, 24, 28, 30*
Torino	8, 6	*1907,* **27, 28,** *29, 39,* **42, 43, 46–49,** *76,* **77,** *85*
Bologna	7, 4	**1925,** *27,* **29,** *32,* **36, 37, 39, 40, 41,** *64, 66*

Italian League Summary (*continued*)

TEAM	TOTALS	CHAMPIONS & RUNNERS-UP (BOLD) (*ITALICS*)
Pro Vercelli	7, 1	**1908, 09, 10,** *11*–**13, 21,** *22*
Roma	3, 7	*1931, 36,* **42,** *81,* **83,** *84,* **86, 2001,** *02, 04*
Lazio	2, 6	*1913, 14, 23, 37,* **74,** *95, 99,* **2000**
Fiorentina	2, 5	**1956,** *57–60,* **69,** *82*
Napoli	2, 4	*1968, 75,* **87,** *88, 89,* **90**
Cagliari	1, 1	**1969,** *70*
Casale	1, 0	**1914**
Novese	1, 0	**1922**
Sampdoria	1, 0	**1991**
Verona	1, 0	**1985**
Vicenza	0, 3	*1911, 12, 78*
Alba	0, 2	*1925, 26*
Internazionale Torino	0, 2	*1898, 99*
Livorno	0, 2	*1920, 43*
US Milanese	0, 2	*1908, 09*
FC Torinese	0, 1	*1900*
Fortitudo	0, 1	*1922*
Parma	0, 1	*1997*
Perugia	0, 1	*1979*
Pisa	0, 1	*1921*
Sampierdarenese	0, 1	*1922*
Savoia	0, 1	*1924*
Udinese	0, 1	*1955*

Italian Cup Record 1922–2004

YEAR	WINNERS	SCORE	RUNNERS-UP
1922	Vado	1-0 (aet)	Udinese
1923–35		*no competition*	
1936	Torino	5-1	Alessandria
1937	Genoa	1-0	Roma
1938	Juventus	3-1, 2-1 (2 legs)	Torino
1939	Internazionale	2-1	Novara
1940	Fiorentina	1-0	Genoa
1941	Venezia	3-3 (aet), (replay) 1-0	Roma
1942	Juventus	1-1 (aet), (replay) 4-1	Milan
1943	Torino	4-0	Venezia
1944–57		*no competition*	
1958	Lazio	1-0	Fiorentina
1959	Juventus	4-1	Internazionale
1960	Juventus	3-2 (aet)	Fiorentina
1961	Fiorentina	2-0	Lazio
1962	Napoli	2-1	Spal
1963	Atalanta	3-1	Torino
1964	Roma	0-0 (aet), (replay) 1-0	Torino
1965	Juventus	1-0	Internazionale
1966	Fiorentina	2-1 (aet)	Catanzaro
1967	Milan	1-0	Padova
1968	Torino	(mini-league format)	Milan
1969	Roma	(mini-league format)	Cagliari
1970	Bologna	(mini-league format)	Torino
1971	Torino	(mini-league format)	Milan
1972	Milan	2-0	Napoli
1973	Milan	1-1 (5-2 pens)	Juventus
1974	Bologna	0-0 (5-4 pens)	Palermo
1975	Fiorentina	3-2	Milan
1976	Napoli	4-0	Verona
1977	Milan	2-0	Internazionale
1978	Internazionale	2-1	Napoli
1979	Juventus	2-1 (aet)	Palermo
1980	Roma	0-0 (3-2 pens)	Torino
1981	Roma	1-1, (replay) 1-1 (5-3 pens)	Torino

Italian Cup Record (*continued*)

YEAR	WINNERS	SCORE	RUNNERS-UP
1982	Internazionale	1-0, 1-1 (2 legs)	Torino
1983	Juventus	0-2, 3-0 (aet) (2 legs)	Verona
1984	Roma	1-1, 1-0 (2 legs)	Verona
1985	Sampdoria	1-0, 2-1 (2 legs)	Milan
1986	Roma	1-2, 2-0 (2 legs)	Sampdoria
1987	Napoli	3-0, 1-0 (2 legs)	Atalanta
1988	Sampdoria	2-0, 1-2 (aet) (2 legs)	Torino
1989	Sampdoria	0-1, 4-0 (2 legs)	Napoli
1990	Juventus	0-0, 1-0 (2 legs)	Milan
1991	Roma	3-1, 1-1 (2 legs)	Sampdoria
1992	Parma	0-1, 2-0 (2 legs)	Juventus
1993	Torino	3-0, 2-5 (2 legs)	Roma
1994	Sampdoria	0-0, 6-1 (2 legs)	Ancona
1995	Juventus	2-0, 1-0 (2 legs)	Parma
1996	Fiorentina	1-0, 2-0 (2 legs)	Atalanta
1997	Vicenza	0-1, 3-0 (aet) (2 legs)	Napoli
1998	Lazio	0-1, 3-1 (2 legs)	Milan
1999	Parma	1-1, 2-2 (2 legs)	Fiorentina
2000	Lazio	2-1, 0-0 (2 legs)	Internazionale
2001	Fiorentina	1-0, 1-1 (2 legs)	Parma
2002	Parma*	1-2, 1-0 (2 legs)	Juventus
2003	Milan	4-1, 2-2 (2 legs)	Roma
2004	Lazio	2-0, 2-2 (2 legs)	Juventus

* Denotes winners on away goals rule.

The San Siro plays host to one of the most hotly-contested derbies in Italian soccer: Milan v Internazionale. The fans of both sides greet the teams with a show with flags, scarves and flares.

Italian Cup Summary

TEAM	TOTALS	WINNERS & RUNNERS-UP (BOLD) (ITALICS)
Juventus	9, 4	**1938, 42, 59, 60, 65,** *73,* **79, 83, 90,** *92,* **95, 2002,** *04*
Roma	7, 4	*1937, 41,* **64, 69, 80, 81, 84, 86, 91,** *93,* **2003**
Fiorentina	6, 3	**1940,** *58, 60,* **61, 66, 75,** *96,* **99, 2001**
Torino	5, 8	**1936,** *38, 43,* **63,** *64,* **68,** *70, 71, 80–82,* **88,** *93*
Milan	5, 7	*1942,* **67,** *68, 71,* **72, 73,** *75,* **77,** *85, 90, 98,* **2003**
Sampdoria	4, 2	**1985,** *86,* **88, 89,** *91,* **94**
Lazio	4, 1	**1958,** *61,* **98, 2000,** *04*
Internazionale	3, 4	**1939,** *59,* **65,** *77, 78, 82,* **2000**
Napoli	3, 4	**1962,** *72, 76, 78,* **87,** *89, 97*
Parma	3, 2	**1992,** *95,* **99, 2001,** *02*
Bologna	2, 0	**1970, 74**
Atalanta	1, 2	**1963,** *87, 96*
Genoa	1, 1	**1937,** *40*
Venezia	1, 1	**1941,** *43*
Vado	1, 0	**1922**
Vicenza	1, 0	**1997**
Verona	0, 3	*1976, 83, 84*
Palermo	0, 2	*1974, 79*
Alessandria	0, 1	*1936*
Ancona	0, 1	*1994*
Cagliari	0, 1	*1969*
Catanzaro	0, 1	*1966*
Novara	0, 1	*1939*
Padova	0, 1	*1967*
Spal	0, 1	*1962*
Udinese	0, 1	*1922*

ITALY

Malta

Malta Football Association
Founded: 1900
Joined FIFA: 1959
Joined UEFA: 1960

THE MALTA FOOTBALL ASSOCIATION was formed in 1900, when the island was still under British rule. It was in turn affiliated to the FA in London, rather than FIFA, for the first half of the century. A league was first played in 1910, and in 1935 the Malta FA Trophy competition was inaugurated. Self-government of the country began in 1947, though membership of FIFA in 1959 (and UEFA in 1960) preceded Malta's full independence, gained in 1964. Despite this, the country played its first World Cup qualifying campaign in an African group in 1960.

League and cup competitions have been dominated by five teams – Floriana, Sliema Wanderers, Valletta, Hamrun Spartans and Hibernians. There are ten teams in the top flight playing each other three times a season (extended from twice in a season in 1996). All games are played in the Ta' Qali national stadium in Valletta. Promotion and relegation is a simple two up, two down system. In addition to the Maltese Trophy Cup (listed here) top teams also compete in the Löwenbrau Super Cup and the Löwenbrau Fives Cup.

Maltese League Record 1910–2004

SEASON	CHAMPIONS	SEASON	CHAMPIONS
1910	Floriana	1952	Floriana
1911	no championship	1953	Floriana
1912	Floriana	1954	Sliema Wanderers
1913	Floriana	1955	Floriana
1914	Hamrun Spartans	1956	Sliema Wanderers
1915	Valletta United	1957	Sliema Wanderers
1916	no championship	1958	Floriana
1917	St George's	1959	Valletta
1918	Hamrun Spartans	1960	Valletta
1919	KOMR Militia	1961	Hibernians
1920	Sliema Wanderers	1962	Floriana
1921	Floriana	1963	Valletta
1922	Floriana	1964	Sliema Wanderers
1923	Sliema Wanderers	1965	Sliema Wanderers
1924	Sliema Wanderers	1966	Sliema Wanderers
1925	Floriana	1967	Hibernians
1926	Sliema Wanderers	1968	Floriana
1927	Floriana	1969	Hibernians
1928	Floriana	1970	Floriana
1929	Floriana	1971	Sliema Wanderers
1930	Sliema Wanderers	1972	Sliema Wanderers
1931	Floriana	1973	Floriana
1932	Valletta United	1974	Valletta
1933	Sliema Wanderers	1975	Floriana
1934	Sliema Wanderers	1976	Sliema Wanderers
1935	Floriana	1977	Floriana
1936	Sliema Wanderers	1978	Valletta
1937	Floriana	1979	Hibernians
1938	Sliema Wanderers	1980	Valletta
1939	Sliema Wanderers	1981	Hibernians
1940	Sliema Wanderers	1982	Hibernians
1941–44	no championship	1983	Hamrun Spartans
1945	Valletta	1984	Valletta
1946	Valletta	1985	Rabat Ajax
1947	Hamrun Spartans	1986	Rabat Ajax
1948	Valletta	1987	Hamrun Spartans
1949	Sliema Wanderers	1988	Hamrun Spartans
1950	Floriana	1989	Sliema Wanderers
1951	Floriana	1990	Valletta

Maltese League Record (*continued*)

SEASON	CHAMPIONS	SEASON	CHAMPIONS
1991	Hamrun Spartans	1999	Valletta
1992	Valletta	2000	Birkirkara
1993	Floriana	2001	Valletta
1994	Hibernians	2002	Hibernians
1995	Hibernians	2003	Sliema Wanderers
1996	Sliema Wanderers	2004	Sliema Wanderers
1997	Valletta		
1998	Valletta		

Maltese Cup Record 1935–2004

YEAR	WINNERS	YEAR	WINNERS
1935	Sliema Wanderers	1972	Floriana
1936	Sliema Wanderers	1973	Gżira United
1937	Sliema Wanderers	1974	Sliema Wanderers
1938	Floriana	1975	Valletta
1939	Melita St Julians	1976	Floriana
1940	Sliema Wanderers	1977	Valletta
1941–44	no competition	1978	Valletta
1945	Floriana	1979	Sliema Wanderers
1946	Sliema Wanderers	1980	Hibernians
1947	Floriana	1981	Floriana
1948	Sliema Wanderers	1982	Hibernians
1949	Floriana	1983	Hamrun Spartans
1950	Floriana	1984	Hamrun Spartans
1951	Sliema Wanderers	1985	Żurrieq
1952	Sliema Wanderers	1986	Rabat Ajax
1953	Floriana	1987	Hamrun Spartans
1954	Floriana	1988	Hamrun Spartans
1955	Floriana	1989	Hamrun Spartans
1956	Sliema Wanderers	1990	Sliema Wanderers
1957	Floriana	1991	Valletta
1958	Floriana	1992	Hamrun Spartans
1959	Sliema Wanderers	1993	Floriana
1960	Valletta	1994	Floriana
1961	Floriana	1995	Valletta
1962	Hibernians	1996	Valletta
1963	Sliema Wanderers	1997	Valletta
1964	Valletta	1998	Hibernians
1965	Sliema Wanderers	1999	Valletta
1966	Floriana	2000	Sliema Wanderers
1967	Floriana	2001	Valletta
1968	Sliema Wanderers	2002	Birkirkara
1969	Sliema Wanderers	2003	Birkirkara
1970	Hibernians	2004	Sliema Wanderers
1971	Hibernians		

San Marino

**Federazione Sammarinese
Giuoco Calcio**
Founded: 1931
Joined FIFA: 1988
Joined UEFA: 1988

San Marino is a tiny independent enclave in northern Italy. Organized soccer dates back to the 1930s, but it was only in 1988 that it joined UEFA and began to play internationals, winning its first match in 2004. The league has 16 teams in two groups of eight. The top three in each progress to an end of season championship play-off.

SEASON	LEAGUE CHAMPIONS
2000	Folgore
2001	Cosmos
2002	Domagnano
2003	Domagnano
2004	Pennarossa

YEAR	CUP WINNERS
2000	Tre Penne
2001	Domagnano
2002	Domagnano
2003	Domagnano
2004	Pennarossa

MALTA, SAN MARINO

Switzerland

Schweizerischer Fussballverband
Founded: 1895
Joined FIFA: 1904
Joined UEFA: 1954

INSTITUTIONALLY, IF NOT SPIRITUALLY, Switzerland is the centre of the soccer universe. The country's peculiar neutrality in international politics makes it the perfect home for many organizations. Since its inception, FIFA has been located in Geneva and in 1955 UEFA based itself in Nyon. But there is something for the spirit too in Switzerland, where soccer has been played since the 1860s. The oldest surviving club is FC St Galen, founded in 1879 in the Germanic speaking part of the country.

The game grew rapidly during the next two decades. The Swiss FA was founded in 1895 and, in an unusually internationalist move for a Swiss institution, became a founding member of FIFA in 1904. During this period nearly all the clubs that have come to dominate Swiss soccer were founded: Grasshoppers from Zurich in 1886, Servette in 1890 and BSC Young Boys in Berne in 1898. A national competition began in 1898. In its most recent format 12 teams play in the top division. The cup is considered a minor affair, with the top clubs only entering later rounds.

* Unofficial championship. ** Third game of play-offs not played.
† Two central leagues were played, followed by two semi-finals and a final won 3-0 by Sankt Gallen.
†† FC Bern won the title but were disqualified for fielding an ineligible player during the qualifying stages.
From 1902–33, except where noted, there was three regional leagues, the winners playing one game against each of the other two in a final mini-league. For the 1908 and 1909 seasons, there were just two regional leagues, East and West, and the winners met in a play-off final. In 1932 and 1933, the league was divided into two groups, the winners of which went into the final round with the winners of a play-off between the group runners-up, plus the Second Division champions. In 1933, Lausanne-Sports managed to win the Second and First division titles in the same year!

Swiss Championship Record 1898–1933

SEASON	CHAMPIONS	SCORE	RUNNERS-UP
1898*	Grasshopper-Club	2-0	La Châtelaine
1899	Anglo-American Club	7-0	Old Boys Basel
1900	Grasshopper-Club	2-0	FC Bern
1901	Grasshopper-Club	2-0	FC Bern
1902	FC Zürich		BSC Young Boys
1903**	BSC Young Boys		FC Zürich
1904	FC Sankt Gallen		Old Boys Basel
1905	Grasshopper-Club		FC La Chaux-de-Fonds, BSC Young Boys Berne (equal)
1906	FC Winterthur		Servette FC Geneve
1907	Servette FC Geneve		Young Fellows Zurich
1908	FC Winterthur	4-1	BSC Young Boys
1909	BSC Young Boys	1-0	FC Winterthur
1910	BSC Young Boys		Servette FC Geneve
1911	BSC Young Boys		FC Zürich
1912	FC Aarau		FC La Chaux-de-Fonds
1913	Montriond Lausanne		Old Boys Basel
1914	FC Aarau		BSC Young Boys
1915†	Brühl Sankt Gallen		Servette FC Geneve
1916	FC Cantonal Neuchâtel		FC Winterthur
1917	FC Winterthur		FC La Chaux-de-Fonds
1918	Servette FC Geneve		BSC Young Boys
1919	Etoile La Chaux-de-Fonds		Servette FC Geneve
1920	BSC Young Boys		Servette FC Geneve
1921	Grasshopper-Club		BSC Young Boys
1922	Servette FC Geneve		FC Luzern
1923††		not awarded	
1924	FC Zürich		Nordstern Basel
1925	Servette FC Geneve		FC Bern
1926	Servette FC Geneve		Grasshopper-Club
1927	Grasshopper-Club		Nordstern Basel
1928	Grasshopper-Club		Nordstern Basel
1929	BSC Young Boys		Grasshopper-Club
1930	Servette FC Geneve		Grasshopper-Club
1931	Grasshopper-Club		Urania Geneve
1932	Lausanne-Sports		FC Zürich
1933	Servette FC Geneve		Grasshopper-Club

Swiss National League Record 1934–2004

SEASON	CHAMPIONS	RUNNERS-UP
1934	Servette FC Geneve	Grasshopper-Club
1935	Lausanne-Sports	Servette FC Geneve
1936	Lausanne-Sports	Young Fellows Zurich
1937	Grasshopper-Club	BSC Young Boys Berne
1938	FC Lugano	Grasshopper-Club
1939	Grasshopper-Club	FC Grenchen
1940	Servette FC Geneve	FC Grenchen
1941	FC Lugano	BSC Young Boys Berne
1942	FC Grenchen	Grasshopper-Club
1943	Grasshopper-Club	FC Lugano
1944	Lausanne-Sports	Servette FC Geneve
1945	Grasshopper-Club	FC Lugano
1946	Servette FC Geneve	FC Lugano
1947	FC Biel-Bienne	Lausanne-Sports
1948	AC Bellinzona	FC Biel-Bienne
1949	FC Lugano	FC Basel
1950	Servette FC Geneve	FC Basel
1951	Lausanne-Sports	FC Chiasso
1952	Grasshopper-Club	FC Zurich
1953	FC Basel	BSC Young Boys Berne
1954	FC La Chaux-de-Fonds	Grasshopper-Club
1955	FC La Chaux-de-Fonds	Lausanne-Sports
1956	Grasshopper-Club	FC La Chaux de Fonds
1957	BSC Young Boys Berne	Grasshopper-Club
1958	BSC Young Boys Berne	Grasshopper-Club
1959	BSC Young Boys Berne	FC Grenchen
1960	BSC Young Boys Berne	FC Biel-Bienne
1961	Servette FC Geneve	BSC Young Boys Berne
1962	Servette FC Geneve	Lausanne-Sports
1963	FC Zürich	Lausanne-Sports
1964	FC La Chaux-de-Fonds	FC Zurich
1965	Lausanne-Sports	BSC Young Boys Berne
1966	FC Zürich	Servette FC Geneve
1967	FC Basel	FC Zurich
1968	FC Zürich	Grasshopper-Club
1969	FC Basel	Lausanne-Sports
1970	FC Basel	Lausanne-Sports
1971	Grasshopper-Club	FC Basel
1972	FC Basel	FC Zurich
1973	FC Basel	Grasshopper-Club
1974	FC Zürich	Grasshopper-Club
1975	FC Zürich	BSC Young Boys Berne
1976	FC Zürich	Servette FC Geneve
1977	FC Basel	Servette FC Geneve
1978	Grasshopper-Club	Servette FC Geneve
1979	Servette FC Geneve	FC Zurich
1980	FC Basel	Grasshopper-Club
1981	FC Zürich	Grasshopper-Club
1982	Grasshopper-Club	Servette FC Geneve
1983	Grasshopper-Club	Servette FC Geneve
1984	Grasshopper-Club	Servette FC Geneve
1985	Servette FC Geneve	FC Aarau
1986	BSC Young Boys Berne	Neuchatel Xamax FC
1987	Neuchâtel-Xamax FC	Grasshopper-Club
1988	Neuchâtel-Xamax FC	Servette FC Geneve
1989	FC Luzern	Grasshopper-Club
1990	Grasshopper-Club	Lausanne-Sports

Swiss National League Record 1934–2003 (*continued*)

SEASON	CHAMPIONS	RUNNERS-UP
1991	Grasshopper-Club	FC Sion
1992	FC Sion	Neuchatel Xamax FC
1993	FC Aarau	BSC Young Boys Berne
1994	Servette FC Geneve	Grasshopper-Club
1995	Grasshopper-Club	FC Lugano
1996	Grasshopper-Club	FC Sion
1997	FC Sion	Neuchatel Xamax FC
1998	Grasshopper-Club	Servette FC Geneve
1999	Servette FC Geneve	Grasshopper-Club
2000	FC Sankt Gallen	Lausanne-Sports
2001	Grasshopper-Club	FC Lugano
2002	FC Basel	Grasshopper-Club
2003	Grasshopper-Club	FC Basel
2004	FC Basel	BSC Young Boys Berne

Swiss League Summary

TEAM	TOTALS	CHAMPIONS & RUNNERS-UP (BOLD) (*ITALICS*)
Grasshopper-Club	**25**, *20*	**1900, 01, 05,** *21, 26,* **27, 28, 29, 30, 31,** *33, 34,* **37, 38, 39,** *42,* **43, 45,** *52, 54, 56, 57, 58, 68,* **71,** *73, 74,* **78,** *80, 81,* **82–84,** *87, 89,* **90, 91,** *94,* **95, 96,** *98,* **99, 2001,** *02,* **03**
Servette FC Geneve	**17**, *16*	*1906,* **07,** *10,* **15,** *18, 19,* **20,** *22,* **25,** *26,* **30,** *33, 34,* **35,** *40,* **44,** *46,* **50,** *61,* **62,** *66, 76–78,* **79,** *82 –84,* **85,** *88,* **94,** *98,* **99**
BSC Young Boys Berne	**11**, *14*	*1902,* **03,** *05 (shared),* **08,** *09–11,* **14,** *18,* **20, 21,** *29,* **37,** *41,* **53,** *57–60,* **61,** *65, 75,* **86,** *93,* **2004**
FC Basel	**10**, *4*	*1949,* **50,** *53,* **67,** *69,* **70,** *71 72, 73, 77,* **80, 2002,** *03,* **04**
FC Zurich	**9**, *8*	**1902,** *03,* **11, 24, 32,** *52,* **63,** *64 66, 67, 68,* **72,** *74–76,* **79,** *81*

This summary only features clubs that have won the Swiss league nine times or more. For a full list of league winners and runners-up please see the league record above. This summary does not include 1898 or 1923.

Swiss Cup Record 1926–2004

SEASON	CHAMPIONS	SCORE	RUNNERS-UP
1926	Grasshopper-Club	2-1	FC Bern
1927	Grasshopper-Club	3-1	FC Young Fellows
1928	Servette FC Geneve	5-1	Grasshopper-Club
1929	Urania Genève Sport	1-0	BSC Young Boys
1930	BSC Young Boys	1-0	FC Aarau
1931	FC Lugano	2-1 (aet)	Grasshopper-Club
1932	Grasshopper-Club	5-1	Urania Genève Sport
1933	FC Basel	4-3	Grasshopper-Club
1934	Grasshopper-Club	2-0	Servette FC Geneve
1935	Lausanne-Sports	10-0	FC Nordstern
1936	FC Young Fellows	2-0	Servette FC Geneve
1937	Grasshopper-Club	10-0	Lausanne-Sports
1938	Grasshopper-Club	2-2(aet), (replay)5-1	Servette FC Geneve
1939	Lausanne-Sports	2-0	FC Nordstern
1940	Grasshopper-Club	3-0	FC Grenchen
1941	Grasshopper-Club	1-1(aet), (replay)2-0	Servette FC Geneve
1942	Grasshopper-Club	0-0(aet), (replay)3-2	FC Basel
1943	Grasshopper-Club	2-1	FC Lugano
1944	Lausanne-Sports	3-0	FC Basel
1945	BSC Young Boys	2-0(aet)	FC Sankt Gallen
1946	Grasshopper-Club	3-0	Lausanne-Sports
1947	FC Basel	3-0	Lausanne-Sports
1948	FC La Chaux-de-Fonds	2-2(aet), (replay) 2-2(aet), (2nd replay) 4-0	FC Grenchen
1949	Servette FC Geneve	3-0	Grasshopper-Club
1950	Lausanne-Sports	1-1 (aet), (replay) 4-0	FC Cantonal Neuchâtel
1951	FC La Chaux-de-Fonds	3-2	FC Locarno
1952	Grasshopper-Club	2-0	FC Lugano
1953	BSC Young Boys	1-1 (aet), (replay) 3-1	Grasshopper-Club

Swiss Cup Record 1926–2003 (*continued*)

SEASON	CHAMPIONS	SCORE	RUNNERS-UP
1954	FC La Chaux-de-Fonds	2-0	FC Fribourg
1955	FC La Chaux-de-Fonds	3-1	FC Thun
1956	Grasshopper-Club	1-0	BSC Young Boys
1957	FC La Chaux-de-Fonds	1-1 (aet), (replay) 3-1	Lausanne-Sports
1958	BSC Young Boys	1-1 (aet), (replay) 4-1	Grasshopper-Club
1959	FC Grenchen	1-0	Servette FC Geneve
1960	FC Luzern	1-0	FC Grenchen
1961	FC La Chaux-de-Fonds	1-0	FC Biel-Bienne
1962	Lausanne-Sports	4-0 (aet)	AC Bellinzona
1963	FC Basel	2-0	Grasshopper-Club
1964	Lausanne-Sports	2-0	FC La Chaux-de-Fonds
1965	FC Sion	2-1	Servette FC Geneve
1966	FC Zürich	2-0	Servette FC Geneve
1967*	FC Basel	w/o	Lausanne-Sports
1968	FC Lugano	2-1	FC Winterthur
1969	FC Sankt Gallen	2-0	AC Bellinzona
1970	FC Zürich	4-1 (aet)	FC Basel
1971	Servette FC Geneve	2-0	FC Lugano
1972	FC Zürich	1-0	FC Basel
1973	FC Zürich	2-0 (aet)	FC Basel
1974	FC Sion	3-2	Neuchâtel-Xamax FC
1975	FC Basel	2-1(aet)	FC Winterthur
1976	FC Zürich	1-0	Servette FC Geneve
1977	BSC Young Boys	1-0	FC Sankt Gallen
1978	Servette FC Geneve	2-2 (aet), (replay) 1-0	Grasshopper-Club
1979	Servette FC Geneve	1-1(aet), (replay)3-2	BSC Young Boys
1980	FC Sion	2-1	BSC Young Boys
1981	Lausanne-Sports	4-3 (aet)	FC Zürich
1982	FC Sion	1-0	FC Basel
1983	Grasshopper-Club	2-2(aet), (replay)3-0	Servette FC Geneve
1984	Servette FC Geneve	1-0	Lausanne-Sports
1985	FC Aarau	1-0	Neuchâtel-Xamax FC
1986	FC Sion	3-1	Servette FC Geneve
1987	BSC Young Boys	4-2 (aet)	Servette FC Geneve
1988	Grasshopper-Club	2-0	FC Schaffhausen
1989	Grasshopper-Club	2-1	FC Aarau
1990	Grasshopper-Club	2-1	Neuchâtel-Xamax FC
1991	FC Sion	3-2	BSC Young Boys
1992	FC Luzern	3-1 (aet)	FC Lugano
1993	FC Lugano	4-1	Grasshopper-Club
1994	Grasshopper-Club	4-0	FC Schaffhausen
1995	FC Sion	4-2	Grasshopper-Club
1996	FC Sion	3-2	Servette FC Geneve
1997	FC Sion	3-3 (aet) 5-4 (pens)	FC Luzern
1998	Lausanne-Sports	2-2 (aet) 4-3 (pens)	FC Sankt Gallen
1999	Lausanne-Sports	2-0	Grasshopper-Club
2000	FC Zürich	2-2 (aet) 3-0 (pens)	Lausanne-Sports
2001	Servette FC Geneve	3-0	FC Yverdon-Sports
2002	FC Basel	2-1 (aet)	Grasshopper-Club
2003	FC Basel	6-0	Neuchâtel-Xamax FC
2004	FC Wil	3-2	Grasshopper-Club

*   Abandoned after 42 minutes at 2-1 and awarded 3-0; Lausanne protested by a sit-in against the penalty that led to 2-1.
    w/o denotes walk over

Swiss Cup Summary

TEAM	TOTALS	CHAMPIONS & RUNNERS-UP (BOLD) (*ITALICS*)
Grasshopper-Club Zurich	**18**, *13*	**1926,** *27, 28,* **31,** *32, 33,* **34, 37, 38,** *40–43,* **46,** *49,* **52,** *53,* **56,** *58, 63, 78,* **83,** *88–90,* **93,** *94, 95, 99,* **2002,** *04*
Lausanne-Sports	**9**, *7*	**1935,** *37,* **39, 44, 46, 47, 50,** *57,* **62,** *64,* **67,** *81,* **84, 98, 99,** *2000*
FC Sion	**9**, *0*	**1965, 74, 80, 82, 86, 91, 95–97**

This summary only features clubs that have won the Swiss cup nine times or more. For a full list of cup winners and runners-up please see the cup record above.

Central Europe

THE SEASONS IN REVIEW 2003–04

IN SWITZERLAND FC BASEL BECAME CHAMPIONS with four games to spare. The team finished 13 points clear of second-placed Young Boys. Christian Gross' side was dominant despite selling one Yakin brother and losing the other to injury. In perhaps his last season, striker Stephane Chapusiat ended the season with 20 goals. Grazer AK took the Austrian title for the first time in the club's 102-year history, fending off challengers Austria Wien. To the delight of coach Walter Schachner, who had been summarily fired by Austria Wien in 2002, Grazer also went on to beat Austria in a thrilling cup final. With the score 2-2 at full time, and 3-3 after extra time, Grazer finally won it 5-4 on penalties.

The pacesetters in Hungary, Ferencváros, did their best to throw away the title, but on a tense final day beat rivals Debreceni, while nearest challengers Újpesti could only manage a draw at MTK. In Poland, Wisła Kraków won the title when second place Legia Warszawa ran out of steam in the final run-in.

Match-fixing allegations

The league in the Czech Republic was won by outsiders Banik Ostrava with games to spare, but the result was immediately thrown into doubt by the still incomplete investigations into match fixing and corruption in Czech soccer. When Ostrava's main rivals this year, Sparta Prague, lost 2-0 away at the otherwise poor Synot side, suspicions were raised. The Synot directors and an assistant referee were caught at a service station near Brno with £3,500 cash on them. The Czech FA has announced that should evidence of malpractice emerge, Sparta could be awarded a walkover in the game and all of Synot's records would be expunged. The results of their investigations have still to be announced.

In Slovakia, the long-time league leaders, Banska Bystrica, faced a late charge from defending champions MSK Žilina whose late-season form came when they appointed a new coach, former national team coach Ladislav Jurkemik. Two draws in the last three games of the season for Bystrica allowed Žilina to finish level on points – with Žilina as champions thanks to a better head-to-head record.

*Ivo Valenta, **President of FC Synot,** faces the press after his hearing at the Czech Football Association in Prague in May 2004. Officials at the club have been accused of bribing referees in the Czech Premier League.*

Austrian Bundesliga Table 2003–04

CLUB	P	W	D	L	F	A	Pts	
Grazer AK	36	21	9	6	62	32	72	Champions
FK Austria Wien	36	21	8	7	63	31	71	
SV Pasching	36	17	12	7	59	41	63	
SK Rapid Wien	36	16	9	11	50	47	57	
Schwarz-Weiß Bregenz	36	11	12	13	47	58	45	
VfB Admira/ Wacker Mödling	36	11	9	16	42	49	42	
SV Austria Salzburg	36	11	5	20	44	48	38	
SV Mattersburg	36	9	10	17	39	61	37	
SK Sturm Graz	36	8	11	17	39	52	35	
FC Kärnten	36	7	11	18	36	62	32	Relegated

Promoted club: FC Wacker Tirol Innsbruck.

Austrian International Club Performances 2003–04

CLUB	COMPETITION	PROGRESS
FK Austria Wien	Champions League	3rd Qualifying Round
	UEFA Cup	1st Round
Grazer AK	Champions League	3rd Qualifying Round
	UEFA Cup	1st Round
SV Salzburg	UEFA Cup	2nd Round
FC Kärnten	UEFA Cup	1st Round

Austrian Top Goalscorers 2003–04

PLAYER	CLUB	NATIONALITY	GOALS
Roland Kollmann	Grazer AK	Austrian	27
Sigur Rushfeldt	FK Austria Wien	Norwegian	25
Roland Linz	VfB Admira WM	Austrian	15
Christian Mayrleb	SV Pasching	Austrian	15

Austrian Cup

2004 FINAL

May 23 – Stadion Wals-Siezenheim, Salzburg

Grazer AK 3-3 FK Austria
(Bazina 45, **Wien**
Kollmann 86, (Gilewicz 28, 99
Aufhauser 106) Dundee 64)

(after extra time)

h/t: 1-1 **Att:** 7,900
Ref: Drabek

Grazer AK won 5-4 on pens

Grazer AK make it a double as they win the Austrian Cup and add it to their league title. They beat Austria Wien in both competitions by the narrowest of margins: penalties in the cup and a single point in the league.

CENTRAL EUROPE

Czech Republic League Table 2003–04

CLUB	P	W	D	L	F	A	Pts	
Banik Ostrava	30	18	9	3	60	25	**63**	Champions League
Sparta Praha	30	16	10	4	48	24	**58**	Champions League
Sigma Olomouc	30	16	7	7	43	24	**55**	UEFA Cup
Slavia Praha	30	15	7	8	43	24	**52**	UEFA Cup*
1. FC Synot	30	14	6	10	43	37	**48**	
Slovan Liberec	30	12	10	8	38	27	**46**	
FC Zlín	30	12	5	13	31	39	**41**	
Ceske Budéjovice	30	11	7	12	38	38	**40**	
FK Teplice	30	9	12	9	32	32	**39**	
FK Jablonec 97	30	8	14	8	27	32	**38**	
Marila Přibram	30	10	7	13	33	37	**37**	
Slezsky FC Opava	30	8	7	15	34	55	**31**	
Chmel Blšany	30	8	6	16	34	54	**30**	
1. FC Brno	30	7	9	14	33	43	**30**	
Viktoria Žižkov	30	6	9	15	18	34	**27**	Relegated
FC Viktoria Plzen	30	4	7	19	23	53	**19**	Relegated

* UEFA Cup place may be withdrawn pending match-fixing allegations.
Promoted clubs: FK Mlada Bodeslav, 1 FK Drnovice.

Czech Rep International Club Performances 2003–04

CLUB	COMPETITION	PROGRESS
Sparta Praha	Champions League	1st Knockout Round
Slavia Praha	Champions League	3rd Qualifying Round
	UEFA Cup	2nd Round
FC Teplice	UEFA Cup	3rd Round
Viktoria Žižkov	UEFA Cup	1st Round

Czech Republic Top Goalscorers 2003–04

PLAYER	CLUB	NATIONALITY	GOALS
Marek Heinz	Banik Ostrava	Czech	19
Lubomir Reiter	Sigma Olomouc	Czech	15
David Lafata	Ceske Budéjovice	Czech	14

Czech Republic Cup

2004 FINAL

May 18 – Strahov Stadium, Prague
Sparta Prague 2-1 Banik Ostrava
(Rezek 51,   (Lika 56)
Johana 84)
h/t: 0-0 **Att:** 6,985
Ref: Vidlák

Champions League here we come. Tiny provincial club Banik Ostrava celebrate their triumph in the Czech league.

Hungarian Champions League Table 2003–04

CLUB	P	W	D	L	F	A	Pts	
Ferencváros	32	16	9	7	44	30	**57**	Champions League
Debreceni VSC	32	16	8	8	51	32	**56**	UEFA Cup
Újpesti FC	32	15	11	6	48	29	**56**	
Balaton FC*	32	14	8	10	34	24	**50**	
Matáv Sopron	32	13	9	10	53	42	**48**	
MTK Hungária FC	32	11	11	10	42	40	**44**	

* Siófok FC were renamed Balaton FC.
Honved take the second UEFA Cup place as losing cup finalists.

In the first half of the season in Hungary, 12 clubs play each other twice. They are then divided into two groups, the top half entering a play-off for places in next season's European competitions and the bottom half entering a relegation play-off. Each team carries the points they accumulated in the first part of the season with them, and play the other five teams in their group twice to determine the final positions.

Hungarian Relegation League Table 2003–04

CLUB	P	W	D	L	F	A	Pts	
Videoton	32	10	10	12	55	51	**40**	
Pécsi Mecsek	32	9	13	10	36	37	**40**	
Zalahús ZTE FC	32	11	6	15	45	47	**39**	
Győri ETO FC	32	10	6	16	36	54	**36**	
Békéscsaba	32	8	8	16	36	50	**32**	*
LFC Haladás	32	4	11	17	19	63	**23**	**

* Békéscsaba remain in top division after winning play-off against 6th team in the 2nd division.
**LFC Haladás stay in top division after winning play-off against 5th team in the 2nd division.
Promoted clubs: Honvéd, Vasas, Kaposvári Rákóczi FC, DVTK Diósgyör (league expanding to 16 clubs for 2004–05).

Hungarian International Club Performances 2003–04

CLUB	COMPETITION	PROGRESS
MTK Hungária	Champions League	3rd Qualifying Round
	UEFA Cup	1st Round
Ferencváros	UEFA Cup	1st Round
Debreceni VSC	UEFA Cup	3rd Round

Hungarian Top Goalscorers 2003–04

PLAYER	CLUB	NATIONALITY	GOALS
Mihaly Toth	Matav Sopron	Hungarian	17
Zoltan Gera	Ferencváros	Hungarian	11
Robert Waltner	Zalahus ZTE FC	Hungarian	10

Hungarian Cup

2004 FINAL

May 5 – Ferenc Puskás Stadium, Budapest
Ferencváros 3-1 Honvéd
(Tököli 36   (Bábik 75)
Gera 68,
Sowunmi 86)
h/t: 1-0 **Att:** 4,000
Ref: Hanacsek

Ferencváros squeezed home to win the Hungarian league by a single point, though the crowd looks desperately thin. With the cup already in the bag, that made it doubles all round.

In Slovenia, Maribor held a one-point advantage over HIT Gorica with one game left. Maribor had won eight straight games to take top spot in the league and then won the cup midweek, despite losing 4-3 in the second leg of the Final; the team won 7-4 on aggregate. But, perhaps drained by the tie, Maribor lost their final league game to lowly NK Mura while Gorica saw off NK Koper to take only the second league title in the club's history.

Polish Champions League Table 2003–04

CLUB	P	W	D	L	F	A	Pts	
Wisła Kraków	26	21	2	3	73	30	65	Champions
Legia Warszawa	26	18	6	2	56	19	60	
Amica Wronki	26	14	6	6	47	25	48	
Groclin-Dyskobolia Grodzisk	26	13	7	6	59	31	46	
Wisła Płock	26	10	8	8	41	39	38	
Lech Poznan	26	10	7	9	43	34	37	
Górnik Zabrze	26	8	9	9	26	33	33	
Górnik Leczna	26	10	3	13	22	38	33	
Odra Wodzisław	26	8	4	14	27	40	28	
Dospel Katowice	26	6	8	12	20	42	26	
Polonia Warszawa	26	6	7	13	25	40	25	
Górnik Polkowice	26	6	5	15	17	37	23	Relegation Play-off*
Lukullus/Swit Nowy Dwór	26	5	7	14	21	42	22	Relegated
Widzew Łódź	26	4	7	15	25	52	19	Relegated

* Górnik Polkowice lost to Cracovia and so were relegated.
Promoted clubs: Cracovia, Zaglebie Lubin, Pogon Szczecin.

Polish International Club Performances 2003–04

CLUB	COMPETITION	PROGRESS
Wisła Kraków	Champions League UEFA Cup	3rd Qualifying Round 2nd Round
Groclin-Dyskobolia Grodzisk	UEFA Cup	3rd Round
GKS Katowice	UEFA Cup	Qualifying Phase
Wisła Płock	UEFA Cup	Qualifying Phase

Polish Top Goalscorers 2003–04

PLAYER	CLUB	NATIONALITY	GOALS
Maciej Zurawski	Wisła Kraków	Polish	19
Ireneusz Jelen	Wisła Płock	Polish	16
Piotr Reiss	Lech Poznan	Polish	13
Marek Saganowski	Legia Warszawa	Polish	13

Polish Cup

2004 FINAL (2 legs)

May 18 – Stadion Lecha, Poznan
Lech Poznan 2-0 Legia Warszawa
(Reiss 17, 35)
h/t: 2-0 **Att:** 26,000
Ref: Slupik

June 1 – Stadion Wojska Polskiego, Warsaw
Legia Warszawa 1-0 Lech Poznan
(Wlodarczyk 6)
h/t: 1-0 **Att:** 15,000
Ref: Fijarczyk

Lech Poznan won 2-1 on aggregate

Dospel Katowice's (in green) third-place finish last year earned them a UEFA Cup spot. However they lost in the Qualifying Phase to Macedonia's Cementarnica 55. Here Katowice's Pavel Adamczky tries an overhead shot.

Slovakian Mars Superliga Table 2003–04

CLUB	P	W	D	L	F	A	Pts	
MSK Žilina	36	17	13	6	62	35	64	Champions League
Dukla Banská Bystrica	36	17	13	6	58	36	64	UEFA Cup
SCP Ružomberok	36	15	10	11	53	47	55	
Spartak Trnava	36	15	8	13	46	46	53	
Laugaricio Trenčín	36	13	9	14	37	43	48	
ZTS Dubnica	36	12	10	14	41	42	46	
Inter Bratislava	36	12	9	15	38	44	45	
Artmedia Petrzalka	36	10	14	12	43	44	44	
Matador Púchov	36	10	9	17	34	54	39	
Slovan Bratislava	36	6	11	19	37	58	29	Relegated

Promoted club: FC Tauris Rimavská Sobota.
Steel Trans Licartovce take the second UEFA Cup place as cup runners-up.

Slovakian International Club Performances 2003–04

CLUB	COMPETITION	PROGRESS
MSK Žilina	Champions League UEFA Cup	3rd Qualifying Round 1st Round
Matador Púchov	UEFA Cup	1st Round
Artmedia Petrzalka	UEFA Cup	1st Round

Slovakian Top Goalscorers 2003–04

PLAYER	CLUB	NATIONALITY	GOALS
Roland Stevko	SCP Ruzomberok	Slovakian	17
Marek Krejci	Artmedia Petrzalka	Slovakian	15
Robert Semenik	Banská Bystrica	Slovakian	15

After trailing Dukla Banská for the whole season, MSK Žilina stepped up in the final rounds to win their third Slovakian league title in a row. Here captain Branislav Lababt lifts the trophy.

Slovakian Cup

2004 FINAL

May 8 – Dunajská Streda
Artmedia **2-0** Steel Trans
Petrzalka   Licartovce
*(Krejci 51,
Mikulic 75)*
h/t: 0-0 **Att:** 2,650
Ref: Jancovic

Slovenian Premier League Table 2003–04

CLUB	P	W	D	L	F	A	Pts	
HIT Gorica	32	15	11	6	55	29	56	Champions League
Olimpija Ljubljana	32	16	7	9	55	39	55	UEFA Cup†
NK Maribor	32	15	9	8	41	34	54	UEFA Cup (cup winners)
FC Koper	32	13	11	8	41	31	50	
Mura Murska Sobota	32	14	7	11	53	54	49	
Primorje Ajdovscina	32	12	12	8	59	36	48	UEFA Cup

† Olimpija Ljubljana were not awarded their UEFA Cup place having failed to register with UEFA. Koper and Sobota also failed to register.

In the first half of the season in Slovenia, 12 clubs play each other twice. They are then divided into two groups, the top half entering a play-off for places in next season's European competitions and the bottom half entering a relegation play-off. Each team carries the points they accumulated in the first part of the season with them, and play the other five teams in their group twice to determine the final positions.

Relegation Table 2003–04

CLUB	P	W	D	L	F	A	Pts	
NK Domzale	32	11	8	13	47	53	41	
Esotech Smartno	32	10	10	12	43	48	40	
Publikum Celje	32	11	6	15	61	52	39	
Ljubljana	32	12	6	14	38	53	39*	
Drava Ptuj	32	7	7	18	34	60	28	Relegation play-off**
Dravograd	32	7	4	21	35	73	24*	Relegated

* Dravograd had 1 point deducted, Ljubljana had 3 points deducted.

**Drava Ptuj beat 2nd division runners-up Bela Krajina in a relegation play-off and so remain at the top level.

Promoted club: NK Rudar Valenje.

Slovenian International Club Performances 2003–04

CLUB	COMPETITION	PROGRESS
NK Maribor	Champions League	2nd Qualifying Round
Publikum Celje	UEFA Cup	1st Round
Olimpija Ljubljana	UEFA Cup	1st Round

Slovenian Top Goalscorers 2003–04

PLAYER	CLUB	NATIONALITY	GOALS
Drazen Zezelj	Primorje Ajdovscina	Slovenian	19
Marko Kmetec	Olimpija Ljubljana	Slovenian	16
Alen Mujanovic	NK Maribor	Slovenian	15
Mladen Kovacevic	HIT Gorcia	Slovenian	15

Slovenian Cup

2004 FINAL (2 legs)

May 19 – Maribor Stadium
NK Maribor 4-0 Dravograd
*(Pekic 5 pen, 17,
Franci 45,
Znuderl 88)*
h/t: 3-0 **Att:** 1,500
Ref: Krajnc

May 26 – Dravograd Stadium
Dravograd 4-3 NK Maribor
*(Gostencnik 6,   (Znuderl 3 pen, 89,
Srsa 61,   Mujanovic 43)
Ljubanic 69,
Frajdl 90)*
h/t: 1-2 **Att:** 700
Ref: Kandare

NK Maribor won 7-4 on aggregate

Marko Kmetec scored 16 goals for Slovenian side Olimpija Ljubljana, but that was only good enough for second place as HIT Gorica took the top spot on the final day of the season.

Swiss Championship Play-off Table 2003–04

CLUB	P	W	D	L	F	A	Pts	
FC Basel	36	26	7	3	86	32	85	Champions League
BSC Young Boys Bern	36	22	6	8	75	48	72	Champions League
Servette FC	36	15	7	14	61	62	52	UEFA Cup
FC Zürich	36	14	8	14	58	52	50	
FC Sankt Gallen	36	14	8	14	54	57	50	
FC Thun	36	13	10	13	51	57	49	
Grasshopper-Club	36	12	5	19	62	74	41	
FC Aarau	36	9	11	16	57	69	38	
Neuchâtel Xamax	36	10	6	20	46	63	36	Relegation play-off *
FC Wil 1900	36	7	8	21	37	73	29	Relegated UEFA Cup (cup winners)

* Neuchâtel Xamax remain at this level after beating Vaduz over 2 legs.
Promoted club: FC Schaffhausen.

Swiss International Club Performances 2003–04

CLUB	COMPETITION	PROGRESS
Grasshopper-Club	Champions League	3rd Qualifying Round
	UEFA Cup	1st Round
Young Boys Bern	UEFA Cup	Qualifying Round
Neuchatel Xamax	UEFA Cup	1st Round
FC Basel	UEFA Cup	2nd Round

Swiss Top Goalscorers 2003–04

PLAYER	CLUB	NATIONALITY	GOALS
Stephane Chapuisat	Young Boys Bern	Swiss	23
Mohamed Kader	Servette FC	Togolese	19
Leandro Fonseca	Young Boys Bern	Brazilian	17
Ricardo Nuñez	Grasshopper-Club	Uruguayan	17

Swiss Cup

2004 FINAL

April 12 – Sankt Jakob-Park, Basel
FC Wil 3-2 Grasshopper-Club
*(Rogerio 5,   (Núñez 8,
Fabinho 30 pen,   Cananas 19)
79 pen)*
h/t: 2-2 **Att:** 22,500
Ref: Wildhaber

FC Wil spent nearly the whole season at the foot of the Swiss league table battling for financial and sporting survival. But they managed a brilliant turnaround in the cup in their very first Final: 2-1 down after 20 minutes they finished up 3-2 victors.

CENTRAL EUROPE

Soccer in Central Europe

1896: Prague-based Czech league established

1906: Poland's oldest club, KS Cracovia, formed

1915: Czech Stredocesky league established

1918: Polish independent republic formed

1919: Formation of Polish FA: Polski Związek Piłki Nóżnej

1922: Formation of Czechoslovak FA

1926: First Polish Cup Final

1934: Czechoslovakia runners-up in World Cup in Italy

1939–44: During war and occupation, Czechoslovak soccer divided into separate leagues and cups

1946–48: Communist takeover and reorganization of Czechoslovak soccer

1949: League and Cup reorganized on a national basis

1954: Czechoslovakian affiliation to UEFA. Polish affiliation to UEFA

1962: Czechoslovakia reach World Cup Final in Chile. Josef Masopust wins European Footballer of the Year award

1993: Czechoslovakia separates into Czech Republic and Slovakia. Independent leagues, cups and FAs created. Separate affiliation to UEFA and FIFA. Legia Warszawa stripped of league title after match-fixing scandal

1996: Czech Republic runners-up in European Championships. Widzew Łódź and Legia Warszawa have their grounds closed for a season after worst incidents of soccer violence in Poland

2003: Czech midfielder Pavel Nedved wins European Footballer of the Year award

Timeline years: 1890, 1895, 1900, 1905, 1910, 1915, 1920, 1925, 1930, 1935, 1940, 1945, 1950, 1955, 1960, 1965, 1970, 1975, 1980, 1985, 1990, 1995, 2000, 2005

1893: Czechoslovakia's oldest clubs, Sparta Praha and Slavia Praha, formed

1901: Formation of Czech FA, Českomoravský Fotbalový Svaz

1906: Czech affiliation to FIFA

1920: Czechoslovakia's first international, v Yugoslavia, won 7-0, venue: Antwerp

1921: Poland's first international, v Hungary, lost 0-1, venue: Budapest. First national league

1923: Polish affiliation to FIFA. Czechoslovakian affiliation to FIFA

1925: National Czechoslovak league established and professionalism introduced

1939–45: No soccer in Poland during the war

1945–46: Polish borders radically redrawn, many Polish clubs transferred to Soviet leagues and some German clubs to the Polish league. Communist reorganization of clubs. League re-established

1951: Polish Cup re-established

1961: Czechoslovak Cup established

1968: Czech Uprising

1976: Czechoslovakia hosts and wins European Championships

Key

- International soccer (Czech Republic)
- International soccer (Poland)
- Affiliation to FIFA
- Affiliation to UEFA
- War

Warta Poznań 1945
Zwiakowiec (1949–55)

Olimpia Poznań 1922

Lech Poznań 1947
Kolejarz (1947–56)

SK Hradec Králové 1905

Slovan Liberec 1958

Teplice 1945

Jablonec 97 1964

SK Kladno 1903

Viktoria Plzeõ 1911

1. FC Union Cheb 1951

FC Marila Příbram 1948
ATK Praha (1948–52)
UDA Praha (1952–56)
Dukla Praha (1956–98)
Dukla Příbram (1998–2000)

SK Pardubice 1911

České Budějovice 1899

Boby Brno 1913
Moravian Nationalism

Sigma Olomouc 1919

Petra Drnovice 1932

SK Líbeň (Folded)

DFC Praha (Folded)

Sparta Praha 1893
AC Sparta (1893–1949), Sparta Bratrstvi, (1949–51), Sparta Sokolovo (1951–53), Spartak Sokolovo (1953–64), Sparta CKD (1964–90)

Olympia

Bohemians Praha 1903
AFK Vršovice (1903–27), Bohemians (1927–39), AFK Bohemia (1939–49), Železničař (1949–51), Spartak Stalingrad (1951–61), Bohemians CKD (1961–90)

Slavia Praha 1893
SK Slavia (1893–1949)
Dynamo Slavia (1949–51)
TJ Slavia (1951–90)

Gdańsk
Lechia Gdańsk 1945
Budowlany (1949–56)

Zawisza Bydgoszcz 1946
Bydgoszcz

TKS Toruń

Szczecin
Pogon Szczecin 1906

Wronki
Amica Wronki 1992

Poznań

Grodzisk
Groclin Dyskobolia Grodzisk 1922

Wrocław

Slask Wrocław 1947
1948–56 Ogniwo

FC Banik Ostrava OKD 192_

TJ Vítkovice 1922

Slezský Opava 1907

Teplice

Liberec

Jablonec nad Nisou

Hradec Králové

PRAGUE (see inset)

Kladno

Plzeň

Příbram

Cheb

CZECH REPUBLIC

Opava

Ostrav_

Pardubice
Olomouc

Žlín

Drnovice

Brno

Budějovice

Svit Žlín 1919

Žilin_

Dubnic_

Trenčín
Prievidza

Trnava

Nitra

Bratislav_

Dunajská Streda

Artmed_
Petrzalka 18_

In_
Bratislava 1_

Slov_
Bratislava 1_

Spartak Trnava 1_

Elbe

Vltava

PRAGUE

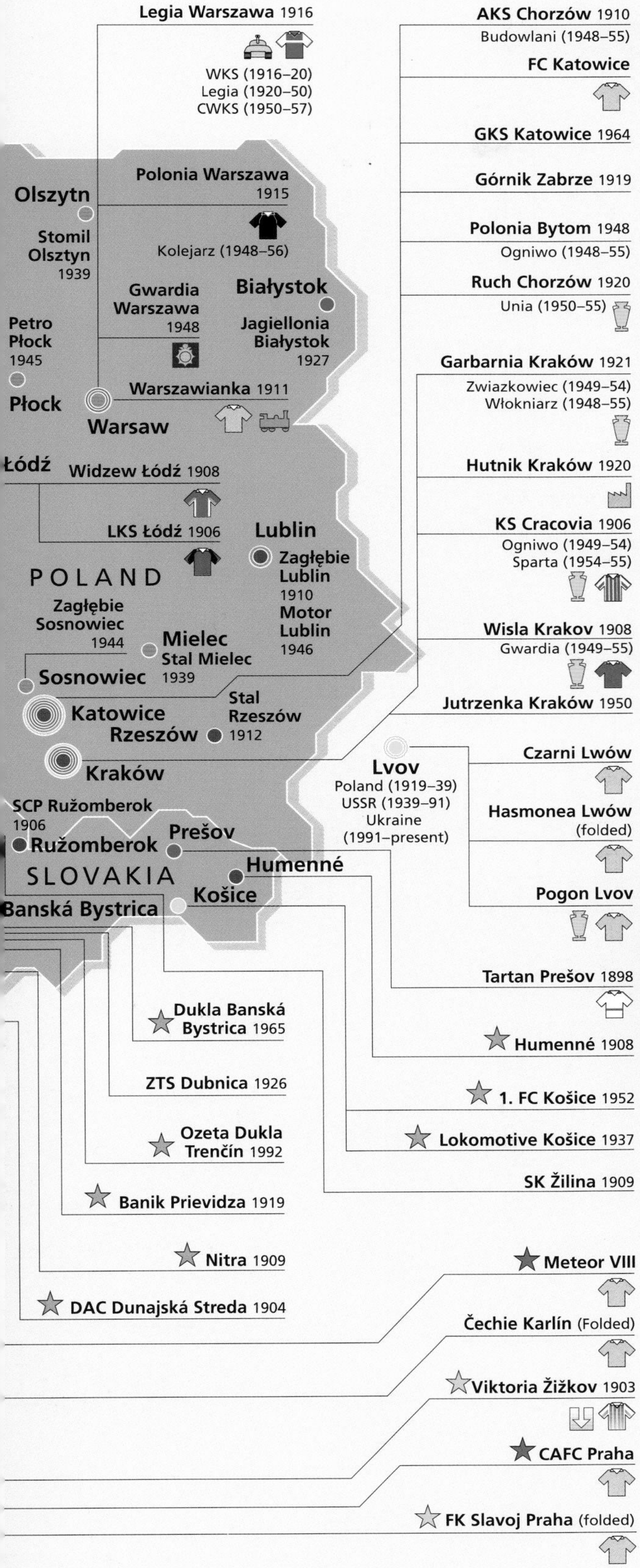

Legia Warszawa 1916
WKS (1916–20)
Legia (1920–50)
CWKS (1950–57)
Polonia Warszawa 1915
Kolejarz (1948–56)
Olszytn
Stomil Olsztyn 1939
Gwardia Warszawa 1948
Białystok
Jagiellonia Białystok 1927
Petro Płock 1945
Płock
Warszawianka 1911
Warsaw
Łódź
Widzew Łódź 1908
LKS Łódź 1906
Lublin
Zagłębie Lublin 1910
Motor Lublin 1946
POLAND
Zagłębie Sosnowiec 1944
Mielec
Stal Mielec 1939
Sosnowiec
Katowice
Stal Rzeszów 1912
Rzeszów
Kraków
SCP Ružomberok 1906
Ružomberok
Prešov
SLOVAKIA
Humenné
Košice
Banská Bystrica
AKS Chorzów 1910
Budowlani (1948–55)
FC Katowice
GKS Katowice 1964
Górnik Zabrze 1919
Polonia Bytom 1948
Ogniwo (1948–55)
Ruch Chorzów 1920
Unia (1950–55)
Garbarnia Kraków 1921
Zwiazkowiec (1949–54)
Włokniarz (1948–55)
Hutnik Kraków 1920
KS Cracovia 1906
Ogniwo (1949–54)
Sparta (1954–55)
Wisla Krakov 1908
Gwardia (1949–55)
Jutrzenka Kraków 1950
Lvov
Poland (1919–39)
USSR (1939–91)
Ukraine
(1991–present)
Czarni Lwów
Hasmonea Lwów (folded)
Pogon Lvov
Tartan Prešov 1898
Humenné 1908
1. FC Košice 1952
Lokomotive Košice 1937
SK Žilina 1909
Dukla Banská Bystrica 1965
ZTS Dubnica 1926
Ozeta Dukla Trenčín 1992
Banik Prievidza 1919
Nitra 1909
DAC Dunajská Streda 1904
Meteor VIII
Čechie Karlín (Folded)
Viktoria Žižkov 1903
CAFC Praha
FK Slavoj Praha (folded)

Central Europe

ORIGINS AND GROWTH OF SOCCER

IN BOHEMIA, PRAGUE PRODUCED the first soccer clubs, Sparta and Slavia, in 1893. A Prague league was running by 1896, followed by the Charity Cup in 1906. With the collapse of the Austro-Hungarian Empire, Czech and Slovak soccer were brought together and with the coming of professionalism in 1925 a new fully national league was established. Under Communist rule Dukla Praha (now Dukla Příbram) broke the Slavia–Sparta stranglehold with support from the Czech army. Slovan Bratislava also rose to challenge the Prague duopoly. With the separation of the Czech Republic and Slovakia, soccer in the region divided once again into separate leagues and cup competitions.

Like Czechoslovakia, Poland's soccer organizations preceded independence. KS Cracovia was formed in 1906 and Wisław (who wore the white star of Polish independence) in 1908, and clubs formed in Warsaw and Katowice before the formation of modern Poland in 1919. The national league was dominated by these three cities until the Second World War. After the war, Polish soccer was given the usual Communist treatment with name changes, and clubs were allocated to, or taken over by, a variety of state institutions. Under this order Polish soccer had its golden era, qualifying for every World Cup between 1974 and 1986, reaching the semi-finals in 1974 and 1982.

Dukla Praha is one of Central Europe's most successful teams. Here the team celebrates a goal against Real Madrid in the 1964 European Cup. However, Dukla lost the tie 6-2 on aggregate.

Central Europe: The main clubs

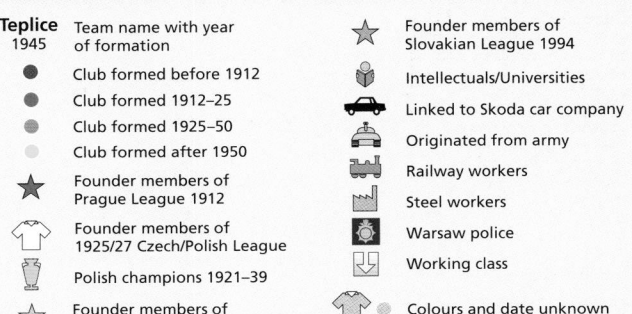

Teplice 1945	Team name with year of formation
●	Club formed before 1912
●	Club formed 1912–25
●	Club formed 1925–50
●	Club formed after 1950
★	Founder members of Prague League 1912
(shirt)	Founder members of 1925/27 Czech/Polish League
(cup)	Polish champions 1921–39
☆	Founder members of Czech League 1994
☆	Founder members of Slovakian League 1994
	Intellectuals/Universities
	Linked to Skoda car company
	Originated from army
	Railway workers
	Steel workers
	Warsaw police
	Working class
	Colours and date unknown

Czech Republic (including former Czechoslovakia)

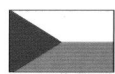

Českomoravský Fotbalový Svaz
Founded: 1901
Joined FIFA: 1906
Joined UEFA: 1954

SOCCER PROSPERED EARLY in the 20th century in this Bohemian province of the Austro-Hungarian Empire; the Prague-based Středočeský League and Czech Charity Cup were up and running before the First World War. With the postwar creation of Czechoslovakia, Bohemian, Moravian and Slovakian soccer were fused to create a professional Czech league in 1925.

During the Second World War, Germany absorbed part of Czechoslovakia, and created a newly independent, but German, satellite: Slovakia. Separate Slovak and Czech leagues and cups were played during the war. The Czechoslovak league was recreated under the Communists in 1946 and remained until the separation of the Czech Republic and Slovakia in 1993, after which two separate national leagues have operated.

Separate cups for the two nations were established under the Communists with a play-off to decide the Czechoslovakian Cup.

Czech League Record 1925–93

SEASON	CHAMPIONS	RUNNERS-UP
1925	SK Slavia Praha	AC Sparta Praha
1926	AC Sparta Praha	SK Slavia Praha
1927	AC Sparta Praha	SK Slavia Praha
1928	Victoria Žižkov	SK Slavia Praha
1929	SK Slavia Praha	Victoria Žižkov
1930	SK Slavia Praha	AC Sparta Praha
1931	SK Slavia Praha	AC Sparta Praha
1932	AC Sparta Praha	SK Slavia Praha
1933	SK Slavia Praha	AC Sparta Praha
1934	SK Slavia Praha	AC Sparta Praha
1935	SK Slavia Praha	AC Sparta Praha
1936	AC Sparta Praha	SK Slavia Praha
1937	SK Slavia Praha	AC Sparta Praha
1938	AC Sparta Praha	SK Slavia Praha
1939	AC Sparta Praha	SK Slavia Praha
1940	SK Slavia Praha	AC Sparta Praha
1941	SK Slavia Praha	SK Plzeň
1942	SK Slavia Praha	SK Prostějov
1943	SK Slavia Praha	AC Sparta Praha
1944	AC Sparta Praha	SK Slavia Praha
1945	*no championship*	
1946	AC Sparta Praha	SK Slavia Praha
1947	SK Slavia Praha	AC Sparta Praha
1948	AC Sparta Praha	SK Slavia Praha
1948*	Dynamo Slavia Praha	Škoda Plzeň
1949	NV Bratislava	Bratrstvi Sparta Praha
1950	NV Bratislava	Bratrstvi Sparta Praha
1951	NV Bratislava	Sparta CKD Praha
1952	Sparta CKD Sokolovo	NV Bratislava
1953	ÚDA Praha	Spartak Sokolovo Praha
1954	Spartak Sokolovo Praha	Baník Ostrava
1955	Slovan Bratislava	ÚDA Praha
1956	Dukla Praha	Slovan Bratislava
1957*		
1958	Dukla Praha	Spartak Sokolovo Praha
1959	RH Bratislava	Dukla Praha
1960	Spartak Hradec Králové	Slovan Bratislava
1961	Dukla Praha	RH Bratislava
1962	Dukla Praha	Slovan Nitra
1963	Dukla Praha	Jednota Trenčín
1964	Dukla Praha	Slovan Bratislava
1965	Sparta Praha	Tatran Prešov
1966	Dukla Praha	Sparta Praha

Czech League Record (*continued*)

SEASON	CHAMPIONS	RUNNERS-UP
1967	Sparta Praha	Slovan Bratislava
1968	Spartak Trnava	Slovan Bratislava
1969	Spartak Trnava	Slovan Bratislava
1970	Slovan Bratislava	Spartak Trnava
1971	Spartak Trnava	VSS Košice
1972	Spartak Trnava	Slovan Bratislava
1973	Spartak Trnava	Tatran Prešov
1974	Slovan Bratislava	Dukla Praha
1975	Slovan Bratislava	Inter Bratislava
1976	Baník Ostrava	Slovan Bratislava
1977	Dukla Praha	Inter Bratislava
1978	ZJS Brno	Dukla Praha
1979	Dukla Praha	Baník Ostrava
1980	Baník Ostrava	ZJS Brno
1981	Baník Ostrava	Dukla Praha
1982	Dukla Praha	Baník Ostrava
1983	Bohemians Praha	Baník Ostrava
1984	Sparta Praha	Dukla Praha
1985	Sparta Praha	Bohemians Praha
1986	FC Vítkovice	Sparta Praha
1987	Sparta Praha	FC Vítkovice
1988	Sparta Praha	Dukla Praha
1989	Sparta Praha	Baník Ostrava
1990	Sparta Praha	Baník Ostrava
1991	Sparta Praha	Slovan Bratislava
1992	Slovan Bratislava	Sparta Praha
1993	Sparta Praha	Slavia Praha

* Between 1948 and 1956 the Czech League was played during the summer months. The 1957–58 season result is therefore given as 1958.

Czech Republic League Record 1994–2004

SEASON	CHAMPIONS	RUNNERS-UP
1994	Sparta Praha	Slavia Praha
1995	Sparta Praha	Slavia Praha
1996	Slavia Praha	Sigma Olomouc
1997	Sparta Praha	Slavia Praha
1998	Sparta Praha	Slavia Praha
1999	Sparta Praha	FK Teplice
2000	Sparta Praha	Slavia Praha
2001	Sparta Praha	Slavia Praha
2002	Slovan Liberec	Sparta Praha
2003	Sparta Praha	Slavia Praha
2004	Baník Ostrava	Sparta Praha

Czech League Summary

TEAM	TOTALS	CHAMPIONS & RUNNERS-UP (BOLD) (*ITALICS*)
Sparta Praha (includes AC Sparta Praha, Bratrstvi Sparta Praha, Sparta CKD Praha, Sparta CKD Sokolovo and Spartak Sokolovo)	**29**, *20*	*1925*, **26, 27, 30, 31, 32**, *33–35*, **36, 37, 38**, *39, 40, 43*, **44, 46**, *47, 48, 49–51*, **52, 53, 54, 58, 65, 66, 67, 84, 85, 86, 87–91**, *92, 93–95*, **97–2001**, *02*, **03**, *04*
Slavia Praha (includes SK Slavia Praha and Dynamo Slavia Praha)	**15**, *18*	**1925**, *26–28*, **29–31**, *32*, **33–35**, *36, 37, 38, 39*, **40–43**, *44*, **46**, *47, 48*, **48***, *93–95*, **96**, *97, 98*, **2000**, *01*, **03**
Marila Příbram (includes ÚDA Praha and Dukla Praha)	**11**, *7*	**1953**, *55*, **56**, *58, 59*, **61–64**, *66*, **74**, *77*, **78, 79, 81, 82**, *84*, **88**

This summary only features the top three clubs in the Czech League. For a full list of league champions and runners-up please see the League Records opposite.

Czech Cup Record 1918–93

YEAR	WINNERS	SCORE	RUNNERS-UP
1918	Sparta Praha	4-1	Slavia Praha
1919	Sparta Praha	2-0	Viktoria Žižkov
1920	Sparta Praha	5-1	Viktoria Žižkov
1921	Viktoria Žižkov	3-0	Sparta Praha
1922	Slavia Praha	3-2	Chechie Karlín
1923	Sparta Praha	3-1	Slavia Praha
1924	Sparta Praha	5-1	AFK Vršovice
1925	Sparta Praha	7-0	CAFC Vinohrady
1926	Slavia Praha	10-0	CAFC Vinohrady
1927	Slavia Praha	1-0	Sparta Praha
1928	Slavia Praha	1-1, (replay) 1-1, (replay) 3-2	Sparta Praha
1929	Viktoria Žižkov	3-1	SK Libeň
1930	Slavia Praha	4-2	SK Kladno
1931	Sparta Praha	3-1	Slavia Praha
1932	Slavia Praha	2-1	Sparta Praha
1933	Viktoria Žižkov	2-1	Sparta Praha
1934	Sparta Praha	6-0	SK Kladno
1935	Slavia Praha	4-1	Bohemians Praha
1936	Sparta Praha	1-1, (replay) 1-0	Slavia Praha
1937–39		*no competition*	
1940	Viktoria Žižkov	5-3	Sparta Praha
1940*	ASO Olomouc	3-1, 2-1 (2 legs)	SK Prostějov
1941	Slavia Praha	13-2	SS Plincner
1941*	Slavia Praha	2-3, 6-3 (2 legs)	Sparta Praha
1942	Bohemians Praha	8-6	Sparta Praha
1942*	Slavia Praha	5-2, 5-5 (2 legs)	Bohemians Praha
1943*	Sparta Praha	3-1, 7-1 (2 legs)	Viktoria Plzeň
1944*	Sparta Praha	4-2, 4-3 (2 legs)	Viktoria Plzeň
1945	Slavia Praha	1-1, 5-2 (2 legs)	SK Rakovník
1946	Sparta Praha	6-0, 3-0 (2 legs)	Slezská Ostrava
1947–50		*no competition*	
1951	Kovosmalt Trnava	1-0	Armaturka Ústí
1952	ATK Praha	4-3	Sokol Hradec Králové
1953–54		*no competition*	
1955	Slovan Bratislava	2-0	ÚDA Praha
1956–59		*no competition*	
1960	RH Brno	3-1	Dynamo Praha
1961	Dukla Praha	3-0	Dynamo Žilina
1962	Slovan Bratislava	1-1, 4-1 (2 legs)	Dukla Praha
1963	Slovan Bratislava	0-0, 9-0 (2 legs)	Dynamo Praha
1964	Spartak Praha Solokovo	4-1	VSS Košice
1965	Dukla Praha	0-0 (aet)(5-3 pens)	Slovan Bratislava
1966	Dukla Praha	2-1, 4-0	Tatran Prešov
1967	Spartak Trnava	2-4, 2-0 (5-4 pens)	Sparta Praha
1968	Slovan Bratislava	0-1, 2-0	Dukla Praha
1969	Dukla Praha	1-1, 1-0	VCHZ Pardubice
1970	TJ Gottwaldov	3-3, 0-0 (4-3 pens)	Slovan Bratislava
1971	Spartak Trnava	2-1, 5-1	Škoda Plzeň
1972	Sparta Praha	0-1, 4-3 (aet)(4-3 pens)	Slovan Bratislava
1973	Baník Ostrava	1-2, 3-1	VSS Košice
1974	Slovan Bratislava	0-1, 1-0 (aet)(4-3 pens)	Slavia Praha
1975	Spartak Trnava	3-1, 1-0	Sparta Praha
1976	Sparta Praha	3-2, 1-0	Slovan Bratislava
1977	Lokomotíva Košice	2-1	Sklo Union Teplice
1978	Baník Ostrava	1-0	Jednota Trenčín
1979	Lokomotíva Košice	2-1	Baník Ostrava
1980	Sparta Praha	2-0	ZTS Košice
1981	Dukla Praha	4-1	Dukla Banská Bystrica
1982	Slovan Bratislava	0-0 (aet)(4-2 pens)	Bohemians Praha
1983	Dukla Praha	2-1	Slovan Bratislava
1984	Sparta Praha	4-2	Inter Bratislava
1985	Dukla Praha	3-2	Lokomotíva Košice
1986	Spartak Trnava	1-1 (aet)(4-3 pens)	Sparta Praha
1987	DAC Dunajská Streda	0-0 (aet)(3-2 pens)	Sparta Praha
1988	Sparta Praha	2-0	Inter Bratislava
1989	Sparta Praha	3-0	Slovan Bratislava
1990	Dukla Praha	1-1 (aet)(5-4 pens)	Inter Bratislava
1991	Baník Ostrava	6-1	Spartak Trnava

Czech Cup Record (*continued*)

YEAR	WINNERS	SCORE	RUNNERS-UP
1992	Sparta Praha	2-1	Tatran Prešov
1993	1. FC Košice	5-1	Sparta Praha

* Denotes results in the short-lived Cesky' Pohár (Czech Cup).

Czech Republic Cup Record 1994–2004

YEAR	WINNERS	SCORE	RUNNERS-UP
1994	Viktoria Žižkov	2-2 (aet)(6-5 pens)	Sparta Praha
1995	SK Hradec Králové	0-0 (aet)(3-1 pens)	Viktoria Žižkov
1996	Sparta Praha	4-0	FC Petra Drnovice
1997	Slavia Praha	1-0 (aet)	FK Dukla Praha
1998	FK Jablonec	2-1 (asdet)	FC Petra Drnovice
1999	Slavia Praha	1-0 (asdet)	FC Slovan Liberec
2000	FC Slovan Liberec	2-1	Baník Ratíškovice
2001	Viktoria Žižkov	2-1 (aet)	Sparta Praha
2002	Slavia Praha	2-1	Sparta Praha
2003	FK Teplice	1-0	FK Jablonec 97
2004	Sparta Praha	2-1	Baník Ostrava

Czech Cup Summary

TEAM	TOTALS	WINNERS & RUNNERS-UP (BOLD) (*ITALICS*)	
Sparta Praha (includes Spartak Praha Sokolovo)	22, 16	**1918–20**, *21*, **23–25**, *27*, *28*, **31**, *32*, *33*, **34**, **36**, **40**, **41***, *42*, **43***, **44***, **46**, **64**, *67*, *72*, *75*, **76**, **80**, **84**, *86*, *87*, **88**, **89**, *92*, *93*, **94**, **96**, *2001*, *02*, **04**	
Slavia Praha (includes Dynamo Praha)	14, 7	*1918*, **22**, **23**, **26–28**, **30**, **31**, **32**, **35**, **36**, **41***, **45**, *60*, *63*, *74*, **97**, **99**, **2002**	
Marila Příbram (includes ÚDA Praha, and Dukla Praha)	8, 3	*1955*, **61**, *62*, **65**, *66*, **68**, **69**, **81**, **83**, **85**, **90**	
Slovan Bratislava (includes Internacional Bratislava)	6, 9	**1955**, **62**, **63**, *65*, **68**, *70*, *72*, **74**, *76*, **82**, *83*, *84*, *88–90*	
Viktoria Žižkov	6, 3	*1919*, *20*, **21**, **29**, **33**, **40**, **94**, **95**, **2001**	
Spartak Trnava	4, 1	**1967**, **71**, **75**, **86**, *91*	
Baník Ostrava	3, 2	**1973**, **78**, *79*, **91**, *2004*	
Lokomotíva Košice	2, 1	**1977**, **79**, *85*	

This summary only features clubs that have won the Czech Cup two or more times. For a full list of league champions and runners-up please see the Cup Record left.

Slovakia

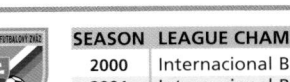

Slovensky Futbalovy Zvaz
Founded: 1938
Joined FIFA: 1994
Joined UEFA: 1993

Though soccer has been played in Slovakia since the late 19th century, it has mostly been part of Czechoslovakian football. When Slovakia gained political independence from Czechoslovakia in 1993, a national 'Superliga' was formed. A Slovakian Cup started in 1970.

SEASON	LEAGUE CHAMPIONS
2000	Internacional Bratislava
2001	Internacional Bratislava
2002	MSK Zilina
2003	MSK Zilina
2004	MSK Zilina

YEAR	CUP WINNERS
2000	Internacional Bratislava
2001	Internacional Bratislava
2002	Koba Senec
2003	Matador Púchov
2004	Artmedia Petrzalka

Poland

Polski Związek Piłki Nóżnej
Founded: 1919
Joined FIFA: 1923
Joined UEFA: 1954

SOCCER ARRIVED IN POLAND before it became a nation state. While the game took off in the cities of Łódź, Kraków and Warsaw in the early 20th century, the modern Polish state did not emerge until after the First World War. Carved out of parts of the German, Russian and Austrian empires, the new Poland quickly acquired a soccer association in 1919, and a national league followed two years later. However, Poland's borders have not stayed still since then, and the Polish league is littered with clubs that are now located in other states. Pogoń Lwów – who won four championships in the 1920s – comes from what was once the Soviet Union and is now the Ukraine. The city of Gdańsk (previously Danzig), home to several top teams, was once part of Germany as were Szczecin and Wrocław (previously Stettin and Breslau).

Cup soccer was slower in coming to Poland, with a single tournament held in 1926 and then nothing until the Communist-initiated Puchar Polski began in 1951. Alongside the new cup competition, Poland's new Communist rulers reorganized soccer at every level with extensive changes of clubs' names and control. The collapse of the Communist regime saw a further swathe of name changes and increasing problems of crowd violence. The latter culminated in October 1996, with a riot between fans of Widzew Łódź and Legia Warszawa, which resulted in each team's stadium being closed for the rest of the season.

The current league consists of an 18-club top flight and two 18-club second divisions, one based in the east of the country and one in the west. Four teams are relegated from the first division, replaced by promotions for the winners and runners-up from the regional leagues. There are currently plans to radically reduce the number of teams in the top flight.

Polish League Record 1921–2004

SEASON	CHAMPIONS	RUNNERS-UP
1921	Cracovia Kraków	Polonia Warszawa
1922	Pogoń Lwów	Warta Poznań
1923	Pogoń Lwów	Wisła Kraków
1924	*no championship*	
1925	Pogoń Lwów	Warta Poznań
1926	Pogoń Lwów	Polonia Warszawa
1927	Wisła Kraków	I.FC Katowice
1928	Wisła Kraków	Warta Poznań
1929	Warta Poznań	Garbarnia Kraków
1930	Cracovia Kraków	Wisła Kraków
1931	Garbarnia Kraków	Wisła Kraków
1932	Cracovia Kraków	Pogoń Lwów
1933	Ruch Chorzów	Pogoń Lwów
1934	Ruch Chorzów	Cracovia Kraków
1935	Ruch Chorzów	Pogoń Lwów
1936	Ruch Chorzów	Wisła Kraków
1937	Cracovia Kraków	AKS Chorzów
1938	Ruch Chorzów	Warta Poznań
1939–45	*no championship*	
1946	Polonia Warszawa	Warta Poznań
1947	Warta Poznań	Wisła Kraków
1948	Cracovia Kraków	Wisła Kraków
1949	Wisła Kraków	Ogniwo Kraków
1950	Wisła Kraków	Ruch Chorzów
1951	Ruch Chorzów*	

Polish League Record (*continued*)

SEASON	CHAMPIONS	RUNNERS-UP
1952	Ruch Chorzów	Ogniwo Kraków
1953	Ruch Chorzów	Wawel Kraków
1954	Polonia Bytom	LKS Łódź
1955	Legia Warszawa	Stal Sosnowiec
1956	Legia Warszawa	Ruch Chorzów
1957	Górnik Zabrze	Gwardia Warsawa
1958	LKS Łódź	Polonia Bytom
1959	Górnik Zabrze	Polonia Bytom
1960	Ruch Chorzów	Legia Warszawa
1961	Górnik Zabrze	Polonia Bytom
1962	Polonia Bytom	Górnik Zabrze
1963	Górnik Zabrze	Ruch Chorzów
1964	Górnik Zabrze	Zagłębie Sosnowiec
1965	Górnik Zabrze	Szombierkj Bytom
1966	Górnik Zabrze	Wisła Kraków
1967	Górnik Zabrze	Zagłębie Sosnowiec
1968	Ruch Chorzów	Legia Warszawa
1969	Legia Warszawa	Górnik Zabrze
1970	Legia Warszawa	Ruch Chorzów
1971	Górnik Zabrze	Legia Warszawa
1972	Górnik Zabrze	Zagłębie Sosnowiec
1973	Stal Mielec	Ruch Chorzów
1974	Ruch Chorzów	Górnik Zabrze
1975	Ruch Chorzów	Stal Mielec
1976	Stal Mielec	GKS Tychy
1977	Śląsk Wrocław	Widzew Łódź
1978	Wisła Kraków	Śląsk Wrocław
1979	Ruch Chorzów	Widzew Łódź
1980	Szombierkj Bytom	Widzew Łódź
1981	Widzew Łódź	Wisła Kraków
1982	Widzew Łódź	Śląsk Wrocław
1983	Lech Poznań	Widzew Łódź
1984	Lech Poznań	Widzew Łódź
1985	Górnik Zabrze	Legia Warszawa
1986	Górnik Zabrze	Legia Warszawa
1987	Górnik Zabrze	Pogoń Szczecin
1988	Górnik Zabrze	GKS Katowice
1989	Ruch Chorzów	GKS Katowice
1990	Lech Poznań	Zagłębie Lubin
1991	Zagłębie Lubin	Górnik Zabrze
1992	Lech Poznań	GKS Katowice
1993	Lech Poznań**	
1994	Legia Warszawa	GKS Katowice
1995	Legia Warszawa	Widzew Łódź
1996	Widzew Łódź	Legia Warszawa
1997	Widzew Łódź	Legia Warszawa
1998	LKS-PTAK Łódź	Polonia Warszawa
1999	Wisła Kraków	Widzew Łódź
2000	Polonia Warszawa	Wisła Kraków
2001	Wisła Kraków	Pogoń Szczecin
2002	Legia Warszawa	Wisła Kraków
2003	Wisła Kraków	Groclin-Dyskobolia Grodzisk
2004	Wisła Kraków	Legia Warszawa

* Ruch Chorzów finished sixth, but as the league programme was not completed it was awarded the title because of its cup win.

** Lech Poznań was awarded the title after Legia Warszawa and LKS Łódź (who finished first and second) were penalized for match-fixing allegations.

Polish League Summary

TEAM	TOTALS	CHAMPIONS & RUNNERS-UP (BOLD) (*ITALICS*)
Ruch Chorzów	**14**, *5*	**1933–36, 38,** *50,* **51–53,** *56,* **60,** *63,* **68,** *70,* **73,** *74,* **75,** *79,* **89**
Górnik Zabrze	**14**, *4*	**1957,** *59,* **61,** *62,* **63–67,** *69,* **71,** *72,* *74,* **85–88,** *91*

Polish League Summary (*continued*)

TEAM	TOTALS	CHAMPIONS & RUNNERS-UP (BOLD) (*ITALICS*)
Wisła Kraków	**9**, *10*	*1923*, **27**, **28**, *1930*, *31*, *36*, *47*, *48*, **49**, **50**, *66*, *78*, *81*, *99*, **2000**, **01**, **02**, **03**, **04**
Legia Warszawa	**7**, *8*	**1955**, **56**, **60**, **68**, **69**, **70**, *71*, **85**, *86*, **94**, **95**, **96**, *97*, **2002**, *04*
Cracovia Kraków	**5**, *1*	**1921**, **30**, **32**, *34*, **37**, *48*
Lech Poznań	**5**, *0*	**1983**, **84**, **90**, **92**, **93**
Widzew Łódź	**4**, *7*	*1977*, *79*, *80*, **81**, **82**, *83*, *84*, *95*, *96*, *97*, *99*
Pogoń Lwów	**4**, *3*	**1922**, **23**, **25**, **26**, *32*, *33*, *35*
Warta Poznań	**2**, *5*	*1922*, **25**, *28*, **29**, *38*, *46*, *47*
Polonia Warszawa	**2**, *3*	*1921*, *26*, **46**, *98*, **2000**
LKS Łódź	**2**, *1*	*1954*, **58**, **98**
Stal Mielec	**2**, *1*	**1973**, **75**, *76*
Polonia Bytom	**2**, *3*	*1954*, **58**, **59**, *61*, *62*
Śląsk Wrocław	**1**, *2*	**1977**, *78*, *82*
Garbarnia Kraków	**1**, *1*	*1929*, **1931**
Szombierkj Bytom	**1**, *1*	*1965*, **80**
Zagłębie Lubin	**1**, *1*	**1990**, *91*
GKS Katowice	**0**, *4*	*1988*, *89*, *92*, *94*
Zagłębie Sosnowiec	**0**, *3*	*1964*, *67*, *72*
Ogniwo Kraków	**0**, *2*	*1949*, *52*
AKS Chorzów	**0**, *1*	*1937*
Groclin-Dyskobolia Grodzisk	**0**, *1*	*2003*
GKS Tychy	**0**, *1*	*1976*
Gwardia Warszawa	**0**, *1*	*1957*
I.FC Katowice	**0**, *1*	*1927*
Pogoń Szczecin	**0**, *1*	*1987*
Stal Sosnowiec	**0**, *1*	*1955*
Wawel Kraków	**0**, *1*	*1953*

Polish Cup Record 1926–2004

YEAR	WINNERS	SCORE	RUNNERS-UP
1926	Wisła Kraków	2-1	Sparta Lwów
1927–50		*no competition*	
1951	Ruch Chorzów	2-0	Wisła Kraków
1952	Polonia Warszawa	1-0	Legia Warszawa
1953		*no competition*	
1954	Gwardia Warszawa	0-0 (aet)(replay)3-1	Wisła Kraków
1955	Legia Warszawa	5-0	Lechia Gdańsk
1956	Legia Warszawa	3-0	Górnik Zabrze
1957	LKS Łódź	2-1	Górnik Zabrze
1958–61		*no competition*	
1962	Zagłębie Sosnowiec	2-1	Górnik Zabrze
1963	Zagłębie Sosnowiec	2-0	Ruch Chorzów
1964	Legia Warszawa	2-1 (aet)	Polonia Bytom
1965	Górnik Zabrze	4-0	Czarni Zagań
1966	Legia Warszawa	2-1 (aet)	Górnik Zabrze
1967	Wisła Kraków	2-0 (aet)	Raków Częstochowa
1968	Górnik Zabrze	3-0	Ruch Chorzów
1969	Górnik Zabrze	2-0	Legia Warszawa
1970	Górnik Zabrze	3-1	Ruch Chorzów
1971	Górnik Zabrze	3-1	Zagłębie Sosnowiec
1972	Górnik Zabrze	5-2	Legia Warszawa
1973	Legia Warszawa	0-0 (aet)(4-2 pens)	Polonia Bytom
1974	Ruch Chorzów	2-0	Gwardia Warszawa
1975	Stal Rzeszów	0-0 (aet)(3-2 pens)	ROW II Rybnik
1976	Śląsk Wrocław	2-0	Stal Mielec
1977	Zagłębie Sosnowiec	1-0	Polonia Bytom
1978	Zagłębie Sosnowiec	2-0	Piast Gliwice
1979	Arka Gdynia	2-1	Wisła Kraków
1980	Legia Warszawa	5-0	Lech Poznań
1981	Legia Warszawa	1-0 (aet)	Pogoń Szczecin
1982	Lech Poznań	1-0	Pogoń Szczecin
1983	Lechia Gdańsk	2-1	Piast Gliwice
1984	Lech Poznań	3-0	Wisła Kraków
1985	Widzew Łódź	0-0 (aet)(3-1 pens)	GKS Katowice
1986	GKS Katowice	4-1	Górnik Zabrze
1987	Śląsk Wrocław	0-0 (aet)(4-3 pens)	GKS Katowice
1988	Lech Poznań	1-1 (aet)(3-2 pens)	Legia Warszawa

Polish Cup Record (*continued*)

YEAR	WINNERS	SCORE	RUNNERS-UP
1989	Legia Warszawa	5-2	Jagiellonia Białystok
1990	Legia Warszawa	2-0	GKS Katowice
1991	GKS Katowice	1-0	Legia Warszawa
1992	Miedz Legnica	1-1 (aet)(4-3 pens)	Górnik Zabrze
1993	GKS Katowice	1-1 (aet)(5-4 pens)	Ruch Chorzów
1994	Legia Warszawa	2-0	LKS Łódź
1995	Legia Warszawa	2-0	GKS Katowice
1996	Ruch Chorzów	1-0	GKS Bełchatów
1997	Legia Warszawa	2-0	GKS Katowice
1998	Amica Wronki	5-3 (aet)	Aluminium Konin
1999	Amica Wronki	1-0	GKS Bełchatów
2000	Amica Wronki	2-2, 3-0 (2 legs)	Wisła Kraków
2001	Polonia Warszawa	2-1, 2-2 (2 legs)	Górnik Zabrze
2002	Wisła Kraków	4-2, 4-0 (2 legs)	Amica Wronki
2003	Wisła Kraków	0-1, 3-0 (2 legs)	Wisła Plock
2004	Lech Poznań	2-0, 0-1 (2 legs)	Legia Warszawa

Polish Cup Summary

TEAM	TOTALS	WINNERS & RUNNERS-UP (BOLD) (*ITALICS*)
Legia Warszawa	**12**, *6*	*1952*, **55**, **56**, **64**, **66**, **69**, *72*, **73**, **80**, **81**, **88**, **89**, **90**, *91*, **94**, **95**, *97*, *2004*
Górnik Zabrze	**6**, *7*	*1956*, *57*, *62*, **65**, *66*, **68–72**, *86*, *92*, **2001**
Wisła Kraków	**4**, *5*	**1926**, *51*, *54*, **67**, *79*, *84*, *2000*, **02**, **03**
Lech Poznań	**4**, *1*	*1980*, **82**, **84**, **88**, **2004**
Zagłębie Sosnowiec	**4**, *1*	**1962**, **63**, *71*, **77**, **78**
GKS Katowice	**3**, *5*	*1985*, **86**, *87*, *90*, **91**, **93**, *95*, *97*
Ruch Chorzów	**3**, *4*	**1951**, *63*, *68*, *70*, **74**, *93*, **96**
Amica Wronki	**3**, *1*	**1998–2000**, *02*
Polonia Warszawa	**2**, *0*	**1952**, **2001**
Śląsk Wrocław	**2**, *0*	**1976**, **87**
Gwardia Warszawa	**1**, *1*	**1954**, *74*
Lechia Gdańsk	**1**, *1*	*1955*, **83**
LKS Łódź	**1**, *1*	**1957**, *94*
Arka Gdynia	**1**, *0*	**1979**
Miedz Legnica	**1**, *0*	**1992**
Stal Rzeszów	**1**, *0*	**1975**
Widzew Łódź	**1**, *0*	**1985**
Polonia Bytom	**0**, *3*	*1964*, *73*, *77*
GKS Bełchatów	**0**, *2*	*1996*, *99*
Piast Gliwice	**0**, *2*	*1978*, *83*
Pogoń Szczecin	**0**, *2*	*1981*, *82*
Aluminium Konin	**0**, *1*	*1998*
Czarni Zagań	**0**, *1*	*1965*
Jagiellonia Białystok	**0**, *1*	*1989*
Raków Częstochowa	**0**, *1*	*1967*
ROW II Rybnik	**0**, *1*	*1975*
Sparta Lwów	**0**, *1*	*1926*
Stal Mielec	**0**, *1*	*1976*
Wisła Plock	**0**, *1*	*2003*

Zbigniew Boniek is widely regarded as the greatest ever Polish soccer player. He made his name with Widzew Łódz, Polish League Champions in 1981 and 82, but it was his performances for the national team in the 1982 World Cup that persuaded Juventus of Italy to pay £1.1 million for him – then a record for a Polish player.

POLAND

307

Soccer in Southeast Europe

SOUTHEAST EUROPE

1894: First Vienna FC formed, oldest independent Austrian soccer club

1897: First Austrian cup competition, Der Challenge Cup, established

1902: Austria's first international, v Hungary, won 5-0, venue: Vienna. Hungary's first international v Austria, lost 0-5, venue: Vienna

1905: Austrian affiliation to FIFA

1908: Macedonian FA formed

1910: First Hungarian Cup Final

1919: Austrian Cup created. Hungary became independent. Yugoslavian FA formed. Yugoslavian affiliation to FIFA

1932: Albanian FA affiliation to FIFA

1936: Austria runners-up in Olympic tournament

1945: Independent Austrian soccer re-established

1952: Hungary winners of Olympic Tounament

1954: Hungarian affiliation to UEFA. Austrian affiliation to UEFA. Albanian and Yugoslavian affiliation to UEFA. Hungary runners-up in World Cup

1964: Hungary winners of Olympic tournament

1968: Hungary winners of Olympic tournament

1991: Croatian FA reformed

1992: Croatian and Slovenian affiliation to FIFA. Bosnian FA formed

1993: Croatian and Slovenian affiliation to UEFA

1994: Macedonian affiliation to FIFA and UEFA

1996: Bosnian affiliation to FIFA and UEFA

2002: Austria and Switzerland to be co-hosts of Euro 2008

Timeline dates: 1890, 1895, 1900, 1905, 1910, 1915, 1920, 1925, 1930, 1935, 1940, 1945, 1950, 1955, 1960, 1965, 1970, 1975, 1980, 1985, 1990, 1995, 2000, 2005

1895: Újpest TE formed, Hungary's oldest surviving soccer club

1901: Formation of Hungarian FA: Magyar Labdarúgó. Formation of Hungarian soccer league

1904: Formation of Austrian FA: Österreichscher Fussball-Bund

1906: Hungarian affiliation to FIFA

1912: Vienna-based league established. First Croatian FA formed

1920: Slovenian FA formed

1926: Professionalism introduced in Hungary

1930: Albanian FA formed

1938: Anschluss declared – forcible incorporation into Greater Germany. Austrian teams enter German championships until 1944.

1938: Hungary reach World Cup Final in France

1946: Communist takeover and reorganization of Hungarian soccer

1953: Hungary beat England 6-3 at Wembley, the first foreign team to do so

1956: Season abandoned due to Hungarian uprising and Soviet invasion

1991: Beginning of the break-up of Yugoslavia and Yugoslavian civil war

Key

	International soccer (Austria)
	International soccer (Hungary)
	Austria/Switzerland Euro 2008 bid
	War
	Affiliation to FIFA
	Affiliation to UEFA

★ First Vienna FC 1894

Wiener SC 1893

★ Cricket FV 1894

★ Wiener AC 1900

★ Wiener AF 1912

★ Rapid Wien 1898
Founded as Wiener Arbeiter-Fussballklub till 1899

Hat factory team
FC Wien 1918
Nicholson (1918–32)

★ FK Austria 1911
Amateure (1911–26), 1973 absorbed Wiener Athletik

SW Bregenz 1920
Bregenz
Lustenau
Austria Lustenau 1914

Kremser FC 1919

Vorwärts Steyr 1919

FC Stahl Linz 1949

Linzer ASK 1908

SV Ried 1912

Sturm Graz 1909

Innsbruck FC Tirol 1914

Salzburg Austria Salzberg 1933

Linz

Ried Im Innkreis

Salzburg

Steyr

Krems

SK Austria 1920
Klagenfurt

VIENNA

Danube

Hertha
Rudolfshi
1. Simmerin SC Wien
Hakoah

FC Admira Mödling 1971
Merger of Admir Wien 1905 and Wacker Wien,190 Moved from Floridsdorf to Mar Enzendorf as FC Admira Wacker th merged with VfB Mödling 1997

VIEN (see in

Maria Enzersdorf
VfB Mödling 1911

SV
Gloggnitz 1922

Graz
Grazer AK 1902

AUSTRIA

SLOVENIA
(see inset)

Varazdin

Zagreb

Istra Pula 1961

Rijeka 1946

Pula

Sibenik 1932

Split

Hajduk Split 1911

Buducnost Banovici

Rudar Kakanj

Boksit Milici

Zeljeznicar Sarajevo 1921

Sarajevo 1946

Lushnja 1927

NK Maribor 1958

SLOVENIA

Feroterm Pohorje 1956

Nova Gorica

Ljubljana

Primorje Ajdovščina 1924

Hit Gorica 1938

Ruse

Celje

Rudar Velenje 1948

Publikum Celje 1946

Sct Olimpija Ljubljana 1911

Dinamo Zagreb 1945
Croatia Zagreb (1993–99)

Zagreb 1949

Varteks Varaždin 1931

Slaven Belupo Koprivnica 1912

Osijek 1946

Ciballia Vinkovci 1947

Marsonia Slavonski Brod 1909

OFK Beograd 1911

Obilic Beograd 1924

Partizan Beograd 1945

Crvena Zvezda Beograd 1945

Cukaricki Beograd 1926

Rad Beograd 1958

Zeleznik Beograd 1930

BELGRADE

Danube

Southeast Europe

ORIGINS AND GROWTH OF SOCCER

SOCCER ARRIVED EARLY in Central and Eastern Europe and rose in popularity quickly with stylish, innovative play. The first soccer association in Vienna was founded by M.D. Nicholson, a Thomas Cook travel agent, in 1904. In Hungary, clubs emerged in the 1880s and 90s, often from gym clubs. MTK was made up of liberal Jewish defectors from a pro-Hapsburg national gym club. A league was founded in 1901 and a cup competition in 1910.

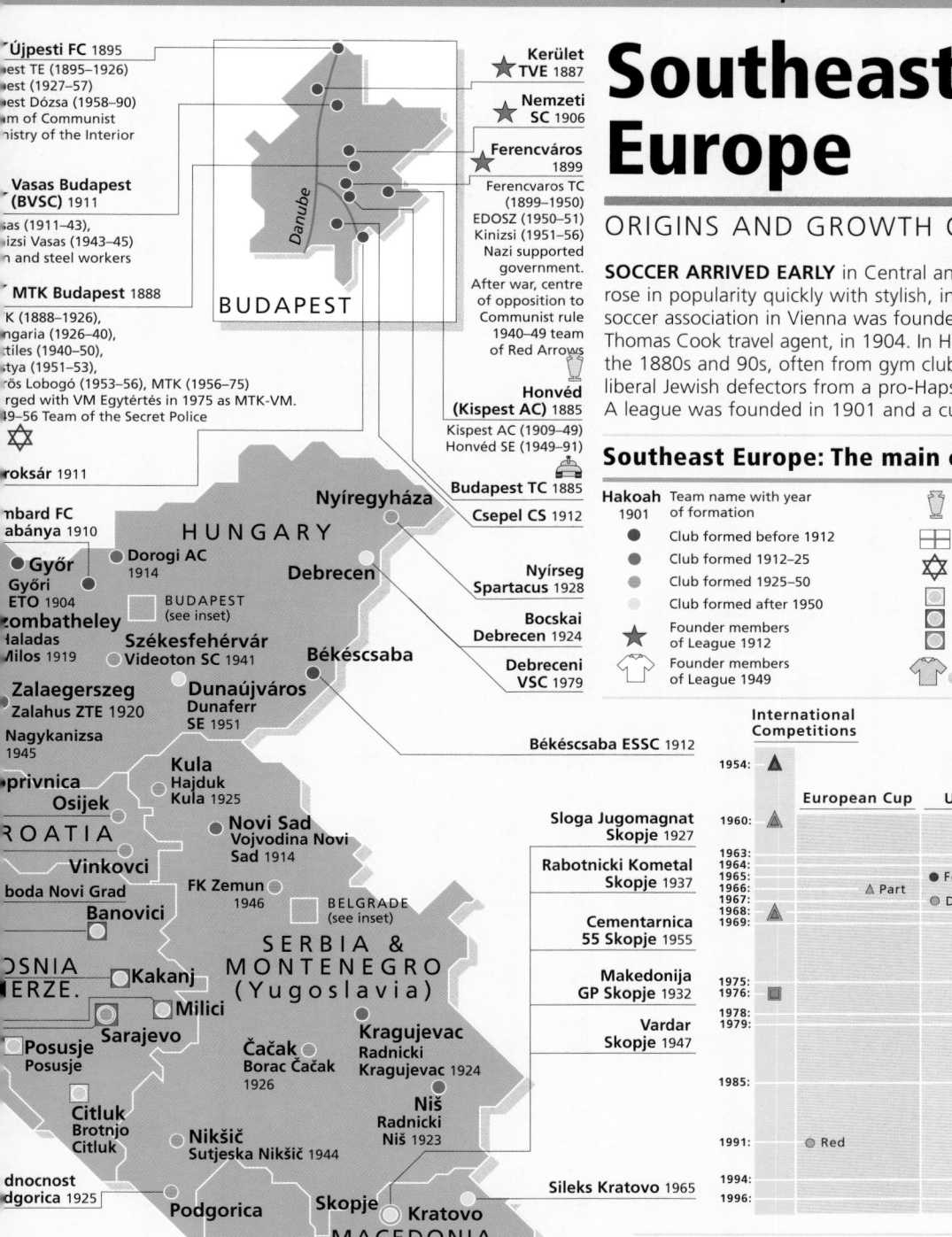

Southeast Europe: The main clubs

Hakoah 1901	Team name with year of formation
●	Club formed before 1912
●	Club formed 1912–25
●	Club formed 1925–50
○	Club formed after 1950
★	Founder members of League 1912
👕	Founder members of League 1949
🏆	Champions 1912–44
🏴󠁧󠁢󠁥󠁮󠁧󠁿	Originated from English football
✡	Jewish origins
◨	Croatian
◨	Muslim
◨	Serbian
👕	Colours and date unknown

Hungary / Budapest clubs

- Újpesti FC 1895
  - Újpest TE (1895–1926)
  - Újpest (1927–57)
  - Újpest Dózsa (1958–90)
  - Team of Communist Ministry of the Interior
- Vasas Budapest (BVSC) 1911
  - Vasas (1911–43),
  - Elözizsi Vasas (1943–45)
  - Iron and steel workers
- MTK Budapest 1888
  - MTK (1888–1926),
  - Hungaria (1926–40),
  - Textiles (1940–50),
  - Bástya (1951–53),
  - Vörös Lobogó (1953–56), MTK (1956–75),
  - merged with VM Egyetértés in 1975 as MTK-VM.
  - 1949–56 Team of the Secret Police
- Soroksár 1911
- Tatabánya FC Bánya 1910
- Győr
  - Győri ETO 1904
- Szombathely
  - Haladás Milos 1919
- Zalaegerszeg
  - Zalahus ZTE 1920
- Nagykanizsa 1945
- Kerület TVE 1887 ★
- Nemzeti SC 1906 ★
- Ferencváros 1899 ★
  - Ferencvaros TC (1899–1950)
  - EDOSZ (1950–51)
  - Kinizsi (1951–56)
  - Nazi supported government. After war, centre of opposition to Communist rule 1940–49 team of Red Arrows
- Honvéd (Kispest AC)
  - Kispest AC (1909–49)
  - Honvéd SE (1949–91)
- Budapest TC 1885
- Csepel CS 1912
- Dorogi AC 1914
- Nyíregyháza
- Debrecen
- Nyírség Spartacus 1928
- Bocskai Debrecen 1924
- Debreceni VSC 1979
- Székesfehérvár
  - Videoton SC 1941
- Dunaújváros
  - Dunaferr SE 1951
- Békéscsaba ESSC 1912

Croatia / Serbia & Montenegro

- Koprivnica
- Osijek
- Vinkovci
- Sloboda Novi Grad
- Banovici
- Kula
  - Hajduk Kula 1925
- Novi Sad
  - Vojvodina Novi Sad 1914
- FK Zemun 1946
- Sloga Jugomagnat Skopje 1927
- Rabotnicki Kometal Skopje 1937
- Cementarnica 55 Skopje 1955
- Makedonija GP Skopje 1932
- Vardar Skopje 1947

Bosnia-Herzegovina / Serbia & Montenegro (Yugoslavia)

- Kakanj
- Milici
- Posusje Posusje
- Sarajevo
- Čitluk Brotnjo Citluk
- Jednocnost Podgorica 1925
- Podgorica
- Čačak Borac Čačak 1926
- Kragujevac Radnicki Kragujevac 1924
- Niš Radnicki Niš 1923
- Nikšič Sutjeska Nikšič 1944
- Sileks Kratovo 1965
- Skopje
- Kratovo

Albania / Macedonia

- Teuta Durrës 1920
- Dinamo Tirana 1950
- Partizani Tirana 1946
- Tirana 1920
- Skumbini Peqin 1924
- Lushnjë
- Miss Ballsh 1972
- Ballsh
- Tomori Berat 1923
- Berat
- Skënderbeu Korçë 1909
- Luftetari (Kampioni) Gjirokastër 1930
- Durrës
- Tirana
- Peqin
- Veles
- Prilep
- Bitola
- Kavadarci
- Korçë
- Gjirokastër
- Borec MHK Veles 1926
- Tikves Kavadarci 1926
- Probeda Prilep 1941
- Pelister Bitola 1945

International Competitions

Year	European Cup	UEFA Cup	European Cup-Winners' Cup
1954:	▲		
1960:	△		
1963:		△ Din	
1964:			▲ MTK
1965:		● Feren	
1966:	△ Part	△ Din	
1967:			
1968:	△	▲ Feren	
1969:		▲ Újpest	
1975:			▲ Feren
1976:	■		△ FK
1978:		▲ Red	
1979:			
1985:		▲ Video	△ Rapid
1991:	○ Red		
1994:		△ Salz	
1996:			△ Rapid

Key

- ▲ World Cup runner-up
- △ European Championships runner-up
- ■ European Championship host
- ○ Austrian competition winner
- △ Austrian competition runner-up
- ● Hungarian competition winner
- ▲ Hungarian competition runner-up
- ○ Yugoslavian competition winner
- △ Yugoslavian competition runner-up

- Din – Dinamo Zagreb
- Feren – Ferencváros
- FK – FK Austria Wien
- MTK – MTK Budapest
- Part – Partizan Beograd
- Rapid – Rapid Wien
- Red – Crvena Zvezda Beograd (Red Star Belgrade)
- Salz – Austria Salzburg
- Újpest – Újpest Dózsa
- Video – Videoton

Austria

Österreichischer Fussball-Bund
Founded: 1904
Joined FIFA: 1905
Joined UEFA: 1954

IN AUSTRIA, EARLY COMPETITIVE SOCCER was firmly centred on the capital, Vienna. A local cup competition – Der Challenge Cup – ran from 1897 to 1911, and included teams invited from Hungary. It was superseded by a Vienna-based league. After the 1938 *Anschluss* with Germany, Austria's top clubs competed in a greater German league as well as their own, and indeed won that competition a number of times. After the Second World War the league was re-established on a national basis, the top flight consisting of ten teams playing each other four times a season.

The Austrian Cup was first played in 1919, and although it lapsed during the Second World War and for nearly a decade afterwards, it has been running annually again since 1959.

AUSTRIA (sidebar)

Austrian League Record 1911–2004

SEASON	CHAMPIONS	RUNNERS-UP
1911	SK Rapid Wien	Wiener Sport-Club
1912	SK Rapid Wien	Wiener Sport-Club
1913	SK Rapid Wien	Wiener Association FC
1914	Wiener Association FC	SK Rapid Wien
1915	Wiener AC	Wiener Association FC
1916	SK Rapid Wien	FAC Wien
1917	SK Rapid Wien	FAC Wien
1918	FAC Wien	SK Rapid Wien
1919	SK Rapid Wien	SC Rudolfshügel Wien
1920	SK Rapid Wien	SV Amateure Wien
1921	SK Rapid Wien	SV Amateure Wien
1922	Wiener Sport-Club	SC Hakoah Wien
1923	SK Rapid Wien	SV Amateure Wien
1924	SV Amateure Wien	First Vienna FC
1925	SC Hakoah Wien	SV Amateure Wien
1926	SV Amateure Wien	First Vienna FC
1927	Admira Wien	Brigittenauer AC Wien
1928	Admira Wien	SK Rapid Wien
1929	SK Rapid Wien	Admira Wien
1930	SK Rapid Wien	Admira Wien
1931	First Vienna FC	Admira Wien
1932	Admira Wien	First Vienna FC
1933	First Vienna FC	SK Rapid Wien
1934	Admira Wien	SK Rapid Wien
1935	SK Rapid Wien	Admira Wien
1936	Admira Wien	First Vienna FC
1937	Admira Wien	FK Austria Wien
1938	SK Rapid Wien	Wiener Sport-Club
1939	Admira Wien	SC Wacker Wien
1940	SK Rapid Wien	SC Wacker Wien
1941	SK Rapid Wien	SC Wacker Wien
1942	First Vienna FC	FC Wien
1943	First Vienna FC	Wiener AC
1944	First Vienna FC	FAC Wien
1945	SK Rapid Wien	SC Wacker Wien
1946	SK Rapid Wien	FK Austria Wien
1947	SC Wacker Wien	SK Rapid Wien
1948	SK Rapid Wien	SC Wacker Wien
1949	FK Austria Wien	SK Rapid Wien
1950	FK Austria Wien	SK Rapid Wien
1951	SK Rapid Wien	SC Wacker Wien
1952	SK Rapid Wien	FK Austria Wien
1953	FK Austria Wien	SC Wacker Wien
1954	SK Rapid Wien	FK Austria Wien
1955	First Vienna FC	Wiener Sport-Club
1956	SK Rapid Wien	SC Wacker Wien

Austrian League Record (*continued*)

SEASON	CHAMPIONS	RUNNERS-UP
1957	SK Rapid Wien	First Vienna FC
1958	Wiener Sport-Club	SK Rapid Wien
1959	Wiener Sport-Club	SK Rapid Wien
1960	SK Rapid Wien	Wiener Sport-Club
1961	FK Austria Wien	First Vienna FC
1962	FK Austria Wien	Linzer ASK
1963	FK Austria Wien	Admira Energie
1964	SK Rapid Wien	FK Austria Wien
1965	Linzer ASK	SK Rapid Wien
1966	Admira Energie	SK Rapid Wien
1967	SK Rapid Wien	Wacker Innsbruck
1968	SK Rapid Wien	Wacker Innsbruck
1969	FK Austria Wien	Wiener Sport-Club
1970	FK Austria Wien	Wiener Sport-Club
1971	Wacker Innsbruck	Austria Salzburg
1972	Wacker Innsbruck	FK Austria Wien
1973	Wacker Innsbruck	SK Rapid Wien
1974	VÖEST Linz	Wacker Innsbruck
1975	Wacker Innsbruck	VÖEST Linz
1976	FK Austria/WAC	Wacker Innsbruck
1977	Wacker Innsbruck	SK Rapid Wien
1978	FK Austria/WAC	SK Rapid Wien
1979	FK Austria Wien	Wiener Sport-Club
1980	FK Austria Wien	VÖEST Linz
1981	FK Austria Wien	SK Sturm Graz
1982	SK Rapid Wien	FK Austria Wien
1983	SK Rapid Wien	FK Austria Wien
1984	FK Austria Wien	SK Rapid Wien
1985	FK Austria Wien	SK Rapid Wien
1986	FK Austria Wien	SK Rapid Wien
1987	SK Rapid Wien	FK Austria Wien
1988	SK Rapid Wien	FK Austria Wien
1989	FC Tirol Innsbruck	FC Admira Wacker
1990	FC Tirol Innsbruck	FK Austria Wien
1991	FC Tirol Innsbruck	FK Austria Wien
1992	FK Austria Wien	SV Austria Salzburg
1993	FK Austria Wien	SV Austria Salzburg
1994	SV Austria Salzburg	FK Austria Wien
1995	SV Austria Salzburg	SK Sturm Graz
1996	SK Rapid Wien	SK Sturm Graz
1997	SV Austria Salzburg	SK Sturm Graz
1998	SK Sturm Graz	SK Rapid Wien
1999	SK Sturm Graz	FC Tirol Innsbruck
2000	FC Tirol Innsbruck	SK Sturm Graz
2001	FC Tirol Innsbruck	SK Rapid Wien
2002	FC Tirol Innsbruck	SK Sturm Graz
2003	FK Austria Wien	Grazer AK
2004	Grazer AK	FK Austria Wien

Austrian League Summary

TEAM	TOTALS	CHAMPIONS & RUNNERS-UP (BOLD) (ITALICS)
SK Rapid Wien	32, 21	1911–13, *14, 16, 17, 18, 19–21,* 23, *28,* 29, 30, *33, 34,* 35, *38,* 40, 41, 45, 46, *47, 48, 49, 50,* 51, 52, *54,* 56, 57, *58, 59,* 60, 64, 65, 66, 67, 68, *73, 77, 78,* 82, 83, *84–86,* 87, 88, 96, *97, 98,* 2001
FK Austria Wien (Includes SV Amateure Wien)	19, 18	1920, 21, 23, 24, 25, 26, *37, 46, 49,* 50, 52, 53, *54,* 61–63, 64, 69, 70, 72, *79–81,* 82, 83, 84–86, *87, 88,* 90, 91, 92, 93, 94, 2003, 04

This summary only features the top two clubs in the Austrian League. For a full list of league champions and runners-up please see the League Record above.

Grazer AK players celebrate their championship victory in 2004.

Austrian Cup Record 1919–2004

YEAR	WINNERS	SCORE	RUNNERS-UP
1919	SK Rapid Wien	3-0	Wiener Sport-Club
1920	SK Rapid Wien	5-2	SV Amateure Wien
1921	SV Amateure Wien	2-1	Wiener Sport-Club
1922	Wiener Association FC	2-1	SV Amateure Wien
1923	Wiener Sport-Club	3-1	SC Wacker Wien
1924	SV Amateure Wien	8-6 (aet)	SK Slovan Wien
1925	SV Amateure Wien	3-1	First Vienna FC
1926	SV Amateure Wien	4-3	First Vienna FC
1927	SK Rapid Wien	3-0	FK Austria Wien
1928	Admira Wien	2-1	Wiener AC
1929	First Vienna FC	3-2	SK Rapid Wien
1930	First Vienna FC	1-0	FK Austria Wien
1931	Wiener AC	16 pts-15 pts (league system)	FK Austria Wien
1932	Admira Wien	6-1	Wiener AC
1933	FK Austria Wien	1-0	Brigittenauer AC Wien
1934	Admira Wien	8-0	SK Rapid Wien
1935	FK Austria Wien	5-1	Wiener AC
1936	FK Austria Wien	3-0	First Vienna FC
1937	First Vienna FC	2-0	Wiener SC
1938	WAC Schwarz-Rot	1-0	Wiener SC
1939–45		no competition	
1946	SK Rapid Wien	2-1	First Vienna FC
1947	Wacker Wien	4-3	FK Austria Wien
1948	FK Austria Wien	2-0	SK Sturm Graz
1949	FK Austria Wien	5-2	Vorwärts Steyr
1950–58		no competition	
1959	Wiener AC	2-0	SK Rapid Wien
1960	FK Austria Wien	4-2	SK Rapid Wien
1961	SK Rapid Wien	3-1	First Vienna FC
1962	FK Austria Wien	4-1	Grazer AK
1963	FK Austria Wien	1-0	Linzer ASK
1964	Admira Energie	1-0	FK Austria Wien
1965	Linzer ASK	1-1, 1-0	Wiener Neustadt
1966	Admira Energie	1-0	SK Rapid Wien
1967	FK Austria Wien	1-2,1-0 (aet)(2 legs)	Linzer ASK
1968	SK Rapid Wien	2-0	Grazer AK
1969	SK Rapid Wien	2-1	Wiener Sport-Club

Austrian Cup Record (*continued*)

YEAR	WINNERS	SCORE	RUNNERS-UP
1970	Wacker Innsbruck	1-0	Linzer ASK
1971	FK Austria Wien	2-1 (aet)	SK Rapid Wien
1972	SK Rapid Wien	1-2, 3-1	Wiener Sport-Club
1973	Wacker Innsbruck*	1-0, 1-2	SK Rapid Wien
1974	FK Austria Wien	2-1, 1-1	Austria Salzburg
1975	Wacker Innsbruck	3-0, 0-2	Sturm Graz
1976	SK Rapid Wien*	1-0, 1-2	Wacker Innsbruck
1977	FK Austria Wien	1-0, 3-0	Wiener Sport-Club
1978	Wacker Innsbruck	1-1, 2-1	VÖEST Linz
1979	Wacker Innsbruck	1-0, 1-1	FC Admira/Wacker
1980	FK Austria Wien	0-1, 2-0	Austria Salzburg
1981	Grazer AK	0-1, 2-0 (aet)(2 legs)	Austria Salzburg
1982	FK Austria Wien	1-0, 3-1	Wacker Innsbruck
1983	SK Rapid Wien	3-0, 5-0	Wacker Innsbruck
1984	SK Rapid Wien*	1-3, 2-0	FK Austria Wien
1985	SK Rapid Wien	3-3 (aet)(4-3 pens)	FK Austria Wien
1986	FK Austria Wien	6-4 (aet)	SK Rapid Wien
1987	SK Rapid Wien	2-0, 2-2	FC Tirol Innsbruck
1988	Kremser SC*	2-0, 1-3	FC Tirol Innsbruck
1989	FC Tirol Innsbruck	0-2, 6-2	FC Admira/Wacker
1990	FK Austria Wien	3-1 (aet)	SK Rapid Wien
1991	SV Stockerau	2-1	SK Rapid Wien
1992	FK Austria Wien	1-0	FC Admira/Wacker
1993	Wacker Innsbruck	3-1	SK Rapid Wien
1994	FK Austria Wien	4-0	FC Linz
1995	SK Rapid Wien	1-0	DSV Leoben
1996	SK Sturm Graz	3-1	FC Admira/Wacker
1997	SK Sturm Graz	2-1	First Vienna FC
1998	SV Ried im Innkreis	3-1	SK Sturm Graz
1999	SK Sturm Graz	1-1 (aet) (4-2 pens)	Linzer ASK
2000	Grazer AK	2-2 (aet) (4-3 pens)	Austria Salzburg
2001	FC Kärnten	2-1 (aet)	FC Tirol Innsbruck
2002	Grazer AK	3-2	SK Sturm Graz
2003	FK Austria Wien	3-0	FC Kärnten
2004	Grazer AK	3-3 (aet)(5-4 pens)	FK Austria Wien

* Denotes winners on away goals rule.

Austrian Cup Summary

TEAM	TOTALS	WINNERS & RUNNERS-UP (BOLD) (*ITALICS*)
FK Austria Wien (includes SV Amateure Wien)	**23**, *10*	*1920*, **21**, **22**, **24**–**26**, *27*, **30**, **31**, **33**, **35**, **36**, *47*, **48**, **49**, **60**, **62**, **63**, *64*, *67*, **71**, **74**, **77**, **80**, **82**, *84*, *85*, **86**, **90**, **92**, **94**, **2003**, *04*
SK Rapid Wien	**14**, *11*	**1919**, **20**, **27**, *29*, **34**, **46**, *59*, **60**, *61*, *66*, *68*, **69**, *71*, **72**, **73**, *76*, **83**–**85**, *86*, *87*, **90**, *91*, *93*, **95**

This summary only features the top two clubs in the Austrian Cup. For a full list of league champions and runners-up please see the Cup Record above.

Liechtenstein

Liechtensteiner Fussballverband
Founded: 1934
Joined FIFA: 1974
Joined UEFA: 1992

YEAR	CUP WINNERS
2000	FC Vaduz
2001	FC Vaduz
2002	FC Vaduz
2003	FC Vaduz
2004	FC Vaduz

It's hard to run a league with only 35,000 inhabitants, and the handful of registered club sides in the Fussballverband play in the lower reaches of the Swiss league. However, Liechtenstein's annual cup has been running since 1946, during which time the trophy has been won 33 times by FC Vaduz.

Slovenia

Nogometna Zveza Slovenije
Founded: 1920
Joined FIFA: 1992
Joined UEFA: 1993

NZS

SEASON	LEAGUE CHAMPIONS
2000	NK Maribor
2001	NK Maribor
2002	NK Maribor
2003	NK Maribor
2004	HIT Gorica

YEAR	CUP WINNERS
2000	SCT Olimpija Ljubljana
2001	HIT Gorica
2002	HIT Gorica
2003	SCT Olimpija Ljubljana
2004	NK Maribor

A separate national league and cup competition have been running in Slovenia since the country's independence in 1991.

Hungary

Magyar Labdarúgó Szövetség
Founded: 1901
Joined FIFA: 1906
Joined UEFA: 1954

THE HUNGARIAN FOOTBALL ASSOCIATION and the league championship were both established in 1901, but drew on a decade's competitive soccer firmly established in Budapest. Hungarian soccer was always quite separate from any other part of the Austro-Hungarian Empire, which disintegrated in 1918. The amateur years (1901–26) were dominated by the Budapest teams MTK Budapest and Ferencváros, and saw the establishment of a national cup competition in 1910. During the Second World War, the league carried on until 1944, with teams from outside Hungary. The 1944 champion, Nagyváradi AC, was from north-western Romania.

After the war, domestic soccer was treated to the usual Communist takeover and reorganization. Not surprisingly, the army-backed team Honvéd dominated the era. The 1956 uprising against both Soviet occupiers and homegrown Communists saw the league abandoned and the rapid departure of star players Puskas, Kocis and Czibor for Spain. The final decades of Communist rule saw Honvéd and Ujpesti in the forefront of the Hungarian league.

The post-Communist era has seen a return of MTK (now called MTK Hungária FC) and Ferencváros to prominence, though woeful finances, betting scandals and stadium violence have left all in the league struggling.

Hungarian Amateur League Record 1901–26

SEASON	CHAMPIONS	RUNNERS-UP
1901	BTC	MUE
1902	BTC	FTC
1903	FTC	BTC
1904	MTK	FTC
1905	FTC	Postas
1906	no championship	
1907	FTC	MAC
1908	MTK	FTC
1909	FTC	MAC
1910	FTC	MTK
1911	FTC	MTK
1912	FTC	MTK
1913	FTC	MTK
1914	MTK	FTC
1915–16	no championship	
1917	MTK	Törekvés
1918	MTK	FTC
1919	MTK	FTC
1920	MTK	KAC
1921	MTK	ÚTE
1922	MTK	FTC
1923	MTK	ÚTE
1924	MTK	FTC
1925	MTK	FTC
1926	FTC	MTK

Hungarian Professional League Record 1927–2004

SEASON	CHAMPIONS	RUNNERS-UP
1927	Ferencváros	Újpest
1928	Ferencváros	Hungária
1929	Hungária	Ferencváros
1930	Újpest	Ferencváros

Hungarian League Record (*continued*)

SEASON	CHAMPIONS	RUNNERS-UP
1931	Újpest	Hungária
1932	Ferencváros	Újpest
1933	Újpest	Hungária
1934	Ferencváros	Újpest
1935	Ujpest	Ferencváros
1936	Hungária	Újpest
1937	Hungária	Ferencváros
1938	Ferencváros	Újpest
1939	Újpest	Ferencváros
1940	Ferencváros	Hungária
1941	Ferencváros	Újpest
1942	Csepeli WMFC	Újpest
1943	Csepeli WMFC	Nagyváradi AC
1944	Nagyváradi AC	Ferencváros
1945	no championship	
1946	Újpest	Vasas
1947	Újpest	Kispest
1948	Csepel	Vasas
1949	Ferencváros	Hungária
1950	Honvéd	EDOSZ
1950*	Honvéd	Textiles
1951	Bástya	Honvéd
1952	Honvéd	Bástya
1953	Vörös Lobogó	Honvéd
1954	Honvéd	Vörös Lobogó
1955	Honvéd	Vörös Lobogó
1956	no championship**	
1957	Vasas SC	Hungária
1958	MTK	Honvéd
1959	Csepel	MTK
1960	Újpest Dozsa	Ferencváros
1961	Vasas SC	Újpest Dozsa
1962	Vasas SC	Újpest Dozsa
1963	Ferencváros	MTK
1963*	Győri V. ETO	Honvéd
1964	Ferencváros	Honvéd
1965	Vasas SC	Ferencváros
1966	Vasas SC	Ferencváros
1967	Ferencváros	Újpest Dozsa
1968	Ferencváros	Újpest Dozsa
1969	Újpest Dozsa	Honvéd
1970	Újpest Dozsa	Ferencváros
1971	Újpest Dozsa	Ferencváros
1972	Újpest Dozsa	Honvéd
1973	Újpest Dozsa	Ferencváros
1974	Újpest Dozsa	Ferencváros
1975	Újpest Dozsa	Honvéd
1976	Ferencváros	Videoton
1977	Vasas SC	Újpest Dozsa
1978	Újpest Dozsa	Honvéd
1979	Újpest Dozsa	Ferencváros
1980	Honvéd	Újpest Dozsa
1981	Ferencváros	Tatabánya
1982	Rába ETO Győr	Ferencváros
1983	Rába ETO Győr	Ferencváros
1984	Honvéd	Rába ETO Győr
1985	Honvéd	Rába ETO Győr
1986	Honvéd	PMSC
1987	MTK-VM	Újpest Dozsa
1988	Honvéd	Tatabánya
1989	Honvéd	Ferencváros
1990	Újpest Dozsa	MTK-VM
1991	Honvéd	Ferencváros
1992	Ferencváros	Vác FC Samsung
1993	Kispest-Honvéd	Vác FC Samsung
1994	Vác FC Samsung	Kispest HFC
1995	Ferencváros	ÚTE
1996	Ferencváros	BVSC

Hungarian League Record (*continued*)

SEASON	CHAMPIONS	RUNNERS-UP
1997	MTK	ÚTE
1998	Újpesti FC	Ferencváros
1999	MTK Hungária FC	Ferencváros
2000	Dunaferr FC	MTK Hungária FC
2001	Ferencváros	Dunaferr FC
2002	Zalahús Zte FC	Ferencváros
2003	MTK Hungária FC	Ferencváros
2004	Ferencváros	Debreceni VSC

* Extra autumn leagues played during these years.
** League championship was abandoned following the Soviet invasion.

Hungarian League Summary

TEAM	TOTALS	CHAMPIONS & RUNNERS-UP (BOLD) (ITALICS)
Ferencváros (includes FTC and EDOSZ)	28, 32	*1902*, **03, 04, 05, 07, 08, 09–13,** *14, 18, 19, 22, 24, 25,* **26–28,** *29, 30,* **32, 34,** *35, 37,* **38, 39, 40, 41,** *44,* **49, 50,** *60,* **63, 64,** *65, 66,* **67, 68,** *70, 71,* **73, 74, 76,** *79,* **81,** *82, 83,89, 91,* **92, 95, 96,** *98,* **99,** *2001, 02,* **03,** *04*
MTK Hungária FC (includes MTK, Hungária, Vörös Lobogó, Bástya, MTK-VM and Textiles)	22, 18	**1904, 08, 10–13, 14,** *17–25,* **26,** *28,* **29,** *31, 33,* **36, 37,** *40,* **49, 50*,** *51, 52,* **53,** *54, 55, 57,* **58,** *59, 63,* **87, 90, 97,** *99,* **2000, 03**
Újpesti FC (includes ÚTE, Újpest and Újpest Dozsa)	19, 18	*1921, 23, 27,* **30, 31,** *32,* **33, 34, 35,** *36, 38, 39,* **41, 42, 46, 47, 60,** *61, 62,* **67, 68,** *69–75, 77,* **78, 79,** *80,* **87,** *90,* **95,** *97,* **98**
Kispest-Honvéd FC (includes Kispest, Kispest HFC and Honvéd)	13, 11	*1947,* **50,** *50*, 51, 52,* **53, 54, 55,** *58,* **63*, 64, 69, 72,** *75, 78,* **80,** *84–86,* **88, 89,** *91,* **93, 94**

* Denotes honours in extra autumn leagues.
This summary only features the top four clubs in the Hungarian League. For a full list of league champions and runners-up please see the League Record above.

Hungarian Cup Record 1910–2004

YEAR	WINNERS	SCORE	RUNNERS-UP
1910	MTK	1-1, (replay) 3-1	BTC
1911	MTK	1-0	MAC
1912	MTK	w/o	FTC
1913	FTC	2-1	BAK
1914	MTK	4-0	MAC
1915–21		*no competition*	
1922	FTC	2-2, (replay) 1-0	ÚTE
1923	MTK	4-1	ÚTE
1924		*no competition*	
1925	MTK	4-0	ÚTE
1926	Kispest AC	1-1, (replay) 3-2 (aet)	Budapest EAC
1927	Ferencváros	3-0	Újpest
1928	Ferencváros	5-1	Attila Miskolc
1929		*no competition*	
1930	Bocskai Debrecen	5-1	Bástya Szeged
1931	Kerület TVE	4-1	Ferencváros
1932	Hungária	1-1, (replay) 4-3	Ferencváros
1933	Ferencváros	1-1	Újpest
1934	Soroksar	2-2, (replay) 1-1, (replay) 2-0	BSZKRT
1935	Ferencváros	2-1	Hungária
1936–40		*no competition*	
1941	Szolnoki MAV	3-0	Salgótarján BTC
1942	Ferencváros	6-2	DIMAVAG
1943	Ferencváros	3-0	Salgótarján BTC
1944	Ferencváros	2-2, (replay) 3-1	Kolozsvári AC

Hungarian Cup Record (*continued*)

YEAR	WINNERS	SCORE	RUNNERS-UP
1945–51		*no competition*	
1952	Bástya	3-2	Dorogi AC
1953–54		*no competition*	
1955	Vasas	3-2	Honvéd
1956	Ferencváros	2-1	Salgótarján BTC
1957–63		*no competition*	
1964	Honvéd	1-0	Győri V. ETO
1965	Győri V. ETO	4-0	Diósgyőri VTK
1966	Győri V. ETO	1-1, (replay) 3-2	Ferencváros
1967	Győri V. ETO	1-0	Salgótarján BTC
1968	MTK	2-1	Honvéd
1969	Újpest Dozsa	3-1	Honvéd
1970	Újpest Dozsa	3-2	Komio Bányász
1971		*no competition*	
1972	Ferencváros	2-1	Tatabánya Bányász
1973	Vasas	4-3	Honvéd
1974	Ferencváros	3-1	Komio Bányász
1975	Újpest Dozsa	3-2	Haladás VSE
1976	Ferencváros	1-0	MTK-VM
1977	Diósgyőri VTK	*	Ferencváros
1978	Ferencváros	4-2	Pécsi MSC
1979	Rába ETO Győr	1-0	Ferencváros
1980	Diósgyőri VTK	3-1	Vasas
1981	Vasas	1-0	Diósgyőri VTK
1982	Újpest Dozsa	2-0	Videoton
1983	Újpest Dozsa	3-2	Honvéd
1984	Siófoki Bányász	2-1	Rába ETO Győr
1985	Honvéd	5-0	Tatabánya Bányász
1986	Vasas	0-0 (5-4 pens)	Ferencváros
1987	Újpest Dozsa	3-2	Pécsi MSC
1988	Békéscsaba ESSC	3-2	Honvéd
1989	Honvéd	1-0	Ferencváros
1990	Pécsi MSC	2-0	Honvéd
1991	Ferencváros	1-0	Vác Izzo FC
1992	Újpest Dozsa	1-0	Vác FC Samsung
1993	Ferencváros	1-1, (replay) 1-1 (5-3 pens)	Szombathely Haladás VSE
1994	Ferencváros	3-0, 2-1 (2 legs)	Honvéd
1995	Ferencváros	2-0, 4-3 (2 legs)	Vác FC Samsung
1996	Honvéd	1-0, 2-0 (2 legs)	BVSC Dreher
1997	MTK Hungária FC	6-0, 2-0 (2 legs)	BVSC Budapest
1998	MTK Hungária FC	1-0	Újpesti FC
1999	Debreceni VSC	2-1	Lombard FC Tatabánya
2000	MTK Hungária FC	3-1	Vasas DH
2001	Debreceni VSC	5-2	Videoton
2002	Újpesti FC	2-1	Szombathely Haladás VSE
2003	Ferencváros	2-1	Debreceni VSC
2004	Ferencváros	3-1	Honvéd

w/o denotes walk over
* A league format was used to determine the winner of the 1977 cup.

Hungarian Cup Summary

TEAM	TOTALS	WINNERS & RUNNERS-UP (BOLD) (ITALICS)
Ferencváros (includes FTC)	20, 8	*1912,* **13,** *22,* **27, 28,** *31, 32,* **33, 35,** *42–44,* **56,** *66,* **72, 74, 76, 77, 78,** *79, 86, 89,* **91,** *93–95,* **2003, 04**
MTK Hungária FC (includes MTK, Hungária, Bástya and MTK-VM)	12, 2	**1910–12, 14,** *23,* **25,** *32,* **35,** *52,* **68,** *76,* **97, 98,** *2000*
Újpesti FC (includes ÚTE, Újpest and Újpest Dozsa)	8, 6	*1922, 23, 25, 27, 33,* **69, 70, 75,** *82,* **83, 87,** *92,* **98,** *2002*

This summary only features the top three clubs in the Hungarian Cup. For a full list of cup winners and runners-up please see the Cup Record above.

Serbia & Montenegro

Football Association of Serbia & Montenegro
Founded: 1919
Joined FIFA: 1919
Joined UEFA: 1993

BEFORE THE FIRST WORLD WAR, clubs existed in Belgrade, Split, Zagreb and elsewhere. After the postwar dismemberment of the Ottoman and Austro-Hungarian Empires, the new state of Yugoslavia was formed. With it, in 1919, came a national FA. A national league was established in 1923 but, like Yugoslavia, it was fragmented by the Second World War. Croatia's alliance with Germany saw the creation of an independent Croatian league which lasted for the duration of the war.

With the end of the war and the triumph of General Tito's Communist partisans, Yugoslavian soccer was reorganized and a national league re-created. It has run continuously ever since, despite war in the 1990s and the departure of Croatian, Bosnian, Slovenian and Macedonian states and clubs. The Yugoslavian FA was renamed the FA of Serbia & Montenegro in 2002.

Yugoslavian League Record 1923–91

SEASON	CHAMPIONS	RUNNERS-UP
1923	Gradanski Zagreb	SASK Sarajevo
1924	Yugoslavia Beograd	Hajduk Split
1925	Yugoslavia Beograd	Gradanski Beograd
1926	Gradanski Zagreb	Yugoslav Beograd
1927	Hajduk Split	BSK Beograd
1928	Concordia Zagreb	Hajduk Split
1929	Hajduk Split	BSK Beograd
1930	Concordia Zagreb	Yugoslav Beograd
1931	BSK Beograd	Concordia Zagreb
1932	Concordia Zagreb	Hajduk Split
1933	BSK Beograd	Hajduk Split
1934	no championship	
1935	BSK Beograd	Yugoslav Beograd
1936	BSK Beograd	Slavia Sarajevo
1937	Gradanski Zagreb	Hajduk Split
1938	HASK Zagreb	BSK Beograd
1939	BSK Beograd	Gradanski Beograd
1940	Gradanski Zagreb	BSK Beograd
1941–46	no championship	
1947	Partizan Beograd	Dinamo Zagreb
1948	Dinamo Zagreb	Hajduk Split
1949	Partizan Beograd	Crvena Zvezda
1950	Hajduk Split	Crvena Zvezda
1951	Crvena Zvezda	Dinamo Zagreb
1952	Hajduk Split	Crvena Zvezda
1953	Crvena Zvezda	Hajduk Split
1954	Dinamo Zagreb	Partizan Beograd
1955	Hajduk Split	BSK Beograd
1956	Crvena Zvezda	Partizan Beograd
1957	Crvena Zvezda	Vojvodina Novi Sad
1958	Dinamo Zagreb	Partizan Beograd
1959	Crvena Zvezda	Partizan Beograd
1960	Crvena Zvezda	Dinamo Zagreb
1961	Partizan Beograd	Crvena Zvezda
1962	Partizan Beograd	Vojvodina Novi Sad
1963	Partizan Beograd	Dinamo Zagreb
1964	Crvena Zvezda	OFK Beograd
1965	Partizan Beograd	FK Sarajevo
1966	Vojvodina Novi Sad	Dinamo Zagreb
1967	FK Sarajevo	Dinamo Zagreb
1968	Crvena Zvezda	Dinamo Zagreb
1969	Crvena Zvezda	Dinamo Zagreb
1970	Crvena Zvezda	Partizan Beograd
1971	Hajduk Split	Željeznicar Sarajevo
1972	Željeznicar Sarajevo	Crvena Zvezda

Yugoslavian League Record (*continued*)

SEASON	CHAMPIONS	RUNNERS-UP
1973	Crvena Zvezda	Velez Mostar
1974	Hajduk Split	Velez Mostar
1975	Hajduk Split	Vojvodina Novi Sad
1976	Partizan Beograd	Hajduk Split
1977	Crvena Zvezda	Dinamo Zagreb
1978	Partizan Beograd	Crvena Zvezda
1979	Hajduk Split	Dinamo Zagreb
1980	Crvena Zvezda	FK Sarajevo
1981	Crvena Zvezda	Hajduk Split
1982	Dinamo Zagreb	Crvena Zvezda
1983	Partizan Beograd	Dinamo Zagreb
1984	Crvena Zvezda	Partizan Beograd
1985	FK Sarajevo	Hajduk Split
1986	Partizan Beograd	Crvena Zvezda
1987	Partizan Beograd	Velez Mostar
1988	Crvena Zvezda	Partizan Beograd
1989	Vojvodina Novi Sad	Crvena Zvezda
1990	Crvena Zvezda	Dinamo Zagreb
1991	Crvena Zvezda	Dinamo Zagreb

Serbia & Montenegro League Record 1992–2004

SEASON	CHAMPIONS	RUNNERS-UP
1992	Crvena Zvezda	Partizan Beograd
1993	Partizan Beograd	Crvena Zvezda
1994	Partizan Beograd	Crvena Zvezda
1995	Vojvodina Novi Sad	Crvena Zvezda
1996	Partizan Beograd	Crvena Zvezda
1997	Partizan Beograd	Crvena Zvezda
1998	FK Obilić	Crvena Zvezda
1999	Partizan Beograd	FK Obilić
2000	Crvena Zvezda	Partizan Beograd
2001	Crvena Zvezda	Partizan Beograd
2002	Partizan Beograd	Crvena Zvezda
2003	Partizan Beograd	Crvena Zvezda
2004	Crvena Zvezda	Partizan Beograd

Serbia & Montenegro League Summary

TEAM	TOTALS	CHAMPIONS & RUNNERS-UP (BOLD) (*ITALICS*)
Crvena Zvezda	22, 17	*1949, 50,* **51,** *52,* **53, 56, 57, 59, 60,** *61,* **64, 68–70,** *72,* **73, 77, 78, 80, 81,** *82,* **84,** *86,* **88,** *89,* **90–92,** *93–98,* **2000,** *01,* **02,** *03,* **04**
Partizan Beograd	18, 11	**1947,** *49,* **54,** *56,* **58,** *59,* **61–63,** *65,* **70,** *76,* **78,** *83,* **84,** *86, 87,* **88,** *92,* **93,** *94,* **96, 97,** *99,* **2000,** *01,* **02,** *03,* **04**
Hajduk Split	9, 10	*1924,* **27, 28,** *29,* **32, 33, 37,** *48,* **50,** *52, 53,* **55,** *71,* **74,** *75, 76,* **79,** *81,* **85**
BSK Beograd	5, 5	*1927,* **29,** *31,* **33,** *35, 36,* **38, 39, 40,** *55*

This summary only features the top four clubs in the Serbia & Montenegro League. For a full list of league champions and runners-up please see the League Record above.

Yugoslavian Cup Record 1947–91

YEAR	WINNERS	SCORE	RUNNERS-UP
1947	Partizan Beograd	2-0	Naša Krila Zemun
1948	Crvena Zvezda	3-0	Partizan Beograd
1949	Crvena Zvezda	3-2	Naša Krila Zemun
1950	Crvena Zvezda	1-1, (replay) 3-0	Dinamo Zagreb
1951	Dinamo Zagreb	2-0, 2-0 (2 legs)	Vojvodina Novi Sad
1952	Partizan Beograd	6-0	Crvena Zvezda
1953	BSK Beograd	2-0	Hajduk Split
1954	Partizan Beograd	4-1	Crvena Zvezda
1955	BSK Beograd	2-0	Hajduk Split

Yugoslavian Cup Record (*continued*)

YEAR	WINNERS	SCORE	RUNNERS-UP
1956		*no competition*	
1957	Partizan Beograd	5-3	Radnicki Beograd
1958	Crvena Zvezda	4-0	Velez Mostar
1959	Crvena Zvezda	3-1	Partizan Beograd
1960	Dinamo Zagreb	3-2	Partizan Beograd
1961	Vardar Skopje	2-1	Varteks Varaždin
1962	OFK Beograd	4-1	Spartak Subotica
1963	Dinamo Zagreb	4-1	Hajduk Split
1964	Crvena Zvezda	3-0	Dinamo Zagreb
1965	Dinamo Zagreb	2-1	Budučnost Titograd
1966	OFK Beograd	6-2 (aet)	Dinamo Zagreb
1967	Hajduk Split	2-1	FK Sarajevo
1968	Crvena Zvezda	7-0	FK Bor
1969	Dinamo Zagreb	3-3, (replay) 3-0	Hajduk Split
1970	Crvena Zvezda	2-2, (replay) 1-0 (aet)	Olimpia Ljubljana
1971	Crvena Zvezda	4-0	Sloboda Turzia
1972	Hajduk Split	2-1	Dinamo Zagreb
1973	Dinamo Zagreb	2-1	Crvena Zvezda
1974	Hajduk Split	1-1, (replay) 2-1	Crvena Zvezda
1975	Hajduk Split	1-0	Borac Banja Luka
1976	Hajduk Split	1-0 (aet)	Dinamo Zagreb
1977	Hajduk Split	2-0 (aet)	Budučnost Titograd
1978	NK Rijeka	1-0 (aet)	Trepca Mitrovica
1979	NK Rijeka	0-0, (replay) 2-1	Partizan Beograd
1980	Dinamo Zagreb	1-1, (replay) 1-0	Crvena Zvezda
1981	Velez Mostar	3-2	Željeznicar Sarajevo
1982	Crvena Zvezda	2-2, (replay) 4-2	Dinamo Zagreb
1983	Dinamo Zagreb	3-2	FK Sarajevo
1984	Hajduk Split	0-0, (replay) 2-1	Crvena Zvezda
1985	Crvena Zvezda	1-1, (replay) 2-1	Dinamo Zagreb
1986	Velez Mostar	3-1	Dinamo Zagreb
1987	Hajduk Split	1-1 (aet)(9-8 pens)	NK Rijeka
1988	Borac Banja Luka	1-0	Crvena Zvezda
1989	Partizan Beograd	6-1	Velez Mostar
1990	Crvena Zvezda	1-0	Hajduk Split
1991	Hajduk Split	1-0	Crvena Zvezda

Serbia & Montenegro Cup Record 1992–2004

YEAR	WINNERS	SCORE	RUNNERS-UP
1992	Partizan Beograd	1-0, 2-2 (2 legs)	Crvena Zvezda
1993	Crvena Zvezda	0-1, 1-0 (5-4 pens)(2 legs)	Partizan Beograd
1994	Partizan Beograd	3-2, 6-1 (2 legs)	Spartak Subotica
1995	Crvena Zvezda	4-0, 0-0 (2 legs)	FK Obilić
1996	Crvena Zvezda	3-0, 3-1 (2 legs)	Partizan Beograd
1997	Crvena Zvezda	0-0, 1-0 (2 legs)	Vojvodina Novi Sad
1998	Partizan Beograd	0-0, 2-0 (2 legs)	FK Obilić
1999	Crvena Zvezda	4-2, 4-0 (2 legs)	Partizan Beograd
2000	Crvena Zvezda	4-0	Napradak Kruševac
2001	Partizan Beograd	1-0	Crvena Zvezda
2002	Crvena Zvezda	1-0	Sartid Smederovo
2003	Sartid Smederovo	1-0	Crvena Zvezda
2004	Crvena Zvezda	1-0	Budučnost Banatski Dvor

Serbia & Montenegro Cup Summary

TEAM	TOTALS	WINNERS & RUNNERS-UP (BOLD) (ITALICS)
Crvena Zvezda	20, 11	1948–50, *52, 54,* **58, 59, 64, 68, 70, 71,** *73, 74, 80,* **82,** *84,* **85,** *88,* **90,** *91, 92, 93,* **95–97,** *99,* **2000,** *01, 02, 03,* **04**
Partizan Beograd	9, 7	**1947,** *48,* **52, 54, 57,** *59, 60,* **79,** *89,* **92,** *93,* **94,** *96,* **98,** *99,* **2001**
Hajduk Split	9, 5	*1953, 55, 63,* **67,** *69,* **72,** *74–77,* **84,** *87,* **90, 91**
Dinamo Zagreb	8, 8	**1950,** *51,* **60,** *63, 64,* **65, 66,** *69,* **72,** *73, 76,* **80,** *82, 83, 85, 86*

This summary only features the top four clubs in the Serbia & Montenegro Cup. For a full list of cup winners and runners-up please see the Cup Record above.

Nikola Zigic of Red Star celebrates with fans after defeating Vojvodina and winning the Serbia and Montenegro national soccer Championships.

Albania

Federata Shqiptarë e Futbollit
Founded: 1930
Joined FIFA: 1932
Joined UEFA: 1954

SEASON	LEAGUE CHAMPIONS
2000	SK Tirana
2001	Vllaznia Shkodër
2002	Dinamo Tiranë
2003	SK Tirana
2004	SK Tirana

YEAR	CUP WINNERS
2000	Teuta Durrës
2001	SK Tirana
2002	SK Tirana
2003	Dinamo Tiranë
2004	Partizani Tiranë

Albania's national league began in 1929 (prior to the formation of the national FA), and the cup competition in 1947. Both tournaments have been dominated by teams from the capital city, Tirana.

Bosnia-Herzegovina

Nogometni Savez Bosne i Hercegovine
Founded: 1992
Joined FIFA: 1996
Joined UEFA: 1996

SEASON	LEAGUE CHAMPIONS
2000	Brotnjo Citluk
2001	Željeznicar Sarajevo
2002	Željeznicar Sarajevo
2003	FK Leotar
2004	Siroki Brijeg

YEAR	CUP WINNERS
2000	Željeznicar Sarajevo
2001	Željeznicar Sarajevo
2002	Sarajevo
2003	Željeznicar Sarajevo
2004	Modrica Maksima

A Bosnian FA was established in 1992 and league soccer in separate Serbian, Muslim and Croat leagues in 1996. In the 2002–03 season all three leagues were integrated into a single national league.

Macedonia

Macedonian Football Union
Founded: 1908
Joined FIFA: 1994
Joined UEFA: 1994

SEASON	LEAGUE CHAMPIONS
2000	Sloga Jugomagnat Skopje
2001	Sloga Jugomagnat Skopje
2002	Vardar Skopje
2003	Vardar Skopje
2004	Pobeda Prilep

YEAR	CUP WINNERS
2000	Sloga Jugomagnat Skopje
2001	Pelister Bitola
2002	Pobeda Prilep
2003	Cementarnica Skopje
2004	Sloga Jugomagnat Skopje

Contemporary Macedonia emerged from the break-up of the former Yugoslavia in 1991. National soccer competitions, cup and league, rapidly followed independence, starting in the 1992–93 season.

Croatia

Croatian Football Federation
Founded: 1912, 1991
Joined FIFA: 1992
Joined UEFA: 1993

CROATIA

UNTIL 1919, CROATIA WAS A PROVINCE of the Austro-Hungarian Empire and soccer spread from its initial Hapsburg centres – Prague, Vienna and Budapest – to the main and now capital city of the country – Zagreb. In 1903, a mixture of students who had studied abroad, and local intellectuals, formed HASK, the first club. Prior to this the main organized sport had been gymnastics or 'sokol', based on the Czech movement in which exercise and national liberation were closely connected. However, unlike some sokol and gymnastic

movements, the Croats took to soccer rapidly and more clubs emerged in Zagreb as well as the other cities and towns. Between 1919 and 1941 Croatia was part of Yugoslavia and its teams competed in the national championship, with Hadjuk Split proving the most successful and the city acquiring a fearsome reputation for soccer fanaticism.

State of independence

After the German invasion of Yugoslavia, a separate Croatia was established and run as a puppet state by the Croat fascist movement, the Ustace. Three national championships were played in these years, but the chaos of the war eventually brought the game to a halt. With Tito and the communists in Belgrade, a new Yugoslavia was formed and once again Croatian teams competed in the national championship with considerable success. In 1991, the Yugoslavian civil war began; Croatia declared independence and a new national soccer association, league and cup were all established. Many of the leading players took the opportunity to go abroad. Soccer and nationalism proved a heady mix in the immediate post-independence years. The new president, Franco Tudjman, took control at leading club Dinamo Zagreb and forced through a name change to Croatia Zagreb – the club only reverting to its former name on his death in 1999.

There are currently 12 teams in the top league who play each other twice in the first phase of the championship. They then split into championship and relegation groups of six, playing twice again to determine final placings. The cup is a two-leg-per-round tournament with the top division teams joining the competition in the later rounds.

Croatian League Record 1940–46 and 1992–2004

SEASON	CHAMPIONS	RUNNERS-UP
1940–41	HSK Hadjuk Split	1.HSK Gradjanski Zagreb
1941	*not completed*	
1942	1.HSK Concordia Zagreb	1.HSK Gradjanski Zagreb
1943	1.HSK Gradjanski Zagreb	HASK Zagreb
1944	*not completed*	
1945	*no competition*	
1946	FD Hajduk Split	FD Dinamo Zagreb
1992*	Hajduk Split	Zagreb
1992–93	Croatia Zagreb	Hajduk Split
1993–94	Hajduk Split	Zagreb
1994–95	Hajduk Split	Croatia Zagreb
1995–96	Croatia Zagreb	Hajduk Split
1996–97	Croatia Zagreb	Hajduk Split
1997–98	Croatia Zagreb	Hajduk Split
1998–99	Croatia Zagreb	NK Rijeka
1999–2000	Dinamo Zagreb	Hajduk Split
2000–01	Hajduk Split	Dinamo Zagreb
2001–02	NK Zagreb	Hajduk Split
2002–03	Dinamo Zagreb	Hajduk Split
2003–04	Hajduk Split	Dinamo Zagreb

Robert Prosinecki played at Real Madrid during the 1990s. *He began his career at Dinamo Zagreb and moved to Red Star Belgrade where he won the European Cup. The leading Yugoslavian player of his era, he had Serb and Croat parentage and opted to play for Croatia.*

Over the years the championship has been decided by various means from a simple league format (1940–41, 1992–95, 1996–97, 1999–2000 and 2001–02) to mini-leagues (1942, 1995–96, 1997–99, 2000–01, 2003–04) and play-offs (1946).

* Championship completed in one year because of war.

One of Croatia's oldest clubs, Hajduk Split, is famed for its production line of talent, selling players from Dalmatia to clubs all over Europe.

Croatian League Summary

TEAM	TOTALS	CHAMPIONS & RUNNERS-UP (BOLD) (ITALICS)
Hajduk Split (includes HSK Hajduk Split, FD Hajduk Split)	7, 7	**1941, 46, 92, 93, 94, 95,** *96–98, 2000,* **01,** *02, 03,* **04**
Dinamo Zagreb (includes FD Dinamo Zagreb, Croatia Zagreb)	7, 4	*1946,* **93,** *95,* **96–2000,** *01,* **03,** *04*
1. HSK Gradjanski Zagreb	1, 2	*1941, 42,* **43**
HSK Concordia Zagreb	1, 0	**1942**
NK Zagreb	1, 0	**2002**
Zagreb	0, 2	*1992, 94*
NK Rijeka	0, 1	*1999*
HASK Zagreb	0, 1	*1943*

Croatian Cup Record 1941 and 1992–2004

YEAR	CHAMPIONS	SCORE	RUNNERS-UP
1941	1. HSK Gradjanski Zagreb	2-2, (replay) 6-2	Concordia Zagreb
1992	INKER Zapresic	1-1, 1-0 (2 legs)	HASK Gradjanski Zagreb
1993	Hajduk Split	4-1, 1-2 (2 legs)	Croatia Zagreb
1994	Croatia Zagreb	2-0, 0-1 (2 legs)	NK Rijeka
1995	Hajduk Split	3-2, 1-0 (2 legs)	Croatia Zagreb
1996	Croatia Zagreb	2-0, 1-0 (2 legs)	Varteks Varazdin
1997	Croatia Zagreb	2-1	NK Zagreb
1998	Croatia Zagreb	1-0, 2-1 (2 legs)	Varteks Varazdin
1999	NK Osijek	2-1 (aet)	HSK Cibalia Vinkovici
2000	Hajduk Split	2-0, 0-1 (2 legs)	Dinamo Zagreb
2001	Dinamo Zagreb	2-0, 1-0 (2 legs)	Hajduk Split
2002	Dinamo Zagreb	1-1, 1-0 (2 legs)	Varteks Varazdin
2003	Hajduk Split	1-0, 4-0 (2 legs)	Uljanik Pula
2004	Dinamo Zagreb*	1-1, 0-0 (2 legs)	Varteks Varazdin

* Won on away goals rule.

Franco Tudjman was a man who likes to mix nationalism and soccer. The ex Yugoslavian army general became president of both the Croatian Republic and Dinamo Zagreb.

Croatian Cup Summary

TEAM	TOTALS	CHAMPIONS & RUNNERS-UP (BOLD) (ITALICS)
Dinamo Zagreb (includes HASK Gradjanski Zagreb, Croatia Zagreb)	7, 4	*1992,* **93, 94, 95,** *96–98,* *2000,* **01, 02,** *04*
Hajduk Split	4, 1	**1993, 95, 2000,** *01,* **03**
1. HSK Gradjanski Zagreb	1, 0	**1941**
INKER Zapresic	1, 0	**1992**
NK Osijek	1, 0	**1999**
Varteks Varazdin	0, 4	*1996, 98, 2002, 04*
HSK Cibalia Vinkovici	0, 1	*1999*
NK Rijeka	0, 1	*1994*
Uljanik Pula	0, 1	*2003*
Concordia Zagreb	0, 1	*1941*
NK Zagreb	0, 1	*1997*

Romania

Federaţia Româna de Fotbal
Founded: 1908
Joined FIFA: 1930
Joined UEFA: 1954

ROMANIANS took to soccer earlier and more enthusiastically than any other Balkan nation, and despite war, revolution and penury, soccer remains an enduring passion in the country. The national FA was set up in 1908, with the considerable support of Prince Carol, heir to the Romanian throne. The first national league was set up in 1910, with play-offs to contest the title until 1934. In 1935, a formal national league and cup competition were established.

The Communist re-creation of Romanian soccer after the Second World War involved considerable change. Cities were generally restricted to a single team; many clubs that had explicitly regional and ethnic connections (Hungarian, Jewish and German teams) were transformed or wound down. The league was cancelled in 1957 to allow the new season to start in the autumn of that year and finish in spring the following year.

Romanian League Record 1910–2004

SEASON	CHAMPIONS	RUNNERS-UP
1910	Olimpia Bucureşti	not known
1911	Olimpia Bucureşti	not known
1912	United FC Ploieşti	not known
1913	Colentina Bucureşti	not known
1914	Colentina Bucureşti	not known
1915	România-Americana	not known
1916	Prahova Ploiesti	not known
1917–19	no championship	
1920	Venus Bucureşti	not known
1921	Venus Bucureşti	not known
1922	Chinezul Timişoara	Victoria Cluj
1923	Chinezul Timişoara	Victoria Cluj
1924	Chinezul Timişoara	CAO Oradea
1925	Chinezul Timişoara	UCAS Petroşani
1926	Chinezul Timişoara	Juventus Bucureşti
1927	Chinezul Timişoara	Coltea Braşov
1928	Coltea Braşov	Jiul Lupeni
1929	Venus Bucureşti	România Cluj
1930	Juventus Bucureşti	Gloria CFR Arad
1931	UDR Reşiţa	SG Sibiu
1932	Venus Bucureşti	UDR Reşiţa
1933	Ripensia Timişoara	Universitatea Cluj
1934	Venus Bucureşti	Ripensia Timişoara
1935	Ripensia Timişoara	CAO Oradea
1936	Ripensia Timişoara	AMEFA Arad
1937	Venus Bucureşti	Rapid Bucureşti
1938	Ripensia Timişoara	Rapid Bucureşti
1939	Venus Bucureşti	Ripensia Timişoara
1940	Venus Bucureşti	Rapid Bucureşti
1941	Unirea Tricolor	Rapid Bucureşti
1942–46	no championship	
1947	IT Arad	Carmen Bucureşti
1948	IT Arad	CFR Timişoara
1949	ICO Oradea	CFR Bucureşti
1950	Flamura Roşie	Lokomotiva Buch
1951	CCA Bucureşti	Dinamo Bucureşti
1952	CCA Bucureşti	Dinamo Bucureşti
1953	CCA Bucureşti	Dinamo Bucureşti
1954	Flamura Roşie	CCA Bucureşti
1955	Dinamo Bucureşti	Flacără Ploieşti
1956	CCA Bucureşti	Dinamo Bucureşti
1957*		
1958	Petrolul Ploieşti	CCA Bucureşti

Romanian League Record (continued)

SEASON	CHAMPIONS	RUNNERS-UP
1960	CCA Bucureşti	Steagul Rosu Braşov
1961	CCA Bucureşti	Dinamo Bucureşti
1962	Dinamo Bucureşti	Petrolul Ploieşti
1963	Dinamo Bucureşti	Steaua Bucureşti
1964	Dinamo Bucureşti	Rapid Bucureşti
1965	Dinamo Bucureşti	Rapid Bucureşti
1966	Petrolul Ploieşti	Rapid Bucureşti
1967	Rapid Bucureşti	Dinamo Bucureşti
1968	Steaua Bucureşti	FC Argeş Piteşti
1969	UT Arad	Dinamo Bucureşti
1970	UT Arad	Rapid Bucureşti
1971	Dinamo Bucureşti	Rapid Bucureşti
1972	FC Argeş Piteşti	UT Arad
1973	Dinamo Bucureşti	Universitatea Craiova
1974	Universitatea Craiova	Dinamo Bucureşti
1975	Universitatea Craiova	ASA Tîrgu Mures
1976	Steaua Bucureşti	Dinamo Bucureşti
1977	Dinamo Bucureşti	Steaua Bucureşti
1978	Steaua Bucureşti	FC Argeş Piteşti
1979	FC Argeş Piteşti	Dinamo Bucureşti
1980	Universitatea Craiova	Steaua Bucureşti
1981	Universitatea Craiova	Dinamo Bucureşti
1982	Dinamo Bucureşti	Universitatea Craiova
1983	Dinamo Bucureşti	Universitatea Craiova
1984	Dinamo Bucureşti	Steaua Bucureşti
1985	Steaua Bucureşti	Dinamo Bucureşti
1986	Steaua Bucureşti	Sportul Studentesc
1987	Steaua Bucureşti	Dinamo Bucureşti
1988	Steaua Bucureşti	Dinamo Bucureşti
1989	Steaua Bucureşti	Dinamo Bucureşti
1990	Dinamo Bucureşti	Steaua Bucureşti
1991	Universitatea Craiova	Steaua Bucureşti
1992	Dinamo Bucureşti	Steaua Bucureşti
1993	Steaua Bucureşti	Dinamo Bucureşti
1994	Steaua Bucureşti	Universitatea Craiova
1995	Steaua Bucureşti	Universitatea Craiova
1996	Steaua Bucureşti	National Bucureşti
1997	Steaua Bucureşti	National Bucureşti
1998	Steaua Bucureşti	Rapid Bucureşti
1999	Rapid Bucureşti	Dinamo Bucureşti
2000	Dinamo Bucureşti	Rapid Bucureşti
2001	Steaua Bucureşti	Dinamo Bucureşti
2002	Dinamo Bucureşti	National Bucureşti
2003	Rapid Bucureşti	Steaua Bucureşti
2004	Dinamo Bucureşti	Steaua Bucureşti

* There were no recorded league champions for 1957 as Romania's soccer league changed from a winter-to-winter season to an autumn-to-spring season.

Romanian League Summary

TEAM	TOTALS	CHAMPIONS & RUNNERS-UP (BOLD) (ITALICS)
Steaua Bucureşti (includes CCA Bucureşti)	21, 11	**1951–53**, *54*, **56**, *58*, **60**, **61**, *63*, **68**, **76**, **77**, *78*, **80**, **84**, **85–89**, *90–92*, *93–98*, **2001**, *03*, **04**
Dinamo Bucureşti	16, 19	*1951–53*, **55**, *56*, **59**, *61*, **62–65**, *67*, **69**, *71*, **73**, **74**, *76*, **77**, *79*, **81**, *82–84*, *85*, *87–89*, *90*, *92*, *93*, **99**, **2000**, *01*, **02**, *04*
Venus Bucureşti	8, 0	**1920**, **21**, **29**, **32**, **34**, **37**, **39**, **40**
Chinezul Timişoara	6, 0	**1922–27**
Universitatea Craiova	5, 5	*1973*, **74**, **75**, **80**, **81**, *82*, *83*, **91**, *94*, *95*
Ripensia Timişoara	4, 2	**1933**, *34*, **35**, **36**, **38**, *39*
UT Arad (includes IT Arad)	4, 1	**1947**, **48**, **69**, **70**, *72*
Rapid Bucureşti	3, 11	*1937*, *38*, *40*, *41*, *64–66*, **67**, *70*, *71*, *98*, **99**, *2000*, **03**
Petrolul Ploieşti	3, 1	**1958**, *59*, **62**, **66**
FC Argeş Piteşti	2, 2	*1968*, **72**, *78*, **79**
Colentina Bucureşti	2, 0	**1913**, **14**
Flamura Roşie	2, 0	**1950**, **54**

Romanian League Summary (*continued*)

TEAM	TOTALS	CHAMPIONS & RUNNERS-UP (BOLD) (*ITALICS*)
Olimpia Bucureşti	2, 0	**1910, 11**
Coltea Braşov	1, 1	*1927*, **28**
Juventus Bucureşti	1, 1	*1926*, **30**
UDR Reşiţa	1, 1	**1931**, *32*
ICO Oradea	1, 0	**1949**
Prahova Ploieşti	1, 0	**1916**
România-Americana	1, 0	**1915**
Unirea Tricolor	1, 0	**1941**
United Ploieşti	1, 0	**1912**
National Bucureşti	0, 3	*1996, 97, 2002*
CAO Oradea	0, 2	*1924, 35*
Victoria Cluj	0, 2	*1922, 23*
AMEFA Arad	0, 1	*1936*
ASA Tîrgu Mureş	0, 1	*1975*
Carmen Bucureşti	0, 1	*1947*
CFR Bucureşti	0, 1	*1949*
CFR Timişoara	0, 1	*1948*
Flacără Ploieşti	0, 1	*1955*
Gloria CFR Arad	0, 1	*1930*
Jiul Lupeni	0, 1	*1928*
Lokomotiva Buch	0, 1	*1950*
România Cluj	0, 1	*1929*
SG Sibiu	0, 1	*1931*
Sportul Studentesc	0, 1	*1986*
Steagul Rosu Braşov	0, 1	*1960*
UCAS Petroşani	0, 1	*1925*
Universitatea Cluj	0, 1	*1933*

Romanian Cup Record 1934–2004

YEAR	WINNERS	SCORE	RUNNERS-UP
1934	Ripensia Timişoara	5-0	Universitatea Cluj
1935	CFR Bucureşti	6-5 (aet)	Ripensia Timişoara
1936	Ripensia Timişoara	5-1	Unirea Tricolor
1937	Rapid Bucureşti	5-1	Ripensia Timişoara
1938	Rapid Bucureşti	3-2	CAMT Timişoara
1939	Rapid Bucureşti	2-0	Sportul Studentesc
1940	Rapid Bucureşti	2-2 (aet), (replay) 4-4 (aet), (replay) 2-2 (aet), (replay) 2-1	Venus Bucureşti
1941	Rapid Bucureşti	4-3	Unirea Tricolor
1942	Rapid Bucureşti	7-1	Universitatea Cluj
1943	Tirnu Severin	4-0	Sportul Studentesc
1944–47		*no competition*	
1948	IT Arad	3-2	CFR Timişoara
1949	CSCA Bucureşti	2-1	CSU Cluj
1950	CCA Bucureşti	3-1	Flamura Roşie
1951	CCA Bucureşti	3-1 (aet)	Flacără Medias
1952	CCA Bucureşti	2-0	Flacără Ploieşti
1953	Flamura Roşie	1-0 (aet)	CCA Bucureşti
1954	Metalul Reşiţa	2-0	Dinamo Bucureşti
1955	CCA Bucureşti	6-3	Progresul Oradea
1956	Progresul Oradea	2-0	Metalul Turzil
1957		*no competition*	
1958	Ştiinţa Timişoara	1-0	Progresul Bucureşti
1959	Dinamo Bucureşti	4-0	Minerul Baia Mare
1960	Progresul Bucureşti	2-0	Dinamo Bucureşti
1961	Arieşul Turda	2-1	Rapid Bucureşti
1962	Steaua Bucureşti	5-1	Rapid Bucureşti
1963	Petrolul Ploieşti	6-1	Siderurgistul Galaţi
1964	Dinamo Bucureşti	5-3	Steaua Bucureşti
1965	Ştiinţa Cluj	2-1	Dinamo Piteşti
1966	Steaua Bucureşti	4-0	IT Arad
1967	Steaua Bucureşti	6-0	Foresta Fălticeni
1968	Dinamo Bucureşti	3-1 (aet)	Rapid Bucureşti
1969	Steaua Bucureşti	2-1	Dinamo Bucureşti
1970	Steaua Bucureşti	2-1	Dinamo Bucureşti
1971	Steaua Bucureşti	3-2	Dinamo Bucureşti

Romanian Cup Record (*continued*)

YEAR	WINNERS	SCORE	RUNNERS-UP
1972	Rapid Bucureşti	2-0	Jiul Petroşani
1973	Chimia Vîlcea	1-1 (aet), (replay) 3-0	Constructorul Galatizi
1974	Jiul Petroşani	4-2	Politehnica Timişoara
1975	Rapid Bucureşti	2-1 (aet)	Universitatea Craiova
1976	Steaua Bucureşti	1-0	CSU Galaţi
1977	Universitatea Craiova	2-1	Steaua Bucureşti
1978	Universitatea Craiova	3-1	Olimpia Satu Mare
1979	Steaua Bucureşti	3-0	Sportul Studentesc
1980	Politehnica Timişoara	2-1 (aet)	Steaua Bucureşti
1981	Universitatea Craiova	6-0	Politehnica Timişoara
1982	Dinamo Bucureşti	3-2	FC Baia Mare
1983	Universitatea Craiova	2-1	Politehnica Timişoara
1984	Dinamo Bucureşti	2-1	Steaua Bucureşti
1985	Steaua Bucureşti	2-1	Universitatea Craiova
1986	Dinamo Bucureşti	1-0	Steaua Bucureşti
1987	Steaua Bucureşti	1-0	Dinamo Bucureşti
1988	Steaua Bucureşti	2-1*	Dinamo Bucureşti
1989	Steaua Bucureşti	1-0	Dinamo Bucureşti
1990	Dinamo Bucureşti	6-4	Steaua Bucureşti
1991	Universitatea Craiova	2-1	FC Bacău
1992	Steaua Bucureşti	1-1 (aet)(3-2 pens)	Politehnica Timişoara
1993	Universitatea Craiova	2-0	Dacia Unirrea Brăila
1994	Gloria Bistraţi	1-0	Universitatea Craiova
1995	Petrolul Ploieşti	1-1 (aet)(5-3 pens)	Rapid Bucureşti
1996	Steaua Bucureşti	3-1	Gloria Bistraţi
1997	Steaua Bucureşti	4-2	National Bucureşti
1998	Rapid Bucureşti	1-0	Universitatea Craiova
1999	Steaua Bucureşti	2-2 (aet)(4-2 pens)	Rapid Bucureşti
2000	Dinamo Bucureşti	2-0	Universitatea Craiova
2001	Dinamo Bucureşti	4-2	Rocar Bucureşti
2002	Rapid Bucureşti	2-1	Dinamo Bucureşti
2003	Dinamo Bucureşti	1-0	National Bucureşti
2004	Dinamo Bucureşti	2-0	Otelul Galati

* Match abandoned at 1-1. However, Romanian FA awarded the match to Steaua as 2-1 victory.

Romanian Cup Summary

TEAM	TOTALS	WINNERS & RUNNERS-UP (BOLD) (*ITALICS*)
Steaua Bucureşti (includes CCA Bucureşti)	20, 7	**1950–52**, *53*, **55**, *62*, *64*, **66, 67, 69–71, 76**, *77*, **79, 80, 84, 85, 86, 87–89, 90, 92, 96, 97, 99**
Dinamo Bucureşti	11, 9	*1954*, **59, 60**, *64*, **68, 69–71**, *82*, **84, 86, 87–89, 90, 2000, 01**, *02*, **03, 04**
Rapid Bucureşti	10, 5	**1937–42**, *61*, **62**, *68*, **72, 75**, *95*, *98*, **99, 2002**
Universitatea Craiova	6, 5	*1975*, **77, 78**, *81*, **83**, *85*, **91, 93**, *94, 98, 2000*
Ripensia Timişoara	2, 2	**1934**, *35*, **36**, *37*
Petrolul Ploieşti	2, 0	**1963, 95**
Politehnica Timişoara	1, 4	*1974*, **80**, *81, 83, 92*
Flamura Roşie	1, 1	**1950**, *53*
Gloria Bistraţi	1, 1	**1994**, *96*
IT Arad	1, 1	**1948**, *66*
Jiul Petroşani	1, 1	*1972*, **74**
Progresul Bucureşti	1, 1	**1958**, *60*
Progresul Oradea	1, 1	**1955**, *56*
Arieşul Turda	1, 0	**1961**
CFR Bucureşti	1, 0	**1935**
Chimia Vîlcea	1, 0	**1973**
CSCA Bucureşti	1, 0	**1949**
Metalul Reşiţa	1, 0	**1954**
Ştiinţa Cluj	1, 0	**1965**
Ştiinţa Timişoara	1, 0	**1958**
Tirnu Severin	1, 0	**1943**

This summary only features the clubs who have won the Romanian Cup. For a full list of runners-up please see the Cup Record above.

ROMANIA

Bulgaria

Bŭlgarski Futbolen Sŭyuz
Founded: 1923
Joined FIFA: 1924
Joined UEFA: 1954

THE FIRST REPORTS OF SOCCER in Bulgaria feature George de Regibus, a Swiss PE teacher, who arrived in 1896 to teach at a boys' middle school in Varna on the Black Sea. Bulgaria remained a province of the tottering Ottoman Empire until independence in 1908. The Ottoman's suspicion of 'the English game' in Istanbul was reproduced in Bulgaria where the game was subject to official disapproval. Yet, despite the chaos of the Balkan Wars (1912–13) and the First World War, Bulgarian soccer began to grow.

Transport chaos

In 1912, Stefan Naumov organised a team in Sofia and arranged the first inter-town match against a side from Plovdiv who won 4-0. More formal clubs quickly followed. In 1913 Slavia, the capital's 'bourgeois' team, was formed, while a group of teenagers founded Levski in 1914. In 1922, 10 clubs created their own city league in Sofia, while a northern league formed around Varna. In 1923, the government created a Bulgarian Sports Federation and soccer acquired a national institutional structure. The following year saw the first, and, thanks to the state of the transport network, unsuccessful attempt to play a national league. But in 1925 national plays-offs were held between city and regional champions and won by Vladislav Varna.

The Second World War forced a reversion to regional competitions in 1940, but only a year was lost to the war in 1944 when the Red Army arrived. It, of course, stayed and, until the 1980s, the major cup competition was called the Soviet Army Cup in its honour. Under the new communist regime soccer was substantially reorganized, and CDNA Sofia, then CSKA Sofia – the army team – became the dominant force in Bulgarian soccer.

Bulgarian League Record 1924–1948

SEASON	CHAMPIONS	SCORE	RUNNERS-UP
1924*	Levski Sofia	0-0	Vladislav Varna
1925	Vladislav Varna	2-0	Levski Sofia
1926	Vladislav Varna	0-0	Slavia Sofia (refused replay)
1927		no championship	
1928	Slavia Sofia	4-0	Vladislav Varna
1929	Botev Plovdiv	1-0	Levski Sofia
1930	Slavia Sofia	4-1	Vladislav Varna
1931	AS 23 Sofia	3-0 w/o	Shipchenski Sokol
1932	Shipchenski Sokol	2-1	Slavia Sofia
1933	Levski Sofia	3-1	Shipchenski Sokol
1934	Vladislav Varna	2-0	Slavia Sofia
1935	Sportklub Sofia	4-0	Ticha Varna
1936	Slavia Sofia	2-0	Ticha Varna
1937	Levski Sofia	1-1, (replay) 3-0 w/o	Levski Ruse
1937–38	Ticha Varna	league format	Vladislav Varna
1938–39	Slavia Sofia	league format	Vladislav Varna
1939–40	JSK Sofia	league format	Levski Sofia
1941	Slavia Sofia	0-0, 2-1 (2 legs)	JSK Sofia
1942	Levski Sofia	2-0, 1-0 (2 legs)	Makedonia Skopje
1943	Slavia Sofia	1-0, 1-0 (2 legs)	Levski Sofia
1944		championship not completed	
1945	Lokomotiv Sofia	3-1, 1-1 (2 legs)	Sportist Sofia

Bulgarian League Record (*continued*)

SEASON	CHAMPIONS	SCORE	RUNNERS-UP
1946	Levski Sofia	1-0, 1-0 (2 legs)	Lokomotiv Sofia
1947	Levski Sofia	1-1, 1-0 (2 legs)	Lokomotiv Sofia
1948	Septemvri Sofia	1-2, 3-1 (2 legs)	Levski Sofia

w/o denotes walk over.
* Final was drawn, championship undecided.
Between 1924–37 and 1941–48 the championship was a knockout cup format.

Republican National League Record 1948–2004

SEASON	CHAMPIONS	RUNNERS-UP
1948–49	Levski Sofia	CSKA Sofia
1950	Levski Sofia	Slavia Sofia
1951	CDNA	Spartak Sofia
1952	CDNA	Spartak Sofia
1953	Levski Sofia	CDNA
1954	CDNA	Slavia Sofia
1955	CDNA	Slavia Sofia
1956	CDNA	Levski Sofia
1957	CDNA	Lokomotiv Sofia
1958	CDNA	Levski Sofia
1958–59	CDNA	Slavia Sofia
1959–60	CDNA	Levski Sofia
1960–61	CDNA	Levski Sofia
1961–62	CDNA	Spartak Plovdiv
1962–63	Spartak Plovdiv	Botev Plovdiv
1963–64	Lokomotiv Sofia	Levski Sofia
1964–65	Levski Sofia	Lokomotiv Sofia
1965–66	CSKA Cherveno zname	Levski Sofia
1966–67	Botev Plovdiv	Slavia Sofia
1967–68	Levski Sofia	CSKA Cherveno zname
1968–69	CSKA Cherveno zname	Levski Sofia
1969–70	Levski-Spartak Sofia	CSKA Septemvrijsko zname
1970–71	CSKA Septemvrijsko zname	Levski-Spartak Sofia
1971–72	CSKA Septemvrijsko zname	Levski-Spartak Sofia
1972–73	CSKA Septemvrijsko zname	Lokomotiv Plovdiv
1973–74	Levski-Spartak Sofia	CSKA Septemvrijsko zname
1974–75	CSKA Septemvrijsko zname	Levski-Spartak Sofia
1975–76	CSKA Septemvrijsko zname	Levski-Spartak Sofia
1976–77	Levski-Spartak Sofia	CSKA Septemvrijsko zname
1977–78	Lokomotiv Sofia	CSKA Septemvrijsko zname
1978–79	Levski-Spartak Sofia	CSKA Septemvrijsko zname
1979–80	CSKA Septemvrijsko zname	Slavia Sofia
1980–81	CSKA Septemvrijsko zname	Levski-Spartak Sofia
1981–82	CSKA Septemvrijsko zname	Levski-Spartak Sofia
1982–83	CSKA Septemvrijsko zname	Levski-Spartak Sofia
1983–84	Levski-Spartak Sofia	CSKA Sofia
1984–85	Levski-Spartak Sofia	CSKA Sofia
1985–86	Beroe Stara Zagora	Botev Plovdiv
1986–87	CFKA Sredets	Levski Sofia
1987–88	FC Vitosha	CSKA Sofia
1988–89	CSKA Sofia	Levski Sofia
1989–90	CSKA Sofia	Slavia Sofia
1990–91	Etar Veliko Turnovo	CSKA Sofia
1991–92	CSKA Sofia	Levski Sofia
1992–93	Levski Sofia	CSKA Sofia
1993–94	Levski Sofia	CSKA Sofia
1994–95	Levski Sofia	Lokomotiv Sofia
1995–96	Slavia Sofia	Levski Sofia
1996–97	CSKA Sofia	Neftohimik Burgas
1997–98	Litex Lovech	Levski Sofia
1998–99	Litex Lovech	Levski Sofia
1999–2000	Levski Sofia	CSKA Sofia
2000–01	Levski Sofia	CSKA Sofia
2001–02	Levski Sofia	Litex Lovech
2002–03	CSKA Sofia	Levski Sofia
2003–04	Lokomotiv Plovdiv	Levski Sofia

BULGARIA

Bulgarian League Summary

TEAM	TOTALS	CHAMPIONS & RUNNERS-UP (BOLD) (ITALICS)
CSKA Sofia (includes Septemvri Sofia, CDNA, CSKA Cherveno zname, CSKA Septemvrijsko zname, CFKA Sredets)	29, 16	**1948**, *49, 51, 52, 53*, **54–62, 66, 68, 69, 70, 71–73, 74, 76, 77–79, 80–83, 84, 85, 87,** *75,* **88, 89, 90, 91, 92,** *93, 94, 97,* **2000, 01, 03**
Levski Sofia (includes Levski-Spartak Sofia FC Vitosha)	23, 29	*1925, 29,* **33,** *37,* **40, 42,** *43,* **46,** *47, 48, 49, 50, 51, 52,* **53,** *56,* **58,** *60, 61,* **64, 65,** *66,* **68, 69, 70,** *71, 72,* **74,** *75, 76, 77, 79,* **81–83,** *84, 85,* **87, 88,** *89,* **92,** *93–95,* **96,** *98, 99,* **2000–02,** *03, 04*
Slavia Sofia	7, 10	*1926,* **28,** *30,* **32,** *34,* **36,** *39,* **41,** *43, 50, 54, 55, 59, 67, 80, 90, 96*
Lokomotiv Sofia (includes JSK Sofia)	4, 6	**1940,** *41,* **45,** *46, 47,* **57,** *64,* **65,** *78,* **95**
Vladislav Varna	3, 4	**1925,** *26,* **28,** *30,* **34,** *38, 39*
Botev Plovdiv	2, 2	**1929,** *63,* **67,** *86*
Litex Lovech	2, 1	**1998,** *99,* **2002**
Shipchenski Sokol	1, 2	**1931,** *32, 33*
Ticha Varna	1, 2	*1935, 36,* **38**
Lokomotiv Plovdiv	1, 1	*1973,* **2004**
Spartak Plovdiv	1, 1	*1962,* **63**
AS 23 Sofia	1, 0	**1931**
Beroe Stara Zagora	1, 0	**1986**
Etar Veliko Turnovo	1, 0	**1991**
Sportklub Sofia	1, 0	**1935**

This summary only features clubs that have won the Bulgarian league. For a full list of league winners and runners-up please see the league record above.

Bulgarian Cup Record 1938–2004

SEASON	CHAMPIONS	SCORE	RUNNERS-UP
1938	FK 13 Sofia	3-0	Levski Ruse
1939	Shipka Sofia	2-0	Levski Ruse
1940	FK 13 Sofia	2-1	Sportklub Plovdid
1941	AS 23 Sofia	4-2	Napreduk Ruse
1942	Levski Sofia	3-1 interrupted, 3-0 w/o	Sportklub Plovdid
1943–45		*no competition*	
1946	Levski Sofia	4-1	Chernolomez Popovo
1947	Levski Sofia	1-0	Botev Plovdiv
1948	Lokomotiv Sofia	1-0	Lokomotiv Plovdiv
1949	Levski Sofia	1-1 (aet), (replay) 2-2, 2-1 (aet)	CDNA
1950	Levski Sofia	1-1 (aet), (replay) 1-1, 1-0 (aet)	CDNA
1951	CDNA	1-0 (aet)	Akademik Sofia
1952	Slavia Sofia	3-1	Spartak Sofia
1953	Lokomotiv Sofia	2-1	Levski Sofia
1954	CDNA	2-1	Slavia Sofia
1955	CDNA	5-2 (aet)	Spartak Plovdiv
1956	Levski Sofia	5-2	Botev Plovdiv
1957	Levski Sofia	2-1	Spartak Pleven
1958	Spartak Plovdiv	1-0	Mineur Pernik
1959	Levski Sofia	1-0	Spartak Plovdiv
1960	Septemvri Sofia	4-3 (aet)	Lokomotiv Plovdiv
1961	CDNA	3-0	Spartak Varna
1962	Botev Plovdiv	3-0	Dunav Ruse
1963	Slavia Sofia	2-0	Botev Plovdiv
1964	Slavia Sofia	3-2	Botev Plovdiv
1965	CSKA Sofia	3-2	Levski Sofia
1966	Slavia Sofia	1-0	CSKA Cherveno zname
1967	Levski Sofia	3-0	Spartak Sofia
1968	Spartak Sofia	3-2	Beroe St. Zagora
1969	CSKA Septemvrijsko z.	2-1	Levski Sofia
1970	Levski-Spartak Sofia	2-1	CSKA Septemvrijsko z.
1971	Levski-Spartak Sofia	3-0	Lokomotiv Plovdiv
1972	CSKA Septemvrijsko z.	3-0	Slavia Sofia
1973	CSKA Septemvrijsko z.	2-1	Beroe St Zagora
1974	CSKA Septemvrijsko z.	2-1 (aet)	Levski-Spartak Sofia
1975	Slavia Sofia	3-2	Lokomotiv Sofia
1976	Levski-Spartak Sofia	4-3 (aet)	CSKA Septemvrijsko z.
1977	Levski-Spartak Sofia	2-1	Lokomotiv Sofia

Bulgarian Cup Record (*continued*)

SEASON	CHAMPIONS	SCORE	RUNNERS-UP
1978	Marek Dupnica	1-0	CSKA Septemvrijsko z.
1979	Levski-Spartak Sofia	4-1	Beroe St Zagora
1980	Slavia Sofia	3-1	Beroe St Zagora
1981	Botev Plovdiv	1-0	Pirin Blagoevgrad
1982*	Lokomotiv Sofia	2-1 (aet)	Lokomotiv Plovdiv
1983*	Lokomotiv Plovdiv	3-1	Chirpan
1984*	Levski-Spartak Sofia	4-0	Dorostol Silistra
1985*	CSKA Septemvrijsko z.	4-0	Cherno More Varna
1986*	CSKA Septemvrijsko z.	2-0	Lokomotiv Sofia
1987*	Levski-Spartak Sofia	3-2	Spartak Pleven
1988*	Levski-Spartak Sofia	2-0	Cherno More Varna
1989*	CSKA Septemvrijsko z.	6-1	Maritza-Iztok Radn.
1990*	CSKA Septemvrijsko z.	2-1	Botev Plovdiv
1981**	CSKA Septemvrijsko z.		Slavia Sofia
1982	Levski-Spartak Sofia	4-0	CSKA Septemvrijsko z.
1983	CSKA Septemvrijsko z.	4-0	Spartak Varna
1984	Levski-Spartak Sofia	1-0	Botev Plovdiv
1985†	CSKA Septemvrijsko z.	2-1	Levski-Spartak Sofia
1986	Levski Sofia	1-0	CSKA Sofia
1987	CSKA Sofia	2-1	Levski Sofia
1988	CSKA Sofia	4-1	Levski Sofia
1989	CSKA Sofia	3-0	Chernomorez Burgas
1990	Sliven	2-0	CSKA Sofia
1991	Levski Sofia	2-1	Botev Plovdiv
1992	Levski Sofia	5-0	Pirin Blagoevgrad
1993	CSKA Sofia	1-0	Botev Plovdiv
1994	Levski Sofia	1-0	Pirin Blagoevgrad
1995	Lokomotiv Sofia	4-2	Botev Plovdiv
1996	Slavia Sofia	abandoned at 1-0, (replay) 4-0 w/o	Levski Sofia
1997	CSKA Sofia	3-1	Levski Sofia
1998	Levski Sofia	5-0	CSKA Sofia
1999	CSKA Sofia	1-0	Litex Lovech
2000	Levski Sofia	2-0	Neftohimik Burgas
2001	Litex Lovech	1-0 (asdet)	Velbazhd Kyustendil
2002	Levski Sofia	3-1	CSKA Sofia
2003	Levski Sofia	2-1	Litex Lovech
2004	Litex Lovetch	2-2 (aet)	CSKA Sofia

* Denotes results in the 'secondary' Soviet Army Cup.
** No final was played in 1981.
† The cup was witheld in 1985. Result not included in the cup summary below.
The Bulgarian Cup was known as the Tzar's Cup between 1938–42, the Soviet Army Cup 1945–81 (although this continued as a 'secondary' tournament until 1990), and the Cup of Bulgaria between 1981–2003.

Bulgarian Cup Summary

TEAM	TOTAL	WINNERS & RUNNERS-UP (BOLD) (ITALICS)
Levski Sofia (also won 3 'secondary' Soviet Army Cups)	24, 8	**1942, 46, 47, 49, 50,** *53,* **56, 57,** *59,* **65,** *67,* **69, 70, 71, 74, 76, 77, 79, 82, 84, 86,** *87,* **88,** *91,* **92, 94, 96, 97, 98, 2000, 02, 03**
CSKA Sofia (also won 4 'secondary' Soviet Army Cups)	17, 12	*1949,* **50, 51, 54, 55, 61, 65,** *66,* **69,** *70, 72–74,* **76,** *78,* **81,** *82, 83,* **86,** *87–89,* **90,** *93,* **97,** *98, 99, 2002,* **04**
Slavia Sofia	7, 3	**1952,** *54,* **63, 64,** *66,* **72,** *75,* **80,** *81,* **96**
Lokomotiv Sofia (also won 1 'secondary' Soviet Army Cup)	3, 2	**1948,** *53,* **75,** *77,* **95**
Botev Plovdiv	2, 8	*1947, 56,* **62,** *63, 64, 81, 84, 91, 93, 95*
Litex Lovech	2, 2	*1999,* **2001,** *03,* **04**
FK 13 Sofia	2, 0	**1938, 40**
Spartak Plovdiv	1, 2	*1955,* **58,** *59*
Spartak Sofia	1, 2	*1952,* **67,** *68*
AS 23 Sofia	1, 0	**1941**
Marek Dupnica	1, 0	**1978**
Septemvri Sofia	1, 0	**1960**
Shipka Sofia	1, 0	**1939**
Sliven	1, 0	**1990**

These totals include the Tzar's Cup, the Soviet Army Cup 1945–81 and the Cup of Bulgaria since 1982.

This summary only features clubs that have won the Bulgarian cup. For a full list of cup winners and runners-up please see the cup record above.

Greece

THE SEASON IN REVIEW 2003–04

THEY HAD TO WAIT UNTIL THE 76TH MINUTE of the last game of the season, but at last, after eight years of waiting, Panathinaikos were on course to win the Greek League and break their rival's Olympiakos' seven-year run at the top. A goal from the Nigerian-Polish substitute, Emmanuel Olisadebe, was enough to give Pana the title, send their opponents Paniliakos down, and prompt a pitch invasion from the 6,000 away fans.

Pana do the double

The season began with almost nobody playing at home. The final run-in to the 2004 Olympics saw all the main Athenian teams forced to play in tiny stadiums while their own were being refurbished. For much of the season Olympiakos had maintained a narrow lead at the top of the table, but a comprehensive 7-0 defeat by Juventus in the Champions League in the autumn suggested a real frailty to the team. When they met challengers Panathinaikos in the Greek Cup Final, that frailty was cruelly exposed as Pana ran out deserved 3-1 winners. When AEK beat Olympiakos 1-0 in the final run-in, Panathinaikos finally took the lead. At the last derby game of the season, a massive riot preceded and followed the match, but a draw meant that Panathinaikos stayed ahead and with key last-minute goals from Olisadebe in games against PAOK and Proodeftiki, they stayed there.

Beyond the top two, PAOK were overjoyed to creep into the Champions League qualifying spot and Aegaleo and Panionios made it to the UEFA Cup. But AEK, Athens's third team, had an utterly dismal season and despite grabbing the last UEFA Cup spot remain so indebted they may not be able to play in the competition. Attempts to rescue the club by ex-striker Demis Nikolaidis were rejected when he insisted that the squad take swingeing pay cuts. Fans, who earlier in the season had forced coach Dusan Bajevic out with threats to him and his family, responded by attacking the club's training ground and players.

Greek League Table 2003–04

CLUB	P	W	D	L	F	A	Pts	
Panathinaikos	30	24	5	1	62	18	77	Champions League
Olympiakos	30	24	3	3	70	19	75	Champions League
PAOK	30	18	6	6	47	27	60	Champions League
AEK Athens	30	16	7	7	57	32	55	UEFA Cup
Aegaleo	30	15	7	8	37	26	52	UEFA Cup
Panionios	30	12	11	7	40	29	47	UEFA Cup
Halkidona	30	13	6	11	40	39	45	
Iraklis	30	12	6	12	40	39	42	
Ionikos	30	9	6	15	33	43	33	
Xanthi	30	8	6	16	28	42	30	
OFI Crete	30	7	8	15	27	44	29	
Kallithea	30	5	12	13	37	42	27	
Aris	30	7	6	17	24	46	27	
Akratitos	30	5	8	17	31	69	23	Relegated*
Paniliakos	30	4	9	17	28	56	21	Relegated
Proodeftiki	30	4	8	18	26	56	20	Relegated

Promoted clubs: Kerkyra, Apollon Kalamarias, Ergotelis*.
* Relegation/promotion decided by play-off.

International Club Performances 2003–04

CLUB	COMPETITION	PROGRESS
AEK Athens	Champions League	Group Stage
Olympiakos	Champions League	Group Stage
Panathinaikos	Champions League	Group Stage
	UEFA Cup	3rd Round
Panionios	UEFA Cup	2nd Round
Aris	UEFA Cup	2nd Round
PAOK	UEFA Cup	2nd Round

Top Goalscorers 2003–04

PLAYER	CLUB	NATIONALITY	GOALS
Dmitrios Papadopoulos	Panathinaikos	Greek	17
Giovanni	Olympiakos	Brazilian	15
Nikos Skarmoutsos	Kallithea	Greek	13

Greek Cup

2004 FINAL

May 8 – Nea Smyrnis, Athens
Panathinaikos 3-1 Olympiakos
(Papadopulos 3, Konstantinou 67, 81)   (Giovanni 65)
h/t: 1-0   **Att:** 7,000
Ref: Gasnaferis

Panathinaikos looked like champions this year, beating big and small teams alike, here (left to right) Michalis Konstantinou, Lucian Sanmartean and Joel Epale celebrate with a goal against Ionikos.

The old national soccer stadium is slowly transformed into an Olympic stadium with a new Calatrava roof. The construction programme for the Athens 2004 Olympics meant that AEK and Olympiakos played away from home for most of the season and the cup final was played at the tiny Panionios stadium.

GREECE

Olympiakos' Ukrainian coach Oleg Protasov didn't last long as he presided over the club's first titleless season for eight years.

AEK coach Dusan Bajevic resigned this season as verbal and physical attacks on him by the club's fans mounted.

Above: AEK were never going to win anything this year but they had the pleasure of denying Olympiakos. Vasilis Lakis scores their winner in the league match, handing top spot in the table to Panathinaikos.

Above left: Tiny Kalithea (in blue), from a working class suburb in southern Athens, performed above themselves to stay up. Here Xenofon Gitas tussles for the ball with Xanthi's Ismail Ba.

Left: Nothing changes. Panathinaikos fans confront the police after a particularly vicious confrontation during their league game with Olympiakos.

Panathinaikos triumphant. Their 3-1 victory over Olympiakos in the Greek Cup Final sealed the club's league and cup double.

323

Soccer in Greece

GREECE

1895: FA rules first translated into Greek — *1895*

1896: Soccer played as exhibition sport at Athens Olympics — *1900*

1899: The Athletics Federation of Greece recognises and takes control of soccer — *1905*

1906: First Athens v Salonika match at the Intermediate Olympics. Game abandoned due to fighting — *1910*

1915

1920: First international, v Sweden, lost 0-9, venue: Antwerp — *1920*

1926: Formation of FA — *1925*
1927: Affiliation to FIFA

1928: National championship established — *1930*

1932: First Greek Cup Final — *1935*

1934: Enter World Cup

1941–45: League abandoned during the war. Cup abandoned until 1947. Regional leagues played 1942–44 — *1940 / 1945*

1950: League abandoned due to civil war — *1950*

1952: League abandoned due to disagreement between top clubs

1954: Affiliation to UEFA — *1955*

1960: Reorganization of National League — *1960*

1962: Cup Final abandoned due to violence between Olympiakios and Panathinaikos fans — *1965*

1963: Second division created

1967: Greek Colonels take power. First live televised soccer. Wave of forced club mergers — *1970*

1967–74: Champions of Cyprus play in Greek first division — *1975*

1971: Panathinaikos runners-up in European Cup — *1980*

1979: Full-time professionalism introduced — *1985*

1980: First appearance in European Championships Finals — *1990*

1981: Karaiskakis Stadium disaster. 21 spectators crushed to death after Olympiakos beat AEK Athens 6-0 — *1995*

1994: First appearance in World Cup finals — *2000*

2002: Collapse of Alpha Digital. Economic crisis leads to players' strike — *2005*

Central Athens goes wild. *All over Greece millions of people poured onto the streets to celebrate Greece's victory over Portugal in the Final of Euro 2004.*

The last time *anyone other than Olympiakos or Panathinaikos, the two giants of Greek domestic soccer, won the Greek league was in 1994 when AEK from Athens finished seven points clear of Panathinaikos. However, Athens' rival Panathinaikos got its revenge by beating AEK 4-2 on penalties to claim the 1994 Greek Cup.*

International Competitions

European Cup

1971:   △ Pan

UEFA Cup

European Cup-Winners' Cup

Key

	International soccer
	Affiliation to FIFA
	Affiliation to UEFA
	War
	Disaster
△	Competition runner-up
•	European Championships winner
Pan	– Panathinaikos

SALONIKA

Makedonikos Thessaloniki 1928

Thermaikos Thessaloniki 1925

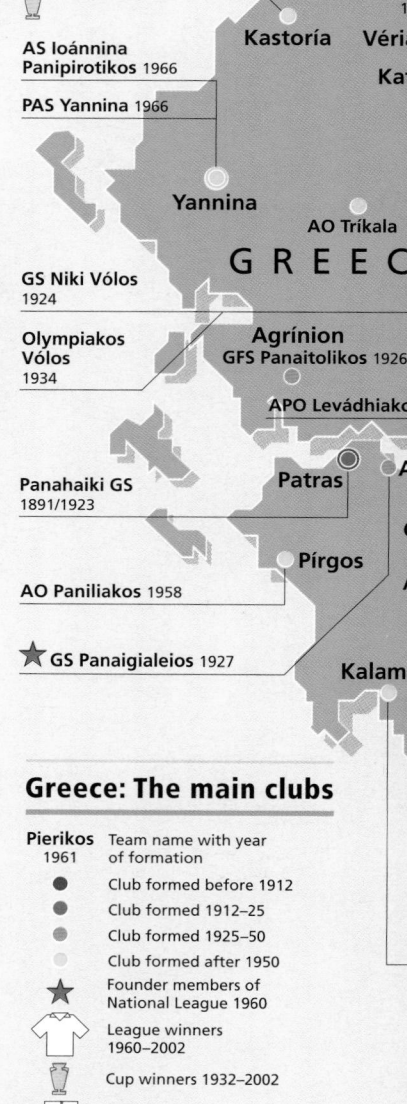

AGS Kastoría 1963

AGS Véroia 1958

Kastoría   **Véria**

AS Ioánnina Panipirotikos 1966

Kateri

PAS Yannina 1966

Yannina

AO Tríkala   **Lá**

GREECE

GS Niki Vólos 1924

Agrínion
GFS Panaitolikos 1926

Olympiakos Vólos 1934

APO Levádhiakos 19

Panahaiki GS 1891/1923

Patras   **Aigí**

Cor

Pírgos   **Arg**

AO Paniliakos 1958

GS Panaigialeios 1927

Kalamáta

Greece: The main clubs

Pierikos 1961 — Team name with year of formation

●	Club formed before 1912
●	Club formed 1912–25
●	Club formed 1925–50
○	Club formed after 1950
★	Founder members of National League 1960
	League winners 1960–2002
	Cup winners 1932–2002
	English origins
	Refugees
	Elite
	Working class
●	Date unknown

★ AS Apollon Kalamarias 1891

★ PAOK Salonica 1926

★ AS ArisThessalonikias 1914

Formed by Greek refugees
from Istanbul

★ GS Iraklis Salonica 1980

Dráma

Xánthi

Sérrai
Pansérraikos 1964

Kavála

SALONIKA
(see inset)

AS Xánthi Skoda 1967

AO Kavála 1965

★ AS Doxa Drámas 1918

Larisa 1964

★ Megas Alexandros Katerínis 1922

AO Pierikos Katerínis 1961

Vólos

Olympiakos Chalkidos

Chalkida

AO Chalkida 1931

ádhia

Elefsina

AO Panelefsiniakos 1931

Mégara

ATHENS/
PIRAEUS
(see inset)

APS Vyzas Mégaron 1928

★ FC Korinthos 1988

Formed from merger of
Pankorinthiakos (1931) and
PAE FC Korinthos (1963)

AO Panargiakos 1926

AO Kalamáta 1967

Iráklion
OFI Crete 1925

Greece

ORIGINS AND GROWTH OF SOCCER

SOCCER ARRIVED IN GREECE via British sailors and traders who played quayside games in the big commercial ports in the late 19th century. The key point of entry was Salonika in the north, which was part of the Ottoman Empire until 1912. The early development of the game suffered from official disapproval; nonetheless it was popular enough for a match to be played between Salonika and Athens at the 1906 Intermediate Olympics – a match that ended in fighting between players and fans and set the tone for subsequent Greek soccer culture.

The growth of soccer and the birth of many clubs was shaped by the turbulent years before and after the First World War, during which the modern Greek nation state emerged. The Ottoman Empire gave up its hold on northern Greece and a massive wave of refugees arrived there from the Turkish mainland. AEK Athens and PAOK Salonica were founded by refugees from Istanbul, and Panionios by refugees from Izmir.

Organization arrives

It was only in 1926 that a national FA was finally formed and a championship was established in which the leading clubs from Athens and Salonika took part. A cup was added in 1932 and the national championship was expanded to include champions from other regions. In 1959, a single national league was created and full-time professionalism finally arrived in 1979.

Both competitions have been dominated by the big teams from Athens with rare successes for provincial teams. Despite enormous domestic support and a great deal of money, the international returns for clubs have been minimal; Panathinaikos' defeat against Ajax in the 1971 European Cup Final is the only highlight. The performance of the national team had been even poorer. However, Greece's unexpected victory at Euro 2004 has changed the status of the national team forever.

GREECE

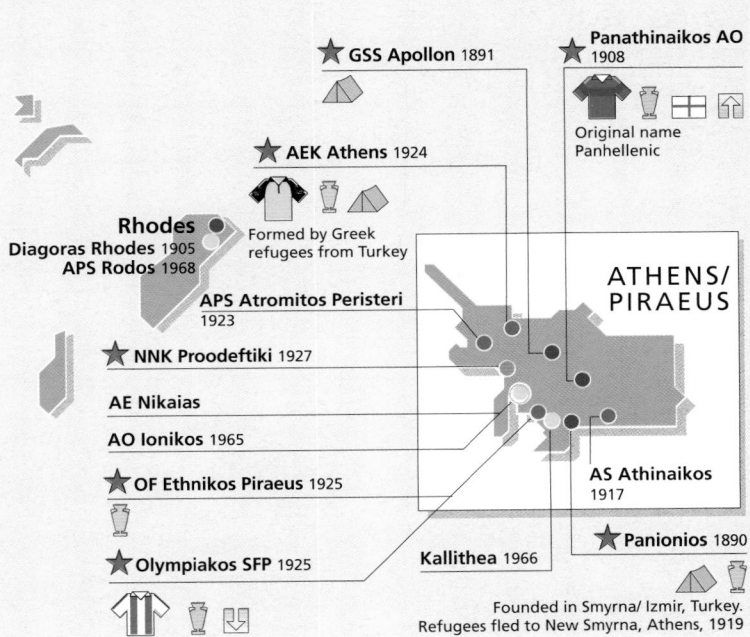

★ GSS Apollon 1891

★ Panathinaikos AO
1908

Original name
Panhellenic

★ AEK Athens 1924

Rhodes
Diagoras Rhodes 1905
APS Rodos 1968

Formed by Greek
refugees from Turkey

APS Atromitos Peristeri
1923

★ NNK Proodeftiki 1927

AE Nikaias

AO Ionikos 1965

★ OF Ethnikos Piraeus 1925

Kallithea 1966

★ Olympiakos SFP 1925

**ATHENS/
PIRAEUS**

AS Athinaikos
1917

★ Panionios 1890

Founded in Smyrna/ Izmir, Turkey.
Refugees fled to New Smyrna, Athens, 1919

Athens

SOCCER CENTER

ATHENS MAY BE THE SPIRITUAL HOME of the Olympics, but in the material world soccer is king. Although Athens is home to a dozen pro and semi-pro teams, the crown is really contested by the big three: Panathinaikos, AEK Athens and Olympiakos. Panathinaikos was originally founded by English bankers and merchants as Panhellenic, and only adopted its Greek name in 1908. Since then Pana has retained an elite following and demeanour. It rose in the 1960s, peaking in 1971 as defeated European Cup finalists (losing 2-0 to Ajax), and also contesting the World Club Cup (losing 3-2 on aggregate to Nacional from Uruguay). Pana is a club with tradition and its older fans gathered around the team's old city centre stadium, Apostolos Nikolaidis, abandoned when the team moved north to the Spiyros Louis. The club has since returned.

Pana acquired proper opposition with the foundation of Olympiakos in 1925, led by the five Andrianopoulos brothers. Lying at the heart of the working-class port district of Piraeus, the club converted the old Olympic velodrome into the Karaiskakis Stadium and played there until the late 1990s. They then played six seasons at the Spiyros Louis before the redevelopment of both stadiums for the 2004 Olympic Games made them homeless and saw Athens' biggest supported team playing at minor stadiums.

The city's third club, AEK Athens (Athlitiki Enosii Konstantinopolous), was founded in 1924 by Greek refugees who had fled from Turkish Constantinople (now Istanbul) and who built the team's original Nea Filadelphia stadium, now called Nikos Goumas. Panionios, to the south-east of the city centre, was actually founded by a community of Greek refugees in 1890 in what was Smyrna and is now Turkish Izmir.

GREECE

OAKA 'SPIYROS LOUIS'

55,000		
	Club:	Greece
	Built:	1982
	Original Capacity:	55,000
	Rebuilt:	2002–04
	Record Attendance:	73,537 Olympiakos v Ajax, 1983
	Significant Matches:	European Cup Finals: 1983, 1994; European Cup-Winners' Cup Final: 1987; Olympic soccer tournament 2004

PERISTERI

PERISTERIO

12,500

Atromito

DIMOTIKO KERATSINIOU

3,000

Ethnikos Piraeus
(1998–)

HAIDARI

Proodeftiki

KORIDALOS

DIMOTIKO AIGALEO

3,500

Aigale

Halkidona

DIMOTIKO NEAPOLIS

8,500

4,360

Ionikos Nikea

KORIDALOS

NIKEA

MOSCHATO

YORGOS KARAISKAKIS

DRAPETSONA

Currently under reconstruction for 2004 Olympic Games. Olympiakos are expected to play here from autumn 2004

32,000

Olympiakos
(1925–97)

Ethnikos Piraeus
(1925–98)

PIRAEUS

SARONIC GULF

Like rivals Olympiakos, Panathinaikos has a fanatical following. Violence on the terraces has been a problem since the 1960s. Local Athens derbies and matches between the top clubs in Athens and Salonika have proved the most troublesome.

AEK ATHENS 1924

League	**1939, 40, 46,** *58–60,* **63,** *65,* **67,** **68,** *70,* **71,** *75, 76,* **78, 79,** *81,* **88,** **89,** *90,* **92–94,** *96, 97, 99, 2002*
Cup	*1932, 39,* **48, 49, 50,** *53,* **56, 64, 66,** *78, 79,* **83,** *94, 95,* **96, 97, 2000, 02**

OLYMPIAKOS 1925

League	**1931, 33, 34,** **36–38, 47, 48,** *49,* **51,** *53,* **54–59,** *61, 62,* **64,** *66,* **67, 68,** *69, 72,* **73–75,** *77,* **79,** **80–83,** *84,* **87,** *89,* **91,** *92,* **95,** **97–2003,** *04*
Cup	*1947,* **51–54,** *55,* **57–61,** *63,* **65,** *66,* **68, 69,** *71,* **73, 74, 75,** *76,* **81,** *86,* **88,** *90,* **92,** *93,* **99,** *2001, 02,* **04**

AEK Athens
(1985–87)

Panathinaikos Olympiakos
(1984–2000) (1997–2002)

PEFKI

KAMATERO

MAROUSI

AEK Athens
(1930–2003)
NIKOS GOUMAS

STADIO OAKA
'SPIYROS LOUIS'
(NATIONAL STADIUM)

IRAKLIO

Currently closed
for reconstruction

32,000

Currently under
reconstruction for
2004 Olympic Games

55,000

VRILISIA

N. LIOSIA

GIPEDO RIZOUPOLIS

16,500

Greece

PANATHINAIKOS 1908

League	**1930,** *31, 32,* **36,** *49,* **53,** *54, 55,* **57,** **60–62,** *63,* **64, 65, 66, 69, 70,** *72,* **74, 77,** *82,* **84, 85, 86, 87,** *90,* **91,** *93, 94,* **95-96,** *98,* **2000,** *01, 03,* **04**
Cup	**1940,** *48, 49,* **55,** *60,* **65,** *67,* **68,** **69,** *72,* **75,** *77,* **82, 84,** *86,* **88, 89,** *91, 93–95,* **97–99,** *2004*
European Cup	*1971*
World Club Cup	*1971*

Apollon **Olympiakos**
Athinon (2002–04)

FILOTHEI

HALANDRI

GALATSI

Olympiakos is sharing with
Apollon 2002–04 due to
stadium redevelopment

AGIOI ANRGYROI

A T H E N S

Panathinaikos
(1922–84, 2000–)

NEO PSICHIKO

HOLARGOS

AMERIKIS SQUARE
Pana's first regular
playing field

APOSTOLOS
NIKOLAIDIS

PAPAGOS

26,000

ZOGRAFOU

VERAN ZEROU STREET
AEK founded in a
sports shop here by
Emilios Ionas and
Kostas Dimoponlos

Original location
of the University of
Athens. George Calafatis,
founder of Panathinaikos,
studied here in the 1890s

KESARIANI

KESARIANI

ACROPOLIS

NEAR EAST

6,000

TAVROS

ELLINKI
PODOSFAIRIKI
OMOSPONDIA
National Football
Association offices

VIRONAS

Ethinikos
Asteras
(1998–)

KALLITHEA

DAFNI

VYRONAS

DIMOTIKO
KALLITHEA

NEA SMYRNIS

AEK Athens
(2003–)

5,000

5,000

12,000

Athinaikos

YMITTOS

Kallithea
FC

Panionios

ILIOUPOLI

PALEO
FALIRO

AEK Athens currently sharing with
Panionios during Nikos Goumas
stadium redevelopment

ALIMOS

PANIONIOS 1890

Cup	**1979, 98**

YORGOS KARAISKAKIS

32,000

Club: Olympiakos (expected to
move here in autumn 2004)
Built: 1895
Rebuilt: 1936, 1999–2002 (abandoned)
Record Attendance: 42,415 Olympiakos v AEK,
7 Apr 1965
Significant Matches: European Cup-Winners' Cup
Final: 1971

Athens

12,000	Capacity of stadium
	Stadium no longer in use for top-flight soccer
	Team colours
E94	Motorway
	Major road
1900	Champions
2000	Runners-up

GREECE

Greece

PLAYERS AND MANAGERS

GREEK PLAYERS AND MANAGERS have not, so far, proved to be great travellers; few have made a mark outside of the domestic game. But at home there have been no shortage of legends. Vyronis was one of the first stars, playing at the 1906 Olympics for Greece, and unusually for the time, picking up his skills with the Swiss side from Servette. Costas Tsiklitaris was a gold medallist at the 1912 Olympics in the long jump as well as a miraculous goalkeeper for Panathinaikos before the First World War – though his career was tragically cut short when he enlisted in the Greek army during the Balkan War 1912–13 and was killed at the front. From the inter-war era, Angelos Messaris is considered to be the leading player – displaying a rare skill and delicacy – though he retired early in 1931 and refused to engage with the game at any level subsequently.

Professionalism arrives late

Professionalism came late to Greece by comparison with most of Europe, but by the 1970s a new crop of Greek players was emerging – good enough to take Panathinaikos to the European Cup Final – featuring the leading scorer of the decade, Antonis Antoniadis. The explosion of TV and European money has seen a wave of foreign players enter the Greek game, including Egyptians, West Africans and the occasional Western European. These conditions created a new set of players in the late 1990s. Some Greeks have overcome their travel sickness – including AEK striker Demis Nikolaidis, and Ajax's Nichlos Macklas. Nikolaidis' departure from the Greek game for Spain was hastened by the threats he received from AEK's ex-president Makis Psomiadis in 2002. Those that stayed have become embroiled in players' strikes

and a desperate fight for money between players and clubs since the collapse of major TV rights deals in 2002.

Foreign influence

While Greece has produced its own managers in club and international soccer, it has also received a steady stream of foreign coaches into the domestic game. In the inter-war and post-war eras, many Britons and central Europeans made the journey south. At Panathinaikos alone these included Yugoslav star Stepan Bobek, Hungarian icon Ferenc Puskas and the Englishman Harry Gane. At the national level Alketas Panagoulias took Greece to two major championships – the 1980 European Championships and the 1994 World Cup.

Greece's international fortunes have been transformed under the leadership of German coach Otto Rehhagel. The old no-nonsense defender from the Bundesliga began by banning officials from the dressing room, taking complete charge of selection and making political peace with the big clubs. He has, amazingly, created an unquenchable team ethic amongst players from a nation of notorious individualists. Their exemplary marking, work rate and counter-attacking abilities has proved brilliantly effective and won them, against all the odds, Euro 2004.

Top 10 International Goalscorers

PLAYER	GOALS	CAPS	FIRST MATCH	LAST MATCH
Nikolaos Anastopoulos	29	73	1977	1988
Dimitris Saravakos	22	78	1982	1994
Dimitris Papaioannou	21	61	1963	1978
Nikos Machlas*	18	60	1993	2002
Themistoklis Nikolaidis*	17	54	1995	2004
Panayotis Tsalohuidis	17	75	1987	1996
Yeorgios Sideris	14	28	1959	1969
Thomas Mavros	11	36	1972	1984
Georgios Georgiadis*	11	58	1994	2004
Vassilis Tsartas*	11	63	1993	2004

* Indicates players still playing at least at club level.

Top 20 International Caps

PLAYER	CAPS	GOALS	FIRST MATCH	LAST MATCH
Efstratos Apostolakis	95	5	1986	1998
Theodoros Zagorakis*	94	0	1994	2004
Dimitris Saravakos	78	22	1982	1994
Anastassios Mitropoulos	76	8	1978	1994
Panayotis Tsalohuidis	75	17	1987	1996
Nikolaos Anastopoulos	73	29	1977	1988
Steilos Manolas	70	6	1982	1994
Yannis Kalitzakis	69	0	1987	1999
Nikos Dabizas*	68	0	1994	2004
Savvas Kofidis	65	1	1982	1994
Dimitris Papaioannou	61	21	1963	1978
Nikos Machlas*	60	18	1993	2002
Nikolaos Sarganis	58	0	1982	1991
Georgios Georgiadis*	58	11	1994	2004
Vassilis Tsartas*	63	11	1993	2004
Yorgos Firos	52	0	1974	1982
Konstandinos Iosifidis	51	2	1974	1982
Petros Mihos	51	0	1982	1988
Dimitris Domazos	50	4	1959	1980
Zisis Vryzas*	50	8	1994	2004
Themistoklis Nikolaidis*	54	17	1995	2004
Antonios Nikopolidis*	48	0	1999	2004
Marinos Ouzonidis	48	4	1995	2001
Ilias Atmatsidis	47	0	1993	2000
Angelos Basinas*	47	3	1999	2004
Nikolaos Tsiantakis	47	2	1988	1994

Greece International Managers

DATES	NAME	GAMES	WON	DRAWN	LOST
1969–71	Lakis Petropoulos	13	2	4	7
1971–73	Billy Bingham	12	1	3	8
1973–76	Alketas Panagoulias	16	5	5	6
1976–77	Lakis Petropoulos	9	1	2	6
1977–81	Alketas Panagoulias	39	11	10	18
1982–84	Christos Archontidis	21	5	3	13
1984–88	Miltos Papapostolou	46	14	15	17
1988–89	Alekos Sofianidis	7	3	1	3
1989–91	Antonis Georgiadis	27	8	9	10
1992	Stefanos Petritsis	1	0	0	1
1992	Antonis Georgiadis	3	3	0	0
1992–94	Alketas Panagoulias	19	6	5	8
1994–97	Kostas Polychroniou	32	17	5	10
1998–99	Anghel Iordaneskou	7	4	2	1
1999–2001	Vassilis Daniil	29	14	8	7
2001	Nikos Christidis	1	0	1	0
2001–	Otto Rehhagel	38	21	8	9

All figures correct as of 4 July 2004.

GREECE

Player of the Year

YEAR	PLAYER	CLUB
1993	Alexandris	AEK
1994	Saravakos	AEK
1995	Georgiadis	Panathinaikos
1996	Alexandris	Olympiakos
1997	Georgiadis	PAOK
1998	Nikolaidis	AEK
1999	Nalitzis Panionos	PAOK
2000	Eleftheropoulos	Olympiakos
2001	Konstantinou	Panathinaikos
2002	Limberopoulos	Panathinaikos
2003	Giannakopoulos	Bolton Wanderers

These awards are taken from the RSSSF website and are estimations based on season MVPs. Records of who won the Greek player of the year award have not been kept during these years.

Top Goalscorers by Season 1959–2004

SEASON	PLAYER	CLUB	GOALS
1959–60	Nestoridis	AEK Athens	33
1960–61	Nestoridis	AEK Athens	27
1961–62	Nestoridis	AEK Athens	29
1962–63	Nestoridis	AEK Athens	23
1963–64	Papaioannou	AEK Athens	29
1964–65	Sideris	Olympiakos	29
1965–66	Papaioannou	AEK Athens	23
1966–67	Sideris	Olympiakos	22
1967–68	Intzoglou	Panionios	24
1968–69	Sideris	Olympiakos	35
1969–70	Antoniadis	Panathinaikos	25
1970–71	Dedes	Panionios	28
1971–72	Antoniadis	Panathinaikos	39
1972–73	Antoniadis	Panathinaikos	22
1973–74	Antoniadis	Panathinaikos	26
1974–75	Antoniadis	Panathinaikos	20
1974–75	Calcadera	Ethnikos Piraeus	20
1975–76	Dedes	AEK Athens	15
1976–77	Papadopoulos	OFI Crete	22
1976–77	Intzoglou	Ethnikos Piraeus	22
1977–78	Mavros	AEK Athens	22
1978–79	Mavros	AEK Athens	31
1979–80	Bajevic	AEK Athens	25
1980–81	Kouis	Aris Salonica	21
1981–82	Haralampidis	Panathinaikos	21
1982–83	Anastopoulos	Olympiakos	29
1983–84	Anastopoulos	Olympiakos	18
1984–85	Mavros	AEK Athens	27
1985–86	Anastopoulos	Olympiakos	19
1986–87	Anastopoulos	Olympiakos	16
1987–88	Nielsen	AEK Athens	21
1988–89	Boda	Olympiakos	20
1989–90	Mavros	Panionios	22
1990–91	Saravakos	Panathinaikos	23
1991–92	Dimitriadis	AEK Athens	27
1992–93	Dimitriadis	AEK Athens	33
1993–94	Alexandris	AEK Athens	24
1993–94	Warzycha	Panathinaikos	24
1994–95	Warzycha	Panathinaikos	29
1995–96	Tsartas	AEK Athens	25
1996–97	Alexandris	Olympiakos	23
1997–98	Warzycha	Panathinaikos	32
1998–99	Nikolaidis	AEK Athens	22
1999–2000	Nalitzis	Panionios/ PAOK Salonica	24
2000–01	Alexandris	Olympiakos	20
2001–02	Alexandris	Olympiakos	19
2002–03	Lymperopoulos	Panathinaikos	16
2003–04	Papadopoulos	Panathinaikos	17

Above: Otto Rehhagel, who, after Bundesliga success with Kaiserslautern, has taken Greece to the pinnacle of European soccer winning Euro 2004 in Portugal.

Above left: Angelos Charisteas of Werder Bremen scored three of Greece's seven goals in Euro 2004 including the winners against France in the quarter-final and Portugal in the Final.

Left: Greece's leading international appearance maker – Efstratos Apostolakis – who went on to coach Panathinaikos.

Below: Dimitris Saravakos, third in the list of all-time Greek international appearances.

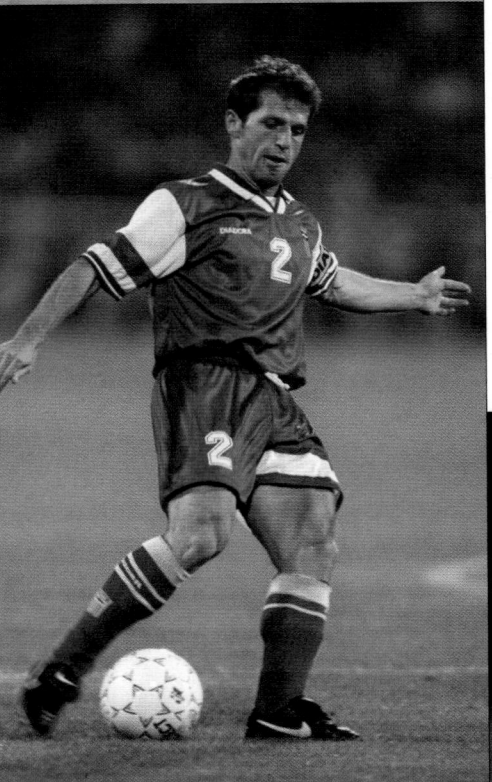

GREECE

Greece

Hellenic Football Federation
Founded: 1926
Joined FIFA: 1927
Joined UEFA: 1954

GREEK SOCCER WAS ORGANIZED AND PLAYED at a regional level before the national level. Local leagues were operating in Athens and Salonika long before a national Greek FA was set up in 1926. In 1928 an Athens-Salonika league was set up, but the national championships were decided by play-offs with regional league champions. In 1960, a fully-fledged national league was created. It became full-time professional in 1979. There are 18 clubs in the top division with a standard three up, three down promotion and relegation system.

The Greek Cup was established in 1932 and now consists of four two-legged rounds followed by a Final. Over the years tournaments have either not been held due to war or have been cancelled due to extensive crowd trouble at Olympiakos v Panathinaikos derbies. In 1962 the Final between these two teams was abandoned by the referee as violence spilled over onto the pitch. In 1964, the two teams met in a semi-final and again the game could not be completed. The tournament was consequently abandoned and the cup was awarded to AEK Athens, winners of the other semi-final.

Greek League Record 1928–2004

SEASON	CHAMPIONS	RUNNERS-UP
1928	Aris Salonica	Ethnikos Piraeus
1929	*no championship*	
1930	Panathinaikos	Aris Salonica
1931	Olympiakos	Panathinaikos
1932	Aris Salonica	Panathinaikos
1933	Olympiakos	Aris Salonica
1934	Olympiakos	Iraklis Salonica
1935	*no championship*	
1936	Olympiakos	Panathinaikos
1937	Olympiakos	PAOK Salonica
1938	Olympiakos	Apollon Athens
1939	AEK Athens	Iraklis Salonica
1940	AEK Athens	PAOK Salonica
1941–45	*no championship*	
1946	Aris Salonica	AEK Athens
1947	Olympiakos	Iraklis Salonica
1948	Olympiakos	Apollon Athens
1949	Panathinaikos	Olympiakos
1950	*no championship*	
1951	Olympiakos	Panionios
1952	*no championship*	
1953	Panathinaikos	Olympiakos
1954	Olympiakos	Panathinaikos
1955	Olympiakos	Panathinaikos
1956	Olympiakos	Ethnikos Piraeus
1957	Olympiakos	Panathinaikos
1958	Olympiakos	AEK Athens
1959	Olympiakos	AEK Athens
1960	Panathinaikos	AEK Athens
1961	Panathinaikos	Olympiakos
1962	Panathinaikos	Olympiakos
1963	AEK Athens	Panathinaikos
1964	Panathinaikos	Olympiakos
1965	Panathinaikos	AEK Athens
1966	Olympiakos	Panathinaikos
1967	Olympiakos	AEK Athens
1968	AEK Athens	Olympiakos
1969	Panathinaikos	Olympiakos
1970	Panathinaikos	AEK Athens

Greek League Record (*continued*)

SEASON	CHAMPIONS	RUNNERS-UP
1971	AEK Athens	Panionios
1972	Panathinaikos	Olympiakos
1973	Olympiakos	PAOK Salonica
1974	Olympiakos	Panathinaikos
1975	Olympiakos	AEK Athens
1976	PAOK Salonica	AEK Athens
1977	Panathinaikos	Olympiakos
1978	AEK Athens	PAOK Salonica
1979	AEK Athens	Olympiakos
1980	Olympiakos	Aris Salonica
1981	Olympiakos	AEK Athens
1982	Olympiakos	Panathinaikos
1983	Olympiakos	Larisa
1984	Panathinaikos	Olympiakos
1985	PAOK Salonica	Panathinaikos
1986	Panathinaikos	OFI Crete
1987	Olympiakos	Panathinaikos
1988	Larisa	AEK Athens
1989	AEK Athens	Olympiakos
1990	Panathinaikos	AEK Athens
1991	Panathinaikos	Olympiakos
1992	AEK Athens	Olympiakos
1993	AEK Athens	Panathinaikos
1994	AEK Athens	Panathinaikos
1995	Panathinaikos	Olympiakos
1996	Panathinaikos	AEK Athens
1997	Olympiakos	AEK Athens
1998	Olympiakos	Panathinaikos
1999	Olympiakos	AEK Athens
2000	Olympiakos	Panathinaikos
2001	Olympiakos	Panathinaikos
2002	Olympiakos	AEK Athens
2003	Olympiakos	Panathinaikos
2004	Panathinaikos	Olympiakos

Greek League Summary

TEAM	TOTALS	CHAMPIONS & RUNNERS-UP (BOLD) (*ITALICS*)
Olympiakos	32, 16	**1931, 33, 34, 36–38, 47, 48, 49, 51, 53, 54–59, 61, 62, 64, 66, 67, 68, 69, 72, 73–75, 77, 79, 80–83, 84, 87, 89, 91, 92, 95, 97–2003, 04**
Panathinaikos	19, 18	**1930**, *31, 32, 36*, **49**, *53, 54, 55, 57*, **60–62**, *63*, **64, 65, 66, 69, 70, 72**, *74, 77, 82*, **84, 85, 86, 87, 90, 91**, *93, 94*, **95, 96**, *98*, **2000**, *01, 03*, **04**
AEK Athens	11, 16	**1939, 40**, *46, 58–60*, **63**, *65*, **67, 68**, *70*, **71**, *75, 76*, **78, 79**, *81*, **88, 89**, *90*, **92–94**, *96, 97, 99*, **2002**
Aris Salonica	3, 3	**1928, 32**, *30, 33, 46, 80*
PAOK Salonica	2, 4	**1937**, *40*, **73, 76**, *78, 85*
Larisa	1, 1	**1983**, *88*
Iraklis Salonica	0, 3	*1934, 39, 47*
Apollon Athens	0, 2	*1938, 48*
Ethnikos Piraeus	0, 2	*1928, 56*
Panionios	0, 2	*1951, 71*
OFI Crete	0, 1	*1986*

Greek Cup Record 1932–2004

YEAR	WINNERS	SCORE	RUNNERS-UP
1932	AEK Athens	5-3	Aris Salonica
1933	Ethnikos Piraeus	2-2, (replay) 2-1	Aris Salonica
1934–38		*no competition*	
1939	AEK Athens	2-1	PAOK Salonica
1940	Panathinaikos	3-1	Aris Salonica
1941–46		*no competition*	
1947	Olympiakos	5-0	Iraklis Salonica
1948	Panathinaikos	2-1	AEK Athens
1949	AEK Athens	0-0, (replay) 2-1 (aet)	Panathinaikos
1950	AEK Athens	4-0	Aris Salonica
1951	Olympiakos	4-0	PAOK Salonica
1952	Olympiakos	2-2, (replay) 2-0	Panionios
1953	Olympiakos	3-2	AEK Athens
1954	Olympiakos	2-0	Doxa Drama
1955	Panathinaikos	2-0	PAOK Salonica
1956	AEK Athens	2-1	Olympiakos
1957	Olympiakos	2-0	Iraklis Salonica
1958	Olympiakos	5-1	Doxa Drama
1959	Olympiakos	2-1	Doxa Drama
1960	Olympiakos	1-1, (replay) 3-0	Panathinaikos
1961	Olympiakos	3-0	Panionios
1962		*not awarded**	
1963	Olympiakos	3-0	Pierikos Katerini
1964	AEK Athens	**	
1965	Olympiakos	1-0	Panathinaikos
1966	AEK Athens	w/o	Olympiakos
1967	Panathinaikos	1-0	Panionios
1968	Olympiakos	1-0	Panathinaikos
1969	Panathinaikos	1-1†	Olympiakos
1970	Aris Salonica	1-0	PAOK Salonica
1971	Olympiakos	3-1	PAOK Salonica
1972	PAOK Salonica	2-1	Panathinaikos
1973	Olympiakos	1-0	PAOK Salonica
1974	PAOK Salonica	2-2 (4-3 pens)	Olympiakos
1975	Olympiakos	1-0	Panathinaikos
1976	Iraklis Salonica	4-4 (6-5 pens)	Olympiakos
1977	Panathinaikos	2-1	PAOK Salonica
1978	AEK Athens	2-0	PAOK Salonica
1979	Panionios	3-1	AEK Athens
1980	Kastoria	5-2	Iraklis Salonica
1981	Olympiakos	3-1	PAOK Salonica
1982	Panathinaikos	1-0	Larisa
1983	AEK Athens	2-0	PAOK Salonica
1984	Panathinaikos	2-0	Larisa
1985	Larisa	4-1	PAOK Salonica
1986	Panathinaikos	4-0	Olympiakos
1987	OFI Crete	1-1 (3-1 pens)	Iraklis Salonica
1988	Panathinaikos	2-2 (4-3 pens)	Olympiakos
1989	Panathinaikos	3-1	Panionios
1990	Olympiakos	4-2	OFI Crete
1991	Panathinaikos	3-0, 2-1 (2 legs)	Athinaikos
1992	Olympiakos	1-1, 2-0 (2 legs)	PAOK Salonica
1993	Panathinaikos	1-0	Olympiakos
1994	Panathinaikos	3-3 (aet)(4-2 pens)	AEK Athens
1995	Panathinaikos	1-0 (aet)	AEK Athens
1996	AEK Athens	7-1	Apollon
1997	AEK Athens	0-0 (5-3 pens)	Panathinaikos
1998	Panionios	1-0	Panathinaikos
1999	Olympiakos	2-0	Panathinaikos
2000	AEK Athens	2-0	Ionikos
2001	PAOK Salonica	4-2	Olympiakos
2002	AEK Athens	2-1	Olympiakos
2003	PAOK Salonica	1-0	Aris Salonica
2004	Panathinaikos	3-1	Olympiakos

w/o denotes walk over

   * Final between Olympiakos and Panathinaikos abandoned at 0-0, cup not awarded.

  ** AEK Athens awarded cup by Greek FA.

   † Panathinaikos won on toss of a coin.

Greek Cup Summary

TEAM	TOTALS	WINNERS & RUNNERS-UP (BOLD) (*ITALICS*)
Olympiakos	20, *11*	**1947**, **51–54**, *55*, **57–61**, **63**, **65**, **66**, *68*, **69**, **71**, **73**, *74*, **75**, *76*, **81**, *86*, *88*, **90**, **92**, *93*, **99**, **2001**, *02*, **04**
Panathinaikos	16, *9*	**1940**, **48**, *49*, **55**, **60**, **65**, *67*, **68**, **69**, *72*, **75**, **77**, **82**, **84**, **86**, **88**, **89**, *91*, **93–95**, *97–99*, **2004**
AEK Athens	13, *5*	**1932**, **39**, **48**, **49**, **50**, *53*, **56**, **64**, *66*, **78**, *79*, **83**, *94*, *95*, **96**, **97**, **2000**, *02*
PAOK Salonica	4, *12*	*1939*, *51*, *55*, *70*, *71*, **72**, *73*, **74**, *77*, *78*, *81*, *83*, *85*, *92*, **2001**, *03*
Panionios	2, *4*	*1952*, *61*, *67*, **79**, *89*, **98**
Aris Salonica	1, *5*	**1932**, *33*, *40*, *50*, **70**, *2003*
Iraklis Salonica	1, *4*	*1947*, *57*, **76**, *80*, *87*
Larisa	1, *2*	*1982*, *84*, **85**
OFI Crete	1, *1*	**1987**, *90*
Ethnikos Piraeus	1, *0*	**1933**
Kastoria	1, *0*	**1980**
Doxa Drama	0, *3*	*1954, 58, 59*
Apollon	0, *1*	*1996*
Athinaikos	0, *1*	*1991*
Ionikos	0, *1*	*2000*
Pierikos Katerini	0, *1*	*1963*

***Olympiakos and Panathinaikos** (in green) have dominated Greek soccer since its early days. Their rivalry is geographical, social and sporting, and often boils over on derby day, resulting in violence and injury.*

Turkey

THE SEASON IN REVIEW 2003–04

'TURKISH SOCCER IS ABOUT AS TRANSPARENT as Romania under Ceausescu' claimed Besiktas coach Mircea Lucescu to the Romanian press, and there was plenty that was murky and unclear in the season's soccer. Outspoken ex-referee and TV commentator Ahmet Cakar was injured in a shooting incident that has yet to be satisfactorily explained. The defeat of the national team by Latvia in the Euro 2004 play-offs could at least be put down to hubris, but the course of the league was another matter.

Beşiktaş come down with the snow

Beşiktaş began the season in electric form, storming to the top of the table, and stretching its lead all the way to the winter break when it stood at 9 points. The team's poor performance in the Champions League at least left the players free to finish the job at home. But almost immediately from the restart Beşiktaş began to disintegrate. Key striker Ilhan Mansiz was inexplicably sold to Japanese club Vissel Kobe and rumours of internal divisions and conflict began to surface. As Fenerbahçe began to finally stir themselves with reasonable but not exceptional performances from van Hooijdonk and Tuncay, Beşiktaş lost an extraordinary game to Samsunspor after having five players sent off. The card-happy referee was incensed by the hail of snowballs that kept coming his way from Beşiktaş fans. Worse was to come when the Turkish authorities ordered that a 1-1 draw between Rizespor and Fenerbahçe be replayed because the referee had forgotten to send off a Rizespor player who had two yellow cards. Fener won the rematch 4-1. But the coup de grace came in April when Fener stamped their authority on the championship, beating Beşiktaş 3-1 away from home.

Galatasaray had one of its worst seasons in a decade, as coach Faith Terim could find neither consistency nor pattern in his squad. Defeat to Fener in the derby game was the last straw. Former star at Gala, the Romanian Gheorghe Hagi, replaced Terim, but the club still finished a disgracefully low sixth and out of the European places. By contrast, Trabzonspor had its best season for years, finishing second in the league, earning a shot at the Champions League, and winning the cup for the second year running.

Turkish police try to keep order as a fence collapses at the goalless draw between Galatasaray and Beşiktaş in October 2003.

Turkish League Table 2003–04

CLUB	P	W	D	L	F	A	Pts	
Fenerbahçe SK	34	23	7	4	82	41	76	Champions League
Trabzonspor K	34	22	6	6	60	38	72	Champions League
Beşiktaş	34	18	8	8	65	45	62	UEFA Cup
Gaziantepspor	34	18	3	13	52	51	57	
Denizlispor	34	17	4	13	52	43	55	
Galatasaray SK	34	15	9	10	56	47	54	
Samsunspor	34	13	7	14	46	47	46	
Malatyaspor	34	11	12	11	51	40	45	
MKE Ankaragücü	34	13	6	15	48	53	45	
Gençlerbirligi	34	12	8	14	56	52	44	UEFA Cup (cup finalists)
Konyaspor	34	10	14	10	53	54	44	
Diyarbakirspor	34	12	7	15	44	54	43	
Akcaabat	34	11	9	14	45	53	42	
Rizespor	34	13	3	18	37	53	42	
Istanbulspor	34	11	8	15	46	45	41	
Bursaspor	34	10	10	14	40	40	40	Relegated
Adanaspor	34	6	4	24	38	73	22	Relegated
Elazigspor	34	5	7	22	37	79	22	Relegated

Promoted clubs: Sakaryaspor AS Adapazarı, Erciyesspor K Kayseri, BB Ankaraspor K (league expanding to 20 clubs for 2004–05 season).

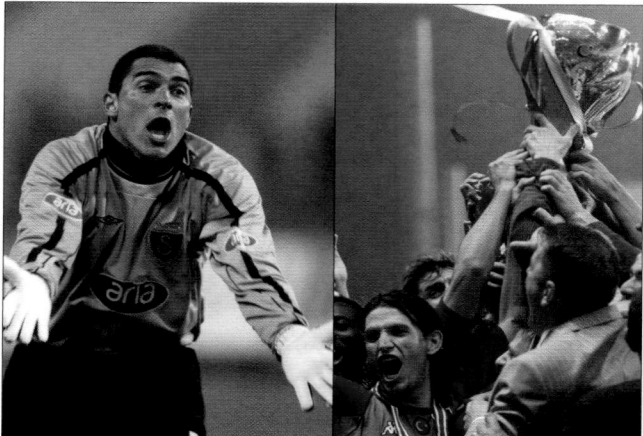

Turkish Cup

2004 FINAL

May 5 – Ataturk Olympic Stadium, Istanbul
Trabzonspor K 4-0 Gençlerbirligi
(Yilmaz 23,
Gokdeniz 70,
77 pen
Ahinful 89 pen)
h/t: 1-0 **Att:** 30,000
Ref: Muftuoglu

Above: Trabzonspor rounded off a really good season with a Turkish Cup Final win over Gençlerbirligi.

Above, left: The injustice of it all: Galatsaray's Colombian goalkeeper Faryd Mondragon questions a penalty decision given in the game with Beşiktaş.

International Club Performances 2003–04

CLUB	COMPETITION	PROGRESS
Beşiktaş	Champions League	Group Stage
	UEFA Cup	3rd Round
Galatasaray SK	Champions League	Group Stage
	UEFA Cup	3rd Round
Gaziantepspor	UEFA Cup	3rd Round
Gençlerbirligi	UEFA Cup	4th Round
Malatyaspor	UEFA Cup	1st Round
Trabzonspor K	UEFA Cup	1st Round

Top Goalscorers 2003–04

PLAYER	CLUB	NATIONALITY	GOALS
Zafer Biryon	Konyaspor	Turkish	24
Pierre van Hooijdonk	Fenerbahçe SK	Dutch	24
Serkan Ayukut	Samsunspor	Turkish	20

Christoph Daum bounces back and takes Fenerbahçe to the title. Here he celebrates his birthday and his team's win over Adanspor.

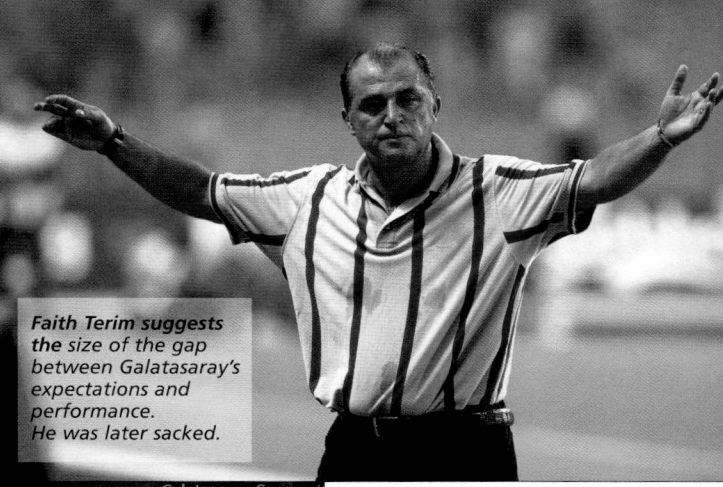

Faith Terim suggests the size of the gap between Galatasaray's expectations and performance. He was later sacked.

Left: Georghe Hagi enters the bear pit. A favourite at the club as a player, Hagi replaced Faith Terim as Galatasaray's manager.

Far left: Turkish national team manager Senol Gunes and Nihat Kahveci leave the pitch after Turkey lost a place at Euro 2004 to Latvia.

Below, left: Mystery transfer of the season: Ilhan Mansiz was sold to Vissel Kobe in Japan and Beşiktaş' fortunes plummeted.

Below: Fenerbahçe are champions: Umit Ozat, Pierre van Hoojidonk and Tuncay Sanli lift the trophy.

TURKEY

Soccer in Turkey

1895: First recorded soccer game played in Izmir — 1895

1900

1903: Beşiktaş, Turkey's oldest club, founded

1905: First Istanbul League started — 1905

1910

1915

1923: Formation of FA: Türkiye Futbol Federasyono. Affiliation to FIFA. First international, v Romania, drawn 2-2, venue: Istanbul — 1920

1925

1924: New Istanbul League established — 1930

1935

1937: National championship by play-off introduced — 1940

1945

1951: Professionalism — 1950

1954: First appearance — 1955

1959: National League

1960

1962: Affiliation to UEFA

1963: First Turkish — 1965

1971: Kayseri Stadium disaster, stand collapses at Kayserispor v Siwas, 44 killed — 1970 / 1975

1980

1985

1990

1996: First appearance in European Championships finals — 1995

2000: Galatasaray win UEFA Cup

2002: Turkey reach World Cup semi-final, its best-ever international performance — 2000 / 2005

Manager Faith Terim has been a key figure in Galatasaray's domination of Turkish soccer during the late 1990s and early 2000s.

Galatasaray's victory against Arsenal in the 2000 UEFA Cup Final was the first major triumph for a Turkish soccer club.

Key

⬚	International soccer	✿	Disaster
⚽	Affiliation to FIFA	○	Competition winner
⚽	Affiliation to UEFA	Gala	Galatasaray

International Competitions

	European Cup	UEFA Cup	European Cup-Winners' Cup
2000:		○ Gala	

Turkey: The main clubs

Altay GK 1914 — Team name with year of formation

- ● Club formed before 1912
- ● Club formed 1912–25
- ● Club formed 1925–50
- ○ Club formed after 1950
- ★ Founder members of National League (1959)
- 👕 Champions (1959–2001)
- 🏆 Cup winners
- 📖 Originated from a school or college

★ **Istanbulspor AS** 1926

★ **Vefa Simtel SK** 1908

★ **Adalet SK** 1946

★ **Kasimpaşa SK** 1921

★ **Feriköy SK** 1927

Sariyer Gençlik SK 1940

★ **Beykoz SK** 1908

ISTANBUL

Izmir

Yeşildirek SK 1951

Bakirköyspor K 1949

Zeytinburnu SK 1953

★ **Karagümrük SK** 1926

Beyoğluspor 1914

★ **Galatasaray SK** 1905

Turkey

ORIGINS AND GROWTH OF SOCCER

WHEN SOCCER FIRST APPEARED on the playing fields of Istanbul in the late 19th century, it was met with suspicion by the ruling authorities. The last Sultan of the Ottoman Empire, already in terminal decline and fearful of Western political and cultural influences, banned his subjects from playing. Not surprisingly, soccer was initially concentrated in the Jewish, Christian and Greek communities of Istanbul. But the game was unstoppable. Beşiktaş was established in 1903 with the support of Osman Pasha, a member of the Sultan's government, Turkish high school students formed Galatasaray in 1905, and Fenerbahçe – the last of Turkey's big three – grew out of St. Joseph's, a French college in the city, in 1907. An Istanbul Sunday amateur league was created in 1905, but the development of organized soccer was held back by the First World War, the subsequent collapse of the Ottoman Empire and the creation of the Turkish Republic. The new republic, declared by Kemal Atatürk in 1923, was led by a diehard Fenerbahçe fan and the formation of a national FA and official regional and Istanbul leagues quickly followed. As transport improved and the quality of the provincial game rose, a national championship was created in 1937, with play-offs between top Istanbul clubs and regional champions.

The game's growing popularity saw professionalism introduced in 1951 and the creation of a fully-fledged national league in 1959. However, it is only in the 1990s that these factors have begun to generate international success with the national team performing well at the 1996 and 2000 European Championships, Galatasaray's victory in the UEFA Cup 2000 and the national team's amazing run to the semi-finals of the 2002 World Cup.

TURKEY

★ Karşiyaka SK 1912

★ Altay GK 1914

★ Altinordu SK 1923

★ Göztepe SK 1925

★ Izmirspor K 1923

Trabzonspor K 1967

Caykur Rizespor 1968

Rizespor K 1953

ISTANBUL (see inset)

Samsunspor K 1965

Orduspor K 1967

Rize

Zonguldak
Zonguldakspor K 1966

Samsun

Adapazari
Sakaryaspor K 1965

Ordu

Giresun
Giresunspor K 1967

Trabzon

Izmit
Kocaelispor K 1966

Karabük
DC Karabukspor 1969

Erzurum
Erzurumspor K 1968

Bursa

Bolu
Boluspor K 1965

ANKARA (see inset)

Yozgat
Yimpas Yozgatspor 1959

T U R K E Y

Bursaspor K 1963

Balikesir
Balikesirspor 1966

Kirikkale
MKE Kirikkalespor K 1967

Van
Vanspor K 1974

Eskişehir
Eskişehirspor K 1965

Kayseri
Kayserispor K 1966

Siirt
Siirt Jet PA 1969

Aydin
Aydinspor K 1966

Diyarbakir

Denizli
Denizlispor K 1966

Konya
Konyaspor K 1981

Kahramanmaraş
Kahramanmaraşspor K 1969

Gaziantep
Gaziantepspor K 1969

Diyarbakirspor K 1968

Antalya
Antalyaspor K 1966

Mersin
Mersin Idmanyurdu SK 1925

Adana

Adanaspor AS SK 1954

Adana Demirspor K 1940

★ Beşiktaş JK 1903

ANKARA

★ Ankara Dermispor 1932

★ Hacettepe SK 1945

★ MKE Ankaragücü SK 1910

Osman Pasha, a member of Sultan's Court, was the club's first patron

★ Gençlerbirligi SK 1923

★ Sekerspor KD 1947

PTT SK 1954

★ Fenerbahçe SK 1907

★ Seker Hilal SK Ankara 1958

Istanbul

SOCCER CENTER

ISTANBUL, IN ITS FORMER LIFE as Constantinople, was the seat of the Byzantine and Ottoman Empires for more than 1,500 years. In 1923, when the Turkish Revolution swept the Ottoman sultanate away, political power migrated to Ankara, but soccer power and the national FA have always remained in Istanbul. It is a power that rests on the presence of Turkey's three leading clubs: Galatasaray and Beşiktaş in the old European centre of the city, and Fenerbahçe across the Bosporus in Asian Turkey. Between them, they have completely dominated Turkish soccer.

English merchants first played soccer in Istanbul in the late 19th century, and by 1904 had set up the first Istanbul league schedule. The Ottoman sultan, Abdülhamid III, banned this pernicious British game from Istanbul as contrary to Islamic law. However, non-Muslims were exempt from the ruling, and clubs began to form across the city, starting in foreign schools and Christian and Jewish areas.

The big three

The social and political allegiances of the big three are not entirely clear cut. Fenerbahçe considers itself the people's team, drawing on the populism of its greatest fan – the leader of the Turkish revolution himself – Kemal Ataturk. While Fenerbahçe is the best-supported club, Galatasaray is the richest, and has made the most of the recent boom in European soccer with success in the UEFA Cup (2000) and flotation on the Turkish stock exchange (2002). Beşiktaş, despite considerable domestic success, is stuck as the city's 'third team'. All three can muster ferocious support at home, which has spilled into violence at both Fener-Gala derbies and at big European games. Visits by Manchester United (1993) and Leeds United (2000), whose teams have been greeted at Istanbul airport with signs reading 'Welcome to Hell', have seen violence and some have ended with fans' deaths.

Beyond the big three, other Istanbul teams have had a presence in the top Turkish division. In the south-west, Zeytinburnu has risen out of the concrete and neglect of one of Istanbul's poorest districts. In the far west of the city, Istanbulspor has won the city league and rose for a time on the money of Istanbul media magnate Cem Uzan. North of the city centre on the banks of the Bosporus, Sariyer GK held onto a mid-table position throughout the 1990s.

For more than 1,500 years the seat of the Ottoman and Byzantine Empires, Istanbul is also the home city of Turkish soccer. A mosque towers over Beşiktaş's Inönü stadium.

TURKEY

BJK INÖNÜ

35,000

Club: Besiktas JK
Built: 1947
Original Capacity: 39,000
Record Attendance: 39,000 Besiktas v Malmö, 1994

IKITELLI

BAYRAMPASA STADI

11,000

Istanbulspor AS

E80

ISTANBULSPOR AS 1926	
Istanbul League 1924–58	1932

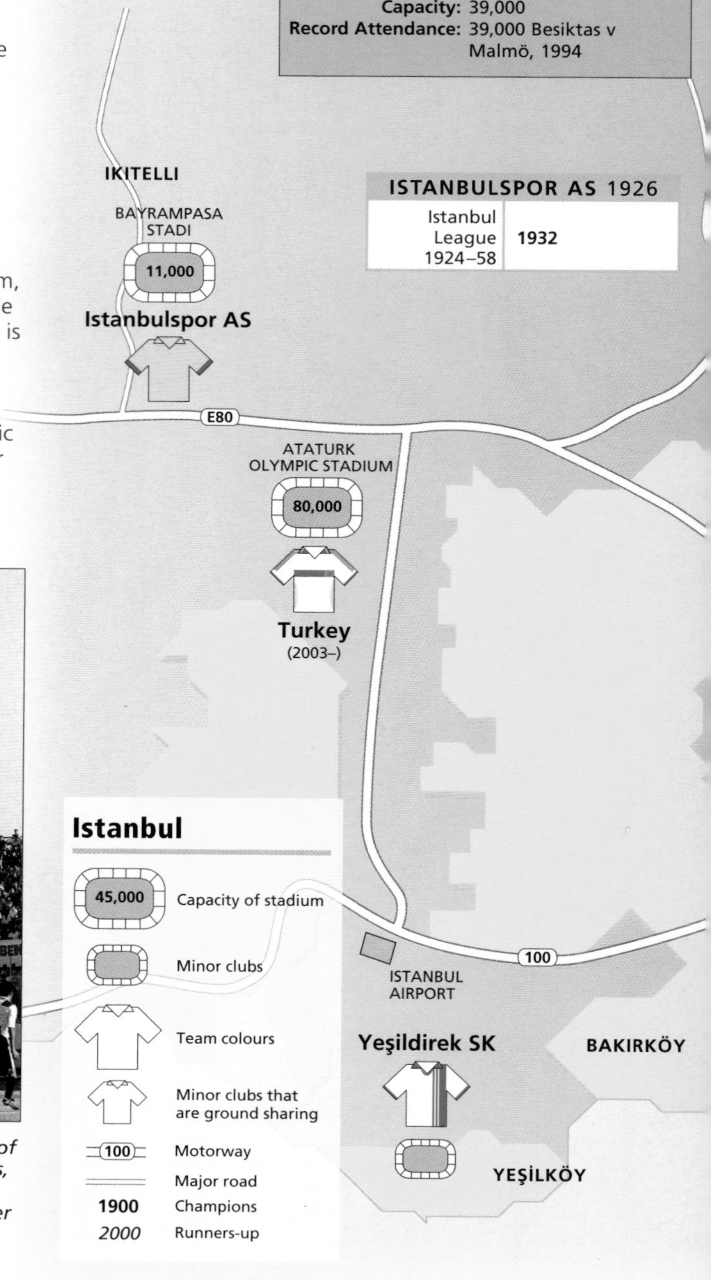

ATATURK OLYMPIC STADIUM

80,000

Turkey
(2003–)

Istanbul

45,000	Capacity of stadium
	Minor clubs
	Team colours
	Minor clubs that are ground sharing
100	Motorway
	Major road
1900	Champions
2000	Runners-up

ISTANBUL AIRPORT

100

Yeşildirek SK

BAKIRKÖY

YEŞİLKÖY

ALI SAMI YEN

 20,000

Club: Galatasaray SK
Built: 1953
Original Capacity: 30,000
Rebuilding planned: 2003–05 (provisional capacity of 41,000)

SÜKRÜ SARACOGLU

54,000

Club: Fenerbahçe SK
Built: 1948
Original Capacity: 25,000
Rebuilt: 1960–81, 1999–2001, 2002–03 (provisional capacity of 63,000)

BOSPORUS CLUBS

Sariyer Gençlik SK

Beykoz SK

YUSUF ZIYA ÖNIS STADI

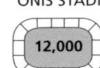 **12,000**

GALATASARAY SK 1905

Istanbul League 1924–58	*1924, 25–27, 29, 30,* **31,** *35, 36, 42,* **49,** *51, 52, 54,* **55, 56, 57, 58**
League 1959–2004	**1961, 62, 63, 66, 69, 71–73,** *75, 79, 86,* **87, 88,** *91,* **93, 94,** **97–2000,** *01, 02, 03*
Cup	**1963–66,** *69,* **73,** *76,* **80,** *82,* **85,** **91,** *93,* **94,** *95,* **96,** *98,* **99, 2000**
UEFA Cup	**2000**

BEŞIKTAŞ JK 1903

Istanbul League 1924–58	*1924,* **33, 34,** *39–43,* **44, 45, 46,** *48,* **49,** *50–52,* **53,** *54, 55*
League 1959–2004	**1960,** *63–65,* **66, 67,** *68,* **74,** *82,* **85, 86,** *87–89,* **90–92,** *93,* **95,** *97, 99, 2000,* **03**
Cup	*1966,* **75,** *77,* **84,** *89, 90,* **93, 94,** *98, 99, 2002*

FENERBAHÇE SK 1907

Istanbul League 1924–58	*1926, 27, 29,* **30, 31,** *33,* **34,** *35–37,* *38–41,* **43, 44,** *45,* **46,** *47,* **48,** *50,* **53,** *56,* **57, 58**
League 1959–2004	**1959,** *60,* **61,** *62,* **64, 65,** *67,* **68,** *70,* **71,** *73,* **74, 75, 76, 77, 78,** *80,* **83,** *84,* **85,** *89,* **90,** *92,* **94,** *96,* **98,** *2001,* **02,** *04*
Cup	*1963,* **65,** *68,* **74,** *79,* **83,** *89,* **96,** *2001*

VEFA SIMTEL SK 1908

Istanbul League 1924–58	*1925, 47*
League 1959–2004	*1959*

TURKEY

Map labels

Galatasaray SK
ALI SAMI YEN

20,000

GALATASARAY HIGH SCHOOL
Galatasaray SK founded by students from the school

I S T A N B U L

GAZIOSMANPAŞA

BALAT
Centre of Istanbul's Jewish community and enthusiastic soccer players at the turn of the century

EYÜP
FERER
Centre of Istanbul's Greek community before the Greco-Turkish war (1920–23) and hotbed of soccer

Kasimpaşa SK

ORTAKÖY

BJK INÖNÜ
Beşiktaş JK
35,000

GALATASARAY ISLAND
Owned by Galatasaray, the club has built a swimming pool and restaurant on the island

BEYOĞLU

DOLMABAHÇE MOSQUE AND PALACE
Housed the Sultan's last harem

Kasimpaşa SK

BEYLERBEYI

BAYRAMPAŞA

FATIH

Haliç

Vefa Simtel SK

ÜSKÜDAR

Vefa Simtel SK

ZEYTINBURNU
10,000

ZEYTINBURNU

EMINÖNÜ

Fenerbahçe SK
(1960–81)

SULTAN'S PALACE

Zeytinburnu SK

Karadeniz Boğazi

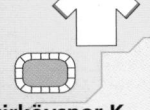
kirköyspor K

MARMARA DENIZI (SEA OF MARMARA)

KADIKÖY

SÜKRÜ SARACOGLU

54,000

Fenerbahçe SK

FENERBAHÇE

E80

Fenerbahçe has played in this area since before the First World War when its ground was known as the Priest's Marsh. The ground was used as part of a chain, smuggling weapons to Ataturk's republican army during the Allied occupation 1918–20. Shortly after the declaration of the Turkish Republic in 1923 Fenerbahçe symbolically defeated a British Army XI 2–1

ERENKÖY 100

Turkey

Türkiye Futbol Federasyonu
Founded: 1923
Joined FIFA: 1923
Joined UEFA: 1962

THE ORIGINS OF ORGANIZED soccer in Turkey are very much centred on Istanbul with a regular Istanbul league created in 1905. However, a combination of disapproval by the ruling Ottoman authorities and the First World War led to two decades of decline. In the immediate aftermath of the Turkish Revolution, a national soccer association was created in 1923, and a new Istanbul league followed a year later.

Between 1937 and 1950 a national championship was contested in play-offs between the top Istanbul clubs and regional champions. Professionalism arrived in 1951, but it took until 1959 to create a single national league. A national cup competition was set up in 1963.

Turkish League Summary

TEAM	TOTALS	CHAMPIONS & RUNNERS-UP (BOLD) (ITALICS)
Fenerbahçe SK	15, 14	**1959**, *60*, **61**, *62*, **64**, **65**, *67*, **68**, **70**, *71*, *73*, **74**, **75**, *76*, *77*, **78**, *80*, **83**, *84*, **85**, **89**, *90*, *92*, *94*, **96**, *98*, **2001**, *02*, **04**
Galatasaray SK	15, 8	*1961*, **62**, **63**, *66*, **69**, **71–73**, *75*, *79*, *86*, *87*, *88*, *91*, **93**, **94**, **97–2000**, *01*, **02**, *03*
Beşiktaş JK	10, 13	*1960*, *63–65*, **66**, *67*, *68*, *74*, **82**, *85*, **86**, *87–89*, **90–92**, *93*, **95**, *97*, *99*, **2000**, *03*
Trabzonspor K	6, 6	**1976**, **77**, **78**, **79–81**, *82*, *83*, *84*, *95*, *96*, *2004*
Eskişehirspor K	0, 3	*1969*, *70*, *72*
Adanaspor K	0, 1	*1981*
Vefa SK	0, 1	*1959*

Turkish League Record 1959–2004

SEASON	CHAMPIONS	RUNNERS-UP
1959	Fenerbahçe SK	Vefa SK
1960	Beşiktaş JK	Fenerbahçe SK
1961	Fenerbahçe SK	Galatasaray SK
1962	Galatasaray SK	Fenerbahçe SK
1963	Galatasaray SK	Beşiktaş JK
1964	Fenerbahçe SK	Beşiktaş JK
1965	Fenerbahçe SK	Beşiktaş JK
1966	Beşiktaş JK	Galatasaray SK
1967	Beşiktaş JK	Fenerbahçe SK
1968	Fenerbahçe SK	Beşiktaş JK
1969	Galatasaray SK	Eskişehirspor K
1970	Fenerbahçe SK	Eskişehirspor K
1971	Galatasaray SK	Fenerbahçe SK
1972	Galatasaray SK	Eskişehirspor K
1973	Galatasaray SK	Fenerbahçe SK
1974	Fenerbahçe SK	Beşiktaş JK
1975	Fenerbahçe SK	Galatasaray SK
1976	Trabzonspor K	Fenerbahçe SK
1977	Trabzonspor K	Fenerbahçe SK
1978	Fenerbahçe SK	Trabzonspor K
1979	Trabzonspor K	Galatasaray SK
1980	Trabzonspor K	Fenerbahçe SK
1981	Trabzonspor K	Adanaspor K
1982	Beşiktaş JK	Trabzonspor K
1983	Fenerbahçe·SK	Trabzonspor K
1984	Trabzonspor K	Fenerbahçe SK
1985	Fenerbahçe SK	Beşiktaş JK
1986	Beşiktaş JK	Galatasaray SK
1987	Galatasaray SK	Beşiktaş JK
1988	Galatasaray SK	Beşiktaş JK
1989	Fenerbahçe SK	Beşiktaş JK
1990	Beşiktaş JK	Fenerbahçe SK
1991	Beşiktaş JK	Galatasaray SK
1992	Beşiktaş JK	Fenerbahçe SK
1993	Galatasaray SK	Beşiktaş JK
1994	Galatasaray SK	Fenerbahçe SK
1995	Beşiktaş JK	Trabzonspor K
1996	Fenerbahçe SK	Trabzonspor K
1997	Galatasaray SK	Beşiktaş JK
1998	Galatasaray SK	Fenerbahçe SK
1999	Galatasaray SK	Beşiktaş JK
2000	Galatasaray SK	Beşiktaş JK
2001	Fenerbahçe SK	Galatasaray SK
2002	Galatasaray SK	Fenerbahçe SK
2003	Beşiktaş JK	Galatasaray SK
2004	Fenerbahçe SK	Trabzonspor K

Turkish Cup Record 1963–2004

YEAR	WINNERS	SCORE	RUNNERS-UP
1963	Galatasaray SK	2-1, 2-1 (2 legs)	Fenerbahçe SK
1964	Galatasaray SK	0-0, w/o (2 legs)	Altay GK
1965	Galatasaray SK	0-0, 1-0 (2 legs)	Fenerbahçe SK
1966	Galatasaray SK	1-0	Beşiktaş JK
1967	Altay GK	2-2*	Göztepe SK
1968	Fenerbahçe SK	2-0, 0-1 (2 legs)	Altay GK
1969	Göztepe SK	1-0, 1-1 (2 legs)	Galatasaray SK
1970	Göztepe SK	1-2, 3-1 (2 legs)	Eskişehirspor K
1971	Eskişehirspor K	0-1, 2-0 (2 legs)	Bursaspor K
1972	MKE Ankaragücü SK	0-0, 3-0 (2 legs)	Altay GK
1973	Galatasaray SK	3-1, 1-1 (2 legs)	MKE Ankaragücü SK
1974	Fenerbahçe SK	0-1, 3-0 (2 legs)	Bursaspor K
1975	Beşiktaş JK	0-1, 2-0 (2 legs)	Trabzonspor K
1976	Galatasaray SK	1-1, 1-1 (5-4 pens) (2 legs)	Trabzonspor K
1977	Trabzonspor K	1-0, 0-0 (2 legs)	Beşiktaş JK
1978	Trabzonspor K	3-0, 0-0 (2 legs)	Demirspor K
1979	Fenerbahçe SK	1-2, 2-0 (2 legs)	Altay GK
1980	Altay GK	1-0, 1-1 (2 legs)	Galatasaray SK
1981	MKE Ankaragücü SK	2-1, 0-0 (2 legs)	Boluspor K
1982	Galatasaray SK	3-0, 1-2 (2 legs)	MKE Ankaragücü SK
1983	Fenerbahçe SK	2-0, 2-1 (2 legs)	Mersin Idmanyurdu SK
1984	Trabzonspor K	2-0	Beşiktaş JK
1985	Galatasaray SK	2-1, 0-0 (2 legs)	Trabzonspor K
1986	Bursaspor K	2-0	Altay GK
1987	Gençlerbirligi SK	5-0, 1-2 (2 legs)	Eskişehirspor K
1988	Sakaryaspor K	2-0, 1-1 (2 legs)	Samsunspor K
1989	Beşiktaş JK	1-0, 2-1 (2 legs)	Fenerbahçe SK
1990	Beşiktaş JK	2-0	Trabzonspor K
1991	Galatasaray SK	3-1	MKE Ankaragücü SK
1992	Trabzonspor K	0-3, 5-1 (2 legs)	Bursaspor K
1993	Galatasaray SK	1-0, 2-2 (2 legs)	Beşiktaş JK
1994	Beşiktaş JK	3-2, 0-0 (2 legs)	Galatasaray SK
1995	Trabzonspor K	3-2, 1-0 (2 legs)	Galatasaray SK
1996	Galatasaray SK	1-0, 1-1 (2 legs)	Fenerbahçe SK
1997	Kocaelispor K	1-0, 1-1 (2 legs)	Trabzonspor K
1998	Beşiktaş JK	1-1, 1-1 (4-2 pens)	Galatasaray SK
1999	Galatasaray SK	0-0, 2-0 (2 legs)	Beşiktaş JK
2000	Galatasaray SK	5-3 (aet)	Antalyaspor
2001	Gençlerbirligi SK	2-2 (aet)(4-1 pens)	Fenerbahçe SK
2002	Kocaelispor	4-0	Beşiktaş JK
2003	Trabzonspor K	3-1	Gençlerbirligi SK
2004	Trabzonspor K	4-0	Gençlerbirligi SK

w/o denotes walk over
* Altay GK won on toss of a coin.

Turkish Cup Summary

TEAM	TOTALS	WINNERS & RUNNERS-UP (BOLD) (ITALICS)
Galatasaray SK	13, 5	1963–66, 69, 73, 76, 80, 82, 85, 91, 93, 94, 95, 96, 98, 99, 2000
Trabzonspor K	7, 5	1975, 76, **77**, **78**, **84**, 85, **90**, 92, 95, 97, **2003**, **04**
Beşiktaş JK	5, 6	1966, 75, **77**, **84**, **89**, **90**, **93**, 94, 98, 99, 2002
Fenerbahçe SK	4, 5	**1963**, 65, **68**, **74**, **79**, **83**, 89, 96, **2001**

This summary only features clubs that have won the Turkish Cup four or more times. For a full list of cup winners and runners-up please see the Cup Record left.

Armenia

Football Federation of Armenia
Founded: 1992
Joined FIFA: 1992
Joined UEFA: 1993

Independent domestic football only came with independence in 1991. Leading clubs Ararat Yerevan, Tsement Ararat and Shirak Gyumri dominate the Armenian game. However, only international matches generate much interest, with tiny crowds at most league games.

SEASON	LEAGUE CHAMPIONS
1998	Tsement Ararat
1999	Shirak Gyumri
2000	Araks Ararat
2001	Pyunik Yerevan
2002	Pyunik Yerevan
2003	Pyunik Yerevan

YEAR	CUP WINNERS
1999	Tsement Ararat
2000	MIKA Ashtarak
2001	MIKA Ashtarak
2002	Pyunik Yerevan
2003	Pyunik Yerevan

Azerbaijan

Association of Football Federations of Azerbaijan
Founded: 1992
Joined FIFA: 1994
Joined UEFA: 1994

The championship was originally decided through mini-leagues. Today, a more conventional system is used. However, a bitter conflict between the clubs and the FA has led to the abandonment of the league.

SEASON	LEAGUE CHAMPIONS
2000	Şamkir
2001	Şamkir
2002	Şamkir
2003	Şamkir
2004	Neftçi Baku

YEAR	CUP WINNERS
2000	Kapaz Gäncä
2001	Şafa Baku
2002	abandoned
2003	abandoned
2004	Neftçi Baku

Cyprus

Kipriaki Omospondia Podosferu

Founded: 1934
Joined FIFA: 1948
Joined UEFA: 1962

The division of the island in 1974 between Greek and Turkish areas also divided the league. Turkish Northern Cyprus has its own organization but is not recognized by FIFA.

SEASON	LEAGUE CHAMPIONS
2000	Anorthosis Famagusta
2001	Omonia Nicosia
2002	APOEL Nicosia
2003	Omonia Nicosia
2004	APOEL Nicosia

YEAR	CUP WINNERS
2000	Omonia Nicosia
2001	Apollon Limassol
2002	Anorthosis Famagusta
2003	Anorthosis Famagusta
2004	AEK Larnaca

Georgia

Georgian Football Federation
Founded: 1990
Joined FIFA: 1992
Joined UEFA: 1992

Uniquely among ex-Soviet republics, Georgia managed to establish a separate national league and cup before formal political independence in 1991. Georgian soccer has been dominated by Dinamo Tbilisi.

SEASON	LEAGUE CHAMPIONS
2000	Torpedo Kutaisi
2001	Torpedo Kutaisi
2002	Torpedo Kutaisi
2003	Dinamo Tbilisi
2004	WIT Georgia

YEAR	CUP WINNERS
2000	Lokomotivi Tbilisi
2001	Torpedo Kutaisi
2002	Lokomotivi Tbilisi
2003	Dinamo Tbilisi
2004	Dinamo Tbilisi

Israel

Israel Football Association
Founded: 1928
Joined FIFA: 1929
Joined UEFA: 1992

An FA was affiliated to the Asian Football Confederation before the creation of Israel in 1948. Political upheavals have affected Israeli soccer since then, but membership of UEFA in 1992 has stabilized the situation.

SEASON	LEAGUE CHAMPIONS
2000	Hapoel Tel-Aviv
2001	Maccabi Haifa
2002	Maccabi Tel-Aviv
2003	Maccabi Tel-Aviv
2004	Maccabi Haifa

YEAR	CUP WINNERS
2000	Hapoel Tel-Aviv
2001	Maccabi Tel-Aviv
2002	Maccabi Tel-Aviv
2003	Hapoel Ramat Gan
2004	Hapoel Bnei Salchin

Kazakhstan

Football Union of Kazakhstan
Founded: 1914
Joined FIFA: 1994
Joined UEFA: 2002

Soccer first arrived in Kazakhstan before the First World War. It was part of the Soviet Union until 1992 when independence was followed by membership of FIFA and the AFC. In 2002, Kazakhstan became UEFA's 53rd and newest member.

SEASON	LEAGUE CHAMPIONS
1999	Irtysh Bastan Pavlodar
2000	Zhenis Astana
2001	Zhenis Astana
2002	Irtysh Bastan Pavlodar
2003	Irtysh Bastan Pavlodar

YEAR	CUP WINNERS
2000	SOPFK Kairat Almaty
2001	Zhenis Astana
2001*	Kairat Almaty
2002	Zhenis Astana
2003	Kairat Almaty

* Transitional season.

Moldova

Federaţia Moldoveneasca de Fotbal

Founded: 1990
Joined FIFA: 1994
Joined UEFA: 1992

Moldova was formed from the break up of the Soviet Union in 1991, with the formation of a national FA and national league and cup competitions preceding a formal state of independence.

SEASON	LEAGUE CHAMPIONS
2000	Zimbru Chişinău
2001	Serif Tiraspol
2002	Serif Tiraspol
2003	Serif Tiraspol
2004	Serif Tiraspol

YEAR	CUP WINNERS
2000	Constructorul Chişinău
2001	Serif Tiraspol
2002	Serif Tiraspol
2003	Zimbru Chişinău
2004	Zimbru Chişinău

Latvia

Football Association of Latvia
Founded: 1921
Joined FIFA: 1923–43, 1991
Joined UEFA: 1992

LATVIAN SOCCER HAS FOLLOWED a similar course to that of its Baltic neighbours: early stirrings before the First World War, a national FA arriving with political independence after the war, and national cup and league competitions beginning soon afterwards. As usual, everything stopped for the Second World War, which saw German invasion and occupation (1940–43) and then occupation by the Red Army. The Soviet Union absorbed Latvia and Latvian soccer was reduced to a rather poor local league for 50 years.

Independence in 1991 brought a truly national league and cup competition and a whole swathe of new clubs that now occupy the top division. The new league was played in two phases to accommodate a winter break. In 1999 Latvia switched to a single-phase season starting in the spring and ending before winter conditions become too harsh. Ten teams play in the top league, playing home and away twice during the course of the year. Whatever the format, contemporary Latvian soccer has been completely dominated by Skonto Riga.

Latvian League Record 1922–2003

SEASON	CHAMPIONS	RUNNERS-UP
1922	Kaiserwald Riga	JKS
1923	Kaiserwald Riga	LJNS
1924	RFK Riga	Cesu VB
1925	RFK Riga	Olimpija Liepaja
1926	RFK Riga	Olimpija Liepaja
1927	Olimpija Liepaja	RFK Riga
1928	Olimpija Liepaja	RFK Riga
1929	Olimpija Liepaja	RFK Riga
1930	RFK Riga	Olimpija Liepaja
1931	RFK Riga	Olimpija Liepaja
1932	ASK Riga	Riga Wanderer
1933	Olimpija Liepaja	RFK Riga
1934	RFK Riga	Riga Wanderer
1935	RFK Riga	Olimpija Liepaja
1936	Olimpija Liepaja	ASK Riga
1937	*no championship*	
1938	Olimpija Liepaja	RFK Riga
1939	Olimpija Liepaja	ASK Riga
1940	RFK Riga	Olimpija Liepaja
1941	*no championship*	
1942	ASK Riga	Olimpija Liepaja
1943	ASK Riga	Olimpija Liepaja
1944	*no championship*	
1945	Dinamo Riga	Daugava Liepaja
1946	Daugava Liepaja	VEF Riga
1947	Daugava Liepaja	VEF Riga
1948	PAK Zhmylov	PAK Goncharov
1949	Metalurgs Liepaja	PAK Zhmylov
1950	AVN Riga	Metalurgs Liepaja
1951	Metalurgs Liepaja	AVN Riga
1952	AVN Riga	Metalurgs Liepaja
1953	Metalurgs Liepaja	Spartak-Elektro
1954	Metalurgs Liepaja	VEF Riga
1955	Darba Rezerves Riga	VEF Riga
1956	Metalurgs Liepaja	RVR Riga
1957	Metalurgs Liepaja	Dinamo Riga
1958	Metalurgs Liepaja	RVR
1959	RER Riga	Metalurgs Liepaja
1960	ASK Riga	Pilots Riga
1961	ASK Riga	Pilots Riga

Latvian League Record 1922–2003 (*continued*)

SEASON	CHAMPIONS	RUNNERS-UP
1962	ASK Riga	Jurmala
1963	ASK Riga	KBRR
1964	ASK Riga	Daugavpils
1965	ASK Riga	Ventspils
1966	Energija Riga	ASK Riga
1967	Energija Riga	ASK Riga
1968	Starts Brotseny	Elektrons Riga
1969	Venta Ventspils	Energija Riga
1970	VEF Riga	Venta Ventspils
1971	VEF Riga	Jurnieks Riga
1972	Jurnieks Riga	VEF Riga
1973	VEF Riga	Starts Brotseny
1974	VEF Riga	Elektrons Riga
1975	VEF Riga	Lielupe Jurmala
1976	Energija Riga	Kimikis Daugavpils
1977	Energija Riga	Elektrons Riga
1978	Kimikis Daugvpils	Elektrons Riga
1979	Elektrons Riga	Energija Riga
1980	Kimikis Daugavpils	Progress
1981	Elektrons Riga	Celtnieks Riga
1982	Elektrons Riga	VEF Riga
1983	VEF Riga	Celtnieks Riga
1984	Torpedo Riga	Celtnieks Riga
1985	Alfa Riga	Kimikis Daugavpils
1986	Torpedo Riga	Celtnieks Riga
1987	Torpedo Riga	Celtnieks Riga
1988	RAF Jelgava	Torpedo Riga
1989	RAF Jelgava	Torpedo Riga
1990	Gauja Valmiera	VEF Riga
1991	Skonto Riga	Pardaugava Riga
1992	Skonto Riga	RAF Jelgava
1993	Skonto Riga	Olimpija Liepaja
1994	Skonto Riga	RAF Jelgava
1995	Skonto Riga	Vilan-D
1996	Skonto Riga	Daugava Riga
1997	Skonto Riga	Daugava Riga
1998	Skonto Riga	Metalurgs Liepaja
1999	Skonto Riga	Metalurgs Liepaja
2000	Skonto Riga	FK Ventspils
2001	Skonto Riga	FK Ventspils
2002	Skonto Riga	FK Ventspils
2003	Skonto Riga	Metalurgs Liepaja

Latvian League Summary

TEAM	TOTAL	WINNERS & RUNNERS-UP (BOLD) (ITALICS)
Skonto Riga	13, 0	**1991–2003**
ASK Riga	9, 4	**1932, 36, 39, 42, 43, 60–65, 66, 67**
RFK Riga	8, 5	**1924–26, 27–29, 30, 31, 33, 34, 35, 38, 40**
Olimpija Liepaja	7, 9	*1925, 26,* **27–29,** *30,* **31,** *33,* **35, 36, 38, 39,** *40, 42, 43, 93*
Metalurgs Liepaja	7, 6	**1949,** *50,* **51,** *52,* **53, 54, 56–58,** *59, 98, 99, 2003*
VEF Riga	6, 7	*1946, 47, 54, 55,* **70, 71, 72, 73–75,** *82,* **83,** *90*
Energija Riga	4, 2	**1966, 67,** *69,* **76, 77,** *79*
Elektrons Riga	3, 4	*1968, 74, 77, 78,* **79, 81, 82**
Torpedo Riga	3, 2	**1984, 86, 87,** *88, 89*
Kimikis Daugavpils	2, 2	**1976,** *78,* **80,** *85*
RAF Jelgava	2, 2	**1988, 89,** *92, 94*
AVN Riga	2, 1	**1950,** *51,* **52**
Daugava Liepaja	2, 1	*1945,* **46, 47**
Kaiserwald Riga	2, 0	**1922, 23**

LATVIA

Skonto Riga's Marian Pahars in action against Moscow Dynamo in the UEFA Cup in 1998. Skonto's domination of Latvian soccer has ensured a berth in European competition for many years, but the team has had little real success on the bigger stage.

Latvian League Summary (*continued*)

TEAM	TOTAL	WINNERS & RUNNERS-UP (BOLD) (*ITALICS*)
Dinamo Riga	1, 1	**1945**, *57*
Jurnieks Riga	1, 1	*1971*, **72**
PAK Zhmylov	1, 1	**1948**, *49*
Starts Brotseny	1, 1	**1968**, *73*
Venta Ventspils	1, 1	**1969**, *70*
Alfa Riga	1, 0	**1985**
Darba Rezerves Riga	1, 0	**1955**
Gauja Valmiera	1, 0	**1990**
RER Riga	1, 0	**1959**

This summary only features clubs that have won the Latvian league. For a full list of league winners and runners-up please see the league record opposite.

Latvian Cup Record 1937–2003

YEAR	WINNERS	SCORE	RUNNERS-UP
1937	RFK Riga	2-0	US
1938	Rigas Vilki	3-1	ASK Riga
1939	RFK Riga	5-1	Olimpija Liepaja
1940–42		no competition	
1943	ASK Riga	0-2, 4-2 (2 legs), (replay) 3-0	Olimpija Liepaja
1944–45		no competition	
1946	Daugava Liepaja	4-2	VEF Riga
1947	Daugava Liepaja	2-1	Daugava Riga
1948	Dinamo Liepaja	3-2	Dinamo Ventspils
1949	Metalurgs Liepaja	4-0	Spartak Riga
1950	AVN Riga	4-0	Metalurgs Liepaja
1951	AVN Riga	6-2	Metalurgs Liepaja
1952	AVN Riga	4-2 (aet)	Metalurgs Liepaja
1953	Metalurgs Liepaja	4-0	Dinamo Riga
1954	Metalurgs Liepaja	2-2, (replay) 5-1	Darba Rezerves
1955	Metalurgs Liepaja	1-1, (replay) 4-2	Darba Rezerves
1956	VEF Riga	1-0	RER Riga
1957	Dinamo Riga	2-2, (replay) 3-2	Metalurgs Liepaja
1958	RER Riga	1-1, (replay) 2-1	Tosmares Liepaja
1959	ASK Riga	7-0	Sloka Jurmala

Latvian Cup Record (*continued*)

YEAR	WINNERS	SCORE	RUNNERS-UP
1960	ASK Riga	1-0	VEF Riga
1961	CSK Brotseny	2-1	Daugavpils
1962	LMR Liepaja	1-0	Kompresors Riga
1963	LMR Liepaja	2-0	RTP Riga
1964	Vulkans	2-1	Tosmares Liepaja
1965	Baltika	2-1	Kompresors Riga
1966	ASK Riga	3-0	Baltika
1967	Juras Osta	2-0	Elektrons Riga
1968	Starts Brotseny	3-2	Venta Ventspils
1969	Elektrons Riga	1-1, (replay) 3-1	Venta Ventspils
1970	Jurnieks Riga	1-0	VEF Riga
1971	VEF Riga	1-0	Elektrons Riga
1972	Jurnieks Riga	1-0	Pilots Riga
1973	Pilots Riga	3-2	Starts Brotseny
1974	Elektrons Riga	1-0	VEF Riga
1975	Lielupe Jurmala	2-1	VEF Riga
1976	Kimikis Daugavpils	1-0	Lielupe Jurmala
1977	Elektrons Riga	1-0	VEF Riga
1978	Elektrons Riga	3-0	Radiotehnikis
1979	Kimikis Daugavpils	4-2	RPI Riga
1980	Elektrons Riga	2-1	Energija Riga
1981	Elektrons Riga	1-0	Kimikis Daugavpils
1982	Energija Riga	2-1	Torpedo
1983	Elektrons Riga	1-0	Energija Riga
1984	Celtnieks Riga	3-1	VEF Riga
1985	Celtnieks Riga	3-0	VEF Riga
1986	Celtnieks Riga	6-0	Gauja Valmiera
1987	VEF Riga	0-0, (replay) 3-2 (pens)	Torpedo
1988	RAF Jelgava	1-0	Gauja Valmiera
1989	Torpedo	1-0	Celtnieks Daugavpils
1990	Daugava-LVFKI	0-0, (replay) 4-2 (pens)	Apgaismes Tehnika
1991	Celtnieks Daugavpils	0-0, (replay) 3-1 (pens)	Skonto Riga
1992	Skonto Riga	1-0 (aet)	Daugava/Kompar
1993	RAF Jelgava	1-0	Pardaugava
1994	Olimpija Liepaja	2-0	DAG Riga
1995	Skonto Riga	3-0	DAG-Liepaja
1996	RAF Jelgava	2-1 (aet)	Skonto Riga
1997	Skonto Riga	2-1	Dinaburg Daugavpils
1998	Skonto Riga	1-0	Metalurgs Liepaja
1999	FK Riga	1-1, (replay) 6-5 (pens)	Skonto Riga
2000	Skonto Riga	4-1	Metalurgs Liepaja
2001	Skonto Riga	2-0	Dinaburg Daugavpils
2002	Skonto Riga	3-0	Metalurgs Liepaja
2003	FK Ventspils	4-0	Skonto Riga

Latvian Cup Summary

TEAM	TOTAL	WINNERS & RUNNERS-UP (BOLD) (*ITALICS*)
Elektrons Riga	7, 2	*1967*, **69**, *71*, **74, 77, 78, 80, 81, 83**
Skonto Riga	7, 4	*1991*, **92, 95, 96, 97, 98, 99, 2000–02**, *03*
Metalurgs Liepaja	4, 7	**1949**, *50–52, 53–55, 57, 98, 2000, 02*
ASK Riga	4, 1	*1938*, **43, 59, 60, 66**
VEF Riga	3, 8	*1946*, **56**, *60, 70*, **71**, *74, 75, 77, 84, 85, 87*
AVN Riga	3, 0	**1950–52**
Celtnieks Riga	3, 0	**1984–86**
RAF Jelgava	3, 0	**1988, 93, 96**
Kimikis Daugavpils	2, 1	**1976, 78**, *81*
Daugava Liepaja	2, 0	**1946, 47**
Jurnieks Riga	2, 0	**1970, 72**
LMR Liepaja	2, 0	**1962, 63**
RFK Riga	2, 0	**1937, 39**

This summary only features clubs that have won the Latvian cup two times or more. For a full list of cup winners and runners-up please see the cup record above.

341

Belarus

Football Federation of the Republic of Belarus
Founded: 1989
Joined FIFA: 1992
Joined UEFA: 1993

BELARUS IS NOW AN INDEPENDENT NATION sandwiched between the western border of Russia and the eastern border of Poland. For nearly all of its history it has been a province of Imperial Russia or a republic of the Soviet Union. Speaking a variant of the Russian language, the Belarusians (or White Russians) imported soccer from Moscow and the Ukraine in the early years of the 20th century. The top Belarusian team – Dinamo Minsk – played in the top Soviet league while most clubs of the region languished in obscure regional leagues.

Independence was established in 1992, and the Belarusians set up their own independent FA and organized a national league and cup competition. Dinamo Minsk has continued to prosper, but other teams are now on the scene as a wave of new post-Communist clubs have emerged and old Soviet-era backers have receded. The top league has 16 teams playing home and away. The league, like many in the region, has switched from having a split season with a winter break to a single season starting in the spring.

Without doubt the best Belarusian player these days is Vasily Baranov. Captain of the national team, he plays his club soccer in Russia for Spartak Moskva.

Belarus League Record 1992–2003

SEASON	CHAMPIONS	SEASON	CHAMPIONS
1992	Dinamo Minsk	1999	FC BATE Borisov
1993	Dinamo Minsk	2000	Slavia Mazyr
1994	Dinamo Minsk	2001	Belshyna Babruisk
1995	Dinamo Minsk	2002	FC BATE Borisov
1995*	Dinamo Minsk	2003	FK Homel
1996	MPKC Mozyr		
1997	Dinamo Minsk		
1998	Dnepr-Transmash Mogilev		

* Extra transitional autumn league – played in order to allow a season to start in spring and end in autumn.

Belarus Cup Record 1992–2004

YEAR	CUP WINNERS	YEAR	CUP WINNERS
1992	Dinamo Minsk	1999	Belshyna Babruisk
1993	Neman-Belkard Grodno	2000	Slavia Mazyr
1994	Dinamo Minsk	2001	Belshyna Babruisk
1995	Dynamo '93	2002	FK Homel
1996	MPKC Mozyr	2003	Dinamo Minsk
1997	Belshyna Babruisk	2004	Shakhtysor Salihorsk
1998	Lokomotiv-96 Vitebsk		

Estonia

Eesti Jalgpalli Liit
Founded: 1921
Joined FIFA: 1923–43, 1992
Joined UEFA: 1992

SOCCER ARRIVED IN ESTONIA via English merchant seamen, having dockside kickabouts with the locals. The earliest converts appear to have been boys' gangs in the capital and port city of Tallinn. It rapidly spread to other Estonian cities before the First World War. In Narva, Russian textile workers adopted the game and played by the newly-imported Russian rules. In the university town of Tartu, German-speaking students and German rules predominated. In Tallinn itself, English coaches and English rules were followed.

Despite the chaos of the First World War, and the arrival of formal independence from the Russian Empire in 1918, a national league was up and running (under a single set of rules) by 1920. A national cup competition was first played in 1938, just in time for all soccer to stop for the war. Like its neighbours the same fate befell Estonian society and soccer: German invasion, Soviet recapture, and absorption as a region into the Soviet Union; Estonia left FIFA in 1943. Independence, a national FA and a new national league and national cup competition were established in 1991. The season was played with a winter break in two phases, but has now switched to a single phase starting in the spring.

FC Flora, the most successful team in the country, provides most of the players for the national team, including midfielder Marko Kristal.

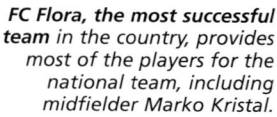

Estonian League Record 1921–2003

SEASON	CHAMPIONS	SEASON	CHAMPIONS
1921	Sport Tallinn	1940	Olümpia Tartu
1922	Sport Tallinn	1941–90	*no national championship*
1923	Kalev Tallinn	1991	TVMK Tallinn
1924	Sport Tallinn	1992	FC Norma Tallinn
1925	Sport Tallinn	1993	FC Norma Tallinn
1926	TJK Tallinn	1994	FC Norma Tallinn
1927	Sport Tallinn	1995	FC Flora Tallinn
1928	TJK Tallinn	1996	FC Lantana Tallinn
1929	Sport Tallinn	1997	FC Lantana Tallinn
1930	Kalev Tallinn	1998	FC Flora Tallinn
1931	Sport Tallinn	1998*	FC Flora Tallinn
1932	Sport Tallinn	1999	FC Levadia Maardu
1933	Sport Tallinn	2000	FC Levadia Maardu
1934	Estonia Tallinn	2001	FC Flora Tallinn
1935	Estonia Tallinn	2002	FC Flora Tallinn
1936	Estonia Tallinn	2003	FC Flora Tallinn
1937	*no championship*		
1938	Estonia Tallinn		
1939	Estonia Tallinn		

* Extra transitional autumn league – played in order to allow a season to start in spring and end in autumn.

Estonian Cup Record 1938–2004

YEAR	CUP WINNERS	YEAR	CUP WINNERS
1938	Sport Tallinn	1996	Tallinna Sadam
1939	TJK Tallinn	1997	Tallinna Sadam
1940	TJK Tallinn	1998	FC Flora Tallinn
1941–90	*no national competition*	1999	FC Levadia Maardu
		2000	FC Levadia Maardu
1991	TVMK Tallinn	2001	Trans Narva
1992	*no competition*	2002	FC Levadia Tallinn
1993	Nikol Tallinn	2003	TVMK Tallinn
1994	FC Norma Tallinn	2004	FC Levadia Tallinn
1995	FC Flora Tallinn		

The Lilleküla stadium, home of FC Flora and of the Estonian national team, was opened in 2003. Its capacity of 15,000 makes it the biggest stadium in the country.

Lithuanian League Record 1922–2003

SEASON	CHAMPIONS	SEASON	CHAMPIONS
1922	LFLS Kaunas	1940–90	*no national championship*
1923	LFLS Kaunas		
1924	Kovas Kaunas	1991	Zalgiris Vilnius
1925	Kovas Kaunas	1992	Zalgiris Vilnius
1926	Kovas Kaunas	1993	Ekranas Panevėžys
1927	LFLS Kaunas	1994	ROMAR Mažeikiai
1928	KSS Klaipėda	1995	Inkaras Kaunas
1929	KSS Klaipėda	1996	Inkaras Kaunas
1930	KSS Klaipėda	1997	Kareda Šiauliai
1931	KSS Klaipėda	1998	Kareda Šiauliai
1932	LFLS Kaunas	1999	Zalgiris Vilnius
1933	Kovas Kaunas	1999*	Zalgiris Kaunas
1934	MSK Kaunas	2000	FBK Kaunas
1935	Kovas Kaunas	2001	FBK Kaunas
1936	Kovas Kaunas	2002	FBK Kaunas
1937	KSS Klaipėda	2003	FBK Kaunas
1938	KSS Klaipėda		
1939	LGSF Kaunas		

* Extra transitional autumn league – played in order to allow a season to start in spring and end in autumn.

Lithuanian Cup Record 1991–2003

YEAR	CUP WINNERS	YEAR	CUP WINNERS
1992	Lietuvos Vilnius	1999	Kareda Šiauliai
1993	Zalgiris Vilnius	2000	Ekranas Panevėžys
1994	Zalgiris Vilnius	2001	Atlantas Klaipėda
1995	Inkaras Kaunas	2002	FBK Kaunas
1996	Kareda Šiauliai	2003	Atlantas Klaipėda
1997	Zalgiris Vilnius	2003*	Zalgiris Vilnius
1998	Ekranas Panevėžys		

* Transitional season.

Lithuania

Lietuvos Futbolo Federacija
Founded: 1922
Joined FIFA: 1923–43, 1992
Joined UEFA: 1992

LITHUANIA IS THE LARGEST and most southerly of the three Baltic States. Like the others, it has spent most of the modern era as part of either the Tsarist Russian Empire or the Communist Soviet Union. Independence came after the First World War in 1918, but it would take another four years of postwar chaos to achieve a national soccer association (affiliated to FIFA in 1923) and a national league competition. The league ran from 1922 to 1939, after which war intervened. Initially occupied by the Germans, Lithuania was recaptured by the Soviets and absorbed into the Soviet Union; a mere region now rather than a nation, Lithuania left FIFA in 1943.

As everywhere, the Communists reorganized Lithuanian soccer in their own image, and most of today's clubs can date their origins to the postwar decades. Although Lithuanian clubs could play in the top Soviet division, very few managed the transition, and a local regional league was played. Lithuania declared independence from the Soviet Union in 1990, which was formally settled in 1991. With independence came a new soccer association, league and cup competition. For all but one season this has been a standard 16-team league format, with the top eight and bottom eight forming mini-leagues in the second half of the season. In the 1996–97 season a two-phase league was tried, but the experiment was not successful.

Goals from striker Martin Opic have been central in FBK Kaunas's recent domination of the Lithuanian league – it has won the championship for the last four years.

LITHUANIA

Russia

THE SEASON IN REVIEW 2003

VALERI GAZZAYEV, THE LUGUBRIOUS COACH of CSKA Moscow, must have a very thick skin. He saw his side lose the championship play-off final to Locomotiv in 2002. The team was beaten again by Locomotiv in the Russian Super Cup Final, this time on penalties. Over the summer he was fired from his 'evening job' as coach of the Russian national team only to see his successor, Georgi Yartsev, steer the squad through the European Championships play-offs and into the finals. Above all, he spent the whole of this season being lambasted by the press for the 'elephant soccer' his sides played – rough, hustling and very physical. But with a game to spare, he and CSKA had the last laugh as the former team of the Red Army won its first post-Communist championship.

New club shines, while old clubs decline

CSKA was almost put into liquidation three seasons ago when the then club president, Shahrudi Dadakhanov, was accused of financing Chechen rebels. The club then passed to businessman Yevgeni Giner, who has brought money and stability to the side. Last year he broke the club's transfer record adding Czech striker Jiri Jarosik to the squad. This year he did it again bringing in the Croat Ivica Olic for £3 million. His purchases are now the most successful strike force in the Russian league. How long they will stay at the club is another matter. Olic openly admitted that he hoped his profile at CSKA would see Roman Abramovich take an interest. A real challenge to CSKA never quite materialized, with Lokomotiv and Dinamo falling away. A late charge from Zenit Sankt-Peterburg was good enough to take second spot. Newly promoted Rubin Kazan was the revelation of the season, coming in third and grabbing a UEFA Cup place, while Spartak underperformed yet again; even victory in the Russian Cup was not enough to save coach Andrei Chernyshov's job.

Russian League Table 2003 – First Level

CLUB	P	W	D	L	F	A	Pts	
CSKA Moskva	30	17	8	5	56	32	59	Champions League
Zenit Sankt-Peterburg	30	16	8	6	48	32	56	UEFA Cup
Rubin Kazan	30	15	8	7	44	29	53	UEFA Cup
Lokomotiv Moskva	30	15	7	8	54	33	52	
Shinnik Yaroslavl	30	12	11	7	43	34	47	
Dinamo Moskva	30	12	10	8	42	29	46	
Saturn Ren TV Moscow Region	30	12	9	9	40	37	45	
Torpedo Moskva	30	11	10	9	42	38	43	
Krylya Sovetov Samara	30	11	9	10	38	33	42	
Spartak Moskva	30	10	6	14	38	48	36	UEFA Cup (cup winners)
FK Rostov	30	8	10	12	30	42	34	
Rotor Volgograd	30	9	5	16	33	44	32	
Spartak-Alania Vladikavkaz	30	9	4	17	23	43	31	
Torpedo-Metallurg Moskva	30	8	5	17	25	39	29	
Uralan Elista	30	6	10	14	23	47	28	Relegated
Chernomorets Novorossiysk	30	6	6	18	30	49	24	Relegated

Promoted clubs: Amkar Perm, Kuban Krasnodar.

Super Cup

2003 FINAL
March 8 – Lokomotiv Stadium, Moscow

Lokomotiv 1-1 CSKA Moskva
Moskva   (Jarosik 41)
(Pimenov 83)

(aet)

h/t: 0-1   **Att:** 15,000
Ref: Ivanov

Lokomotiv Moskva won
4-3 on pens

Above: CSKA's Czech striker Jiri Jarosik jumps highest in the Super Cup Final. But Jarosik's first-half goal was not enough. Lokomotiv equalized late in the second half and went on to win a penalty shootout.

Right: CSKA take a lap of honour after beating Rotor Volgograd and winning its first post-Soviet championship.

Top Goalscorers 2003

PLAYER	CLUB	NATIONALITY	GOALS
Dmitriy Loskov	Lokomotiv Moskva	Russian	14
Aleksandr Kerzhakov	Zenit Sankt-Peterburg	Russian	13
Valeriy Yesipov	Rotor Volgograd	Russian	13
Aleksei Medvedev	Saturn Ren TV Moscow Region	Russian	11
Pereira dos Santos	Rubin Kazan	Brazilian	11

International Club Performances 2003–04

CLUB	COMPETITION	PROGRESS
CSKA Moskva	Champions League	Qualifying Phase 2
Lokomotiv Moskva	Champions League	Eighth-finals
Torpedo Moskva	UEFA Cup	2nd Round
Spartak Moskva	UEFA Cup	3rd Round

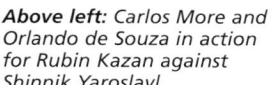

Pavel Mares scores for Zenit St-Peterburg against Spartak. Zenit went on to win 2-1 and affirm the declining fortunes of the once dominant Moscow club.

Above left: Carlos More and Orlando de Souza in action for Rubin Kazan against Shinnik Yaroslavl.

Above right: Georgi Yartsev grimaces his way to the European Championships in Portugal 2004.

Left: Valeri Gazzayev shows off his armoured skin and moustache combination.

Below: Luis Pereira and Moizes Pineiro of Spartak lift the Russian Cup – but it was small consolation as the side plummeted to an unheard of tenth in the league.

Russian Cup

2003 FINAL

June 15 – Lokomotiv Stadium, Moscow
Spartak 1-0 FK Rostov
Moskva
(Yegor Titov 28)
h/t: 1-0   **Att:** 25,000
Ref: Yegorov

Ukraine

THE SEASON IN REVIEW 2003–04

AS WITH LAST SEASON THE UKRAINIAN LEAGUE was a two-horse race between Dynamo Kyiv and Shakhtar Donetsk – the end result was no different either. Dynamo won the title on the last day of the season with a 2-0 victory over Volyn Lutsk, leaving them three points clear of their rivals. Halfway through the season it looked as if the positions would be reversed with Shakhtar reaching the winter break nine points clear.

But, in a replay of last year's form, the second half of the season saw Shakhtar begin to flag, regularly throwing points away. Dynamo steadily made up the ground between them, slipping into a narrow lead in the final quarter of the season. Shakhtar's imperious president, Rinat Akhmetov, sacked German coach Bernd Schuster, replacing him with the Romanian Mircea Lucescu, who had recently departed Turkish club Beşiktaş after a disastrous mid-season collapse. Despite a late recovery, it was too much for Shakhtar, who effectively surrendered their title challenge when Dynamo beat them 4-2 at home in the season's most exhilarating game – Dynamo's first victory at Donetsk for eight years.

Cup compensation for Shakhtar

There was compensation for Shakhtar in the Ukrainian cup as the team won its third title in four seasons, beating Dnipro Dnipropetrovsk 2-0 in a particularly bad-tempered and fractious Final. A stormy first half saw both sides reduced to ten men after Shakhtar had snatched an early lead with a header from their highly rated young striker Olexiy Belik in the second minute. Shakhtar captain Anatoly Timoshchuk finished matters off with a solo goal in the 89th minute. Internationally, however, there was little cheer for Ukraine as, once again, the national team failed to qualify for the European Championships; Shakhtar lost in the Champions League qualifying rounds and Dynamo failed to make it out of the Group Stage.

Above: Ukraine miss the party. In the run-up to Euro 2004 Ukraine were confined to friendlies against the qualifiers. Here Andrei Vorobei challenges for a high ball with Lilian Turam and Mikael Silvestre of France in Paris.

Right: Oleg Blokhin smiles, but the Ukrainian national team is no laughing matter after missing out on Euro 2004. Blokhin raised more than smiles when he selected seven Dnipro players for the team which played Slovakia in April. The game ended in a 1-1 draw.

Ukrainian Premier League Table 2003–04

CLUB	P	W	D	L	F	A	Pts	
Dynamo Kyiv	30	23	4	3	68	20	73	Champions League
Shakhtar Donetsk	30	22	4	4	62	19	70	Champions League Qualifying
Dnipro Dnipropetrovsk	30	16	9	5	44	23	57	UEFA Cup
Metalurg Donetsk	30	14	10	6	51	34	52	UEFA Cup
Chornomorets Odesa	30	11	12	7	38	33	45	
Obolon Kyiv	30	11	8	11	34	35	41	
Borysfen Boryspil	30	11	8	11	25	29	41	
Illichivets Mariupol	30	10	10	10	34	36	40	UEFA Cup (Fair Play)
Arsenal Kyiv	30	10	7	13	38	44	37	
Kryvbas Kryvyj Rih	30	10	6	14	26	41	36	
Metalurg-Zaporizhzhja**	30	8	8	14	26	40	32	
Tavrija Simferopol	30	7	11	12	22	28	32	
SC Volyn-1 Lutsk	30	7	8	15	25	44	29	
Vorskla-Naftohaz Poltava†	30	6	9	15	26	49	27	
Karpaty Lviv	30	6	8	16	22	39	26	Relegated
Zirka Kirovohrad	30	3	8	19	16	43	14*	Relegated

Promoted clubs: Metalist Kharkiv, Zakarpaty Uzhhorod.

Top Goalscorers 2003–04

PLAYER	CLUB	NATIONALITY	GOALS
Georgi Demetradze	Metalurg Donetsk	Georgian	18
Oleksander Kosyrin	Chornomorets Odesa	Ukrainian	14
Maksim Shatskikh	Dynamo Kyiv	Uzbekistani	10
Zvonomir Vukic	Shakhtar Donetsk	Serbia & Montenegran	10

International Club Performances 2003–04

CLUB	COMPETITION	PROGRESS
Dynamo Kyiv	Champions League	Group Stage
Shakhtar Donetsk	Champions League	3rd Qualifying Round
	UEFA Cup	1st Round
Metalurg Donetsk	UEFA Cup	1st Round
Dnipro Dnipropetrovsk	UEFA Cup	3rd Round

* Zirka had 3 points deducted for not paying wages to one of their players.

**Metalurg Zaporizhzhja were relegated in 2003, but because FC Oleksandrija became defunct the Ukrainian Football Federation reinstalled them in the Premier League for 2003–04.

† Vorskla Poltava changed name to Vorskla-Naftohaz Poltava.

Far left: Uzbekistani striker Maksim Shatskikh was champions Dynamo Kyiv's top scorer this season with 10 goals.

Left: Bernd Schuster was fired as coach of Shakhtar Dontesk after a disastrous string of results in the spring.

Below: Schuster's replacement was the Romanian Mircea Lucescu fresh from a controversial season at Beşiktaş in Turkey. In his first game in charge Shakhtar responded with a 5-1 victory against Kaparty Lviv.

Bottom: Players of Shakhtar Donetsk celebrate the team's victory over Dnipro Dnipropetrovsk in the Ukrainian Cup Final in Kiev.

Ukrainian Cup

2004 FINAL

May 30 – Olympic Stadium, Kyiv
Shakhtar 2-0 Dnipro
Donetsk   Dnipropetrovsk
(Belyk 2,
Tymoschuk 89)
h-t: 1-0 **Att:** 68,000
Ref: Burenko

Soccer in Russia

1887: Soccer first introduced into Russia — **1885**

1893: First recorded soccer match played at the Semenovsky Velodrome in St Petersburg — **1890**

1898: Football Association established in St Petersburg — **1895 / 1900**

1901: First St Petersburg league established — **1905**

1912: Formation of FA: All-Russia Football Union. Affiliated to FIFA as Russia. First Russian international, v Finland, lost 1-2, venue: Stockholm — **1910 / 1915**

1922–24: Key Moscow clubs all established: Spartak, Lokomotiv, Dinamo, CSKA, Torpedo — **1920 / 1925**

1936: National league championship established — **1930 / 1935**

1941–44: League abandoned, Cup not played 1940–43 due to war — **1940 / 1945**

1952: First international as Soviet Union, v Bulgaria, won 2-1, venue: Kotka, Finland — **1950 / 1955**

1960: Soviet Union win inaugural European Championships in Paris — **1960**

1974: Withdrew from World Cup after refusing to play-off with Chile — **1965 / 1970 / 1975**

1982: Disaster at Luzhniki Stadium, 340 crushed to death at Spartak Moskva v Haarlem in UEFA Cup 2nd Round match — **1980 / 1985**

1992: Secession of central Asian FAs, re-establishment of Russian league and cup. Establishment of Russian Football Federation — **1990 / 1995**

2002: Top division renamed Premiere League. Squad names and numbers introduced for first time. Riots in central Moscow after dismal World Cup showing — **2000 / 2005**

1910: First Moscow league established

1911: First women's soccer match played in Moscow, Pushkino v Sport

1924: First Soviet international, v Turkey, won 3-0, venue: Moscow

1945: Dinamo Moscow visit Britain, the first foreign tour by a Soviet team

1946: Affiliation to FIFA as Soviet Union

1954: Affiliation to UEFA

1961: Dinamo Kiev become first non-Muscovite club to win the league

1985: Sokolniki Sports Palace disaster. Twenty killed in stampede at World Football Youth Championships

1991: Last Soviet League, secession of Ukrainian, Caucasian and Baltic FAs. Last Soviet international. Played as CIS until 1994, then as Russia

Key

- International soccer
- Affiliation to FIFA
- Affiliation to UEFA
- War
- Disaster

RUSSIA

Russia: The main clubs

Dinamo Minsk 1928 — Team name with year of formation

- Club formed 1912–25
- Club formed 1925–50
- Club formed after 1950

LITHUANIA (1922) Ind. 1991 — Country, formation of national FA, and independence from USSR

- Founder members of National League, 1936
- Soviet era champions
- Soviet era Cup winners
- Army
- Car factory
- Electrical workers
- Independent club
- KGB
- Railway workers
- Aviation industry origins
- Working class origins

Metalist Kharkov 1944
Lokomotiv (1944–56)
Avangard (1956–66)

Dnipro Dnipropetrovsk 1936
Stal (1936–48), Metallurg (1948–62)

Zarja Lugansk 1938
Jerjinec (1938–64)
Zarja Voroschilovgrad (1964–90)

Shakhtar Donetsk 1936
Stachanovec Stalino (1935–47)
Shachter Stalino (1947–61)

Zenit Sankt-Peterburg 1931
Stalin Leningrad (1931–40)
Zenit Leningrad (1940–91)

Elektrik Leningrad 1931

Dinamo Sankt Petersburg 1925
Dinamo Leningrad (1925–40)

Lokomotiv Moskva 1923
Korthen Kazanska (1923–36)

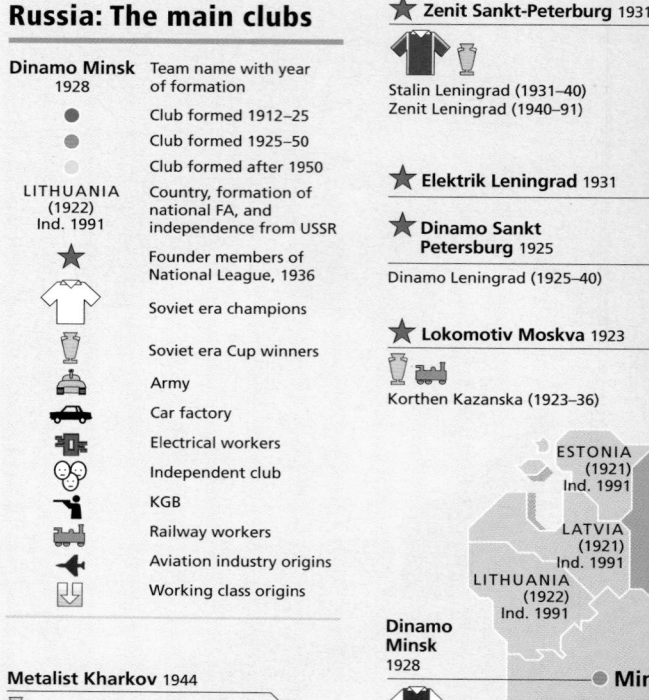

ESTONIA (1921) Ind. 1991
LATVIA (1921) Ind. 1991
LITHUANIA (1922) Ind. 1991
Dinamo Minsk 1928
BELARUS (1991) Ind. 1992
Mins...
SKA Karpati Lvov 1963
Lvov
Kie...
UKRAINE (1991) Ind. 1991
MOLDOVA (1991) Ind. 1991

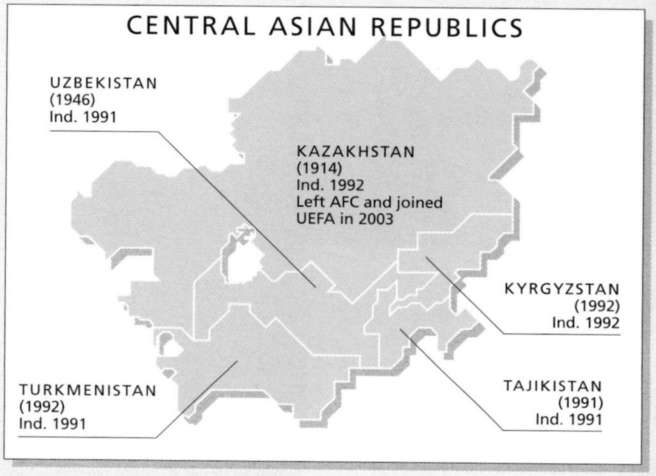

CENTRAL ASIAN REPUBLICS

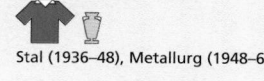

UZBEKISTAN (1946) Ind. 1991

KAZAKHSTAN (1914) Ind. 1992 Left AFC and joined UEFA in 2003

KYRGYZSTAN (1992) Ind. 1992

TURKMENISTAN (1992) Ind. 1991

TAJIKISTAN (1991) Ind. 1991

Russia (including the former Soviet Union)

ORIGINS AND GROWTH OF SOCCER

THE EARLIEST REPORTS OF SOCCER IN RUSSIA are of games played by British traders and bankers, gradually joined by Russian students, cadets and clerks. In 1894, Harry Charnock, general manager of the Morozov Mill, east of Moscow, introduced the game to his workers who played as Orekhovoclub Sport. In 1896, a set of rules was first translated into Russian and the following year, Sport, the first Russian club, was established in St. Petersburg. The popularity of soccer rose rapidly in the years before the First World War with leagues formed in St. Petersburg (1901), Moscow (1912), and finally an all-Russian FA in 1912.

In the chaotic years of revolution and civil war after 1917, the military initially took over all soccer clubs, and began a drive to bring the game to Central Asia. During the 1920s, however, under the New Economic Policy, competitive sport was officially frowned upon and the game remained disorganized. But under Stalin it was revived, new clubs were established, each explicitly linked to a state institution (the secret police, the army, railway unions, cooperatives etc.) and a seven-team league began in 1936. Moscow remained the centre of the Soviet game but new teams and powers emerged after the Second World War in Kiev, Tbilisi and Leningrad. Crowds remained huge in the 1950s and 60s, and though political interference was rife, soccer provided a peculiarly depoliticized space in Soviet life. With the break up of the Soviet Union soccer associations, leagues and cups have all fragmented. The economic decline of Russia has left the game in deep trouble.

RUSSIA

Spartak Moskva 1922
Moskovski Klub Sporta (1922–35)

Torpedo Moskva 1924
Proletarskkaja Kuznica (1924–36)
Zil Motors factory team

Dinamo Moskva 1923
Roots of club in Orekhovoclub Sport

CSKA Moskva 1923
Previously Society of Ski Enthusiasts, (1901–23). Offical formation as football club, Olls (1923), OPVV (1923–28), CDKA (1928–50), CDSA (1950–58), CSK-MO (1958–59)

Petersburg
ngrad (1924–91)

Yaroslavl
Shinnik Yaroslavl 1957

R U S S I A

Nizhniy Novgorod
Lokomotiv Nizhniy Novgorod 1987

Krylya Sovetov Samara 1943
Krylya Sovetov Kuybyshev (1943–52), Zenit Sovetov Kuybyshev (1952–53), Krylya Sovetov Kuybyshev (1953–91)

Moscow
Ramenske
Saturn Ramenske 1958

Kazan
Rubin Kazan 1936

Samara
(Kubeyshev till 1991)

Dynamo Kyiv 1927

Voronezh
Fakel Voronezh 1954

Kharkiv

Volgograd
Stalingrad (1925–45)

nipropetrovs'k

Luhans'k

Donets'k

Rostov na Donu

Rotor Volgograd 1933
Traktor Stalingrad (1933–48)
Torpedo Stalingrad (1948–57)
Stal Stalingrad (1957–61)
Stalvolgograd (1961–71)
Barikardy Vologograd (1971–75)

Elista
Uralan Elista 1958

Novorossiysk

Anzhi Makhachkala 1992

Sochi

Vladikavkaz

Makhachkala

GEORGIA (1990) Ind. 1991

Tbilisi

Alania Vladikavkaz 1921
SK Terksoi Oblasti (1921) then ORK Imeni Lenina, Spartak Ordzhonikidze (1937–94), Spartak-Alania (1994–96)

AZERBAIJAN (1991) Ind. 1991

Yerevan

ARMENIA (1934) Ind. 1991

Dinamo Tbilisi 1925
Dinamo Iberyia (1990–93)

Zhemchuzhina Sochi 1990

Chernomorets Novorossiisk 1960
Tsement (1960–70), did not exist (1970–77), Tsement (1978–91), Gekris (1992–93)

Rostselmash Rostov na Donu 1930
SKVO (1938–60)

Ararat Yerevan 1937
Dinamo Yerevan (1937–54)
Spartak Yerevan (1954–62)

Key

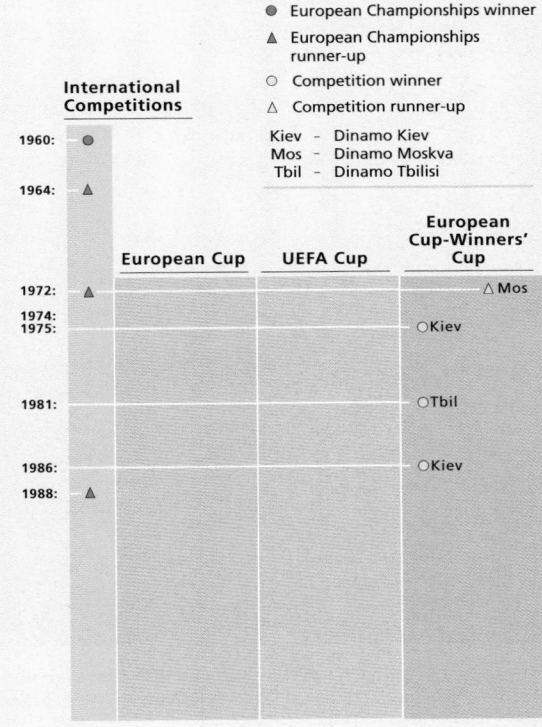

● European Championships winner
▲ European Championships runner-up
○ Competition winner
△ Competition runner-up

Kiev – Dinamo Kiev
Mos – Dinamo Moskva
Tbil – Dinamo Tbilisi

International Competitions

	European Cup	UEFA Cup	European Cup-Winners' Cup
1960: ●			
1964: ▲			
1972: ▲			△ Mos
1974:			○ Kiev
1975:			
1981:			○ Tbil
1986:			○ Kiev
1988: ▲			

Moscow

SOCCER CENTER

MOSCOW'S SOCCER HISTORY began in 1894 when Harry Charnock, the English manager of the Morozov mill, arranged for a company soccer pitch to be created and a team established. Though Charnock failed to break the link between his Russian workers' leisure time and their consumption of vodka (as he had hoped), he certainly established soccer in the wider culture. Before the First World War, a Moscow league was up and running, and indigenous Russian teams began to outnumber the English and other foreign teams in the capital. However, the political upheavals of the time pretty much stopped soccer in its tracks. By the mid-1920s, the Bolsheviks had come to recognize the power and popularity of the game, and with their usual unpleasant thoroughness began its nationwide reorganization. All of Moscow's five main clubs date from this era, and all have been linked to one arm of the Soviet state or another.

The influence of state institutions

Dinamo Moskva, in the north-west of the city, had its roots in Charnock's Orekhovo Club, but when Felix Dzerzhinsky – future leader of the KGB – took charge in 1923, it became a team sponsored by the secret police. CSKA, further to the west, was the Red Army's side; Lokomotiv was tied to the railway workers' union; and Torpedo in the south was for many years part of the great Zil automobile empire. The collapse of Zil in the face of Mercedes and BMW has seen only a shadow outfit continue as Torpedo Zil (renamed Torpedo Metallurg in 2003), while the main team has tried to reinvent itself at the Luzhniki stadium.

Spartak was notionally attached to a food producers' co-operative, and was the only team to achieve any kind of autonomy from state institutions. Led by Nikolai Starostin, who spent three years in prison camps for his temerity in challenging CSKA and Dinamo at the height of Stalin's rule, Spartak has not surprisingly been the people's choice. In post-Communist Moscow, Spartak has been the only side to regularly attract significant crowds, and dominated the new Russian league until Lokomotiv's breakthrough in 2002 and CSKA's in 2003.

Felix Dzerzhinsky, leader of the Russian secret police, took charge of Dinamo Moskva in 1923. His statue, which stood in Red Square, was torn down during the political unrest of 1991.

MOSCOW STADIUM DISASTERS

Moscow is second only to Glasgow in the number of tragedies and disasters endured by the soccer-watching public. In October 1982, Spartak Moskva was playing at the then Lenin (now Luzhniki) stadium, in a second-round UEFA Cup match against Haarlem of the Netherlands. With the score at 1-0, Spartak scored a late second goal to make the tie safe, sparking a surge in one very cramped section of open and icy terracing. How many were killed and injured in the ensuing crush is uncertain, as the Soviet authorities banned any domestic reporting. Initial reports suggested 70 dead and 100 injured but plausible claims of 340 dead have been made. In August 1985, at a World Youth Championship match between the Soviet Union and Canada at the Sokolniki Sports Palace, at least 20 people were killed in a panic-stricken stampede after the lights failed. In the late 1980s, persistent and regular rioting and fighting between CSKA and Spartak fans at the Luzhniki saw a number of deaths and injuries.

After years of being Moscow's fourth of fifth team, Lokomotiv's 2002 championship triumph has finally brought glory to its compact Lokomotiv Stadium. Once the railway workers' team, Lokomotiv's stadium is embellished with a neon engine and classical Soviet era script.

Nikolai Starostin, revered founder, star player and 'club leader' of Spartak Moskva, was associated with the club from its foundation in 1922 to his death in 1996. He was arrested by Stalin in 1942 and spent three years in the gulag prison camps for his association with the club.

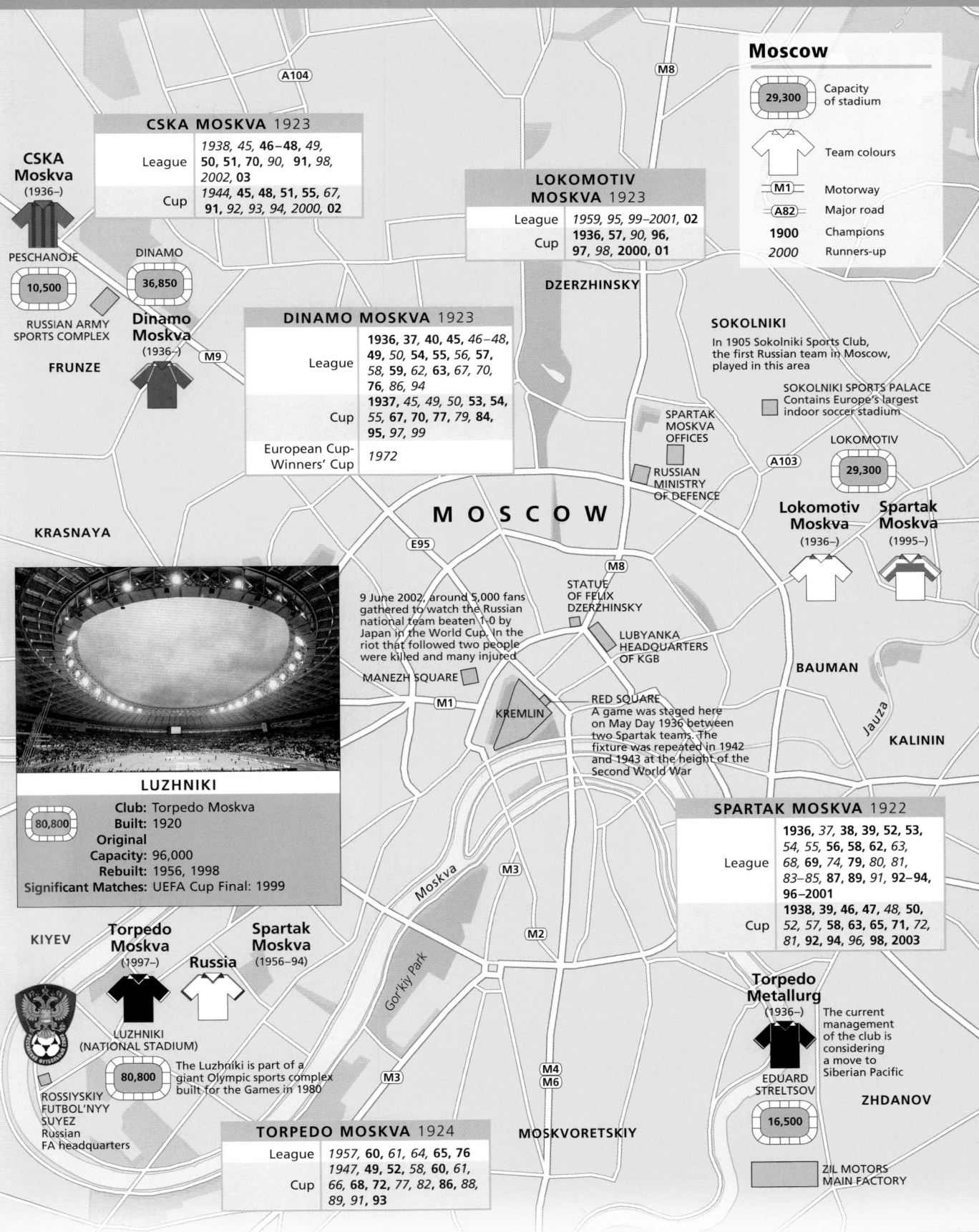

Moscow

29,300	Capacity of stadium
	Team colours
M1	Motorway
A82	Major road
1900	Champions
2000	Runners-up

CSKA MOSKVA 1923

League	*1938, 45,* **46–48,** *49,* **50, 51, 70, 90,** *91,* **98,** *2002,* **03**
Cup	*1944,* **45, 48, 51, 55,** *67,* **91, 92, 93, 94, 2000, 02**

CSKA Moskva (1936–)

PESCHANOJE

10,500

RUSSIAN ARMY SPORTS COMPLEX

FRUNZE

DINAMO

36,850

Dinamo Moskva (1936–)

M9

LOKOMOTIV MOSKVA 1923

League	*1959, 95, 99–2001, 02*
Cup	**1936, 57, 90, 96, 97, 98, 2000, 01**

DZERZHINSKY

DINAMO MOSKVA 1923

League	**1936, 37, 40, 45,** *46–48,* **49, 50, 54, 55, 56, 57,** *58,* **59,** *62,* **63,** *67,* **70,** *76,* *86,* **94**
Cup	**1937,** *45, 49, 50,* **53, 54,** *55,* **67, 70, 77,** *79,* **84,** *95, 97, 99*
European Cup-Winners' Cup	*1972*

KRASNAYA

MOSCOW

E95

SOKOLNIKI

In 1905 Sokolniki Sports Club, the first Russian team in Moscow, played in this area

SOKOLNIKI SPORTS PALACE
Contains Europe's largest indoor soccer stadium

A103

LOKOMOTIV

29,300

Lokomotiv Moskva (1936–)

Spartak Moskva (1995–)

SPARTAK MOSKVA OFFICES

RUSSIAN MINISTRY OF DEFENCE

STATUE OF FELIX DZERZHINSKY

M8

LUBYANKA HEADQUARTERS OF KGB

BAUMAN

Jauza

KALININ

9 June 2002, around 5,000 fans gathered to watch the Russian national team beaten 1-0 by Japan in the World Cup. In the riot that followed two people were killed and many injured

MANEZH SQUARE

M1

KREMLIN

RED SQUARE
A game was staged here on May Day 1936 between two Spartak teams. The fixture was repeated in 1942 and 1943 at the height of the Second World War

LUZHNIKI

80,800

Club: Torpedo Moskva
Built: 1920
Original Capacity: 96,000
Rebuilt: 1956, 1998
Significant Matches: UEFA Cup Final: 1999

KIYEV

Torpedo Moskva (1997–)

LUZHNIKI (NATIONAL STADIUM)

Russia

Spartak Moskva (1956–94)

Moskva

Gor'kiy Park

M3

M2

SPARTAK MOSKVA 1922

League	**1936,** *37,* **38, 39, 52, 53,** *54, 55,* **56, 58,** *62,* **63,** *68, 69,* **74, 79, 80, 81,** *83–85,* **87, 89, 91,** *92–94,* **96–2001**
Cup	**1938, 39, 46, 47,** *48,* **50,** *52,* **57, 58, 63, 65, 71,** *72,* **81, 92, 94,** *96,* **98, 2003**

80,800

The Luzhniki is part of a giant Olympic sports complex built for the Games in 1980

ROSSIYSKIY FUTBOL'NYY SUYEZ
Russian FA headquarters

Torpedo Metallurg (1936–)

The current management of the club is considering a move to Siberian Pacific

EDUARD STRELTSOV

16,500

ZHDANOV

TORPEDO MOSKVA 1924

League	*1957,* **60,** *61,* **64,** *65,* **76**
Cup	*1947, 49, 52, 58,* **60,** *61,* **66,** *68,* **72,** *77, 82,* **86,** *88, 89,* **91, 93**

MOSKVORETSKIY

ZIL MOTORS MAIN FACTORY

Russia and Ukraine

THE VYSSHAYA LIGA AND THE VISCHCHA LIGA 1992–2003

WITH THE BREAK-UP OF the Soviet Union in 1991, Soviet soccer also broke into separate national leagues. Out of the chaos emerged the Vysshaya Liga in Russia and the Vischcha Liga in the Ukraine. In the new Russia, teams dependent for funding and support on the old order – especially Dinamo and CSKA from Moscow – found the post-Communist going hard. Spartak Moskva, always the outsider, quickly aligned itself with sponsors Gazprom – the oil and gas giant spirited away from the wreckage of the Soviet state by ruthless carpetbaggers – and has comprehensively dominated the league under chain-smoking coach Oleg Romantsev, winning the league nine times in ten years. Challengers have arisen in the provinces, where ambitious local officials and politicians have backed Alania Vladikavkaz and Rotor Volgograd. In Moscow, Torpedo and Lokomotiv have nurtured local talent and crept their way into contention. Rotor has boasted Russia's finest striker of the era in Oleg Veretennikov, who has refused to move to a bigger club and who was the victim of an unprovoked acid attack in 1997.

Dominance of Dynamo

Post-Communist Ukraine has proved to be an even tighter soccer monopoly than that found in Russia, with the first nine championship going to Dynamo Kyiv, many with barely a threat to the leaders during the whole season. Under Soviet-era boss Valeri Lobanovsky, Dynamo proved fantastically connected to money and power in the new Ukraine, and has such resources that its reserves regularly win the Second Division championship but are barred from promotion.

By contrast, many smaller teams are in such terrible financial circumstances that they have refused promotion (like Torpedo Zaporizhya in 1999). CSKA Kyiv has left the army and been bought up by the city council.

The old order finally passed when Shakhtar Donetsk from the Ukraine's coal mining region pipped Dynamo to the 2002 title. Dynamo's season was undercut by the death of manager Valeri Lobanovsky while Shakhtar thrived under the leadership of new manager Nevio Scala.

Valeri Lobanovsky (left) was the epitome of tactics and organisation of Soviet soccer. His Dynamo Kyiv team played hyper-disciplined running soccer and dominated the Soviet league for a decade in the mid-1970s and 1980s.

CSKA Moskva
1998, 2002, **03**

Dinamo Moskva
1994

Lokomotiv Moskva
1995, 99–2001, **02**

Zenit Sankt-Peterburg
2003

St. Petersburg

Moscow

Spartak Moskva
1992–94, 96–2001

R U S S I A

Dynamo Kyiv
1993–2001, *02, 03*

Shakhtar Donetsk
1994, 97–2001, **02, 03**

Kiev

U K R A I N E

Volgograd

Rotor Volgograd
1993, 97

Chornomorets Odesa
1995, 96

Dnipropetrovsk
Odesa

Donetsk

Alania Vladikavkaz
1992, *95,* **96**

Dnipro Dnipropetrovsk
1993

Vladikavkaz

Vysshaya Liga and Vischcha Liga

Dynamo Kyiv — Team name

League champions/ runners-up

1982, *83* — Champions in bold / Runners-up in italics

● **Moscow** — City of origin

Russian League Positions 1992–2003

TEAM	1992	1993	1994	1995	1996	1997	1998	1999	2000	2001	2002	2003
Kamaz-Chally Nab. Chelny		10	6	9	14	18						
Baltika Kaliningrad					7	9	15					
Textilschik Kamyshin	10	4	7	10	17							
Rubin Kazan												3
Kuban Krasnodar	18											
Lada Togliatti			16		18							
Anzhi Makhachkala									4	13	15	
Asmaral Moskva	7	18										
CSKA Moskva	5	9	10	6	5	12	2	3	8	7	2	1
Dinamo Moskva	3	3	2	4	4	3	9	5	5	9	8	6
Lokomotiv Moskva	4	5	3	2	6	5	3	2	2	2	1	4
Spartak Moskva	1	1	1	3	1	1	1	1	1	1	3	10
Torpedo Moskva	11	7	11	5	12	11	11	4	3	4	4	8
Torpedo Metallurg										14	14	14
Okean Nakhodka	13	16										
Lokomotiv Nizhniy Novgorod	6	11	8	12	8	17		11	15			
Chernomorets Novorossiisk			11	13	6	10	14	6	16			16
Amkar Perm												
FK Rostov	8	17		14	11	13	6	7	12	12		11
Zenit Sankt-Peterburg	16				10	8	5	8	7	3	10	2
Krylya Sovetov Samara	14	14	13	15	9	7	12	12	14	5	5	9
Sokol Saratov									8	16		
Zhemchuzhina Sochi		13	9	13	15	14	13	15				
Dinamo Stravropol	15	12	15									
Saturn Ren TV Moscow Region								10	9	6	7	7
Dinamo-Gazovik Tyumen	20		12	16								
FK Tyumen					15	16						
Uralan Elista						7	9	16			13	15
Spartak-Alania Vladikavkaz	2	6	5	1	2	10	8	6	10	11	12	13
Luch Vladivostok		15										
Rotor Volgograd	12	2	4	7	3	2	4	13	11	10	9	12
Fakel Voronezh	17				16				13	15		
Shinnik Yaroslavl	19					4	14	16			6	5
Uralmash Yekaterinburg	9	8	14	8	16							

Veteran Oleg Veretennikov celebrates another goal for Rotor Volgograd on his way to a record 141 goals in the Vysshaya Liga.

Ukrainian League Positions 1992–2003

TEAM	1992–93	1993–94	1994–95	1995–96	1996–97	1997–98	1998–99	1999–2000	2000–01	2001–02	2002–03
Stal' Alchevsk									13		
Borysfen Boryspil											
Bukovyna Cherivtsi	12	17									
Dnipro Dnipropetrovsk	2	4	3	3	4	4	12	11	3	6	4
Metalurg Donetsk						6	14	7	5	3	3
Shakhtar Donetsk	4	2	4	10	2	2	2	2	2	1	2
Prikarpattya Ivano-Frankivsk		11	11	13	10	15	14				
Metalist Kharkov	5	18					6	5	9	5	16
Kremin Kremenchuk	9	15	10	9	15						
Kryvbas Kryvi-Rih	8	6	6	14	12	8	3	3	11	9	12
Arsenal Kyiv				4	11	13	7	10	6	12	5
Dynamo Kyiv	1	1	1	1	1	1	1	1	1	2	1
Obolon Kyiv											14
Zirka Kyrovohrad					6	10	11	11	16		
Zarja Lugans'k	15	14	16	18							
Volun-1 Luts'k	11	11	15	17							6
SKA Karpati Lvov	6	5	8	8	5	3	4	9	10	8	7
Ilichivets Mariupol						12	5	8	4	10	10
SK Mykolajv			13	16			16				
Chornomorets Odesa	3	3	2	2	7	15		15			8
FC Olexandriya										13	13
Vorskla Poltava					3	5	10	4	12	11	11
Veres Rivne	16	12	18								
Temp Shepetivka		9	17								
Tavriya Simferopol	10	8	5	12	6	14	9	13	7	7	9
Nyva Ternopil		7	12	13	9	7	13	12	14		
Zakarpattya Uzhgorod										14	
Nyva Vynnytsya	14	10	14	15	16						
Metalurg Zaporizhzhya	7	16	9	5	8	9	8	6	8	4	15
Torpedo Zaporizhzhya	13	13	7	7	14	16					

Key to League Positions Tables

- League champions
- Other teams playing in league
- Season promoted to league
- Season of relegation from league
- `5` Final position in league

Russia (including the former Soviet Union)

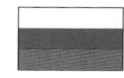

Rossiyskiy Futbol'nyy Soyuz
Founded: 1912, 1991
Joined FIFA: 1912, 1992
Joined UEFA: 1954

ALTHOUGH SOCCER HAD arrived in Moscow by the turn of the 19th century, it was slow to spread beyond the major Russian cities. A national soccer association, founded in 1912, was unable to create a national league from the small-scale affairs in Moscow and St. Petersburg. The re-creation of a domestic soccer programme under the Communists was slow, as they found it hard to arrange and play national league soccer in a country so geographically huge, so bereft of functioning transportation and in a state of social upheaval. But, by 1936, the trains were reliable enough and the clubs settled enough for an all-Soviet league and cup to be established.

With a break for the war, these competitions continued until 1991, but the 1991–92 season saw both state and league fragment with the emergence of independent Baltic (Lithuania, Latvia, Estonia) and Caucasian (Georgia, Armenia, Azerbaijan) states, as well as the Ukraine, Moldova, Belarus and Kazakhstan (for details of these leagues see pages 338–43). The Central Asian republics of the former Soviet Union soon followed (Turkmenistan, Kyrgyzstan, Tajikistan and Uzbekistan). Details of these leagues can be found on pages 476–77.

Soviet Union League Record 1936–91

SEASON	CHAMPIONS	RUNNERS-UP
1936	Dinamo Moskva	Dinamo Kiev
1936*	Spartak Moskva	Dinamo Moskva
1937	Dinamo Moskva	Spartak Moskva
1938	Spartak Moskva	CDKA Moskva
1939	Spartak Moskva	Dinamo Tbilisi
1940	Dinamo Moskva	Dinamo Tbilisi
1941–44	no championship	
1945	Dinamo Moskva	CDKA Moskva
1946	CDKA Moskva	Dinamo Moskva
1947	CDKA Moskva	Dinamo Moskva
1948	CDKA Moskva	Dinamo Moskva
1949	Dinamo Moskva	CDKA Moskva
1950	CDKA Moskva	Dinamo Moskva
1951	CDKA Moskva	Dinamo Tbilisi
1952	Spartak Moskva	Dinamo Kiev
1953	Spartak Moskva	Dinamo Tbilisi
1954	Dinamo Moskva	Spartak Moskva
1955	Dinamo Moskva	Spartak Moskva
1956	Spartak Moskva	Dinamo Moskva
1957	Dinamo Moskva	Torpedo Moskva
1958	Spartak Moskva	Dinamo Moskva
1959	Dinamo Moskva	Lokomotiv Moskva
1960	Torpedo Moskva	Dinamo Kiev
1961	Dinamo Kiev	Torpedo Moskva
1962	Spartak Moskva	Dinamo Moskva
1963	Dinamo Moskva	Spartak Moskva
1964	Dinamo Tbilisi	Torpedo Moskva
1965	Torpedo Moskva	Dinamo Kiev
1966	Dinamo Kiev	SKA Rostov-na-Donu
1967	Dinamo Kiev	Dinamo Moskva
1968	Dinamo Kiev	Spartak Moskva
1969	Spartak Moskva	Dinamo Kiev
1970	CSKA Moskva	Dinamo Moskva
1971	Dinamo Kiev	Ararat Yerevan
1972	Zarja Vorosch'grad	Dinamo Kiev
1973	Ararat Yerevan	Dinamo Kiev
1974	Dinamo Kiev	Spartak Moskva

Soviet Union League Record (*continued*)

SEASON	CHAMPIONS	RUNNERS-UP
1975	Dinamo Kiev	Shakhtar Donetsk
1976	Dinamo Moskva	Ararat Yerevan
1976*	Torpedo Moskva	Dinamo Kiev
1977	Dinamo Kiev	Dinamo Tbilisi
1978	Dinamo Tbilisi	Dinamo Kiev
1979	Spartak Moskva	Shakhtar Donetsk
1980	Dinamo Kiev	Spartak Moskva
1981	Dinamo Kiev	Spartak Moskva
1982	Dinamo Minsk	Dinamo Kiev
1983	Dnipro Dnipropetrovsk	Spartak Moskva
1984	Zenit Leningrad	Spartak Moskva
1985	Dinamo Kiev	Spartak Moskva
1986	Dinamo Kiev	Dinamo Moskva
1987	Spartak Moskva	Dnipro Dnipropetrovsk
1988	Dnipro Dnipropetrovsk	Dinamo Kiev
1989	Spartak Moskva	Dnipro Dnipropetrovsk
1990	Dinamo Kiev	CSKA Moskva
1991	CSKA Moskva	Spartak Moskva

* Extra transitional autumn league – played in order to allow a season to start in spring and end in autumn.

Soviet Union League Summary

TEAM	TOTALS	CHAMPIONS & RUNNERS-UP (BOLD) (*ITALICS*)
Dinamo Kiev	**13**, *11*	*1936, 52, 60,* **61,** *65,* **66–68,** *69,* **71,** *72, 73,* **74, 75,** *76,* **77,** *78,* **80, 81,** *82,* **85, 86, 88,** *90*
Spartak Moskva	**12**, *12*	*1936,* **37, 38, 39,** *52, 53,* **54,** *55,* **56,** *58,* **62,** *63,* **68, 69,** *74,* **79,** *80, 81, 83–85,* **87,** *89,* **91**
Dinamo Moskva	**11**, *11*	**1936,** *36,* **37,** *40,* **45,** *46–48,* **49,** *50,* **54, 55,** *56, 57, 58,* **59,** *62, 63,* **67,** *70,* **76,** *86*

This summary only features the top three clubs in the Soviet Union League. For a full list of league champions and runners-up please see the League Record above.

Soviet Union Cup Record 1936–92

YEAR	WINNERS	SCORE	RUNNERS-UP
1936	Lokomotiv Moskva	2-0	Dinamo Tbilisi
1937	Dinamo Moskva	5-2	Dinamo Tbilisi
1938	Spartak Moskva	3-2	Elektrik Leningrad
1939	Spartak Moskva	3-1	Stalinets Leningrad
1940–43		no competition	
1944	Zenit Leningrad	2-1	CDKA Moskva
1945	CDKA Moskva	2-1	Dinamo Moskva
1946	Spartak Moskva	3-2	Dinamo Tbilisi
1947	Spartak Moskva	2-0	Torpedo Moskva
1948	CDKA Moskva	3-0	Spartak Moskva
1949	Torpedo Moskva	2-1	Dinamo Moskva
1950	Spartak Moskva	3-0	Dinamo Moskva
1951	CDSA Moskva	2-1	Komanda Kalinin
1952	Torpedo Moskva	1-0	Spartak Moskva
1953	Dinamo Moskva	1-0	Kriliya Kuybyshev
1954	Dinamo Moskva	2-1	Spartak Yerevan
1955	CDSA Moskva	2-1	Dinamo Moskva
1956		no competition	
1957	Lokomotiv Moskva	1-0	Spartak Moskva
1958	Spartak Moskva	1-0	Torpedo Moskva

Soviet Union Cup Record (*continued*)

YEAR	WINNERS	SCORE	RUNNERS-UP
1959		*no competition*	
1960	Torpedo Moskva	4-3	Dinamo Tbilisi
1961	Shakhtar Donetsk	3-1	Torpedo Moskva
1962	Shakhtar Donetsk	2-0	Znarnia Truda O-Z
1963	Spartak Moskva	2-1	Shakhtar Donetsk
1964	Dinamo Kiev	1-0	Kriliya Kuybyshev
1965	Spartak Moskva	0-0, (replay) 2-1	Dinamo Minsk
1966	Dinamo Kiev	2-0	Torpedo Moskva
1967	Dinamo Moskva	3-0	CSKA Moskva
1968	Torpedo Moskva	1-0	Pakhtakor Tashkent
1969	SKA Karpati Lvov	2-1	SKA Rostov-na-Donu
1970	Dinamo Moskva	2-1	Dinamo Tbilisi
1971	Spartak Moskva	2-2, (replay) 1-0	SKA Rostov-na-Donu
1972	Torpedo Moskva	0-0, (replay) 1-1 (aet)(5-1 pens)	Spartak Moskva
1973	Ararat Yerevan	2-1	Dinamo Kiev
1974	Dinamo Kiev	3-0	Zarja Voroshilovgrad
1975	Ararat Yerevan	2-1	Zarja Voroshilovgrad
1976	Dinamo Tbilisi	3-0	Ararat Yerevan
1977	Dinamo Moskva	1-0	Torpedo Moskva
1978	Dinamo Kiev	2-1	Shakhtar Donetsk
1979	Dinamo Tbilisi	0-0 (aet)(5-4 pens)	Dinamo Moskva
1980	Shakhtar Donetsk	2-1	Dinamo Tbilisi
1981	SKA Rostov-na-Donu	1-0	Spartak Moskva
1982	Dinamo Kiev	1-0	Torpedo Moskva
1983	Shakhtar Donetsk	1-0	Metalist Kharkov
1984	Dinamo Moskva	2-0	Zenit Leningrad
1985	Dinamo Kiev	2-1	Shakhtar Donetsk
1986	Torpedo Moskva	1-0	Shakhtar Donetsk
1987	Dinamo Kiev	3-3 (aet)(4-2 pens)	Dinamo Minsk
1988	Metalist Kharkov	2-0	Torpedo Moskva
1989	Dnipro Dnipropetrovsk	1-0	Torpedo Moskva
1990	Dinamo Kiev	6-1	Lokomotiv Moskva
1991	CSKA Moskva	3-2	Torpedo Moskva
1992	Spartak Moskva	2-0	CSKA Moskva

Soviet Union Cup Summary

TEAM	TOTALS	WINNERS & RUNNERS-UP (BOLD) (*ITALICS*)
Spartak Moskva	10, 5	**1938, 39, 46, 47,** *48,* **50,** *52,* **57, 58, 63, 65, 71,** *72,* **81, 92**
Dinamo Kiev	8, 1	**1964, 66,** *73,* **74, 78, 82, 85, 87, 90**
Dinamo Moskva	7, 5	**1937,** *45,* **49,** *50,* **53, 54, 55,** *67,* **70,** *77,* **79,** *84*
Torpedo Moskva	6, 9	*1947,* **49,** *52,* **58,** *60, 61, 66, 68, 72,* **77,** *82,* **86,** *88, 89, 91*
CSKA Moskva (includes CDKA Moskva, CDSA Moskva)	5, 3	*1944,* **45, 48, 51, 55,** *67,* **91,** *92*

This summary only features the clubs that have won the Soviet Union Cup five times or more. For a full list of cup winners and runners-up please see the Cup Record above.

Russian League Record 1992–2003

SEASON	CHAMPIONS	RUNNERS-UP
1992	Spartak Moskva	Alania Vladikavkaz
1993	Spartak Moskva	Rotor Volgograd
1994	Spartak Moskva	Dinamo Moskva
1995	Alania Vladikavkaz	Lokomotiv Moskva
1996	Spartak Moskva	Alania Vladikavkaz
1997	Spartak Moskva	Rotor Volgograd
1998	Spartak Moskva	CSKA Moskva
1999	Spartak Moskva	Lokomotiv Moskva
2000	Spartak Moskva	Lokomotiv Moskva
2001	Spartak Moskva	Lokomotiv Moskva
2002	Lokomotiv Moskva	CSKA Moskva
2003	CSKA Moskva	Zenit Sankt-Peterburg

Russian League Summary

TEAM	TOTALS	CHAMPIONS & RUNNERS-UP (BOLD) (*ITALICS*)
Spartak Moskva	9, 0	**1992–94, 96–2001**
Lokomotiv Moskva	1, 4	*1995, 99–2001,* **02**
Alania Vladikavkaz	1, 2	**1992,** *95, 96,*
CSKA Moskva	1, 2	*1998, 2002,* **03**
Rotor Volgograd	0, 2	*1993, 97*
Dinamo Moskva	0, 1	*1994*
Zenit Sankt-Peterburg	0, 1	*2003*

Russian Cup Record 1993–2004

YEAR	WINNERS	SCORE	RUNNERS-UP
1993	Torpedo Moskva	1-1 (aet)(5-3 pens)	CSKA Moskva
1994	Spartak Moskva	2-2 (aet)(4-2 pens)	CSKA Moskva
1995	Dinamo Moskva	0-0 (aet)(8-7 pens)	Rotor Volgograd
1996	Lokomotiv Moskva	3-2	Spartak Moskva
1997	Lokomotiv Moskva	2-0	Dinamo Moskva
1998	Spartak Moskva	1-0	Lokomotiv Moskva
1999	Zenit Sankt-Peterburg	3-1	Dinamo Moskva
2000	Lokomotiv Moskva	3-2 (aet)	CSKA Moskva
2001	Lokomotiv Moskva	1-1 (aet)(4-3 pens)	Anzhi Makhachkala
2002	CSKA Moskva	2-0	Zenit Sankt-Peterburg
2003	Spartak Moskva	1-0	FK Rostov
2004	TEREK Groznyi	1-0	Krylya Sovetov Samara

Russian Cup Summary

TEAM	TOTALS	WINNERS & RUNNERS-UP (BOLD) (*ITALICS*)
Lokomotiv Moskva	4, 1	**1996, 97, 98,** *2000,* **01**
Spartak Moskva	3, 1	**1994,** *96,* **98, 2003**
CSKA Moskva	1, 3	*1993, 94, 2000,* **02**
Dinamo Moskva	1, 2	**1995,** *97, 99*
Zenit Sankt-Peterburg	1, 1	**1999,** *2002*
TEREK Groznyi	1, 0	**2004**
Torpedo Moskva	1, 0	**1993**
Anzhi Makhachkala	0, 1	*2001*
FK Rostov	0, 1	*2003*
Krylya Sovetov Samara	0, 1	*2004*
Rotor Volgograd	0, 1	*1995*

Ukraine

Football Federation of Ukraine
Founded: 1991
Joined FIFA: 1992
Joined UEFA: 1992

Ukrainian soccer has until recently been played in the shadow of the institutions and competitions of the Soviet Union. A separate national league and cup were established after independence was gained from the USSR in 1991. The league has since been dominated by Dynamo Kyiv.

SEASON	LEAGUE CHAMPIONS
2000	Dynamo Kyiv
2001	Dynamo Kyiv
2002	Shakhtar Donetsk
2003	Dynamo Kyiv
2004	Dynamo Kyiv

YEAR	CUP WINNERS
2000	Dynamo Kyiv
2001	Shakhtar Donetsk
2002	Shakhtar Donetsk
2003	Dynamo Kyiv
2004	Shakhtar Donetsk

THE CONMEBOL NATIONS

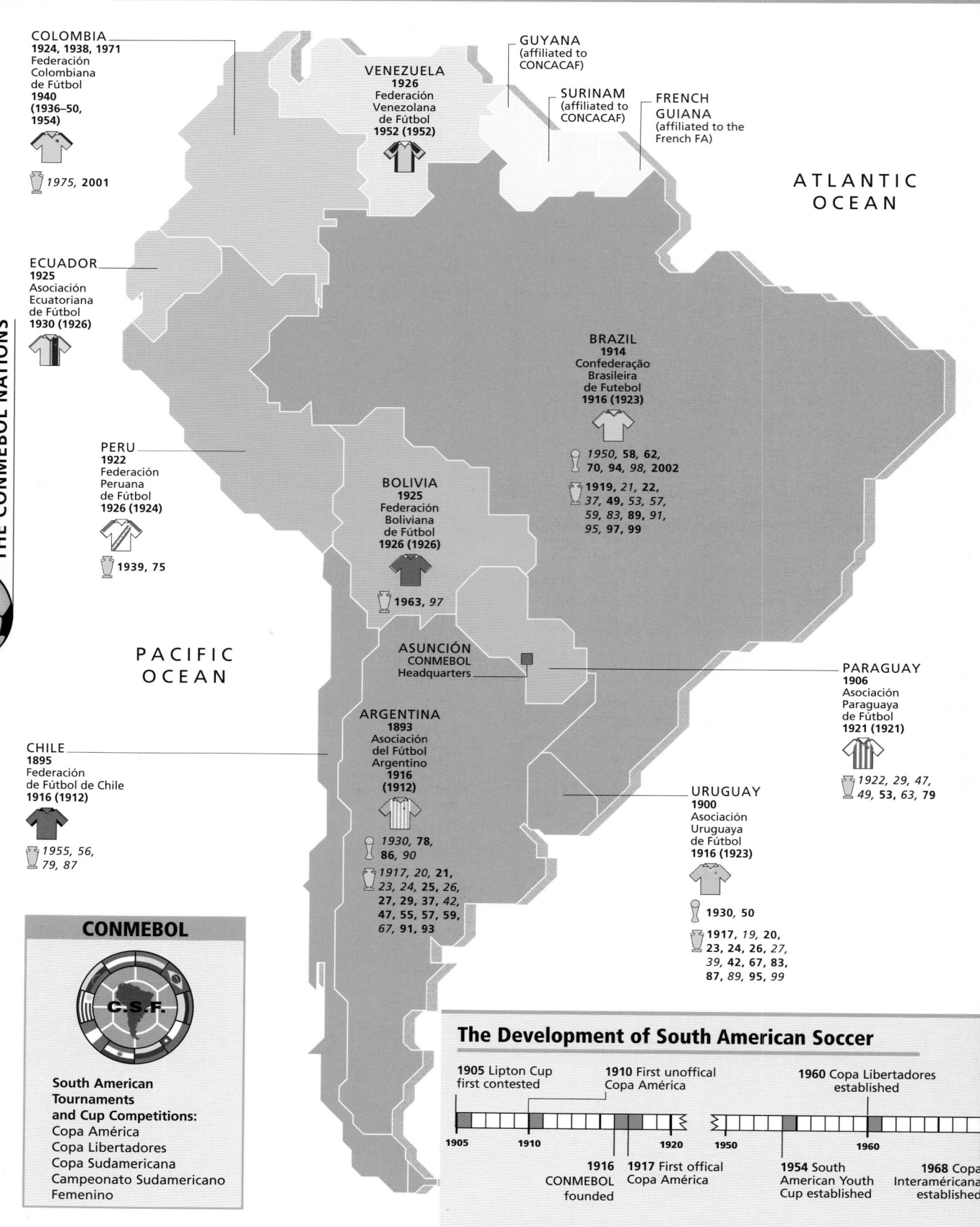

COLOMBIA
1924, 1938, 1971
Federación
Colombiana
de Fútbol
1940
**(1936–50,
1954)**

1975, 2001

GUYANA
(affiliated to
CONCACAF)

VENEZUELA
1926
Federación
Venezolana
de Fútbol
1952 (1952)

SURINAM
(affiliated to
CONCACAF)

**FRENCH
GUIANA**
(affiliated to the
French FA)

A T L A N T I C
O C E A N

ECUADOR
1925
Asociación
Ecuatoriana
de Fútbol
1930 (1926)

BRAZIL
1914
Confederação
Brasileira
de Futebol
1916 (1923)

1950, **58, 62,
70, 94,** *98,* **2002**

1919, *21,* **22,**
37, **49,** *53, 57,
59, 83,* **89,** *91,*
95, **97,** *99*

PERU
1922
Federación
Peruana
de Fútbol
1926 (1924)

1939, 75

BOLIVIA
1925
Federación
Boliviana
de Fútbol
1926 (1926)

1963, *97*

P A C I F I C
O C E A N

ASUNCIÓN
CONMEBOL
Headquarters

PARAGUAY
1906
Asociación
Paraguaya
de Fútbol
1921 (1921)

1922, 29, **47,**
49, 53, *63,* **79**

ARGENTINA
1893
Asociación
del Fútbol
Argentino
**1916
(1912)**

1930, **78,
86, 90**

1917, *20,* **21,**
23, 24, **25, 26,**
27, *29, 37,* **42,**
47, 55, 57, 59,
67, **91, 93**

URUGUAY
1900
Asociación
Uruguaya
de Fútbol
1916 (1923)

1930, *50*

1917, *19,* **20,**
23, 24, *26,* **27,**
39, **42,** *67,* **83,**
87, *89,* **95,** *99*

CHILE
1895
Federación
de Fútbol de Chile
1916 (1912)

*1955, 56,
79, 87*

CONMEBOL

C.S.F.

**South American
Tournaments
and Cup Competitions:**
Copa América
Copa Libertadores
Copa Sudamericana
Campeonato Sudamericano
Femenino

The Development of South American Soccer

1905 Lipton Cup
first contested

1910 First unoffical
Copa América

1960 Copa Libertadores
established

1905 · 1910 · 1920 · 1950 · 1960

1916
CONMEBOL
founded

1917 First offical
Copa América

1954 South
American Youth
Cup established

1968 Copa
Interamérica
established

The CONMEBOL Nations

Date of affiliation to CONMEBOL	Formation of National FA —	**COUNTRY**
		1916
	Date of affiliation to CONMEBOL —	Name of Football Association
▢ Founder member		**1916 (1912)**
▢ 1917–29	Team colours	
▢ 1930–49	World Cup —	🏆 **1990** — Winners in bold
▢ 1950–present	Copa América —	🏆 *2000* — Runners-up in italic

Date of affiliation to CONMEBOL, Date of affiliation to FIFA

(Official tournaments only)

Above: *Fallen giants: Colo Colo (right), Chile's leading club, went bankrupt in 2002. This is just the tip of an iceberg of debt and financial irregularities in South American soccer.*
Below: *Ecuador qualified for the World Cup finals in 2002 for the first time in its history. After decades of discrimination, it was the national team's first predominantly black squad.*

1971 Unofficial South American Footballer of the Year award established

1991 Teams from CONCACAF first invited to Copa América. South American Women's Championship established

2002 Copa Sudamericana replaced Copa Mercosur and Merconorte

1996 Last Copa de Oro

1980   1990   2000

1986 CONMEBOL South American Footballer of the Year Award established

1992 Copa CONMEBOL established

1993 Copa de Oro established

1998 Copa Mercosur and Copa Merconorte established

The CONMEBOL Nations

CONMEBOL (Confederación Sudamericana de Fútbol) was founded in 1916 and is the first and oldest of the world's regional soccer confederations. In 1905 Argentina and Uruguay contested the Lipton Cup for the first time. In July 1916, an informal international soccer tournament was held in Buenos Aires, Argentina, between the hosts, Chile, Uruguay and Brazil, part of a festival celebrating 100 years of independence from Spain. Recognizing the growing power and influence of the European-based and controlled FIFA (founded 1904), Héctor Gomez, a Uruguayan educationalist, took the opportunity to gather representatives of the four soccer associations and created CONMEBOL.

Since then CONMEBOL has grown to represent all of the South American nations minus Surinam and Guyana (members of CONCACAF) and French Guiana (which remains affiliated to the French FA). Its headquarters is in the Paraguayan capital, Asunción, from where it exerts considerable influence over FIFA as well as more local soccer matters. Its major international tournament, the Copa América, had been played on a varying but approximately biennial basis since 1916. Since then other international club tournaments have been established, including the prestigious Copa Libertadores in 1960, and a variety of less successful, made-for-television tournaments. Most recently CONMEBOL has dissolved the Copas Mercosur and Merconorte to create a single continental club tournament, the Copa Sudamericana. Although launched without Brazilian participation in 2001–02, it has been a success and Brazilian teams are now taking part in the tournament.

Ronaldo celebrates Brazil's fifth World Cup victory in 2002. Brazil now looks set to host the tournament in 2014.

Calendar of Events	
Club Tournaments	Copa Libertadores 2004–05 Copa Sudamericana 2004–05
International Tournaments	Qualifying Tournament for 2006 World Cup

South America

THE SEASONS IN REVIEW 2003, 2003–04

JUST FOR ONCE IT WAS THE YEAR OF THE UNDERDOG in South American international club soccer. Buenos Aires giants Boca Juniors and River Plate shared the domestic honours and could have made a clean sweep of the continent's cups. But both were beaten in their respective Finals. In the Copa Sudamericana Cienciano went to Buenos Aires for the first leg and came away with a 3-3 draw. The second leg could not be played at Cienciano's Cuzcu Stadium high in the Andes Mountains as it was too small to meet CONMEBOL regulations. So they were forced to play in a newly refurbished stadium in Arequipa. Undeterred, they stole a goal from River to win the trophy. In the Copa Libertadores, Once Caldas cut it even finer, forcing a 0-0 draw in Argentina and a 1-1 draw at home before Boca's nerves disintegrated and the Colombians won on penalties.

This refreshing sporting change was not matched by events off the field where the seemingly perennial crisis of Latin American soccer continued unabated. Low attendances across the continent were exemplified at Libertad – one of the biggest teams in Paraguay – who had less than 200 people at one of their home league games. Although the grim economic realities of South American urban life continue to eat away at the audience, problems of violence and disorder make matters even worse.

In Ecuador, the upsurge of interest in soccer since the country's successful appearance at the World Cup in 2002 has been accompanied by an upsurge of both crowds and fighting. In Peru, games at Universitario have descended into small riots. Internal political unrest continually disrupted the schedule of the Bolivian championship and the utterly bankrupt Chilean game was disfigured by an enormous riot at the Santiago derby between Colo Colo and Universidad.

Copa Sudamericana

2003 FINAL (2 legs)

Dec 10 – Monumental, Buenos Aires
River Plate 3-3 Cienciano
(Agentina) (Peru)
(López 28, 50, *(Portilla 26, 79,*
Marcelo Salas 85) *Carty 67)*
h/t: 1-1 **Att:** 43,296
Ref: Simon (Brazil)

19 December – Universidad Nacional, Arequipa
Cienciano 1-0 River Plate
(Lugo 78)
h/t: 0-0 **Att:** 44,000
Ref: Méndez (Uruguay)
Cienciano won 4-3 on aggregate

Below: The bitter taste of defeat: River players (left to right) Marcelo Gallardo, Eduardo Coudet and Daniel Montenegro leave the pitch after their two-leg defeat by Cienciano.

Bottom: Uruguayan head coach Juan Ramon Carrasco addresses his team at a training session in Chile. His ultra-attacking approach made him popular with the fans but his lack of regard for defence saw the team beaten 3-0 at home by Venezuela in a World Cup qualifier. He was promptly sacked.

Top 10 South American Leagues

COUNTRY	CHAMPIONS	RUNNERS-UP
Argentina – Apertura	Boca Juniors	San Lorenzo
Argentina – Clausura	River Plate	Boca Juniors
Bolivia – Apertura*	The Strongest	Bolivar
Bolivia – Clausura*	The Strongest	Jorge Wilstermann
Brazil – National Championship*	Cruzeiro	Santos
Chile – Apertura*	Cobreola	Colo Colo
Chile – Clausura*	Cobreola	Colo Colo
Colombia – Apertura*	Once Caldas	Atlético Júnior
Colombia – Clausura*	Deportes Tolima	Deportivo Cali
Ecuador – Apertura*	Barcelona	LDU
Ecuador – Clausura*	LDU	Barcelona
Ecuador – National Championship*	LDU	Barcelona
Paraguay – Apertura*	Libertad	Guaraní
Paraguay – Clausura*	Libertad	Olimpia
Paraguay – National Championship*	Libertad	Guaraní
Peru – Apertura*	Sporting Cristal	Alianza Lima
Peru – Clausura*	*abandoned*	
Peru – National Championship*	Alianza Lima	Sporting Cristal
Uruguay – Apertura*	Nacional	Peñarol
Uruguay – Clausura*	Peñarol	Liverpool
Uruguay – National Championship*	Peñarol	Nacional
Venezuela – Apertura	Caracas FC	Deportivo Táchira
Venezuela – Clausura	Caracas FC	Deportivo Táchira
Venezuela – National Championship	Caracas FC	Deportivo Táchira

* Results for 2003 season.

SOUTH AMERICA

Cienciano players celebrate as they beat River Plate in the Final of the Copa Sudamericana. It is the first time a Peruvian team has ever won an international club competition.

Top right: *Argentinian coach Néstor Clausen of The Strongest celebrates with champagne as his team win the Bolivian Clausura – their second title of the year.*

Middle, left: *Players and fans of Libertad celebrate as a clean sweep of titles earned them the Paraguayan National Championship.*

Above: *Riot police stalk the stands of Santiago's Monumental Stadium. In a match between Colo Colo and Universidad, a piece of wood thrown from the crowd injured Universidad player Nelson Pinto. A riot followed during which police made 168 arrests.*

Left: *Cobreola players (left to right) Rodrigo Melendez, Patricio Glaz and Fernando Martel celebrate with the Chilean Clausura trophy after beating Colo Colo over two legs in the Final.*

Copa América

TOURNAMENT OVERVIEW

INTERNATIONAL SOCCER started early in South America with Argentina and Uruguay contesting the Lipton Cup (donated by Sir Thomas Lipton, the English tea merchant) beginning in 1905, and the Newton Cup from 1906. With regular international soccer across the River Plate and the opening of a rail link to Chile, the Argentine FA invited Uruguay, Chile and Brazil to Buenos Aires for a four-way tournament in 1910 (this is now thought of as the first 'unofficial' Copa América, as CONMEBOL was not formed until 1916). The Brazilians decided not to show, but the tournament went ahead with victories for Uruguay and Argentina over Chile. For the deciding match, 40,000 fans gathered at Gimnasia's stadium – and promptly burnt down a stand. The game was abandoned. The next day, a heavily policed rematch at Racing Club's ground saw Argentina win 4-1.

The second tournament was held in 1916 to celebrate the centenary of Argentinian independence. This time the Brazilians did show, but Uruguay won the title. In 1917, the holders hosted and won the first official championships in Montevideo. Two years later it was the turn of Brazil, and Rio aristocrats Fluminense built a new stadium to stage the matches. In a final play-off with Uruguay, Freidenreich, the Brazilian striker, ended the match with a goal after 43 minutes of extra time. Brazil won again in 1922, but the 1920s really belonged to Uruguay and Argentina. After a six-year gap (1929–35), while domestic struggles over professionalism were worked out, the tournament resumed appropriately with Uruguayan (1935) and Argentinian (1937) victories.

Argentina and Brazil dominant

A protracted players' strike in Argentina saw the team withdraw from both the 1949 and 1953 tournaments, but over the era as a whole it was the dominant side. Peru's victory in 1939, and Bolivia's in 1963, gave the continent's minnows a look-in. By the early 1960s the popularity of the tournament was declining as the Copa Libertadores took off and club versus country disputes over player availability sharpened. With Argentina and Brazil fielding consistently weak teams, the tournament took an eight-year break (1967–75) before recommencing as a finals-only event.

The tournament was relaunched in 1987 with all matches held in a single host country during the European close season to maximize player availability and TV and sponsorship money. The perennial problem of creating a tournament format with ten teams was solved in 1993 by inviting two outside nations – Mexico and the USA. This format has been replicated since with appearances for South Korea, Costa Rica and Japan as well. In the modern era, Argentina and Brazil have won when they have fielded their strongest sides, but their weaker teams have let the Uruguayans and the Colombians in.

Unofficial tournaments

YEAR	WINNERS	RUNNERS-UP	THIRD PLACE
1910	Argentina	Uruguay	Chile
1916	Uruguay	Argentina	Brazil
1935	Uruguay	Argentina	Brazil
1941	Argentina	Uruguay	Chile
1945	Argentina	Brazil	Chile
1946	Argentina	Brazil	Paraguay
1956	Uruguay	Chile	Argentina
1959	Uruguay	Argentina	Brazil

Copa América: winners and runners-up

TEAM COLOURS	COUNTRY	TOTAL WINS, YEARS	TOTAL RUNNERS-UP, YEARS
15	Argentina	**15:** 1910*, 21, 25, 27, 29, 37, 41*, 45*, 46*, 47, 55, 57, 59, 91, 93	**10:** 1916*, 17, 20, 23, 24, 26, 35*, 42, 59*, 67
14	Uruguay	**14:** 1916*, 17, 20, 23, 24, 26, 35*, 42, 56*, 59*, 67, 83, 87, 95	**7:** 1910*, 19, 27, 39, 41*, 89, 99
6	Brazil	**6:** 1919, 22, 49, 89, 97, 99	**11:** 1921, 25, 37, 45*, 46*, 53, 57, 59, 83, 91, 95
2	Paraguay	**2:** 1953, 79	**5:** 1922, 29, 47, 49, 63
2	Peru	**2:** 1939, 75	0
1	Bolivia	**1:** 1963	**1:** 1997
1	Colombia	**1:** 2001	**1:** 1975
0	Chile	0	**4:** 1955, 56*, 79, 87
0	Mexico	0	**2:** 1993, 2001

* honours in unofficial tournaments

COPA AMÉRICA

VENEZUELA

COLOMBIA

ECUADOR

PERU

1939 **1927**

1927 **1939**

BRAZIL

**1919,
22** **1921,
25, 37** **1917,
20, 42**

1919 **1922**

BOLIVIA

PARAGUAY

**1922,
29** **1923,
24, 25,
39**

CHILE

1926

1920

1926

PACIFIC
OCEAN

URUGUAY

**1917,
20, 23,
24, 26,
42** **1919,
27, 39** **1921,
22, 29,
37**

1917 **1923** **1924** **1942**

ARGENTINA

**1921,
25, 27,
29, 37** **1917,
20, 23,
24, 26,
42** **1919**

1921 **1925**

1929 **1937**

ATLANTIC
OCEAN

Artur Freidenreich *was the
first great black Brazilian
soccer player. He scored the
winner for Brazil against
Uruguay in the 1919 Copa
América Final in Rio.*

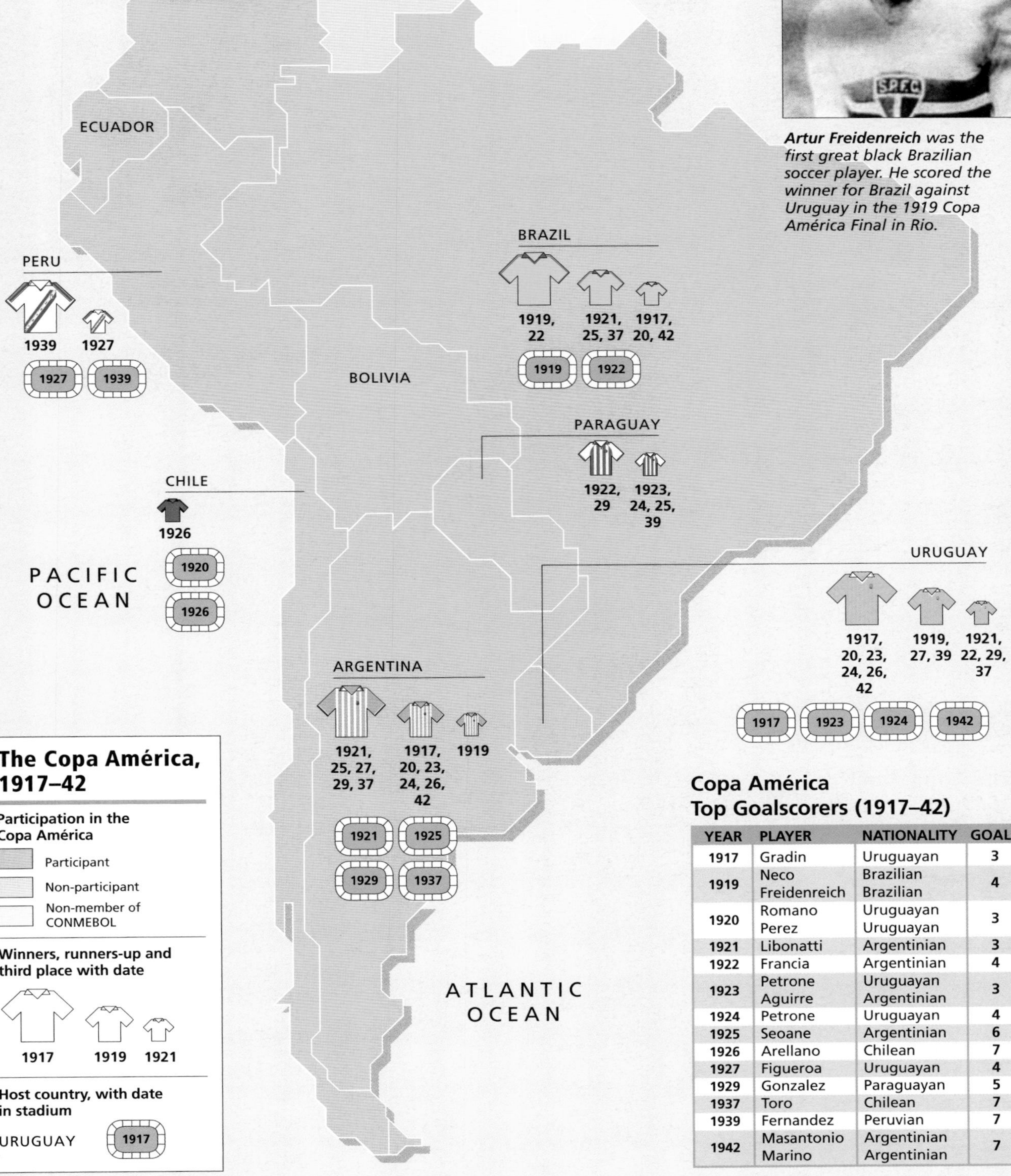

The Copa América,
1917–42

**Participation in the
Copa América**

Participant

Non-participant

Non-member of
CONMEBOL

**Winners, runners-up and
third place with date**

1917 **1919** **1921**

**Host country, with date
in stadium**

URUGUAY **1917**

Copa América
Top Goalscorers (1917–42)

YEAR	PLAYER	NATIONALITY	GOALS
1917	Gradin	Uruguayan	3
1919	Neco	Brazilian	4
	Freidenreich	Brazilian	
1920	Romano	Uruguayan	3
	Perez	Uruguayan	
1921	Libonatti	Argentinian	3
1922	Francia	Argentinian	4
1923	Petrone	Uruguayan	3
	Aguirre	Argentinian	
1924	Petrone	Uruguayan	4
1925	Seoane	Argentinian	6
1926	Arellano	Chilean	7
1927	Figueroa	Uruguayan	4
1929	Gonzalez	Paraguayan	5
1937	Toro	Chilean	7
1939	Fernandez	Peruvian	7
1942	Masantonio	Argentinian	7
	Marino	Argentinian	

COPA AMÉRICA

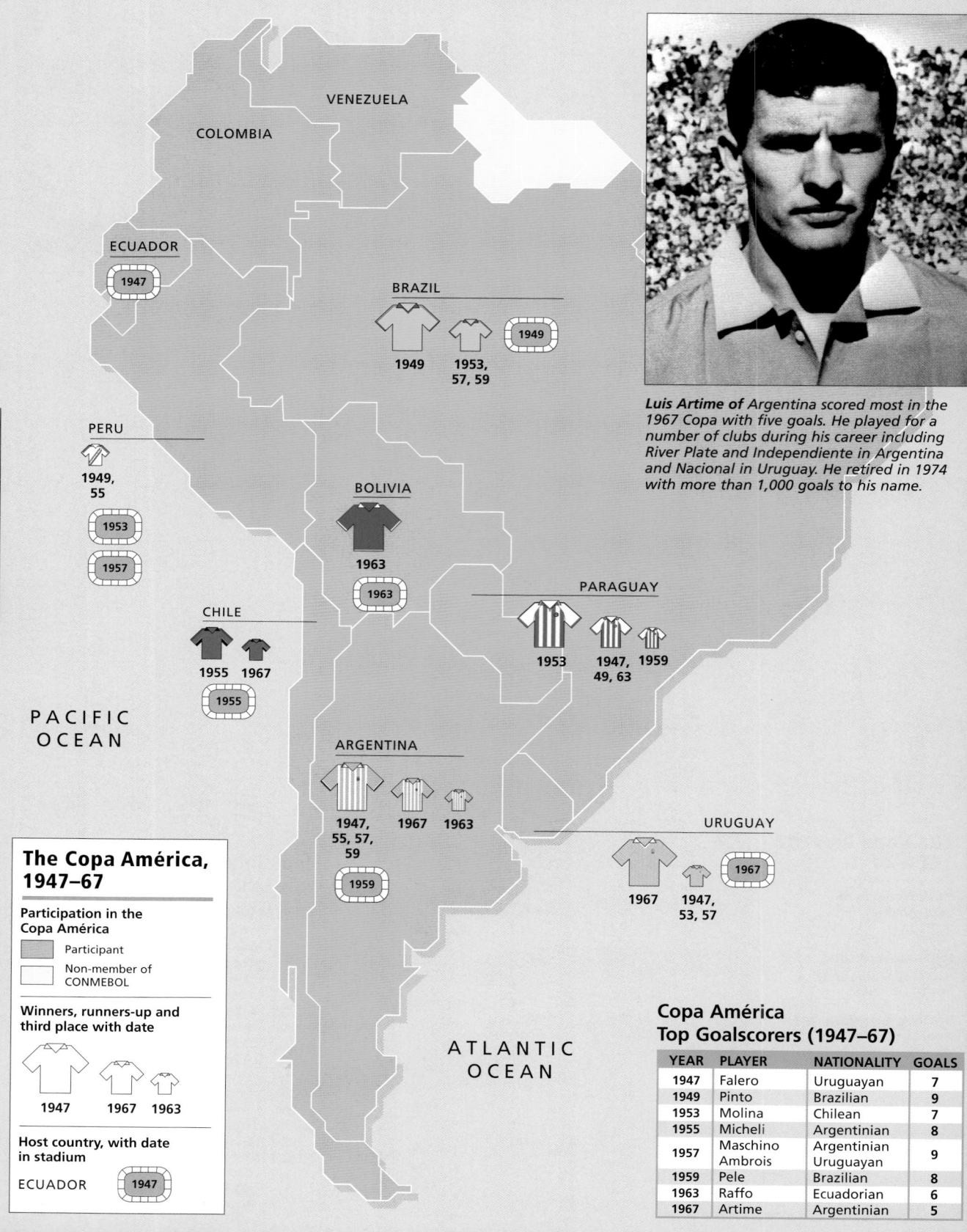

Luis Artime of Argentina scored most in the 1967 Copa with five goals. He played for a number of clubs during his career including River Plate and Independiente in Argentina and Nacional in Uruguay. He retired in 1974 with more than 1,000 goals to his name.

VENEZUELA

COLOMBIA

ECUADOR — 1947

BRAZIL — 1949 / 1953, 57, 59 / 1949

PERU — 1949, 55 / 1953 / 1957

BOLIVIA — 1963 / 1963

CHILE — 1955 / 1967 / 1955

PARAGUAY — 1953 / 1947, 49, 63 / 1959

ARGENTINA — 1947, 55, 57, 59 / 1967 / 1963 / 1959

URUGUAY — 1967 / 1947, 53, 57 / 1967

PACIFIC OCEAN

ATLANTIC OCEAN

The Copa América, 1947–67

Participation in the Copa América

- Participant
- Non-member of CONMEBOL

Winners, runners-up and third place with date

1947 1967 1963

Host country, with date in stadium

ECUADOR 1947

Copa América Top Goalscorers (1947–67)

YEAR	PLAYER	NATIONALITY	GOALS
1947	Falero	Uruguayan	7
1949	Pinto	Brazilian	9
1953	Molina	Chilean	7
1955	Micheli	Argentinian	8
1957	Maschino Ambrois	Argentinian Uruguayan	9
1959	Pele	Brazilian	8
1963	Raffo	Ecuadorian	6
1967	Artime	Argentinian	5

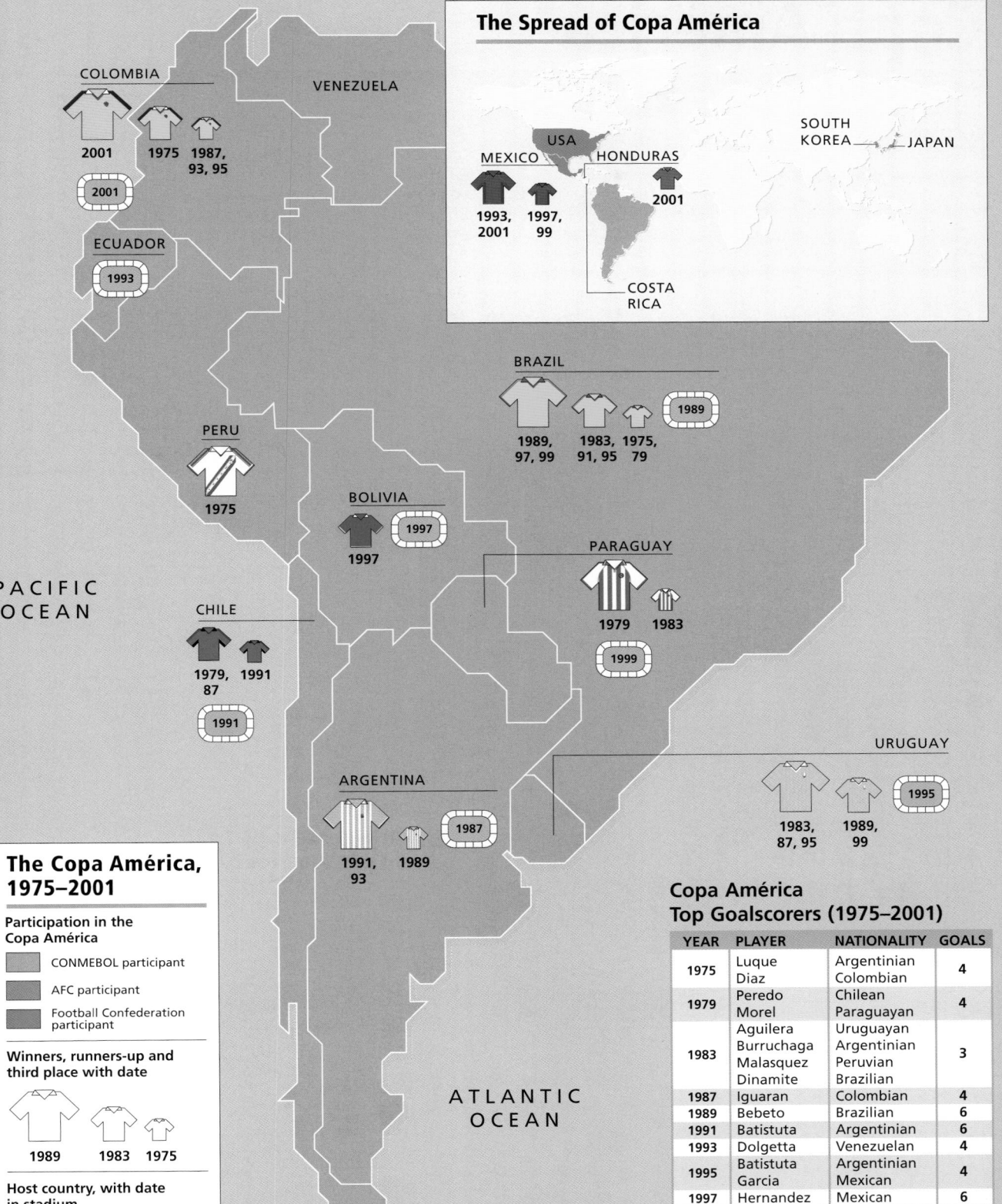

COLOMBIA

2001   1975   1987,
               93, 95

2001

ECUADOR

1993

VENEZUELA

The Spread of Copa América

MEXICO   USA   HONDURAS

1993,   1997,   2001
2001   99

COSTA
RICA

SOUTH
KOREA   JAPAN

PERU

1975

BRAZIL

1989,   1983,   1975,   1989
97, 99   91, 95   79

BOLIVIA

1997   1997

PARAGUAY

1979   1983

1999

PACIFIC
OCEAN

CHILE

1979,   1991
87

1991

ARGENTINA

1991,   1989
93

1987

URUGUAY

1983,   1989,   1995
87, 95   99

COPA AMÉRICA

ATLANTIC
OCEAN

The Copa América, 1975–2001

Participation in the Copa América

CONMEBOL participant

AFC participant

Football Confederation participant

Winners, runners-up and third place with date

1989   1983   1975

Host country, with date in stadium

ARGENTINA   1987

Copa América Top Goalscorers (1975–2001)

YEAR	PLAYER	NATIONALITY	GOALS
1975	Luque Diaz	Argentinian Colombian	4
1979	Peredo Morel	Chilean Paraguayan	4
1983	Aguilera Burruchaga Malasquez Dinamite	Uruguayan Argentinian Peruvian Brazilian	3
1987	Iguaran	Colombian	4
1989	Bebeto	Brazilian	6
1991	Batistuta	Argentinian	6
1993	Dolgetta	Venezuelan	4
1995	Batistuta Garcia	Argentinian Mexican	4
1997	Hernandez	Mexican	6
1999	Rivaldo Ronaldo	Brazilian Brazilian	5
2001	Aristizábal	Colombian	6

Copa América

TOURNAMENT REVIEW 2001

COLOMBIA LOST THE right to host the 1986 World Cup because of fears of disruption and chaos created by the endemic violence born of a massive narcotics industry. It went on to almost lose the 2001 Copa América to a wave of bombings and shootings that heralded yet another breakdown of the country's fragile peace process. Throughout May and early June, the civil war between the government, left-wing paramilitaries FARC and right-wing paramilitaries erupted with bombings in Bogotá, Cali and Medellín. Twelve people were killed and over 200 injured in the cities due to host two groups and the Final. However, the CSF (South American Football Confederation) repeatedly confirmed Colombia as hosts as president Andrés Pastrana promised massive troop deployments during the tournament.

In late June, Hernán Mejía Campuzano, vice-president of the Colombian Football Federation, was kidnapped by FARC paramilitaries. The CSF, panicked, announced that the Copa would now take place with an alternative host. Campuzano was promptly released, and headed straight for a meeting of the CSF executive in Buenos Aires. There, on 30 June, the Copa was returned to Colombia, but was to be played in 2002. Finally, on 5 July, under pressure from both Colombian president Andrés Pastrana and Brazilian TV company Traffic, the CSF announced that the Copa would go ahead as planned in Colombia, kicking off just six days later. Pastrana had gone on national TV declaring that the cup was essential to the maintenance of national pride and solidarity. Traffic threatened lawsuits resulting from loss of return on the $7 million it had invested in the TV rights.

COPA AMÉRICA

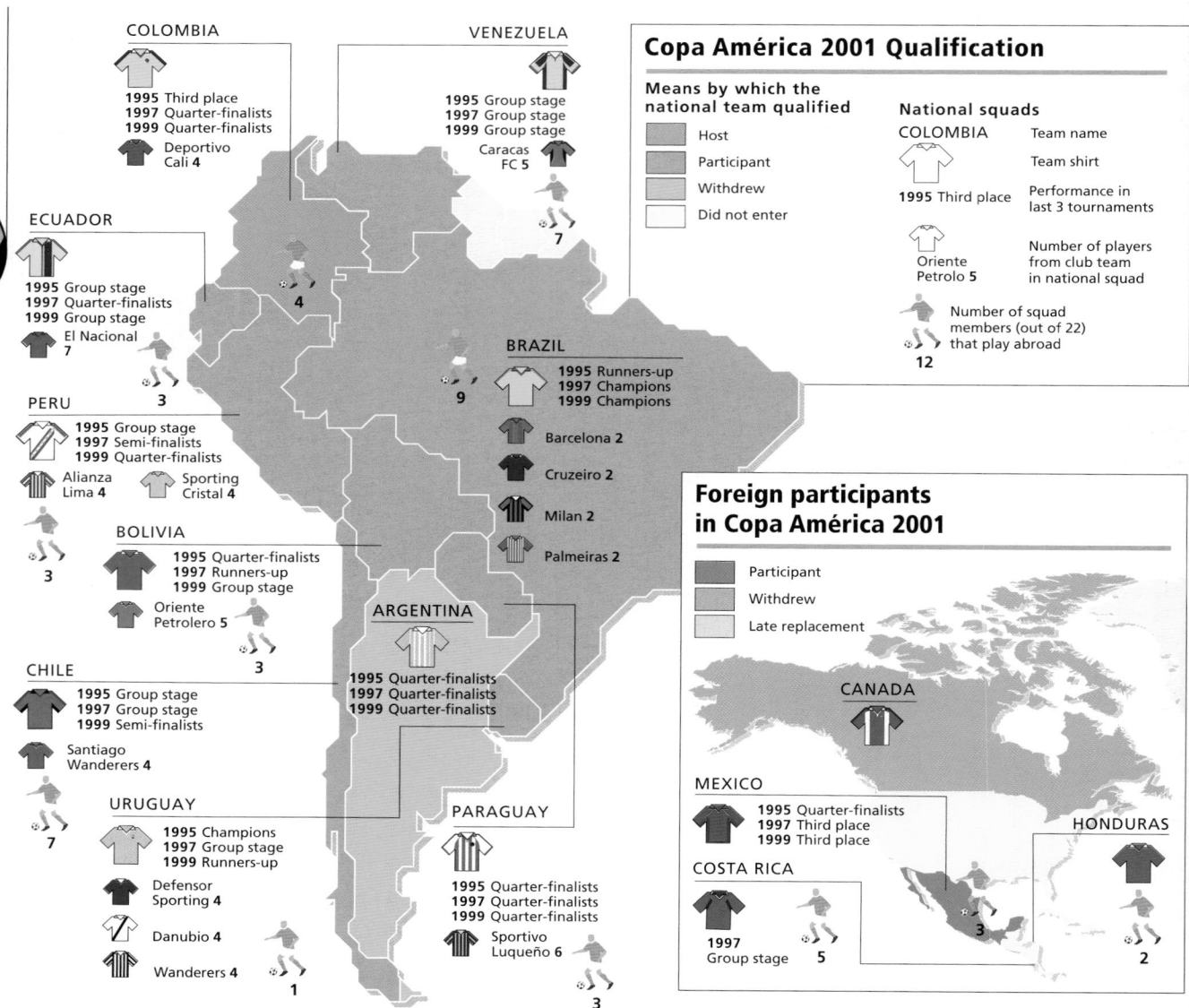

COLOMBIA
1995 Third place
1997 Quarter-finalists
1999 Quarter-finalists
Deportivo Cali 4

VENEZUELA
1995 Group stage
1997 Group stage
1999 Group stage
Caracas FC 5
7

ECUADOR
1995 Group stage
1997 Quarter-finalists
1999 Group stage
El Nacional 7
3
4

PERU
1995 Group stage
1997 Semi-finalists
1999 Quarter-finalists
Alianza Lima 4
Sporting Cristal 4
3

BOLIVIA
1995 Quarter-finalists
1997 Runners-up
1999 Group stage
Oriente Petrolero 5
3

BRAZIL
1995 Runners-up
1997 Champions
1999 Champions
Barcelona 2
Cruzeiro 2
Milan 2
Palmeiras 2
9

ARGENTINA
1995 Quarter-finalists
1997 Quarter-finalists
1999 Quarter-finalists

CHILE
1995 Group stage
1997 Group stage
1999 Semi-finalists
Santiago Wanderers 4
7

URUGUAY
1995 Champions
1997 Group stage
1999 Runners-up
Defensor Sporting 4
Danubio 4
Wanderers 4
1

PARAGUAY
1995 Quarter-finalists
1997 Quarter-finalists
1999 Quarter-finalists
Sportivo Luqueño 6
3

Copa América 2001 Qualification

Means by which the national team qualified
- Host
- Participant
- Withdrew
- Did not enter

National squads

COLOMBIA — Team name

— Team shirt

1995 Third place — Performance in last 3 tournaments

Oriente Petrolo 5 — Number of players from club team in national squad

12 — Number of squad members (out of 22) that play abroad

Foreign participants in Copa América 2001

- Participant
- Withdrew
- Late replacement

CANADA

MEXICO
1995 Quarter-finalists
1997 Third place
1999 Third place

COSTA RICA
1997 Group stage
5
3

HONDURAS
2

Not everyone was convinced by the CSF and by Pastrana's assurances. Argentina and Canada, who were due to play group games in Medellín, thought better of it and withdrew. Costa Rica and Honduras agreed to make up the numbers.

If the political prospects for the tournament looked poor, the sporting prospects were not that much better. The long South American World Cup qualification tournament had already stolen much of the Copa's thunder. Argentina, the strongest of the South American sides, was not present, Uruguay sent a reserve squad, and no settled Brazilian squad existed to be sent. Barranquilla, a humid port on the coast, and Bogotá, high up in the Andes, both presented serious problems of acclimatization for the players.

A massive police presence was promised by President Pastrana in order to persuade the CSF to allow Colombia to host the tournament.

Copa América 2001: The Venues

45,600 PASCUAL GUERRERO	Tournament stadium with capacity and name
● Cali	Location of stadium
🌵	Scene of bomb attacks

Barranquilla — 50,220 METROPOLITANO
— 52,800 ATANASIO GIRARDOT
Medellín 🌵
Manizales
34,000 HERNÁN RAMÍREZ VILLEGAS — **Pereira**
Bogotá 🌵 — 46,310 EL CAMPÍN
29,000 CENTENARIO — **Arménia**
Cali 🌵
COLOMBIA
45,600 PASCUAL GUERRERO
35,000 PALOGRANDE

The Development of Copa América 2001

May Bombs In Medellín and Bogotá kill 12 and injure hundreds

25 June Hernán Campuzano, vice-president of the FCF, kidnapped by FARC guerrillas

28 June CONMEBOL announces tournament to be held elsewhere; Colombia threatens to withdraw unless it is played in Colombia

5 July CONMEBOL announce tournament to take place on original dates

9 July Costa Rica agrees to participate

11 July Tournament begins

May — June — July

4 May Car bomb in Cali injures dozens including Colombian players and coaches

26 June CONMEBOL ratifies Colombia as hosts for Copa América

27 June CONMEBOL suspends decision, Campuzano released

30 June Colombia reinstated as hosts, but tournament postponed to 2002

6 July Argentina withdraws

7 July Canada withdraws

10 July Honduras agrees to participate

THE GROUP STAGES

In Group A, Colombia and Chile outclassed Ecuador and Venezuela. Colombia, under Francisco Maturana, fielded a young team with an experienced defence, including Mario Yepes and Ivan Córdoba. In Group B, the poor form of Brazil continued, beaten by Mexico and threatened for much of the game by an experimental Paraguayan side. In Group C, late arrivals Costa Rica and Honduras hit form and qualified along with Uruguay.

COLOMBIA A CHILE
ECUADOR VENEZUELA

BRAZIL B MEXICO
PERU PARAGUAY

COSTA RICA C HONDURAS
URUGUAY BOLIVIA

GROUP A

Chile 4-1 Ecuador
Colombia 2-0 Venezuela
Chile 1-0 Venezuela
Colombia 1-0 Ecuador
Ecuador 4-0 Venezuela
Colombia 2-0 Chile

	P	W	D	L	F	A	Pts
Colombia	3	3	0	0	5	0	9
Chile	3	2	0	1	5	3	6
Ecuador	3	1	0	2	5	5	3
Venezuela	3	0	0	3	0	7	0

GROUP B

Peru 3-3 Paraguay
Mexico 1-0 Brazil
Brazil 2-0 Peru
Paraguay 0-0 Mexico
Peru 1-0 Mexico
Brazil 3-1 Paraguay

	P	W	D	L	F	A	Pts
Brazil	3	2	0	1	5	2	6
Mexico	3	1	1	1	1	1	4
Peru	3	1	1	1	4	5	4
Paraguay	3	0	2	1	4	6	2

GROUP C

Uruguay 1-0 Bolivia
Costa Rica 1-0 Honduras
Uruguay 1-1 Costa Rica
Honduras 2-0 Bolivia
Costa Rica 4-0 Bolivia
Honduras 1-0 Uruguay

	P	W	D	L	F	A	Pts
Costa Rica	3	2	1	0	6	1	7
Honduras	3	2	0	1	3	1	6
Uruguay	3	1	1	1	2	2	4
Bolivia	3	0	0	3	0	7	0

COPA AMÉRICA

THE QUARTER-FINALS

Chile and Peru gave Mexico and Colombia easy quarter-final victories, though the Peruvians held out against a rampant Colombian attack for the first 50 minutes. It required an inspired shot from Aristizábal to break the deadlock and a header ten minutes later to seal it. Costa Rica and Uruguay met again after drawing 1-1 in the group stage – Uruguay went through to the last four winning 2-1. The big upset came in the Brazil v Honduras tie. The Hondurans were expected to play for a draw and penalties, but their passing and movement were too much for a lethargic, leaden Brazil, and they triumphed 2-0.

22 July – Pereira
Attendance 20,000

Chile **0-2** Mexico
h/t: 0-1

	Scorers	
		Arellano 17, Osorno 78
□ □	Yellow cards	□ □ □
	Red cards	

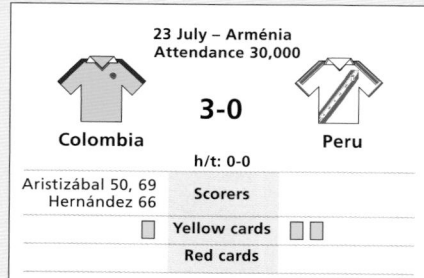

22 July – Arménia
Attendance 29,000

Costa Rica **1-2** Uruguay
h/t: 0-0

Wanchope 52	Scorers	Lemos 60 (pen) Lima 87
□ □ □ □	Yellow cards	□ □ □
	Red cards	

23 July – Arménia
Attendance 30,000

Colombia **3-0** Peru
h/t: 0-0

Aristizábal 50, 69 Hernández 66	Scorers	
□	Yellow cards	□ □
	Red cards	

23 July – Manizales
Attendance 30,000

Brazil **0-2** Honduras
h/t: 0-0

	Scorers	Belletti 57 o.g. Martínez S. 88
□ □	Yellow cards	□ □
■	Red cards	■

THE SEMI-FINALS

Colombia proved too strong for Honduras with the team's stars Freddy Grisales and Victor Hugo Aristizábal combining to put the hosts 2-0 ahead and so progress to the Final. Throughout the tournament Grisales gave Colombia's midfield energy and purpose while Aristizábal scored six goals – the biggest tally in a Copa América since Pele in 1959. Mexico was compact and composed in the victory over Uruguay, but picked up injuries and suspensions to key players, late red cards for García Aspe and Vidrio proving costly in the Final.

25 July – Pereira
Attendance 20,000

Mexico **2-1** Uruguay
h/t: 1-1

Borgetti 14 García Aspe 67 (pen)	Scorers	Morales R. 32
□ □ □ □	Yellow cards	□ □ □ □
■ ■	Red cards	■ ■

26 July - Manizales
Attendance 40,000

Colombia **2-0** Honduras
h/t: 1-0

Bedoya 6 Aristizábal 63	Scorers	
□ □	Yellow cards	□ □ □ □
	Red cards	

THIRD PLACE PLAY-OFF

Honduras continued to show great form in the third-fourth play-off match, and the team's teenage winger, Fabian Estoyanoff, ran the Uruguayan right-wing ragged. But Uruguay dug in and found equalizers to both the Honduran strikes. However, when it came to penalties, the Honduran players held their nerve.

July 29 - Bogotá
Attendance 47,000

Uruguay **2-2** Honduras
(after extra time)
Honduras won 5-4 on pens
h/t: 2-2 f/t: 2-2

Bizera 21 Martínez 44	Scorers	Martínez S. 14 Izaguirre 41
□ □ □ □	Yellow cards	□ □
	Red cards	

THE FINAL

Without captain Aspe and centre-backs Vidrio and Márquez, Mexico barely troubled Colombia in the Final. Cue a short burst of national celebration that the tournament had been peaceful and well supported and had ended in a home victory. It is a shame but no surprise that since the tournament Colombian politics and peace negotiations have shown no sign of following a similar path.

The Colombian squad celebrates its victory by holding up the Copa América trophy in a shower of red, yellow and blue ticker tape. A peaceful tournament and a home victory more than justified the decision to award the Copa to Colombia.

The Winning Goal

With 64 minutes on the clock, Colombia was awarded a free kick on the right-hand side of the pitch. Ivan López curled in a cross and Colombian captain Ivan Córdoba leapt over the Mexican defence to head powerfully into the net past keeper Oscar Pérez.

The Starting Line-Up

July 29 - El Campín, Bogotá
Attendance 47,000

MEXICO	Referee	COLOMBIA
Formation: 3-5-2	Ubaldo Aquino (Paraguay)	**Formation: 4-4-2**
Manager		**Manager**
Javier Aguirre		Francisco Maturana

Substitutes

Mexico			Colombia
Sánchez	**1**	**8**	Ferriera
Victorino	**10**	**11**	Arriaga
Osorno	**11**	**12**	Calero
Reyes	**16**	**16**	González
Hierro	**17**	**18**	Castillo
Zepeda	**19**	**21**	Diaz
Martinez	**22**	**23**	Molina

Highlights of the Game

KEY

Player booked ▢ — Substitution
Player sent off ▪ — Goal

MEXICO — KICK OFF 0 mins — **COLOMBIA**

1 min: Play interrupted briefly as a parachutist drifted onto the pitch crashing into the sideline advertising placards

5 min: Victor Aristizábal hits the post

20 min: Bedoya

28 min: Vargas

31 min: Castillo on, Aristizábal off after a collision with goalie Oscar Pérez almost draws a penalty

35 min: Coach Javier Aguirre refused to leave the bench after being sent off for stepping out of coach's area

45 mins

HALF-TIME: 0-0

54 min: Victorino on, Arellano off

65 min: Ivan Córdoba puts Colombia ahead

67 min: Osorno on, Johan Rodríguez off

70 min: Ramón Carlos Morales

74 min: Zepeda on, Alberto Rodríguez off

79 min: Juan Rodríguez sent off for a violent tackle

87 min: Molina on, Hernández off

90 min: Gerardo Torrado sent off for violent conduct

90 mins
+ 3 mins injury time

93 min: Molina

FULL-TIME: 0-1

2: Ivan Córdoba rises above the Mexican defenders to power his header past Oscar Pérez

1: Ivan López crosses from a free-kick into a packed penalty area

Colombian full-back Ivan Córdoba rises to meet Ivan López's free kick and heads the only goal of the Final of Copa América 2001.

Copa América

THE COPA AMÉRICA is the oldest continental soccer tournament. Unofficial tournaments were played as far back as 1910 and 1916, with the first official tournament held in 1917. The small number of South American nations and the vast differences in the strength of teams across the continent have produced an ever-changing range of tournament formats.

Most of the early tournaments were based on a mini-league format with play-offs in the event of ties. In 1975 CONMEBOL radically changed the format by playing the first rounds of the competition all over South America. Three groups of three played for three semi-final places, the fourth slot going to the reigning champions. Public interest, already at a low level, dipped even further with this bizarre elongated format, and in 1987 the tournament was re-established in a single host nation over two or three weeks.

In 1989 and 1991 two leagues of five were played to produce four semi-finalists, and from 1993 the tournament was enlarged, with two places being given to teams invited from the rest of the Americas and Asia: the USA, Costa Rica, Mexico and Japan have all participated. Twelve teams allow for a model based on three groups of four with winner, runners-up and the two best-placed third teams going on to knockout quarter-finals. Due to fixture congestion and the complexities of holding a bi-annual tournament, CONMEBOL have cancelled the 2003 tournament and the next Copa América will be played in Peru in 2004.

1910 ARGENTINA*
1 Argentina
2 Uruguay
3 Chile

1916 ARGENTINA*
1 Uruguay
2 Argentina
3 Brazil

1917 URUGUAY
1 Uruguay
2 Argentina
3 Brazil

1919 BRAZIL
1 Brazil (after play-off)
2 Uruguay
3 Argentina

PLAY-OFF
May 29 – das Laranjeiras, Rio de Janeiro
Brazil 1-0 Uruguay
(Friedenreich 122)
(after extra time)
h/t: 0-0 **90 mins:** 0-0
Att: 28,000 **Ref:** Barbera (Argentina)

1920 CHILE
1 Uruguay
2 Argentina
3 Brazil

1921 ARGENTINA
1 Argentina
2 Brazil
3 Uruguay

1922 BRAZIL
1 Brazil (after play-off)
2 Paraguay
3 Uruguay

PLAY-OFF
October 22 – das Laranjeiras, Rio de Janeiro
Brazil 3-1 Paraguay
(Neco 11,   (G. Rivas 60)
Formiga 48, 89)
h/t: 1-0 **Att:** 20,000
Ref: Guevara (Chile)

1923 URUGUAY
1 Uruguay
2 Argentina
3 Paraguay

1924 URUGUAY
1 Uruguay
2 Argentina
3 Paraguay

1925 ARGENTINA
1 Argentina
2 Brazil
3 Paraguay

1926 CHILE
1 Uruguay
2 Argentina
3 Chile

1927 PERU
1 Argentina
2 Uruguay
3 Peru

1929 ARGENTINA
1 Argentina
2 Paraguay
3 Uruguay

1935 PERU*
1 Uruguay
2 Argentina
3 Peru

1937 ARGENTINA
1 Argentina (after play-off)
2 Brazil
3 Uruguay

PLAY-OFF
February 1 – Gasómetro, Buenos Aires
Argentina 2-0 Brazil
(De la Mata 109,
122)
(after extra time)
h/t: 0-0 **90 mins:** 0-0
Att: 80,000 **Ref:** Macias (Argentina)

1939 PERU
1 Peru
2 Uruguay
3 Paraguay

1941 CHILE*
1 Argentina
2 Uruguay
3 Chile

1942 URUGUAY
1 Uruguay
2 Argentina
3 Brazil

1945 CHILE*
1 Argentina
2 Brazil
3 Chile

1946 ARGENTINA*
1 Argentina
2 Brazil
3 Paraguay

1947 ECUADOR
1 Argentina
2 Paraguay
3 Uruguay

1949 BRAZIL
1 Brazil (after play-off)
2 Paraguay
3 Peru

PLAY-OFF
May 11 – São Januario, Rio de Janeiro
Brazil 7-0 Paraguay
(Ademir 17,
27, 48,
Tesourinha 43, 70,
Jair 72, 89)
h/t: 3-0 **Att:** 55,000
Ref: Berrick (England)

1953 PERU
1 Paraguay (after play-off)
2 Brazil
3 Uruguay

PLAY-OFF
April 1 – Nacional, Lima
Paraguay 3-2 Brazil
(A. Lopez 14,   (Baltazar 56, 65)
Gavilan 17,
R. Fernández 41)
h/t: 3-0 **Att:** 35,000
Ref: Dean (England)

1955 CHILE
1 Argentina
2 Chile
3 Peru

1956 URUGUAY*
1 Uruguay
2 Chile
3 Argentina

1957 PERU
1 Argentina
2 Brazil
3 Uruguay

1959 ARGENTINA
1 Argentina
2 Brazil
3 Paraguay

1959 ECUADOR*
1 Uruguay
2 Argentina
3 Brazil

1963 BOLIVIA
1 Bolivia
2 Paraguay
3 Argentina

1967 URUGUAY
1 Uruguay
2 Argentina
3 Chile

1975 FINAL** (2 legs)
October 16 – El Campín, Bogotá
Colombia 1-0 Peru
(P. Castro)
Att: 50,000 **Ref:** Comesaña (Argentina)

October 22 – Nacional, Lima
Peru 2-0 Colombia
(Zárate,
Ramírez)
Att: 50,000 **Ref:** Silvagno (Chile)

PLAY-OFF
October 28 – Olímpico, Caracas
Peru 1-0 Colombia
(Sotil 25)
h/t: 1-0 **Att:** 30,000
Ref: Barreto (Uruguay)

Copa América Winners

Argentina
1910, 21, 25, 27, 29,
37, 41*, 45*, 46* 47,
55, 57, 59, 91, 93

Uruguay
1916*, 17, 20, 23, 24,
26, 35*, 42, 56*, 59*,
67, 83, 87, 95

Brazil
1919, 22, 49,
89, 97, 99

Peru
1939, 75

Paraguay
1953, 79

Bolivia
1963

Colombia
2001

1979 FINAL** (2 legs)

November 28 – Defensores del Chaco,
Asunción
Paraguay 3-0 Chile
*(C. Romero 12, 65,
M. Morel 36)*
h/t: 2-0 **Att:** 40,000
Ref: Da Rosa (Uruguay)

December 5 – Nacional, Santiago
Chile 1-0 Paraguay
(Rivas 10)
h/t: 1-0 **Att:** 55,000
Ref: Barreto (Uruguay)

PLAY-OFF

December 11 – José Amalfitani, Buenos Aires
Paraguay 0-0 Chile
h/t: 0-0 **Att:** 6,000
Ref: Coelho (Brazil)
Paraguay won on goal difference

1983 FINAL**(2 legs)

October 27 – Centenario, Montevideo
Uruguay 2-0 Brazil
*(Francescoli
41 pen, Diogo 80)*
h/t: 1-0 **Att:** 65,000
Ref: Ortiz (Paraguay)

November 4 – Fonte Nova, Salvador
Brazil 1-1 Uruguay
(Jorginho 23)   (Aguilera 77)
h/t: 1-0 **Att:** 95,000
Ref: Perez (Peru)
Uruguay won 3-1 on aggregate

1987 ARGENTINA

THIRD PLACE PLAY-OFF

July 11 – Monumental, Buenos Aires
Colombia 2-1 Argentina
*(G. Gomez 8,   (Caniggia 86)
Galeano 27)*
h/t: 2-0 **Att:** 15,000
Ref: Corujo (Venezuela)

FINAL

July 12 – Monumental, Buenos Aires
Uruguay 1-0 Chile
(Bengochea 56)
h/t: 0-0 **Att:** 35,000
Ref: Romualdo Arppi (Brazil)

1989 BRAZIL

1 Brazil
2 Uruguay
3 Argentina

1991 CHILE

1 Argentina
2 Brazil
3 Chile

1993 ECUADOR

THIRD PLACE PLAY-OFF

July 3 – Reales Tamarindos, Portoviejo
Colombia 1-0 Ecuador
(Valencia 84)
h/t: 0-0 **Att:** 18,000
Ref: Arbolda (Venezuela)

FINAL

July 4 – Monumental, Guayaquil
Argentina 2-1 Mexico
(Batistuta 65, 84)   (Galindo 76 pen)
h/t: 0-0 **Att:** 40,000
Ref: Marcio Rezende (Brazil)

1995 URUGUAY

THIRD PLACE PLAY-OFF

July 22 – Campus Municipal, Maldonado
Colombia 4-1 United States
*(Quinonez 31,   (Moore 53 pen)
Valderrama 38,
Asprilla 50,
Rincon 76)*
h/t: 2-0 **Att:** 2,500
Ref: Imperatore (Chile)

FINAL

July 23 – Centenario, Montevideo
Uruguay 1-1 Brazil
(Bengoechea 48)   (Tulio 30)
(after extra time)
90 mins: 0-0 **Att:** 58,000
Ref: Brizio Carter (Mexico)
Uruguay won 5-3 on pens

1997 BOLIVIA

THIRD PLACE PLAY-OFF

June 28 – Jesús Bermúdez, Oruro
Mexico 1-0 Peru
(Hernández 82)
Ref: Borgesano (Venezuela)

FINAL

June 29 – Hernando Siles, La Paz
Brazil 3-1 Bolivia
*(Edmundo 40,   (E. Sanchez 44)
Ronaldo 79,
Ze Roberto 90)*
h/t: 1-1 **Att:** 50,000
Ref: Nieves (Uruguay)

1999 PARAGUAY

THIRD PLACE PLAY-OFF

July 17 – Defensores del Chaco, Asunción
Mexico 2-1 Chile
*(Palencia 26,   (Palacios 81)
Zepeda 86)*
Att: 4,000 **Ref:** Elizondo (Argentina)

* Unofficial.
** No fixed venues for these tournaments; matches were played home and away.

FINAL

July 18 – Defensores del Chaco, Asunción
Brazil 3-0 Uruguay
*(Rivaldo 20, 27,
Ronaldo 46)*
h/t: 2-0 **Att:** 40,000
Ref: Ruiz (Colombia)

2001 COLOMBIA

THIRD PLACE PLAY-OFF

28 July – El Campín, Bogotá
Honduras 2-2 Uruguay
*(Martínez 14, 45)   (Bizera 22,
Izaguirre 42)*
h/t: 2-2 **Att:** 47,000
Ref: Hidalgo (Peru)
Honduras won 5-4 on pens

FINAL

29 July – El Campín, Bogotá
Colombia 1-0 Mexico
(I. Cordoba 65)
h/t: 0-0 **Att:** 47,000
Ref: Aquino (Paraguay)

*The **1999 Copa América Final** between Brazil and Uruguay took place in the Defensores del Chaco stadium in Asunción, Paraguay. Brazil won 3-0 with two goals from Rivaldo and one from Ronaldo. Mexico beat Chile 2-1 in the same stadium to claim third place.*

Copa Libertadores

TOURNAMENT REVIEW 2004

IT MUST BE THE YEAR OF THE UNDERDOG when a Venezuelan team – Deportivo Táchira – can make a very rare appearance in the quarter-finals of the Copa Libertadores after dispatching former champions Uruguay's Nacional. Boca Juniors were looking to spoil the party and make it four out of five Copa Libertadores triumphs, but the cup and the season belonged to the tiny Colombian team Once Caldas. They made their way to the Final by beating Ecuador's Barcelona and then two Brazilian giants: last year's Copa runners-up Santos in the quarter-finals and then São Paulo in the semis. The Colombians proved to be very tough competitors away from home. In both away legs in Brazil Once Caldas ground out draws before stealing a goal and a victory at home.

Boca Juniors found the knockout stages just as tough. Peru's Sporting Cristal were dispensed with in the second round but Brazil's São Caetano proved tougher with Boca only squeezing through on penalties. That set Boca up for a semi-final clash with Buenos Aires opponents River Plate. In keeping with the violent and unpredictable nature of Argentinian soccer this season, the two games were disorderly affairs. Away fans were banned from both legs but the trouble merely moved onto the field. Boca just managed a 1-0 win at home in the first leg, despite two River players and one of their own being shown red cards for violent conduct. The game was held up for nearly ten minutes while both sides protested the sendings off. The second leg proved equally eventful. River held a 1-0 lead but lost the advantage as Sambueza was sent off for abusing the referee. With all their substitutes used an injury to Rojas left them with just nine men. Tevez duly equalized for Boca but his wild celebrations saw him sent off as well, leaving River the glimpse of a chance. Nastui's 90th-minute strike took the game to extra time and penalties, where Boca finally triumphed.

The Final went true to form. Once Caldas defended heroically to get a 0-0 draw in Argentina and despite the fury of Boca's attacks kept them to 1-1 in the return leg in Colombia. Boca's nerve finally shattered as they missed four penalties in a row, leaving Once Caldas with the trophy for the first time in their history.

GROUP STAGE

GROUP 1

CLUB	P	W	D	L	F	A	Pts	
América (Mexico)	6	4	1	1	11	5	13	Second Round
São Caetano (Brazil)	6	2	2	2	10	8	8	Play-off
Peñarol (Uruguay)	6	2	2	2	9	7	8	
The Strongest (Bolivia)	6	1	1	4	4	14	4	

GROUP 2

CLUB	P	W	D	L	F	A	Pts	
Once Caldas (Colombia)	6	4	1	1	11	6	13	Second Round
Unión Atlético Maracaibo (Venezuela)	6	2	2	2	10	9	8	Play-off
Vélez Sarsfield (Argentina)	6	2	1	3	7	9	7	
Fénix (Uruguay)	6	1	2	3	6	10	5	

GROUP 3

CLUB	P	W	D	L	F	A	Pts	
Cruzeiro (Brazil)	6	4	1	1	15	6	13	Second Round
Santos Laguna (Mexico)	6	3	3	0	10	6	12	Second Round
Caracas FC (Venezuela)	6	2	0	4	8	12	6	
Universidad de Concepción (Chile)	6	0	2	4	7	16	2	

GROUP 4

CLUB	P	W	D	L	F	A	Pts	
São Paulo (Brazil)	6	5	0	1	11	7	15	Second Round
LDU (Ecuador)	6	4	0	2	13	3	12	Second Round
Alianza Lima (Peru)	6	3	0	3	6	8	9	
Cobreloa (Chile)	6	0	0	6	3	15	0	

GROUP 5

CLUB	P	W	D	L	F	A	Pts	
Nacional (Uruguay)	6	3	3	0	7	4	12	Second Round
Independiente (Argentina)	6	2	2	2	9	7	8	Play-off
Cienciano (Peru)	6	2	1	3	10	12	7	
El Nacional (Ecuador)	6	1	2	3	6	9	5	

GROUP 6

CLUB	P	W	D	L	F	A	Pts	
River Plate (Argentina)	6	3	2	1	10	6	11	Second Round
Deportivo Táchira (Venezuela)	6	2	4	0	8	4	10	Second Round
Deportes Tolima (Colombia)	6	1	2	3	6	9	5	
Libertad (Paraguay)	6	1	2	3	5	10	5	

GROUP 7

CLUB	P	W	D	L	F	A	Pts	
Santos (Brazil)	6	5	1	0	16	6	16	Second Round
Barcelona (Ecuador)	6	2	2	2	9	6	8	Play-off
Guaraní (Paraguay)	6	1	3	2	6	7	6	
Jorge Wilstermann (Bolivia)	6	0	2	4	5	17	2	

GROUP 8

CLUB	P	W	D	L	F	A	Pts	
Boca Juniors (Argentina)	6	4	0	2	10	4	12	Second Round
Deportivo Cali (Colombia)	6	3	0	3	9	9	9	Second Round
Bolívar (Bolivia)	6	3	0	3	7	9	9	
Colo Colo (Chile)	6	2	0	4	6	10	6	

GROUP 9

CLUB	P	W	D	L	F	A	Pts	
Sporting Cristal (Peru)	6	3	1	2	13	9	10	Second Round
Rosario Central (Argentina)	6	3	1	2	8	8	10	Second Round
Coritiba (Brazil)	6	2	2	2	7	8	8	
Olimpia (Paraguay)	6	1	2	3	7	10	5	

Venezuela on the up: Deportivo Táchira (right) were unbeaten in the Group Stage of this year's competition but fell to the Brazilians São Paulo in the quarter-finals.

COPA LIBERTADORES

WORST RUNNERS-UP PLAY-OFF

São Caetano **2-2** Independiente
São Caetano won 4-2 on pens
São Caetano proceed to Second Round

Barcelona **6-1** Unión Atlético Maracaibo
Barcelona proceed to Second Round

SECOND ROUND (2 legs)

São Caetano **2-1** América
América **1-1** São Caetano
São Caetano won 3-2 on aggregate

Barcelona **0-0** Once Caldas
Once Caldas **1-1** Barcelona
Once Caldas won 4-2 on pens

Deportivo Cali **1-0** Cruzeiro
Cruzeiro **2-1** Deportivo Cali
Deportivo Cali won 3-0 on pens

Rosario Central **1-0** São Paulo
São Paulo **2-1** Rosario Central
São Paulo won 5-4 on pens

Deportivo Táchira **3-0** Nacional
Nacional **2-2** Deportivo Táchira
Deportivo Táchira won 5-2 on aggregate

Santos Laguna **0-1** River Plate
River Plate **1-2** Santos Laguna
River Plate won 4-2 on pens

LDU **4-2** Santos
Santos **2-0** LDU
Santos won 5-3 on pens

Sporting Cristal **2-3** Boca Juniors
Boca Juniors **2-1** Sporting Cristal
Boca Juniors won 5-3 on aggregate

QUARTER-FINALS (2 legs)

São Paulo **3-0** Deportivo Táchira
Deportivo Táchira **1-4** São Paulo
São Paulo won 7-1 on aggregate

Santos **1-1** Once Caldas
Once Caldas **1-0** Santos
Once Caldas won 2-1 on aggregate

River Plate **1-0** Deportivo Cali
Deportivo Cali **1-3** River Plate
River Plate won 4-1 on aggregate

São Caetano **0-0** Boca Juniors
Boca Juniors **1-1** São Caetano
Boca Juniors won 4-3 on pens

SEMI-FINALS (2 legs)

São Paulo **0-0** Once Caldas
Once Caldas **2-1** São Paulo
Once Caldas won 2-1 on aggregate

Boca Juniors **1-0** River Plate
River Plate **2-1** Boca Juniors
Boca Juniors won 5-4 on pens

2004 FINAL (2 legs)

June 23 – La Bombonera, Buenos Aires
Boca Juniors **0-0** Once Caldas
(Argentina)   (Colombia)
h/t: 0-0 **Att:** 58,000
Ref: Mendez (Uruguay)

June 30 – Palogrande, Manizales
Once Caldas **1-1** Boca Juniors
(Viafara 7)   (Burdisso 51)
(after extra time)
h/t: 1-0 **90 mins:** 1-1
Att: 40,000 **Ref:** Chandia (Chile)
Once Caldas won 2-0 on penalties

Below: América fans scale the fences and breach the moat during their Second Round match against Brazil's São Caetano at the Azteca Stadium in Mexico City.

Right: The result? América and Toluca play in an empty Azteca Stadium. As punishment for the trouble against São Caetano, América were ordered to play their home games behind closed doors.

Boca and River players were involved in an almighty 8-minute scuffle during their semi-final encounter.

Top Goalscorers 2004

PLAYER	CLUB	GOALS
Luis Fabiano	Sao Paulo	8
Fernando Cavenaghi	River Plate	6

Above: Once Caldas Campeón. The team celebrate with the Copa Libertadores trophy after beating Boca Juniors in the Final.

Above left: Rolando Schiavi of Boca Juniors (in blue) climbs above Jorge Agudelo of Once Caldas during the first leg of the Final in Buenos Aires.

Copa Libertadores

COPA LIBERTADORES

TOURNAMENT OVERVIEW

SOUTH AMERICA'S first international club competition was held in 1948 in Chile, staged by Santiago's leading club Colo Colo. The winners were Brazil's Vasco da Gama, but the event proved a financial disaster and was not repeated. But by the late 1950s the success of UEFA's European Cup and the offer of a World Club Cup between European and South American champions spurred clubs and federations into action. The Copa Libertadores was launched at a meeting in Montevideo in 1960.

The opening match was played in April 1960 between San Lorenzo and Bahia ending in a 3-0 win for the home side. San Lorenzo went on to meet the eventual winners, Peñarol, of Montevideo. The format was so popular with the Uruguayan crowds that San Lorenzo played both legs of the tie in Montevideo. Peñarol beat Olimpia of Paraguay to take the title and then beat Palmeiras to win again in 1961. Peñarol were the Real Madrid of the Copa Libertadores – the team that recognized and reaped the massive commercial potential of the new tournament.

Shifting power base

But when Peñarol's reign was terminated in 1962 by Pele's Santos, the tournament suddenly acquired glamour. In the Final, Santos had won 2-1 at Peñarol. But just after half-time in the return leg, Peñarol led 3-2. A stone thrown from the crowd knocked the referee unconscious and the game was suspended for an hour. At the restart what appeared to be a Santos equalizer was ruled out when the linesman was also knocked unconscious. The game finally finished after almost three and a half hours, and after much wrangling the score was left 3-2 to Peñarol. In a play-off at the Monumental in Buenos Aires Santos won 3-0.

The shifting power base of South American club soccer can be traced through the Copa Libertadores results. Following Santos' second win (1963), the cup stayed with Uruguayan and Argentinian teams until Cruzeiro's victory in 1976. Argentinian teams dominated the 1980s, but in the 1990s Brazilian clubs regained their prowess. In recent years Boca Juniors has been undisputed master of the Copa Libertadores, winning three of the last five tournaments.

Racing Club of Argentina won its only Copa Libertadores in 1967, beating Nacional of Uruguay in the Final. Its line-up featured Raffo (front row, far right) whose 14 goals made him the tournament's leading scorer that year.

Copa Libertadores – Top Goalscorers (1960–2004)

YEAR	SCORER	TEAM	COUNTRY	GOALS
1960	Spencer	Peñarol	Uruguay	7
1961	Panzutto	Independiente Santa Fé	Colombia	4
1962	Spencer	Peñarol	Uruguay	6
	Coutinho	Santos	Brazil	
	Raymondi	Emelec	Ecuador	
1963	Sanfillipo	Boca Juniors	Argentina	7
1964	Rodríguez	Independiente	Argentina	6
1965	Pelé	Santos	Brazil	8
1966	Onega	River Plate	Argentina	17
1967	Raffo	Racing Club	Argentina	14
1968	Tupãzinho	Palmeiras	Brazil	11
1969	Ferrero	Santiago Wanderers	Chile	8
1970	Bertocchi	Liga Universitaria Quito	Ecuador	9
	Mas	River Plate	Argentina	
1971	Castronovo	Peñarol	Uruguay	10
	Artime	Nacional	Uruguay	
1972	Toninho	São Paulo	Brazil	6
	Cubillas	Alianza Lima	Peru	
	Rojas	Alianza Lima	Peru	
	Ramírez	Universitario de Deportes	Peru	
1973	Caszely	Colo Colo	Chile	9
1974	Morena	Peñarol	Uruguay	7
	Terto	São Paulo	Brazil	
	Rocha	São Paulo	Brazil	
1975	Morena	Peñarol	Uruguay	8
	Ramírez	Universitario de Deportes	Peru	
1976	Palhinha*	Cruzeiro	Brazil	13
1977	Scotta	Deportivo Cali	Colombia	5
	Silva	Portuguesa FC	Venezuela	
1978	Scotta	Deportivo Cali	Colombia	8
	La Rosa	Alianza Lima	Peru	
1979	Miltão	Guaraní	Brazil	6
	Oré	Universitario de Deportes	Peru	
1980	Victorino	Nacional	Uruguay	6
1981	Zico	Flamengo	Brazil	11
1982	Morena	Peñarol	Uruguay	7
1983	Luzardo	Nacional	Uruguay	8
1984	Tita	Flamengo	Brazil	8
1985	Sánchez	Blooming	Bolivia	11
1986	De Lima	Deportivo	Ecuador	9
1987	Gareca	América de Cali	Colombia	7
1988	Iguarán	Millonarios	Colombia	5
1989	Aguillera	Peñarol	Uruguay	10
	Amarilla	Olimpia	Paraguay	
1990	Samaniego	Olimpia	Paraguay	7
1991	Gaúcho	Flamengo	Brazil	8
1992	Palhinha**	São Paulo	Brazil	7
1993	Almada	Universidad Católica	Chile	9
1994	Rivas	Minervén	Venezuela	7
1995	Jardel	Grêmio	Brazil	12
1996	De Ávila	América de Cali	Colombia	11
1997	Acosta	Universidad Católica	Chile	11
1998	Sergio João	Bolívar	Bolivia	10
1999	Bonilla	Deportivo Cali	Colombia	6
	Baiano	Corinthians	Brazil	
	Gauchinho	Cerro Porteño	Paraguay	
	Morán	Estudiantes de Mérida	Venezuela	
	Sosa	Nacional	Uruguay	
	Zapata	Deportivo Cali	Colombia	
2000	Luizão	Corinthians	Brazil	14
2001	Lopes	Palmeiras	Brazil	9
2002	Mendes	Grêmio	Brazil	10
2003	Oliveira	Santos	Brazil	9
	Delgado	Boca Juniors	Argentina	
2004	Fabiano	São Paulo	Brazil	8

* Wanderlei Eustáquio de Oliveira. ** Jorge Ferreira da Silva

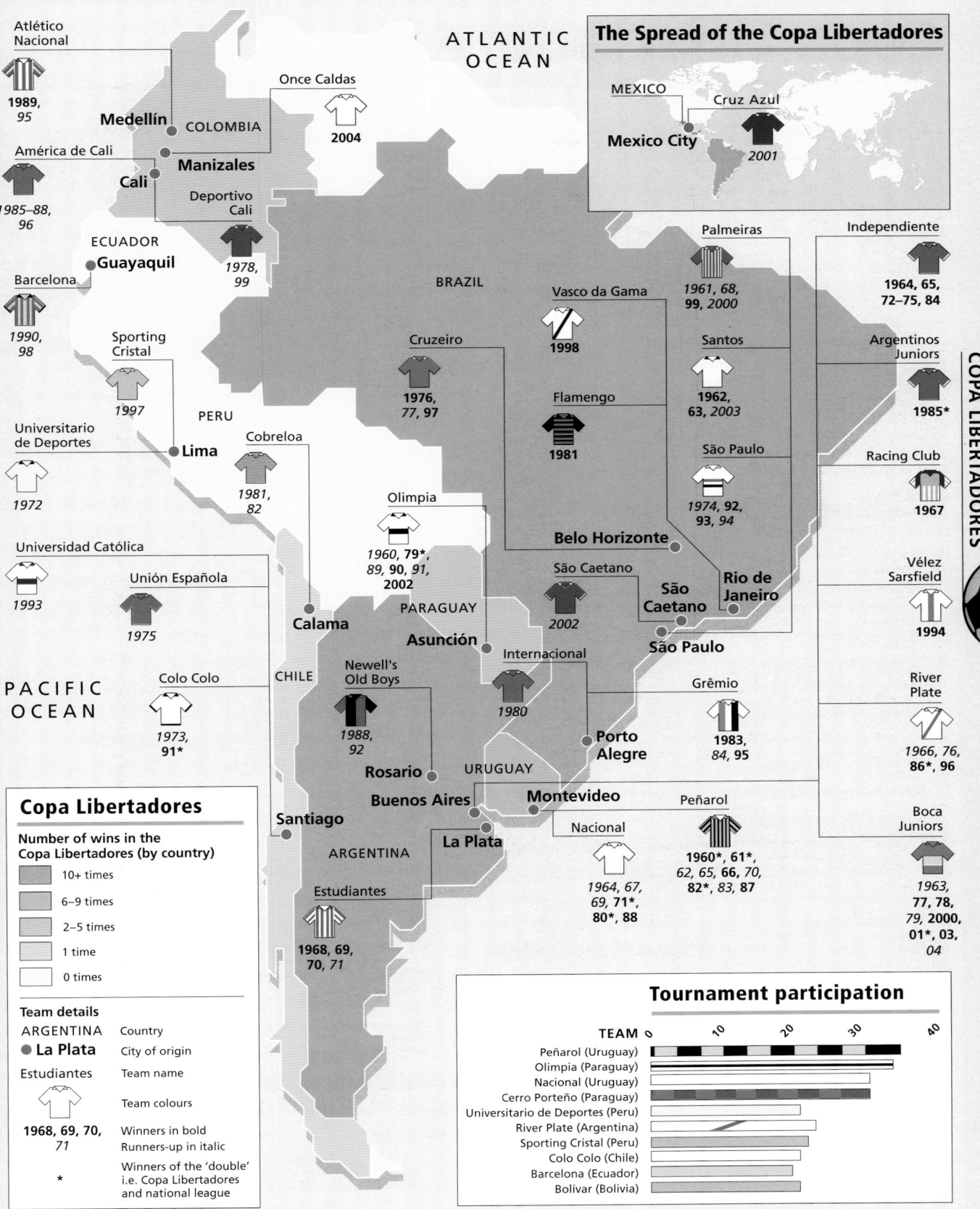

ATLANTIC OCEAN

Atlético Nacional
1989, *95*
Medellín

COLOMBIA

Once Caldas
2004

América de Cali
1985–88, *96*
Cali

Manizales

Deportivo Cali
1978, *99*

ECUADOR
Guayaquil

Barcelona
1990, *98*

Sporting Cristal
1997

PERU

Universitario de Deportes
1972

Lima

Cobreloa
1981, *82*

Universidad Católica
1993

Unión Española
1975

PACIFIC OCEAN

Colo Colo
1973, **91***

CHILE

Calama

Newell's Old Boys
1988, *92*

Rosario

Santiago

ARGENTINA

Buenos Aires

La Plata

Estudiantes
1968, 69, 70, *71*

BRAZIL

Cruzeiro
1976, 77, 97

Vasco da Gama
1998

Flamengo
1981

Olimpia
1960, **79***, **89, 90, 91, 2002**

Asunción

PARAGUAY

Belo Horizonte

São Caetano
2002

São Caetano

Internacional
1980

Grêmio
1983, *84*, **95**

Porto Alegre

URUGUAY

Montevideo

Nacional
1964, 67, 69, **71***, *80***, **88**

Palmeiras
1961, 68, 99, *2000*

Santos
1962, 63, *2003*

São Paulo
1974, 92, 93, 94

São Paulo

Rio de Janeiro

Peñarol
1960*, **61***, **62, 65, 66**, *70*, **82***, *83*, **87**

Independiente
1964, 65, 72–75, 84

Argentinos Juniors
1985*

Racing Club
1967

Vélez Sarsfield
1994

River Plate
1966, 76, 86*, *96*

Boca Juniors
1963, 77, 78, *79*, **2000**, *01***, *03, 04*

COPA LIBERTADORES

Copa Libertadores

Number of wins in the Copa Libertadores (by country)

- 10+ times
- 6–9 times
- 2–5 times
- 1 time
- 0 times

Team details

ARGENTINA	Country
● **La Plata**	City of origin
Estudiantes	Team name
	Team colours
1968, 69, 70, *71*	Winners in bold / Runners-up in italic
*	Winners of the 'double' i.e. Copa Libertadores and national league

Tournament participation

TEAM	0	10	20	30	40
Peñarol (Uruguay)					
Olimpia (Paraguay)					
Nacional (Uruguay)					
Cerro Porteño (Paraguay)					
Universitario de Deportes (Peru)					
River Plate (Argentina)					
Sporting Cristal (Peru)					
Colo Colo (Chile)					
Barcelona (Ecuador)					
Bolívar (Bolivia)					

Copa Libertadores

THE COPA LIBERTADORES is the oldest and most prestigious South American international club championship. When first played, in 1960, it was contested by national champions in a knockout competition with matches played over two legs. From 1962, it consisted of three mini-leagues of three to decide three semi-finalists to meet the previous year's champions. In 1968, it expanded to 20 teams with two places allocated to each member of CONMEBOL. Five leagues of four produced eight quarter-finalists who met the previous year's champion in three further mini-leagues of three. In 1988, the format switched to two-leg knockouts for the quarter-finals, semi-finals and Final. The Final is now determined by aggregate scores, but had, until 1988, been determined by aggregate points over the final matches. Extra time and penalties are used to decide tied fixtures.

Each nation chooses its own method of filling its two places in the competition; for example, in Uruguay, the top six clubs play an end-of-season mini-league, while in Chile one place goes to the national champion and a second to the winner of a play-off among the next four teams in the league.

1960 FINAL (2 legs)
June 12 – Centenario, Montevideo
Peñarol 1-0 Olimpia
(Uruguay) (Paraguay)
(Spencer 79)

June 19 – Sajonia, Asunción
Olimpia 1-1 Peñarol
(Recalde 28) (Cubilla 83)
Peñarol won on points aggregate

1961 FINAL (2 legs)
June 9 – Centenario, Montevideo
Peñarol 1-0 Palmeiras
(Uruguay) (Brazil)
(Spencer 89)

June 11 – Pacaembú, São Paulo
Palmeiras 1-1 Peñarol
(Nardo 77) (Sasia 2)
Peñarol won on points aggregate

1962 FINAL (2 legs)
July 28 – Centenario, Montevideo
Peñarol 1-2 Santos
(Uruguay) (Brazil)
(Spencer 18) (Coutinho 29, 70)

Aug 2 – Villa Belmiro, Santos
Santos 2-3 Peñarol
(Dorval 27, (Spencer 73,
Mengalvio 50) Sasia 18, 48)

PLAY-OFF
Aug 30 – Monumental, Buenos Aires
Santos 3-0 Peñarol
(Coutinho 11
Pele 48, 89)

1963 FINAL (2 legs)
September 3 – Maracaná, Rio de Janeiro
Santos 3-2 Boca Juniors
(Brazil) (Argentina)
(Coutinho 2, 21, (Sanfilippo
Lima 28) 43, 89)

September 11 – La Bombonera, Buenos Aires
Boca Juniors 1-2 Santos
(Sanfilippo 46) (Coutinho 50,
Pele 82)
Santos won on points aggregate

1964 FINAL (2 legs)
Aug 6 – Centenario, Montevideo
Nacional 0-0 Independiente
(Uruguay) (Argentina)

Aug 12 – La Doble Visera, Avellaneda
Independiente 1-0 Nacional
(Rodriguez 35)

Independiente won
on points aggregate

1965 FINAL (2 legs)
April 9 – La Doble Visera, Avellaneda
Independiente 1-0 Peñarol
(Argentina) (Uruguay)
(Bernao 83)

April 12 – Centenario, Montevideo
Peñarol 3-1 Independiente
(Goncalves 14, (De la Mata 88)
Reznik 43,
Rocha 46)

PLAY-OFF
April 15 – Estadio Nacional, Santiago
Independiente 4-1 Peñarol
(Acevedo 10, (De la Mata 88)
Bernao 27,
Avallay 33,
Mura 82)

1966 FINAL (2 legs)
May 12 – Centenario, Montevideo
Peñarol 2-0 River Plate
(Uruguay) (Argentina)
(Abaddie 75,
Joya 85)

May 18 – Monumental, Buenos Aires
River Plate 3-2 Peñarol
(D. Onega 38, (Rocha 32,
Sarnari 52, Spencer 50)
E. Onega 73)

PLAY-OFF
May 20 – Estadio Nacional, Santiago
Peñarol 4-2 River Plate
(Spencer 57, 101, (D. Onega 37,
Abbadie 72, Solari 42)
Rocha 109)

(after extra time)

1967 FINAL (2 legs)
August 15 – Mozart Y Cuyo, Avellaneda
Racing Club 0-0 Nacional
(Argentina) (Uruguay)

August 25 – Centenario, Montevideo
Nacional 0-0 Racing Club

PLAY-OFF
August 29 – Estadio Nacional, Santiago
Racing Club 2-1 Nacional
(Cardozo 14, (Esparrago 79)
Raffo 43)

1968 FINAL (2 legs)
May 2 – La Plata, La Plata
Estudiantes 2-1 Palmeiras
(Argentina) (Brazil)
(Veron 83, (Servillio 50)
Flores 87)

May 7 – Pacaembú, São Paulo
Palmeiras 3-1 Estudiantes
(Tupazinho 10, 68, (Veron 72)
Reinaldo 54)

PLAY-OFF
May 15 – Centenario, Montevideo
Estudiantes 2-0 Palmeiras
(Ribaudo 13,
Veron 82)

1969 FINAL (2 legs)
May 15 – Centenario, Montevideo
Nacional 0-1 Estudiantes
(Uruguay) (Argentina)
(Flores 66)

May 22 – La Plata, La Plata
Estudiantes 2-0 Nacional
(Flores 31, (Veron 72)
Conigliaro 37)
Estudiantes won on points aggregate

1970 FINAL (2 legs)
May 21 – La Plata, La Plata
Estudiantes 1-0 Peñarol
(Uruguay) (Argentina)
(Togneri 87)

June 2 – Centenario, Montevideo
Peñarol 0-0 Estudiantes
Estudiantes won on points aggregate

1971 FINAL (2 legs)
May 26 – La Plata, La Plata
Estudiantes 1-0 Nacional
(Uruguay) (Argentina)
(Romeo 60)

June 2 – Centenario, Montevideo
Nacional 1-0 Estudiantes
(Masnik 17)

PLAY-OFF
June 9 – Estadio Nacional, Lima
Nacional 2-0 Estudiantes
(Esparrago 22,
Artime 65)

1972 FINAL (2 legs)
May 17 – Estadio Nacional, Lima
Universitario 0-0 Independiente
de Deportes (Argentina)
(Peru)

May 24 – Cordero, Avellaneda
Independiente 2-1 Universitario
(Maglioni 6, 60) **de Deportes**
(Rojas 79)
Independiente won on points aggregate

1973 FINAL (2 legs)
May 22 – Cordero, Avellaneda
Independiente 1-1 Colo Colo
(Argentina) (Chile)
(Mendoza 75) (Caszely 71)

May 29 – Estadio Nacional, Santiago
Colo Colo 0-0 Independiente

PLAY-OFF
June 6 – Centenario, Montevideo
Independiente 2-1 Colo Colo
(Mendoza 25, (Caszely 39)
Giachello 107)

1974 FINAL (2 legs)
October 12 – Pacaembú, São Paulo
São Paulo 2-1 Independiente
(Brazil) (Argentina)
(Rocha 48, (Saggioratto 28)
Mirandinha 50)

October 16 – Cordero, Avellaneda
Independiente 2-0 São Paulo
(Bochini 34,
Balbuena 48)

PLAY-OFF
October 19 – Estadio Nacional, Santiago
Independiente 1-0 São Paulo
(Pavoni 37)

1975 FINAL (2 legs)
June 18 – Estadio Nacional, Santiago
Unión Española 1-0 Independiente
(Chile) (Argentina)
(Ahumada 87)

June 25 – Cordero, Avellaneda
Independiente 3-1 Unión Española
(Rojas 1, (Las Heras 56)
Pavoni 58,
Bertoni 83)

PLAY-OFF
June 29 – Defensores del Chaco, Asunción
Independiente 2-0 Unión Española
(Ruiz Moreno 29,
Bertoni 65)

1976 FINAL (2 legs)
July 21 – Mineirão, Belo Horizonte
Cruzeiro 4-1 River Plate
(Brazil) (Argentina)
(Nelinho 22, (Mas 62)
Palinha 29, 40,
Waldo 80)

July 28 – Monumental, Buenos Aires
River Plate 2-1 Cruzeiro
(J.J. Lopez 10, (Palinha 48)
Gonzalez 76)

PLAY-OFF
July 30 – Estadio Nacional, Santiago
Cruzeiro 3-2 River Plate
(Nelinho 24, (Mas 59,
Ronaldo 55, Urquiza 64)
Joazinho 88)

1977 FINAL (2 legs)
September 6 – La Bombonera, Buenos Aires
Boca Juniors 1-0 Cruzeiro
(Argentina) (Brazil)
(Veglio 3)

September 11 – Mineirão, Belo Horizonte
Cruzeiro 1-0 Boca Juniors
(Nelinho 76)

PLAY-OFF

September 14 – Centenario, Montevideo
Cruzeiro 0-0 Boca Juniors
Boca Juniors won 5-4 on pens

1978 FINAL (2 legs)

November 23 – Pascual Guerrero, Cali
Deportivo Cali 0-0 Boca Juniors
(Colombia)   (Argentina)

November 28 – La Bombonera, Buenos Aires
Boca Juniors 4-0 Deportivo Cali
(Perotti 15, 85
Mastrangelo 60
Salinas 71)
Boca Juniors won on points aggregate

1979 FINAL (2 legs)

July 22 – Defensores del Chaco, Asunción
Olimpia 2-0 Boca Juniors
(Paraguay)   (Argentina)
(Aquino 3
Piazza 27)

July 27 – La Bombonera, Buenos Aires
Boca Juniors 0-0 Olimpia
Olimpia won on points aggregate

1980 FINAL (2 legs)

July 30 – Biera Rio, Porto Alegre
Internacional 0-0 Nacional
(Brazil)   (Uruguay)

August 6 – Centenario, Montevideo
Nacional 1-0 Internacional
(Victorino 35)
Nacional won on points aggregate

1981 FINAL (2 legs)

November 13 – Maracanã, Rio de Janeiro
Flamengo 2-1 Cobreloa
(Brazil)   (Chile)
(Zico 12, 30)   (Merello 65)

November 20 – Estadio Nacional, Santiago
Cobreloa 1-0 Flamengo
(Merello 79)

PLAY-OFF

November 23 – Centenario, Montevideo
Flamengo 2-0 Cobreloa
(Zico 18, 79)

1982 FINAL (2 legs)

November 26 – Centenario, Montevideo
Peñarol 0-0 Cobreloa
(Uruguay)   (Chile)

November 30 – Estadio Nacional, Santiago
Cobreloa 0-1 Peñarol
(Morena 89)
Peñarol won on points aggregate

1983 FINAL (2 legs)

July 22 – Centenario, Montevideo
Peñarol 1-1 Grêmio
(Uruguay)   (Brazil)
(Morena 35)   (Tita 12)

July 28 – Olimpico, Porto Alegre
Grêmio 2-1 Peñarol
(Caio 9,   (Morena 70)
Cesar 87)
Grêmio won on points aggregate

1984 FINAL (2 legs)

July 24 – Olimpico, Porto Alegre
Grêmio 0-1 Independiente
(Brazil)   (Argentina)
(Burruchaga 24)

July 27 – Cordero, Avellaneda
Independiente 0-0 Grêmio
Independiente won on points aggregate

1985 FINAL (2 legs)

October 17 – La Bombonera, Buenos Aires
Argentinos 1-0 América de Cali
Juniors   (Colombia)
(Argentina)
(Comisso 40)

October 22 – Pascual Guerrero, Cali
América de Cali 1-0 Argentinos
(Ortiz 3)   **Juniors**

PLAY-OFF

October 24 – Defensores del Chaco, Asunción
Argentinos 1-1 América de Cali
Juniors   *(Gareca 42)*
(Comisso 37)
Argentinos Juniors won 5-4 on pens

1986 FINAL (2 legs)

October 22 – Pascual Guerrero, Cali
América de Cali 1-2 River Plate
(Colombia)   (Argentina)
(Cabanas 47)   (Funes 22,
Alonso 25)

October 29 – Monumental, Buenos Aires
River Plate 1-0 América de Cali
(Funes 70)
River Plate won on points aggregate

1987 FINAL (2 legs)

October 21 – Pascual Guerrero, Cali
América de Cali 2-0 Peñarol
(Colombia)   (Uruguay)
(Battaglia 21,
Cabanas 35)

October 28 – Centenario, Montevideo
Peñarol 2-1 América de Cali
(Aguirre 58,   (Cabanas 19)
Villar 86)

PLAY-OFF

October 31 – Estadio Nacional, Santiago
Peñarol 1-0 América de Cali
(Aguirre 119)

1988 FINAL (2 legs)

October 19 – Parque de la Independencia, Rosario
Newell's 1-0 Nacional
Old Boys   (Uruguay)
(Argentina)
(Gabrich 60)

October 26 – Centenario, Montevideo
Nacional 3-0 Newell's
(Vargas 10,   **Old Boys**
Ostolaza 30,
De Leon 81)
Nacional won 3-1 on aggregate

1989 FINAL (2 legs)

May 24 – El Bosque, Asunción
Olimpia 2-0 Atlético
(Paraguay)   **Nacional**
(Bobadilla 36,   (Colombia)
Sanabria 60)

May 31 – El Campin, Bogotá
Atlético 2-0 Olimpia
Nacional
(Amarilla 46,
Usurriaga 64)
Atlético Nacional won 5-4 on pens

1990 FINAL (2 legs)

October 3 – El Bosque, Asunción
Olimpia 2-0 Barcelona
(Paraguay)   (Ecuador)
(Amarilla 47,
Samaniego 65)

October 10 – Modelo, Guayaquil
Barcelona 1-1 Olimpia
(Trobbiani 61)   (Amarilla 80)
Olimpia won 3-1 on aggregate

1991 FINAL (2 legs)

May 29 – Defensores del Chaco, Asunción
Olimpia 0-0 Colo Colo
(Paraguay)   (Chile)

June 5 – Estadio Nacional, Santiago
Colo Colo 3-0 Olimpia
(Perez 13, 18,
Herrera 85)
Colo Colo won 3-0 on aggregate

1992 FINAL (2 legs)

June 10 – Parque de la Independencia, Rosario
Newell's 1-0 São Paulo
Old Boys   (Brazil)
(Argentina)
(Berizzo 38)

June 17 – Pacaembú, São Paulo
São Paulo 1-0 Newell's
(Rai 65)   **Old Boys**
São Paulo won 3-2 on pens

1993 FINAL (2 legs)

May 19 – Pacaembú, São Paulo
São Paulo 5-1 Universidad
(Brazil)   **Católica**
(Lopez o.g. 31,   (Chile)
Dinho 41,   (Almada 85 pen)
Gilmar 55,
Rai 61,
Muller 65)

May 26 – San Carlos de Aponquindo, Santiago
Universidad 2-0 São Paulo
Católica
(Lunari 9,
Almada 16 pen)
São Paulo won 5-3 on aggregate

1994 FINAL (2 legs)

August 24 – José Amalfitani, Buenos Aires
Vélez Sarsfield 1-0 São Paulo
(Argentina)   (Brazil)
(Asad 35)

August 31 – Pacaembú, São Paulo
São Paulo 1-0 Vélez Sarsfield
(Muller 32 pen)
Vélez Sarsfield won 5-3 on pens

1995 FINAL (2 legs)

August 24 – Olimpico, Porto Alegre
Grêmio 3-1 Atlético
(Brazil)   **Nacional**
(Marulanda o.g.   (Colombia)
36, Jardel 40,   (Angel 71)
Paulo Nunes 56)

August 30 – Atanasio Girardot, Medellín
Atlético 1-1 Grêmio
Nacional   *(Dinho 85)*
(Aristizabal 13)
Grêmio won 4-2 on aggregate

1996 FINAL (2 legs)

June 19 – Pascual Guerrero, Cali
América de Cali 1-0 River Plate
(Colombia)   (Argentina)
(De Avila 72)

June 26 – Monumental, Buenos Aires
River Plate 2-0 América de Cali
(Crespo 7, 14)
River Plate won 2-1 on aggregate

1997 FINAL (2 legs)

August 6 – San Martin de Porres, Lima
Sporting Cristal 0-0 Cruzeiro
(Peru)   (Brazil)

August 13 – Mineirão, Belo Horizonte
Cruzeiro 1-0 Sporting Cristal
(Elivelton 75)
Cruzeiro won 1-0 on aggregate

1998 FINAL (2 legs)

August 12 – São Januario, Rio de Janeiro
Vasco da Gama 2-0 Barcelona
(Brazil)   (Ecuador)
(Donizete 7,
Luizao 33)

August 26 – Monumental Isidro Romero, Guayquil
Barcelona 1-2 Vasco da Gama
(De Avila 79)   (Luizao 24,
Donizete 45)
Vasco da Gama won 4-1 on aggregate

1999 FINAL (2 legs)

June 2 – Pascual Guerrero, Cali
Deportivo Cali 1-0 Palmeiras
(Colombia)   (Brazil)
(Bonilla 42)

June 16 – Morumbi, São Paulo
Palmeiras 2-0 Deportivo Cali
(Evair 63 pen,   (Zapata 69 pen)
Oseas 75)
Palmeiras won 2-1 on aggregate

2000 FINAL (2 legs)

June 14 – La Bombonera, Buenos Aires
Boca Juniors 2-2 Palmeiras
(Argentina)   (Brazil)
(Arruabarrena   (Pena 43,
22, 61)   Euller 63)

June 21 – Parque Antarctica, São Paulo
Palmeiras 0-0 Boca Juniors
Boca Juniors won 4-2 on pens

2001 FINAL (2 legs)

June 20 – Azteca, Mexico City
Cruz Azul 0-1 Boca Juniors
(Mexico)   (Argentina)
(Delgado 79)

June 28 – La Bombonera, Buenos Aires
Boca Juniors 0-1 Cruz Azul
(Palencia 45)
Boca Juniors won 3-1 on pens

2002 FINAL (2 legs)

July 24 – Defensores del Chaco, Asunción
Olimpia 0-1 São Caetano
(Paraguay)   (Brazil)
(Ailton 61)

July 31 – Pacaembú, São Paulo
São Caetano 1-2 Olimpia
(Ailton 31)   (Córdoba 49,
Báez 58)
Olimpia won 4-2 on pens

2003 FINAL (2 legs)

June 25 – La Bombonera, Buenos Aires
Boca Juniors 2-0 Santos
(Argentina)   (Brazil)
(Delgado 32, 83)

July 2 – Morumbi, São Paulo
Santos 1-3 Boca Juniors
(Alex 70)   (Tevez 21,
Delgado 84,
Schiavi 95 pen)
Boca Juniors won 5-1 on aggregate

2004 FINAL (2 legs)

June 23 – La Bombonera, Buenos Aires
Boca Juniors 0-0 Once Caldas
(Argentina)   (Colombia)

June 30 – Palogrande, Manizales
Once Caldas 1-1 Boca Juniors
(Viafara 7)   (Burdisso 51)
(after extra time)
Once Caldas won 2-0 on penalties

COPA LIBERTADORES

Colombia

THE SEASON IN REVIEW 2003

IN THE APERTURA the small provincial team from Manizales, Once Caldas, made the running and took the championship and a place in the Copa Libertadores for 2004. Colombia's representatives in the 2003 edition of the tournament, América and Independiente Medellín, fielded virtually reserve sides in their domestic games. It almost paid off as both made it to the semi-finals. América was able to stay with the pace, but the strategy kept Independiente out of the play-offs.

The surprise of the season was newly promoted Centauros Villavicencio who opened with a six-game unbeaten run and qualified for the play-offs at its first attempt. Demand for tickets was so great that the Second Phase game against Millonarios, which Centauros won 3-1, was a lockout. The Final saw Once Caldas beat Atlético Júnior by a single goal over three hours and take the team's first championship for 54 years.

Records fall

The Clausura was overshadowed by Atlético Júnior's last-day qualification for the play-offs; two celebrating fans hurtled to their deaths as a stand collapsed beneath them; 34 were injured. Records were broken, as Deportes Quindío's Ivan Valenciano became Colombia's highest-ever league scorer with over 213 goals. Atlético Huila's Fernando Uribe became, at 15 years and 3 months, the league's youngest-ever scorer. Neither removed their shirts when celebrating as the Colombian authorities, under sponsor pressure, had banned the practice – as heaven forbid sponsors' logos were being hidden at the most important moments of the game.

The Final saw Deportivo Cali take on Tolima. Tolima, along with Quindío, had been contemplating leaving the league at the beginning of the season such was the club's financial situation, but the team sensationally recovered to win its first-ever championship on penalties after a tied play-off Final.

Colombian Apertura League Table 2003

CLUB	P	W	D	L	F	A	Pts	
Once Caldas	18	10	5	3	26	15	**35**	Qualified for Second Phase
CD Millonarios	18	8	7	3	23	14	**31**	Qualified for Second Phase
América de Cali	18	8	7	3	31	23	**31**	Qualified for Second Phase
Centauros Villavicencio	18	7	8	3	24	21	**29**	Qualified for Second Phase
Deportivo Cali	18	8	4	6	27	23	**28**	Qualified for Second Phase
Atlético Júnior	18	8	3	7	19	18	**27**	Qualified for Second Phase
Unión Magdalena	18	7	5	6	22	22	**26**	Qualified for Second Phase
Deportes Pereira	18	7	5	6	22	25	**26**	Qualified for Second Phase
Atlético Huila	18	6	8	4	22	22	**26**	
CD Independiente Medellín	18	7	4	7	29	23	**25**	
Atlético Bucaramanga	18	6	7	5	21	20	**25**	
Deportes Tolima	18	6	4	8	24	24	**22**	
Envigado FC	18	6	4	8	20	23	**22**	
Atlético Nacional	18	6	2	10	17	20	**20**	
Deportivo Pasto	18	4	7	7	15	18	**19**	
Independiente Santa Fe	18	5	3	10	15	23	**18**	
Corporación Tuluá	18	3	8	7	17	25	**17**	
Deportes Quindío	18	3	4	11	13	28	**13**	

Second Phase – Group A

CLUB	P	W	D	L	F	A	Pts	
Once Caldas	6	4	2	0	14	3	**14**	Qualified for Final
Deportivo Cali	6	3	2	1	10	5	**11**	
América de Cali	6	2	0	4	6	12	**6**	
Unión Magdalena	6	0	2	4	3	13	**2**	

Second Phase – Group B

CLUB	P	W	D	L	F	A	Pts	
Atlético Júnior	6	4	0	2	9	5	**12**	Qualified for Final
Deportes Pereira	6	3	0	3	9	7	**9**	
CD Millonarios	6	2	1	3	7	9	**7**	
Centauros Villavicencio	6	2	1	3	5	9	**7**	

Apertura Championship Play-off

2003 FINAL (2 legs)

June 5 – Estadio Metropolitano, Barranquilla
Atlético Júnior 0-0 Once Caldas
h/t: 0-0 **Att:** 42,600
Ref: Duque

June 8 – Estadio Palogrande, Manizales
Once Caldas 1-0 Atlético Júnior
(Galván 74)
h/t: 0-0 **Att:** 40,000
Ref: Cervantes

Once Caldas won 1-0 on aggregate

Top, left: *He's back. Faustino Asprilla came home in 2003, playing for the struggling Tuluá.*

Top, right: *Deportes Quindío's Ivan Valenciano celebrates again during the season that saw him become the Colombian league's all-time top scorer with 213 goals.*

Above: *Independiente Medellín go out to Brazilian club Santos in the semi-finals of the 2003 Copa Libertadores. International duty cost Medellín dear in the league; it finished tenth in the Apertura and failed to make the play-off final in the Clausura.*

COLOMBIA

Colombian Clausura League Table 2003

CLUB	P	W	D	L	F	A	Pts	
Deportivo Cali	18	10	4	4	34	18	34	Qualified for Second Phase
Atlético Nacional	18	9	5	4	23	14	32	Qualified for Second Phase
Unión Magdalena	18	9	1	8	20	18	28	Qualified for Second Phase
CD Independiente Medellín	18	8	4	6	20	15	28	Qualified for Second Phase
Deportivo Pasto	18	8	4	6	20	19	28	Qualified for Second Phase
Deportes Tolima	18	7	6	5	22	17	27	Qualified for Second Phase
CD Millonarios	18	8	2	8	21	21	26	Qualified for Second Phase
Atlético Júnior	18	7	4	7	24	28	25	Qualified for Second Phase
Deportes Pereira	18	6	7	5	20	18	25	
Deportes Quindío	18	6	7	5	21	20	25	
América de Cali	18	6	7	5	23	23	25	
Atlético Huila	18	6	6	6	23	25	24	
Independiente Santa Fe	18	5	9	4	15	13	24	
Once Caldas	18	4	6	8	20	26	18	
Envigado FC	18	3	9	6	18	21	18	
Atlético Bucaramanga	18	4	5	9	24	30	17	
Corporación Tuluá	18	4	5	9	16	26	17	
Centauros Villavicencio	18	4	5	9	15	27	17	

Second Phase – Group A

CLUB	P	W	D	L	F	A	Pts	
Deportivo Cali	6	3	3	0	10	6	12	Qualified for Final
CD Millonarios	6	3	1	2	9	7	10	
Unión Magdalena	6	2	3	1	7	6	9	
Deportivo Pasto	6	0	1	5	4	11	1	

Second Phase – Group B

CLUB	P	W	D	L	F	A	Pts	
Deportes Tolima	6	3	1	2	8	7	10	Qualified for Final (on away goals)
Atlético Júnior	6	3	1	2	8	7	10	
Atlético Nacional	6	3	0	3	8	8	9	
CD Independiente Medellín	6	2	0	4	8	10	6	

NB: NO RELEGATION OR PROMOTION FOR 2003. Current system is to relegate the worst-performing team over the previous 3 seasons every 3 years, as per 2002, and to promote the best performing team in the 2nd division over the same period.

Clausura Championship Play-off

2003 FINAL (2 legs)

December 17 – Manuel Murillo Toro, Ibagué
Deportes **2-0** Deportivo
Tolima   Cali
(Pereira 51, 83)
h/t: 0-0 **Att:** 18,956
Ref: Betancurt

December 21 – Pascual Guerrero, Cali
Deportivo **3-1** Deportes
Cali   Tolima
(Díaz 15,   *(Bedoya o.g. 34)*
Preciado 20,
Murillo 39)
h/t: 3-1 **Att:** 14,000
Ref: Ruiz

Tolima won 4-2 on penalties

Top: Luis Garcia, coach of Deportes Tolima, turns a blind eye to his team's drinking. Tolima's championship was Garcia's fourth.

Above: Once Caldas poses for the camera as Apertura champions.

Arnulfo Valentierra, Once Caldas striker and top scorer in the Apertura 2003.

Top Goalscorers 2003

NAME	CLUB	GOALS
APERTURA		
Arnulfo Valentierra	Once Caldas	13
Julián Vásquez	América de Cali	11
Leonardo Fabio Moreno	América de Cali	10
CLAUSURA		
Orlando Ballesteros	Atlético Bucaramanga	13
Milton Rodríguez	Deportivo Pereira	13

International Club Performances 2003

CLUB	COMPETITION	PROGRESS
Deportivo Cali	Copa Libertadores	2nd Round
Independiente Medellín	Copa Libertadores	Semi-finals
América de Cali	Copa Libertadores	Semi-finals
Deportivo Pasto	Copa Sudamericana	1st stage, preliminary phase
Atlético Nacional	Copa Sudamericana	Semi-finals

Soccer in Colombia

COLOMBIA

Early 1880s: Soccer introduced to Colombia, mainly on Atlantic coast — 1880

1890

1900

1910

1924: First federation formed. Liga de Football del Atlántico started in Barranquilla — 1920

1936: Affiliation to FIFA

1938: Formation of national FA: Associación Colombiana de Fútbol. First international, v Mexico, lost 1-3, venue: Mexico City — 1930

1940: Affiliation to CONMEBOL — 1940

1948: National professional league, the *DiMayor*, established — 1950

1948–53: *El Dorado*. National federation suspended from FIFA, massive import of foreign players

1968: League format shifts to Apertura and Clausura Championships with a mini-league for the top teams at the end of the year — 1960

1971: National FA reformed — 1970

1981: 18 die and 45 injured in crush at match between Deportes Tolima and Deportivo Cali in Ibagué

1982: 22 die and 200 injured in crush at derby between Deportivo and América in Cali — 1980

1984: Colombia withdraws from hosting World Cup

1989: League season abandoned after the assassination of a referee — 1990

1993: Colombia qualify for World Cup, beating Argentina 5-0 in Buenos Aires, 30 die in celebrations in Bogotá — 2000

1994: The national team's Andres Escobar shot dead in Medellín

2001: Colombia beat Mexico to win the Copa América — 2010

In 2002 a seven-tonne statue of Carlos Valderrama, one of Colombia's greatest ever players, was unveiled outside the Estadio Eduardo Santos in Santa Marta. Valderrama started his career here in 1981 with Union Magdalena.

Key

- International soccer
- ⚽ Affiliation to FIFA
- ⚽ Affiliation to CONMEBOL
- Disaster
- ■ Copa América host
- ● Copa América winner
- ▲ Copa América runner-up
- ○ Competition winner
- △ Competition runner-up

Amér – América de Cali
Atl N – Atlético Nacional
D Cali – Deportivo Cali
Indep – Independiente Santa Fé
Mill – Millonarios

	International Competitions	Copa CONMEBOL (1992–99)	Copa Merconorte (1998–2001)
	Copa Libertadores	Copa Sudamericana (2002–)	
1975:	▲		
1978:	△D Cali		
1985:	△ Amér		
1986:	△ Amér		
1987:	△ Amér		
1989:	○Atl N		
1995:	△ Atl N		
1996:	△ Amér	△Indep	
1998:		○Atl N	△D Cali
1999:	△D Cali	○Amér	△Indep
2000:		○Atl N	△Mill
2001:	● ■	○Mill	
2002:		△Atl N	

Atlético Júnior 1924/1948
 (1948)

Sporting Barranquilla 1950

Deportivo Barranquilla 1949

Deportivo 'Unicosta' 1995

Once Caldas 1948
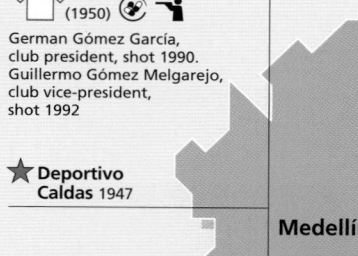 (1950)
German Gómez García, club president, shot 1990.
Guillermo Gómez Melgarejo, club vice-president, shot 1992

Deportivo Caldas 1947

Atlético Manizales 1954

Deportes Quindío 1947
(1953)

Corporación Tuluá 1967

Escuela Sarimento Lora 1984

Barranquilla
Cartagena
Real Cartagena 1971

Medellín
Envigado

Manizales
Armenia **Pereira**

Tuluá
Cali **Ibagué**
Deportes Tolima 1955

Neiva
Atlético Huila 1990

Pasto
● **Deportivo Pasto** 1949

Asociación 1962

Boca Júniors 1939
 (1951, 52)

Deportivo Cali 1928
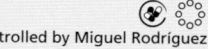 (1949)

América de Cali 1924
Controlled by Miguel Rodríguez Orejuelas, Cali cartel

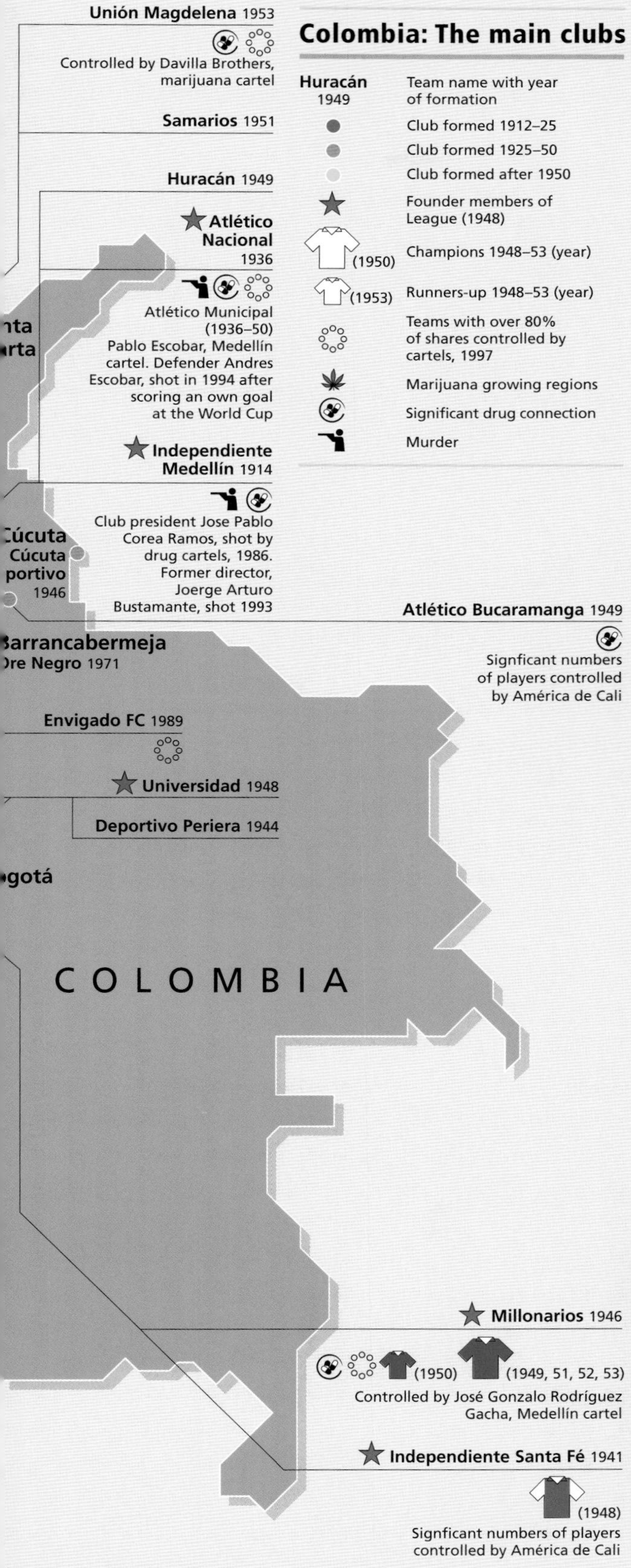

Colombia: The main clubs

Unión Magdelena 1953
Controlled by Davilla Brothers, marijuana cartel

Samarios 1951

Huracán 1949

Atlético Nacional 1936

Atlético Municipal (1936–50)
Pablo Escobar, Medellín cartel. Defender Andres Escobar, shot in 1994 after scoring an own goal at the World Cup

Independiente Medellín 1914

Club president Jose Pablo Corea Ramos, shot by drug cartels, 1986. Former director, Joerge Arturo Bustamante, shot 1993

Cúcuta
Cúcuta portivo 1946

Barrancabermeja
Dre Negro 1971

Envigado FC 1989

Universidad 1948

Deportivo Periera 1944

gotá

COLOMBIA

Millonarios 1946
(1950) (1949, 51, 52, 53)
Controlled by José Gonzalo Rodríguez Gacha, Medellín cartel

Independiente Santa Fé 1941
(1948)
Signficant numbers of players controlled by América de Cali

Atlético Bucaramanga 1949
Signficant numbers of players controlled by América de Cali

Legend

Huracán 1949	Team name with year of formation
●	Club formed 1912–25
●	Club formed 1925–50
●	Club formed after 1950
★	Founder members of League (1948)
👕 (1950)	Champions 1948–53 (year)
👕 (1953)	Runners-up 1948–53 (year)
°°°	Teams with over 80% of shares controlled by cartels, 1997
🌿	Marijuana growing regions
⚽	Significant drug connection
🔫	Murder

Colombia

ORIGINS AND GROWTH OF SOCCER

SOCCER BEGAN IN COLOMBIA in the early 1880s and the first recorded game was played in 1888. The early areas of soccer strength were in the country's northern ports and the first regular league, the Liga de Football del Atlántico, started in Barranquilla in 1924. FIFA membership followed in 1936, a national FA was set up in 1938, CONMEBOL membership in 1940 (after initially flirting with membership of the Central American Federation) and, in 1948, a new national professional league, the *DiMayor*, was established.

Almost immediately, conflict broke out between the FA and the big clubs, Millonarios and Independiente Santa Fé from Bogotá, who refused to pay transfer fees to foreign clubs. The struggle resulted in the formation of a rebel league. The extra money meant that Colombian clubs could offer massive wages and signing-on fees. They attracted star players from across the world, in particular a huge contingent from Argentina, including Alfredo di Stefano, who moved north as their long-running dispute with the Argentinian FA over the formation of a player's union remained deadlocked. The era from 1948–53, known as *El Dorado*, saw massive crowds and huge interest in soccer. But FIFA suspended Colombia from all international club competitions in 1949 and forced the Colombians to accept the global rules on transfers in 1954.

Drug money

In the 1970s, as Colombia's export-based industries collapsed during the global recession, the Colombian drug industry began its explosive growth and became the most powerful economic and political force in the country. Colombian clubs' finances were in disarray and their purchase provided both social status and an instrument for money laundering for the different drug cartels. The Cali cartel took over América, Pablo Escobar's Medellín cartel bought Atlético Nacional and took control of Millonarios in Bogotá. Despite repeated efforts to normalize the game in Colombia, the role of cartels and drug money in soccer is unresolved. The 1989 season was cancelled after the shooting of referee, Alvaro Ortega, on cartel orders, while assassinations, kidnapping, match-fixing and money laundering appear to be endemic. Colombia was forced to pull out of hosting the 1986 World Cup and the 2001 Copa América almost collapsed after a spate of bombings and shootings.

Colombian fans remember full-back Andres Escobar, who was shot dead in Medellín after returning from the 1994 World Cup. He had scored an own goal in a shock 2-1 defeat by the United States.

COLOMBIA

Colombia

APERTURA AND CLAUSURA 1994–2003

IN 1989, THREE PRESIDENTIAL CANDIDATES were assassinated in Colombia; Gonzalo Rodriguez-Gacha, a hit man for the Medellín drugs cartel and effective owner of Bogotá's Millonarios, was killed in a shootout with police; Miguel Rodriguez Orejuela, leader of the Cali drugs cartel and owner of América de Cali, was in prison; and the soccer season was cancelled at the play-off stage after referee Alvaro Ortega was shot in Medellín. Ortega, it was said, had failed to ensure the right result in the Medellín derby that season. In 1991, the Colombian FA appeared to be overhauling soccer's connections to what Colombians call *el narcotráfico*. Reform arrived in the shape of a new national league incorporating promotion and relegation, but the chaos continued. Pablo Escobar, leader of the Medellín cartel and owner of Atlético Nacional, was finally arrested by police in 1992. He escaped, only to be shot a year later. Juan José Bellini, former president of the Colombian FA and director of América, was imprisoned in 1997 on drug trafficking and corruption charges. A similar fate befell directors at Unión Magdalena and Millonarios.

Matters are no different today, and the last decade has seen Colombian soccer played under conditions of civil war and endemic violence. The country has been divided between the drug cartels, the left-wing paramilitaries FARC, an assortment of right-wing paramilitary groups, the military, the government and, most recently, the US government and army. Money laundering through soccer clubs continues, and the combination of drugs money, narcotics and gambling has ensured that players, club directors and referees are regularly threatened and even killed. Most recently, the Copa América 2001 was almost lost by Colombia after a spate of bombings and shootings in the big cities.

Colombian League Positions Table 1994–2003

SEASON

TEAM	1994 A	1994 C	Play-Offs	1995	1995-96 A	1995-96 C	Play-Offs	1996-97 A	1996-97 C	Play-Offs	1998 A	1998 C	Play-Offs	1999 A	1999 C	Play-Offs	2000 A	2000 C	Play-Offs	2001 A	2001 C	Play-Offs	2002 A	Play-Offs	2002 C	Play-Offs	2003 A	Play-Offs	2003 C	Play-Offs
Atlético Júnior	10	4	QF	C	3(B)	8		7	4(A)		7	7(A)		4	4		6	3	RU	8	12		12		17		6	RU	11	Q
Atlético Nacional	1	1	C	3	1(B)	3	SF	2	4(B)		2	1(B)	QF	2	6	C	5	7		12	3		3	RU	8	Q	14		2	Q
Atlético Bucaramanga	14	15			6(A)	13		8	2(A)	RU	14	4(B)		9	9		15	10		15	16		6	Q	5	Q	11		16	
América de Cali	2	10	SF	2	2(B)	2	SF	1	6(A)	C	8	5(B)	QF	1	10	RU	2	1	C	7	5	C	8	C	4	Q	3	Q	10	
Deportivo Cali	6	6	QF	4	1(A)	1	C	3	1(B)		5	2(A)	C	7	5		1	15		2	4	QF	1	Q	1	Q	5	Q	1	RU
Real Cartagena																	10	13		13	14		17		14					
Cúcuta Deportivo	7	9		16				16																						
Deportivo 'Unicosta'									8(B)			8(B)																		
Envigado FC	4	8	QF	12	6(B)	7		12	5(B)		13	4(A)		14	12		8	12		10	7		4	Q	18		13		14	
Atlético Huila	8	7		15	4(B)	16					8	7(B)		16	16		11	11		14	15		14		15		9		12	
Independiente Medellín	9	3	SF	7	8(A)	12		5	8(A)		4	2(B)	QF	8	3		13	9		5	10	RU	16		3	C	10		4	Q
Millonarios	5	2	RU	14	4(A)	6	RU	15	2(B)		9	5(A)	QF	11	1		4	4		9	2	QF	13		16		2	Q	7	Q
Once Caldas	3	5	QF	8	5(A)	5		10	5(A)		1	1(A)	RU	3	7		12	6		3	1	QF	9		10		1	C	15	
Deportivo Pasto														12	8		14	8		16	6		5	Q	2	RU	15		5	Q
Deportivo Pereira	16	13		6	7(B)	11		14	7(B)											11	11		10		13		8	Q	8	
Deportes Quindío	15	11		10	7(A)	14		12	1(A)		11	3(A)	QF	13	15		16	14			11		11				18		9	
Independiente Santa Fé	12	14		5	5(B)	15		11	7(A)		3	8(A)	QF	10	13		9	2	SF	6	9	QF	2	Q	9		16		13	
Deportes Tolima				9	2(A)	4		4	3(A)		10	6(B)		5	11		3	6	SF	4	8	QF	18		7	Q	12		6	C
Corporación Tuluá	13	16		11	8(B)	9		9	6(B)		12	3(B)		6	2		7	16		1	13	QF	15		12		17		17	
Unión Magdalena	11	12		13	3(A)	10		6	3(B)		15	6(A)		15	14								7	Q	6	Q	7	Q	3	Q
Centauros Villavicencio																											4	Q	18	

(A) = Group A   (B) = Group B

Except for 1995, the season is divided into two leagues, Apertura and Clausura (marked A and C on the table), also called Torneo Mustang I and II. The winners played off to decide the championship. In 2002, a new system was devised in which both the Apertura and Clausura had two phases. The first is a regular league, the top eight clubs (marked Q) qualifying for a second phase in which two groups of four play each other. The winners of each group meet in a play-off for the championship.

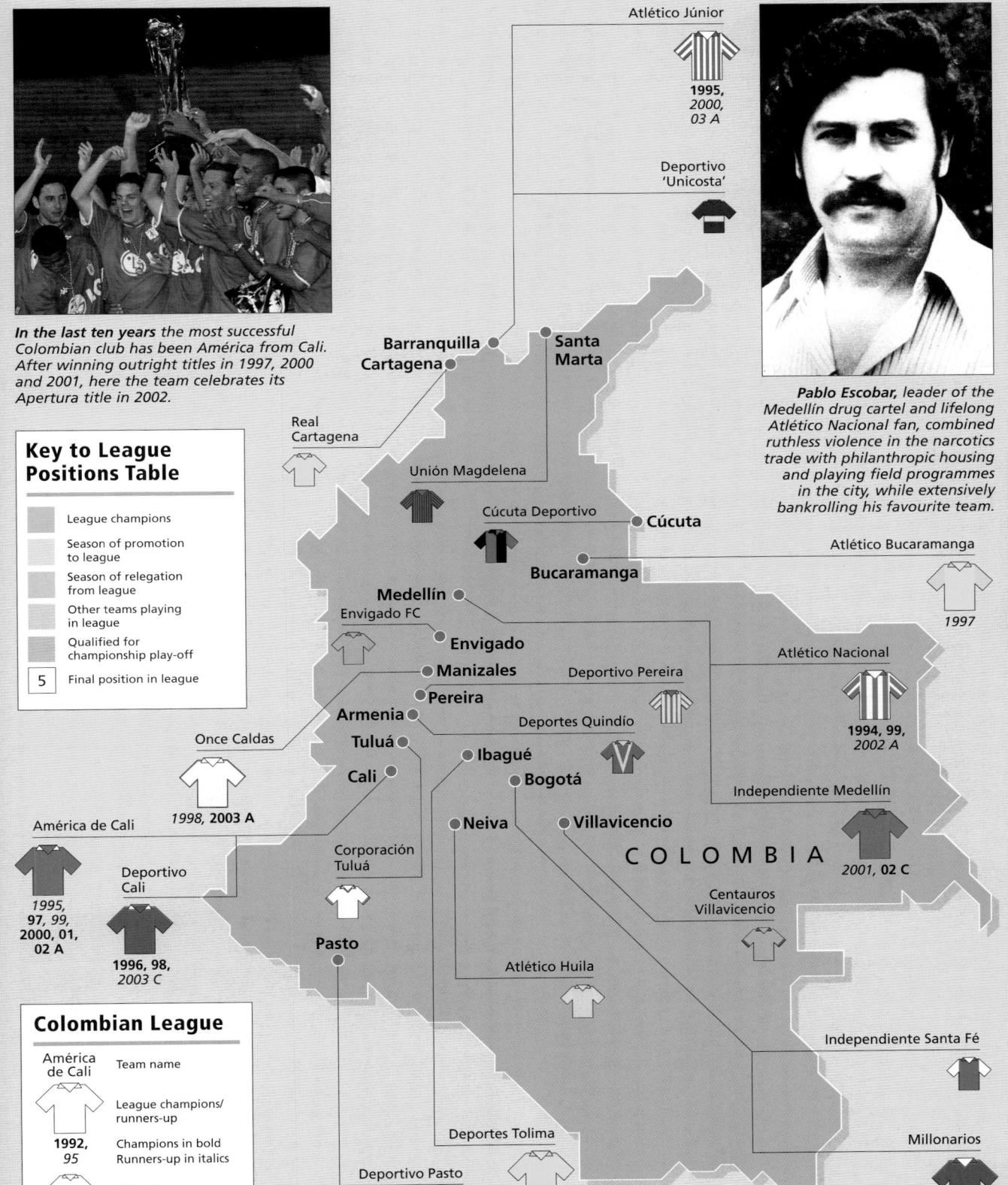

In the last ten years the most successful Colombian club has been América from Cali. After winning outright titles in 1997, 2000 and 2001, here the team celebrates its Apertura title in 2002.

Pablo Escobar, leader of the Medellín drug cartel and lifelong Atlético Nacional fan, combined ruthless violence in the narcotics trade with philanthropic housing and playing field programmes in the city, while extensively bankrolling his favourite team.

COLOMBIA

Key to League Positions Table

- League champions
- Season of promotion to league
- Season of relegation from league
- Other teams playing in league
- Qualified for championship play-off
- 5 — Final position in league

Atlético Júnior
1995, 2000, 03 A

Deportivo 'Unicosta'

Barranquilla
Cartagena
Santa Marta

Real Cartagena

Unión Magdelena

Cúcuta Deportivo — Cúcuta

Atlético Bucaramanga
1997

Medellín
Envigado FC
Envigado
Manizales
Pereira
Armenia
Tuluá
Cali

Bucaramanga

Deportivo Pereira

Atlético Nacional
1994, 99, 2002 A

Deportes Quindío

Ibagué
Bogotá

Independiente Medellín
2001, 02 C

Once Caldas
1998, **2003 A**

América de Cali
1995, 97, 99, 2000, 01, 02 A

Deportivo Cali
1996, 98, 2003 C

Corporación Tuluá

Pasto

Neiva
Villavicencio

C O L O M B I A

Centauros Villavicencio

Atlético Huila

Independiente Santa Fé

Colombian League

América de Cali — Team name

League champions/ runners-up

1992, 95 — Champions in bold / Runners-up in italics

Other teams in the league

● Cali — City of origin

Deportes Tolima

Deportivo Pasto
2002 C

2003 C

Millonarios
1994, 96

Colombia

Federación Colombiana de Fútbol
Founded: 1924, reformed 1938, 1971
Joined FIFA: 1936–1950, 1954
Joined CONMEBOL: 1940

SOCCER WAS A LATE DEVELOPER in Colombia, with the first regular competition only established in the city of Barranquilla in 1924, and a national organization only created in 1938. But it would take until 1948 for the first professional national league to be set up: the *DiMayor*. The league broke away from the Colombian FA in 1950, before rejoining it and FIFA (which it had been a member of between 1936 and 1950) in 1954. It retained a simple format until 1968 when it switched to a season consisting of Apertura (opening), Clausura (closing) and play-off championships. The 1989 national championship has no recorded victor as the season was abandoned following the assassination of a referee and widespread allegations of drug-money handling, illegal gambling and match fixing throughout the game. Colombia has no significant national cup competition. In 2002 the league went back to an Apertura and Clausura format with no play-offs.

Colombian League Record 1948–2003

SEASON	CHAMPIONS	RUNNERS-UP
1948	Independiente Santa Fé	Atlético Júnior
1949	Millonarios	Deportivo Cali
1950	Once Caldas	Millonarios
1951	Millonarios	Boca Júniors
1952	Millonarios	Boca Júniors
1953	Millonarios	Atlético Quindio
1954	Atlético Nacional	Atlético Quindio
1955	Independiente Medellín	Atlético Nacional
1956	Atlético Quindio	Millonarios
1957	Independiente Medellín	Deportes Tolima
1958	Independiente Santa Fé	Millonarios
1959	Millonarios	Independiente Medellín
1960	Independiente Santa Fé	América de Cali
1961	Millonarios	Independiente Medellín
1962	Millonarios	Deportivo Cali
1963	Millonarios	Independiente Santa Fé
1964	Millonarios	Cucuta Deportivo
1965	Deportivo Cali	Atlético Nacional
1966	Independiente Santa Fé	Independiente Medellín
1967	Deportivo Cali	Millonarios
1968	Unión Magdalena	Deportivo Cali
1969	Deportivo Cali	América de Cali
1970	Deportivo Cali	Atlético Júnior
1971	Independiente Santa Fé	Atlético Nacional
1972	Millonarios	Deportivo Cali
1973	Atlético Nacional	Millonarios
1974	Deportivo Cali	Atlético Nacional
1975	Independiente Santa Fé	Millonarios
1976	Atlético Nacional	Deportivo Cali
1977	Atlético Júnior	Deportivo Cali
1978	Millonarios	Deportivo Cali
1979	América de Cali	Independiente Santa Fé
1980	Atlético Júnior	Deportivo Cali
1981	Atlético Nacional	Deportes Tolima
1982	América de Cali	Deportes Tolima
1983	América de Cali	Atlético Júnior
1984	América de Cali	Millonarios
1985	América de Cali	Deportivo Cali
1986	América de Cali	Deportivo Cali
1987	Millonarios	América de Cali
1988	Millonarios	Atlético Nacional
1989	*not awarded**	
1990	América de Cali	Atlético Nacional

Colombian League Record (*continued*)

SEASON	CHAMPIONS	RUNNERS-UP
1991	Atlético Nacional	América de Cali
1992	América de Cali	Atlético Nacional
1993	Atlético Júnior	Independiente Medellín
1994	Atlético Nacional	Millonarios
1995	Atlético Júnior	América de Cali
1996	Deportivo Cali	Millonarios
1997	América de Cali	Atlético Bucaramanga
1998	Deportivo Cali	Once Caldas
1999	Atlético Nacional	América de Cali
2000	América de Cali	Atlético Júnior
2001	América de Cali	Independiente Medellín
2002 A	América de Cali	Atlético Nacional
2002 C	Independiente Medellín	Deportivo Pasto
2003 A	Once Caldas	Atlético Júnior
2003 C	Deportes Tolima	Deportivo Cali

* The 1989 season was abandoned due to alleged criminal activities and the killing of a referee.

Colombian League Summary

TEAM	TOTALS	CHAMPIONS & RUNNERS-UP (BOLD) (*ITALICS*)
Millonarios	13, 9	**1949, 50, 51–53, 56, 58, 59, 61–64, 67,** *72, 73, 75,* **78,** *84,* **87, 88,** *94, 96*
América de Cali	12, 6	*1960, 69, 79,* **82–86,** *87,* **90,** *91, 92,* **95,** *97,* **99, 2000, 01, 02 A**
Deportivo Cali	7, 11	**1949,** *62,* **65,** *67, 68,* **69, 70,** *72,* **74,** *76–78, 80, 85, 86,* **96,** *98,* **2003 C**
Atlético Nacional	7, 8	**1954,** *55,* **65,** *71,* **73,** *74,* **76,** *81,* **88,** *90,* **91,** *92,* **94,** *99, 2002 A*
Independiente Santa Fé	6, 2	**1948,** *58,* **60,** *63,* **66,** *71,* **75,** *79*
Atlético Júnior	4, 5	*1948, 70,* **77,** *80, 83,* **93,** *95,* **2000,** *03 A*
Independiente Medellín	3, 5	**1955,** *57,* **59,** *61,* **66,** *93,* **2001,** *02 C*
Once Caldas	2, 1	*1950, 98,* **2003 A**
Deportes Tolima	1, 3	*1957, 81, 82,* **2003 C**
Atlético Quindio	1, 2	**1953,** *54,* **56**
Unión Magdalena	1, 0	**1968**
Boca Júniors	0, 2	*1951, 52*
Atlético Bucaramanga	0, 1	*1997*
Cúcuta Deportivo	0, 1	*1964*
Deportivo Pasto	0, 1	*2002 C*

Millonarios from Bogotá is the most successful club in Colombia. The team poses for the cameras after winning the 1952 league title.

Venezuela

Federación Venezolana de Fútbol
Founded: 1926
Joined FIFA: 1952
Joined CONMEBOL: 1952

AN ORGANIZED NATIONAL LEAGUE was set up in Caracas in 1921. However, the game has failed to take off, given the popularity of the national sport of baseball, and this has left Venezuela as the weakest of the ten soccer nations in South America. League teams turned professional in 1955 but have had very little success in the Copa Libertadores. The national team has also failed to make an impact in the Copa América.

Venezuelan Amateur League Record 1921–54

SEASON	CHAMPIONS	RUNNERS-UP
1921	América	Centro Atlético
1922	Centro Atlético	América
1923	América	Centro Atlético
1924	Centro Atlético	Vargas (La Guaira)
1925	Loyola SC	Venzóleo
1926	Centro Atlético	Venzóleo
1927	Venzóleo	Centro Atlético
1928	Deportivo Venezuela	Centro Atlético
1929	Deportivo Venezuela	Unión SC
1930	Centro Atlético	Unión SC
1931	Deportivo Venezuela	Centro Atlético
1932	Unión SC	Dos Caminos SC
1933	Deportivo Venezuela	Dos Caminos SC
1934	Unión SC	Dos Caminos SC
1935	Unión SC	Dos Caminos SC
1936	Dos Caminos SC	Centro Atlético
1937	Dos Caminos SC	Litoral SC
1938	Dos Caminos SC	Litoral SC
1939	Unión SC	Litoral SC
1940	Unión SC	Dos Caminos SC
1941	Litoral SC	Dos Caminos SC
1942	Dos Caminos SC	Loyola SC
1943	Loyola SC	Litoral SC
1944	Loyola SC	Dos Caminos SC
1945	Dos Caminos SC	Loyola SC
1946	Deportivo Español	Centro Atlético
1947	Unión SC	Universidad Central
1948	Loyola SC	Unión SC
1949	Dos Caminos SC	Universidad Central
1950	Unión SC	La Salle FC
1951	Universidad Central	Loyola SC
1952	La Salle FC	Loyola SC
1953	Universidad Central	La Salle FC
1954	Deportivo Vasco	Loyola SC

Venezuelan Professional League Record 1955–2004

SEASON	CHAMPIONS	RUNNERS-UP
1955	La Salle FC	Deportivo Español
1956	Banco Obrero	La Salle FC
1957	Universidad Central	La Salle FC
1958	Deportivo Portugués	Deportivo Español
1959	Deportivo Español	Deportivo Portugués
1960	Deportivo Portugués	Deportivo Español
1961	Deportivo Italia	Banco Agricola y Pecuario
1962	Deportivo Portugués	Universidad Central
1963	Deportivo Italia	Deportivo Portugués
1964	Deportivo Galicia	Tiquire Flores
1965	Lara FC	Deportivo Italia
1966	Deportivo Italia	Deportivo Galicia
1967	Deportivo Portugués	Deportivo Galicia
1968	Unión Deportivo Canarias	Deportivo Italia
1969	Deportivo Galicia	Valencia FC

Venezuelan League Record (*continued*)

SEASON	CHAMPIONS	RUNNERS-UP
1970	Deportivo Galicia	Deportivo Italia
1971	Valencia FC	Deportivo Italia
1972	Deportivo Italia	Deportivo Galicia
1973	Portuguesa FC	Valencia FC
1974	Deportivo Galicia	Portuguesa FC
1975	Portuguesa FC	Deportivo Galicia
1976	Portuguesa FC	Estudiantes de Mérida
1977	Portuguesa FC	Estudiantes de Mérida
1978	Portuguesa FC	Deportivo Galicia
1979	Deportivo Táchira	Deportivo Galicia
1980	Estudiantes de Mérida	Portuguesa FC
1981	Deportivo Táchira	Estudiantes de Mérida
1982	Atlético San Cristóbal	Deportivo Táchira
1983	Universidad de Los Andes	Portuguesa FC
1984	Deportivo Táchira	Deportivo Italia
1985	Estudiantes de Mérida	Deportivo Táchira
1986	Unión Atlético Táchira	Estudiantes de Mérida
1987	CS Maritimo	Unión Atlético Táchira
1988	CS Maritimo	Unión Atlético Táchira
1989	Mineros de Guayana	Pepeganga Margarita
1990	CS Maritimo	Unión Atlético Táchira
1991	Universidad de Los Andes	CS Maritimo
1992	Caracas FC	Minervén
1993	CS Maritimo	Minervén
1994	Caracas FC	Trujillanos
1995	Caracas FC	Minervén
1996	Minervén	Mineros de Guayana
1997	Caracas FC	Atlético Zulia
1998	Atlético Zulia	Estudiantes de Mérida
1999	ItalChacoa	Unión Atlético Táchira
2000	Deportivo Táchira	ItalChacao
2001	Caracas FC	Trujillanos
2002	Nacional Táchira	Estudiantes de Mérida
2003	Caracas FC	Unión Atlético Maracaibo
2004 A	Caracas FC	Deportivo Táchira
2004 C	Caracas FC	Deportivo Táchira

Venezuelan League Summary

TEAM	TOTALS	CHAMPIONS & RUNNERS-UP (BOLD) (*ITALICS*)	
Caracas FC	**8**, 0	**1992, 94, 95, 97, 2001, 03, 04C**	
Unión SC	**7**, 3	*1929, 30,* **32,** *34, 35,* **39, 40,** *47,* **48,** *50*	
Dos Caminos SC	**6**, 7	*1932–35,* **36–38,** *40, 41,* **42,** *44, 45,* **49**	
Portuguesa FC	**5**, 3	**1973,** *74,* **75–78,** *80,* **83**	
Centro Atlético	**4**, 7	*1921,* **22, 23,** *24,* **26,** *27, 28,* **30,** *31, 36, 46*	
Deportivo Galicia	**4**, 6	**1964,** *66, 67,* **69, 70,** *72,* **74, 75,** *78, 79*	
Deportivo Italia	**4**, 5	**1961,** *63,* **65,** *66,* **68,** *70, 71,* **72,** *84*	
Loyola SC	**4**, 5	**1925,** *42,* **43, 44,** *45,* **48,** *51,* **52,** *54*	
Deportivo Táchira	**4**, 4	**1979,** *81,* **82,** *84,* **85, 2000,** *04A, 04C*	
Deportivo Portugués	**4**, 2	**1958,** *59,* **60,** *62,* **63,** *67*	
CS Maritimo	**4**, 1	**1987,** *88,* **90,** *91,* **93**	
Deportivo Venezuela	**4**, 0	**1928, 29, 31, 33**	
Universidad Central	**3**, 3	*1947, 49,* **51,** *53,* **57,** *62*	

This summary only features clubs that have won the Venezuelan league three or more times. For a full list of league champions and runners-up please see the League Records above.

VENEZUELA

 # Bolivia

Federación Boliviana de Fútbol
Founded: 1925
Joined FIFA: 1926
Joined CONMEBOL: 1926

BOLIVIAN SOCCER CAN BE TRACED back to the formation of the first team, Oruro Royal Club, in 1896. Its first matches were against the clubs Nimbles Sports and Northern, formed by workers on the La Paz to Antofagasta railway. Soccer spread to the major cities high in the Andes over the next decade. Local leagues were formed and early national competitions between local league champions ran from 1914 to 1925. An official national tournament was held in 1926 after the creation of a national soccer federation. Teams from the capital La Paz, like Bolivar and The Strongest, dominated during the early years. They have been challenged more recently by the Cochabamba team, Jorge Wilstermann and the Santa Cruz teams, Oriente Petrolero and Blooming.

Professionalism arrived in 1951 and between 1954 and 1957 a *Torneo Integrado* was held between the champions of the three major leagues in La Paz, Cochabamba and Oruro. In 1958 a national league was finally established.

The season is split into two with an Apertura (opening) championship played at the beginning of the year, and a Clausura (closing) championship played at the end. The Apertura is a regular league with teams playing each other home and away. The Clausura consists of two groups of six teams playing each other home and away which reduces to two groups of four then four semi-finalists. The national champions were the winners of a two-leg play-off between the Apertura and Clausura winners; this has now been abandoned. Relegation is decided on a points average over the previous two seasons.

A cup competition – La Copa Simón Bolívar – has also run intermittently in Bolivia. Between 1960 and 1976 the winners became the Bolivian entrant to the Copa Libertadores. It was revived in 1989 as a way of organizing promotion from the regional to the national leagues.

Bolivian Cup Record 1960–76

YEAR	WINNERS	YEAR	WINNERS
1960	Jorge Wilstermann	1969	CD Universitario
1961	Deportivo Municipal	1970	Chaco Petrolero
1962–63	no competition	1971	Oriente Petrolero
1964	The Strongest	1972	Jorge Wilstermann
1965	Deportivo Municipal	1973	Jorge Wilstermann
1966	Bolívar	1974	The Strongest
1967	Jorge Wilstermann	1975	Guabirá
1968	Bolívar	1976	Bolívar

Bolivian Cup Record 1989–2003

YEAR	WINNERS	YEAR	WINNERS
1989	Enrique Happ	1998	Unión Central
1990	Universidad	1999	Atlético Pompeya
1991	Enrique Happ	2000	Iberoamericano
1992	Enrique Happ	2001	San José
1993	Real Santa Cruz	2002	Aurora
1994	Stormers	2003	La Paz
1995	Municipal		
1996	Blooming		
1997	Real Potosí		

 # Ecuador

Asociación Ecuatoriana de Fútbol
Founded: 1925
Joined FIFA: 1926
Joined CONMEBOL: 1930

THE FIRST ECUADORIAN CLUB, CS Pastria, was formed in the port city of Guayaquil in 1908, around a decade after visiting sailors had first played soccer in Ecuador. Local tournaments were organized in Guayaquil before and after the First World War, culminating in a short-lived city league which existed between 1922 and 1929.

Soccer spread slowly to the interior of the country and it was only in 1957 that the national soccer federation was reconstituted and a national league established. The league has been dominated by teams from Guayaquil (Barcelona and Emelec) and Quito (Deportivo, El Nacional and Liga Deportivo Universitaria).

In previous years the league had an awesomely complex structure. In the top division, Primera A, 12 teams competed home and away for the Apertura championship: the winners qualifying for the Copa Libertadores. In the Clausura championship the teams were first divided into three groups of four playing home and away. The winners and runners-up of each group then went into a group of six and the third and fourth placed teams went into a second group of six. The winners of the first mini-league then played-off against the winners of the Apertura to determine the overall national champions. The bottom two teams from the second mini-league were relegated. However, the league has now been simplified with the top six clubs from the Apertura and the Clausura playing-off in a final mini-league to decide the national champions.

Bolivian League Record 1958–2003

SEASON	CHAMPIONS	SEASON	CHAMPIONS
1958	Jorge Wilstermann	1982	Bolívar
1959	Jorge Wilstermann	1983	Bolívar
1960	Jorge Wilstermann	1984	Blooming
1961	Deportivo Municipal	1985	Bolívar
1962	Chaco Petrolero	1986	The Strongest
1963	The Strongest/Aurora	1987	Bolívar
1964	The Strongest	1988	Bolívar
1965	Deportivo Municipal	1989	The Strongest
1966	Bolívar	1990	Oriente Petrolero
1967	Jorge Wilstermann	1991	Bolívar
1968	Bolívar	1992	Bolívar
1969	CD Universitario	1993	The Strongest
1970	CD Chaco Petrolero	1994	Bolívar
1971	Oriente Petrolero	1995	CS San José
1972	Jorge Wilstermann	1996	Bolívar
1973	Jorge Wilstermann	1997	Bolívar
1974	The Strongest	1998	Blooming
1975	Guabirá	1999	Blooming
1976	Bolívar	2000	Jorge Wilstermann
1977	The Strongest	2001	Oriente Petrolero
1978	Bolívar	2002	Bolívar
1979	Oriente Petrolero	2003 A	The Strongest
1980	Jorge Wilstermann	2003 C	The Strongest
1981	Jorge Wilstermann		

Ecuadorian League Record 1957–2003

SEASON	CHAMPIONS	SEASON	CHAMPIONS
1957	Emelec	1964	Deportivo
1958	no championship	1965	9 du Octubre
1959	no championship	1966	Barcelona
1960	Barcelona	1967	El Nacional
1961	Emelec	1968	Deportivo
1962	Everest	1969	LDU
1963	Barcelona	1970	Barcelona

BOLIVIA, ECUADOR

Ecuadorian League Record (*continued*)

SEASON	CHAMPIONS	SEASON	CHAMPIONS
1971	Barcelona	1989	Barcelona
1972	Emelec	1990	Barcelona
1973	El Nacional	1991	Valdez
1974	El Nacional	1992	El Nacional
1975	LDU	1993	Barcelona
1976	Deportivo	1994	Emelec
1977	El Nacional	1995	Barcelona
1978	El Nacional	1996	El Nacional
1979	Emelec	1997	Barcelona
1980	Barcelona	1998	LDU
1981	LDU	1999	LDU
1982	El Nacional	2000	Olmedo
1983	El Nacional	2001	Emelec
1984	El Nacional	2002	Emelec
1985	Barcelona	2003	LDU
1986	El Nacional		
1987	Barcelona		
1988	Emelec		

Peru

Federación Peruana de Fútbol
Founded: 1922
Joined FIFA: 1924
Joined CONMEBOL: 1926

SOCCER WAS INTRODUCED TO PERU at the turn of the 19th century by British residents in the capital Lima. Many teams grew out of expatriate tennis and cricket clubs. A local league was formed in 1912, but it was only in 1922 that a national soccer federation was established.

A formalized Lima-based league was set up in 1926 and in 1931 Peruvian soccer went professional. In 1966 the league was expanded to encompass the strongest teams from the regional competitions. In 1972 the league changed again with a Lima-based metropolitan league and a network of regional leagues producing qualifiers for a national championship tournament. Lima teams have consistently led Peruvian soccer: Universitario de Deportes, Sporting Cristal, Alianza Lima, Sport Boys and Deportivo Municipal, all come from the capital.

In 1976 a single national league was established but with a fantastically complex structure. Again split into two leagues – Apertura and Clausura – the championship is decided via a play-off between the two champions, unless one club has won both. The winners claim a place in the Copa Libertadores. The six teams with the highest points total across the season (excluding the champions) then compete in an end-of-season play-off league to determine Peru's second spot in the competition. The two clubs with the overall lowest points total are relegated. The winners of the Lima regional league and the winners of the Copa Perú (a tournament between regional champions) are promoted to the top division.

Peruvian League Record 1926–2003

SEASON	CHAMPIONS	SEASON	CHAMPIONS
1926	Sport Progreso	1933	Alianza Lima
1927	Alianza Lima	1934	Universitario de Deportes
1928	Alianza Lima	1935	Sport Boys
1929	Universitario de Deportes	1936	*no championship*
1930	Atlético Chalaco	1937	Sport Boys
1931	Alianza Lima	1938	Deportivo Municipal
1932	Alianza Lima	1939	Universitario de Deportes

Peruvian League Record (*continued*)

SEASON	CHAMPIONS	SEASON	CHAMPIONS
1940	Deportivo Municipal	1973	Desensor Lima
1941	Universitario de Deportes	1974	Universitario de Deportes
1942	Sport Boys	1975	Alianza Lima
1943	Deportivo Municipal	1976	Unión Huaral
1944	FC Sucre	1977	Alianza Lima
1945	Universitario de Deportes	1978	Alianza Lima
1946	Universitario de Deportes	1979	Sporting Cristal
1947	Atlético Chalaco	1980	Sporting Cristal
1948	Alianza Lima	1981	Melgar FBC
1949	Universitario de Deportes	1982	Universitario de Deportes
1950	Deportivo Municipal	1983	Sporting Cristal
1951	Sport Boys	1984	Sport Boys
1952	Alianza Lima	1985	Universitario de Deportes
1953	FC Sucre	1986	Colegio San Agustín
1954	Alianza Lima	1987	Universitario de Deportes
1955	Alianza Lima	1988	Sporting Cristal
1956	Sporting Cristal	1989	Unión Huaral
1957	Centro Iqueño	1990	Universitario de Deportes
1958	Sport Boys	1991	Sporting Cristal
1959	Universitario de Deportes	1992	Universitario de Deportes
1960	Universitario de Deportes	1993	Universitario de Deportes
1961	Sporting Cristal	1994	Sporting Cristal
1962	Alianza Lima	1995	Sporting Cristal
1963	Alianza Lima	1996	Sporting Cristal
1964	Universitario de Deportes	1997	Alianza Lima
1965	Alianza Lima	1998	Universitario de Deportes
1966	Universitario de Deportes	1999	Universitario de Deportes
1967	Universitario de Deportes	2000	Universitario de Deportes
1968	Sporting Cristal	2001	Alianza Lima
1969	Universitario de Deportes	2002	Sporting Cristal
1970	Sporting Cristal	2003	Alianza Lima
1971	Universitario de Deportes		
1972	Sporting Cristal		

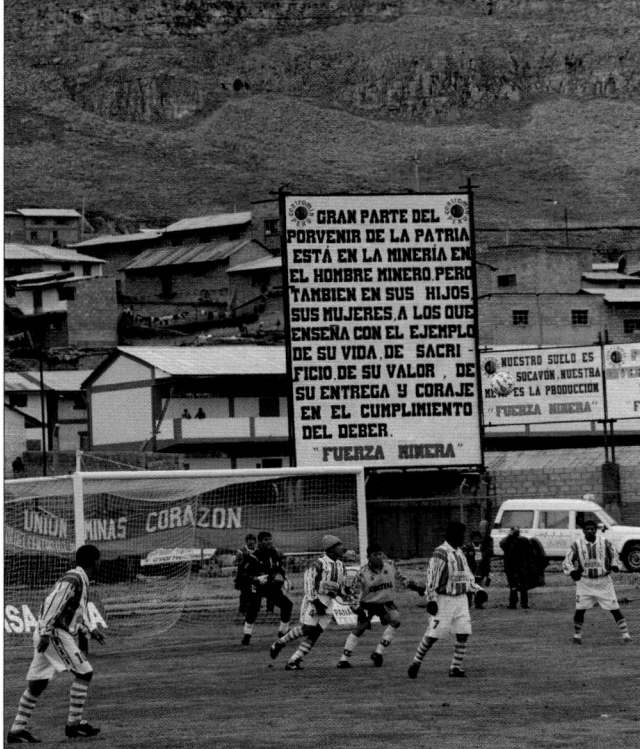

Peruvian soccer club Union Minas, *which plays at 4,380m in the Andes near the border with Bolivia, holds the record for the professional team which plays at the highest altitude in the world. Half-time refreshment for the players comes in the form of oxygen.*

PERU

Brazil

THE SEASON IN REVIEW 2003

THE VERY CORE OF BRAZILIAN public life was in flux in 2003. To begin with, for the very first time a left-of-centre president was sworn into office – Luiz Inacio Lula da Silva, known as 'Lula'. Perhaps even more surprisingly, the Brazilian National Championship kicked off as a simple home and away, three points for win, no frills, no play-off, standard league tournament. The two are not entirely unconnected because the reorganization of the league is a small step in the reform of the often dismal and chaotic state of Brazilian domestic soccer, which Lula's administration had been promising to reform.

New order, old stench

On the other hand, the reassuring stench of the old order remained in the air. Richard Teixeira was re-elected as head of the Brazilian FA – the CBF – and spent most of the year either ensconced in FIFA's offices in Zurich or in the CBF's own suburban Rio bunker. Neither Teixeira nor any of the other 16 senior soccer figures recommended for criminal investigation and prosecution by the Brazilian senate in 2001 have received even more than a cursory glance from the Brazilian criminal justice system. Nonetheless, the new government passed the Supporters Statute in May 2003, requiring clubs to publish real attendance data, allocate numbered places to ticket holders, take full legal responsibility for fights and accidents and ensure that the required number of ambulances are present at games. Even this minimal set of reforms evoked a volcanic and petulant response from club directors. Predictably led by Vasco's president Eurico Miranda, the directors threatened a lock out at the start of the National Championship but in the face of criticism from every quarter of Brazilian society the rebellion collapsed.

Brazilian National Championship 2003

CLUB	P	W	D	L	F	A	Pts	
Cruzeiro	46	31	7	8	102	47	**100**	Copa Libertadores, Copa Sudamericana
Santos	46	25	12	9	93	60	**87**	Copa Libertadores, Copa Sudamericana
São Paulo	46	22	12	12	81	67	**78**	Copa Libertadores, Copa Sudamericana
São Caetano	46	19	14	13	53	37	**74***	Copa Libertadores, Copa Sudamericana
Coritiba	46	21	10	15	67	58	**73**	Copa Libertadores, Copa Sudamericana
Internacional	46	20	10	16	59	57	**72***	Copa Sudamericana
Atlético Mineiro	46	19	15	12	76	62	**72**	Copa Sudamericana
Flamengo	46	18	12	16	66	73	**66**	Copa Sudamericana
Goiás	46	18	11	17	78	63	**65**	Copa Sudamericana
Paraná	46	18	11	17	85	75	**65**	Copa Sudamericana
Figueirense	46	17	14	15	62	54	**65**	Copa Sudamericana
Atlético Paranaense	46	17	10	19	67	72	**61**	
Guarani	46	17	10	19	64	72	**61**	
Criciúma	46	17	9	20	57	69	**60**	
Corinthians	46	15	12	19	61	63	**59***	
Vitória	46	15	11	20	50	64	**56**	
Vasco da Gama	46	13	15	18	57	69	**54**	
Juventude	46	12	14	20	55	70	**53***	
Fluminense	46	13	11	22	52	77	**52***	
Grêmio	46	13	11	22	54	68	**50**	Copa Sudamericana
Ponte Preta	46	11	18	17	63	73	**50***	
Paysandu	46	15	12	19	74	77	**49***	
Fortaleza	46	12	13	21	58	74	**49**	Relegated
Bahia	46	12	10	24	59	92	**46**	Relegated

* Points totals were adjusted during the season in response to teams fielding ineligible players. The net effect of these awards were as follows: São Caetano +3; Internacional +2; Corinthians +2; Juventude +3; Fluminense +2; Ponte Preta -1; Paysandu -8

Promoted clubs: Palmeiras, Botafago-RJ.

Brazilian State Championships 2003

STATE	CHAMPIONS
Bahia	Vitória
Ceará	Fortaleza
Goiás	Goiás
Minas Gerais	No championship in 2003
Paraná	Coritiba FC
Rio de Janeiro	Vasco da Gama
Rio Grande do Sul	SC Internacional
Rio-São Paulo	No championship in 2003 – participating clubs in 2002 now in São Paulo Championship
São Paulo	Corinthians

Top Goalscorers 2003

PLAYER	CLUB	NATIONALITY	GOALS
Dimba	Goiás	Brazilian	31
Renaldo	Paraná	Brazilian	30
Luis Fabiano	São Paulo	Brazilian	29
Alex	Cruzeiro	Brazilian	23
Aristizábal	Cruzeiro	Colombian	21

Left: Diego and Robinho – Santos managed to hang on to its teenage stars for another season but the club could only finish runners-up in both the National Championship and the Copa Libertadores.

Right: Grêmio v Vasco. Grêmio managed to work its way through four coaches in half a season – between them they kept the club one point clear of relegation.

Igor Soares (top) of Atlético Paranaense jumps for the ball with Igor Freire of Flamengo during their league game at the Maracana.

Above: Brazilian striker Romario of Fluminense fights with fan Ricardo Gomes after a training session in Rio de Janeiro. Romario reacted after Gomes threw chickens onto the pitch in protest at Fluminense's poor showing in this season's league tournament.

Below left: Oswaldo de Oliveira, fired as Corinthians and Flamengo coach, was just one of over 40 managerial casualties during the Brazilian championship.

Below right: Santos coach Emerson Leao gives the orders.

BRAZIL

The story of the championship was simple. Having won the Minas Gerias state championship and the Copa do Brazil in an unbeaten run of 36 games that began last season, Cruzeiro's form just got better. Wanderley Luxemburgo's squad could not stop scoring – with goals coming from a prolific front-line including Daevid, Alex and Colombian forward Victor Aristizábal. Cruzeiro's only real challengers were Santos and São Paulo. In fact, Santos knocked them off the top of the table at the halfway mark, but Cruzeiro's 3-0 win in the crucial game between the sides ensured the gap became insurmountable. São Paulo played brilliantly in the first half the season, but, like the rest of the league, its squad was dismembered by the mid-season transfer market as over 50 players left Brazil for Europe. São Paulo lost Kaka to Milan and Reinaldo to PSG. Grêmio's season imploded as sales to cover debt left the squad looking very threadbare.

Courtroom victories and other dramas

While the top clubs accumulated points on the field, some of the stragglers resorted to the courtroom to get theirs. Corinthians and Internacional clawed back points in a post-match tribunal from games against small clubs Paysandu and Ponte Preta respectively. In both cases the smaller clubs had apparently fielded ineligible players – though the CBF could not explain how they had slipped through the fine mesh of its administrative net. Big Rio club Fluminense never looked like doing anything except getting relegated – but there was plenty of incidental entertainment on the way. The club welcomed back its errant star Romario who, not content with drawing a handsome salary and skipping training, has been taking control of transfers, tactics and coaching and assaulting protesting fans. Scheduling decisions designed to accommodate the ever-present TV giant Globo helped keep crowds at a record low. Only 13,000 turned up to see Corinthians take on Flamengo at the Maracana, a match between two of the country's best-supported sides. However, the appalling state of the country's stadiums and the continuing outbreaks of violence remain the central problems for Brazilian domestic soccer. Again Vasco da Gama led the way in the violence stakes as its supporters mounted a massive attack on the Coritiba team bus during the club's visit to Rio for a league match.

International Club Performances 2003

CLUB	COMPETITION	PROGRESS
Corinthians	Copa Libertadores	2nd Round
	Copa Sudamericana	1st Stage
Paysandu	Copa Libertadores	2nd Round
Grêmio	Copa Libertadores	Quarter-finals
	Copa Sudamericana	1st Stage
Santos	Copa Libertadores	Runners-up
	Copa Sudamericana	Quarter-finals
Internacional	Copa Sudamericana	1st Stage
Flamengo	Copa Sudamericana	1st Stage
Atlético Mineiro	Copa Sudamericana	1st Stage
Cruzeiro	Copa Sudamericana	1st Stage
Palmeiras	Copa Sudamericana	1st Stage
Vasco da Gama	Copa Sudamericana	1st Stage
Fluminense	Copa Sudamericana	2nd Stage
São Caetano	Copa Sudamericana	2nd Stage
São Paulo	Copa Sudamericana	Semi-finals

Copa do Brasil

2003 FINAL (2 legs)

June 8 – Maracana Stadium, Rio de Janeiro
Flamengo 1-1 Cruzeiro
(Fernando   (Alex 76)
Baiano 90)
h/t: 0-0 **Att:** 73,104
Ref: Simon

June 11 – Mineirao Stadium, Belo Horizonte
Cruzeiro 3-1 Flamengo
(Deivid 1,   (Fernando
Aristizabal 15,   Baiano 64)
Luisao 28)
h/t: 3-0 **Att:** 80,000
Ref: De Oliviera

Cruzeiro won 4-2 on aggregate

Coach Wanderley Luxemburgo is back on the winning trail with Cruzeiro after being booted out of his jobs with the Brazilian national team for losing too many matches and Corinthians for not paying his taxes.

Cruzeiro's captain Alex de Souza raises the Copa do Brazil trophy after a 3-1 win over Flamengo in the second leg at the Mineirao Stadium in Belo Horizonte.

Below: Alex raises the Brazilian championship trophy after Cruzeiro swept Paysandu aside to clinch the title – Alex's goals proved inspirational this season, but how long can he be kept at home?

Bottom: Cruzeiro fans celebrate the club's league title after the final home game of the season in Belo Horizonte.

Ze Carlos da Silva of Flamengo (right) performs a scissors-kick next to Edu Dracena of Cruzeiro, during the first leg of the Copa do Brazil Final at the Maracana in Rio de Janeiro. The match ended in a 1-1 draw.

BRAZIL

Soccer in Brazil

1894: Charles Miller returns to Brazil from England with first imported soccer equipment. First recorded match, São Paulo

1898: First club, Associacao Atletica of Mackenzie College, São Paulo founded

1901: São Paulo League, Campeonata Paulista de Futebol, established

1905: Bahia State League (first provincial league) established

1906: Rio League established

1914: CBD founded: Confederação Brasileira de Desportos. First international v Argentina, lost 3-0, venue: Buenos Aires

1916: Affiliation to CONMEBOL

1923: Affiliation to FIFA

1933: Professionalism legalized

1950: Rio-São Paulo Tournament established. Brazil hosted World Cup and was beaten 2–1 by Uruguay in the Final in front of the biggest ever soccer crowd – c. 200,000

1959: Brazilian Cup established

1967: Rio-São Paulo Tournament replaced by Taca de Prata

1968: Brazilian Cup discontinued

1971: Fully-fledged National League established, replaces Taca de Prata

1980: CBF (Confederação Brasileira de Futbol) replaces CBD

1982: First women's international, v Spain

1989: Brazilian Cup re-established

1993: Pele, Minister of Sport, fails to reform the game

2000: Massive judicial investigation launched into the finances of Brazilian soccer. National championship replaced by one-off João Havelange Tournament

2003: National Championships reformed, Play-offs abandoned

Timeline years: 1890, 1895, 1900, 1905, 1910, 1915, 1920, 1925, 1930, 1935, 1940, 1945, 1950, 1955, 1960, 1965, 1970, 1975, 1980, 1985, 1990, 1995, 2000, 2005

Complete with his 'Miss World Cup' sash, *Gylmar the Brazilian goalkeeper is held up in triumph after victory in the 1962 World Cup Final against Czechoslovakia in Chile.*

International Competitions

Year		Copa Libertadores	Copa CONMEBOL	Copa Mercosur
1919:	● ■			
1921:	▲			
1922:	● ■			
1925:	▲			
1937:	▲			
1945:	▲			
1946:	▲			
1949:	● ■			
1950:	▲ ■			
1953:	▲			
1957:	▲			
1958:	●			
1959:	●			
1961:		△ Palm		
1962:	●	○ Santos		
1963:		○ Santos		
1968:		△ Palm		
1970:	●			
1974:		△ São P		
1976:		○ Cruz		
1977:		△ Cruz		
1980:		△ Inter		
1981:		○ Flam		
1983:	▲ ■	○ Grêm		
1984:		△ Grêm		
1989:	● ■			
1991:	▲			
1992:		○ São P	○ Atl M	
1993:		○ São P	○ Bota	
1994:	●	△ São P	○ São P	
1995:	▲	○ Grêm		△ Atl M
1997:	●	○ Cruz	○ Atl M	
1998:	●	○ Vasco	○ Santos	○ Palm △ Cruz
1999:	●	○ Palm		○ Flam △ Palm
2000:		△ Palm		○ Vasco △ Palm
2001:				△ Flam
2002:	●	△ São C		
2003:		△ Santos		

Key

- International soccer
- Affiliation to FIFA
- Affiliation to CONMEBOL
- Women's soccer
- ♀ World Cup host
- ● World Cup winner
- ▲ World Cup runner-up
- ■ Copa América host
- ● Copa América winner
- ▲ Copa América runner-up
- ○ Competition winner
- △ Competition runner-up

Atl M – Atlético Mineiro
Bota – Botafogo
Cruz – Cruzeiro
Flam – Flamengo
Grêm – Grêmio
Inter – Internacional
Palm – Palmeiras
São C – São Caetano
São P – São Paulo
Vasco – Vasco da Gama

Atlética Ponte Preta 1900

Guarani FC 1911

RORAIM (1995)

AMAZONAS (1914)

ACRE (1989)

RONDÔNIA (1945)

Coritiba 1909

Paraná Clube 1989
Merger of Colorado and Pinheiros

Atlético Paranaense 1924

Criciúma EC 1947

Comerciaro (1978)

Brazil: The main clubs

Santos 1912	Team name with year of formation
●	Club formed before 1912
●	Club formed 1912–25
○	Club formed 1925–50
○	Club formed after 1950
PARÁ (1913)	State (year of championship foundation)
	Founded 1900–10
	Founded 1910–20
	Founded 1920–50
	Founded 1950–80
	Founded 1980–95
	Team colours
	English origins
	German origins
	Italian origins
	Portuguese origins
	Lower class
	Upper class
	Originated from a cricket club
	Originated from a rowing club
	Railway company origins

Brazil

ORIGINS AND GROWTH OF SOCCER

THE EARLIEST REPORTS OF SOCCER in Brazil are of British and Dutch sailors playing on the Rio dockside in the 1870s and of British and Brazilian railway workers in São Paulo in 1882. But the written record begins with Charles Miller. Brazilian-born of English coffee-merchant parentage, Miller was educated in England. With a game for Hampshire against the Corinthians under his belt, he returned to Brazil in 1894 with a collection of footballs and a raging enthusiasm. Collecting together Englishmen from the São Paulo Railway, the local gas company and the London and Brazilian bank, he organized the first 'official' soccer match in São Paulo in 1895. Within five years teams had sprung up in São Paulo and Rio, drawing on German colleges and gym clubs, Portuguese immigrants, English companies, as well as members of elite cricket and rowing clubs.

The race issue

São Paulo's Campeonata Paulista de Futebol was the first organized tournament which started in 1901, followed by leagues in Bahia (1904) and Rio de Janeiro (1905). A national association running all sports, the CBD, was set up in 1914 with a soccer section. The elite and predominantly white origins of Brazilian soccer soon came into conflict with the mass popularity of the game on the issue of race. Carlos Alberto, a mulatto of mixed race, played for Fluminense in 1916 with rice flour on his face to lighten his complexion. In 1921, President Pesoa called for an all-white team to represent Brazil in the Copa América.

But in 1923, Vasco da Gama won the Rio Championship with a team dominated by black and mixed-race players. Rio's big teams, flushed with fear for their sporting and social status, organized an alternative league and sought to exclude black players by making the signing of a team sheet a pre-condition of participation. But the sporting and economic logic was against exclusion, and as players of all races began moving to Italy and elsewhere, professionalism was introduced into the Rio Championships in 1933 and quickly spread.

The 1970 World Cup-winning Brazilian team is regarded by many as the finest soccer team ever. The side that faced Italy in the Final included: (back row left to right) Carlos Alberto, Brito, Piazza, Felix, Clodoaldo, Everaldo, Gerson; (front row) Jairzinho, Rivelino, Tostão, Pele and Paulo Cesar.

Map labels

Unión São João 1981

EC Vitória 1899
Club de Cricket Victoria (1899–1946)

EC Bahia 1931
Merger of Atlética de Bahia and Club Bahiano de Tenis

América FC 1915

SC Recife 1905

AMAPÁ (1944)

RIO GRANDE DO NORTE (1920)

Araras

MARANHÃO (1918)

CEARÁ (1920)

Natal

PARÁ (1913)

PIAUÍ (1918)

PARAIABA (1917)

Recife

B R A Z I L

PERNAMBUCO (1915)

ALAGOAS (1927)

TOCANTINS (1993)

SERGIPE (1918)

Salvador

MATO GROSSO (1974)

DISTRITO FEDERAL (1973)

BAHIA (1905)

Brasília
SE Gama 1975

Goiás EC 1943 **Goiânia**

GOAIS (1944)

MINAS GERAIS

ESPÍRITO SANTO (1940)

Atlético Bragantino 1928

Belo Horizonte

Bragança Paulista **Rio de Janeiro**

RIO DE JANEIRO (1906)

Campinas

MATO GROSSO DO SUL (1979)

São Caetano

São Caetano 1989

Atlético Mineiro 1908

SÃO PAULO (1902)

São Paulo

Curitiba

Santos 1912

Cruzeiro EC 1921

Palestra Italia (1921–42)

PARANÁ (1915)

SANTA CATARINA (1927)

SC Corinthians 1910

Flamengo 1895

Criciúma

RIO GRANDE DO SUL (1919)

Botafogo SP 1918

Caxias du Sul

Porto Alegre

Portuguesa de Desportos 1920

CR Vasco da Gama 1898

Atlética das Palmeiras 1914

Societa Palestra Italia (1914–42)

EC Juventude 1913

São Paulo FC 1935

Fluminense 1902

SC Internacional 1909

Grêmio 1903

Botafogo 1914

São Paulo

SOCCER CENTER

BRAZIL

SÃO PAULO IS THE INDUSTRIAL and commercial heart of Brazil. After an English public school education, Charles Miller (son of a coffee merchant family) returned to São Paulo in 1894 with some soccer balls. In 1895, he organized a game among British workers at the São Paulo Railway Company, the London and Brazilian Bank and the Gas Company on the Varzea do Carmo. More games were organized between soccer sections formed by the British at São Paulo Athletic Club and Mackenzie College. The word spread and Germans from the city's gymnastic clubs created SC Germania. Together with another club, CA Paulistino, these teams formed the city's first league in 1901. Within a year, São Paulo had over 60 clubs and the game began to spread beyond its European elite circles.

The five big teams of the professional era emerged a decade or so after this initial explosion. In 1910, Corinthians was founded by railway workers in Bom Retiro, and named after the English amateurs who had recently toured the city. In 1912, the Rio team América relocated to the port area of the city. After considering various names, like 'Africa' and 'Concordia', it settled on the area's name, Santos, for its new club. In 1914, the city's Italian immigrant population created Club Sociedada Esportivo Palestra Italia. During the Second World War, anti-Italian sentiment saw the side change its name to Palmeiras. The Portuguese community followed with the creation of Portuguesa from the merger of five clubs (Lusiadas, Portugal Marinhense, 5 de Outobro, Luzitano and Marques de Pombal).

Professionalism and disaster

These four clubs were among those teams which were paying their players and pushing for the development of a professional game in the 1920s. The last of the big five, São Paulo, rose out of the ashes of an earlier team of the same name. São Paulo 'I' was formed in 1930, when CA Paulistino stopped playing soccer in protest over the adoption of professionalism, and the club's players joined AA de Palmeiras. The venture folded in 1935 and São Paulo 'II' drew on what was left of the team to start again. By then a professional city league had been created.

The decades that followed were a peak for São Paulo soccer – a rash of stadium building, including the city government's funding of the Pacaembu, and the arrival of Pele at Santos. The club's victories in the Copa Libertadores in the early 1960s at last allowed the city to eclipse Rio. Forty years on, Corinthians are the city's leading club, but their financial situation is dire. Santos have been revived by their young stars Diego and Robinho and their championship victory in 2002.

São Paulo, Brazil's industrial and commercial heartland, has witnessed decades of explosive economic and demographic growth that has created extremes of wealth (in the central business district featured here) and poverty in the sprawling shanty towns of the city's periphery: perfect conditions for the creation of massive fan bases.

CÍCERO POMPEU DE TOLEDO – MORUMBI

80,000	
Club:	São Paulo
Built:	1960
Original Capacity:	120, 000
Record Attendance:	138,032 Corinthians v Ponte Preta, 1977
Significant Matches:	2000 Club World Championship: six group matches

SÃO PAULO
SEE ENLARGEMENT FOR MORE DETAIL

AA Portuguesa Santos

URBANO CALDEIRA 'VILA BELMIRO'
18,500

ULRICO MURSA
15,000

SANTOS

ATLANTIC OCEAN

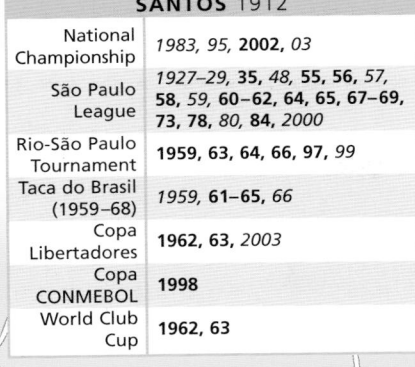

SANTOS 1912

National Championship	*1983, 95,* **2002,** *03*
São Paulo League	*1927–29,* **35,** *48,* **55, 56, 57, 58, 59,** *60–62,* **64, 65,** *67–69,* **73, 78,** *80,* **84,** *2000*
Rio-São Paulo Tournament	**1959, 63, 64, 66, 97,** *99*
Taca do Brasil (1959–68)	*1959,* **61–65,** *66*
Copa Libertadores	**1962, 63,** *2003*
Copa CONMEBOL	**1998**
World Club Cup	**1962, 63**

CORINTHIANS 1910

National Championship	*1976,* **90, 94, 98, 99,** *2002*
São Paulo League	**1914,** *18,* **22–24,** *25,* **28–30,** *36,* **37–39, 41,** *42, 43,* **45–47, 51, 52, 54, 55,** *62,* **66, 68,** *74, 77,* **79,** *82, 83, 84, 87,* **88,** *91,* **93, 95, 97, 98, 99, 2001,** *03*
Rio-São Paulo Tournament	**1950, 53, 54,** *63,* **66,** *93,* **2002,** *03*
Copa do Brasil (1989–2004)	**1995,** *2001,* **02**
FIFA Club World Championship	**2000**

LIMAO · CASA VERDE

Palmeiras

PALESTRA ITÁLIA 'PARQUE ANTÁRCTICA'
32,000

Rio Tiete

VILA GUILHERME · VILA MARIA

OSWALDO TEIXEIRA DUARTE 'CANDIDÉ'
22,000

Via Presidente Dutra

ALFREDO SCHURING 'PARQUE SÃO JORGE'
15,000

Corinthians

LAPA

PERDIZES

BOM RETIRO · PARI

Portuguesa

CONDO RODOLFO CRESPI
9,000

'PACAEMBU'
Paulo Machado de Carvalho.
This municipal stadium is used for big games by all the city's leading clubs
40,000

SANTA CECILIA

VILA MADALENA

CONSOLACAO

REPUBLICA

SÃO PAULO

BRAS

Juventus

ALTO DA MOOCA

BELA VISTA

São Paulo AC

CAMBUCI

PINHEIROS

JARDIM AMERICA

São Paulo

CÍCERO POMPEU DE TOLEDO 'MORUMBI'
80,000

BUTANTA

JARDIM PAULISTA

SC Germania

FEDERAÇÃO PAULISTA DE FUTEBOL STATE FA HEADQUARTERS

IPIRANGA

Rio Tiete

Avenida Reboucas

Avenida Brasil

Avenida Paulista

BROOKLIN PAULISTANA
Birth place of Rivellino

BRAZIL

PORTUGUESA 1920

National Championship	*1996*
São Paulo League	**1935, 36,** *40, 60, 73, 75, 85*
Rio-São Paulo Tournament	**1952, 55,** *65*

SÃO PAULO 1935

National Championship	*1971, 73,* **77,** *81,* **86,** *89, 90,* **91**
São Paulo League	*1930,* **31,** *32–34,* **38,** *41,* **43, 44, 45, 46, 48, 49,** *50,* **52, 53,** *56,* **57,** *58,* **63,** *67,* **70, 71,** *72,* **75,** *78,* **80, 81,** *82, 83,* **85, 87, 89, 91, 92,** *94, 96, 97,* **98, 2000,** *03*
Rio-São Paulo Tournament	*1965, 98,* **2001,** *02, 03*
Copa do Brasil (1989–2004)	*2000*
Copa Libertadores	*1974,* **92, 93,** *94*
Copa CONMEBOL	**1994**
Supercopa	**1993,** *97*
World Club Cup	**1992, 93**

PALMEIRAS 1914

National Championship	**1972, 73,** *78,* **93, 94,** *97*
São Paulo League	**1920,** *21,–23,* **26, 27,** *31,* **32–34, 35, 36,** *37,* **39, 40,** *42,* **44,** *47,* **49, 50,** *51,* **53, 54,** *59,* **61, 63, 64, 65, 66,** *69–71,* **72, 74, 76,** *86,* **92, 93, 94, 95, 96,** *99*
Rio-São Paulo Tournament	**1931, 51,** *55,* **61, 62,** *65,* **93, 2000**
Taca do Brasil (1959–68)	**1960, 67**
Copa do Brasil (1989–2004)	*1996,* **98**
Copa Libertadores	*1961, 68,* **99,** *2000*
Copa Mercosur	**1998,** *99, 2000*
World Club Cup	*1999*

São Paulo

32,000	Capacity of stadium
	Minor clubs
	Stadium no longer in use for top-flight soccer
	Team colours
	Early São Paulo teams
	Major road
1900	Champions
2000	Runners-up

Rio de Janeiro

SOCCER CENTER

UNCONFIRMED REPORTS TELL OF British sailors playing soccer in Rio's docks throughout the late 19th century. The expatriate British elite played cricket (in Paissandu and Rio Cricket Sud in Niteroi) and formed rowing clubs. After a match between São Paulo and Rio in 1901, a rash of soccer clubs were set up among the expatriates: Fluminense in 1902, América and Botafogo in 1904. Fluminense attracted the pinnacle of society, students from the Alfredo Gomez College formed Botafogo, and Bangu were in effect the works' team of the British managers at a textile firm in the suburbs. In 1906 a local tournament, the Carioca, was established. In 1911, defectors from Fluminense joined Flamengo rowing club to create a Flamengo soccer section.

The literacy test

At first, elite control of Rio soccer was more absolute than in São Paulo, and the white expatriates, professionals and students of these clubs dominated the game. But in 1923, Vasco da Gama, a team formed by Portuguese immigrants, came into the top division, fielding four black players among poor white players. The key difference was that they were professionals, and the team was unstoppable. The big elite clubs left the

league and formed their own (LMDT), which ran the following year without Vasco. But the crowds went to Vasco, and the club – along with two others – was eventually asked to join the LMDT. However, pre-match paperwork in the league required literacy of all players, and Vasco's advantage was eradicated until the literacy test was abolished in 1929. By the early 1930s, all the clubs were paying players in an intense competitive struggle, and inevitably a professional league was established in 1933 – known to this day as the Carioca.

Although Vasco is a perennial challenger, and often the victor, the Flamengo-Fluminense rivalry is the key to soccer in Rio. In a single game, this local derby condenses the divisions of class and race in the city; Fluminense (the aristocracy) versus Flamengo (the people). It is this intensity for soccer, reflected citywide, that saw the creation of the world's largest soccer stadium – the Maracana – and the national disaster of defeat in the 1950 World Cup. Today, the clubs share power in Rio with the Confederação Brasileira de Futebol, who chose to locate here rather than in the capital Brasília, and the nation's gigantic TV company – Globo. The rising tide of accusations of corruption, match fixing and interference are now lapping at the doors of the presidents of the major Rio clubs and the Rio FA.

BRAZIL

MARIO FILHO – MARACANA

95,095

Clubs:	Botafogo, Flamengo, Fluminense
Built:	1950
Original Capacity	180,000
Rebuilt:	1993–98
Record Attendance:	183,341 1969 Brazil v Paraguay, World Cup
Significant Matches:	1950 World Cup: seven matches including final pool match; Copa América: 1989 final pool matches

BANGU 1904

National Championship	1985
Rio League (Carioca)	1916, **33**, 51, 59, 64, 65, **66**, 67, 85

DUQUE DE CAXIAS
Birthplace of Jairzinho

116

040

Olaria AC

RUA BARIRI

18,000

Soccer in Rio reflects the divisions of class and race in the city. This is embodied in the Fla-Flu derby which pits the people (in the shape of Flamengo) against the aristocracy (in the shape of Fluminense).

465

MENDHANHA   MOCA BONITA

15,000

MADUREIRA

ANICETO MOSCOSO

10,000

Baia de Gunabara

RAMOS

210

101

ÍTALO DEL CIMA

25,000

Bangu

CAMPO GRANDE

BANGU

Madureira

PILARES

EDSON PASSOS

15,000

CENTRO

NITEROI
Birthplace of Gerson

RIO DE JANEIRO

Campo Grande

JACAREPAGUA

América

108

COPACABANA
SEE CENTRAL RIO
FOR MORE DETAIL

AMÉRICA 1904

Rio League (Carioca)	1911, **13**, 14, **16**, 17, 21, **22**, 28, 29, 31, 35, 50, 54, 55, **60**

101

071

ATLANTIC OCEAN

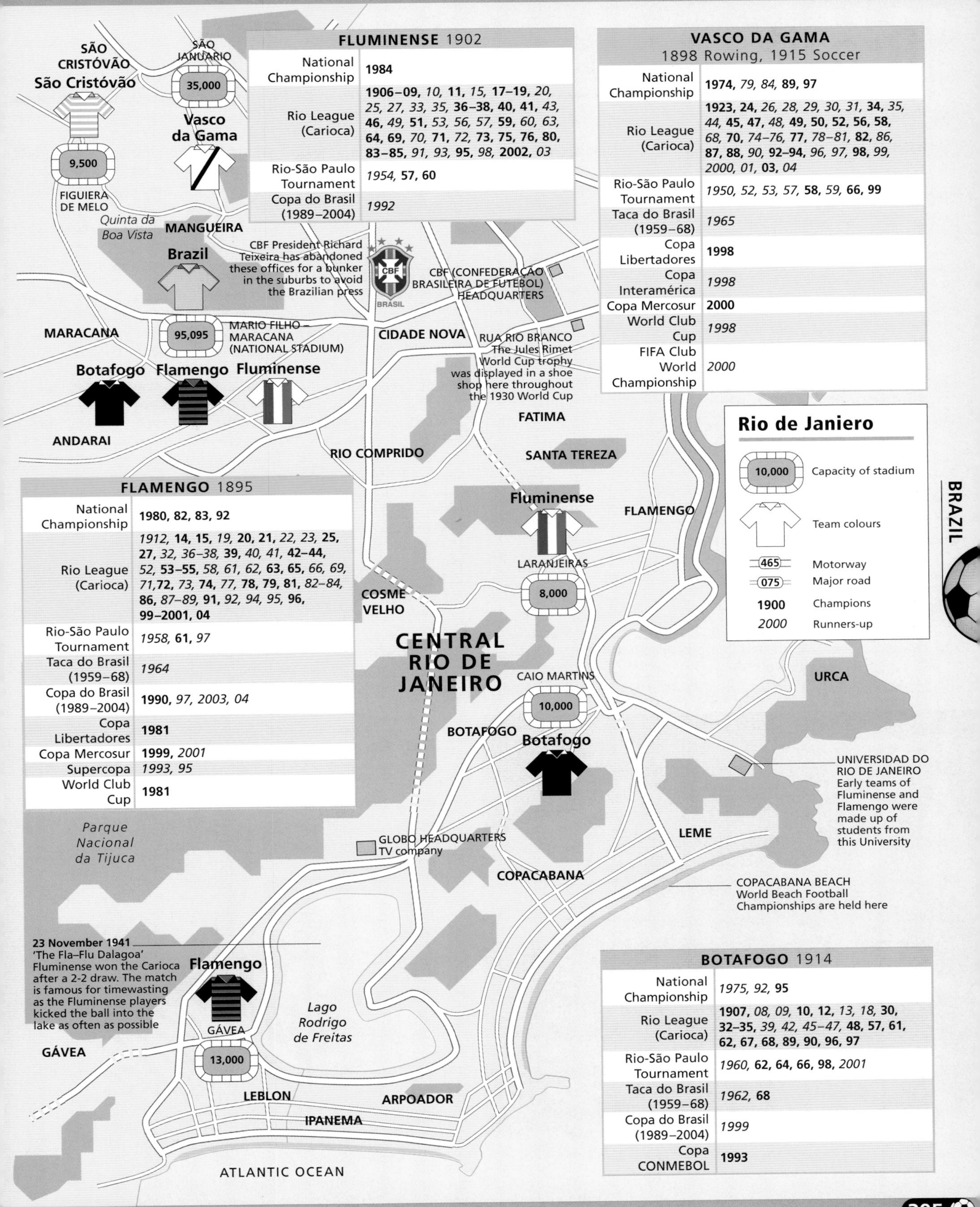

SÃO CRISTÓVÃO
São Cristóvão
9,500
FIGUEIRA DE MELO

SÃO JANUARIO
35,000
Vasco da Gama
Quinta da Boa Vista

MANGUEIRA

Brazil

MARACANA

95,095
MARIO FILHO – MARACANA (NATIONAL STADIUM)

Botafogo Flamengo Fluminense

ANDARAI

FLUMINENSE 1902

National Championship	**1984**
Rio League (Carioca)	**1906–09**, *10*, **11**, *15*, **17–19**, *20*, *25*, *27*, *33*, *35*, **36–38**, **40**, **41**, *43*, **46**, *49*, **51**, *53*, **56**, **57**, **59**, *60*, *63*, **64**, **69**, *70*, **71**, *72*, **73**, *75*, **76**, **80**, **83–85**, *91*, **93**, *95*, *98*, **2002**, *03*
Rio-São Paulo Tournament	**1954**, **57**, **60**
Copa do Brasil (1989–2004)	*1992*

CBF President Richard Teixeira has abandoned these offices for a bunker in the suburbs to avoid the Brazilian press

CBF (CONFEDERAÇÃO BRASILEIRA DE FUTEBOL) HEADQUARTERS
CBF BRASIL

CIDADE NOVA

RUA RIO BRANCO
The Jules Rimet World Cup trophy was displayed in a shoe shop here throughout the 1930 World Cup

FATIMA

RIO COMPRIDO

SANTA TEREZA

VASCO DA GAMA
1898 Rowing, 1915 Soccer

National Championship	**1974**, *79*, **84**, **89**, **97**
Rio League (Carioca)	**1923**, **24**, *26*, *28*, *29*, *30*, **31**, **34**, *35*, *44*, **45**, **47**, *48*, **49**, **50**, **52**, **56**, **58**, *68*, **70**, *74–76*, **77**, *78–81*, **82**, *86*, **87**, **88**, *90*, *92–94*, *96*, **97**, **98**, *99*, **2000**, *01*, *03*, **04**
Rio-São Paulo Tournament	**1950**, *52*, *53*, *57*, **58**, *59*, *66*, **99**
Taca do Brasil (1959–68)	*1965*
Copa Libertadores	**1998**
Copa Interamérica	**1998**
Copa Mercosur	**2000**
World Club Cup	*1998*
FIFA Club World Championship	*2000*

Rio de Janiero

10,000	Capacity of stadium
	Team colours
465	Motorway
075	Major road
1900	Champions
2000	Runners-up

Fluminense
LARANJEIRAS
8,000

FLAMENGO

COSME VELHO

CENTRAL RIO DE JANEIRO

FLAMENGO 1895

National Championship	**1980**, **82**, **83**, **92**
Rio League (Carioca)	*1912*, **14**, **15**, *19*, **20**, **21**, *22*, *23*, **25**, **27**, *32*, *36–38*, **39**, *40*, *41*, *42–44*, *52*, **53–55**, *58*, *61*, *62*, **63**, *65*, *66*, *69*, *71*, **72**, *73*, **74**, *77*, **78**, *79*, *81*, *82–84*, **86**, *87–89*, *91*, *92*, *94*, *95*, **96**, *99–2001*, **04**
Rio-São Paulo Tournament	*1958*, **61**, *97*
Taca do Brasil (1959–68)	*1964*
Copa do Brasil (1989–2004)	**1990**, *97*, **2003**, *04*
Copa Libertadores	**1981**
Copa Mercosur	**1999**, *2001*
Supercopa	*1993*, **95**
World Club Cup	**1981**

CAIO MARTINS
10,000

BOTAFOGO
Botafogo

URCA

UNIVERSIDAD DO RIO DE JANEIRO
Early teams of Fluminense and Flamengo were made up of students from this University

Parque Nacional da Tijuca

GLOBO HEADQUARTERS
TV company

LEME

COPACABANA

COPACABANA BEACH
World Beach Football Championships are held here

23 November 1941
'The Fla–Flu Dalagoa' Fluminense won the Carioca after a 2-2 draw. The match is famous for timewasting as the Fluminense players kicked the ball into the lake as often as possible

Flamengo
GÁVEA
13,000

GÁVEA

Lago Rodrigo de Freitas

LEBLON   ARPOADOR

IPANEMA

ATLANTIC OCEAN

BOTAFOGO 1914

National Championship	*1975*, *92*, **95**
Rio League (Carioca)	**1907**, **08**, **09**, **10**, *12*, **13**, *18*, **30**, **32–35**, *39*, *42*, *45–47*, **48**, *57*, **61**, *62*, **67**, **68**, *89*, *90*, *96*, **97**
Rio-São Paulo Tournament	*1960*, *62*, **64**, *66*, *98*, *2001*
Taca do Brasil (1959–68)	*1962*, **68**
Copa do Brasil (1989–2004)	*1999*
Copa CONMEBOL	**1993**

Brazil

BRAZIL

FANS AND OWNERS

FOR MOST OF THEIR EXISTENCE Brazilian soccer clubs have operated in the legal twilight zone. As they have grown and their income has risen, they have become the perfect vehicles for those seeking influence, prestige and money. The chaotic, corrupt and opaque character of these clubs was supposed to be resolved by the Pele Law, passed in 1998 by the then Minister of Sport. The new law stated that Brazilian clubs were to become either civil or commercial companies regulated by law or, alternatively, they could spin off their professional arms as separate entities and outside investors could buy into them, bringing in modern management and much needed investment. The Pele Law also sought to modernize the archaic and inequitable player-club contracts and was therefore fiercely opposed by the leading teams or the Clube dos Treze, as they are better known. The 'Club of 13' was formed in 1997 to squeeze a better TV deal out of Globo, which they did. However, this being Brazil, the 13 are really 17.

Financial partners
Since the Pele Law came into force only a few clubs have explored the possibility of recruiting financial partners, and many of the schemes have ended in disaster. The American bank Hicks Muse, Tate and First (HMTF), operating as Pan-American Sports Teams, bought into Cruzeiro and Corinthians, while ISL, FIFA's marketing agents until their spectacular bankruptcy in mid-2001, bought into Grêmio and Flamengo. Nations Bank investment in Vasco da Gama has already been dissolved, while Parmalat has pulled out of its long-standing relationship with Palmeiras. But investors have rightly been cautious, as the Dias-Althoff report into Brazilian soccer in 2002 revealed that corruption and waste are endemic and numerous

leading figures in the clubs, state soccer authorities and the CBF have been recommended for criminal prosecution, though as yet none have been brought to trial. In 2004 under President Lula the Federal Government passed a fans' statute that required minimum levels of hygiene and safety at Brazilian soccer grounds.

Violence on and off the pitch
The anarchy and viciousness of Brazil's clubs is paralleled by many of their fans. The big clubs have all acquired organized and often violent supporters' groups called *Torcida Organizada*. Equipped with firecrackers, noise bombs and, increasingly, with guns, these groups have ensured that violence inside and outside the grounds has been on the rise. In 2000, Vagner Jose Lima was killed when armed São Paulo fans attacked a small group of Corinthians supporters in the Bexiga district. São Paulo fans standing by their broken-down bus were shot at by a passing bus full of Santos fans. In 2001, Santos fans broke into the squad's training camp, attacking and berating the players for their poor performances. Four shootings were reported at the Bahia v Vitória derby in Salvador and shootings at Flamengo matches are common. Television coverage of, and judicial intervention in the violence is minimal as Globo seeks to protect its investments. But, whatever they show, the viciousness of the contemporary Brazilian game, dominated by fouling and diving, is mirrored in the stands. The concentration of power and money in the leading clubs is paralleled by the level of support for the big clubs. As the *Placar* survey shows, Flamengo, Corinthians, São Paulo, Vasco and Palmeiras are way out in front, with fans not only in their home towns but in other major cities.

Corinthians is the best supported club in São Paulo and retains its core working-class support.

Club Support in Brazil 2001

Santos 2.4%
Botafogo 2.7%
SC Recife 1.6%
Santa Cruz 1.5%
EC Bahia 2.5%
Fluminense 2.7%
SC Internacional 2.9%
Cruzeiro EC 3.9%
Atlético Mineiro 4.0%
Grêmio 4.5%
Palmeiras 7.2%
Other 13.1%
Flamengo 19.1%
Information supplied by *Placar* magazine
CR Vasco da Gama 8.4%
São Paulo FC 9.1%
SC Corinthians 14.4%

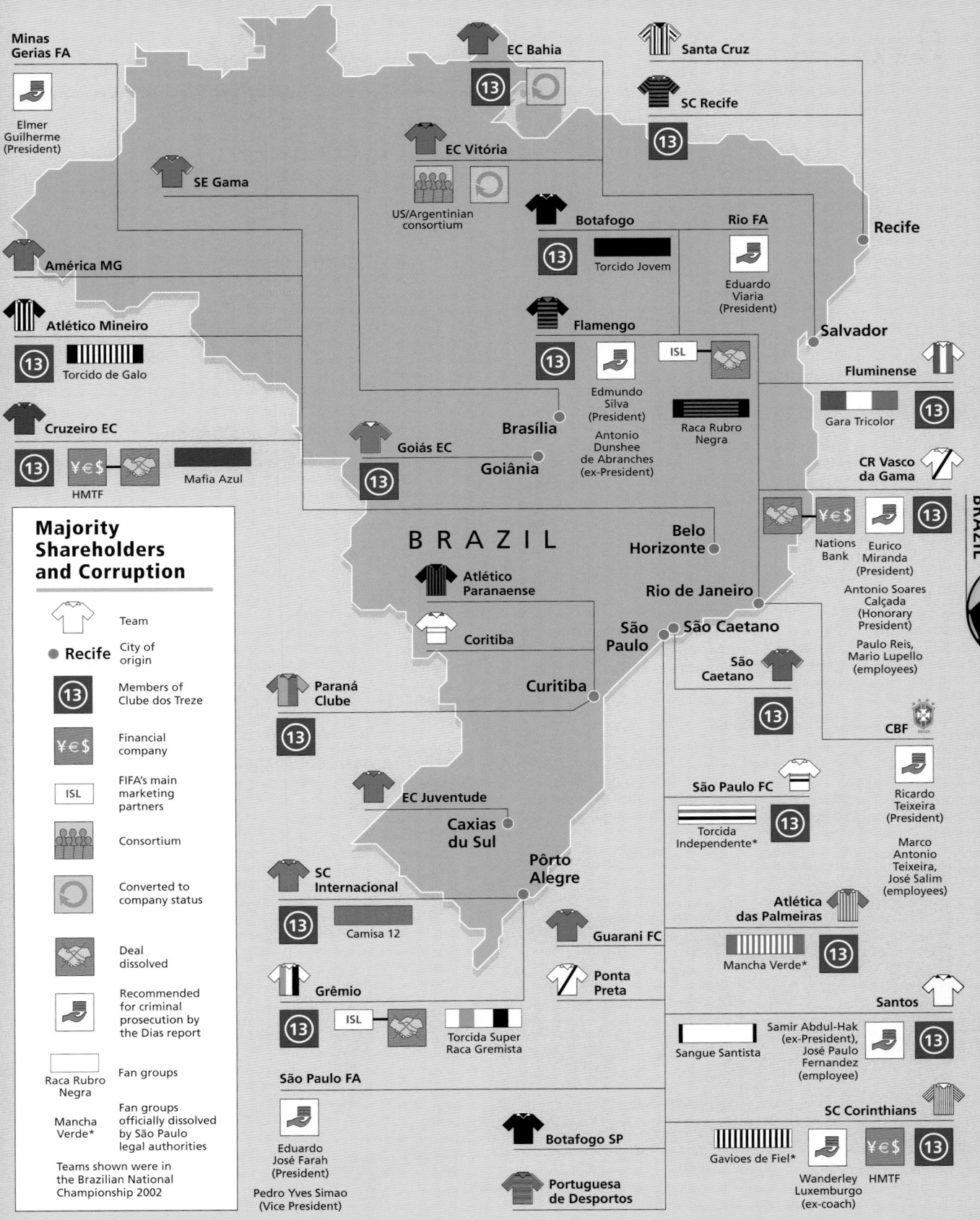

Minas Gerias FA

Elmer Guilherme (President)

SE Gama

América MG

Atlético Mineiro

Torcido de Galo

Cruzeiro EC

HMTF

Mafia Azul

EC Bahia

EC Vitória

US/Argentinian consortium

Santa Cruz

SC Recife

Botafogo

Torcido Jovem

Rio FA

Eduardo Viaria (President)

Flamengo

Edmundo Silva (President)

Antonio Dunshee de Abranches (ex-President)

ISL

Raca Rubro Negra

Recife

Salvador

Fluminense

Gara Tricolor

Goiás EC

Brasília

Goiânia

B R A Z I L

Belo Horizonte

CR Vasco da Gama

Nations Bank

Eurico Miranda (President)

Antonio Soares Calçada (Honorary President)

Paulo Reis, Mario Lupello (employees)

Majority Shareholders and Corruption

Team	
Recife	City of origin
13	Members of Clube dos Treze
¥€$	Financial company
ISL	FIFA's main marketing partners
	Consortium
	Converted to company status
	Deal dissolved
	Recommended for criminal prosecution by the Dias report
Raca Rubro Negra	Fan groups
Mancha Verde*	Fan groups officially dissolved by São Paulo legal authorities

Teams shown were in the Brazilian National Championship 2002

Atlético Paranaense

Coritiba

Paraná Clube

EC Juventude

Caxias du Sul

SC Internacional

Camisa 12

Grêmio

ISL

Torcida Super Raca Gremista

São Paulo FA

Eduardo José Farah (President)

Pedro Yves Simao (Vice President)

Rio de Janeiro

São Paulo

São Caetano

São Caetano

Curitiba

Pôrto Alegre

Guarani FC

Ponta Preta

Botafogo SP

Portuguesa de Desportos

CBF

Ricardo Teixeira (President)

Marco Antonio Teixeira, José Salim (employees)

São Paulo FC

Torcida Independente*

Atlética das Palmeiras

Mancha Verde*

Santos

Sangue Santista

Samir Abdul-Hak (ex-President), José Paulo Fernandez (employee)

SC Corinthians

Gavioes de Fiel*

Wanderley Luxemburgo (ex-coach)

HMTF

BRAZIL

Brazil

PLAYERS AND MANAGERS

SOCCER BEGAN IN BRAZIL as a game of the rich, white elite; black and mixed-race players were dissuaded, banned or disguised with make-up by the leading clubs until the rise of the predominantly black and very successful Vasco da Gama from Rio de Janeiro in the 1930s. Since the advent of professionalism, black players have dominated the game and the popular archetype on which their style of play is based is described as the *Malandro*: the wide boy from the *favellas*, who waltzes through life on a stream of trickery and cunning, guile and style, and who moves with the grace of the *capoeira* master (a black Brazilian version of *t'ai chi*). From the heady mix of black Brazilian urban culture sprang two generations of extraordinarily gifted, stylish players: Garrincha, Gerson, Pele, Jairzhino, Rivelino and Carlos Alberto, and with them came the 'Beautiful Game' as well as three World Cups.

Exodus

The great Brazilian teams of this golden era played their club soccer almost exclusively in Brazil, but with the steady decline of the Brazilian economy, an exodus of talent to Europe and Japan has become a tidal wave. Today's leading Brazilian players (Cafu, Ronaldo, Roberto Carlos and Rivaldo) all play their soccer in Spain and Italy.

It is not only the Brazilian economy that has been in decline. The World Cup of 1970 represented the high point of Brazilian soccer. Despite a flickering renaissance in the early 1980s around players like Zico, Socrates and old-style manager Tele Santana, there has been a steady erosion of the *Malandro* as international and club managers have insisted on aggression, defence, persistent fouling and winning at any cost, exemplified by the dour, mechanical Brazilian team under Phil Scolari who only just scraped into the 2002 World Cup Finals – winning the tournament will have brought a welcome check to this despondent outlook. Brazilian managers have also been caught in the web of corruption that has engulfed Brazilian soccer, including ex-national coach Wanderley Luxemburgo, who was sacked in 2000 and was investigated by both police and the Senate.

Mario Zagallo held the Brazilian manager's job between 1995 and 1998. He is the longest-lasting manager of a national team that has had 125 managers since it first played an international match.

Top 10 International Caps

PLAYER	CAPS	GOALS	FIRST MATCH	LAST MATCH
Marcos Evangelista de Moeis **'Cafu'***	126	5	1990	2004
Roberto Carlos da Silva*	104	8	1992	2004
Claudio **Taffarel**	101	0	1987	1998
Djalma **do Santos**	98	3	1952	1968
Gylmar dos Santos Neves **'Gilmar'**	94	0	1953	1969
Carlos Caetano Beldorn Verri **'Dunga'**	91	6	1982	1998
Edson Arantes do Nascimento **'Pele'**	91	77	1957	1971
Roberto **Rivelino**	91	25	1965	1978
Nascimento dos Santos **Aldair***	81	3	1989	2001
Jair Ventura Filho **'Jairzinho'**	81	33	1963	1982

Top 10 International Goalscorers

PLAYER	GOALS	CAPS	FIRST MATCH	LAST MATCH
Edson Arantes do Nascimento **'Pele'**	77	91	1957	1971
Romario da Souza Faria*	54	68	1987	2001
Ronaldo Luis Nazario da Lima*	53	79	1994	2004
Artur Antunes Coimbra **'Zico'**	48	71	1971	1989
Jose Roberto Gama de Oliveira **'Bebeto'**	38	75	1985	1998
Rivaldo Vito Borba Ferreira*	34	74	1993	2003
Jair Ventura Filho **'Jairzinho'**	33	81	1963	1982
Ademir Marques de Menezes	32	39	1945	1953
Eduardo Goncalves de Andrade **'Tostao'**	31	53	1966	1972
Thomaz Soaras da Silva **'Zizinho'**	30	55	1942	1957

* Indicates players still playing at least at club level.
Bold indicates players recognized by either their first name, last name or nickname. Nicknames are indicated between inverted commas.

Brazil International Managers*

DATES	NAME	GAMES	WON	DRAWN	LOST
1979–80	Jaime Valente	12	7	2	3
1980–82	Tele Santana and	38	29	6	3
	Carlos Alberto Parreira	6	3	3	0
1983	Gilson Nunes,	3	2	0	1
	Carlos Alberto Parreira	7	1	4	2
	and Cleber Camerino	9	7	2	0
1984	Edu Antunes	3	1	1	1
	and Cleber Camerino	6	4	1	1
1985	Evaristo de Macedo	6	3	0	3
1985–86	Tele Santana	17	11	3	3
1986	Jair Pereira	4	2	2	0
1987–88	Carlos Alberto Silva	45	29	11	5
1989–90	Sebastiao Lazaroni	35	21	7	7
1990–91	Falcão	17	6	7	4
1991–92	Ernesto Paulo	8	4	1	3
1992–94	Carlos Alberto Parreira	45	26	14	4
1994–95	Mario Zagallo	3	3	0	0
1995	Pupo Giminez	5	3	2	0
1995–98	Mario Zagallo	90	65	17	8
1998–2000	Wanderley Luxemburgo	34	22	7	5
2000–01	Emerson Leao	10	3	4	3
2001–02	Luis Filipe Scolari	26	19	1	6
2002–04	Carlos Alberto Parreira	21	9	9	3

* Only includes managers who have been in charge on a regular basis.
All figures correct as of 6 June 2004.

Player of the Year

YEAR	PLAYER	CLUB
1973	Ancheta	Grêmio
1973	Cejas	Santos
1974	Zico	Flamengo
1975	Waldir Peres	São Paulo
1976	Elias Figueroa	Internacional
1977	Toninho Cerezo	Atlético Mineiro
1978	Falcão	Internacional
1979	Falcão	Internacional
1980	Toninho Cerezo	Atlético Mineiro
1981	Jesus	Grêmio
1982	Zico	Flamengo
1983	Costa	Atlético Paranaense
1984	Costa	Vasco da Gama
1985	Mahrino	Bangu Atlético
1986	Careca	São Paulo
1987	Renato Gaucho	Flamengo
1988	Taffarel	Internacional
1989	Rocha	São Paulo
1990	Sampaio	Santos
1991	Mauro da Silva	Bragantino
1992	Junior	Flamengo
1993	Sampaio	Palmeiras
1994	Marcio Amoroso	Guarani
1995	Giovanni	Santos
1996	Djalminha	Palmeiras
1997	Edmundo	Vasco da Gama
1998	Edilson	Corinthians
1999	Marcelinho	Corinthians
2000	Romario	Vasco da Gama
2001	Alex Mineiro	Atlético Paranaense
2002	Kaka	São Paulo
2003	Alex	Cruzeiro

Awarded by *Placar* magazine as the Bola de Ouro.

Jairzinho was the first player ever to have scored in every round of the World Cup Finals on the way to victory. Here he celebrates the last goal of his record-breaking feat in the Final of the 1970 tournament against Italy in Mexico City.

Championship-Winning Managers

YEAR	MANAGER	CLUB
1971	Santana	Atlético Mineiro
1972	Brandao	Palmeiras
1973	Brandao	Palmeiras
1974	Travaglini	Vasco da Gama
1975	Minelli	Internacional
1976	Minelli	Internacional
1977	Minelli	São Paulo
1978	Silva	Guarani
1979	Andrade	Internacional
1980	Coutinho	Flamengo
1981	Andrade	Grêmio
1982	Torres	Flamengo
1983	Parriera	Flamengo
1984	Andrade	Coritiba
1985	Pepe	São Paulo
1986	Carlinhos	Flamengo
1987	Picerni	Sport Club Recife
1988	Macedo	Bahia
1989	Rosa	Vasco da Gama
1990	Batista	Corinthians
1991	Santana	São Paulo
1992	Carlinhos	Flamengo
1993	Luxemburgo	Palmeiras
1994	Luxemburgo	Palmeiras
1995	Autuori	Botafogo
1996	Scolari	Grêmio
1997	Lopes	Vasco da Gama
1998	Luxemburgo	Corinthians
1999	Oliveira	Corinthians
2000	Santana	Vasco da Gama
2001	Geninho	Atlético Paranaense
2002	Leao	Santos
2003	Luxemburgo	Cruzeiro

BRAZIL

Top Goalscorers 1971–2003

SEASON	PLAYER	CLUB	GOALS
1971	Dario	Atlético Mineiro	15
1972	Dario	Atlético Mineiro	17
1972	Pedro Rocha	São Paulo	17
1973	Ramon	Santa Cruz	21
1974	Roberto Dinamite	Vasco da Gama	16
1975	Flávio	Internacional	16
1976	Dario	Internacional	16
1977	Reinaldo	Atlético Mineiro	28
1978	Paulinho	Vasco da Gama	19
1979	Roberto Cesar	Cruzeiro	12
1980	Zico	Flamengo	21
1981	Nunes	Flamengo	16
1982	Zico	Flamengo	20
1983	Serginho	Santos	22
1984	Roberto Dinamite	Vasco da Gama	16
1985	Edmar	Guarani	20
1986	Careca	São Paulo	25
1987	Muller	São Paulo	10
1988	Nilson	Internacional	15
1989	Túlio	Goiás	11
1990	Charles	Bahia	11

SEASON	PLAYER	CLUB	GOALS
1991	Paulinho	Santos	15
1992	Bebeto	Vasco da Gama	18
1993	Guga	Santos	15
1994	Túlio	Botafogo	19
1994	Amoroso	Guarani	19
1995	Túlio	Botafogo	23
1996	Nunes	Grêmio	16
1997	Edmundo	Vasco da Gama	29
1998	Viola	Santos	21
1999	Guilherme	Atlético Mineiro	28
2000	Adhemar	São Cãetano	22
2001	Alex Mineiro	Atlético Paranaense	21
2002	Fabiano	São Paulo	19
2002	Fabri	Grêmio	19
2003	Dimba	Guarani	31

Romario da Souza Faria has been one of Brazil's leading goalscorers since the late 1980s. He began his career with Vasco da Gama, moved to Europe to play for PSV and Barcelona, before returning home to Vasco via Flamengo. His continued success was underlined when he was voted Brazilian Player of the Year in 2000.

Brazil

THE CAMPEONATO BRASILEIRO 1971–2003

BRAZIL WAS THE LAST major soccer-playing nation to organize a national club tournament – the enormous size of the country, poor transport links and the huge inequalities in wealth and soccer skills were major obstacles to overcome. However, in 1967, the Torneio Rio-São Paulo (between the leading clubs of the leading soccer cities) was expanded to include other state champions and renamed the Taça Roberto Gomes Pedrosa. In line with the then military dictatorship's desire for all things national, the Campeonato Brasileiro was first organized by the CBD in 1971. It began as a 20-team league with the top clubs going into a play-off round. Since then its format has changed every single year for almost three decades. Numbers of divisions, methods of qualification and classification, relegation and promotion have wildly fluctuated. Ticket sales were included in the classifications system in 1974, and in 1975 an extra point was awarded for winning matches by more than two goals. A struggle over TV money in 1987 saw two national tournaments – the big clubs' Copa União and the CBF's yellow module – played side-by-side.

In 1996, leading Rio club Fluminense was relegated but managed to maintain its position in the top flight by having the following year's league expanded by four clubs. However, this just delayed the inevitable as big clubs kept playing badly, so a two-season averaging system for relegation was introduced to try and bypass any awkward seasons. Nevertheless, Botafogo still managed to be relegated in 1999. The club went straight to the soccer authorities and won back two points from a game earlier in the season against São Paulo who had fielded an ineligible player. That meant that the small club Gama had to take the drop. Gama headed for the courts and was reinstated only to see FIFA ban the club from CBF leagues for having the temerity to resort to national courts rather than FIFA itself.

The deadlock was broken by the big clubs who organized a national championship – the monstrously complex 116-team Copa João Havelange – that began in 2000 with Gama and Botafogo both playing in the top division. Emblematic of the state of Brazilian soccer, a dreary, poorly attended championship culminated in a chaotic Final between Vasco and São Cãetano. Massive overcrowding in Vasco's stadium for the second leg led to a huge terrace crush, the game was abandoned and hundreds were injured.

Since then reform has finally come to the Campeonato. The new government, under Lula da Silva, is regulating the game more tightly and the championship itself has, for the first time, assumed a conventional format without play-offs.

São Caetano continue to defy the odds, as the tiny São Paulo state team, nicknamed the Azulao, reached the National Championship play-off Final in 2001 and quarter-finals in 2002.

What goes down stays down. Palmeiras goalkeeper Marcos and defender Cesar watch another ball fly past. Palmeiras' disastrous form in 2002 saw the club's sports psychologist resign, the team relegated and, most miraculous of all, it stayed relegated despite a last-minute attempt to get them reinstated.

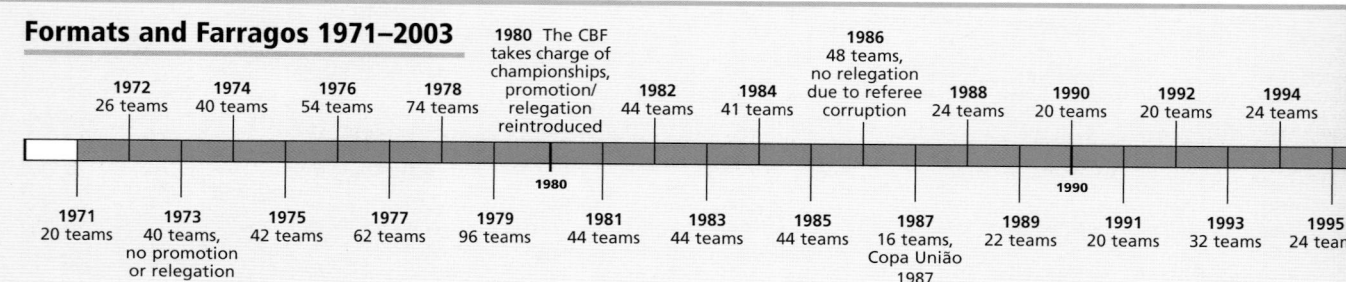

Formats and Farragos 1971–2003

1980 The CBF takes charge of championships, promotion/ relegation reintroduced

1986 48 teams, no relegation due to referee corruption

1972 26 teams	**1974** 40 teams	**1976** 54 teams
1978 74 teams	**1982** 44 teams	**1984** 41 teams
1988 24 teams	**1990** 20 teams	**1992** 20 teams
1994 24 teams		

1971 20 teams	**1973** 40 teams, no promotion or relegation	**1975** 42 teams
1977 62 teams	**1979** 96 teams	**1981** 44 teams
1983 44 teams	**1985** 44 teams	**1987** 16 teams, Copa União 1987
1989 22 teams	**1991** 20 teams	**1993** 32 teams
1995 24 team		

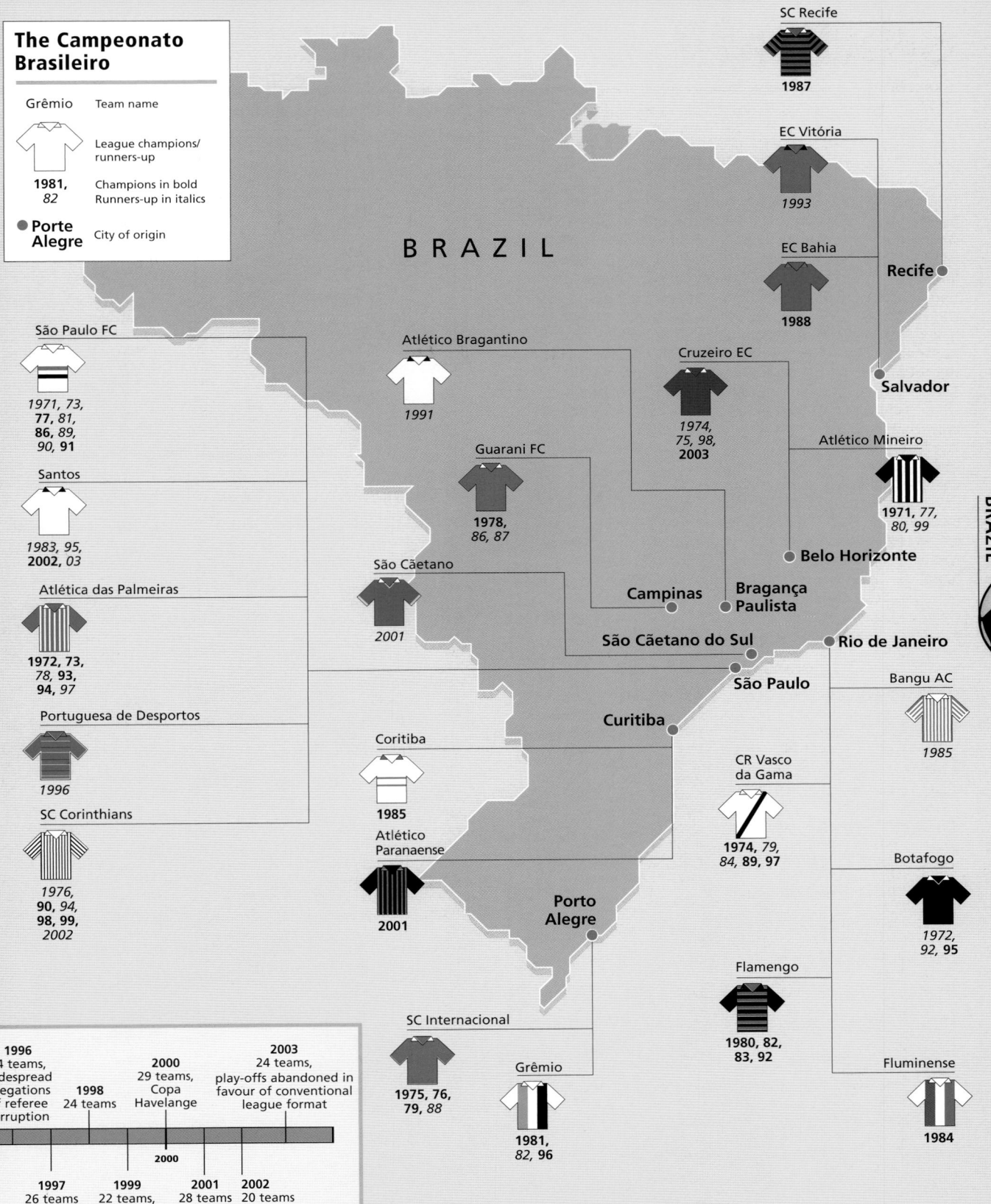

The Campeonato Brasileiro

Grêmio — Team name

League champions/runners-up

1981, *82* — Champions in bold / Runners-up in italics

● **Porte Alegre** — City of origin

B R A Z I L

SC Recife — **1987**

EC Vitória — *1993*

EC Bahia — **1988**

Recife

São Paulo FC — *1971, 73,* **77, 81,** **86,** *89,* **90, 91**

Santos — *1983, 95,* **2002,** *03*

Atlética das Palmeiras — **1972, 73,** *78,* **93,** **94,** *97*

Portuguesa de Desportos — *1996*

SC Corinthians — *1976,* **90, 94,** **98, 99,** *2002*

Atlético Bragantino — *1991*

Guarani FC — **1978,** *86, 87*

São Cãetano — *2001*

Cruzeiro EC — *1974,* *75, 98,* **2003**

Atlético Mineiro — *1971, 77,* **80, 99**

Salvador

Belo Horizonte

Campinas

Bragança Paulista

São Cãetano do Sul

Rio de Janeiro

São Paulo

Bangu AC — *1985*

Curitiba

Coritiba — **1985**

Atlético Paranaense — **2001**

CR Vasco da Gama — **1974,** *79,* **84, 89,** *97*

Botafogo — *1972,* *92,* **95**

Porto Alegre

Flamengo — **1980, 82,** **83, 92**

Fluminense — **1984**

SC Internacional — **1975, 76,** *79, 88*

Grêmio — **1981,** *82,* **96**

BRAZIL

1996
24 teams, widespread allegations of referee corruption

1997
26 teams

1998
24 teams

1999
22 teams, the Gama scandal

2000
29 teams, Copa Havelange

2000

2001
28 teams

2002
20 teams

2003
24 teams, play-offs abandoned in favour of conventional league format

Brazil

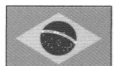

Confederação Brasileira de Futebol
Founded: 1914
Joined FIFA: 1923
Joined CONMEBOL: 1916

THE ORGANIZATION OF Brazilian soccer parallels the uneven geography of this enormous nation. League soccer began at state rather than national level. The Campeonata Paulista de Futebol began in São Paulo in 1901. Rio's league, the Liga Metropolitan de Football, followed in 1905. For the first half of the 20th century Brazilian soccer was dominated by these two leagues, and a series of inter-city cups established the effective national champions. Simultaneously, state leagues were established all over the country, with significant areas of soccer strength developing beyond Rio and São Paulo.

With the creation of the Copa Libertadores de América, the Taca do Brasil was established as a national cup competition to determine Brazil's entrants. It was discontinued in 1968, replaced first by the Taca de Prata (or Roberto Gomes Pedrosa Cup) and then by a fully-fledged national league in 1971. The formats of the latter have changed in a complex and Byzantine fashion to ensure, irrespective of performance, regular pay days for the biggest clubs. Finally, in 2003, a conventional league format – with no play-offs – was agreed for the National Championship. In 1989 a new national cup competition, the Copa do Brasil, was established with equally shifting formats and the winners also enter the Copa Libertadores alongside the national champions.

State leagues continue to run in the early part of the season ensuring an unrelenting schedule of soccer all year round.

São Paulo Championship Record 1902–2004

SEASON	CHAMPIONS	SEASON	CHAMPIONS
1902	São Paulo Athletic	1935	Santos/Portuguesa
1903	São Paulo Athletic	1936	Palestra Itália/Portuguesa
1904	São Paulo Athletic	1937	Corinthians
1905	Atlético Paulistano	1938	Corinthians
1906	Germania	1939	Corinthians
1907	Internacional	1940	Palestra Itália
1908	Atlético Paulistano	1941	Corinthians
1909	Atlética das Palmeiras	1942	Palmeiras
1910	Atlética das Palmeiras	1943	São Paulo
1911	São Paulo Athletic	1944	Palmeiras
1912	Americano	1945	São Paulo
1913	Americano/Atlético Paulista	1946	São Paulo
1914	Corinthians/Atlética São Bento	1947	Palmeiras
1915	Germania/Atlética das Palmeiras	1948	São Paulo
1916	Corinthians/Atlética Paulista	1949	São Paulo
1917	Atlético Paulistano	1950	Palmeiras
1918	Atlético Paulistano	1951	Corinthians
1919	Atlético Paulistano	1952	Corinthians
1920	Palestra Itália	1953	São Paulo
1921	Atlético Paulistano	1954	Corinthians
1922	Corinthians	1955	Santos
1923	Corinthians	1956	Santos
1924	Corinthians	1957	São Paulo
1925	Atlética São Bento	1958	Santos
1926	Palestra Itália/Atlético Paulista	1959	Palmeiras
1927	Palestra Itália/Atlético Paulista	1960	Santos
1928	Corinthians/Internacional	1961	Santos
1929	Corinthians/Atlético Paulista	1962	Santos
1930	Corinthians	1963	Palmeiras
1931	São Paulo	1964	Santos
1932	Palestra Itália	1965	Santos
1933	Palestra Itália	1966	Palmeiras
1934	Palestra Itália	1967	Santos

São Paulo Championship Record (*continued*)

SEASON	CHAMPIONS	SEASON	CHAMPIONS
1968	Santos	1987	São Paulo
1969	Santos	1988	Corinthians
1970	São Paulo	1989	São Paulo
1971	São Paulo	1990	Atlético Bragantino
1972	Palmeiras	1991	São Paulo
1973	Santos/Portuguesa	1992	São Paulo
1974	Palmeiras	1993	Palmeiras
1975	São Paulo	1994	Palmeiras
1976	Palmeiras	1995	Corinthians
1977	Corinthians	1996	Palmeiras
1978	Santos	1997	Corinthians
1979	Corinthians	1998	São Paulo
1980	São Paulo	1999	Corinthians
1981	São Paulo	2000	São Paulo
1982	Corinthians	2001	Corinthians
1983	Corinthians	2002	Ituano
1984	Santos	2003	Corinthians
1985	São Paulo	2004	São Caetano
1986	Atlética Internacional		

Rio Championship (Carioca) Record 1906–2004

SEASON	CHAMPIONS	SEASON	CHAMPIONS
1906	Fluminense	1950	Vasco da Gama
1907	Fluminense/Botafogo	1951	Fluminense
1908	Fluminense	1952	Vasco da Gama
1909	Fluminense	1953	Flamengo
1910	Botafogo	1954	Flamengo
1911	Fluminense	1955	Flamengo
1912	Botafogo/Paissandu	1956	Vasco da Gama
1913	América	1957	Botafogo
1914	Flamengo	1958	Vasco da Gama
1915	Flamengo	1959	Fluminense
1916	América	1960	América
1917	Fluminense	1961	Botafogo
1918	Fluminense	1962	Botafogo
1919	Fluminense	1963	Flamengo
1920	Flamengo	1964	Fluminense
1921	Flamengo	1965	Flamengo
1922	América	1966	Bangu Atlético
1923	Vasco da Gama	1967	Botafogo
1924	Vasco da Gama	1968	Botafogo
1925	Flamengo	1969	Fluminense
1926	São Cristovoa	1970	Vasco da Gama
1927	Flamengo	1971	Fluminense
1928	América	1972	Flamengo
1929	Vasco da Gama	1973	Fluminense
1930	Botafogo	1974	Flamengo
1931	América	1975	Fluminense
1932	Botafogo	1976	Fluminense
1933	Botafogo/Bangu Atlético	1977	Vasco da Gama
1934	Botafogo/Vasco da Gama	1978	Flamengo
1935	Botafogo/America	1979	Flamengo
1936	Fluminense	1979*	Flamengo
1937	Fluminense	1980	Fluminense
1938	Fluminense	1981	Flamengo
1939	Flamengo	1982	Vasco da Gama
1940	Fluminense	1983	Fluminense
1941	Fluminense	1984	Fluminense
1942	Flamengo	1985	Fluminense
1943	Flamengo	1986	Flamengo
1944	Flamengo	1987	Vasco da Gama
1945	Vasco da Gama	1988	Vasco da Gama
1946	Fluminense	1989	Botafogo
1947	Vasco da Gama	1990	Botafogo
1948	Botafogo	1991	Flamengo
1949	Vasco da Gama	1992	Vasco da Gama

BRAZIL

Rio Championship (Carioca) Record (*continued*)

SEASON	CHAMPIONS
1993	Vasco da Gama
1994	Vasco da Gama
1995	Fluminense
1996	Flamengo
1996*	Botafogo
1997	Botafogo
1998	Vasco da Gama

SEASON	CHAMPIONS
1999	Flamengo
2000	Flamengo
2001	Flamengo
2002	Fluminense
2003	Vasco da Gama
2004	Flamengo

* Extra tournament.

Rio-São Paulo Tournament Record 1933–2004

SEASON	CHAMPIONS	RUNNERS-UP
1933	Palestra Itália	
1934–49	*no competition*	
1950	Corinthians	Vasco da Gama
1951	Palmeiras	Corinthians
1952	Portuguesa	Vasco da Gama
1953	Corinthians	Vasco da Gama
1954	Corinthians	Fluminense
1955	Portuguesa	Palmeiras
1956	*no competition*	
1957	Fluminense	Vasco da Gama
1958	Vasco da Gama	Flamengo
1959	Santos	Vasco da Gama
1960	Fluminense	Botafogo
1961	Flamengo	Palmeiras
1962	Botafogo	Palmeiras
1963	Santos	Corinthians
1964	Santos/Botafogo	
1965	Palmeiras	Portuguesa/São Paulo
1966	Corinthians/Santos/ Vasco da Gama/Botafogo	
1967–92	*no competition*	
1993	Palmeiras	Corinthians
1994–96	*no competition*	
1997	Santos	Flamengo
1998	Botafogo	São Paulo
1999	Vasco da Gama	Santos
2000	Palmeiras	Atlético Mineiro
2001	São Paulo	Botafogo
2002	Corinthians	São Paulo
2003	Corinthians	São Paulo
2004	*no competition*	

Brazilian National Championship Record 1971–2003

SEASON	CHAMPIONS	RUNNERS-UP
1971	Atlético Mineiro	São Paulo
1972	Palmeiras	Botafogo
1973	Palmeiras	São Paulo
1974	Vasco da Gama	Cruzeiro
1975	Internacional	Cruzeiro
1976	Internacional	Corinthians
1977	São Paulo	Atlético Mineiro
1978	Guarani	Palmeiras
1979	Internacional	Vasco da Gama
1980	Flamengo	Atlético Mineiro
1981	Grêmio	São Paulo
1982	Flamengo	Grêmio
1983	Flamengo	Santos
1984	Fluminense	Vasco da Gama
1985	Coritiba	Bangu Atlético
1986	São Paulo	Guarani
1987	Sport Club Recife	Guarani
1988	Bahia	Internacional
1989	Vasco da Gama	São Paulo
1990	Corinthians	São Paulo
1991	São Paulo	Atlético Bragantino
1992	Flamengo	Botafogo
1993	Palmeiras	Vitória
1994	Palmeiras	Corinthians
1995	Botafogo	Santos

Brazilian National Championship Record (*continued*)

SEASON	CHAMPIONS	RUNNERS-UP
1996	Grêmio	Portuguesa
1997	Vasco da Gama	Palmeiras
1998	Corinthians	Cruzeiro
1999	Corinthians	Atlético Mineiro
2000	Vasco da Gama	São Cãetano
2001	Atlético Paranaense	São Cãetano
2002	Santos	Corinthians
2003	Cruzeiro	Santos

Brazilian National Championship Summary

TEAM	TOTALS	CHAMPIONS & RUNNERS-UP (BOLD) (*ITALICS*)
Palmeiras	4, 2	**1972, 73,** *78,* **93, 94,** *97*
Vasco da Gama	4, 2	**1974,** *79, 84,* **89,** *97,* **2000**
Flamengo	4, 0	**1980, 82, 83, 92**
São Paulo	3, 5	*1971,* **73,** *77,* **81,** *86, 89, 90,* **91**
Corinthians	3, 3	*1976,* **90,** *94,* **98, 99,** *2002*
Internacional	3, 1	**1975,** *76,* **79,** *88*
Grêmio	2, 1	**1981,** *82,* **96**
Atlético Mineiro	1, 3	**1971,** *77, 80, 99*
Cruzeiro	1, 3	**1974,** *75, 98,* **2003**
Santos	1, 3	*1983, 95,* **2002,** *03*
Botafogo	1, 2	*1972, 92,* **95**
Guarani	1, 2	**1978,** *86, 87*
Atlético Paranaense	1, 0	**2001**
Bahia	1, 0	**1988**
Coritiba	1, 0	**1985**
Fluminense	1, 0	**1984**
Sport Club Recife	1, 0	**1987**

This summary only features clubs that have won the Brazilian National Championship. For a full list of league champions and runners-up please see the League Record above.

Copa do Brasil Record 1989–2004

YEAR	WINNERS	SCORE	RUNNERS-UP
1989	Grêmio	0-0, 2-1 (2 legs)	Sport Club Recife
1990	Flamengo	1-0, 0-0 (2 legs)	Goias
1991	Criciuma	1-1, 0-0 (2 legs)	Grêmio
1992	Internacional	1-2, 1-0 (2 legs)	Fluminense
1993	Cruzeiro	0-0, 2-1 (2 legs)	Grêmio
1994	Grêmio	0-0, 1-0 (2 legs)	Ceara
1995	Corinthians	2-1, 1-0 (2 legs)	Grêmio
1996	Cruzeiro	1-1, 2-1 (2 legs)	Palmeiras
1997	Grêmio	0-0, 2-2 (2 legs)	Flamengo
1998	Palmeiras	0-1, 2-0 (2 legs)	Cruzeiro
1999	Juventude	2-1, 0-0 (2 legs)	Botafogo
2000	Cruzeiro	0-0, 2-1 (2 legs)	São Paulo
2001	Grêmio	2-2, 3-1 (2 legs)	Corinthians
2002	Corinthians	2-1, 1-1 (2 legs)	Brasiliense
2003	Cruzeiro	1-1, 3-1 (2 legs)	Flamengo
2004	Santo André	2-2, 2-0 (2 legs)	Flamengo

Copa do Brasil Summary

TEAM	TOTALS	WINNERS & RUNNERS-UP (BOLD) (*ITALICS*)
Grêmio	4, 3	**1989,** *91,* **93, 94,** *95,* **97, 2001**
Cruzeiro	4, 1	**1993, 96, 98, 2000,** *03*
Corinthians	2, 1	**1995,** *2001,* **02**
Flamengo	1, 3	**1990,** *97, 2003, 04*
Palmeiras	1, 1	*1996,* **98**
Criciuma	1, 0	**1991**
Internacional	1, 0	**1992**
Juventude	1, 0	**1999**
Santo André	1, 0	**2004**

This summary only features clubs that have won the Copa do Brasil. For a full list of winners and runners-up please see the Record above.

BRAZIL

Argentina

THE SEASON IN REVIEW 2003–04

THE DEPTH AND FEROCITY OF VIOLENCE and disorder in Argentinian soccer defies the normal explanations. Argentina is far from the poorest or most unstable society in Latin America, yet the persistence and intensity of soccer-related problems has reached such a peak that one of the country's leading judges, Mariano Berges, actually called a halt to the season in an attempt to regain control over the situation.

In late August a game between Chacarita Juniors and Boca Juniors was abandoned during the second half as fighting in the stands became too ferocious to continue. Judge Berges banned the Federal Police from providing security at championship games and thus no matches could be played at all. Although a number of government commissions have investigated the problem, a range of laws has been passed, CCTV has been introduced and clubs have been pressurized to stop giving tickets and transport to the hardcore barra bravas groups, the violence has continued both inside and outside the stadiums. CCTV footage has revealed that at Boca special turnstiles through which banned fans leaders can pass unchallenged, and tickets and payment are strictly optional, remain in use. The Apertura was eventually allowed to restart after a month's absence. Judge Berges began another commission into hooliganism aided by the government's promise to establish special units and courts for prosecuting and trying fans charged with violent behaviour.

The Apertura went to Boca who won with some ease, wrapping things up with two games to spare. Coach Carlos Bianchi fielded an attacking trio of Guillermo Barros Schelotto, Carlos Tévez, and the Brazilian Pedro Iarley, and Boca scored plenty of goals all season. They sealed their triumph with a 2-0 win over rivals River Plate. Their early victory allowed them to play the reserves for the final two games and head for the World Club Cup Final

Top: A Brazilian at Boca: Boca striker Pedro Iarley takes on Quilmes' Rodrigo Brana.

Middle: Chacarita Juniors fans start trouble at their Apertura game with Boca. Minutes later the game was abandoned as fighting broke out across the stadium. As a result the entire league programme was suspended for a month.

Right: Rafael di Zeo, a leading figure among Boca's barra bravas, regularly appeared inside the Bombonera from which he has been banned.

Above: Raul Gamez, President of Vélez Sarsfield, who spent much of his season trying to persuade cult Paraguayan goalkeeper José Luis Chilavert to return to the club.

Apertura League Table 2003–04

CLUB	P	W	D	L	F	A	Pts
Boca Juniors	19	11	6	2	31	11	39
San Lorenzo	19	11	3	5	26	13	36
Banfield	19	9	5	5	27	18	32
Quilmes	19	8	7	4	20	13	31
Rosario Central	19	8	7	4	28	26	31
Newell's Old Boys	19	7	8	4	27	20	29
Arsenal	19	6	8	5	18	16	26
River Plate	19	7	5	7	23	24	26
Colón	19	5	9	5	23	24	24
Talleres	19	6	6	7	27	30	24
Estudiantes	19	6	5	8	18	20	23
Racing Club	19	4	10	5	23	23	22
Lanús	19	4	10	5	21	23	22
Independiente	19	5	7	7	15	19	22
Vélez Sarsfield	19	5	7	7	20	28	22
Chacarita Juniors	19	5	9	5	20	19	21*
Gimnasia LP	19	5	6	8	14	22	21
Olimpo	19	5	5	9	17	23	20
Atlético de Rafaela	19	3	8	8	19	28	17
Nueva Chicago	19	2	5	12	14	31	11

* 3 points deducted due to crowd disturbances at a Boca Juniors game.

Apertura Top Goalscorers

PLAYER	CLUB	GOALS
Ernesto Farías	Estudiantes LP	13
Julian Vásquez	Newell's Old Boys	11
Alberto Acosta	San Lorenzo	10
Fernando Cavenaghi	River Plate	9

ARGENTINA

River Plate coach Manuel Pellegrini feels the strain as his team slip to another defeat in a disappointing Apertura campaign.

Top: *The Rosario derby: Newell's Old Boys (in red and black) take on Rosario Central.*

Left: *Alberto Acosta's ten goals for San Lorenzo helped lift them into second spot in the Apertura.*

Above: *Boca Juniors' players (left to right) Diego Cagna, Raul Cascini, Carlos Tevez (in white) and Clemente Rodriguez celebrate clinching the Apertura championship.*

in Tokyo reasonably refreshed. They duly beat Milan on penalties winning the trophy for the third time in their history.

Despite their 'millionarios' tag, River Plate have considerable financial difficulties. During the summer of 2003 they sold their best youngsters, bought in old ex-players, suffered a lot of injuries and not only finished the Apertura in mid-table but also lost their Copa Sudamericana Final to Cienciano – a team from the Peruvian mountains. Coach Manuel Pellegrini, like the majority of coaches in the top division, was fired. Other clubs were also diverted by money troubles. Argentinos Juniors were forced to trade a big stake in the future value of their star Lucas Biglia for a miserly short-term injection of cash. Talleres and Rosario Central have hocked the future value of their entire junior squads to soccer agents and entrepreneurs.

The star of the Clausara was the increasingly eccentric Estudiantes coach Carlos Bilardo. His odd and erratic behaviour included publicly engaging in bets with his strikers over how many goals they would score; putting his squad through an 11-hour training session set to music – they duly lost 4-1 to Independiente – and showing up in the dug out at River Plate with a fluted glass, champagne and an ice bucket. Alcohol is strictly prohibited in Argentina's stadiums and though he claimed it was merely a soft drink the police took him away. With no half-time team talk Estudiantes lost 3-0. His only challenger in the eccentric stakes was Maradona who once again fell seriously ill and was admitted to hospital for much of the championship. Games at every stadium in the country were decked out with flags and banners, his image, and messages of support.

The title race was between Boca and River once again although Talleres, who at one point looked a certainty for relegation, bankruptcy and collapse, turned on an extraordinary run of form to take them to the top of the table midway thought the season. River found their form again and Fernando Cavenaghi and Marcelo Salas made for a match-winning front-line. Boca got the better of River in their fantastically bad-tempered Copa Libertadores semi-final. Boca squeezed through on penalties, but their draining two-leg Final against Once Caldas proved too much for the squad as both Libertadores and Clausura slipped from their grasp. River took the championship, their first for three years.

Clausura League Table 2003–04

CLUB	P	W	D	L	F	A	Pts
River Plate	19	12	4	3	41	21	40
Boca Juniors	19	10	6	3	34	17	36
Talleres	19	10	5	4	30	19	35
Banfield	19	9	5	5	27	17	32
Vélez Sarsfield	19	9	4	6	31	21	31
Quilmes	19	7	8	4	21	16	29
Arsenal	19	7	8	4	21	22	29
Racing Club	19	8	4	7	29	29	28
San Lorenzo	19	6	8	5	18	16	26
Atlético de Rafaela	19	7	5	7	25	24	26
Colón	19	7	4	8	20	26	25
Newell's Old Boys	19	4	10	5	28	25	22
Independiente	19	5	7	7	21	27	22
Estudiantes LP	19	5	6	8	20	30	21
Lanús	19	5	5	9	22	28	20
Olimpo	19	4	7	8	18	28	19
Gimnasia LP	19	3	8	8	21	26	17
Nueva Chicago	19	2	11	6	18	27	17
Chacarita Juniors	19	3	8	8	21	34	17
Rosario Central	19	2	7	10	16	29	13

Relegated clubs: Chacarita Juniors, Nueva Chicago, Talleres, Atlético de Rafaela.
Promoted clubs: Instituto, Almagro, Argentinos Juniors, Huracán TA.

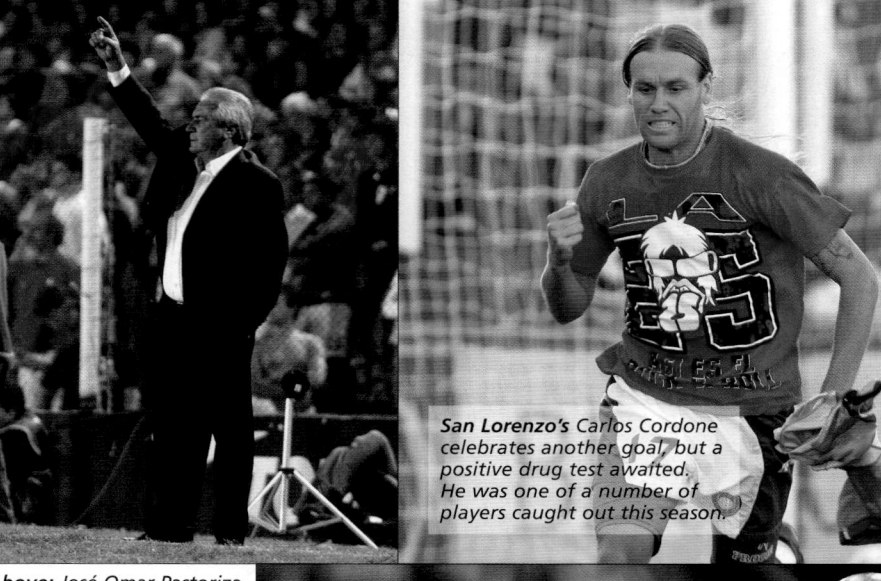

San Lorenzo's Carlos Cordone celebrates another goal, but a positive drug test awaited. He was one of a number of players caught out this season.

Above: José Omar Pastoriza was the fourth coach appointed at Independiente this season – the result was another disappointing mid-table finish.

Clausura Top Goalscorers

PLAYER	CLUB	GOALS
Rolando Zarate	Vélez Sarsfield	13
Aldo Osorio	Talleres	10
Fernando Cavenaghi	River Plate	9

International Club Performances 2004 (unless otherwise stated)

CLUB	COMPETITION	PROGRESS
Boca Juniors	Copa Libertadores	Runners-up
	Copa Sudamericana 2003	Quarter-finals
River Plate	Copa Libertadores	Semi-finals
	Copa Sudamericana 2003	Runners-up
Vélez Sarsfied	Copa Libertadores	Group Stage
	Copa Sudamericana 2003	Preliminary Stage
Rosario Central	Copa Libertadores	2nd Round
	Copa Sudamericana 2003	Preliminary Stage
Independiente	Copa Libertadores	Worst runners-up play-off
	Copa Sudamericana 2003	Preliminary Stage
Colón	Copa Sudamericana 2003	Preliminary stage

Boca keeper Wilfredo Caballero makes a save from Newell's Old Boys' Jairo Patino.

ARGENTINA

Left: Boca coach Carlos Bianchi just missed out on a third Copa Libertadores this year and then announced his retirement after six years with the Buenos Aires club.

Far left: Boca fans plead for Maradona to recover before their Copa Libertadores game against Bolivar.

Below: Time gentlemen please: Carlos Bilardo drinks up on the touchline – just one example of the Estudiantes coach's increasingly bizarre behaviour this year.

Bottom left: Talleres players (left to right) Ariel Donet, Aldo Osorio and Luciano De Bruna celebrate another goal. Talleres' third-place finish was not enough for them to avoid relegation via the play-offs.

River Plate players (left to right) Maximiliano Lopez, Franco Costanzo, Franco Miranda and Javier Madcherano celebrate their final-day victory in the Clausura after beating Atlético de Rafela to claim the trophy.

Soccer in Argentina

ARGENTINA

1860s: British sailors bring soccer to Buenos Aires — `1860`

— `1865`

1865: Buenos Aires Football Club (now defunct) founded

`1870`

1882: Alexander Watson Hutton arrives in Buenos Aires — `1875`

`1880`

1887: Quilmes and Gimnasia y Esgrima (La Plata) (oldest surviving clubs) founded — `1885`

`1890`

1891: First championship played in Buenos Aires

1893: Argentine Association Football League first played — `1895`

`1900`

1901: First international, v Uruguay, won 3–2, venue: Montevideo — `1905`

1906: First provincial league formed: Liga Santiaguena de Futbol — `1910`

1912: Rival Federacion Argentina de Football League set up — `1915`
Affiliation to FIFA

`1920`

1914: Federacion Argentina de Football League disbanded — `1925`

1916: Affiliation

1919: Associacion Amateurs founded as separate league in Buenos Aires — `1930`

`1935`

1926: Last season of Associacion Amateurs — `1940`

1931: Professionalism introduced and professional league established — `1945`

1948: Players' strike: mass exodus of professionals to Colombia — `1950`

`1955`

1950 and 1954: President Peron bans national team from World Cup — `1960`

1967: National and Metropolitan (Buenos Aires) championships run in same season — `1965`

`1970`

1968: Buenos Aires: 74 died, 150 injured in crush and stand collapse at River v Boca match — `1975`

1978: Argentina win World Cup in Buenos Aires — `1980`

1986: Single national championship established — `1985`

`1990`

1992: National championship shifts to Apertura and Clausura format — `1995`

`2000`

`2005`

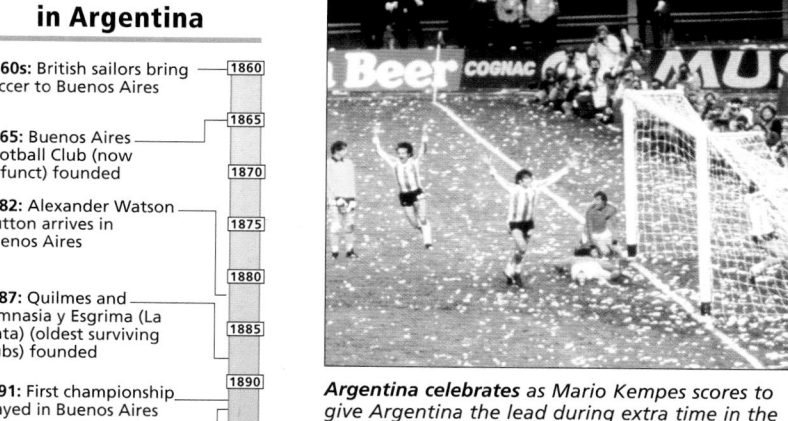

Argentina celebrates as Mario Kempes scores to give Argentina the lead during extra time in the 1978 World Cup Final in Buenos Aires.

International Competitions

Year		
1910:	●	■
1916:	▲	■
1917:	▲	
1920:	▲	
1921:	●	■
1923:	▲	
1924:	▲	
1925:	▲	
1926:	●	
1927:	●	
1929:	●	■
1930:	▲	
1935:	▲	
1937:	●	■
1941:	●	
1942:	▲	
1945:	●	
1946:	●	■
1947:	●	
1955:	●	
1957:	●	
1959*:	●▲	■

Key

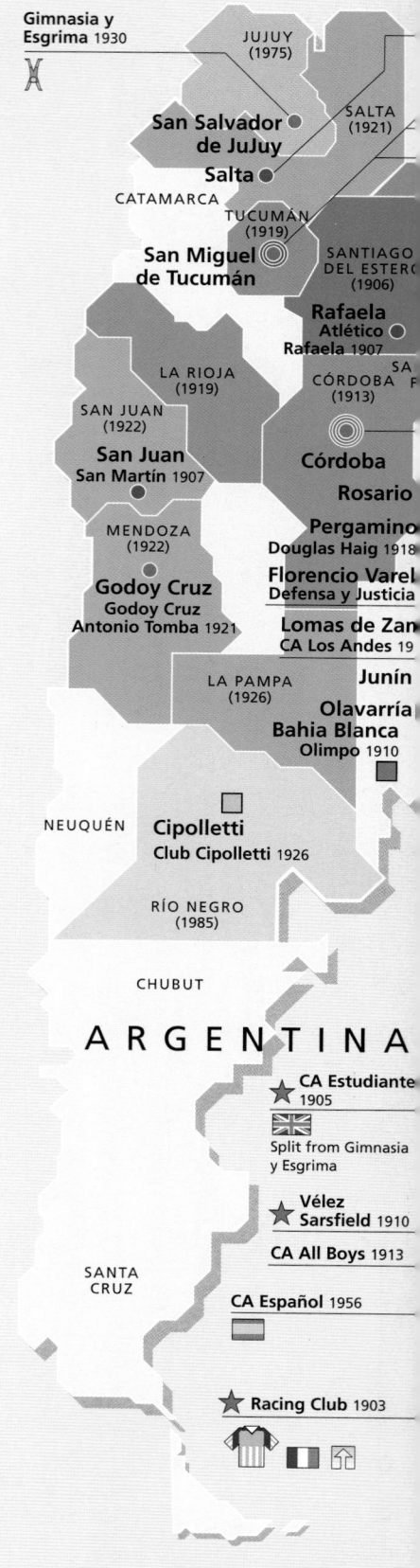

International soccer	
Affiliation to FIFA	
Affiliation to CONMEBOL	
Disaster	
■	World Cup host
●	World Cup winner
▲	World Cup runner-up
■	Copa América host
●	Copa América winner
▲	Copa América runner-up
○	Competition winner
△	Competition runner-up

* An extra unofficial tournament was held in 1959. See pages 360–61

Argen	Argentinos Juniors
Boca	CA Boca Juniors
Estud	CA Estudiantes
Indep	CA Independiente
Newell	CA Newell's Old Boys
River	CA River Plate
Rosario	CA Rosario Central
Racing	Racing Club
San L	San Lorenzo
Vélez	Vélez Sarsfield
Lanús	CA Lanús

Copa Libertadores

Year	winner	runner-up
1963:		△Boca
1964:	○Indep	
1965:	○Indep	
1966:		△River
1967:	○Racing	
1968:	○Estud	
1969:	○Estud	
1970:	○Estud	
1971:		△Estud
1972:	○Indep	
1973:	○Indep	
1974:	○Indep	
1975:	○Indep	
1976:		△River
1977:	○Boca	
1978:	○Boca	
1979:		△Boca
1984:		
1985:	○Indep	
1986:	○Argen	
1987:	○River	
1988:		△Newell
1990:		
1991:		△Newell
1992:		
1994:	○Vélez	
1995:		
1996:	○River	
1997:		
1998:		
2000:	○Boca	
2001:	○Boca	
2002:	○Boca	
2003:		
2004:		△Boca

Copa CONMEBOL

Year	winner	runner-up
1995:	○Rosario	
1996:	○Lanús	
1997:		△Lanús
1998:		△Rosario

Copa Sudamericana

Year	winner	runner-up
2003:	○San L	
2004:		△River

Gimnasia y Esgrima 1930

JUJUY (1975)

San Salvador de JuJuy

SALTA (1921)

Salta

CATAMARCA

TUCUMÁN (1919)

San Miguel de Tucumán

SANTIAGO DEL ESTERO (1906)

Rafaela Atlético **Rafaela** 1907

LA RIOJA (1919)

SA CÓRDOBA F (1913)

SAN JUAN (1922)

San Juan San Martín 1907

Córdoba

Rosario

MENDOZA (1922)

Pergamino Douglas Haig 1918

Florencio Varel Defensa y Justicia

Godoy Cruz Godoy Cruz Antonio Tomba 1921

Lomas de Zam CA Los Andes 19

LA PAMPA (1926)

Junín

Olavarría

Bahia Blanca Olimpo 1910

NEUQUÉN

Cipolletti Club Cipolletti 1926

RÍO NEGRO (1985)

CHUBUT

A R G E N T I N A

★ **CA Estudiante** 1905

Split from Gimnasia y Esgrima

★ **Vélez Sarsfield** 1910

CA All Boys 1913

SANTA CRUZ

CA Español 1956

★ **Racing Club** 1903

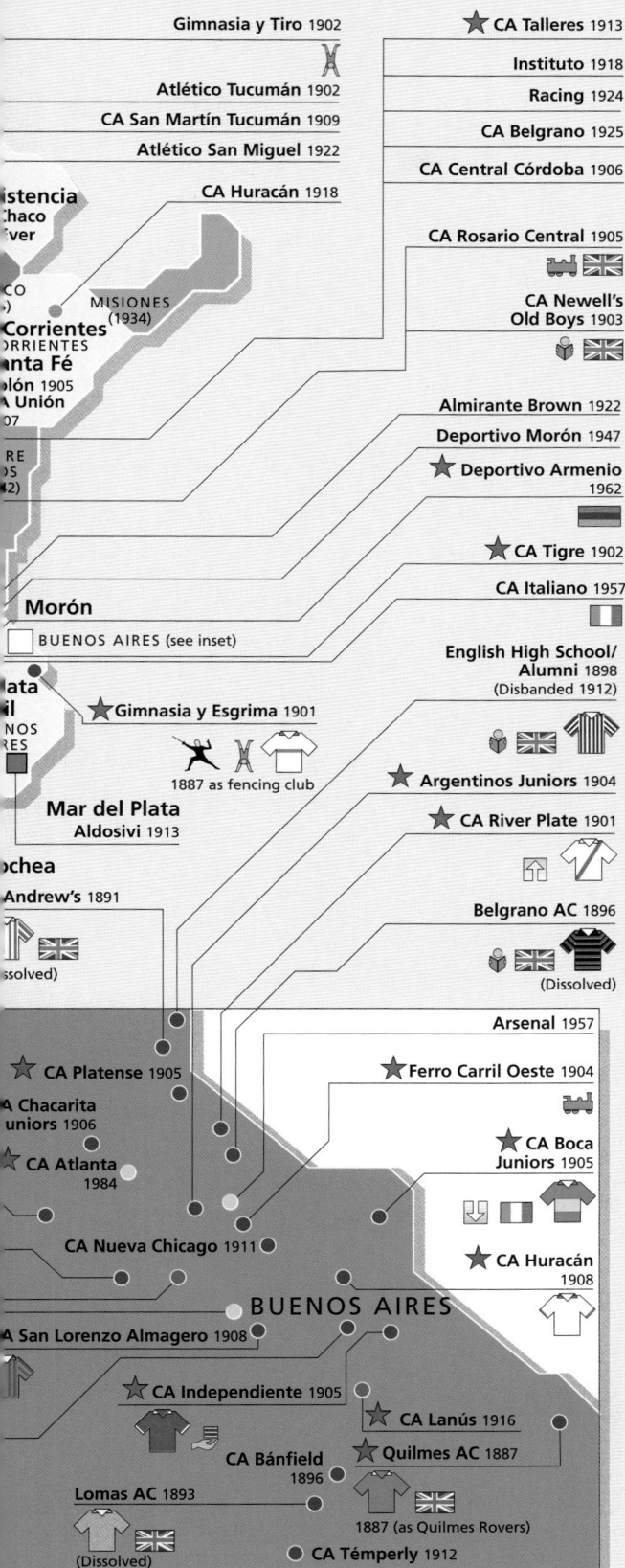

Argentina

ORIGINS AND GROWTH OF SOCCER

IN THE LAST QUARTER of the 19th century, Buenos Aires had a vibrant British community of around 40,000 people, with their own network of banks, schools and social events. It was in this outpost of Britain's informal empire that Buenos Aires Football Club was founded in 1867. In 1882, Alexander Watson Hutton arrived to teach at St Andrew's Scottish School. In 1884, he founded his own English high school, hired a games master and started soccer both there and at other schools in the city. A championship was first played between these teams in 1891. In 1893, under Hutton's leadership, five clubs founded the Argentine Association Football League, a championship which has continued unbroken to the present day.

The growth of the sport was rapid. By 1901, the AAFL were organizing four divisions in Buenos Aires alone. Outside the capital the first club was Lobos Athletic (1892), while Newell's Old Boys (1903) and Rosario Central (1905) established soccer in Rosario, Argentina's second city. Regular internationals with Uruguay across the River Plate began in 1901. In the first decade of the 20th century soccer became progressively less British and more Argentinian. The biggest clubs (Racing, Boca and River Plate) emerged from immigrant and indigenous groups. The AFA began to publish rules in Spanish. The transition of power and influence became clear when the annual match between Argentinos and Británicos saw Británicos lose 5-1, a defeat from which it never recovered.

The national organization of soccer was bedevilled by successive splits (1912–14, 1919–27) and the formation of alternative national organizations and rival leagues. Matters were settled due to pressure from the onset of professionalism, the need to stop the best players going to play in Italy, and the need to rationalize impossibly large leagues and uneven competition between clubs. In 1931, a national professional league of 18 big clubs was established.

Argentina: The main clubs

Colón 1905	Team name with year of formation		Pre-professional champions
●	Club formed before 1912		Armenian origins
●	Club formed 1912–25		British origins
●	Club formed 1925–50		French origins
○	Club formed after 1950		Italian origins
JUJUY (1975)	State (year of Championship foundation)		Spanish origins
			Railway workers
	Founded 1900–10		Originated from a fencing club
	Founded 1901–20		Originated from a gymnastics club
	Founded 1920–50		Originated from a school
	Founded 1950–80		Shop workers
	Founded 1980–95		
	No championship		Elite
☐	City with regional league (colour coded as above)		Working class
★	Founder members of pre-professional league		Colours unknown

Buenos Aires

SOCCER CENTER

SOME OF THE HISTORY OF BUENOS AIRES can be seen
in the pattern and density of the soccer clubs that stud this
enormous city of over 11 million people. In the 1860s, Buenos
Aires had a population of just 170,000, of whom maybe 40,000
were Britons organizing and servicing a massive wave of British
investment in Argentina. Schools, colleges, social and athletics
clubs sprung up. As early as 1867, a British Buenos Aires
Football Club had been set up, only to switch to rugby in 1887.
The arrival of Alexander Watson Hutton at St. Andrews Scottish
School in 1882, and at the English High School in 1884,
was a catalyst. Teams at his schools began to play old boys
clubs, and in 1891 a local championship was held. It was
repeated in 1893 and has been played ever since.

The decline of British influence

In the following decade, dozens of British clubs appeared all
over the city, some beginning to attract spectators. But in 1901,
an Argentinian fencing and gymnastic club in La Plata –
Argentina's new administrative centre to the south of Buenos
Aires – formed a soccer section. Although the league was still
dominated by British teams like Alumni, Lomas Athletic and
Belgrano, the shift to Spanish-speaking players and Argentinian
teams gathered pace quickly. The city's biggest clubs were
founded in a few short years: River Plate in 1901, Racing Club
in 1903, Boca Juniors and Independiente in 1905. By 1912, the
AFA was using Spanish, and Alumni, for one, had disbanded.

Simultaneously, Buenos Aires grew explosively. By 1914, it
had grown almost ten-fold with 1.5 million inhabitants, and
it has barely stopped since. Its regular, grid-like structure created
a series of neighbourhoods with clear boundaries, which have
often been populated with specific immigrant groups or social
classes, and every neighbourhood has acquired its own soccer
team. The names speak for themselves: Deportivo Italiano,
Deportivo Armenio, Deportivo Español, the list goes on.
Everything about Buenos Aires' development was accelerated.
British teams, including Southampton, Nottingham Forest,
Tottenham and Everton, were regularly touring the city before
the First World War. International matches with Uruguay were
played regularly, and the first informal South American
championship was held in the city in 1910.

The big city teams

The 1920s were consumed by the struggle over payments
and professionalism until, in 1931, a professional league was
established and the biggest teams in the city came to define
and dominate the game. River Plate and Boca Juniors were
both founded in Boca, the poor docks area in the city centre.
River, which was formed from the merger of Santa Rosa and
Rosales, migrated north and settled in the Retiro district of
the city, acquiring a mass following with a distinctly elite tone.
Boca, founded by an Irishman and a group of Italian students,
has stayed close to its roots in the district. Alternately the two
strongest teams through this era, their derby matches remain
the highpoint of the city's season. Further south in the industrial
zone of Avellaneda, Racing Club and Independiente play the
city's other major derby. Independiente was founded by
employees of the City of London department store.

ARGENTINA

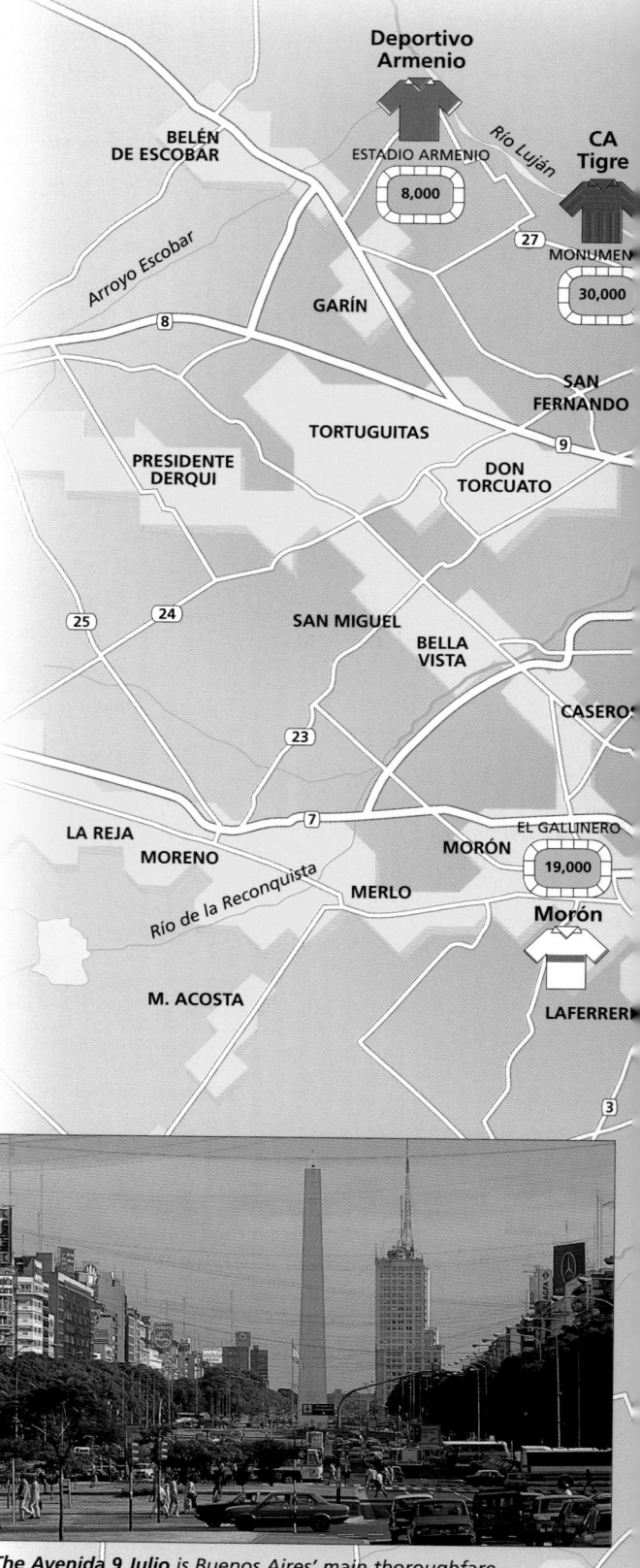

*The Avenida 9 Julio is Buenos Aires' main thoroughfare.
The spiritual home of Argentinian soccer since the 1860s,
the city houses some 30 professional soccer teams.*

Buenos Aires

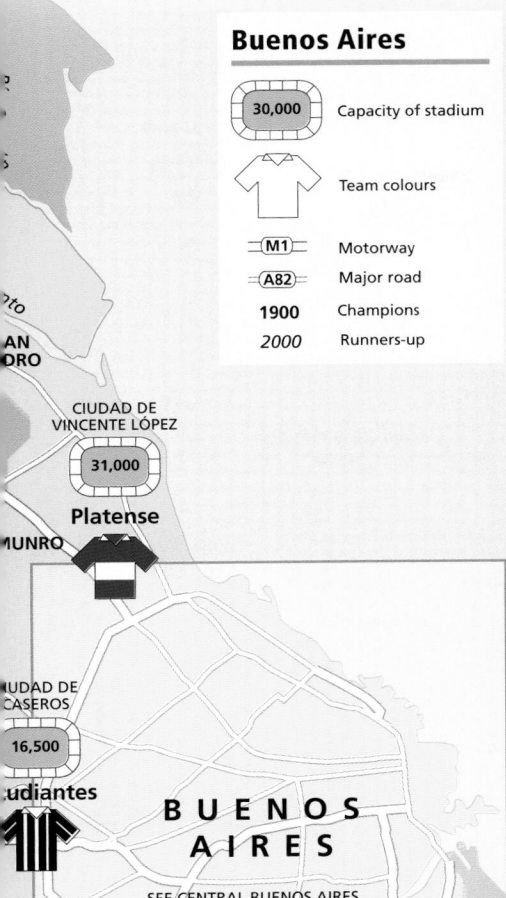

30,000	Capacity of stadium
(shirt)	Team colours
M1	Motorway
A82	Major road
1900	Champions
2000	Runners-up

Buenos Aires, together with Montevideo across the mouth of the River Plate, is the cradle of soccer in South America. It was in these two great cities that the first South American international matches took place in the early years of the 20th century.

ARGENTINA

RIO DE LA PLATA

GIMNASIA Y ESGRIMA 1901

Amateur League (1891–1930)	**1929**
FAF League (1912–14)	*1913*
AAF League (1919–26)	*1924*
Apertura League (1992–2004)	*1999*
Clausura League (1992–2004)	*1995, 96, 2002*

ESTUDIANTES LA PLATA 1905

Amateur League (1891–1930)	*1919, 30*
FAF League (1912–14)	**1913**, *14*
Metropolitan League (1967–85)	**1967**, *68*, **82**
National League (1967–85)	*1967, 75*, **83**
Copa Libertadores	**1968–70**, *71*
Copa Interamerica	**1969**
World Club Cup	**1968**, *69, 70*

QUILMES 1887

Amateur League (1891–1930)	*1895*, **1912**
Metropolitan League (1967–85)	**1978**
National League (1967–85)	*1982*

CIUDAD DE VINCENTE LÓPEZ

31,000

Platense

MUNRO

CIUDAD DE CASEROS

16,500

...udiantes

BUENOS AIRES

SEE CENTRAL BUENOS AIRES FOR MORE DETAIL

CA Banfield

FLORENCIO SOLÁ

16,500

TALLERES

30,000

Talleres

Quilmes

CENTENARIO

33,000

DON BOSCO

QUILMES

FRAGATA SARMIENTO

10,000

EDUARDO GALLARDÓN

35,000

MONTE GRANDE

Los Andes

CA Italiano

Almirante Brown

BERAZATEGUI

JOSÉ MARÍA EZEIZA

205

LONGCHAMPS

GLEW

TRISTÁN SUÁREZ

53

2

VILLA ELISA

Estudiantes La Plata

LUIS JORGE HIRSCHI

26,000

36

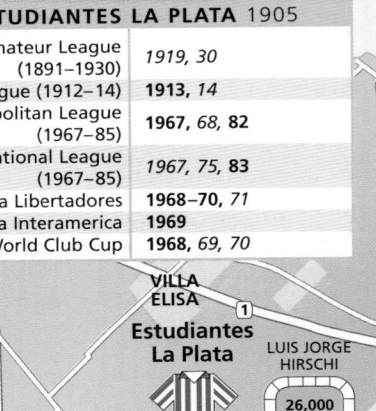

Gimnasia y Esgrima

JUAN CARLOS ZERILLO

33,000

ENSENADA

LA PLATA

1

11

Racing, who took the name of a Parisian team of the time, was founded by French immigrants and attracted a well-heeled fan base that included the Peron family, a connection that took them all the way to the top, winning three championships in a row between 1949 and 1951.

Corruption rears its head

Argentina's long economic decline saw the city's leading clubs accumulate significant debts. In 1967, the government baled them out, but at the price of reorganizing the season and introducing provincial clubs from Rosario and Sante Fé into the competition. Under the Military Junta (1976–83), the city's clubs became more closely enmeshed with political factions in the government. On the bright side, a major clean up and stadium renovation programme was carried out in the run up to the 1978 World Cup. However, the economy has continued to falter, and the problem of massive corruption continues to plague the city's teams, while the spread of poverty fuels the criminal gangs that now run the clubs' *ultra* fan groups.

La Boca, once a poor area around the city's docks and the original home of both Boca Juniors and River Plate, is now an attractive and bohemian artists' quarter which attracts tourists by the thousand.

ESTADIO DR CAMILO CICHERO, LA BOMBONERA

57,395	**Club:** Boca Juniors **Built:** 1940 **Original Capacity:** 60,000 **Rebuilt:** 1949–53, 1995

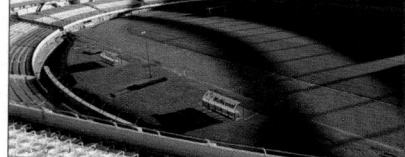

ESTADIO ANTONIO VESPUCIO LIBERTI DE NUNEZ, 'MONUMENTAL'

76,687	**Clubs:** River Plate, Argentina **Built:** 1938 **Original Capacity:** 100,000, Argentina v Brazil, Copa América, 4 April 1959 **Rebuilt:** 1973 **Significant Matches:** Copa América: 1959, 87; 1978 World Cup

CENTRAL BUENOS AIRES

Chacarita Juniors

PRESIDENTE PERÓN

24,300

DEFENSOR DE BELGRANO

8,500

Belgrano

Parque Sarmiento

CHACARITA JUNIORS 1906

Metropolitan League (1967–85)	1969

ARGENTINOS JUNIORS 1904

Amateur League (1891–1930)	1926
Metropolitan League (1967–85)	1980, 84
National League (1967–85)	1985
Copa Libertadores	1985
Copa Interamerica	1986
World Club Cup	1985

DON LEON KOLBOVSKI

24,144

Atlanta

ESTADIO ARGENTINOS JUNIORS

25,000

Argentinos Juniors

Vélez Sarsfield

CA All Boys

12,000

ISLAS MALVINAS

JOSE AMALFITANI 'EL FORTIN'

49,747

Constructed on a lagoon filled with the rubble of the railway industry

Neuva Chicago

NUEVA CHICAGO

28,500

In the early 20th century, this area was home to Argentina's meat-packing industry, which rivalled that of Chicago. The area was quickly populated by immigrants

NUEVA ESPAÑA

32,500

CA Español

Parque Almirante Guillermo Browr

VÉLEZ SARSFIELD 1910

AAF League (1919–26)	1919
Argentine League (1931–66, 86–91)	1953
Metropolitan League (1967–85)	1971, 79
National League (1967–85)	**1968**, 85
Apertura League (1992–2004)	1994, 96
Clausura League (1992–2004)	1992, 93, 96, 98
Copa Libertadores	**1994**
Copa Interamerica	**1996**
Supercopa	**1996**
World Club Cup	**1994**

SAN LORENZO 1908

Amateur League (1891–1930)	**1927**
AAF League (1919–26)	**1923, 24,** 25, 26
Argentine League (1931–66, 86–91)	1931, 33, 36, 41, 42, 46, 57, 59, 61, 88
Metropolitan League (1967–85)	**1968, 72, 83**
National League (1967–85)	1971, **72, 74**
Apertura League (1992–2004)	1995, 2004
Clausura League (1992–2004)	**1995, 2001**
Copa Sudamericana	**2002**

THE LOCAL DERBY

BOCA — **RIVER**

291 matches played

105 Boca Juniors wins
93 River Plate wins
93 draws

0 50 100 150 200 250

NUMBER OF MATCHES
(all first-class games up to May 2004)

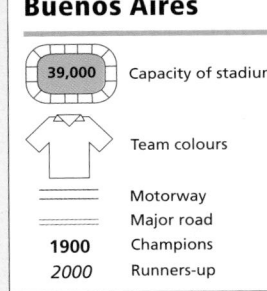

Central Buenos Aires

39,000	Capacity of stadium
	Team colours
	Motorway
	Major road
1900	Champions
2000	Runners-up

RIVER PLATE 1901

Amateur League (1891–1930)	*1909, 17, 18*
AAF League (1919–26)	*1920, 21, 22*
Argentine League (1931–66, 86–91)	**1932, 36, 37,** *38, 39,* **41, 42,** *43,* **44, 45,** *47,* **48, 49,** *52,* **53,** *55–57,* **60,** *62, 63,* **65, 66, 86, 90**
Metropolitan League (1967–85)	*1969, 70,* **75,** *77,* **79, 80**
National League (1967–85)	*1968, 69, 72, 73,* **75,** *76, 78,* **79, 81,** *84*
Apertura League (1992–2004)	**1992,** *93,* **94, 95, 97, 98, 2000,** *01, 02, 03*
Clausura League (1992–2004)	**1997,** *99,* **2000,** *01,* **02,** *04*
Copa Libertadores	*1966, 76, 86, 96*
Copa Interamerica	**1987**
Supercopa	**1991, 97**
World Club Cup	**1986,** *96*
Copa Sudamericana	*2003*

BOCA JUNIORS 1905

Amateur League (1891–1930)	**1919, 20, 23, 24, 26,** *27–29,* **30**
Argentine League (1931–66, 86–91)	**1931,** *33,* **34, 35, 40, 43, 44,** *45–47,* **50, 54, 58, 62, 64, 65, 89, 91**
Metropolitan League (1967–85)	*1973,* **76,** *78,* **81**
National League (1967–85)	**1969, 70, 76**
Apertura League (1992–2004)	*1992,* **93, 98, 99, 2001,** *03,* **04**
Clausura League (1992–2004)	**1999,** *2003,* **04**
Copa Libertadores	*1963,* **77, 78, 79, 2000, 01, 03**
Copa Interamerica	*1978*
Supercopa	**1989,** *94*
World Club Cup	**1977, 2000, 01, 03**

HURACÁN 1908

Amateur League (1891–1930)	**1921, 22,** *23,* **25, 28**
Metropolitan League (1967–85)	**1973,** *75,* **76**
Clausura League (1992–2004)	*1994*

INDEPENDIENTE 1905

FAF League (1912–14)	*1912*
AAF League (1919–26)	**1922,** *23,* **26**
Argentine League (1931–66, 86–91)	*1932,* **34, 35, 37, 38, 39, 40, 48,** *54,* **60, 63, 64, 89, 90**
Metropolitan League (1967–85)	**1970, 71,** *77,* **82, 83**
National League (1967–85)	**1967, 77, 78,** *83*
Apertura League (1992–2004)	*1997,* **2003**
Clausura League (1992–2004)	*1993,* **94,** *2000*
Copa Libertadores	**1964, 65, 72–75, 84**
Copa Interamerica	**1973, 74, 76**
Supercopa	*1989,* **94, 95**
World Club Cup	*1964, 65, 72,* **73,** *74,* **84**

ESTADIO ANTONIO VESPUCIO LIBERTI DE NUNEZ, "MONUMENTAL" (NATIONAL STADIUM)

76,687

River Plate

Argentina

Parque tres de Febrero

Avenida Pte. F. Alcorta

Autopista A. Illia

RIO DE LA PLATA

Atlanta bought the land for this stadium from Chacarita Juniors and evicted the team, creating an undying enmity between the clubs. The area around the stadium housed Buenos Aires' main Jewish community.

Ferro Carril Oeste (1998–)

ARQ. RICARDO ETCHEVERRY

24,205

Avenida Rivadavia

Avenida 9 De Julio

PLAZA DEL MAYO
Relatives of 'the Disappeared' gathered here to protest and received significant press coverage during the 1978 World Cup Finals

Boca Juniors

Avenida J. B. Alberdi

Avenida San Juan

Avenida Directorio

Autopista 25 Mayo

San Lorenzo

Avenida Saenz

ESTADIO DR CAMILO CICHERO, LA BOMBONERA

57,395

TOMÁS ADOLFO DUCÓ

48,292

Avenida Vélez Sarsfield

PEDRO BIDEGAÍN, 'EL NUEVO GASOMETRO'

43,000

Huracán

Racing Club

Independiente

PRESIDENTE PERÓN

56,200

DOBLE VISERA DE CEMENTO

57,901

Lanús

ESTADIO DEL VIADUCTO

10,000

LA FORTALEZA

46,519

Arsenal di Sarandi

FERRO CARRIL OESTE 1904

Metropolitan League (1967–85)	*1981,* **84**
National League (1967–85)	*1981,* **82, 84**

RACING CLUB 1903

Amateur League (1891–1930)	**1913–18**
AAF League (1919–26)	**1919,** *20,* **21, 25**
Argentine League (1931–66, 86–91)	**1949–51,** *52,* **55, 58, 59,** *61,* **66**
Metropolitan League (1967–85)	*1967,* **72**
National League (1967–85)	*1980*
Apertura League (1992–2004)	*1996,* **2002**
Copa Libertadores	**1967**
Supercopa	**1988,** *92*
World Club Cup	**1967**

LANÚS 1916

Amateur League (1891–1930)	*1897*
Argentine League (1931–66, 86–91)	*1956*
Clausura League (1992–2004)	*1998*
Copa CONMEBOL	**1996,** *97*

Argentina

FANS AND OWNERS

ARGENTINA'S CLUBS ARE IN CRISIS. With the exception of Colón from Santa Fé, every single club in the Argentinian first division is in debt. With the massive devaluation of the Peso and the emergency changes to banking in Argentina, these debts have become larger, though exactly how large nobody knows. Players and creditors go regularly unpaid, and at both national and club level players' strikes and lawsuits have been endemic. Yet money has still been flooding into the clubs. Player sales, overwhelmingly to Europe, have earned the clubs over half a billion dollars since 1975 ($360 million of which has been made in the last five years), television deals have improved massively, and although attendances have passed their peak, they are still significant.

So where has the money gone? Mostly it has been spent on massive, ludicrously paid squads, and been lost to corruption and skimming on all the transfers by club officials and agents. Racing Club was the first to collapse under the weight of debt, declaring bankruptcy in 2000, and allowed by government fiat to keep playing and trading until a private buyer could be found. Although still in debt, Racing, now owned by Fernando Marin and his company Blanquiceleste, is on an upward financial and soccer-playing curve, while San Lorenzo, Boca and River Plate are all over $30 million in debt. These big clubs remain in the hands of small cliques of members and are constantly prey to internal feuding and struggles over elected officials. Some, like Boca, continue to count wealthy patrons among their boards, but most are administratively and financially crippled. The absence of transparent financial accounts from these murky institutions means that the data available on levels of debt is likely to underestimate the difficulties of Argentinian clubs.

The *barra bravas*

Another place that the money has gone is to the *barra bravas* – the organized supporters clubs attached to every team. The *barras* emerged in the 1950s as a combination of local street gangs and die-hard fans. Their fearsome and noisy displays at the stadiums and their small-scale criminal organization made them perfect vehicles for manipulation by club officials. An understanding between the two saw the *barras* at each club's disposal when it required its own players and coaches controlled, and when votes were required in the fierce politicking during elections for club boards. In return, the *barras* received match tickets (often resold) and cash. As a consequence, a lot of the data available on attendances needs to be scrutinized carefully. Free tickets are not recorded in the data, and indeed some of the sales of cheaper seats go unrecorded.

The older leadership of the *barras* began to disappear in the 1990s, when firearms, flares, noise bombs and drugs became standard equipment. *Barra* groups now have less to do with soccer and have become a network of career professionals, providing income for poor urban men with an interest in organized crime. The gangs regularly hijack buses to go to games, fleecing fans and food-sellers on the way, and shootings near grounds have become a regular feature of the weekend's fixtures. The clubs, police and judiciary have been slow to act and, while CCTV in the top division is bringing some change, the violence seems to be migrating to the lower divisions.

ARGENTINA

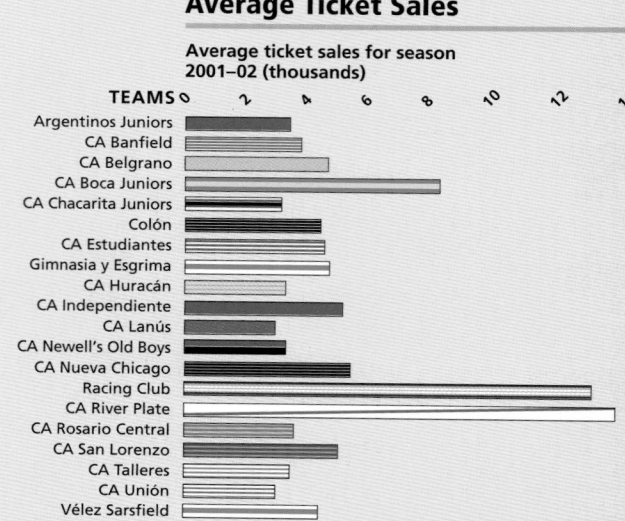

Club Debts 2000–01

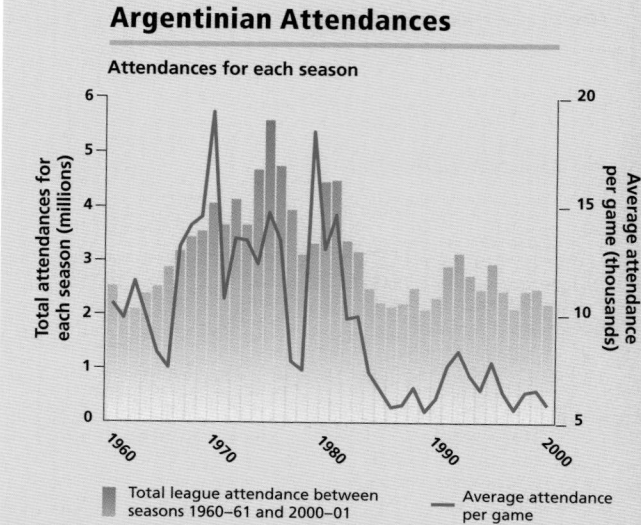

Average Ticket Sales

Average ticket sales for season 2001–02 (thousands)

Club members get in free at their own stadium and there are no conventional attendance records.

Argentinian Attendances

Attendances for each season

Total league attendance between seasons 1960–61 and 2000–01

Average attendance per game

Colón

La Banda de Rulo,
La Barra del Tablon,
La Banda del Santa Rosa

CA Unión

La Barra
de la Bombas

CA Talleres

Las Violetas, La Fiel,
Los Bulldogs,
La Barra de Juan

Santa Fé

CA Belgrano

Cordoba

Los Piratas,
La Banda del 2004,
La Banda del Jeton,
La Banda del Mosquito

Rosario

CA Newell's Old Boys

Cacho, Pimpi,
El Preso,
El Sapo, La lata,
Los Anticannals,
La San Roque

Rosario Central

BUENOS AIRES
(see inset)

La Banda del Chapero,
La Banda de los Pillines

La Plata

Gimnasia y Esgrima

La 22

A R G E N T I N A

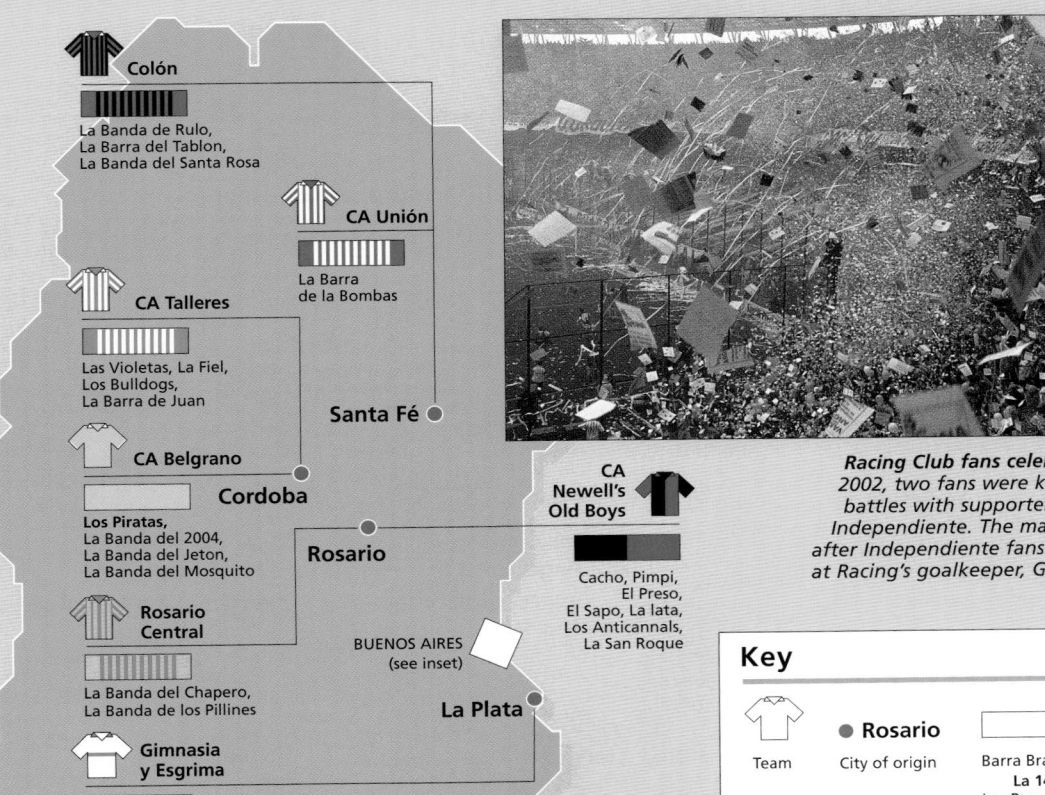

Racing Club fans celebrate, but in February 2002, two fans were killed in running street battles with supporters of Avellaneda rivals Independiente. The match itself was delayed after Independiente fans threw a smoke bomb at Racing's goalkeeper, Gustavo Campagnuolo.

Key

	● **Rosario**	
Team	City of origin	Barra Bravas
		La 14 Main groups in bold
		Los Ranas Lesser groups in roman

Teams shown were members
of the Primera Division 2001–02

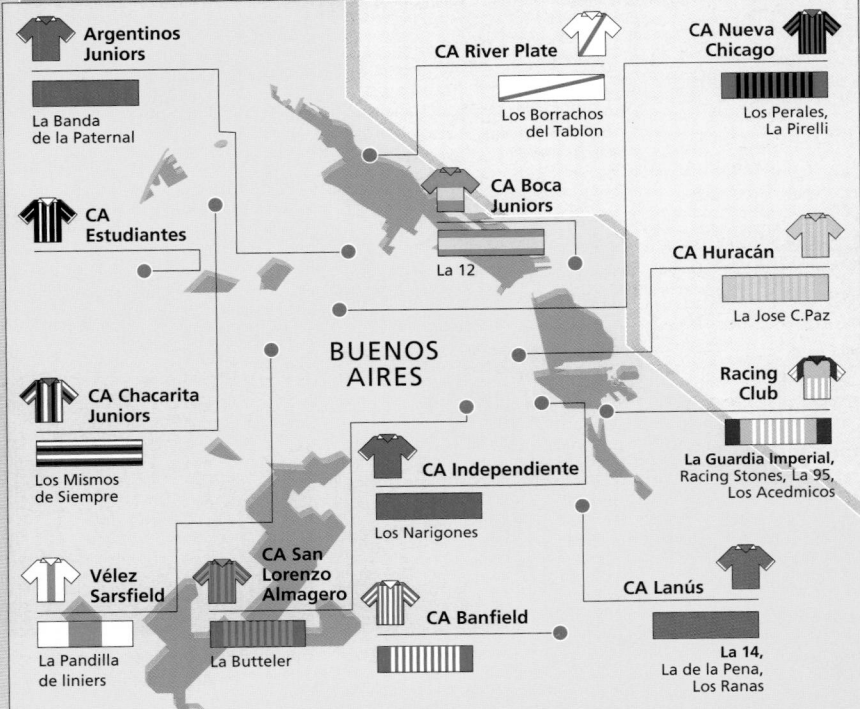

Argentinos Juniors

La Banda
de la Paternal

CA River Plate

Los Borrachos
del Tablon

CA Nueva Chicago

Los Perales,
La Pirelli

CA Boca Juniors

La 12

CA Estudiantes

CA Huracán

La Jose C.Paz

BUENOS AIRES

CA Chacarita Juniors

Los Mismos
de Siempre

Racing Club

La Guardia Imperial,
Racing Stones, La 95,
Los Acedmicos

CA Independiente

Los Narigones

Vélez Sarsfield

CA San Lorenzo Almagero

CA Lanús

La Pandilla
de liniers

La Butteler

CA Banfield

La 14,
La de la Pena,
Los Ranas

Fernando Marin, owner of legal firm Blanquiceleste and now Racing Club, may be the first of a new generation of private owners of Argentinian clubs.

Argentina

PLAYERS AND MANAGERS

PLAYERS AND MANAGERS in Argentina appear to come from one of two schools of soccer: open, silky and stylish on the one hand; defensive, caustic and rough on the other. In the person of Maradona the two can be seen in an individual. These two sides of Argentinian soccer style are best expressed in the contrasting styles of the two managers that led Argentina to World Cup victories: César Menotti in 1978 and Carlos Bilardo in 1986. Menotti came from the city of Rosario and inherited its traditions of stylish soccer and radical politics. Although to some onlookers he was compromised by winning the 1978 cup for the Junta he despised, his claim that his team played in the old style of a lost Argentina was read as a coded condemnation of the generals. Bilardo, by contrast, built an altogether rougher, tougher team in the mould of the spiky and aggressive Estudiantes team of the 1960s in which he played and for whom gamesmanship and trickery were the essence of the game.

From a trickle to a flood

Although soccer's popularity in Argentina has never wavered, the smooth running of both soccer and the economy certainly have. Not surprisingly, Argentinian soccer is marked by waves of emigration and unrest among its players. In the late 1940s, a prolonged players' strike saw a mass exodus of stars to the newly reinvigorated Colombian professional league and subsequently many left for Spain and Italy, claiming citizenship there on the basis of their grandparents' origins. Alfredo di Stefano, the leading player of his age, played only a handful of games for Argentina before decamping to Real Madrid and the Spanish national team. By the 1990s, the steady flow had turned into a rush as almost the entire national squad earned their wages around the Mediterranean, while at the end of 2001 their compatriots at home were on strike again, chasing unpaid wages from bankrupt clubs.

Top 10 International Goalscorers

PLAYER	GOALS	CAPS	FIRST MATCH	LAST MATCH
Gabriel Batistuta*	56	78	1991	2002
Diego Maradona	34	91	1977	1994
Luis Artime	24	16	1961	1967
Hernan Crespo*	23	46	1995	2004
Leopoldo Luque	22	45	1975	1981
Daniel Passarella	22	70	1976	1986
Hermino Masantonio	21	19	1935	1942
Jose Sanfillipo	21	30	1956	1962
Mario Kempes	20	43	1973	1982
Rene Jenjaudro Pontoni	19	29	1942	1947

* Indicates players still playing at least at club level.

Argentina International Managers

DATES	NAME	GAMES	WON	DRAWN	LOST
1940–58	Guillermo Stábile	110	74	18	18
1959	Victorio Luis Spinetto	6	5	1	0
1959	José Manuel Moreno	5	2	1	2
1960	Guillermo Stábile	10	6	1	3
1960–61	Victorio Luis Spinetto	10	5	3	2
1961	José D'Amico	2	1	0	1
1962	Juan Carlos Lorenzo*	5	2	2	1
1962	Jim López	2	1	1	0
1963	Horacio Amable Torres	8	4	1	3
1963	José D'Amico	2	1	0	1
1964–65	José Maria Minella*	15	9	5	1
1966	Juan Carlos Lorenzo	6	2	2	2
1967	Jim López	5	4	0	1
1967	Carmelo Faraone	2	0	0	2
1967–68	Renato Cesarini	5	1	1	3
1968	José Maria Minella	8	2	3	3
1969	Humberto Maschio	4	1	3	0
1969	Adolfo Alfredo Pedernera	4	1	1	2
1970–72	Juan José Pizzuti	23	10	8	5
1972–73	Omar Enrique Sivori	13	8	2	3
1974	Vladislao Wenceslao Cap	10	4	3	3
1974–82	César Luis Menotti	84	51	17	16
1983–90	Carlos Salvador Bilardo	70	36	23	11
1990–94	Alfio Oscar Basile	43	23	14	6
1994–98	Daniel Alberto Passarella	56	35	11	10
1999–	Marcelo Alberto Bielsa	64	39	15	10

* One match under different manager.
All figures correct as of 6 June 2004.

Top 20 International Caps

PLAYER	CAPS	GOALS	FIRST MATCH	LAST MATCH
Diego Simeone*	106	11	1988	2003
Oscar Ruggeri	97	7	1983	1994
Diego Maradona	91	34	1977	1994
Ariel Ortega*	86	17	1993	2003
Roberto Ayala*	84	3	1994	2004
Javier Zanetti*	80	4	1994	2004
Gabriel Batistuta*	78	56	1991	2002
America Gallego	73	3	1975	1982
Daniel Passarella	70	22	1976	1986
Alberto Tarantini	61	1	1974	1982
Jorge Olguin	60	0	1976	1982
Roberto Sensini*	60	0	1987	2000
Jorge Burruchaga	59	13	1983	1990
Ubaldo Fillol	58	0	1974	1985
Juan Sebastian Veron*	56	9	1996	2004
Rene Houseman	55	13	1973	1979
Claudio Javier Lopez*	55	10	1995	2004
Osvaldo Ardiles	53	8	1975	1982
Ricardo Giusti	53	0	1983	1990
Claudio Caniggia*	50	16	1987	2002

César Menotti's Argentina played some of the best soccer ever in the finals of its victorious 1978 World Cup campaign.

Carlos Bilardo led an aggressive and tricky Argentina, complete with Diego Maradona, to World Cup glory in Mexico in 1986.

ARGENTINA

Player of the Year

YEAR	PLAYER	CLUB
1970	Yazalde	Independiente
1971	Pastoriza	Independiente
1972	Bargas	Chacarita Juniors
1973	Brindisi	Huracán
1974	Raimondo	Independiente
1975	Scotta	San Lorenzo
1976	Passarella	River Plate
1977	Fillol	River Plate
1978	Kempes	Valencia [Sp]
1979	Maradona	Argentinos Juniors
1980	Maradona	Argentinos Juniors
1981	Maradona	Boca Juniors
1982	Gatti	Boca Juniors
1983	Bochini	Independiente
1984	Marcico	Ferro Carril Oeste
1985	Francescoli	River Plate
1986	Maradona	Napoli [Ita]
1987	Fabbri	Racing Club
1988	Paz	Racing Club
1989	Moreno	Independiente
1990	Goycochea	Racing Club/ Millonarios
1991	Ruggeri	Vélez Sarsfield
1992	Islas	Independiente
1993	Bello	River Plate
1994	Montoya	Boca Juniors
1995	Francescoli	River Plate
1996	Chilavert	Vélez Sarsfield
1997	Salas	River Plate
1998	Batistuta	Fiorentina [Ita]
1999	Saviola	River Plate
2000	Riquelme	Boca Juniors
2001	Riquelme	Boca Juniors
2002	Milito	Independiente
2003	Tévez	Boca Juniors

Awarded by the Argentinian Association of Sports Journalists.

Top Goalscorers 1931–2004

SEASON	PLAYER	CLUB	GOALS
1930–31	Zozaya	Estudiantes	33
1931–32	Ferreyra	River Plate	43
1932–33	Varallo	Boca Juniors	34
1933–34	Barrera	Racing Club	34
1934–35	Cosso	Vélez Sarsfield	33
1935–36	Barrera	Racing Club	32
1936–37	Erico	Independiente	47
1937–38	Erico	Independiente	43
1938–39	Erico	Independiente	40
1939–40	Langara	San Lorenzo	33
1939–40	Benitez Caceres	Racing Club	33
1940–41	Canteli	Newell's Old Boys	30
1941–42	Martino	San Lorenzo	25
1942–43	Arrieta	Lanús	23
1942–43	Labruna	River Plate	23
1942–43	Frutos	Platense	23
1943–44	Mellone	Huracán	26
1944–45	Labruna	River Plate	25
1945–46	Boye	Boca Juniors	24
1946–47	di Stefano	River Plate	27
1947–48	Santos	Rosario Central	21
1948–49	Simes	Racing Club	26
1948–49	Pizzuti	Banfield	26
1949–50	Papa	San Lorenzo	24
1950–51	Vernazza	River Plate	22
1951–52	Ricagni	Huracán	28
1952–53	Pizzuti	Racing Club	22
1952–53	Benavidez	San Lorenzo	22

Top Goalscorers (*continued*)

SEASON	PLAYER	CLUB	GOALS
1953–54	Berni	San Lorenzo	19
1953–54	Conde	Vélez Sarsfield	19
1953–54	Borello	Boca Juniors	19
1954–55	Massei	Rosario Central	21
1955–56	Castro	Rosario Central	17
1955–56	Grillo	Independiente	17
1956–57	Zarate	River Plate	22
1957–58	Sanfilippo	San Lorenzo	28
1958–59	Sanfilippo	San Lorenzo	31
1959–60	Sanfilippo	San Lorenzo	34
1960–61	Sanfilippo	San Lorenzo	26
1961–62	Artime	River Plate	25
1962–63	Artime	River Plate	25
1963–64	Veira	San Lorenzo	17
1964–65	Carone	Vélez Sarsfield	19
1965–66	Artime	Independiente	23
1967 M	Acosta	Lanús	18
1967 N	Artime	Independiente	11
1968 N	Obberti	Los Andes	13
1968 N	Wehbe	Vélez Sarsfield	13
1969 M	Machado da Silva	Racing Club	14
1969 N	Fischer	San Lorenzo	14
1969 N	Bulla	Platense	14
1970 M	Mas	River Plate	16
1970 N	Bianchi	Vélez Sarsfield	18
1971 M	Bianchi	Vélez Sarsfield	36
1971 N	Obberti	Newell's Old Boys	10
1971 N	Luniz	Juventud Antoniana	10
1972 M	Brindisi	Huracán	21
1972 N	Morete	River Plate	14
1973 M	Mas	River Plate	17
1973 M	Curioni	Boca Juniors	17
1973 M	Pena	Estudiantes	17
1973 N	Gomez Voglino	Atlanta	18
1974 M	Morete	River Plate	18
1974 N	Kempes	Rosario Central	25
1975 M	Scotta	San Lorenzo	32
1975 N	Scotta	San Lorenzo	28
1976 M	Kempes	Rosario Central	21
1976 N	Eresuma	San Lorenzo	12
1976 N	Luduena	Talleres	12
1976 N	Marchetti	Unión	12
1977 M	Alvarez	Argentinos Juniors	27
1977 N	Letanu	Estudiantes	13
1978 M	Andreuchi	Quilmes	22
1978 M	Maradona	Argentinos Juniors	22
1978 N	Reinaldi	Talleres	18
1979 M	Fortunato	Estudiantes	14
1979 M	Maradona	Argentinos Juniors	14
1979 N	Maradona	Argentinos Juniors	12
1980 M	Maradona	Argentinos Juniors	25
1980 N	Maradona	Argentinos Juniors	17
1981 M	Chaparro	Instituto	20
1981 N	Bianchi	Vélez Sarsfield	15
1982 N	Juarez	FC Oeste	22
1982 M	Morete	Independiente	20
1983 N	Husillos	Loma Negra	11
1983 M	Ramos	Newell's Old Boys	30

Top Goalscorers (*continued*)

SEASON	PLAYER	CLUB	GOALS
1984 N	Pasculli	Argentinos Juniors	9
1984 M	Francescoli	River Plate	24
1985 N	Comas	Vélez Sarsfield	12
1986†	Francescoli	River Plate	25
1986–87	Palma	Rosario Central	20
1987–88	Rodriguez	Deportivo Español	18
1988–89	Gorosito	San Lorenzo	20
1988–89	Dertycia	Argentinos Juniors	20
1989–90	Cozzoni	Newell's Old Boys	23
1990–91	Gonzalez	Vélez Sarsfield	18
1991–92 A	Diaz	River Plate	14
1991–92 C	Latorre	Boca Juniors	9
1992–93 A	Acosta AF	San Lorenzo	12
1992–93 C	Da Silva	River Plate	13
1993–94 A	Martinez	Boca Juniors	12
1993–94 C	Crespo	River Plate	11
1993–94 C	Espina	Platense	11
1994–95 A	Francescoli	River Plate	12
1994–95 C	Flores	Vélez Sarsfield	14
1995–96 A	Calderon	Estudiantes	13
1995–96 C	Lopez	Lanús	12
1996–97 A	Reggi	FC Oeste	11
1996–97 C	Martinez	Boca Juniors	15
1997–98 A	Da Silva	Rosario Central	15
1997–98 C	Sosa	Gimnasia	17
1998–99 A	Palermo	Boca Juniors	20
1998–99 C	Calderon	Independiente	17
1999–2000 A	Saviola	River Plate	15
1999–2000 C	Fuentes	Colón	17
2000–01 A	Angel	River Plate	13
2000–01 C	Romeo	San Lorenzo	15
2001–02 A	Cardetti	River Plate	17
2001–02 C	Cavenaghi	River Plate	15
2002–03 A	Silvera	Independiente	16
2002–03 C	Figueroa	Rosario Central	17
2003–04 A	Farias	Estudiantes LP	13
2003–04 C	Zarate	Vélez Sarsfield	13

M Metropolitan League   **N** National League
† Reverted to a single league   **C** Clausura League
A Apertura League

ARGENTINA

Claudio Caniggia remained playing at the top level for more than 15 years. His clubs included River Plate, Boca Juniors, Verona, SL Benfica and Rangers in Scotland.

Argentina

PRIMERA DIVISION 1985–2003

THE MID-1980s BEGAN with a reform of the old league system in which two separate tournaments – a Torneo Nacional and a Torneo Metropolitano – were played side-by-side. In 1985, a single national league kicked off. The increased representation of provincial sides (outside Buenos Aires) was confirmed with a series of titles for the two big Rosario teams, Rosario Central in 1987 and Newell's Old Boys in 1988 and 91. Newell's Old Boys built the club's success on an extensive scouting network and intensive youth policy, which produced strikers like Ariel Cozzoni. However, the big Buenos Aires clubs continued to win championships with one each for River Plate, Independiente and Boca Juniors, as well as victories for these teams plus Racing Club and San Lorenzo in the Liguilla – the qualifying tournament for the lucrative Copa Libertadores.

The financial screw

In 1992, another reorganization took place, with the national league being split into two separate 17-game leagues: the Apertura and Clausura. Competition has been open with championships going to River Plate, Boca Juniors, Independiente, San Lorenzo and Vélez Sarsfield. Although the financial screw has been on most clubs for the last decade, the big Buenos Aires clubs have pulled ahead of the others with bigger squads, more players imported from other Latin American countries and more lucrative sales of stars to top European clubs. During the 1990s, River Plate fielded Hernan Crespo, Oscar Ruggeri, Marcello Salas and Enzo Francescoli. Vélez Sarsfield, under coach Carlos Bianchi, starred Paraguayan goalkeeper José Luis Chilavert and striker José Flores and took back-to-back championships and a Copa Libertadores.

Most recently, Boca Juniors, also under Bianchi, has built a series of inspiring squads. Whenever the team has won a competition, however, the squad has been dismantled to pay the bills. Occasional challengers have included Gimnasia from La Plata, Racing Club and Lanús. Teams from Santa Fé and Córdoba have also reached the top flight and managed to hang in there. Nearly all clubs in Argentina are now in deep financial crisis, and almost every stadium is blighted by violence on match days.

Ten years of waiting is over: Gabriel Milito and Independiente fans celebrate winning the 2002–03 Apertura after beating San Lorenzo 3-0 to clinch the title. Milito has since signed for Real Zaragoza in Spain.

Champions' Winning Margin 1985–91

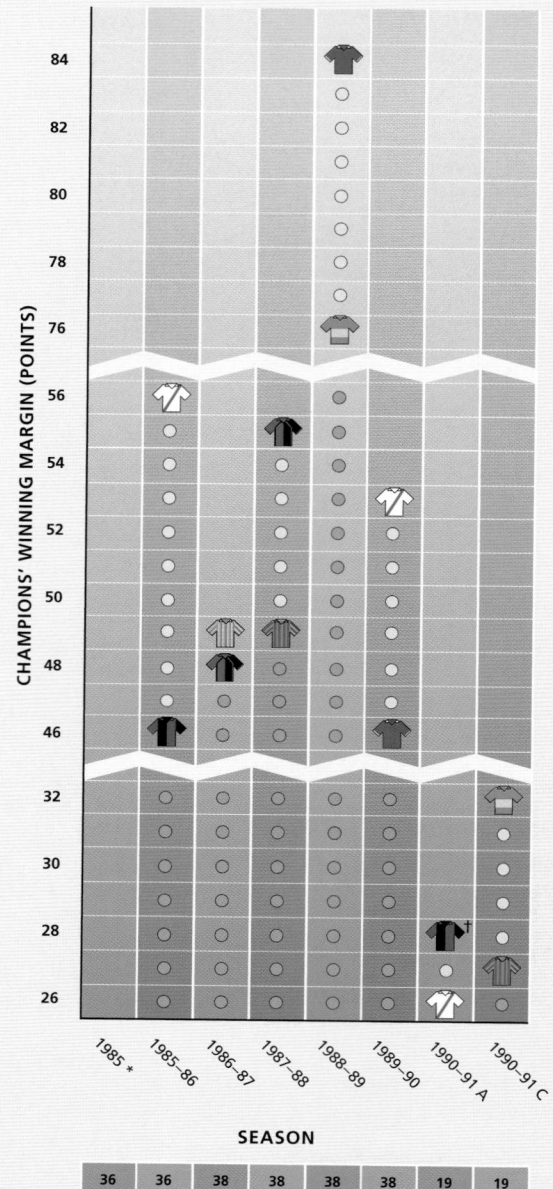

CHAMPIONS' WINNING MARGIN (POINTS)

SEASON: 1985 *, 1985–86, 1986–87, 1987–88, 1988–89, 1989–90, 1990–91 A, 1990–91 C

| 36 | 36 | 38 | 38 | 38 | 38 | 19 | 19 |

Total games played by each team (2 points awarded for a win except in 1989–90, when 3 points were awarded for a win and 2 points for a win on penalties)

* Championship decided by play-off
† Newell's Old Boys won national title by play-off for 1991

 Boca Juniors   Independiente   Newell's Old Boys

 River Plate   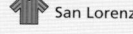 Rosario Central   San Lorenzo

Argentinian Players Transferred Abroad 1985–2001

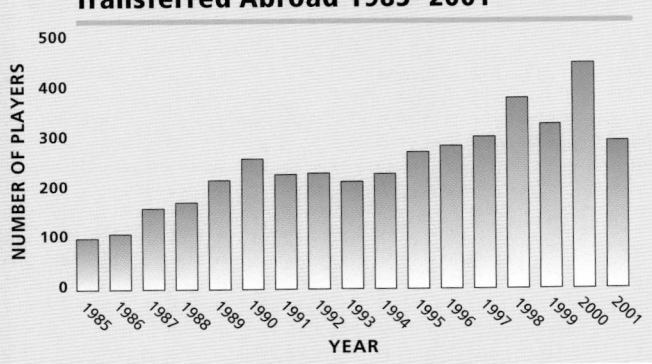

NUMBER OF PLAYERS — YEAR (1985–2001)

Income from Foreign Transfers 1985–2001

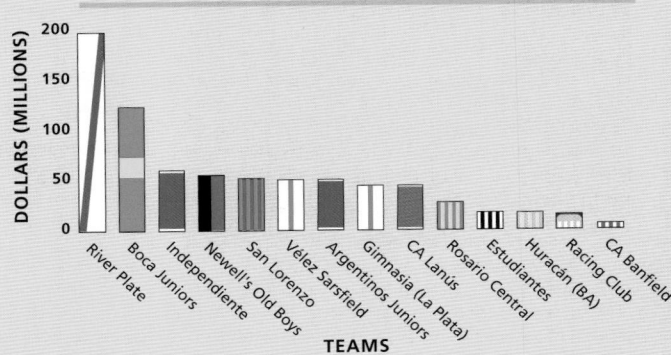

DOLLARS (MILLIONS) — TEAMS: River Plate, Boca Juniors, Independiente, Newell's Old Boys, San Lorenzo, Vélez Sarsfield, Argentinos Juniors, Gimnasia (La Plata), CA Lanús, Rosario Central, Estudiantes, Huracán (BA), Racing Club, CA Banfield

Argentinian League Positions 1985–1991

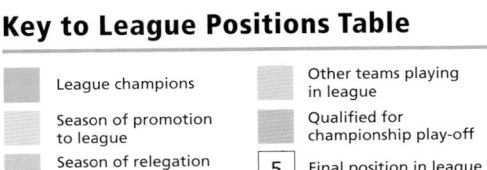

Key to League Positions Table

- League champions
- Season of promotion to league
- Season of relegation from league
- Other teams playing in league
- Qualified for championship play-off
- 5 Final position in league

* In the 1990–91 season the winners of the Apertura, Newell's Old Boys, and the winners of the Clausura, Boca Juniors, played-off for the national title. Newell's Old Boys won the title after a penalty shootout.

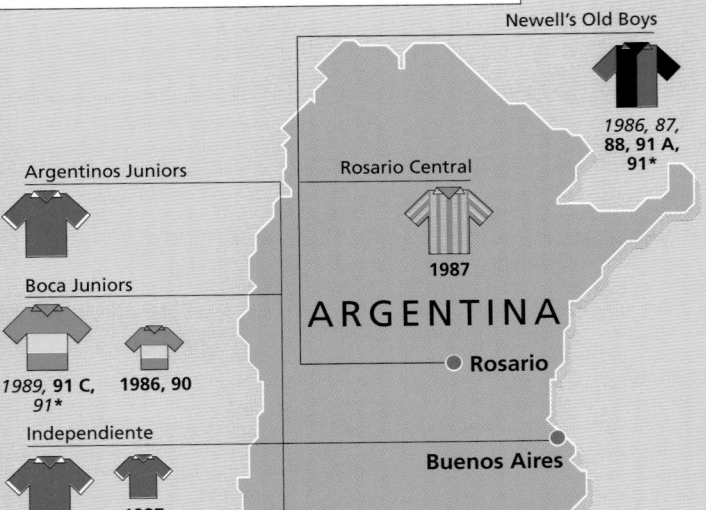

Map labels

Newell's Old Boys — 1986, 87, 88, 91 A, 91*

Rosario Central — 1987

Argentinos Juniors

Boca Juniors — 1989, 91 C, 91* / 1986, 90

Independiente — 1989, 90 / 1987

Racing Club — 1988

River Plate — 1986, 90, 91 A / 1989

San Lorenzo — 1988, 91 C / 1991

ARGENTINA · Rosario · Buenos Aires

Primera Division 1986–91

Independiente	Team name
1989, 90	League champions/runners-up — Champions in bold, Runners-up in italics
	Winners of Copa Libertadores Liguilla
● Buenos Aires	City of origin

League positions table

TEAM	1985	1985-86	1986-87	1987-88	1988-89	1989-90	1990-91 A	1990-91 C
Argentinos Juniors	1	4	17	7	7	9	4	18
Deportivo Armenio				13	19			
CA Banfield					18			
CA Belgrano								
Boca Juniors		5	4	12	2	3	8	1
CA Chacarita Juniors	19							
CA Chaco For Ever						17	14	19
Deportivo Español	2	14	7	3	19	18	17	
CA Estudiantes	16	12	16	7	16	7	9	
Ferro Carril Oeste	6	5	14	18	6	4	16	
Gimnasia y Esgrima (La Plata)	9	12	5	10	6	4	14	
Huracán (Buenos Aires)	13						8	6
Independiente	9	3	11	1	2	10	5	
Instituto	11	8	14	20	20			
CA Italiano		20						
CA Lanús							20	12
Deportivo Mandiyú				12	10		17	3
Newell's Old Boys	2	2	1	12	10		1*	8
CA Quilmes								
CA Platense	16	18	10	15	10	14	9	
Racing	18	15	17	15	17			
Racing Club		5	3	9	6	13	3	
River Plate	1	10	4	4	1	2	9	
Rosario Central			1	7	12	3	4	15
San Lorenzo	6	5	2	5	15	10	2	
CA San Martín					17			
CA Unión Santa Fé	14	16	18		10	18	12	
CA Talleres	8	11	20		6	10	10	20
CA Témperley	15	18						
Vélez Sarsfield	2	12	8	6	11	5	3	6

SEASON

ARGENTINA

River Plate and the club's fans remain the most powerful force in Argentinian soccer. However, despite big crowds and big transfers, the club remains mired in an ever deepening pit of debt.

Carlos Bianchi finally returned Boca Juniors to winning ways in the late 1990s after a lean era. Since his appointment, the club has won three championships and two Copa Libertadores.

Juan Román Riquelme of Boca Juniors was South American Footballer of the Year in 2001.

ARGENTINA

Key to League Positions Table

- League champions
- Season of promotion to league
- Season of relegation from league
- Other teams playing in league
- **5** Final position in league
- **A** Apertura
- **C** Clausura

Argentinian League Positions 1992–2003

SEASON

TEAM	92-93 A	92-93 C	93-94 A	93-94 C	94-95 A	94-95 C	95-96 A	95-96 C	96-97 A	96-97 C	97-98 A	97-98 C	98-99 A	98-99 C	99-00 A	99-00 C	00-01 A	00-01 C	01-02 A	01-02 C	02-03 A	02-03 C
Almagro																	18	10				
Argentinos Juniors	18	10	11	13	5	20	16	20			8	8	6	11	12	16	17	4	11	16		
Arsenal																					8	14
CA Banfield			9	7	8	13	19	18	20	19									18	7	12	13
CA Belgrano	7	13	16	9	6	15	20	13			19	9	18	14	16	16	9	18				
Boca Juniors	1	6	4	7	13	4	2	5	10	9	2	6	1	1	3	1	3	3	3	2	2	
CA Chacarita Juniors															8	15	9	6	8	17	4	19
Colón							13	9	8	2	14	16	5	12	16	3	10	13	4	11	7	6
Deportivo Español	11	4	18	14	18	4	17	11	18	16	17	19										
CA Estudiantes	7	13	20	15			9	3	10	16	10	11	11	15	10	17	7	9	6	9	19	8
Ferro Carril Oeste	4	16	10	15	14	13	17	9	14	10	12	11	17	19	19	20						
Gimnasia y Esgrima (Jujuy)			17	12	8	14	10	20	14	4	19	9	19	19								
Gimnasia y Esgrima (La Plata)	16	10	10	15	8	2	13	2	6	13	4	3	2	8	3	9	3	18	7	2	16	10
Gimnasia y Tiro			16	19																		
Huracán (Buenos Aires)	4	6	11	2	14	19	5	7	18	14	19	18	16	20			8	7	19	4	20	20
CA Huracán (Corrientes)									17	15												
Independiente	15	2	4	1	11	9	13	12	2	4	7	10	14	5	8	2	14	17	10	20	1	17
Instituto															16	11						
CA Lanús	7	15	4	9	6	9	2	3	2	10	11	2	4	16	10	11	15	14	12	12	11	12
CA Los Andes																	19	19				
Deportivo Mandiyú	12	10	13	20	19	18																
Newell's Old Boys	20	17	13	9	4	15	11	17	8	2	18	8	6	7	12	5	13	12	14	6	10	15
CA Nueva Chicago																			13	13	18	9
Olimpo																					17	5
CA Platense	18	18	13	5	14	7	11	14	15	8	9	14	20	18								
Quilmes																						
Racing Club	16	6	2	9	11	6	2	7	4	7	13	15	3	13	6	18	20	5	1	5	6	11
Atlético de Rafaela																						
River Plate	2	3	1	5	1	9	7	14	1	1	1	6	14	2	1	1	2	2	2	1	3	1
Rosario Central	12	6	18	3	8	7	10	6	5	18	3	13	6	4	2	13	12	20	16	14	13	4
San Lorenzo	2	4	7	3	1	5	19	6	4	6	3	4	3	5	1	5	8	9	7			
CA San Martín	12	19																				
CA Unión Santa Fé									16	10	14	19	6	5	12	8	11	15	17	15	14	18
CA Talleres	7	20			20	15									5	10	4	11	20	19	15	16
Vélez Sarsfield	6	1	2	18	3	3	1	1	13	5	4	1	11	13	7	5	6	8	15	10	5	3

Relegation is determined by averaging out points over three seasons rather than a points total over a single season.

ARGENTINA

Gimnasia y Esgrima (Jujuy)

Gimnasia y Tiro

CA Belgrano

Instituto

CA Talleres

CA San Martin

San Salvador de JuJuy

Salta

Colón

1997 C

Atlético de Rafaela

CA Unión Santa Fé

Córdoba

San Juan

Santa Fé

Rosario

Rosario Central

2000 A

Newell's Old Boys

Bahia Blanca

Olimpo

CA Los Andes

Lomas de Zamora

La Plata

Gimnasia y Esgrima

1995 C, 96 C, 99 A, 2002 C

Racing Club

1996 A, **2002 A**

River Plate

1993 A, **94 A, 95 A,** 97 A, 97 C, **98 A,** *99 C,* **2000 A,** *00 C,* **01 A,** *01 C,* **02 A, 02 C, 03 C**

Arsenal

CA Huracán

Deportivo Mandiyú

Corrientes

CA Chacarita Juniors

CA Platense

Buenos Aires

San Lorenzo

1995 A, 95 C, **2001 C**

Vélez Sarsfield

1993 C, *94 A,* **96 A,** *96 C,* **98 C**

Almagro

CA Banfield

Deportivo Español

Ferro Carril Oeste

CA Nueva Chicago

Quilmes

Argentinos Juniors

Boca Juniors

1993 A, 98 A, **99 A,** *99 C,* **2001 A,** *03 A,* **03 C**

CA Estudiantes

Huracán

1994 C

CA Lanús

1998 C

Independiente

1993 C, **94 C,** *97 C,* **2000 C,** *03 A*

A R G E N T I N A

Primera Division 1992–2003

Independiente — Team name

League champions/ runners-up

1989, *90* — Champions in bold Runners-up in italics

Other teams in the Primera Division

Buenos Aires — City of origin

The 35-year wait: Racing Club players celebrate their goal, away at Vélez Sarsfield, which gave them the final point needed to take the club's first national championship for 35 years in 2002.

Argentina

Asociación del Fútbol Argentino
Founded: 1893
Joined FIFA: 1912
Joined CONMEBOL: 1916

THE ARGENTINE LEAGUE championship is, outside of the UK, the world's oldest league. It was established in 1891 by expatriate Briton Alexander Hutton under the auspices of the Argentine Association Football League (AAFL). English teams and colleges (Alumni, Lomas Athletic and English High School) dominated the early years of the league until Racing Club's victory in 1913 signalled a shift of power to Argentinian clubs. This division in Argentine soccer was reflected in two splits that created parallel soccer associations and league championships in the years 1912–14 and 1919–26.

Professionalism and a professional league were established in 1931. For the next four decades, Argentine soccer was dominated by the big five from Buenos Aires (Boca Juniors, Independiente, Racing Club, River Plate and San Lorenzo). From 1967 to 1985 the championship was divided into two consecutive leagues, the Metropolitan and National. A single league was re-established in the mid-1980s and an extra tournament for the top teams was created – the Pre-Libertadores Liguilla – with a place in the lucrative Copa Libertadores at stake. Both tournaments were replaced in the early 1990s by the division of the season into two short leagues – the Apertura (opening) and Clausura (closing) championships.

Cup soccer has never proved popular in Argentina and, despite cups being donated by government ministers and Swedish ambassadors, no tournament has ever lasted very long.

Argentine Amateur League Record 1891–1930

SEASON	CHAMPIONS
1891	St Andrew's
1892	no championship
1893	Lomas Athletic
1894	Lomas Athletic
1895	Lomas Athletic
1896	Lomas Athletic
1897	Lomas Athletic
1898	Lomas Athletic
1899	Belgrano Athletic
1900	English High School
1901	Alumni
1902	Alumni
1903	Alumni
1904	Belgrano Athletic
1905	Alumni
1906	Alumni
1907	Alumni
1908	Belgrano
1909	Alumni
1910	Alumni
1911	Alumni
1912	Quilmes
1913	Racing Club
1914	Racing Club
1915	Racing Club
1916	Racing Club
1917	Racing Club
1918	Racing Club
1919	Boca Juniors
1920	Boca Juniors
1921	Huracán

SEASON	CHAMPIONS
1922	Huracán
1923	Boca Juniors
1924	Boca Juniors
1925	Huracán
1926	Boca Juniors
1927	San Lorenzo
1928	Huracán
1929	Gimnasia Y Esgrima
1930	Boca Juniors

FAF League Record 1912–14

SEASON	CHAMPIONS
1912	Estudianil Porteno
1913	Estudiantes LP
1914	Estudianil Porteno

AAF League Record 1919–26

SEASON	CHAMPIONS
1919	Racing Club
1920	River Plate
1921	Racing Club
1922	Independiente
1923	San Lorenzo
1924	San Lorenzo
1925	Racing Club
1926	Independiente

Argentine Professional League Record 1931–66

SEASON	CHAMPIONS	RUNNERS-UP
1931	Boca Juniors	San Lorenzo
1932	River Plate	Independiente
1933	San Lorenzo	Boca Juniors
1934	Boca Juniors	Independiente
1935	Boca Juniors	Independiente
1936	River Plate	San Lorenzo
1937	River Plate	Independiente
1938	Independiente	River Plate
1939	Independiente	River Plate
1940	Boca Juniors	Independiente
1941	River Plate	San Lorenzo
1942	River Plate	San Lorenzo
1943	Boca Juniors	River Plate
1944	Boca Juniors	River Plate
1945	River Plate	Boca Juniors
1946	San Lorenzo	Boca Juniors
1947	River Plate	Boca Juniors
1948	Independiente	River Plate
1949	Racing Club	River Plate
1950	Racing Club	Boca Juniors
1951	Racing Club	Banfield
1952	River Plate	Racing Club
1953	River Plate	Vélez Sarsfield
1954	Boca Juniors	Independiente
1955	River Plate	Racing Club
1956	River Plate	Lanús
1957	River Plate	San Lorenzo
1958	Racing Club	Boca Juniors
1959	San Lorenzo	Racing Club
1960	Independiente	River Plate
1961	Racing Club	San Lorenzo
1962	Boca Juniors	River Plate
1963	Independiente	River Plate
1964	Boca Juniors	Independiente
1965	Boca Juniors	River Plate
1966	Racing Club	River Plate

Metropolitan League Record 1967–85

SEASON	CHAMPIONS	RUNNERS-UP
1967	Estudiantes	Racing Club
1968	San Lorenzo	Estudiantes
1969	Chacarita Juniors	River Plate
1970	Independiente	River Plate
1971	Independiente	Vélez Sarsfield
1972	San Lorenzo	Racing Club
1973	Huracán	Boca Juniors
1974	Newell's Old Boys	Rosario Central
1975	River Plate	Huracán
1976	Boca Juniors	Huracán
1977	River Plate	Independiente
1978	Quilmes	Boca Juniors
1979	River Plate	Vélez Sarsfield
1980	River Plate	Argentinos Juniors
1981	Boca Juniors	Ferro Carril Oeste
1982	Estudiantes	Independiente
1983	Independiente	San Lorenzo
1984	Argentinos Juniors	Ferro Carril Oeste
1985	no championship	

ARGENTINA

National League Record 1967–85

SEASON	CHAMPIONS	RUNNERS-UP
1967	Independiente	Estudiantes
1968	Vélez Sarsfield	River Plate
1969	Boca Juniors	River Plate
1970	Boca Juniors	Rosario Central
1971	Rosario Central	San Lorenzo
1972	San Lorenzo	River Plate
1973	Rosario Central	River Plate
1974	San Lorenzo	Rosario Central
1975	River Plate	Estudiantes
1976	Boca Juniors	River Plate
1977	Independiente	Talleres
1978	Independiente	River Plate
1979	River Plate	Unión Santa Fé
1980	Rosario Central	Racing Club
1981	River Plate	Ferro Carril Oeste
1982	Ferro Carril Oeste	Quilmes
1983	Estudiantes	Independiente
1984	Ferro Carril Oeste	River Plate
1985	Argentinos Juniors	Vélez Sarsfield

Argentine League Record 1986–91

SEASON	CHAMPIONS	RUNNERS-UP
1986	River Plate	Newell's Old Boys
1987	Rosario Central	Newell's Old Boys
1988	Newell's Old Boys	San Lorenzo
1989	Independiente	Boca Juniors
1990	River Plate	Independiente
1991*	Newell's Old Boys	Boca Juniors

Apertura League Record 1992–2004

SEASON	CHAMPIONS	RUNNERS-UP
1992	River Plate	Boca Juniors
1993	Boca Juniors	River Plate
1994	River Plate	Vélez Sarsfield
1995	River Plate	San Lorenzo
1996	Vélez Sarsfield	Racing Club
1997	River Plate	Independiente
1998	River Plate	Boca Juniors
1999	Boca Juniors	Gimnasia y Esgrima LP
2000	River Plate	Rosario Central
2001	Boca Juniors	River Plate
2002	Racing Club	River Plate
2003	Independiente	Boca Juniors
2004	Boca Juniors	San Lorenzo

Clausura League Record 1992–2004

SEASON	CHAMPIONS	RUNNERS-UP
1992	Newell's Old Boys	Vélez Sarsfield
1993	Vélez Sarsfield	Independiente
1994	Independiente	Huracán
1995	San Lorenzo	Gimnasia y Esgrima LP
1996	Vélez Sarsfield	Gimnasia y Esgrima LP
1997	River Plate	Colón
1998	Vélez Sarsfield	Lanús
1999	Boca Juniors	River Plate
2000	River Plate	Independiente
2001	San Lorenzo	River Plate
2002	River Plate	Gimnasia y Esgrima LP
2003	River Plate	Boca Juniors
2004	River Plate	Boca Juniors

* In the 1990–91 season the winners of the Apertura, Newell's Old Boys, and the winners of the Clausura, Boca Juniors, played-off for the national title. Newell's Old Boys won the title after a penalty shoot-out.

Argentine League Summary 1931–2004

TEAM	TOTALS	CHAMPIONS & RUNNERS-UP (BOLD) (ITALICS)
River Plate	32, 25	**1932, 36, 37,** *38, 39,* **41, 42, 43, 44, 45, 47, 48, 49, 52, 53, 55–57,** *60, 62, 63, 65, 66, 68†, 69†, 69*, 70*, 72†, 73†,* **75*,** *75†, 76†,* **77*,** *78†,* **79†, 79*, 80*, 81†,** *84†,* **86, 90, 92§,** *93§,* **94§, 95§, 97†,** *97§,* **98†,** *99#,* **2000§, 2000#,** *01§, 01#, 02§,* **02#,** *03#,* **04#**
Boca Juniors	20, 15	*1931,* **33, 34, 35, 40, 43, 44,** *45–47, 50, 54, 58, 62, 64, 65, 69†,* **70†,** *73*, 76*, 76†,* **78*,** *81*,* **89, 91, 92§,** *93§, 98§, 99§,* **99#, 2001§,** *03§,* **03#, 04§,** *04#*
Independiente	14, 14	*1932, 34, 35, 37,* **38, 39, 40,** *48, 54, 60, 63,* **64,** *67†,* **70*, 71*,** *77*, 77†, 78†, 82*,* **83*,** *83†,* **89, 90,** *93#, 94#, 97§,* **2000#,** *03§*
San Lorenzo	9, 11	*1931, 33,* **36, 41, 42, 46, 57,** *59, 61,* **68*,** *71†,* **72*,** *72†, 74†,* **83*,** *88,* **95#,** *95§,* **2001#,** *04§*
Racing Club	7, 7	**1949–51,** *52,* **55,** *58, 59,* **61, 66,** *67*, 72*,* **80†,** *96§,* **2002§**
Vélez Sarsfield	5, 6	*1953,* **68†,** *71*, 79*, 85†,* **92#,** *93#, 94§,* **96§,** *96#,* **98#**
Rosario Central	4, 4	**1970†,** *71†,* **73†,** *74†, 74*,* **80†,** *87,* **2000§**
Newell's Old Boys	4, 2	**1974*,** *86,* **87, 88,** *91,* **92#**
Estudiantes	3, 3	**1967*,** *67†,* **68*,** *75†,* **82*,** *83†*
Ferro Carril Oeste	2, 3	*1981*,* **81†,** *82†,* **84†,** *84*￼*
Argentinos Juniors	2, 1	**1980*,** *84*,* **85†**
Huracán	1, 3	**1973*,** *75*, 76*,* **94#**
Quilmes	1, 1	**1978*,** *82†*
Chacarita Juniors	1, 0	**1969***
Gimnasia y Esgrima (La Plata)	0, 4	*1995#, 96#, 99§, 2002#*
Lanús	0, 2	*1956, 98#*
Banfield	0, 1	*1951*
Colón	0, 1	*1997#*
Talleres	0, 1	*1977†*
Unión Santa Fé	0, 1	*1979†*

* denotes winners/runners-up of Metropolitan League
† denotes winners/runners-up of National League
§ denotes winners/runners-up of Apertura League
# denotes winners/runners-up of Clausura League

Pre-Libertadores Liguilla Record 1986–91

SEASON	CHAMPIONS
1986	Boca Juniors
1987	Independiente
1988	Racing Club
1989	River Plate
1990	Boca Juniors
1991	San Lorenzo

Pre-Libertadores Liguilla Summary

TEAM	TOTAL	WINNERS
Boca Juniors	2	1986, 90
River Plate	1	1989
Independiente	1	1987
Racing Club	1	1988
San Lorenzo	1	1991

ARGENTINA

Uruguay

THE SEASON IN REVIEW 2003

THE URUGUAYAN SEASON opened, in traditional manner, with the creation of a new format for the First Division. Last year's Torneo Clasificatorio and short Apertura and Clausura leagues were abandoned in favour of two simple 18-team, 17-game leagues; though an early season liguilla was also played to decide qualification for Continental tournaments. The outcome of the Apertura was never in question. Nacional started at a canter, winning 14 and drawing 2 of its opening 16 games. It lost the final game to Danubio 3-2, but had already claimed the title. Peñarol's challenge ended when it lost the derby game 3-1, but, undeterred, it turned to its lawyers instead, and appealed to the league to cancel the championship, alleging that Nacional's seven-goal striker Sebastian Abreu was incorrectly registered with the FA. After being banned, reinstated, banned and reinstated, Abreu saw out the first half of the season before heading back to Mexico.

Nacional's season was transformed in its Copa Sudamericana tie with Paraguayan side Libertad, when it threw away a three-goal lead from the opening leg and went out of the tournament. Its subsequent form in the Clausura was abject, finishing an unheard of 9th. However, it is not unconnected that Nacional began the second half of the season without three key strikers – Abreu, Carlos Juarez and Gabriel Alvez – all of whom had been sold. Peñarol had the unfamiliar experience of being chased by other teams and Fénix, Miramar Misiones and Liverpool all played well. But, under coach Diego Aguirre, Peñarol saw them all off to take the Clausura and went on to beat a deflated Nacional in the championship play-off. The star of Peñarol's season was goalkeeper and captain José Luis Chilavert, who in his final year at the club became the main taker of penalties and free kicks.

Apertura Torneo – Final Table

CLUB	P	W	D	L	F	A	Pts	
Nacional	17	14	2	1	34	9	44	Apertura winners
Peñarol	17	12	2	3	43	20	38	
Danubio	17	10	4	3	34	19	34	
Montevideo Wanderers	17	10	3	4	40	28	33	
CA Fénix	17	9	2	6	41	38	29	
Cerro	17	8	4	5	25	21	28	
Maldonado (Maldonado)	17	8	4	5	24	26	28	
Defensor Sporting Club	17	8	3	6	28	23	27	
Liverpool	17	8	3	6	24	24	27	
Miramar Misiones	17	6	4	7	28	27	22	
Bella Vista	17	6	3	8	23	22	21	
Central Español	17	6	3	8	15	22	21	
Tacuarembó FC (Tacuarembó)	17	5	5	7	25	26	20	
Villa Española	17	4	5	8	31	37	17	
River Plate	17	3	4	10	18	27	13	
CA Plaza (Colonia)	17	2	6	9	17	26	12	
Colonia (Juan Lacaze, CO)	17	2	3	12	13	36	9	
Juventud (Las Piedras)	17	1	2	14	11	43	5	

The structure of the season
The Uruguayan season acquired a new structure for 2003. The championship now involves two 18-team (17-match) leagues: the Apertura and the Clausura. The winners of the two leagues then play-off to decide the championship. However, at the end of the season an aggregate table is made up from the two leagues and if the winners of that aggregate league is neither the Apertura winners nor the Clausura winners then they too go into the championship play-off. The champions and the runners-up both get a place in the Copa Libertadores, while the champions also get a place in the Copa Sudamericana. The aggregate table is also used to decide who gets relegated, with the two lowest placed clubs from Montevideo and the lowest placed Interior club going down. A post-season Liguilla featuring the next best eight teams (apart from those involved in the championship play-off) then decides who gets the other place in the Copa Libertadores (winners) and the in the Copa Sudamericana (runners-up).

An uncontrollable passion – Montevideo team Fénix made it to the Libertadores – here striker Germán Hornos celebrates after scoring in the group stage game against Bolivian club the Strongest.

Captain Alejandro Lembo lifts the Apertura trophy after Nacional made it 16 matches without defeat, beating Deportivo Maldonado 3-2 in the penultimate match of the campaign.

URUGUAY

Clausura Torneo – Final Table

CLUB	P	W	D	L	F	A	Pts	
Peñarol	17	12	3	2	30	13	**39**	Clausura winners
Liverpool	17	9	4	4	23	15	**31**	
Fénix	17	8	5	4	21	16	**29**	
Defensor Sporting Club	17	8	4	5	30	20	**28**	
Miramar Misiones	17	8	4	5	26	21	**28**	
Cerro	17	7	6	4	22	17	**27**	
River Plate	17	8	3	6	26	25	**27**	
Danubio	17	7	6	4	21	21	**27**	
Nacional	17	7	5	5	29	23	**26**	
Bella Vista	17	7	5	5	23	22	**26**	
Maldonado (Maldonado)	17	6	5	6	16	14	**23**	
Colonia (Juan Lacaze, CO)	17	6	5	6	24	23	**23**	
Central Español	17	7	1	9	17	20	**22**	
Montevideo Wanderers	17	4	7	6	19	24	**19**	
Tacuarembó FC (Tacuarembó)	17	4	5	8	19	23	**17**	
CA Plaza (Colonia)	17	2	5	10	16	30	**11**	
Villa Española	17	1	5	11	14	29	**8**	
Juventud (Las Piedras)	17	2	2	13	17	37	**8**	

All teams from Montevideo unless otherwise stated.
Relegated clubs: River Plate, Villa Española (Montevideo), Juventud (Interior).
Promoted clubs: CS Cerrito, CA Rentistas, Rocha FC.

Championship Play-off

2003 SEMI-FINAL
December 4 – Estadio Centenario, Montevideo
Peñarol 1-0 Nacional
(Bizera 45)
h/t: 1-0   **Att:** 40,000
Ref: Méndez

The championship final is normally between the aggregate table winners and the semi-final winners. But as Peñarol won both the aggregate table and the semi-final, it became champions without the need for another match.

Top Goalscorers 2003

PLAYER	CLUB	NATIONALITY	GOALS
Alexander Medina	Liverpool	Uruguayan	22
Carlos Bueno	Peñarol	Uruguayan	18
Julio Ramirez	Montevideo Wanderers	Uruguayan	16

International Club Performances 2003

CLUB	COMPETITION	PROGRESS
Peñarol	Copa Libertadores	Group Stage
Nacional	Copa Libertadores	2nd Round
Fénix	Copa Libertadores	Group Stage
Danubio	Copa Sudamericana	1st Stage, Preliminary Phase
Nacional	Copa Sudamericana	2nd Stage, Preliminary Phase

Copa Libertadores Qualifiers 2004

TEAM AND QUALIFICATION
Peñarol as champions
Nacional as runners-up
Fénix as winners of Pre-Libertadores Liguilla

Copa Sudamericana Qualifiers 2004

TEAM AND QUALIFICATION
Peñarol as champions
Danubio as runners-up of Pre-Libertadores Liguilla

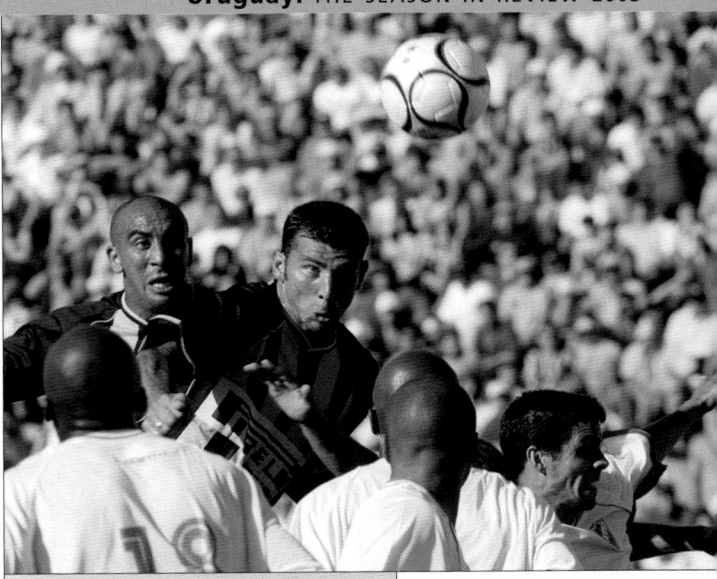

Above: Gabriel Cedres avenges Peñarol's Apertura defeat in the Nacional-Penarol derby. His header opened the scoring in Peñarol's 3-1 Clausura victory. Marcella da Suoza looks on.

Left: Captain, goalkeeper, penalty taker and all-round Peñarol hero José Luis Chilavert waves goodbye after winning the Clausura. Now 38, Chilavert is finally calling it a day.

Below: Peñarol celebrates its championship victory after beating Nacional 1-0 in the play-off with a goal from Joe Bizera deep in first-half injury time.

Montevideo

SOCCER CENTER

URUGUAY

AT THE HEART OF MONTEVIDEO'S soccer landscape is the Centenario stadium, built for the first World Cup in 1930. Described by Jules Rimet as a 'temple of football', it is shared by the city's two biggest clubs: Peñarol and Nacional (who retain smaller grounds as well). It sits in the centre of a city that saw some of the earliest club championships and international matches in Latin America, and which hosts almost every team in the Uruguayan top division (and almost half the population of the country). Together with Buenos Aires, across the mouth of the River Plate, Montevideo is the cradle of soccer in Latin America.

The substantial expatriate British community, mostly involved in shipping and banking, was playing soccer informally in the 1880s and setting up schools and sports clubs across the city. Albion Cricket Club, formed in 1891, created a soccer section in 1893. British railway engineers set up CURCC (Central Uruguayan Railways Cricket Club) in 1891 and took to soccer soon after. The team first split from the company and then transformed itself into Peñarol in 1913. Peñarol is one half of the most successful double act in world soccer. Together with its rival, Nacional, they have won over 80 per cent of the Uruguayan championships ever played.

Nacional v Peñarol

Nacional was set up in 1899 by local students in self-conscious opposition to the foreigners running CURCC. Since this time, the team's social and political affiliations have always remained with the nationalist elite. In 1903, the Uruguayan FA put the Nacional squad in the national colours in a representative match against Argentinian Buenos Aires. Nacional still celebrates the occasion annually. Peñarol continues to be associated with the poorest, immigrant strands of Montevideo society. The annual derby matches are keenly contested. A similar derby is played out in a smaller way in the western suburb of Cerro, which has been absorbed into the city in the last few decades. Older, more middle-class residents have remained true to the area's original team, Rampla Juniors, while the new working-class immigrants tend to favour the recently-arrived Cerro.

Beyond the big two, Montevideo spawned an enormous number of clubs encouraged by the opening of Grand Central Park in 1900 by a tramway company who wanted people to use the park for soccer. Although over a hundred years of soccer history have passed, British influences linger on in many of the clubs' names – Liverpool, Racing, Wanderers and River Plate. In recent years there have been significant challenges to the big two, most notably from Danubio, Defensor Sporting and Fénix.

PARQUE SUERO COLÓN

2,000

Colón

FERROCARRIL

Racing Club

CENTRAL RAILWAYS WORKSHOPS
Peñarol founded here

BELLA VISTA 1920	
Amateur League (1900–1931)	*1924*
National League (1932–2003)	**1990**

NEUVO PARIS

OSVALDO ROBERTO

8,500

SAYAGO

Montevideo Wanderers

Liverpool FC

PRADO

Bella Vista

BELVEDERE

BELVEDERE

PARQUE ALFREDO VIERA

Cerro

9,500

PARQUE JOSÉ NASAZZI

15,000

LUIS TROCCOLI

15,000

CERRO NORTE

25,000

PARQUE ABRAHAM PALADINO

LA TEJA

PARQUE CAPURRO

CAPURRO

CERRO 1922	
National League (1932–2003)	*1960*

8,000

10,000

Fénix

CA Progreso

VILLA DEL CERRO

AGUADA

OLIMPICO

9,500

Rampla Juniors

RAMPLA JUNIORS 1914	
Amateur League (1900–1931)	*1923*, **27**, **28**
National League (1932–2003)	*1932, 40, 64*

CIUDAD VIEJA

CA PROGRESO 1917	
National League (1932–2003)	**1989**

Montevideo docks: River Plate was originally founded in the Customs House in the docks area of the city at the beginning of the 20th century.

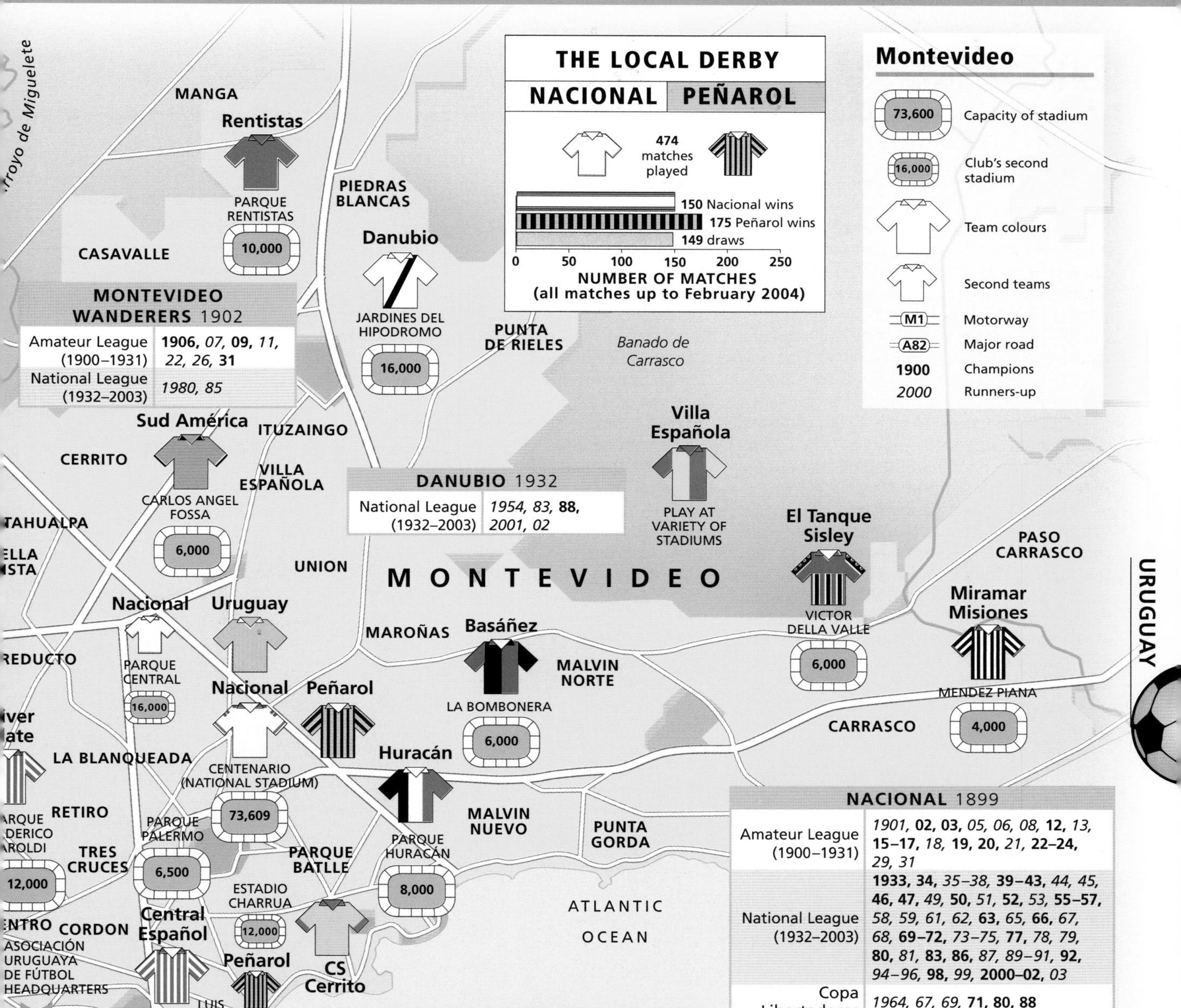

URUGUAY

MANGA

Rentistas

PARQUE
RENTISTAS

10,000

CASAVALLE

MONTEVIDEO WANDERERS 1902

Amateur League (1900–1931)	**1906,** *07,* **09, 11,** *22, 26,* **31**
National League (1932–2003)	*1980, 85*

Sud América

CERRITO

CARLOS ANGEL
FOSSA

6,000

TAHUALPA

ELLA
STA

UNION

PIEDRAS
BLANCAS

Danubio

JARDINES DEL
HIPODROMO

16,000

PUNTA
DE RIELES

ITUZAINGO

VILLA
ESPAÑOLA

DANUBIO 1932

National League (1932–2003)	*1954, 83,* **88,** *2001, 02*

THE LOCAL DERBY

NACIONAL	PEÑAROL

474
matches
played

150 Nacional wins
175 Peñarol wins
149 draws

| 0 | 50 | 100 | 150 | 200 | 250 |

NUMBER OF MATCHES
(all matches up to February 2004)

Banado de
Carrasco

Villa
Española

PLAY AT
VARIETY OF
STADIUMS

Montevideo

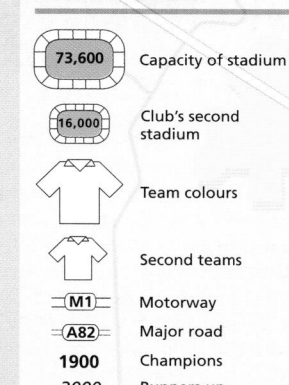

73,600	Capacity of stadium
16,000	Club's second stadium
	Team colours
	Second teams
M1	Motorway
A82	Major road
1900	Champions
2000	Runners-up

El Tanque
Sisley

VICTOR
DELLA VALLE

6,000

PASO
CARRASCO

Miramar
Misiones

MENDEZ PIANA

CARRASCO

4,000

MONTEVIDEO

Nacional   Uruguay

PARQUE
CENTRAL

16,000

REDUCTO

iver
ate

LA BLANQUEADA

Nacional   Peñarol

CENTENARIO
(NATIONAL STADIUM)

73,609

RETIRO

ARQUE
DERICO
AROLDI

12,000

PARQUE
PALERMO

6,500

TRES
CRUCES

ENTRO CORDON
ASOCIACIÓN
URUGUAYA
DE FÚTBOL
HEADQUARTERS

AUF

**Central
Español**

PARQUE
BATLLE

ESTADIO
CHARRUA

12,000

Peñarol

LUIS
FRANZINI

18,000

PUNTA
CARRETAS

Defensor
Sporting

MAROÑAS

Basáñez

LA BOMBONERA

6,000

Huracán

PARQUE
HURACÁN

8,000

CS
Cerrito

MALVIN
NORTE

MALVIN
NUEVO

PUNTA
GORDA

ATLANTIC

OCEAN

NACIONAL 1899

Amateur League (1900–1931)	*1901,* **02, 03,** *05, 06, 08,* **12, 13,** *15–17,* **18, 19, 20,** *21,* **22–24,** *29,* **31**
National League (1932–2003)	**1933, 34,** *35–38,* **39–43,** *44, 45, 46,* **47,** *49,* **50,** *51,* **52,** *53,* **55–57,** *58, 59,* **61,** *62,* **63,** *65,* **66,** *67, 68,* **69–72,** *73–75,* **77,** *78, 79,* **80,** *81,* **83, 86,** *87,* **89–91,** *92, 94–96,* **98,** *99,* **2000–02,** *03*
Copa Libertadores	*1964, 67, 69,* **71,** *80,* **88**
Copa Interamérica	**1972,** *81,* **89**
Supercopa	*1990*
World Club Cup	**1971,** *80,* **88**

PEÑAROL 1899

Amateur League (1900–1931)	**1900, 01,** *02, 03, 05,* **07,** *09, 10, 11,* **12,** *14–17,* **18, 20, 21, 26,** *27,* **28, 29**
National League (1932–2003)	**1932,** *33, 34,* **35–38,** *39,* **41–43, 44, 45, 46,** *47,* **49, 50, 51,** *52,* **53, 54,** *55–57,* **58–62,** *63,* **64, 65, 66, 67, 68,** *69–72,* **73–75, 76, 77,** *78, 79,* **81, 82,** *84,* **85,** *86,* **88,** *93–97,* **98, 99,** *2000,* **03**
Copa Libertadores	**1960, 61,** *62,* **65,** *66,* **70,** *82, 83,* **87**
Copa CONMEBOL	*1993, 94*
World Club Cup	*1960,* **61, 66, 82,** *87*

DEFENSOR SPORTING 1913

National League (1932–2003)	**1976,** *82,* **87,** *91,* **93,** *97*

CENTRAL ESPAÑOL 1905

National League (1932–2003)	**1984**

CENTENARIO

73,609

Clubs: Nacional, Peñarol, Uruguay
Built: 1930
**Original
Capacity:** 80,000
Significant Matches: 1930 World Cup: nine
matches, including semi-final
and Final;
Copa América: 1942, 56, 67,
and Finals 83, 95

Uruguay

PRIMERA DIVISIÓN PROFESIONAL 1984–2003

THE 1980s BEGAN chaotically in Uruguay, with a brutal military government presiding over economic decline and urban disorder. With very strict controls and limits placed on conventional politics, many leading political figures migrated into the administration of soccer, including Julio Maria Sanguinetti, future Uruguayan president and then-president of Peñarol. Similarly, Tabaré Vázquez, future leader of the leftist Encuentro Progresista party, was president of Progresso. The *junta*, recognizing the popular appeal of the sport, were prepared to bale out clubs as the economic squeeze destroyed their balance sheets.

Military rule ended and democratic elections were held in 1984, and for a time it seemed that the old order of Peñarol and Nacional championship victories had been swept aside. That year the title went unexpectedly to the tiny Montevideo club Central Español, led by the top-scoring striker José Villareal. Indeed, the country's lesser lights won a whole string of championships in the late 1980s. Defensor took two, aided by the free-scoring Gerardo Miranda, followed by Danubio and Bella Vista.

The 1990s saw Peñarol and Nacional take back their stranglehold on the league, though Defensor amalgamated with a popular basketball club to become Defensor Sporting and won the Clausura in 1997. The club has maintained its challenge to the big two by shrewd spending, an active youth policy and lucrative forays into the Copa Libertadores. However, nearly all other clubs, big and small, struggled financially throughout the 1990s, and only the sale of players overseas (some 400 in the late 1990s) and the sale of bonds to long-suffering fans kept clubs afloat. In 1998, Frontera Riviera became the first side from outside Montevideo to be promoted to the top flight. The growing strength of provincial soccer was recognized by changes in the structure of the Uruguayan league. Places were guaranteed to clubs from outside Montevideo, and relegation systems changed to ensure a Montevideo-provincial balance.

Primera División Profesional

Peñarol	Team name
	League champions/runners-up
1985, *88*	Champions in bold Runners-up in italics
	Other teams in the Primera División Profesional
● Rocha	City of origin

Of the smaller clubs Danubio (in red and blue) has proved the most successful. Victories have come in the 2001 Apertura and the 2002 Clausura but the main championship prize still eludes them.

Key to League Positions Table

- League champions
- Season of promotion to league
- Season of relegation from league
- Other teams playing in league
- Teams in relegation league (Clasificatorio)
- 5 Final position in league

Uruguayan League Positions 1984–2003

SEASON

TEAM	1984	1985	1986	1987	1988	1989	1990	1991	1992	1993	1994 A	1994 C	1995 A	1995 C	1996 A	1996 C	1997 A	1997 C	1998 A	1998 C	1999 A	1999 C	2000 A	2000 C	2001 A	2001 C	2002 A	2002 C	2003 A	2003 C
Basáñez											3	12	13	8																
Bella Vista (Montevideo)	5	13	5	3	11	5	1	9	5	11	13	11								2	6	4	8	7	9	8	10		11	10
Bella Vista (Paysandú)																			13	11	15	12	9	9						
Central Español	1	8	3	10	9	12	4	6	13		12	5	5	12	12	7											9	10	12	13
CS Cerrito																														
Cerro	12	4	10	9	8	4	12	7	11	6	4	3	7	11	10	11	11	5			6	10	5	7					6	6
Deportivo Colonia																													17	12
Danubio	4	11	9	6	1	7	6	5	3	3	11	10	10	5	4	5	9	12	11	5	3	3	2	4	1	2	7	1	3	8
Defensor Sporting	8	12	8	1	3	6	8	1	6	2	1	6	4	6	2	4	4	1	4	7	2	4	3	2	5	4	6	4	8	4
El Tanque Sisley								14																						
Fénix			12																						6	8	3	3	5	3
Frontera Riviera																					11	9	16	15						
Huracán	9	10	7	12	4	10	14	11		12					5	3	8	7	10	9	8	5	18	13						
Juventud																					12	11	10	6					18	18
Liverpool FC				5	11	7	8	10	9	9	7	2	7	9	10	5	4	12	8	15	6	14	17						9	2
Deportivo Maldonado																					9	13	9	14			4	9	7	11
Miramar Misiones	13		11	12																									10	5
Nacional	3	5	1	2	7	2	2	2	1	4	6	2	3	1	3	1	1	6	1	1*	1	2	1	3*	3	1*	1	5*	1	9
Peñarol	2	1	2	8	2	3	4	4	1	2	1*	1	2*	1	6*	3	2*	3	4	5	1*	4	1	2	3	2	2	2	2	1*
CA Plaza																											8	6	16	16
CA Progreso	10	6	6	7	13	1	11	12	9	5	8	13	11	10																
Racing Club						5	10	8	13										12	10					11	8				
Rampla Juniors	7	7	11	13							8	10	9	12	3	6	2	6	11	7	10	14	12							
Rentistas					9	9	13	12											10	8	8	2	7	15	6	10				
River Plate		3	13	4	10	13	13			2	10	7	8	4	7	8	2	3	5	3	10	7	10	6					15	7
Rocha																							13	16						
Sud América	11	9										8	13	11	12															
Deportivo Tacuarembó																					12	14	8	5	7	7			13	15
Villa Española																	9	11						17			10	7	14	17
Montevideo Wanderers	6	2	4	5	6	8	10	3	7	7	5	4	6	9	8	9	7	6	12						4	5	5	8	4	14

*Denotes championship play-off winners.

Since 1993 the season has been divided into two leagues, Apertura and Clausura (marked A and C), the winners of which play off to decide the championship. In 1997 Nacional (winners of the Apertura) and Peñarol (the team with the most points overall) played off for the championship. For 2001 and 2002 the championship began with Torneo Clasificatorio. The top 10 teams then played the Apertura and Clausura for the national championship. The remainder played in a relegation league. In 2003 it reverted to a traditional Apertura and Clausura with a play-off Final.

URUGUAY

Uruguay

Asociación Uruguaya de Fútbol
Founded: 1900
Joined FIFA: 1923
Joined CONMEBOL: 1916

THE FIRST RECORDED SOCCER MATCHES IN URUGUAY took place in autumn 1878 in Montevideo between teams made up of British residents and visiting British sailors. The first club, Albion FC, was set up in 1886 by an Englishman, William Pool. A national soccer association was founded in 1900 and an amateur league soon followed, although it was initially restricted to only four clubs from Montevideo – Albion FC, Central Uruguayan Railways Cricket Club (later to become Peñarol), Uruguay Athletic Club and Deutsche Fussball Klub. Club numbers steadily expanded and though again restricted to the capital city the first three decades of the 20th century were a golden era for Uruguayan soccer. Enormous domestic interest was sustained and enhanced by amazing international successes: victory at the 1924 and 1928 Olympic Games – both held in Europe – and hosting and winning the 1930 World Cup. On the back of this wave of economic and sporting success, professionalism and a reconstituted national league were established in 1932.

Since then Uruguayan soccer has been dominated by two teams – Nacional and Peñarol, both from the capital Montevideo – more completely than any other significant soccer nation. Between them they have won the national championship over 80 times, ceding the title to only eight other clubs in over a century. In fact, all the country's major clubs are based in Montevideo and concern has often been aired about its metropolitan bias. To counter the effect of this bias a regional league system run by the Organization del Futbol del Interior has been established to ensure continued interest in the sport outside the capital.

The league is currently split into two halves – the Apertura (opening) and Clausura (closing) championships. A play-off between the two champions for the national title is held at the end of the season, unless the same team wins both championships. The national champions get a place in the Copa Libertadores. The next eight clubs from an aggregate table (across both championships) play in a post-season liguilla (mini-league) to decide the other entrants for the Copa Libertadores and the Copa Sudamericana. The two worst teams from Montevideo and the worst team from the interior (again from the aggregate table) are relegated.

Uruguayan League Record 1900–2003

SEASON	CHAMPIONS	SEASON	CHAMPIONS
1900	Peñarol	1915	Nacional
1901	Peñarol	1916	Nacional
1902	Nacional	1917	Nacional
1903	Nacional	1918	Peñarol
1904	*no championship*	1919	Nacional
1905	Peñarol	1920	Nacional
1906	Wanderers	1921	Peñarol
1907	Peñarol	1922	Nacional
1908	River Plate	1923	Nacional
1909	Wanderers	1924	Nacional
1910	River Plate	1925	*no championship*
1911	Peñarol	1926	Peñarol
1912	Nacional	1927	Rampla Juniors
1913	River Plate	1928	Peñarol
1914	River Plate	1929	Peñarol

Uruguayan League Record (*continued*)

SEASON	CHAMPIONS	SEASON	CHAMPIONS
1930	*no championship*	1968	Peñarol
1931	Wanderers	1969	Nacional
1932	Peñarol	1970	Nacional
1933	Nacional	1971	Nacional
1934	Nacional	1972	Nacional
1935	Nacional	1973	Peñarol
1936	Peñarol	1974	Peñarol
1937	Peñarol	1975	Peñarol
1938	Peñarol	1976	Defensor
1939	Nacional	1977	Nacional
1940	Nacional	1978	Peñarol
1941	Nacional	1979	Peñarol
1942	Nacional	1980	Nacional
1943	Nacional	1981	Peñarol
1944	Peñarol	1982	Peñarol
1945	Peñarol	1983	Nacional
1946	Nacional	1984	Central Español
1947	Nacional	1985	Peñarol
1948	*no championship*	1986	Nacional
1949	Peñarol	1987	Defensor
1950	Nacional	1988	Danubio
1951	Peñarol	1989	Progreso
1952	Nacional	1990	Bella Vista
1953	Peñarol	1991	Defensor
1954	Peñarol	1992	Nacional
1955	Nacional	1993	Peñarol
1956	Nacional	1994	Peñarol
1957	Nacional	1995	Peñarol
1958	Peñarol	1996	Peñarol
1959	Peñarol	1997	Peñarol
1960	Peñarol	1998	Nacional
1961	Peñarol	1999	Peñarol
1962	Peñarol	2000	Nacional
1963	Nacional	2001	Nacional
1964	Peñarol	2002	Nacional
1965	Peñarol	2003	Peñarol
1966	Nacional		
1967	Peñarol		

Chile

Federación de Fútbol de Chile
Founded: 1895
Joined FIFA: 1912
Joined CONMEBOL: 1916

SOCCER ARRIVED IN CHILE in the late 19th century via visiting British sailors in the coastal ports of Valparaíso and Viña del Mar. The first clubs were formed in the early 1890s, the earliest being Santiago Wanderers formed in Valparaíso in 1892. It was soon joined by others, especially in the capital Santiago, and in 1895 a national FA was founded.

The geography of Chile – very long, very thin – militated against the formation of a regular national tournament and regional leagues quickly developed instead.

At the prompting of the most successful clubs, a national league was established in 1933 and professionalism legalized. However, it was not until the 1950s that teams from outside Santiago entered the league, and not until 1971 that Unión San Felipe won the title for a provincial city.

The national league ran as a conventional single league until 1997 when the season was split into two championships – Apertura and Clausura. In 1998, the league reverted to a single championship format, with the top four behind the champions playing-off for Chile's second slot in the Copa Libertadores. In 2002 the league reverted to separate Apertura and Clausura tournaments. It was not until 1991 that a Chilean club, Colo Colo, won the Copa Libertadores. A national cup competition – the Copa Chile – was established in 1958 (but was not played between 1962–73). The last tournament was played in 2001.

Paraguay

Asociación Paraguaya de Fútbol
Founded: 1906
Joined FIFA: 1921
Joined CONMEBOL: 1921

THE TOP DIVISION IN PARAGUAY has 13 clubs playing an Apertura and a Clausura championship each year. The Apertura consists of a short league with each team playing the others once. Until 1997 draws were not allowed and penalty shootouts took place if the scores were level at the end of 90 minutes (victory by this method was only worth two points as against three for a normal time win). Out of this league, the top six teams form two mini-leagues which produce the contestants for a two-leg play-off Final. The Clausura is a normal league with clubs playing each other home and away. The national championship is decided by a two-leg play-off between Apertura and Clausura champions.

Chilean League Record 1933–2003

SEASON	CHAMPIONS	SEASON	CHAMPIONS
1933	Magallanes	1971	Unión San Felipe
1934	Magallanes	1972	Colo Colo
1935	Magallanes	1973	Unión Española
1936	Audax Italiano	1974	Huachipato
1937	Colo Colo	1975	Unión Española
1938	Magallanes	1976	Everton
1939	Colo Colo	1977	Unión Española
1940	Universidad de Chile	1978	Palestino
1941	Colo Colo	1979	Colo Colo
1942	Santiago Morning	1980	Cobreloa
1943	Unión Española	1981	Colo Colo
1944	Colo Colo	1982	Cobreloa
1945	Green Cross	1983	Colo Colo
1946	Audax italiano	1984	Universidad Católica
1947	Colo Colo	1985	Cobreloa
1948	Audax italiano	1986	Colo Colo
1949	Universidad Católica	1987	Universidad Católica
1950	Everton	1988	Cobreloa
1951	Unión Española	1989	Colo Colo
1952	Everton	1990	Colo Colo
1953	Colo Colo	1991	Colo Colo
1954	Universidad Católica	1992	Cobreloa
1955	Palestino	1993	Colo Colo
1956	Colo Colo	1994	Universidad de Chile
1957	Audax italiano	1995	Universidad de Chile
1958	Santiago Wanderers	1996	Colo Colo
1959	Universidad de Chile	1997 A	Universidad Católica
1960	Colo Colo	1997 C	Colo Colo
1961	Universidad Católica	1998	Colo Colo
1962	Universidad de Chile	1999	Universidad de Chile
1963	Colo Colo	2000	Universidad de Chile
1964	Universidad de Chile	2001	Santiago Wanderers
1965	Universidad de Chile	2002 A	Universidad de Chile
1966	Universidad Católica	2002 C	Colo Colo
1967	Universidad de Chile	2003 A	Cobreloa
1968	Santiago Wanderers	2003 C	Cobreloa
1969	Universidad de Chile		
1970	Colo Colo		

Chilean Cup Record 1958–2001

YEAR	WINNERS	YEAR	WINNERS
1958	Colo Colo	1986	Cobreloa
1959	Santiago Wanderers	1987	Cobresal
1960	no competition	1988	Colo Colo
1961	Santiago Wanderers	1989	Colo Colo
1962–73	no competition	1990	Colo Colo
1974	Colo Colo	1991	Universidad Católica
1975	Palestino	1992	Unión Española
1976	no competition	1993	Unión Española
1977	Palestino	1994	Colo Colo
1978	no competition	1995	Universidad Católica
1979	Universidad de Chile	1996	Colo Colo
1980	Deportes Iquique	1997	no competition
1981	Colo Colo	1998	Universidad de Chile
1982	Colo Colo	1999	no competition
1983	Universidad Católica	2000	Universidad de Chile
1984	Everton	2001	Universidad de Chile
1985	Colo Colo		

Paraguayan League Record 1906–2003

SEASON	CHAMPIONS	SEASON	CHAMPIONS
1906	Guaraní	1957	Olimpia
1907	Guaraní	1958	Olimpia
1908	no championship	1959	Olimpia
1909	Nacional	1960	Olimpia
1910	Libertad	1961	Cerro Porteño
1911	Nacional	1962	Olimpia
1912	Olimpia	1963	Cerro Porteño
1913	Cerro Porteño	1964	Guaraní
1914	Olimpia	1965	Guaraní
1915	Cerro Porteño	1966	Cerro Porteño
1916	Olimpia	1967	Guaraní
1917	Libertad	1968	Olimpia
1918	Cerro Porteño	1969	Guaraní
1919	Cerro Porteño	1970	Cerro Porteño
1920	Libertad	1971	Olimpia
1921	Guaraní	1972	Cerro Porteño
1922	no championship	1973	Cerro Porteño
1923	Guaraní	1974	Cerro Porteño
1924	Nacional	1975	Olimpia
1925	Olimpia	1976	Libertad
1926	Nacional	1977	Cerro Porteño
1927	Olimpia	1978	Olimpia
1928	Olimpia	1979	Olimpia
1929	Olimpia	1980	Olimpia
1930	Libertad	1981	Olimpia
1931	Olimpia	1982	Olimpia
1932–34	no championship	1983	Olimpia
1935	Cerro Porteño	1984	Guaraní
1936	Olimpia	1985	Olimpia
1937	Olimpia	1986	Sol de América
1938	Olimpia	1987	Cerro Porteño
1939	Cerro Porteño	1988	Olimpia
1940	Cerro Porteño	1989	Olimpia
1941	Cerro Porteño	1990	Cerro Porteño
1942	Nacional	1991	Sol de América
1943	Libertad	1992	Cerro Porteño
1944	Cerro Porteño	1993	Olimpia
1945	Libertad	1994	Cerro Porteño
1946	Nacional	1995	Olimpia
1947	Olimpia	1996	Cerro Porteño
1948	Olimpia	1997	Olimpia
1949	Guaraní	1998	Olimpia
1950	Cerro Porteño	1999	Olimpia
1951	Sportivo Luqueño	2000	Olimpia
1952	Presidente Hayes	2001	Cerro Porteño
1953	Sportivo Luqueño	2002	Libertad
1954	Cerro Porteño	2003	Libertad
1955	Cerro Porteño		
1956	Olimpia		

SOCCER YEARBOOK: THE CAF NATIONS

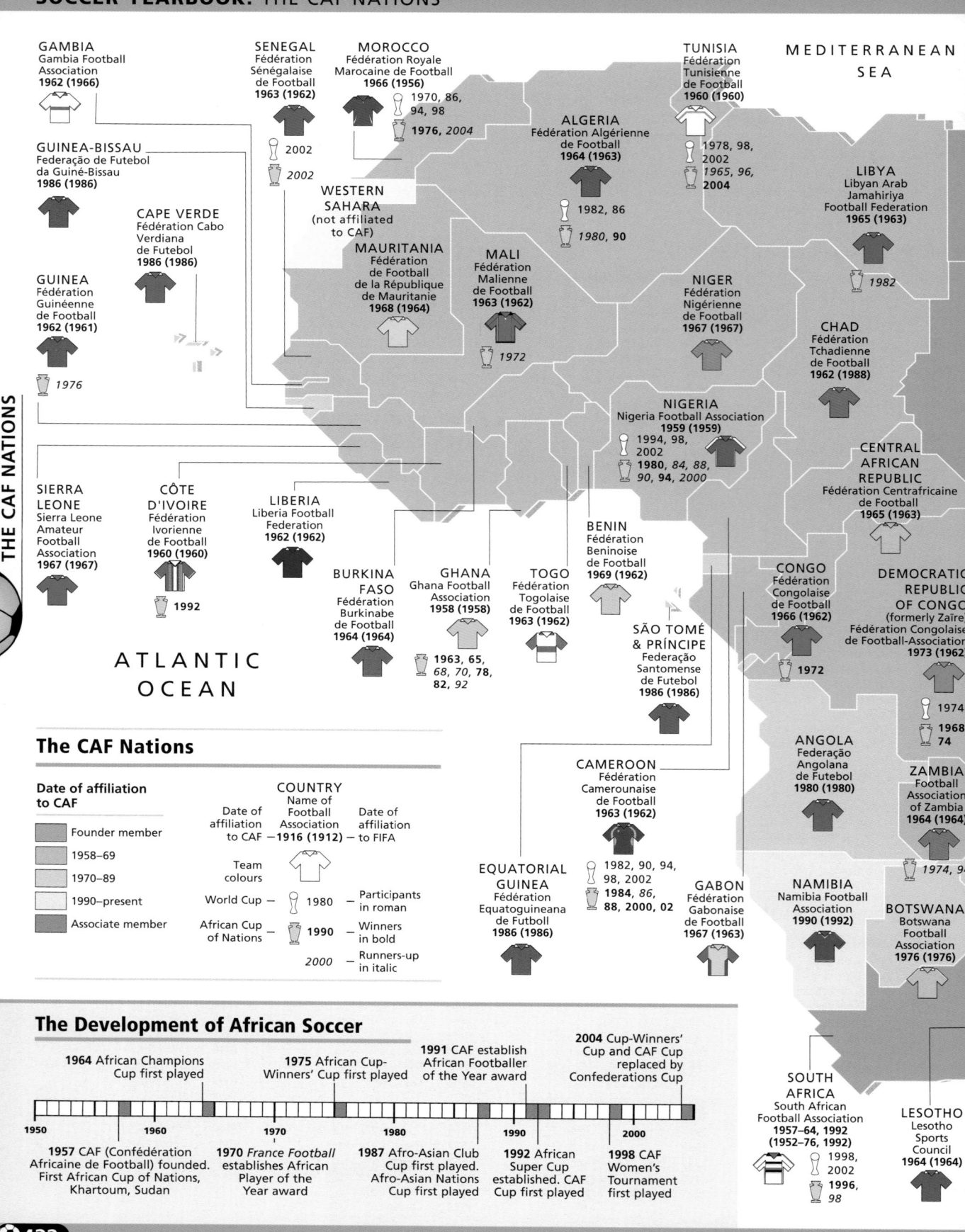

The CAF Nations

EGYPT
Egyptian Football
Association
1957 (1923)

1934, 90

**1957, 59,
62, 86, 98**

Cairo
CAF
Headquarters

UGANDA
Federation of
Uganda Football
Associations
1959 (1959)

1978

ERITREA
Eritrean National
Football Federation
1994 (1998)

DJIBOUTI
Fédération
Djiboutienne
de Football
1986 (1994)

SUDAN
Sudan Football
Association
1957 (1948)

*1959, 63,
70*

ETHIOPIA
Ye'Ityopiya Football
Federechin
1957 (1953)

SOMALIA
Somalia Football
Federation
1968 (1960)

1957, 62

RWANDA
Fédération Rwandaise
de Football Amateur
1976 (1976)

KENYA
Kenya Football
Federation
1968 (1960)

BURUNDI
Fédération
de Football
du Burundi
1972 (1972)

TANZANIA
Football Association
of Tanzania
1960 (1964)

**INDIAN
OCEAN**

SEYCHELLES
Seychelles Football
Association
1986 (1986)

MALAWI
Football Association
of Malawi
1968 (1967)

MAURITIUS
Mauritius Football
Association
1962 (1962)

MOZAMBIQUE
Federação Moçambicana
de Futebol
1978 (1978)

MADAGASCAR
Fédération Malagasy
de Football
1963 (1962)

RÉUNION
Ligue de la
Réunion
**Associate 1992
(not affiliated)**

ZIMBABWE
Zimbabwe Football
Association
1980 (1965–70, 1980)

SWAZILAND
National Football
Association of
Swaziland
1976 (1976)

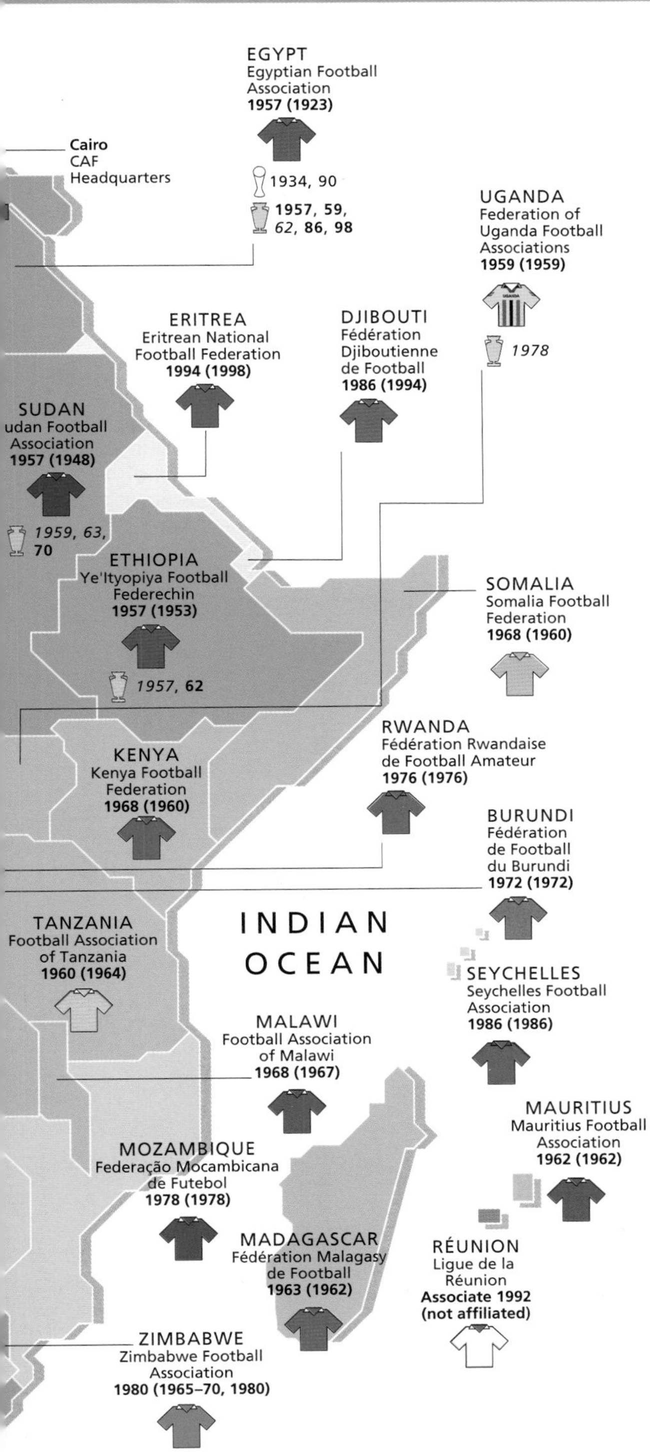

CAF

**African Tournaments
and Cup Competitions:**
African Cup of Nations
African Champions League
Confederations Cup
CAF Super Cup

CAF (CONFEDERATION AFRICAINE DE FOOTBALL) was first proposed in 1956 by representatives of the only independent nations then in Africa: Egypt, Ethiopia, Sudan and South Africa. With FIFA support the organization was inaugurated in Khartoum in 1957 and then based in Cairo, Egypt. Politics intervened in CAF's development immediately when the South Africans proposed sending either an all-black or all-white team to the first African Cup of Nations in Sudan. South Africa was then suspended and remained outside the CAF until 1992.

With only three members CAF's global and continental influence was small but the wave of decolonization that swept Africa from the late 1950s rapidly increased its membership, while the quality and popularity of African soccer has steadily enhanced CAF's status and power at the FIFA table. CAF votes and influence were central to the success of João Havelange in winning the FIFA presidency in 1974 and African representation at the World Cup has climbed to five places.

Despite the size of the continent, the expense of travel and the often-shaky finances of local soccer associations, CAF established three international club tournaments (now reduced to two) and the biennial African Cup of Nations. Within CAF there are also five regional federations: the Arab Football Union, Confederation of East and Central African Football Associations, Confederation of Southern African Football Federations, Union of Football Associations of Central Africa and West African Football Union, each of which organizes its own cup competition.

Chaotic scenes like this one, as people jostle for a good view before a league match between Hearts of Oak and Asante Kotoko in Accra Stadium in Ghana, are commonplace at African football matches.

Calendar of Events

Club Tournaments	African Champions League 2005
	Confederations Cup 2005
	CAF Super Cup 2005
International	Qualifying tournament for 2006
Tournaments	African Nations Cup
	Qualifying Tournament for 2006 World Cup

Africa

THE SEASONS IN REVIEW 2002–03, 2003–04

AFRICA

IN A SEASON THAT COULD BOAST an African Nation's Cup, a CAF presidential election and Nigeria's first triumph in African club competition in almost 40 years, one fundamental act will be remembered in African soccer. In May 2004 Africa was awarded its first World Cup, to be held in South Africa in 2010. Egypt, Libya and Tunisia had also tabled bids, but only Morocco was a serious challenger to the South Africans, losing the FIFA vote 14-10.

Fortunately, FIFA was not swayed by performances on the field in the 2004 African Nation's Cup held in Tunisia; South Africa was ignominiously bundled out at the group stage, while a young Moroccan team made it all the way to the Final, where it lost to the hosts. Cameroon, the defending champion, was knocked out in the quarter-finals, despite boasting the talents of the African Player of the Year – Samuel Eto'o – who has prospered in Spain with Real Mallorca. More worrying for the West Africans, their much-hyped one-piece kit used at the tournament was ruled illegal by Sepp Blatter and, after losing an appeal, the national team had six points docked from its total in the 2006 World Cup qualifying tournament. Sanity prevailed and the ban was rescinded at FIFA's centenary congress.

Rwandan pride restored

Cameroon was not the only soccer association to cross swords with FIFA. The world soccer body found itself either actively involved in restructuring or threatening to suspend soccer associations in Kenya, Uganda, Zimbabwe and Tanzania. The problems included financial mismanagement, rival executive committees and government interference. By contrast, Rwandan soccer continued to be a source of national pride and unity as the national team attended its first Nation's Cup and the army team, APR, made an exceptional showing in the Champions League.

Top 16 African Leagues

COUNTRY	CHAMPIONS	RUNNERS-UP	CUP WINNERS
Algeria*	JS Kabylie	USM Alger	USM Alger
Angola	AS Aviaçaõ	Petro Atlético	Inter Luanda
Cameroon	Cotonsport	Canon Yaoundé	Cotonsport
Cote d'Ivoire	ASEC Mimosas	Africa Sports	ASEC Mimosas
DR Congo	AS Vita	SC Cilu	DC Motema Pembe
Egypt*	Zamalek	Al Ahly	Al Mokaoulom
Ghana	Asante Kotoko	Hearts of Oak	
Kenya	Tusker	Nzoia Sugar	Chemelil Sugar
Morocco	Hassania US d'Agadir	Raja de Casablanca	FAR Rabat
Nigeria	Enyimba	Julius Berger	Lobi Stars
Senegal	Jeanne d'Arc	ASC Diaraf	AS Douanes
South Africa*	Kaiser Chiefs	Ajax Cape Town	Moroka Swallows
Tanzania*	Simba FC	Prisons	Simba FC
Tunisia*			CA Bizertin
Zambia	Zanaco	Green Buffalos	Power Dynamos
Zimbabwe	Amazulu	Highlanders	Dynamos

* Data for season 2003–04, the rest correct to summer 2003.

The Finals of Africa's two minor club trophies maintained the stranglehold of North African clubs as first Raja Casablanca beat Cameroon's Cotonport in the CAF Cup and Nigeria's Julius Berger lost the Final of the last edition of the Cup-Winners' Cup to Tunisia's Etoile de Sahel. But Enyimba finally broke the Nigerian jinx and won the African Champions League. In its home city of Aba, the team bankrolled by the Abia state government beat Al Ismaily 2-0. It lost the return leg in Cairo by a single goal as the game degenerated into an on-field brawl. The trophy presentation was delayed for half an hour as fans rioted in the stands. Subsequently, Ismaily has accused Enyimba of fielding two ineligible players in the Final; the case remains unresolved, sitting on the desks of CAF's executive committee.

CAF Cup

2003 FINAL (2 legs)

November 9 – Casablanca, Morocco
Raja 2-0 Cotonsport
Casablanca   (Cameroon)
(Morocco)
Bidodan 11,
Diallo 72)
h/t: 1-0 **Att:** 80,000
Ref: Ndoye (Senegal)

November 23 – Garoua, Cameroon
Cotonsport 0-0 Raja
Casablanca
h/t: 0-0 **Att:** 30,000
Ref: El-Beltagy (Egypt)
Raja Casablanca won 2-0 on aggregate

Cup-Winners' Cup

2003 FINAL (2 legs)

November 15 – Abeokuta, Nigeria
Julius Berger 2-0 Étoile
(Nigeria)   du Sahel
(Ezeh 7,   (Tunisia)
Idahor 47)
h/t: 1-0 **Att:** 15,000
Ref: Shelmani (Libya)

December 6 – Sousse, Tunisia
Étoile 3-0 Julius Berger
du Sahel
(Obiakor 2,
60, 87)
h/t: 1-0 **Att:** 28,000
Ref: Felix (Zimbabwe)
Étoile du Sahel won 3-2 on aggregate

Champions League

2003 FINAL (2 legs)

November 30 – Aba, Nigeria
Enyimba 2-0 Al Ismaily
(Nigeria)   (Egypt)
(Nwanna 28,
Anumnu 49)
h/t: 1-0 **Att :** 25,000
Ref: Tessema (Ethiopia)

December 12 – Ismailiya, Egypt
Al Ismaily 1-0 Enyimba
(Abd Rabbou
27 pen)
h/t: 1-0 **Att:** 30,000
Ref: Maillet (Seychelles)
Enyimba won 2-1 on aggregate

Super Cup

2004 FINAL

February 22 – Aba, Nigeria
Enyimba 1-0 Étoile
(Nigeria)   du Sahel
(Osim 20)   (Tunisia)
h/t : 1-0 **Att:** 20,000
Ref: Divine (Cameroon)

Below: Raja Casablanca took the CAF Cup back to Morocco after grinding out a 0-0 draw with Cotonsport in Garoua, Cameroon. Two goals in the first leg in Casablanca secured them the trophy.

Left: Enyimba broke the jinx and won Nigeria's first African Champions Cup. The team lost on the night to Ismaily, but won on aggregate. Enyimba's celebrations were followed by a riot and pitch invasion by the Egyptian fans.

Below left: Enyimba's Obinna Nwaneri (right) and Ugah Okpara lift the 2004 African Super Cup, making it three trophies in a row for the Nigerian and African Champions.

Nigerian Ogochakwu Obiakor celebrates his hat-trick for Tunisian club Etoile du Sahel in their victorious Cup-Winners' Cup Final against Julius Berger.

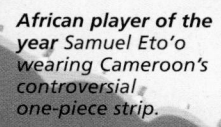

African player of the year Samuel Eto'o wearing Cameroon's controversial one-piece strip.

AFRICA

GUINEA-BISSAU
[1974]
Federação de Futebol
da Guiné-Bissau
1974 (1975)

GAMBIA
[1965]
Gambia Football
Association
1952 (1973)

BURKINA FASO
[1960]
Fédération Burkinabe
de Football
1960 (1965)

MOROCCO
[1956]
Fédération Royale
Marocaine de Football
1955 (1916)

TUNISIA
[1956]
Fédération Tunisienne
de Football
1956 (1921)

WESTERN SAHARA
(not affiliated
to CAF, claimed
by Morocco)

Rabat

Tizi-Ouzou

Tunis

MEDITERRANEA
SEA

Casablanca

GUINEA
[1958]
Fédération
Guinéenne
de Football
1959 (1965)

SENEGAL
[1960]
Fédération Sénégalaise
de Football
1960 (1968)

ALGERIA
[1962]
Fédération Algérienne
de Football
1962 (1920)

LIBYA
[1951]
Libyan Arab Jamahiriya
Football Federation
1962 (1964)

SIERRA LEONE
[1961]
Sierra Leone
Amateur
Football
Association
1923 (1978)

CAPE VERDE
[1975]
Fédération Cabo
Verdiana
de Futebol
1982 (1985)

MAURITANIA
[1960]
Fédération de Football de la
République de Mauritanie
1961 (1976)

MALI
[1960]
Fédération Malienne
de Football
1960 (1966)

NIGER
[1960]
Fédération Nigérienne
de Football
1967 (1966)

CHAD
[1960]
Fédération Tchadienne
de Football
1962 (1990)

COTE D'IVOIRE
[1960]
Fédération Ivorienne
de Football
1960 (1960)

Kumasi

Lagos

NIGERIA
[1960]
Nigeria Football
Association
1935 (1972)

Yaoundé

LIBERIA
[1947]
Liberia Football
Federation
1936 (1965)

Abidjan

Accra

CAMEROON
[1960]
Fédération Camerounaise
de Football
1960 (1961)

**DEMOCRATIC
REPUBLIC
OF CONGO**
(Zaïre)
[1960]
Fédération
Congolaise
de Football-
Association
1919 (1923)

GHANA
[1957]
Ghana Football
Association
1957 (1957)

BENIN
[1957]
Fédération
Beninoise
de Football
1968 (1969)

**SÃO TOMÉ
& PRÍNCIPE**
[1975]
Federação Santomense
de Futebol
1975 (1977)

TOGO
[1960]
Fédération Togolaise
de Football
1960 (1965)

EQUATORIAL GUINEA
[1968]
Fédération
Equatoguineana
de Futboll
1976 (1979)

CONGO
[1960]
Fédération
Congolaise
de Football
1962 (1965)

ANGOLA
[1975]
Federação Angolana
de Futebol
1977 (1979)

GABON
[1960]
Fédération Gabonaise
de Football
1962 (1968)

NAMIBIA
[1992]
Namibia Football
Association
1992 (1987)

ZAMBIA
[1964]
Football Association
of Zambia
1929 (1962)

BOTSWANA
[1966]
Botswana Football
Association
1970 (1978)

ATLANTIC
OCEAN

SOUTH AFRICA
[1961]
South African
Football Association
1892 (1971)

LESOTHO
[1966]
Lesotho Sports
Council
1932 (1970)

The CAF Nations

COUNTRY
[date of independence]
Name of national
Football
Foundation   Association   Foundation of
of national FA — **1916 (1912)** — national league

The top 15 teams in post-colonial Africa

Al Ahly Egypt Cairo 1907	**Espérance Sportive** Tunisia Tunis 1910	**Orlando Pirates** South Africa Soweto 1937
Asante Kotoko Ghana Kumasi 1926	**FAR Rabat** Morocco Rabat 1946	**Tonnerre Yaoundé** Cameroon Yaoundé 1938
ASEC Abidjan Côte d'Ivoire Abidjan 1948	**Hearts of Oak** Ghana Accra 1911	**TP Mazembe** DR Congo Lubumbashi 1939
Canon Yaoundé Cameroon Yaounde 1930	**JS Kabylie** Algeria Tizi-Ouzou 1946	**WAC Casablanca** Morocco Casablanca 1939
Club Africain Tunisia Tunis 1920	**Mamelodi Sundowns** South Africa Pretoria 1970	**Zamalek** Egypt Cairo 1925

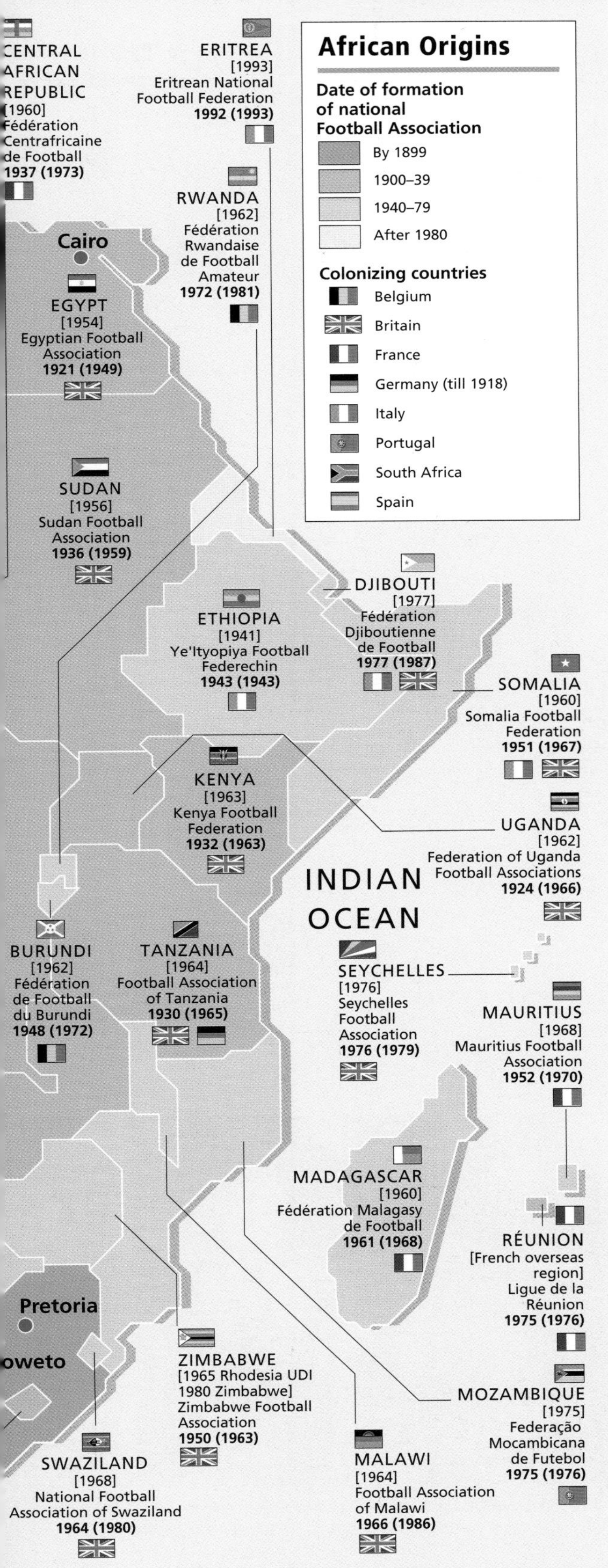

African Origins

CENTRAL AFRICAN REPUBLIC
[1960]
Fédération Centrafricaine de Football
1937 (1973)

ERITREA
[1993]
Eritrean National Football Federation
1992 (1993)

RWANDA
[1962]
Fédération Rwandaise de Football Amateur
1972 (1981)

Cairo

EGYPT
[1954]
Egyptian Football Association
1921 (1949)

SUDAN
[1956]
Sudan Football Association
1936 (1959)

ETHIOPIA
[1941]
Ye'Ityopiya Football Federechin
1943 (1943)

DJIBOUTI
[1977]
Fédération Djiboutienne de Football
1977 (1987)

SOMALIA
[1960]
Somalia Football Federation
1951 (1967)

KENYA
[1963]
Kenya Football Federation
1932 (1963)

UGANDA
[1962]
Federation of Uganda Football Associations
1924 (1966)

INDIAN OCEAN

BURUNDI
[1962]
Fédération de Football du Burundi
1948 (1972)

TANZANIA
[1964]
Football Association of Tanzania
1930 (1965)

SEYCHELLES
[1976]
Seychelles Football Association
1976 (1979)

MAURITIUS
[1968]
Mauritius Football Association
1952 (1970)

MADAGASCAR
[1960]
Fédération Malagasy de Football
1961 (1968)

RÉUNION
[French overseas region]
Ligue de la Réunion
1975 (1976)

Pretoria

oweto

ZIMBABWE
[1965 Rhodesia UDI
1980 Zimbabwe]
Zimbabwe Football Association
1950 (1963)

MOZAMBIQUE
[1975]
Federação Moçambicana de Futebol
1975 (1976)

SWAZILAND
[1968]
National Football Association of Swaziland
1964 (1980)

MALAWI
[1964]
Football Association of Malawi
1966 (1986)

Date of formation of national Football Association

	By 1899
	1900–39
	1940–79
	After 1980

Colonizing countries

	Belgium
	Britain
	France
	Germany (till 1918)
	Italy
	Portugal
	South Africa
	Spain

Africa

ORIGINS AND GROWTH OF SOCCER

SOCCER ARRIVED IN AFRICA via the usual routes – British sailors, missionaries, traders and administrators – but it was, of course, filtered through the various colonial establishments that ran the continent at the turn of 19th century. French, Belgian and Portuguese colonialists also imported soccer into the continent in the early years of the 20th century. As a consequence, organized soccer remained in schools and colleges for the most part, and independent national soccer associations and teams did not exist in most of the continent. The exception was the creation of the South African FA in 1892.

During the inter-war years, soccer began to gain a substantial following among Africans. By the 1920s, leagues had developed across North Africa (Egypt, Tunisia, Algeria and Morocco) and matches were played between French colonies. Egypt, the strongest soccer-playing nation, played at the 1920 Olympics and the first World Cup in 1930. In the 1930s, Nigerian soccer acquired organized leagues and in the 1950s inter-colony matches were played in British West Africa. Belgian Congo (later Zaïre, or Democratic Republic of Congo) and Ghana also acquired formal soccer leagues in this era, but in these countries it was the European colonists that retained administrative control.

Not surprisingly, the development of African soccer in the postwar years is intimately connected to the process of decolonization and the establishment of new states. CAF, formed from the only independent African nations in 1957 (Egypt, Ethiopia, Sudan and South Africa), held its first tournament that year to celebrate Sudanese independence, and almost immediately expelled South Africa for its continuing racial segregation of soccer teams and players.

The enormous popularity and domestic political significance of soccer in Africa since independence can be seen from politicians' desire to be associated with the game (the Zambian national team was known as the 'Kenneth Kaunda XI'), the political reorganization of clubs and leagues (in Algeria, all teams were allocated to nationalized industrial groupings in the1970s) and political battles over the control of national FAs. Soccer has continued to be strong in North Africa, but has more recently been challenged by the rise of Nigeria, Ghana, DR Congo, Cameroon and South Africa as significant soccer nations.

AFRICA

Hugely successful domestically, Al Ahly from Cairo was voted CAF Club of the Century in 2000, having attained three victories in the African Champions League and four in the African Cup-Winners' Cup.

The African Cup of Nations

TOURNAMENT OVERVIEW

THE COURSE OF THE AFRICAN CUP OF NATIONS inevitably parallels many aspects of Africa's postwar history. Prior to the massive wave of decolonization that swept the continent in the 1960s, only four nations were entered in the first tournament, in Sudan in 1957: Ethiopia, Egypt, South Africa and Sudan. South Africa was forced to withdraw by CAF because it refused to send a mixed-race team, and Egypt won the trophy easily, beating Ethiopia 4-0 in the Final.

In 1963 and 1965, Ghana, the first new nation to achieve independence in this era, announced West Africa's soccer-playing prowess by winning both Finals against North African opposition. From Ghana, the baton passed to Central Africa, with the two Congos winning three of the next four tournaments.

In 1965, CAF ruled that each squad could only play two overseas-based players and the rule remained in force until 1982. By then, the rapidly increasing African presence in European leagues left the tournament without many of the leading stars of African soccer. The tournament further accommodated the power of European soccer by switching the finals to January, taking advantage of player availability during European soccer's mid-season break. Across this period, the growing strength of African soccer saw the tournament acquire a qualifying round and expand from four to eight participants in the finals. In 1992, it expanded again to 12 teams and in 1996 to 16.

With access to European-based players, the championships have been dominated by West Africa since the 1980s, with Ghana, Nigeria and Cameroon all taking the prize. There was a look-in for a resurgent post-Apartheid South Africa in 1996, Egypt in 1998 and an all-North African Final in 2004.

The African Cup of Nations (1956–2004)

YEAR	WINNERS	SCORE	RUNNERS-UP
1957	Egypt	4-0	Ethiopia
1959	Egypt	*final tournament*	Sudan
1962	Ethiopia	4-2	Egypt
1963	Ghana	3-0	Sudan
1965	Ghana	3-2	Tunisia
1968	Congo-Kinshasa	1-0	Ghana
1970	Sudan	1-0	Ghana
1972	Congo	3-2	Mali
1974	Zaïre	2-2, replay 2-0	Zambia
1976	Morocco	*final tournament*	Guinea
1978	Ghana	2-0	Uganda
1980	Nigeria	3-0	Algeria
1982	Ghana	1-1 (7-6 pens)	Libya
1984	Cameroon	3-1	Nigeria
1986	Egypt	0-0 (5-4 pens)	Cameroon
1988	Cameroon	1-0	Nigeria
1990	Algeria	1-0	Nigeria
1992	Côte d'Ivoire	0-0 (11-10 pens)	Ghana
1994	Nigeria	2-1	Zambia
1996	South Africa	2-0	Tunisia
1998	Egypt	2-0	South Africa
2000	Cameroon	2-2 (4-3 pens)	Nigeria
2002	Cameroon	0-0 (3-2 pens)	Senegal
2004	Tunisia	2-1	Morocco

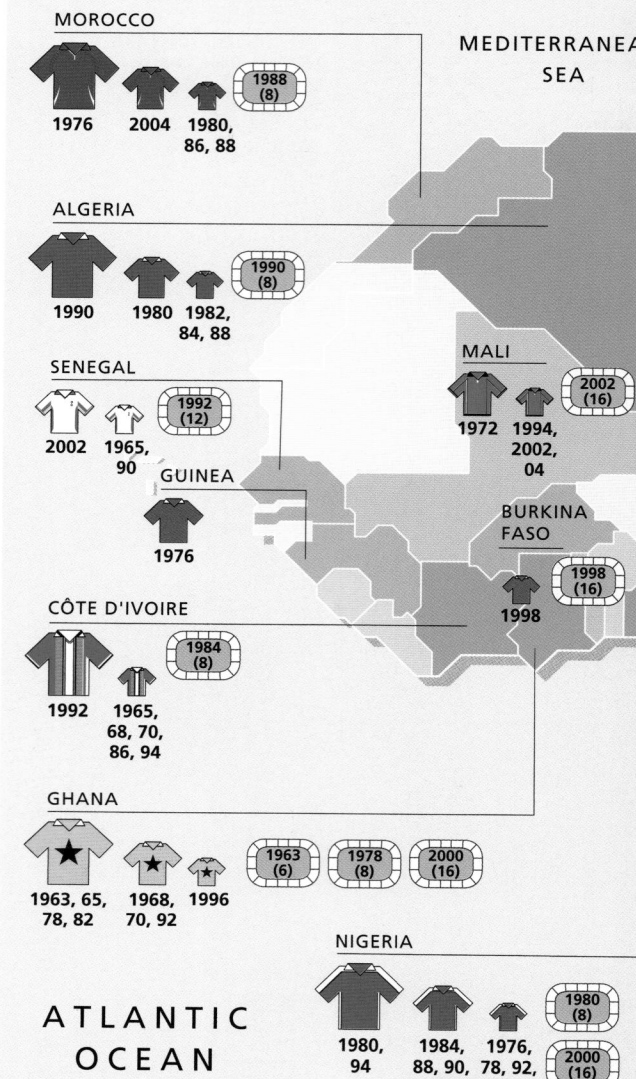

MOROCCO
1976 2004 1980, 86, 88 (1988 (8))

ALGERIA
1990 1980 1982, 84, 88 (1990 (8))

MALI
1972 1994, 2002, 04 (2002 (16))

SENEGAL
2002 1965, 90 (1992 (12))

GUINEA
1976

BURKINA FASO
1998 (1998 (16))

CÔTE D'IVOIRE
1992 1965, 68, 70, 86, 94 (1984 (8))

GHANA
1963, 65, 78, 82 1968, 70, 92 1996 (1963 (6)) (1978 (8)) (2000 (16))

NIGERIA
1980, 94 1984, 88, 90, 2000 1976, 78, 92, 2002, 04 (1980 (8)) (2000 (16))

MEDITERRANEAN SEA

ATLANTIC OCEAN

The African Cup of Nations *has been contested since 1957, but in recent years its colourful spectacle and top quality football has raised the tournament's profile.*

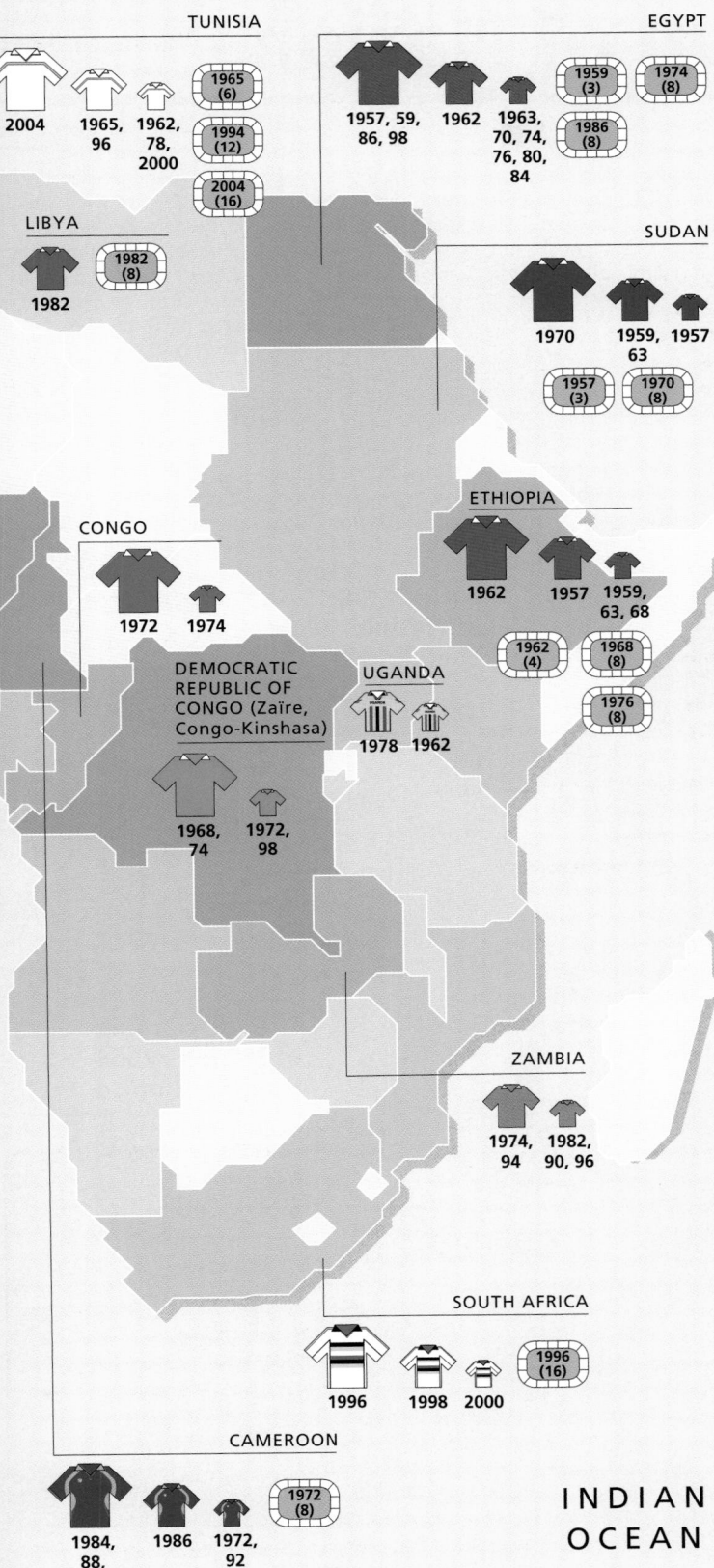

The African Cup of Nations Top Goalscorers

YEAR	SCORER	NATIONALITY	GOALS
1957	El Diba	Egyptian	5
1959	Al-Gohari	Egyptian	3
1962	Badawi	Egyptian	3
	W. Mengistou	Ethiopian	
1963	Chazli	Egyptian	6
1965	Acheampong	Ghanaian	3
	O. Kofi	Ghanaian	
	Mangle	Côte d'Ivoire	
1968	Pokou	Côte d'Ivoire	6
1970	Pokou	Côte d'Ivoire	8
1972	F. Keita	Malian	5
1974	Ndaye	Zairean	9
1976	N'jo Léa	Guinean	4
1978	Omondi	Ugandan	4
1980	Labied	Moroccan	3
	Odegbami	Nigerian	
1982	Alhassan	Ghanaian	4
1984	Abou Zeid	Egyptian	4
1986	Milla	Cameroon	4
	A. Traore	Côte d'Ivoire	
1988	Abdelhamid	Egyptian	2
	Belloumi	Algerian	
	Milla	Cameroon	
	A. Traore	Côte d'Ivoire	
1990	Menad	Algerian	4
1992	Yekini	Nigerian	4
1994	Yekini	Nigerian	5
1996	K. Bwalya	Zambian	5
1998	H. Hassan	Egyptian	7
	McCarthy	South African	
2000	Bartlett	South African	5
2002	Aghahowa	Nigerian	3
	Mboma	Cameroon	
	Olembe	Cameroon	
2004	Dos Santos	Tunisian	4
	Kanouté	Malian	
	Mboma	Cameroon	
	Okocha	Nigerian	

INDIAN OCEAN

The African Cup of Nations

Participation in the African Nations Cup

- 10+ times
- 6–9 times
- 2–5 times
- 1 time
- 0 times

Winners, runners-up and semi-finalists with date

1980 1980 1980

Host country, with date of tournament and number of participants in brackets

CAMEROON 1976 (4)

The African Cup of Nations

TOURNAMENT REVIEW 2004

THE 24TH AFRICAN NATIONS CUP was held in January 2004 in Tunisia. Making their debut at the Nation's Cup were Benin, Rwanda and Zimbabwe – with the last two winning games during the tournament – a feat also achieved by Kenya. Togo and Burkina Faso are more regular participants but all went home disappointed with their performances. The DRC's campaign predictably exploded as the financial and administrative chaos of its build-up seeped onto the pitch. Two other giants played well below expectation – Egypt and South Africa – both looked leaden-footed and departed at the group stage.

Algeria played with great spirit and brought by far the largest travelling contingent of fans – over 20,000 saw them lose to last-minute goals by Morocco in Sfax and promptly rioted. Guinea took Mali to the verge of extra time in their quarter-final and the team's small group of fans played with the biggest sound and best rhythms of any side. Senegal and Cameroon followed them out at the quarter-final stage. In a stadium full of smoke and flares, the former was hustled out by hosts Tunisia in a bad-tempered match that saw 10 minutes of extra time. Cameroon, who never looked hungry enough to win, fell to the Nigerian's in the best game of the tournament.

In the semi-finals the Tunisians held their nerve against Nigeria, winning on penalties, while Morocco showed discipline and flair in annihilating Mali 4-0. But it was not enough to displace the Tunisians who had predictably pushed home advantage beyond the limits. Ball boys failed to return opposition balls, time wasting and diving went unpunished; and under Frenchman Roger Lemerre Tunisia found goals in the Final from the recently assimilated dos Santos and the wily Jaziri. Morocco's first-half strike from Mokhtari was just not enough.

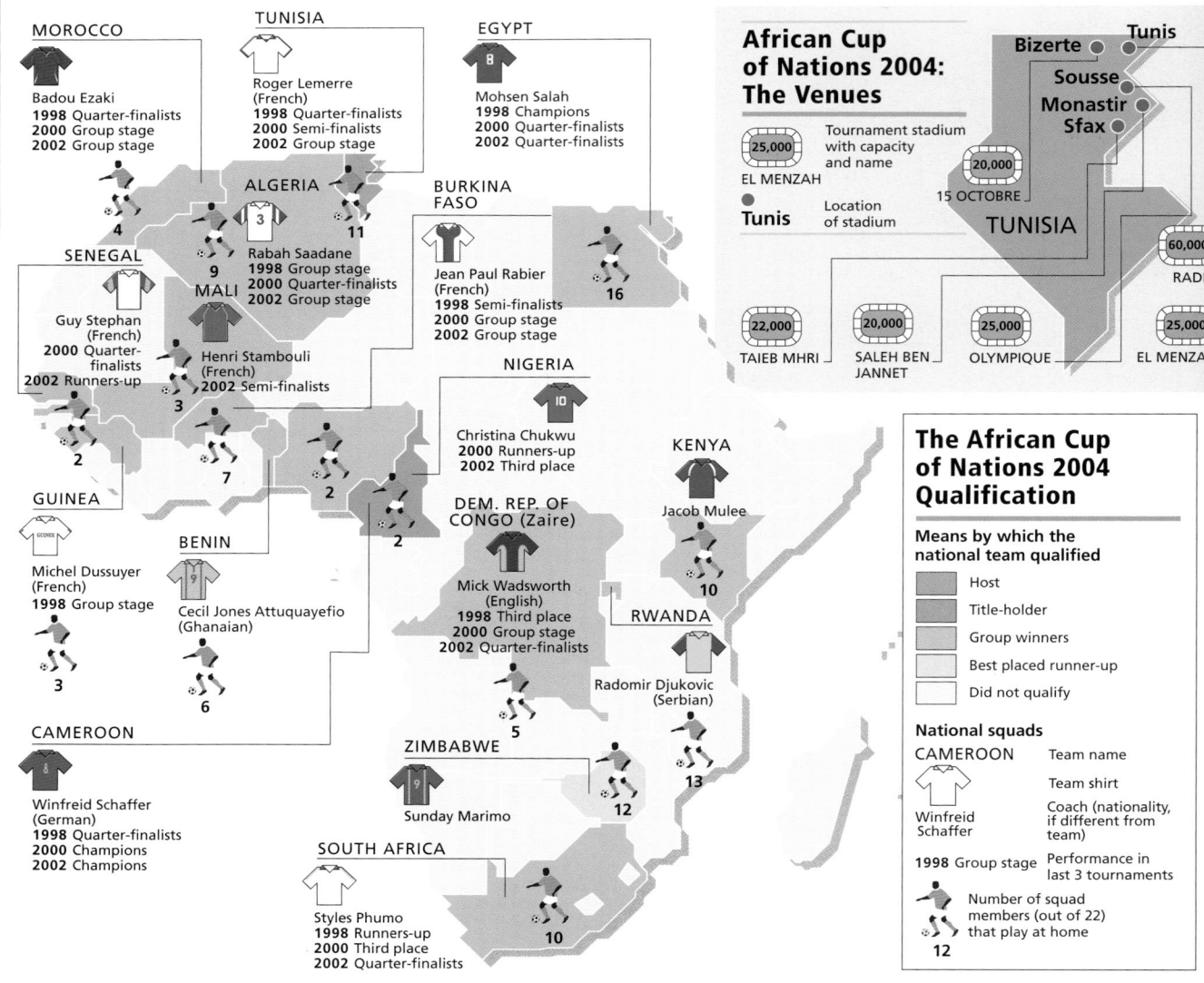

MOROCCO
Badou Ezaki
1998 Quarter-finalists
2000 Group stage
2002 Group stage

TUNISIA
Roger Lemerre (French)
1998 Quarter-finalists
2000 Semi-finalists
2002 Group stage

EGYPT
Mohsen Salah
1998 Champions
2000 Quarter-finalists
2002 Quarter-finalists

ALGERIA
Rabah Saadane
1998 Group stage
2000 Quarter-finalists
2002 Group stage

BURKINA FASO
Jean Paul Rabier (French)
1998 Semi-finalists
2000 Group stage
2002 Group stage

SENEGAL
Guy Stephan (French)
2000 Quarter-finalists
2002 Runners-up

MALI
Henri Stambouli (French)
2002 Semi-finalists

NIGERIA
Christina Chukwu
2000 Runners-up
2002 Third place

KENYA
Jacob Mulee

GUINEA
Michel Dussuyer (French)
1998 Group stage

BENIN
Cecil Jones Attuquayefio (Ghanaian)

DEM. REP. OF CONGO (Zaire)
Mick Wadsworth (English)
1998 Third place
2000 Group stage
2002 Quarter-finalists

RWANDA
Radomir Djukovic (Serbian)

CAMEROON
Winfreid Schaffer (German)
1998 Quarter-finalists
2000 Champions
2002 Champions

ZIMBABWE
Sunday Marimo

SOUTH AFRICA
Styles Phumo
1998 Runners-up
2000 Third place
2002 Quarter-finalists

African Cup of Nations 2004: The Venues

25,000 – Tournament stadium with capacity and name
EL MENZAH
Tunis – Location of stadium

Tunis
Bizerte
Sousse
Monastir
Sfax

TUNISIA

20,000 – 15 OCTOBRE
60,000 – RAD
22,000 – TAIEB MHRI
20,000 – SALEH BEN JANNET
25,000 – OLYMPIQUE
25,000 – EL MENZA

The African Cup of Nations 2004 Qualification

Means by which the national team qualified
- Host
- Title-holder
- Group winners
- Best placed runner-up
- Did not qualify

National squads
CAMEROON – Team name
(team shirt) – Team shirt
Winfreid Schaffer – Coach (nationality, if different from team)
1998 Group stage – Performance in last 3 tournaments
Number of squad members (out of 22) that play at home
12

THE AFRICAN CUP OF NATIONS

THE GROUP STAGES

GROUP A

Tunisia **2-1** Rwanda
DR Congo **1-2** Guinea
Rwanda **1-1** Guinea
Tunisia **3-0** DR Congo
Tunisia **1-1** Guinea
Rwanda **1-0** DR Congo

	P	W	D	L	F	A	Pts
Tunisia	3	2	1	0	6	2	7
Guinea	3	1	2	0	4	3	5
Rwanda	3	1	1	1	3	3	4
DR Congo	3	0	0	3	1	6	0

GROUP B

Senegal **0-0** Burkina Faso
Kenya **1-3** Mali
Senegal **3-0** Kenya
Burkina Faso **1-3** Mali
Senegal **1-1** Mali
Burkina Faso **0-3** Kenya

	P	W	D	L	F	A	Pts
Mali	3	2	1	0	7	3	7
Senegal	3	1	2	0	4	1	5
Kenya	3	1	0	2	4	6	3
Burkina Faso	3	0	1	2	1	6	1

GROUP C

Zimbabwe **1-2** Egypt
Cameroon **1-1** Algeria
Cameroon **5-3** Zimbabwe
Algeria **2-1** Egypt
Cameroon **0-0** Egypt
Algeria **1-2** Zimbabwe

	P	W	D	L	F	A	Pts
Cameroon	3	1	2	0	6	4	5
Algeria	3	1	1	1	4	4	4
Egypt	3	1	1	1	3	3	4
Zimbabwe	3	1	0	2	6	9	3

GROUP D

Nigeria **0-1** Morocco
South Africa **2-0** Benin
Nigeria **4-0** South Africa
Morocco **4-0** Benin
Morocco **1-1** South Africa
Nigeria **2-1** Benin

	P	W	D	L	F	A	Pts
Morocco	3	2	1	0	6	1	7
Nigeria	3	2	0	1	6	2	6
South Africa	3	1	1	1	3	5	4
Benin	3	0	0	3	1	6	0

THE QUARTER-FINALS

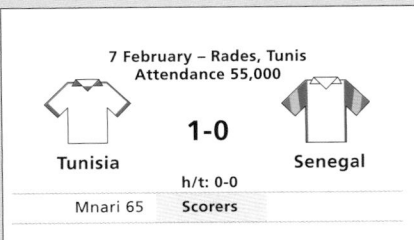

7 February – Rades, Tunis
Attendance 55,000

Tunisia **1-0** **Senegal**
h/t: 0-0

	Scorers	
Mnari 65		

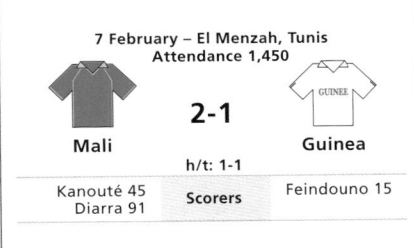

7 February – El Menzah, Tunis
Attendance 1,450

Mali **2-1** **Guinea**
h/t: 1-1

	Scorers	
Kanouté 45		Feindouno 15
Diarra 91		

8 February – Saleh Ben Jannet, Monastir
Attendance 18,000

Cameroon **1-2** **Nigeria**
h/t: 1-1

	Scorers	
Eto'o 42		Okocha 45
		Utaka 73

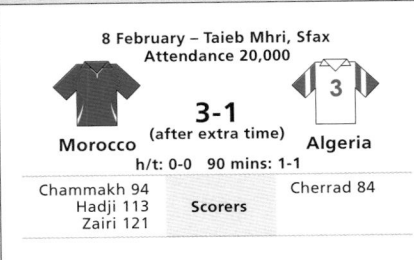

8 February – Taieb Mhri, Sfax
Attendance 20,000

Morocco **3-1** (after extra time) **Algeria**
h/t: 0-0   90 mins: 1-1

	Scorers	
Chammakh 94		Cherrad 84
Hadji 113		
Zairi 121		

THE SEMI-FINALS

11 February – Rades, Tunis
Attendance 57,000

Tunisia **1-1** **Nigeria**
h/t: 0-0

	Scorers	
Badra 82 pen		Okocha 67 pen

Tunisia won 5-3 on pens

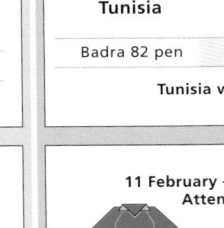

11 February – Olympique, Sousse
Attendance 25,000

Mali **0-4** **Morocco**
h/t: 0-1

	Scorers	
		Mokhtari 14, 58
		Hadji 80
		Nabil Baha 91

THIRD PLACE PLAY-OFF

13 February – Saleh Ben Jannet, Monastir
Attendance 2,500

Nigeria **2-1** **Mali**
h/t: 1-0

	Scorers	
Okocha 17		Atouba 70
Odemwingie 47		

THE FINAL

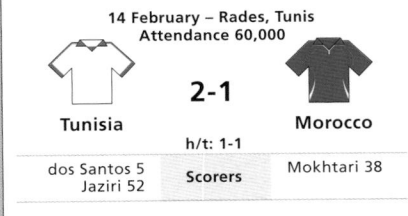

14 February – Rades, Tunis
Attendance 60,000

Tunisia **2-1** **Morocco**
h/t: 1-1

	Scorers	
dos Santos 5		Mokhtari 38
Jaziri 52		

Tunisia's Francileudo dos Santos (right)
heads home the opening goal after five
minutes of the Final against Morocco.

The African Cup of Nations

ESTABLISHED ALONGSIDE the Confederation Africaine de Football (CAF) in 1957, the African Cup of Nations is the continent's main international tournament. Its timing has varied but has now been set for January to ensure that the increasingly large number of Africans who play in European leagues can attend during what is for many nations a midwinter break.

The early tournaments were small affairs with no qualifying rounds. Indeed, given the refusal of the CAF to accept an exclusively black or exclusively white South African team in 1957, the first tournament consisted of only two games. As the wave of decolonization crossed Africa in the late 1950s and 1960s the number of rounds, games and entrants steadily rose. Qualifying rounds were first introduced for the sixth tournament in 1968. By the early 1990s the final tournament had 12 entrants and this has now grown to 16.

1957 SUDAN

SEMI-FINALS
Ethiopia w/o South Africa
South Africa disqualified because of apartheid
Egypt **2-1** Sudan

FINAL
February 16 – Khartoum
Egypt **4-0** Ethiopia
(El Diba 4)
Att: 15,000 **Ref:** Youssef (Sudan)

1959 EGYPT

FINAL TOURNAMENT
May 22 – Cairo
Egypt **4-0** Ethiopia
(Gohri 29, 42, 73,
Cherbini 64)
May 22 – Cairo
Sudan **1-0** Ethiopia
(Drissa 40)
May 29 – Cairo
Egypt **2-1** Sudan
(Issam 12, 89)   (Manzul 65)

1 Egypt
2 Sudan
3 Ethiopia

1962 ETHIOPIA

SEMI-FINALS
Ethiopia **4-2** Tunisia
Egypt **2-1** Uganda

THIRD PLACE PLAY-OFF
January 20 – Addis Ababa
Tunisia **3-0** Uganda
(Djedidi,
Moncef Chérif,
Meddeb)

FINAL
January 21 – Addis Ababa
Ethiopia **4-2** Egypt
(Girma 74,   (Badawi 35, 75)
Menguistou
84, 117,
Italo 101)
(after extra time)
h/t: 0-1 **90 mins:** 2-2
Att: 20,000 **Ref:** Brooks (Uganda)

1963 GHANA

THIRD PLACE PLAY-OFF
November 30 – Accra
Egypt **3-0** Ethiopia
(Raidh,
Taha,
Chazli)

FINAL
December 1 – Accra
Ghana **3-0** Sudan
(Aggrey-Fynn
62 pen,
Mfum 72, 82)
h/t: 0-0 **Att:** 50,000
Ref: Abdelkader (Tunisia)

1965 TUNISIA

THIRD PLACE PLAY-OFF
November 21 – Zouiten, Tunis
Côte d'Ivoire **1-0** Senegal
(Yobone 35)

FINAL
November 21 – Zouiten, Tunis
Ghana **3-2** Tunisia
(Odoi 37, 96,   (Chetali 47,
O. Kofi 79)   Chaibi 67)
(after extra time)
h/t: 1-0 **Att:** 30,000
Ref: Chekaimi (Algeria)

1968 ETHIOPIA

SEMI-FINALS
Congo- **3-2** Ethiopia
Kinshasa*
(after extra time)
Ghana **4-3** Côte d'Ivoire

THIRD PLACE PLAY-OFF
January 21 – Addis Ababa
Côte d'Ivoire **1-0** Ethiopia
(Pokou 28)

FINAL
January 21 – Addis Ababa
Congo- **1-0** Ghana
Kinshasa*
(Kalala 66)
h/t: 0-0 **Att:** 12,000
Ref: Al Diba (Egypt)

1970 SUDAN

SEMI-FINALS
Ghana **2-1** Côte d'Ivoire
(after extra time)
Sudan **2-1** Egypt
(after extra time)

THIRD PLACE PLAY-OFF
February 16 – Khartoum
Egypt **3-1** Côte d'Ivoire
(Chazli 3, 14, 50)   (Pokou 72)

FINAL
February 16 – Khartoum
Sudan **1-0** Ghana
(El Issed 12)
h/t: 1-0 **Att:** 35,000
Ref: Tesfaye (Ethiopia)

1972 CAMEROON

SEMI-FINALS
Congo **1-0** Cameroon
Mali **4-3** Zaïre
(after extra time)

THIRD PLACE PLAY-OFF
March 4 – Yaoundé
Cameroon **5-2** Zaïre
(Akono 4 pen,   (Kakoko 13,
Ndongo 31,   Mayanga 17)
Owona 32,
Mouthé 34,
Ndoga 42)

FINAL
March 5 – Yaoundé
Congo **3-2** Mali
(M'bono 57, 59,   (Diakhité 42,
M'Pelé 63)   M. Traoré 75)
h/t: 0-1 **Att:** 5,000
Ref: Aoussi (Algeria)

1974 EGYPT

SEMI-FINALS
Zaïre **3-2** Egypt
Zambia **4-2** Congo
(after extra time)

THIRD PLACE PLAY-OFF
March 11 – Cairo
Egypt **4-0** Congo
(M. Abdou 5,
Chehata 18, 80,
Abugreisha 82)

FINAL
March 12 – Cairo
Zaïre **2-2** Zambia
(Ndaye 65, 117)   (Kaushi 40,
Sinyangwe 120)
(after extra time)
h/t: 0-1 **90 mins:** 1-1
Att: 5,000 **Ref:** Gamar (Libya)

REPLAY
March 14 – Cairo
Zaïre **2-0** Zambia
(Ndaye 30, 76)
h/t: 1-0 **Att:** 1,000
Ref: Gamar (Libya)

1976 ETHIOPIA

FINAL PHASE
March 9 – Addis Ababa
Guinea **1-1** Nigeria
(P. Camara 88)   (Lawal 52)
March 9 – Addis Ababa
Morocco **2-1** Egypt
(Faras 23,   (A. Rehab 34)
Zahraoui 88)
March 11 – Addis Ababa
Morocco **2-1** Nigeria
(Faras 82,   (B. Otu 50)
Guezzar 87)
March 11 – Addis Ababa
Guinea **4-2** Egypt
(Léa 24, 65,   (Abdou 33,
Ghanem o.g. 53,   Siaguy 86)
Morciré 62)
March 14 – Addis Ababa
Nigeria **3-2** Egypt
(Ilerika 35, 62,   (Al-Khatib 7,
Lawal 82)   Ussama 41)
March 14 – Addis Ababa
Morocco **1-1** Guinea
(Baba 86)   (Chérif 33)

1 Morocco
2 Guinea
3 Nigeria

1978 GHANA

SEMI-FINALS
Ghana **1-0** Tunisia
Uganda **2-1** Nigeria

THIRD PLACE PLAY-OFF
March 16 – Accra
Nigeria **v/o** Tunisia
Tunisia withdrew at 1-1 after 30 mins.
Match awarded 2-0 to Nigeria

FINAL
March 18 – Accra
Ghana **2-0** Uganda
(Afriye 38, 64)
h/t: 1-0 **Att:** 40,000
Ref: El Ghoul (Libya)

1980 NIGERIA

SEMI-FINALS
Nigeria **1-0** Morocco
Egypt **2-2** Algeria
(after extra time)
Algeria won 4-2 on pens

THIRD PLACE PLAY-OFF
March 21 – Lagos
Morocco **2-0** Egypt
(Labied 9, 78)

FINAL
March 22 – Lagos
Nigeria **3-0** Algeria
(Odegbami 2, 42,
Lawal 50)
h/t: 2-0 **Att:** 80,000
Ref: Tesfaye (Ethiopia)

The African Cup of Nations Winners

Egypt
1957, 59, 86, 98

Ethiopia
1962

Ghana
1963, 65, 78, 82

Congo
1972

Sudan
1970

DR Congo (Zaïre)
1968, 74

Morocco
1976

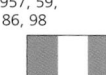

Nigeria
1980, 94

Cameroon
1984, 88, 2000, 02

Algeria
1990

Côte d'Ivoire
1992

South Africa
1996

Tunisia
2004

1982 LIBYA

SEMI-FINALS
Ghana **3-2** Algeria
(after extra time)
Libya **2-1** Zambia

THIRD PLACE PLAY-OFF
March 18 – Tripoli
Zambia **2-0** Algeria
(Kaumba 2, Munshya 25)

FINAL
March 19 – Tripoli
Ghana **1-1** Libya
(Al Hassan 35)   (Beshari 70)
(after extra time)
h/t: 0-1 **90 mins:** 1-1 **Att:** 50,000
Ref: Sohan Ramlochun (Mauritania)
Ghana won 7-6 on pens

1984 CÔTE D'IVOIRE

SEMI-FINALS
Nigeria **2-2** Egypt
(after extra time)
Nigeria won 8-7 on pens

Cameroon **0-0** Algeria
(after extra time)
Cameroon won 5-4 on pens

THIRD PLACE PLAY-OFF
March 17 – Abidjan
Algeria **3-1** Egypt
*(Madjer 67,   (Abdelghani
Belloumi 70,   74 pen)
Yahi 88)*

FINAL
March 17 – Abidjan
Cameroon **3-1** Nigeria
*(Ndjeya 32,   (Lawal 10))
Abega 79,
Ebongue 84)*
h/t: 1-1 **Att:** 50,000
Ref: Bennaceur (Tunisia)

1986 EGYPT

SEMI-FINALS
Egypt **1-0** Morocco
Cameroon **1-0** Côte d'Ivoire
(after extra time)

THIRD PLACE PLAY-OFF
March 20 – Cairo
Côte d'Ivoire **3-2** Morocco
*(Ben Salah 8,   (Rhiati 44,
Kaondio   Sahil 85)
38 pen, 68)*

FINAL
March 21 – Cairo
Egypt **0-0** Cameroon
(after extra time)
h/t: 0-0 **90 mins:** 0-0
Att: 100,000 **Ref:** Bennaceur (Tunisia)
Egypt won 5-4 on pens

1988 MOROCCO

SEMI-FINALS
Cameroon **1-0** Morocco
Nigeria **1-1** Algeria
(after extra time)
Nigeria won 9-8 on pens

THIRD PLACE PLAY-OFF
March 26 – Casablanca
Algeria **1-1** Morocco
(Belloumi 87)   (Nader 67)
(after extra time)
Algeria won 4-3 on pens

FINAL
March 27 – Casablanca
Cameroon **1-0** Nigeria
(Kunde 55)
h/t: 1-0 **Att:** 50,000
Ref: Idrissa (Senegal)

1990 ALGERIA

SEMI-FINALS
Algeria **2-1** Senegal
Nigeria **2-0** Zambia

THIRD PLACE PLAY-OFF
March 15 – Algiers
Zambia **1-0** Senegal
(Chikabala 73)

FINAL
March 16 – Algiers
Algeria **1-0** Nigeria
(Oudjani 38)
h/t: 1-0 **Att:** 80,000
Ref: not known

1992 SENEGAL

SEMI-FINALS
Côte d'Ivoire **0-0** Cameroon
(after extra time)
Côte d'Ivoire won 3-1 on pens

Ghana **2-1** Nigeria

THIRD PLACE PLAY-OFF
January 21 – Dakar
Nigeria **2-1** Cameroon
*(Ekpo 75,   (Maboang 85)
Yekini 88)*
h/t: 2-1 **Att:** 2,000
Ref: Zeli (Côte d'Ivoire)

FINAL
January 26 – Dakar
Ghana **0-0** Côte d'Ivoire
(after extra time)
h/t: 0-0 **90 mins:** 0-0
Att: 60,000 **Ref:** Sene (Ghana)
Côte d'Ivoire won 11-10 on pens

1994 TUNISIA

SEMI-FINALS
Nigeria **2-2** Côte d'Ivoire
(after extra time)
Nigeria won 4-2 on pens
Zambia **4-0** Mali

THIRD PLACE PLAY-OFF
April 10 – Tunis
Côte d'Ivoire **3-1** Mali
*(Koné 2,   (Diallo 46)
Ouattara 68,
Sié 70)*

FINAL
April 10 – Tunis
Nigeria **2-1** Zambia
(Amunike 5, 46)   (Litana 3)
h/t: 1-1 **Att:** 25,000
Ref: Lim Kee Chong (Mauritius)

1996 SOUTH AFRICA

SEMI-FINALS
Tunisia **4-2** Zambia
South Africa **3-0** Ghana

THIRD PLACE PLAY-OFF
Zambia **1-0** Ghana

FINAL
Feb 3 – Johannesburg
South Africa **2-0** Tunisia
(Williams 73, 74)
h/t: 0-0 **Att:** 80,000
Ref: Massembe (Uganda)

1998 BURKINA FASO

SEMI-FINALS
South Africa **2-1** DR Congo
(after extra time)
Egypt **2-0** Burkina Faso

THIRD PLACE PLAY-OFF
March 27 – Municipal, Ouagadougou
DR Congo **4-4** Burkina Faso
DR Congo won 4-1 on pens

FINAL
February 28 – 4 Août, Ouagadougou
Egypt **2-0** South Africa
*(A. Hassan 5,
T. Mostafa 13)*
h/t: 2-0 **Att:** 40,000
Ref: Belgola (Morocco)

2000 GHANA/NIGERIA

SEMI-FINALS
Nigeria **2-0** South Africa
Cameroon **3-0** Tunisia

THIRD PLACE PLAY-OFF
February 12 – Accra
South Africa **2-2** Tunisia
*(Bartlett 11,   (Zitouni 28, 90)
Novente 62)*
South Africa won 4-3 on pens

FINAL
February 13 – Lagos
Cameroon **2-2** Nigeria
*(Eto'o 26,   (Chukwu 44,
Mboma 31)   Okocha 47)*
h/t: 1-2 **90 mins:** 2-2
Att: 40,000
Ref: Daami (Tunisia)
Cameroon won 4-3 on pens

2002 MALI

SEMI-FINALS
Senegal **2-1** Nigeria
Mali **0-3** Cameroon

THIRD PLACE PLAY-OFF
February 9 – Mopti
Mali **0-1** Nigeria
(Aiyegbeni 29)

FINAL
February 10 – Bamako
Cameroon **0-0** Senegal
h/t: 0-0 **90 mins:** 0-0
Att: 50,000
Ref: Al Ghandour (Egypt)
Cameroon won 3-2 on pens

2004 TUNISIA

SEMI-FINALS
Tunisia **1-1** Nigeria
(after extra time)
Tunisia won 5-3 on pens
Morocco **4-0** Mali

THIRD PLACE PLAY-OFF
February 13 – Monastir
Nigeria **2-1** Mali
*(Okocha 17,   (Atouba 70)
Odemwingie 47)*

FINAL
February 14 – Tunis
Tunisia **2-1** Morocco
*(dos Santos 5,   (Mokhtari 38)
Jaziri 52)*
h/t: 1-1 **Att:** 60,000
Ref: Ndoye (Senegal)

The African Champions League

TOURNAMENT OVERVIEW

IN A REVERSE OF EUROPEAN SOCCER'S development, where continental club competitions preceded international tournaments, the African Champions Cup (as it was first known) followed the African Cup of Nations by seven years. It was first played in 1964, with the strongest support coming from Ghana, whose pan-Africanist president donated the tournament's Kwame Nkrumah trophy. Fourteen clubs played for the right to attend a finals tournament in Accra. The Ghanaian side, Real Republicans (closely associated with President Nkrumah and dissolved two years later after his fall), performed poorly, and the first champions were the Cameroonian side Oryx Douala. No tournament was played in 1965, and in 1966 it was played as a straight knockout over two legs.

For the first decade the cup belonged to Central and West African clubs. The Zaïrians Tout Puissant Englebert, Asante Kotoko of Ghana and Hafia Conakry from Guinea all won the title at least once during those early years, interspersed by Cameroonian and Congolese triumphs. TP Englebert's first victory came after two drawn legs against Asante Kotoko, who then refused a further play-off to decide the Final. After this incident, aggregate scores and then penalties were introduced to decide tied matches.

In the 1980s and 90s, the power base of African club soccer shifted north of the Sahara. Egyptian, Moroccan, Algerian and Tunisian teams have taken the title 17 times since 1981. Orlando Pirates' victory in 1995, after many years of South African exclusion, suggested the balance of power might tip again, but the recent victories of Hearts of Oak and Raja Casablanca suggests not. Following European developments, the tournament became the African Champions League in 1997 and acquired a mini-league format at the quarter-finals stage.

Asante Kotoko of Kumasi, Ghana, appeared in seven African Champions League finals between 1967 and 1993, winning the trophy in 1970 and 1983. The team is pictured here before the 1993 Final against the Egyptian side Zamalek.

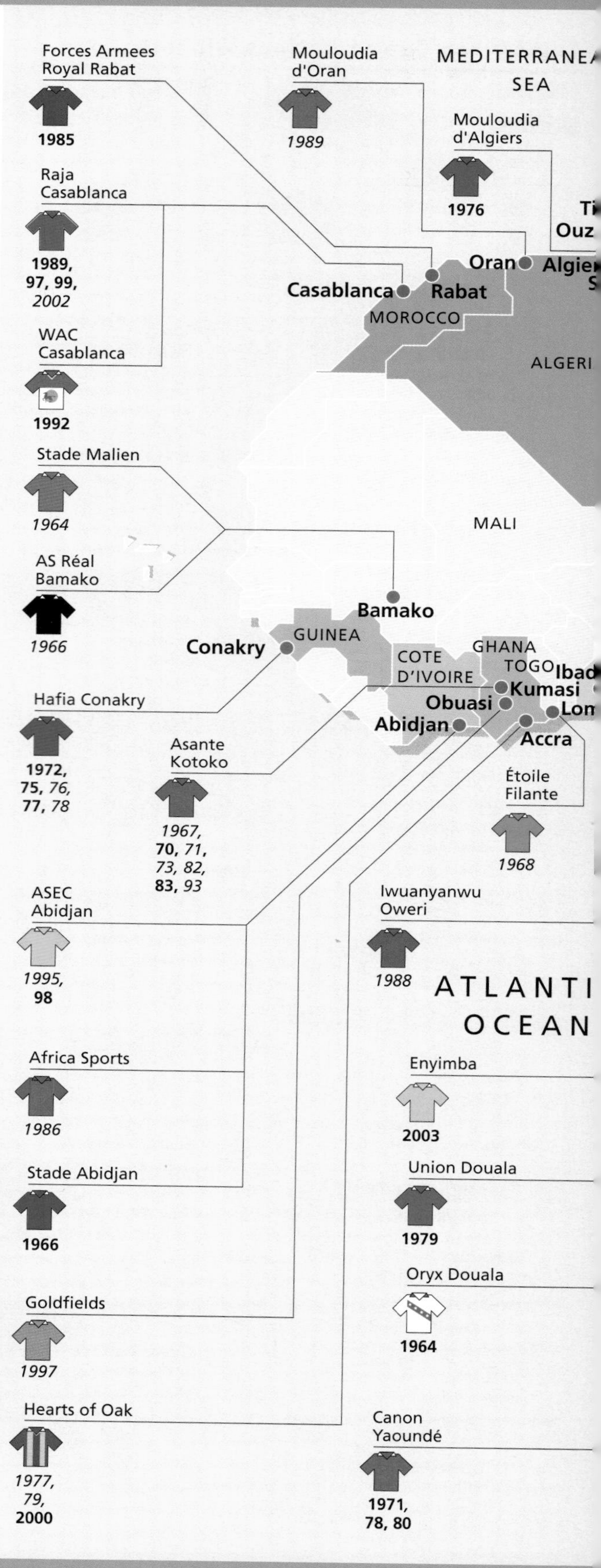

Forces Armees Royal Rabat
1985

Mouloudia d'Oran
1989

MEDITERRANEA SEA

Mouloudia d'Algiers
1976

Raja Casablanca
1989, 97, 99, *2002*

Casablanca   Rabat
MOROCCO

Oran   Algier

Ti Ouz

Algier S

ALGERI

WAC Casablanca
1992

Stade Malien
1964

MALI

AS Réal Bamako
1966

Bamako

GUINEA

Conakry

GHANA
TOGO Ibad

COTE D'IVOIRE

Kumasi
Obuasi   Lon

Hafia Conakry
1972, 75, 76, 77, 78

Abidjan

Accra

Asante Kotoko
1967, 70, 71, 73, 82, 83, **93**

Étoile Filante
1968

ASEC Abidjan
1995, **98**

Iwuanyanwu Oweri
1988

ATLANTI OCEAN

Africa Sports
1986

Enyimba
2003

Stade Abidjan
1966

Union Douala
1979

Goldfields
1997

Oryx Douala
1964

Hearts of Oak
1977, 79, **2000**

Canon Yaoundé
1971, 78, **80**

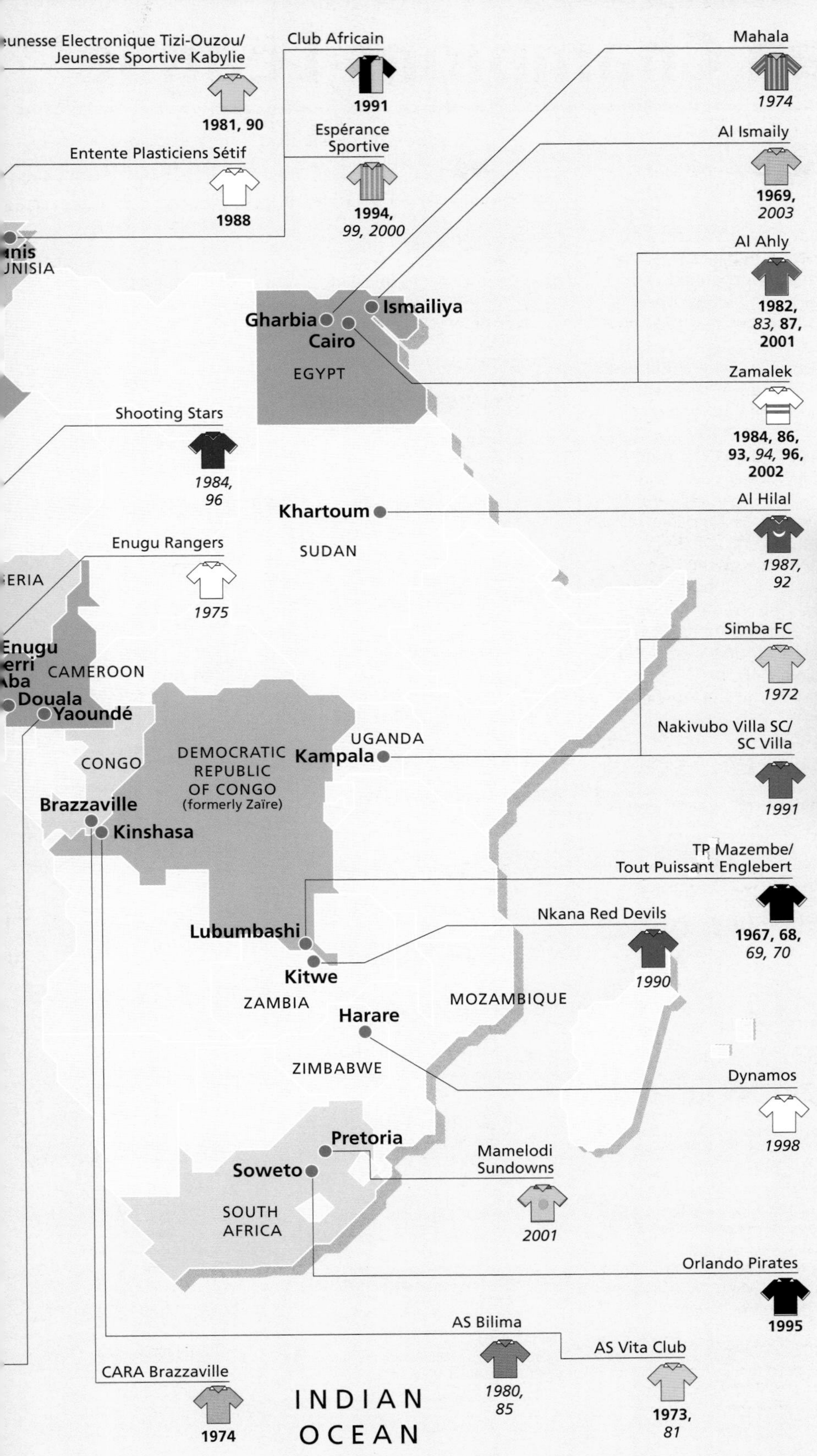

Jeunesse Electronique Tizi-Ouzou/
Jeunesse Sportive Kabylie

1981, 90

Club Africain

1991

Espérance
Sportive

1994,
99, 2000

Entente Plasticiens Sétif

1988

Tunis
TUNISIA

Mahala

1974

Al Ismaily

1969,
2003

Al Ahly

1982,
83, **87,**
2001

Gharbia • • **Ismailiya**
Cairo
EGYPT

Zamalek

1984, 86,
93, *94,* **96,**
2002

Shooting Stars

1984,
96

Al Hilal

1987,
92

Khartoum •
SUDAN

Enugu Rangers

1975

NIGERIA

Simba FC

1972

Nakivubo Villa SC/
SC Villa

1991

Enugu
Berri
Aba
Douala • CAMEROON
• **Yaoundé**

CONGO

DEMOCRATIC
REPUBLIC
OF CONGO
(formerly Zaïre) **Kampala** •
UGANDA

Brazzaville •
• **Kinshasa**

TP Mazembe/
Tout Puissant Englebert

1967, 68,
69, 70

Lubumbashi •
Kitwe •
ZAMBIA

Nkana Red Devils

1990

MOZAMBIQUE

Harare •
ZIMBABWE

Dynamos

1998

Pretoria •
Soweto •
SOUTH
AFRICA

Mamelodi
Sundowns

2001

Orlando Pirates

1995

CARA Brazzaville

1974

AS Bilima

1980,
85

AS Vita Club

1973,
81

INDIAN
OCEAN

Zamalek's Hassan twins, Hossam on the left and Ibrahim on the right, clasp the African Champions League trophy in 2002, 15 years after they won the cup together with arch rivals Al Ahly.

The African Champions
League 1964–2003

COUNTRY	WINNERS	RUNNERS-UP
Egypt	9	4
Morocco	5	1
Cameroon	5	0
Algeria	4	1
Ghana	3	8
Democratic Republic of Congo	3	5
Guinea	3	2
Côte D'Ivoire	2	2
Tunisia	2	2
Nigeria	1	4
South Africa	1	1
Congo	1	0
Mali	0	2
Sudan	0	2
Uganda	0	2
Togo	0	1
Zambia	0	1
Zimbabwe	0	1

The African Champions League

THE OLDEST INTERNATIONAL African club competition is the African Champions League with its Sékou Touré Trophy. The competition was first played in 1964 with 14 participating clubs. The final four played in a three-day Final in Accra, Ghana. With a wave of decolonisation and state formation sweeping Africa in the 1960s, the tournament steadily expanded with all matches from the preliminary rounds being played over two legs. Aggregate points gave way to aggregate scores as a method of deciding draws. Replays were played for tied Finals, but in 1976 penalties were introduced. Since 1997, the quarter-finals have been played as two leagues of four teams, all playing each other home and away. The group winners progress to a two-leg Final.

The African Cup-Winners' Cup was started in 1975 for African domestic cup winners. If the cup winner was also in the African Champions League, the place went to the defeated cup finalists. Winners were awarded the Nelson Mandela Trophy. In 1992, a third African competition was created – the CAF Cup – for national league runners-up (or third- and fourth-placed teams if clubs above them were involved in other international competitions). As with the Cup-Winners' Cup, all matches were played over two legs, and tied matches were decided on aggregate goals, away goals and, finally, penalties. The winners received the Moshood Abiola Cup. As of 2004 these two tournaments have been merged into the African Confederations Cup.

1964 FINAL
February 7 – Accra, Ghana
Oryx Douala 2-1 Stade Malien
(Cameroon)   (Mali)

1965 FINAL
no tournament

1966 FINAL (2 legs)
December 11 – Bamako, Mali
Réal Bamako 3-1 Stade Abidjan
(Mali)   (Côte d'Ivoire)

December 25 – Abidjan, Côte d'Ivoire
Stade Abidjan 4-1 Réal Bamako

Stade Abidjan won 5-4 on aggregate

1967 FINAL (2 legs)
November 19 – Kumasi, Ghana
Asante Kotoko 1-1 TP Englebert
(Ghana)   (Zaïre*)

November 26 – Kinshasa, Zaïre*
TP Englebert 2-2 Asante Kotoko

TP Englebert won after Asante Kotoko refused a play-off

1968 FINAL (2 legs)
March 16 – Kinshasa, Zaïre*
TP Englebert 5-0 Étoile Filante
(Zaïre*)   (Togo)

March 30 – Lomé, Togo
Étoile Filante 4-1 TP Englebert

TP Englebert won 6-4 on aggregate

1969 FINAL (2 legs)
December 22 – Kinshasa, Zaïre*
TP Englebert 2-2 Al Ismaily
(Zaïre*)   (Egypt)

January 9 – Cairo, Egypt
Al Ismaily 3-1 TP Englebert

Al Ismaily won 5-3 on aggregate

1970 FINAL (2 legs)
January 10 – Kumasi, Ghana
Asante Kotoko 1-1 TP Englebert
(Ghana)   (Zaïre*)

January 24 – Kinshasa, Zaïre*
TP Englebert 1-2 Asante Kotoko

Asante Kotoko won 3-2 on aggregate

1971 FINAL (2 legs)
December 5 – Kumasi, Ghana
Asante Kotoko 3-0 Canon Yaoundé
(Ghana)   (Cameroon)

December 19 – Yaoundé, Cameroon
Canon Yaoundé 2-0 Asante Kotoko

Result to be decided on points, not goal, aggregate so went to play-off

December 21 – Yaoundé, Cameroon
Canon Yaoundé 1-0 Asante Kotoko

Match abandoned at 1-0, result stood, Canon Yaoundé winners

1972 FINAL (2 legs)
December 10 – Conakry, Guinea
Hafia Conakry 4-2 Simba FC
(Guinea)   (Uganda)

December 22 – Kampala, Uganda
Simba FC 2-3 Hafia Conakry

Hafia Conakry won 7-4 on aggregate

1973 FINAL (2 legs)
November 25 – Kumasi, Ghana
Asante Kotoko 4-2 AS Vita Club
(Ghana)   (Zaïre*)

December 16 – Kinshasa, Zaïre*
AS Vita Club 3-0 Asante Kotoko

AS Vita Club won 5-4 on aggregate

1974 FINAL (2 legs)
November 29 – Brazzaville, Congo
CARA 4-2 Mahala
Brazzaville   (Egypt)
(Congo)

December 13 – Mahalla, Egypt
Mahala 1-2 CARA
        Brazzaville

CARA Brazzaville won 6-3 on aggregate

1975 FINAL (2 legs)
December 7 – Conakry, Guinea
Hafia Conakry 2-1 Enugu Rangers
(Guinea)   (Nigeria)

December 20 – Lagos, Nigeria
Enugu Rangers 1-2 Hafia Conakry

Hafia Conakry won 4-1 on pens

1976 FINAL (2 legs)
December 5 – Conakry, Guinea
Hafia Conakry 3-0 Mouloudia
(Guinea)   **d'Algiers**
        (Algeria)

December 12 – Algiers, Algeria
Mouloudia 3-0 Hafia Conakry
d'Algiers

Mouloudia d'Algiers won 4-1 on pens

1977 FINAL (2 legs)
December 4 – Accra, Ghana
Hearts of Oak 0-1 Hafia Conakry
(Ghana)   (Guinea)

December 18 – Conakry, Guinea
Hafia Conakry 3-2 Hearts of Oak

Hafia Conakry won 4-2 on aggregate

1978 FINAL (2 legs)
December 3 – Conakry, Guinea
Hafia Conakry 0-0 Canon Yaoundé
(Guinea)   (Cameroon)

December 17 – Yaoundé, Cameroon
Canon Yaoundé 2-0 Hafia Conakry

Canon Yaoundé won 2-0 on aggregate

1979 FINAL (2 legs)
December 2 – Accra, Ghana
Hearts of Oak 1-0 Union Douala
(Ghana)   (Cameroon)

December 16 – Yaoundé, Cameroon
Union Douala 1-0 Hearts of Oak

Union Douala won 5-3 on pens

1980 FINAL (2 legs)
November 30 – Yaoundé, Cameroon
Canon Yaoundé 2-2 AS Bilima
(Cameroon)   (Zaïre*)

December 14 – Kinshasa, Zaïre*
AS Bilima 0-3 Canon Yaoundé

Canon Yaoundé won 5-2 on aggregate

1981 FINAL (2 legs)
November 27 – Tizi-Ouzou, Algeria
JE Tizi-Ouzou 4-0 AS Vita Club
(Algeria)   (Zaïre*)

December 13 – Kinshasa, Zaïre*
AS Vita Club 0-1 JE Tizi-Ouzou

JE Tizi-Ouzou won 5-0 on aggregate

1982 FINAL (2 legs)
November 28 – Cairo, Egypt
Al Ahly 3-0 Asante Kotoko
(Egypt)   (Ghana)

December 12 – Kumasi, Ghana
Asante Kotoko 1-1 Al Ahly

Al Ahly won 4-1 on aggregate

1983 FINAL (2 legs)
November 27 – Cairo, Egypt
Al Ahly 0-0 Asante Kotoko
(Egypt)   (Ghana)

December 11 – Kumasi, Ghana
Asante Kotoko 1-0 Al Ahly

Asante Kotoko won 1-0 on aggregate

1984 FINAL (2 legs)
November 23 – Cairo, Egypt
Zamalek 2-0 Shooting Stars
(Egypt)   (Nigeria)

December 8 – Lagos, Nigeria
Shooting Stars 0-0 Zamalek

Zamalek won 2-0 on aggregate

1985 FINAL (2 legs)
November 30 – Rabat, Morocco
FAR Rabat 5-2 AS Bilima
(Morocco)   (Zaïre*)

December 22 – Lubumbashi, Zaïre*
AS Bilima 1-1 FAR Rabat

FAR Rabat won 6-3 on aggregate

1986 FINAL (2 legs)
November 28 – Cairo, Egypt
Zamalek 2-0 Africa Sports
(Egypt)   (Côte d'Ivoire)

December 21 – Abidjan, Côte d'Ivoire
Africa Sports 2-0 Zamalek

Zamalek won 4-2 on pens

1987 FINAL (2 legs)
November 29 – Khartoum, Sudan
Al Hilal 0-0 Al Ahly
(Sudan)   (Egypt)

December 18 – Cairo, Egypt
Al Ahly 2-0 Al Hilal

Al Ahly won 2-0 on aggregate

1988 FINAL (2 legs)
November 26 – Ibadan, Nigeria
Iwuanyanwu 1-0 Entente
Owerri   Sétif
(Nigeria)   (Algeria)

December 9 – Constantine, Algeria
Entente 4-0 Iwuanyanwu
Sétif   Owerri

Entente Sétif won 4-1 on aggregate

1989 FINAL (2 legs)
December 3 – Casablanca, Morocco
Raja 2-0 Mouloudia
Casablanca   d'Oran
(Morocco)   (Algeria)

December 15 – Oran, Algeria
Mouloudia 1-0 Raja
d'Oran   Casablanca

Raja Casablanca won 4-2 on pens

1990 FINAL (2 legs)
November 30 – Algiers, Algeria
JS Kabylie 1-0 Nkana Red
(Algeria)   Devils
                (Zaïre*)

December 22 – Lusaka, Zambia
Nkana Red 1-0 JS Kabylie
Devils

JS Kabylie won 5-3 on pens

1991 FINAL (2 legs)
November 23 – Tunis, Tunisia
Club Africain 5-1 Nakivubo
(Tunisia)   Villa SC
                (Zaïre*)

December 14 – Kampala, Uganda
Nakivubo 1-1 Club Africain
Villa SC

Club Africain won 6-2 on aggregate

1992 FINAL (2 legs)
November 29 – Casablanca, Morocco
WAC 2-0 Al Hilal
Casablanca   (Sudan)
(Morocco)

December 13 – Khartoum, Sudan
Al Hilal 0-0 WAC
            Casablanca

WAC Casablanca won 2-0 on aggregate

1993 FINAL (2 legs)
November 26 – Kumasi, Ghana
Asante Kotoko 0-0 Zamalek
(Ghana)   (Egypt)

December 10 – Cairo, Egypt
Zamalek 0-0 Asante Kotoko

Zamalek won 7-6 on pens

1994 FINAL (2 legs)
December 4 – Cairo, Egypt
Zamalek 0-0 Espérance
(Egypt)   Sportive
                (Tunisia)

December 17 – Tunis, Tunisia
Espérance 3-1 Zamalek
Sportive

Espérance Sportive won 3-1 on aggregate

1995 FINAL (2 legs)
Johannesburg, South Africa
Orlando 2-2 ASEC Abidjan
Pirates
(South Africa)   (Côte d'Ivoire)

Abidjan, Côte d'Ivoire
ASEC Abidjan 0-1 Orlando
            Pirates

Orlando Pirates won 3-2 on aggregate

1996 FINAL (2 legs)
Lagos, Nigeria
Shooting Stars 2-1 Zamalek
(Nigeria)   (Egypt)

Cairo, Egypt
Zamalek 2-1 Shooting Stars

Zamalek won 5-4 on pens

1997 FINAL (2 legs)
November 30 – Obuasi, Ghana
Goldfields 1-0 Raja
(Ghana)   Casablanca
                (Morocco)

December 14 – Casablanca, Morocco
Raja 1-0 Goldfields
Casablanca

Raja Casablanca won 5-4 on pens

1998 FINAL (2 legs)
November 28 – Harare, Zimbabwe
Dynamos 0-0 ASEC
(Zimbabwe)   Abidjan
                (Côte d'Ivoire)

December 12 – Abidjan, Côte d'Ivoire
ASEC 4-2 Dynamos
Abidjan

ASEC Abidjan won 4-2 on aggregate

1999 FINAL (2 legs)
November 27 – Casablanca, Morocco
Raja 0-0 Espérance
Casablanca   Sportive
(Morocco)   (Tunisia)

December 12 – Tunis, Tunisia
Espérance 0-0 Raja
Sportive   Casablanca

Raja Casablanca won 4-3 on pens

2000 FINAL (2 legs)
December 2 – Tunis, Tunisia
Espérance 1-2 Hearts of Oak
Sportive   (Ghana)
(Tunisia)

December 17 – Accra, Ghana
Hearts of Oak 3-1 Espérance
                Sportive

Hearts of Oak won 5-2 on aggregate

2001 FINAL (2 legs)
December 8 – Pretoria, South Africa
Mamelodi 1-1 Al Ahly
Sundowns   (Egypt)
(South Africa)

December 21 – Cairo, Egypt
Al Ahly 3-0 Mamelodi
                Sundowns

Al Ahly won 4-1 on aggregate

2002 FINAL (2 legs)
November 30 – Casablanca, Morocco
Raja 0-0 Zamalek
Casablanca   (Egypt)
(Morocco)

December 13 – Cairo, Egypt
Zamalek 1-0 Raja
                Casablanca

Zamalek won 1-0 on aggregate

2003 FINAL (2 legs)
November 30 – Aba, Nigeria
Enyimba 2-0 Al Ismaily
(Nigeria)   (Egypt)

December 12 – Ismailiya, Egypt
Al Ismaily 1-0 Enyimba

Enyimba won 2-1 on aggregate

The African Cup-Winners' Cup and CAF Cup

The African Cup-Winners' Cup 1975–2003

YEAR	WINNERS	RUNNERS-UP
1975	Tonnerre Yaoundé (Cameroon)	Stella Club (Côte d'Ivoire)
1976	Shooting Stars (Nigeria)	Tonnerre Yaoundé (Cameroon)
1977	Enugu Rangers (Nigeria)	Canon Yaoundé (Cameroon)
1978	Horoya AC (Guinea)	Milaha Athletic (Algeria)
1979	Canon Yaoundé (Cameroon)	Gor Mahia (Kenya)
1980	TP Mazembe (Zaïre*)	Africa Sports (Côte d'Ivoire)
1981	Union Douala (Cameroon)	Stationery Stores (Nigeria)
1982	Al Mokaoulom (Egypt)	Power Dynamos (Zambia)
1983	Al Mokaoulom (Egypt)	Agaza Lomé (Togo)
1984	Al Ahly (Egypt)	Canon Yaoundé (Cameroon)
1985	Al Ahly (Egypt)	Leventis United (Nigeria)
1986	Al Ahly (Egypt)	AS Sogara (Gabon)
1987	Gor Mahia (Kenya)	Espérance Sportive (Tunisia)
1988	CA Bizerte (Tunisia)	Rancher Bees (Nigeria)
1989	Al Merreikh (Sudan)	Bendel United (Nigeria)
1990	BCC Lions (Nigeria)	Club Africain (Tunisia)
1991	Power Dynamos (Zambia)	BCC Lions (Nigeria)
1992	Africa Sports (Côte d'Ivoire)	Vital'O FC (Burundi)
1993	Al Ahly (Egypt)	Africa Sports (Côte d'Ivoire)
1994	DC Motema Pembe (Zaïre*)	Kenya Breweries (Kenya)
1995	JS Kabylie (Algeria)	Julius Berger (Nigeria)
1996	Arab Contractors (Egypt)	AC Sodigraf (Zaïre*)
1997	Étoile du Sahel (Tunisia)	FAR Rabat (Morocco)
1998	Espérance Sportive (Tunisia)	Primeiro de Agosto (Angola)
1999	Africa Sports (Côte d'Ivoire)	Club Africain (Tunisia)

The African Cup-Winners' Cup (continued)

YEAR	WINNERS	RUNNERS-UP
2000	Zamalek (Egypt)	Canon Yaoundé (Cameroon)
2001	Kaizer Chiefs (South Africa)	Inter Clube (Angola)
2002	WAC Casablanca (Morocco)	Asante Kotoko (Ghana)
2003	Etoile du Sahel (Tunisia)	Julius Berger (Nigeria)

The CAF Cup 1992–2003

YEAR	WINNERS	RUNNERS-UP
1992	Shooting Stars (Nigeria)	Nakivubo Villa SC (Uganda)
1993	Stella Club (Côte d'Ivoire)	Simba FC (Tanzania)
1994	Bendel Insurance (Nigeria)	Primeiro de Maio (Angola)
1995	Étoile du Sahel (Tunisia)	AS Kaloum Stars (Guinea)
1996	KAC Marrakech (Morocco)	Étoile du Sahel (Tunisia)
1997	Espérance Sportive (Tunisia)	Petro Atlético (Angola)
1998	CS Sfax (Tunisia)	ASC Jeanne d'Arc (Senegal)
1999	Étoile du Sahel (Tunisia)	WAC Casablanca (Morocco)
2000	JS Kabylie (Algeria)	Al Ismaily (Egypt)
2001	JS Kabylie (Algeria)	Étoile du Sahel (Tunisia)
2002	JS Kabylie (Algeria)	Tonnerre Yaoundé (Cameroon)
2003	Raja Casablanca (Morocco)	Cotonsport (Cameroon)

* Zaïre is now known as the Democratic Republic of Congo.

THE AFRICAN CHAMPIONS LEAGUE, AFRICAN CUP-WINNERS' CUP, CAF CUP

Egypt

Egyptian Football Asscoiation
Founded: 1921
Joined FIFA: 1923
Joined CAF: 1957

SOCCER ARRIVED IN Egypt during the British armed occupation at the turn of the 19th century. No British clubs from the era survive, but the dominant force in Egyptian soccer, the Cairo-based Al Ahly, was founded in 1907. The club has come to represent the republican strand of Egyptian nationalist politics, a fact confirmed when Nasser was made honorary president of the club in 1954. The team's eternal rival – Zamalek – was founded in 1911 as Kaser-el-nil, becoming Al Mukhtalat in 1925. Its allegiance became clear when the soccer fanatic King Farouk lent his support and name to the club in 1940. When Farouk was deposed in 1952, the club became Zamalek.

The prescience of Egyptian soccer can be seen from the early formation of the Egyptian FA (1921), preceding national independence by a year. A cup was donated that year by the king to create the first national competition. In 1920, Egypt played at the Olympic Games in Antwerp, the first African nation ever to do so. In 1924 in Amsterdam, Egypt made it to the quarter-finals, and in 1928, the semi-finals. Egypt was the first African side to play in the World Cup Finals (1934) and supplied the first African referee to the World Cup in 1966.

During the Second World War, Egyptian and Allied military teams played extensively, and in 1949, a national league was created alongside the cup. Politics has never been far from Egyptian soccer and in 1958 the army took over the national FA and professionalized the game through the back door. With the outbreak of the Arab-Israeli Six-Day War in 1967, Egyptian domestic soccer was regularly disrupted until after the Yom Kippur War in the 1970s. Enormous and fanatical support has tragically been accompanied by a series of disasters including a riot at the 1966 Cairo derby between Zamalek and Al Ahly that saw over 300 injured when the military took control of the stadium. In 1974, a wall collapsed at Zamalek during a friendly match against Dukla Praha killing 49 people.

Egyptian League Record 1949–2004

SEASON	CHAMPIONS	SEASON	CHAMPIONS
1949	Al Ahly	1974	no championship
1950	Al Ahly	1975	Al Ahly
1951	Al Ahly	1976	Al Ahly
1952	no championship	1977	Al Ahly
1953	Al Ahly	1978	Zamalek
1954	Al Ahly	1979	Al Ahly
1955	no championship	1980	Al Ahly
1956	Al Ahly	1981	Al Ahly
1957	Al Ahly	1982	Al Ahly
1958	Al Ahly	1983	Al Mokaoulom
1959	Al Ahly	1984	Zamalek
1960	Zamalek	1985	Al Ahly
1961	Al Ahly	1986	Al Ahly
1962	Al Ahly	1987	Al Ahly
1963	Al Tersana	1988	Zamalek
1964	Zamalek	1989	Al Ahly
1965	Zamalek	1990	no championship
1966	Olympia	1991	Al Ismaily
1967	Al Ismaily	1992	Zamalek
1968–72	no championship	1993	Zamalek
1973	Mahala	1994	Al Ahly

Egyptian League Record (continued)

SEASON	CHAMPIONS	SEASON	CHAMPIONS
1995	Al Ahly	2001	Zamalek
1996	Al Ahly	2002	Al Ismaily
1997	Al Ahly	2003	Zamalek
1998	Al Ahly	2004	Zamalek
1999	Al Ahly		
2000	Al Ahly		

Cup of Egypt 1949–2004

YEAR	WINNERS	YEAR	WINNERS
1949	Al Ahly	1980	no competition
1950	Al Ahly	1981	Al Ahly
1951	Al Ahly	1982	no competition
1952	Zamalek	1983	Al Ahly
1953	Al Ahly	1984	Al Ahly
1954	Al Tersana	1985	Al Ahly
1955	Zamalek	1986	Al Tersana
1956	Al Ahly	1987	no competition
1957	Zamalek	1988	Zamalek
1958	Zamalek and Al Ahly*	1989	Al Ahly
1959	Zamalek	1990	Al Mokaoulom
1960	Zamalek	1991	Al Ahly
1961	Al Ahly	1992	Al Ahly
1962	Zamalek	1993	Al Ahly
1963	Al Ittihad	1994	no competition
1964	Quanah	1995	Al Mokaoulom
1965	Al Tersana	1996	Al Ahly
1966	Al Ahly	1997	Al Ismaily
1967	Al Tersana	1998	Al Masry
1968–72	no competition	1999	Zamalek
1973	Al Ittihad	2000	Al Ismaily
1974	no competition	2001	Al Ahly
1975	Zamalek	2002	Zamalek
1976	Al Ittihad	2003	Al Ahly
1977	Zamalek	2004	Al Mokaoulom
1978	Al Ahly		
1979	Zamalek		

* Cup shared.

Zamalek from Cairo is the second best supported team in Egypt. The club enjoyed the support of King Farouk during the 1940s. It remains the most dangerous rival of neighbours Al Ahly.

Soccer in Egypt

League champions 3 times or more — **1966**	
League champions 1–2 times — **1966**	
Other teams — 1966	
Cup of Egypt winners — 1966	
● Cairo	City of origin
○	African Champions League
●	African Cup-Winners' Cup
●	CAF Cup
1973	Winners in bold
1973	Runners-up in italics
*	Title shared

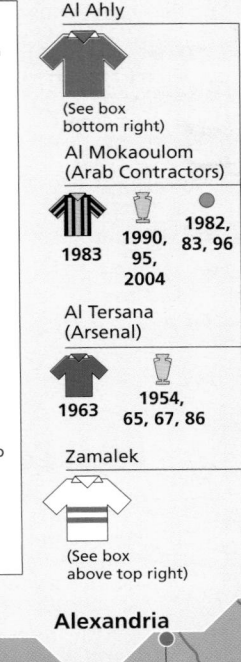

Al Ahly
(See box bottom right)

Al Mokaoulom (Arab Contractors)
1983 — **1990, 95, 2004** — **1982, 83, 96**

Al Tersana (Arsenal)
1963 — **1954, 65, 67, 86**

Zamalek
(See box above top right)

Tanta

Mahala
1974 — **1973**

Al Mansurah

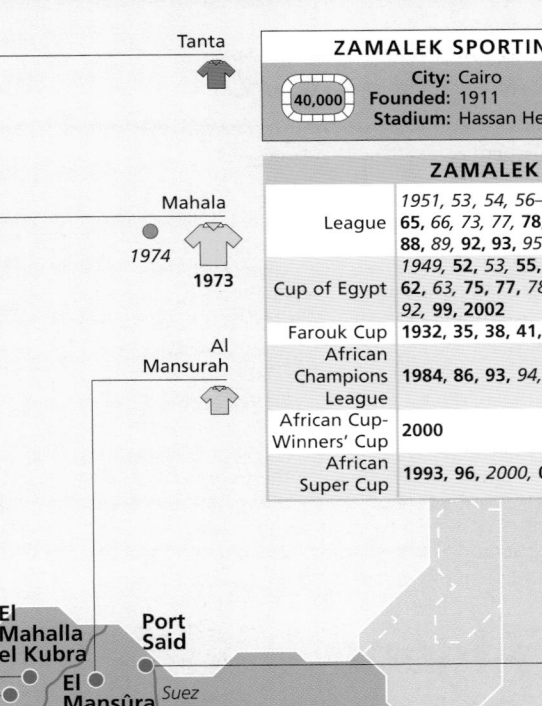

ZAMALEK SPORTING CLUB

40,000

City: Cairo
Founded: 1911
Stadium: Hassan Helmi

ZAMALEK	
League	*1951, 53, 54, 56–59, 60, 61–63,* **64, 65,** *66,* **73, 77, 78,** *79–83,* **84, 85–87, 88, 89, 92, 93,** *95–99,* **2001, 03, 04**
Cup of Egypt	*1949, 52, 53,* **55,** *57, 58*, **59, 60, 62,** *63,* **75, 77,** *78,* **79, 88,** *92,* **99, 2002**
Farouk Cup	**1932, 35, 38, 41,** *43*, **44,** *48*
African Champions League	**1984, 86, 93,** *94,* **96, 2002**
African Cup-Winners' Cup	**2000**
African Super Cup	**1993, 96,** *2000,* **03**

Alexandria ●

El Mahalla el Kubra

Port Said

Al Masry
1998

El Mansûra

Suez Canal

Tanta

Ismailiya ●

Quanah
1964

Cairo ●

Olympia

1966

Al Ittihad (Union Recreation)
1963, 73, 76

Al Ismaily
2000 — ○ *1969, 2003* — **1997, 2000** — **1967, 91, 2002**

Nile

Jubilant Al Ismaily players celebrate after their 4-0 victory over Al Mokaoulom in the 2000 Cup of Egypt Final. Four goals in 13 minutes of the second half sealed their triumph.

AL AHLY NATIONAL SPORTING CLUB

20,000

City: Cairo
Founded: 1907
Stadium: Mokhtar el Tetch

AL AHLY	
League	**1949–51, 53, 54, 56–59, 61, 62,** *67,* **75–77,** *78,* **79–82, 84, 85–87, 88, 89, 91, 93,** *94–2000,* **01–04**
Cup of Egypt	**1949–51,** *52,* **53, 56, 58**, *59,* **61, 66,** *73, 76,* **78, 81, 83–85, 89, 91–93, 96, 97, 2001, 03**
Farouk Cup	**1924, 25,** *26,* **27, 28, 30, 31, 37, 40,** *41,* **42,** *43*, **44, 45–47**
African Champions League	**1982,** *83,* **87, 2001**
African Cup-Winners' Cup	**1984–86, 93**
African Super Cup	*1993,* **2001, 02**

Lake Nasser

North Africa

APART FROM EGYPT (see pages 448-49) soccer arrived in North Africa at the turn of the 19th century via the colonial administration of French North Africa. Within a quarter of a century, leagues were up and running in Algeria (1920s), Morocco (1916) and Tunisia (1921). In the ex-Italian colony of Libya a league was finally established in 1964. Under French control a North African Club Championship was established (1919–49), and before independence internationals were played in the North African Cup (1919–30). In Algeria, separate regional leagues were played until independence (in Algiers, Constantine and Oran).

Successive club name changes indicate the degree of political involvement in soccer in Algeria; JS Kabylie was formally known as JE Tizi-Ouzou in an attempt to suppress the club's identification with regionalist sentiments. In Morocco royal and military patronage is evident in the leading clubs' names.

Algeria

Fédération Algérienne de Football
Founded: 1962
Joined FIFA: 1963
Joined CAF: 1964

Algerian League Record 1963–2004

SEASON	CHAMPIONS	SEASON	CHAMPIONS
1963	USM Algiers	1985	JE Tizi-Ouzou
1964	USM Annaba	1986	JE Tizi-Ouzou
1965	CR Belcourt	1987	Entente Sétif
1966	CR Belcourt	1988	Mouloudia d'Oran
1967	NA Hussein-Dey	1989	JE Tizi-Ouzou
1968	Entente Sétif	1990	KS Kabylie
1969	CR Belcourt	1991	MO Constantine
1970	CR Belcourt	1992	Mouloudia d'Oran
1971	Mouloudia d'Oran	1993	Mouloudia d'Oran
1972	Mouloudia d'Algiers	1994	US Chaouia
1973	JS Kabylie	1995	JS Kabylie
1974	JS Kabylie	1996	USM Alger
1975	Mouloudia d'Algiers	1997	CS Constantine
1976	Mouloudia d'Algiers	1998	USM El Harrach
1977	JS Kawkabi	1999	MC Alger
1978	Mouloudia d'Algiers	2000	CR Belouizdad
1979	Mouloudia d'Algiers	2001	CR Belouizdad
1980	JE Tizi-Ouzou	2002	USM Alger
1981	RS Kouba	2003	USM Alger
1982	JE Tizi-Ouzou	2004	JS Kabylie
1983	JE Tizi-Ouzou		
1984	GCR Mascara		

Algerian Cup Record 1963–2004

YEAR	WINNERS	YEAR	WINNERS
1963	Entente Sétif	1972	Hamra-Annaba
1964	Entente Sétif	1973	Mouloudia d'Algiers
1965	MC Saida	1974	USM Maison Carrée
1966	CR Belcourt	1975	Mouloudia d'Oran
1967	Entente Sétif	1976	Mouloudia d'Algiers
1968	Entente Sétif	1977	JS Kawkabi
1969	CR Belcourt	1978	CM Belcourt
1970	CR Belcourt	1979	MS Hussein-Dey
1971	Mouloudia d'Algiers	1980	Entente Sétif

Algerian Cup Record (continued)

YEAR	WINNERS	YEAR	WINNERS
1981	USK Algiers	1994	JS Kabylie
1982	DNC Algiers	1995	CR Belouizdad
1983	Mouloudia d'Algiers	1996	USM Alger
1984	Mouloudia d'Oran	1997	USM Alger
1985	Mouloudia d'Oran	1998	WA Tlemoen
1986	JE Tizi-Ouzou	1999	USM Alger
1987	USM El-Harrach	2000	MC Ouargla
1988	USK Algiers	2001	USM Alger
1989	no competition	2002	WA Tlemcen
1990	Entente Sétif	2003	USM Alger
1991	USM Bel Abbés	2004	USM Alger
1992	JS Kabylie		
1993	no competition		

Morocco

Fédération Royale Marocaine de Football
Founded: 1955
Joined FIFA: 1956
Joined CAF: 1966

Moroccan League Record 1916–2004

SEASON	CHAMPIONS	SEASON	CHAMPIONS
1916	CA Casablanca	1963	FAR Rabat
1917	US Marocaine	1964	FAR Rabat
1918	US Marocaine	1965	MAS Fès
1919	US Marocaine	1966	WAC Casablanca
1920	Olympique Marocaine	1967	FAR Rabat
1921	Olympique Marocaine	1968	FAR Rabat
1922	Olympique Marocaine	1969	WAC Casablanca
1923	US Fès	1970	FAR Rabat
1924	Olympique Marocaine	1971	RS Settat
1925	US Fès	1972	ADM Casablanca
1926	US Athletic	1973	KAC Kenitra
1927	Stade Marocaine	1974	RBM Beni Mellal
1928	no championship	1975	MC Oujda
1929	US Athletic	1976	WAC Casablanca
1930	Stade Marocaine	1977	WAC Casablanca
1931	US Marocaine	1978	WAC Casablanca
1932	US Marocaine	1979	MAS Fès
1933	US Marocaine	1980	Chebab Mohammedia
1934	US Marocaine	1981	KAC Kenitra
1935	US Marocaine	1982	KAC Kenitra
1936	Olympique Marocaine	1983	MAS Fès
1937	Olympique Marocaine	1984	FAR Rabat
1938	US Marocaine	1985	MAS Fès
1939	US Marocaine	1986	WAC Casablanca
1940	US Marocaine	1987	FAR Rabat
1941	US Marocaine	1988	Raja Casablanca
1942	US Marocaine	1989	FAR Rabat
1943	US Marocaine	1990	WAC Casablanca
1944	Stade Marocaine	1991	WAC Casablanca
1945	Racing Avant-Garde	1992	KAC Marrakech
1946	US Marocaine	1993	WAC Casablanca
1947	US Athletic	1994	Olympic Casablanca
1948	WAC Casablanca	1995	COD Meknes
1949	WAC Casablanca	1996	Raja Casablanca
1950	WAC Casablanca	1997	Raja Casablanca
1951	WAC Casablanca	1998	Raja Casablanca
1952–56	no championship	1999	Raja Casablanca
1957	WAC Casablanca	2000	Raja Casablanca
1958	KAC Marrakech	2001	Raja Casablanca
1959	EJS Casablanca	2002	Hassania US d'Agadir
1960	KAC Kenitra	2003	Hassania US d'Agadir
1961	FAR Rabat	2004	Raja Casablanca
1962	FAR Rabat		

Moroccan Cup Record 1957–2003

YEAR	WINNERS	YEAR	WINNERS
1957	MC Oujda	1981	WAC Casablanca
1958	MC Oujda	1982	Raja Casablanca
1959	FAR Rabat	1983	CLAS Casablanca
1960	MC Oujda	1984	FAR Rabat
1961	KAC Kenitra	1985	FAR Rabat
1962	MC Oujda	1986	FAR Rabat
1963	KAC Marrakech	1987	KAC Marrakech
1964	KAC Marrakech	1988	*no competition*
1965	KAC Marrakech	1989	WAC Casablanca
1966	COD Meknes	1990–91	*no competition*
1967	FUS Rabat	1992	Olympic Casablanca
1968	Raja Casablanca	1993	KAC Marrakech
1969	RS Settat	1994	WAC Casablanca
1970	WAC Casablanca	1995	FAR Rabat
1971	FAR Rabat	1996	Raja Casablanca
1972	Chabab Mohammedia	1997	WAC Casablanca
1973	FUS Rabat	1998	WAC Casablanca
1974	Raja Casablanca	1999	FAR Rabat
1975	Chabab Mohammedia	2000	Majd Casablanca
1976	FUS Rabat	2001	WAC Casablanca
1977	Raja Casablanca	2002	Raja Casablanca
1978	WAC Casablanca	2003	FAR Rabat
1979	WAC Casablanca		
1980	MAS Fès		

Tunisia

Fédération Tunisienne de Football
Founded: 1956
Joined FIFA: 1960
Joined CAF: 1960

Tunisian League Record 1921–2004

SEASON	CHAMPIONS	SEASON	CHAMPIONS
1921	Racing Club	1956	CS Hammam-Lif
1922	Stade Gauloise	1957	Stade Tunisien
1923	Stade Gauloise	1958	Étoile du Sahel
1924	Racing Club	1959	Espérance Sportive
1925	Sporting Club	1960	Espérance Sportive
1926	Stade Gauloise	1961	Stade Tunisien
1927	Sporting Club	1962	Stade Tunisien
1928	Avant Garde	1963	Étoile du Sahel
1929	US Tunisienne	1964	Club Africain
1930	US Tunisienne	1965	Stade Tunisien
1931	Italia de Tunis	1966	Étoile du Sahel
1932	US Tunisienne	1967	Club Africain
1933	Sfax Railway	1968	Sfax Railway
1934	Italia de Tunis	1969	CS Sfax
1935	Italia de Tunis	1970	Espérance Sportive
1936	Italia de Tunis	1971	CS Sfax
1937	Savoia de la Goulette	1972	Étoile du Sahel
1938	CS Gabesien	1973	Club Africain
1939–40	*no championship*	1974	Club Africain
1941	Espérance Sportive	1975	Espérance Sportive
1942–43	*no championship*	1976	Espérance Sportive
1944	CA Bizerte	1977	JS Kairouan
1945	CA Bizerte	1978	CS Sfax
1946	Club Africain	1979	Club Africain
1947	Club Africain	1980	Club Africain
1948	CA Bizerte	1981	CS Sfax
1949	Étoile du Sahel	1982	Espérance Sportive
1950	CS Hammam-Lif	1983	CS Sfax
1951–55	*no championship*	1984	CA Bizerte

Tunisian League Record (*continued*)

SEASON	CHAMPIONS	SEASON	CHAMPIONS
1985	Espérance Sportive	1996	Club Africain
1986	Étoile du Sahel	1997	Espérance Sportive
1987	Étoile du Sahel	1998	Espérance Sportive
1988	Espérance Sportive	1999	Espérance Sportive
1989	Espérance Sportive	2000	Espérance Sportive
1990	Club Africain	2001	Espérance Sportive
1991	Espérance Sportive	2002	Espérance Sportive
1992	Club Africain	2003	Espérance Sportive
1993	Espérance Sportive	2004	Espérance Sportive
1994	Espérance Sportive		
1995	CS Sfax		

Tunisian Cup Record 1922–2003

YEAR	WINNERS	YEAR	WINNERS
1922	Avant Garde	1968	Club Africain
1923	Racing Club	1969	Club Africain
1924	Stade Gauloise	1970	Club Africain
1925	Sporting Club	1971	CS Sfax
1926	Stade Gauloise	1972	Club Africain
1927-28	*no competition*	1973	Club Africain
1929	US Tunisienne	1974	Étoile du Sahel
1930	US Tunisienne	1975	Étoile du Sahel
1931	Racing Club	1976	Club Africain
1932	US Tunisienne	1977	AS Marsa
1933	US Tunisienne	1978	*no competition*
1934	US Tunisienne	1979	Espérance Sportive
1935	Italia de Tunis	1980	Espérance Sportive
1936	Stade Gauloise	1981	Étoile du Sahel
1937	Sporting Club	1982	CA Bizerte
1938	Espérance Sportive	1983	Étoile du Sahel
1939–40	*no competition*	1984	AS Marsa
1941	US Ferryville	1985	CS Hammam-Lif
1942–43	*no competition*	1986	Espérance Sportive
1944	Olympique Tunis	1987	CA Bizerte
1945	Patrie FC Bizerte	1988	COT Tunis
1946	CS Hammam-Lif	1989	Club Africain
1947	CS Hammam-Lif	1990	AS Marsa
1948	CS Hammam-Lif	1991	Étoile du Sahel
1949	CS Hammam-Lif	1992	Club Africain
1950	CS Hammam-Lif	1993	Olympique Beja
1951–55	*no competition*	1994	AS Marsa
1956	Stade Tunisien	1995	CS Sfaxien
1957	Étoile de Tunis	1996	Étoile du Sahel
1958	Stade Tunisien	1997	Espérance Sportive
1959	Étoile du Sahel	1998	Club Africain
1960	Stade Tunisien	1999	Espérance Sportive
1961	AS Marsa	2000	Club Africain
1962	Stade Tunisien	2001	CS Hammam-Lif
1963	Étoile du Sahel	2002	*abandoned*
1964	Espérance Sportive	2003	Stade Tunisien
1965	Club Africain		
1966	Stade Tunisien		
1967	Club Africain		

Libya

Libyan Arab Jamahiriya Football Federation
Founded: 1962
Joined FIFA: 1963
Joined CAF: 1965

SEASON	LEAGUE CHAMPIONS
2000	Al Ahly
2001	Al Medina
2002	Al Ittihad
2003	Al Ittihad
2004	Al Olympique

NORTH AFRICA

West Africa

WHILE NORTH AFRICA WAS SLIGHTLY earlier in its adoption of soccer and both Central and Southern Africa have significant league and cup competitions, African soccer has been most enduringly strong in West Africa. At the head of the pack have been Nigeria (see pages 454-55), Guinea, Côte d'Ivoire, Ghana and Senegal. In Ghana and Nigeria soccer arrived with British imperial administrations in the early 20th century. Ghana's oldest and most successful team, Hearts of Oak, was founded in 1911. City-based and regional tournaments began in the 1920s and, post-independence, a national league was established in 1957 and a cup in 1958.

In French West Africa (including what are now Guinea, Senegal and Côte d'Ivoire) many soccer clubs were established in the 1930s. Côte d'Ivoire's leading clubs, Africa Sports, Stella Abidjan and Stade Abidjan, were all founded in 1936. In Côte d'Ivoire and Senegal national league and cup competitions followed independence in 1960.

The Senegalese are coming

But while Côte d'Ivoire's clubs have won both the African Champions League and the CAF Cup, Senegalese teams have yet to take an African championship. The national team did, however, reach the Final of the 2002 African Nations Cup in Mali beating Nigeria in the semi-final. In the Final it lost to Cameroon on penalties. The team started the tournament in confident mood having qualified in sensational style for the 2002 World Cup Finals where many pundits rightly tipped it to perform well, and it certainly didn't disappoint, with a stunning overall performance. The 5-0 thrashing of Namibia in the last game of the qualifying tournament saw the team through to the Finals and hopes of a bright future.

Guinea's national league began in 1965 and is dominated by Hafia Conrakry, three times winners of the African Champions League during the 1970s, but its fortunes have been on the wane in recent years.

Founded in 1911 Hearts of Oak, from Accra, is the most successful club in Ghana. Its greatest international success came in 2000 when it won the African Champions League, beating Espérance Sportive of Tunisia in the Final.

Ghana

Ghana Football Association
Founded: 1957
Joined FIFA: 1958
Joined CAF: 1958

Ghanaian League Record 1957–2003

SEASON	CHAMPIONS	SEASON	CHAMPIONS
1957	Hearts of Oak	1982	Asante Kotoko
1958	Hearts of Oak	1983	Asante Kotoko
1959	Asante Kotoko	1984	Hearts of Oak
1960	Eleven Wise FC	1985	Hearts of Oak
1961	Real Republicans	1986	Asante Kotoko
1962	Real Republicans	1987	Asante Kotoko
1963	Asante Kotoko	1988	Asante Kotoko
1964	Asante Kotoko	1989	Hearts of Oak
1965	Asante Kotoko	1990	Hearts of Oak
1966	BA United	1991	Asante Kotoko
1967	Asante Kotoko	1992	Asante Kotoko
1968	Asante Kotoko	1993	Asante Kotoko
1969	Asante Kotoko	1994	Goldfields
1970	Great Olympics	1995	Goldfields
1971	Hearts of Oak	1996	Goldfields
1972	Asante Kotoko	1997	Hearts of Oak
1973	Hearts of Oak	1998	Hearts of Oak
1974	Great Olympics	1999	Hearts of Oak
1975	Asante Kotoko	2000	Hearts of Oak
1976	Hearts of Oak	2001	Hearts of Oak
1977	Sekondi Hasaacas	2002	Hearts of Oak
1978	Hearts of Oak	2003	Asante Kotoko
1979	Hearts of Oak		
1980	Asante Kotoko		
1981	Asante Kotoko		

Ghanaian Cup Record 1958–2001

YEAR	CUP WINNERS	YEAR	CUP WINNERS
1958	Asante Kotoko	1984	Asante Kotoko
1959	Cornerstones	1985	Sekondi Hasaacas
1960	Asante Kotoko	1986	Okwahu United
1961	*no competition*	1987	Hearts of Oak
1962	Real Republicans	1988	Hearts of Oak
1963	Real Republicans	1989	Hearts of Oak
1964	Real Republicans	1990	Asante Kotoko
1965	Real Republicans	1991	Asante Kotoko
1966–68	*no competition*	1992	Voradep
1969	Cape Coast Dwarfs	1993	Goldfields
1970–72	*no competition*	1994	Hearts of Oak
1973	Hearts of Oak	1995	Hearts of Oak
1974	Hearts of Oak	1996	Hearts of Oak
1975	Great Olympics	1997	Ghaphoa
1976	Asante Kotoko	1998	Asante Kotoko
1977	*no competition*	1999	Hearts of Oak
1978	Asante Kotoko	2000	Hearts of Oak
1979	Hearts of Oak	2001	Asante Kotoko
1980	Sekondi Hasaacas		
1981	Hearts of Oak		
1982	Eleven Wise FC		
1983	Great Olympics		

Benin

Fédération Beninoise de Football
Founded: 1962
Joined FIFA: 1962
Joined CAF: 1969

SEASON	LEAGUE CHAMPIONS
1999	Dragons de l'Ouémé
2000	*no official championship*
2001	*no official championship*
2002	Dragons de l'Ouémé
2003	Dragons de l'Ouémé

Benin (continued)

YEAR	CUP WINNERS
1999	Mogas 90
2000	Mogas 90
2001	Buffles de Borgou
2002	Jeunesse Sportive Pobé
2003	Mogas 90

Burkina Faso

Fédération Burkinabe de Football
Founded: 1960
Joined FIFA: 1964
Joined CAF: 1964

SEASON	LEAGUE CHAMPIONS
2000	USFA
2001	Etoile Filante
2002	Etoile Filante
2003	ASFA Yennenga
2004	ASFA Yennenga

YEAR	CUP WINNERS
1999	Etoile Filante
2000	Etoile Filante
2001	Etoile Filante
2002	USFA
2003	Etoile Filante

Cape Verde

Fédération Cabo Verdiana de Futebol
Founded: 1982
Joined FIFA: 1986
Joined CAF: 1986

SEASON	LEAGUE CHAMPIONS
1999	Amarante
2000	Derby FC
2001	Onze Unidos
2002	Sporting Clube da Praia
2003	Académico di Sal

Côte d'Ivoire

Fédération Ivorienne de Football
Founded: 1960
Joined FIFA: 1960
Joined CAF: 1960

SEASON	LEAGUE CHAMPIONS
1999	Africa Sports
2000	ASEC Abidjan
2001	ASEC Abidjan
2002	ASEC Abidjan
2003	ASEC Mimosas

Côte d'Ivoire (continued)

YEAR	CUP WINNERS
1999	ASEC Abidjan
2000	Stade Abidjan
2001	Alliance Bouaké
2002	Africa Sports
2003	ASEC Mimosas

Gambia

Gambia Football Association
Founded: 1952
Joined FIFA: 1966
Joined CAF: 1962

SEASON	LEAGUE CHAMPIONS
1999	Ports Authority
2000	Real Banjul
2001	Wallidan
2002	Wallidan
2003	Armed Forces

Guinea

Fédération Guinéenne de Football
Founded: 1959
Joined FIFA: 1961
Joined CAF: 1962

SEASON	LEAGUE CHAMPIONS
1998	AS Kaloum Stars
1999	*not held*
2000	Horoya AC
2001	Horoya AC
2002	Satellite FC

YEAR	CUP WINNERS
1999	Horoya AC
2000	Fello Stars Labé
2001	*unknown*
2002	Hafia Conakry
2003	Etoile de Guinée

Guinea-Bissau

Federação de Futebol da Guiné-Bissau
Founded: 1974
Joined FIFA: 1986
Joined CAF: 1986

SEASON	LEAGUE CHAMPIONS
2000	Sporting Clube de Bissau
2001	*no championship*
2002	Sporting Clube de Bissau
2003	UDIB
2004	Sporting Clube de Bissau

Liberia

Liberia Football Federation
Founded: 1936
Joined FIFA: 1962
Joined CAF: 1962

SEASON	LEAGUE CHAMPIONS
1999	LPRC Oilers
2000	Mighty Barolle
2001	Mighty Barolle
2002	LPRC Oilers
2003	*abandoned*

Mali

Fédération Malienne de Football
Founded: 1960
Joined FIFA: 1962
Joined CAF: 1963

SEASON	LEAGUE CHAMPIONS
1999	Djoliba AC
2000	Stade Malien
2001	Stade Malien
2002	Stade Malien
2003	Stade Malien

YEAR	CUP WINNERS
1999	Stade Malien
2000	Cercle Olympique
2001	Stade Malien
2002	Cercle Olympique
2003	Djoliba AC

Mauritania

Fédération de Football de la République de Mauritanie
Founded: 1961
Joined FIFA: 1964
Joined CAF: 1968

SEASON	LEAGUE CHAMPIONS
1999	SDPA Rosso
2000	Mauritel
2001	FC Nouadhibou
2002	FC Nouadhibou
2003	NASR

Niger

Fédération Nigérienne de Football
Founded: 1967
Joined FIFA: 1967
Joined CAF: 1967

Niger (continued)

SEASON	LEAGUE CHAMPIONS
2000	JS Ténéré
2001	JS Ténéré
2002	*no championship*
2003	Sahel SC
2004	Sahel SC

Senegal

Fédération Sénégalaise de Football
Founded: 1960
Joined FIFA: 1962
Joined CAF: 1963

SEASON	LEAGUE CHAMPIONS
1999	ASC Jeanne D'Arc
2000	ASC Diaraf
2001	ASC Jeanne D'Arc
2002	ASC Jeanne D'Arc
2003	ASC Jeanne D'Arc

YEAR	CUP WINNERS
1999	ASEC Ndiambour
2000	Porte Autonome
2001	SONACOS
2002	AS Douanes
2003	AS Douanes

Sierra Leone

Sierra Leone Amateur Football Association
Founded: 1923
Joined FIFA: 1967
Joined CAF: 1967

SEASON	LEAGUE CHAMPIONS
1999	East End Lions
2000	Mighty Blackpool
2001	Mighty Blackpool
2002	*no championship*
2003	*no championship*

Togo

Fédération Togolaise de Football
Founded: 1960
Joined FIFA: 1962
Joined CAF: 1963

SEASON	LEAGUE CHAMPIONS
1998	*no competition*
1999	Semassi
2000	*not completed*
2001	Dynamic Togolais
2002	AS Douane

Nigeria

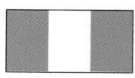

Nigeria Football Association
Founded: 1935
Joined FIFA: 1959
Joined CAF: 1959

NIGERIA

THE FIRST RECORDED SOCCER IN NIGERIA dates from 1904 when a team of Nigerian students from Hope Waddell Training Institute in Calabar beat a team from the British warship HMS Thistle 3-2. Initially however, most teams were made up of white colonial administrators and soldiers. But by 1919 mixed European and African teams, such as Diamonds FC from Lagos, were competing for the War Memorial Cup. In 1931, the Lagos and District Amateur FA was created, followed by a national Nigerian soccer association in 1935 and a national FA Cup in 1945.

The organization of Nigerian soccer was dominated almost exclusively by white Europeans, but on the field the best players were all Nigerian. In 1949, a Nigerian Select XI toured Britain and the first official Nigerian international match was played later that year against Sierra Leone. Membership of CAF and FIFA came in 1959, preceding independence from Britain by a year. For the first post-independence international, the national strip was changed and the Red Devils became the Green Eagles.

Biafran secession

Like everything else in Nigerian life, soccer was disrupted for the four years of the civil war (1967–70) and the secession of the state of Biafra. It was only in 1972 that a formal national league was created, won in its first year by the Mighty Jets from Jos. At the same time, from the ashes of Biafran independence, Enugu Rangers was founded, and politically and sportingly it has been the region's torchbearer. From its inception, Nigerian soccer has relied on public and private corporations to run soccer clubs; among the leading teams have been Lagos Railways (now defunct), Bendel Insurance and Stationery Stores. Other once-powerful sides, such as Leventis United and Abiola Babes, have disappeared since their rich benefactors pulled out. However, they have been replaced by Nigeria's new entrepreneurs and, increasingly, by state governments.

Nigerian soccer has proved increasingly successful on the international stage, with regular appearances at the World Cup, victories in the African Cup of Nations and a number of African club triumphs. However, problems with corruption, financial insecurity, the drain of talent to Europe and phenomenally dangerous stadiums have beset the game in recent years.

Stationery Stores from Lagos won the Nigerian Cup four times and the league title in 1992 before the company that sponsored it went out of business and the team folded.

Nigerian League Record 1972–2003

SEASON	CHAMPIONS	SEASON	CHAMPIONS
1972	Mighty Jets	1989	Iwuanyanwu Owerri
1973	Bendel Insurance	1990	Iwuanyanwu Owerri
1974	Rangers International	1991	Julius Berger
1975	Rangers International	1992	Stationery Stores
1976	Shooting Stars	1993	Iwuanyanwu Owerri
1977	Rangers International	1994	BCC Lions
1978	Racca Rovers	1995	Shooting Stars
1979	Bendel Insurance	1996	Udoji United
1980	Shooting Stars	1997	Eagle Cement
1981	Rangers International	1998	Shooting Stars
1982	Rangers International	1999	Lobi Stars
1983	Shooting Stars	2000	Julius Berger
1984	Rangers International	2001	Enyimba
1985	New Nigeria Bank	2002	Enyimba
1986	Leventis United	2003	Enyimba
1987	Iwuanyanwu Owerri		
1988	Iwuanyanwu Owerri		

Nigerian FA Challenge Cup 1945–2003

YEAR	WINNERS	YEAR	WINNERS
1945	Marine	1976	Rangers International
1946	Lagos Railways	1977	Shooting Stars
1947	Marine	1978	Bendel Insurance
1948	Lagos Railways	1979	Shooting Stars
1949	Lagos Railways	1980	Bendel Insurance
1950	GO Union	1981	Rangers International
1951	Lagos Railways	1982	Stationery Stores
1952	Lagos PAN Bank	1983	Rangers International
1953	Kano Pillars	1984	Leventis United
1954	Calabar Rovers	1985	Abiola Babes
1955	Port Harcourt	1986	Leventis United
1956	Lagos Railways	1987	Abiola Babes
1957	Lagos Railways	1988	Iwuanyanwu Owerri
1958	Port Harcourt	1989	BCC Lions
1959	Ibadan Lions	1990	Stationery Stores
1960	Lagos EDN	1991	El Kanemi Warriors
1961	Ibadan Lions	1992	El Kanemi Warriors
1962	Police	1993	BCC Lions
1963	Port Harcourt	1994	BCC Lions
1964	Lagos Railways	1995	Shooting Stars
1965	Lagos EDN	1996	Julius Berger
1966	Ibadan Lions	1997	BCC Lions
1967	Stationery Stores	1998	Wikki Tourists
1968	Stationery Stores	1999	Plateau United
1969	Ibadan Lions	2000	Niger Tornadoes
1970	Lagos EDN	2001	Dolphin FC
1971	Shooting Stars	2002	Julius Berger
1972	Bendel Insurance	2003	Lobi Stars
1973	*no winner*		
1974	Rangers International		
1975	Rangers International		

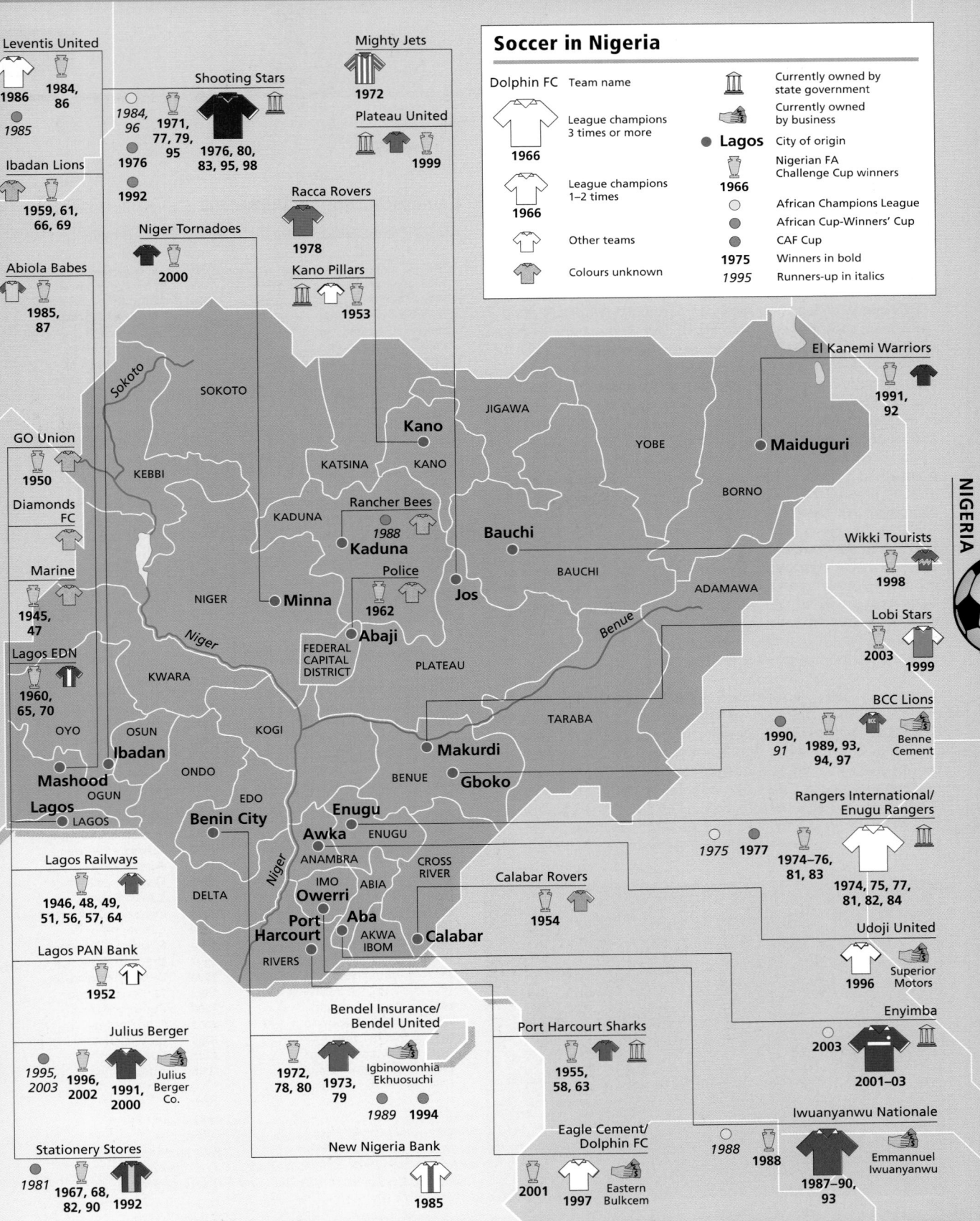

Leventis United
1986 · 1984, 86
1985

Shooting Stars
1984, 96 · 1971, 77, 79, 95 · 1976, 80, 83, 95, 98
1976
1992

Mighty Jets
1972

Plateau United
1999

Soccer in Nigeria

Dolphin FC — Team name
1966

League champions 3 times or more
1966

League champions 1–2 times
1966

Other teams

Colours unknown

Currently owned by state government

Currently owned by business

Lagos — City of origin

Nigerian FA Challenge Cup winners
1966

African Champions League

African Cup-Winners' Cup

CAF Cup

1975 Winners in bold

1995 Runners-up in italics

Ibadan Lions
1959, 61, 66, 69

Niger Tornadoes
2000

Racca Rovers
1978

Kano Pillars
1953

El Kanemi Warriors
1991, 92

Abiola Babes
1985, 87

GO Union
1950

Diamonds FC

Marine
1945, 47

Lagos EDN
1960, 65, 70

Rancher Bees
1988

Police
1962

Wikki Tourists
1998

Lobi Stars
2003 · 1999

BCC Lions
1990, 91 · 1989, 93, 94, 97 · Benne Cement

Mashood
Lagos

Rangers International/ Enugu Rangers
1975 · 1977 · 1974–76, 81, 83 · 1974, 75, 77, 81, 82, 84

Lagos Railways
1946, 48, 49, 51, 56, 57, 64

Udoji United
1996 · Superior Motors

Lagos PAN Bank
1952

Calabar Rovers
1954

Enyimba
2003 · 2001–03

Julius Berger
1995, 2003 · 1996, 2002 · 1991, 2000 · Julius Berger Co.

Bendel Insurance/ Bendel United
1972, 78, 80 · 1973, 79 · Igbinowonhia Ekhuosuchi
1989 · 1994

Port Harcourt Sharks
1955, 58, 63

Iwuanyanwu Nationale
1988 · 1988 · 1987–90, 93 · Emmannuel Iwuanyanwu

Stationery Stores
1981 · 1967, 68, 82, 90 · 1992

New Nigeria Bank
1985

Eagle Cement/ Dolphin FC
2001 · 1997 · Eastern Bulkcem

Map cities
Sokoto · SOKOTO · KEBBI · KATSINA · KADUNA · Kano · KANO · JIGAWA · YOBE · Maiduguri · BORNO · NIGER · Rancher Bees · Kaduna · Bauchi · BAUCHI · ADAMAWA · Minna · Police · Jos · FEDERAL CAPITAL DISTRICT · Abaji · PLATEAU · Benue · KWARA · OYO · OSUN · KOGI · TARABA · Ibadan · ONDO · BENUE · Makurdi · Gboko · OGUN · EDO · Benin City · Enugu · Awka · ANAMBRA · ENUGU · CROSS RIVER · Lagos · LAGOS · DELTA · Niger · IMO · ABIA · Owerri · Aba · AKWA IBOM · Calabar · Port Harcourt · RIVERS

Cameroon

Fédération Camerounaise de Football
Founded: 1960
Joined FIFA: 1962
Joined CAF: 1963

CAMEROON WAS ORIGINALLY created and colonized by the Germans, from 1884 onwards. However, soccer did not follow until the expulsion of the Germans in 1916 by the British and French, who then received successive League of Nations and UN mandates to run the country. In the 1920s soccer developed among Africans in the colonial education system, and in the 1930s and 40s clubs and local competitions were established.

Political, sporting and social life in Cameroon is dictated by a series of linguistic and cultural divisions. Around a quarter of the population lives in the former British zone in the north-west – anglophone Cameroon. Its team is unquestionably PWD (Public Works Department) from Bamenda. The club's president in the late 1980s and early 90s was Ni John Frundi, founder and leader of the main opposition party, the SDF, and challenger in the bitter 1992 presidential elections. Rumours and accusations of corruption and match-fixing against the club abound among the politically and demographically dominant French-speaking parts of Cameroon.

Province and ethnicity

The rest of the country is formally francophone but is itself divided by province and ethnicity. The Bamileke from western Cameroon are allied with Racing Club Bafoussam at home and with Union Sportive and Diamant Yaoundé as migrants in the big cities. The Bassa and Douala from the Littoral province are tied to Dynamo Douala and the Beti from Centre province are concentrated in and around Yaoundé, supporting Canon and Tonnerre. In 1967, legislation was passed to disband ethnically-orientated organizations of all kinds, but soccer was exempted after huge public protest. Despite this, the national team is a multi-ethnic affair and a significant source of national unity, but, as ever, only when things are going well. The fantastic performance of the Cameroon national team at the 1990 World Cup, the best performance by an African team up to that time, was certainly used by President Biya in his bitter but successful campaign to retain the presidency in 1992.

Cameroon League 1961–2003

SEASON	CHAMPIONS	SEASON	CHAMPIONS
1961	Oryx Douala	1984	Tonnerre Yaoundé
1962	Caiman Douala	1985	Canon Yaoundé
1963	Oryx Douala	1986	Canon Yaoundé
1964	Oryx Douala	1987	Tonnerre Yaoundé
1965	Oryx Douala	1988	Tonnerre Yaoundé
1966	Diamant Yaoundé	1989	Racing Club Bafoussam
1967	Oryx Douala	1990	Union Sportive
1968	Caiman Douala	1991	Canon Yaoundé
1969	Union Sportive	1992	Racing Club Bafoussam
1970	Canon Yaoundé	1993	Racing Club Bafoussam
1971	Aigle Royale Nkongsamba	1994	Aigle Royale Nkongsamba
1972	Léopards Douala	1995	Racing Club Bafoussam
1973	Léopards Douala	1996	Unisport
1974	Canon Yaoundé	1997	Cotonsport
1975	Caiman Douala	1998	Cotonsport
1976	Union Sportive	1999	Sable Batié
1977	Canon Yaoundé	2000	Fovu Baham
1978	Union Sportive	2001	Cotonsport
1979	Canon Yaoundé	2002	Canon Yaoundé
1980	Canon Yaoundé	2003	Cotonsport
1981	Tonnerre Yaoundé		
1982	Canon Yaoundé		
1983	Tonnerre Yaoundé		

Cameroon Cup 1956–2003

YEAR	WINNERS	YEAR	WINNERS
1956	Oryx Douala	1981	Dynamo Douala
1957	Canon Yaoundé	1982	Dragon Douala
1958	Tonnerre Yaoundé	1983	Canon Yaoundé
1959	Caiman Douala	1984	Dihep Nkam
1960	Lion Yaoundé	1985	Union Sportive
1961	Union Sportive	1986	Canon Yaoundé
1962	Lion Yaoundé	1987	Tonnerre Yaoundé
1963	Oryx Douala	1988	Panthère Sportive
1964	Diamant Yaoundé	1989	Tonnerre Yaoundé
1965	Lion Yaoundé	1990	Prévoyance Yaoundé
1966	Lion Yaoundé	1991	Tonnerre Yaoundé
1967	Canon Yaoundé	1992	Olympique Mvoylé
1968	Oryx Douala	1993	Canon Yaoundé
1969	Union Sportive	1994	Olympique Mvoylé
1970	Oryx Douala	1995	Canon Yaoundé
1971	Diamant Yaoundé	1996	Racing Club Bafoussam
1972	Diamant Yaoundé	1997	Union Sportive
1973	Canon Yaoundé	1998	Dynamo Douala
1974	Tonnerre Yaoundé	1999	Canon Yaoundé
1975	Canon Yaoundé	2000	Kumbo Strikers
1976	Canon Yaoundé	2001	Fovu Baham
1977	Canon Yaoundé	2002	Mount Cameroon
1978	Canon Yaoundé	2003	Cotonsport
1979	Dynamo Douala		
1980	Union Sportive		

After its strong showing at Italia '90, Cameroon, shown here in 1992, has established itself as the strongest national team in Africa. Despite a convincing victory in the 2002 African Nations Cup, its World Cup campaign later in the year saw a disappointing first-round exit.

CAMEROON

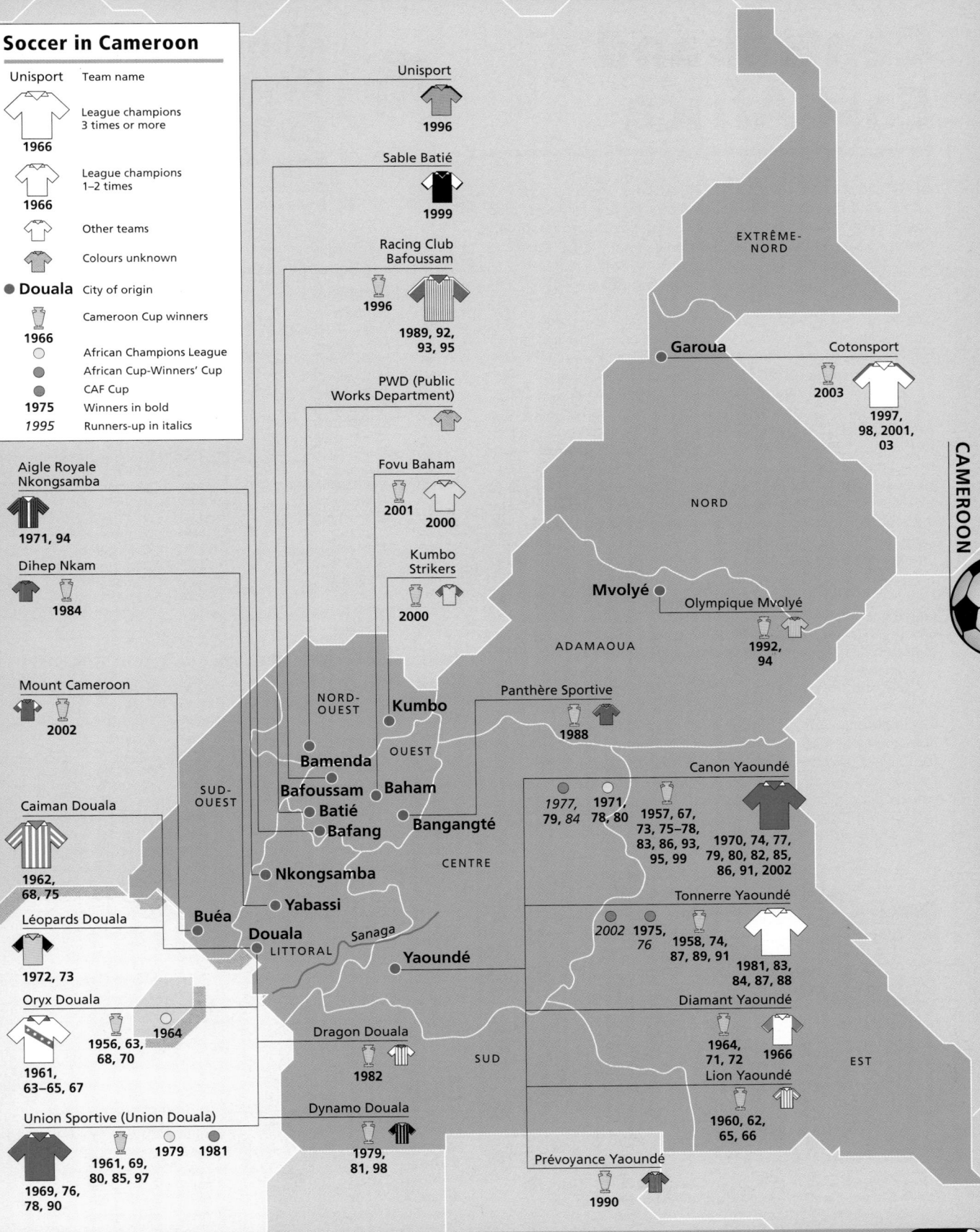

Soccer in Cameroon

Unisport	Team name
1966	League champions 3 times or more
1966	League champions 1–2 times
	Other teams
	Colours unknown
● **Douala**	City of origin
1966	Cameroon Cup winners
○	African Champions League
●	African Cup-Winners' Cup
●	CAF Cup
1975	Winners in bold
1995	Runners-up in italics

Unisport
1996

Sable Batié
1999

Racing Club Bafoussam
1996
1989, 92, 93, 95

PWD (Public Works Department)

Fovu Baham
2001
2000

Kumbo Strikers
2000

Aigle Royale Nkongsamba
1971, 94

Dihep Nkam
1984

Mount Cameroon
2002

Caiman Douala
1962, 68, 75

Léopards Douala
1972, 73

Oryx Douala
1956, 63, 68, 70   1964
1961, 63–65, 67

Union Sportive (Union Douala)
1961, 69, 80, 85, 97   1979   1981
1969, 76, 78, 90

Dragon Douala
1982

Dynamo Douala
1979, 81, 98

EXTRÊME-NORD

Garoua   Cotonsport
2003
1997, 98, 2001, 03

NORD

Mvolyé   Olympique Mvolyé
1992, 94

ADAMAOUA

Kumbo

NORD-OUEST

Bamenda

OUEST

Bafoussam   **Baham**
Batié
Bafang   **Bangangté**

Panthère Sportive
1988

Canon Yaoundé
1977, 79, 84   *1971, 78, 80*   **1957, 67, 73, 75–78, 83, 86, 93, 95, 99**   **1970, 74, 77, 79, 80, 82, 85, 86, 91, 2002**

Tonnerre Yaoundé
2002   *1975, 76*   **1958, 74, 87, 89, 91**   **1981, 83, 84, 87, 88**

Diamant Yaoundé
1964, 71, 72   1966

Lion Yaoundé
1960, 62, 65, 66

CENTRE

Nkongsamba

Yabassi

Buéa

Douala
LITTORAL

Sanaga

Yaoundé

SUD-OUEST

SUD

EST

Prévoyance Yaoundé
1990

CAMEROON

Central and East Africa

CENTRAL AND EAST AFRICA

ALTHOUGH EAST AND CENTRAL AFRICA are considered a single region by CAF, they are, in soccer-playing terms, worlds apart. Central Africa has produced African club and national champions as well as World Cup qualifying national teams. East Africa's trophy cabinet is, by contrast, rather bare.

Central Africa's three key soccer-playing nations are Cameroon (see pages 456-57), the Democratic Republic of Congo (or DRC, formerly known as Zaïre and the Belgian Congo) and Congo (formally known as Congo-Brazzaville and the French Congo). In the Belgian Congo, as it was then known, Africa's second oldest football association was established in the capital Léopoldville (now Kinshasa) in 1919, although a city league had been up and running since 1916. Zaïrian football's golden age lasted from independence in 1960 to the mid-1970s. The country's leading club, TP Englebert, won two and then lost two consecutive African Champions League Finals between 1967 and 1970, while the national side was the first sub-Saharan team to make it to the World Cup (1974). International matches were played between French and Belgian Congo from 1923 to 1950 in the Stanley Pool Championship (Stanley Pool is a lake that separates the capitals of the states).

Football first arrived in East Africa via British workers and colonists in Kenya, Uganda, Tanzania and Zanzibar. Kenya's oldest club, Mombassa FC, dates from 1906. The Gossage Cup, an international tournament between the four countries, was held between 1927 and 1972. Post-independence, national leagues were created. Kenya's Gor Mahia won the region's only African club championship – the Cup-Winners' Cup – in 1987, while two Ugandan teams have made it to the Final of the Champions League (Simba FC in 1972, and SC Villa in 1991). But otherwise, both at club and international level, the region's footballing record is weak. In Sudan, the 1930s saw the formation of leading Khartoum clubs Al Hilal and El Mourada. In Ethiopia a mixture of English and Italian influences introduced football during the 1930s, and a national league and football association accompanied independence in 1943.

SC Villa from Kampala (seen here in white) is one of Uganda's leading teams. Formerly known as Nakivubo Villa, the team has ten Ugandan league championships to its name.

Democratic Republic of Congo (formerly Zaïre)

Fédération Congolaise de Football-Association
Founded: 1919
Joined FIFA: 1962
Joined CAF: 1973

Democratic Republic of Congo League Record 1964–2003

SEASON	CHAMPIONS	SEASON	CHAMPIONS
1964	CS Imana	1985	US Tshinkunku
1965	Dragons	1986	FC Lupopo
1966	TP Englebert	1987	DC Motema Pembe
1967	TP Englebert	1988	AS Vita Club
1968	FC St. Eloi	1989	DC Motema Pembe
1969	TP Englebert	1990	FC Lupopo
1970	AS Vita Club	1991	Mikishi
1971	AS Vita Club	1992	US Bilombe
1972	AS Vita Club	1993	AS Vita Club
1973	AS Vita Club	1994	DC Motema Pembe
1974	CS Imana	1995	AS Bantous
1975	AS Vita Club	1996	*not known*
1976	TP Mazembe	1997	AS Vita Club
1977	AS Vita Club	1998	DC Motema Pembe
1978	CS Imana	1999	DC Motema Pembe
1979	AS Bilima	2000	TP Mazembe
1980	AS Vita Club	2001	TP Mazembe
1981	FC Lupopo	2002	FC Lupopo
1982	AS Bilima	2003	AS Vita Club
1983	Sanga Balende		
1984	AS Bilima		

Democratic Republic of Congo Cup Record 1964–2003

YEAR	WINNERS	YEAR	WINNERS
1964	DC Motema Pembe	1986	Kalamu
1965	AS Bilima	1987	Kalamu
1966	TP Mazembe	1988	Kalamu
1967	TP Mazembe	1989	Kalamu
1968	FC Lupopo	1990	DC Motema Pembe
1969–70	*no competition*	1991	DC Motema Pembe
1971	AS Vita Club	1992	US Bilombe
1972	AS Vita Club	1993	DC Motema Pembe
1973	AS Vita Club	1994	DC Motema Pembe
1974	DC Motema Pembe	1995	AC Sodigraf
1975	AS Vita Club	1996	AS Dragons
1976	TP Mazembe	1997	AS Dragons
1977	AS Vita Club	1998	AS Dragons
1978	DC Motema Pembe	1999	AS Dragons
1979	TP Mazembe	2000	TP Mazembe
1980	Lubumbashi Sport	2001	AS Vita Club
1981	AS Vita Club	2002	US Kenya
1982	AS Vita Club	2003	DC Motema Pembe
1983	AS Vita Club		
1984	DC Motema Pembe		
1985	DC Motema Pembe		

Burundi

Fédération de Football du Burundi
Founded: 1948
Joined FIFA: 1972
Joined CAF: 1972

SEASON	LEAGUE CHAMPIONS
1999	Vital'O FC
2000	Vital'O FC
2001	Prince Louis FC
2002	*suspended*
2003	*abandoned*

Central African Republic

Fédération Centrafricaine de Football
Founded: 1937
Joined FIFA: 1963
Joined CAF: 1965

SEASON	LEAGUE CHAMPIONS
1999	*cancelled*
2000	Olympique Réal
2001	Olympique Réal
2002	*abandoned*
2003	AS Tempête Mocat

Chad

Fédération Tchadienne de Football
Founded: 1962
Joined FIFA: 1988
Joined CAF: 1962

SEASON	LEAGUE CHAMPIONS
1998	AS Coton Chad
1999	Renaissance
2000	FC Tourbillon
2001	FC Tourbillon
2002	*unknown*

Congo

Fédération Congolaise de Football
Founded: 1962
Joined FIFA: 1962
Joined CAF: 1966

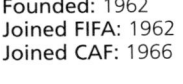

SEASON	LEAGUE CHAMPIONS
1999	Vita Club Mokanda
2000	Etoile du Congo
2001	Etoile du Congo
2002	AS Police
2003	Saint Michel de Ouenzé

Djibouti

Fédération Djiboutienne de Football
Founded: 1977
Joined FIFA: 1994
Joined CAF: 1986

SEASON	LEAGUE CHAMPIONS
2000	CDE
2001	Force Nationale de Police
2002	AS Boreh
2003	Gendarmerie Nationale
2004	Gendarmerie Nationale

Equatorial Guinea

Fédération Equatoguineana de Futboll
Founded: 1976
Joined FIFA: 1986
Joined CAF: 1986

SEASON	LEAGUE CHAMPIONS
1999	Akonangui FC
2000	CD Ela Nguema
2001	Akonangui FC
2002	CD Ela Nguema
2003	Atlético de Malabo

Eritrea

Eritrean National Football Federation
Founded: 1992
Joined FIFA: 1998
Joined CAF: 1994

SEASON	LEAGUE CHAMPIONS
1999	Red Sea FC
2000	Red Sea FC
2001	Hintsa
2002	Red Sea FC
2003	Anseba Sports Club

Ethiopia

Ye'Ityopiya Football Federechin
Founded: 1943
Joined FIFA: 1953
Joined CAF: 1957

SEASON	LEAGUE CHAMPIONS
2000	St. George
2001	Mebrat Hail
2002	St. George
2003	St. George
2004	Awassa Kenema

Gabon

Fédération Gabonaise de Football
Founded: 1962
Joined FIFA: 1963
Joined CAF: 1967

SEASON	LEAGUE CHAMPIONS
1999	FC 105
2000	Mangasport
2001	FC 105
2002	US Nzambi
2003	US Bitam

Kenya

Kenya Football Federation
Founded: 1932
Joined FIFA: 1960
Joined CAF: 1968

SEASON	LEAGUE CHAMPIONS
1999	Tusker FC
2000	Tusker FC
2001	Oserian Fastac
2002	Oserian Fastac
2003	Ulinzi Stars

Madagascar

Fédération Malagasy de Football
Founded: 1961
Joined FIFA: 1962
Joined CAF: 1963

SEASON	LEAGUE CHAMPIONS
1999	AS Fortior
2000	AS Fortior
2001	Stade Olympique de l'Emyrne
2002	AS Adema
2003	Ecoredipharm

Rwanda

Fédération Rwandaise de Football Amateur
Founded: 1972
Joined FIFA: 1976
Joined CAF: 1976

SEASON	LEAGUE CHAMPIONS
1999	FC APR
2000	FC APR
2001	FC APR
2002	Rayon Sports
2003	FC APR

São Tomé and Principe

Federação Santomense de Futebol
Founded: 1975
Joined FIFA: 1986
Joined CAF: 1986

SEASON	LEAGUE CHAMPIONS
1999	Sporting Praia Cruz
2000	Inter Bom-Bom
2001	Bairros Unidos FC
2002	*cancelled*
2003	Inter Bom-Bom

Somalia

Somalia Football Federation
Founded: 1951
Joined FIFA: 1960
Joined CAF: 1968

SEASON	LEAGUE CHAMPIONS
1999	*no championship*
2000	Elman FC
2001	Elman FC
2002	Elman FC
2003	Elman FC

Sudan

Sudan Football Association
Founded: 1936
Joined FIFA: 1948
Joined CAF: 1957

SEASON	LEAGUE CHAMPIONS
1999	Al Hilal
2000	Al Merreikh
2001	Al Merreikh
2002	Al Merreikh
2003	Al Hilal

Tanzania

Football Association of Tanzania
Founded: 1930
Joined FIFA: 1964
Joined CAF: 1960

SEASON	LEAGUE CHAMPIONS
1999	Prisons
2000	Young Africans
2001	Simba SC
2002	Simba SC
2003	*not awarded*

Uganda

Federation of Uganda Football Associations
Founded: 1924
Joined FIFA: 1959
Joined CAF: 1959

SEASON	LEAGUE CHAMPIONS
1999	SC Villa
2000	SC Villa
2001	SC Villa
2002	SC Villa
2003	SC Villa

Southern Africa

IN ECONOMICS, POLITICS and in soccer, South Africa (see pages 462-63) is the giant of Southern Africa and the rest of the region has long lived in its shadow. The apartheid regime led to South Africa's exclusion from FIFA, CAF and global soccer in general until 1994, but throughout those years of exclusion, soccer retained a strong foothold in the country. So much so that the constant drain of players to their rich neighbour has limited the development of soccer in nearby Lesotho and Swaziland, while civil war has disrupted the game in Zimbabwe, Angola and Mozambique.

Railway workers

The most stable soccer-playing nation in the region, Zambia, acquired a colonial FA in 1929 in the Northern Rhodesian FA. A national league and cup competition was set up following independence in 1962. In 1991, Zambian giants Power Dynamos won the Cup-Winners' Cup, the nation's only African championship victory. Like Zambia, soccer reached Zimbabwe with the arrival of British railway workers in the late 19th century, and a national league and cup were operating by the early 1960s. A Rhodesian FA was set up by Ian Smith's government in the wake of the declaration of independence in 1965, but was suspended by FIFA in 1970. The achievement of black majority rule in 1980 saw Zimbabwe's re-admission to FIFA, and a professional national league began in 1992.

Race politics also shamed soccer in Malawi. Before independence in 1966, a Nyasaland African FA (for black teams) and a Nyasaland FA (for white teams) ensured racially segregated soccer was played throughout the country.

Portuguese influence brought soccer to both Angola and Mozambique and in the shape of Mozambique's Eusebio created Africa's first global soccer-playing star during the 1960s. But a chaotic process of Portuguese decolonization during 1975, as well as civil war, has left the region's societies and footballing cultures alike weak and disorganized.

Zimbabwean champions Dynamos, from Harare, took on ASEC Abidjan from Côte d'Ivoire in the 1998 African Champions League Final but lost 4-2 in the second leg after a 0-0 draw in the first leg.

Zimbabwe

Zimbabwe Football Association
Founded: 1950
Joined FIFA: 1965–70, 1980
Joined CAF: 1980

Zimbabwean League Record 1962–2003

SEASON	CHAMPIONS	SEASON	CHAMPIONS
1962	Bulawayo Rovers	1984	Black Rhinos
1963	Dynamos	1985	Dynamos
1964	St. Pauls	1986	Dynamos
1965	Dynamos	1987	Black Rhinos
1966	St. Pauls	1988	Zimbabwe Saints
1967	Tornados	1989	Dynamos
1968	Sables	1990	Highlanders
1969	Sables	1991	Dynamos
1970	Dynamos	1992	Black Aces
1971	Arcadia United	1993	Zimbabwe Highlanders
1972	Sables	1994	Dynamos
1973	Metal Box	1995	Dynamos
1974	Sables	1996	CAPS United
1975	Chibuku	1997	Dynamos
1976	Dynamos	1998	no championship
1977	Zimbabwe Saints	1999	Zimbabwe Highlanders
1978	Dynamos	2000	Zimbabwe Highlanders
1979	CAPS United	2001	Zimbabwe Highlanders
1980	Dynamos	2002	Zimbabwe Highlanders
1981	Dynamos	2003	AmaZulu
1982	Dynamos		
1983	Dynamos		

Zimbabwean Cup Record 1962–2003

YEAR	WINNERS	YEAR	WINNERS
1962	Bulawayo Rovers	1984	Black Rhinos
1963	Salisbury Callies	1985	Dynamos
1964	no competition	1986	Highlanders
1965	Salisbury City Wanderers	1987	Zimbabwe Saints
		1988	Dynamos
1966	Mangula	1989	Dynamos
1967	Salisbury Callies	1990	Highlanders
1968	Arcadia United	1991	Wankie FC
1969	Arcadia United	1992	CAPS United
1970	Wankie	1993	Tanganda
1971	Chibuku	1994	Blackpool
1972	Mangula	1995	Chapungu
1973	Wankie	1996	Dynamos
1974	Chibuku	1997	CAPS United
1975	Salisbury Callies	1998	CAPS United
1976	Dynamos	1999	unknown
1977	Zimbabwe Saints	2000	Dynamos
1978	Zisco Steel	2001	Zimbabwe Highlanders
1979	Zimbabwe Saints	2002	Masvingo United
1980	CAPS United	2003	Dynamos
1981	CAPS United		
1982	CAPS United		
1983	CAPS United		

Angola

Federação Angolana de Futebol
Founded: 1977
Joined FIFA: 1980
Joined CAF: 1980

SEASON	LEAGUE CHAMPIONS
1999	Primeiro de Agosto
2000	Petro Atlético
2001	Petro Atlético
2002	Atlético Sport Aviação
2003	Atlético Sport Aviação

Angola (continued)

YEAR	CUP WINNERS
1999	Sagrada Esperança
2000	Petro Atlético
2001	Sonangol
2002	Petro Atlético
2003	Inter Club Luanda

Botswana

Botswana Football Association
Founded: 1970
Joined FIFA: 1976
Joined CAF: 1976

SEASON	LEAGUE CHAMPIONS
2000	Mogoditshane Fighters
2001	Mogoditshane Fighters
2002	Botswana Defence Force
2003	Mogoditshane Fighters
2004	Botswana Defence Force

YEAR	CUP WINNERS
1999	Mogoditshane Fighters
2000	Mogoditshane Fighters
2001	TASC
2002	Tafic GF
2003	Mogoditshane Fighters

Lesotho

Lesotho Sports Council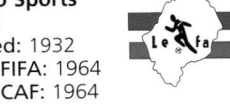
Founded: 1932
Joined FIFA: 1964
Joined CAF: 1964

SEASON	LEAGUE CHAMPIONS
1999	RL Defence Force
2000	Lesotho Prison Service
2001	RL Defence Force
2002	Lesotho Prison Service
2003	Matlama FC

YEAR	CUP WINNERS
1998	Arsenal
1999	*not known*
2000	RL Defence Force
2001	*not known*
2002	*not known*

Malawi

Football Association of Malawi
Founded: 1966
Joined FIFA: 1967
Joined CAF: 1968

Malawi (continued)

SEASON	LEAGUE CHAMPIONS
1999	Bata Bullets
2000	Bata Bullets
2001	Total Big Bullets
2002	Total Big Bullets
2003	Bakili Bullets

Mauritius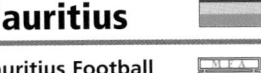

Mauritius Football Association
Founded: 1952
Joined FIFA: 1962
Joined CAF: 1962

SEASON	LEAGUE CHAMPIONS
2000	*no championship*
2001	Olympique de Moka
2002	AS Port-Louis 2000
2003	AS Port-Louis 2000
2004	AS Port-Louis 2000

YEAR	CUP WINNERS
2000	*abandoned*
2001	USBBRH
2002	AS Port-Louis 2000
2003	Savanne SC
2004	Savanne SC

Mozambique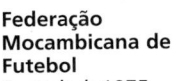

Federação Mocambicana de Futebol
Founded: 1975
Joined FIFA: 1978
Joined CAF: 1978

SEASON	LEAGUE CHAMPIONS
1999	Ferroviário Maputo
2000	Costa do Sol
2001	Costa do Sol
2002	Ferroviário Maputo
2003	Maxaquene

YEAR	CUP WINNERS
1999	Costa do Sol
2000	Costa do Sol
2001	Maxaquene
2002	Costa do Sol
2003	Ferroviário Nampula

Namibia

Namibia Football Association
Founded: 1992
Joined FIFA: 1992
Joined CAF: 1990

Namibia (continued)

SEASON	LEAGUE CHAMPIONS
1999	Black Africans Nashua
2000	Blue Waters
2001	*league format change*
2002	Liverpool
2003	Chief Santos

YEAR	CUP WINNERS
2000	Chief Santos
2001	*format change*
2002	Orlando Pirates
2003	Civics FC
2004	Black Africa

Seychelles

Seychelles Football Association
Founded: 1976
Joined FIFA: 1986
Joined CAF: 1986

SEASON	LEAGUE CHAMPIONS
1999	St. Michel United
2000	St. Michel United
2001	Red Star
2002	La Passe FC & St. Michel United (shared)
2003	St. Michel United

YEAR	CUP WINNERS
1999	Red Star
2000	Sunshine SC
2001	St. Michel United
2002	Anse Réunion
2003	St. Louis

The Zambian team which beat Mauritius 3-0 in Port Louis in a Nations Cup match on 25 April 1993. Two days later, en route to Senegal for a World Cup qualifier, the whole team was killed when their plane crashed off the coast of Gabon.

Swaziland

National Football Association of Swaziland
Founded: 1964
Joined FIFA: 1976
Joined CAF: 1976

SEASON	LEAGUE CHAMPIONS
2000	Mbabane Highlanders
2001	Mbabane Highlanders
2002	Manzini Wanderers
2003	Manzini Wanderers
2004	Mhlambanyatsi Rovers

YEAR	CUP WINNERS
2000	Mhlume United
2001	Eleven Men in Flight
2002	*abandoned*
2003	*unknown*
2004	Green Mamba

Zambia

Football Association of Zambia
Founded: 1929
Joined FIFA: 1964
Joined CAF: 1964

SEASON	LEAGUE CHAMPIONS
1999	Nkana FC
2000	Power Dynamos
2001	Nkana FC
2002	Zanaco
2003	Zanaco

YEAR	CUP WINNERS
1999	Zamsure
2000	Nkana FC
2001	Power Dynamos
2002	Zanaco
2003	Power Dynamos

South Africa

SOUTH AFRICAN
FOOTBALL ASSOCIATION

South African Football Association
Founded: 1892, 1991
Joined FIFA: 1952–76, 1992
Joined CAF: 1957–64, 1992

THE HISTORY OF SOCCER in South Africa is inevitably tied to the politics of race in the country. The first recorded game in South Africa took place in Natal in 1866 and the province also produced the first club – the white Pietermaritzburg Country – founded in 1879. Three further white clubs were quickly formed – Natal Wasps, Durban Alphas and Umgeni Stars – and in 1882 they formed the Natal FA. In 1891, a Cape Town FA was formed by four British military clubs, and a national organization, FASA (Football Association of South Africa), was formed in 1892. Western province joined in 1896 and Transvaal in 1899.

For all these organizational changes, soccer was always secondary to rugby in the affections of white South Africans, but among the black population, soccer was always the dominant sport. In 1898, the first black club – Orange Free State Bantu FC – was founded, and an Orange Free State FA was set up in 1930 in Bloemfontein, the centre of African national politics; a Natal Bantu FA followed in 1931. All of these associations provided a crucial training ground for black administrators and politicians, including the ANC leader Albert Luthili. However, the sporting heart of black soccer was

Johannesburg and the mining towns of the Rand where the Transvaal Pirates, Swallows and Evergreen Mighty Greens flourished. Subsequently, the region has provided the other dominant forces in South African soccer – the Orlando Pirates, Mamelodi Sundowns and Kaizer Chiefs.

With the imposition of strict apartheid in 1948, the racial and political divide in soccer solidified. The SASF was formed in 1952 representing African and coloured soccer and it formally declared itself a non-racial organization in 1963. The older FASA remained resolutely white and was eventually expelled from CAF and FIFA for refusing to field mixed-race international sides. Domestically, a whites-only national professional league (the NPFL) ran from 1959, while the black NPSL was formed in 1971. The two effectively merged in 1978, the economics of township crowds weighing more heavily than the politics of racial separation. During the state of emergency in the 1980s, soccer matches and grounds provided a location for political rallies of all kinds and the ANC celebrated the release of political prisoners in 1989 and 1990 at the FNB Stadium in Johannesburg. In 1992, South Africa was readmitted to FIFA and CAF.

The Kaizer Chiefs from Johannesburg (in white) and the Mamelodi Sundowns from Pretoria are among the top teams in a strong South African soccer league.

South African League and Cup Winners 1971–2004

YEAR	LEAGUE CHAMPIONS (NPSL till 1984 then NSL)	CUP WINNERS	TOP EIGHT CUP WINNERS (NPSL till 1984 then NSL)
1971	Orlando Pirates	Kaizer Chiefs	
1972	Amazulu	Kaizer Chiefs	Orlando Pirates
1973	Orlando Pirates	Orlando Pirates	Orlando Pirates
1974	Kaizer Chiefs	Orlando Pirates	Kaizer Chiefs
1975	Orlando Pirates	Orlando Pirates	Moroka Swallows
1976	Orlando Pirates	Kaizer Chiefs	Kaizer Chiefs
1977	Kaizer Chiefs	Orlando Pirates	Kaizer Chiefs
1978	Lusitano Club	Wits University	Orlando Pirates
1979	Kaizer Chiefs	Kaizer Chiefs	Moroka Swallows
1980	Highlands Park	Orlando Pirates	Witbank Black Aces
1981	Kaizer Chiefs	Kaizer Chiefs	Kaizer Chiefs
1982	Durban City	Kaizer Chiefs	Kaizer Chiefs
1983	Durban City	Moroka Swallows	Orlando Pirates
1984	Kaizer Chiefs	Kaizer Chiefs	Wits University
1985	Bush Bucks	Bloemfontein Celtic	Kaizer Chiefs
1986	Rangers FC	Mamelodi United	Arcadia
1987	Jomo Cosmos	Kaizer Chiefs	Kaizer Chiefs
1988	Mamelodi United	Orlando Pirates	Mamelodi United
1989	Kaizer Chiefs	Moroka Swallows	Kaizer Chiefs
1990	Mamelodi United	Jomo Cosmos	Mamelodi United
1991	Kaizer Chiefs	Moroka Swallows	Kaizer Chiefs
1992	Kaizer Chiefs	Kaizer Chiefs	Kaizer Chiefs
1993	Mamelodi United	Witbank Aces	Orlando Pirates
1994	Orlando Pirates	Vaal Professionals	Kaizer Chiefs
1995	Cape Town Spurs	Cape Town Spurs	Wits University
1996	Kaizer Chiefs	Orlando Pirates	Orlando Pirates
1997	Manning Rangers	*no competition*	*no competition*
1998	Mamelodi Sundowns	Mamelodi Sundowns	*no competition*
1999	Mamelodi Sundowns	Supersport United	*no competition*
2000	Mamelodi Sundowns	Kaizer Chiefs	Orlando Pirates
2001	Orlando Pirates	Santos	Kaizer Chiefs
2002	Santos	*no competition*	Santos
2003	Orlando Pirates	Santos	*competition discontinued*
2004	Kaizer Chiefs	Moroka Swallows	

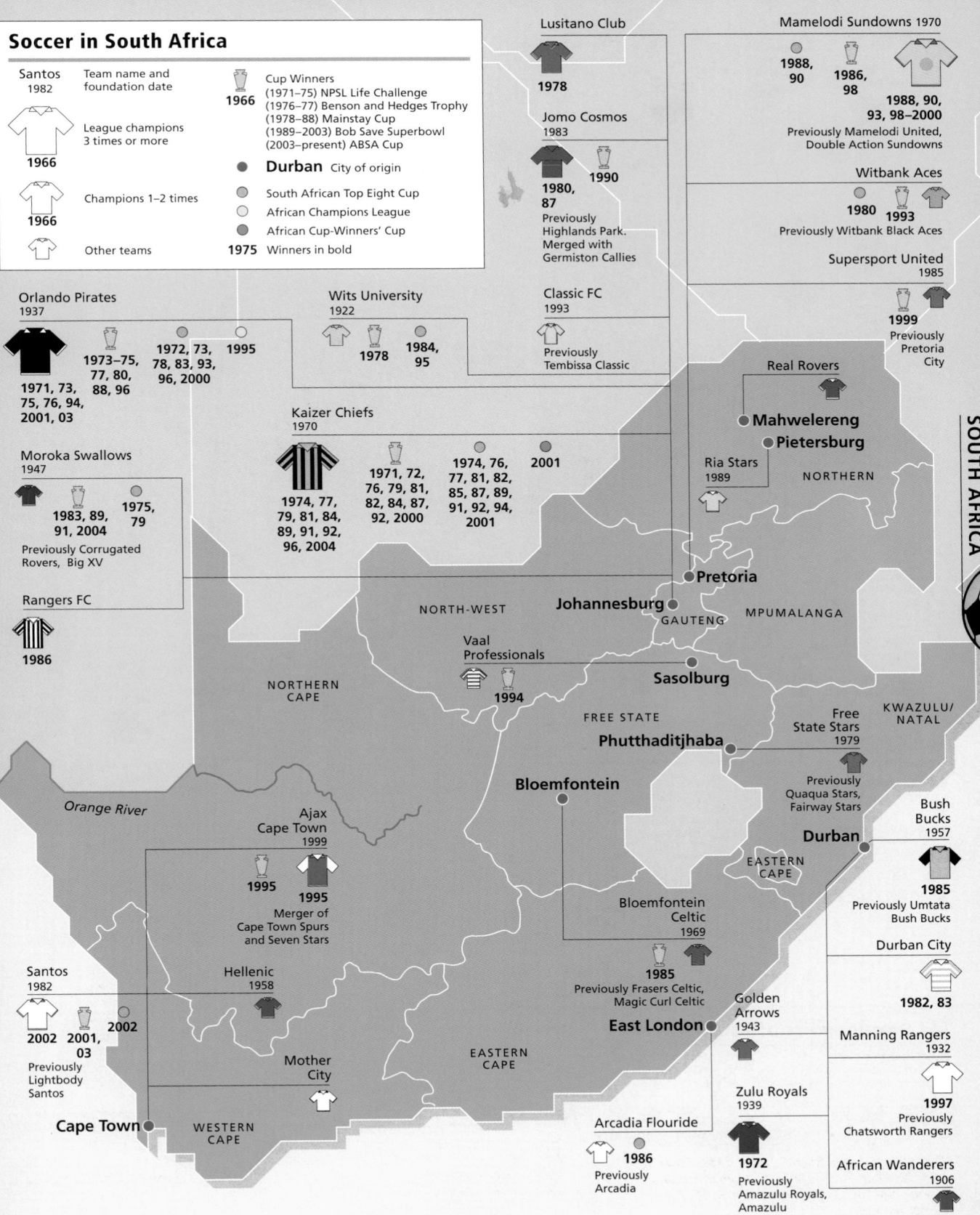

Soccer in South Africa

Santos
1982 — Team name and foundation date

1966 — Cup Winners
(1971–75) NPSL Life Challenge
(1976–77) Benson and Hedges Trophy
(1978–88) Mainstay Cup
(1989–2003) Bob Save Superbowl
(2003–present) ABSA Cup

1966 — League champions 3 times or more

1966 — Champions 1–2 times

— Other teams

Durban City of origin

South African Top Eight Cup

African Champions League

African Cup-Winners' Cup

1975 — Winners in bold

Lusitano Club
1978

Jomo Cosmos
1983
1990
1980, 87
Previously Highlands Park. Merged with Germiston Callies

Mamelodi Sundowns 1970
1988, 90
1986, 98
1988, 90, 93, 98–2000
Previously Mamelodi United, Double Action Sundowns

Witbank Aces
1980 1993
Previously Witbank Black Aces

Supersport United
1985
1999
Previously Pretoria City

Orlando Pirates
1937
1973–75, 77, 80, 88, 96
1971, 73, 75, 76, 94, 2001, 03
1972, 73, 78, 83, 93, 96, 2000
1995

Wits University
1922
1978
1984, 95

Classic FC
1993
Previously Tembisa Classic

Kaizer Chiefs
1970
1971, 72, 76, 79, 81, 82, 84, 87, 92, 2000
1974, 77, 79, 81, 84, 89, 91, 92, 96, 2004
1974, 76, 77, 81, 82, 85, 87, 89, 91, 92, 94, 2001
2001

Real Rovers
Mahwelereng
Pietersburg

Ria Stars
1989

NORTHERN

Moroka Swallows
1947
1983, 89, 91, 2004
1975, 79
Previously Corrugated Rovers, Big XV

Rangers FC
1986

Pretoria

NORTH-WEST
Johannesburg
GAUTENG
MPUMALANGA

Vaal Professionals
1994

Sasolburg

NORTHERN CAPE

FREE STATE

Phutthaditjhaba

Free State Stars
1979
Previously Quaqua Stars, Fairway Stars

KWAZULU/ NATAL

Orange River

Bloemfontein

Ajax Cape Town
1999
1995
1995
Merger of Cape Town Spurs and Seven Stars

EASTERN CAPE

Bush Bucks
1957
1985
Previously Umtata Bush Bucks

Durban

Durban City
1982, 83

Bloemfontein Celtic
1969
1985
Previously Frasers Celtic, Magic Curl Celtic

Santos
1982
2002 2001, 03
Previously Lightbody Santos

Hellenic
1958
2002

Manning Rangers
1932

Golden Arrows
1943

East London

Mother City

EASTERN CAPE

Zulu Royals
1939

Cape Town
WESTERN CAPE

Arcadia Flouride
1986
Previously Arcadia

1972
Previously Amazulu Royals, Amazulu

1997
Previously Chatsworth Rangers

African Wanderers
1906

SOUTH AFRICA

463

THE AFC NATIONS

LEBANON
Fédération
Libanaise
de Football
Association
1964 (1935)

KUWAIT
Kuwait
Football
Association
1962 (1962)

1982

1976,
80

BAHRAIN
Bahrain Football
Association
1970 (1966)

KAZAKHSTAN
Football Union
of Kazakhstan
1994* (1994)

*As of 2002
joined UEFA

KYRGYZSTAN
Federation of
Kyrgyz Republic
1994 (1994)

MONGOLIA
Mongolian
Football
Federation
1998 (1998)

ISRAEL
Israel Football
Association
1956–75 (1928)
Joined UEFA
in 1992

1970

1956,
60, **64**
68

SYRIA
Association
Arabe Syrienne
de Football
1969 (1937)

TURKMENISTAN
Football Federation
of Turkmenistan
1994 (1994)

UZBEKISTAN
Uzbekistan
Football Federation
1994 (1994)

TAJIKISTAN
Tajikistan
National Football
Federation
1994 (1994)

CHINA
Chinese Football
Association
1974 (1931–58, 1979)

2002

1984

IRAQ
Iraq
Football
Association
1971 (1950)

IRAN
Football Federation
of the Islamic
Republic of Iran
1958 (1945)

AFGHANISTAN
The Football Federation
of Afghanistan
1954 (1948)

BHUTAN
Bhutan
Football
Federation
1993 (2000)

LAOS
Fédération
Lao de
Football
1980 (1952)

JORDAN
Jordan
Football
Association
1970 (1958)

1986

1978, 98
1968,
72, 76

PAKISTAN
Pakistan
Football
Federation
1954 (1948)

NEPAL
All Nepal
Football
Association
1971 (1970)

MYANMAR
Myanmar
Football
Federation
1954 (1957)

PALESTINE
Palestinian
Football
Federation
1998 (1998)

SAUDI ARABIA
Saudi Arabian
Football Federation
1972 (1959)

1994, 98,
2002
1984, 88,
92, 96,
2000

UAE
United Arab
Emirates
Football
Association
1974 (1972)

INDIA
All India
Football
Federation
1954 (1948)

1964

BANGLADESH
Bangladesh
Football
Federation
1974 (1974)

THAILAND
Football
Association
of Thailand
1957 (1925)

R E D
S E A

OMAN
Oman
Football
Association
1979 (1980)

1990

1996

QATAR
Qatar Football
Association
1972 (1970)

YEMEN
Yemen Football
Association
North 1980 (1980)
South 1967 (1967)

Kuala Lumpur
AFC
Headquarters

MALAYSIA
Persatuan
Bolasepak Malaysia
1958 (1956)

SINGAPORE
Football
Association
of Singapore
1954 (1952)

MALDIVES
Football
Association
of the Maldives
1986 (1986)

**SRI
LANKA**
Football
Federation
of Sri Lanka
1958 (1950)

I N D I A N
O C E A N

The AFC Nations

**Date of affiliation
to AFC**

Founder member

1955–69

1970–89

1990–present

COUNTRY

Date of
affiliation
to AFC — **1916** (1912) — Date of
affiliation
to FIFA

Name of
Football
Association

Team
colours

World Cup — 1980 — Participants
in roman

Asian Cup — 1990 — Winners
in bold

2000 — Runners-up
in italic

The Development of Asian Soccer

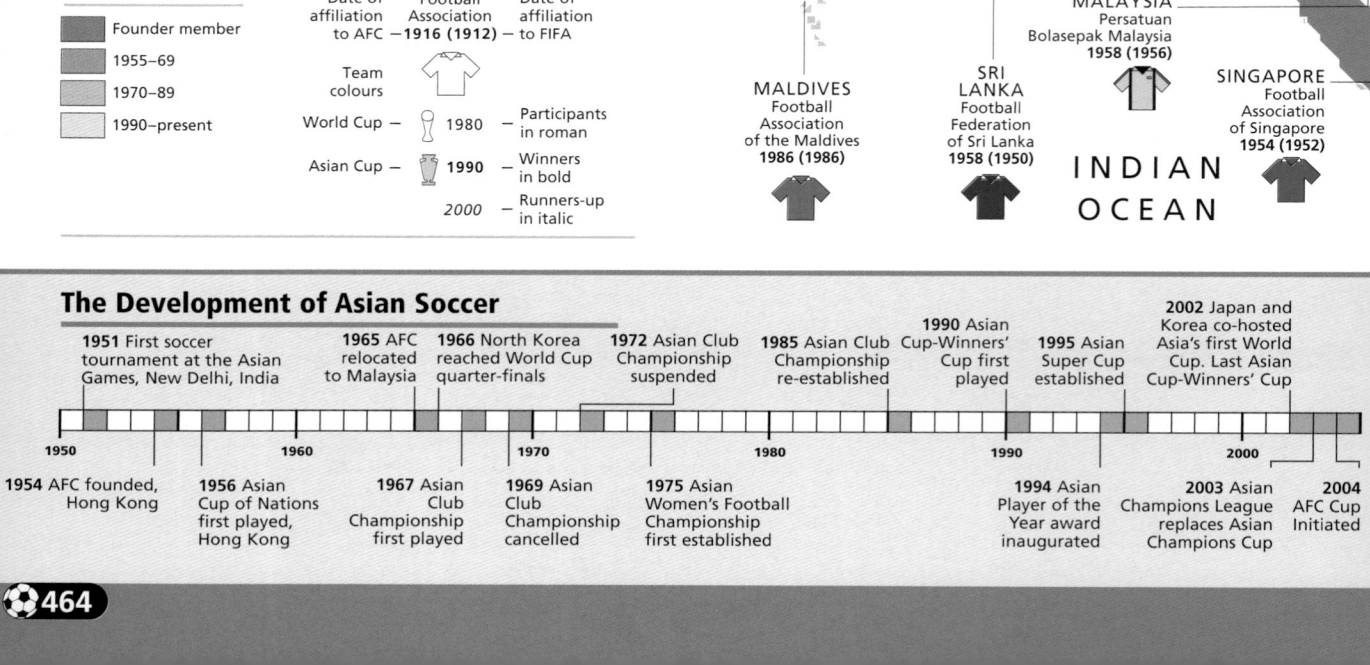

1951 First soccer
tournament at the Asian
Games, New Delhi, India

1965 AFC
relocated
to Malaysia

1966 North Korea
reached World Cup
quarter-finals

1972 Asian Club
Championship
suspended

1985 Asian Club
Championship
re-established

1990 Asian
Cup-Winners'
Cup first
played

1995 Asian
Super Cup
established

2002 Japan and
Korea co-hosted
Asia's first World
Cup. Last Asian
Cup-Winners' Cup

1950   1960   1970   1980   1990   2000   2004

1954 AFC founded,
Hong Kong

1956 Asian
Cup of Nations
first played,
Hong Kong

1967 Asian
Club
Championship
first played

1969 Asian
Club
Championship
cancelled

1975 Asian
Women's Football
Championship
first established

1994 Asian
Player of the
Year award
inaugurated

2003 Asian
Champions League
replaces Asian
Champions Cup

2004
AFC Cup
Initiated

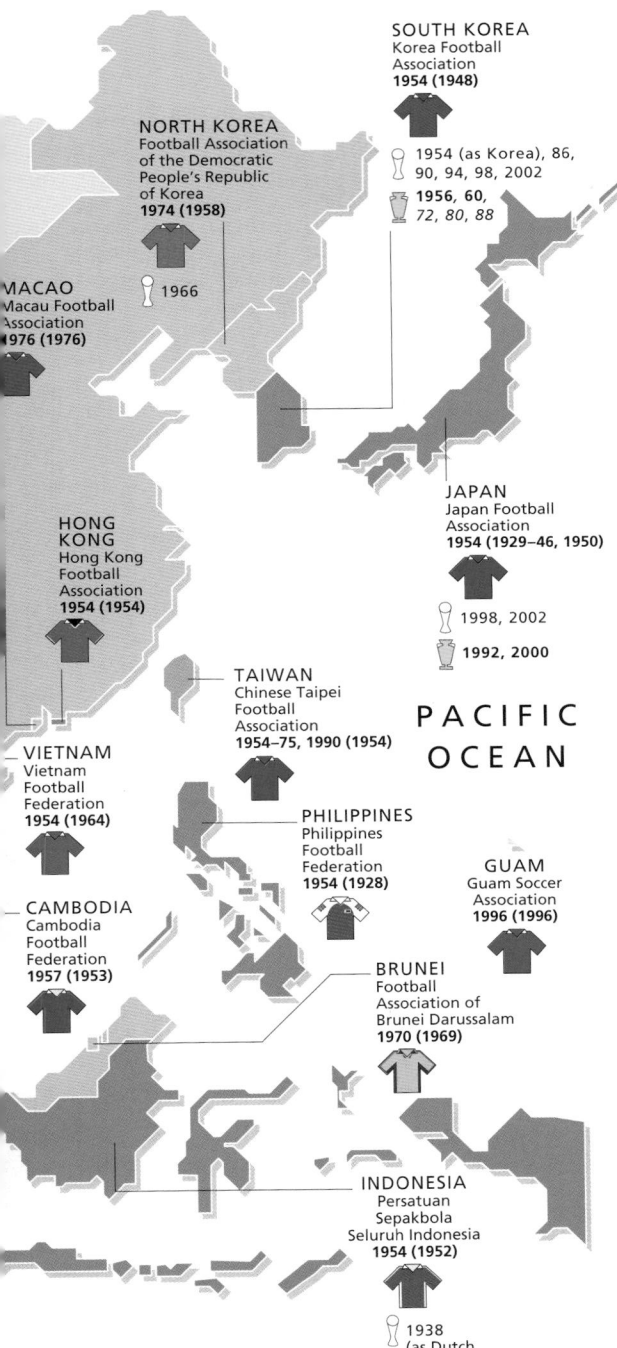

SOUTH KOREA
Korea Football
Association
1954 (1948)

1954 (as Korea), 86,
90, 94, 98, 2002

1956, 60,
72, 80, 88

NORTH KOREA
Football Association
of the Democratic
People's Republic
of Korea
1974 (1958)

1966

MACAO
Macau Football
Association
1976 (1976)

HONG KONG
Hong Kong
Football
Association
1954 (1954)

JAPAN
Japan Football
Association
1954 (1929–46, 1950)

1998, 2002

1992, 2000

TAIWAN
Chinese Taipei
Football
Association
1954–75, 1990 (1954)

PACIFIC OCEAN

VIETNAM
Vietnam
Football
Federation
1954 (1964)

PHILIPPINES
Philippines
Football
Federation
1954 (1928)

GUAM
Guam Soccer
Association
1996 (1996)

CAMBODIA
Cambodia
Football
Federation
1957 (1953)

BRUNEI
Football
Association of
Brunei Darussalam
1970 (1969)

INDONESIA
Persatuan
Sepakbola
Seluruh Indonesia
1954 (1952)

1938
(as Dutch
East Indies)

AFC

**Asian Tournaments
and Cup Competitions:**
Asian Cup
Asian Games
Asian Champions League
AFC Cup
Asian Women's Championship

AFC
Asian Football Confederation

The AFC Nations

THE AFC (ASIAN FOOTBALL CONFEDERATION) is the ruling FIFA affiliated body for Asian soccer. Prior to the AFC's formation international soccer was played at the 1951 and 1954 Asian Games. The Manila Games of 1954 provided the opportunity for representatives of Asian soccer to form the AFC, based in Hong Kong until relocating to Malaysia in 1965. The AFC's Asian Cup, open to professionals and amateurs, has superseded the Asian Games as the continent's premier international tournament.

The enormous size and diversity of Asia has presented organizational dilemmas. International tournaments involve vast travelling distances for often poor clubs and leagues, and most competitions have used regionally-based qualifying rounds. Travel aside, the AFC (which included Israel and Taiwan among its members) has been beset by international politics. Indonesia refused travel visas for both nations' teams at the 1962 Asian Games and pressure continued over the next decade for both nations to be expelled. China protested Taiwan's presence and Middle Eastern nations objected to Israel. At the 1974 Asian Games North Korea and Iran refused to play Israel; two years later Israel and Taiwan were expelled. In the 1990s AFC has been busy with the modernization and commercialization of Asian soccer and the promotion of its international club tournaments.

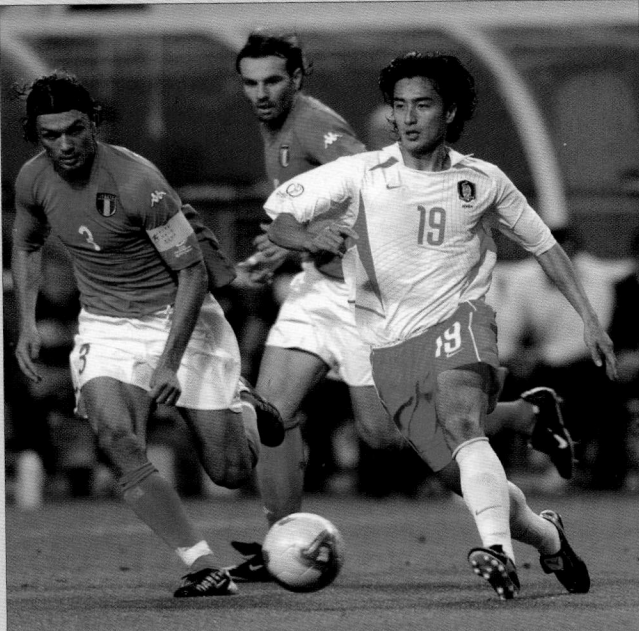

The future of Asian soccer: Ahn Jung-hwan's goal against Italy in the 2002 World Cup was one of the highpoints of the tournament. South Korea's fourth-place finish was the best ever by an Asian team.

Calendar of Events	
Club Tournaments	Asian Champions League 2005 AFC Cup 2005
International Tournaments	Qualifying Tournament for 2006 World Cup

Asia

THE SEASONS IN REVIEW 2003, 2003–04

THIS YEAR SAW THE 50TH ANNIVERSARY OF the Asian Football Confederation founded in Kuala Lumpur in 1954. Peter Velappan, the confederation's general secretary, has been arguing that Asia's time has come. The success of the 2002 World Cup in Japan and Korea has established Asia's global soccer profile. Now its growth will draw on the continent's enormous population, its increasing wealth and the sheer rise in numbers of young people. The AFC's Vision Asia programme of soccer modernisation is to be the instrument of change – supporting domestic soccer and creating new competitions, and the 2004 Asian Cup to be held in China should further boost the game in the world's biggest market.

Immense task, considerable obstacles

However, the task remains immense and the obstacles considerable. The 2003 Asian Champions League was delayed for four months by the SARS epidemic in China. When the all clear was given, UAE's Al Ain took a 4-2 lead in its semi-final with Dalian Shide to China, where it lost 3-4, winning on aggregate by a single goal. This meant that none of the biggest East Asian countries with their lucrative television markets were represented in the final where Al Ain met the Thai team BEC Tero Sasana. Al Ain took a two-goal lead to Thailand where it lost 1-0, although not without the help of some questionable refereeing and a clear late penalty appeal from BEC. In addition, the sheer enormity and variety of Asia means that the Asian Champions League must compete with popular regional champion's leagues in the Far East and Middle East.

In Qatar the weakness of domestic soccer due to its tiny population has been addressed by the state attempting to purchase players' allegiances and citizenship. Alongside a massive influx of aging European stars (like Gabriel Batistuta and Frank Le Boeuf) into Qatari soccer, the government was on the verge of making Brazilians Ailton (Werder Bremen), Leandro and Dede (Borussia Dortmund) Qataris until FIFA intervened to ban the practice. At the other end of the money and stability scale, soccer in Iraq has managed to continue throughout the US-UK occupation and the national team has been able to compete in qualifying competitions too. Peace, however, did not break out everywhere. In a group match in the Champions League in 2004, a game between Al Qadisiya from Kuwait and Al Sadd from Kuwait descended into a brawl on the final whistle. Players and officials traded punches and 24 people have been banned from participating in the event by the AFC.

Persik Kediri (in purple) took the Indonesian championship by five clear points. However, the team faltered in the Asian Champions League in a big way, losing 15-0 against Korean champions Seongnam Ilhwa Chunma in a Group Stage match.

Top 16 Asian Leagues

COUNTRY	CHAMPIONS	RUNNERS-UP	CUP WINNERS
China*	Shanghai Shenhua	Shanghai Imternational	Beijing Hyundai Cars
India	East Bengal Club	Dempo Sports Club	Salgaocar SC
Indonesia*	Persik Kediri	PSM Makassar	no cup
Iran	Paas	Esteghlal	Zob-Ahan*
Japan*	Yokohama F. Marinos	Jubilo Iwata	Jubilo Iwata
Malaysia*	Perak	Kedah	Selangor
Oman	Al Nasr	Muscat	Rowi*
Qatar	Al Sadd	Qatar SC	Khor
Saudi Arabia	Al Shabab	Al Ittihad	Al Ittihad
Singapore*	Home United	Geylang United	Home United
South Korea*	Seongnam Ilhwa Chunma	Ulsan Hyundai Horang-I	Chonbuk Hyundai Motors
Syria*	Al-Jaish	Al Ittihad	no cup
Thailand	Krung Thai Bank	Port Authority of Thailand	no cup
UAE	Al Ain	Al Ahly	Al Ahly
Uzbekistan*	Pachtakor Tashkent	Neftchi Ferghana	Pachtakor Tashkent
Vietnam	Hoang Anh Gia Lai	Sông Da Nam Dinh	Binh Dinh*

* Results for 2003 seasons. Remainder are 2003–04 seasons.

Asian Champions League

2002–03
FINAL (2 legs)

October 3 – Sheik Thanon Stadium, Riyadh

Al Ain 2-0 BEC-Tero
(UAE)   Sasana
(Johar 38,   (Thailand)
Omar 74)

h/t: 1-0 **Att:** 20,000
Ref: Kwon Jong Chul (Korea)

October 11 – Rajamangala Stadium, Bangkok

BEC-Tero 1-0 Al Ain
Sasana
(Chaiman 60 pen)

h/t: 0-0 **Att:** 35,000
Ref: Saad Kameel (Kuwait)

Al Ain won 2-1 on aggregate

Honduran striker Martinze shows how it's done as he helps new Chinese Champions Shanghai Shenhua to the top of the table.

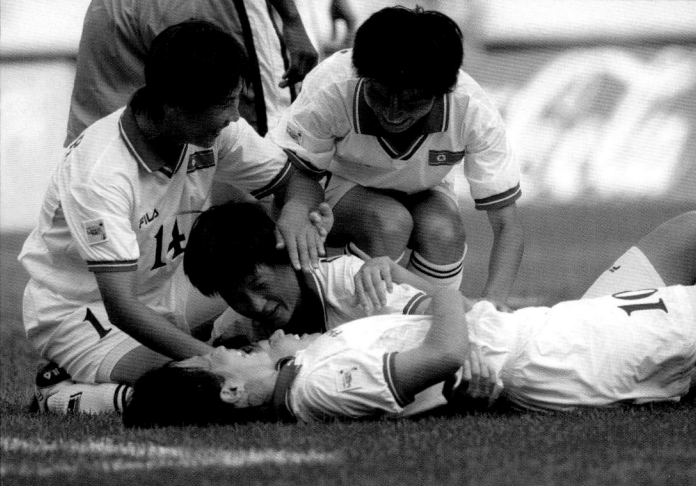

Above, left: East Bengal players seem suitably downhearted after losing the 116th Durand Cup Final to Salgaocar of Goa. India's FA Cup competition is the third oldest in the world after England and Scotland.

Above: North Korea's women's team made its first appearance in a Women's World Cup this year. Pyol-Hui, on the ground, is mobbed by team-mates after scoring the team's second goal against Nigeria.

Far left: Salem Jawhar Salmeen can only be described as pleased. His club, Al Ain from the UAE, has just won the Asian Champions Cup, despite losing the second leg to BEC Tero Sasana in Bangkok.

Left: The 2003 Asian Footballer of the Year, Mehdi Mahdavikia, playing in midfield for Hamburg. The talented Iranian won himself a transfer to Bayern München during 2004.

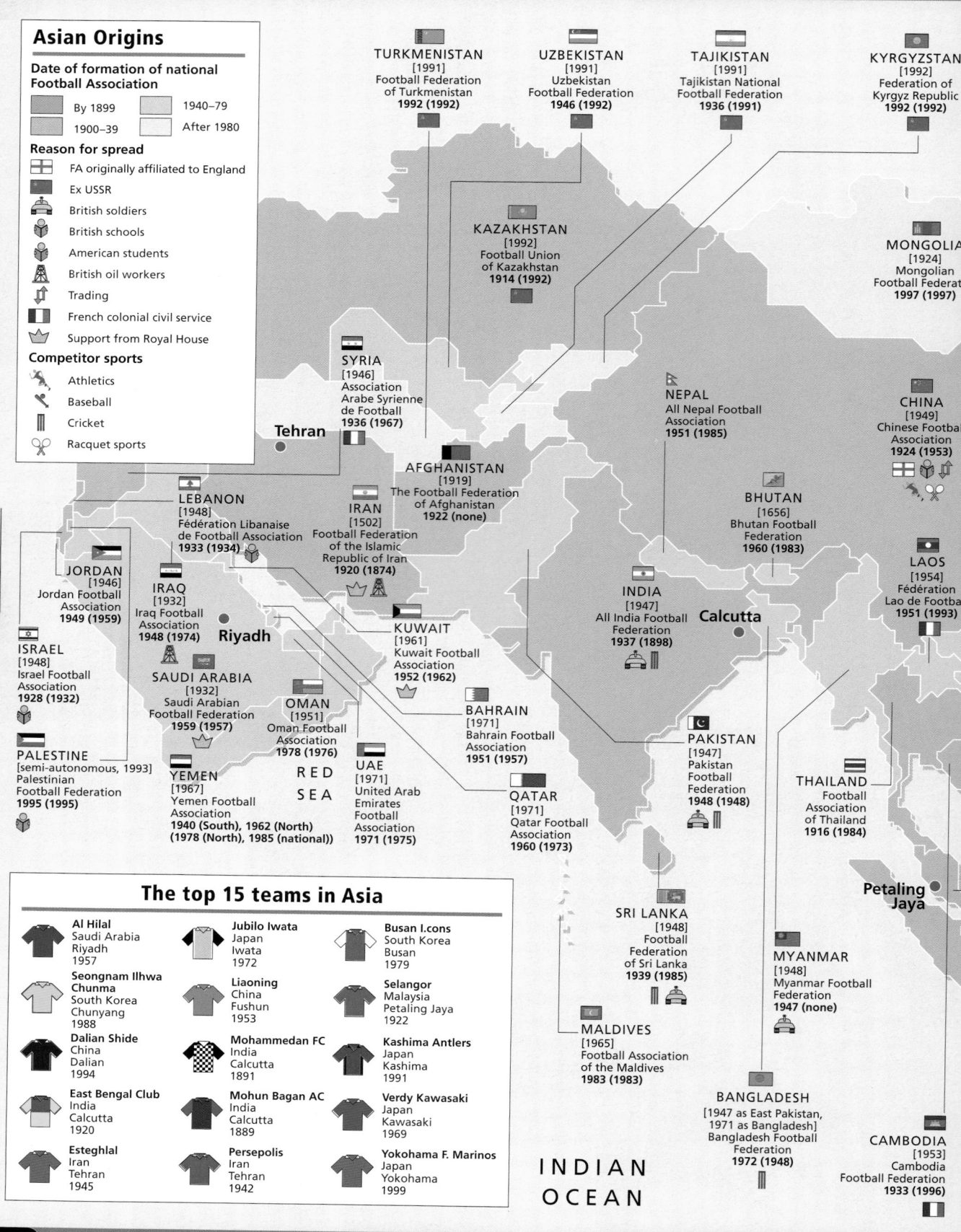

Asian Origins

Date of formation of national Football Association

By 1899	1940–79
1900–39	After 1980

Reason for spread

- FA originally affiliated to England
- Ex USSR
- British soldiers
- British schools
- American students
- British oil workers
- Trading
- French colonial civil service
- Support from Royal House

Competitor sports

- Athletics
- Baseball
- Cricket
- Racquet sports

ASIA

TURKMENISTAN
[1991]
Football Federation
of Turkmenistan
1992 (1992)

UZBEKISTAN
[1991]
Uzbekistan
Football Federation
1946 (1992)

TAJIKISTAN
[1991]
Tajikistan National
Football Federation
1936 (1991)

KYRGYZSTAN
[1992]
Federation of
Kyrgyz Republic
1992 (1992)

KAZAKHSTAN
[1992]
Football Union
of Kazakhstan
1914 (1992)

MONGOLIA
[1924]
Mongolian
Football Federation
1997 (1997)

SYRIA
[1946]
Association
Arabe Syrienne
de Football
1936 (1967)

Tehran

NEPAL
All Nepal Football
Association
1951 (1985)

CHINA
[1949]
Chinese Football
Association
1924 (1953)

LEBANON
[1948]
Fédération Libanaise
de Football Association
1933 (1934)

AFGHANISTAN
[1919]
The Football Federation
of Afghanistan
1922 (none)

IRAN
[1502]
Football Federation
of the Islamic
Republic of Iran
1920 (1874)

BHUTAN
[1656]
Bhutan Football
Federation
1960 (1983)

LAOS
[1954]
Fédération
Lao de Football
1951 (1993)

JORDAN
[1946]
Jordan Football
Association
1949 (1959)

IRAQ
[1932]
Iraq Football
Association
1948 (1974)

KUWAIT
[1961]
Kuwait Football
Association
1952 (1962)

INDIA
[1947]
All India Football
Federation
1937 (1898)

Calcutta

Riyadh

ISRAEL
[1948]
Israel Football
Association
1928 (1932)

SAUDI ARABIA
[1932]
Saudi Arabian
Football Federation
1959 (1957)

OMAN
[1951]
Oman Football
Association
1978 (1976)

BAHRAIN
[1971]
Bahrain Football
Association
1951 (1957)

PAKISTAN
[1947]
Pakistan
Football
Federation
1948 (1948)

PALESTINE
[semi-autonomous, 1993]
Palestinian
Football Federation
1995 (1995)

YEMEN
[1967]
Yemen Football
Association
**1940 (South), 1962 (North)
(1978 (North), 1985 (national))**

UAE
[1971]
United Arab
Emirates
Football
Association
1971 (1975)

**RED
SEA**

QATAR
[1971]
Qatar Football
Association
1960 (1973)

THAILAND
Football
Association
of Thailand
1916 (1984)

**Petaling
Jaya**

SRI LANKA
[1948]
Football
Federation
of Sri Lanka
1939 (1985)

MYANMAR
[1948]
Myanmar Football
Federation
1947 (none)

MALDIVES
[1965]
Football Association
of the Maldives
1983 (1983)

BANGLADESH
[1947 as East Pakistan,
1971 as Bangladesh]
Bangladesh Football
Federation
1972 (1948)

CAMBODIA
[1953]
Cambodia
Football Federation
1933 (1996)

**INDIAN
OCEAN**

The top 15 teams in Asia

Al Hilal
Saudi Arabia
Riyadh
1957

**Seongnam Ilhwa
Chunma**
South Korea
Chunyang
1988

Dalian Shide
China
Dalian
1994

East Bengal Club
India
Calcutta
1920

Esteghlal
Iran
Tehran
1945

Jubilo Iwata
Japan
Iwata
1972

Liaoning
China
Fushun
1953

Mohammedan FC
India
Calcutta
1891

Mohun Bagan AC
India
Calcutta
1889

Persepolis
Iran
Tehran
1942

Busan I.cons
South Korea
Busan
1979

Selangor
Malaysia
Petaling Jaya
1922

Kashima Antlers
Japan
Kashima
1991

Verdy Kawasaki
Japan
Kawasaki
1969

Yokohama F. Marinos
Japan
Yokohama
1999

Asia

ORIGINS AND GROWTH OF SOCCER

SOCCER ARRIVED IN ASIA through the tentacles of the formal and informal British Empire as the nation's sailors, missionaries and teachers played soccer in the late 19th century in Japan and Korea. But these limited expatriate communities could not sustain formal clubs and leagues.

The story in China and India, however, was different.

In Calcutta, clerks in Indian public service and teams from the British Army were playing regularly in the first decade of the 20th century and were soon joined by the locals, some of whom formed India's first indigenous club, Mohan Bagan, in 1889. The team was soon contesting the Indian Football Association Shield. British traders in Shanghai are on record as playing soccer as early as 1879, and in 1887 Shanghai Football Club was formed from the Shanghai Athletic Club. A Briton, John Prentice, set up another club – Engineers – and donated a cup contested by the various émigré teams in the city. Further south, Hong Kong FC was founded by Britons in 1886, and in 1896 the Hong Kong Shield was first contested in a tournament between civilian and military teams. Soccer was also played in Singapore in this era and by the early 20th century Shanghai had acquired its own FA (affiliated to London) and the Chinese themselves were beginning to play and form teams. Chinese soccer was represented in this era by the South China Athletic Association founded in 1904, which went on to represent China at the inaugural Far East Asian Olympic Games in 1913. Chinese resentment against European control of soccer culminated in 1931 when the nationalist Kuomintang government ordered all Chinese clubs to leave foreign leagues.

By the Second World War soccer had spread through the rest of Southeast Asia, though its popularity was limited. A more enthusiastic response came from Southwest Asia where both Iran and Iraq took up the game with royal and government patronage, a process that was repeated in the 1970s when oil wealth made the active promotion of soccer in the Gulf States possible. French colonists brought the game to Syria, while the British and Jewish emigrants brought the game to Palestine. In Central Asia, soccer primarily arrived via the Soviet occupiers who had taken control of the region in the 1930s.

ASIA

The British Army was playing soccer regularly in India during the first decade of the 20th century. This picture shows action from an inter-regimental tournament played at Simla in 1907.

The AFC Nations

COUNTRY
[date of independence]
Name of national
Football
Foundation — Association — Foundation of
of national FA — **1916 (1912)** — national league

NORTH KOREA
[1945]
Football Association
of the Democratic
People's Republic
of Korea
1945 (1985)

SOUTH KOREA
[1945]
Korea Football
Association
1928 (1983)

JAPAN
Japan Football
Association
1921 (1965)

Dalian

Chunyang
Busan

Kashima
Kawasaki
Yokohama
Iwata

MACAO
[to China 2000]
Macau Football
Association
1939 (1973)

PACIFIC
OCEAN

...shun

TAIWAN
[1949]
Chinese Taipei
Football Association
1936 (1994)

HONG KONG
[to China 1997]
Hong Kong
Football Association
1914 (1946)

GUAM
[Unincorporated
territory of the USA]
Guam Soccer
Association
1975 (1994)

VIETNAM
[1954]
Vietnam Football
Federation
1962 (1981)

PHILIPPINES
[1946]
Philippines Football
Federation
1907 (1967)

BRUNEI
[1984]
Football Association
of Brunei Darussalam
1959 (none)

SINGAPORE
[1949]
Football Association
of Singapore
1892 (1981)

INDONESIA
[1949]
Persatuan Sepakbola
Seluruh Indonesia
1930 (1981)

MALAYSIA
[1957]
Persatuan
Bolasepak Malaysia
1933 (1921)

The Asian Cup & Asian Games

TOURNAMENT OVERVIEWS

ALONE AMONG THE SOCCER REGIONS, Asia has two significant international competitions: the soccer tournament of the multi-sport, amateur-only Asian Games, first held in 1951, and the AFC-controlled Asian Cup, first held in 1956. The Asian Games have provided space for some of the older but perhaps weaker soccer-playing nations to shine with early victories going to India, Burma (now Myanmar) and Taiwan, as well as the traditionally stronger countries of Israel and South Korea. Opportunities for the underdogs remain, with Uzbekistan winning the 1994 Games in Hiroshima. At the Tehran Games held in 1974, the host Iran beat Israel in its last appearance in Asian tournaments, as Israel was expelled from AFC the following year.

Shifting patterns

As soccer has become progressively richer and steadily more professionalized in Asia, the Asian Cup, open to professionals, has come to assume greater prestige in the region. Initially the final tournaments were held as mini-leagues, with the South Koreans and Israelis again dominating the early tournaments. Politics continued to haunt the tournament, with Pakistan and Afghanistan refusing to play Israel in the inaugural finals. From the 1970s, the soccer balance of power has steadily shifted, with victories going west – to Iran and Saudi Arabia (three-time winners in 1984, 88 and 96) and the UAE. More recently, the reinvigoration of Japanese soccer and the creation of the J.League has seen two Japanese victories (1992 and 2000).

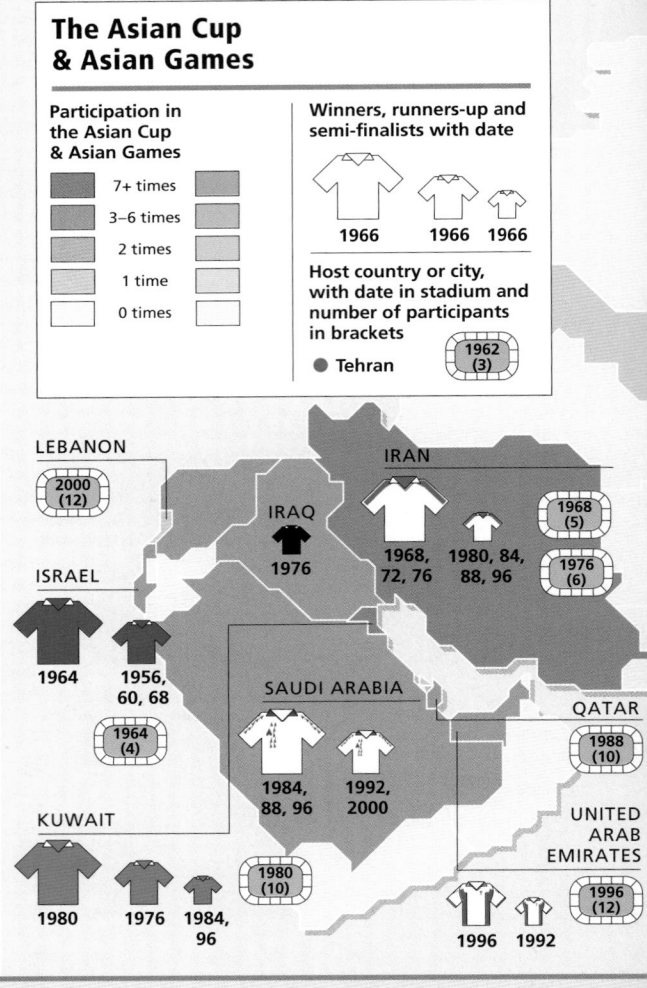

The Asian Cup & Asian Games

Participation in the Asian Cup & Asian Games

- 7+ times
- 3–6 times
- 2 times
- 1 time
- 0 times

Winners, runners-up and semi-finalists with date

1966   1966   1966

Host country or city, with date in stadium and number of participants in brackets

● Tehran   1962 (3)

LEBANON 2000 (12)

IRAQ 1976

ISRAEL 1964 | 1956, 60, 68

IRAN | 1968, 72, 76 | 1980, 84, 88, 96 | 1968 (5) | 1976 (6)

SAUDI ARABIA 1984, 88, 96 | 1992, 2000 | 1964 (4)

QATAR 1988 (10)

KUWAIT 1980 | 1976 | 1984, 96 | 1980 (10)

UNITED ARAB EMIRATES 1996 (12) | 1996 | 1992

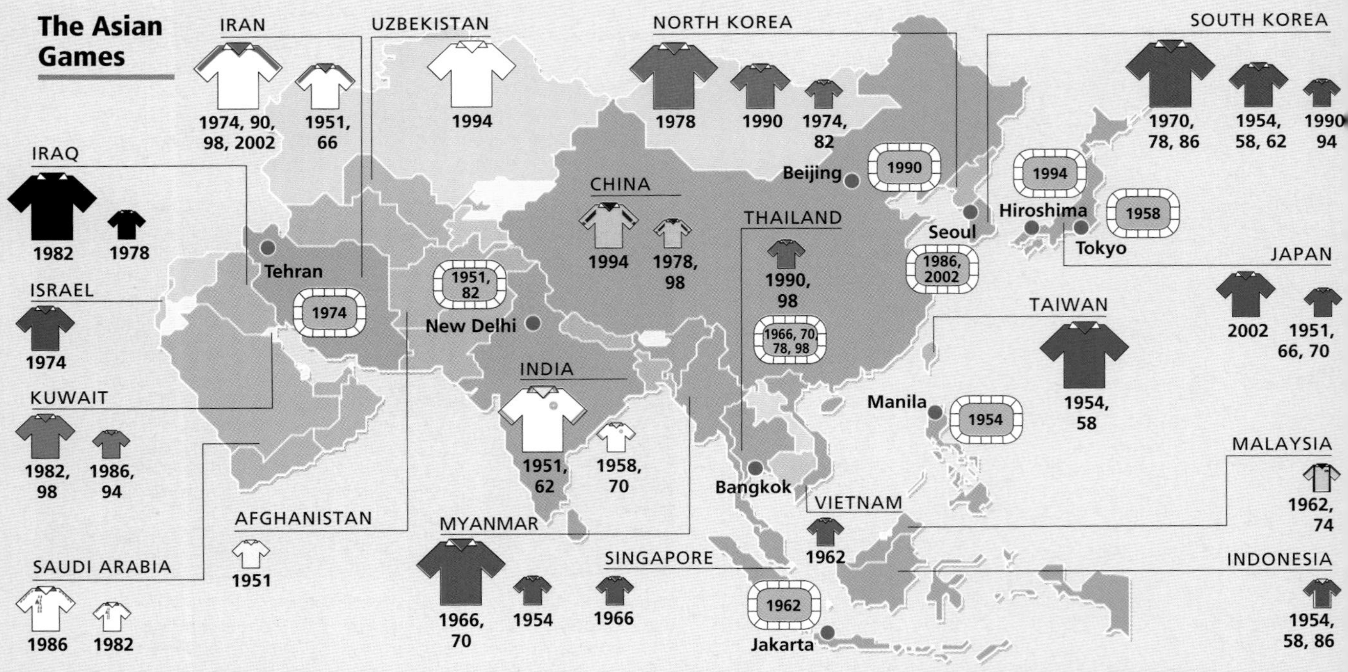

The Asian Games

IRAN 1974, 90, 98, 2002 | 1951, 66

UZBEKISTAN 1994

NORTH KOREA 1978 | 1990 | 1974, 82

SOUTH KOREA 1970, 78, 86 | 1954, 58, 62 | 1990, 94

IRAQ 1982 | 1978

Tehran | 1974

ISRAEL 1974

CHINA 1994 | 1978, 98

THAILAND 1990, 98

Beijing | 1990

Seoul | 1986, 2002

Hiroshima | 1994

Tokyo | 1958

JAPAN 2002 | 1951, 66, 70

KUWAIT 1982, 98 | 1986, 94

New Delhi | 1951, 82

INDIA 1951, 62 | 1958, 70

1966, 70, 78, 98

Manila | 1954

TAIWAN 1954, 58

AFGHANISTAN 1951

SAUDI ARABIA 1986 | 1982

MYANMAR 1966, 70 | 1954 | 1966

SINGAPORE 1962 | Jakarta

Bangkok

VIETNAM 1962

MALAYSIA 1962, 74

INDONESIA 1954, 58, 86

The Asian Cup

JAPAN
1992 (8)
1992, 2000

NORTH KOREA
1980

CHINA
2004 (16)
1984   1976, 88, 92, 2000

TAIWAN
1960, 68

SOUTH KOREA
1960 (4)
1956, 60   1972, 80, 88   1964, 2000

MYANMAR
1968

INDIA
1964

HONG KONG
1956 (4)
1956, 64

THAILAND
1972 (6)
1972

CAMBODIA
1972

VIETNAM
1956, 60

SINGAPORE
1984 (10)

The Saudi Arabian players celebrate victory over the UAE in a penalty shootout to win the Asian Cup in 1996. It was the team's third victory in four tournaments.

Sergey Lebedev scored one of Uzbekistan's goals in the 4-2 win over China in the 1994 Asian Games Football Final.

The Asian Games (1951–2002)

YEAR	WINNERS	SCORE	RUNNERS-UP
1951	India	1-0	Iran
1954	Taiwan	5-2	South Korea
1958	Taiwan	3-2	South Korea
1962	India	2-1	South Korea
1966	Myanmar	1-0	Iran
1970	Myanmar	0-0 (title shared)	South Korea
1974	Iran	1-0	Israel
1978	South Korea	0-0 (title shared)	North Korea
1982	Iraq	1-0	Kuwait
1986	South Korea	2-0	Saudi Arabia
1990	Iran	0-0 (4-1 pens)	North Korea
1994	Uzbekistan	4-2	China
1998	Iran	2-0	Kuwait
2002	Iran	2-1	Japan

The Asian Cup (1956–2000)

YEAR	WINNERS	SCORE	RUNNERS-UP
1956	South Korea	*	Israel
1960	South Korea	*	Israel
1964	Israel	*	India
1968	Iran	*	Israel
1972	Iran	2-1	South Korea
1976	Iran	1-0	Kuwait
1980	Kuwait	3-0	South Korea
1984	Saudi Arabia	2-0	China
1988	Saudi Arabia	0-0 (4-3 pens)	South Korea
1992	Japan	1-0	Saudi Arabia
1996	Saudi Arabia	0-0 (asdet) (4-2 pens)	United Arab Emirates
2000	Japan	1-0	Saudi Arabia

* Tournament decided on league basis, no final match.

The Asian Champions League

THE ASIAN CHAMPIONS LEAGUE

TOURNAMENT OVERVIEW

THE ENORMOUS GEOGRAPHICAL SIZE OF ASIA and the relative weakness and unevenness of club soccer made the establishment of a regular international club tournament difficult. The AFC first decided to create a tournament modelled on the European Cup in 1962 called the Asian Club Championship, but it took five years to set up. In the event, only six clubs took part in a finals tournament held in Bangkok, Thailand, in 1967. Eventual champions, Hapoel Tel Aviv, only played a single match – the Final – after a series of byes, beating the Malaysian side Selangor 2-1. Ten teams competed in 1969, again in Bangkok, with Maccabi Tel Aviv beating the Korean side Yangzee 1-0 to claim the title.

Hapoel appeared in the Final again in 1970, but lost 2-1 to the Iranian army team, Taj Club. The following year Maccabi got to the Final and was set to meet Al Shorta from Iraq, but the Iraqis refused to play the match for political reasons and Maccabi was awarded the trophy. Israeli dominance of the competition ended in 1975 when the country's teams were expelled from AFC because of the war in the Middle East. Continuing political problems meant that the competition was abandoned until 1985, but then it was revamped with a proper geographically-based series of qualifying rounds and a six-team final tournament held that year in Jeddah in Saudi Arabia.

Since then the Asian soccer landscape has transformed. The competition has been dominated since 1985 by teams from Japan and South Korea. But there has also been success for the rapidly strengthening teams from the Gulf, like Al Sadd from Qatar in 1989, Al Hilal and Al Nassr from Saudi Arabia in the 1990s; for the revamped clubs of post-revolutionary Iran, like Esteghlal and Pas Club; for the back-to-back winners Thai Farmers Bank (in 1994 and 95); and for the Chinese, for whom Liaoning from Shenyang took the title in 1990.

In 2002, the AFC reorganised the tournament merging it with the now discontiued Asian Cup-Winners' Cup (see page 475), and have renamed it the Asian Champions League.

***Thai Farmers Bank**, from Bangkok, won the Asian Club Championship in 1994 and 95.*

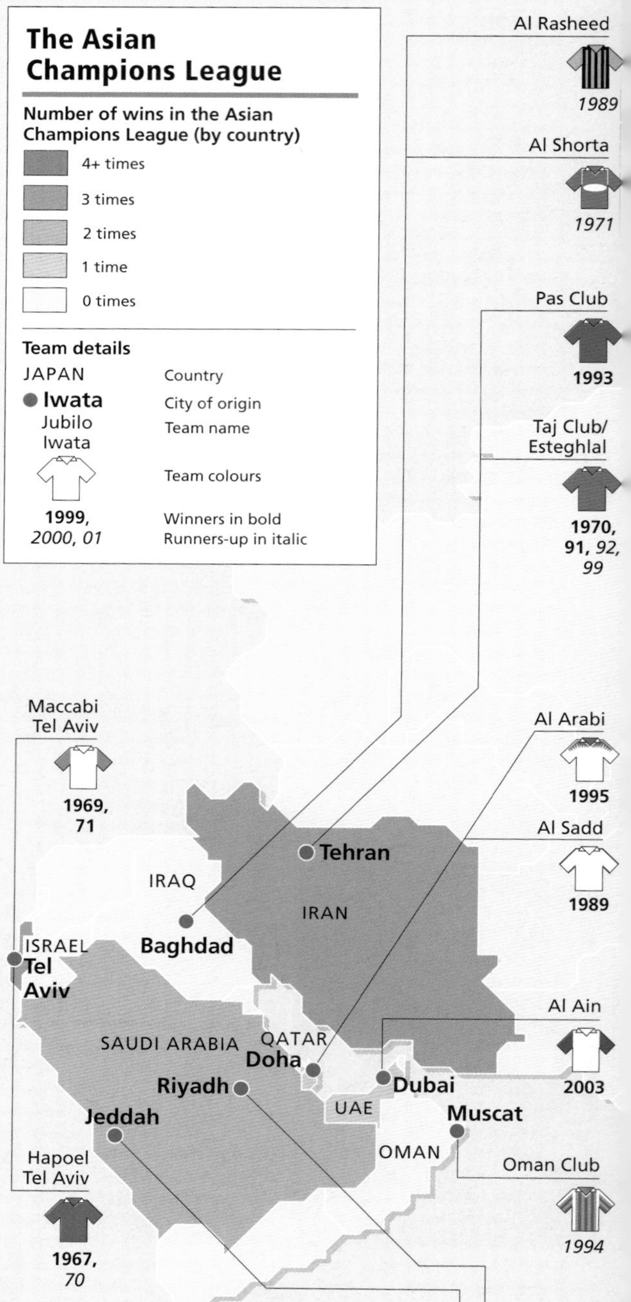

The Asian Champions League

Number of wins in the Asian Champions League (by country)

- 4+ times
- 3 times
- 2 times
- 1 time
- 0 times

Team details

JAPAN	Country
● **Iwata**	City of origin
Jubilo Iwata	Team name
	Team colours
1999, *2000, 01*	Winners in bold / Runners-up in italic

Al Rasheed — *1989*

Al Shorta — *1971*

Pas Club — **1993**

Taj Club/ Esteghlal — **1970,** 91, *92,* 99

Al Arabi — *1995*

Al Sadd — **1989**

Al Ain — 2003

Oman Club — 1994

Al Ahly — *1986*

Maccabi Tel Aviv — **1969,** 71

Tehran — IRAQ — IRAN — Baghdad — ISRAEL — **Tel Aviv** — SAUDI ARABIA — QATAR — **Doha** — **Riyadh** — UAE — **Jeddah** — **Dubai** — **Muscat** — OMAN

Hapoel Tel Aviv — **1967,** 70

The Asian Champions League

COUNTRY	WINNERS	RUNNERS-UP
South Korea	6	3
Japan	3	3
Iran	3	2
Israel	3	1
Saudi Arabia	2	5
Thailand	2	1
China	1	2
Qatar	1	1
UAE	1	0
Iraq	0	2
Malaysia	0	1
Oman	0	1

Sami Al Jaber (left) of Saudi Arabian club Al Hilal kisses the Asian Club Championship Cup after the team's 3-2 victory over Japan's Jubilo Iwata in the 2000 Final in Riyadh.

The Asian Cup-Winners' Cup 1991–2002

YEAR	WINNERS	RUNNERS-UP
1991	Piroozi (Iran)	Muharraq (Bahrain)
1992	Nissan Motors (Japan)	Al Nassr (Saudi Arabia)
1993	Nissan Motors (Japan)	Piroozi (Iran)
1994	Al Qadisiya (Saudi Arabia)	South China (Hong Kong)
1995	Yokohama Flugels (Japan)	Al Shabab (Saudi Arabia)
1996	Bellmare Hiratsuka (Japan)	Talaba (Iraq)
1997	Al Hilal (Saudi Arabia)	Nagoya Grampus Eight (Japan)
1998	Al Nassr (Saudi Arabia)	Suwon Samsung Bluewings (Japan)
1999	Al Ittihad (Saudi Arabia)	Chunnam Dragons (South Korea)
2000	Shimizu S-Pulse (Japan)	Al Zawra (Iraq)
2001	Al Shabab (Saudi Arabia)	Dalian Shide (China)
2002	Al Hilal (Saudi Arabia)	Chonbuk Hyundai Motors (South Korea)

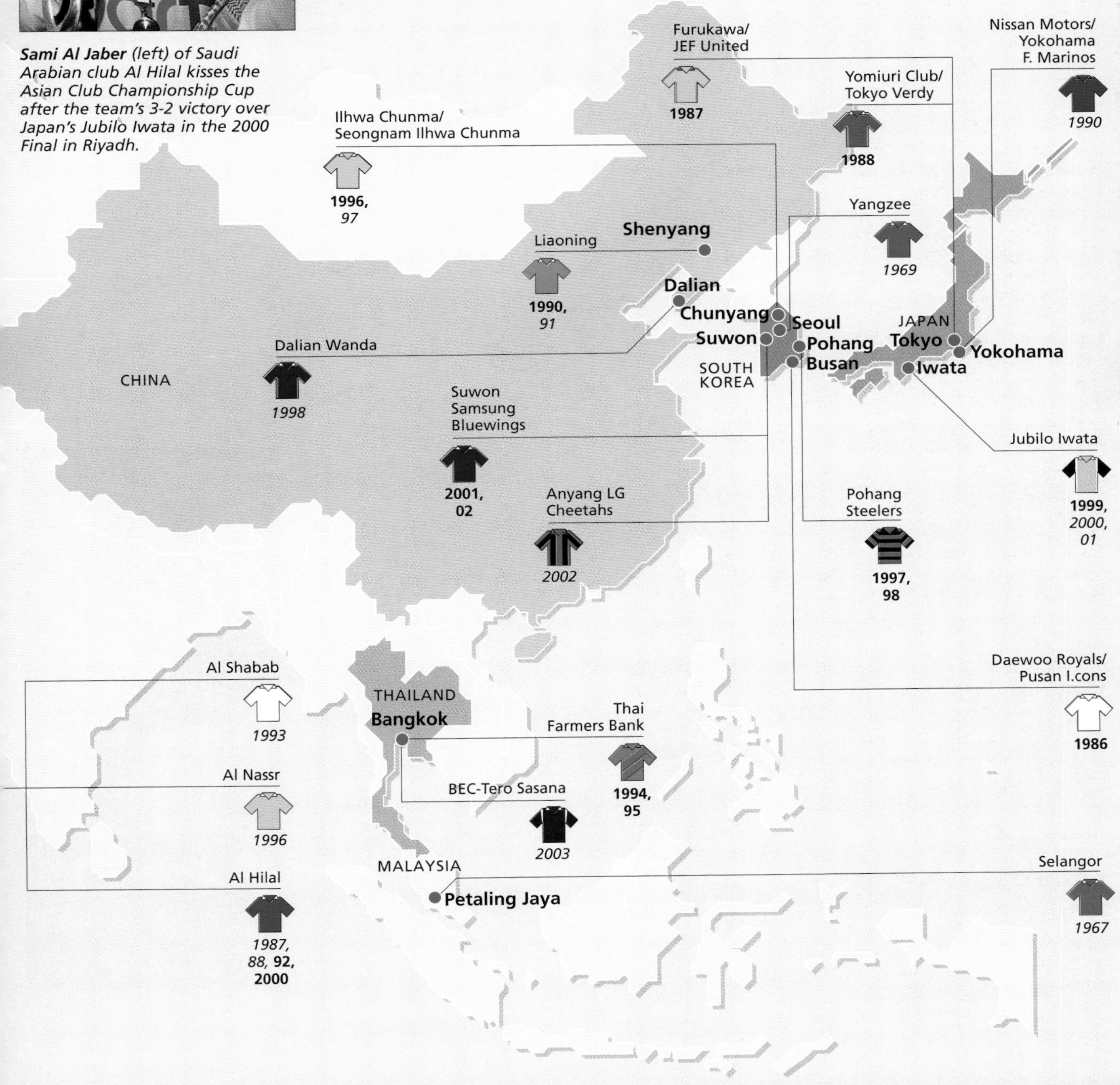

Furukawa/
JEF United
1987

Yomiuri Club/
Tokyo Verdy
1988

Nissan Motors/
Yokohama
F. Marinos
1990

Ilhwa Chunma/
Seongnam Ilhwa Chunma
**1996,
97**

Liaoning
**1990,
91**

Shenyang

Yangzee
1969

Dalian
Chunyang
Suwon

Seoul
Pohang
Busan

JAPAN
Tokyo
Yokohama
Iwata

SOUTH
KOREA

CHINA

Dalian Wanda
1998

Suwon
Samsung
Bluewings
**2001,
02**

Anyang LG
Cheetahs
2002

Pohang
Steelers
**1997,
98**

Jubilo Iwata
**1999,
*2000,
01***

Al Shabab
1993

THAILAND
Bangkok

Thai
Farmers Bank
**1994,
95**

Daewoo Royals/
Pusan I.cons
1986

Al Nassr
1996

BEC-Tero Sasana
2003

MALAYSIA
● **Petaling Jaya**

Al Hilal
**1987,
88, 92,
2000**

Selangor
1967

THE ASIAN CHAMPIONS LEAGUE

The Asian Cup

The Asian Cup Winners

South Korea
1956, 60

Israel
1964

Iran
1968, 72, 76

Kuwait
1980

Saudia Arabia
1984, 88, 96

Japan
1992, 2000

ASIA HAS TWO MAJOR international soccer competitions. The Asian Cup is the competition run by the FIFA affiliate AFC (Asian Football Confederation) while the other soccer tournament is played at the Asian Games, which is a multi-sports competition. The Asian Games were first held in 1951 and have continued every four years, without qualifying tournaments and a group/knockout stage format. The Asian Cup began in 1956 and is also played on a four-year cycle, but from 1960 it has had a pre-tournament qualifying round based on geographical zones. It has become the pre-eminent Asian soccer competition.

Decolonization and international politics have continued to influence the entrants and outcome of the tournaments. Taiwan's place in Asian soccer has been contested by China, and vice-versa, with both claiming to be the sole Chinese representative. Israel's place in Asian soccer has been equally problematic. Israel achieved a bye into the 1956 Asian Cup as neither Pakistan or Afghanistan would play them. Again Israel reached the 1974 Asian Games Final in Tehran without touching a ball, after North Korea and Kuwait refused to play them. In the end both Taiwan and Israel were expelled from the AFC in 1975. Israel now plays within UEFA.

1956 HONG KONG*
1 South Korea
2 Israel
3 Hong Kong

1960 SOUTH KOREA*
1 South Korea
2 Israel
3 Taiwan

1964 ISRAEL*
1 Israel
2 India
3 South Korea

1968 IRAN*
1 Iran
2 Myanmar
3 Israel

1972 THAILAND**
SEMI-FINALS
Iran **2-1** Cambodia
South Korea **1-1** Thailand
South Korea won 2-1 on pens

THIRD PLACE PLAY-OFF
Thailand **2-2** Cambodia
Thailand won 5-3 on pens

FINAL
May 19 – Bangkok
Iran **2-1** South Korea
(Jabary 48,   *(Lee Whae-taek 65)*
Khalani 107)
(after extra time)
h/t: 0-0 90 mins: 1-1
Att: 8,000

1976 IRAN
SEMI-FINALS
Iran **2-0** China
Kuwait **3-2** Iraq

THIRD PLACE PLAY-OFF
China **1-0** Iraq

FINAL
June 13 – Tehran
Iran **1-0** Kuwait
Att: 40,000

1980 KUWAIT
SEMI-FINALS
Kuwait **2-1** Iran
South Korea **2-1** North Korea

THIRD PLACE PLAY-OFF
Iran **3-0** North Korea

FINAL
September 28 – Kuwait City
Kuwait **3-0** South Korea
Att: 35,000

1984 SINGAPORE
SEMI-FINALS
Saudi Arabia **1-1** Iran
Saudi Arabia won 5-4 on pens
China **1-0** Kuwait

THIRD PLACE PLAY-OFF
Kuwait **1-1** Iran
Kuwait won 5-3 on pens

FINAL
December 16 – Singapore
Saudi Arabia **2-0** China
(Shaye Nafisah 10,
Majed
Abdullah 47)
h/t: 1-0 Att: 40,000

1988 QATAR
SEMI-FINALS
Saudi Arabia **1-0** Iran
South Korea **2-1** China
(after extra time)

THIRD PLACE PLAY-OFF
Iran **0-0** China
Iran won 3-0 on pens

FINAL
December 19 – Doha
Saudi Arabia **0-0** South Korea
(after extra time)
h/t: 0-0 90 mins: 0-0
Att: 25,000
Saudi Arabia won 4-3 on pens

1992 JAPAN
SEMI-FINALS
Japan **3-2** China
Saudi Arabia **2-0** UAE

THIRD PLACE PLAY-OFF
China **1-1** UAE
China won 4-3 on pens

FINAL
November 8 – Hiroshima
Japan **1-0** Saudi Arabia
(Takagi 6)
h/t: 1-0 Att: 40,000
Ref: Al Sharif (Syria)

1996 UNITED ARAB EMIRATES
SEMI-FINALS
Iran **0-0** Saudi Arabia
Saudi Arabia won 4-3 on pens
UAE **1-0** Kuwait

THIRD PLACE PLAY-OFF
Iran **1-1** Kuwait
Iran won 3-2 on pens

FINAL
December 21 – Abu Dhabi
UAE **0-0** Saudi Arabia
(after extra time)
h/t: 0-0 90 mins: 0-0 Att: 60,000
Ref: Mohammed Nazri Abdullah
(Malaysia)
Saudi Arabia won 4-2 on pens

2000 LEBANON
SEMI-FINALS
Saudi Arabia **2-1** South Korea
Japan **3-2** China

THIRD PLACE PLAY-OFF
South Korea **1-0** China

FINAL
October 28 – Beirut
Japan **1-0** Saudi Arabia
(Mochizuki 29)
h/t: 1-0 Att: 57,600
Ref: Ali Bujsaim (UAE)

* League format.
** Finals tournament.

Ryuzo Morioka, the Japanese captain, celebrates victory in the 2000 Asian Nations Cup Final after Japan defeated Saudi Arabia 1-0 in Beirut.

THE ASIAN CUP

The Asian Champions League

THE ASIAN CLUB CHAMPIONSHIP, now rebranded as the Asian Champions League, is the leading international club competition in Asia. Originally conceived by the Asian Football Confederation in 1962, it took five years to launch the competition, which began as a six-team tournament played out in Bangkok. Geography has always dogged the competition, with Asia's enormous size making schedules difficult to arrange, and the inclusion of Israel in the AFC created significant conflicts with other members. In 1971, the Iraqi club Al Shorta, or Police Club, refused to play Maccabi Tel Aviv in the Final. The competition was only played again in 1985 by which time Israel had left the AFC.

The competition is open to national champions in all members of AFC. The early rounds are played on a geographical basis, dividing into East and West Asia. Semi-finals and a Final tournament are then staged in a single nation.

The other international club tournament in Asia has now been discontinued. From 2003, the Asian Cup-Winners' Cup will no longer be held, but for the last ten years it has been a significant event in the Asian soccer calendar. It was open to cup winners of all AFC member states, or losing finalists if the cup winner was entered for the Asian Club Championship. Early rounds were played over two legs with a small finals tournament (semi-finals, Final, third place play-off) in a single host city. The competition began in 1990 with 18 entrants, and by the mid-90s it was attracting more prize money and more teams. The last seven Finals were won by either Japanese or South Korean teams, except for the Saudi Al Hilal in 2000.

^1967 FINAL
December 19 – Bangkok, Thailand
Hapoel 2-1 Selangor
Tel Aviv   (Malaysia)
(Israel)

1968–69 FINAL
January 30 – Bangkok, Thailand
Maccabi 1-0 Yangzee
Tel Aviv   (South Korea)
(Israel)

1970 FINAL
April 10 – Tehran, Iran
Taj Club 2-1 Hapoel
(Iran)   Tel Aviv
(Israel)

1971 FINAL
April 2 – Bangkok, Thailand
Maccabi w/o Al Shorta
Tel Aviv   (Iraq)
(Israel)
Al Shorta withdrew from this match, awarded to Maccabi

1972 FINAL
tournament cancelled

1985–86 FINAL
January 24, 1986 – Jeddah, Saudi Arabia
Daewoo 3-1 Al Ahly
Royals   (Saudi Arabia)
(South Korea)

1986–87 TOURNAMENT
December, 1986 – Riyadh, Saudi Arabia
Al Talaba **2-2** Liaoning
Furukawa **4-3** Al Hilal
Furukawa **2-0** Al Talaba
Al Hilal **1-0** Liaoning
Furukawa **1-0** Liaoning
Al Hilal **2-1** Al Talaba

	P	W	D	L	F	A	Pts
1 Furukawa	3	3	0	0	7	3	**6**
2 Al Hilal	3	2	0	1	6	5	**4**
3 Liaoning	3	0	1	2	2	4	**1**
4 Al Talaba	3	0	1	2	3	6	**1**

1987–88 FINAL
Yomiuri Club w/o Al Hilal
(Japan)   (Saudi Arabia)
Al Hilal withdrew before 1st leg

1988–89 FINAL (2 legs)
March 31
Al Rasheed 3-2 Al Sadd
(Iraq)   (Qatar)

April 6
Al Sadd 1-0 Al Rasheed
Al Sadd won on away goals rule

1989–90 FINAL (2 legs)
April 22
Liaoning 2-1 Nissan Motors
(China)   (Japan)

April 29
Nissan Motors 1-1 Liaoning

1990–91 FINAL
July 29 – Dhaka, Bangladesh
Esteghlal 2-1 Liaoning
(Iran)   (China)

1991–92 FINAL
December 22, 1991 – Doha, Qatar
Al Hilal 1-1 Esteghlal
(Saudi Arabia)   (Iran)
(Hussein   *(Amir Abbas 58)*
Al Habashi 73)
(after extra time)
Al Hilal won 4-3 on pens

1992–93 FINAL
January 22 – Bahrain
Pas Club 1-0 Al Shabab
(Iran)   (Saudi Arabia)

1993–94 FINAL
February 7 – Bangkok, Thailand
Thai Farmers 2-1 Oman Club
Bank   (Oman)
(Thailand)   *(Zahir Salim 44)*
(Thawan
Thamniyai 4,
Sing Totavee 18)

1994–95 FINAL
January 29 – Bangkok, Thailand
Thai Farmers 1-0 Al Arabi
Bank   (Qatar)
(Thailand)
(Natipong
Sritong-in 82)

1995–96 FINAL
December 29 – Riyadh, Saudi Arabia
Ilhwa 1-0 Al Nassr
Chunma   (Saudi Arabia)
(South Korea)
(Lee Tae
Hong 110)
(after extra time)

1996–97 FINAL
March 9 – Kuala Lumpur, Malaysia
Pohang 2-1 Ilhwa
Steelers   Chunma
(South Korea)   (South Korea)
(Park Tae-ha 77,   *(Park Ji-ho 79)*
Hong Jong-kyong
118 pen)

1997–98 FINAL
April 5 – Hong Kong
Pohang 0-0 Dalian Wanda
Steelers   (China)
(South Korea)
Pohang Steelers won 6-5 on pens

1998–99 FINAL
April 30 – Tehran, Iran
Jubilo Iwata 2-1 Esteghlal
(Japan)   (Iran)
(Suzuki 36,   *(Dinmohammadi*
Nakayama 45)   *66)*

1999–2000 FINAL
April 22 – Riyadh, Saudi Arabia
Al Hilal 3-2 Jubilo Iwata
(Saudi Arabia)   (Japan)
(Ricardo   *(Nakayama 18,*
3, 89, 102)   *Takahara 19)*

2000–01 FINAL
May 26 – Suwon, South Korea
Suwon Samsung 1-0 Jubilo Iwata
Bluewings   (Japan)
(South Korea)
(Sandro dos
Santos 15)

2001–02 FINAL
April 5 – Tehran, Iran
Suwon Samsung 0-0 Anyang LG
Bluewings   Cheetahs
(South Korea)   (South Korea)
Suwon Samsung won 4-2 on pens

2002–03 FINAL (2 legs)
October 3 – Dubai, UAE
Al Ain 2-0 BEC-Tero
(UAE)   Sasana
(Johar 38,   (Thailand)
Omar 74)

October 11 – Bangkok, Thailand
BEC-Tero 1-0 Al Ain
Sasana
(Chaiman 60 pen)
Al Ain won on 2-1 on aggregate

Al Ain's Salem Jawhar Salmeen (centre) celebrates with the trophy after the 2003 Asian Champions League Final in Bangkok.

THE ASIAN CHAMPIONS LEAGUE

Southwest Asia

SOCCER BECAME POPULAR IN IRAN and Iraq well before the Second World War, with active royal support from the Shahs of Iran. Under the last Shah a programme of modernization and the importation of foreign coaches gave the game a huge boost. A national league was established in 1960, and became semi-professional in 1974. But soccer's development in Iran was stopped in its tracks by the Islamic revolution in 1978. The league only recommenced at the end of the Iran-Iraq War in 1988, and women were banned from matches until 1994. Nonetheless the depth of Iranian soccer saw them qualify for the 1998 World Cup. To their north, the states of Central Asia acquired soccer after their inclusion in the Soviet Union and all established independent FAs and national leagues in the wake of the break-up of the Soviet Union in 1991.

Late starters, quick developers

Soccer arrived in the Near East with French and British protectorate status and colonial administrations after the First World War. National leagues were established in Lebanon in 1934, Jordan in 1959 and Syria in 1981. The Gulf states, by contrast, have proved to be late starters and quick developers. With oil money to hand and active royal and state promotion, national leagues were established in Bahrain in 1957, Kuwait in 1962, Qatar in 1973, UAE in 1975 and Saudi Arabia in 1979, although the national King's Cup tournament has been running there since 1957. All of these states have actively imported players from all over the world. Qatar has gone as far as to offer massive financial inducements to players to take Qatari citizenship and play for the national team. As yet they have failed to secure any major names.

It has been virtually impossible to get information about soccer in Afghanistan in recent years. Since the fall of the regime Afghanistan has re-entered international soccer competitions. The Taleban discouraged competitiveness, so winners and losers alike were not recorded.

Afghanistan

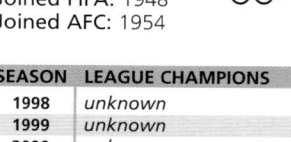

The Football Federation of Afghanistan
Founded: 1922
Joined FIFA: 1948
Joined AFC: 1954

SEASON	LEAGUE CHAMPIONS
1998	*unknown*
1999	*unknown*
2000	*unknown*
2001	*unknown*
2002	*disrupted*

Bahrain

Bahrain Football Association
Founded: 1951
Joined FIFA: 1966
Joined AFC: 1970

SEASON	LEAGUE CHAMPIONS
2000	West Riffa
2001	Muharraq
2002	Muharraq
2003	West Riffa
2004	Muharraq

YEAR	CUP WINNERS
1999	East Riffa
2000	East Riffa
2001	Al Ahli
2002	Muharraq
2003	Al Ahli

Iran

Football Federation of the Islamic Republic of Iran
Founded: 1920
Joined FIFA: 1945
Joined AFC: 1958

SEASON	LEAGUE CHAMPIONS
2000	Piroozi
2001	Esteghlal
2002	Piroozi
2003	Sepehan Isfahan
2004	Paas Tehran

Iran *(continued)*

YEAR	CUP WINNERS
1999	Piroozi
2000	Esteghlal
2001	Fajr Sepasi
2002	Esteghlal
2003	Zob-Ahan

Iraq

Iraq Football Association
Founded: 1948
Joined FIFA: 1950
Joined AFC: 1971

SEASON	LEAGUE CHAMPIONS
1999	Al Zawra
2000	Al Zawra
2001	Al Zawra
2002	Al Talaba
2003	*abandoned*

YEAR	CUP WINNERS
1999	Al Zawra
2000	Al Zawra
2001	*no competition*
2002	Al Talaba
2003	Al Talaba

Jordan

Jordan Football Association
Founded: 1949
Joined FIFA: 1958
Joined AFC: 1970

SEASON	LEAGUE CHAMPIONS
2000	Al Faysali
2001	Al Faysali
2002	*league format change*
2003	Al Faysali
2004	Al Faysali

YEAR	CUP WINNERS
2000	Al Wihdat
2001	Al Faysali
2002	*format change*
2003	Al Faysali
2004	Al Faysali

Argentinian striker Gabriel Batistuta is one of a number of big name players who have moved to Qatar to end their careers – he signed for Al Arabi in 2002. More recently players like Stefan Effenberg and Christoph Dugarry have trodden the same path.

Kuwait

Kuwait Football Association
Founded: 1952
Joined FIFA: 1962
Joined AFC: 1962

SEASON	LEAGUE CHAMPIONS
1999	Al Qadisiya
2000	Al Salmiya
2001	Al Kuwait
2002	Al Arabi
2003	Al Qadisiya

YEAR	CUP WINNERS
1998	Kazmah
1999	Al Arabi
2000	Al Arabi
2001	Al Salmiya
2002	Al Kuwait

Kyrgyzstan

Federation of Kyrgyz Republic
Founded: 1992
Joined FIFA: 1994
Joined AFC: 1994

SEASON	LEAGUE CHAMPIONS
1999	Dinamo Bishkek
2000	SKA-PVO Bishkek
2001	SKA-PVO Bishkek
2002	SKA-PVO Bishkek
2003	Jashtyk Ak Altyn Kara-Su

YEAR	CUP WINNERS
1999	SKA-PVO Bishkek
2000	SKA-PVO Bishkek
2001	SKA-PVO Bishkek
2002	SKA-PVO Bishkek
2003	SKA-PVO Bishkek

Lebanon

Fédération Libanaise de Football Association
Founded: 1933
Joined FIFA: 1935
Joined AFC: 1964

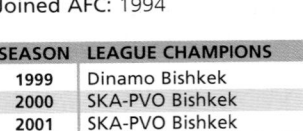

SEASON	LEAGUE CHAMPIONS
2000	Al Nejmeh
2001	*abandoned*
2002	Al Nejmeh
2003	Olympic Beirut
2004	Al Nejmeh

Oman

Oman Football Association
Founded: 1978
Joined FIFA: 1980
Joined AFC: 1979

SEASON	LEAGUE CHAMPIONS
2000	Al Arouba
2001	Dhofar
2002	Al Arouba
2003	Rowi
2004	Al Nasr

Palestine

Palestinian Football Federation
Founded: 1995
Joined FIFA: 1998
Joined AFC: 1998

SEASON	LEAGUE CHAMPIONS
1999	*not known*
2000	Khadamat Rafah
2001	*abandoned*
2002	*no championship*
2003	*no championship*

Qatar

Qatar Football Association
Founded: 1960
Joined FIFA: 1970
Joined AFC: 1972

SEASON	LEAGUE CHAMPIONS
2000	Al Sadd
2001	Al Wakra
2002	Al Etehad
2003	Qatar FC
2004	Al Sadd

Saudi Arabia

Saudi Arabian Football Federation
Founded: 1959
Joined FIFA: 1959
Joined AFC: 1972

SEASON	LEAGUE CHAMPIONS
2000	Al Ittihad
2001	Al Ittihad
2002	Al Hilal
2003	Al Ittihad
2004	Al Shabab

Saudi Arabia *(continued)*

YEAR	CUP WINNERS
2000	Al Hilal
2001	Al Ittihad
2002	Al Ahly
2003	Al Hilal
2004	Al Ittihad

Syria

Association Arabe Syrienne de Football
Founded: 1936
Joined FIFA: 1937
Joined AFC: 1969

SEASON	LEAGUE CHAMPIONS
1999	Al Jaish
2000	Jabla
2001	Al Jaish
2002	Al Jaish
2003	Al Jaish

YEAR	CUP WINNERS
1999	Jabla
2000	Al Jaish
2001	Hottin
2002	Al Jaish
2003	*unknown*

Tajikistan
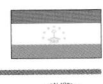

National Football Federation Tajikistan
Founded: 1936
Joined FIFA: 1994
Joined AFC: 1994

SEASON	LEAGUE CHAMPIONS
1999	Varzob Dushanbe
2000	Varzob Dushanbe
2001	Regar-TadAZ Tursunzade
2002	Regar-TadAZ Tursunzade
2003	Regar-TadAZ Tursunzade

Turkmenistan

Football Federation of Turkmenistan
Founded: 1992
Joined FIFA: 1994
Joined AFC: 1994

SEASON	LEAGUE CHAMPIONS
1999	Nisa Ashkhabad
2000	Kopétdag Ashkhabad
2001	Nisa Ashkhabad
2002	Shagadam Turkmenbashy
2003	Nisa Ashkhabad

United Arab Emirates

United Arab Emirates Football Association
Founded: 1971
Joined FIFA: 1972
Joined AFC: 1974

SEASON	LEAGUE CHAMPIONS
2000	Al Ain
2001	Al Wahda
2002	Al Ain
2003	Al Ain
2004	Al Ain

YEAR	CUP WINNERS
2000	Al Wahda
2001	Al Ain
2002	Al Ahly
2003	Sharjah
2004	Al Ahly

Uzbekistan

Uzbekistan Football Federation
Founded: 1946
Joined FIFA: 1994
Joined AFC: 1994

SEASON	LEAGUE CHAMPIONS
1999	Dustlik Tashkent
2000	Dustlik Tashkent
2001	Neftchi Ferghana
2002	Pachtakor Tashkent
2003	Pachtakor Tashkent

YEAR	CUP WINNERS
1999	*no competition*
2000	Dustlik Tashkent
2001	Pachtakor Tashkent
2002	Pachtakor Tashkent
2003	Pachtakor Tashkent

Yemen

Yemen Football Association
Founded: 1940 (South), 1962 (North). 1990
Joined FIFA: 1967 (South), 1980 (North). 1990
Joined AFC: 1967 (South), 1980 (North). 1990

SEASON	LEAGUE CHAMPIONS
2000	Al Ahli
2001	Al Ahli
2002	Al Wahda
2003	Al Sha'ab Ibb
2004	Al Sha'ab Ibb

South and East Asia

SOCCER'S DEEPEST ROOTS in Asia are in India, where the game was extensively played by the British Army and the imperial administration. Calcutta is the home of Indian soccer and its local league championship has been running since 1898. More recently the spread of the game across the nation has seen the creation of the Santosh Trophy in 1971 (contested by state teams and the Indian Army) and the Federation Cup – a nationwide competition for clubs – in 1977. The National Football League was created in 1996. After the partition of British India in 1947, national FAs and leagues were established in what was West Pakistan (now Pakistan) and East Pakistan (now Bangladesh). In the case of Bangladesh the league was originally confined to Dhaka but went national in 2000.

Soccer in China began among English expatriates in Shanghai and Hong Kong at the turn of the 20th century. A separate national Chinese FA was founded in Beijing in 1924 and affiliated to FIFA in 1931. The Chinese FA left FIFA from 1958 to 1979 in protest at FIFA's recognition of Taiwan. A national league was founded in 1926 and disrupted by 30 years of invasion, civil war and revolution. Re-established in 1953, abandoned during the Cultural Revolution (1966–72), the league went professional in 1993. In contrast, Hong Kong's professional league dates from 1945 and is the oldest pro-league in Asia.

Soccer came to the Philippines via Spanish sailors in the late 19th century and an FA was set up in 1907. British soldiers brought soccer to Malaysia and, with Singaporean teams included, league and cup competitions have run since 1921. Thailand's league dates from 1916 and a pro-league from 1995. The Dutch brought soccer to Indonesia, and in 1930 seven regional associations and leagues were established which proved a basis strong enough for the country to appear as the Dutch East Indies in the 1938 World Cup Finals. A national league was created in 1979 and went professional in 1994. The French brought soccer to Vietnam, Cambodia and Laos. Cambodia's league dates from the 1950s, Vietnam's from 1981, after the conclusion of its wars of independence, and in Laos a national league was set up in 1997.

Mohun Bagan from Calcutta. The city rivalry with East Bengal is the most intense in Asian soccer. Mohun represents the indigenous West Bengalies of the city, and East Bengal Bangladesh's migrants.

Bangladesh

Bangladesh Football Federation
Founded: 1972
Joined FIFA: 1974
Joined AFC: 1974

SEASON	LEAGUE CHAMPIONS
2000	Muktijoddha SKC
2001	Abahani Ltd
2002	Mohammedan SC
2003	*league format change*
2004	Brothers Union

Bhutan

Bhutan Football Federation
Founded: 1960
Joined FIFA: 2000
Joined AFC: 1993

SEASON	LEAGUE CHAMPIONS
1999	Kamglung
2000	Phuentsholing FC
2001	Druk Star FC
2002	Rigzung FC
2003	Drukpol

Brunei

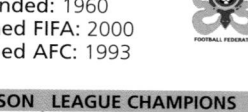

Football Association of Brunei Darussalam
Founded: 1959
Joined FIFA: 1969
Joined AFC: 1970

SEASON	LEAGUE CHAMPIONS
2002*	DPMM FC
2003	Wijaya United

* First-ever Brunei league. Previously no unified national championship.

Cambodia

Cambodia Football Federation
Founded: 1933
Joined FIFA: 1953
Joined AFC: 1957

SEASON	LEAGUE CHAMPIONS
1998	Royal Dolphins
1999	Royal Dolphins
2000	National Police
2001	*unknown*
2002	*no competition*

China

Chinese Football Association
Founded: 1924
Joined FIFA: 1931–58, 1979
Joined AFC: 1974

SEASON	LEAGUE CHAMPIONS
1999	Shandong Luneng Taishin
2000	Dalian Shide
2001	Dalian Shide
2002	Dalian Shide
2003	Shanghai Shenhua

Guam

Guam Soccer Association
Founded: 1975
Joined FIFA: 1996
Joined AFC: 1996

SEASON	LEAGUE CHAMPIONS
1999	Coors Light Silver Bullets
2000	Coors Light Silver Bullets
2001	Staywell Zoom S. Bullets
2002	Guam Shipyard
2003	Guam Shipyard

Hong Kong

Hong Kong Football Association
Founded: 1914
Joined FIFA: 1954
Joined AFC: 1954

SEASON	LEAGUE CHAMPIONS
2000	South China
2001	Happy Valley
2002	Happy Valley
2003	Happy Valley
2004	Sun Hei

India

All India Football Federation
Founded: 1937
Joined FIFA: 1948
Joined AFC: 1954

SEASON	LEAGUE CHAMPIONS
2000	Mohun Bagan AC
2001	East Bengal Club
2002	Mohun Bagan AC
2003	East Bengal Club
2004	East Bengal Club

Indonesia
 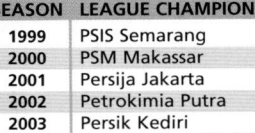

Persatuan Sepakbola Seluruh Indonesia
Founded: 1930
Joined FIFA: 1952
Joined AFC: 1954

SEASON	LEAGUE CHAMPIONS
1999	PSIS Semarang
2000	PSM Makassar
2001	Persija Jakarta
2002	Petrokimia Putra
2003	Persik Kediri

Laos

Fédération Lao de Football
Founded: 1951
Joined FIFA: 1952
Joined AFC: 1980

SEASON	LEAGUE CHAMPIONS
1999	*unknown*
2000	Vientiane Municipality
2001	*unknown*
2002	Telecom & Transportation
2003	Telecom & Transportation

Macão

Macão Football Association
Founded: 1939
Joined FIFA: 1976
Joined AFC: 1976

SEASON	LEAGUE CHAMPIONS
1999	GD Lam Pak
2000	Polícia de Segurança Pública
2001	GD Lam Pak
2002	Monte Carlo
2003	Monte Carlo

Malaysia

Persatuan Bolasepak Malaysia
Founded: 1933
Joined FIFA: 1956
Joined AFC: 1958

SEASON	LEAGUE CHAMPIONS
1999	Penang
2000	Selangor
2001	Penang
2002	Perak
2003	Perak

Maldives

Football Association of the Maldives
Founded: 1983
Joined FIFA: 1986
Joined AFC: 1986

SEASON	LEAGUE CHAMPIONS
1999	Club Valencia
2000	Victory SC
2001	Victory SC
2002	Victory SC
2003	Victory SC

Mongolia

Mongolian Football Federation
Founded: 1997
Joined FIFA: 1998
Joined AFC: 1998

SEASON	LEAGUE CHAMPIONS
1999	ITI Bank Bars
2000	Erchim
2001	Khangarid
2002	Erchim
2003	Khangarid

Myanmar
 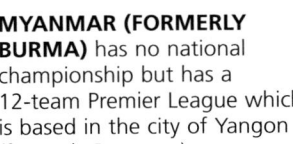

Myanmar Football Federation
Founded: 1947
Joined FIFA: 1957
Joined AFC: 1954

MYANMAR (FORMERLY BURMA) has no national championship but has a 12-team Premier League which is based in the city of Yangon (formerly Rangoon).

Nepal
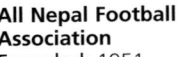

All Nepal Football Association
Founded: 1951
Joined FIFA: 1970
Joined AFC: 1971

YEAR	CUP WINNERS
1998	Mahendra Police
1999	Mahendra Police
2000	*no competition*
2001	Eastern Region
2002	*no competition*

North Korea

Football Association of the Democratic People's Republic of Korea
Founded: 1945
Joined FIFA: 1958
Joined AFC: 1974

SEASON	LEAGUE CHAMPIONS
1998	Locomotive
1999	Locomotive
2000	Locomotive
2001	*unknown*
2002	*unknown*

Pakistan

Pakistan Football Federation
Founded: 1948
Joined FIFA: 1948
Joined AFC: 1954

SEASON	LEAGUE CHAMPIONS
2000	Allied Bank Limited
2001	WAPDA
2002	*league format change*
2003	WAPDA
2004	*cancelled*

Philippines

Philippines Football Federation
Founded: 1907
Joined FIFA: 1928
Joined AFC: 1954

YEAR	CUP WINNERS
2000	*unknown*
2001	*unknown*
2002	*unknown*
2003	*unknown*
2004	NCR

Singapore

Football Association of Singapore
Founded: 1892
Joined FIFA: 1952
Joined AFC: 1954

SEASON	LEAGUE CHAMPIONS
1999	Home United
2000	Singapore Armed Forces
2001	Geyland United
2002	Singapore Armed Forces
2003	Home United

Sri Lanka

Football Federation of Sri Lanka
Founded: 1939
Joined FIFA: 1950
Joined AFC: 1958

SEASON	LEAGUE CHAMPIONS
2000	Ratnams SC
2001	Saunders SC
2002	Saunders SC
2003	Negombo Youth SC
2003*	Blue Stars SC

* Season change from autumn/spring to spring/autumn.

Taiwan

Chinese Taipei Football Association
Founded: 1936
Joined FIFA: 1954
Joined AFC: 1954–75, 1990

SEASON	LEAGUE CHAMPIONS
1998	Tai-power
1999	Tai-power
2000	Tai-power
2001	Tai-power
2002	*unknown*

Thailand

Football Association of Thailand
Founded: 1916
Joined FIFA: 1925
Joined AFC: 1957

SEASON	LEAGUE CHAMPIONS
2000	BEC Tero Sasana
2001	BEC Tero Sasana
2002	*league format change*
2003	Krung Thai Bank
2004	Krung Thai Bank

Vietnam

Vietnam Football Federation
Founded: 1962
Joined FIFA: 1964
Joined AFC: 1954

SEASON	LEAGUE CHAMPIONS
2000	Song Lam Nghe An
2001	Song Lam Nghe An
2002	Cang Saigon
2003	Hoang Anh Gia Lai
2004	Hoang Anh Gia Lai

SOUTH AND EAST ASIA

South Korea

THE SEASON IN REVIEW 2003

IT WAS ALWAYS GOING TO BE a testing year for Korean domestic soccer. Would the K-League be able to sustain the massive rise in interest and attendances that followed South Korea's 2002 World Cup success? And would anyone be able to mount a sustained challenge to the winner of the last two championships – Seongnam Ilhwa Chunma? In both cases the answer was no. Despite the enlargement of the league with two new teams entering the fray – Daegu FC and Gwangju Sangmu Phoenix – and a marathon 44 games per team, total attendances dropped from last year's 2.65 million to 2.4 million. More worryingly, Seongnam were completely unstoppable. They led for most of the season and won the championship by 17 points. Even so, at one point attendance for their homes games dropped below 2,000.

Seongnam are certainly better funded than most K-League sides, but they also performed with an admirable consistency. Their key striker, Kim Do-hoon, took the golden boot with a record-breaking 28 goals from 40 games – though he was pressed considerably harder than his team. Two Brazilians scored 27 apiece: Dodo for Ulsan Hyundai, and Magno Alves of Chonbuk Motors. Chonbuk did, however, manage a cup victory over Chunnam Dragons. After seeing a two-goal lead eradicated by a brace of goals from Chunnam's Shin Byeong-Ho, Chonbuk held their nerve to win a penalty shootout.

Seventy points adrift

Further down the league, Daejon Citizen's sixth place was a credible improvement and their 5-1 victory over Seongnam in the early rounds of the cup suggests real promise for the future. Busan I.cons were disappointed with ninth place under new English coach Ian Porterfield. Down at the bottom, new boys Daegu FC and Bucheon SK were adrift with Bucheon virtually out of sight 70 points behind the champions – a fact that may have influenced their sponsors, the communications conglomerate SK, to drop their deal and name from the club.

Right: Magno Alves, Chonbuk Motors' Brazilian striker, tied for second place in the race for the Korean Golden Boot with 27 goals.

Korean FA Cup

2003 FINAL
November 30 – Seoul World Cup Stadium

Chonbuk 2-2 Chunnam

Hyundai Dragons
Motors *(Shin Byeong-Ho*
(Edmilson Dias de 51, 65)
Lucena 9, 47)

(asdet)
h/t: 1-0 **Att:** 20,000
Ref: Son Jong-doek
Chonbuk Hyundai Motors won
4-2 on pens

Below: Chonbuk Hyundai Motors lift the Korean FA Cup after beating Chunnam Dragons in a penalty shootout at the Seoul World Cup Stadium in November 2003.

South Korean K-League Table 2003

CLUB	P	W	D	L	F	A	Pts	
Seongnam Ilhwa Chunma	44	27	10	7	85	50	**91**	Asian Champions League
Ulsan Hyundai Horang-i	44	20	13	11	63	44	**73**	
Suwon Samsung Bluewings	44	19	15	10	59	46	**72**	
Chunnam Dragons	44	17	20	7	65	48	**71**	
Chonbuk Hyundai Motors	44	18	15	11	72	58	**69**	Asian Champions League (cup winners)
Daejeon Citizen	44	18	11	15	50	51	**65**	
Pohang Steelers	44	17	13	14	53	46	**64**	
Anyang LG Cheetahs	44	14	14	16	69	68	**56**	
Busan I.cons	44	13	10	21	41	71	**49**	
Gwangju Sangmu Phoenix	44	13	7	24	41	60	**46**	
Daegu FC	44	7	16	21	38	60	**37**	
Bucheon SK	44	3	12	29	39	73	**21**	

No promotion or relegation this season.

Top Goalscorers 2003

PLAYER	CLUB	NATIONALITY	GOALS
Kim Do-hoon	Seongnam Ilhwa Chunma	Korean	28
Magno Alves	Chonbuk Hyundai Motors	Brazilian	27
Ricardo Lucas 'Dodo'	Ulsan Hyundai Horang-I	Brazilian	27
Itamar Batista da Silva	Chunnam Dragons	Brazilian	23

International Club Performances 2003

CLUB	COMPETITION	PROGRESS
Seongnam Ilhwa Chunma	Asian Champions League	Group Stage
Taejon Citizen	Asian Champions League	Group Stage
Seongnam Ilhwa Chunma	East Asian Champions Cup	3rd Place

SOUTH KOREA

Left: Gwangju stand to attention. One of the new clubs in the K-League this season, Gwangju Sangmu Phoenix are run by the South Korean army. A poor first season saw them finish third from bottom.

Below, left: Daegu FC (in blue) play SK Bucheon in the battle at the bottom. Both sides can be thankful that there was no relegation this season as the league seeks to expand. However, Bucheon finished 70 points behind Seongnam and must seek to improve.

Below: Ulsan's Brazilian striker Dodo – a headline writer's dream – scored 27 goals and so avoided any extinction references this season.

Kim Do-hoon claimed his second Korean Golden Boot this year, scoring 28 goals in his first season with Seongnam Ilhwa Chunma's .

Seongnam Ilhwa Chunma celebrate their third league title in a row finishing 18 points clear of their nearest rivals.

South Korea

KFA

Korea Football Association
Founded: 1928
Joined FIFA: 1948
Joined AFC: 1954

SOUTH KOREA

FOR MOST OF the first half of the 20th century the whole Korean peninsula was occupied and colonized by the Japanese but a national FA was established in Seoul in 1928 and amateur soccer flourished in the cities. After the Second World War, the peninsula was divided into North and South (Soviet and US occupation zones, respectively), a division solidified by the stalemate of the Korean War (1949–53). The Korea Football Association joined FIFA in 1948 and was a founder member of the AFC (Asian Football Confederation) in 1954. Soccer struggled as baseball was the dominant spectator sport. However, in the early 1980s, with the financial support of Chaebol (a number of large Korean companies), a professional league was established. Chaebol have not been the only investors in Korean clubs. The religious foundation of the Moonies own Songnam Ilhwa Chunma. Alongside the league a number of cup competitions have been held, some sporadically. A Korean FA Cup began in 1996 to ensure Korean representation in the AFC's Asian Cup-Winners' Cup. The league has ten clubs, with the top six going into a championship play-off at the end of the season.

Honours have been spread around the country since the inception of the professional league and South Korean clubs have proved very successful in international club competitions, with four victories in the Asian Club Championship – including an all-South Korean Final in 1997 when the reigning champions Ilhwa Chunma were beaten by the Pohang Steelers. Two South Korean teams also contested the 2002 Final: Suwon Samsung Bluewings and Anyang LG Cheetahs. The Bluewings won 4-2 on penalties.

South Korean K-League Record 1983–2003

SEASON	CHAMPIONS	RUNNERS-UP
1983	Hallelujah	Daewoo
1984	Daewoo Royals	Yukong Elephants
1985	LG Hwangso	POSCO Atoms
1986	POSCO Atoms	LG Hwangso
1987	Daewoo Royals	Yukong Elephants
1988	POSCO Atoms	Hyundai Horang-i
1989	Yukong Elephants	LG Hwangso
1990	LG Hwangso	Daewoo Royals
1991	Daewoo Royals	Hyundai Horang-i
1992	POSCO Atoms	Ilhwa Chunma
1993	Ilhwa Chunma	LG Cheetahs
1994	Ilhwa Chunma	Yukong Elephants
1995	Ilhwa Chunma	Pohang Atoms
1996	Ulsan Hyundai Horang-i	Suwon Samsung Bluewings
1997	Pusan Daewoo Royals	Chunnam Dragons
1998	Suwon Samsung Bluewings	Ulsan Hyundai Horang-i
1999	Suwon Samsung Bluewings	Pusan Daewoo Royals
2000	Anyang LG Cheetahs	Puchon SK
2001	Seongnam Ilhwa Chunma	Anyang LG Cheetahs
2002	Seongnam Ilhwa Chunma	Ulsan Hyundai Horang-i
2003	Seongnam Ilhwa Chunma	Ulsan Hyundai Horang-i

South Korean FA Cup Record 1996–2003

YEAR	WINNERS	SCORE	RUNNERS-UP
1996	Pohang Atoms	0-0 (7-6 pens)	Suwon Samsung Bluewings
1997	Chunnam Dragons	1-0	Chonan Ilhwa Chunma
1998	Anyang LG Cheetahs	2-1	Ulsan Hyundai Horang-i
1999	Chonan Ilhwa Chunma	3-0	Chonbuk Hyundai Dinos
2000	Chonbuk Hyundai Motors	2-0	Songnam Ilhwa Chunma
2001	Taejon Citizen	1-0	Pohang Steelers
2002	Suwon Samsung Bluewings	1-0	Pohang Steelers
2003	Chonbuk Hyundai Motors	2-2 (4-2 pens)	Chunnam Dragons

Top Goalscorers 1983–2003

YEAR	SCORER	TEAM	NATIONALITY	GOALS
1983	Park Yun-gi	Yukong Elephants	Korean	9
1984	Baek Jong-cheol	Hyundai Horang-i	Korean	16
1985	Piyapong Pue-on Kim Yong-se	LG Hwangso Yukong Elephants	Korean Korean	12
1986	Jeong Hae-won	Daewoo Royals	Korean	10
1987	Choi Sang-guk	POSCO Atoms	Korean	15
1988	Lee Gi-geun	POSCO Atoms	Korean	12
1989	Cho Gueng-yeon	POSCO Atoms	Korean	20
1990	Yun Sang-cheol	LG Cheetahs	Korean	12
1991	Lee Gi-geun	POSCO Atoms	Korean	16
1992	Im Geun-jae	LG Cheetahs	Korean	10
1993	Caha Sang-hae	POSCO Atoms	Korean	10
1994	Yun Sang-cheol	LG Cheetahs	Korean	21
1995	Roh Sang-rae	Chunnam Dragons	Korean	15
1996	Shin Tae-yong	Chonan Ilhwa Chunma	Korean	18
1997	Kim Hyun-seok	Ulsan Hyundai Horang-i	Korean	9
1998	Yoo Sang-chul	Ulsan Hyundai Horang-i	Korean	14
1999	Sasa Drakulic	Suwon Samsung Bluewings	Yugoslavian	14
2000	Kim Do-hoon	Chonbuk Hyundai Motors	Korean	12
2001	Sandro Dos Santos	Suwon Samsung Bluewings	Brazilian	13
2002	Edmilson dias de Lucera	Chonbuk Hyundai Motors	Brazilian	14
2003	Kim Do-hoon	Seongnam Ilhwa Chunma	Korean	28

Adidas K-Cup Record 1992–2002

YEAR	WINNERS
1992	Ilhwa Chunma
1993	POSCO Atoms
1994	Yukong Elephants
1995	Hyundai Horang-i
1996	Puchon Yukong
1997	Pusan Daewoo Royals
1998	no competition

YEAR	WINNERS
1999	Suwon Samsung Bluewings
2000	Suwon Samsung Bluewings
2001	Suwon Samsung Bluewings
2002	Seongnam Ilhwa Chunma

In 2003 Seongnam Ilhwa Chunma won their third consecutive South Korean league title.

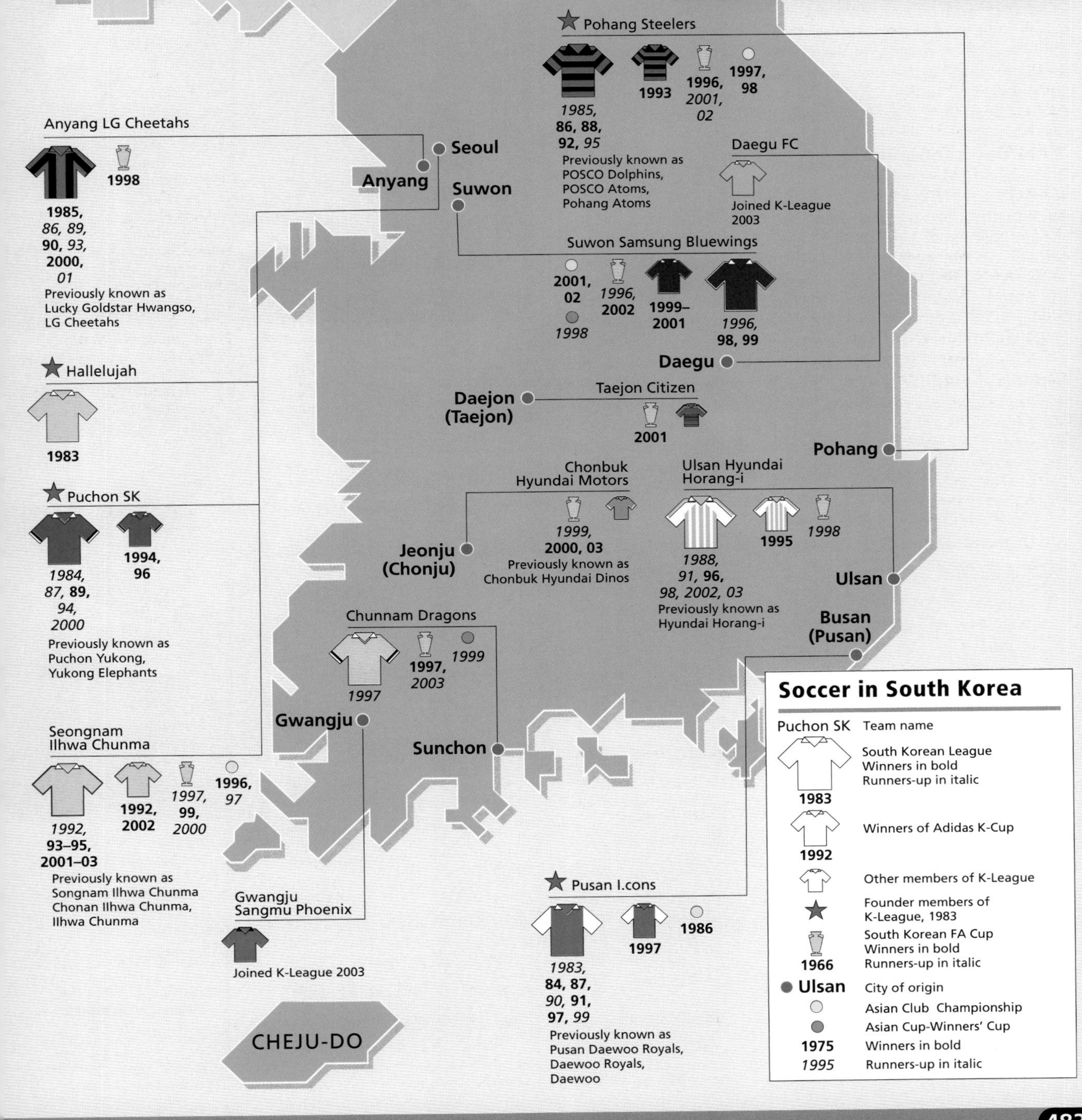

SOUTH KOREA

NORTH KOREA

☆ Pohang Steelers

1985, 86, 88, 92, 95

1993

1996, 2001, 02

○ **1997, 98**

Previously known as POSCO Dolphins, POSCO Atoms, Pohang Atoms

Daegu FC

Joined K-League 2003

Anyang LG Cheetahs

1998

1985, 86, 89, 90, 93, **2000, 01**

Previously known as Lucky Goldstar Hwangso, LG Cheetahs

● **Seoul**

Anyang

Suwon

Suwon Samsung Bluewings

2001, 02

1996, 2002

1999–2001

1996, 98, 99

○ *1998*

Daegu ●

★ Hallelujah

1983

Daejon (Taejon) ●

Taejon Citizen

2001

Pohang ●

★ Puchon SK

1984, 87, **89,** *94,* **2000**

1994, 96

Previously known as Puchon Yukong, Yukong Elephants

Chonbuk Hyundai Motors

1999, **2000, 03**

Previously known as Chonbuk Hyundai Dinos

Jeonju (Chonju) ●

Ulsan Hyundai Horang-i

1988, 91, 96, 98, 2002, 03

Previously known as Hyundai Horang-i

1995

1998

Ulsan ●

Busan (Pusan) ●

Seongnam Ilhwa Chunma

1992, **1992, 2002**

1997, 99, 2000

○ **1996, 97**

1992, 93–95, **2001–03**

Previously known as Songnam Ilhwa Chunma Chonan Ilhwa Chunma, Ilhwa Chunma

Chunnam Dragons

1997, 2003

1997

● *1999*

Gwangju ●

Sunchon ●

Gwangju Sangmu Phoenix

Joined K-League 2003

★ Pusan I.cons

1983, **84, 87, 90, 91, 97, 99**

○ **1986**

1997

Previously known as Pusan Daewoo Royals, Daewoo Royals, Daewoo

CHEJU-DO

Soccer in South Korea

Puchon SK — Team name

1983 — South Korean League Winners in bold Runners-up in italic

1992 — Winners of Adidas K-Cup

Other members of K-League

★ — Founder members of K-League, 1983

1966 — South Korean FA Cup Winners in bold Runners-up in italic

● **Ulsan** — City of origin

○ — Asian Club Championship

● — Asian Cup-Winners' Cup

1975 — Winners in bold

1995 — Runners-up in italic

Japan

THE SEASON IN REVIEW 2003

The First Stage of the J-League saw unfancied JEF from Ichihara lead the league under Croat coach Ivica Osim. However, the team's lead crumbled over the last three games and the normal order of things returned. Yokohama Marinos reversed last year's top placings, winning the championship and putting Jubilo Iwata in second place. Tokyo Verdy made a commendable comeback over the year after a disastrous start – the arrival of Argentinian Ossie Ardiles as coach and the goals of Cameroonian Patrick Mboma dragging them out of the depths of the relegation zone. Kashima Antlers' league form seemed to suffer from its heady victory in the early season East Asian Champions League.

Final day shenanigans

The Second Stage was a more closely fought affair with up to ten teams in contention at any one time. The final day's games began with Jubilo Iwata heading the table and playing third-placed Yokohama Marinos at home. Gral opened the scoring in the second minute for Jubilo and victory looked certain when Marino's keeper Tatsuya Enomoto was sent off after 13 minutes. But Marinos found a second-half equalizer and with injury time looming, the score was 1-1. A point saved, but Jubilo was still champions-elect. Then, with seconds to spare, Marinos' Tatsuhiko scored a second. Kashima Antlers, who had begun the day in second place, then looked set to be champions as the team was leading Urawa Red Diamonds 2-1 as well. But, while Yokohama hung on, the Brazilian Emerson found a last-minute equalizer for Urawa and Yokohama were champions. Jubilo ended up in third place as JEF United sneaked into second spot on goal difference.

Above: Champions for two minutes, on the final day of the season, Kashima Antlers (right) was 2-1 up at Urawa Red Diamonds and top of the J-league. But Yokohama's comeback and Urawa's last-minute goal saw them drop to fourth place.

Urawa Red Diamonds striker Tatsuya Tanaka relishes his goal in the 2003 League Cup Final – Urawa cruised past Kashima 4-0.

J-League Division 1 Table 2003

| FIRST STAGE | | | | | | | |
CLUB	P	W	D	L	F	A	Pts
Yokohama F. Marinos	15	10	2	3	29	16	32
Jubilo Iwata	15	9	4	2	34	17	31
JEF United Ichihara	15	8	3	4	33	20	27
FC Tokyo	15	7	4	4	14	11	25
Cerezo Osaka	15	8	1	6	29	29	25
Urawa Red Diamonds	15	7	3	5	25	23	24
Nagoya Grampus Eight	15	5	8	2	19	16	23
Kashima Antlers	15	7	2	6	23	21	23
Kashiwa Reysol	15	6	3	6	19	19	21
Tokyo Verdy 1969	15	6	1	8	28	32	19
Shimizu S-Pulse	15	5	3	7	20	18	18
Gamba Osaka	15	4	4	7	26	29	16
Vissel Kobe	15	5	1	9	18	34	16
Oita Trinita	15	4	3	8	20	21	15
Vegalta Sendai	15	3	3	9	17	28	12
Kyoto Purple Sanga	15	3	1	11	14	34	10

| SECOND STAGE | | | | | | | | |
CLUB	P	W	D	L	F	A	Pts	
Yokohama F. Marinos	15	7	5	3	27	17	26	Asian Champions League
JEF United Ichihara	15	7	5	3	24	18	26	
Jubilo Iwata	15	7	5	3	22	17	26	Asian Champions League
Kashima Antlers	15	6	7	2	21	19	25	
FC Tokyo	15	6	6	3	32	20	24	
Urawa Red Diamonds	15	6	5	4	29	19	23	
Gamba Osaka	15	6	5	4	24	17	23	
Nagoya Grampus Eight	15	6	4	5	30	26	22	
Tokyo Verdy 1969	15	5	6	4	28	25	21	
Shimizu S-Pulse	15	6	3	6	19	26	21	
Kashiwa Reysol	15	3	7	5	16	20	16	
Cerezo Osaka	15	4	3	8	26	27	15	
Vissel Kobe	15	3	5	7	17	29	14	
Kyoto Purple Sanga	15	3	4	8	14	26	13	Relegated
Vegalta Sendai	15	2	6	7	14	28	12	Relegated
Oita Trinita	15	1	8	6	7	16	11	

Yokohama F. Marinos are champions as winners of both stages. Promoted clubs: Albirex Niigata, Sanfrecce Hiroshima.

League Cup

2003 FINAL

November 3 – Tokyo National Stadium

Kashima 0-4 Urawa Red
Antlers   Diamonds
(Koji 13,
Emerson 48, 86,
Tatsuya 56)
h/t: 0-1 Att: 51,758
Ref: Masayoshi Okada

Left: Yokohama F. Marinos skipper Daisuke Oku receives the J-league trophy from League chairman Masaru Suzuki on the last day of the Second Stage. As the Marinos won both Stages of the championship no play-off was required.

Below: Rodrigo Gral laps it up after scoring the winner for Jubilo Iwata in the Cup Final against Cerezo Osaka. Ten minutes later he was sent off for a second bookable offence.

Bottom: Celebrations followed, but in reality it was a disappointing season for Jubilo.

Emperor's Cup

2003 FINAL

January 1, 2004 – Tokyo National Stadium
Cerezo Osaka 0-1 Jubilo Iwata
(Gral 71)
h/t: 0-0 **Att:** 51,500
Ref: Toshimitsu Yoshida

Yokohama coach Takeshi Okada takes the plaudits after his team's triumphant season. The former national team coach made Manager of the Year after the Marinos' two-stage league double.

Top Goalscorers 2003

PLAYER	CLUB	NATIONALITY	GOALS
Ueslei	Nagoya Grampus Eight	Brazilian	22
Rodrigo Gral	Jubilo Iwata	Brazilian	21
Emerson	Urawa Red Diamonds	Brazilian	18

International Club Performances 2003

CLUB	COMPETITION	PROGRESS
Kashima Antlers	Asian Champions League	Group Stage
Shimizu S-Pulse	Asian Champions League	Group Stage
Kashima Antlers	East Asian Champions Cup	Winners
Jubilo Iwata	East Asian Champions Cup	4th Place

Japan

THE J-LEAGUE 1993–2003

A NATIONAL SOCCER LEAGUE had been played in Japan since 1965, but the JSL was always a corporate amateur affair. Until the late 1980s there were no official professional contracts and teams were all sponsored by Japan's industrial giants as a combination of company welfare, advertising and philanthropy. With international club success in the 1980s coming to Japan (Furukawa Electric won the Asian Club Championship in 1987), the Japanese FA decided to organize a professional league.

The J-League was launched in 1993, with a capital injection of around $20 million. The top teams of the old JSL were revamped, corporate names were banned and hometown affiliations emphasized in clubs names and outlook. Riding the end of Japan's massive consumer binge of the early 1990s, the J-League proved enormously popular. Massive TV coverage, marketing and a slew of foreign players saw gate takings and income rise for four years. Brazilians, Italians and Eastern Europeans all made their way there towards the end of their careers, and more recently African players have followed in their footsteps.

Early years of the J-League

The early years of the J-League belonged to the leading teams of the JSL era: Yomiuri Club became Verdy Kawasaki and won the championship in 1993 and 94, and Nissan Motors became Yokohama Marinos and beat Verdy in the 1995 championship play-off. The late 90s saw a shift of power with titles alternating between two clubs with no pre-J-League pedigree, Kashima Antlers and Jubilo Iwata, before Kashima moved up a gear to take a treble of domestic trophies in 2000. Gamba Osaka, JEF United Ichihara, Nagoya Grampus Eight and Sanfrecce Hiroshima have proved the leagues underachievers.

Despite a dip in the late 1990s, as consumer indifference and economic stagnation set in, the quality of play and the size of crowds have risen again with the World Cup going to Japan in 2002. Distinctive fan cultures and solid gates have emerged at Shimizu S-Pulse, Uruwa Red Diamonds and Consadole Sapporo. Perhaps most importantly, a soccer gambling system – the Toto – was introduced in 2000 and has proved to be a massive commercial success.

The J-League: leading investors

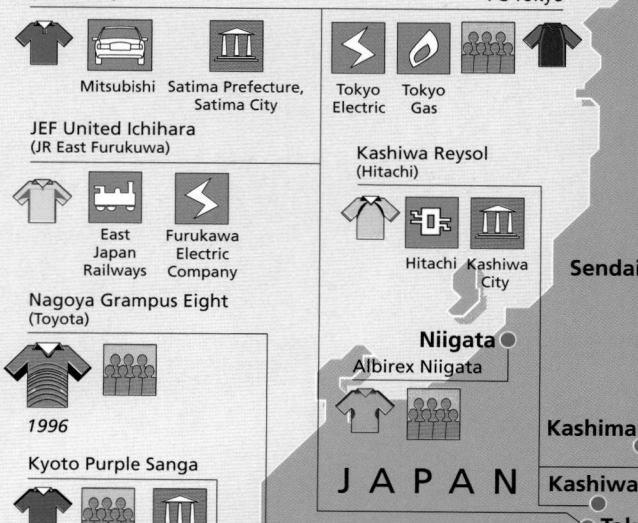

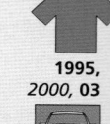

Uruwa Red Diamond fans have created the most distinctive fan culture in the J-League, and the one most at odds with key elements of Japanese culture. Early fan groups were the first to boo their own players for poor performances and create an intimidating atmosphere for visiting teams.

Yokohama F. Marinos' defender Yuji 'Bomberhead' Nakazawa lifts the J-League championship trophy after his team's two-stage triumph in 2003.

Sapporo

Consadole Sapporo (Toshiba)

Vegalta Sendai

Miyagi Prefecture, Sendai City

Kashima Antlers (Sumitomo Honda)

Sumitomo Metals — *1993, 96, 97, 98, 2000, 01*

Tokyo Verdy

Nippon Television

Verdy Kawasaki (Yomiuri Club)

Nippon Television — **1993, 94, 95**

Kawasaki Frontale

Fujitsu

Key to League Positions Table

F/S	Denotes First/Second stages
	League champions
	Season of promotion to league
	Season of relegation from league
	Other teams playing in league
5	Final position in league

JAPAN

Japanese League Positions 1993–2003

SEASON

TEAM	1993 F	1993 S	1994 F	1994 S	1995 F	1995 S	1996	1997 F	1997 S	1998†F	1998†S	1999 F	1999 S	2000 F	2000 S	2001 F	2001 S	2002 F	2002 S	2003 F	2003 S
Avispa Fukuoka							15	17	15	18	15	11	15	14	6	12	15				
Bellmare Hiratsuka			7	2	7	14	11	4	9	12	12	16	16								
Sanfrecce Hiroshima	6	5	1	4	10	12	14	10	13	13	9	6	8	10	11	13	3	15	14		
JEF United Ichihara	5	9	6	9	6	7	9	15	14	11	18	15	11	11	16	2	5	8	11	3	2
Jubilo Iwata			11	7	5	9	4	6	1*	1	2	1	12*	5	3	1	2	1	1**	2	3
Kashima Antlers	1	4	3	5	8	6	1	1	4	5	1*	9	6	8	1*	11	1*	5	3	7	4
Kashiwa Reysol					14	5	5	3	10	10	8	4	4	4	2	6	7	14	9	9	11
Kawasaki Frontale														15	15						
Verdy Kawasaki	2	1*	4	1*	2	1	7	16	12	6	17	2	10	9	10						
Vissel Kobe								14	17	17	14	12	7	7	14	10	13	13	10	13	13
Kyoto Purple Sanga							16	13	16	15	11	14	9	16	12			6	7	16	14
Albirex Niigata																					
Nagoya Grampus Eight	9	8	8	12	4	2	2	12	5	3	6	8	2	12	7	3	6	3	13	7	8
Oita Trinita																				14	16
Cerezo Osaka							9	10	13	11	8	9	13	5	5	2	9	14	16	5	12
Gamba Osaka	8	6	10	10	11	13	12	8	2	14	16	10	13	13	4	5	11	4	2	12	7
Consadole Sapporo										16	10					8	14	16	16		
Vegalta Sendai																		9	15	15	15
Shimizu S-Pulse	4	2	2	6	12	4	10	7	6	2	5	3	1	3	13	4	4	2	11	12	10
Tokyo Verdy																16	9	12	4	10	9
FC Tokyo														6	8	9	8	10	5	4	5
Uruwa Red Diamonds	10	10	12	11	3	8	6	9	7	3	9	13	14			7	12	11	8	6	6
Yokohama Flugels	7	7	5	8	13	11	3	2	11	8	7										
Yokohama F. Marinos	3	3	9	3	1	3*	8	5	3	4	4	7	3	1	5	15	10	2	6	1	1**

*Denotes championship play-off winners. Except 1996, season is divided into two stages, First and Second, with a play-off to decide the championship.

**Champions won both stages, so there was no play-off.

†First year of promotion and relegation.

Japan

Japan Football Association
Founded: 1921
Joined FIFA: 1929–46, 1950
Joined AFC: 1954

A RUDIMENTARY VERSION of soccer has been played in Japan for over 1,500 years. The rapid modernization of Japan on Western lines after the Meiji restoration (1868) saw modern soccer established in schools and universities in the early years of the 20th century. In 1921, the first national cup competition was established, modelled on the English FA Cup. Breaking for the war, it was replaced in 1946 by the Emperor's Cup. An additional cup competition, the Japan Soccer League Cup, was launched in 1976 and renamed the J-League Cup in 1992. Winners of this competition enter the Asian Cup-Winners' Cup.

National league soccer started in 1965, based on teams supported by industrial groups (Toyota, Hitachi, Nissan etc.). Although popular, the league was always second to baseball in Japan. In 1993, with enormous new commercial backing, the old structures were abandoned and Japanese league soccer was relaunched as the J-League in a ten-team premier league, later expanded to 16. A second division was added in 1999. Teams score three points for a win, two points for a win in extra time (drawn games always go to extra time) and one for a draw. Until 1998, drawn games after extra time were decided by a penalty shootout. The season was then divided into opening and closing championships with play-offs to decide the winners.

Japanese League Record 1965–2003

SEASON	CHAMPIONS	RUNNERS-UP
1965	Toyo Industrial	Yahata Steel
1966	Toyo Industrial	Yahata Steel
1967	Toyo Industrial	Furukawa Electric
1968	Toyo Industrial	Yanmar Diesel
1969	Mitsubishi Heavy Industrial	Toyo Industrial
1970	Toyo Industrial	Mitsubishi Heavy Industrial
1971	Yanmar Diesel	Mitsubishi Heavy Industrial
1972	Hitachi	Yanmar Diesel
1973	Mitsubishi Heavy Industrial	Hitachi
1974	Yanmar Diesel	Mitsubishi Heavy Industrial
1975	Yanmar Diesel	Mitsubishi Heavy Industrial
1976*		
1977	Furukawa Electric	Mitsubishi Heavy Industrial
1978	Fujita Industrial	Mitsubishi Heavy Industrial
1978†	Mitsubishi Heavy Industrial	Yanmar Diesel
1979	Fujita Industrial	Yomiuri Club
1980	Yanmar Diesel	Fujita Industrial
1981	Fujita Industrial	Yomiuri Club
1982	Mitsubishi Heavy Industrial	Yanmar Diesel
1983	Yomiuri Club	Nissan Motors
1984	Yomiuri Club	Nissan Motors
1985*		
1986	Furukawa Electric	Nippon Kokan
1987	Yomiuri Club	Nippon Kokan
1988	Yamaha Motors	Nippon Kokan
1989	Nissan Motors	All Nippon Airways
1990	Nissan Motors	Yomiuri Club
1991	Yomiuri Club	Nissan Motors
1992	Yomiuri Club	Nissan Motors
1993	Verdy Kawasaki	Kashima Antlers
1994	Verdy Kawasaki	Sanfrecce Hiroshima
1995	Yokohama Marinos	Verdy Kawasaki
1996	Kashima Antlers	Nagoya Grampus Eight
1997	Jubilo Iwata	Kashima Antlers
1998	Kashima Antlers	Jubilo Iwata

Japanese League Record (*continued*)

SEASON	CHAMPIONS	RUNNERS-UP
1999	Jubilo Iwata	Shimizu S-Pulse
2000	Kashima Antlers	Yokohama Marinos
2001	Kashima Antlers	Jubilo Iwata
2002	Jubilo Iwata**	Yokohama Marinos
2003	Yokohama F. Marinos**	Jubilo Iwata

* There is no result as the season changed its start and finish date.
† Two seasons were played in this year.
** No play-offs needed as champions won both stages.

Japanese League Summary

TEAM	TOTALS	CHAMPIONS & RUNNERS-UP (BOLD) (*ITALICS*)
Verdy Kawasaki (includes Yomiuri Club)	7, 4	*1979, 81,* **83, 84, 87,** *90,* **91–94,** *95*
Sanfrecce Hiroshima (includes Toyo Industrial)	5, 2	**1965–68,** *69,* **70,** *94*
Mitsubishi Heavy Industrial	4, 6	**1969,** *70, 71,* **73,** *74, 75, 77, 78,* **78†,** *82*
Yokohama F. Marinos (includes Yokohama Marinos and Nissan Motors)	4, 6	*1983, 84,* **89,** *90, 91, 92,* **95,** *2000, 02,* **03**
Yanmar Diesel	4, 4	**1968,** *71, 72,* **74, 75,** *78,* **80,** *82*
Jubilo Iwata (includes Yamaha Motors)	4, 3	**88, 97, 98,** *99,* **2001,** *02,* **03**
Kashima Antlers	4, 2	**1993,** *96,* **97, 98, 2000,** *01*
Fujita Industrial	3, 1	**1978, 79,** *80,* **81**
Furukawa Electric	2, 1	**1967,** *77,* **86**
Hitachi	1, 1	**1972,** *73*
Nippon Kokan	0, 3	*1986–88*
Yahata Steel	0, 2	*1965, 66*
All Nippon Airways	0, 1	*1989*
Nagoya Grampus Eight	0, 1	*1996*
Shimizu S-Pulse	0, 1	*1999*

Japanese Cup Record 1921–2003

YEAR	WINNERS	SCORE	RUNNERS-UP
1921	Tokyo Shukyu-dan	1-0	Mikage Shukyu-dan
1922	Nagoya Shukyu-dan	1-0	Hiroshima Koto-shihan
1923	Astra Club	2-1	Nagoya Shukyu-dan
1924	Rijo FC	4-1	All Mikage Shihan Club
1925	Rijo FC	3-0	Tokyo University
1926		no competition	
1927	Kobe-Ichi Jr. Highschool Club	2-0	Rijo FC
1928	Waseda University WMW	6-1	Kyoto University
1929	Kwangaku Club	3-0	Housei University
1930	Kwangaku Club	3-0	Keio University BRB
1931	Tokyo University LB	5-1	Kobun Jr. Highschool
1932	Keio Club	5-1	Yoshino Club
1933	Tokyo University LB	4-1	Sendai Football Club
1934		no competition	
1935	All Keio Club	6-1	Tokyo Bunri University
1936	Keio University BRB	3-2	Fusei Senmon
1937	Keio University BRB	*	Kobe Commercial University
1938	Waseda University WMW	4-1	Keio University BRB
1939	Keio University BRB	3-2	Waseda University WMW

JAPAN

Japanese Cup Record (*continued*)

YEAR	WINNERS	SCORE	RUNNERS-UP
1940	Keio University BRB	1-0	Waseda University WMW
1941–45		*no competition*	
1946	Tokyo University LB	6-2	Kobe Keizai-dai Club
1947–48		*no competition*	
1949	Tokyo University LB	5-2	Kwangaku Club
1950	All Kwangaku	6-1	Keio University BRB
1951	Keio University BRB	3-2	Osaka Club
1952	All Keio University	6-2	Osaka Club
1953	All Kwangaku	5-4	Osaka Club
1954	Keio University BRB	5-3 (aet)	Toyo Industrial
1955	All Kwangaku	4-3	Chudai Club
1956	Keio University BRB	4-2	Yahata Steel
1957	Chuo University	2-1	Toyo Industrial
1958	Kwangaku Club	2-1	Yahata Steel
1959	Kwangaku Club	1-0	Chuo University
1960	Furukawa Electric	4-0	Keio University BRB
1961	Furukawa Electric	3-2	Chuo University
1962	Chuo University	2-1	Furukawa Electric
1963	Waseda University WMW	3-0	Hitachi
1964†	Yahata Steel	0-0 (aet)	Furukawa Electric
1965	Toyo Industrial	3-2	Yahata Steel
1966	Waseda University WMW	3-2 (aet)	Toyo Industrial
1967	Toyo Industrial	1-0	Mitsubishi Heavy Industrial
1968	Yanmar Diesel	1-0	Mitsubishi Heavy Industrial
1969	Toyo Industrial	4-1	Rikkyo University
1970	Yanmar Diesel	2-1 (aet)	Toyo Industrial
1971	Mitsubishi Heavy Industrial	3-1	Yanmar Diesel
1972	Hitachi	2-1	Yanmar Diesel
1973	Mitsubishi Heavy Industrial	2-1	Hitachi
1974	Yanmar Diesel	2-1	Eidai Industrial
1975	Hitachi	2-0	Fujita Industrial
1976	Furukawa Electric	4-1	Yanmar Diesel
1977	Fujita Industrial	4-1	Yanmar Diesel
1978	Mitsubishi Heavy Industrial	1-0	Toyo Industrial
1979	Fujita Industrial	2-1	Mitsubishi Heavy Industrial
1980	Mitsubishi Heavy Industrial	1-0	Tanabe Medecine
1981	NKK	2-0	Yomiuri Club
1982	Yamaha Motors	1-0 (aet)	Fujita Industrial
1983	Nissan Motors	2-0	Yanmar Diesel
1984	Yomiuri Club	2-0	Furukawa Electric
1985	Nissan Motors	2-0	Fujita Industrial
1986	Yomiuri Club	2-1	NKK
1987	Yomiuri Club	2-0	Mazda
1988	Nissan Motors	3-1 (aet)	Fujita Industrial
1989	Nissan Motors	3-2	Yamaha Motors
1990	Matsushita	0-0 (aet)(4-3 pens)	Nissan Motors
1991	Nissan Motors	4-1 (aet)	Yomiuri Club
1992	Yokohama Marinos	2-1 (aet)	Verdy Kawasaki
1993	Yokohama Flugels	6-2 (aet)	Kashima Antlers
1994	Bellmare Hiratsuka	2-0	Cerezo Osaka
1995	Nagoya Grampus Eight	3-0	Sanfrecce Hiroshima
1996	Verdy Kawasaki	3-0	Sanfrecce Hiroshima
1997	Kashima Antlers	3-0	Yokohama Flugels
1998	Yokohama Flugels	2-1	Shimizu S-Pulse
1999	Nagoya Grampus Eight	2-0	Sanfrecce Hiroshima
2000	Kashima Antlers	3-2 (asdet)	Shimizu S-Pulse
2001	Shimizu S-Pulse	3-2	Cerezo Osaka
2002	Kashima Antlers	1-0	Urawa Red Diamonds
2003	Jubilo Iwata	1-0	Cerezo Osaka

Japanese Cup Summary

TEAM	TOTALS	WINNERS & RUNNERS-UP (BOLD) (*ITALICS*)
Keio University BRB (includes Tokyo Bunri)	7, 5	*1930, 35,* **36, 37, 38, 39, 40, 50, 51, 54, 56,** *60*
Yokohama Marinos (includes Nissan Motors)	6, 1	**1983, 85, 88, 89,** *90,* **91, 92**
Urawa Red Diamonds (includes Mitsubishi Heavy Industrial)	4, 4	*1967, 68,* **71,** *73,* **78,** *79,* **80,** *2002*
Verdy Kawasaki (Includes Yomiuri Club)	4, 3	*1981,* **84,** *86,* **87,** *91, 92,* **96**
Furukawa Electric	4, 2	**1960, 61,** *62,* **64†,** *76,* **84**
Waseda University WMW	4, 2	*1928,* **38, 39, 40,** *63,* **66**
Kwangaku Club	4, 1	*1929,* **30,** *49,* **58, 59**
Tokyo University LB	4, 1	*1925,* **31,** *33,* **46, 49**
Cerezo Osaka (includes Yanmar Diesel)	3, 8	**1968,** *70,* **71,** *72,* **74,** *76, 77, 83, 94, 2001, 03*
Sanfrecce Hiroshima (includes Toyo Industrial and Mazda)	3, 8	*1954, 57,* **65,** *66,* **67,** *69, 70, 78, 87, 95, 96, 99*
Bellmare Hiratsuka (includes Fujita Industrial)	3, 4	*1975,* **77,** *79,* **82,** *85, 88,* **94**
Kashima Antlers	3, 1	*1993,* **97, 2000,** *02*
All Kwangaku	3, 0	**1950, 53, 55**
Chuo University	2, 2	**1957,** *59,* **61,** *62*
Hitachi	2, 2	*1963,* **72, 73,** *75*
Jubilo Iwata (includes Yamaha Motors)	2, 1	**1982,** *89,* **2003**
Rijo FC	2, 1	**1924, 25,** *27*
Yokohama Flugels	2, 1	*1993,* **97, 98**
Nagoya Grampus Eight	2, 0	**1995, 99**
Yahata Steel	1, 3	*1956, 58,* **64†,** *65*
Shimizu S-Pulse	1, 2	*1998, 2000,* **01**
Nagoya Shukyu-dan	1, 1	**1922,** *23*
NKK	1, 1	**1981,** *86*
All Keio Club	1, 0	**1935**
All Keio University	1, 0	**1952**
Astra Club	1, 0	**1923**
Keio Club	1, 0	**1932**
Kobe-Ichi Jr. Highschool Club	1, 0	**1927**
Matsushita	1, 0	**1990**
Tokyo Shukyu-dan	1, 0	**1921**
Osaka Club	0, 3	*1951–53*
All Mikage Shihan Club	0, 1	*1924*
Chudai Club	0, 1	*1955*
Eidai Industrial	0, 1	*1974*
Fusei Senmon	0, 1	*1936*
Hiroshima Koto-shihan	0, 1	*1922*
Housei University	0, 1	*1929*
Kobe Commercial University	0, 1	*1937*
Kobe Keizai-dai Club	0, 1	*1946*
Kobun Jr Highschool	0, 1	*1931*
Kyoto University	0, 1	*1928*
Mikage Shukyu-dan	0, 1	*1921*
Rikkyo University	0, 1	*1969*
Sendai Football Club	0, 1	*1933*
Tanabe Medecine	0, 1	*1980*
Yoshino Club	0, 1	*1932*

* Final score unknown.

† This year the title was tied, as extra time did not produce a champion.

JAPAN

NORTHERN MARIANA ISLANDS
[Commonwealth Territory of USA]
Northern Mariana Islands Football Association
associate (not affiliated)

WESTERN SAMOA
[1962]
Western Samoa Football Association
1986 (1986)

MARSHALL ISLANDS
(not affiliated to OFC)

AMERICAN SAMOA
[Unincorporated territory of the USA]
American Samoa Football Association
1994 (1998)

INDIAN OCEAN

PALAU
(not affiliated to OFC)

MICRONESIA
(not affiliated to OFC)

SOLOMON ISLANDS
[1978]
Solomon Islands Football Federation
1988 (1988)

PAPUA NEW GUINEA
[1975]
Papua New Guinea Football Association
1966 (1963)

TOKELAU
(not affiliated to OFC)

TUVALU
(not affiliated to OFC)

WALLIS & FUTUNA
(not affiliated to OFC)

VANUATU
[1980]
Vanuatu Football Association
1988 (1988)

AUSTRALIA
[1901]
Australian Soccer Federation
1966–72, 78 (1963)

1974

1980, 96, 98, 2000, 02

NEW CALEDONIA
[French Overseas Territory]
Fédération Néo-Calédonienne de Football
provisional (associate)

FIJI
[1970]
Fiji Football Association
1966 (1963)

TONGA
[1970]
Tonga Football Association
1994 (1994)

NEW ZEALAND
[1926]
New Zealand Football Association
1966 (1948)

Auckland
OFC Headquarters

NIUE ISLANDS
[Territory in Free Association with New Zealand]
Niue Islands Football Association
associate (not affiliated)

1982

1973, 98, 2000, 02

Former OFC President Charles Dempsey caused a storm by abstaining in the ballot to decide the hosts of the 2006 World Cup effectively giving the hosting rights to Germany ahead of South Africa.

OFC Nations Cup (1973–2002)

YEAR	WINNERS	SCORE	RUNNERS-UP
1973	New Zealand	2-0	Tahiti
1980	Australia	4-2	Tahiti
1996	Australia	6-0, 5-0 (2 legs)	Tahiti
1998	New Zealand	1-0	Australia
2000	Australia	2-0	New Zealand
2002	New Zealand	1-0	Australia

The OFC Nations

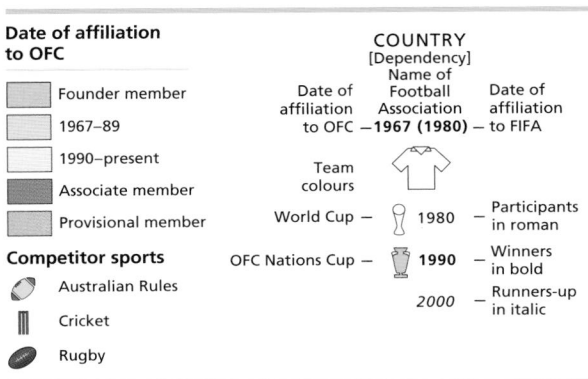

Date of affiliation to OFC

▪	Founder member
▪	1967–89
▪	1990–present
▪	Associate member
▪	Provisional member

Competitor sports

🏉 Australian Rules
▮ Cricket
🏉 Rugby

COUNTRY
[Dependency]
Name of
Football
Association
Date of
affiliation
to OFC **1967 (1980)** Date of
affiliation
to FIFA

Team colours 👕

World Cup 🏆 1980 — Participants in roman

OFC Nations Cup 🏆 1990 — Winners in bold

2000 — Runners-up in italic

The OFC Nations

THE OFC (OCEANIA FOOTBALL CONFEDERATION) was the last of the world's soccer confederations to be formed. Hardly surprising given that in the major countries of the region rugby (union and league), Australian Rules and cricket have provided very stiff competition for soccer, as indeed they have in Fiji and the smaller Pacific societies. Prior to OFC's formation in 1966 Australia and others had played in Asian World Cup qualifiers.

OFC consists of Australia, New Zealand, Papua New Guinea and the island states, statelets, archipelagoes and dependencies of the vast Pacific Ocean. Soccer's organization and strengths in the region are very asymmetrical. The Oceania Games, the Oceania qualifying rounds of the World Cup, has been dominated by Australia, where postwar immigrant communities from Europe have given the game a huge boost. The relative weakness of the region's other clubs and leagues mean that no international club tournament was held until 2000. Australia sought to rejoin Asia in the 1970s given the paucity of local competition, but was refused. Since then Oceania has campaigned vigorously for its own berth at the World Cup finals, but its efforts have been rebuffed and the confederation's representatives still have to play-off against UEFA or CONMEBOL sides for their place.

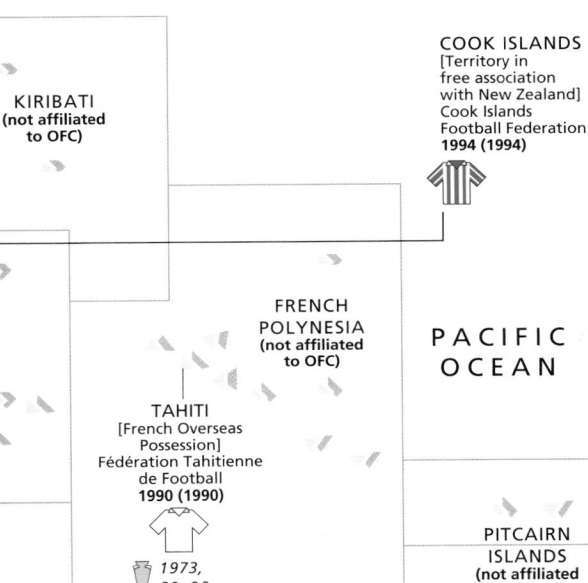

COOK ISLANDS
[Territory in free association with New Zealand]
Cook Islands Football Federation
1994 (1994)

KIRIBATI
(not affiliated to OFC)

FRENCH POLYNESIA
(not affiliated to OFC)

PACIFIC OCEAN

TAHITI
[French Overseas Possession]
Fédération Tahitienne de Football
1990 (1990)

🏆 *1973, 80, 96*

PITCAIRN ISLANDS
(not affiliated to OFC)

OFC

Oceania Tournaments and Cup Competitions:
OFC Nations Cup
OFC Club Championship
OFC Women's Tournament

Two goal hero: Commins Menapi of the Solomon Islands is carried off by his teammates after scoring twice in a 2-2 draw with Australia in the OFC Nations Cup in Adelaide in June 2004. The result earns the Solomon Islands a place in the championship play-off against Australia later in the year.

The Development of Oceanian Soccer

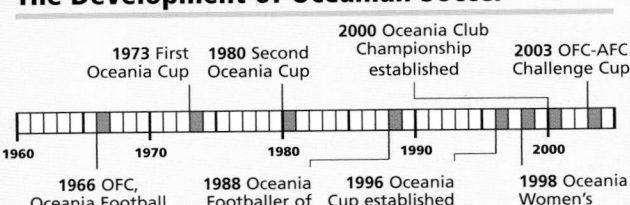

1973 First Oceania Cup

1980 Second Oceania Cup

2000 Oceania Club Championship established

2003 OFC-AFC Challenge Cup

1960 · 1970 · 1980 · 1990 · 2000

1966 OFC, Oceania Football Confederation founded

1988 Oceania Footballer of the Year Award established

1996 Oceania Cup established as biennial tournament

1998 Oceania Women's Tournament established

Calendar of Events	
Club Tournaments	OFC Club Championship 2005
International	OFC Nations Cup 2004
Tournaments	OFC-AFC Challenge Cup 2005
	Qualifying Tournament for 2006 World Cup

Oceania

SOCCER HAS ALWAYS STRUGGLED in Oceania, competing, especially in the most populated areas, with Australian Rules soccer and both rugby codes. Although a national FA was set up in Australia in 1882, soccer was only played at an amateur regional level. But its popularity was sustained and expanded by the new wave of European immigration to Australia in the mid-20th century – Italians, Hungarians, Croats and Greeks prominent among the soccer migrants and the names of the top clubs in the 1970s and 80s. In recent years the Australian Soccer Federation has encouraged more ethnically-neutral names in pursuit of the mainstream Australian sports dollar. A national league and a national cup competition were created in 1977. However, no team from Tasmania has ever been part of the league and it was nearly 23 years after starting that a team from Western Australia took part.

New Zealand's national league competition (although a split between leagues on each of the North and South Islands with a play-off between the winners for the national championship) dates from 1970s, and the main cup competition, the Chatham Cup (with a trophy donated by the Royal Navy ship HMS *Chatham*), has been played since 1923.

Australia

Australia Soccer Federation
Founded: 1961
Joined FIFA: 1963
Joined OFC: 1966–72, 1978

Australian League Record 1977–2004

SEASON	CHAMPIONS	RUNNERS-UP
1977	Sydney City	Marconi Fairfield
1978	West Adelaide	Sydney City
1979	Marconi Fairfield	Heidelberg United
1980	Sydney City	Heidelberg United
1981	Sydney City	South Melbourne
1982	Sydney City	Saint George
1983	Saint George	Sydney City
1984	South Melbourne	Sydney Olympic
1985	Brunswick	Sydney City
1986	Adelaide City	Sydney Olympic
1987	APIA Leichhardt	Preston
1988	Marconi Fairfield	Sydney Croatia
1989	Marconi Fairfield	Sydney Olympic
1990	Sydney Olympic	Marconi Fairfield
1991	South Melbourne	Melbourne Croatia
1992	Adelaide City	Melbourne Croatia
1993	Marconi Fairfield	Adelaide City
1994	Adelaide City	Melbourne Knights
1995	Melbourne Knights	Adelaide City
1996	Melbourne Knights	Marconi Fairfield
1997	Brisbane Strikers	Sydney United
1998	South Melbourne	Carlton
1999	South Melbourne	Sydney United
2000	Wollongong Wolves	Perth Glory
2001	Wollongong Wolves	South Melbourne
2002	Sydney Olympic Sharks	Perth Glory
2003	Perth Glory	Sydney Olympic Sharks
2004	Perth Glory	Parramatta Power

Australian Cup Record 1977–1997

YEAR	WINNERS	SCORE	RUNNERS-UP
1977	Brisbane City	1-1 (aet)(5-3 pens)	Marconi Fairfield
1978	Brisbane City	2-1	Adelaide City
1979	Adelaide City	3-2	Saint George
1980	Marconi Fairfield	0-0, 3-0 (2 legs)	Heidelberg United
1981	Brisbane Lions	3-1	West Adelaide
1982	APIA Leichhardt	2-1	Heidelberg United
1983	Sydney Olympic	1-0, 1-0 (2 legs)	Heidelberg United
1984	Newcastle Rosebud	1-0	Melbourne Croatia
1985	Sydney Olympic	2-1	Preston
1986	Sydney City	3-2	West Adelaide
1987	Sydney Croatia	1-0, 1-0	South Melbourne
1988	APIA Leichhardt	0-0 (aet)(5-3 pens)	Brunswick
1989	Adelaide City	2-0	Sydney Olympic
1990	South Melbourne	4-1	Sydney Olympic
1991	Parramatta Eagles	1-0	Preston Macedonia
1992	Adelaide City	2-1	Marconi Fairfield
1993	Heidelberg United	2-1	Parramatta Eagles
1994	Parramatta Eagles	2-0	Sydney United
1995	Melbourne Knights	6-0	Heidelberg United
1996	South Melbourne	3-1	Newcastle Breakers
1997	Collingwood Warriors	1-0	Marconi Fairfield

New Zealand

New Zealand Football Association
Founded: 1938
Joined FIFA: 1948
Joined OFC: 1966

New Zealand League Record 1970–2003

SEASON	CHAMPIONS	RUNNERS-UP
1970	Blockhouse Bay	Eastern Suburbs
1971	Eastern Suburbs	Mount Wellington
1972	Mount Wellington	Blockhouse Bay
1973	Christchurch United	Mount Wellington
1974	Mount Wellington	Christchurch United
1975	Christchurch United	North Shore United
1976	Wellington Diamond United	Mount Wellington
1977	North Shore United	Stop Out
1978	Christchurch United	Mount Wellington
1979	Mount Wellington	Christchurch United
1980	Mount Wellington	Gisborne City
1981	Wellington Diamond United	Dunedin City
1982	Mount Wellington	North Shore United
1983	Manurewa	North Shore United
1984	Gisborne City	Papatoetoe
1985	Wellington United	Gisborne City
1986	Mount Wellington	Miramar Rangers
1987	Christchurch United	Gisborne City
1988	Christchurch United	Mount Wellington
1989	Napier City Rovers	Mount Manganui
1990	Waitakere City	Mount Wellington
1991	Christchurch United	Miramar Rangers
1992	Waitakere City	Waikato United
1993	Napier City Rovers	Waitakere City
1994	North Shore United	Napier City Rovers
1995	Waitakere City	Waikato United
1996	Waitakere City	Miramar Rangers
1997	Waitakere City	Napier City Rovers
1998	Napier City Rovers	Central United
1999	Central United	Dunedin Technical
2000	Napier City Rovers	University Mount Wellington
2001	Central United	Miramar Rangers
2002	Miramar Rangers	Napier City Rovers
2003	Miramar Rangers	East Auckland

New Zealand Cup Record 1986–2003

YEAR	WINNERS	SCORE	RUNNERS-UP
1986	North Shore United	0-1, 4-1 (2 legs)	Mount Manganui
1987	Gisborne City	5-1, 2-2 (2 legs)	Christchurch United
1988	Christchurch United	2-2, 1-1 (away goals)	Waikato United
1989	Christchurch United	7-1	Rotorua City
1990	Mount Wellington	3-3 (aet)(4-2 pens)	Christchurch United
1991	Christchurch United	2-1	Wellington United
1992	Miramar Rangers	3-1	Waikato United
1993	Napier City Rovers	6-0	Rangers
1994	Waitakere City	1-0	Wellington Olympic
1995	Waitakere City	4-0	North Shore United
1996	Waitakere City	3-1	Mount Wellington
1997	Central United	3-2 (aet)	Napier City Rovers
1998	Central United	5-0	Dunedin Technical
1999	Dunedin Technical	4-0	Waitakere City
2000	Napier City Rovers	4-1	Central United
2001	University Mount Wellington	3-3 (5-4 pens)	Central United
2002	Napier City Rovers	2-0	Tauranga City United
2003	Uni-Mt Wellington	3-1	Melville United

American Samoa

American Samoa Football Association
Founded: 1971
Joined FIFA: 1998
Joined OFC: 1994

SEASON	LEAGUE CHAMPIONS
1999	Konika Machine FC
2000	Wild Wild West
2001	PanSa Soccer Club
2002	PanSa Soccer Club
2003	Manumea

Cook Islands

Cook Islands Football Federation
Founded: 1971
Joined FIFA: 1994
Joined OFC: 1994

SEASON	LEAGUE CHAMPIONS
2000	Avatiu FC
2001	Sokattack Nikao
2002	Tupapa FC
2003	Tupapa FC
2004	Tupapa FC

YEAR	CUP WINNERS
2000	Tupapa FC
2001	Avatiu FC
2002	Tupapa FC
2003	Niaho
2004	Niaho

Fiji

Fiji Football Asociation
Founded: 1938
Joined FIFA: 1963
Joined OFC: 1966

SEASON	LEAGUE CHAMPIONS
1999	Ba
2000	Nadi
2001	Ba
2002	Ba
2003	Olympians

YEAR	CUP WINNERS
1999	Nadi
2000	Ba
2001	Rewa
2002	Nadi
2003	Ba

New Caledonia

Fédération Néo-Caledonienne de Football
Founded: 1960
Joined FIFA: 1966
Provisional member only

SEASON	LEAGUE CHAMPIONS
1999	FC Gaitcha
2000	JS Baco
2001	JS Baco
2002	AS Mont-Dore
2003	AS Magenta

New Caledonia (continued)

YEAR	CUP WINNERS
1999	JS Traput
2000	AS Magenta
2001	AS Magenta
2002	AS Magenta
2003	AS Magenta

Papua New Guinea

Papua New Guinea Football Asociation
Founded: 1962
Joined FIFA: 1963
Joined OFC: 1966

SEASON	LEAGUE CHAMPIONS
1999	Guria
2000	Unitech
2001	Sobou Lae
2002	Sobou Lae
2003	Sobou Lae

Solomon Islands

Solomon Islands Football Federation
Founded: 1988
Joined FIFA: 1988
Joined OFC: 1988

SEASON	LEAGUE CHAMPIONS
1999	Rangers
2000	Lauga United
2001	Koloale
2002	*unknown*
2003	Koloale

Tahiti

Fédération Tahitienne de Football
Founded: 1938
Joined FIFA: 1990
Joined OFC: 1990

SEASON	LEAGUE CHAMPIONS
2000	AS Vénus
2001	AS Pirae
2002	AS Vénus
2003	AS Pirae
2004	Manu-Ura

YEAR	CUP WINNERS
2000	AS Pirae
2001	AS Dragon
2002	AS Pirae
2003	Manu-Ura
2004	Tefana

Tonga

Tonga Football Association
Founded: 1965
Joined FIFA: 1994
Joined OFC: 1994

SEASON	LEAGUE CHAMPIONS
1999	SC Lotoha'apai
2000	SC Lotoha'apai
2001	SC Lotoha'apai
2002	SC Lotoha'apai
2003	SC Lotoha'apai

Vanuatu

Vanuatu Football Association
Founded: 1934
Joined FIFA: 1988
Joined OFC: 1988

SEASON	LEAGUE CHAMPIONS
1998	Tafea FC
1999	Tafea FC
2000	Tafea FC
2001	Fara
2002	Tupuji Imere

Western Samoa

Western Samoa Football Association
Founded: 1968
Joined FIFA: 1986
Joined OFC: 1986

SEASON	LEAGUE CHAMPIONS
1999	Moata'a
2000	Titavi FC
2001	Gold Star
2002	Strickland Brothers
2003	Gold Star

YEAR	CUP WINNERS
1999	Moaula
2000	Gold Star
2001	Strickland Brothers
2002	Vaivase-tai
2003	Strickland Brothers

OCEANIA

CONCACAF

Date of affiliation to CONCACAF

- Founder member
- 1962–69
- 1970–89
- 1990–present

COUNTRY

Date of affiliation to CONCACAF — **1916 (1912)** — Date of affiliation to FIFA

Name of Football Association

Team colours

World Cup — 1980 — Participants in roman

Gold Cup 1991– present (CONCACAF Championship 1963–89, CCCF Championship 1941–61) — 1990 — Winners in bold

2000 — Runners-up in italic

CANADA
The Canadian Soccer Association
1978 (1912–28, 1946)
1986
1985, 2000

BERMUDA
Bermuda Football Association
1966 (1962)

New York
Football Confederation Headquarters

DOMINICAN REPUBLIC
Federación Dominicana de Fútbol
1964 (1958)

UNITED STATES OF AMERICA
United States Soccer Federation
1961 (1913)
1930, 34, 50, 90, 94, 98, 2002
1989, **91**, *93*, *98*, **2002**

BELIZE
Belize National Football Association
1986 (1986)

BAHAMAS
The Bahamas Football Association
1981 (1968)

TURKS AND CAICOS ISLANDS
Football Association of Turks and Caicos
1998 (1998)

GULF OF MEXICO

CUBA
Associación de Fútbol de Cuba
1961 (1933)
1938

MEXICO
Federación Mexicana de Fútbol Asociación AC
1961 (1929)
1930, 50, 54, 58, 62, 66, 70, 78, 86, 94, 98, 2002
1965, *67*, **71**, **77**, **93**, **96**, **98**, **2003**

EL SALVADOR
Federación Salvadoreña de Fútbol
1962 (1938)
1970, 82
1941, **43**, *63*, *81*

CAYMAN ISLANDS
Cayman Islands Football Association
1992 (1992)

JAMAICA
Jamaica Football Association
1961 (1962)
1998

GUATEMALA
Federación Nacional de Fútbol de Guatemala
1961 (1933)
1943, *46*, *48*, **65**, *67*, *69*

PACIFIC OCEAN

HONDURAS
Federación Nacional Autónoma de Fútbol de Honduras
1961 (1951)
1953, **81**, *85*, *91*

NICARAGUA
Federación Nicaraguense de Fútbol
1968 (1950)

COSTA RICA
Federación Constarricense de Fútbol
1962 (1921)
1990, 2002
1941, *46*, **48**, **51**, **53**, **55**, **60**, *61*, **63**, **69**, **89**, *2002*

PANAMA
Federación Nacional de Fútbol de Panama
1961 (1938)
1951

CARIBBEAN SEA

HAITI
Fédération Haïtienne de Football
1961 (1933)
1974
1957, *61*, *71*, *73*, *77*

The Development of Soccer in America

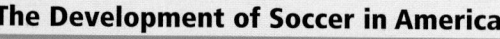

1941 CCCF Championship first played, San José, Costa Rica

1961 CONCACAF (Confederación Norte-Centroamerica y del Caribe de Fútbol) founded, based in New York, replaces CCCF

1991 CONCACAF Gold Cup, CONCACAF Women's Championship and CONCACAF Cup-Winners' Cup first played

2001 Football Confederation's Giants Cup established and abandoned

1930   1940   1950   1960   1970   1980   1990   2000

1938 CCCF (Confederación Centroamerica y del Caribe Fútbol) founded

1962 CONCACAF Champions Cup first played

1963 CONCACAF Championship first played, San Salvador, El Salvador

1998 CONCACAF Cup-Winners' Cup abandoned

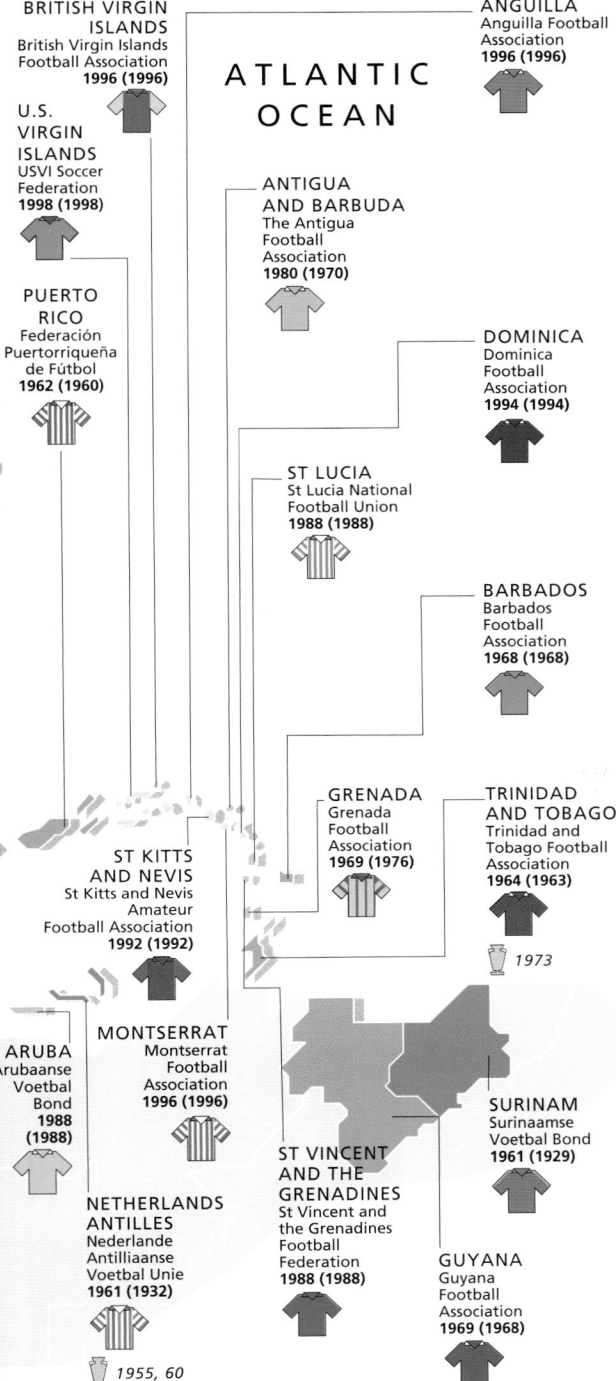

BRITISH VIRGIN ISLANDS
British Virgin Islands Football Association
1996 (1996)

U.S. VIRGIN ISLANDS
USVI Soccer Federation
1998 (1998)

PUERTO RICO
Federación Puertorriqueña de Fútbol
1962 (1960)

ATLANTIC OCEAN

ANGUILLA
Anguilla Football Association
1996 (1996)

ANTIGUA AND BARBUDA
The Antigua Football Association
1980 (1970)

DOMINICA
Dominica Football Association
1994 (1994)

ST LUCIA
St Lucia National Football Union
1988 (1988)

BARBADOS
Barbados Football Association
1968 (1968)

GRENADA
Grenada Football Association
1969 (1976)

TRINIDAD AND TOBAGO
Trinidad and Tobago Football Association
1964 (1963)
1973

ST KITTS AND NEVIS
St Kitts and Nevis Amateur Football Association
1992 (1992)

ARUBA
Arubaanse Voetbal Bond
1988 (1988)

MONTSERRAT
Montserrat Football Association
1996 (1996)

NETHERLANDS ANTILLES
Nederlandse Antilliaanse Voetbal Unie
1961 (1932)
1955, 60

ST VINCENT AND THE GRENADINES
St Vincent and the Grenadines Football Federation
1988 (1988)

SURINAM
Surinaamse Voetbal Bond
1961 (1929)

GUYANA
Guyana Football Association
1969 (1968)

CONCACAF

North and Central American Tournaments and Cup Competitions:
CONCACAF Gold Cup
CONCACAF Women's Gold Cup
CONCACAF Champions Cup

The CONCACAF Nations

THE ORGANIZATION OF SOCCER in North and Central America reflects the basic divisions and conflicts of the region. North America (USA and Canada) is on a different sporting and economic plane from the rest of the region. Mexico remains the singular dominant soccer-playing power in the area, unsure whether to remain a big fish in a small pool or take a chance by joining the stronger soccer nations of South America.

Before the Second World War these divisions were reflected in the formation of both CCCF (Confederación Centroamerica y del Caribe de Fútbol) in 1938, made up of Central American and Caribbean nations, and NAFC (North American Football Confederation) in 1939, made up of Mexico, USA and Cuba. The NAFC held only two tournaments and its influence as a governing body dwindled. CCCF, without either Mexico or the USA, remained marginal.

In 1961 CONCACAF (Confederación Norte-Centroamerica y del Caribe de Fútbol) was created out of these former federations and was initially based in Guatemala City.

Over the last few decades one of CONCACAF's central missions has been to raise the profile of soccer in the USA in the hope of providing competition for Mexico and a steady flow of interest and money into the region's rather weak and one-sided international club competitions. As such CONCACAF was transformed into the more Anglo-sounding Football Confederation, its headquarters moved to New York and its regional tournament has been renamed the Gold Cup. It has now reverted to being called CONCACAF.

While the US has now both a stable professional league and held the 1994 World Cup, Mexican clubs have migrated south to CONMEBOL's Copa Libertadores. In response, the Football Confederation has abandoned some of its tournaments and joined with CONMEBOL to create the Copa Pan-Americana.

A member of the CONCACAF executive since 1990, Chuck Blazer, now General Secretary, has been the power behind the non-stop merry-go-round of ever-changing tournament formats.

Calendar of Events	
Club Tournaments	CONCACAF Champions Cup 2005
International Tournaments	Qualifying Tournament for 2006 World Cup

CONCACAF

THE SEASONS IN REVIEW 2003, 2003–04

CONCACAF'S SEASON REFLECTED THE REGION'S perennial problems. Their domestic league aside Mexican teams are more interested in South American competitions than in CONCACAF competitions. Most of the Confederation is made up of desperately poor islands and Central American states. In Guatemala, like many other countries, government interference in the FA saw FIFA and CONCACAF suspend the organization, while the civil unrest in Haiti that followed the ousting of President Aristide saw the domestic soccer programme interrupted, though both leagues were eventually completed. Of course, soccer in the northern giants the USA and Canada remains a strictly minority affair. Professional women's soccer, which had got underway in the USA, folded just before the Women's World Cup as sponsorship money ran out. But there were signs of hope too. The Gold Cup 2003 was played as a cross-border affair in the USA and Mexico and Mexican clubs are reaching out to Hispanics in the States. Several clubs played a small mid-season tournament in California and Texas while Guadalajara are setting up a team in the MLS to be called Chivas USA.

International tournaments develop

The 2003 Gold Cup saw a victory for Mexico over an invited young Brazilian team in a taut Final, while the losing semi-finalists, the USA and Costa Rica, fought out an unusually good third place play-off game. CONCACAF's leadership have also proved adept at playing the political game in world soccer, securing a steady flow of development funds to the region and securing a place for the winners of its Champions Cup in the newly created World Club Championship.

After years of trying to find an attractive formula for its international competitions that could actually attract reasonable

audiences and the interest of the big Mexican clubs, CONCACAF has settled for a single Champions Cup tournament in which the small islands and states play-off for places against teams from the bigger countries. Just to keep things a little out of kilter this season saw two Finals – the 2003 edition played late and won by Toluca from Mexico and the 2004 Final in May. The latter was an all-Costa Rican affair, and reflects the increasing strength of the Tico's domestic game. Alajuelense beat Chicago Fire and Mexicans Pachuca on their way to the Final, while their local rivals Saprissa got past Monterrey and the San Jose Earthquakes. The two-legged Final looked close after the first game ended in a 1-1 draw, but in the second leg Alajuelense cruised home 4-0, breaking the US-Mexican dominance that has seen their clubs win the competition ever year for a decade.

Above: Chivas midfielder Ramon Ramirez (in stripes) shields the ball from Pachuca's Caballero. Ramirez will be one of the first players to head north if Chivas USA are accepted into the MLS.

Top 12 CONCACAF Leagues

COUNTRY	CHAMPIONS	RUNNERS-UP
Belize†	Kulture Yabra	Builders Hardware Bandits
Costa Rica – Apertura	Saprissa	Herediano
Costa Rica – Clausura	Herediano	Saprissa
Costa Rica – National Championship	Saprissa	Herediano
El Salvador – Apertura	CD FAS	CD Águila
EL Salvador – Clausura	Alianza	CD FAS
Guatemala – Apertura	Municipal	Comunicaciones
Guatemala – Clausura	Cobán Imperial	Municipal
Haiti – Ouverture*	Don Bosco	Cavaly
Haiti – Clôture*	Roulado	Victory FC
Honduras – Apertura	Real España	Olimpia
Honduras – Clausura	Olimpia	Marathón
Jamaica	Tivoli Gardens	Harbour View
Mexico – Apertura	Pachuca	Tigres
Mexico – Clausura	UNAM Pumas	Guadalajara
Nicaragua – Apertura	Real Estelí FC	Diriangén FC
Nicaragua – Clausura	Real Estelí FC	Diriangén FC
Panama – Apertura*	Tauro FC	Deportivo Árabe Unido
Panama – Clausura*	Tauro FC	Alianza
Panama – National Championship*	Tauro FC	
Trinidad and Tobago*	San Juan Jabloteh	W Communication
USA*	San Jose Earthquakes	Chicago Fire

* Results for 2003 season.

† Top teams have withdrawn from the Belize FA to form a pirate league but it is not recognised by CONCACAF.

Below: In search of the Yankee dollar: Tigres' keeper Compagnuolo saves from América's Blanco in the mid-season Mexican Liguilla played in California and Texas.

Freddy Adu (left), the 15-year-old wunderkind, opens his professional career with DC United.

Canada celebrate their 1-0 quarter-final victory over the Chinese in the 2003 Women's World Cup.

Above: *Vicente Sanchez of Toluca (in red) takes on the Morelia defence in the 2003 CONCACAF Champions Cup Final.*

Below: *Alajuelense make it look easy after their 4-0 crushing of fellow Costa Rican's Saprissa gives them victory in the 2004 CONCACAF Champions Cup Final.*

CONCACAF Champions Cup

2002–03	2003–04
FINAL (2 legs)	FINAL (2 legs)
Sep 17 – Estadio Morelos, Morelia, Mexico	May 5, 2004 – Estadio Rosabal Cordero, Herédia, Costa Rica
CA Monarcas 3-3 CD Toluca Morelia (Mexico) (Mexico) (López 6, 82, (Navia 44, 63, Lozano 13) Álvarez 69) **h/t:** 1-2 **Att :** 7,000 **Ref:** Archundia (Mexico)	**Deportivo 1-1 LD Alajuelense** Saprissa (Costa Rica) (Costa Rica) (López 32) (Solis 61) **h/t:** 0-1 **Att :** 8,000 **Ref:** Batres (Guatemala)
Oct 8 – Estadio Nemesio Diez, Toluca, Mexico	May 12, 2004 – Estadio Alejandro Morera Soto, Alajuela, Costa Rica
CD Toluca 2-1 CA Monarcas (Da Silva 35, Morelia Sanchez 54) (Álvarez 81) **h/t:** 1-0 **Att :** 7,000 **Ref:** Alcala (Mexico)	**LD Alajuelense 4-0 Deportivo** (Ledesma 6, Saprissa Alpízar 24, 40, López 76) **h/t:** 3-0 **Att:** 13,000 **Ref:** Pineda (Honduras)
CD Toluca won 5-4 on aggregate	Alajuelense won 5-1 on aggregate

The biggest trophy in world soccer? Mexico try to hoist the 2003 Gold Cup after beating Brazil 1-0.

NORTH & CENTRAL AMERICA AND THE CARIBBEAN

Soccer is not new to North America having been played there since the 1870s. It thrived during the 1920s, especially in New England, with teams such as the Fall River Marksmen (in stripes) and Bethlehem Steel drawing big crowds and generating widespread interest in the game.

CANADA
[1867]
The Canadian
Soccer Association
1912 (1961)

UNITED STATES OF AMERICA
[1776]
United States
Soccer Federation
1913 (1967/8)

Washington DC

Los Angeles

DOMINICAN REPUBLIC
[1865]
Federación
Dominicana
de Fútbol
1953 (1991)

BAHAMAS
[1973]
The Bahamas
Football Association
1967 (1996)

CAYMAN ISLANDS
[British dependent territory]
Cayman Islands
Football Association
1966 (1996)

CUBA
[1901]
Asociación de
Fútbol de Cuba
1924 (1912)

GULF OF
MEXICO

PACIFIC
OCEAN

MEXICO
[1836]
Federación Mexicana
de Fútbol Asociación AC
1927 (1941)

JAMAICA
[1962]
Jamaica Football
Association
1910 (1974)

Kingston

CARIBBEAN
SEA

TURKS AND CAICOS ISLANDS
[British Crown Colony]
Football Association
of Turks and Caicos
1996 (1999)

Guadalajara

Mexico
City

Guatemala
City

Tegucigalpa

San
Salvador

Alajuela

San
José

BELIZE
[1981]
Belize National
Football Association
1980 (1991)

HONDURAS
[1838]
Federación Nacional
Autónoma de
Fútbol de Honduras
1951 (1965)

GUATEMALA
[1838]
Federación Nacional de
Fútbol de Guatemala
1919 (1926)

EL SALVADOR
[1841]
Federación
Salvadoreña
de Fútbol
1935 (1972)

NICARAGUA
[1838]
Federación
Nicaraguense
de Fútbol
1931 (1963)

COSTA RICA
[1838]
Federación
Constarricense
de Fútbol
1921 (1921)

The top 15 teams in North & Central America and the Caribbean

Alajuelense Costa Rica Alajuela 1919	**DC United** USA Washington DC 1996	**Joe Public FC** Trinidad Port of Spain 1996
Alianza FC El Salvador San Salvador 1959	**Cruz Azul** Mexico Mexico City 1927	**Necaxa** Mexico Mexico City 1923
América Mexico Mexico City 1916	**Comunicaciones** Guatemala Guatemala City 1939	**Robin Hood** Surinam Paramaribo *not known*
Olimpia Honduras Tegucigalpa 1926	**CSD Municipal** Guatemala Guatemala City 1936	**Santos** Jamaica Kingston *not known*
LA Galaxy Los Angeles USA 1996	**Guadalajara** Mexico Guadalajara 1906	**Saprissa** Costa Rica San José 1935

The CONCACAF Nations

COUNTRY
[date of independence]
Name of national
Football
Foundation   Association   Foundation of
of national FA — **1916 (1912)** — national league

North & Central America and the Caribbean

ORIGINS AND GROWTH OF SOCCER

IN NORTH AMERICA and the Caribbean the question remains: why has soccer developed in such a limited way? It was played in the USA through colleges and universities, in particular in the 1870s, but it soon fell behind in popularity to American football and baseball. The main areas of soccer strength were the New England industrial towns, New York, Los Angeles and St Louis.

However, for the most part soccer remained a game played by recent immigrants (Hispanic and European). Even when it did prosper (a professional national league ran through the 1920s and the USA made the semi-finals of the 1930 World Cup) the game was plagued by conflicts between professionals and amateurs, splits among the various leagues and, with the depression of the 1930s, the economic decimation of its main areas of support. The relative failure of men's soccer left open space in which American women's soccer could prosper in the 1970s. In Canada, Scottish immigrants led to the establishment of soccer in the 1880s, but again with little success.

The success of baseball within the USA was repeated all over the region. US military forces brought the game to Cuba, Nicaragua, Panama, Puerto Rico and the Dominican Republic. In Venezuela, baseball arrived with the US oil industry, which practically ran the country in the early years of the 20th century. In the Caribbean, cricket's popularity always restricted the growth of soccer (as the popularity of basketball does today), with the exception of Haiti whose early independence was paralleled by the creation of the first FA in the region. In Mexico (and later in Guatemala, Costa Rica, El Salvador and Honduras) soccer has truly prospered, introduced in the late 19th century by both British and Spanish expatriates.

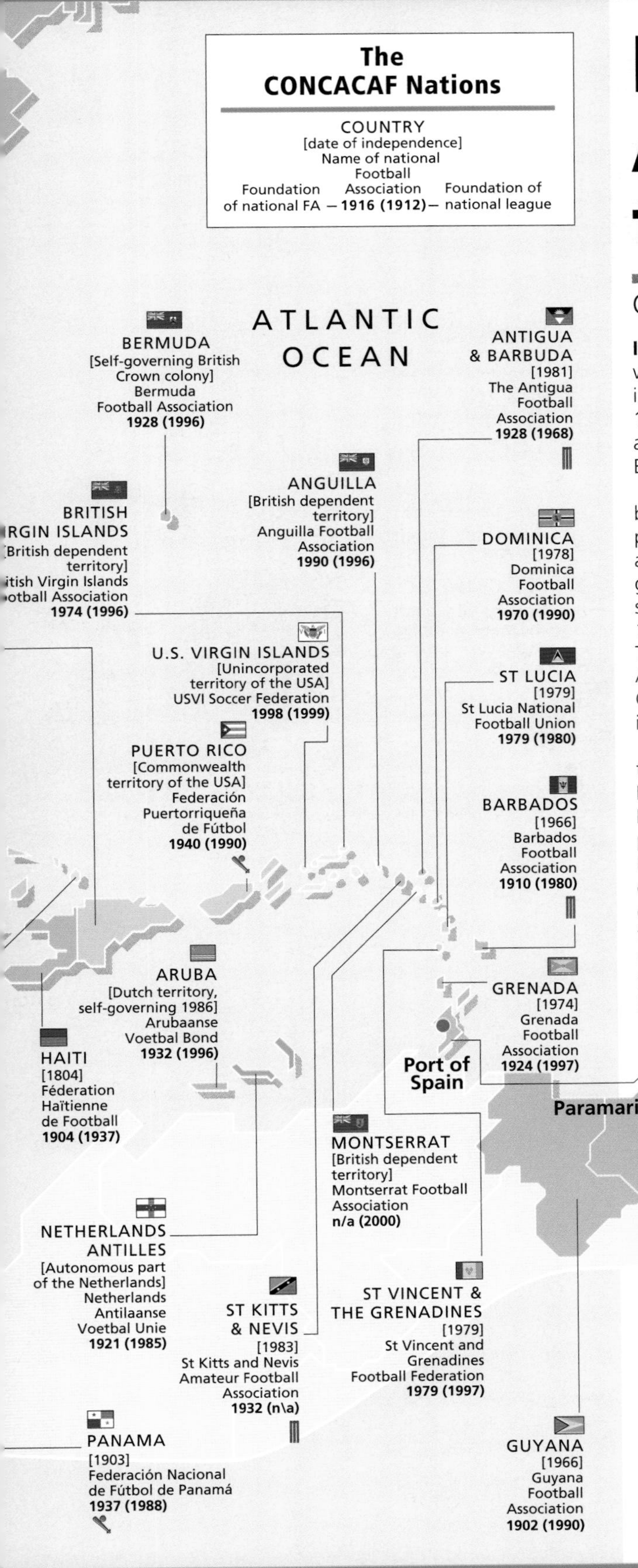

ATLANTIC OCEAN

BERMUDA
[Self-governing British Crown colony]
Bermuda Football Association
1928 (1996)

ANTIGUA & BARBUDA
[1981]
The Antigua Football Association
1928 (1968)

ANGUILLA
[British dependent territory]
Anguilla Football Association
1990 (1996)

BRITISH VIRGIN ISLANDS
[British dependent territory]
British Virgin Islands Football Association
1974 (1996)

DOMINICA
[1978]
Dominica Football Association
1970 (1990)

U.S. VIRGIN ISLANDS
[Unincorporated territory of the USA]
USVI Soccer Federation
1998 (1999)

ST LUCIA
[1979]
St Lucia National Football Union
1979 (1980)

PUERTO RICO
[Commonwealth territory of the USA]
Federación Puertorriqueña de Fútbol
1940 (1990)

BARBADOS
[1966]
Barbados Football Association
1910 (1980)

GRENADA
[1974]
Grenada Football Association
1924 (1997)

ARUBA
[Dutch territory, self-governing 1986]
Arubaanse Voetbal Bond
1932 (1996)

Port of Spain

Paramaribo

HAITI
[1804]
Féderation Haïtienne de Football
1904 (1937)

TRINIDAD & TOBAGO
[1962]
Trinidad and Tobago Football Association
1908 (1990)

MONTSERRAT
[British dependent territory]
Montserrat Football Association
n/a (2000)

NETHERLANDS ANTILLES
[Autonomous part of the Netherlands]
Netherlands Antilaanse Voetbal Unie
1921 (1985)

ST KITTS & NEVIS
[1983]
St Kitts and Nevis Amateur Football Association
1932 (n\a)

ST VINCENT & THE GRENADINES
[1979]
St Vincent and Grenadines Football Federation
1979 (1997)

SURINAM
[1975]
Surinaamse Voetbal Bond
1920 (1950)

PANAMA
[1903]
Federación Nacional de Fútbol de Panamá
1937 (1988)

GUYANA
[1966]
Guyana Football Association
1902 (1990)

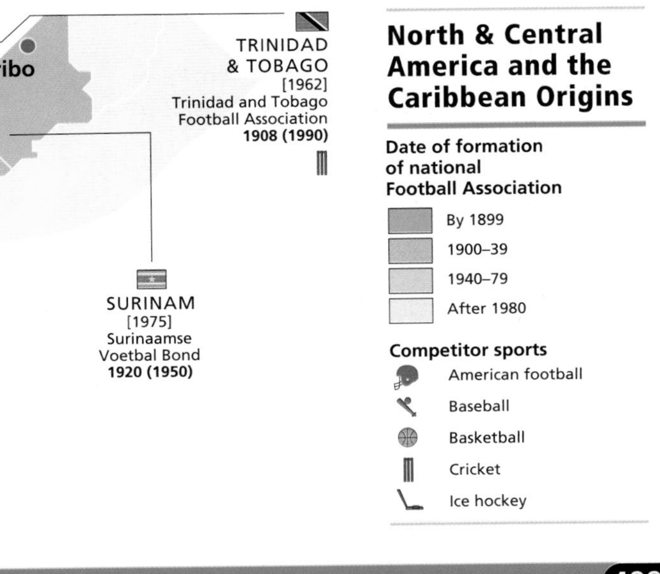

North & Central America and the Caribbean Origins

Date of formation of national **Football Association**

	By 1899
	1900–39
	1940–79
	After 1980

Competitor sports

	American football
	Baseball
	Basketball
	Cricket
	Ice hockey

The CONCACAF and Gold Cups

TOURNAMENT OVERVIEW

THE FIRST INTERNATIONAL soccer tournament in the region was held as part of a local Olympic tournament in Havana in 1930. The organizing committee held two further games in 1935 and 1938 from which came the idea of an independent soccer tournament and organization. CCCF (Confederacion Centroamericano y del Caribe de Futbol) was set up in 1938 and held its first tournament in Costa Rica in 1941. The tournament's profile remained low for the next 30 years: the cost of participation was too high for most of the Caribbean teams, making it an exclusively Central American affair. The region's main soccer power, Mexico, did not participate, throwing its lot in with the US and Cuba in the North American Football Confederation.

This division was finally overcome with the formation of CONCACAF in 1963, which embraced the whole of the Americas outside CONMEBOL, and the first CONCACAF championship was held the same year. Low participation rates led to the 1973, 1977, 1981, 1985 and 1989 tournaments serving as qualifiers for the World Cups, but to no avail. With the accession of Trinidadian Jack Warner to the presidency of CONCACAF in 1991, the tournament was relaunched and rebranded as the Gold Cup. The name, designed to be more recognizable in the American market, was accompanied by increased sponsorship, invitations to Asian and South American teams and the promise of more tournaments hosted by the US.

The CONCACAF Championships and the Gold Cup

Participation in the tournament 1963–2003

7+ times	
5–6 times	
3–4 times	
1–2 times	
0 times	

Winners, runners-up and third place with date

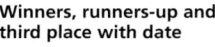

1993 1993 1993

1993*   Third place tie

World Cup qualifiers 1973–89

1967   date

Host country, with date in stadium and number of participants in brackets

COSTA RICA

1969 (6)   1993† Tournament co-hosted

The CONCACAF Championships 1963–89

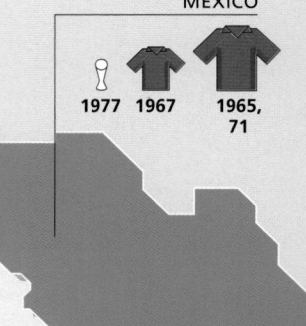

MEXICO

1977 1967 1965, 71

Nations invited to the Gold Cup 1991–2003

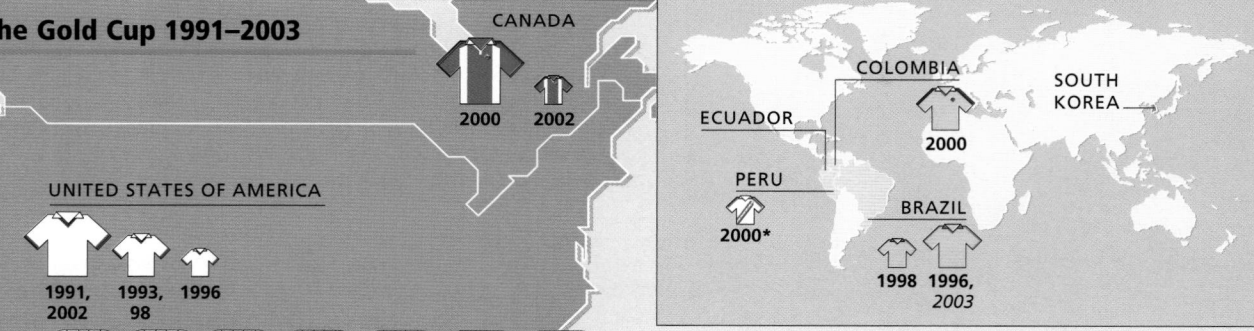

COLOMBIA
2000

ECUADOR

SOUTH KOREA

PERU
2000*

BRAZIL
1998 1996, *2003*

The Gold Cup 1991–2003

CANADA
2000 2002

UNITED STATES OF AMERICA
1991, 2002   1993, 98   1996

1991 (8) 1993† (8) 1996 (9) 1998 (10) 2000 (12) 2002 (12) 2003† (12)

ATLANTIC OCEAN

PACIFIC OCEAN

MEXICO
1993, 96, 98, 2003   1991

1993† (8)

2003† (12)

2002 1993*

GULF OF MEXICO

GUATEMALA

EL SALVADOR

COSTA RICA

JAMAICA
1993*

HONDURAS
1991

PANAMA

HAITI

CUBA

CARIBBEAN SEA

TRINIDAD & TOBAGO
2000*

MARTINIQUE

ST VINCENT AND THE GRENADINES

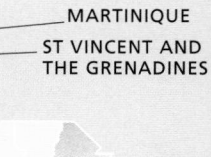
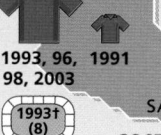

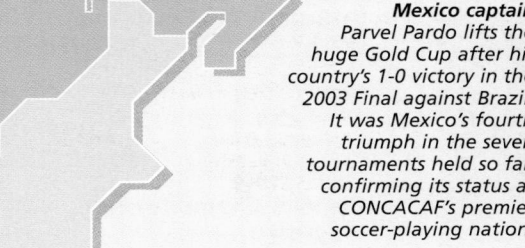

CANADA
1985

UNITED STATES
OF AMERICA

Mexico captain
Parvel Pardo lifts the
huge Gold Cup after his
country's 1-0 victory in the
2003 Final against Brazil.
It was Mexico's fourth
triumph in the seven
tournaments held so far,
confirming its status as
CONCACAF's premier
soccer-playing nation.

ATLANTIC
OCEAN

GULF OF
MEXICO

GUATEMALA
1967   1965,
        69
1965
(6)

CUBA

JAMAICA

HAITI
1971   1973

NETHERLANDS
ANTILLES
1963,
69

TRINIDAD
& TOBAGO
1971
(6)

SURINAM

HONDURAS
1981   1967
1967,
81 (6)

CARIBBEAN
SEA

NICARAGUA

PANAMA

EL SALVADOR
1963
(9)
1963

COSTA RICA
1963,   1965,   1989
69   71
1969
(6)

The Gold Cup 1991–2003

YEAR	WINNERS	SCORE	RUNNERS-UP
1991	USA	0-0 (4-3 pens)	Honduras
1993	Mexico	4-0	USA
1996	Mexico	2-0	Brazil
1998	Mexico	1-0	USA
2000	Canada	2-0	Colombia
2002	USA	2-0	Costa Rica
2003	Mexico	1-0	Brazil

CONCACAF's efforts at marketing the Gold Cup to the American
public have been rewarded with a huge upsurge of interest, the
inclusion of countries like Brazil and high attendances at matches.

USA

THE SEASON IN REVIEW 2003

IT WAS A YEAR OF quiet consolidation in the MLS. Now shrunk down to only ten teams, six of which are owned by the industrialist Philip Anschutz while two are run by the league itself, the competition did well to maintain public interest and attendances; while the trend towards more soccer-only stadiums – including LA Galaxy's new 27,000-seat arena – have helped create a better atmosphere at games. MLS certainly fared better than the women's game in the US, which saw the national team lose its World Cup crown, and, worse, the world's first professional women's league – WUSA – closed down two weeks before the tournament kicked off in September.

Final goal fest

The men's game has its own problems: with only ten teams in the two conferences, an eight-team play-off system means that the league has to grind through 30 games just to lose two teams. Dallas Burn was the poorest team by a long way, while Columbus Crew was unlucky to lose out on a play-off place by a single point.

In the knockout play-off series the San Jose v Los Angeles clash was the pick of the matches, with San Jose turning over a 2-0 deficit from the first leg. But as Los Angeles scored twice in the second leg too, it took three more goals in extra time from the Earthquakes to take them into the Western Conference Final with Kansas City Wizards – where again the team won in extra time. Its opponents in the MLS Cup Final, Chicago Fire, held the league's best record going into the play-offs, and dispatched DC United with some ease before sneaking past New England Revolution in the Eastern Conference Final. The championship play-off itself was nothing if not a goal fest – San Jose won 4-2, adding a second MLS title to its 2001 triumph.

Eastern Division Final Table 2003

CLUB	P	W	D	L	F	A	Pts	
Chicago Fire	30	15	8	7	53	43	**53**	Play-offs
New England Revolution	30	12	9	9	55	47	**45**	Play-offs
NY/NJ MetroStars	30	11	9	10	40	40	**42**	Play-offs
DC United	30	10	9	11	38	36	**39**	Play-offs
Columbus Crew	30	10	8	12	44	44	**38**	

Western Division Final Table 2003

CLUB	P	W	D	L	F	A	Pts	
San Jose Earthquakes	30	14	9	7	45	35	**51**	Play-offs
Kansas City Wizards	30	11	9	10	48	44	**42**	Play-offs
Colorado Rapids	30	11	7	12	40	45	**39**	Play-offs
Los Angeles Galaxy	30	9	9	12	35	35	**36**	Play-offs
Dallas Burn	30	6	5	19	35	64	**23**	

Top Goalscorers 2003

PLAYER	CLUB	NATIONALITY	GOALS
John Spencer	Colorado Rapids	Scottish	15
Carlos Ruiz	Los Angeles Galaxy	Guatemalan	15
Taylor Twellman	New England Revolution	American	15

International Performances 2003

CLUB	COMPETITION	PROGRESS
San Jose Earthquakes	CONCACAF Champions Cup	1st Round
New England Revolution	CONCACAF Champions Cup	1st Round
Columbus Crew	CONCACAF Champions Cup	Quarter-finals
Los Angeles Galaxy	CONCACAF Champions Cup	Quarter-finals

Eastern Championship Play-offs

CONFERENCE SEMI-FINALS (2 legs)
Metro Stars **0-2** New England Revolution
DC United **0-2** Chicago Fire
New England **1-1** Metro Stars Revolution
Chicago **2-0** DC United Fire (aet)

FINAL
Chicago Fire **1-0** New England Revolution (aet)

Western Championship Play-offs

CONFERENCE SEMI-FINALS (2 legs)
Los Angeles **2-0** San Jose Galaxy Earthquakes
Colorado **1-1** Kansas City Rapids Wizards
Kansas City **2-0** Colorado Wizards Rapids
San Jose **5-2** Los Angeles Earthquakes Galaxy (aet)

FINAL
San Jose **3-2** Kansas City Earthquakes Wizards (aet)

MLS Championship

2003 FINAL
November 23 – The Home Depot Centre, Carson, California
Chicago Fire 2-4 San Jose
(Beasley 49, **Earthquakes** Rooner o.g. 54) (Ekelund 5, Donovan 38, 71, Mulrooney 50)
h/t: 0-2 **Att:** 27,000
Ref: Hall

Right: Damani Ralph, a 22-year-old Jamaican, whose 11 goals sharpened the cutting edge of Chicago Fire's front-line.

Below: Freddie Adu, the MLS teenage sensation, rejected overtures from Manchester United and Juventus to sign his first professional deal with DC United. Adu will be the youngest recorded soccer professional in the USA.

USA

*Uruguayan Jose Cancela,
one of the leading lights at
New England Revolution,
flicks the ball away from
DC United's Bryan Namoff.*

Above: *Hristo Stoitchkov,
ex-Bulgarian international and
player-coach at DC United.
Stoitchkov's main contribution
to MLS this season was to
shatter the leg of a young
opponent in a bone-crunching
early-season tackle. MLS let him
off with the mildest ticking off
and the puniest of fines.*

Far left: *San Jose Earthquakes'
Landon Donovan shows superb
control as he dribbles past
Chicago Fire defender
Jim Curtin in the MLS Final.*

Left: *Donovan celebrates
his brace of goals at the
final whistle of the
Championship Final.*

Below: *The San Jose
Earthquakes squad celebrates
its second MLS Championship
victory in three years.*

 # USA

United States Soccer Federation
Founded: 1913
Joined FIFA: 1913
Joined CONCACAF: 1961

IT IS CLAIMED THAT the Pilgrim Fathers saw native Americans playing a rudimentary form of soccer, Passuckquakkohowog, in Massachusetts in 1620, and there was some kind of soccer played at American colleges as early as the 1820s. However, when the game split between handling and kicking codes, it was the handling game that prevailed and went on to dominate college and then professional sports. In competition with American football, baseball, basketball and ice hockey, soccer has always had a marginal place in American culture.

A series of amateur cups were created at the turn of the 19th century and a single season of professional league soccer was played in 1894. The first sustainable professional league was created in 1921, and lasted until the early 1930s. The majority of the teams in the league came from the East Coast and attracted

newly arrived immigrant populations. With the ASL's demise, a national professional game had to wait for the 1968 merger of the United Soccer Association and the National Professional Soccer League for the formation of the NASL. The NASL survived until 1984 and indeed thrived in the mid-70s as a steady stream of exotic foreign players (at the end of their careers) took up the increasingly attractive financial rewards of US soccer.

The decline of audiences and sponsorship money in the early 1980s left the USA without a national professional league. However, soccer continued to grow, especially among women. By hosting the World Cup in 1994, the USA was committed to re-establishing a professional league, and MLS – Major League Soccer – was created in 1996, while pre-existing smaller leagues merged to create unified Second and Third Divisions.

The ASL Record 1922–32

SEASON	CHAMPIONS	RUNNERS-UP
1922	Philadelphia Field Club	New York Field Club
1923	J & P Coats	Bethlehem Steel
1924	Fall River Marksmen	Bethlehem Steel
1925	Fall River Marksmen	Bethlehem Steel
1926	Fall River Marksmen	New Bedford Whalers
1927	Bethlehem Steel	Boston Wonder Workers
1928	Boston Wonder Workers	New Bedford Whalers
1929	Fall River Marksmen*	
1929†	Fall River Marksmen	Providence Gold Bugs
1930	Fall River Marksmen	New Bedford Whalers
1930†	Fall River Marksmen	New Bedford Whalers
1931	New York Giants	New Bedford Whalers
1932	*incomplete*	

* No play-off.
† Autumn league played.

The NASL Record 1967–84

YEAR	WINNERS	PLAY-OFF	RUNNERS-UP
1967*	Los Angeles Wolves	5-4	Washington Whips
1967**	Oakland Clippers	0-1, 4-1	Baltimore Bays
1968†	Atlanta Chiefs	0-0, 3-0	San Diego Toros
1969††	Kansas City Spurs		Tampa Bay Rowdies
1970	Rochester Lancers	3-0, 3-1	Washington Darts
1971	Dallas Tornado	1-2, 4-1, 2-0	Atlanta Chiefs
1972	New York Cosmos	2-1	St. Louis Stars
1973	Philadelphia Atoms	2-0	Dallas Tornado
1974	Los Angeles Aztecs	4-3	Dallas Tornado
1975	Tampa Bay Rowdies	2-0	Portland Timbers
1976	Toronto Metros-Croatia	3-0	Minnesota Kicks
1977	New York Cosmos	2-1	Seattle Sounders
1978	New York Cosmos	3-1	Tampa Bay Rowdies
1979	Vancouver Whitecaps	2-1	Tampa Bay Rowdies
1980	New York Cosmos	3-0	Fort Lauderdale Strikers
1981	Chicago Sting	1-0	New York Cosmos
1982	New York Cosmos	1-0	Seattle Sounders
1983	Tulsa Roughnecks	2-0	Toronto Blizzard
1984	Chicago Sting	2-0	Toronto Blizzard

* USA   ** NPSL   † NASL   †† No play-off

Vancouver Royals
Vancouver Royal Canadians
Vancouver Whitecaps
Vancouver
Seattle
Seattle Sounders

1979
Golden Bay Earthquakes

1977, 82

Oakland Clippers
Portland Timbers
Portland
1967
Oakland Stompers
San Francisco Gales
1975

Los Angeles Galaxy

San Jose Earthquakes

1996, 99, 2001, 02
San Francisco
California Surf
Los Angeles Aztecs

2001, 03
Las Vegas Quicksilver
Las Vegas

1974
Los Angeles Wolves
San Jose
Los Angeles
San Diego Sockers
San Diego Toros

1967
Los Angeles Toros
San Diego
1968

PACIFIC OCEAN

The MLS Record 1996–2003

YEAR	WINNERS	PLAY-OFF	RUNNERS-UP
1996	DC United	3-2	Los Angeles Galaxy
1997	DC United	2-1	Colorado Rapids
1998	Chicago Fire	2-0	DC United
1999	DC United	2-0	Los Angeles Galaxy
2000	Kansas City Wizards	1-0	Chicago Fire
2001	San Jose Earthquakes	2-1 (aet)	Los Angeles Galaxy
2002	Los Angeles Galaxy	1-0 (asdet)	New England Revolution
2003	San Jose Earthquakes	4-2	Chicago Fire

Soccer in the USA

DC United Team name

MLS Winners or runners-up
1996

Other members of MLS

NASL Winners or runners-up
1967

● **Tulsa** City of origin

1928 Winners in bold
1927 Runners-up in italic

The ASL

Boston Wonder Workers
1927, **1928**

Pawtucket

Providence

Fall River

Providence Gold Bugs
1929†

New York Giants
1931

New York Field Club
1922

New York

New Bedford

Bethlehem

Bethlehem Steel
1923–25, **1927**

New Bedford Whalers
1926, 28, 30, 30† , **31***

Philadelphia Field Club
1922

● **Philadelphia**

Fall River Marksmen
1924–26, 29, *29†*,
30, 30†

J & P Coats
Later known as Pawtucket Rangers
1923

* Merger of New Bedford Whalers and Fall River Marksmen
† Autumn league honours

Due to the paucity of domestic competition, Canada's leading professional soccer teams have regularly been members of American leagues.

● **Edmonton**
Edmonton Drillers

Calgary
Calgary Boomers

Chicago Mustangs
Chicago Spurs
Chicago Sting
1981, 84
Chicago Fire
998, 2000, 03

Denver
Colorado Rapids
RAPIDS
1997
Colorado Caribous
Denver Dynamos

Minnesota Kicks
1976
Minnesota Strikers

Minneapolis

Toronto Metros-Croatia
1976
Previously known as Toronto Metros

Toronto Blizzard
Toronto Falcons
1983, 84
Toronto City

Chicago

Detroit
Detroit Cougars
Detroit Express

Columbus
Columbus Crew

Kansas City

Tulsa
Tulsa Roughnecks
1983

Dallas
Houston Hurricane
Houston Stars
Houston

San Antonio
San Antonio Thunder

Dallas Burn

Dallas Tornado
1971, *73, 74*

Kansas City Spurs
1969
Kansas City Wizards
2000

St. Louis Stars
Saint Louis *1972*

Memphis
Memphis Rogues

Montreal Olympique
Montreal Manic

Montreal

Rochester Lancers
1970

Toronto

Rochester

Cleveland Stokers

Cleveland

Baltimore

Washington DC

New York

Philadelphia

Atlanta Chiefs
1968, *71*
Atlanta Apollos

Atlanta

Jacksonville
Jacksonville Tea Men

Tampa Bay
Tampa Bay Mutiny
Folded 2002
Tampa Bay Rowdies
1969, *75, 78, 79*

Miami Toros
1974
Miami Fusion
Folded 2002

Team America

Washington Darts
1970

Fort Lauderdale

Miami

Fort Lauderdale Strikers
1980

New England Tea Men
Boston Minutemen
Boston Beacons
New England Revolution
2002

Connecticut Bicentennials

New York Cosmos
1972, 77, 78, *80*, **81**, *82*
NY/NJ MetroStars

Philadelphia Atoms
1973
Philadelphia Fury
Philadelphia Spartans
Pittsburgh Phantoms

Baltimore Comets
Baltimore Bays
1967

Washington Diplomats
Washington Whips
1967

DC United
1996, 97, 98, *99*,

Boston

Hartford

New York

Philadelphia

USA

ATLANTIC OCEAN

GULF OF MEXICO

Mexico

THE SEASON IN REVIEW 2003–04

ONCE AGAIN, DESPITE THE BIG MONEY TEAMS in Mexican soccer, it was small teams from small cities that took the glory. The final rounds of the Apertura saw Pachuca and Tigres make their way to the Final. Pachuca swept past Necaxa and Atlante, while Tigres saw off the mighty Cruz Azul and Toluca. Pachuca won the first leg 3-1 and Tigres self-destructed in the second leg, finishing an aggressive game with only eight players on the field, although Pachuca also had a player sent off. Though they won 1-0, Tigres' last-minute consolation goal was too little too late.

Jaguares make the running

The Clausura saw the emergence of Jaguares de Chiapas as a real force in Mexican soccer. Based in the tiny provincial city of Tuxtla in a conflict-ridden zone of southern Mexico, sell-out crowds saw the team give its best performances since promotion two years ago. But the championship also saw the rise and rise of UNAM Pumas under the legendary Mexican player Hugo Sanchez. His youthful, hard-running, counter-attacking team beat Cruz Azul and Atlas in the play-offs to make the Final against Guadalajara. The first leg of the Final was a 1-1 draw and the rematch a long, nail-biting, goalless affair. The penalties that followed were no different, as both sides scored their opening four spot kicks. Pumas scored its fifth, only for Guadalajara midfielder Rafael Medina to step up and miss, handing the title to Pumas.

Apertura 2003–04 Tables

GROUP 1								
CLUB	P	W	D	L	F	A	Pts	
Pachuca	19	10	6	3	28	19	36	Qualified
Toluca	19	8	3	8	33	24	27	Play-off
Monterrey	19	5	7	7	29	29	22	
Puebla	19	5	5	9	23	30	20	
Atlas	19	5	4	10	29	32	19	

GROUP 2								
CLUB	P	W	D	L	F	A	Pts	
Tigres	19	11	5	3	38	20	38	Qualified
Cruz Azul	19	7	6	6	30	30	27	Play-off
Morelia	19	7	4	8	25	29	25	
Jaguares Chiapas	19	5	6	8	21	34	21	
San Luis	19	2	5	12	20	39	11	

GROUP 3								
CLUB	P	W	D	L	F	A	Pts	
Pumas	19	11	5	3	34	23	38	Qualified
Santos Laguna	19	8	7	4	41	29	31	Qualified
Tecos UAG	19	9	4	6	31	29	31	Play-off
América	19	8	4	7	34	26	28	
Gallos Blancos	19	1	4	14	16	44	7	

GROUP 4								
CLUB	P	W	D	L	F	A	Pts	
Atlante	19	8	7	4	32	21	31	Qualified
Necaxa	19	7	9	3	23	18	30	Qualified
Guadalajara	19	9	2	8	30	28	29	Play-off
Veracruz	19	8	3	8	34	38	27	
Irapuato	19	6	4	9	23	32	22	

Apertura Top Goalscorers 2003–04

PLAYER	CLUB	NATIONALITY	GOALS
Luis Gabriel Rey	Atlante	Colombian	15
José Cardozo	Toluca	Paraguayan	13
Carlos María Morales	Atlas	Uruguayan	12
Emilio Mora	Veracruz	Mexican	12

Apertura 2003–04 Play-offs

PLAY-OFFS FOR QUARTER-FINAL (2 legs)
Toluca **4-0** Guadalajara
Guadalajara **4-2** Toluca
Toluca won 6-2 on aggregate

Cruz Azul **1-0** Tecos
Tecos **1-3** Cruz Azul
Cruz Azul won 4-1 on aggregate

QUARTER-FINALS (2 legs)
Cruz Azul **0-1** Tigres
Tigres **1-2** Cruz Azul
Aggregate score 2-2
Tigres qualified on season record

Toluca **2-2** Pumas
Pumas **0-2** Toluca
Toluca won 4-2 on aggregate

Atlante **3-1** Santos Laguna
Santos Laguna **2-2** Atlante
Atlante won 5-3 on aggregate

Necaxa **1-3** Pachuca
Pachuca **1-2** Necaxa
Pachuca won 4-3 on aggregate

SEMI-FINALS (2 legs)
Toluca **1-0** Tigres
Tigres **2-0** Toluca
Tigres won 2-1 on aggregate

Atlante **0-0** Pachuca
Pachuca **2-1** Atlante
Pachuca won 2-1 on aggregate

Below: The legendary Hugo Sanchez issues orders. They seemed to work as he coached UNAM Pumas to their first Mexican title in 13 years.

FINAL (2 legs)
December 17 – Estadio Hidalgo, Pachuca
Pachuca 3-1 Tigres
(Sanchez o.g. 23,   (Soares 59)
Bautista 77,
Gabriel de Anda
86 pen)
h/t: 1-0   **Att:** 30,000
Ref: Alcala

December 20 – Estadio Universitario, Monterrey
Tigres 1-0 Pachuca
(Silvera 90)
h/t: 0-0   **Att:** 45,000
Ref: Rodriguez
Pachuca won 3-2 on aggregate

Angel Sosa of Necaxa (in red) in action against Queretaro. Necaxa played their first season away from Mexico City this year and were rewarded with big home crowds.

Pachuca players celebrate with the Apertura trophy after their victory over Tigres.

Clausura 2003–04 Tables

GROUP 1							
CLUB	P	W	D	L	F	A	Pts
Toluca	19	8	6	5	31	25	**30**	Qualified
Atlas	19	6	9	4	28	25	**27**	Qualified
Pachuca	19	6	8	5	32	33	26	Play-off
Puebla	19	5	5	9	27	29	20	
Monterrey	19	2	12	5	28	30	18	

GROUP 2							
CLUB	P	W	D	L	F	A	Pts
Jaguares Chiapas	19	12	6	1	35	20	**42**	Qualified
Cruz Azul	19	6	5	8	36	34	23	Play-off
Tigres	19	6	5	8	37	39	23	
Morelia	19	6	4	9	25	35	22	
San Luis	19	4	6	9	23	35	18	

GROUP 3							
CLUB	P	W	D	L	F	A	Pts
Pumas	19	12	5	2	42	19	**41**	Qualified
América	19	9	5	5	34	27	**32**	Qualified
Gallos Blancos	19	5	9	5	24	27	24	
Santos Laguna	19	6	3	10	31	30	21	
Tecos UAG	19	5	3	11	32	40	18	

GROUP 4							
CLUB	P	W	D	L	F	A	Pts
Guadalajara	19	10	4	5	30	23	**34**	Qualified
Atlante	19	7	6	6	29	26	**27**	Qualified
Irapuato	19	6	8	5	23	30	26	
Necaxa	19	5	6	8	22	26	21	
Veracruz	19	4	5	10	25	41	17	

Relegated club: San Luis. Promoted club: Club Dorados de Sinaloa.

Clausura Top Goalscorers 2003–04

PLAYER	CLUB	NATIONALITY	GOALS
Bruno Marioni	Pumas	Argentinian	16
Néstor Silvera	Tigres	Argentinian	16
Salvador Cabañas	Jaguares Chiapas	Chilean	15
Robert de Pinho	Atlas	Brazilian	15
Marcelo Delgado	Cruz Azul	Argentinian	13

International Club Performances 2004

CLUB	COMPETITION	PROGRESS
América	Copa Libertadores	2nd Round
Santos Laguna	Copa Libertadores	2nd Round
Pachuca	CONCACAF Champions Cup	Quarter-finals
Monterrey	CONCACAF Champions Cup	Semi-finals

Clausura 2003–04 Play-offs

PLAY-OFF FOR QUARTER-FINAL (2 legs)

Cruz Azul **2-1** Pachuca
Pachuca **0-2** Cruz Azul
Cruz Azul won 4-1 on aggregate

QUARTER-FINALS (2 legs)

Cruz Azul **2-1** Jaguares
Jaguares **2-2** Cruz Azul
Cruz Azul won 4-3 on aggregate

Atlante **2-0** Guadalajara
Guadalajara **3-1** Atlante
Guadalajara won on season record

Toluca **3-2** América
América **0-1** Toluca
Toluca won 4-2 on aggregate

Atlas **1-1** Pumas
Pumas **3-1** Atlas
Pumas won 4-2 on aggregate

SEMI-FINALS (2 legs)

Toluca **1-0** Guadalajara
Guadalajara **2-0** Toluca
Guadalajara won 2-1 on aggregate

Cruz Azul **0-0** Pumas
Pumas **3-2** Cruz Azul
Pumas won 3-2 on aggregate

Below left: Midfielder 'Chelito' Delgado (left) scored almost half Cruz Azul's goals as they made the semi-finals of the Clausura.

FINAL (2 legs)

June 10 – Estadio Jalisco, Guadalajara
Guadalajara 1-1 Pumas
(Ramon Morales 86) *(Jose Luis Lopez 76)*

h/t: 0-0 **Att:** 50,000 **Ref:** Guerra

June 13 – Estadio Olímpico Universitario, Mexico City
Pumas 0-0 Guadalajara
(after extra time)
Att: 65,000 **Ref:** Pineda
Pumas won 5-4 on pens

Nestor Silvera scored 16 goals for Tigres in the Clausura.

Bruno Marioni, Pumas top-scoring Argentinian striker, lifts the Mexican Clausura championship trophy aloft.

Soccer in Mexico

MEXICO

1900: First club, Pachuca founded — 1900

1903: First Mexico City League played — 1905

1908: Copa Tower first played — 1910

— 1915

1919: Copa Eliminatoria first played, replaced Copa Tower — 1920

1923: First International, v Guatemala, won 3–2, venue: Guatemala City — 1925

1927: FMF founded Federación Mexicana de Fútbol — 1930

1929: Affiliation to FIFA

1932: Last Copa Eliminatoria played. Copa Mexico first played — 1935

1943: Guadalajara announce Mexican only policy for their squad — 1940

1944: Primera Fuerza, national professional league established — 1945

1950: Second Division created — 1950

— 1955

1961: Affiliation to CONCACAF. Televisa buy América — 1960

1966: Azteca built and opened — 1965

1970: League shifts format to small leagues and play-offs — 1970

— 1975

1985: Azteca disaster. Ten killed and 29 injured in crowd crush at UNAM v América, Mexican Cup Final

1990: Banned from the World Cup for fielding under- and over-age players in youth tournaments — 1985

1993: Mexico first invited to Copa América — 1990

1996: League shifts format to Apertura and Clausura Championships with play-offs — 1995

1999: Mexican clubs first invited to Copa Libertadores — 2000

2001: Cruz Azul reach Final of Copa Libertadores — 2005

The Azteca Stadium *(capacity 110,000) in Mexico City is home to several clubs including the country's most popular team, América, and has hosted two World Cup Finals, in 1970 and 1986.*

Key

- International soccer
- Affiliation to CONCACAF
- Affiliation to FIFA
- Disaster
- World Cup host
- CONCACAF Championship/Gold Cup winner
- △ CONCACAF Championship/Gold Cup runner-up
- ▲ Copa América runner-up

- ○ Competition winner
- △ Competition runner-up

Amér	América
Atlan	Atlante
Cruz	Cruz Azul
Guad	CD Guadalajara
Monte	Monterrey
Mor	Monarcas Morelia
Nec*	Necaxa (as Atlético Español)
Tol	CD Toluca
UAG	UAG 'Los Tecos'
Univ	Universidad de Guadelajara

International Competitions

CONCACAF Champions Cup

Year		CONCACAF Champions Cup	CONCACAF Cup-Winners' Cup	Copa Libertadores
1962:1963:		○ Guad		
		△ Guad		
1965:	●			
1967:	△			
1968:		○ Tol		
1969:		○ Cruz		
1970:	■	○ Cruz		
1971:	●	○ Cruz		
1975:		○ Nec*		
1977:	●	○ Amér		
1978:		○ Univ		
1980:		○ UNAM		
1982:		○ UNAM		
1983:		○ Atlan		
1986:1987:	■	○ Amér		
1989:		○ UNAM		
1990:		○ Amér		
1991:		○ Puebla		
1992:		○ Amér		
1993:	▲ ●	△ León	○ Monte	
1994:		△ Atlan	○ Necaxa	
1995:			○ UAG	
1996:	●	○ Cruz		
1997:		○ Cruz		
1998:	●		Tol	
2001:	▲			△ Cruz
2003:	● Tol	△ Mor		

CD Guadalajara 1906

Union FC (1906–08)

CD Atlas Guadalajara 1916

UAG, 'Los Tecos' 1971

Universidad de Guadalajara 1974

Purchased franchise from Torreón 1974. Withdrew from league soccer 1994

Mexico: The main clubs

CF Puebla 1943 — Team name with year of formation

- ● Club formed before 1912
- ● Club formed 1912–25
- ● Club formed 1925–50
- ○ Club formed after 1950
- ★ Founder members Mexico City League 1902
- Founder members Professional League 1943
- Amateur champions
- English origins
- Spanish origins
- Scottish origins
- Belgian founder
- Franchise purchase
- Originated from a school or college
- Working class
- Colours and date unknown

Mexico

ORIGINS AND GROWTH OF SOCCER

SOCCER FIRST ARRIVED IN MEXICO CITY in the late 19th century via the expatriate British population and the French and Spanish immigrant communities. British mining engineers from the Compañia Real del Monte set up Pachuca Athletic Club, Mexico's first, in 1900. They contested the first championship with clubs of similar origins – Athletic, British Club, Reforma, Rovers, Mexico City Cricket Club and the Scottish-dominated champions Orizaba, all based in or near Mexico City.

Most of the British expatriate population left Mexico during the First World War and the game became dominated by Spanish speakers. A wave of Spanish clubs were formed at this time: Asturias, Real España, Cataluña and Aurora. Indigenous Mexican clubs were not far behind: Guadalajara was founded as Union FC in 1906, while América was formed as a merger of two clubs (Record FC and Colón FC) in 1916. At the same time, its eternal rival, Atlante, was founded as Sinaloa, changing its name to Lusitania and U-53, before settling on the current name in 1920. A national soccer association was founded in 1927 and affiliated to FIFA in 1929.

Cup and league established

The rapid growth of soccer in Mexico can be seen from the early development of national cup tournaments (the Copa Tower 1908–19, the Copa Eliminatoria 1920–32, and the Copa Mexico 1932–43) and the early arrival of professionalism in 1933. League soccer remained based on local and regional leagues until a single national league was established in 1944.

Mexico has been unable to translate these early strengths into enduring international success. It is easily the most powerful soccer nation in the CONCACAF region, but because of North American indifference and Central American and Caribbean weakness, neither its club teams nor its national team have been properly tested. Hosting two World Cups and regularly qualifying for others has not yielded a serious challenge for the trophy. The recent entry of Mexican clubs in the hitherto South American Copa Libertadores is the latest effort to break away from being a big fish in a small pond.

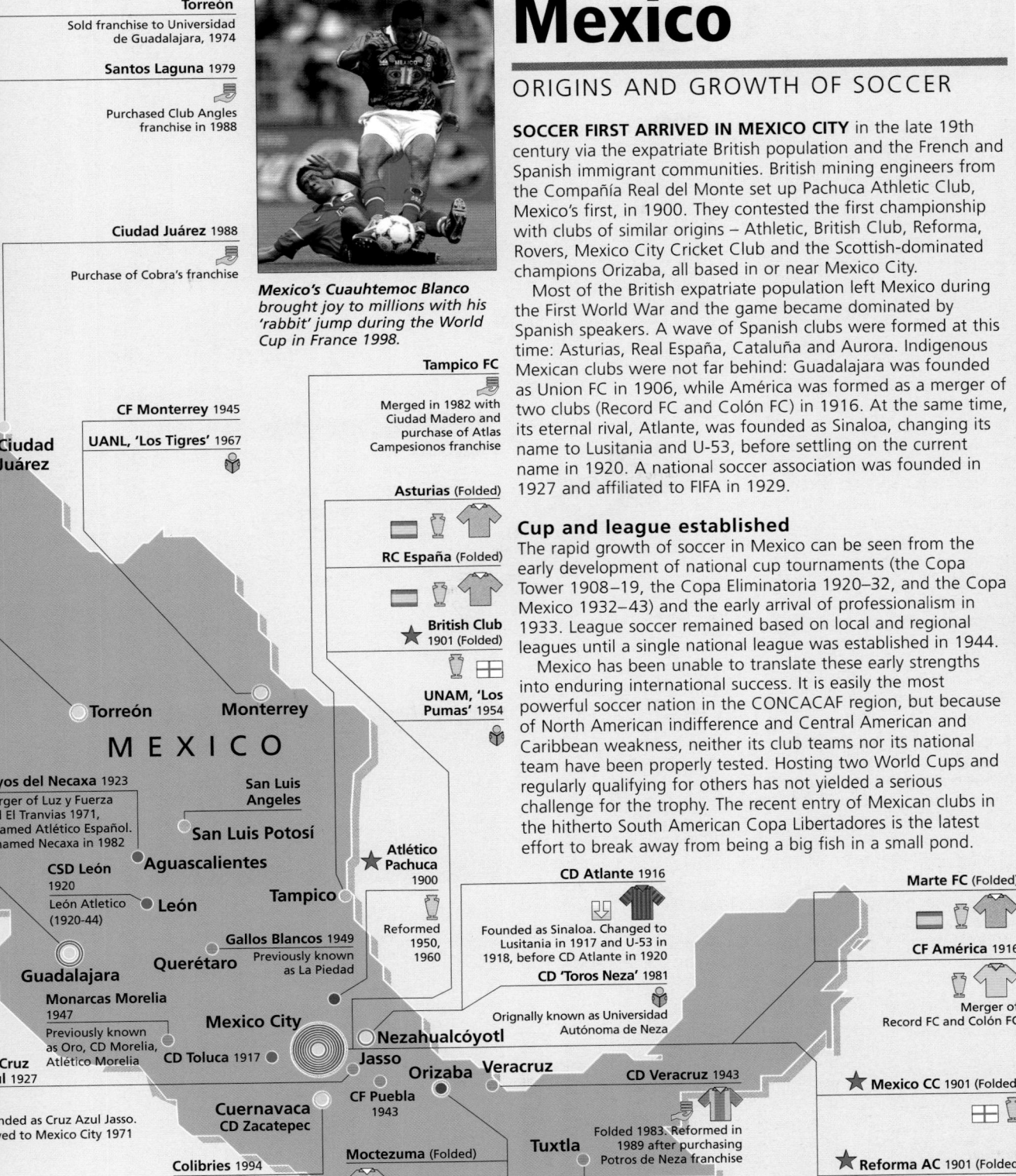

Mexico's Cuauhtemoc Blanco brought joy to millions with his 'rabbit' jump during the World Cup in France 1998.

MEXICO

Torreón
Sold franchise to Universidad de Guadalajara, 1974

Santos Laguna 1979
Purchased Club Angles franchise in 1988

Ciudad Juárez 1988
Purchase of Cobra's franchise

CF Monterrey 1945
UANL, 'Los Tigres' 1967

Ciudad Juárez

Tampico FC
Merged in 1982 with Ciudad Madero and purchase of Atlas Campesionos franchise

Asturias (Folded)

RC España (Folded)

British Club 1901 (Folded)

UNAM, 'Los Pumas' 1954

Torreón   **Monterrey**

MEXICO

ayos del Necaxa 1923
Merger of Luz y Fuerza nd El Tranvias 1971, enamed Atlético Español. enamed Necaxa in 1982

San Luis Angeles

San Luis Potosí

CSD León 1920
León Atletico (1920-44)

Aguascalientes

León

Tampico

Atlético Pachuca 1900
Reformed 1950, 1960

CD Atlante 1916
Founded as Sinaloa. Changed to Lusitania in 1917 and U-53 in 1918, before CD Atlante in 1920

Marte FC (Folded)

CF América 1916
Merger of Record FC and Colón FC

Gallos Blancos 1949
Previously known as La Piedad

Querétaro

CD 'Toros Neza' 1981
Orignally known as Universidad Autónoma de Neza

Guadalajara

Monarcas Morelia 1947
Previously known as Oro, CD Morelia, Atlético Morelia

Mexico City

CD Toluca 1917

Nezahualcóyotl

Jasso

D Cruz zul 1927
ounded as Cruz Azul Jasso. oved to Mexico City 1971

Cuernavaca
CD Zacatepec

Colibries 1994
Purchase of franchise Atlético Cuernavaca. Relocated 2002. Previously known as Atlético Celaya

Moctezuma (Folded)

Orizaba Charleston (Folded)

CF Puebla 1943

Orizaba   **Veracruz**

CD Veracruz 1943
Folded 1983. Reformed in 1989 after purchasing Potros de Neza franchise

Tuxtla

Jaguares de Chiapas 1915
Previously known as FD Irapuato. Relocated 2002

Mexico CC 1901 (Folded)

Reforma AC 1901 (Folded)

MEXICO

Mexico City

SOCCER CENTER

MEXICO

AT THE TURN OF THE CENTURY, Mexico City was host to a considerable mercantile and financial British community. Soccer clubs, like Reforma and Mexico Cricket Club, sprang up across the city and a city league began in 1902. The First World War and the Mexican Revolution saw most of the British drift away along with their teams, to be replaced by a mixture of Spanish immigrant and indigenous Mexican teams. It is only the latter that have survived the coming of professionalism.

The centralization of political power and the sharp social divisions of Mexican society are reflected in the city's soccer. The capital's clubs, particularly Cruz Azul, América and Necaxa – teams with national followings outside of Mexico City – all represent a specific strand of Mexican society. Cruz Azul, the solidly working-class team, was founded in Jasso in 1927, before being bought by a cement company and transferred to the south of Mexico City. UNAM, or Los Pumas as the team is more often known, sprang from the National Autonomous University of Mexico. The university no longer runs the team but it continues to field student players and is most widely known for giving youth its chance on the pitch. The club's supporters lean towards the younger, more intellectual, left-wing strands of Mexican life. América, by contrast, is the team of the ruling order and support for the club is often interpreted as an act of social climbing and aspiration. Atlante, originally from the poorest part of the inner city, is the people's team, representing the most marginalized members of Mexican society, while the ever-expanding suburbs have their team in Toros Neza to the west of the city.

The influence of Televisa

The concentration of power in Mexican soccer can be seen from the three clubs that have played at the Azteca Stadium. Televisa, the nation's biggest media company with business in every part of the Americas, owns the stadium and all the clubs. In 1961, the company bought the long-faded América, spent more money, (including the purchase of the first major wave of foreign players in Mexico) and, through relentless promotion, created a national following for the club. Televisa has since strengthened its grip on Mexican soccer by buying the Azteca itself, Necaxa in 1983 (which has now moved out of the city to the richer demographic fields of Aguascalientes) and Atlante in 1996. It has seen off all rivals to its pre-eminent position in TV coverage of Mexican soccer, helped gain host status for Mexico in two World Cups (1970 and 1986), and kept very close to the PRI – the political party that ruled Mexico uninterrupted from 1929 to 2000.

THE NATIONAL DERBY 'El Superclássico'

AMÉRICA	GUADALAJARA

 171 matches played

61 América wins
56 Guadalajara wins
54 draws

0   50   100   150   200   250

NUMBER OF MATCHES
(all matches up to May 2004)

Guadalajara is 360 miles/580 kms
north-west of Mexico City

UNAM 'LOS PUMAS' 1954

National League (1944–2004)	*1968,* **77,** *78, 79,* **81,** *85, 88,* **91, 2004 C**
Cup	**1975**
CONCACAF Champions Cup	**1980, 82, 89**
Interamerican Cup	**1981,** *90*

AZTECA

Clubs:	América, Necaxa, Mexico
Built:	1966
Original Capacity:	112,000
Rebuilt:	1986
Significant Matches:	1970 World Cup: ten matches including semi-final, 3rd place play-off, Final; 1986 World Cup: nine matches including semi-final and Final; 1993 Gold Cup

106,000

Televisa, Mexico's leading TV company, is based in Mexico City, from where it runs its soccer empire. It owns two of the city's big clubs, América and Atlante, as well as the Azteca Stadium.

5

NAUCALPÁN

Bosque
Chapultep

COACALCO

In 2002 Necaxa moved from Mexico City to Aguascalientes in Central Mexico

Necaxa

Sierra de Guadalupe

ECATEPEC

NECAXA 1923

Amateur League (1903–43)	**1933, 35, 37, 38**
National League (1944–2004)	*1974*, **95, 96,** *97*(w), *98*(s), **99**(w), *2002*(s)
Cup	**1960, 66, 95,** *99*
CONCACAF Champions Cup	**1975, 99**
Interamerican Cup	*1976*

Mexico City

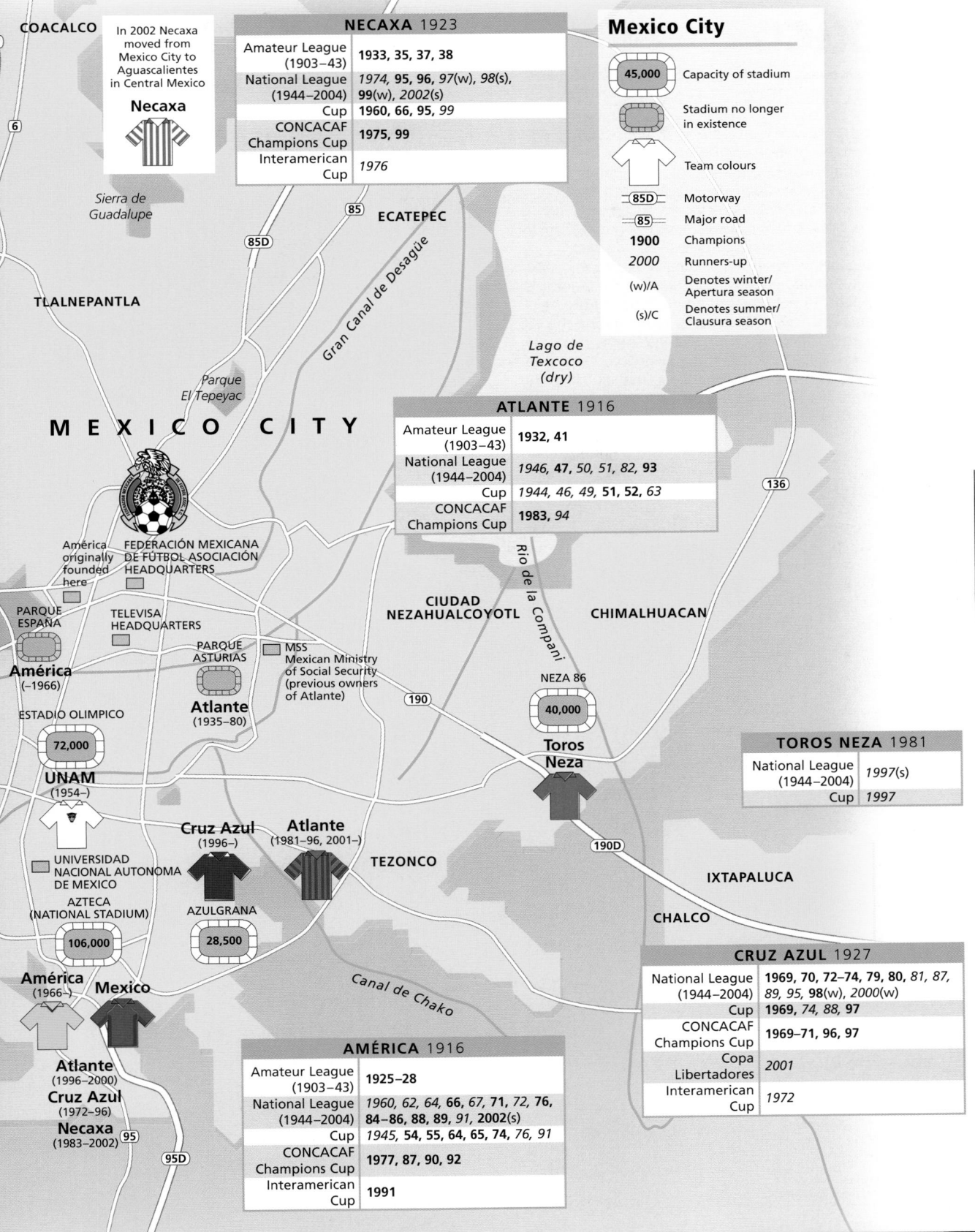

45,000	Capacity of stadium
	Stadium no longer in existence
	Team colours
85D	Motorway
85	Major road
1900	Champions
2000	Runners-up
(w)/A	Denotes winter/ Apertura season
(s)/C	Denotes summer/ Clausura season

MEXICO

Gran Canal de Desagüe

Lago de Texcoco (dry)

TLALNEPANTLA

Parque El Tepeyac

M E X I C O   C I T Y

América originally founded here

FEDERACIÓN MEXICANA DE FÚTBOL ASOCIACIÓN HEADQUARTERS

PARQUE ESPAÑA

América (–1966)

TELEVISA HEADQUARTERS

PARQUE ASTURIAS

Atlante (1935–80)

MSS Mexican Ministry of Social Security (previous owners of Atlante)

CIUDAD NEZAHUALCOYOTL

CHIMALHUACAN

Río de la Compani

ATLANTE 1916

Amateur League (1903–43)	**1932, 41**
National League (1944–2004)	*1946*, **47,** *50, 51, 82*, **93**
Cup	*1944, 46, 49,* **51, 52,** *63*
CONCACAF Champions Cup	**1983,** *94*

NEZA 86

40,000

Toros Neza

ESTADIO OLIMPICO

72,000

UNAM (1954–)

UNIVERSIDAD NACIONAL AUTONOMA DE MEXICO

Cruz Azul (1996–)

Atlante (1981–96, 2001–)

TEZONCO

IXTAPALUCA

CHALCO

TOROS NEZA 1981

National League (1944–2004)	*1997*(s)
Cup	*1997*

AZTECA (NATIONAL STADIUM)

106,000

AZULGRANA

28,500

América (1966–)

Mexico

Atlante (1996–2000)

Cruz Azul (1972–96)

Necaxa (1983–2002)

Canal de Chako

AMÉRICA 1916

Amateur League (1903–43)	**1925–28**
National League (1944–2004)	*1960, 62, 64,* **66, 67, 71, 72, 76, 84–86, 88, 89,** *91,* **2002**(s)
Cup	*1945,* **54, 55, 64, 65, 74,** *76, 91*
CONCACAF Champions Cup	**1977, 87, 90, 92**
Interamerican Cup	**1991**

CRUZ AZUL 1927

National League (1944–2004)	**1969, 70, 72–74, 79, 80,** *81, 87, 89,* **95, 98**(w), *2000*(w)
Cup	**1969,** *74, 88,* **97**
CONCACAF Champions Cup	**1969–71,** *96,* **97**
Copa Libertadores	*2001*
Interamerican Cup	*1972*

Mexico

PRIMERA DIVISIÓN 1981–2003

THE 1980s BEGAN with media giants Televisa determined to make CF América – its key soccer property – the best team in Mexico. A change of strip and an open chequebook did the trick and in 1984, under Carlos Reynos, América took the title, pipping long-standing rival CD Guadalajara to the post. Four out of the next six titles followed, CF Monterrey winning in 1986 and Guadalajara getting one back the following year.

The Mexican league has been through a variety of changes. It has always concluded with the top eight or ten teams playing off (over two legs) to determine the title, but leagues, mini-leagues and groups have all been used to determine the top teams, while relegation is decided on a Byzantine, multiple-season averaging system. In 1996, the league was split into two separate halves – a winter and a summer championship. But whatever system has been used, league soccer in Mexico has proved a very attractive business proposition. Since the 1980s

In recent years, smaller provincial teams like Monarcas Morelia (in hoops), seen here in action against UAG (in checks), have risen to challenge the traditional giants of Mexican soccer. Morelia's breakthrough moment came in 2001 when the team beat another small club, Toluca, to take the Winter Championship.

Televisa has been joined by rival TV Azteca as multiple club proprietors, while cement, loan, brewing and petrochemical companies have all bought into Mexican clubs. Franchises (or membership of the league) can and have been bought and sold, enabling rich but relegated teams to buy their way back up.

MEXICO

MEXICO

Tecos UAG
1994

CD Atlas
1999s

Universidad de Guadalajara
1990

CD Guadalajara
1983, 84, 87, 97s, 99w

Ciudad Juárez

Santos Laguna
1994, 97w, 2000s, 01s

Torreón

CSD Léon
1992, 98w

Union de Curtidores

León

Gallos Blancos
(formerly La Piedad)

Irapuato AC

Irapuato

Guadalajara

Monarcas Morelia
(formerly Atlético Morelia)
2001w, 03w, 03s

CD Toluca
1998s, 99s, 2000s, 01w, 03w

Colibries
(formerly Atlético Celaya)
1996

CD Zacatepec

Morelia

Toluca

Cuernavaca

CF Monterrey
Mexico 86, 93, 2003s

UANL (Tigres)
1982, 2002w

Real San Luis FC

Monterrey

UAT

Atlético Potosino

San Luis Potosí

Ciudad Victoria

Tampico

Querétaro

Mexico City

Pachuca de Soto

Jasso

CF Puebla
1983, 90, 92

Tampico FC

Deportivo Neza

Querétaro
(formerly Tampico-Madero)
Prode 85, Mexico 86

Atlético Pachuca
2000w, 01s, 02w

CD Toros Neza
1997s

CD Veracruz

Nezahualcóyotl

Veracruz

Jaguares de Chiapas
(formerly CD Veracruz, FD Irapuato)

UNAM (Pumas)
1985, 88, 91

CD Atlante
1982, 93

Necaxa
1995, 96, 97w, 98s, 99w, 2002s

CF América
1984, 85, Prode 85, 88, 89, 91, 2002s

CD Cruz Azul

Tuxla
1987, 89, 95, 98w, 2000w

Primera División

CF América — Team name

League champions/ runners-up

1984, 91 — Champions in bold Runners-up in italics

Other teams in the Primera División

● **Mexico City** — City of origin

w — winter season
s — summer season

América has continued to be a perennial contender and 2002 saw the team champions again at last. Honours have also been shared between outsiders CD Atlante and CSD Léon, who both took surprise titles in the early 1990s; Televisa's other key team, Necaxa, who won three titles in the 1990s; and Cruz Azul, who finally delivered on its promise, winning in 1998. In the late 1990s, the real surprises came from the smaller provincial teams: Toluca, Pachuca, Atlético Morelia and Santos Laguna.

Key to League Positions Table

▦	League champions
▦	Season of promotion to league
▦	Season of relegation from league
▦	Other teams playing in league
▦	Qualified for championship play-off

Mexican League Positions 1981–2003

TEAM	1981-82	1982-83	1983-84	1984-85	Prode 85	Mexico 86	1986-87	1987-88	1988-89	1989-90	1990-91	1991-92	1992-93	1993-94	1994-95	1995-96	1996-97w	1996-97s	1997-98w	1997-98s	1998-99w	1998-99s	1999-2000w	1999-2000s	2000-01w	2000-01s	2001-02w	2001-02s	2002-03w	2002-03s
CF América	SF	SF	C	C	C	SF	QF	C	C	SF	RU		SF	SF	SF	SF		QF	SF	SF		QF	SF		QF	SF			C	QF
CD Atlante	RU	QF	QF		SF	QF						QF	C	QF			QF	QF	SF	QF							QF			QF
CD Atlas				SF										QF		QF	QF		QF	SF	SF	RU	SF	QF	SF			QF		QF
Colibríes (formerly Atlético Celaya)																RU														
CD Cruz Azul			SF	QF	QF	QF	RU		RU		QF	SF	QF	QF	RU	QF			C	QF	QF	SF	RU		QF		SF		QF	
Gallos Blancos (formerly La Piedad)																												QF		
CD Guadalajara		RU	RU	QF	QF	SF	C	QF		SF	QF			SF		QF	C	QF		RU	QF	QF	SF		QF			QF	QF	QF
Universidad de Guadalajara	QF	SF		QF	QF			SF			RU	QF																		
Irapuato AC																														
Jaguares de Chiapas (formerly CD Veracruz, FD Irapuato)																														
Ciudad Juárez																														
CSD Léon			SF										C	SF					RU						QF					
CF Monterrey	QF		QF			C	QF				QF		RU		QF										QF					C
Monarcas Morelia (formerly Atlético Morelia)				QF	QF	SF	SF				QF			QF					SF	QF		QF	QF			C		QF	RU	RU
Necaxa	QF						QF		SF	QF			C	C	RU	SF	RU	C	QF	QF	QF	QF			QF	RU				
Deportivo Neza	SF																													
CD Toros Neza																	SF	RU	QF											
Atlético Pachuca																								C		QF	RU	C		
Atlético Potosino		QF																												
CF Puebla		C		QF	SF	QF	SF	QF		C	SF	RU		QF		SF		QF							QF	SF				
Querétaro (formerly Tampico-Madero)				RU	RU																									
Real San Luis FC																														
Santos Laguna															RU	QF		C	QF		QF		SF		RU	SF	C	QF	SF	SF
Tampico FC																														
Tecos UAG		QF	QF				QF	QF					QF	C	QF				QF	QF		QF					QF		QF	
CD Toluca		QF						QF		QF				SF			QF		C	QF	C	QF	C	RU			SF	QF	C	QF
UANL (Tigres)	C		QF				QF			QF			QF												QF	RU				SF
UAT							QF																							
UNAM (Pumas)			SF	RU				RU		SF	C	QF			QF			QF			SF			SF				SF	SF	
Union de Curtidores																														
CD Veracruz													QF			SF														SF
CD Zacatepec	QF																													

MEXICO

In Mexico, the championship is decided by play-offs, involving eight or ten teams.

In 1986, two shorter championships called Prode 85 and Mexico 86 were held before and after the World Cup. They are counted as official championships.

Since 1996–97 the season has been divided into two, with winter and summer championships.

Mexico

Federación Mexicana de Fútbol Asociación AC
Founded: 1927
Joined FIFA: 1929
Joined CONCACAF: 1961

MEXICO DOMINATES SOCCER in the Central American region. The national team has qualified for the finals of ten of the 15 World Cup tournaments, including Italia '90, when they were barred from the qualifying tournament by FIFA for having breached age regulations in a youth tournament. The country's unrivalled position has meant that the development of soccer has been hindered through lack of decent opposition.

Domestic competitions, however, have been hotly contested for a century. The first amateur league was established in 1903 by five clubs in Mexico City. The Primera Fuzera, based in Mexico City, ran alongside two provincial amateur leagues: Liga de Occidente and Liga Veracruzana. In 1943 the three competitions were fused to form a professional league and a second division was added in 1950. In 1970, the league format was changed to two then four groups, with a series of multi-leg play-off rounds to decide the championship.

Meanwhile, the Mexican Cup went through three incarnations during its amateur phase. These were the Copa Tower, which existed between 1908 and 1919; the Copa Eliminatoria between 1920 and 1932 (this tournament only accepted clubs that played in the Primera Fuerza); and the Copa Mexico between 1932 and 1943, a tournament that accepted clubs from all over the country. The Cup finally turned professional in 1944.

Mexican League Record 1944–2004

SEASON	CHAMPIONS	RUNNERS-UP
1944	Asturias	España
1945	España	Puebla
1946	Veracruz	Atlante
1947	Atlante	León
1948	León	Oro
1949	León	Atlas
1950	Veracruz	Atlante
1951	Atlas	Atlante
1952	León	Guadalajara
1953	Tampico	Zacatepec
1954	Marte	Oro
1955	Zacatepec	Guadalajara
1956	León	Oro
1957	Guadalajara	Toluca
1958	Zacatepec	Toluca
1959	Guadalajara	León
1960	Guadalajara	América
1961	Guadalajara	Oro
1962	Guadalajara	América
1963	Oro	Guadalajara
1964	Guadalajara	América
1965	Guadalajara	Oro
1966	América	Atlas
1967	Toluca	América
1968	Toluca	UNAM
1969	Cruz Azul	Guadalajara
1970	Guadalajara	Cruz Azul
1970*	Cruz Azul	Guadalajara
1971	América	Toluca
1972	Cruz Azul	América
1973	Cruz Azul	León
1974	Cruz Azul	Atlético Español

Mexican League Record (*continued*)

SEASON	CHAMPIONS	RUNNERS-UP
1975	Toluca	León
1976	América	Unión de Guadalajara
1977	UNAM	Unión de Guadalajara
1878	UANL	UNAM
1979	Cruz Azul	UNAM
1980	Cruz Azul	UANL
1981	UNAM	Cruz Azul
1982	UANL	Atlante
1983	Puebla	Guadalajara
1984	América	Guadalajara
1985	América	UNAM
1986†	América	Tampico-Madero
1986†	Monterrey	Tampico-Madero
1987	Guadalajara	Cruz Azul
1988	América	UNAM
1989	América	Cruz Azul
1990	Puebla	Unión de Guadalajara
1991	UNAM	América
1992	León	Puebla
1993	Atlante	Monterrey
1994	UAG	Santos Laguna
1995	Necaxa	Cruz Azul
1996	Necaxa	Atlético Celaya
1997 (w)§	Santos Laguna	Necaxa
1997 (s)	Guadalajara	Toros Neza
1998 (w)	Cruz Azul	León
1998 (s)	Toluca	Necaxa
1999 (w)	Necaxa	Guadalajara
1999 (s)	Toluca	Atlas
2000 (w)	Pachuca	Cruz Azul
2000 (s)	Toluca	Santos Laguna
2001 (w)	Morelia	Toluca
2001 (s)	Santos Laguna	Pachuca
2002 (w)	Pachuca	Tigres
2002 (s)	América	Necaxa
2003 (w)	Toluca	Morelia
2003 (s)	Monterrey	Morelia
2004 (w)	Pachuca	Tigres
2004 (s)	UNAM	Guadalajara

* A short tournament was played before or after the 1970 World Cup in Mexico. It is counted as a championship.

† Due to the 1986 World Cup in Mexico, the 1985–86 season was cancelled and replaced by two short tournaments.

§ From 1997 a championship was played in both winter (**w**) and summer (**s**).

Mexican League Summary

TEAM	TOTALS	CHAMPIONS & RUNNERS-UP (BOLD) (ITALICS)
Guadalajara	10, 9	*1952, 55,* **57,** *59–62,* **63, 64, 65, 69, 70,** *70, 83, 84, 87, 97 (s), 99 (w), 2004 (s)*
América	9, 6	*1960, 62, 64, 66, 67,* **71,** *72,* **76, 84–86†, 88, 89, 91, 2002 (s)**
Cruz Azul	8, 6	**1969,** *70,* **70, 72–74, 79, 80, 81,** *87,* **89, 95, 98 (w),** *2000 (w)*
Toluca	7, 4	*1957, 58,* **67,** *68,* **71, 75, 98 (s), 99 (s), 2000 (s),** *01 (w),* **03 (w)**
León	5, 5	**1947,** *48,* **49,** *52,* **56,** *59,* **73,** *75,* **92,** *98 (w)*
UNAM	4, 5	**1968,** *77,* **78, 79,** *81,* **85,** *88,* **91,** *2004 (s)*
Necaxa (includes Atlético Español)	3, 4	*1974,* **95, 96, 97 (w),** *98 (s),* **99,** *2002 (s)*
Pachuca	3, 1	**2000 (w),** *01,* **02 (w), 04 (w)**
Atlante	2, 4	*1946,* **47,** *50, 51,* **82, 93**
Puebla	2, 2	*1945,* **83, 90,** *92*
Santos Laguna	2, 2	*1994,* **97 (w),** *2000 (s),* **01 (s)**

Mexican League Summary (*continued*)

TEAM	TOTALS	CHAMPIONS & RUNNERS-UP (BOLD) (*ITALICS*)
Monterrey	2, 1	**1986†, 93**, *2003 (s)*
UANL	2, 1	**1978, 80**, *82*
Zacatepec	2, 1	*1953*, **55, 58**
Veracruz	2, 0	**1946, 50**
Oro	1, 5	**1948**, *54, 56, 61, 63, 65*
Atlas	1, 3	**1949**, *51, 66, 99 (s)*
Morelia	1, 2	**2001 (w)**, *03 (w)*, **03 (s)**
Tampico-Madero (includes Tampico)	1, 2	**1953**, *86†, 86†*
España	1, 1	*1944*, **45**
Asturias	1, 0	**1944**
Marte	1, 0	**1954**
UAG	1, 0	**1994**
Unión de Guadalajara	0, 3	*1976, 77, 90*
Tigres	0, 2	*2002 (w), 04 (w)*
Atlético Celaya	0, 1	*1996*
Toros Neza	0, 1	*1997 (s)*

(w) denotes winter season
(s) denotes summer season
† Due to the 1986 World Cup in Mexico, the league was replaced with two short tournaments. They both counted as championships.

Mexican Cup Record 1944–99

YEAR	WINNERS	SCORE	RUNNERS-UP
1944	España	**6-2**	Atlante
1945	Puebla	**6-4**	América
1946	Atlas	**5-4 (aet)**	Atlante
1947	Moctezuma	**4-3**	Oro
1948	Veracruz	**3-1**	Guadalajara
1949	León	**3-0**	Atlante
1950	Atlas	**3-1 (aet)**	Veracruz
1951	Atlante	**1-0**	Guadalajara
1952	Atlante	**2-0**	Puebla
1953	Puebla	**4-1**	León
1954	América	**1-1 (aet)(3-2 pens)**	Guadalajara
1955	América	**1-0**	Guadalajara
1956	Toluca	**2-1**	Irapuato
1957	Zacatepec	**2-1**	León
1958	León	**5-2 (aet)**	Zacatepec
1959	Zacatepec	**2-1**	León
1960	Atlético Español	**2-2 (aet)(10-9 pens)**	Tampico
1961	Tampico	**1-0**	Toluca
1962	Atlas	**3-3, (replay) 1-0**	Tampico
1963	Guadalajara	**2-1**	Atlante
1964	América	**1-1 (aet)(5-4 pens)**	Monterrey
1965	América	**4-0**	Morelia
1966	Atlético Español	**3-3, (replay) 1-0**	León
1967	León	**2-1**	Guadalajara
1968	Atlas	**2-1**	Veracruz
1969	Cruz Azul	**2-1 (aet)**	Monterrey
1970	Guadalajara	**3-2, 2-1 (2 legs)**	Torreón
1971	León	**0-0 (aet) (10-9 pens)**	Zacatepec
1972	León	**Final Group**	Puebla
1973		*no competition*	
1974	América	**2-1, 1-1 (2 legs)**	Cruz Azul
1975	UNAM	**Final Group**	Unión de Guadalajara
1976	UANL	**2-0, 1-2 (2 legs) won on away goals**	América
1977–87		*no competition*	
1988	Puebla	**0-0, 1-1 (2 legs)**	Cruz Azul
1989	Toluca	**2-1, 1-1 (2 legs)**	Unión de Guadalajara
1990	Puebla	**4-1, 0-2 (2 legs)**	UANL
1991	Unión de Guadalajara	**1-0, 0-0 (2 legs)**	América

Mexican Cup Record (*continued*)

YEAR	WINNERS	SCORE	RUNNERS-UP
1992	Monterrey	**4-2**	Ciudad Juarez
1993–94		*no competition*	
1995	Necaxa	**2-0**	Veracruz
1996	UANL	**1-1, 1-0 (2 legs)**	Atlas
1997	Cruz Azul	**2-0**	Toros Neza
1998		*no competition*	
1999	Tigres	**2-0**	Necaxa
2000		*tournament discontinued*	

Mexican Cup Summary

TEAM	TOTALS	WINNERS & RUNNERS-UP (BOLD) (*ITALICS*)
León	5, 4	**1949**, *53, 57*, **58, 59, 66, 67, 71, 72**
América	5, 3	*1945*, **54, 55, 64, 65**, *74, 76*, **91**
Puebla	4, 2	**1945**, *52*, **53**, *72*, **88, 90**
Atlas	4, 1	**1946, 50, 62, 68**, *96*
Necaxa (includes Atlético Español)	3, 1	**1960, 66**, *95*, **99**
Guadalajara	2, 5	*1948, 51, 54, 55*, **63**, *67*, **70**
Atlante	2, 4	*1944, 46, 49*, **51, 52**, *63*
Cruz Azul	2, 2	**1969**, *74*, **88**, *97*
Zacatepec	2, 2	**1957**, *58*, **59**, *71*
Toluca	2, 1	**1956**, *61*, **89**
UANL	2, 1	**1976**, *90*, **96**
Veracruz	1, 3	**1948**, *50, 68, 95*
Monterrey	1, 2	*1964, 69*, **92**
Tampico	1, 2	*1960*, **61**, *62*
Unión de Guadalajara	1, 2	*1975, 89*, **91**
España	1, 0	**1944**
Moctezuma	1, 0	**1947**
Tigres	1, 0	**1999**
UNAM	1, 0	**1975**
Ciudad Juarez	0, 1	*1992*
Irapuato	0, 1	*1956*
Morelia	0, 1	*1965*
Oro	0, 1	*1947*
Toros Neza	0, 1	*1997*
Torreón	0, 1	*1970*

Necaxa 1999–2000: *four times Mexican champions, the team was founded in Mexico City in 1923. Bought by Spanish businessmen in 1971, it played as Atlético Español until TV giant, Televisa, bought it in 1982 and renamed it Necaxa. The team has recently relocated outside Mexico City to Aguascalientes, 150 miles northeast.*

MEXICO

Canada

The Canadian Soccer Association
Founded: 1912
Joined FIFA: 1912–28, 1946
Joined CONCACAF: 1978

DESPITE SOCCER'S EARLY ARRIVAL, Canada proved stony ground for the development of the game. Clubs were forming in the last quarter of the 19th century and national cup and league competitions were established in 1912 and 1922 respectively, but the transition to a regular national professional league has proved elusive.

The game's lacklustre progression may be attributed to three factors. Firstly, the country's vast size makes the administration of a single, national competition difficult. Secondly, soccer faces fierce competition from the major North American sports of ice hockey, gridiron, baseball and basketball. Thirdly, as the names of leading clubs suggest, soccer has been a game for recent, non-Anglo immigrants: Toronto Scots and Ulsters, Eintracht Vancouver, Vancouver Croatia and Scarborough Azzurri, and has yet to really enter the mainstream.

The first attempt to create a modern professional league was the Eastern Canada Professional Soccer League. It lasted only five years, 1961–65, forcing top Canadian teams to play in various US leagues in the 1970s and 80s. A further attempt to professionalize and commercialize the game came with the Canadian Soccer League in 1987. It was disbanded in 1992. Again leading clubs have been forced into American pro leagues. The semi-professional Canadian Professional Soccer League was re-established in Ontario in 1998 and has so far survived and expanded into Quebec. Currently, plans exist for the amalgamation of the CPSL and the top professional clubs playing in America to form a national league.

In 2000 Canada (in white) won the Gold Cup, beating Colombia 2-0 in the Final in Los Angeles. This was a major achievement for a team whose players almost all play outside their native country.

Canadian Soccer League Record 1987–1992

SEASON	CHAMPIONS	SEASON	CHAMPIONS
1987	Calgary Kickers	1990	Vancouver 86ers
1988	Vancouver 86ers	1991	Vancouver 86ers
1989	Vancouver 86ers	1992	Winnipeg Fury

Canadian Professional Soccer League Record 1998–2003

SEASON	CHAMPIONS	SEASON	CHAMPIONS
1998	St. Catharine's	2002	Ottawa
1999	Toronto Olympians	2003	Brampton
2000	Toronto Croatia		
2001	St. Catharine's		

Canadian Challenge Cup Record 1913–2002

YEAR	WINNERS	YEAR	WINNERS
1913	Norwood Wanderers	1965	Vancouver Firefighters
1914	Norwood Wanderers	1966	British Columbia
1915	Winnipeg Scots	1967	Toronto
1916–18	no competition	1968	Toronto Royals
1919	Montreal Grand	1969	Columbus Vancouver
1920	Westinghouse Ontario	1970	no competition
1921	Toronto Scots	1971	Eintracht Vancouver
1922	Hillhurst Calgary	1972	New Westminster Blues
1923	Naniamo Wanderers	1973	Vancouver Firefighters
1924	Weston University	1974	Calgary Springer Kickers
1925	Toronto Ulsters	1975	London Boxing Club Victoria
1926	Weston University	1976	Victoria West SC
1927	Naniamo Wanderers	1977	Columbus Vancouver
1928	New Westminster Royals	1978	Columbus Vancouver
1929	CNR Montreal	1979	Victoria West SC
1930	New Westminster Royals	1980	St. John Drydock
1931	New Westminster Royals	1981	Toronto Ciociaro
1932	Toronto Scots	1982	Victoria West SC
1933	Toronto Scots	1983	Vancouver Firefighters
1934	Verduns Montreal	1984	Victoria West SC
1935	Aldreds Montreal	1985	Vancouver Croatia
1936	New Westminster Royals	1986	Hamilton Steelers
1937	Johnston Nationals	1987	Lucania SC
1938	North Shore Vancouver	1988	Holy Cross
1939	Radials Vancouver	1989	Scarborough Azzurri
1940–45	no competition	1990	Vancouver Firefighters
1946	Toronto Ulster United	1991	Norvan SC
1947	St. Andrews Vancouver	1992	Norvan SC
1948	Carsteel Montreal	1993	West Side Rino
1949	North Shore Vancouver	1994	Edmonton Ital-Canadians
1950	Vancouver City	1995	Mistral-Estrie
1951	Ulster United Toronto	1996	Westside CIBC
1952	Steelco Montreal	1997	Edmonton Ital-Canadians
1953	New Westminster Royals	1998	RDP Condores
1954	Scottish Winnipeg	1999	Calgary CSFC
1955	New Westminster Royals	2000	Luciana Winnipeg
1956	Halecos Vancouver	2001	Halifax King of Donair
1957	Ukrainia SC Montreal	2002	Manifoba
1958	New Westminster Royals		
1959	Alouettes Montreal		
1960	New Westminster Royals		
1961	Concordia Montreal		
1962	Scottish Winnipeg		
1963	no competition		
1964	Columbus Vancouver		

Central America

SOCCER IN CENTRAL AMERICA has had to compete with American sports, primarily baseball, for the affections and interest of fans and patrons. Where American influence (especially military influence) and occupation has been strongest, baseball has proved the winner, and soccer has been a minority sport in both Nicaragua and Panama. The region's strongest leagues have been traditionally in Costa Rica, Guatemala, Honduras and El Salvador. Soccer took off in the 1920s with leagues and clubs established in all of them. The Costa Rican league dates from 1921, the Salvadorian from 1926, and Guatemala began in 1919. Honduras has had formal tournaments since the 1920s but a properly constituted national league did not take off until 1965. All of these countries operate a complex national league system in which an opening championship (the Apertura) is followed by a closing (Clausura) championship. These are sometimes followed by a knockout competitions between the top six or eight teams in the league or with a final play-off between the winners of the two phases.

The centrality of soccer to popular culture and national identity in the region can be seen from an infamous event – the Futbal War. In 1969, El Salvador beat Honduras 3-2 in a World Cup qualifying match in Mexico City, following an unresolved two-leg play-off between the sides. This acted as the final trigger in a long-running border dispute between the states, and El Salvador invaded Honduras. Although little was resolved, over 2,000 people perished in the conflict.

The big Costa Rican derby is between Alajuelense (left) and Saprissa. Both teams are based in the capital San José and have dominated soccer in the country for many years with almost 50 championships between them in 80 years.

Belize

Belize National Football Association
Founded: 1980
Joined FIFA: 1986
Joined CONCACAF: 1986

SEASON	LEAGUE CHAMPIONS
1999	Juventus
2000	Sagitún
2001	Kulture Yabra
2002	Kulture Yabra
2003	*no championship*

Costa Rica

Federación Costarricense de Fútbol
Founded: 1921
Joined FIFA: 1921
Joined CONCACAF: 1962

SEASON	LEAGUE CHAMPIONS
2000	Alajuelense
2001	Alajuelense
2002	Alajuelense
2003	Alajuelense
2004	Saprissa

El Salvador

Federación Salvadoreña de Fútbol
Founded: 1935
Joined FIFA: 1938
Joined CONCACAF: 1962

SEASON	LEAGUE CHAMPIONS
2000 A	Aguila
2000 C	Luis Angel Firpo
2001 A/C	Aguila
2002 A	Alianza
2002 C	CD Fas
2003 A	CD Fas
2003 C	San Salvador
2004 A	CD Fas
2004 C	Alianza

A = Apertura   C = Clausura.

Guatemala

Federación Nacional de Fútbol de Guatemala
Founded: 1919
Joined FIFA: 1933
Joined CONCACAF: 1961

SEASON	LEAGUE CHAMPIONS
2001 A	Municipal
2001 C	Comunicaciones
2002 A	Municipal
2002 C	Municipal
2003 A	Comunicaciones
2003 C	Comunicaciones
2004 A	Municipal
2004 C	Coban Imperial

A = Apertura   C = Clausura.

YEAR	CUP WINNERS
2000	*unknown*
2001	*unknown*
2002	Jalapa
2003	Municipal
2004	Municipal

Guyana

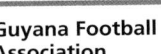

Guyana Football Association
Founded: 1902
Joined FIFA: 1968
Joined CONCACAF: 1969

SEASON	LEAGUE CHAMPIONS
1998	Santos FC
1999	*unknown*
2000	*no championship*
2001	Fruta Conquerors
2002	*no championship*

YEAR	CUP WINNERS
2000	Topp XX
2001	Topp XX
2002	Victoria Kings
2003	Fruta Conquerors
2004	Camptown

Honduras

Federación Nacional Autónoma de Fútbol de Honduras
Founded: 1951
Joined FIFA: 1951
Joined CONCACAF: 1961

SEASON	LEAGUE CHAMPIONS
2002 A	Motagua
2002 C	Marathon
2003 A	Olympia
2003 C	Marathon
2004 A	Real España
2004 C	Olympia

A = Apertura   C = Clausura.

Nicaragua

Federación Nicaraguense de Fútbol
Founded: 1931
Joined FIFA: 1950
Joined CONCACAF: 1968

SEASON	LEAGUE CHAMPIONS
2000	FC Diriangén
2001	Deportivo Walter Ferreti
2002	Jalapa
2003	FC Real Estelí
2004	FC Real Estelí

Panama

Federación Nacional de Fútbol de Panamá
Founded: 1937
Joined FIFA: 1938
Joined CONCACAF: 1961

SEASON	LEAGUE CHAMPIONS
1999	Deportivo Árabe Unido
2000	Tauro FC
2001	Panamá Viejo FC
2002	Plaza Amador
2003	Tauro FC

Surinam

Surinaamse Voetbal Bond
Founded: 1920
Joined FIFA: 1929
Joined CONCACAF: 1961

SEASON	LEAGUE CHAMPIONS
1999	SNL
2000	Transvaal
2001	*no championship*
2002	Voorwaarts
2003	FCS National

The Caribbean

SOCCER IN THE CARIBBEAN has always been in fierce competition for players, fans and money with cricket, baseball and, increasingly, with basketball. Small populations and generally low incomes have made the competition fiercer and squeezed the space for soccer in the region. The strongest soccer-playing traditions and leagues have been in Haiti, Cuba, Jamaica and Trinidad and Tobago.

Cuban soccer dates from the first decade of the 20th century, when it was played among Spaniards and Cubans educated in Britain. A league was established in the 1920s, and the first floodlit stadium in the region was built in Havana in 1928 – a subsequent wave of interest culminated in Cuba's appearance in the quarter-finals of the 1938 World Cup.

Soccer in Haiti dates from the same era with a national FA created in 1904, which became FIFA's first Caribbean member in 1933. Its most successful clubs, Violette Athlétique Club and Racing Club Haïtien, were founded in 1918 and 1923. Haiti was the first Caribbean nation to qualify for the World Cup Finals in 1974.

Jamaica's national FA was first established in 1910, joining FIFA after independence in 1962. Drawing on the increasingly large and dispersed global Jamaican diaspora, the national team qualified for the World Cup in 1998.

Trinidad and Tobago's national FA is even older (founded in 1908), though international success has eluded them both at club and national level.

THE CARIBBEAN

Anguilla

Anguilla Football Association
Founded: 1990
Joined FIFA: 1996
Joined CONCACAF: 1996

SEASON	LEAGUE CHAMPIONS
1999	Attackers
2000	no competition
2001	Roaring Lions
2002	Roaring Lions
2003	Roaring Lions

Antigua and Barbuda

The Antigua Football Association
Founded: 1928
Joined FIFA: 1970
Joined CONCACAF: 1980

SEASON	LEAGUE CHAMPIONS
2000	Empire
2001	Empire
2002	Parham FC
2003	Parham FC
2004	Bassa FC

Aruba

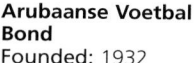

Arubaanse Voetbal Bond
Founded: 1932
Joined FIFA: 1988
Joined CONCACA: 1988

SEASON	LEAGUE CHAMPIONS
1999	SV Estrella
2000	Deportivo Nacional
2001	Deportivo Nacional
2002	RCA
2003	Deportivo Nacional

Bahamas

The Bahamas Football Association
Founded: 1967
Joined FIFA: 1968
Joined CONCACAF: 1981

SEASON	LEAGUE CHAMPIONS
2000	Abacom United FC
2001	Cavalier FC
2002	unfinished
2003	Bears FC
2004	Bears FC

Barbados

Barbados Football Association
Founded: 1910
Joined FIFA: 1968
Joined CONCACAF: 1968

SEASON	LEAGUE CHAMPIONS
2000	Notre Dame SC
2001	Paradise
2002	Notre Dame SC
2003	Paradise
2004	Notre Dame SC

YEAR	CUP WINNERS
1999	Pride of Gall Hill
2000	Paradise
2001	Notre Dame
2002	Youth Milan
2003	Paradise

Bermuda

Bermuda Football Association
Founded: 1928
Joined FIFA: 1962
Joined CONCACAF: 1966

SEASON	LEAGUE CHAMPIONS
2000	PHC Zebras
2001	Dandy Town Hornets SC
2002	North Village
2003	North Village
2004	Dandy Town Hornets SC

British Virgin Islands

British Virgin Islands Football Association
Founded: 1974
Joined FIFA: 1996
Joined CONCACAF: 1996

SEASON	LEAGUE CHAMPIONS
1999	Veterans
2000	HBA Panthers
2000/01	HBA Panthers
2001	Future Stars United
2002	HBA Panthers

YEAR	CUP WINNERS
1999	unknown
2000	Rangers
2001	Rangers
2002	unknown
2003	Virgin Gorda

Cayman Islands

Cayman Islands Football Association
Founded: 1966
Joined FIFA: 1992
Joined CONCACAF: 1992

SEASON	LEAGUE CHAMPIONS
2000	Western Union FC
2001	Scholars International
2002	Georgetown SC
2003	Scholars International
2004	Latinos

Cuba

Associación de Fútbol de Cuba
Founded: 1924
Joined FIFA: 1933
Joined CONCACAF: 1961

SEASON	LEAGUE CHAMPIONS
2000	FC Pinar del Río
2001	Ciudad de la Habana
2002	Ciego de Ávila
2003	FC Villa Clara
2003*	Ciego de Ávila

* Season change from autumn/spring to spring/autumn.

Dominica

Dominica Football Association
Founded: 1970
Joined FIFA: 1994
Joined CONCACAF: 1994

SEASON	LEAGUE CHAMPIONS
1999	Harlem Bombers
1999	Harlem Bombers
2000	Harlem Bombers
2002	Saint Joseph
2003	Harlem Bombers

Dominican Republic

Federación Dominicana de Fútbol
Founded: 1953
Joined FIFA: 1958
Joined CONCACAF: 1964

SEASON	LEAGUE CHAMPIONS
2000	unknown
2001	CD Pantoja
2002	Baninter
2003	Baninter
2004	Casa de España

Grenada

Grenada Football Association
Founded: 1924
Joined FIFA: 1976
Joined CONCACAF: 1969

SEASON	LEAGUE CHAMPIONS
1999	St. Andrews Football League Grenville
2000	Grenada Boys Secondary School St. George's
2001	Grenada Boys Secondary School St. George's
2002	QPR FC
2003	Hurricane FC

Haiti

Féderation Haïtienne de Football
Founded: 1904
Joined FIFA: 1933
Joined CONCACAF: 1961

SEASON	LEAGUE CHAMPIONS
2000	Racing Club Haïtien
2001	FICA
2002 O	Roulado
2002 C	Racing Club Haïtien
2003 O	Don Bosco
2003 C	Roulado
2004 O	Don Bosco
2004 C	Roulado

O = Ouverture   C = Clôture.

Jamaica

Jamaica Football Association
Founded: 1910
Joined FIFA: 1962
Joined CONCACAF: 1961

SEASON	LEAGUE CHAMPIONS
2000	Harbour View
2001	Arnett Gardens FC
2002	Arnett Gardens FC
2003	Hazard United
2004	Tivoli Gardens

Montserrat

Montserrat Football Association
Founded: *unknown*
Joined FIFA: 1996
Joined CONCACAF: 1996

Montserrat *(continued)*

SEASON	LEAGUE CHAMPIONS
1999	*abandoned*
2000	Royal Montserrat Police Force
2001	Royal Montserrat Police Force
2002	*unknown*
2003	Royal Montserrat Police Force

Netherlands Antilles

Nederlande Antilliaanse Voetbal Unie
Founded: 1921
Joined FIFA: 1932
Joined CONCACAF: 1961

SEASON	LEAGUE CHAMPIONS
1999	Sithoc FC
2000	*unknown*
2001	Jong Colombia Boca Sami
2002	Centro SD Barber
2003	Centro SD Barber

Puerto Rico

Federación Puertorriqueña de Fútbol
Founded: 1940
Joined FIFA: 1960
Joined CONCACAF: 1962

SEASON	LEAGUE CHAMPIONS
1998	Académicos de Quintana
1999	CF Nacional
2000	Académicos de Quintana
2001	Académicos de Quintana
2002	Académicos de Quintana

St Kitts and Nevis

St Kitts and Nevis Amateur Football Association
Founded: 1932
Joined FIFA: 1992
Joined CONCACAF: 1992

SEASON	LEAGUE CHAMPIONS
2000	*no championship*
2001	Garden Hotspurs FC
2002	Cayon Rockets
2003	Village Superstars
2004	Newtown United

St Lucia

St Lucia National Football Union
Founded: 1979
Joined FIFA: 1988
Joined CONCACAF: 1988

SEASON	LEAGUE CHAMPIONS
1998	Mabouya Valley Rovers
1999	Roots Alley Ballers
2000	Roots Alley Ballers
2001	VSADC
2002	VSADC

St Vincent and the Grenadines
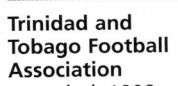

St Vincent and Grenadines Football Federation
Founded: 1979
Joined FIFA: 1988
Joined CONCACAF: 1988

SEASON	LEAGUE CHAMPIONS
1997	ASC Le Geldar
1998	AS Jahouvey Mana
1999	AJ Saint-Georges
2000	AJ Saint-Georges
2001	Conquering Lions

Trinidad and Tobago

Trinidad and Tobago Football Association
Founded: 1908
Joined FIFA: 1963
Joined CONCACAF: 1964

Trinidad and Tobago *(continued)*

SEASON	LEAGUE CHAMPIONS
1999	Defence Force
2000	William's Connection FC
2001	William's Connection FC
2002	San Juan Jabloteh
2003	San Juan Jabloteh

Turks and Caicos Islands

Football Association of Turks and Caicos
Founded: 1996
Joined FIFA: 1998
Joined CONCACAF: 1998

SEASON	LEAGUE CHAMPIONS
2000	Masters
2001	SWA Sharks
2002	Beaches FC
2003	Caribbean All Stars
2004	KPMG United

U.S. Virgin Islands

USVI Soccer Federation
Founded: 1998
Joined FIFA: 1998
Joined CONCACAF: 1998

SEASON	LEAGUE CHAMPIONS
2000	UWS Upsetters
2001	UWS Upsetters
2002	Haitian Stars
2003	Waitikibuli United

Joe Public FC, based in Port of Spain, was runner-up in the Trinidad and Tobago League Championship in 1997, but the following year it took the title, and since then has remained one of the main teams on the island.

Index

INDEX

INDEX

ACKNOWLEDGEMENTS

THANKS TO:
Sarah Bond for love, support and telling me to make it happen.
Andy Jones for inspiration. Johnny Acton, Barbara Wyllie and Sophie Woodward for research and Johnny for endless conversation and discussion.
Bob Bickerton for truly the most extraordinary knowledge of football colours one could imagine. Eric Weil for invaluable assistance with Latin America.
Soccer Investor for letting me wander through their library and illuminating me every Wednesday.
Historians, press officers, information officers, librarians, statisticians, archivists at national and regional FAs, leagues and clubs,
as well as hundreds and hundreds of fans' websites of so many clubs that I don't even know where to start.
Thanks also for help with pictures and facts to Irina Andrievskaya, Agustín Beltrame, Patricia Quijano Dark, Svetlana N. Drazhnikova, Emily Lewis,
David Litterer, Jen Little, Tim Maitland, Emmanuel Maradas, Nick McCormack, Olexi Scherbak, Sergey Ukladov, Joel Wainwright.
For invaluable correspondence and corrections thanks to Ewen Anderson, the encyclopedic Peter Law and Efthymios.

BIBLIOGRAPHY

WEBSITES
www.european-football-statistics.co.uk
www.fifa.com
www.rsssf.com
www.transfermarkets.co.uk
www.uefa.com
www.worldstadiums.com

YEARBOOKS AND ENCYCLOPEDIAS
Football Asia, Kuala Lumpur, Asian Football Confederation, annual.
Ballard J. and Suff P., **The Dictionary of Football**, Boxtree, Basingstoke, 1999.
Creswell P. and Evans S., **European Football: A Fan's Handbook**, Rough Guide, London, 1998.
Deloitte and Touche Annual Review of Football Finance, Manchester, annual.
Il Calcio Italiano Analisi Economico, Deloitte and Touche, Milan, annual.
Hammond M. (ed.), **The European Football Yearbook**, Sports Projects, Birmingham, annual.
Jelinek R. and Tomes J., **Prvni Fotbalovy Atlas Sveta**, Inforkart, Prague, 2000.
Oliver G., **The Guinness Book of World Soccer**, 2nd Edition, Guinness, Enfield, 1995.
Presti S. (ed.), **Annuario del Calcio Mondiale**, SET, Torino, annual.
Radnedge K., **The Complete Encyclopedia of Football**, Carlton Books, London, 1999.
Ricci F. (ed.), **Pro-Sports African Football Yearbook**, Fillipo Maria Ricci, Rome, annual.
Rollin J., **The Rothmans Football Yearbook**, Headline Books, London, annual.
FA Premier League National Fan Survey, Sir Norman Chester Centre for Football Research, Leicester, annual survey.
Van Hoof S., Parr M., Yamenetti C., **The North and Latin American Football Guide**, Heart Books, Rijmenam, annual.

MAGAZINES AND NEWSPAPERS
African Football, AS, A Bola, Calcio 2000, Don Balon, L'Equipe, Football Asia, France Football, Gazzetta dello Sport, Guido Sportivo, Kicker, Lance, Marca, Placar, Soccer Analyst, Soccer Investor, Voetbal International, When Saturday Comes, World Soccer. The Daily Telegraph, The Financial Times, The Independent.

OVERVIEWS, GLOBAL HISTORIES, COLLECTIONS
Armstrong G. and Giullianoti R. (eds.), **Entering the Field: New Perspectives on World Football**, Berg, Oxford, 1997.
Armstrong G. and Giullianoti R. (eds.), **Football Cultures and Indentities**, Macmillan, Basingstoke, 1998.
Armstrong G. and Giullianoti R. (eds.), **Fear and Loathing in World Football**, Berg, Oxford, 2001.
Finn G. and Giullianoti R. (eds.), **Football Cultures: Local Contest, Global Visions**, Cass, London, 2000.
Giulianotti R., **Football: A Sociology of the Global Game**, Polity Press, Cambridge, 1999.
Glanville B., **The Story of the World Cup**, Faber, London, 2001.
Inglis S., **The Football Grounds of England and Wales**, Willow, London, 1983.
Inglis S,. **The Football Grounds of Europe**, Willow, London, 1990.
Inglis S., **Sightlines: A Stadium Odyssey**, Yellow Jersey, London, 2000.
Kuper S., **Football Against the Enemy**, Orion, London, 1994.
Murray B., **The World's Game: A History of Soccer**, University of Illinois Press, Urbana, 1994.
Sugden J. and Tomlinson A., **Who Rules the People's Game? FIFA and the contest for World Football**, Polity Press, Cambridge, 1998.
Sugden J. and Tomlinson A., **Hosts and Champions: Soccer Cultures, National Identities and the USA World Cup**, Arena, Aldershot, 1994.
Walvin J., **The People's Game: The History of Football Revisited**, Mainstream, London, 1994.

BRAZIL
Bellos A., **Futbol: The Brazillian Way of Life**, Bloomsbury, London, 2002.
Lever J., **Soccer Madness**, University of Chicago Press, Chicago, 1983.

FRANCE
Ruhn C. (ed.), **Le Foot: The Legends of French Football**, Abacus, London, 2000.
Holt R., **Sport and Society in Modern France**, Macmillan, Basingstoke, 1981.

ITALY
Manna A. and Gibbs M., **The Day Italian Football Died**, Breedon Books, Derby, 2000.
Parks T., **A Season with Verona**, Secker and Warburg, London, 2002.

JAPAN
Birchall J., **Ultra Nippon: How Japan Reinvented Football**, Headline, London, 2000.
Moffet S., **Japanese Rules: Why Japan Needed Football and How it Got it**, Yellow Jersey, London, 2002.

LATIN AMERICA
Mason T., **Passion of the People? Football in South America**, Verso, London, 1995.
Taylor C., **The Beautiful Game: A Journey Through Latin American Football**, Phoenix, London, 1998.

NETHERLANDS
Winner D., **Brilliant Orange: The Neurotic Genius of Dutch Football**, Bloomsbury, London, 2000.

SPAIN
Burns J., **Barça, A People's Passion**, Bloomsbury, London, 1999.
Hall P., **Morbo: The Story of Spanish Football**, When Saturday Comes, London, 2001.

USSR
Edleman R., **Serious Fun: A History of Spectator Sports in the Soviet Union**, Oxford University Press, Oxford, 1993.

PICTURE CREDITS